HALL'S CONTEMPLATIONS.

TO THE HIGH AND MIGHTY PRINCE,

HENRY, PRINCE OF WALES.

MOST GRACIOUS PRINCE,—THIS work of mine, which, if my hopes and desires fail me not, time may hereafter make great, I have presumed to dedicate to your Highness. I dare say, these meditations, how rude soever they may fall from my pen, in regard of their subject are fit for a Prince. Here your Highness shall see how the great pattern of Princes, the KING OF HEAVEN, hath ever ruled the world; how his substitutes, earthly kings, have ruled it under him, and with what success either of glory or ruin. Both your peace and war shall find here holy and great examples. And if history and observation be the best counsellors of your youth, what story can be so wise and faithful as that which God hath written for men, wherein you see both what had been done, and what should be? What observation so worthy as that which is both raised from God, and directed to him? If the propriety which your Highness justly hath in the Work and Author, may draw your princely eyes and heart the rather to these holy speculations, your servant shall be happier in this favour than in all your outward bounty; as one to whom your spiritual progress deserves to be dearer than his own life; and whose daily suit is, that God would guide your steps aright in this slippery age, and continue to rejoice all good hearts in the view of your gracious proceedings.

Your Highness's humbly devoted servant,

JOSEPH HALL.

JOSEPH HALL, D.D.

CONTEMPLATIONS

ON THE

HISTORICAL PASSAGES

OF THE

OLD AND NEW TESTAMENTS.

BY THE

RIGHT REV. JOSEPH HALL, D.D.

BISHOP OF NORWICH.

WITH

A MEMOIR OF THE AUTHOR.

BY

JAMES HAMILTON, M.B.S.

A NEW EDITION, REVISED AND CORRECTED.

Eugene, Oregon

Wipf and Stock Publishers
199 W 8th Ave, Suite 3
Eugene, OR 97401

Contemplations on the Historical Passages of the Old and New Testaments
With a Memoir of the Author
By Hall, Joseph and Hamilton, James
ISBN: 1-59752-201-5
Publication date 5/17/2005
Previously published by T. Nelson and Sons, 1854

CONTENTS.

LIFE OF BISHOP HALL vii

BOOK I.
	Page
1. The Creation	1
2. Man	4
3. Paradise	6
4. Cain and Abel	8
5. The Deluge	10

BOOK II.
1. Noah	12
2. Babel	13
3. Abraham	15
4. Isaac offered	16
5. Lot and Sodom	18

BOOK III.
1. Jacob and Esau	20
2. Jacob and Laban	23
3. Dinah	25
4. Judah and Thamar	26
5. Joseph	28

BOOK IV.
1. The Affliction of Israel	33
2. Birth and Breeding of Moses	35
3. Moses Called	38
4. The Plagues of Egypt	41

BOOK V.
1. The Waters of Marah	45
2. The Quails and Manna	47
3. The Rock of Rephidim	50
4. The Foil of Amalek, or Moses' hand lifted up	53
5. The Law	55
6. The Golden Calf	58

BOOK VI.
1. The Veil of Moses	63
2. Nadab and Abihu	66
3. Aaron and Miriam	68
4. The Searchers of Canaan	70
5. Korah's Conspiracy	73

BOOK VII.
1. Aaron's Censer and Rod	75
2. The Brazen Serpent	78
3. Balaam	80
4. Phineas	84
5. The Death of Moses	87

BOOK VIII.
1. Rahab	89
2. Jordan divided	92
3. The Siege of Jericho	94
4. Achan	96
5. The Gibeonites	99

BOOK IX.
1. The Rescue of Gibeon	102
2. The Altar of the Reubenites	104
3. Ehud and Eglon	106
4. Jael and Sisera	108
5. Gideon's Calling	110
6. Gideon's Preparation and Victory	113
7. The Revenge of Succoth and Penuel	116
8. Abimelech's Usurpation	119

BOOK X.
1. Jephthah	121
2. Samson conceived	124
3. Samson's Marriage	127
4. Samson's Victory	131
5. Samson's End	134
6. Micah's Idolatry	137

BOOK XI.
1. The Levite's Concubine	139
2. The Desolation of Benjamin	143
3. Naomi and Ruth	145
4. Boaz and Ruth	148
5. Hannah and Peninnah	151
6. Eli and Hannah	152
7. Eli and his Sons	154

BOOK XII.
1. The Ark and Dagon	158
2. Ark's Revenge and Return	161
3. The Removal of the Ark	163
4. Meeting of Saul and Samuel	165
5. Inauguration of Saul	169
6. Samuel's Contestation	171
7. Saul's Sacrifice	173
8. Jonathan's Victory and Saul's Oath	175

BOOK XIII.
1. Saul and Agag	178
2. The Rejection of Saul, and the Choice of David	180
3. David called to the Court	183
4. David and Goliah	184
5. Jonathan's Love, and Saul's Envy	188
6. Michal's Wife	190
7. David and Abimelech	193

BOOK XIV.
1. Saul in David's Cave	195
2. Nabal and Abigail	197
3. David and Achish	200
4. Saul and the Witch of Endor	203
5. Ziklag spoiled and revenged	205
6. The Death of Saul	208
7. Abner and Joab	210

BOOK XV.
1. Uzziah, and the Ark removed	213
2. Mephibosheth and Ziba	216
3. Hanun, and David's Ambassadors	218
4. David with Bathsheba and Uriah	221
5. Nathan and David	224
6. Amnon and Tamar	226
7. Absalom's Return and Conspiracy	229

CONTENTS.

BOOK XVI.
1. Shimei cursing ... 232
2. Ahithophel ... 234
3. The Death of Absalom ... 236
4. Sheba's Rebellion ... 239
5. The Gibeonites revenged ... 242
6. The Numbering of the People ... 244

BOOK XVII.
1. Adonijah defeated ... 247
2. David's End, and Solomon's Beginning 249
3. The Execution of Joab and Shimei ... 252
4. Solomon's Choice, with his Judgment upon the two Harlots ... 254
5. The Temple ... 256
6. Solomon and the Queen of Sheba ... 259
7. Solomon's Defection ... 261

BOOK XVIII.
1. Rehoboam ... 264
2. Jeroboam ... 267
3. The Seduced Prophet ... 270
4. Jeroboam's Wife ... 273
5. Asa ... 276
6. Elijah with the Sareptan ... 279
7. Elijah with the Baalites ... 283
8. Elijah running before Ahab, fleeing from Jezebel ... 287

BOOK XIX.
1. Ahab and Benhadad ... 291
2. Ahab and Naboth ... 295
3. Ahab and Micaiah, or the Death of Ahab 299
4. Ahaziah sick, and Elijah revenged ... 302
5. The Rapture of Elijah ... 306
6. Elisha healing the Waters—cursing the Children—relieving the Kings ... 310
7. Elisha with the Shunamite ... 314
8. Elisha with Naaman ... 318
9. Elisha raising the Iron, blinding the Assyrians ... 324
10. The Famine of Samaria relieved ... 327

BOOK XX.
1. The Shunamite suing to Jehoram—Elisha conferring with Hazael ... 330
2. Jehu with Jehoram and Jezebel ... 334
3. Jehu killing the Sons of Ahab, and the Priests of Baal ... 338
4. Athaliah and Joash ... 342
5. Joash with Elisha dying ... 345
6. Uzziah Leprous ... 348
7. Ahaz with his New Altar ... 351
8. The utter Destruction of the Kingdom of Israel ... 352
9. Hezekiah and Sennacherib ... 354
10. Hezekiah sick, recovered, visited ... 358
11. Manasseh ... 362
12. Josiah's Reformation ... 366
13. Josiah's Death, with the Desolation of the Temple and Jerusalem ... 369

BOOK XXI.
1. Zerubbabel and Ezra ... 372
2. Nehemiah building the Walls of Jerusalem ... 378
3. Nehemiah redressing the Extortion of the Jews ... 382
4. Ahasuerus feasting—Vashti cast off—Esther chosen ... 385
5. Haman disrespected by Mordecai Mordecai's Message to Esther ... 389
6. Esther suing to Ahasuerus ... 394
7. Mordecai honoured by Haman ... 397
8. Haman hanged—Mordecai advanced ... 399

FROM THE NEW TESTAMENT.

BOOK I.
1. The Angel and Zachary ... 404
2. The Anunciation of Christ ... 408
3. The Birth of Christ ... 410
4. The Sages and the Star ... 413
5. The Purification ... 416
6. Herod and the Infants ... 418

BOOK II.
1. Christ among the Doctors ... 421
2. Christ's Baptism ... 424
3. Christ tempted ... 426
4. Simon called ... 433
5. The Marriage in Cana ... 435
6. The Good Centurion ... 438

BOOK III.
1. The Widow's Son raised ... 441
2. The Ruler's Son cured ... 443
3. The Dumb Devil ejected ... 444
4. Matthew called ... 449
5. Christ among the Gergesenes, or Legion and the Gadarene Herd ... 451

BOOK IV.
1. The Faithful Canaanite ... 460
2. The Deaf and Dumb Man cured ... 465
3. Zaccheus ... 467
4. John Baptist beheaded ... 475
5. The Five Loaves and Two Fishes ... 482
6. The Walk upon the Waters ... 487
7. The Bloody Issue healed ... 493
8. Jairus and his Daughter ... 498
9. The Motion of the two fiery Disciples repelled ... 500
10. The Ten Lepers ... 503
11. The Pool of Bethesda ... 507
12. The Transfiguration of Christ ... 512
13. The Same ... 516
14. The Same ... 522
15. The Woman taken in Adultery ... 524
16. The Thankful Penitent ... 528
17. Martha and Mary ... 534
18. The Beggar that was born blind cured 537
19. The Stubborn Devil ejected ... 541
20. The Widow's Mites ... 544
21. The Ambition of the two Sons of Zebedee ... 545
22. The Tribute-money paid ... 548
23. Lazarus dead ... 550
24. Lazarus raised ... 554
25. Christ's Procession to the Temple ... 560
26. The Fig-tree cursed ... 564
27. Christ betrayed ... 565
28. The Agony ... 569
29. Peter and Malchus, or Christ apprehended ... 571
30. Christ before Caiaphas ... 574
31. Christ before Pilate ... 576
32. The Crucifixion ... 581
33. The Resurrection ... 589
34. The Ascension ... 598

LIFE

OF

BISHOP HALL.

In a posthumous volume, entitled "The Shaking of the Olive Tree," first appeared two autobiographical tracts, — the one, "Observations of some Specialties of Divine Providence in the Life of Joseph Hall, Bishop of Norwich;" the other, "Hard Measure," setting forth the sufferings of his later years. With much good taste, these sketches have been frequently reprinted, where a more formal Life might have been expected; and in the present instance, the same course might have been pursued with advantage. But as some passages in these fragments refer to subjects of trivial or temporary importance, and other sources of information are open, we have endeavoured, by omitting the one, to find place for the other.

Bishop Hall's object in leaving the chief events of his life on record, was worthy of the man. "Not out of a vain affectation of my own glory, which I know how little it can avail me when I am gone hence, but out of a sincere desire to give glory to my God, whose wonderful providence I have noted in all my ways, have I recorded some remarkable passages of my fore-past life. What I have done is worthy of nothing but silence and forgetfulness; but what God hath done for me is worthy of everlasting and thankful memory."

JOSEPH HALL was born July 1, 1574, at Bristow Park, in the parish of Ashby de la Zouch, Leicestershire. His parentage was "honest and well-allowed." His father held an office under the Earl of Huntingdon, which enabled him to procure a good education for his twelve children, and warranted his ambition that one of them should enter the ministry, at a time when a University was not the only avenue to the Church. But the instructions and impressions which Joseph received from his mother were a better qualification than the lessons of all his teachers; and the consciousness of their value in after days invested the memory of the gentle giver with an affection doubly filial. Winifred Bambridge was the Monica of Bishop Hall. A body always feeble, and often anguish-stricken, was the appropriate tenement of a spirit sorrowful and sorely exercised. But happily, the clouds which at one time shaded the piety of this excellent woman, did not render it forbidding to the more genial temper of her son. He rejoiced in the light, when others would have complained of the halo, nor refused to be conducted to the kingdom by a guide whose countenance was sometimes sad. And he at last had the satisfaction of seeing her set free from these vexing thoughts, and deriving the joy of a religion of hope. "What with these trials, so had she profited in the school of Christ, that it was hard for any friend to come from her discourse no whit holier. How often have I blessed the memory of those divine passages of experimental divinity which I have heard from her mouth! What day did she pass without a large task of private devotion, whence she would still come forth with a countenance of undissembled mortification! Never any lips have read to me such feeling lectures of piety; neither have I known any soul that more accurately practised them than her own. Temptations, desertions, and spiritual comforts were her usual theme; shortly, for I can hardly take off my pen from so exemplary a subject, her life and death were saint-like."

It was at the public school of his native village that he received the elements of his education. After spending " some years, not altogether indiligently, under the ferule of such masters as the place afforded, and attaining some competent ripeness for the University," as he was now fifteen years of age, it became a subject of much deliberation to his father, and anxious interest to himself, where he should next be sent. His father's fortune, not so large as his family, rendered the University almost unattainable; and Joseph's schoolmaster, in his zeal for so meritorious a pupil, had privately negociated with Mr. Pelset, a clerical friend, famed for his talents and the eloquence with which he displayed them, to receive him into his house as his scholar; — Mr. Pelset undertaking, " within one seven years, to send him forth, no less furnished with arts, languages, and grounds of theoretical divinity, than the carefullest tutor in the strictest college of either University." The scheme, when unfolded to his father, so completely adapted itself to his circumstances and desires, that he speedily took the requisite steps for securing its advantages. " There, and now were all my hopes of my future life upon blasting. The indentures were preparing, the time was set, my suits were addressed for the journey. What was the issue? O God! thy providence made and found it. Thou knowest how heartily and sincerely, in those my young years, I did cast myself upon thy hands; with what faithful resolution I did in this particular occasion resign myself over to thy disposition, earnestly begging of thee in my fervent prayers, to order all things to the best; and confidently waiting upon thy will for the event. Certainly, never did I in all my life more clearly roll myself upon the Divine Providence, than I did in this business; and it succeeded accordingly."

While these measures were in progress, his elder brother had occasion to visit Cambridge, and was kindly entertained by his townsman Nathaniel Gilby, a Fellow of Emanuel College. The majestic structures, the learned leisure, and the old renown of Cambridge, won this brother " to a great love and reverence of an academical life," and powerfully enforced Mr. Gilby's earnest persuasions by all means to send his younger brother thither. Under these influences he returned to Ashby, and with Mr. Gilby's message reported in the most glowing terms his own impressions. On his knees he begged that his father would not drown the expectations of the youthful aspirant " in a shallow country channel;" and concluded by beseeching him, if the cost were the hindrance, to sell part of the land which should otherwise be his own inheritance. An appeal thus urged could not be resisted, and with an honest enthusiasm the governor of Ashby exclaimed, " Cost what it will, to the University he shall go." The decision was opportunely made, for instantly a knock at the door announced a messenger from Mr. Pelset, to tell that he was waiting for his pupil, and would expect him on the morrow. Mr. Hall told the servant that he was some minutes too late, and informing him of his change of purpose, dismissed him with a courteous message to his master, whilst Joseph welcomed the change in his destination with tears of joy.

He had spent only two years in Emanuel College, when his father, " whose not very large cistern was to feed many pipes besides his," was prevailed on to recall him, that he might become the master of that school where he had shortly before been scholar. His extreme disappointment at this premature interruption of his studies was so evident as to move the pity of an uncle, by whose generosity he was enabled to resume his place at college, where he soon after obtained a scholarship. But, though other four years terminated his right to this maintenance, they had not abated his literary enthusiasm, and had only exalted into passion his love for the haunts of learning. There was only one capacity in which he could prolong his residence, and from that he was precluded by the statutes. These allowed of only a single fellow from any shire and the Leicestershire fellowship was preoccupied by his townsman and tutor Mr. Gilby. Here, not for the first time, he experienced the blessing of a faithful friend.

For in conversation with the Earl of Huntingdon, his class-fellow Mr. Cholmley so represented his worth and accomplishments, as to engage in his behalf the warm interest of his father's patron. The Earl was much concerned to hear that his hopes of a fellowship were forestalled; but on learning the reason, resolved on a remedy. He sent for Mr. Gilby, and offered to make him his chaplain, on terms which gained his ready assent. Mr. Gilby tendered his resignation at Cambridge; it was accepted, and three days of public competition for the vacant fellowship were named. The examination proceeded, and at the close of the second day word arrived that the Earl of Huntingdon was dead. Joseph Hall instantly repaired to the Master of the College, and entreated him, in regard for his friend now thrown destitute, to stay the election. He represented that his own youth less required the situation, and held out better prospects of provision in other ways. But he was told, that the place having been declared vacant, the election must proceed, and that his tutor " must wait upon the providence of God for his disposing elsewhere." " Then was I with a cheerful unanimity chosen into that society, which if it had any equals, I dare say had none beyond it, for good order, studious carriage, strict government, austere piety; in which I spent six or seven years more, with such contentment as the rest of my life hath in vain striven to yield. Now was I called to public disputations often, with no ill success; for never durst I appear in any of those exercises of scholarship, till I had from my knees looked up to heaven for a blessing, and renewed my actual dependence upon that divine hand. In this while, two years together I was chosen to the rhetoric lecture in the public schools, when I was encouraged with a sufficient frequence of auditors; but finding that well-applauded work somewhat out of my way, not without a secret blame of myself for so much excursion, I fairly gave up that task in the midst of those poor acclamations to a worthy successor, Dr. Dod, and betook myself to those serious studies, which might fit me for the high calling whereunto I was destined, wherein, after I had carefully bestowed myself for a time, I took the boldness to enter into sacred orders; the honour whereof having once attained, I was no niggard of that talent which God had entrusted to me, preaching often, as occasion was offered, both in country villages abroad, and at home in the most awful auditory of the University."

The rhetoric lecture was not the only avocation of this tranquil period. Mr. Hall then first adventured in the field of authorship; but either from deference to an ecclesiastical censure strangely passed upon it, or because he had afterwards learned so completely to count all things but loss for Christ, we do not find him making any subsequent reference to a publication which has procured him applause among many who are ignorant of his nobler works.* It was in his 23d year that he gave to the world his Satires, and introduced a species of composition new to British literature. The circumstance of his being the first English satirist would entitle the *Virgidemium* to a place of importance in the history of our national poetry; but the united suffrages of skilful critics — with one formidable exception, and personal animosity made Milton here an incompetent judge—have awarded it other claims. Its greatest fault is obscurity—an obscurity which the learned notes of Warton and Singer have only partially dispelled — the more provoking as having been purposely assumed by one of the most perspicuous of writers, and not unjustly punished by the comparative neglect to which it has consigned the production. It was Hall's very natural mistake, with no models but the ancient satirists, to consider their style of intricacy and innuendoes essential; and so completely was he possessed by this misconception, that he thinks it incumbent to apologize for the excessive perspicuity of his verses.

* Warton observes, not with his usual judgment, that " the poet is better known than the prelate or the polemic." So far is this from being the case, that of many thousands who have read Bishop Hall's Meditations and Sermons with pleasure and advantage, few have ever heard that he was a poet, and still fewer that his poems were once proscribed by authority, as unfit to be circulated or read.—*Chalmers' Biog. Dict.* Art. *Hall.*

But more than the meaning is enigmatical. By clothing the elliptical sententiousness of Persius in the antiquated phraseology of Chaucer, he has locked his sense in a double cipher. In one respect he improved upon his patterns, as his successors have degenerated from him — in the freedom from offensive personalities which distinguishes his Satires — the "biting" and the "toothless" alike. It was his noble determination " to mar his own verse rather than another's name." The faithful delineation of manners gives us an acquaintance with the times beyond the reach, though not beyond the province of history,—whilst the couplets are not loaded with inglorious names, which nothing but such distinction could have saved from forgetfulness. Widely severed as were the peculiarities of Pope — perspicuous, modernized, and personal—we do not wonder that these Satires should have been the subjects of his minute and frequent study when he at last discovered them, and that he should have expressed regret that " he had not seen them sooner." " Whether we consider the age of the man or of the world, they appear to be equally wonderful," is the verdict of an accomplished critic.* Nor can we withhold the more specific and discriminating sentence of one, whose large acquaintance with the imagery and diction of his father-poets has made him the too fastidious judge of his own. " In his Satires," says Mr. Campbell, "he discovered not only the early vigour of his own genius, but the powers and pliability of his native tongue. * * * In the point, and volubility, and vigour of Hall's numbers, we might frequently imagine ourselves perusing Dryden. This may be exemplified in the harmony and picturesqueness of the following description of a magnificent rural mansion, which the traveller approaches in the hopes of reaching the seat of ancient hospitality, but finds it deserted by its selfish owner :—

>   Beat the broad gates ; a goodly hollow sound,
>   With double echoes, doth again rebound;
>   But not a dog doth bark to welcome thee,
>   Nor churlish porter canst thou chafing see.
>   All dumb and silent, like the dead of night,
>   Or dwelling of some sleepy Sybarite ;
>   The marble pavement hid with desert weed,
>   With house-leek, thistle, dock, and hemlock seed.
>   *   *   *   *   *   *
>   Look to the tow'red chimnies, which should be
>   The wind-pipes of good hospitality,
>   Through which it breatheth to the open air,
>   Betokening life and liberal welfare ;
>   Lo, there th' unthankful swallow takes her rest,
>   And fills the tunnel with her circled nest.

" His Satires are neither cramped by personal hostility, nor spun out to vague declamations on vice, but give us the form and pressure of the times, exhibited in the faults of coeval literature, and in the foppery or sordid traits of prevailing manners. The age was undoubtedly fertile in eccentricity. * * * From the literature of the age, Hall proceeds to its manners and prejudices, and among the latter derides the prevalent confidence in alchymy and astrology. To us this ridicule appears an ordinary effort of reason; but it was in him a common sense above the level of the times."†

To do justice to " the vigorous and musical couplets of this old poet," we must extract the opening passage of the 3d book, which our readers may like none the worse for its entire freedom from obscurity. No classical description of the golden age can surpass the playful ingenuity of the following : —

>   Time was, and that was term'd the time of gold,
>   When world and time were young that now are old,
>   (When quiet Saturn sway'd the mace of lead,
>   And pride was yet unborn and yet unbred.)
>   Time was, that while the autumn fall did last,
>   Our hungry sires gap'd for the falling mast.
>   Could no unhusked acorn leave the tree,
>   But there was challenge made whose it might be.

* Edinburgh Review, vol. xxxi. p. 481.
† Campbell's Specimens of the British Poets, vol. ii. pp. 257-9.

> But if some nice and licorous appetite
> Desir'd more dainty dish of rare delight,
> They scal'd the stored crab with bended knee,
> Till they had sated their delicious eye:
> Or search'd the hopeful thicks of hedgy rows,
> For briery berries, or haws, or sourer sloes:
> Or when they meant to fare the fin'st of all
> They lick'd oak-leaves besprent with honey-fall.
> As for the thrice three-angled beech nut-shell
> Or chesnut's armed husk and hid kernell,
> No squire durst touch, the law would not afford,
> Kept for the court, and for the king's own board.

These Satires, though the principal, were not the only poetical effusions of our author. During his college days he complied with a prevailing taste, and composed a multitude of occasional poems, threnodies and gratulatory odes. From one of the earliest we transcribe a few stanzas, of which the euphonic pomp and well-adjusted expressions may help to reconcile us to an imagery which the long-forgotten occasion has rendered extravagant. The whole elegy on Dr. Whitaker seems to have been penned with ink from Cocytus, and is such as Chatterton, in one of his most dismal moods, would have delighted to imitate:—

> Bind ye my brows with mourning cyparisse,
>   And palish twigs of deadly poplar tree,
> Or if some sadder shades ye can devise,
>   Those sadder shades veil my light-loathing eye;
> I loathe the laurel bands I loved best,
> And all that maketh mirth and pleasant rest.
> Thou flattering sun that ledst this loathed light,
>   Why didst thou in thy saffron robes arise?
> Or fold'st not up the day in dreary night?
>   And wak'st the western world's amazed eyes?
> And never more rise from the ocean,
> To wake the morn, or chase night-shades again.
> Hear we no bird of day or dawning morn,
>   To greet the sun, or glad the waking ear:
> Sing out, ye screech-owls, louder than aforn,
>   And ravens black of night, of death, of drear:
> And all ye barking fowls yet never seen,
> That fill the moonless night with hideous din.

That we may not return to this subject—in later years Hall employed his muse on a dearer but more arduous theme, a metrical translation of the Psalms. The first ten appeared with the title, "Some few of David's Psalms, metaphrased for a taste of the rest." We could have wished that his success had been more commensurate with his laudable design; but the "Metaphrase" wants the vigour, the pathos, the melody, in short the poetry of his youthful productions. There have been those who could call forth rich music from a lyre of their own, without being able to retune the harp of David; nor can we wonder that the chords which refused the enchantments of Milton and Byron, should have been silent beneath the touch of Hall.

Having obtained orders, his own inclinations and the rules of the society to which he belonged, made him desirous of some extra-collegiate appointment. At that time a school had recently been opened at Tivérton in Devon, provided with an ample endowment, and left principally under the patronage of the Lord Chief-Justice Popham. He applied to the master of Emanuel College to recommend a governor for the new erection. Dr. Chaderton without any hesitation nominated Mr. Hall, and immediately carried him to London, that he might introduce him to the Chief-Justice. The illustrious judge was so fascinated by the indications of genius and accomplishments which this interview revealed, that before they parted, the one had promised his influence, and the other signified his readiness to accept. On leaving his Lordship, Mr. Hall had not proceeded far when he was accosted by a messenger in the street, who put a letter into his hand. Dr. Chaderton remarking a change in the countenance of his friend as he perused his despatches, asked what the matter might be?

Mr. Hall answered by handing him the letter, which contained a very pressing invitation from Lady Drury to the Rectory of Halsted in Suffolk. "Sir," said Mr. Hall, "methinks God pulls me by the sleeve, and tells me it is his will I should rather go to the east than to the west." "Nay," said Dr. Chaderton, "I should rather think that God would have you go westward, for that he hath contrived your engagement before the tender of this letter, which therefore coming too late, may receive a fair and easy answer." "Pardon my dissent," was Mr. Hall's reply; "I well know that divinity was the end whereto I was destined by my parents, and this I have so constantly proposed to myself, that I never meant other than to pass through this western school to it; but I see that God, who found me ready to go the farther way about, now calls me the nearest and directest way to that sacred end." To this the good Doctor had nothing farther to oppose, and though it was the frustration of his journey to London, he recognized the finger of God, and joyfully relinquished his protegée to the better care of Providence. All that remained was to satisfy Lord Popham. This Mr. Hall undertook; and not only was his apology as frankly sustained as it was candidly given, but he was enabled to recompense the former kindness of a friend. For, remembering by whose representations to the Earl of Huntingdon he had obtained his fellowship, he stated the qualifications of Mr. Cholmley so effectually, that the vacant place was transfered to him, and they " two, who came together to the University, must now leave it at once."*

His next step in life is too important not to be told, and his own account is too characteristic to admit of any other relating it. "Being now settled in that sweet and civil country of Suffolk, near to St. Edmund's-Bury, my first work was to build up my house, which was then extremely ruinous; which done, the uncouth solitariness of my life, and the extreme incommodity of that single housekeeping, drew my thoughts, after two years, to condescend to the necessity of a married estate, which God no less strangely provided for me. For walking from the church on Monday in the Whitsun-week, with a grave and reverend minister, Mr. Grandidge, I saw a comely modest gentlewoman standing at the door of that house where we were invited to a wedding-dinner, and inquiring of that worthy friend whether he knew her, ' Yes, quoth he, I know her well, and have bespoken her for your wife.' When I further demanded an account of that answer, he told me she was the daughter of a gentleman whom he much respected, Mr. George Winniff of Bretenham ; that out of an opinion had of the fitness of that match for me, he had already treated with her father about it, whom he found very apt to entertain it, advising me not to neglect the opportunity; and not concealing the just praises of the modesty, piety, good disposition, and other virtues that were lodged in that seemly presence, I listened to the motion as sent from God, and at last upon due prosecution happily prevailed, enjoying the comfortable society of that meet help for the space of forty-nine years."

The increasing comforts of Halsted Rectory could not hinder him from listening soon after to a proposal made by Sir Edmund Bacon, that he should accompany him in a continental tour. The amount of enterprise and resources which such an expedition then demanded can scarcely now be understood. In those days the travelling retinue of a nobleman resembled the Mecca caravan, and he marched under an escort which showed that he was taking his pleasure in an enemy's country. Mr. Hall possessed a high degree of that noble curiosity which compels some to labour in the fire for knowledge, whilst others, waiting till wisdom come, are contentedly ignorant. No one in reading his works can fail to be struck with the indications of a busy, quick, and observant eye. Many of his most striking and original remarks are the result of sagaciously noting, and dexterously applying what passes before the eyes of other men too often to appear uncommon, that is, to appear in any way *remarkable*. But the pro-

* From the above narrative, it will be seen that Mr. Campbell has committed an oversight in stating that Hall " was some time master of the school at Tiverton, in Devonshire."—*British Poets*, II. 260. He was never actually appointed.

spect of exploring a field then so seldom traversed dilated his mind with absolute ecstasy, and he rejoiced in the ungathered harvest of knowledge which it promised. Above all, he wished to visit a Roman Catholic country. He longed to behold popery in reality; not the crippled crouching thing which prolonged a skulking existence in England, but the stalwart galled and raging Apollyon that stalked tremendously through Europe. Sir Edmund travelled in the protection of the English ambassador, and for farther concealment, Mr. Hall exchanged his canonicals for the silken robes and gay colours of a fashionable English gentleman. And notwithstanding the frequent debates into which his zeal betrayed him amongst jesuits and friars, the suspicious excellence of his Latin, and the sturdy protestantism, which only "the hulk of a tall Brabanter" saved from martyrdom at the procession of John the Baptist, he passed undetected from Calais to Brussels, from Nemours to Spa, and then, returning, to Antwerp and Middleburgh. It was our traveller's anxiety to view the ancient college of this last city, which lost him his voyage home. He left his party at Flushing, and lingered so long at Middleburgh, that his friends availed themselves of a favourable wind, and he arrived in time to look after their vessel far at sea. " Sadly returning to Middleburgh, he waited long for an inconvenient and tempestuous passage." In his epistles he has given an account of this expedition, an extract from which will serve the additional purpose of enabling the reader to compare his earlier — more quaint, dense, and cramp — with his later style. His six Decads of Epistles are the first specimens of that familiar and delightful composition since so common in our language. He claims this merit for himself, and we do not know of any British author who published letters of his own before him.

" Besides my hopes, not my desires, I travelled of late; for knowledge partly, and partly for health. There was nothing that made not my journey pleasant, save the labour of the way: which yet was so sweetly deceived by the society of Sir Edmund Bacon, (a gentleman truly honourable, beyond all titles), that I found small cause to complain. The sea brooked not me, nor I it; an unquiet element, made only for wonder and use, not for pleasure. Alighted once from that wooden conveyance, and uneven way, I bethought myself how fondly our life is committed to an unsteady and reeling piece of wood, fickle winds, restless waters, while we may set foot on stedfast and constant earth. Lo, then everything taught me, everything delighted me; so ready are we to be affected with these foreign pleasures, which at home we should overlook. I saw much as one might in such a span of earth in so few months. The time favoured me: for now newly had the key of peace opened those parts which war had before closed; closed (I say) to all English, save either fugitives or captives. All civil occurrences (as what fair cities, what strange fashions, entertainments, dangers, delights, we found), are fit for other ears and winter evenings. What I noted, as a divine, within the sphere of my profession, my paper shall not spare in some part to report.

" Along our way, how many churches saw we demolished! Nothing left, but rude heaps, to tell the passenger there hath been both devotion and hostility. Fury hath done that there, which Covetousness would do with us; would do, but shall not: the truth within shall save the walls without. And, to speak truly (whatever the vulgar exclaim), Idolatry pulled down those walls, not rage. If there had been no Hollander to raze them, they would have fallen alone rather than hide so much impiety under their guilty roof. These are spectacles, not so much of cruelty as justice; cruelty of man, justice of God. But (which I wondered at) churches fall and jesuits' colleges rise everywhere. There is no city where those are not either rearing or built. Whence cometh this? Is it, for that devotion is not so necessary as policy? Those men (as we say of the fox) fare best where they are most cursed. None so much spited of their own, none so hated of all, none so opposed by ours; and yet these ill weeds grow. Whosoever lives long shall see them feared of their own, who now hate them; shall see these seven lean kine devour all the fat beasts that feed on the meadows of Tiber.

"At Brussels I saw some English women profess themselves vestals, with a thousand rites, I know not whether more ridiculous or magical. Poor souls! they could not be fools enough at home. It would have made you to pity, laugh, disdain (I know not which more), to see by what cunning sleights and fair pretences that weak sex was fetched into a wilful bondage; and (if these two can agree) willingly constrained to serve a master whom they must and cannot obey. What follows hence? Late sorrow, secret mischief, misery irremediable.

"I talked there, in more boldness perhaps than wisdom, with Costerus, a famous jesuit, an old man, more testy than subtile, and more able to wrangle than satisfy. Our discourse was long and roving; and on his part full both of words and vehemency. He spake as at home, I as a stranger: yet so as he saw me modestly peremptory. The particulars would swell my letter too much: it is enough that the truth lost less than I gained.

"At Ghent, a city that commands reverence for age and wonder for the greatness, we fell upon a capuchin novice, who wept bitterly because he was not allowed to make himself miserable. His head had now felt the razor, his back the rod: all that laconical discipline pleased him well, which another being condemned to, would justly account a torment. What hindered then? Piety to his mother would not permit this which he thought piety to God. He could not be a willing beggar, unless his mother would beg unwillingly. He was the only heir of his father, the only stay of his mother: the comfort of her widowhood depended on this her orphan; who now naked must enter into the world of the capuchins, as he came first into this, leaving his goods to the division of the fraternity — the least part whereof should have been hers, whose he wished all. Hence those tears. These men for devout, the jesuits for learned and pragmatical, have engrossed all opinion from other orders. O hypocrisy! No capuchin may take or touch silver. This metal is as very an anathema to them, as the wedge of gold to Achan; at the offer whereof he starts back, as Moses from the serpent: yet he carries a boy with him, that takes and carries it, and never complains of either metal or measure. I saw and laughed at it, and by this open trick of hypocrisy suspected more, more close.

"At Nemours, on a pleasant and steep hill-top, we found one that was termed a married hermit; approving his wisdom above his fellows, that could make choice of so cheerful and sociable a solitariness. Whence, after a delightful passage up the sweet river *Mosa*, we visited the populous and rich city of *Leodium* (Liege). I would those streets were more moist with wine than with blood; wherein no day, no night is not dismal to some. No law, no magistrate lays hold on the known murderer if himself list; for three days after this fact, the gates are open and justice shut: private violence may pursue him, public justice cannot: whence some of more hot temper carve themselves revenge; others take up with a small pecuniary satisfaction. O England, thought I, happy for justice, happy for security! There you shall find in every corner a maumet (image); at every door a beggar, in every dish a priest. From thence we passed to the Spa, a village famous for her medicinal and mineral waters, compounded of iron and copperas; the virtue whereof yet the simple inhabitant ascribes to their beneficial saint, whose heavy foot hath made an ill-shaped impression in a stone of the upper well: — a water more wholesome than pleasant, and yet more famous than wholesome.

"One thing I may not omit without sinful oversight; a short but memorable story; which the graphier of that town (though of different religion) reported to more ears than ours. When the last inquisition tyrannized in those parts, and helped to spend the faggots of Ardenne, one of the rest, a confident confessor, being led far to his stake, sung psalms along the way, in a heavenly courage and victorious triumph. The cruel officer, envying his last mirth, and grieving to see him merrier than his tormentors, commanded him silence. He sings still, as desirous to improve his last breath to the best. The view of his approaching glory bred his joy; his joy breaks forth into a cheerful confession. The enraged sheriff causes his tongue to be cut off near the roots. Bloody wretch! It had been good music to have heard his shrieks; but to hear his music was torment. The poor martyr dies in silence, rests in peace. Not many months after, our butcherly officer hath a son born with his tongue hanging down upon his chin, like a deer after long chase, which never could be gathered up within the bounds of his lips. O the divine hand, full of justice, full of revenge!'

" Let me tell you yet, ere I take off my pen, two wonders more, which I saw in that wonder of cities, Antwerp;—one a solemn mass in a shambles, and that on God's day; while the house was full of meat, of butchers, of buyers; some kneeling, others bargaining, most talking, all busy. It was strange to see one house sacred to God and the belly, and how these two services agreed. The priests did eat flesh, the butchers sold flesh, in one roof at one instant. The butcher killed and sold it by pieces; the priest did sacrifice, and orally devour it whole.* The other,—an Englishman, so madly devout that he had wilfully housed up himself as an anchorite, the worst of all prisoners. There sat he, pent up for his farther merit, half hunger-starved for the charity of the citizens. It was worth seeing how manly he could bite in his secret want, and dissemble his over-late repentance. I cannot commend his mortification, if he wish to be in heaven; yea in purgatory, to be delivered from thence. I durst not pity him, because his durance was willing, and as he hoped meritorious; but such encouragement as he had from me, such thank shall he have from God, who, instead of an *Euge* which he looks for, shall angrily challenge him with ' who required this?'"

The interview with Father Costerus, to which Mr. Hall alludes in the foregoing letter, has been recorded elsewhere, and is characteristic of the times. It often happens that the prevailing notions of the day supply arguments for some great truth, to which controversialists resort more eagerly, and on which they are disposed to lay greater stress, than on those proofs which are alike weighty and conclusive in every age. It has been said that Baxter, in his book on the Immortality of the Soul, perplexed the sceptics of his time by a reference to ghosts and apparitions more than by all his other reasonings; and if they were so inconsistent in their credulity, we can scarcely conceive anything fairer or more irresistible as an *argumentum ad homines*, however inefficacious it may be in the altered belief of the present generation. It was similar ground which our protestant divine occupied in common with his popish antagonist, without any suspicion of its soundness. An English barrister, a proselyte to popery, and resident at Brussels, was narrating to Sir Edmund Bacon, in a style of extravagant hyperbole, the wonders lately performed by our Lady at Zichem; and to silence the shrewd objections of the worthy knight, had instanced a cure miraculously wrought upon himself. At this moment Mr. Hall entered the apartment, and, there being nothing in his dress to indicate his profession, joined freely in the conversation. "Put case this report of your's be granted for true, I beseech you teach me what difference there is betwixt these miracles and those which were wrought by Vespasian, by some vestals with charms and spells; the rather that I have noted in the late published report, some patient prescribed to come upon a Friday, and some to wash in such a well before their approach, and divers other such charm-like operations." The confident tone of the lawyer was suddenly lowered by this unexpected interrogatory, and he excused himself from a reply, saying, " I do not profess this kind of scholarship; but we have in the city many famous divines, with whom if it would please you to confer, you might sooner receive satisfaction." Mr. Hall asked who was considered the most eminent divine of the place. The English gentleman named Father Costerus, and undertook to secure him a conference, to which Mr. H. gladly

* We need scarcely say that the author alludes to that monstrous tenet of popery, transubstantiation.

acceded. Accordingly, in the afternoon the zealous Romanist returned to announce that the father had agreed to the conference, and to accompany him to the Jesuits' College. There arrived, the porter opened the gate, and ejaculating a *Deo gratias*, admitted the stranger. He did not remain long in the hall till Costerus joined him. After a friendly salutation, the priest ran on in a long and formal oration on the unity of that church in which only men can be saved, when Mr. Hall took advantage of the first moment which civility allowed to interrupt him. "Sir, I beseech you mistake me not. My nation tells you of what religion I am. I come not hither out of any doubt of my professed belief, or any purpose to change it; but moving a question to this gentleman concerning the pretended miracles of the time, he pleased to refer me to yourself for my answer; which motion of his I was the more willing to embrace, for the fame that I have heard of your learning and worth. And if you can give me satisfaction herein, I am ready to receive it." So seating themselves at a table in the end of the hall, they prepared for a vigorous encounter. The jesuit commenced by giving his view of the distinction between miracles diabolical and divine. This did not satisfy Mr. Hall, and he stated his objections. Upon this his opponent diverged into a vehement assault on the English church, which he protested could not yield one miracle. Mr. Hall reclaimed, that in his church they had manifest proofs of the ejection of devils by fasting and prayer. "If it can be proved," cried Costerus, "that ever any devil was dispossessed in your church, I shall quit my religion." In the long and keen debate which followed, Mr. Hall started many questions to which his antagonist could give no satisfactory answers. They soon obtained an additional auditor in Father Baldwin, an English jesuit, who came in and seated himself on a form at the other end of the table, and seemed not a little mortified that a gentleman of his nation should leave the college as unenlightened as he came. The next morning the persevering lawyer arrived with a message from this father, expressing his disappointment that an Englishman should have preferred a conference with a foreigner, when he would have been happy to have his acquaintance and to give him satisfaction. Mr. Hall would as willingly have made arrangements for this interview as for the former, had not a secret signal from Sir Edmund reminded him that they came to travel, not to argue, and that their safe-conduct would not be strengthened by an additional debate. Father Baldwin's message was therefore politely declined, Mr. Hall having no hope of converting the priest, and being resolved that no papist should alter him.

It may be worth while to mention, as justifying an objection to the English ritual strongly urged by the Presbyterians of that day, that in his voyage up the Maese, Mr. Hall had what he calls "a dangerous conflict" with a Sorbonist of the Carmelite order, on the subject of the Eucharist. This friar was trying to persuade the company, from the circumstance of their kneeling at the sacrament, that the English protestants recognised the doctrine of transubstantiation. By what arguments Mr. Hall confuted the calumny we do not know; but the debate waxed so hot, that Sir Edmund was constrained to interfere, and call away his polemical friend from a discussion more manly than discreet, in a country where all argument against the established religion was prohibited by law: — not, however, till the prior indicated his suspicions to the bystanders, by significantly telling them that he had once prepared a suit of green satin for his travels in England. Mr. Hall was afterwards employed by his Majesty King James, to persuade the people of Scotland into kneeling at the communion. It does not appear that he executed his commission with great alacrity; and when he found his church claimed by Roman Catholics on the ground of this ceremony, he might well have shown indulgence for those Presbyterians who saw in it a remnant of popery.

At Spa he composed the second of his three centuries of "Meditations and Vows." We know what lofty musings have arisen in poetic minds in the forests and by the "waves" of Ardenne; but the thoughts of our traveller took their rise in heaven.

As the productions of an able pen, these Meditations reflect lustre on the talents of their author, and give him as good a claim to be styled, as he has often been, the Christian Seneca, as a Latin father to be called the Christian Cicero. Each embodies some brief reflection, and closes with a practical resolution: in this last respect, reminding us of perhaps the most instructive document in the life of that wise self-observer, President Edwards. They are precious, as revealing thoughts which had long dwelt in a sanctified bosom, as recording the animadversions of one who was no less sagacious in reading the hearts of others than strict in watching his own, and as contributing wise directions to others advancing in the same heavenward journey. No reader need grudge a few extracts, should they bring him acquainted with a work, never to be forgotten, but perhaps not sufficiently known in practical divinity: —

"As there is a foolish wisdom, so there is a wise ignorance, in not prying into God's ark, in not inquiring into things not revealed. I would fain know all that I need, and all that I may. I leave God's secrets to himself. It is happy for me that God makes me of his court, though not of his council."

"The devil himself devised that slander of early holiness, *A young saint, an old devil.* Sometimes young devils have proved old saints, never the contrary: but true saints in youth do always form angels in their age. I will strive to be ever good; but if I should not find myself best at last, I should fear I was never good at all."

"As we say, There would be no thieves, if there were no receivers; so would there not be so many open mouths to detract and slander, if there were not so many open ears to entertain them. If I cannot stop another man's mouth from speaking ill, I will either open my mouth to reprove it, or else I will stop mine ears from hearing it; and let him see in my face that he hath no room in my heart."

"I am a stranger even at home: therefore if the dogs of the world bark at me, I neither care nor wonder."

"I care not for any companion, but such as may teach me somewhat, or learn somewhat of me; but these shall much pleasure me, neither know I whether more. For though it be an excellent thing to learn, yet I learn but to teach others."

"If I die, the world shall miss me but a little; I shall miss it less. Not it me — because it hath such store of better men: not I it — because it hath so much ill, and I shall have so much happiness."

"I acknowledge no Master of Requests in heaven but one — Christ my Mediator. I know I cannot be so happy as not to need him; nor so miserable that he should contemn me. Good prayers never come weeping home: I am sure I shall either receive what I ask, or what I should ask."

"I never loved those salamanders that are never well but when they are in the fire of contention. I will rather suffer a thousand wrongs than offer one: I will suffer a hundred, rather than return one: I will suffer many ere I complain of one, and endeavour to right it by contending. I have ever found that to strive with my superior is furious; with my equal, doubtful; with my inferior, sordid and base; with any, full of unquietness."

"Sudden extremity is a notable trial of faith. The faithful, more quickly than any casualty, can lift up his heart to his stay in heaven: whereas the worldling stands amazed and distraught with the evil, because he hath no refuge to fly unto. When, therefore, some sudden stitch girds me in the side, like to be the messenger of death; or when the sword of my enemy, in an unexpected assault, threatens my body; I will seriously note how I am affected: so the suddenest evil, as it shall not come unlooked-for, shall not go away unthought of. If I find myself courageous and heavenly-minded, I will rejoice in the truth of God's grace in me; knowing that one drachm of tried faith is worth a whole pound of speculative; and that which once stood by me will never fail me. If dejected and heartless, herein I will acknowledge cause of humiliation, and with all care and diligence seek to store myself against the danger following.

"I will be ever doing something, that either God when he cometh, or Satan when he tempteth, may find me busied."

"Each day is a new life, and an abridgment of the whole. I will so live, as if I counted every day my first and my last; as if I began to live but then, and should live no more afterwards."

"Rareness causes wonder. If the sun should arise but once on the earth, I doubt every man would be a Persian, and fall down and worship it."

"The proud man hath no God; the envious man hath no neighbour; the angry man hath not himself."

"I observe three seasons wherein a wise man differs not from a fool: in his infancy, in sleep, and in silence; for in the two former we are all fools, and in silence all are wise. Surely, he is not a fool that hath unwise thoughts, but he that utters them. Even concealed folly is wisdom, and sometimes wisdom uttered is folly. While others care how to speak, my care shall be how to hold my peace."

"Extremity distinguisheth friends. Worldly pleasures, like physicians, give us over when once we lie a-dying; and yet the deathbed had most need of comforts. Christ Jesus standeth by his in the pangs of death, and after death at the bar of judgment, not leaving them either in their bed or in their grave."

The living at Halsted was small, and, notwithstanding the moderate desires of the incumbent, so inadequate that he was forced "to write books to buy books." He applied to the patron for an augmentation of ten pounds *per annum*—a demand in itself not exorbitant, and only just, when it is remembered that Sir Robert Drury, by an abuse of power then frequent, was appropriating to his own uses a portion of the minister's emoluments. Sir Robert's refusal to comply with Mr. Hall's request, prepared him to accept any preferment that might be offered him. And he soon had more than he desired. For during a visit to London he was sought out by a friend, who came to tell him the high acceptance which his Meditations had obtained at the court of Prince Henry, and to urge him to embrace an opportunity of preaching before his Highness. Mr. Hall was then confined to his lodgings in Drury Lane by a severe cold. "I strongly pleaded my indisposition of body, and my inpreparation for any such work, together with my bashful fears, and utter unfitness for such a presence. My averseness doubled his importunity; in fine, he left me not till he had my engagement to preach the Sunday following at Richmond. He made way for me to that awful pulpit, and encouraged me by the favour of his noble lord the Earl of Essex. I preached: through the favour of my God, that sermon was not so well given as taken; insomuch as that sweet prince signified his desire to hear me again the Tuesday following; which done, that labour gave more contentment than the former, so as that prince both gave me his hand, and commanded me to his service. My patron seeing me, upon my return to London, looked after by some great persons, began to wish me at home, and told me that some or other would be snatching me up. I answered, it was in his power to prevent: Would he be pleased to make my maintenance but so competent as in right it should be, I would never stir from him. Instead of condescending, it pleased him to fall into an expostulation of the rate of competencies, affirming the variableness thereof according to our own estimation, and our either raising or moderating the causes of our expenses. I showed him the insufficiency of my means; but a harsh and unpleasing answer so disheartened me, that I resolved to embrace the first opportunity of my remove.

"Now whilst I was taken up with these anxious thoughts, a messenger came to me from my Lord Denny, my after most honourable patron, entreating me from his Lordship to speak with him. No sooner came I thither, than after a glad and noble welcome, I was entertained with the earnest offer of Waltham. The conditions were, like the mover of them, free and bountiful. I received them as from the munificent hand of my God; and returned full of the cheerful acknowledgments of a gracious providence over me. Too late now did my former noble patron relent, and offer me those terms which had before fastened me for ever. I returned home happy in a new master, and in a new patron; betwixt whom I divided myself and my labours, with much comfort, and no less acceptation.

"In the second year of mine attendance on his highness, when I came for my dismission from that monthly service, it pleased the prince to command me a longer stay; and at last upon mine allowed departure, by the mouth of Sir Thomas Challoner, his governor, to tender unto me a motion of more honour and favour than I was worthy of; which was, that it was his highness' pleasure and purpose to have me continually resident at the court as a constant attendant, whilst the rest held on their wonted vicissitudes; for which purpose his highness would obtain for me such preferments as should yield me full contentment. I returned my humblest thanks, and my readiness to sacrifice myself to the service of so gracious a master; but being conscious to myself of my unanswerableness to so great expectation, and loath to forsake so dear and noble a patron, who had placed much of his heart upon me, I did modestly put it off, and held close to my Waltham; where in a constant course I preached a long time (as I had done also at Halsted before) thrice in the week; yet never durst I climb into the pulpit to preach any sermon, whereof I had not before, in my poor and plain fashion, penned every word in the same order wherein I hoped to deliver it, although in the expression I listed not to be a slave to syllables."

His attendance at court did not long detain him from the undivided performance of his pastoral duties at Waltham; for the hopes of the nation were quickly prostrated by the death of the amiable prince, which occurred Nov. 6, 1612; and on the first day of the following year Mr. Hall discharged the last office of a love which had supplanted the deference of the courtier, by preaching a farewell sermon to the prince's household, then dissolved at St. James's. The discourse contains repeated testimonies of the grateful and affectionate admiration with which the chaplain cherished the memory of his illustrious patron — testimonies which royal station has seldom so justly merited. But history has recorded the engaging character of King James's eldest son so fully, as to supersede any extracts from this ardent eulogy. The closing sentences, however, possess a pathos and an appropriateness to the text (Rev. xxi. 3) which will justify their insertion here:—"But what if we shall meet here no more?—what if we shall no more see one another's face? Brethren, we shall once meet together above; we shall once see the glorious face of God, and never look off again. Let it not overgrieve us to leave these tabernacles of stone, since we must shortly lay down these tabernacles of clay, and enter into tabernacles not made with hands, eternal in the heavens. Till then, farewell, my dear brethren, farewell in the Lord. Go in peace, and live as those that have lost such a master, and as those that serve a Master whom they cannot lose. And the God of peace go with you, and prosper you in all your ways, and so fix this tabernacle in you upon earth, that you may be received into those tabernacles of the New Jerusalem, and dwell with him for ever in that glory which he hath provided for all that love him. Amen."

The sixteen years which Mr. Hall spent at Waltham were among the most pleasant of his life, for they were the least distracted. His circumstances freed him from worldly solicitudes; the national convulsions which agitated his old age, of which he was sometimes the sorrowful witness, and sometimes the unoffending victim, had not commenced; his home was the shining abode of that happiness, a beam of which occasionally brightens upon his pages; and in that home no apartment was more loved or frequented than his study. What Hall has already described, no other should attempt to tell; and we do not believe that any reader ever complained of the length of the following letter, which gives in brief the distribution of this good man's time for many years together. It will possess an additional value to those whose distinguished prerogative has placed them in situations of like advantage:—

"Every day is a little life, and our whole life is but a day repeated: whence it is that old Jacob numbered his life by days, and Moses desired to be taught this point of holy arithmetic, to number not his years but his days. Those, therefore, that dare lose a day are dangerously prodigal, those that dare misspend it desperate. All days are his who gave time a beginning and continuance; yet some he hath made ours, not to command but to use. In none may we forget him: in some we must forget all besides him. First, therefore, I desire to awake at those hours, not when I will, but when I must: pleasure is not a fit rule for rest, but health; neither do I consult so much with the sun, as with mine own necessity, whether of body or in that of the mind. If this vassal could well serve me waking, it should never sleep; but now it must be pleased that it may be serviceable. Now, when sleep is rather driven away than leaves me, I would ever awake with God; my first thoughts are for Him who hath made the night for rest, and the day for travail; and as he gives, so blesses both. If my heart be early seasoned with his presence, it will savour of him all day after. While my body is dressing, not with an effeminate curiosity, nor yet with rude neglect, my mind addresses itself to her ensuing task, bethinking what is to be done, and in what order, and marshalling (as it may) my hours with my work. That done, after some while's meditation, I walk up to my masters and companions, my books; and sitting down amongst them with the best contentment, I dare not reach forth my hand to salute any of them, till I have first looked up to heaven, and craved favour of Him to whom all my studies are duly referred; without whom I can neither profit nor labour. After this, out of no great variety, I call forth those which may best fit my occasions, wherein I am not too scrupulous of age. Sometimes I put myself to school to one of those ancients whom the Church hath honoured with the name of Fathers, whose volumes I confess not to open without a secret reverence of their holiness and gravity; sometimes to those later Doctors, who want nothing but age to make them classical; always to God's book. That day is lost, whereof some hours are not improved in those divine monuments: others I turn over out of choice, these out of duty. Ere I can have sate unto weariness, my family, having now overcome all household distractions, invite me to our common devotions; not without some short preparation. These, heartily performed, send me up with a more strong and cheerful appetite to my former work, which I find made easy to me by intermission and variety. Now, therefore, can I deceive the hours with change of pleasures, that is, of labours. One while my eyes are busied, another while my hand, and sometimes my mind takes the burden from them both. One hour is spent in textual divinity, another in controversy; histories relieve them both. Now, when my mind is weary of others' labours, it begins to undertake its own: sometimes it meditates, and winds up for future use; sometimes it lays forth its conceits into present discourse, sometimes for itself, often for others. Neither know I whether it works or plays in these thoughts; I am sure no sport hath more pleasure, no work more use. Only the decay of a weak body makes me think these delights insensibly laborious. Thus could I all day (as ringers use) make myself music with changes, were it not that this faint monitor interrupts me still in the midst of my busy pleasures, and enforces me both to respite and repast. I must yield to both; while my body and mind are joined together in these unequal couples, the better must follow the weaker. Before my meals, therefore, and after, I let myself loose from all thoughts, and now would forget that I ever studied. A full mind takes away the body's appetite, no less than a full body makes a dull and unwieldy mind. Company, discourse, recreations, are now seasonable and welcome. These prepare me for a diet, not gluttonous but medicinal. The palate may not be pleased, but the stomach, nor that for its own sake; neither would I think any of these comforts worth respect in themselves, but in their use, in their end, so far as they may enable me to better things. If I see any dish to tempt my palate, I fear a serpent in that apple, and would please myself by a wilful denial. I rise capable of more, not desirous; not now immediately from my trencher to my book, but after some intermission. Moderate speed is a sure help to all proceedings; where those things which are prosecuted with violence of endeavour or desire, either succeed not, or continue not.

"After my later meal, my thoughts are slight: only my memory may be charged with her task of recalling what was committed to her custody in the day; and my heart is busy in examining my hands and mouth, and all other senses, of that day's behaviour. And now the evening is come, no tradesman doth more carefully take in his wares, clear his shop-board, and shut his windows, than I would shut up my thoughts and clear my mind. That student shall live miserably, who, like a camel, lies down under his burden. All this done, calling together my family, we end the day with God. How miserable is the condition of those men who spend the time as if it were given them, and not lent! as if hours were waste creatures, and such as should never be accounted for! as if God would take this for a good bill of reckoning, *Item,* spent upon my pleasures, 40 years!

"Such are my common days; but God's day calls for another respect. The same sun arises on this day, and enlightens it: yet, because the Sun of righteousness arose upon it, and gave a new life to the world in it, and drew the strength of God's moral precept unto it; therefore justly do we sing with the Psalmist, ' This is the day which the Lord hath made.' Now I forget the world, and in a sort myself; and deal with my wonted thoughts, as great men use, who at some times of their privacy, forbid the access of all suitors. Prayer, meditation, reading, hearing, preaching, singing, good conference, are the business of this day, which I dare not bestow on any work or pleasure, but heavenly. I hate superstition on the one side, and looseness on the other; but I find it hard to offend in too much devotion, easy in profaneness. The whole week is sanctified by this day; and according to my care of this day, is my blessing on the rest."

So intent was he on these beloved employments that, to secure leisure for study, he is said* to have restricted himself at one time to a single meal in the day. He was not a solitary instance of the like abstinence among his contemporaries. But that he was not criminally negligent of his health may be inferred from various circumstances. He wisely imitated Isaac, " who went out in the evening to meditate."† And not only did he from time to time indulge himself with " his other soul," music; but like many other worthies formed for patient contemplation, he occasionally took down the angle, and by the river side pursued the calling symbolical of his own. To the remonstrances of a considerate friend he answers —" Fear not my immoderate studies. I have a body that controls me enough in these courses; my friends need not. There is nothing whereof I could sooner surfeit, if I durst neglect my body to satisfy my mind; but while I affect knowledge, my weakness checks me, and says, ' Better a little learning, than no health.' I yield, and patiently abide myself debarred of my chosen felicity."

The quiet tenor of his life at Waltham was thrice interrupted by a call from his Majesty, to bear a part in undertakings of public interest. The first was in 1616, when he went to France to grace the splendid retinue of the British ambassador, Viscount Doncaster. Had the festivities of that brilliant occasion possessed any attractions for our sober-minded theologian, he was effectually precluded from enjoying them by a dangerous sickness, which overtook him soon after his arrival, and lasted with his stay. When the time arrived for the return of the ambassador, he was kindly invited by the illustrious Du Moulin to reside with him till his recovery should be established. " I thanked him,",says Dr. Hall, " but resolved if I could but creep homewards to put myself upon the journey. A litter was provided, but of so little ease, that Simeon's penitential lodging, or a malefactor's stocks, had been less penal. I crawled down from my close chamber into that carriage, ' in which you seemed to me

* Lloyd's Memoirs, p. 419.   † Art of Divine Meditation, Chap. X.

to be conveyed as in a coffin;'* as Mr. Moulin wrote to me afterward; that misery had I endured in all the long passage from Paris to Dieppe, being left alone to the surly muleteers, had not the providence of my good God brought me to St. German's, upon the very setting out of those coaches, which had staid there upon that morning's entertainment of my lord ambassador. How glad was I that I might change my seat and my company. In the way, beyond all expectation, I began to gather some strength; whether the fresh air or the desires of my home revived me, so much and so sudden reparation ensued, as was sensible to myself, and seemed strange to others. Being shipped at Dieppe, the sea used us hardly, and after a night and a great part of the day following, sent us back well wind-beaten, to that bleak haven whence we set forth, forcing us to a more pleasing land-passage, through the coasts of Normandy and Picardy; towards the end whereof my former complaint returned upon me, and landing with me, accompanied me to and at my long-desired home." On his return, he found that, during his absence, the king had conferred upon him the deanery of Worcester.

Early in the following year he was called to accompany his Majesty on his famous expedition into Scotland, for the purpose of establishing Episcopacy.† It was James's fortune to have at his command men whose consciences acquiesced in, whose talents vindicated, and whose worth commended the measures which his vanity suggested, and his obstinacy enforced. The ceremonies, afterwards obnoxiously distinguished as the Five Articles of Perth, were the main cause of the royal pedant's progress into Scotland on this occasion. He did one thing wisely when he took in his train an Episcopalian so sincere, so learned, and so reasonable as Dr. Hall. His words had more persuasiveness than his master's ordinances; and though we do not know that he came any speed, the meekness and earnestness with which he argued the question, were better fitted to overcome the presbyterian prejudices of Scotchmen, than the domineering arrogance of one whose arguments owed all their weight to his station. He respected the presbyterian ministers, and they recompensed his good opinion with their cordial esteem. His more imperious and less logical brethren envied and misrepresented his reputation. As he says himself—" The great love and respect that I found, both from the ministers and people, brought me no small envy from some of our own. Upon a commonly received supposition, that his Majesty would have no farther use of his chaplains, after his remove from Edinburgh (forasmuch as the divines of the country, whereof there is great store and worthy choice, were allotted to every station), I easily obtained, through the solicitation of my ever-honoured Lord of Carlisle, to return with him before my fellows. No sooner was I gone, than suggestions were made to his Majesty of my over plausible demeanour and doctrine to that already prejudice people, for which his Majesty, after a gracious acknowledgment of my good service then done, called me upon his return to a favourable and mild account; not more freely professing what informations had been given against me, than his own full satisfaction with my sincere and just answer; as whose excellent wisdom well saw, that such winning carriage of mine could be no hinderance to those his great designs. At the same time his Majesty, having secret notice that a letter was coming to me from Mr. W. Struthers, a reverend and learned divine of Edinburgh, concerning the five points they proposed and urged to the Church of Scotland, was pleased to impose upon me an earnest charge, to give him a full answer in satisfaction to those his modest doubts; and at large to declare my judgment concerning these required observations, which I speedily performed with so great approbation of his Majesty, that it pleased him to command a transcript thereof, as I was informed, publicly to be read in their most famous university; the effect whereof his Majesty vouchsafed to signify afterwards unto some of my best friends, with allowance beyond my hopes."

* In quâ videbaris mihi efferri, tanquam in sandapilâ.
† For an account of his Majesty's doings on this occasion, see Calderwood's History, pp. 673, et seq.

In 1618, the Synod of Dort assembled to pronounce a judgment on the controversies introduced by the new sect of Arminians.* As they desired the attendance of divines from the various reformed churches, Dr. Hall was one of four deputed to represent the Church of England. But he had not attended two months, when the deleterious influence of a Dutch atmosphere, and the sleepless nights of a garrison town, reduced his delicate frame to such a state of weakness that he became unfit to give his presence regularly, and came to the reluctant conclusion that he must withdraw. Before setting out, he complied with a request of the Synod, and preached before them a sermon in Latin, which he was enabled to do with unexpected vigour, having enjoyed during the previous night his first sound rest after a wakeful fortnight. At first he only retired to the Hague, in the hope that a change of place, and the attentions which he received in the house of the ambassador, might recruit his exhausted strength; but experiencing no salutary result, he accepted his Majesty's recal. "Returning by Dort, I sent in my sad farewell to that grave assembly, who by common vote sent to me the president of the Synod, and the assistants, with a respectful and gracious valediction. Neither did the Deputies of my Lords the States neglect to visit me; and after a noble acknowledgment of more good service from me than I durst own, dismissed me with an honourable retribution, and sent after me a rich medal of gold, the portraiture of the Synod, for a precious monument of their respects to my poor endeavours, who failed not, whilst I was at the Hague, to impart unto them my poor advice concerning the proceeding of that synodical meeting. The difficulties of my return in such weakness were many and great; wherein, if ever, God manifested his special providence to me, in overruling the cross accidents of that passage, and, after many dangers and despairs, contriving my safe arrival." The gold medal was transmitted to him from the States, through the eminent scholar Daniel Heinsius, and from all the gratifying circumstances attending its presentation, was a memorial which he justly valued. It is conspicuously introduced in his portrait preserved in Emanuel College. Dr. Hall had never occasion to be ashamed of his connexion with the venerable Synod of Dort, notwithstanding the aspersions heaped upon it as soon as its sittings had terminated, and propagated to the present day. Amongst other calumnies, his colleagues were accused of a conspiracy against the Arminians, and of having taken an oath before-hand to vote down the remonstrants. The slander might have refuted itself; but Dr. Hall published a letter which effectually dispelled it, and we are not aware that this falsehood has ever been revived.

The errors which this Synod condemned, but did not cure, soon crossed the German Ocean, to divide the churches of Britain. "Sides were taken, and pulpits rang everywhere of these opinions." The pacific spirit of this holy man was wounded, when he heard the watchwords of Arminian controversy passed as freely and angrily in England as they had ever been in Holland. When the convocation of the Church met in 1623, Dr. Hall preached a sermon in Latin before it, of which an English translation by his son is preserved among his other works. Its tone is as conciliatory as might have been anticipated from the known tendencies of the author, and its very title is nobly indicative of his designs and feelings,—"Noah's dove bringing an olive of peace to the tossed ark of Christ's church." He laboured in other ways to restore the unity of which he mourned the departure; and published, as "a project of pacification," some remarks "on the five busy articles, commonly known by the name of Arminius." In this his mediatory interference met with no better reward than did that of Richard Baxter in a similar controversy a short time after; for it brought upon him the suspicions of many, and the open hostility of some in either party. As

* A full account of this famous Synod will be found in Hales's Golden Remains, and in Brandt's History of the Reformation in the Low Countries. But perhaps there is none better than the Articles of the Synod, with a historical preface, translated by the late Mr. Scott of Aston-Sandford.

he calmly remarks, " I was scorched a little with this flame, which I desired to quench."

Hitherto Dr. Hall had sustained the lighter responsibilities and easier labours of a parish priest. When he had adventured in controversy, no other necessity was laid upon him than the love which he bore to truth, and concern at beholding the best cause the worst supported. He had enjoyed frequent, if not long, intervals of that contemplative leisure after which his soul habitually thirsted. He was now called to govern a church where his ambition had only been to serve; but the period of his elevation was one when the office of a bishop was least likely to be courted. His episcopate extended over the most tempestuous period which the English hierarchy has encountered. The vessel was heaving when he was summoned to his post; and the billow which bore him to the shore was that which swept over the wreck.

It was in 1627 that Dr. Hall was consecrated Bishop of Exeter. He had previously declined the see of Gloucester. He entered on this high station aware of the suspicions from many quarters which attended him: " for some that sate at the stern of the Church had him in great jealousy for too much favour of Puritanism." He had early intelligence that certain persons were set as spies to watch over him. However, he formed his resolution, and walked wisely according to its rule. In his diocese he found some who did not comply with the ecclesiastical canons; but by his prudent and gainly conduct he reclaimed all the refractory, except two who retired from his jurisdiction. What greatly tended to secure harmony within his extensive charge, was the honourable determination which he formed at the outset, and to which he steadily adhered, of never imposing any new orders or rites on his clergy. This, with the full toleration of week-day lectures and extra-canonical services, and the favourable notice which he took of the more diligent among the clergy, secured for his diocese an invidious pre-eminence over those around it, and brought on him the resentment of his more narrow-minded brethren on the bench, as well as the hostility of the less exemplary within his own cure. At court he was informed against, and "was three several times upon his knees to his Majesty, to answer these great criminations;" insomuch that he "plainly told the Lord Archbishop of Canterbury, that rather than he would be obnoxious to these slanderous tongues of his misinformers, he would cast up his rochet." The unanimity and attachment of his clergy were his sufficient compensation for the obloquy which others so unworthily cast upon him. But a doubtful oath imposed in 1640,* and which this conscientious prelate could not tender to his clergy, gave rise to dissensions, through the officious interposition of some strangers. The majority still adhered to him; but, the firebrands being now scattered, he foresaw a conflagration. In this conjuncture he was the more ready to accept the offer of a translation to Norwich, made to him in the year following (1641), by King Charles. With his promotion to this see he closes his *Specialties*. " But how I took the Tower in my way; and how I have been dealt with since my repair hither, I could be lavish in the sad report, ever desiring my good God to enlarge my heart in thankfulness to him, for the sensible experience I have had of his fatherly hand over me, in the deepest of all my afflictions, and to strengthen me for whatsoever other trials he shall be pleased to call me unto; that being found faithful unto the death, I may obtain that crown of life, which he has ordained for all those that overcome."

The value of Bishop Hall's services, and the perils of his situation, will be better understood when it is remembered that Laud was at this time the primate of England. Among the other inflictions of that arbitrary and unprincipled prelate, was the famous " Book of Spirits." This he revived, and required that it should be read from every pulpit in England. Those who resisted were silenced for their puritanism; but the piety and independence of Hall rescued the clergy of his diocese. And although the archbishop, in the plenitude of his zeal against evangelical religion, had summoned be-

* The synodical or *et cetera* oath.

fore the Star Chamber some pious individuals, who had founded lectureships and purchased impropriations for the supply of destitute parishes, and compelled them, at a prodigious sacrifice, to relinquish their scheme, Bishop Hall had the intrepidity to protect within his bounds the obnoxious lecturers.

His moderation, however, did not save him from the storm which at this time burst after long threatening, and carried the episcopal order before it. The circumstance which implicated him was, at the worst, an act of unadvisedness. When the Parliament met towards the close of 1641, the popular indignation against the bishops had risen so high, that the House of Lords was beset by an armed mob of many thousands, who, by the cry of " No bishops!" gave unequivocal indications of their object. Such of the order as happened to be present, including the Archbishop of York and the subject of this memoir, felt that their lives were in jeopardy, and escaped with difficulty to their homes; — some under the protection of the Earl of Manchester, others by secret and circuitous routes, and the rest by remaining till the night was far advanced. Having been so narrowly rescued, the bishops felt no inclination to expose themselves again to similar danger, and were induced to sign a document prepared by the Archbishop of York, petitioning the King and Parliament to guarantee their safety in attending on their legislative duties, and protesting against all enactments which might pass during their absence. This protest was instantly laid hold of by their enemies as a most unconstitutional and treasonable declaration, and made the ground of an impeachment against the twelve who had signed it. " We poor souls," says Hall, " who little thought that we had done anything that might deserve a chiding, are now called to our knees at the bar, and charged severally with high treason, being not a little astonished at the suddenness of this crimination, compared with the perfect innocency of our own intentions. But now traitors we are in all haste, and must be dealt with accordingly. For on January 30, (1642), in all the extremity of frost, at eight o'clock in the dark evening, are we voted to the Tower; only two of our number had the favour of the black rod by reason of their age, which though desired by a noble lord on my behalf, would not be yielded: wherein I acknowledge and bless the gracious providence of God; for had I been gratified, I had been undone both in body and purse, the rooms being strait, and the expense beyond the reach of my estate. The news of our crime and imprisonment soon flew over the city, and was entertained by our well-wishers with ringing of bells and bonfires; who now gave us up (not without great triumph) for lost men, railing on our perfidiousness, and adjudging us to what foul deaths they pleased."

At this time of surprise and peril, with the exultations of his enemies ringing in his ears, and an impeachment for his life hanging over him, Bishop Hall addressed a letter to a private friend, so full of the noble sentiments and indignant utterance which conscious rectitude inspires, in harmony with Christian humility, that we regret being compelled to give only extracts:—

" My intentions and this place are such strangers, that I cannot enough marvel how they met. But, howsoever, I do in all humility kiss the rod wherewith I smart, as well knowing whose hand it is that wields it. To that infinite justice who can be innocent? but to my king and country never heart was, or can be more clear; and I shall beshrew my hand if it shall have (against my thoughts) justly offended either; and if either say so, I reply not; as having learned not to contest with those that can command legions.

" You tell me in what fair terms I stood not long since with the world; how large room I had in the hearts of the best men: but can you tell me how I lost it? Truly I have in the presence of God narrowly searched my own bosom; I have impartially ransacked this fag-end of my life, and curiously examined every step of my ways; and I cannot, by the most exact scrutiny of my saddest thoughts, find what it is that I have done to forfeit that good estimation wherewith you say I was once blessed.

"Can my enemies say, that I bore up the reins of government too hard, and exercised my jurisdiction in a rigorous and tyrannical way, insolently lording it over my charge? Malice itself, perhaps, would, but dare not speak it; or if it should, the attestation of so numerous and grave a clergy would choke such impudence. Let them witness whether they were not still entertained, with an equal return of reverence, as if they had been all bishops with me, or I only a presbyter with them. Let them say whether aught here looked despotical, or sounded rather of imperious command than of brotherly complying; whether I have not rather from some beholders undergone the censure of a too humble remissness, as stooping too low beneath the eminence of episcopal dignity; whether I have not suffered as much in some opinions, for the winning mildness of my administration, as some others for a rough severity.

"Can they say that I barred the free course of religious exercises, by the suppression of painful and peaceable preachers? If shame will suffer any man to object it, let me challenge him to instance but in one hand. Nay, the contrary is so famously known in the western parts, that every mouth will herein justify me. What free admission and encouragement have I always given to all the sons of peace, that came with God's message in their mouths! What mis-suggestions have I waved! How have I often and publicly professed, that as well might we complain of too many stars in the sky, as too many orthodox preachers in the church!

"Can they challenge me as a close and back-stair friend to Popery or Arminianism, who have in so many pulpits, and so many presses, cried down both? Surely the very paper that I have spent in the refutation of both these, is enough to stop more mouths than can be guilty of this calumny.

"Lastly, since no man can offer to upbraid me with too much pomp, which is wont to be the common eye-sore of our envied profession, can any man pretend to a ground of taxing me of too much worldliness? Surely, of all the vices forbidden in the decalogue, there is no one which my heart, upon due examination can less fasten upon me than this. He that made it, knows that he hath put into it a true disregard (save only for necessary use) of the world, and all that it can boast of, whether for profit, pleasure, or glory. No, no; I know the world too well to doat upon it. It were too great a shame for a philosopher, a Christian, a divine, a bishop, to have his thoughts grovelling here upon earth; for mine, they scorn the employment, and look upon all these sublunary distractions with no other eyes than contempt.

"To shut up all, and to surcease your trouble, I write not this as one that would pump for favour and reputation from the disaffected multitude (for I charge you that what passes privately betwixt us may not fall under common eyes), but only with this desire and intention, to give you true grounds, when you shall hear my name mentioned with a causeless offence, to yield me a just and charitable vindication. Go you on still to do the office of a true friend, yea, the duty of a just man; in speaking in the cause of the dumb, in righting the innocent, in rectifying the misguided; and lastly, the service of a faithful and christian patriot, in helping the times with the best of your prayers, which is the daily task of your much devoted and thankful friend, — Jos. Norvic."

After a bill had passed both Houses, and obtained the royal assent, for depriving the bishops of their seats in parliament, the Commons proceeded to impeach the twelve who had signed the protestation, at the bar of the Lords, on a charge of high treason. But finding that there was no likelihood of obtaining a conviction of a crime so serious, they assumed a lower ground. A bill was introduced and passed by both Houses, declaring the bishops delinquents of a high nature, depriving them of their ecclesiastical authority, and assigning to each a stated yearly maintenance. The bishops were then released, on giving bond to a great amount.

It was in the month of June that Bishop Hall found himself once more at large, after a confinement of five months. During this time he had not been idle. For besides taking his rotation with his brethren in preaching on the Lord's day, and corresponding with his friends, he wrote his work entitled, "The Free Prisoner." On his release, he instantly repaired to Norwich, the seat of his new bishopric, and was received with more respect than he anticipated from the temper of the times. He preached on the Sabbath following his arrival to a crowded audience, and continued his services unmolested till the month of March following (1643). The ordinance of sequestration was then issued, and the commissioners of Parliament came to inform the Bishop that he must abandon his palace, and that they were required to seize on all his estate, real and personal. They went to the extent of their warrant, "not leaving so much as a dozen of trenchers, or his children's pictures, out of their curious inventory." But before the time fixed for the public sale of his goods arrived, a pious lady, unknown to the Bishop, redeemed his furniture, until he should be able to repurchase it; and a benevolent divine of his diocese rendered an additional service, by paying the estimated value of his library. Being now deprived of every source of income, he applied to the committee on sequestrations for the annuity granted by Parliament; but he was told that an order had come down inhibiting any such allowance. In answer, however, to a petition from his wife, a smaller yearly payment was assigned to her; though, by a most unrighteous exaction, out of this scanty fund the Bishop had to defray assessments and monthly payments for lands which were no longer his. At last, after his endurance had been sorely tried, by witnessing the defacing of his cathedral, and the demolition of its splendid organ, he was ejected from the palace, which his straitened means rendered no longer a suitable habitation. A generous neighbour relinquished his house for the accommodation of the Bishop and his family, where he only remained till he procured the lease of a small property at Higham, in the neighbourhood of Norwich.

Of his subsequent life, spent in retirement and without molestation, we know little; but that little is enough to prove that its latter end was worthy of its beginning. He continued to preach until his infirmities and legal prohibitions had disabled him. Then "as oft and long as he was able, this learned Gamaliel was not only content, but very diligent to sit at the feet of the youngest of his disciples, as diligent a hearer as he had been a preacher." After the death of Charles I, he continued to observe with his family a weekly fast because of it. Though his fortune was so greatly reduced, a number of poor widows were his weekly pensioners. In 1652 he lost his wife, and then he wrote a tract, almost his last, entitled, " Songs in the Night." From this interesting memorial we see how this grey-headed saint went down to his grave "sorrowing yet rejoicing." " Have I lost my goods and foregone a fair estate? Had all the earth been mine, what is it to heaven? Had I been the lord of all the world, what were this to a kingdom of glory?

" Have I parted with a dear consort; the sweet companion of my youth; the tender nurse of my age; the partner of my sorrows for these forty-eight years? She is but stept a little before me to that happy rest, which I am panting towards, and wherein I shall speedily overtake her. In the meantime and ever, my soul is espoused to that glorious and immortal Husband from whom it shall never be parted.

" Am I bereaved of some of my dear children, the sweet pledges of our matrimonial love; whose parts and hopes promised me comfort in my declined age? Why am I not rather thankful it hath pleased my God, out of my loins, to furnish heaven with some happy guests? Why do I not, instead of mourning for their loss, sing praises to God for preferring them to that eternal blessedness?

" Am I afflicted with bodily pains and sickness, which banishes all sleep from my eyes, and exercises me with a lingering torture? Ere long this momentary distemper shall end in an everlasting rest."

And so it was; for though his painful malady was prolonged for four years more, they will appear but a " moment" now. The grace which enabled him to overcome at last, strengthened him to bear throughout. One who saw has recorded, that "though sorely afflicted with bodily diseases, he bore them all with as much patience as hath been seen in any flesh, except that of the Saviour." And when his time drew near, many of the noble, and learned, and pious, gathered to his chamber to implore his dying prayers, and bear away his dying benediction. After much time spent in devotion, and many words of gracious exhortation, he summoned the expiring energies of nature to make the last confession of his faith; and when so engaged, his strength departed, the agonies of death came over him, and then he fell asleep. He died on the 8th of September 1656, when he had reached his 82d year.

His will assigned the *churchyard* as his burying place; adding as his reason, " I do not hold God's house a meet repository for the dead bodies of the greatest saints." He bequeathed £30 to each widow in the village where he was born, and in that where he died.

Here our sketch should have ended. But on looking back, we feel conscious of an involuntary injury to the memory of this great man, in having presented, even with his own assistance, a view of his character so exclusively external. We are aware that publications, parochial and diocesan cares, the business of the nation, the defence of orthodoxy, journeys of observation or of diplomacy — in short, that the whole *busy* work of existence formed but in part the life of Bishop Hall. His was eminently A LIFE OF CONTEMPLATION.

He fell upon a time when the Church of England contained many men whose genius and piety would have immortalized and sainted them in an earlier age. With a theology less accurate and a devotion less enlightened than signalized their puritan successors, and with a piety less strenuous and sanguine than that which poured in animation through the stern and athletic orthodoxy of our covenanting fathers, a jealous sincerity, a serene quietism, and an unflinching self-denial, were the commanding characteristics of their religion, which made it awful and interesting to others, and safe for themselves. It wanted in the activity of life and the diffusiveness of Christianity. It was introverted, not aggressive. It mused and soliloquized. It was monastic, and dwelt alone. It was more amiable in its forbearance, than meritorious for its services. In its narrow channel it flowed deep, but it seldom overflowed.

The idolatry of one party has injured them with another; but the day is coming that will restore to each his own. In its first outburst, the noise of faction will overwhelm the voice of piety, still and small, but it cannot last so long. And now that the rancour of raging polemics is settling down into forgetfulness, the memorial and the works of these excellent of the earth are reviving, and posterity, more just to them than they were to themselves, is admitting the claims of either party to attributes of worth which they could not discern in one another.

For ourselves, with leanings all away from prelacy, we would commemorate with as much alacrity as we have felt delight in contemplating the singular devotion and exalted genius which distinguished many a high churchman of the first Charles's reign — the exemplars of an age only moving regret by the contrasted littleness of our own. To specify all the instances would not be easy; and it is hard to select a few. But there was *George Herbert*, the gentle, the elegant — majestically humble, gravely gay—as antithetic in his character as in his own quaint poesy — passing no week without music, and no day without showing mercy — converting life into one Sabbath, and fulfilling his invocation to that sacred day, when it and he " flew hand in hand to heaven." *Jeremy Taylor*, too, soaring in ether with a load of learning which would have kept another grovelling — now casting a look of hope to the ancient models, anon dashed by the contemplation of his own ideal — beside the waters of Lough Neagh, musing on the mysterious tower of its romantic island, and its more mysterious antiquity, till his " thoughts wandered through eternity;" or amid the ruins of its monastery listening for the reviving echoes of its wonted orisons, until his dreaming fancy beheld in the evening light of autumn its tapers rekindled, and in the falling shadows marshalled anew the sacerdotal procession—an imagination revelling in all the picturesque and sublime of religion, and a heart responding with harmonious impulse to its loftiest requirements. There was *Nicholas Ferrar* — the Church-of-England man—closing his eyes on propitious fortune and radiant beauty, and that nothing earthly might distract his gaze, and no rest short of heaven allure his sense, immured in a protestant convent—meting to himself scanty slumbers on the hard pillow of an anchoret — with his goods feeding all the needy except himself, and indulging no luxury save the midnight music of the choristers whom he retained to "praise God nightly" in the oratory of Little Gidding. And *Henry Hammond*, economizing his time by the abundance of his prayers, and increasing his wealth by the wise munificence of his charities—living for his friends, reducing kindness to a law, and welcoming the interruption which called for its exercise—amidst bodily sufferings, producing works of research and judgment, demanding but sufficient to destroy the most vigorous health—"omne jam tulerat punctum, cùm Mors, quasi suum adjiciens calculum, terris abstulit." Among these and many more,* almost as ascetic in his life, but above them all in the largeness of his views and the soundness of his creed, we recognise the gifted author of the following " Contemplations."

The " art of heavenly meditation," was that which he had chiefly studied. Even among his contemporaries, there were few who combined such density of expression with such amplitude of thought — few who had studied the Fathers so diligently, and who could command them so readily — few who had drunk so deeply the classic inspiration—few who had entered into the meaning of Scripture, with the same spirit of quick apprehension and thorough appreciation—and fewer still who had learned to dwell so much on high. The spirit that taught the prophets to speak, taught him to understand. In his company we feel that we are not attended by a perfunctory and hireling guide,— but by one whose profession is his passion, whose familiarity with sacred things is reverential — whose insight is the result of love and long acquaintance.

He was a man of peace, and delighted in the retirement without which it is seldom enjoyed. " The court is for honour, the city for gain, the country for quietness ; a blessing that need not, in the judgment of the wisest, yield to the other two. Yea, how many have we known that having nothing but a coat of thatch to hide them from heaven, yet have pitied the careful pomp of the mighty? How much more may they who have full hands and quiet hearts pity them both?" " What a heaven," as he elsewhere exclaims, " lives a scholar in, that at once in one close room can daily converse with all the glorious martyrs and fathers! — that can single out at pleasure, either sententious Tertullian, or grave Cyprian, or learned Jerome, or flowing Chrysostom, or divine Ambrose, or devout Bernard,— or who alone is all these—heavenly Augustin, and talk with them, and hear their wise and holy counsels, verdicts, resolutions : yea, to rise higher, with courtly Isaiah, with learned Paul, with all their fellow-prophets, apostles : yet more, like another Moses, with God himself!" In such retirement passed the chosen hours of our author, and refreshed by such converse he penned his Contemplations.

> More sweet than odours caught by him who sails
> Near spicy shores of Araby the blest,
> A thousand times more exquisitely sweet,
> The freight of holy feeling which we meet,
> In thoughtful moments, wafted by the gale
> From fields where good men walk, or bowers wherein they rest."✝

* See Walton's Life of Herbert — Heber's Life of Taylor — Peckard's Life of Ferrar—and Fell's Life of Hammond. For others of the same period, the reader is referred to Lloyd's Memoirs, Walton's Lives, and Dr. C. Wordsworth's interesting collection of " Ecclesiastical Biography."
✝ Wordsworth.

The Work now laid before him, the reader will find richly freighted with this "holy feeling." Its value does not consist alone nor chiefly in the acute expositions of Scripture incidentally introduced — in the descriptive vivacity which paints the Bible scenes to the eye of fancy, or enacts its history anew — in the apothegmatical *naïveté*, which deals out so calmly yet so pointedly the eager observations of a penetrating eye, on the various wisdom and folly, virtues and vices, with which a long life had made him familiar. Nor is it only in the ardent enforcement of Christian duty, and eloquent statement of Christian privilege, that this book bespeaks the attention of the serious reader. It presents in one view the Bible, and a mind rich in feeling and accomplishments, lovingly exploring and reverently interpreting the Bible; nay, as it were, fraternizing and amalgamating with it. These Contemplations will not be read with advantage by one who peruses them as a common book, as hastily and as unconcerned; nor will they be read aright without adverting continually to the peculiar mode of their execution, to their author and their end. In the former particular, they closely resemble the Confessions of his favourite Augustin, consisting of reflections and ejaculations, so mingled as to blend devotion with instruction. The author, whom we have already attempted to pourtray, recurs to our imagination as the gentle, self-denied, and benignant parish priest, whom his neighbours met and eyed reverentially as he took his stated evening walk, cheerful at times, but oftener pensive, in the fields near Waltham parsonage — a man of that calm resolution and ardent faith, which could at any warning have followed the Saviour whom he loved to prison and to death, and whose aspirations often soared so high as to forget the Meshech where he sojourned. And the *end* will be answered, if we who read them, learn for ourselves to live the same divine life, and acquire the same skill in heavenly meditation — an art little esteemed and less practised in an age which would not be too busy if it thought as much as it toils; and an art concerning which a great proficient* has left a testimony which may compensate for our omissions, and form the appropriate introduction to the work that follows.

"Be acquainted with this heavenly work, and thou wilt in some degree be acquainted with God; thy joys will be spiritual, prevalent, and lasting, according to the nature of their blessed object; thou wilt have comfort in life and death: when thou hast neither wealth, nor health, nor the pleasure of this world, yet wilt thou have comfort: without the presence or help of any friend, without a minister, without a book, when all means are denied thee, or taken from thee, yet mayest thou have vigorous, real comfort. Thy graces will be mighty, active, and victorious; and daily joy, which is thus fetched from heaven, will be thy strength. Thou wilt be as one that stands on the top of an exceeding high mountain; he looks down on the world as if it were quite below him — fields and woods, cities and towns, seem to him but little spots. Thus despicably wilt thou look on all things here below. The greatest princes will seem but as grasshoppers; the busy, contentious, covetous world, but as a heap of ants. Men's threatenings will be no terror to thee, nor the honours of this world any strong enticement: temptations will be more harmless, as having lost their strength; and afflictions less grievous as having lost their sting; and every mercy will be better known, and better relished."

* Baxter.

CONTEMPLATIONS.

BOOK I.

CONTEMPLATION I.—THE CREATION.

WHAT can I see, O God, in thy creation, but miracles of wonders? Thou madest something of nothing, and of that something all things. Thou, which wast without a beginning, gavest a beginning to time, and to the world in time. It is the praise of us men, if, when we have matter, we can give fashion: thou gavest a being to the matter, without form; thou gavest a form to that matter, and a glory to that form. If we can finish but a slight and imperfect matter according to a former pattern, it is the height of our skill: but to begin that which never was, whereof there was no example, whereto there was no inclination, wherein there was no possibility of that which it should be, is proper only to such power as thine: the infinite power of an infinite Creator! With us, not so much as a thought can arise without some matter; but here, with thee, all matter arises from nothing. How easy is it for thee to repair all out of something, which couldst thus fetch all out of nothing! Wherein can we now distrust thee, that hast proved thyself thus omnipotent? Behold, to have made the least clod of nothing, is more above wonder, than to multiply a world! But now the matter doth not more praise thy power, than the form thy wisdom. What beauty is here! what order! What order in working! what beauty in the work!

Thou mightest have made all the world perfect in an instant, but thou wouldst not. That will, which caused thee to create, is reason enough why thou didst thus create. How should we deliberate in our actions, which are so subject to imperfection; since it pleased thine infinite perfection (not out of need) to take leisure? Neither did thy wisdom herein proceed in time only, but in degrees: at first thou madest nothing absolute; first, thou madest things which should have being without life; then, those which should have life and being; lastly, those which have being, life, reason: So we ourselves, in the ordinary course of generation, first live the life of vegetation, then of sense; of reason afterwards. That instant wherein the heaven and the earth were created in their rude matter, there was neither day nor light: but presently thou madest both light and day. While we have this example of thine, how vainly do we hope to be perfect at once! It is well for us, if, through many degrees, we can rise to our consummation.

But, alas! what was the very heaven itself without light? How confused! how formless! like to a goodly body without a soul, like a soul without thee. Thou art light, and in thee is no darkness. Oh! how incomprehensibly glorious is the light that is in thee, since one glimpse of this created light gave so lively a glory to all thy workmanship! This even the brute creatures can behold! that, not the very angels,—that shines forth only to the other supreme world of immortality; this to the basest part of thy creation. There is one cause of our darkness on earth and of the utter darkness of hell;—the restraint of thy light. Shine thou, O God, into the vast corners of my soul, and in thy light I shall see light.

But whence, O God, was that first light? The sun was not made till the fourth day —light the first. If man had been, he might have seen all lightsome; but, whence it had come, he could not have seen; as, in some great pond, we see the banks full; we see not the springs from whence the water ariseth. Thou madest the sun; madest the light without the sun, before the sun, that so light might depend upon thee, and not upon thy creature. Thy power will not be limited to means. It was easy to thee to make an heaven without sun, light without an heaven, day without a sun, time without a day. It is good reason thou shouldst be the Lord of thine own works. All means serve thee: why do we, weak wretches, distrust thee, in the want of those means which thou canst either command or forbear? How plainly wouldst thou teach us, that we creatures need not one another, so long as we have thee! One day we shall have light again without the sun: Thou shalt be our sun: thy presence shall be our light: " Light is sown for the righteous." The sun and light is but for the world below itself: thine only for above. Thou givest this light to the sun, which the sun gives to the world: that light which thou shalt once give us, shall make us shine like the sun in glory.

Now this light, which for three days was thus dispersed through the whole heavens, it pleased thee, at last, to gather and unite into one body of the sun. The whole heaven was our sun, before the sun was created: but now one star must be the treasury of light to the heaven and earth. How thou lovest the union and reduction of all things of one kind to their own head and centre! so the waters must, by thy command, be gathered into one place, the sea: so the upper waters must be severed by these airy limits from the lower: so heavy substances hasten downward, and light mount up: so the general light of the first days must be called into the compass of one sun: so thou wilt once gather thine elect from all coasts of heaven, to the participation of one glory. Why do we abide our thoughts and affections scattered from thee, from thy saints, from thine anointed? Oh! let this light, which thou hast now spread abroad in the hearts of all thine, once meet in thee. We are as thy heavens, in this their first imperfection; be thou our sun, unto which our light may be gathered.

Yet this light was by thee interchanged with darkness, which thou mightest as easily have commanded to be perpetual. The continuance, even of the best things, cloyeth and wearieth: there is nothing but thyself, wherein there is not satiety. So pleasing is the vicissitude of things, that the intercourse even of those occurrents, which in their own nature are less worthy gives more contentment than the unaltered estate of better. The day dies into night, and rises into the morning again, that we might not expect any stability here below, but in perpetual successions. It is always day with thee above: the night savoureth only of mortality. Why are we not here spiritually, as we shall be hereafter? Since thou hast made us children of the light, and of the day, teach us to walk ever in the light of thy presence, not in the darkness of error and unbelief.

Now, in this thine enlightened frame, how fitly, how wisely are all the parts disposed; that the method of the creation might answer the matter and the form both Behold all purity above; below, the dregs and lees of all. The higher I go, the more perfection; each element superior to other, not more in place than dignity; that, by these stairs of ascending perfection, our thoughts might climb unto the top of all glory, and might know thine imperial heaven, no less glorious above the visible than those above the earth. Oh! how miserable is the place of our pilgrimage, in respect of our home! Let my soul tread awhile in the steps of thine own proceedings; and so think as thou wroughtest. When we would describe a man, we begin not at the feet, but the head. The head of thy creation is the heaven; how high! how spacious! how glorious! It is a wonder that we can look up to so admirable a height, and that the very eye is not tired in the way. If this ascending line could be drawn right forwards, some, that have calculated curiously, have found it five hundred years' journey unto the starry heaven. I do not examine their art; O Lord, I wonder rather at thine, which hast drawn so large a line about this little point of earth: for, in the plainest rules of art and experience, the compass must needs be six times as much as half the height. We think one island great, but the earth immeasurable. If we were in that heaven, with these eyes, the whole earth (were it equally enlightened) would seem as little to us, as now the least star in the firmament seems to us upon earth: and, indeed, how few stars are so little as it? And yet, how many void and ample spaces are there beside all the stars? The hugeness of this thy work, O God, is little inferior for admiration to the majesty of it. But, oh, what a glorious heaven is this which thou hast spread over our heads! With how precious a vault hast thou walled in this our inferior world! What worlds of light hast thou set above us! Those things which we see are wondrous; but those, which we believe and see not, are yet more. Thou dost but set out these unto view, to shew us what there is within. How proportionable are thy works to thyself! Kings erect not cottages, but set forth their magnificence in sumptuous buildings; so hast thou done, O King of Glory! If the lowest pavement of that heaven of thine be so glorious, what shall we think of the better parts yet unseen? And if this sun of thine be of such brightness and majesty, oh! what is the glory of the Maker of it? And yet if some other of thy stars were let down as low as it, those other stars would be suns to us; which now thou hadst rather to have admired in their distance. And if such a sky be prepared for the use and benefit even of thine enemies also upon earth, how happy shall those eternal tabernacles be, which thou hast sequestered for thine own?

Behold then in this high and stately building of thine, I see three stages: this lowest heaven for fowls, for vapours, for meteors: the second for the stars: the third for thine angels and saints. The first is thine outward court, open for all: the second is the body of thy covered temple, wherein are those candles of heaven perpetually burning: the third is thine holy of holies. In the first is tumult and vanity: in the second, immutability and rest: in the third, glory and blessedness. The first we feel, the second we see, the third we believe. In these two lower is no felicity; for neither the fowls nor stars are happy. It is the third heaven alone, where thou, O blessed Trinity! enjoyest thyself, and thy glorified spirits enjoy thee. It is the manifestation of thy glorious presence, that makes heaven to be itself. This is the privilege of thy children, that they here, seeing thee (which art invisible) by the eye of faith, have already begun that heaven, which the perfect sight of thee shall make perfect above. Let my soul then let these heavens alone, till it may see as it is seen. That we may descend to this lowest and meanest region of heaven, wherewith our senses are more acquainted; what marvels do even here meet with us? There are thy clouds, thy bottles of rain, vessels as thin as the liquor which is contained in them: there they hang and move, though weighty with their burden: how they are upheld, and why they fall, here, and now, we know not, and wonder. Those thou makest one while, as some airy seas, to hold water: another while as some airy furnaces, whence thou scatterest thy sudden fires unto all the parts of the earth, astonishing the world with the fearful noise of that eruption: out of the midst of water thou fetchest fire, and hard stones out of the midst of thin vapours: another while, as some steel glasses, wherein the sun looks, and shews his face in the variety of those colours which he hath not; there are thy streams of light, blazing and falling stars, fires darted up and down in many forms, hollow openings, and (as it were) gulfs in the sky, bright circles about the moon and other planets, snows, hail: in all which it is enough to admire thine hand, though we cannot search out thine action. There are thy subtile winds, which we hear and feel, yet neither can see their substance, nor know their causes; whence, and whither they pass, and what they are, thou knowest. There are thy fowls of all shapes, colours, notes, natures: whilst I compare these with the inhabitants of that other heaven, I find those stars and spirits like one another: these meteors and fowls, in as many varieties as there are several creatures. Why is this? Is it because Man (for whose sake these are made) delights in change, thou in constancy? or is it, that in these thou mayest shew thine own skill, and their imperfection? There is no variety in that which is perfect, because there is but one perfection? and so much shall we grow nearer to perfectness, by how much we draw nearer to unity and uniformity. From thence, if we go down to the great deep, the womb of moisture, the well of fountains, the great pond of the world; we know not whether to wonder at the element itself, or the guests which it contains. How doth that sea of thine roar and foam and swell, as if it would swallow up the earth? Thou stayest the rage of it by an insensible violence; and, by a natural miracle, confinest his waves: why it moves, and why it stays, it is to us equally wonderful: what living mountains (such are thy whales) roll up and down in those fearful billows: for greatness of number, hugeness of quantity, strangeness of shapes, variety of fashions, neither air nor earth can compare with the waters. I say nothing of thy hid treasures, which thy wisdom hath reposed in the bowels of the earth and sea: how secretly and how basely are they laid up! secretly, that we might not seek them; basely, that we might not over-esteem them: I need not dig so low as these metals, mineries, quarries, which yield riches enough of observation to the soul. How many millions of wonders doth the very face of the earth offer me? Which of these herbs, flowers, trees, leaves, seeds, fruits, is there; what beast, what worm, wherein we may not see the footsteps of a Deity, wherein we may not read infiniteness of power, of skill, and must be forced to confess, that he which made the angels and stars of heaven, made also the vermin on the earth? O God, the heart of man is too strait to admire enough even that which he treads upon! What shall we say to thee, the Maker of all these? O Lord, how wonderful are thy works in all the world! in wisdom hast thou made them all: and in all these thou spakest, and they were done. Thy will is thy word, and thy word is thy deed. Our tongue, and hand, and heart are different: all are one in thee, which art simply one, and infinite. Here needed no helps, no instruments: what could be present with the Eternal? What needed, or what could be added to the Infinite? Thine hand is not shortened, thy word is still equally effectual: say thou the word, and my soul shall be made new again; say thou the word, and my body shall be repaired from his dust: for all things obey thee. O Lord, why do I not yield to the word of thy counsel; since I must yield, as all thy creatures, to the word of thy command?

CONTEMPLATION II.—OF MAN.

But, O God! what a little lord hast thou made over this great world? The least corn of sand is not so small to the whole earth, as man is to the heaven. When I see the heavens, the sun, moon, and stars, O God, what is man? Who would think thou shouldst make all these creatures for one, and that one well-near the least of all? Yet none but he can see what thou hast done; none but he can admire and adore thee in what he seeth: How had he need to do nothing but this, since he alone must do it! Certainly the price and virtue of things consist not in the quantity: one diamond is worth more than many quarries of stone; one loadstone hath more virtue than mountains of earth. It is lawful for us to praise thee in ourselves. All thy creation hath not more wonder in it, than one of us: other creatures thou madest by a simple command; Man, not without a divine consultation;— others at once; man thou didst first form, then inspire:—others in several shapes, like to none but themselves; man, after thine own image:—others with qualities fit for service; man, for dominion. Man had his name from thee; they had their names from man. How should we be consecrated to thee above all others, since thou hast bestowed more cost on us than others! What shall I admire first? thy providence in the time of our creation; or thy power and wisdom in the act? First, thou madest the great house of the world, and furnishedst it; then thou broughtest in thy tenant to possess it. The bare walls had been too good for us, but thy love was above our desert: thou, that madest ready the earth for us before we were, hast, by the same mercy, prepared a place in heaven for us, while we are on earth. The stage was first fully prepared, then was man brought forth thither, as an actor, or spectator, that he might neither be idle nor discontent. Behold, thou hadst addressed an earth for use, an heaven for contemplation. After thou hadst drawn that large and real map of the world, thou didst thus abridge it into this little table of man: he alone consists of heaven and earth, soul and body. Even this earthly part, which is vile in comparison of the other, as it is thine, O God, I dare admire it, though I can neglect it as mine own; for, lo! this heap of earth hath an outward reference to heaven. Other creatures grovel down to their earth, and have all their senses intent upon it; this is reared up towards heaven, and hath no more power to look beside heaven than to tread beside the earth. Unto this, every part hath his wonder. The head is nearest to heaven, as in place, so in resemblance, both for roundness of figure, and for those divine guests which have their seat in it: There dwell those majestical powers of reason, which make a man; all the senses, as they have their original from thence, so they do all agree there to manifest their virtue. How goodly proportions hast thou set in the face! such as, though ofttimes we can give no reason when they please, yet transport us to admiration. What living glasses are those which thou hast placed in the midst of this visage, whereby all objects from far are clearly represented to the mind! and because their tenderness lies open to dangers, how hast thou defenced them with hollow bones, and with prominent brows, and lids! and lest they should be too much bent on what they ought not, thou hast given them peculiar nerves to pull them up towards the seat of their rest. What a tongue hast thou given him; the instrument not of taste only, but of speech! how sweet and excellent voices are formed by that little loose film of flesh! what an incredible strength hast thou given to the weak bones of the jaws! what a comely and tower-like neck, therefore most sinewy because smallest! and lest I be infinite, what able arms and active hands hast thou framed him, whereby he can frame all things to his own conceit! In every part, beauty, strength, convenience meet together. Neither is there any whereof our weakness cannot give reason why it should be no otherwise. How hast thou disposed of all the inward vessels, for all offices of life, nourishment, digestion, generation! No vein, sinew, artery, is idle. There is no piece in this exquisite frame, whereof the place, use, form, doth not admit wonder, and exceed it. Yet this body, if it be compared to the soul, what is it, but as a clay wall that encompasses a treasure; as a wooden box of a jeweller; as a coarse case to a rich instrument; or as a mask to a beautiful face? Man was made last, because he was worthiest. The soul was inspired last, because yet more noble. If the body have this honour to be the companion of the soul, yet withal it is the drudge. If it be the instrument, yet also the clog of that divine part, the companion for life, the drudge for service, the instrument for action, the clog in respect of contemplation. These external works are effected by it; the internal, which are more noble, hindered; contrary to the bird, which sings most in her cage, but flies most and highest at liberty. This my soul teaches me of itself, that itself cannot conceive, how capable, how active it is. It can pass by her nimble thoughts from heaven to earth in a moment: it can be all things, can comprehend all things; know that which is, and conceive that which never was, never shall be. Nothing can fill it, but thou which art infinite; nothing can limit it, but thou which art everywhere. O God, which madest it, replenish it, possess it, dwell thou in it, which hast appointed it to dwell in clay. The body was made of earth common to his fellows; the soul inspired immediately from God. The body lay senseless upon the earth like itself: the breath of life gave it what it is, and that breath was from thee. Sense, motion, reason, are infused into it at once. From whence then was this quickening breath? No air, no earth, no water, was here used to give help to this work. Thou that breathedst upon man, and gavest him the Holy Spirit, didst also breathe upon the body, and gavest it a living spirit. We are beholden to nothing but thee for our soul. Our flesh is from flesh; our spirit is from the God of spirits. How should our souls rise up to thee, and fix themselves in their thoughts upon thee, who alone created them in their infusion, and infused them in their creation? How should they long to return back to the fountain of their being, and author of being glorious? Why may we not say, that this soul, as it came from thee, so it is like thee? As thou, so it is one, immaterial, immortal, understanding spirit, distinguished into three powers, which all make up one spirit. So thou, the wise Creator of all things, wouldst have some things to resemble their Creator. These other creatures are all body; man is body and spirit. The angels are all spirit, not without a kind of spiritual composition: thou art alone after thine own manner, simple, glorious, infinite: no creature can be like thee in thy proper being, because it is a creature. How should our finite, weak, compounded nature, give any perfect resemblance of thine? Yet of all visible creatures, thou vouchsafest man the nearest correspondence to thee: not so much in the natural faculties, as in those divine graces, wherewith thou beautifiest his soul.

Our knowledge, holiness, righteousness, was like the first copy from which they were drawn. Behold, we were not more like thee in these, than now we are unlike ourselves in their loss. O God, we now praise ourselves to our shame, for the better we were, we are the worse; as the sons of some prodigal, or tainted ancestors, tell of the lands and lordships which were once theirs. Only do thou whet our desires, answerably to the readiness of thy mercies, that we may redeem what we have lost; that we may recover in thee, what we have lost in ourselves. The fault shall be ours, if our damage prove not beneficial.

I do not find that man, thus framed, found the want of an helper. His fruition of God gave him fulness of contentment: the sweetness which he found in the contemplation of this new workmanship, and the glory of the Author, did so take him up, that he had neither leisure nor cause of complaint. If man had craved an helper, he had grudged at the condition of his creation, and had questioned that which he had, perfection of being. But he that gave him his being, and knew him better than himself, thinks of giving him comfort in the creature, while he sought none but in his Maker. He sees our wants, and forecasts our relief, when we think ourselves too happy to complain. How ready will he be to help our necessities, that thus provides for our perfection!

God gives the nature to his creatures;

man must give the name; that he might see they were made for him, they shall be to him what he will. Instead of their first homage, they are presented to their new lord, and must see of whom they hold. He that was so careful of man's sovereignty in his innocence, how can he be careless of his safety in his renovation?

If God had given them their names, it had not been so great a praise of Adam's memory to recall them, as it was now of his judgment (at first sight) to impose them: he saw the inside of all the creatures at first, (his posterity sees but their skins ever since;) and by this knowledge he fitted their names to their dispositions. All that he saw were fit to be his servants, none to be his companions. The same God that finds the want, supplies it. Rather than man's innocency shall want an outward comfort, God will begin a new creation: not out of the earth, which was the matter of man; not out of the inferior creatures, which were the servants of man; but out of himself, for dearness, for equality. Doubtless, such was man's power of obedience, that if God had bidden him yield up his rib, waking, for his use, he had done it cheerfully: but the bounty of God was so absolute, that he would not so much as consult with man's will, to make him happy. As man knew not while he was made, so shall he not know while his other self is made out of him: that the comfort might be greater, which was seen before it was expected.

If the woman should have been made, not without the pain or will of the man, she might have been upbraided with her dependence and obligation. Now she owes nothing but to her Creator; the rib of Adam sleeping can challenge no more of her than the earth can of him. It was an happy change to Adam of a rib for an helper; what help did that bone give to his side! God had not made it, if it had been superfluous: and yet if man could not have been perfect without it, it had not been taken out.

Many things are useful and convenient, which are not necessary; and if God had seen man might not want it, how easy had it been for him, which made the woman of that bone, to turn the flesh into another bone! but he saw man could not complain of the want of that bone, which he had so multiplied, so animated.

O God, we can never be losers by thy changes; we have nothing but what is thine. Take from us thine own, when thou wilt: we are sure thou canst not but give us better.

CONTEMPLATION III.—OF PARADISE.

MAN could no sooner see, than he saw himself happy: his eye-sight and reason were both perfect at once, and the objects of both were able to make him as happy as he would. When he first opened his eyes, he saw heaven above him, earth under him, the creatures around him, God before him; he knew what all these things meant, as if he had been long acquainted with them all. He saw the heavens glorious, but afar off: his Maker thought it requisite to fit him with a paradise nearer home. If God had appointed him immediately to heaven, his body had been superfluous; it was fit his body should be answered with an earthen image of that heaven, which was for his soul. Had man been made only for contemplation, it would have served as well to have been placed in some vast desert, on the top of some barren mountain; but the same power which gave him a heart to meditate, gave him hands to work, and work fit for his hands. Neither was it the purpose of the Creator, that man should but live. Pleasure may stand with innocence. He that rejoiced to see all he had made to be good, rejoiceth to see all that he hath made to be well. God loves to see his creatures happy; our lawful delight is his: they know not God, that think to please him with making themselves miserable.

The idolaters thought it a fit service for Baal, to cut and lance themselves: never any holy man looked for thanks from the true God by wronging himself. Every earth was not fit for Adam, but a garden, a paradise. What excellent pleasures, and rare varieties, have men found in gardens, planted by the hands of men! and yet all the world of men cannot make one twig, or leaf, or spire of grass. When he that made the matter undertakes the fashion, how must it needs be, beyond our capacity, excellent! No herb, no flower, no tree, was wanting there, that might be for ornament or use; whether for sight, or for scent, or for taste. The bounty of God wrought further than to necessity, even to comfort and recreation: Why are we niggardly to ourselves, when God is liberal? But for all this, if God had not there conversed with man, no abundance could have made him blessed.

Yet, behold! that which was man's storehouse, was also his work-house; his pleasure was his task: paradise served not only to feed his senses, but to exercise his hands. If happiness had consisted in doing nothing, man had not been employed; all his delights could not have made him happy in an idle life. Man therefore is no sooner made, than he is set to work: neither greatness nor perfection can privilege a folded hand; ne must labour because he was happy; how much more we, that we may be! This first labour of his was, as without necessity, so without pains, without weariness: How much more cheerfully we go about our businesses, so much nearer we come to our paradise.

Neither did these trees afford him only action for his hands, but instruction to his heart; for here he saw God's sacraments grow before him: all other trees had a natural use; these two in the midst of the garden a spiritual. Life is the act of the soul, knowledge the life of the soul; the tree of knowledge, and the tree of life, then, were ordained as earthly helps of the spiritual part. Perhaps he which ordained the end, immortality of life, did appoint this fruit as the means of that life. It is not for us to inquire after the life we had, and the means we should have had. I am sure it served to nourish the soul by a lively representation of that living tree, whose fruit is eternal life, and whose leaves serve to heal the nations.

O infinite mercy! man saw his Saviour before him, ere he had need of a Saviour: he saw in whom he should recover an heavenly life, ere he lost the earthly. But after he had tasted of the tree of knowledge, he might not taste of the tree of life; that immortal food was not for a mortal stomach: yet then did he most savour that invisible tree of life, when he was most restrained from the other.

O Saviour! none but a sinner can relish thee; my taste hath been enough seasoned with the forbidden fruit, to make it capable of thy sweetness; sharpen thou as well the stomach of my soul by repenting; by believing, so shall I eat, and, in despite of Adam, live for ever. The one tree was for confirmation, the other for trial; one showed him what life he should have, the other what knowledge he should not desire to have. Alas! he that knew all other things, knew not this one thing, that he knew enough: how divine a thing is knowledge, whereof even innocency itself is ambitious! Satan knew what he did: if this bait had been gold, or honour, or pleasure, man had contemned it: who can hope to avoid error, when even man's perfection is mistaken? He looked for speculative knowledge; he should have looked for experimental: he thought it had been good to know evil; good was large enough to have perfected his knowledge, and therein his blessedness.

All that God made was good, and the Maker of them much more good; they good in their kinds, he good in himself. It would not content him to know God and his creatures; his curiosity affected to know that which God never made, evil of sin, and the evil of death, which indeed himself made by desiring to know them: now we know evil well enough, and smart with knowing it. How dear hath this lesson cost us, that in some cases it is better to be ignorant! and yet do the sons of Eve inherit this saucy appetite of their grandmother: how many thousand souls miscarry with the presumptuous affectation of forbidden knowledge!

O God, thou hast revealed more than we can know, enough to make us happy; teach me a sober knowledge and a contented ignorance.

Paradise was made for man, yet there I see the serpent: what marvel is it, if my corruption find the serpent in my closet, in my table, in my bed, when our holy parents found him in the midst of paradise? No sooner he is entered but he tempteth; he can no more be idle than harmless. I do not see him at any other tree; he knew there was no danger in the rest: I see him at the tree forbidden. How true a serpent he is in every point! in his insinuation to the place, in his choice of the tree, in his assault of the woman, in his plausibleness of speech to avoid terror, in his question to move doubt, in his reply to work distrust, in his protestation of safety, in his suggestion to envy and discontent, in his promise of gain!

And if he was so cunning at the first, what shall we think of him now, after so many thousand years' experience? Only thou, O God! and these angels that see thy face, are wiser than he. I do not ask why, when he left his goodness, thou didst not bereave him of his skill: still thou wouldst have him an angel, though an evil one; and thou knowest how to ordain his craft to thine own glory. I do not desire thee to abate of his subtilty, but to make me wise: let me beg it, without presumption, make me wiser than Adam. Even thine image which he bore, made him not (through his own weaknesss) wise enough to obey thee: thou offeredst him all fruits, and restrainedst but one; Satan offered him but one, and restrained not the rest. When he chose rather to be at Satan's feeding than thine, it was just with thee to turn him out of thy gates with a curse: why shouldst thou feed a rebel at thine own board?

And yet we transgress daily, and thou shuttest not heaven against us: how is it that we find more mercy than our forefather? His strength is worthy of severity, our weakness finds pity. That God, from whose face he fled in the garden, now makes him with shame to flee out of the garden: those angels that should have kept him, now keep the gates of paradise against him. It is not so easy to recover happiness, as to keep it or lose it; yea, the same cause that drave man from paradise hath also withdrawn paradise from the world.

That fiery sword did not defend it against those waters wherewith the sins of men drowned the glory of that place: neither now do I care to seek where that paradise was which we lost: I know where that paradise is, which we must care to seek, and hope to find. As man was the image of God, so was that earthly paradise an image of heaven; both the images are defaced, both the first patterns are eternal: Adam was in the first, and stayed not: in the second, is the second Adam, which said, "This day shalt thou be with me in paradise." There was that chosen vessel, and heard and saw what could not be expressed: by how much the third heaven exceeds the richest earth, so much doth that paradise, whereto we aspire, exceed that which we have lost.

CONTEMPLATION IV.—OF CAIN AND ABEL.

Look now, O my soul! upon the two first brethren, perhaps twins, and wonder at their contrary dispositions and estates. If the privileges of nature had been worth any thing, the first-born child should not have been a reprobate.

Now, that we may ascribe all to free grace, the elder is a murderer, the younger a saint: though goodness may be repaired in ourselves, yet it cannot be propagated to ours: now might Adam see the image of himself in Cain, for after his own image begot he him; Adam slew his posterity, Cain his brother. We are too like one another, in that wherein we are unlike to God: even the clearest grain sends forth that chaff from which it was fanned ere the sowing: yet is this Cain a possession. The same Eve that mistook the fruit of the garden, mistook also the fruit of her own body; her hope deceived her in both: so, many good names are ill bestowed; and our comfortable expectations in earthly things do not seldom disappoint us.

Doubtless their education was holy; for Adam, though in paradise he could not be innocent, yet was a good man out of paradise: his sin and fall now made him circumspect; and since he saw that his act had bereaved them of that image of God, which he once had for them, he could not but labour, by all holy endeavours, to repair it in them, that so his care might make amends for his trespass. How plain is it that even good breeding cannot alter destiny! That which is crooked, can none make straight: who would think that brethren, and but two brethren, should not love each other? Dispersed love grows weak, and fewness of objects useth to unite affections: if but two brothers be left alive of many, they think that the love of all the rest should survive in them; and now the beams of their affection are so much the hotter, because they reflect mutually in a right line upon each other: yet behold, here are but two brothers in a world, and one is the butcher of the other. Who can wonder at dissensions among thousands of brethren, when he sees so deadly opposition betwixt two, the first roots of brotherhood? Who can hope to live plausibly and securely amongst so many Cains, when he sees one Cain the death of one Abel? The same devil that set enmity betwixt man and God, sets enmity betwixt man and man; and yet God said, "I will put enmity between thy seed and her seed." Our hatred of the serpent and his seed is from God; their hatred of the holy seed is from the serpent: behold here at once, in one person, the seed of the woman and of the serpent; Cain's natural parts are of the woman, his vicious qualities of the serpent: the woman gave him to be a brother, the serpent to be a manslayer; all uncharitableness, all quarrels are of one author: we cannot entertain wrath, and not give place to the devil. Certainly, so deadly an act must needs be deeply grounded.

What, then, was the occasion of this capital malice? Abel's sacrifice is accepted: what was this to Cain? Cain's is rejected: what could Abel remedy this? O envy! the corrosive of all ill minds, and the root of all desperate actions. The same cause that moved Satan to tempt the first man to destroy himself and his posterity, the same moves the second man to destroy the third.

It should have been Cain's joy to see his brother accepted: it should have been his sorrow to see that himself had deserved a rejection; his brother's example should have excited and directed him. Could Abel have stayed God's fire from descending? or should he (if he could) reject God's acceptation, and displease his Maker to content a brother? Was Cain ever the farther from a blessing, because his brother obtained mercy? How proud and foolish is malice! which grows thus mad for no other cause but because God or Abel is not less good. It hath been an old and happy danger to be holy; indifferent actions must be careful to avoid offence; but I care not what devil or what Cain be angry that I do good, or receive good.

There was never any nature without envy: every man is born a Cain, hating that goodness in another which he neglected in himself. There was never envy that was not bloody; for if it eat not another's heart, it will eat our own; but unless it be restrained, it will surely feed itself with the blood of others, ofttimes in act, always in affection. And that God, which (in good) accepts the will for the deed, condemns the will for the deed in evil. If there be an evil heart, there will be an evil eye; and if both these, there will be an evil hand.

How early did martyrdom come into the world! The first man that died, died for religion: who dare measure God's love by outward events, when he sees wicked Cain standing over bleeding Abel, whose sacrifice was first accepted, and now himself is sacrificed! Death was denounced to man as a curse; yet, behold! it first lights upon a saint: how soon was it altered by the mercy of that just hand which inflicted it! If death had been evil and life good, Cain had been slain, and Abel had survived. Now that it begins with him that God loves, "O death, where is thy sting!"

Abel says nothing — his blood cries. Every drop of innocent blood hath a tongue, and is not only vocal, but importunate. What a noise, then, did the blood of my Saviour make in heaven, who was himself the shepherd and the sacrifice, the man that was offered, and the God to whom it was offered! The Spirit that heard both, says, "It spake better things than the blood of Abel." Abel's blood called for revenge — his for mercy: Abel's pleaded his own innocency — his the satisfaction for all the believing world: Abel's procured Cain's punishment — his freed all repentant souls from punishment; better things indeed than the blood of Abel; better, and therefore that which Abel's blood said was good. It is good that God should be avenged of sinners. Execution of justice upon offenders is no less good than rewards of goodness.

No sooner doth Abel's blood speak unto God, than God speaks to Cain. There is no wicked man to whom God speaks not, if not to his ear, yet to his heart. What speech was this? Not an accusation, but an inquiry; yet such an inquiry as would infer an accusation. God loves to have a sinner accuse himself; and therefore hath he set his deputy in the breast of man· neither doth God love this more than nature abhors it. Cain answers stubborn.y: the very name of Abel wounds him no less than his hand had wounded Abel: consciences that are without remorse, are not without horror: wickedness makes men desperate. The murderer is angry with God, as of late, for accepting his brother's oblation; so now, for listening to his blood.

And now he dares answer God with a question, "Am I my brother's keeper?" where he should have said, Am not I my brother's murderer? Behold, he scorneth to keep whom he feared not to kill. Good duties are base and troublesome to wicked minds, while even violences of evil are pleasant. Yet this miscreant, which neither had grace to avoid his sin nor to confess it, now that he is convinced of sin, and cursed for it, how he howleth, how he exclaimeth! He that cares not for the act of his sin, shall care for the smart of his punishment. The damned are weary of their torments, but in vain. How great a madness is it to complain too late! He that would not keep his brother, is cast out from the protection of God; he that feared not to kill his brother, fears now that whosoever meets him will kill him. The troubled conscience projecteth fearful things, and sin makes even cruel men cowardly. God saw it was too much favour for him to die; he therefore wills that which Cain wills. Cain would live; it is yielded him, but for a curse. How often doth God hear sinners in anger! He shall live, banished from God, carrying his hell in his bosom, and the brand of God's vengeance in his forehead. God rejects him, the earth repines at him, men abhor him; himself now wishes that death which he feared, and no man dare pleasure him with a murder. How bitter is the end of sin, yea, without end! Still Cain finds that he killed himself more than his brother. We should never sin if our foresight were but as good as our sense; the issue of sin would appear a thousand times more horrible than the act is pleasant.

CONTEMPLATION V.—OF THE DELUGE.

The world was grown so foul with sin, that God saw it was time to wash it with a flood: and so close did wickedness cleave to the authors of it, that when they were washed to nothing, yet it would not off; yea, so deep did it stick in the very grain of the earth, that God saw it meet to let it soak long under the waters. So, under the law, the very vessels that had touched unclean water, must either be rinsed or broken. Mankind began but with one; and yet he that saw the first man, lived to see the earth peopled with a world of men; yet man grew not so fast as wickedness. One man could soon and easily multiply a thousand sins—never man had so many children: so that when there were men enough to store the earth, there were as many sins as would reach up to heaven; whereupon the waters came down from heaven, and swelled up to heaven again. If there had not been so deep a deluge of sin, there had been none of the waters; from whence, then, was this superfluity of iniquity? Whence but from the unequal yoke with infidels? These marriages did not beget men so much as wickedness; from hence religious husbands both lost their piety, and gained a rebellious and godless generation.

That which was the first occasion of sin, was the occasion of the increase of sin: A woman seduced Adam—women betrayed the sons of God: the beauty of the apple betrayed the woman—the beauty of these women betrayed this holy seed: Eve saw, and lusted—so did they; this also was a forbidden fruit—they lusted, tasted, sinned, died. The most sins begin at the eyes; by them commonly Satan creeps into the heart: that soul can never be in safety that hath not covenanted with his eyes.

God needed not have given these men any warning of his judgment; they gave him no warning of their sins, no respite; yet that God might approve his mercies to the very wicked, he gives them an hundred and twenty years' respite of repenting. How loath is God to strike, that threats so long! He that delights in revenge surprises his adversary; whereas he that gives long warnings desires to be prevented. If we were not wilful, we should never smart.

Neither doth he give them time only, but a faithful teacher. It is a happy thing when he that teacheth others is righteous. Noah's hand taught them as much as his tongue. His business in building the ark was a real sermon to the world, wherein at once were taught mercy and life to the believer, and to the rebellious, destruction.

Methinks I see those monstrous sons of Lamech coming to Noah, and asking him what he means by that strange work? whether he meant to sail upon the dry land? To whom, when he reports God's purpose and his, they go away laughing at his idleness, and tell one another in sport, that too much holiness hath made him mad: yet cannot they all flout Noah out of his faith; he preaches, and builds, and finishes. Doubtless more hands went to this work than his. Many a one wrought upon the ark, which yet was not saved in the ark. Our outward works cannot save us without our faith; we may help to save others, and perish ourselves. What a wonder of mercy is this that I here see! One poor family called out of a world, and, as it were, eight grains of corn fanned from a whole barnful of chaff. One hypocrite was saved with the rest, for Noah's sake; not one righteous man was swept away for company: for these few was the earth preserved still under the waters, and all kinds of creatures upon the waters; which else had been all destroyed. Still the world stands for their sakes for whom it was preserved, else fire should consume that which could not be cleansed by water.

This difference is strange: I see the savagest of all creatures, lions, tigers, bears, by an instinct from God, come to seek the ark (as we see swine, foreseeing a storm, run home crying for shelter),—men I see not: reason once debauched is worse than brutishness. God hath use even of these fierce and cruel beasts, and glory by them; even they, being created for man, must live by him, though to his punishment. How gently do they offer and submit themselves to their preserver! renewing that obeisance to this repairer of the world, which they, before sin, yielded to him that first stored the world. He that shut them into the ark when they were entered, shut their mouths also when they did enter. The lions fawn upon Noah and Daniel. What heart cannot the Maker of them mollify!

The unclean beasts God would have to live, the clean to multiply; and therefore he sends to Noah seven of the clean, of the unclean two. He knew the one would annoy man with their multitude, the other would enrich him. Those things are worthy of most respect, which are of most use.

But why seven? Surely that God, that created seven days in the week, and made one for himself, did here preserve, of seven clean beasts, one for himself for sacrifice. He gives us six for one in earthly things, that in spiritual we should be all for him.

Now the day is come, all the guests are entered, the ark is shut, and the windows of heaven opened. I doubt not but many of those scoffers, when they saw the violence of the waves descending and ascending, according to Noah's prediction, came wading middle-deep unto the ark, and importunately craved that admittance which they once denied; but now, as they formerly rejected God, so are they justly rejected of God. Ere vengeance begin, repentance is seasonable; but if judgment be once gone out, we cry too late. While the gospel solicits us, the doors of the ark are open; if we neglect the time of grace, in vain shall we seek it with tears. God holds it no mercy to pity the obstinate. Others, more bold than they, hope to overrun the judgment; and, climbing up to the high mountains, look down upon the waters with more hope than fear. And now when they see their hills become islands, they climb up into the tallest trees; there with paleness and horror at once look for death, and study to avoid it, whom the waves overtake at last, half dead with famine and half with fear. Lo! now from the tops of the mountains they descry the ark floating upon the waters, and behold with envy that which before they beheld with scorn.

In vain doth he fly whom God pursues. There is no way to fly from his judgments, but to fly to his mercy by repentance. The faith of the righteous cannot be so much derided, as their success is magnified. How securely doth Noah ride out this uproar of heaven, earth, and waters! He hears the pouring down of the rain above his head; the shrieking of men, and roaring and bellowing of beasts on both sides of him; the raging and threats of the waves under him; he saw the miserable shifts of the distressed unbelievers; and, in the meantime, sits quietly in his dry cabin, neither feeling nor fearing evil. He knew that he which owned the waters would steer him; that he who shut him in would preserve him. How happy a thing is faith! what a quiet safety, what an heavenly peace doth it work in the soul, in the midst of all the inundation of evil!

Now, when God hath fetched again all the life which he had given to his unworthy creatures, and reduced the world unto its first form, wherein waters were over the face of the earth, it was time for a renovation of all things to succeed this destruction. To have continued this deluge long, had been to punish Noah that was righteous. After forty days, therefore, the heavens clear up; after an hundred and fifty, the waters sink down. How soon is God weary of punishing, which is never weary of blessing! But may not the ark rest suddenly? If we did not stay some while under God's hand, we should not know how sweet his mercy is, and how great our thankfulness should be. The ark, though it was Noah's fort against the waters, yet it was his prison; he was safe in it, but pent up: he that gave him life by it, now thinks time to give him liberty out of it.

God doth not reveal all things to his best servants. Behold, he that told Noah, an hundred and twenty years before, what day he should go into the ark, yet foretells him not now in the ark what day the ark should rest upon the hills, and he should go forth. Noah therefore sends out his intelligencers, the raven and the dove, whose wings in that vaporous air might easily descry further than his sight. The raven, of quick scent, of gross feed, of tough constitution; no fowl was so fit for discovery: the likeliest things always succeed not. He neither will venture far into that solitary world for fear of want, nor yet come into the ark for love of liberty, but hovers about in uncertainties. How many carnal minds fly out of the ark of God's church, and embrace the present world; rather choosing to feed upon the unsavoury carcases of sinful pleasures, than to be restrained within the strait lists of Christian obedience!

The dove is sent forth, a fowl both swift and simple. She, like a true citizen of the ark, returns, and brings faithful notice of the continuance of the waters, by her restless and empty return; by her olive-leaf, of the abatement. How worthy are those messengers to be welcome, which with innocence in their lives, bring glad tidings of peace and salvation in their mouths!

Noah rejoices and believes; yet still he waits seven days more. It is not good to devour the favours of God too greedily; but so take them in, that we may digest them. O strong faith of Noah, that was not weary with this delay! Some man would have so longed for the open air, after so long closeness, that, upon the first notice of safety, he would have uncovered and voided the ark. Noah stays seven days ere he will open, and well-near two months ere he will forsake the ark; and not then unless God that commanded to enter, had bidden him depart. There is no action good without faith; no faith without a word,

Happy is that man which in all things (neglecting the counsels of flesh and blood) depends upon the commission of his Maker!

BOOK II.

CONTEMPLATION I.—OF NOAH.

No sooner is Noah come out of the ark, but he builds an altar: not an house for himself, but an altar to the Lord. Our faith will ever teach us to prefer God to ourselves: delayed thankfulness is not worthy of acceptation. Of those few creatures that are left, God must have some; they are all his: yet his goodness will have man know that it was he, for whose sake they were preserved. It was a privilege to those very brute creatures, that they were saved from the waters, to be offered up in fire unto God. What a favour is it to men, to be reserved from common destructions, to be sacrificed to their Maker and Redeemer.

Lo, this little fire of Noah, through the virtue of his faith, purged the world, and ascended up into those heavens from which the waters fell, and caused a glorious rainbow to appear therein for his security: all the sins of the former world were not so unsavoury unto God, as this smoke was pleasant. No perfume can be so sweet as the holy obedience of the faithful. Now God that was before annoyed with the ill savour of sin, smells a sweet savour of rest. Behold here a new and second rest! First, God rested from making the world, now he rests from destroying it; even while we cease not to offend, he ceases from a public revenge. His word was enough; yet withal he gives a sign, which may speak the truth of his promise to the very eyes of men. Thus he doth still in his blessed sacraments, which are as real words to the soul. The rainbow is the pledge of our safety, which even naturally signifies the end of a shower: all the signs of God's institution are proper and significant.

But who would look, after all this, to have found righteous Noah, the father of the new world, lying drunken in his tent! Who could think that wine should overthrow him that was preserved from the waters! that he, who could not be tainted with the sinful examples of the former world, should begin the example of a new sin of his own! What are we men if we be but ourselves! While God upholds us, no temptation can move us: when he leaves us, no temptation is too weak to overthrow us. What living man had ever so noble proofs of the mercy, of the justice of God: Mercy upon himself, justice upon others! What man had so gracious approbation from his Maker? Behold, he of whom in an unclean world, God said, Thee only have I found righteous, proves now unclean when the world was purged. The preacher of righteousness unto the former age, the king, priest, and prophet of the world renewed, is the first that renews the sins of that world which he had reproved, and which he saw condemned for sin. God's best children have no fence for sins of infirmity. Which of the saints have not once done that, whereof they are ashamed? God, that lets us fall, knows how to make as good use of the sins of his holy ones, as of their obedience. If we had not such patterns, who could choose but despair at the sight of his sins?

Yet we find Noah drunken but once. One act can no more make a good heart unrighteous, than a trade of sin can stand with regeneration. But when I look to the effect of this sin, I cannot but blush and wonder. Lo! this sin is worse than sin: other sins move shame, but hide it; this displays it to the world.

Adam had no sooner sinned, but he saw and abhorred his own nakedness, seeking to hide it even with bushes. Noah had no sooner sinned, but he discovers his nakedness, and hath not so much rule of himself as to be ashamed. One hour's drunkenness betrays that which more than six hundred years' sobriety had modestly concealed. He that gives himself to wine, is not his own: what shall we think of this vice, which robs a man of himself, and lays a beast in his room? Noah's nakedness is seen in wine. It is no unusual quality, in this excess, to disclose secrets. Drunkenness doth both make imperfections, and show those we have to others' eyes: so would God have it, that we might be doubly ashamed both of those weaknesses which we discover, and of that weakness which moved us to discover. Noah is uncovered but in the midst of his own tent: it had been sinful, though no man had seen it. Unknown sins have their guilt and shame, and are justly attended with known punishments. Ungracious Cham saw it and laughed: his father's shame should have been his; the deformity of those parts from which he had his being, should have begotten in him a secret horror and dejection. How many graceless men make sport at the causes of their humiliation! Twice had Noah given him life; yet neither the name of a father and preserver, nor age nor virtue, could shield him from the contempt of his own. I see that even God's ark may nourish monsters. Some filthy toads may lie under the stones of the temple: God preserves some men in judgment. Better had it been for Cham to have perished in the waters, than to live unto his father's curse. Not content to be a witness of this filthy sight, he goes on to be a proclaimer of it. Sin doth ill in the eye, but worse in the tongue. As all sin is a work of darkness, so it should be buried in darkness. The report of sin is ofttimes as ill as the commission; for it can never be blazoned without uncharitableness; seldom without infection. Oh the unnatural, and more than Chamish impiety of those sons, which rejoice to publish the nakedness of their spiritual parents, even to their enemies!

Yet it was well for Noah that Cham could tell it to none but his own; and those, gracious and dutiful sons. Our shame is the less, if none know our faults but our friends. Behold how love covereth sins! These good sons are so far from going forward to see their father's shame, that they go backward to hide it. The cloak is laid on both their shoulders; they both go back with equal paces, and dare not so much as look back, lest they should unwillingly see the cause of their shame, and will rather adventure to stumble at their father's body, than to see his nakedness. How did it grieve them to think, that they, which had so often come to their holy father with reverence, must now in reverence turn their backs upon him! that they must now clothe him in pity, which had so often clothed them in love! And, which adds more to their duty, they covered him and said nothing. This modest sorrow is their praise, and our example. The sins of those we love and honour, we must hear of with indignation, fearfully and unwillingly believe, acknowledge with grief and shame, hide with honest excuses, and bury in silence.

How equal a regard is this both of piety and disobedience! Because Cham sinned against his father, therefore he shall be plagued in his children: Japheth is dutiful to his father, and finds it in his posterity. Because Cham was an ill son to his father, therefore his sons shall be servants to his brethren: because Japheth set his shoulder to Shem's, to bear the cloak of shame, therefore shall Japheth dwell in the tents of Shem, partaking with him in blessings as in duty. When we do but what we ought, yet God is thankful to us; and rewards that, which we should sin if we did not. Who could ever yet show me a man rebelliously undutiful to his parents, that hath prospered in himself, and his seed?

CONTEMPLATION II.—OF BABEL.

How soon are men and sins multiplied! within one hundred years, the world is as full of both, as if there had been no deluge. Though men could not but see the fearful monuments of the ruin of their ancestors, yet how quickly had they forgotten a flood! Good Noah lived to see the world both populous and wicked again: and doubtless ofttimes repented to have been the preserver of some, whom he saw to traduce the vices of the former world to the renewed. It could not but grieve him to see the destroyed giants revive out of his own loins, and to see them of his flesh and blood tyrannise over themselves. In his sight Nimrod, casting off the awe of his holy grandfather, grew imperious and cruel, and made his own kinsmen servants. How easy a thing it is for a great spirit to be the head of a faction, when even brethren will stoop to servitude! And now, when men are combined together, evil and presumptuous motions find encouragement in multitudes, and each man takes a pride in seeming forwardest: we are the cheerfuller in good, when we have the assistance of company; much more in sinning, by how much we are more prone to evil than good. It was a proud word—" Come, let us build a city and a tower, whose top may reach to heaven."

They were newly come down from the hills unto the plains, and now think of raising up of an hill of building in the plain. When their tents were pitched upon the mountains of Armenia, they were as near to heaven as their tower could make them; but their ambition must needs aspire to an height of their own raising. Pride is ever discontented, and still seeks matter of boasting in her own works.

How fondly do men reckon without God! " Come let us build;" as if there had been no stop but in their own will; as if both earth and time had been theirs. Still do all natural men build Babel, forecasting their own plots so resolutely, as if there were no power to countermand them. It is just with God, that peremptory determinations seldom prosper: whereas those things, which are fearfully and modestly undertaken, commonly succeed.

" Let us build us a city." If they had

taken God with them, it had been commendable; establishing of societies is pleasing to him that is the God of order: but a tower whose top may reach to heaven, was a shameful arrogance, an impious presumption. Who would think, that we little ants, that creep upon this earth, should think of climbing up to heaven, by multiplying of earth?

Pride ever looks at the highest. The first man would know as God; these would dwell as God: covetousness and ambition know no limits. And what if they had reached up to heaven? Some hills are as high as they could hope to be, and yet are no whit the better; no place alters the condition of nature. An angel is glorious, though he be upon earth; and man is but earth though he be above the clouds. The nearer they had been to heaven, the more subject they had been to the violences of heaven, to thunders, lightnings, and those other higher inflammations: what had this been, but to thrust themselves into the hands of the revenger of all wicked insolences! God loves that heaven should be looked at, and affected with all humble desires, with the holy ambitions of faith, not with the proud imaginations of our own achievements.

But wherefore was all this? not that they loved so much to be neighbours to heaven, as to be famous upon earth. It was not commodity that was here sought, not safety, but glory. Whither doth not thirst of fame carry men, whether in good or evil? It makes them seek to climb to heaven; it makes them not fear to run down headlong to hell. Even in the best things, desire of praise stands in competition with conscience, and brags to have the more clients. One builds a temple to Diana, in hope of glory, intending it for one of the great wonders of the world; another, in hope of fame, burns it. He is a rare man that hath not some Babel of his own, whereon he bestows pains and cost, only to be talked of. If they had done better things in a vain-glorious purpose, their act had been accursed: if they had built houses to God, if they had sacrificed, prayed, lived well; the intent poisons the action: But now both the act and the purpose are equally vain, and the issue is as vain as either.

God hath a special indignation at pride above all sins, and will cross our endeavours, not for that they are evil, (what hurt could be in laying one brick upon another?) but for that they are proudly undertaken. He could have hindered the laying of the first stone, and might as easily have made a trench for the foundation, the grave of the builders; but he loves to see what wicked men would do, and to let fools run themselves out of breath. What monument should they have had of their own madness, and his powerful interruption, if the walls had risen to no height? To stop them, then, in the midst of their course, he meddles not with either their hands or their feet, but their tongues; not by pulling them out, not by loosing their strings, not by making them say nothing, but by teaching them to say too much. Here is nothing varied but the sound of letters; even this frustrates the work, and befools the workmen. How easy is it for God ten thousand ways to correct and forestall the greatest projects of men! He that taught Adam the first words, taught them words that never were. One calls for brick, the other looks him in the face, and wonders what he commands, and how and why he speaks such words as were never heard, and instead thereof brings him mortar, returning him an answer as little understood; each chides with other, expressing his choler, so as he only can understand himself. From heat they fall to quiet entreaties, but still with the same success. At first every man thinks his fellow mocks him; but now perceiving this serious confusion, their only answer was silence, and ceasing: they could not come together, for no man could call them to be understood; and if they had assembled, nothing could be determined, because one could never attain to the other's purpose: no, they could not have the honour of a general dismission, but each man leaves his trowel and station, more like a fool than he undertook it: so commonly actions begun in glory shut up in shame. All external actions depend upon the tongue. No man can know another's mind, if this be not the interpreter. Hence, as there were many tongues given to stay the building of Babel, so there were as many given to build the New Jerusalem, the evangelical church. How dear hath Babel cost all the world! At the first, when there was but one language, men did spend their time in arts; (so was it requisite at the first settling of the world, and so came early to perfection): but now we stay so long (of necessity) upon the shell of tongues, that we can hardly have time to chew the sweet kernel of knowledge. Surely men would have grown too proud, if there had been no Babel. It falls out ofttimes that one sin is a remedy of a greater. Division of tongues must needs slacken any work. Multiplicity of languages had not been given by the Holy Ghost, for a blessing to the church, if the world had not been before possessed with multiplicity of languages for a punishment. Hence it is, that the building of our Sion rises no faster, because our tongues are divided. Happy were the church of God, if we all spake but one language: while we differ, we can build nothing but Babel; difference of tongues caused their Babel to cease, but it builds ours.

CONTEMPLATION III.—OF ABRAHAM.

It was fit that he which should be the father and pattern of the faithful, should be thoroughly tried; for in a set copy every fault is important, and may prove a rule of error. Of ten trials which Abraham passed, the last was the sorest. No son of Abraham can hope to escape temptations, while he sees that bosom in which he desires to rest, so assaulted with difficulties. Abraham must leave his country and kindred, and live amongst strangers. The calling of God never leaves men where it finds them. The earth is the Lord's, and all places are alike to the wise and faithful. If Chaldea had not been grossly idolatrous, Abraham had not left it; no bond must tie us to the danger of infection.

But whither must he go? To a place he knew not, to men that knew not him. It is enough comfort to a good man, wheresoever he is, that he is acquainted with God: we are never out of our way, while we follow the calling of God. Never any man lost by his obedience to the Highest. Because Abraham yielded, God gives him the possession of Canaan. I wonder more at his faith in taking this possession, than in leaving his own. Behold, Abraham takes possession for that seed which he had not; which in nature he was not like to have: of that land whereof he should not have one foot, wherein his seed should not be settled for almost five hundred years after. The power of faith can prevent time, and make future things present. If we be the true sons of Abraham, we have already (while we sojourn here on earth) the possession of our land of promise; while we seek our country, we have it.

Yet even Canaan doth not afford him bread, which yet he must believe shall flow with milk and honey to his seed. Sense must yield to faith. Woe were us, if we must judge of our future estate by the present. Egypt gives relief to Abraham, when Canaan cannot. In outward things, God's enemies may fare better than his friends. Thrice had Egypt preserved the church of God; in Abraham, in Jacob, in Christ. God ofttimes makes use of the world for the behoof of his, though without their thanks; as contrarily he uses the wicked for scourges to his own inheritance, and burns them; because in his good they intended evil.

But what a change is this! Hitherto hath Sarah been Abraham's wife; now Egypt hath made her his sister; fear hath turned him from a husband to a brother: no strength of faith can exclude some doubtings. God hath said, I will make thee a great nation: Abraham saith, the Egyptians will kill me. He that lived by his faith, yet shrinketh and sinneth. How vainly shall we hope to believe without all fear, and to live without infirmities! Some little aspersions of unbelief cannot hinder the praise and power of faith. Abraham believed, and it was imputed to him for righteousness. He that through inconsiderateness doubted twice of his own life, doubted not of the life of his seed, even from the dead and dry womb of Sarah; yet it was more difficult that his posterity should live in Sarah, than that Sarah's husband should live in Egypt: this was above nature, yet he believes it. Sometimes the believer sticks at easy trials, and yet breaks through the greatest temptations without fear. Abraham was old, ere this promise and hope of a son, and still the older, the more incapable; yet God makes him wait twenty-five years for performance. No time is long to faith, which hath learned to defer hopes without fainting and irksomeness.

Abraham heard this news from the angel, and laughed; Sarah heard it, and laughed: they did not more agree in their desire, than differ in their affection. Abraham laughed for joy; Sarah for distrust. Abraham laughed, because he believed it would be so; Sarah, becasue she believed it could not be. The same act varies in the manner of doing, and the intention of the doer. Yet Sarah laughed but within herself, and is bewrayed. How God can find us out in secret sins! How easily did she now think, that he, which could know of her inward laughter, could know of her conception! and now she that laughed, and believed not, believeth and feareth.

What a lively pattern do I see in Abraham, and Sarah, of a strong faith, and a weak; of strong in Abraham, and weak in Sarah! She to make God good of his word to Abraham, knowing her own barrenness, substitutes an Hagar; and, in an ambition of seed, persuades to polygamy. Abraham had never looked to obtain the promise by any other than a barren womb, if his own wife had not importuned him to take another. When our own apparent means fail, weak faith is put to the shifts, and projects strange devices of her own, to attain her end. She will rather conceive by another womb, than be childless. When she hears of an impossibility to nature, she doubteth, and yet hides her diffidence; and, when she must believe, feareth, because she did distrust. Abraham hears and believes, and expects and rejoices: he saith not, I am old and weak; Sarah is old and barren: where are the many nations that shall come from these withered loins? It is enough to him that God hath said it: he sees not the means, he sees the promise. He knew that God would rather raise him up seed from the very stones that he trode upon, than himself should want a large and happy issue.

There is no faith where there is either means or hopes. Difficulties and impossibilities are the true objects of belief. Hereupon God adds to his name, that which he would fetch from his loins, and made his name as ample as his posterity. Never any man was a loser by believing: faith is ever recompensed with glory.

Neither is Abraham content only to wait for God, but to smart for him. God bids him cut his own flesh; he willingly sacrifices this parcel of his skin and blood to him that was the owner of all. How glad he is to carry this painful mark of the love of his Creator! How forward to seal this covenant with blood, betwixt God and him! not regarding the soreness of his body, in comparison of the confirmation of his soul. The wound was not so grievous as a signification was comfortable. For herein he saw, that from his loins should come that blessed seed, which should purge his soul from all corruption. Well is that part of us lost which may give assurance of the salvation of the whole. Our faith is not yet sound, if it have not taught us to neglect pain for God, and more to love his sacraments than our own flesh.

CONTEMPLATION IV.—OF ISAAC SACRIFICED.

But all these are but easy tasks of faith: all ages have stood amazed at the next; not knowing whether they should more wonder at God's command, or Abraham's obedience. Many years had that good patriarch waited for his Issac; now at last he hath joyfully received him, and that with this gracious acclamation, " In Isaac shall thy seed be called, and all nations blessed." Behold the son of his age, the son of his love, the son of his expectation; he that might not endure a mock from his brother, must now endure the kmife of his father: " Take thine only son Isaac whom thou lovest, and get thee to the land of Moriah, and offer him there for a burnt-offering."

Never any gold was tried in so hot a fire. Who but Abraham would not have expostulated with God? What! doth the God of mercies now begin to delight in blood? Is it possible that murder should become piety? Or if thou wilt needs take pleasure in a human sacrifice, is there none but Isaac fit for thine altar? none but Abraham to offer him? Shall these hands destroy the fruits of mine own loins? Can I not be faithful, unless I be unnatural? Or if I must needs be the monster of all parents, will not Ishmael yet be accepted? O God! where is thy mercy? where is thy justice? Hast thou given me but one only son, and must I now slay him? Why did I wait so long for him? Why didst thou give him me? Why didst thou promise me a blessing in him? What will the heathen say, when they shall hear of this infamous massacre? How can thy name, and my profession, escape a perpetual blasphemy? With what face shall I look upon my wife Sarah, whose son I have murdered? How shall she entertain the executioner of Isaac? Or who will believe that I did this from thee? How shall not all the world spit at this holy cruelty, and say, There goes the man that cut the throat of his own son! Yet if he were an ungracious or rebellious child, his deserts might give some colour to this violence: but to lay hands on so dear, so dutiful, so hopeful a son, is incapable of all pretences.

But grant that thou, which art the God of nature, mayest either alter or neglect it; what shall I say to the truth of thy promises? Can thy justice admit contradictions? Can thy decrees be changeable? Canst thou promise and disappoint? Can these two stand together—Isaac shall live to be the father of nations, and Isaac shall now die by the hand of his father? When Isaac is once gone, where is my seed, where is my blessing? O God, if thy commands and purposes be capable of alteration, alter this bloody sentence, and let thy first word stand.

These would have been the thoughts of a weak heart. But God knew that he spake to an Abraham, and Abraham knew that he had to do with a God: faith had taught him not to argue but obey. In a holy wilfulness he either forgets nature or despises her: he is sure that what God commands is good, that what he promises is infallible; and therefore is careless of the means, and trusts to the end.

In matters of God, whosoever consults with flesh and blood, shall never offer up his Isaac to God. There needs no counsellor when we know God is the commander; here is neither grudging, nor deliberating, nor delaying; his faith would not suffer him so much as to be sorry for that he must do. Sarah herself may not know of God's charge and her husband's purpose, lest her affection should have overcome her faith; lest her weakness, now grown importunate, should have said, Disobey God, and die. That which he must do, he will do; he that hath learned not to regard the life of his son, had learned not to regard the sorrow of his wife. It is too much tenderness to respect the censures and constructions of others, when we have a direct word from God. The good patriarch rises early, and addresses himself to his sad journey. And now must he travel three whole days to this execution; and still must Isaac be in his eye, whom all this while he seems to see bleeding upon the pile of wood which he carries. There is nothing so miserable as to dwell under the expectation of a great evil. That misery which must be, is mitigated with speed, and aggravated with delay. All this while, if Abraham had repented him, he had leisure to return. There is no small trial, even in the very time of trial. Now, when they are come within sight of the chosen mountain, the servants are dismissed. What a devotion is this that will abide no witnesses! He will not suffer two of his own vassals to see him do that, which soon after all the world must know he hath done; is not Abraham afraid of that piety, which the beholders could not see without horror, without resistance, which no ear could hear of without abomination. What stranger could have endured to see the father carry the knife and fire, instruments of that death which he had rather suffer than inflict; the son securely carrying that burden which must carry him?

But if Abraham's heart could have known how to relent, that question of his dear, innocent, and religious son had melted it into compassion: " My father, behold the fire and the wood, but where is the sacrifice?" I know not whether that word (my father) did not strike Abraham as deep as the knife of Abraham could strike his son: yet doth he not so much as think, O miserable man, that may not at once be a son to such a God, and father to such a son! Still he persists, and conceals; and, where he meant not, prophesies, " My son, God shall provide a lamb for the burnt-offering."

The heavy tidings were loath to come forth. It was a death to Abraham to say what he must do. He knows his own faith to act this; he knows not Isaac's to endure it. But now when Isaac hath helped to build the altar, whereon he must be consumed, he hears (not without astonishment) the strange command of God, the final will of his father: My son, thou art the lamb, which God hath provided for this burnt-offering. If my blood would have excused thee, how many thousand times had I rather to give thee my own life, than take thine! Alas! I am full of days, and now, of long, lived not but in thee. Thou mightest have preserved the life of thy father, and have comforted his death; but the God of us both hath chosen thee. He, that gave thee unto me miraculously, bids me, by an unusual means, return thee unto him. I need not tell thee that I sacrifice all my worldly joys, yea and myself, in thee; but God must be obeyed: neither art thou too dear for him that calls thee. Come on, my son, restore the life that God hath given thee by me. Offer thyself willingly to these flames; send up thy soul cheerfully unto thy glory; and know, that God loves thee above others, since he requires thee alone to be consecrated in sacrifice to himself.

Who cannot imagine with what perplexed mixtures of passions, with what changes of countenance, what doubts, what fears, what amazement, good Isaac received this sudden message from the mouth of his father! how he questioned, how he pleaded! But when he had somewhat digested his thoughts, and considered that the author was God, the actor Abraham, the action a sacrifice, he now approves himself the son of Abraham: now he encourages the trembling hands of his father, with whom he strives in this praise of forwardness and obedience: now he offers his hands and feet to the cords, his throat to the knife, his body to the altar; and, growing ambitious of the sword and fire, entreats his father to do that which he would have done, though he had dissuaded him. O holy emulation of faith! O blessed agreement of the sacrificer and oblation! Abraham is as ready to take as Isaac to give: he binds those dear hands, which are more straitly bound with the cords of duty and resolution; he lays his sacrifice upon the wood, which now before-hand burnt inwardly with the heavenly fire of zeal and devotion.

And now having kissed him his last, not without mutual tears, he lifts up his hand to fetch the stroke of death at once, not so much as thinking, perhaps, God will relent after the first wound. Now the stay of Abraham, the hope of the church, lies bleeding under the hand of a father. What bowels can choose but yearn at this spectacle! Which of the savagest heathens, that had been now upon the hill of Moriah, and had seen (through the bushes) the sword of a father hanging over the throat of such a son, would not have been more perplexed in his thoughts than that unexpected sacrifice was in those briars? Yet he, whom it nearest concerned, is least touched: faith hath wrought the same in him which cruelty would in others, not to be moved. He contemns all fears, and overlooks all impossibilities. His heart tells him, that the same hand which raised Isaac from the dead womb of Sarah, can raise him again from the ashes of his sacrifice. With this confidence was the hand of Abraham now falling upon the throat of Isaac, who had given himself for dead, and rejoiced in the change; when suddenly the angel of God interrupts him, forbids him, commends him. The voice of God was never so welcome, never so sweet, never so seasonable as now: it was the trial that God intended, not the fact: Isaac is sacrificed, and is yet alive; and now both of them are more happy in that they would have done, than they could have been distressed if they had done it. God's charges are ofttimes harsh in the beginnings and proceeding, but in the conclusion always comfortable. True spiritual comforts are commonly late and sudden. God defers on purpose, that our trials may be perfect, our deliverance welcome, our recompense glorious. Isaac had never been so precious to his father, if he had not been recovered from death; if he had not been as miraculously restored as given. Abraham had never been so blessed in his seed, if he had not neglected Isaac for God.

The only way to find comfort in an earthly thing, is to surrender it (in a faithful carelessness) into the hands of God. Abraham came to sacrifice: he may not go away with dry hands. God cannot abide that good purposes should be frustrate, lest either he should not do that for which he came, or should want means of speedy thanksgiving for so gracious a disappointment. Behold, a ram stands ready for the sacrifice, and, as it were, proffers himself to this happy exchange. He that made that beast, brings him thither, fastens him there. Even in small things there is a great providence. What mysteries there are in every act of God! The only Son of God, upon this very hill, is laid upon the altar of the cross, and so becomes a true sacrifice for the world; that yet he is raised without impeachment, and exempted from the power of death. The Lamb of God, which takes away the sins of the world, is here really offered and accepted. One Saviour in two figures; in the one dying, restored in the other. So Abraham, while he exercises his faith, confirms it; and rejoices more to foresee the true Isaac in that place offered to death for his sins, than to see the carnal Isaac preserved from death for the reward of his faith. Whatsoever is dearest to us upon earth, is our Isaac: happy are we, if we can sacrifice it to God. Those shall never rest with Abraham, that cannot sacrifice with Abraham.

CONTEMPLATION V.—OF LOT AND SODOM.

BEFORE Abraham and Lot grew rich, they dwelt together; now their wealth separates them; their society was a greater good than their riches. Many a one is a loser by his wealth. Who would account those things good which make us worse? It had been the duty of young Lot to offer rather than to choose, to yield rather than contend. Who would not here think Abraham the nephew, and Lot the uncle? It is no disparagement for greater persons to begin treaties of peace. Better doth it beseem every son of Abraham to win with love, than to sway with power. Abraham yields over this right of his choice; Lot takes it: and behold, Lot is crossed in that which he chose, Abraham was blessed in that which was left him. God never suffers any man to lose by an humble remission of his right in a desire for peace.

Wealth had made Lot not only undutiful but covetous: he sees the goodly plains of Jordan, the richness of the soil, the commodity of the rivers, the situation of the cities; and now not once inquiring into the conditions of the inhabitants, he is in love with Sodom. Outward appearances are deceitful guides to our judgment or affections. They are worthy to be deceived that value things as they seem. It is not long after that Lot pays dear for his rashness. He fled for quietness with his uncle, and finds war with strangers. Now he is carried prisoner with all his substance, by great enemies: Abraham must rescue him, of whom he was forsaken. That wealth, which was the cause of his former quarrels, is made a prey to merciless heathens: that place, which his eye covetously chose, betrays his life and goods. How many Christians, while they have looked at gain, have lost themselves!

Yet this ill success hath neither driven out Lot nor amended Sodom; he still loves his commodity, and the Sodomites their sins. Wicked men grow worse with afflictions, as water grows more cold after a heat: and as they leave not sinning, so God leaves not plaguing them, but still follows them with succession of judgments. In how few years hath Sodom forgot she was spoiled and led captive! If that wicked city had been warned by the sword, it had escaped the fire; but now this visitation hath not made ten good men in those five cities. How fit was this heap for the fire, which was all chaff? Only Lot vexed his righteous soul with the sight of their uncleanness: he vexed his own soul, for who bade him stay there? Yet because he was vexed, he is delivered. He escapeth their judgment, from whose sins he escaped. Though he would be a guest of Sodom, yet, because he would not entertain their sins, he becomes an host to the angels. Even the good angels are the executioners of God's judgment. There cannot be a better or more noble act, than to do justice upon obstinate malefactors.

Who can be ashamed of that which did not misbeseem the very angels of God! Where should the angels lodge but with Lot! The houses of holy men are full of these heavenly spirits, when they know not: they pitch their tents in ours, and visit us when we see not; and, when we feel not, protect us. It is the honour of God's saints to be attended by angels. The filthy Sodomites now flock together, stirred up with the fury of envy and lust, and dare require to do that in troops, which, to act single, had been too abominable to imagine natural. Continuance and society in evil makes wicked men outrageous and impudent. It is not enough for Lot to be the witness, but he must be the bawd also: " Bring forth these men that we may know them."

Behold even the Sodomites speak modestly, though their acts and intents be villanous. What a shame is it for those which profess purity of heart, to speak filthily! The good man craves and pleads the laws of hospitality; and, when he sees headstrong purposes of mischief, chooses rather to be an ill father than an ill host. His intention was good, but his offer was faulty. If, through his allowance, the Sodomites had defiled his daughters, it had been his sin: if through violence they had defiled his guests, it had been only theirs. There can be no warrant for us to sin, lest others should sin. It is for God to prevent sins with judgments; it is not for men to prevent a greater sin with a less. The best minds, when they are troubled, yield inconsiderate motions, as water that is violently stirred, sends up bubbles: God meant better to Lot, than to suffer his weak offer to be accepted. Those which are bent upon villany are more exasperated by dissuasion, as some strong streams, when they are resisted by flood-gates, swell over the banks.

Many a one is hardened by the good word of God, and instead of receiving the counsel, rages at the messenger. When men are grown to that pass, that they are no whit better by afflictions, and worse with admonitions, God finds it time to strike. Now Lot's guests begin to show themselves angels, and first deliver Lot in Sodom, then from Sodom; first strike them with blindness, whom they will after consume with fire. How little did the Sodomites think that vengeance was so near them! While they went groping in the streets, and cursing those whom they could not find, Lot with the angels is in secure light, and sees them miserable, and foresees them burning. It is the use of God, to blind and besot those whom he means to destroy. The light which they shall see shall be fiery, which shall be the beginning of an everlasting darkness, and a fire unquenchable. Now they have done sinning, and God begins to judge. Wickedness hath but a time; the punishment of wickedness is beyond all time. The residue of the night was both short and dangerous; yet good Lot, though sought for by the Sodomites, and newly pulled into his house by the angels, goes forth of his house to seek his sons-in-law. No good man would be saved alone. Faith makes us charitable with neglect of all peril. He warns them like a prophet, and advises them like a father, but both in vain: he seems to them as if he mocked, and they do more than seem to mock him again. Why should to-morrow differ from other days? Who ever saw it rain fire? Or whence should that brimstone come? Or if such showers must fall, how shall nothing burn but this valley? So to carnal men, preaching is foolishness, devotion idleness, the prophets madmen, Paul a babbler. These men's incredulity is as worthy of the fire, as the others' uncleanness. " He that believes not is condemned already."

The messengers of God do not only hasten Lot, but pull him by a gracious violence out of that impure city. They thirsted at once after vengeance upon Sodom, and Lot's safety; they knew God could not strike Sodom till Lot was gone out, and that Lot could not be safe within those walls. We are all naturally in Sodom: if God did not haul us out, while we linger, we should be condemned with the world. If God meet with a very good field, he pulls up the weeds, and lets the corn grow; if indifferent, he lets the corn and weeds grow together; if very ill, he gathers the few ears of corn, and burns the weeds.

Oh! the large bounty of God, which reacheth not to us only, but to ours! God saves Lot for Abraham's sake, and Zoar for Lot's sake. If Sodom had not been too wicked, it had escaped. Were it not for God's dear children that are intermixed with the world, it could not stand. The wicked owe their lives unto those few good, whom they hate and persecute. Now at once the sun rises upon Zoar, and fire falls down upon Sodom. Abraham stands upon the hill, and sees the cities burning. It is fair weather with God's children, when it is foulest with the wicked. Those which burned with the fire of lust, are now consumed with the fire of vengeance. They sinned against nature; and now against the course of nature, fire descends from heaven and consumes them. Lot may not so much as look at the flame, whether for the stay of his passage, or the horror of the sight, or trial of his faith, or fear of commiseration. Small precepts from God are of importance. Obedience is as well tried, and disobedience as well punished, in little as in much. His wife doth but turn back her head; whether in curiosity, or unbelief, or love and compassion of the place, she is turned into a monument of disobedience. What doth it avail her not to be turned into ashes in Sodom, when she is turned into a pillar of salt in the plain? He that saved a whole city cannot save his own wife: God cannot abide small sins in those whom he hath obliged. If we displease him, God can as well meet with us out of Sodom. Lot, now come into Zoar, marvels at the stay of her, whom he might not before look back to call; and soon after returning to seek her, beholds this change with wonder and grief. He finds salt instead of flesh, a pillar instead of a wife. He finds Sodom consumed, and her standing; and is more amazed with this, by how much it was both more near him, and less expected.

When God delivers us from destruction, he doth not secure us from all afflictions. Lot hath lost his wife, his allies, his substance, and now betakes himself to an uncomfortable solitariness.

Yet though he fled from company, he could not fly from sin. He who could not be tainted with uncleanness in Sodom, is overtaken with drunkenness and incest in a cave. Rather than Satan shall not want baits, his own daughters will prove Sodomites. Those which should have comforted betrayed him. How little are some hearts moved with judgments! The ashes of Sodom, and the pillar of salt, were not yet out of their eye, when they dare think of lying with their own father. They knew, that whilst Lot was sober, he could not be unchaste. Drunkenness is the way to all bestial affections and acts. Wine knows no difference either of persons or sins. No doubt, Lot was afterwards ashamed of his incestuous seed, and now wished he had come alone out of Sodom: yet even this unnatural bed was blessed with increase; and one of our Saviour's worthy ancestors sprung after from this line. God's election is not tied to our means, neither are blessings or curses ever traduced. The chaste bed of holy parents hath ofttimes bred a monstrous generation; and contrarily, God hath raised sometimes an holy seed from the drunken bed of incest, or fornication. It hath been seen, that weighty ears of corn have grown out of the compass of the tilled field: thus will God magnify the freedom of his own choice, and let us know that we are not born, but made, good.

BOOK III.

CONTEMPLATION I.—OF JACOB AND ESAU.

OF all the patriarchs, none made so little noise in the world as Isaac; none lived either so privately, or so innocently: neither know I whether he approved himself a better son or an husband; for the one he gave himself over to the knife of his father, and mourned three years for his mother; for the other he sought not to any handmaid's bed, but, in a chaste forbearance, reserved himself for twenty years' space, and prayed. Rebecca was so long barren. His prayers proved more effectual than his seed. At last she conceived, as if she had been more than the daughter-in-law to Sarah, whose son was given her, not out of the power of nature, but out of her husband's faith.

God is oft better to us than we would. Isaac prays for a son: God gives him two at once. Now she is no less troubled with the strife of the children in her womb, than before with the want of children. We know not when we are pleased: that which we desire ofttimes discontents us more in the fruition: we are ready to complain both full and fasting. Before Rebecca conceived, she was at ease. Before spiritual regeneration there is all peace in the soul: no sooner is the new man formed in us, but the flesh conflicts with the spirit. There is no grace where is no unquietness. Esau alone would not have striven. Nature will ever agree with itself. Never any Rebecca conceived only an Esau, or was so happy as to conceive none but a Jacob: she must be the mother of both, that she may have both joy and exercise. This strife began early: every true Israelite begins his war with his being. How many actions which we know not of, are not without presage and signification!

These two were the champions of two nations: the field was their mother's womb; their quarrel precedency and superiority. Esau got the right of nature, Jacob of grace; yet that there might be some pretence of equality, lest Esau should outrun his brother into the world, Jacob holds him fast by the heel; so his hand was born before the other's foot. But, because Esau is some minutes the elder, that the younger might have better claim to that which God had promised, he buys that which he could not win. If either by strife, or purchase, or suit, we can attain spiritual blessings, we are happy. If Jacob had come forth first, he had not known how much he was bound to God for the favour of his advancement.

There was never any meat, except the forbidden fruit, so dear bought as this broth of Jacob; in both, the receiver and eater is accursed. Every true son of Israel will be content to purchase spiritual favours with earthly; and that man hath in him too much of the blood of Esau, who will not rather die than forego his birthright.

But what hath careless Esau lost, if, having sold his birthright, he may obtain the blessing? Or what hath Jacob gained, if his brother's venison may countervail his pottage? Yet thus hath old Isaac decreed, who was now not more blind in his eyes, than his affections. God had forewarned him that the elder should serve the younger, yet Isaac goes about to bless Esau.

It was as hard for Abraham to reconcile God's promise and Isaac's sacrifice, as for Isaac to reconcile the superiority of Jacob with Esau's benediction; for God's hand was in that; in this, none but his own. The dearest of God's saints have been sometimes transported with natural affections. He saw himself preferred to Ishmael, though the elder. He saw his father wilfully forgetting nature at God's command, in binding him for sacrifice. He saw Esau lewdly matched with heathens, and yet he will remember nothing but Esau is my first-born. But how gracious is God, that when we would, will not let us sin! and so orders our actions, that we do not what we will, but what we ought!

That God which had ordained the lordship to the younger, will also contrive for him the blessing: what he will have effected, shall not want means. The mother shall rather defeat the son, and beguile the father, than the father shall beguile the chosen son of his blessing. What was Jacob to Rebecca, more than Esau? or what mother doth not more affect the elder? But now God inclines the love of the mother to the younger, against the custom of nature, because the father loves the elder, against the promise. The affections of the parents are divided: that the promise might be fulfilled, Rebecca's craft shall answer Isaac's partiality; Isaac would unjustly turn Esau into Jacob; Rebecca doth as cunningly turn Jacob into Esau: her desire was good; her means were unlawful. God doth ofttimes effect his just will by our weaknesses; yet neither thereby justifying our infirmities, nor blemishing his own actions.

Here was nothing but counterfeiting; a feigned person, a feigned name, feigned venison, a feigned answer, and yet behold a true blessing; but to the man, not to the means. Those were so unsound, that Jacob himself doth more fear their curse, than hope for their success. Isaac was now both simple and old; yet, if he had perceived the fraud, Jacob had been more sure of a curse, than he could be sure that he should not be perceived.

Those which are plain-hearted in themselves, are the bitterest enemies to deceit in others. Rebecca, presuming upon the oracle of God and her husband's simplicity, dare be his surety for the danger, his counsellor for the carriage of the business, his cook for the diet, yea, dresses both the meat and the man; and now puts words into his mouth, the dish into his hand, the garments upon his back, the goat's hair upon the open parts of his body, and sends him in, thus furnished for the blessing, standing, no doubt, at the door, to see how well her device succeeded. And if old Isaac should, by any of his senses, have discerned the guile, she had soon stept in and undertaken the blame, and urged him with that known will of God concerning Jacob's dominion, and Esau's servitude, which either age or affection had made him forget.

And now she wishes she could borrow Esau's tongue as well as his garments, that she might securely deceive all the senses of him which had suffered himself to be more dangerously deceived with his affection. But this is past her remedy: her son must name himself Esau with the voice of Jacob. It is hard if our tongue do not bewray what we are, in spite of our habit. This was enough to work Isaac to a suspicion, to an inquiry, not to an incredulity. He that is good of himself, will hardly believe evil of another, and will rather distrust his own senses than the fidelity of those he trusted. All the senses are set to examine; none sticketh at the judgment, but the ear: to deceive that, Jacob must second his dissimulation with three lies at one breath: I am Esau;—as thou badest me;—my venison. One sin entertained, fetcheth in another; and if it be forced to lodge alone, either departeth or dieth. I love Jacob's blessing, but I hate his lie. I would not do that wilfully which Jacob did weakly, upon condition of a blessing. He that pardoned his infirmity would curse my obstinateness.

Good Isaac sets his hands to try whether his ears informed him aright; he feels the hands of him whose voice he suspected: that honest heart could not think that the skin might more easily be counterfeited than the lungs. A small satisfaction contents those whom guiltiness hath not made scrupulous. Isaac believes, and blesses the younger son in the garments of the elder. If our heavenly father smell upon our backs the savour of our elder brother's robes, we cannot depart from him unblessed.

No sooner is Jacob gone away, full of the joy of his blessing, than Esau comes in, full of the hope of the blessing; and now he cannot repent him to have sold that in his hunger for pottage, which in his pleasure he shall buy again with venison. The hopes of the wicked fail them when they are at highest; whereas God's children find those comforts in extremity which they durst not expect.

Now he comes in, blowing and sweating for his reward, and finds nothing but a repulse. Lewd men, when they think they have earned of God, and come proudly to challenge favour, receive no answer but—"Who art thou?" Both the father and the son wonder at each other; the one with fear, the other with grief. Isaac trembled, and Esau wept; the one upon conscience, the other upon envy. Isaac's heart now told him, that he should not have purposed the blessing where he did; and that it was due to him unto whom it was given, and not purposed. Hence he durst not reverse that which he had done with God's will, besides his own: for now he saw that he had done unwilling justice. God will find both time and means to reclaim his own, to prevent their sins, to manifest and reform their errors. Who would have looked for tears from Esau? Or who dare trust tears when he sees them fall from so graceless eyes?

It was a good word, "Bless me also, my father." Every miscreant can wish himself well: no man would be miserable if it were enough to desire happiness. Why did he not rather weep to his brother for the pottage, than to Isaac for a blessing? If he had not then sold, he had not needed now to beg. It is just with God to deny us those favours which we were careless in keeping, and which we undervalued in enjoying. Esau's tears find no place for Isaac's repentance; except it were, that he hath done that by wile which he should have done upon duty.

No motive can cause a good heart to repent that he hath done well. How happy a thing it is to know the seasons of grace, and not to neglect them! How desperate to have known and neglected them! These tears were both late and false; the tears of rage, of envy, of carnal desire. Worldly sorrow causeth death. Yet while Esau howls out thus for a blessing, I hear him cry out, of his father's store, "Hast thou but one blessing, my father?" Of his brother's subtilty, "Was he not rightly called Jacob?" I do not hear him blame his own deserts. He did not see, while his father was deceived, and his brother crafty, that God was just, and himself incapable. He knew himself profane, and yet claims a blessing

Those that care not to please God, yet care for the outward favours of God, and are ready to murmur if they want them; as if God were bound to them and they free. And yet so merciful is God, that he hath second blessings for those that love him not, and gives them all they care for. That one blessing of special love is for none but Israel; but those of common kindness are for them that can sell their birthright. This blessing was more than Esau could be worthy of: yet, like a second Cain, he resolves to kill his brother, because he was more accepted. I know not whether he were a worse son or brother; he hopes for his father's death, and purposes his brother's, and vows to shed blood instead of tears. But wicked men cannot be so ill as they would: that strong wrestler, against whom Jacob prevailed, prevailed with Esau, and turned his wounds into kisses. An host of men came with Esau; an army of angels met Jacob. Esau threatened, Jacob prayed; his prayers and presents have melted the heart of Esau into love. And now, instead of the grim and stern countenance of an executioner, Jacob sees the face of Esau as the face of God. Both men and devils are stinted; the stoutest heart cannot stand out against God. He that can wrestle earnestly with God, is secure from the harms of men. Those minds which are exasperated with violence, and cannot be broken with fear, yet are bowed with love: when the ways of a man please God, he will make his enemies at peace with him.

CONTEMPLATION II.—OF JACOB AND LABAN.

Isaac's life was not more retired and quiet, than Jacob's was busy and troublesome. In the one I see the image of contemplation; of action in the other. None of the patriarchs saw so evil days as he; from whom justly hath the church of God therefore taken her name. Neither were the faithful ever since called Abrahamites, but Israelites. That no time might be lost, he began his strife in the womb; after that, he flies for his life from a cruel brother to a cruel uncle. With a staff goes he over Jordan alone, doubtful and comfortless, not like the son of Isaac. In the way, the earth is his bed, and the stone his pillow; yet even there he sees a vision of angels. Jacob's heart was never so full of joy as when his head lay hardest. God is most present with us in our greatest dejection, and loves to give comfort to those that are forsaken of their hopes.

He came far to find out an hard friend, and of a nephew becomes a servant. No doubt, when Laban heard of his sister's son, he looked for the camels and attendance that came to fetch his sister Rebecca; not thinking that Abraham's servant could come better furnished than Isaac's son: but now, when he saw nothing but a staff, he looks upon him, not as an uncle, but a master; and while he pretends to offer him a wife as the reward of his service, he craftily requires his service as the dowry of his wife.

After the service of a hard apprenticeship hath earned her whom he loved, his wife is changed, and he is in a sort forced to an unwilling adultery. His mother had before, in a cunning disguise, substituted him, who was the younger son, for the elder; and now, not long after, his father-in-law, by a like fraud, substitutes to him the elder daughter for the younger. God comes oftentimes home to us in our own kind; and even by the sin of others pays us our own, when we look not for it. It is doubtful whether it were a greater cross to marry whom he would not, or to be disappointed of her whom he desired. And now he must begin a new hope, where he made account of fruition. To raise up an expectation once frustrate, is more difficult than to continue a long hope drawn on with likelihoods of performance: yet, thus dear is Jacob content to pay for Rachel fourteen years' servitude. Commonly God's children come not easily by their pleasures. What miseries will not love digest and overcome? And if Jacob were willingly consumed with heat in the day, and frost in the night, to become the son-in-law to Laban, what should we refuse to be the sons of God?

Rachel, whom he loved, is barren: Leah, which was despised, is fruitful. How wisely God weighs out to us our favours and crosses in an equal balance; so tempering our sorrows that they may not oppress, and our joys that they may not transport us! Each one hath some matter of envy to others, and of grief to himself.

Leah envies Rachel's beauty and love: Rachel envies Leah's fruitfulness: yet Leah would not be barren, nor Rachel blear-eyed. I see in Rachel the image of her grandmother Sarah, both in her beauty of person, in her actions, in her success. She also will needs suborn her handmaid to make her a mother, and at last, beyond hope, herself conceiveth. It is a weak greediness in us to affect God's blessings by unlawful means. What a proof and praise had it been of her faith, if she had stayed God's leisure, and would rather have endured her barrenness than her husband's polygamy! Now she shows herself the daughter of Laban: the father for covetousness, the daughters for emulation, have drawn sin into Jacob's bed: he offended in yielding, but they more in soliciting him, and therefore the fact is not imputed to Jacob, but to them. In those sins which Satan draws us into, the blame is ours: in those which we move each other into, the most fault and punishment lies upon the tempter. None of the patriarchs divided his seed into so many wombs as Jacob; none was so much crossed in his seed.

Thus, rich in nothing but wives and children, was he now returning to his father's house, accounting his charge his wealth. But God meant him yet more good. Laban sees that both his family and his flocks were well increased by Jacob's service. Not his love, therefore, but his gain, makes him loath to part. Even Laban's covetousness is made by God the means to enrich Jacob.

Behold, his strait master entreats him to that recompense, which made his nephew mighty and himself envious. God, considering his hard service, paid him wages out of Laban's folds. Those flocks and herds had but a few spotted sheep and goats, until Jacob's covenant; then (as if the fashion had been altered) they all ran into parted colours; the most and best (as if they had been weary of their former owner) changed the colours of their young, that they might change their master.

In the very shapes and colours of brute creatures there is a divine hand, which disposeth them to his own ends. Small and unlikely means shall prevail, where God intends an effect. Little peeled sticks of hazel or poplar, laid in the troughs, shall enrich Jacob with an increase of his spotted flocks: Laban's sons might have tried the same means, and failed. God would have Laban know, that he put a difference betwixt Jacob and him; that as for fourteen years he had multiplied Jacob's charge of cattle to Laban, so now, for the last six years, he would multiply Laban's flock to Jacob: and if Laban had the more, yet the better were Jacob's. Even in these outward things, God's children have many times sensible tastes of his favours above the wicked.

I know not whether Laban were a worse uncle, or father, or master: he can like well Jacob's service, not his wealth. As the wicked have no peace with God, so the godly have no peace with men: for if they prosper not, they are despised; if they prosper, they are envied. This uncle, whom his service had made his father, must now, upon his wealth, be fled from as an enemy, and like an enemy pursues him: if Laban had meant to have taken a peaceable leave, he had never spent seven days' journey in following his innocent son. Jacob knew his churlishness, and therefore resolved rather to be unmannerly than injured. Well might he think that he, whose oppression changed his wages so often in his stay, would also abridge his wages in the parting; now therefore he wisely prefers his own estate to Laban's love. It is not good to regard too much the unjust discontentment of worldly men, and to purchase unprofitable favour with too great loss.

Behold, Laban follows Jacob with one troop, Esau meets him with another, both with hostile intentions: both go on to the utmost point of their execution; both are prevented ere the execution. God makes fools of the enemies of his church; he lets them proceed, that they may be frustrate; and, when they are gone to the utmost reach of their tether, he pulls them back to their task with shame. Lo now, Laban leaves Jacob with a kiss; Esau meets him with a kiss: of the one he hath an oath, tears of the other, peace with both. Who shall need to fear man that is in league with God?

But what a wonder is this! Jacob received not so much hurt from all his enemies, as from his best friend. Not one of his hairs perished by Laban or Esau, yet he lost a joint by the angel, and was sent halting to his grave. He that knows our strength, yet will wrestle with us for our exercise, and loves our violence and importunity.

O happy loss of Jacob! he lost a joint and won a blessing. It is a favour to halt from God, yet this favour is seconded with a greater. He is blessed, because he would rather halt than leave ere he was blessed. If he had left sooner, he had not halted, but he had not prospered. That man shall go away sound, but miserable, that loves a limb more than a blessing. Surely if Jacob had not wrestled with God, he had been foiled with evils. How many are the troubles of the righteous!

Not long after, Rachel, the comfort of his life, dieth. And when? but in her travail, and in her travel to his father. When he had now before digested in his thoughts the joy and gratulation of his aged father for so welcome a burden, his children (the staff of his age) wound his soul to the death. Reuben proves incestuous, Judah adulterous, Dinah ravished, Simeon and Levi murderous, Er and Onan stricken dead, Joseph lost, Simeon imprisoned, Benjamin, the death of his mother, the father's right hand, endangered; himself driven by famine, in his old age, to die amongst the Egyptians, a people that held it abomination to eat with him. If that angel with whom he strove, and who therefore strove for him, had not delivered his soul out of all adversity, he had been supplanted with evils, and had been so far from gaining the name of Israel, that he had lost the name of Jacob. Now, what son of Israel can hope for good days, when he hears his father's were so evil? It is enough for us, if, when we are dead, we can rest with him in the land of promise. If the angel of the covenant once bless us, no pain, no sorrows, can make us miserable.

CONTEMPLATION III.—OF DINAH.

I FIND but one only daughter of Jacob, who must needs therefore be a great darling to her father; and she so miscarries, that she causes her father's grief to be more than his love. As her mother Leah, so she hath a fault in her eyes, which was curiosity. She will needs see and be seen; and while she doth vainly see, she is seen lustfully. It is not enough for us to look to our own thoughts, except we beware of the provocations of others. If we once wander out of the lists that God hath set us in our callings, there is nothing but danger. Her virginity had been safe, if she had kept home; or if Shechem had forced her in her mother's tent, this loss of her virginity had been without her sin; now she is not innocent that gave the occasion.

Her eyes were guilty of the temptation; only to see, is an insufficient warrant to draw us into places of spiritual hazard. If Shechem had seen her busy at home, his love had been free from outrage; now the lightness of her presence gave encouragement to his inordinate desires. Immodesty of behaviour makes way to lust, and gives life unto wicked hopes: yet Shechem bewrays a good nature, even in filthiness. He loves Dinah after his sin, and will needs marry her whom he had defiled. Commonly lust ends in loathing. Amnon abhors Thamar as much after his act, as before he loved her; and beats her out of doors, whom he was sick to bring in. But Shechem would not let Dinah fare the worse for his sin. And now he goes about to entertain her with honest love, whom the rage of his lust had dishonestly abused. Her deflowering shall be no prejudice to her, since her shame shall redound to none but him; and he will hide her dishonour with the name of a husband. What could he now do but sue to his father, to her's, to herself, to her brethren; entreating that, with humble submission, which he might have obtained by violence? Those actions which are ill begun, can hardly be salved up with late satisfactions; whereas good entrances give strength unto the proceedings, and success to the end.

The young man's father doth not only consent, but solicit; and is ready to purchase a daughter either with substance or pain. The two old men would have ended the matter peaceably; but youth commonly undertakes rashly, and performs with passion. The sons of Jacob think of nothing but revenge, and (which is worst of all) begin their cruelty with craft, and hide their craft with religion. A smiling malice is most deadly; and hatred doth most rankle the heart when it is kept in and dissembled. "We cannot give our sister to an uncircumcised man." Here was God in the mouth, and Satan in the heart. The bloodiest of all projects have ever wont to be coloured with religion; because the worse any thing is, the better show it desires to make; and contrarily, the better colour is put upon any vice, the more odious it is; for as every simulation adds to an evil, so the best adds most evil. Themselves had taken the daughters and sisters of uncircumcised men; yea, Jacob himself did so: why might not an uncircumcised man obtain their sister? Or, if there be a difference of giving and taking, it had been well if it had not been only pretended. It had been a happy ravishment of Dinah, that should have drawn a whole country into the bosom of the church. But here was a sacrament intended, not to the good of the soul, but to the murder of the body. It was a hard task for Hamor and Shechem, not only to put the knife to their own foreskins, but to persuade a multitude to so painful a condition.

The sons of Jacob dissemble with them, they with the people. "Shall not their flocks and substance be ours?" Common profit is pretended; whereas only Shechem's pleasure is meant. No motive is so powerful to the vulgar sort, as the name of commodity: the hope of this makes them prodigal of their skin and blood; not the love to the sacrament, not the love to Shechem: sinister respects draw more to the profession of religion than conscience. If it were not for the loaves and fishes, the train of Christ would be less. But the sacraments of God, misreceived, never prosper in the end. These men are content to smart, so they may gain.

And now, that every man lies sore of his own wound, Simeon and Levi rush in armed, and wound all the males to death. "Cursed be their wrath, for it was fierce; and their rage, for it was cruel." Indeed, filthiness should not have been wrought in Israel; yet murder should not have been wrought by Israel: if they had been fit judges, (which were but bloody executioners) how far doth the punishment exceed the fault? To punish above the offence, is no less injustice than to offend. One offendeth, and all feel the revenge: yea all (though innocent) suffer that revenge, which he that offended deserved not. Shechem sinneth, but Dinah tempted him. She that was so light, as to wander abroad alone, only to gaze, I fear was not over difficult to yield; and if, having wrought her shame, he had driven her home with disgrace to her father's tent, such tyrannous lust had justly called for blood: but now he craves, and would pay dear for but leave to give satisfaction.

To execute rigour upon a submissive offender, is more merciless than just. Or if the punishment had been both just and proportionable from another, yet from them which had vowed peace and affinity, it was shamefully unjust. To disappoint the trust of another, and to neglect our own promise and fidelity for private purposes, adds faithlessness unto our cruelty. That they were impotent, it was through their circumcision: what impiety was this, instead of honouring a holy sign, to take an advantage by it! What shrieking was there now in the streets of the city of the Hivites! And how did the beguiled Shechemites, when they saw the swords of the two brethren, die cursing the sacrament in their hearts, which had betrayed them! Even their curses were the sins of Simeon and Levi, whose fact, though it were abhorred by their father, yet it was seconded by their brethren. Their spoil makes good the others' slaughter. Who would have looked to have found this outrage in the family of Jacob! How did that good patriarch, when he saw Dinah come home blubbered and wringing her hands, Simeon and Levi sprinkled with blood, wish that Leah had been barren as long as Rachel! Good parents have grief enough (though they sustain no blame) for their children's sins. What great evils arise from small beginnings! The idle curiosity of Dinah hath bred all this mischief; ravishment follows upon her wandering; upon her ravishment, murder; upon the murder, spoil. It is holy and safe to be jealous of the first occasions of evil, either done or suffered.

CONTEMPLATION IV.—OF JUDAH AND THAMAR.

I FIND not many of Jacob's sons more faulty than Judah; who yet is singled out from all the rest, to be the royal progenitor of Christ, and to be honoured with the dignity of the birth-right, that God's election might not be of merit, but of grace: else, howsoever he might have sped alone, Thamar had never been joined with him in this line. Even Judah marries a Canaanite; it is no marvel though his seed prosper not. And yet, that good children may not be too much discouraged with their unlawful propagation, the fathers of the promised seed are raised from an incestuous bed. Judah was very young, scarce from under the rod of his father, yet he takes no other counsel for his marriage, but from his own eyes, which were, like his sister Dinah's, roving and wanton. What better issue could be expected from such beginnings? Those proud Jews, that glory so much of their pedigree and name from this patriarch, may now choose whether they will have their mother a Canaanite or a harlot; even in these things ofttimes the birth follows the belly. His eldest son Er is too wicked to live; God strikes him dead ere he can leave any issue, not abiding any scions to grow out of so bad a stock. Notorious sinners God reserves to his own vengeance. He doth not inflict sensible judgments upon all his enemies, lest the wicked should think there were no punishment abiding for them elsewhere. He doth inflict such judgments upon some, lest he should seem careless of evil. It were as easy for him to strike all dead, as one: but he had rather all should be warned by one; and would have his enemies find him merciful, as well as his children just: his brother Onan sees the judgment, and yet follows his sins. Every little thing discourages us from good: nothing can alter the heart that is set upon evil. Er was not worthy of any love; but, though he were a miscreant, yet he was a brother. Seed should have been raised to him. Onan justly loses his life with his seed, which he would rather spill, than lend to a wicked brother. Some duties we owe to humanity, more to our nearness of blood. Ill deservings of others can be no excuse for our injustice, for our uncharitableness. That which Thamar required, Moses afterward, as from God, commanded, the succession of brothers into the barren bed. Some laws God spake to his church, long ere he wrote them: while the author is certainly known, the voice and the finger of God are worthy of equal respect. Judah had lost two sons, and now doth but promise the third, whom he sins in not giving. It is the weakness of nature, rather to hazard a sin than a danger, and to neglect our own duty, for wrongful suspicion of others: though he had lost his son in giving him, yet he should have given him. A faithful man's promise is his debt, which no fear of damage can dispense with.

But whereupon was his slackness? Judah feared that some unhappiness in the bed of Thamar was the cause of his son's miscarriage; whereas it was their fault, that Thamar was both a widow and childless. Those that are but the patients of evil, are many times burdened with suspicions; and therefore are ill thought of, because they fare ill. Afflictions would not be so heavy, if they did not lay us open unto uncharitable conceits.

What difference God puts betwixt sins of wilfulness and infirmity! The son's pollution is punished with present death; the father's incest is pardoned, and in a sort prospereth.

Now Thamar seeks by subtilty, that which she could not have by award of justice. The neglect of due retributions drives men to indirect courses; neither know I whether they sin more in righting themselves wrongfully, or the other in not righting them. She therefore takes upon her the habit of a harlot, that she might perform the act: if she had not wished to seem a whore, she had not worn that attire, nor chosen that place. Immodesty of outward fashion or gesture bewrays evil desires. The heart that means well, will never wish to seem ill: for commonly we affect to show better than we are. Many harlots will put on the semblances of chastity, of modesty; never the contrary. There is no trusting those, which do not wish to appear good. Judah esteems her by her habit; and now the sight of a harlot hath stirred up in him a thought of lust. Satan finds well, that a fit object is half a victory.

Who would not be ashamed to see a son of Jacob thus transported with filthy affections! At the first sight he is inflamed; neither yet did he see the face of her whom he lusted after; it was motive enough to him that she was a woman: neither could the presence of his neighbour, the Adullamite, compose those wicked thoughts, or hinder his unchaste acts.

That sin must needs be impudent which can abide a witness: yea, so hath his lust besotted him, that he cannot discern the voice of Thamar, that he cannot foresee the danger of his shame in parting with such pledges. There is no passion, which doth not for the time bereave a man of himself. Thamar had learned not to trust him without a pawn: he had promised his son to her as a daughter, and failed; now he promised a kid to her, as an harlot, and performeth it. Whether his pledge constrained him, or the power of his word, I inquire not. Many are faithful in all things, save those which are the greatest and dearest. If his credit had been as much endangered in the former promise, he had kept it. Now hath Thamar requited him. She expected long the enjoying of his promised son, and he performed not. But here he performs the promise of the kid, and she stays not to expect it. Judah is sorry that he cannot pay the hire of his lust, and now feareth lest he shall be beaten with his own staff, lest his signet should be used to confirm and seal his reproach; resolving not to know them, and wishing they were unknown of others. Shame is the easiest wages of sin, and the surest which ever begins first in ourselves. Nature is not more forward to commit sin, than willing to hide it.

I hear as yet of no remorse in Judah, but fear of shame. Three months hath his sin slept; and now, when he is securest, it awakes and baits him. News is brought him that Thamar begins to swell with her conception; and now he swells with rage, and calls her forth to the flame like a rigorous judge, without so much as staying for the time of her deliverance, that his cruelty in this justice should be no less ill, than the injustice of occasioning it. If Judah had not forgotten his sin, his pity had been more than his hatred to this of his daughter's. How easy is it to detest those sins in others, which we flatter in ourselves! Thamar doth not deny the sin, nor refuse punishment; but calls for that partner in her punishment, which was partner in the sin. The staff, the signet, the handkerchief, accuse and convince Judah; and now he blushes at his own sentence, much more at his act, and cries out, "She is more righteous than I!" God will find a time to bring his children upon their knees, and to wring from them penitent-confessions. And, rather than he will not have them soundly ashamed, he will make them the trumpets of their own reproach.

Yet doth he not offer himself to the flame with her, but rather excuses her by himself. This relenting in his own case, shamed his former zeal. Even in the best men, nature is partial to itself. It is good so to sentence others' frailties, that yet we remember our own, whether those that have been, or may be. With what shame, yea with what horror, must Judah needs look upon the great belly of Thamar, and on her two sons, the monuments of his filthiness!

How must it needs wound his soul, to hear them call him both father and grandfather; to call her mother and sister! If this had not cost him many a sigh, he had no more escaped his father's curse, than Reuben did: I see the difference, not of sins, but of men. Remission goes not by the measure of the sin, but the quality of the sinner; yea, rather, the mercy of the forgiver. "Blessed is the man (not that sins not, but) to whom the Lord imputes not his sin."

CONTEMPLATION V. — OF JOSEPH.

I MARVEL not that Joseph had the double portion of Jacob's land, who had more than two parts of his sorrows. None of his sons did so truly inherit his afflictions; none of them was either so miserable or so great: suffering is the way to glory. I see in him not a clearer type of Christ, than of every Christian. Because we are dear to our Father, and complain of sins, therefore are we hated of our carnal brethren. If Joseph had not meddled with his brother's faults, yet he had been envied for his father's affection; but now malice is met with envy. There is nothing more thankless or dangerous than to stand in the way of a resolute sinner. That which doth correct and oblige the penitent, makes the wilful mind furious and revengeful.

All the spite of his brethren cannot make Joseph cast off the livery of his father's love. What need we care for the censures of men, if our hearts can tell us that we are in favour with God?

But what meant young Joseph to add unto his own envy by reporting his dreams? The concealment of our hopes or abilities hath not more modesty than safety. He that was envied for his dearness, and hated for his intelligence, was both envied and hated for his dreams. Surely God meant to make the relation of these dreams a means to effect that which the dreams imported. We men work by likely means: God by contraries. The main quarrel was, "Behold, this dreamer cometh!" Had it not been for his dreams, he had not been sold: if he had not been sold, he had not been exalted. So Joseph's state had not deserved envy, if his dreams had not caused him to be envied. Full little did Joseph think, when he went to seek his brethren, that this was the last time he should see his father's house. Full little did his brethren think, when they sold him naked to the Ishmaelites, to have once seen him in the throne of Egypt. God's decree runs on; and while we either think not of it, or oppose it, is performed.

In an honest and obedient simplicity, Joseph comes to inquire of his brethren's health, and now may not return to carry news of his own misery: whilst he thinks of their welfare, they are plotting his destruction: "Come, let us slay him." Who would have expected this cruelty in them, which should be the fathers of God's church! It was thought a favour, that Reuben's entreaty obtained for him, that he might be cast into the pit alive, to die there. He looked for brethren, and behold, murderers: every man's tongue, every man's fist, was bent against him. Each one strives who shall lay the first hand upon that changeable coat which was dyed with their father's love and their envy: and now they have stript him naked, and hauling him by both arms, as it were, cast him alive into his grave. So, in pretence of forbearance, they resolve to torment him with a lingering death. The savagest robbers could not have been more merciless: for now, besides (what in them lies), they kill their father in their brother. Nature, if it once degenerate, grows more monstrous and extreme, than a disposition born to cruelty.

All this while, Joseph wanted neither words nor tears; but, like a passionate suppliant (bowing his bare knees to them whom he dreamed should bow to him), entreats and persuades, by the dear name of their brotherhood, by their profession of one common God, for their father's sake, for their own souls' sake, not to sin against his blood. But envy hath shut out mercy, and makes them not only forget themselves to be brethren, but men. What stranger can think of poor innocent Joseph, crying naked in that desolate and dry pit (only saving that he moistened it with tears), and not be moved! Yet his hard-hearted brethren sit them down carelessly, with the noise of his lamentation in their ears, to eat bread, not once thinking, by their own hunger, what it was for Joseph to be famished to death.

Whatsoever they thought, God never meant that Joseph should perish in that pit; and therefore he sends the very Ishmaelites to ransom him from his brethren: the seed of him that persecuted his brother Isaac, shall now redeem Joseph from his brethren's persecution. When they came to fetch him out of the pit, he now hoped for a speedy despatch: that since they seemed not to have so much mercy as to prolong his life, they would not continue so much cruelty as to prolong his death.

And now, when he hath comforted himself with hope of the favour of dying, behold death exchanged for bondage! How much is servitude, to an ingenuous nature, worse than death! for this is common to all; that, to none but the miserable. Judah meant this well, but God better. Reuben saved him from the sword; Judah from famishing. God will ever raise up some secret favourers to his own, amongst those that are most malicious. How well was this favour bestowed! If Joseph had died for hunger in the pit, both Jacob and Judah, and all his brethren, had died for hunger in Canaan. Little did the Ismaelitish merchants know what a treasure they bought, carried, and sold; more precious than all their balm and myrrhs. Little did they think that they had in their hands the lord of Egypt, the jewel of the world. Why should we contemn any man's meanness, when we know not his destiny?

One sin is commonly used for the veil of another: Joseph's coat is sent home dipped in blood, that, while they should hide their own cruelty, they might afflict their father, no less than their brother. They have devised this real lie, to punish their old father, for his love, with so grievous a monument of his sorrow.

He that is mourned for in Canaan as dead, prospers in Egypt under Potiphar; and of a slave, is made ruler. Thus God meant to prepare him for a greater charge; he must first rule Potiphar's house, then Pharaoh's kingdom: his own service is his least good, for his very presence procures a common blessing: a whole family shall fare the better for one Joseph. Virtue is not looked upon alike with all eyes: his fellows praise him, his master trusts him, his mistress affects him too much. All the spite of his brethren was not so great a cross to him, as the inordinate affection of his mistress. Temptations on the right hand are now more perilous, and hard to resist, by how much they are more plausible and glorious; but the heart that is bent upon God, knows how to walk steadily and indifferently betwixt the pleasures of sin and fears of evil. He saw this pleasure would advance him: he knew what it was to be a minion of one of the greatest ladies of Egypt, yet resolves to contemn. A good heart will rather lie in the dust, than rise by wickedness: "How shall I do this, and sin against God?"

He knew that all the honours of Egypt could not buy off the guilt of one sin; and therefore abhors not only her bed, but her company. He that will be safe from the acts of evil, must wisely avoid the occasions. As sin ends ever in shame, when it is committed, so it makes us past shame, that we may commit it. The impudent strumpet dare not only solicit, but importune, and in a sort force the modesty of her good servant: she lays hold on his garment: her hand seconds her tongue.

Good Joseph found it now time to fly, when such an enemy pursued him: how much had he rather leave his cloak than his virtue! and to suffer his mistress to spoil him of his livery, rather than he should blemish her honour, or his master's in her, or God in either of them!

This second time is Joseph stript of his garment: before, in the violence of envy, now, of lust; before, of necessity, now, of choice; before, to deceive his father, now, his master: for behold, the pledge of his fidelity, which he left in those wicked hands, is made an evidence against him, of that which he refused to do: therefore did he leave his cloak, because he would not do that of which he is accused and condemned, because he left it. What safety is there against great adversaries, when even arguments of innocence are used to convince of evil! Lust yielded unto is a pleasant madness; but is a desperate madness when it is opposed: no hatred burns so furiously as that which arises from the quenched coals of love.

Malice is witty to devise accusations of others, out of their virtue and our own guiltiness. Joseph either pleads not, or is not heard.

Doubtless he denied the fact, but he dare not accuse the offender. There is not only the praise of patience, but ofttimes of wisdom, even in unjust sufferings. He knew that God would find a time to clear his innocence, and to regard his chaste faithfulness.

No prison would serve him but Pharaoh's. Joseph had lain obscure, and not been known to Pharaoh, if he had not been cast into Pharaoh's dungeon. The afflictions of God's children turn ever to their advantages. No sooner is Joseph a prisoner, than a guardian of the prisoners. Trust and honour accompany him wheresoever he is: in his father's house, in Potiphar's, in the jail, in the court; still he hath both favour and rule.

So long as God is with him, he cannot but shine, in spite of men. The walls of that dungeon cannot hide his virtues, the irons cannot hold them. Pharaoh's officers are sent to witness his graces, which he may not come forth to show. The cupbearer admires him in the jail, but forgets him in the court. How easily doth our own prosperity make us either forget the deservings or miseries of others! But as God cannot neglect his own, so least of all in their sorrows. After two years more of Joseph's patience, that God, which caused him to be lifted up out of the former pit to be sold, now calls him out of the dungeon to honour. He now puts a dream into the head of Pharaoh; he puts the remembrance of Joseph's skill into the head of the cup-bearer; who, to pleasure Pharaoh, not to requite Joseph, commends the prisoner for an interpreter. He puts an interpretation in the mouth of Joseph: he puts this choice into the heart of Pharaoh, of a miserable prisoner, to make him the ruler of Egypt. Behold, one hour hath changed his fetters into a chain of gold, his rags into fine linen, his stocks into a chariot, his jail into a palace, Potiphar's captive into his master's lord, the noise of his chains into *ABRECH. He, whose chastity refused the wanton allurements of the wife of Potiphar, had now given him to his wife the daughter of Potipherah. Humility goes before honour: serving and suffering are the best tutors to government. How well are God's children paid for their patience! How happy are the issues of the faithful! Never any man repented him of the advancement of a good man.

Pharaoh hath not more preferred Joseph, than Joseph hath enriched Pharaoh: if Joseph had not ruled, Egypt and all the bordering nations had perished. The providence of so faithful an officer hath both given the Egyptians their lives, and the money, cattle, lands, bodies of the Egyptians, to Pharaoh. Both have reason to be well pleased. The subjects owe to him their lives; the king his subjects, and his dominions. The bounty of God made Joseph able to give more than he received: it is like, the seven years of plenty were not confined to Egypt; other countries adjoining were no less fruitful; yet, in the seven years of famine, Egypt had corn when they wanted.

See the difference betwixt a wise, prudent frugality, and a vain, ignorant expense of the benefits of God. The sparing hand is both full and beneficial; whereas the lavish is not only empty, but injurious.

Good Jacob is pinched with the common famine. No piety can exempt us from the evils of neighbourhood. No man can tell, by outward events, which is the patriarch, and which the Canaanite.

Neither doth his profession lead him to the hope of a miraculous preservation. It is a vain tempting of God, to cast ourselves upon an immediate provision with neglect of common means. His ten sons must now leave their flocks, and go down into Egypt, to be their father's purveyors. And now they go to buy of him whom they had sold; and bow their knees to him, for his relief, which had bowed to them before for his own life. His age, his habit, the place, the language, kept Joseph from their knowledge; neither had they called off their minds from their folds, to inquire of matters of foreign state, or to hear that an Hebrew was advanced to the highest honour of Egypt. But he cannot but know them, whom he left at their full growth, whose tongue and habit and number were all one; whose faces had left so deep an impression in his mind at their unkind parting. It is wisdom sometimes to conceal our knowledge, that we may not prejudice truth.

He that was hated of his brethren, for being his father's spy, now accuses his brethren for common spies of the weakness of Egypt: he could not, without their suspicion, have come to a perfect intelligence of his father's estate and theirs, if he had not objected to them that which was not. We are always bound to go the nearest way to truth. It is more safe, in cases of inquisition, to fetch far about: that he might seem enough an Egyptian, he swears heathenishly: how little could they suspect this oath would proceed from the son of him, which swore by the fear of his father Isaac! How oft have sinister respects drawn weak goodness to disguise itself, even with sins!

It was no small joy to Joseph, to see this late accomplishment of his ancient dream; to see these suppliants (I know not whether more brethren or enemies) grovelling before him in an unknown submission: and now it doth him good to seem merciless to them, whom he had found

* Bow the knee.

wilfully cruel: to hide his love from them which had showed their hate to him, and to think how much he favoureth them, and how little they know it: and as, sporting himself in their seeming misery, he pleasantly imitates all those actions reciprocally unto them, which they in despite and earnest had done formerly to him; he speaks roughly, rejects their persuasions, puts them in hold, and one of them in bonds. The mind must not always be judged by the outward face of the actions. God's countenance is ofttimes as severe, and his hand as heavy to them whom he best loveth. Many a one, under the habit of an Egyptian, hath the heart of an Israelite. No song could be so delightful to him, as to hear them, in a late remorse, condemn themselves before him, of their old cruelty towards him, who was now their unknown witness and judge.

Nothing doth so powerfully call home the conscience as affliction, neither need there any other art of memory for sin, besides misery. They had heard Joseph's deprecation of their evil with tears, and had not pitied him; yet Joseph doth but hear their mention of this evil which they had done against him, and pities them with tears: he weeps for joy to see their repentance, and to compare his safety and happiness with the cruelty which they intended, and did, and thought they had done.

Yet he can abide to see his brother his prisoner, whom no bonds could bind so strong, as his affection bound him to his captive. Simeon is left in pawn, in fetters; the rest return with their corn, with their money, paying nothing for their provision but their labour; that they might be as much troubled with the beneficence of that strange Egyptian lord, as before with his imperious suspicion. Their wealth was now more irksome to them than their need; and they fear God means to punish them more in this superfluity of money, than in the want of victuals. "What is this that God hath done to us?" It is a wise course to be jealous of our gain; and more to fear, than desire abundance.

Old Jacob, that was not used to simple and absolute contentments, receives the blessing of seasonable provision, together with the affliction of that heavy message, the loss of one son, and the danger of another; and knows not whether it be better for him to die with hunger, or with grief, for the departure of that son of his right hand. He drives off all till the last. Protraction is a kind of ease in evils that must come.

At length (as no plea is so importunate as that of famine) Benjamin must go: one evil must be hazarded for the redress of another. What would it avail him, to see whom he loved miserable? How injurious were that affection, to keep his son so long in his eye, till they should see each other die for hunger!

The ten brothers return into Egypt, loaded with double money in their sacks, and a present in their hands: the danger of mistaking is requited, by honest minds, with more than restitution. It is not enough to find our own hearts clear in suspicious actions, except we satisfy others. Now hath Joseph what he would, the sight and presence of his Benjamin, whom he therefore borrows of his father for a time, that he might return him with a greater interest of joy: and now he feasts them whom he formerly threatened, and turns their fear into wonder. All unequal love is not partial; all the brethren are entertained bountifully, but Benjamin hath a five-fold portion. By how much his welcome was greater, by so much his pretended theft seemed more heinous; for good turns aggravate unkindness, and our offences are increased with our obligations. How easy is it to find advantages, where there is a purpose to accuse! Benjamin's sack makes him guilty of that whereof his heart was free. Crimes seem strange to the innocent. Well might they abjure this fact, with the offer of bondage and death: for they, which carefully brought again that which they might have taken, would never take that which was not given them. But thus Joseph would yet dally with his brethren, and make Benjamin a thief, that he might make him a servant, and fright his brethren with the peril of that their charge, that he might double their joy and amazedness, in giving them two brothers at once. Our happiness is greater and sweeter, when we have well feared and smarted with evils.

But now when Judah seriously reported the danger of his old father, and the sadness of his last complaint, compassion and joy will be concealed no longer, but break forth violently at his voice and eyes. Many passions do not well abide witnesses, because they are guilty to their own weakness. Joseph sends forth his servants, that he might freely weep. He knew he could not say I am Joseph, without an unbeseeming vehemence.

Never any word sounded so strangely as this in the ears of the patriarchs. Wonder, doubt, reverence, joy, fear, hope, guiltiness, struck them at once. It was time for Joseph to say, "Fear not:" no marvel if they stood with paleness and silence before him, looking on him, and on each other. The more they considered, they wondered more; and the more they believed, the more they feared. For these words, "I am Joseph," seemed to sound thus much to their guilty thoughts:—You are murderers, and I am a prince in spite of you. My power, and this place, give me all opportunities of revenge: my glory is your shame, my life your danger; your sins live together with me. But now the tears and gracious words of Joseph have soon assured them of pardon and love, and have bidden them turn their eyes from their sin against their brother, to their happiness in him, and have changed their doubts into hopes and joys, causing them to look upon him without fear, though not without shame. His loving embracements clear their hearts of all jealousies, and hasten to put new thoughts into them of favour, and of greatness; so that now forgetting what evil they did to their brother, they are thinking of what good their brother may do to them. Actions, salved up with a free forgiveness, are as not done: and as a bone once broken is stronger after well setting, so is love after reconcilement.

But as wounds once healed leave a scar behind them, so remitted injuries leave commonly in the actors a guilty remembrance, which hindered these brethren from that freedom of joy, which else they had conceived. This was their fault, not Joseph's, who strives to give them all security of his love, and will be as bountiful as they were cruel. They send him naked to strangers; he sends them in new and rich liveries to their father: they took a small sum of money for him; he gives them great treasures: they sent his torn coat to his father; he sends variety of costly raiments to his father, by them: they sold him to be the load of camels; he sends them home with chariots. It must be a great favour, that can appease the conscience of a great injury. Now they return home, rich and joyful, making themselves happy to think how glad they should make their father with this news.

That good old man would never have hoped, that Egypt could have afforded such provision as this—"Joseph is yet alive." This was not food, but life to him. The return of Benjamin was comfortable; but that his dead son was yet alive, after so many years' lamentation, was tidings too happy to be believed, and was enough to endanger that life with excess of joy, which the knowledge thereof doubled. Overexcellent objects are dangerous in their sudden apprehensions. One grain of that joy would have safely cheered him, whereof a full measure overlays his heart with too much sweetness. There is no earthly pleasure whereof we may not surfeit: of the spiritual we can never have enough.

Yet his eyes revive his mind, which his ears had thus astonished. When he saw the chariots of his son, he believed Joseph's life, and refreshed his own. He had too much before, so that he could not enjoy it: now he saith, "I have enough; Joseph my son is yet alive."

They told him of his honour; he speaks of his life: life is better than honour. To have heard that Joseph lived a servant, would have joyed him more, than to hear that he died honourably. The greater blessing obscures the less. He is not worthy of honour, that is not thankful for life.

Yet Joseph's life did not content Jacob, without his presence: "I will go down and see him, ere I die." The sight of the eye is better than to walk in desires. Good things pleasure us not in their being, but in our enjoying.

The height of all earthly contentment appeared in the meeting of these two, whom their mutual loss had more endeared to each other. The intermission of comforts hath this advantage, that it sweetens our delight more in the return, than was abated in the forbearance. God doth ofttimes hide away our Joseph for a time, that we may be more joyous and thankful in his recovery. This was the sincerest pleasure that ever Jacob had, which therefore God reserved for his old age.

And if the meeting of earthly friends be so unspeakably comfortable, how happy shall we be in the light of the glorious face of God our heavenly Father! of that of our blessed Redeemer, whom we sold to death by our sins; and which now, after that noble triumph, hath all power given him in heaven and earth!

Thus did Jacob rejoice, when he was to go out of the land of promise to a foreign nation, for Joseph's sake; being glad that he should lose his country for his son. What shall our joy be, who must go out of this foreign land of our pilgrimage, to the home of our glorious inheritance, to dwell with none but our own, in that better and more lightsome Goshen, free from all the encumbrances of this Egypt, and full of all the riches and delights of God! The guilty conscience can never think itself safe: so many years' experience of Joseph's love could not secure his brethren of remission. Those that know they have deserved ill, are wont to misinterpret favours, and think they cannot be beloved. All that while, his goodness seemed but concealed and sleeping malice, which they feared in their father's last sleep would awake, and bewray itself in revenge: still, therefore, they plead the name of their father, though dead, not daring to use their own. Good meanings cannot be more wronged than with suspicion. It grieves Joseph to see their fear, and to find they had not forgotten their own sin, and to hear them so passionately crave that which they had.

"Forgive the trespass of the servants of thy father's God." What a conjuration of pardon was this! What wound could be either so deep, or so festered, as this plaster could not cure! They say not, the sons of thy father, for they knew Jacob was dead, and they had degenerated; but the servants of thy father's God. How much stronger are the bonds of religion than of nature! If Joseph had been rancorous, this deprecation had charmed him; but now it dissolves him into tears: they are not so ready to acknowledge their old offence, as he to protest his love; and if he chide them for any thing, it is for that they thought they needed to entreat; since they might know it could not stand with the fellow-servant of their father's God to harbour maliciousness, to purpose revenge. "Am not I under God?" And fully to secure them, he turns their eyes from themselves to the decree of God, from the action to the event; as one that would have them think there was no cause to repent of that which proved so successful.

Even late confession finds forgiveness. Joseph had long ago seen their sorrow; never but now heard he their humble acknowledgment. Mercy stays not for outward solemnities. How much more shall that infinite goodness pardon our sins, when he finds the truth of our repentance!

BOOK IV.

CONTEMPLATION I.—OF THE AFFLICTION OF ISRAEL.

EGYPT was long an harbour to the Israelites; now it proves a jail: the posterity of Jacob finds too late, what it was for their forefathers to sell Joseph a slave into Egypt. Those whom the Egyptians honoured before as lords, now they contemn as drudges. One Pharaoh advances, whom another labours to depress. Not seldom the same man changes copies: but if favours outlive one age, they prove decrepit and heartless. It is a rare thing to find posterity heirs of their father's love. How should men's favour be but like themselves, variable and inconstant? There is no certainty but in the favour of God, in whom can be no change, whose love is entailed upon a thousand generations.

Yet if the Israelites had been treacherous to Pharaoh, if disobedient, this great change of countenance had been just: now the only offence of Israel is, that he prospereth. That which should be the motive of their gratulation and friendship, is the cause of their malice. There is no more hateful sight to a wicked man, than the prosperity of the conscionable. None but the Spirit of that true harbinger of Christ, can teach us to say with contentment, "He must increase, but I must decrease."

And what if Israel be mighty and rich? "If there be war, they may join with our enemies, and get them out of the land." —Behold, they are afraid to part with those whom they are grieved to entertain: either staying or going is offence enough to those that seek quarrels: there were no wars, and yet they say, If there be wars. The Israelites had never given cause of fear to revolt, and yet they say, "Lest they join to our enemies," to those enemies which we may have: so they make their certain friends slaves, for fear of uncertain enemies. Wickedness is ever cowardly, and full of unjust suspicions: it makes a man fear, where no fear is; fly, when none pursues him. What difference there is betwixt David and Pharaoh! The faith of the one says, "I will not be afraid for ten thousand that should beset me:" the fear of the other says, "Lest if there be war, they join with our enemies;" therefore should he have made much of the Israelites, that they might be his: his favour might have made them firm. Why might they not as well draw their swords for him? Weak and base minds ever incline to the worse, and seek safety rather in an impossibility of hurt, than in the likelihood of just advantage. Favours had been more binding than cruelties: yet the foolish Egyptian had rather have impotent servants, than able friends. For their welfare alone Pharaoh owes Israel a mischief; and how will he pay it?

"Come let us work wisely." Lewd men call wicked policies wisdom, and their success happiness. Herein Satan is wiser than they, who both lays the plot, and makes them such fools as to mistake villany and madness for the best virtue.

Injustice is upheld by violence, whereas just governments are maintained by love. Taskmasters must be set over Israel; they should not be the true seed of Israel, if they were not still set to wrestle with God in afflictions: heavy burdens must be laid upon them. Israel is never but loaded: the destiny of one of Jacob's sons is common to all, to lie down betwixt their burdens. If they had seemed to breathe them in Goshen sometimes, yet even there it was no small misery to be foreigners, and to live among idolaters; but now the name of a slave is added to the name of a stranger. Israel hath gathered some rust in idolatrous Egypt, and now he must be scoured: they had borne the burden of God's anger if they had not borne the burdens of the Egyptians.

As God afflicted them with another mind than the Egyptians (God to exercise them, the Egyptians to suppress them), so causes he the event to differ. Who would not have thought with these Egyptians, that so extreme misery should not have made the Israelites unfit, both for generation and resistance? Moderate exercise strengthens, extreme destroys nature: that God, which many times works by contrary means, caused them to grow with depression, with persecution to multiply. How can God's church but fare well, since the very malice of their enemies benefits them! O the sovereign goodness of our God, that turns all our poisons into cordials! God's vine bears the better with bleeding.

And now the Egyptians could be angry with their own maliciousness, that this was the occasion of multiplying them whom they hated and feared; to see that this service gained more to the workmen than to their masters: the stronger therefore the Israelites grew, the more impotent grew the malice of their persecutors. And since their own labour strengthens them, now tyranny will try what can be done by the violence of others. Since the present strength cannot be subdued, the hopes of succession must be prevented: women must be suborned to be murderers; and those whose office is to help the birth must destroy it.

There was less suspicion of cruelty in that sex, and more opportunity of doing mischief. The male children must be born, and die at once. What can be more innocent than the child that hath not lived so much as to cry, or to see light? It is fault enough to be the son of an Israelite. The daughters may live for bondage, for lust; a condition so much (at the least) worse than death, as their sex was weaker. O marvellous cruelty, that a man should kill a man for his sex's sake! Whosoever hath loosed the reins unto cruelty, is easily carried into incredible extremities.

From burdens they proceed to bondage, and from bondage to blood: from an unjust vexation of their body, to an inhuman destruction of the fruit of their body. As the sins of the concupiscible part, from slight motions, grow on to foul executions, so do those of the irascible. There is no sin whose harbour is more unsafe than that of malice: but ofttimes the power of tyrants answers not their will. Evil commanders cannot always meet with equally mischievous agents.

The fear of God teaches the midwives to disobey an unjust command; they well knew how no excuse it is for evil, I was bidden. God said to their hearts, " Thou shalt not kill." This voice was louder than Pharaoh's. I commend their obedience in disobeying; I dare not commend their excuse. There was as much weakness in their answer, as strength in their practice: as they feared God in not killing, so they feared Pharaoh in dissembling. Ofttimes those that make conscience of greater sins are overtaken with less. It is well and rare, if we can come forth of a dangerous action without any soil; and if we have escaped the storm, that some after-drops wet us not.

Who would not have expected that the midwives should be murdered, for not murdering? Pharaoh could not be so simple to think these women trusty; yet his indignation had no power to reach to their punishment. God prospered the midwives: who can harm them? Even the not doing of evil is rewarded with good. And why did they prosper? Because they feared God — not for their dissimulation, but their piety; so did God regard their mercy, that he regarded not their infirmity. How fondly do men lay the thank upon the sin, which is due to the virtue! True wisdom teaches to distinguish God's actions, and to ascribe them to the right causes: pardon belongs to the lie of the midwives, and remuneration to their goodness; prosperity to their fear of God.

But that which the midwives will not, the multitude shall do. It were strange if wicked rulers should not find some or other instruments of violence; all the people must drown whom the women saved: cruelty hath but smoked before, now it flames up; secret practising hath made it shameless, that now it dare proclaim tyranny. It is a miserable state, where every man is made an executioner. There can be no greater argument of an ill cause, than a bloody persecution; whereas truth upholds herself by mildness, and is promoted by patience. This is their act; what was their issue? The people must drown their males, themselves are drowned: they die by the same means by which they caused the Israelitish infants to die. That law of retaliation which God will not allow to us, because we are fellow-creatures, he justly practiseth in us. God would have us read our sins in our judgments, that we might both repent of our sins and give glory to his justice.

Pharaoh raged before; much more now, that he received a message of dismission. The monitions of God make ill men worse: the waves do not beat, nor roar any where so much as at the bank which restrains them. Corruption, when it is checked, grows mad with rage: as the vapour in a cloud would not make that fearful report, if it met not with opposition. A good heart yields at the stillest voice of God: but the most gracious motions of God harden the wicked. Many would not be so desperately settled in their sins, if the world had not controlled them. How mild a message was this to Pharaoh, and yet how galling! "We pray thee let us go." God commands him that which he feared. He took pleasure in the present servitude of Israel: God calls for a release. If the suit had been for mitigation of labour, for preservation of their children, it might have carried some hope, and have found some favour: but now God requires that which he knows will as much discontent Pharaoh, as Pharaoh's cruelty could discontent the Israelites; "Let us go." How contrary are God's precepts to natural minds! And indeed, as they love to cross him in their practice, so he loves to cross them in their commands before, and his punishments afterwards. It is a dangerous sign of an ill heart to feel God's yoke heavy.

Moses talks of sacrifice. Pharaoh talks of work. Any thing seems due work to a carnal mind, saving God's service; nothing superfluous, but religious duties. Christ tells us, there is but one thing necessary; nature tells us, there is nothing but that needless: Moses speaks of devotion, Pharaoh of idleness. It hath been an old use, as to cast fair colours upon our own vicious actions, so to cast evil aspersions upon the good actions of others. The same devil that spoke in Pharaoh, speaks still in our scoffers, and calls religion hypocrisy; conscionable care, singularity. Every vice hath a title, and every virtue a disgrace.

Yet while possible tasks were imposed, there was some comfort: their diligence might save their back from stripes. The conceit of a benefit to the commander, and hope of impunity to the labourer, might give a good pretence to great difficulties. But to require tasks not feasible is tyrannical, and doth only pick a quarrel to punish. They could neither make straw, nor find it, yet they must have it. Do what may be, is tolerable; but do what cannot be, is cruel. Those which are above others in place, must measure their commands, not by their own wills, but by the strength of their inferiors. To require more of a beast than he can do, is inhuman. The task is not done; the taskmasters are beaten: the punishment lies where the charge is; they must exact it of the people, Pharaoh of them. It is the misery of those which are trusted with authority, that their inferiors' faults are beaten upon their backs. This was not the fault to require it of the taskmasters, but to require it by the taskmasters of the people. Public persons do either good or ill with a thousand hands, and with no fewer shall receive it.

CONTEMPLATION II.—OF THE BIRTH AND BREEDING OF MOSES.

It is a wonder that Amram, the father of Moses, would think of the marriage-bed in so troublesome a time, when he knew he should beget children either to slavery or slaughter. Yet even now, in the heat of this bondage, he marries Jochebed. The drowning of his sons was not so great an evil, as his own burning; the thraldom of his daughters not so great an evil, as the subjection unto sinful desires. He therefore uses God's remedy for his sin, and refers the sequel of his danger to God. How necessary is this intimation for those which have not the power of containing! Perhaps he would have thought it better to live childless: but Amram and Jochebed durst not incur the danger of a sin, to avoid the danger of a mischief. No doubt, when Jochebed, the mother of Moses, saw a man-child born of her, and him beautiful and comely, she fell into extreme passion to think that the executioner's hand should succeed the midwife's. All the time of her conception, she could not but fear a son; now she sees him, and thinks of his birth and death at once: her second throes are more grievous than her first. The pains of travail in others are somewhat mitigated with hope, and countervailed with joy, that a man-child is born; in her they are doubled with fear. The remedy of others is her complaint. Still she looks when some fierce Egyptian would come in, and snatch her new-born infant out of her bosom, whose comeliness had now also added to her affection.

Many times God writes presages of majesty and honour, even in the faces of children. Little did she think that she held in her lap the deliverer of Israel. It is good to hazard in greatest appearances of danger. If Jochebed had said, If I bear a son, they will kill him, where had been the great rescuer of Israel? Happy is that resolution which can follow God hood-winked, and let him dispose of the event. When she can no longer hide him in her womb, she hides him in her house, afraid lest every one of his cryings should guide the executioners to his cradle. And now she sees her treasure can be no longer hid, she ships him in a bark of bulrushes, and commits him to the mercy of the waves, and (which was more merciless) to the danger of an Egyptian passenger, yet doth she not leave him without a guardian.

No tyranny can forbid her to love him whom she is forbidden to keep. Her daughter's eyes must supply the place of her arms. And if the weak affection of a mother were thus effectually careful, what shall we think of Him whose love, whose compassion, is (as himself) infinite? His eye, his hand, cannot but be with us, even when we forsake ourselves. Moses had never a stronger protection about him, no, not when all his Israelites were pitched about his tent in the wilderness, than now when he lay sprawling alone upon the waves: no water, no Egyptian, can hurt him. Neither friend nor mother dare own him, and now God challenges his custody. When we seem most neglected and forlorn in ourselves, then is God most present, most vigilant.

His providence brings Pharaoh's daughter thither to wash herself. Those times looked for no great state: a princess comes to bathe herself in the open stream. She meant only to wash herself: God fetches her thither to deliver the deliverer of his people. His designs go beyond ours. We know not (when we set our foot over our threshold) what he hath to do with us. This event seemed casual to this princess, but predetermined and provided by God before she was. How wisely and sweetly God brings to pass his own purposes, in our ignorance and regardlessness! She saw the ark, opens it, finds the child weeping: his beauty and his tears had God provided for the strong persuasions of mercy. This young and lively oratory prevailed. Her heart is struck with compassion, and yet her tongue could say, "It is a Hebrew child."

See here the merciful daughter of a cruel father! It is an uncharitable and injurious ground, to judge of the child's disposition by the parent's. How well doth pity beseem great personages, and most in extremities! It had been death to another to rescue the child of a Hebrew; in her it was safe and noble. It is a happy thing when great ones improve their places to so much more charity, as their liberty is more.

Moses' sister finding the princess compassionate, offers to procure a nurse, and fetches the mother: and who can be so fit a nurse as a mother? She now with glad hands receives her child, both with authority and reward. She would have given all her substance for the life of her son; and now she hath a reward to nurse him. The exchange of the name of a mother for the name of a nurse, hath gained her both her son and his education, and with both a recompense. Religion doth not call us to a weak simplicity, but allows us as much of the serpent as of the dove. Lawful policies have from God both liberty in the use, and blessing in the success.

The good lady did not breed him as some child of alms, or as some wretched outcast, for whom it might be favour enough to live, but as her own son, in all the delicacies, in all the learning of Egypt. Whatsoever the court or the school could put into him, he wanted not; yet all this could not make him forget that he was a Hebrew. Education works wondrous changes, and is of great force either way. A little advancement hath so puffed some up above themselves, that they have not only forgot their friends, but scorned their parents. All the honours of Egypt could not win Moses not to call his nurse mother, or wean him from a willing misery with the Israelites. If we had Moses' faith, we could not but make his choice. It is only our infidelity that binds us so to the world, and makes us prefer the momentary pleasures of sin unto that everlasting recompense of reward.

He went forth and looked on the burdens of Israel. What needed Moses to have afflicted himself with the afflictions of others? Himself was at ease and pleasure in the court of Pharaoh. A good heart cannot endure to be happy alone, and must needs, unbidden, share with others in their miseries. He is no true Moses that is not moved with the calamities of God's church. To see an Egyptian smite a Hebrew, it smote him, and moved him to smite. He hath no Israelitish blood in him that can endure to see an Israelite stricken either with hand or tongue.

Here was his zeal: where was his authority? Doubtless, Moses had an instinct from God of his magistracy, else how should he think they would have understood what himself did not? Oppressions may not be righted by violence, but by law. The redress of evil, by a person unwarranted, is evil. Moses knew that God had called him; he knew that Pharaoh knew it not; therefore he hides the Egyptian in the sand. Those actions which may be approved unto God, are not always safe with men: as contrarily, too many things go current with men, which are not approved of God.

Another Hebrew is stricken, but by a Hebrew: the act is the same, the agents differ; neither doth their profession more differ than Moses' proceedings. He gives blows to the one, to the other words. The blows to the Egyptians were deadly; the words to the Hebrew gentle and plausible. As God makes a difference betwixt the chastisements of his own and punishments of strange children, so must wise governors learn to distinguish of sins and judgments according to circumstances. How mildly doth Moses admonish! " Sirs, ye are brethren." If there had been but a dram of good nature in these Hebrews, they had relented · now it is strange to see, that being so universally vexed with their common adversary, they should yet vex one another. One would have thought that a common opposition should have united them more; yet now private grudges do thus dangerously divide them. Blows enough were not dealt by the Egyptians, their own must add to the violence. Still Satan is thus busy, and Christians are thus malicious, that (as if they wanted enemies) they fly on one another's faces. While we are in this Egypt of the world, all unkind strifes would easily be composed, if we did not forget that we are brethren.

Behold an Egyptian in the skin of an Hebrew: how dogged an answer doth Moses receive to so gentle a reproof! Who would not have expected that this Hebrew had been enough dejected with the common affliction? But vexations may make some more miserable, not more humble; as we see sicknesses make some tractable, others more froward. It is no easy matter to bear a reproof well, if never so well tempered. No sugar can bereave a pill of its bitterness. None but the gracious can say, " Let the righteous smite me." Next to the not deserving a reproof, is the well taking of it. But who is so ready to except and exclaim as the wrong doer? The patient replies not. One injury draws on another, first to his brother, then to his reprover. Guiltiness will make a man stir upon every touch. He that was wronged could incline to reconciliation. Malice makes men incapable of good counsel; and there are none so great enemies to justice as those who are enemies to peace.

With what impatience doth a galled heart receive an admonition! This unworthy Israelite is the pattern of a stomachful offender: first he is moved to choler in himself, then he calls for the authority of the admonisher. A small authority will serve for a loving admonition. It is the duty of men, much more of Christians, to advise against sin; yet this man asks, " Who made thee a judge?" for but finding fault with his injury. Then he aggravates and misconstrues: " Wilt thou kill me?" when Moses meant only to save both. It was the death of his malice only that was intended, and the safety of his person. And lastly, he upbraids him with former actions: " Thou killedst the Egyptian." What if he did? what if unjustly? What was this to the Hebrew? Another man's sin is no excuse for ours. A wicked heart never looks inward to itself, but outward to the quality of the reprover: if that afford exception, it is enough; as a dog runs first to revenge on the stone. What matter is it to me who he be that admonisheth me? Let me look home into myself: let me look to his advice. If that be good, it is more shame to me to be reproved by an evil man. As a good man's allowance cannot warrant evil, so an evil man's reproof may remedy evil. If this Hebrew had been well pleased, Moses had not heard of his slaughter; now in choler all will out; and if this man's tongue had not thus cast him in the teeth with blood, he had been surprised by Pharaoh, ere he could have known that the fact was known.

Now he grows jealous, flees, and escapes. No friend is so commodious, in some cases, as an adversary. This wound, which the Hebrew thought to give Moses, saved his life. As it is good for a man to have an enemy, so it shall be our wisdom to make use of his most choleric objections. The worst of an enemy may prove most sovereign to ourselves. Moses flees. It is no discomfort for a man to flee when his conscience pursues him not. Where God's warrant will not protect us, it is good for the heels to supply the place of the tongue.

Moses, when he may not in Egypt, will be doing justice in Midian. In Egypt, he delivers the oppressed Israelite; in Midian, the wronged daughters of Jethro. A good man will be doing good wheresoever he is: his trade is a compound of charity and justice. As, therefore, evil dispositions cannot be changed with airs, no more will good. Now then he sits him down by a well in Midian. There he might have to drink, but where to eat he knew not. The case was altered with Moses; to come from the dainties of the court of Egypt, to the hunger of the fields of Midian. It is a lesson that all God's children must learn to take out, to want, and to abound. Who can think strange of penury, when the great governor of God's people once had nothing? Who would not have thought, in this case, Moses should have been heartless and sullen; so cast down with his own complaints, that he should have had no feeling of others: yet how hot is he upon justice! No adversity can make a good man neglect good duties. He sees the oppression of the shepherds, the image of that other he left behind him in Egypt. The maids (daughters of so great a peer) draw water for their flocks; the inhuman shepherds drive them away. Rudeness hath no respect, either to sex or condition. If we lived not under laws, this were our case: might would be the measure of justice. We should not so much as enjoy our own water. Unjust courses will not ever prosper. Moses shall rather come from Egypt to Midian to beat the shepherds, than they shall vex the daughters of Jethro. This act of justice was not better done than taken. Reuel requites it kindly with an hospitable entertainment. A good nature is ready to answer courtesies: we cannot do too much for a thankful man. And if a courteous heathen reward the watering of a sheep in this bountiful manner, how shall our God recompense but a cup of cold water that is given to a disciple? This favour hath won Moses, who now consents to dwell with him, though out of the church. Curiosity, or whatsoever idle occasions, may not draw us (for our residence) out of the bounds of the church of God; danger of life may. We love not the church if we easily leave it: if in a case of life, we leave it not (upon opportunity) for a time of respite, we love not ourselves. The first part of Moses' requital was his wife, one of those whom he had formerly protected.

I do not so much marvel that Jethro gave him his daughter (for he saw him valiant, wise, learned, nobly bred), as that Moses would take her, a stranger both in blood and religion. I could plead for him necessity; his own nation was shut up to him. If he would have tried to fetch a daughter of Israel, he had endangered to leave himself behind. I could plead some correspondence in common principles of religion; for doubtless Moses' zeal could not suffer him to smother the truth in himself: he should have been an unfaithful servant, if he had not been his master's teacher. Yet neither of these can make this match either safe or good. The event bewrays it dangerously inconvenient. This choice had like to have cost him dear: she stood in his way for circumcision; God stands in his way for revenge. Though he was now in God's message, yet might he not be forborn in this neglect. No circumstance either of the dearness of the solicitor, or our own engagement, can bear out a sin with God. Those, which are unequally yoked, may not ever look to draw one way. True love to the person cannot long agree with dislike of the religion. He had need to be more than a man, that hath a Zipporah in his bosom, and would have true zeal in his heart. All this while, Moses' affection was not so tied to Midian, that he could forget Egypt. He was a stranger in Midian: what was he else in Egypt? Surely either Egypt was not his home, or a miserable one; and yet, in reference to it, he calls his son Gershom, a stranger there. Much better were it to be a stranger there, than a dweller in Egypt. How hardly can we forget the place of our abode or education, although never so homely: and if he so thought of his Egyptian home, where was nothing but bondage and tyranny, how should we think of that home of ours above, where is nothing but rest and blessedness?

CONTEMPLATION III.—OF MOSES' CALLING.

FORTY years was Moses a courtier, and forty years (after that) a shepherd. That great men may not be ashamed of honest vocations, the greatest that ever were, have been content to take up with mean trades. The contempt of honest callings, in those which are well-born, argues pride without wit. How constantly did Moses stick to his hook! and yet a man of great spirits, of excellent learning, of curious education; and, if God had not (after his forty 'years' service) called him off, he had so ended his days. Humble resolutions are so much more heroical, as they fall into higher subjects.

There can be no fitter disposition for a leader of God's people, than constancy in his undertakings, without either weariness or change. How had he learned to subdue all ambitious desires, and to rest content with his obscurity! So he might have the freedom of his thoughts, and full opportunity of holy meditations, he willingly leaves the world to others, and envies not his proudest acquaintance of the court of Pharaoh. He that hath true worth in himself, and familiarity with God, finds more pleasure in the deserts of Midian, than others can do in the palaces of kings.

While he is tending his sheep, God appeared unto him. God never graces the idle with his visions. When he finds us in our callings, we find him in the tokens of his mercy. Satan appears to the idle man in manifold temptations; or rather presents himself, and appears not. God was ever with Moses, yet was he not seen till now. He is never absent from his; but sometimes he makes their senses witnesses of his presence. In small matters may be greater wonders. That a bush should burn, is no marvel; but that it should not consume in burning, is justly miraculous. God chooseth not ever great subjects wherein to exercise his power; it is enough that his power is great in the smallest. When I look upon this burning bush with Moses, methinks I can never see a worthier and more lively emblem of the church: that in Egypt was in the furnace, yet wasted not. Since then, how oft hath it been flaming, never consumed! The same power that enlightens it, preserves it; and to none but his enemies is he a consuming fire. Moses was a great philosopher: but small skill would have served to know the nature of fire, and of the bush; that fire meeting with combustible matter, could not but consume. If it had been some solid wood, it would have yielded later to the flame; but bushes are of so quick despatch, that the joy of the wicked is compared to a fire of thorns. He noted a while, saw it continued, and began to wonder. It was some marvel how it should come there: but how it should continue without supply, yea, without diminution of matter, was truly admirable. Doubtless he went oft about it, and viewed it on all sides; and now, when his eye and mind could meet with no likely causes so far off, resolves, I will go see it. His curiosity led him nearer; and what could he see but a bush in a flame, which he saw at first unsatisfied? It is good to come to the place of God's presence, howsoever: God may perhaps speak to thy heart, though thou come but for novelty. Even those which have come upon curiosity, have been oft taken. Absence is without hope. If Moses had not come, he had not been called out of the bush.

To see a fire not consuming the bush, was much: but to hear a speaking fire, this was more; and to hear his own name out of the mouth of the fire, it was most of all. God makes way for his greatest messages by astonishment and admiration; as, on the contrary, carelessness carries us to a mere unproficiency under the best means of God. If our hearts were more awful, God's messages would be more effectual to us.

In that appearance, God meant to call Moses to come; yet when he is come, inhibits him —" Come not hither." We must come to God; we must not come too near him. When we meditate of the great mysteries of his word, we come to him. We come too near him when we search into his counsels. The sun and the fire say of themselves, Come not too near; how much more the light which none can attain unto? We have all our limits set us. The Gentiles might come into some outer courts, not into the inmost; the Jews might come into the inner court, not into the temple; the priests and Levites into the temple, not into the holy of holies; Moses to the hill, not to the bush. The waves of the sea had not more need of bounds than man's presumption. Moses must not come close to the bush at all; and, where he may stand, he may not stand with his shoes on. There is no unholiness in clothes. God prepared them for man at first, and that of skins, lest any exception should be taken at the hides of dead beasts. This rite was significant. What are the shoes but worldly and carnal affections? If these be not cast off when we come to the holy place, we make ourselves unholy. How much less should we dare to come with resolutions of sin? This is not only to come with shoes on, but with shoes bemired with wicked filthiness; the touch whereof profanes the pavement of God, and makes our presence odious.

Moses was the son of Amram, Amram of Kohath, Kohath of Levi, Levi of Jacob, Jacob of Isaac, Isaac of Abraham. God puts together both ends of his pedigree: " I am the God of thy father, and of Abraham, Isaac, Jacob." If he had said only,

I am thy God, it had been Moses' duty to attend awfully; but now, that he says, "I am the God of thy father, and of Abraham," &c., he challenges reverence by prescription. Any thing that was our ancestors' pleases us; their houses, their vessels, their coat-armour; how much more their God! How careful should parents be to make holy choices! Every precedent of theirs are so many monuments and motives to their posterity. What a happiness it is to be born of good parents! Hence God claims an interest in us, and we in him, for their sake. As many a man smarteth for his father's sin, so the goodness of others is crowned in a thousand generations. Neither doth God say, I was the God of Abraham, Isaac, Jacob:—but I am. The patriarchs still live after so many thousand years of dissolution. No length of time can separate the souls of the just from their Maker. As for their body, there is still a real relation betwixt the dust of it and the soul; and if the being of this part be more defective, the being of the other is more lively, and doth more than recompense the wants of that earthly half.

God could not describe himself by a more sweet name than this—" I am the God of thy father, and of Abraham," &c. Yet Moses hides his face for fear. If he had said, I am the glorious God that made heaven and earth, that dwells in light inaccessible, whom the angels cannot behold; or, I am God the avenger, just and terrible, a consuming fire to mine enemies; here had been just cause of terror.

But, why was Moses so frighted with a familiar compellation? God is no less awful to his own in his very mercies, (great is thy mercy that thou mayest be feared) for to them no less majesty shines in the favours of God, than in his judgments and justice. The wicked heart never fears God, but thundering or shaking the earth, or raining fire from heaven; but the good can dread him in his very sunshine: his loving deliverances and blessings affect them with awfulness. Moses was the true son of Jacob, who, when he saw nothing but visions of love and mercy, could say, " How dreadful is this place!"

I see Moses now at the bush, hiding his face at so mild a representation; hereafter we shall see him in this very mount, betwixt heaven and earth, in thunder, lightning, smoke, earthquakes, speaking mouth to mouth with God, barefaced and fearless. God was then more terrible, but Moses was less strange. This was his first meeting with God: further acquaintance makes him familiar, and familiarity makes him bold. Frequency of conversation gives us freedom of access to God, and makes us pour out our hearts to him as fully and as fearlessly as to our friends. In the meantime, now at first he made not so much haste to see, but he made as much haste to hide his eyes. Twice did Moses hide his face; once for the glory which God put upon him, which made him so shine that he could not be beheld of others; once for God's own glory, which he could not behold. No marvel. Some of the creatures are too glorious for mortal eyes; how much more, when God appears to us in the easiest manner, must his glory needs overcome us! Behold the difference betwixt our present and future estate. Then the more majesty of appearance, the more delight. When our sin is quite gone, all our fear at God's presence shall be turned into joy. God appeared to Adam before his sin with comfort, but in the same form, which, after his sin, was terrible. And if Moses cannot abide to look upon God's glory, when he descends to us in mercy, how shall wicked ones abide to see his fearful presence when he sets upon vengeance! In this fire he flamed, and consumed not; but in his revenge, our God is a consuming fire.

First, Moses hides himself in fear, now in modesty. " Who am I ?" None in all Egypt or Midian was comparatively fit for this embassage. Which of the Israelites had been brought up a courtier, a scholar, an Israelite by blood, by education an Egyptian, learned, wise, valiant, experienced? Yet, " Who am I ?" The more fit any man is for whatsoever vocation, the less he thinks himself. Forwardness argues insufficiency. The unworthy thinks still, Who am I not? Modest beginnings give hopeful proceedings and happy endings. Once before, Moses had taken upon him, and laid about him; hoping then they would have known, that by his hand God meant to deliver Israel: but now, when it comes to the point, " Who am I ?" God's best servants are not ever in an equal disposition to good duties. If we find differences in ourselves sometimes, it argues that grace is not our own. It is our frailty that those services which we are forward to aloof off, we shrink at near hand, and fearfully misgive. How many of us can bid defiances to death, and suggest answers to absent temptations, which, when they come home to us, we fly off, and change our note, and, instead of action, expostulate!

CONTEMPLATION IV. — THE PLAGUES OF EGYPT.

It is too much honour for flesh and blood to receive a message from heaven; yet here God sends a message to man, and is repulsed. Well may God ask, Who is man, that I should regard him? But for man to ask, Who is the Lord? is a proud and a bold blasphemy. Thus wild is nature at the first; but ere God hath done with Pharaoh, he will be known of him, he will make himself known by him to all the world. God might have swept him away suddenly. How unworthy is he of life, who with the same breath that he receives, denies the giver of it! But he would have him convinced, ere he was punished. First, therefore, he works miracles before him, then upon him. Pharaoh was now, from a staff of protection and sustentation to God's people, turned to a serpent that stung them to death. God shows himself, in this real emblem, doing that suddenly before him, which Satan had wrought in him by leisure: and now, when he crawls, and winds, and hisses, threatening peril to Israel, he shows him how in an instant he can turn him into a senseless stick, and make him, if not useful, yet fearless. The same God which wrought this, gives Satan leave to imitate it. The first plague that he meant to inflict upon Pharaoh is delusion. God can be content the devil should win himself credit, where he means to judge; and holds the honour of a miracle well lost, to harden an enemy: yet, to show that his miracle was of power, the other's of permission, Moses' serpent devours theirs. How easily might the Egyptians have thought, that he which caused their serpent not to be, could have kept it from being: and that they, which could not keep his serpent from devouring, could not secure them from being consumed! But wise thoughts enter not into those that must perish. All God's judgments stand ready, and wait but till they be called for. They need but a watch-word to be given them. No sooner is the rod lift up, but they are gone forth into the world: presently the waters run into blood; the frogs and lice crawl about, and all the other troops of God come rushing in upon his adversaries. All creatures conspire to revenge the injuries of God. If the Egyptians look upward, there they have thunder, lightning, hail, tempests: one while, no light at all: another while, such fearful flashes, as had more terror than darkness. If they look under them, there they see their waters changed into blood, their earth swarming with frogs and grasshoppers: if about them, one while the flies fill their eyes and ears; another while they see their fruits destroyed, their cattle dying, their children dead. If, lastly, they look upon themselves, they see themselves loathsome with lice, painful and deformed with scabs, biles, and blotches.

First, God begins his judgments with waters. As the river of Nilus was to Egypt, instead of heaven, to moisten and fatten the earth, so their confidence was more in it than in heaven. Men are sure to be punished most, and soonest, in that which they make a co-rival with God. They had before defiled the river with the blood of innocents; and now it appears to them in it's own colour. The waters will no longer keep their counsel. Never any man delighted in blood, which had not enough of it ere his end: they shed but some few streams, and now behold whole rivers of blood. Neither was this more a monument of their slaughter past, than an image of their future destruction. They were afterwards overwhelmed in the Red Sea: and now, beforehand, they see the rivers red with blood. How dependent and servile is the life of man, that cannot either want one element, or endure it corrupted! It is hard to say, whether there were more horror or annoyance in this plague. They complain of thirst, and yet doubt whether they should die or quench it with blood. Their fish (the chief part of their sustenance) dies with the infection, and infecteth more by being dead. The stench of both is ready to poison the inhabitants; yet Pharaoh's curiosity carries him away quite from the sense of the judgment. He had rather send for his magicians to work feats, than to humble himself under God for the removal of this plague; and God plagues his curiosity with deceit: those whom he trusts shall undo him with prevailing. The glory of a second miracle shall be obscured by a false imitation, for a greater glory to God in the sequel.

The rod is lift up again. Behold, that Nilus, which they had before adored, was never so beneficial as it is now troublesome; yielding them not only a dead, but a living annoyance: it never did so store them with fish as it now plagues them with frogs. Whatsoever any man makes his god, besides the true one, shall be once his tormentor. Those loathsome creatures leave their own element to punish them which rebelliously detained Israel from their own. No bed, no table, can be free from them: their dainty ladies cannot keep them out of their bosoms; neither can the Egyptians sooner open their mouths than they are ready to creep into their throats, as if they would tell them, that they came on purpose to revenge the wrongs of their Maker. Yet even this wonder also is Satan allowed to imitate. Who can marvel to see the best virtues counterfeited by wicked men, when he sees the devil emulating the miraculous power of God? The feats that Satan plays may harden, but cannot benefit. He that hath leave to bring frogs, hath neither leave nor power to take them away, nor to take away the stench from them. To bring them, was but to add to the judgment; to remove them, was an act of mercy. God doth commonly use Satan in executing of judgment, never in the works of mercy to men.

Yet even by thus much is Pharaoh hardened, and the sorcerers grown insolent. When the devil and his agents are in the height of their pride, God shames them in a trifle. The rod is lift up. The very dust receives life. Lice abound everywhere, and make no difference betwixt beggars and princes. Though Pharaoh and his courtiers abhorred to see themselves lousy, yet they hoped this miracle would be more easily imitable: but now the greater possibility, the greater foil. How are the great wonder-mongers of Egypt abashed, that they can neither make lice of their own, nor deliver themselves from the lice that are made! Those that could make serpents and frogs, could not either make or kill lice; to show them that those frogs and serpents were not their own workmanship. Now Pharaoh must needs see how impotent a devil he served, that could not make that vermin which every day arises voluntarily out of corruption. Jannes and Jambres cannot now make those lice (so much as by delusion) which, at another time, they cannot choose but produce unknowing, and which now they cannot avoid. That spirit which is powerful to execute the greatest things when he is bidden, is unable to do the least when he is restrained. Now these co-rivals of Moses can say, "This is the finger of God." Ye foolish enchanters, was God's finger in the lice, not in the frogs, not in the blood, not in the serpent? And why was it rather in the less than in the greater? Because ye did imitate the other, not these: as if the same finger of God had not been before in your imitation, which was now in your restraint; as if ye could have failed in these, if ye had not been only permitted the other. While wicked minds have their full scope, they never look up above themselves; but when once God crosses them in their proceedings, their want of success teaches them to give God his own. All these plagues, perhaps, had more horror than pain in them. The frogs creep upon their clothes, the lice upon their skins: but those stinging hornets which succeed them, shall wound and kill. The water was annoyed with the first plague, the earth with the second and third; this fourth fills the air, and, besides corruption, brings smart. And that they may see this winged army comes from an angry God (not either from nature or chance), even the very flies shall make a difference betwixt Egypt and Goshen. He which gave them their being, sets them their stint. They cannot more sting an Israelite than favour an Egyptian. The very wings of flies are directed by a providence, and do acknowledge their limits. Now Pharaoh finds how impossible it is for him to stand out with God, since all his power cannot rescue him from lice and flies.

And now his heart begins to thaw a little: "Go, do sacrifice to your God in this land;" or (since that will not be accepted) "go into the wilderness, but not far." But how soon it knits again! Good thoughts make but a thoroughfare of carnal hearts; they can never settle there: yea, his very misgiving hardens him the more, that now neither the murrain of his cattle, nor the botches of his servants can stir him a whit. He saw his cattle struck dead with a sudden contagion; he saw his sorcerers (after their contestation with God's messengers) struck with a scab in their very faces, and yet his heart is not struck. Who would think it possible, that any soul could be secure in the midst of such variety and frequence of judgments? These very plagues have not more wonder in them, than their success hath. To what a height of obduration will sin lead a man, and, of all sins, incredulity! Amidst all these storms Pharaoh sleepeth, till the voice of God's mighty thunders, and hail mixed with fire, roused him up a little.

Now, as betwixt sleeping and waking, he starts up, and says, "God is righteous, I am wicked; Moses, pray for us;" and presently lays down his head again. God hath no sooner done thundering, than he hath done fearing. All this while you never find him careful to prevent any one evil, but desirous still to shift it off, when he feels it; never holds constant to any good motion; never prays for himself, but carelessly wills Moses and Aaron to pray for him; never yields God his whole demand, but higgleth and dodgeth, like some hard chapmen, that would get a release with the cheapest. First, they shall not go; then, Go, and sacrifice, but in Egypt; next, Go, sacrifice in the wilderness, but not far off; after, Go, ye that are men; then, Go, you and your children only; at last, Go all, save your sheep and cattle. Wheresoever mere nature is, she is still improvident of future good, sensible of present evil, inconstant in good purposes, unable through unacquaintance, and unwilling to speak for herself; niggardly in her grants and uncheerful. The plague of the grasshoppers startled him a little, and the more through the importunity of his servants; for when he considered the fish destroyed with the first blow, the cattle with the fifth, the corn with the seventh, the fruit and leaves with this eighth, and nothing now left him but a bare fruitless earth to live upon (and that covered over with locusts), necessity drove him to relent for an advantage: " Forgive me this once; take from me this death only."

But as constrained repentance is ever short and unsound, the west wind, together with the grasshoppers, blows away his remorse; and now is he ready for another judgment. As the grasshoppers took away the sight of the earth from him, so now a gross darkness takes away the sight of heaven too. Other darknesses were but privative; this was real and sensible. The Egyptians thought this night long, (how could they choose, when it was six in one?) and so much the more, for that no man could rise to talk with other, but was necessarily confined to his own thoughts. One thinks the fault in his own eyes, which he rubs oftentimes in vain. Others think, that the sun is lost out of the firmament, and is now withdrawn for ever; others, that all things are returning to their first confusion: all think themselves miserable, past remedy, and wish (whatsoever had befallen them) that they might have had but light enough to see themselves die.

Now Pharaoh proves like to some beasts that grow mad with baiting. Grace often resisted turns to desperateness. " Get thee from me; look thou see my face no more; whensoever thou comest in my sight, thou shalt die." As if Moses could not plague him as well in absence; as if he that could not take away the lice, flies, frogs, grasshoppers, could, at his pleasure, take away the life of Moses that procured them. What is this but to run upon the judgments, and run away from the remedies? Evermore, when God's messengers are abandoned, destruction is near. Moses will see him no more, till he see him dead upon the sands; but God will now visit him more than ever. The fearfullest plagues God still reserves for the upshot: all the former do but make way for the last. Pharaoh may exclude Moses and Aaron, but God's angel he cannot exclude. Insensible messengers are used, when the visible are debarred.

Now God begins to call for the blood they owed him: in one night every house hath a carcase in it, and, which is more grievous, of their first-born, and, which is yet more fearful, in an instant. No man could comfort another; every man was too full of his own sorrow, helping rather to make the noise of the lamentation more doleful and astonishing. How soon hath God changed the note of this tyrannical people! Egypt was never so stubborn in denying passage to Israel, as now importunate to entreat it. Pharaoh did not more force them to stay before, than now to depart: whom lately they would not permit, now they hire to go. Their rich jewels of silver and gold were not too dear for them whom they hated; how much rather had they to send them away wealthy, than to have them stay to be their executors! Their love to themselves obtained of them the enriching of their enemies; and now they are glad to pay them well for their old work, and their present journey. God's people had staid like slaves; they go away like conquerors, with the spoil of those that hated them, armed for security, and wealthy for maintenance.

Old Jacob's seventy souls which he brought down into Egypt, in spite of their bondage and bloodshed, go forth six hundred thousand men, besides children. The world is well mended with Israel since he went with his staff and his scrip over Jordan. Tyranny is too weak, where God bids " Increase and multiply." I know not where else the good herb overgrows the weeds; the church outstrips the world. I fear, if they had lived in ease and delicacy, they had not been so strong, so numerous. Never any true Israelite lost by his affliction. Not only for the action, but the time, Pharaoh's choice meets with God's. That very night, when the hundred and thirty years were expired, Israel is gone: Pharaoh neither can, nor can will to keep them any longer; yet in this, not fulfilling God's will, but his own. How sweetly doth God dispose of all second causes, that, while they do their own will, they do his!

The Israelites are equally glad of this haste. Who would not be ready to go, yea to fly out of bondage? They have what they wished; it was no staying for a second invitation. The loss of an opportunity is many times unrecoverable. The love of their liberty made the burden of their dough light. Who knew whether the variable mind of Pharaoh might return to a denial, and, after all his stubbornness, repent of his obedience? It is foolish to hazard, where there is certainty of good offers, and uncertainty of continuance. They go therefore, and the same God that fetched them out, is both their guide and protector. How carefully doth he choose their way! not the nearer, but the safer. He would not have his people so suddenly change from bondage to war.

It is the wondrous mercy of God, that he hath respect, as to his own glory, so to our infirmities. He intends them wars hereafter, but after some longer breathing and more preparation; his goodness so orders all, that evils are not ready for us, till we be ready for them. And as he chooses, so he guides their way. That they might not err in that sandy and untracted wilderness, himself goes before them: who could but follow cheerfully, when he sees God lead him! He that led the wise men by a star, leads Israel by a cloud. That was a higher object, therefore he gives them a higher and more heavenly conduct: this was more earthly; therefore he contents himself with a lower representation of his presence: a pillar of cloud and fire; a pillar for firmness, of cloud and fire for visibility and use. The greater light extinguishes the less; therefore in the day he shows them not fire, but a cloud. In the night nothing is seen without light; therefore he shows them not the cloud but fire. The cloud shelters them from heat by day; the fire digests the rawness of the night. The same God is both a cloud and a fire to his children, ever putting himself into those forms of gracious respects that may best fit their necessities.

As good motions are long ere they can enter into hard hearts, so they seldom continue long. No sooner were the backs of Israel turned to depart, than Pharaoh's heart and face is turned after them, to fetch them back again. It vexes him to see so great a command, so much wealth, cast away in one night, which now he resolves to redeem, though with more plagues. The same ambition and covetousness, that made him wear out so many judgments, will not leave him, till it have wrought out his full destruction. All God's vengeances have their end, the final perdition of his enemies, which they cannot rest till they have attained. Pharaoh therefore, and his Egyptians, will needs go fetch their bane. They well knew that Israel was fitter to serve than to fight; weary with their servitude, not trained up to war, not furnished with provision for a field: themselves, captains and soldiers by profession, furnished with horses and chariots of war. They gave themselves therefore the victory beforehand, and Israel either for spoil or bondage. Yea, the weak Israelites gave up themselves for dead, and are already talking of their graves. They see the sea before them; behind them the Egyptians: they know not which is most merciless, and are stricken with the fear of both. O God, how couldst thou forbear so distrustful a people! They had seen all thy wonders in Egypt, and in their Goshen; they saw even now thy pillar before them, and yet they did more fear Egypt than believe thee. Thy patience is no less miracle than thy deliverance. But instead of removing from them, the cloudy pillar removes behind them, and stands betwixt the Israelites and Egyptians; as if God would have said, they shall first overcome me, O Israel, ere they touch thee. Wonder did now justly strive with fear in the Israelites; when they saw the cloud remove behind them, and the sea remove before them. They were not used to such bulwarks. God stood behind them in the cloud, the sea reared them up walls on both sides of them. That, which they feared would be their destruction, protected them. How easily can God make the cruellest of his creatures both our friends and patrons!

Yet here was faith mixed with unbelief. He was a bold Israelite that set the first foot into the channel of the sea; and every step that they set in that moist way, was a new exercise of their faith. Pharaoh sees all this, and wonders; yet hath not the wit or grace to think (though the pillar tell him so much), that God made a difference betwixt him and Israel. He is offended with the sea for giving way to his enemies, and yet sees not why he may not trust it as well as they. He might well have thought, that he which gave light in Goshen, when there was darkness in Egypt, could as well distinguish in the sea; but he cannot now either consider, or fear: it is his time to perish. God makes him fair way, and lets him run smoothly on, till he come to the midst of the sea; not one wave may rise up against him, to wet so much as the hoof of his horse. Extraordinary favours to wicked men are the forerunners of their ruin.

Now, when God sees the Egyptians too far to return, he finds time to strike them with their last terror. They know not why, but they would return too late. Those chariots, in which they trusted, now fail them, as having done service enough to carry them into perdition. God pursues them, and they cannot flee from him. Wicked men make equal haste, both to sin and from judgment: but they shall one day find, that it is not more easy to run into sin, than impossible to run away from judgment: the sea will show them that it regards the rod of Moses, not the sceptre of Pharaoh; and now (as glad to have got the enemies of God at such an advantage) shuts her mouth upon them, and swallows them up in her waves; and, after she hath made sport with them awhile, casts them upon her sand, for a spectacle of triumph to their adversaries.

What a sight was this to the Israelites, when they were now safe on the shore, to see their enemies come floating after them upon the billows, and to find among the carcases upon the sands, their known oppressors, which now they can tread upon with exultation! They did not cry more loud before than now they sing. Not their faith, but their sense, teaches them now to magnify that God, after their deliverance, whom they hardly trusted for their deliverance.

BOOK V.

CONTEMPLATION I.—THE WATERS OF MARAH.

ISRAEL was not more loath to come to the Red Sea than to part from it. How soon can God turn the horror of any evil into pleasure! One shore resounded with shrieks of fear; the other with timbrels, and dances, and songs of deliverance. Every main affliction is our Red Sea, which, while it threats to swallow, preserves us. At last our songs shall be louder than our cries. The Israelitish dames, when they saw their danger, thought they might have left their timbrels behind them. How unprofitable a burden seemed those instruments of music! Yet now they live to renew that forgotten minstrelsy and dancing, which their bondage had so long discontinued; and well might those feet dance upon the shore, which had walked through the sea. The land of Goshen was not so bountiful to them as these waters: that afforded them a servile life; this gave them at once freedom, victory, riches, bestowing upon them the remainder of that wealth which the Egyptians had but lent. It was a pleasure to see the floating carcases of their adversaries; and every day offers them new booties: it is no marvel, then, if their hearts were tied to these banks. If we find but a little pleasure in our life, we are ready to doat upon it. Every small contentment glues our affections to that we like; and if here our imperfect delights hold us so fast that we would not be loosed, how forcible shall those infinite joys be above, when our souls are once possessed of them.

Yet if the place had pleased them more, it is no marvel they were willing to follow Moses; that they durst follow him in the wilderness, whom they followed through the sea. It is a great confirmation to any people, when they have seen the hand of God with their guide. O Saviour, which hast undertaken to carry me from the spiritual Egypt to the land of promise, how faithful, how powerful have I found thee! how fearlessly should I trust thee! how cheerfully should I follow thee through contempt, poverty, death itself! "Master, if it be thou, bid us come unto thee."

Immediately before, they had complained of too much water; now they go three days without. Thus God meant to punish their infidelity, with the defect of that whose abundance made them to distrust. Before they saw all water, no land; now, all dry and dusty land, and no water. Extremities are the best trials of men; as in bodies, those that can bear sudden changes of heats and cold without complaint, are the strongest. So much as an evil touches upon the mean, so much help it yields towards patience. Every degree of sorrow is a preparation of the next: but when we pass to extremes without the mean, we want the benefit of recollection, and must trust to our present strength. To come from all things to nothing, is not a descent but a downfall; and it is a rare strength and constancy, not to be maimed at least. These headlong evils, as they are the sorest, so they must be most provided for; as, on the contrary, a sudden advancement from a low condition to the height of honour is most hard to manage. No man can marvel how that tyrant blinded his captives, when he hears that he brought them immediately out of a dark dungeon into rooms that were made bright and glorious. We are not worthy to know for what we are reserved. No evil can amaze us, if we can overcome sudden extremities.

The long deferring of a good, though tedious, yet makes it the better when it comes. Well did the Israelites hope, that the waters, which were so long in finding, would be precious when they were found: yet behold they are crossed, not only in their desires, but in their hopes; for, after three days' travel, the first fountains they find are bitter waters. If these wells had not run pure gall, they could not have so much complained. Long thirst will make bitter waters sweet. Yet such were these springs, that the Israelites did not so much like their moisture as abhor their relish. I see the first handsel that God gives them, in their voyage to the land of promise, thirst and bitterness. Satan gives us pleasant entrances into his ways, and reserves the bitterness for the end. God inures us to our worst at first, and sweetens our conclusion with pleasure.

The same God that would not lead Israel through the Philistines' land, lest they should shrink at the sight of war, now leads them through the wilderness, and fears not to try their patience with bitter potions. If he had not loved them, the Egyptian furnace, or sword, had prevented their thirst, or the sea whereof their enemies drunk dead; and yet see how he diets them! Never any have had so bitter draughts upon earth, as those he loves best. The palate is an ill judge of the favours of God. O my Saviour, thou didst drink a more bitter cup from the hands of thy Father, than that which thou refusedst of the Jews, or than that which I can drink from thee!

Before, they could not drink if they would; now, they might and would not. God can give us blessings with such a tang, that the fruition shall not much differ from the want. So many a one hath riches, not grace to use them; many have children, but such as they prefer barrenness. They had said before, Oh that we had any water! Now, Oh that we had good water! It is good so to desire blessings from God, that we may be the better for enjoying them; so to crave water, that it may not be sauced with bitterness.

Now, these fond Israelites, instead of praying, murmur; instead of praying to God, murmur against Moses. "What hath the righteous done?" He made not either the wilderness dry, or the waters bitter: yea, if his conduct were the matter, what one foot went he before them without God? The pillar led them, and not he; yet Moses is murmured at. It is the hard condition of authority, that when the multitude fare well, they applaud themselves; when ill, they repine against their governors. Who can hope to be free, if Moses escape not? Never any prince so merited of a people. He thrust himself upon the pikes of Pharaoh's tyranny—he brought them from a bondage worse than death—his rod divided the sea, and shared life to them, death to their pursuers. Who would not have thought these men so obliged to Moses, that no death could have opened their mouths, or raised their hands against him? Yet now, the first occasion of want makes them rebel. No benefit can stop the mouth of impatience. If our turn be not served for the present, former favours are either forgotten or contemned. No marvel if we deal so with men, when God receives this measure from us. One year of famine, one summer of pestilence, one moon of unseasonable weather, makes us overlook all the blessings of God; and more to mutiny at the sense of our evil, than to praise him for our varieties of good: whereas, favours well bestowed leave us both mindful and confident, and will not suffer us either to forget or distrust. O God, I have made an ill use of thy mercies, if I have not learnt to be content with thy corrections.

Moses was in the same want of water with them, in the same distaste of bitterness; and yet they say to Moses, What shall we drink? If they had seen him furnished with full vessels of sweet water, and themselves put over to this unsavoury liquor, envy might have given some colour to this mutiny; but now their leader's common misery might have freed him from their murmurs. They held it one piece of the late Egyptian tyranny, that a task was required of them (which the imposers knew they could not perform) to make brick when they have no straw; yet they say to Moses, What shall we drink? Themselves are grown exactors, and are ready to menace more than stripes, if they have not their ends without means. Moses took not upon him their provision, but their deliverance; and yet, as if he had been the common victualler of the camp, they ask, What shall we drink? When want meets with impatient minds, it transports them to fury; every thing disquiets, and nothing satisfies them.

What course doth Moses now take? That which they should have done, and did not. They cried not more fervently to him than he to God. If he were their leader, God was his. That which they unjustly required of him, he justly requires of God that could do it. He knew whence to look for redress of all complaints: this was not his charge, but his Maker's, which was able to maintain his own act. I see and acknowledge the harbour that we must put into in all our ill weather. It is to thee, O God, that we must pour out our hearts, who only canst make our bitter waters sweet.

Might not that rod which took away the liquid nature from the waters, and made them solid, have also taken away the bitter quality from these waters, and made them sweet, since to flow is natural unto the water, to be bitter is but accidental? Moses durst not employ his rod without a precept; he knew the power came from the commandment. We may not presume on likelihoods, but depend upon warrants; therefore Moses doth not lift up his rod to the waters, but his hand and voice to God.

The hand of faith never knocked at heaven in vain. No sooner hath Moses showed his grievance, than God shows him the remedy; yet an unlikely one, that it might be miraculous. He that made the waters, could have given them any savour. How easy is it for him that made the matter to alter the quality! It is not more hard to take away than to give. Who doubts but the same hand that created them, might have immediately changed them? Yet that almighty power will do it by means. A piece of wood must sweeten the waters. What relation hath wood to water? or that which hath no savour, to the redress of bitterness? Yet here is no more possibility of failing, than proportion to the success. All things are subject to the command of their Maker. He that made all of nothing, can make every thing of any thing. There is so much power in every creature as he will please to give. It is the praise of Omnipotency to work by improbabilities; Elisha with salt, Moses with wood, shall sweeten the bitter waters. Let no man despise the means when he knows the author.

God taught his people by actions, as well as words. This entrance showed them their whole journey, wherein they should taste of much bitterness; but at last, through the mercy of God, sweetened with comfort. Or did it not represent themselves rather in the journey, in the fountains of whose hearts were the bitter waters of manifold corruptions? yet their unsavoury souls are sweetened by the graces of his Spirit. O blessed Saviour, the wood of thy cross, that is, the application of thy sufferings, is enough to sweeten a whole sea of bitterness! I care not how unpleasant a potion I find in this wilderness, if the power and benefit of thy precious death may season it to my soul.

CONTEMPLATION II.—THE QUAILS AND MANNA.

THE thirst of Israel is well quenched; for, besides the change of the waters of Marah, their station is changed to Elim, where were twelve fountains for their twelve tribes. And now they complain as much of hunger.

Contentation is a rare blessing; because it arises either from a fruition of all comforts, or a not desiring of some which we have not. Now, we are never so bare as not to have some benefits; never so full, as not to want something, yea, as not to be full of wants. God hath much ado with us. Either we lack health, or quietness, or children, or wealth, or company, or ourselves in all these. It is a wonder these men found not fault with the want of sauce to their quails, or with their old clothes, or their solitary way. Nature is moderate in her desires; but conceit is insatiable. Yet who can deny hunger to be a sore vexation? Before, they were forbidden sour bread; but now, what leaven is so sour as want? When means hold out, it is easy to be content. While their dough and other cakes lasted, while they were gathering of the dates of Elim, we hear no news of them. Who cannot pray for his daily bread when he hath it in his cupboard? But when our own provision fails us, then not to distrust the provision of God is a noble trial of faith. They should have said, He that stopt the mouth of the sea, that it could not devour us, can as easily stop the mouth of our stomachs. It was no easier matter to kill the firstborn of Egypt, by his immediate hand, than to preserve us. He that commanded the sea to stand still and guard us, can as easily command the earth to nourish us. He that made the rod a serpent, can as well make these stones bread. He that brought armies of frogs and caterpillars to Egypt, can as well bring whole drifts of birds and beasts to the desert. He that sweetened the waters with wood, can as well refresh our bodies with the fruits of the earth. Why do we not wait on him, whom we have found so powerful? Now they set the mercy and love of God upon a wrong last, while they measure it only by their present sense. Nature is jocund and cheerful while it prospereth: let God withdraw his hand, no sight, no trust. Those can praise him with timbrels for a present favour, that cannot depend upon him in the want of means for a future. We all are never weary of receiving, soon weary of attending.

The other mutiny was of some few malcontents, perhaps those strangers, which sought their own protection under the wing of Israel; this, of the whole troop. Not that none were free: Caleb, Joshua, Moses, Aaron, Miriam, were not yet tainted. Usually God measures the state of any church or country by the most; the greater part carries both the name and censure. Sins are so much the greater as they are more universal: so far is evil from being extenuated by the multitude of the guilty, that nothing can more aggravate it. With men, commonness may plead for favour; with God, it pleads for judgment. Many hands draw the cable with more violence than few. The leprosy of the whole body is more loathsome than that of a part.

But what do these mutineers say? Oh that we had died by the hand of the Lord! And whose hand was this, O ye fond Israelites, if you must perish by famine? God carried you forth; God restrained his creatures from you; and, while ye are ready to die, thus ye say, Oh that we had died by the hand of the Lord!

It is the folly of men, that in immediate judgments they can see God's hand; not in those whose second causes are sensible: whereas God holds himself equally interested in all, challenging that there is no evil in the city but from him. It is but one hand, and many instruments, that God strikes us with. The water may not lose the name, though it comes by channels and pipes from the spring. It is our faithlessness, that in visible means we see not him that is invisible.

And when would they have wished to die? When they sat by the flesh-pots of Egypt? Alas! what good would their flesh-pots have done them in their death? If they might sustain their life, yet what could they avail them in dying? For, if they were unpleasant, what comfort was it to see them?—if pleasant, what comfort to part from them? Our greatest pleasures are but pains in their loss. Every mind affects that which is like itself. Carnal minds are for the flesh-pots of Egypt, though bought with servitude: spiritual are for the presence of God, though redeemed with famine; and would rather die in God's presence, than live without him, in the sight of delicate or full dishes.

They loved their lives well enough. I heard how they shrieked when they were in danger of the Egyptians; yet now they say, Oh that we had died! not, Oh that we might live by the flesh-pots; but, Oh that we had died! Although life be naturally sweet, yet a little discontentment makes us weary. It is a base cowardliness, so soon as ever we are called from the garrison to the field, to think of running away. Then is our fortitude worthy of praise, when we can endure to be miserable.

But what, can no flesh-pots serve but those of Egypt? I am deceived if that land afforded them any flesh-pots save their own. Their landlords of Egypt held it abomination to eat of their dishes, or to kill that which they did eat. In those times, then, they did eat of their own; and why not now? They had droves of cattle in the wilderness; why did they not take of them? Surely, if they would have been as good husbands of their cattle as they were of their dough, they might have had enough to eat without need of murmuring: for if their back-burdens of dough lasted for a month, their herds might have served them many years. All grudging is odious, but most when our hands are full. To whine in the midst of abundance, is a shameful unthankfulness.

When a man would have looked that the anger of God should have appeared in fire, now, behold, his glory appears in a cloud. Oh the exceeding long-suffering of God, that hears their murmurings! and, as if he had been bound to content them, instead of punishing, pleases them! as a kind mother would deal with a crabbed child, who rather stills him with the breast, than calls for the rod. One would have thought, that the sight of the cloud of God should have dispelled the cloud of their distrust; and this glory of God should have made them ashamed of themselves, and afraid of him: yet I do not hear them once say, What mighty and gracious God have we distrusted! Nothing will content an impotent mind but fruition. When a heart is hardened with any passion, it will endure much ere it will yield to relent.

Their eyes saw the cloud; their ears heard the promise; the performance is speedy and answerable. Needs must they

THE QUAILS AND MANNA.

be convinced, when they saw God as glorious in his work as in his presence; when they saw his word justified by his act. God tells them aforehand what he will do, that their expectation might stay their hearts. He doth that which he foretold, that they might learn to trust him ere he performed. They desired meat, and receive quails: they desired bread, and have manna. If they had had of the coarsest flesh, and of the basest pulse, hunger would have made it dainty: but now God will pamper their famine; and gives them meat of kings, and bread of angels. What a world of quails were but sufficient to serve six hundred thousand persons! They were all strong, all hungry; neither could they be satisfied with single fowls. What a table hath God prepared in the desert, for abundance, for delicacy! Never prince was so served in his greatest pomp, as these rebellious Israelites in the wilderness. God loves to over-deserve of men, and to exceed not only their sins, but their very desires, in mercy. How good shall we find him to those that please him, since he is so gracious to offenders! If the most graceless Israelites be fed with quails and manna, O what goodness is that he hath laid up for them that love him! As, on the contrary, if the righteous scarce be saved, where will the sinners appear! O God, thou canst, thou wilt make this difference. Howsoever, with us men, the most crabbed and stubborn oftentimes fare the best; the righteous Judge of the world frames his remunerations as he finds us: and if his mercy sometimes provoke the worst to repentance by his temporal favours, yet he ever reserves so much greater reward for the righteous, as eternity is beyond time, and heaven above earth.

It was not of any natural instinct, but from the overruling power of their Creator, that these quails came to the desert. Needs must they come whom God brings. His hand is in all the motions of his meanest creatures. Not only we, but they, move in him. As not many quails, so not one sparrow falls without him. How much more are the actions of his best creature, man, directed by his providence! How ashamed might these Israelites have been, to see these creatures so obedient to their Creator, as to come and offer themselves to their slaughter; while they went so repiningly to his service and their own preferment! Who can distrust the provision of the great Housekeeper of the world, when he sees how He can furnish his tables at pleasure? Is he grown now careless, or we faithless rather? Why do we not repose upon his mercy? Rather than we shall want, when we trust him, he will fetch quails from all the coasts of heaven to our board. O Lord, thy hand is not shortened to give; let not ours be shortened or shut in receiving.

Elijah's servitors, the ravens, brought him his full service of bread and flesh at once, each morning and evening. But these Israelites have their flesh at even, and their bread in the morning. Good reason there should be a difference: Elijah's table was upon God's direct appointment; the Israelites' upon their mutiny. Although God will relieve them with provision, yet he will punish their impatience with delay; so shall they know themselves his people that they shall find they were murmurers. Not only in the matter, but in the order, God answers their grudging: first they complain of the want of flesh-pots, then of bread. In the first place, therefore, they have flesh, bread after. When they have flesh, yet they must stay a time ere they can have a full meal, unless they would eat their meat breadless, and their bread dry. God will be waited on, and will give the consummation of his blessings at his leisure. In the evening of our life, we have the first pledges of his favour: but in the morning of our resurrection, must we look for our perfect satiety of the true manna, the bread of life.

Now the Israelites sped well with their quails; they did eat and digest, and prosper: not long after, they have quails with a vengeance; the meat was pleasant, but the sauce was fearful. They let down the quails at their mouth, but they came out at their nostrils. How much better had it been to have died of hunger, through the chastisement of God, than of the plague of God, with the flesh betwixt their teeth! Behold, they perish of the same disease then, whereof they now recover. The same sin repeated is death, whose first act found remission. Relapses are desperate, where the sickness itself is not. With us men, once goes away with a warning; the second is but whipping; the third is death. It is a mortal thing to abuse the lenity of God. We should be presumptuously mad, to hope that God will stand us for a sinning-stock, to provoke him how we will. It is more mercy than he owes us, if he forbear us once; it is his justice to plague us the second time. We may thank ourselves, if we will not be warned.

Their meat was strange, but nothing so much as their bread. To find quails in a wilderness was unusual; but for bread to come down from heaven was yet more.

They had seen quails before, though not in such number; manna was never seen till now. From this day, till their settling in Canaan, God wrought a perpetual miracle in this food. A miracle in the place: other bread rises up from below; this fell down from above: neither did it ever rain bread till now; yet so did this heavenly shower fall, that it is confined to the camp of Israel. A miracle in the quantity: that every morning should fall enough to fill so many hundred thousand mouths and maws. A miracle in the composition: that it is sweet like honey-cakes round like corianders, transparent as dew. A miracle in the quality: that it melted by one heat, by another hardened. A miracle in the difference of the fall: that (as if it knew times, and would teach them as well as feed them) it fell double in the even of the Sabbath, and on the Sabbath fell not. A miracle in the putrefaction and preservation: that it was full of worms, when it was kept beyond the due hour for distrust; full of sweetness when it was kept a day longer for religion; yea, many ages, in the ark, for a monument of the power and mercy of the Giver. A miracle in the continuance and ceasing: that this shower of bread followed their camp in all their removals, till they came to taste of the bread of Canaan; and then withdrew itself, as if it should have said, Ye need no miracles, now ye have means.

They had the types; we have the substance. In this wilderness of the world, the true manna is rained upon the tents of our hearts. He that sent the manna, was the manna which he sent. He hath said, "I am the manna that came down from heaven."— Behold, their whole meals were sacramental. Every morsel they did eat was spiritual. We eat still of their manna: still he comes down from heaven. He hath substance enough for worlds of souls, yet only is to be found in the lists of the true church; he hath more sweetness than the honey and the honeycomb. Happy are we, if we can find him so sweet as he is.

The same hand that rained manna upon their tents, could have rained it into their mouths, or laps. God loves we should take pains for our spiritual food. Little would it have availed them, that the manna lay about their tents, if they had not gone forth and gathered it, beaten it, baked it. Let salvation be never so plentiful, if we bring it not home, and make it ours by faith, we are no whit the better. If the work done, and means used, had been enough to give life, no Israelite had died. Their bellies were full of that bread, whereof one crumb gives life; yet they died many of them in displeasure. As in natural, so in spiritual things, we may not trust to means. The carcase of the sacrament cannot give life, but the soul of it, which is the thing represented. I see each man gather, and take his just measure out of the common heap. We must be industrious, and helpful each to other; but, when we have done, Christ is not partial. If our sanctification differ, yet our justification is equal in all.

He that gave a homer to each, could have given an ephah. As easily could he have rained down enough for a month, or a year, at once, as for a day. God delights to have us live in a continual dependence upon his providence, and each day renew the acts of our faith and thankfulness. But what a covetous Israelite was that, which, in a foolish distrust, would be sparing the charges of God, and reserving that for morning, which he should have spent upon his supper! He shall know, that even the bread that came down from heaven can corrupt. The manna was from above; the worms and stink from his diffidence. Nothing is so sovereign, which, being perverted, may not annoy instead of benefiting us.

Yet I see some difference between the true and typical manna: God never meant that the shadow and the body should agree in all things. The outward manna reserved was poison; the spiritual manna is to us, as it was to the ark, not good, unless it be kept perpetually. If we keep it, it shall keep us from putrefaction. The outward manna fell not at all on the Sabbath. The spiritual manna, though it baulks no day, yet it falls double on God's day; and if we gather it not then, we famish. In that true Sabbath of our glorious rest, we shall for ever feed on that manna which we have gathered in this, even of our life.

CONTEMPLATION III.—THE ROCK OF REPHIDIM.

Before, Israel thirsted and was satisfied; after that, they hungered and were filled; now they thirst again. They have bread and meat, but want drink. It is a marvel if God do not evermore hold us short of something, because he would keep us still in exercise. We should forget at whose cost we live, if we wanted nothing. Still God observes a vicissitude of evil and good; and the same evils that we have passed return upon us in their courses. - Crosses are not of the nature of those diseases which they say a man can have but once. Their first seizure doth but make way for their re-entry. None but our last enemy comes once for all: and I know not if that; for even in living, we die daily. So must we take our leaves of all afflictions, that we reserve a lodging for them, and expect their return.

All Israel murmured when they wanted bread, meat, water; and yet all Israel departed from the wilderness of Sin to Rephidim, at God's command. The very worst men will obey God in something; none but the good in all. He is rarely desperate, that makes a universal opposition to God. It is an unsound praise that is given a man for one good action. It may be safely said of the very devils themselves, that they do something well: they know and believe, and tremble. If we follow God and murmur, it is all one as if we had staid behind.

Those distrust his providence in their necessity, that are ready to follow his guidance in their welfare. It is a harder matter to endure an extreme want, than to obey a hard commandment. Sufferings are greater trials than actions. How many have we seen jeopard their lives, with cheerful resolution, which cannot endure in cold blood to lose a limb with patience? Because God will have his thoroughly tried, he puts them to both; and if we cannot endure both to follow him from Sin and to thirst in Rephidim, we are not sound Israelites.

God led them on purpose to this dry Rephidim. He could as well have conducted them to another Elim, to convenient waterings; or He, that gives the waters of all their channels, could as well have derived them to meet Israel: but God doth purposely carry them to thirst. It is not for necessity that we fare ill, but out of choice. It were all one with God to give us health, as sickness; abundance, as poverty. The treasury of his riches hath more store than his creature can be capable of. We should not complain, if it were not good for us to want.

This should have been a contentment able to quench any thirst: " God hath led us hither." If Moses, out of ignorance, had misguided us, or we by chance had fallen upon these dry deserts, though this were no remedy of our grief, yet it might be some ground of our complaint. But now the counsel of so wise and merciful a God hath drawn into this want; and shall not he as easily find the way out? " It is the Lord, let him do what he will." There can be no more forcible motive to patience, than the acknowledgment of a divine hand that strikes us. It is fearful to be in the hand of an adversary; but who would not be confident of a father? Yet, in our frail humanity, choler may transport a man from the remembrance of nature; but when we feel ourselves under the discipline of a wise God (that can temper our afflictions to our strength, to our benefit), who would not rather murmur at himself that he should swerve towards impatience? Yet these sturdy Israelites wilfully murmur, and will not have their thirst quenched with faith, but with water: " Give us water."

I looked to hear when they would have entreated Moses to pray for them: but, instead of entreating, they contend; and, instead of prayers, I find commands: " Give us water." If they had gone to God without Moses, I should have praised their faith; but now they go to Moses without God, I hate their stubborn faithlessness. To seek to the second means, with neglect of the first, is the fruit of a false faith.

The answer of Moses is, like himself, mild and sweet. Why contend ye with me? " Why tempt ye the Lord?"—in the first expostulation condemning them of injustice; since not he, but the Lord, hath afflicted them: in the second, of presumption; that since it was God that tempted them by want, they should tempt him by murmuring. In the one, he would have them see their wrong; in the other, their danger. As the act came not from him, but from God, so he puts it off to God from himself. " Why tempt ye the Lord?" The opposition which is made to the instruments of God, redounds ever to his person. He holds himself smitten through the sides of his ministers. So hath God incorporated these respects, that our subtilty cannot divide them.

But what temptation is this? " Is the Lord among us, or no?" Infidelity is crafty and yet foolish; crafty in her insinuations, foolish in her conceits. They imply, " If we were sure the Lord were with us, we would not distrust." They conceive doubts of his presence, after such confirmations. What could God do more to make them know him present, unless every moment should have renewed miracles? The plagues of Egypt and the division of the sea were so famous, that the very inns of Jericho rang of them. Their waters were lately sweetened; the quails were yet in their teeth; the manna was yet in their eye; yea, they saw God in the pillar of the cloud: and yet they say, " Is the Lord amongst us?" No argument is enough to an incredulous heart; not reason, sense, nor experience. How

F

much better was that faith of Thomas, that would believe his eyes and hands, though his ears he would not! O the deep infidelity of these Israelites, that saw and believed not!

And how will they know if God be amongst them? as if he could not be with them, and they be athirst. Either God must humour carnal minds, or be distrusted. If they prosper, though it be with wickedness, God is with them: if they be thwarted in their own designs, straight, " Is God with us?" It was the way to put God from them, to distrust and murmur. If he had not been with them, they had not lived. If he had been in them, they had not mutinied. They can think him absent in their want, and cannot see him absent in their sin; and yet wickedness, not affliction, argues him gone: yet then is he most present, when he most chastises.

Who would not have looked, that this answer of Moses should have appeased their fury? As what can still him, that will not be quiet to think he hath God for his adversary? But, as if they would wilfully war against heaven, they proceed; yet with no less craft than violence, bending their exception to one part of the answer, and smoothly omitting what they could not except against. They will not hear of tempting God; they maintain their strife with Moses, both with words and stones. How malicious, how heady is impatience! The act was God's; they cast it upon Moses: " Wherefore hast thou brought us?" The act of God was merciful: they make it cruel; " To kill us and our children;" as if God and Moses meant nothing but their ruin, who intended nothing but their life and liberty. Foolish men! what needed this journey to death? Were they not as obnoxious to God in Egypt? Could not God by Moses as easily have killed them in Egypt, or in the sea, as their enemies? Impatience is full of misconstruction. If it be possible to find out any gloss, to corrupt the text of God's actions, they shall be sure not to escape untainted.

It was no use expostulating with an unreasonable multitude. Moses runs straight to him that was able at once to quench their thirst and their fury; " What shall I do to this people?" It is the best way to trust God with his own causes. When men will be intermeddling with his affairs, they undo themselves in vain. We shall find difficulties in all great enterprises: if we be sure we have begun them from God, we may securely cast all events upon his providence, which knows how to dispose, and how to end them.

Moses perceived rage, not in the tongues only, but in the hands of the Israelites: " Yet a while longer, and they will stone me." Even the leader of God's people feared death, and sinned not in fearing. Life is worthy to be dear to all; especially to him whom public charge hath made necessary. Mere fear is not sinful; it is impotence and distrust that accompany it, which make it evil. How well is that fear bestowed, that sends us the more importunately to God! Some men would have thought of flight: Moses flies to his prayers; and that not for revenge, but for help. Who but Moses would not have said, This twice they have mutinied, and been pardoned; and now again thou seest, O Lord, how madly they rebel, and how bloodily they intend against me! Preserve me, I beseech thee, and plague them. I hear none of this; but, imitating the long suffering of his God, he seeks to God for them, which sought to kill him for the quarrel of God.

Neither is God sooner sought than found. All Israel might see Moses go towards the rock: none but the elders might see him strike it. Their unbelief made them unworthy of this privilege. It is no small favour of God to make us witnesses of his great works: that he crucifies his Son before us, that he fetches the water of life out of the true rock in our sight, is a high prerogative: if his rigour would have taken it, our infidelity had equally excluded us, whom now his mercy hath received.

Moses must take his rod: God could have done it by his will, without a word, or by his word, without the rod; but he will do by means, that which he can as easily do without. There was no virtue in the rod, none in the stroke; but all in the command of God. Means must be used, and yet their efficacy must be expected out of themselves.

It doth not suffice God to name the rod, without a description: " Whereby thou smotest the river." Wherefore but to strengthen the faith of Moses, that he might well expect this wonder, from that which he had tried to be miraculous. How could he but firmly believe, that the same means which turned the waters into blood, and turned the sea into a wall, could as well turn the stone into water? Nothing more raises up the heart in present affiance, than the recognition of favours, or wonders passed. Behold, the same rod that brought plagues to the Egyptians, brings deliverances to Israel. By the same means can God save and condemn; like as the same sword defends and kills.

That power which turned the wings of the quails to the wilderness, turned the course of the water through the rock. He might, if he had pleased, have caused a spring to well out of the plain earth; but he will now fetch it out of the stone, to convince and shame their infidelity.

What is more hard and dry than the rock? what more moist and supple than water? That they may be ashamed to think they distrusted, lest God could bring them water out of the clouds or springs, the very rock shall yield it.

And now, unless their hearts had been more rocky than this stone, they could not but have resolved them into tears for this diffidence.

I wonder to see these Israelites fed with sacraments: their bread was sacramental, whereof they communicated every day. Lest any man should complain of frequence, the Israelites received daily; and now their drink was sacramental, that the ancient church may give no warrant of a dry communion.

Twice, therefore, hath the rock yielded them water of refreshing; to signify that the true spiritual Rock yields it always. The rock that followed them was Christ. Out of thy side, O Saviour, issued that bloody stream, whereby the thirst of all believers is comfortably quenched. Let us but thirst (not with repining, but with faith); this rock of thine shall abundantly flow forth to our souls, and follow us, till this water be changed into that new wine, which we shall drink with thee in thy Father's kingdom.

CONTEMPLATION IV.—THE FOIL OF AMALEK: OR THE HAND OF MOSES LIFT UP.

No sooner is Israel's thirst slacked, than God hath an Amalekite ready to assault them. The Almighty hath choice of rods to whip us with, and will not be content with one trial. They would needs be quarrelling with Moses without a cause; and now God sends the Amalekites to quarrel with them. It is just with God, that they which would be contending with their best friends, should have work enough of contending with enemies.

In their passage out of Egypt, God would not lead them the nearest way, by the Philistines' land, lest they should repent at the sight of war; now they both see and feel it. He knows how to make the fittest choice of the times of evil, and withholds that one while, which he sends another, not without a just reason why he sends and withholds it: and though to us they come ever, as we think, unseasonably, and at some times more unfitly than others, yet He that sends them knows their opportunities.

Who would not have thought a worse time could never have been picked for Israel's war than now? In the feebleness of their troops, when they were wearied, thirsty, unweaponed; yet now must the Amalekites do that which before the Philistines might not do. We are not worthy, not able to choose for ourselves.

To be sick, and die in the strength of youth, in the minority of children; to be pinched with poverty, or miscarriage of children in our age,—how harshly unseasonable it seems! But the infinite wisdom that orders our events, knows how to order our times. Unless we will be shameless unbelievers, O Lord, we must trust thee with ourselves and our seasons, and know, that not that which we desire, but that which thou hast appointed, is the fittest time for our sufferings.

Amalek was Esau's grandchild, and these Israelites the sons of Jacob. The abode of Amalek was not so far from Egypt, but they might well hear what became of their cousins of Israel: and now, doubtless out of envy, watched their opportunity of revenge for their old grudge. Malice is commonly hereditary and runs in the blood, and, as we used to say of runnet, the older it is, the stronger.

Hence is that foolish hostility which some men unjustly nourish upon no other grounds than the quarrels of their forefathers. To wreak our malice upon posterity, is, at the best, but the humour of an Amalekite.

How cowardly and how crafty was this skirmish of Amalek! They do not bid them battle in fair terms of war, but without all noise of warning, come stealing upon the hindmost, and fall upon the weak and scattered remnants of Israel.

There is no looking for favour at the hands of malice: the worst that either force or fraud can do, must be expected of an adversary; but much more of our spiritual enemy, by how much his hatred is deeper. Behold, this Amalek lies in ambush to hinder our passage unto our land of promise, and subtilely takes all advantages of our weaknesses. We cannot be wise or safe if we stay behind our colours, and strengthen not those parts where is most peril of opposition.

I do not hear Moses say to his Joshua, Amalek is come up against us, it matters not whether thou go against him or not; or if thou go, whether alone or with company; or if accompanied, whether with many or few, strong or weak; or if strong men, whether they fight or no; I will pray on the hill: but, "Choose us out men, and go fight."

Then only can we pray with hope when we have done our best. And though the means cannot effect that which we desire, yet God will have us use the likeliest means on our part to effect it. Where it comes immediately from the charge of God, any means are effectual: one stick of wood shall fetch water out of the rock; another shall fetch bitterness out of the water; but in those projects which we make for our own purposes, we must choose those helps which promise most efficacy. In vain shall Moses be upon the hill, if Joshua be not in the valley. Prayer without means is a mockery of God.

Here are two shadows of one substance: the same Christ in Joshua fights against our spiritual Amalek, and in Moses spreads out his arms upon the hill; and, in both, conquers. And why doth he climb up the hill rather than pray in the valley? Perhaps that he might have the more freedom to his thoughts, which, following the sense, are so much more heavenly, as the eyes see more of heaven. Though virtue lies not in the place, yet choice must be made of those places which may be the most help to our devotion; perhaps that he might be in the eye of Israel.

The presence and sight of the leader gives heart to the people: neither doth any thing more move the multitude than example. A public person cannot hide himself in the valley; but yet it becomes him best to show himself upon the hill.

The hand of Moses must be raised, but not empty; neither is it his own rod that he holds, but God's. In the first meeting of God with Moses, the rod was Moses', it is like, for the use of his trade; now the propriety is altered: God hath so wrought by it, that now he challenges it, and Moses dare not call it his own.

Those things which it pleases God to use for his own service, are now changed in their condition. The bread of the sacrament was once the baker's; now it is God's: the water was once every man's; now it is the laver of regeneration. It is both unjust and unsafe to hold those things common wherein God hath a peculiarity.

At other times, upon occasion of the plagues, and of the quails, and of the rock, he was commanded to take the rod in his hand; now he doth it unbidden. He doth it not now for miraculous operation, but for encouragement.

For when the Israelites should cast up their eyes to the hill, and see Moses and his rod (the man and the means that had wrought so powerfully for them), they could not but take heart to themselves, and think, There is the man that delivered us from the Egyptian; why not now from the Amalekite? There is the rod which turned waters to blood, and brought varieties of plagues on Egypt; why not now on Amalek?

Nothing can more hearten our faith, than the view of the monuments of God's favour: if ever we have found any word or act of God cordial to us, it is good to fetch it forth oft to the eye. The renewing of our sense and remembrance makes every gift of God perpetually beneficial.

If Moses had received a command, that rod, which fetched water from the rock, could as well have fetched the blood of the Amalekites out of their bodies. God will not work miracles always; neither must we expect them unbidden.

Not as a standard-bearer, so much as a suppliant, doth Moses lift up his hand. The gesture of the body should both express and further the piety of the soul. This flesh of ours is not a good servant, unless it help us in the best offices. The God of spirits doth more respect the soul of our devotion; yet it is both unmannerly and irreligious to be misgestured in our prayers. The careless and uncomely carriage of the body helps both to signify and make a profane soul.

The hand and the rod of Moses never moved in vain; though the rod did not strike Amalek, as it had done the rock, yet it smote heaven, and fetched down victory. And that the Israelites might see the hand of Moses had a greater stroke in the fight than all theirs, the success must rise and fall with it. Amalek rose, and Israel fell, with his hand falling; Amalek fell and Israel rises with his hand raised. O the wondrous power of the prayers of faith! All heavenly favours are derived to us from this channel of grace. To these are we beholden for our peace, preservations, and all the rich mercies of God which we enjoy. We could not want, if we could ask.

Every man's hand would not have done this, but the hand of a Moses. A faithless man may as well hold his hand and tongue still: he may babble, but prays not;

he prays ineffectually, and receives not: only the prayer of the righteous availeth much; and only the believer is righteous.

There can be no merit, no recompense answerable to a good man's prayer; for heaven, and the ear of God, is open to him; but the formal devotions of an ignorant and faithless man, are not worth that crust of bread which he asks: yea, it is presumption in himself; how should it be beneficial to others? It profanes the name of God, instead of adoring it.

But how justly is the fervency of the prayer added to the righteousness of the person! When Moses' hand slackened, Amalek prevailed. No Moses can have his hand ever up; it is a title proper to God, that his hands are stretched out still, whether to mercy or vengeance. Our infirmity will not suffer any long intention, either of body or mind. Long prayers can hardly maintain their vigour, as in tall bodies the spirits are diffused. The strongest hand will languish with long extending: and when our devotion tires, it is seen in the success; then straight our Amalek prevails. Spiritual wickednesses are mastered by vehement prayer, and, by heartlessness in prayer, overcome us.

Moses had two helps — a stone to sit on, and a hand to raise his; and his sitting and holpen hand is no less effectual. Even in our prayers will God allow us to respect our own infirmities. In cases of our necessity, he regards not the posture of body, but the affections of the soul.

Doubtless Aaron and Hur did not only raise their hands, but their minds with his. The more cords, the easier draught. Aaron was brother to Moses: there cannot be a more brotherly office, than to help one another in our prayers, and to excite our mutual devotions. No Christian may think it enough to pray alone. He is no true Israelite, that will not be ready to lift up the weary hands of God's saints.

All Israel saw this: or if they were so intent upon the slaughter and spoil, that they observed it not, they might hear it after from Aaron and Hur. Yet this contents not God: it must be written. Many other miracles had God done before, not one directly commanded to be recorded: the other were only for the wonder; this for the imitation of God's people. In things that must live by report, every tongue adds or detracts something. The word once written is both unalterable and permanent.

As God is careful to maintain the glory of his miraculous victory, so is Moses desirous to second him; God by a book, and Moses by an altar, and a name. God commands to enrol it in parchment; Moses registers it in the stones of his altar, which he raises not only for future memory, but for present use. That hand which was weary of lifting up, straight offers a sacrifice of praise to God. How well it becomes the just to be thankful! Even very nature teacheth us men to abhor ingratitude in small favours: how much less can that fountain of goodness abide to be laded at with unthankful hands! O God, we cannot but confess our deliverances! Where are our altars? Where are our sacrifices? Where is our Jehovah-nissi? I do not more wonder at thy power in preserving us, than at thy mercy, which is not weary of casting away favours upon the ungrateful.

CONTEMPLATION V.— OF THE LAW.

It is but about seven weeks since Israel came out of Egypt: in which space God had cherished their faith by five several wonders: yet now he thinks it time to give them statutes from heaven, as well as bread. The manna and water from the rock (which was Christ in the gospel) were given before the law; the sacraments of grace before the legal covenant. The grace of God preventeth our obedience; therefore should we keep the law of God, because we have a Saviour. O the mercy of our God, which, before we see what we are bound to do, shows us our remedy, if we do it not! How can our faith disannul the law, when it was before it? It may help to fulfil that which shall be; it cannot frustrate that which was not. The letters which God had written in our fleshy tables, were now (as those which are carved in some barks) almost grown out: he saw it time to write them in dead tables, whose hardness should not be capable of alteration. He knew that the stone would be more faithful than our hearts.

O marvellous accordance betwixt the two testaments! In the very time of their delivery, there is the same agreement which is in the substance. The ancient Jews kept our feasts, and we still keep theirs. The feast of the passover is the time of Christ's resurrection; then did he pass from under the bondage of death. Christ is our passover; the spotless lamb, whereof not a bone must be broken. The very day wherein God came down in fire and thunder to deliver the law, even the same day came also the Holy Ghost down upon the disciples in fiery tongues, for the propagation of the gospel. That other was in fire and smoke; obscurity was mingled with terror: this was in fire without smoke, befitting the light and clearness of the gospel; fire, not in flashes, but in tongues; not to terrify, but to instruct. The promulgation of the law makes way for the law of the gospel. No man receives the Holy Ghost, but he which hath felt the terrors of Sinai.

God might have imposed upon them a law by force; they were his creatures, and he could require nothing but justice. It had been but equal, that they should be compelled to obey their Maker; yet that God which loves to do all things sweetly, gives the law of justice in mercy, and will not imperiously command, but craves our assent for that, which it were rebellion not to do.

How gentle should be the proceeding of fellow-creatures who have an equality of being, with an inequality of condition! when their infinite Maker requests, where he might constrain! God will make no covenant with the unwilling; how much less the covenant of grace, which stands all upon love? If we stay till God offer violence to our will, or to us against our will, we shall die strangers from him. The church is the spouse of Christ: he will enjoy her love by a willing contract, not by a ravishment. The obstinate have nothing to do with God. The title of all converts is, a willing people.

That Israel inclined to God, it was from God. He inquires after his own gifts in us, for our capacity of more. They had not received the law, unless they had first received a disposition fit to be commanded. As there was an inclination to hear, so there must be a preparation for hearing. God's justice had before prepared his Israelites by hunger, thirst, fear of enemies; his mercy had prepared them by deliverances, by provisions of water, meat, bread; and yet, besides all the sight of God in his miracles, they must be three days prepared to hear him. When our souls are at the best, our approach to God requires particular addresses; and if three days were little enough to prepare them to receive the law, how is all our life short enough to prepare for the reckoning of our observing it? And if the word of a command expected such readiness, what shall the word of promise, the promise of Christ and salvation?

The murrain of Egypt was not so infectious as their vices; the contagion of these stuck still by Israel. All the water of the Red Sea, and of Marah, and that which gushed out of the rock, had not washed it off. From these they must now be sanctified. As sin is always dangerous, so most when we bring it into God's sight: it envenometh both our persons and services, and turns our good into evil. As, therefore, we must be always holy, so most when we present ourselves to the holy eyes of our Creator. We wash our hands every day; but, when we are to sit with some great person, we scour them with balls. And if we must be so sanctified only to receive the law, how holy must we be to receive the grace promised in the gospel?

Neither must themselves only be cleansed, but their very clothes: their garments smelt of Egypt, even they must be washed. Neither can clothes be capable of sin, nor can water cleanse from sin. The danger was neither in their garment nor their skins; yet they must be washed, that they might learn by their clothes with what souls to appear before their God. Those garments must be washed, which should never wax old, that now they might begin their age in purity; as those which were in more danger of being foul than bare. It is fit that our reverence to God's presence should appear in our very garments, that both without and within we may be cleanly; but little would neatness of vestures avail us with a filthy soul. The God of spirits looks to the inner man, and challenges the purity of that part which resembles himself: "Cleanse your hands, ye sinners; and purge your hearts, ye double-minded."

Yet even when they were washed and sanctified, they may not touch the mount, not only with their feet, but with their eyes. The smoke keeps it from their eyes, the marks from their feet. Not only men, that had some impurity at their best, are restrained, but even beasts, which are not capable of any unholiness. Those beasts which must touch his altars, yet might not touch his hill. And if a beast touch it, he must die; yet so, as no hands may touch that which hath touched the hill. Unreasonableness might seem to be an excuse in these creatures; that, therefore, which is death to a beast, must needs be capital to them, whose reason should guide them to avoid presumption. Those Israelites which saw God every day in the pillar of fire, and the cloud, must not come near him in the mount. God loves at once familiarity and fear; familiarity in our conversation, and fear in his commands. He loves to be acquainted with men in the walks of their obedience; yet he takes state upon him in his ordinances, and will be trembled at in his word and judgments.

I see the difference of God's carriage to

men in the law, and in the gospel. There, the very hill where he appeared may not be touched by the purest Israelite. Here, the hem of his garment is touched by the woman that had the flux of blood; yea, his very face was touched with the lips of Judas. There, the very earth was prohibited them, on which he descended. Here, his very body and blood is proffered to our touch and taste. O the marvellous kindness of our God! How unthankful are we, if we do not acknowledge this mercy above his ancient people! They were his own; yet strangers, in comparison of our liberty. It is our shame and sin, if, in these means of entireness, we be no better acquainted with God than they, which in their greatest familiarity were commanded aloof.

God was ever wonderful in his works, and fearful in his judgments; but he was never so terrible in the execution of his will, as now in the promulgation of it. Here was nothing but a majestical terror in the eyes, in the ears, of the Israelites, as if God meant to show them by this how fearful he could be. Here was the lightning darted in their eyes, the thunders roaring in their ears, the trumpet of God drowning the thunder-claps, the voice of God out-speaking the trumpet of the angel; the cloud enwrapping, the smoke ascending, the fire flaming, the mount trembling, Moses climbing and quaking, paleness and death in the face of Israel, uproar in the elements, and all the glory of heaven turned into terror. In the destruction of the first world, there were clouds without fire; in the destruction of Sodom, there was fire raining without clouds: but here was fire, smoke, clouds, thunder, earthquakes, and whatsoever might work more astonishment than ever was in any vengeance inflicted.

And if the law were thus given, how shall it be required? If such were the proclamation of God's statutes, what shall the sessions be? I see and tremble at the resemblance. The trumpet of the angel called unto the one: the voice of an archangel, the trumpet of God, shall summon us to the other. To the one, Moses (that climbed up that hill, and alone saw it) says, " God came with ten thousands of his saints." In the other, " Thousand thousands shall minister to him, and ten thousand thousands shall stand before him." In the one, mount Sinai only was on a flame; all the world shall be so in the other. In the one, there was fire, smoke, thunder, and lightning; in the other a fiery stream shall issue from him, wherewith the heavens shall be dissolved, and the elements shall melt away with a noise. O God, how powerful art thou to inflict vengeance upon sinners, who didst thus forbid sin! And if thou wert so terrible a lawgiver, what a judge shalt thou appear! What shall become of the breakers of so fiery a law? O where shall those appear, that are guilty of the transgressing that law, whose very delivery was little less than death? If our God should exact his law but in the same rigour wherewith he gave it, sin could not quit the cost. But now the fire, wherein it was delivered, was but terrifying; the fire, wherein it shall be required, is consuming. Happy are those that are from under the terrors of that law, which was given in fire, and in fire shall be required!

God would have Israel see, that they had not to do with some impotent commander, that is fain to publish his laws, without noise, in dead paper, which can more easily enjoin than punish, or descry than execute; and therefore, before he gives them a law, he shows them that he can command heaven, earth, fire, air, in revenge of the breach of the law, that they could not but think it deadly to displease such a lawgiver, or violate such dreadful statutes; that they might see all the elements examples of that obedience which they should yield unto their Maker.

This fire, wherein the law was given, is still in it, and will never out: hence are those terrors which it flashes in every conscience that hath felt remorse of sin. Every man's heart is a Sinai, and resembles to him both heaven and hell: " The sting of death is sin, and the strength of sin is the law."

That they might see he could find out their closest sins, he delivers his law in the light of fire from out of the smoke. That they might see what is due to their sins, they see fire above, to represent the fire that should be below them. That they might know he could waken their security, the thunder and louder voice of God speaks to their hearts. That they might see what their hearts should do, the earth quakes under them. That they might see they could not shift their appearance, the angel calls them together. O royal law, and mighty lawgiver! how could they think of having any other God, that had such proofs of this! How could they think of making any resemblance of him, whom they saw could not be seen, and whom they saw, in not being seen, infinite! How could they think of daring to profane his name, whom they heard to name himself, with that voice, Jehovah! How could they think of standing with him for a day, whom they saw to command that heaven which makes and measures day! How could they think of disobeying his deputies, whom they saw so able to revenge! How could they think of killing, when they were half dead with the fear of him that could kill both body and soul! How could they think of the flames of lust, that saw such fires of vengeance! How could they think of stealing from others, that saw whose the heaven and the earth were, to dispose of at his pleasure! How could they think of speaking falsely, that heard God speak in so fearful a tone! How could they think of coveting others' goods, that saw how weak and uncertain right they had to their own! Yea, to us was this law so delivered, to us in them. Neither had their been such state in the promulgation of it, if God had not intended it for eternity. We men, that so fear the breach of human laws, for some small mulcts of forfeiture, how should we fear thee, O Lord, that canst cast body and soul into hell!

CONTEMPLATION VI.— OF THE GOLDEN CALF.

It was not much above a month since Israel made their covenant with God; since they trembled to hear him say, " Thou shalt have no other God but me;" since they saw Moses part from them, and climb up the hill to God; and now they say, " Make us gods: we know not what is become of this Moses." O ye mad Israelites, have ye so soon forgotten that fire and thunder which you heard and saw? Is that smoke vanished out of your mind, as soon as out of your sight? Could your hearts cease to tremble with the earth? Can ye, in the very sight of Sinai, call for other gods? And for Moses, was it not for your sakes that he thrust himself into the midst of that smoke and fire, which ye feared to see afar off? Was he not now gone after so many sudden embassages, to be your lieger with God? If ye had seen him take his heels, and run away from you into the wilderness, what could ye have said or done more? Behold, our better Moses was with us awhile upon earth: he is now ascended into the mount of heaven to mediate for us: shall we now think of another Saviour? Shall we not hold it our happiness, that he is for our sakes above?

And what if your Moses had been gone for ever? Must ye therefore have gods made? If ye had said, Choose us another governor, it had been a wicked and unthankful motion: ye were too unworthy of a Moses, that could so soon forget him. But to say, " Make us gods," was absurdly impious. Moses was not your god, but your governor; neither was the presence of God tied to Moses. You saw God still, when he was gone, in his pillar, and in his manna; and yet ye say, " Make us gods." Every word is full of senseless wickedness. How many gods would you have? or what gods are those that can be made! Or, whatever the idolatrous Egyptians did, with what face can ye, after so many miraculous obligations, speak of another god? Had the voice of God scarce done thundering in your ears? Did ye so lately hear and see him to be an infinite God? Did ye quake to hear him say, out of the midst of the flames, " I am Jehovah thy God; thou shalt have no gods but me?" Did ye acknowledge God your Maker; and do ye now speak of making of gods? If ye had said, Make us another man to go before us, it had been an impossible suit. Aaron might help to mar you and himself; he could not make one hair of a man: and do ye say, " Make us gods?" And what should these gods do? " Go before you?" How could they go before you, that cannot stand alone? Your help makes them to stand, and yet they must conduct you. O the impatient ingratitude of carnal minds! O the sottishness of idolatry! Who would not have said, Moses is not with us; but he is with God for us? He stays long. He that called him withholds him. His delay is for our sakes, as well as his ascent. Though we see him not, we will hope for him. His favours to us have deserved not to be rejected: or, if God will keep him from us, he that withholds him, can supply him. He that sent him, can lead us without him; his fire and cloud is all-sufficient. God hath said, and done enough for us, to make us trust him. We will, we can, have no other God; we care not for any other guide. But, behold, here is none of this. Moses stays but some five and thirty days, and now he is forgotten, and is become but " this Moses;" yea, God is forgotten with him; and, as if God and Moses had been lost at once, they say, " Make us gods." Natural men must have God at their beck: and if he come not at a call, he is cast off, and they take themselves to their own shifts; like as the Chinese whip their gods when they answer them not: whereas his holy ones 'wait long, and seek him; and not only in their sinking, but from the bottom of the deeps, call upon him; "and though he kill them, will trust in him."

Superstition besots the minds of men, and blinds the eye of reason; and first makes them not men, ere it makes them idolaters. How else could he that is the image of God, fall down to the images of creatures? How could our forefathers have so doated upon stocks and stones, if they had been themselves? As the Syrians were first blinded, and then led into the midst of Samaria, so are idolaters first bereaved of their wits and common sense, and afterwards are carried brutishly into all palpable impiety.

Who would not have been ashamed to hear this answer from the brother of Moses. "Pluck off your ear-rings?" He should have said, "Pluck this idolatrous thought out of your hearts." And now, instead of chiding, he soothes them. And, as if he had been no kin to Moses, he helps to lead them back again from God to Egypt. The people importuned him, perhaps with threats. He that had waded through all the menaces of Pharaoh, doth he now shrink at the threats of his own? Moses is not afraid of the terrors of God: his faith, that carried him through the water, led him up to the fire of God's presence; while his brother Aaron fears the faces of those men, which he lately saw pale with the fear of their glorious Lawgiver: as if he, that forbade other gods, could not have maintained his own act and agent against men. Sudden fears, when they have possessed weak minds, lead them to shameful errors. Importunity or violence may lessen, but they cannot excuse a fault. Wherefore was he a governor, but to depress their disordered motions? Facility of yielding to a sin, or wooing it with our voluntary suit, is a higher stair of evil; but even at last to be won to sin, is damnable. It is good to resist any onset of sin; but one condescent loses all the thanks of our opposition. What will it avail a man that others are plagued for soliciting him, while he smarteth for yielding? If both be in hell, what ease is it to him that another is deeper in the pit?

What now did Aaron? Behold, he that alone was allowed to climb up the trembling and fiery hill of Sinai with Moses, and heard God say, "Thou shalt not make to thyself any graven image, for I am a jealous God," as if he meant particularly to prevent this act, within one month calls for their ear-rings, makes the graven image of a calf, erects an altar, consecrates a day to it, calls it their god, and weeps not to see them dance before it. It is a miserable thing, when governors humour the people in their sins, and instead of making up the breach, enlarge it. Sin will take heart by the approbation of the meanest looker on; but if authority once second it, it grows impudent: as contrarily, where the public government opposes evil, though it be under-hand practised, not without fear, there is life in that state.

Aaron might have learned counsel of his brother's example. When they came to him with stones in their hands, and said, "Give us water," he ran as roundly to God with prayers in his mouth: so should Aaron have done, when they said, "Give us gods;" but he weakly runs to their ear-rings, that which should be made their god, not to the true God which they had, and forsook. Who can promise to himself freedom from gross infirmities, when he that went up into the mount comes down, and doth that in the valley which he heard forbidden in the hill?

I see yet, and wonder at the mercy of that God which had justly called himself jealous. This very Aaron, whose infirmity had yielded to so foul an idolatry, is after chosen by God to be a priest to himself. He that had set up an altar to the calf, must serve at the altar of God. He that had melted and carved out the calf for a god, must sacrifice calves and rams and bullocks unto the true God. He that consecrated a day to the idol, is himself consecrated to him which was dishonoured by the idol. The grossest of all sins cannot prejudice the calling of God; yea, as light is best seen in darkness, the mercy of God is most magnified in our unworthiness.

What a difference God puts between persons and sins! While so many thousand Israelites were slain, that had stomachfully desired the idol, Aaron, that in weakness condescended, is both pardoned the fact, and afterwards laden with honour from God. Let no man take heart to sin from mercy. He that can purpose to sin upon the knowledge of God's mercy in the remission of infirmities, presumes, and makes himself a wilful offender. It is no comfort to the wilful that there is remission to the weak and penitent.

The ear-rings are plucked off. Egyptian jewels are fit for an idolatrous use. This very gold was contagious. It had been better the Israelites had never borrowed these ornaments, than that they should pay them back to the idolatry of their first owners. What cost the superstitious Israelites are content to be at for this lewd devotion! The riches and pride of their outward habit are they willing to part with to their molten god; as glad to have their ears bare, that they might fill their eyes. No gold is too dear for their idol: each man is content to spoil his wives and children of that whereof they spoiled the Egyptians.

Where are those worldlings that cannot abide to be at any cost for their religion? which could be content to do God chargeless service? These very Israelites that were ready to give gold, not out of their purses, but from their very ears, to misdevotion, shall once condemn them. O sacrilege succeeding to superstition! Of old they were ready to give gold to the false service of God; we, to take away gold from the true. How do we see men prodigal to their lusts and ambitions, and we hate not to be niggards to God!

This gold is now grown to a calf. Let no man think that form came forth casually, out of the melted ear-rings. This shape was intended by the Israelites, and perfected by Aaron. They brought this god in their hearts with them out of Egypt, and now they set it up in their eyes. Still doth Egypt hurt them. Servitude was the least evil that Israel receives from Egypt; for that sent them still to the true God, but this idolatrous example led them to a false. The very sight of evil is dangerous; and it is hard for the heart not to run into those sins, to which the eye and ear are inured. Not out of love, but custom, we fall into some offences.

The Israelites wrought so long in the furnaces of the Egyptians' brick, that they have brought forth a molten calf. The black calf with the white spots, which they saw worshipped in Egypt, hath stolen their hearts; and they which before would have been at the Egyptian flesh-pots, would now be at their devotions. How many have fallen into a fashion of swearing, scoffing, drinking, out of the usual practice of others; as those that live in an ill air are infected with diseases. A man may pass through Ethiopia unchanged, but he cannot dwell there and not be discoloured.

Their sin was bad enough: let not our uncharitableness make it worse. No man may think they have so put off humanity, and sense, with their religion, as to think that calf a god, or that this idol, which they saw yesterday made, did bring them out of Egypt three months ago: this were to make them more beasts than that calf which this image represented. Or, if they should have been so insensate, can we think that Aaron could be thus desperately mad? The image and the holy day were both to one deity: "To-morrow is the holy day of the Lord your God." It was the true God they meant to worship in the calf; and yet at best this idolatry is shameful. It is no marvel if this foul sin seeks pretences; yet no excuse can hide the shame of such a face. God's jealousy is not stirred only by the rivality of a false god, but of a false worship. Nothing is more dangerous than to mint God's services in our own brain.

God sends down Moses to remedy this sin. He could as easily have prevented, as redressed it. He knew ere Moses came up what Israel would do ere he came down; likeas he knew the two tables would be broken, ere he gave them. God most wisely permits and ordinates sin to his own ends, without our excuse: and though he could easily by his own hands remedy evils, yet he will do it by means both ordinary and subordinate. It is not for us to look for any immediate redress from God, when we have a Moses, by whom it may be wrought. Since God himself expects this from man, why should man expect it from God?

Now might Moses have found a time to have been even with Israel for all their unthankfulness, and mutinous insurrections: "Let me alone: I will consume them, and make of thee a mighty nation." Moses should not need to solicit God for revenge: God solicits him, in a sort, for leave to revenge. Who would look for such a word from God to man, "Let me alone?" As yet Moses had said nothing: before he opens his mouth, God prevents his importunity, as foreseeing that holy violence which the requests of Moses would offer to him. Moses stood trembling before the majesty of his Maker; and yet hears him say, "Let me alone." The mercy of our God hath, as it were, obliged his power to the faith of men. The fervent prayers of the faithful hold the hands of the Almighty. As I find it said afterwards of Christ, That "he could do no miracles there, because of their unbelief:" so now I hear God (as if he could not do execution upon Israel, because of Moses' faith) say, "Let me alone, that I may consume them."

We all naturally affect propriety, and like our own so much better, as it is freer from partners. Every one would be glad to say, with that proud one, " I am, and there is none beside me:" so much the more sweetly would this message have sounded to nature, " I will consume them and make of thee a mighty nation." How many endeavour that, not without danger of curses and uproar, which was voluntarily tendered unto Moses! Whence are our depopulations and inclosures, but for that men cannot abide either fellows or neighbours? But how graciously doth Moses strive with God, against his own preferment! If God had threatened, " I will consume thee, and make of them a mighty nation," I doubt whether he could have been more moved. The more a man can leave himself behind him, and aspire to a care of community, the more spiritual he is. Nothing makes a man so good a patriot as religion.

Oh the sweet disposition of Moses, fit for him that should be familiar with God! He saw they could be content to be merry and happy without him: he would not be happy without them. They had professed to have forgotten him: he slacks not to sue for them. He that will ever hope for good himself, must return good for evil unto others.

Yet, it was not Israel so much that Moses respected, as God in Israel. He was thrifty and jealous for his Maker; and would not have him lose the glory of his mighty deliverances; nor would abide a pretence for any Egyptian dog to bark against the powerful work of God: " Wherefore shall the Egyptians say?" If Israel could have perished without dishonour to God, perhaps his hatred to their idolatry would have overcome his natural love, and he had let God alone. Now so tender is he over the name of God, that he would rather have Israel escape with a sin, than God's glory should be blemished in the opinions of men by a just judgment. He saw that the eyes and tongues of all the world were intent upon Israel, a people so miraculously fetched from Egypt, whom the sea gave way to; whom heaven fed; whom the rock watered; whom the fire and cloud guarded; which heard the audible voice of God. He knew withal, how ready the world would be to misconstrue, and how the heathens would be ready to cast imputations of levity or impotence upon God; and therefore says, " What will the Egyptians say?" Happy is that man which can make God's glory the scope of all his actions and desires; neither cares for his own welfare, nor fears the miseries of others, but with respect to God in both. If God had not given Moses this care of his glory, he could not have had it: and now his goodness takes it so kindly, as if himself had received a favour from his creature; and, for a reward of the grace he had wrought, promises not to do that which he threatened. But what needs God to care for the speech of the Egyptians — men, infidels? And if they had been good, yet their censure should have been unjust. Shall God care for the tongues of men; the holy God for the tongues of infidels? The very Israelites, now they were from under the hands of Egypt, cared not for their words; and shall the God of heaven regard that which is not worth the regard of men? Their tongues could not talk against God, but from himself; and if it could have been the worse for him, would he have permitted it? But, O God, how dainty art thou of thine honour, that thou canst not endure the worst of men should have any colour to taint it! What, do we men stand upon our justice and innocence, with neglect of all unjust censures, when that infinite God, whom no censures can reach, will not abide that the very Egyptians should falsely tax his power and mercy! Wise men must care, not only to deserve well, but to hear well, and to wipe off, not only crimes, but censures.

There was never so precious a monument as the tables written with God's own hand. If we see but the stone which Jacob's head rested on, or on which the foot of Christ did once tread, we look upon it with more than ordinary respect. With what eye should we have beheld this stone, which was hewed, and written with the very finger of God? Any manuscript scroll, written by the hand of a famous man, is laid up amongst our jewels: what place then should we have given to the handwriting of the Almighty?

That which he hath dictated to his servants the prophets, challenges just honour from us: how doth that deserve veneration, which his own hand wrote immediately?

Prophecies and evangelical discourses he hath written by others; never did he write any thing himself, but these tables of the law; nor did he ever speak any thing audibly to the whole of mankind, but it. The hand, the stone, the law, were all his. By how much more precious this record was, by so much was the fault greater of defacing it. What king holds it less than rebellion to tear his writing and blemish his seal? At the first, he engraved his image in the table of man's heart; Adam blurred the image, but, through God's mercy, saved the tablet. Now he writes his will in the tables of stone; Moses breaks the tables, and defaces the writing. If they had been given him for himself, the author, the matter had deserved, that as they were written in stone for permanency, so they should be kept for ever; and, as they were everlasting in use, so they should be in preservation. Had they been written in clay, they could but have been broken; but now they were given for all Israel, for all mankind. He was but the messenger, not the owner. Howsoever therefore Israel had deserved, by breaking this covenant with God, to have this monument of God's covenant with them broken by the same hand that wrote it; yet how durst Moses thus carelessly cast away the treasure of all the world, and by his hands undo that which was with such cost and care done by his Creator? How durst he fail the trust of that God, whose pledge he received with awe and reverence? He that expostulated with God, to have Israel live and prosper, why would he deface the rule of their life, in the keeping whereof they should prosper? I see that forty days' talk with God cannot bereave a man of passionate infirmity. He that was the meekest upon earth, in a sudden indignation abandons that, which in cold blood he would have held faster than his life. He forgets the law written, when he saw it broken. His zeal for God hath transported him from himself, and his duty to the charge of God. He more hated the golden calf, wherein he saw engraven the idolatry of Israel, than he honoured the tables of stone, wherein God had engraven his commandments; and more longed to deface the idol, than he cared to preserve the tables. Yet that God, which so sharply revenged the breach of one law upon the Israelites, checks not Moses for breaking both the tables of the law. The law of God is spiritual. The internal breach of one law is so heinous, that, in comparison of it, God scarce counts the breaking of the outward tables a breach of the law. The goodness of God winks at the errors of honest zeal, and so loves the strength of good affections, that it passeth over their infirmities. How highly God doth esteem a well-governed zeal, when his mercy crowns it with all the faults!

The tables had not offended: the calf had, and Israel in it. Moses takes revenge on both; he burns and stamps the calf to powder, and gives it Israel to drink, that they might have it in their belly, instead of their eyes. How he hasteth to destroy the idol, wherein they sinned! that, as an idol is nothing, so it might be brought to nothing; and atoms and dust is nearest to nothing: that, instead of going before Israel, it might pass through them, so as the next day they might find their god in their excrements, to the just shame of Israel, when they should see their new god cannot defend himself from being either nothing, or worse.

Who can but wonder, to see a multitude of so many hundred thousands (when Moses came running down the hill) to turn their eyes from their god, to him; and, on a sudden, instead of worshipping their idol, to batter it in pieces, in the very height of the novelty. Instead of building altars and kindling fires to it, to kindle a hotter fire than that wherewith it was melted, to consume it? instead of dancing before it, to abhor and deface it? instead of singing, to weep before it? there was never a more stiff-necked people: yet I do not hear any one man of them say, He is but one man; we are many: how easily may we destroy him, rather than he our god? If his brother durst not resist our motion in making it, why will we suffer him to dare to resist the keeping of it? It is our act, and we will maintain it. Here was none of this, but an humble obeisance to the basest and bloodiest revenge that Moses shall impose. God hath set such an impression of majesty in the face of lawful authority, that wickedness is confounded in itself to behold it. If from hence visible powers were not more feared than the invisible God, the world would be overrun with outrage. Sin hath a guiltiness in itself, that, when it is seasonably checked, it pulls in its head, and seeks rather a hiding-place than a fort.

The idol is not capable of a further revenge. It is not enough, unless the idolaters smart. The gold was good, if the Israelites had not been evil: so great a sin cannot be expiated without blood. Behold, that meek spirit which, in his plea with God would rather perish himself, than Israel should perish, arms the Levites against their brethren, and rejoices to see thousands of the Israelites bleed, and blesses their executioners.

It was the mercy of Moses that made him cruel. He had been cruel to all, if some had not found him cruel. They are merciless hands which are not sometimes imbrued in blood. There is no less charity than justice, in punishing sinners with death: God delights no less in a killing mercy than in a pitiful justice. Some tender hearts would be ready to censure the rigour of Moses. Might not Israel have repented, and lived? Or, if they must die, must their brethren's hand be upon them? if their throats must be cut by their brethren, shall it be done in the very heat of their sin? But they must learn a difference betwixt pity and fondness, mercy and injustice. Moses had a heart as soft as theirs, but more hot; as pitiful, but wiser. He was a good physician, and saw that Israel could not live, unless he bled; he therefore lets out this corrupt blood, to save the whole body. There cannot be a better sacrifice to God, than the blood of malefactors; and this first sacrifice so pleased God in the hands of the Levites, that he would have none but them sacrifice to him for ever. The blood of the idolatrous Israelites cleared that tribe from the blood of the innocent Shechemites.

BOOK VI.

CONTEMPLATION I.—THE VEIL OF MOSES.

It is a wonder that neither Moses nor any Israelite gathered up the shivers of the former tables. Every shred of that stone, and every letter of that writing, had been a relic worthy laying up; but he well saw how headlong the people were to superstition, and how unsafe it were to feed that disposition in them.

The same zeal that burnt the calf to ashes, concealed the ruins of this monument. Holy things, besides their use, challenge no further respect. The breaking of the tables did as good as blot out all the writing; and the writing defaced left no virtue in the stone, no reverence to it.

If God had not been friends with Israel, he had not renewed his law. As the Israelites were wilfully blind if they did not see God's anger in the tables broken, so could they not but hold it a good sign of grace, that God gave them his testimonies.

There was nothing wherein Israel outstripped all the rest of the world more than in this privilege; the pledge of his covenant, the law written with God's own hand. Oh what a favour, then, is it, where God bestows his gospel upon any nation! That was but a killing letter; this is the power of God to salvation.

Never is God thoroughly displeased with any people, where that continues. For likeas those which purpose love, when they fall of, call for their tokens back again, so, when God begins once perfectly to mislike, the first thing he withdraws is his gospel.

Israel recovers this favour, but with an abatement. "Hew thee two tables." God made the first tables; the matter, the form was his: now Moses must hew the next. As God created the first man after his own image; but that once defaced, Adam begat Cain after his own; or as the first temple razed, a second was built: yet so far short, that the Israelites wept at the sight of it. The first works of God are still the best: those that he secondarily works by us, decline in their perfection. It was reason, that though God had forgiven Israel, they should still find they had sinned. They might see the footsteps of displeasure in the differences of the agent.

When God had told Moses before, "I will not go before Israel, but my angel shall lead them," Moses so noted the difference, that he rested not, till God himself undertook their conduct; so might the Israelites have noted some remainders of offence, while, instead of that which his own hand did formerly make, he saith now, "Hew thee." And yet these second tables are kept reverently in the ark, when the other lay mouldered in shivers upon Sinai: likeas the repaired image of God in our regeneration is preserved, perfected, and laid up at last safe in heaven; whereas the first image of our created innocence is quite defaced: so the second temple had the glory of Christ's exhibition, though meaner in frame. The merciful respects of God are not tied to glorious outsides, or the inward worthiness of things or persons: "He hath chosen the weak and simple to confound the wise and mighty."

Yet God did this work by Moses. Moses hewed, and God wrote. Our true Moses repairs that law of God, which we, in our nature, had broken; he revives it for us, and it is accepted of God, no less than if the first characters of his law had been still entire. We can give nothing but the table; it is God that must write in it. Our hearts are but a bare board, till God, by his finger, engrave his law in them. Yea, Lord, we are a rough quarry; hew thou us out, and square us fit for thee to write upon.

Well may we marvel to see Moses, after this oversight, admitted to this charge again. Who of us would not have said, Your care indeed deserves trust: you did so carefully keep the first tables, that it would do well to trust you with such another burden?

It was good for Moses that he had to do with God, not with men. The God of mercy will not impute the slips of our infirmity to the prejudice of our faithfulness. He, that after the mis-answer of the one talent, would not trust the evil servant with a second, because he saw a wilful neglect, will trust Moses with his second law, because he saw fidelity in the worst error of his zeal. Our charity must learn, as to forgive, so to believe where we have been deceived: not that we should wilfully beguile ourselves in an unjust credulity, but that we should search diligently into the disposition of persons, and grounds of their actions. Perhaps none may be so sure as they that have once disappointed us. Yea, Moses brake the first; therefore he must hew the second. If God had broken them, he would have repaired them. The amends must be where the fault was. Both God and his church look for a satisfaction in that wherein we have offended.

It was not long since Moses' former fast of forty days: when he then came down from the hill, his first question was not for meat; and now going up again to Sinai, he takes not any repast with him. That God, which sent the quails to the host of Israel, and manna from heaven, could have fed him with dainties. He goes up confidently, in a secure trust of God's provision. There is no life to that of faith. "Man lives not by bread only." The vision of God did not only satiate, but feast him. What a blessed satiety shall there be when we shall see him as he is; and he shall be all in all to us; since this very frail mortality of Moses was sustained and comforted but with representations of his presence!

I see Moses the receiver of the law, Elias the restorer of the law, Christ the fulfiller of the old law, and author of the new, all fasting forty days; and these three great fasters I find together glorious in Mount Tabor. Abstinence merits not; for religion consists not in the belly, either full or empty. What are meats or drinks to the kingdom of God, which is, like himself, spiritual? But it prepares best for good duties. Full bellies are fitter for rest. Not the body, so much as the soul, is more active with emptiness. Hence solemn prayer takes ever fasting to attend it, and so much the rather speeds in heaven when it is so accompanied. It is good so to diet the body, that the soul may be fattened.

When Moses came down before, his eyes sparkled with anger, and his face was both interchangeably pale and red with indignation; now it is bright with glory. Before, there were the flames of fury in it; now, the beams of majesty. Moses had before spoken with God: why did not his face shine before? I cannot lay the cause upon the inward trouble of his passions, for this brightness was external. Whither shall we impute it, but to his more entireness with God?

The more familiar acquaintance we have with God, the more do we partake of him. He that passes by the fire, may have some gleams of heat; but he that stands by it, hath his colour changed. It is not possible a man should have any long conference with God, and be no whit affected. We are strangers from God,—it is no wonder if our faces be earthly; but he that sets himself apart to God, shall find a kind of majesty and awful respect put upon him in the minds of others.

How did the heart of Moses shine with illumination, when his face was thus lightsome! And if the flesh of Moses, in this base composition, so shined by conversing with God forty days in Sinai, what shall our glory be when clothed with incorruptible bodies? We shall converse with him for ever in the highest heaven.

Now his face only shone; afterwards the three disciples saw all his body shining. The nature of a glorified body, the clearer vision, the immediate presence of that fountain of glory, challenge a far greater resplendence to our faces than his. O God, we are content that our faces be blemished a while with contempt, and blubbered with tears. How can we but shine with Moses, when we shall see thee more than Moses!

The brightness of Moses' face reflected not upon his own eyes; he shone bright, and knew not of it. He saw God's face glorious; he did not think others had so seen his. How many have excellent graces, and perceive them not! Our own sense is an ill judge of God's favours to us · those that stand by, can convince us in that which we deny to ourselves. Here below, it is enough if we can shine in the eyes of others; above, we shall shine and know it. At this instant, Moses sees himself shine; then he needed not. God meant not that he should more esteem himself, but that he should be more honoured of the Israelites. That other glory shall be for our own happiness, and therefore requires our knowledge.

They that did but stand still to see anger in his face, ran away to see glory in it. Before, they had desired that God would not speak to them any more but by Moses; and now, that God doth but look upon them in Moses, they are afraid: and yet there was not more difference betwixt the voices than the faces of God and Moses. This should have drawn Israel to Moses so much the more, to have seen this impression of divinity in his face.

That which should have comforted, affrights them: yea, Aaron himself, that before went up into the mount to see and speak with God, now is afraid to see him that had seen God. Such a fear there is in guiltiness,—such confidence in innocency. When the soul is once cleared from sin, it shall run to that glory with joy, the least glimpse whereof now appals it, and sends it away in terror. How could the Israelites now choose but think, How shall we abide to look God in the face, since our eyes are dazzled with the face of Moses! And well may we still argue, if the image of God, which he hath set in the fleshy forehead of authority, daunt us, how shall we stand before the dreadful tribunal of heaven!

Moses marvels to see Israel run away from their guide, as from their enemy, and looks back to see if he could discern any new cause of fear; and not conceiving how his mild face could affright them, calls them to stay and return.

O my people, whom do ye fly? It is for your sakes that I ascended, stayed, came down. Behold, here are no armed Levites to strike you, no Amalekites, no Egyptians to pursue you, no fires and thunders to dismay you. I have not that rod of God in my hand, which you have seen to command the elements; or if I had, so far am I from purposing any rigour against you, that I now lately have appeased God towards you; and, lo! here the pledges of his reconciliation. God sends me to you for good; and do you run from your best friend? Whither will ye go from me, or without me? Stay, and hear the charge of that God from whom we cannot fly.

They perceive his voice the same, though his face were changed, and are persuaded to stay, and return and hear him, whom they dare not see; and now, after many doubtful paces, approaching nearer, dare tell him he was grown too glorious.

Good Moses, finding that they durst not look upon the sun of his face, clouds it with a veil; choosing rather to hide the work of God in him, than to want an opportunity of revealing God's will to his people. I do not hear him stand upon terms of reputation: if there be glory in my face, God put it there; he would not have placed it so conspicuously if he had meant it should be hid. Hide ye your faces rather, which are blemished with your sin, and look not that I should wrong God and myself, to seem less happy, in favour of your weakness. But without all self-respects, he modestly hides his glorified face, and cares not their eyes should pierce so far as to his skin, on condition that his words may pierce into their ears. It is good for a man sometimes to hide his graces; some talents are best improved by being laid up. Moses had more glory by his veil than by his face. Christian modesty teaches a wise man not to expose himself to the fairest show, and to live at the utmost pitch of his strength.

There is many a rich stone laid up in the bowels of the earth, many a fair pearl laid up in the bosom of the sea, that never was seen, nor ever shall be. There is many a goodly star, which, because of height, comes not within our account. How did our true Moses, with the veil of his flesh, hide the glory of his deity, and put on vileness, besides the laying aside of majesty, and shut up his great and divine miracles with, "See you tell no man!" How far are those spirits from this, which care only to be seen, and wish only to dazzle others' eyes with admiration, not caring for unknown riches! But those yet more, which desire to seem above themselves, whether in parts or graces, whose veil is fairer than their skin. Modest faces shall shine through their veils, when the vain-glorious shall bewray their shame through their covering.

That God which gave his law in smoke, delivered it again through the veil of Moses. Israel could not look to the end of that which should be abolished: for the same cause had God a veil upon his face, which hid his presence in the holy of holies. Now, as the veil of God did rend when he said, "It is finished;" so the veil of Moses was then pulled off. We clearly see Christ the end of the law. Our Joshua, that succeeded Moses, speaks to us bare-faced. What a shame is it there should be a veil upon our hearts, when there is none on his face!

When Moses went to speak with God, he pulled off his veil: it was good reason he should present to God that face which he had made: there had been more need of his veil to hide the glorious face of God from him, than to hide his from God: but his faith and thankfulness serve for both these uses. Hypocrites are contrary to Moses: he showed his worst to men, his best to God; they show their best to men, their worst to God: but God sees both their veil and their face; and I know not whether he more hates their veil of dissimulation, or their face of wickedness.

CONTEMPLATION II.—OF NADAB AND ABIHU.

THAT God, which showed himself to men in fire when he delivered his law, would have men present their sacrifices to him in fire; and this fire he would have his own, that there might be a just circulation in this creature; as the water sends up those vapours which it receives down again in rain. Hereupon it was, that fire came down from God unto the altar; that as the charge of the sacrifice was delivered in fire and smoke, so God might signify the acceptation of it, in the like fashion wherein it was commanded. The Baalites might lay ready their bullock upon the wood, and water in their trench; but they might sooner fetch the blood out of their bodies, and destroy themselves, than one flash out of heaven to consume the sacrifice.

That devil, which can fetch down fire from heaven, either maliciously or to no purpose (although he abound with fire, and did as fervently desire this fire, in emulation to God, as ever he desired mitigation of his own), yet now he could no more kindle a fire for the idolatrous sacrifice, than quench the flames of his own torment. Herein God approves himself only worthy to be sacrificed unto, that he creates the fire for his own service; whereas the impotent idols of the heathen must fetch fire from their neighbour's kitchen, and themselves are fit matter for their borrowed fire.

The Israelites, that were led too much with sense, if they had seen the bullock consumed with a fire fetched from a common hearth, could never have acknowledged what relation the sacrifice had to God; had never perceived that God took notice of the sacrifice: but now they see the fire coming out from the presence of God, they are convinced both of the power and acceptation of the Almighty; they are at once amazed and satisfied to see the same God answer by fire, which before had spoken by fire. God doth not less approve our evangelical sacrifices than theirs under the law: but as our sacrifices are spiritual, so are the signs of his acceptation. Faith is our guide, as sense was theirs. Yea, even still doth God testify his approbation by sensible evidences. When by a lively faith and fervent zeal our hearts are consecrated to God, then doth this heavenly fire come down upon our sacrifices: then are they holy, living, acceptable.

This flame that God kindled, was not as some momentary bonfire, for a sudden and short triumph, nor as a domestic fire, to go out with the day; but is given for a perpetuity, and neither must die nor be quenched. God, as he is himself eternal, so he loves permanency and constancy of grace in us: if we be but a flash and away, God regards us not. All promises are to perseverance. Sure, it is but an elementary fire that goes out; that which is celestial continues. It was but some presumptuous heat in us that decays upon every occasion.

But he that miraculously sent down this fire at first, will not renew the miracle every day by a like supply: it began immediately from God; it must be nourished by means. Fuel must maintain that fire which came from heaven; God will not work miracles every day: if he hath kindled his Spirit in us, we may not expect he shall every day begin again: we have the fuel of the word and sacraments, prayers and meditations, which must keep it in for ever. It is from God that these helps can nourish his graces in us, likeas every flame of our material fire hath a concourse of providence; but we may not expect new infusions: rather know, that God expects of us an improvement of those habitual graces we have received.

While the people, with fear and joy, see God lighting his own fire, fire from heaven, the two sons of Aaron, in a careless presumption, will be serving him with a common flame; as if he might not have leave to choose the forms of his own worship. If this had been done some ages after, when the memory of the original of this heavenly fire had been worn out, it might have been excused with ignorance; but now, when God had newly sent his fire from above, newly commanded the continuance of it, either to let it go out, or, while it still flamed, to fetch profane coals to God's altar, could savour of no less than presumption and sacrilege. When we bring zeal without knowledge, misconceits of faith, carnal affections, the devices of our will-worship, superstitious devotions, into God's service, we bring common fire to his altar: these flames were never of his kindling; he hates both altar, fire, priest, and sacrifice. And now, behold, the same fire which consumed the sacrifice before, consumes the sacrificers. It was the sign of his acceptation, in consuming the beast, but, while it destroyed men, the fearful sign of his displeasure. By the same means can God bewray both love and hatred. We would have pleaded for Nadab and Abihu; they are but young men, the sons of Aaron, not yet warm in their function: let both age, and blood, and inexperience, excuse them as yet. No pretences, no privileges, can bear off a sin with God. Men think either to patronise or mitigate evils by their feigned reasons. That none may hope the plea either of birth, or of youth, or of the first commission of evil, may challenge pardon; I see here young men, sons of the ruler of Israel, for the first offence struck dead.

Yea, this made God the more to stomach, and the rather to revenge this impiety, because the sons of Aaron did it. God hath both pardoned and graced their father; he had honoured them, of the thousands of Israel, culling them out of his altar; and now, as their father set up a false god, so they bring false fire unto the true God.

If the sons of infidels live godlessly, they do their kind; their punishment shall be (though just) yet less; but if the children of religious parents, after all Christian nurture, shall shame their education, God takes it more heinously, and revenges it more sharply. The more bonds of duty, the more plagues of neglect.

If, from the agents, we look to the act itself; set aside the original descent, and what difference was there betwixt these fires? Both looked alike, heated alike, ascended alike, consumed alike; both were fed with the same material wood; both vanished into smoke; there was no difference, but in the commandment of God.

If God had enjoined ordinary fire, they had sinned to look for celestial. Now he commanded only the fire which he sent; they sinned in sending up incense in that fire which he commanded not. It is a dangerous thing, in the service of God, to decline from his own institutions. We have to do with a power which is wise to prescribe his own worship, just to require what he hath prescribed, powerful to revenge that which he hath not required.

If God had struck them with some leprosy in their forehead, as he did their aunt Miriam, soon after, or with some palsy, or lingering consumption, the punishment had been grievous. But he, whose judgments are ever just, sometimes secret, saw fire the fittest revenge for a sin of fire; his own fire fittest to punish strange fire; a sudden judgment fit for a present and exemplary sin: he saw, that if he had winked at this, his service had been exposed to profanation.

It is wisdom in governors to take sin at the first bound, and so to revenge it, that their punishments may be preventions. Speed of death is not always a judgment: suddenness, as it is ever justly suspicable, so then certainly argues anger, when it finds us in an act of sin. Leisure of repentance is an argument of favour. When God gives a man law, it implies that he would not have judgment surprise him.

Doubtless, Aaron looked somewhat heavily on this sad spectacle: it could not but appal him to see his two sons dead before him; dead in displeasure, dead suddenly, dead by the immediate hand of God. And now he could repent him of his new honour to see it succeed so ill with the sons of his loins; neither could he choose but see himself stricken in them. But his brother Moses, that had learned not to know either nephews or brother, when they stood in his way to God, wisely turned his eyes from the dead carcases of his sons, to his respect of the living God. My brother, this event is fearful, but just; these were thy sons, but they sinned; it was not for God, it is not for thee, to look so much who they were, as what they did. It was their honour and thine, that they were chosen to minister before the Lord. He that called them, justly required their sanctification and obedience. If they have profaned God and themselves, can thy natural affection so miscarry thee, that thou couldst wish their impunity, with the blemish of thy Maker? Our sons are not ours, if they disobey our Father: to pity their misery is to partake of their sin. If thou grudge at their judgment, take heed lest the same fire of God come forth upon this strange fire of nature. Show now whether thou more lovest God, or thy sons. Show whether thou be a better father, or a son.

Aaron, weighing these things, holds his peace, not out of an amazement or sullenness, but out of patient and humble submission; and seeing God's pleasure, and their desert, is content to forget that he had sons. He might have had a silent tongue, and a clamorous heart. There is no voice louder in the ears of God, than a speechless repining of the soul. Heat is more increase with keeping in; but Aaron's silence was no less inward: he knew how little he should get by brawling with God. If he breathed out discontentment, he saw God could speak fire to him again; and therefore he quietly submits to the will of God, and held his peace, because the Lord had done it. There is no greater proof of grace, than to smart patiently, and humbly and contentedly to rest the heart in the justice and wisdom of God's proceeding; and to be so far from chiding, that we dispute not. Nature is froward; and though she well knows we meddle not with our match, when we strive with our Maker, yet she pricks us forward to this idle quarrel; and bids us, with Job's wife, curse and die.

G

If God either chide or smite, as servants are charged to their masters, we may not answer again; when God's hand is on our back, our hand must be on our mouth; else, as mothers do their children, God shall whip us so much the more for crying.

It is hard for a stander-by, in this case, to distinguish betwixt hard-heartedness and pity. There Aaron sees his sons lie: he may neither put his hand to them to bury them, nor shed a tear for their death. Never parent can have juster cause of mourning, than to see his sons dead in their sin; if prepared and penitent, yet who can but sorry for their end? But to part with children to the danger of a second death, is worthy of more than tears. Yet Aaron must learn so far to deny nature, that he must more magnify the justice of God, than lament the judgment. Those whom God hath called to his immediate service, must know that he will not allow them the common passions and cares of others. Nothing is more natural than sorrow for the death of our own: if ever grief be seasonable, it becomes a funeral. And if Nadab and Abihu had died in their beds, this favour had been allowed them, the sorrow of their father and brethren; for when God forbids solemn mourning to his priests over the dead, he excepts the cases of this nearness of blood. Now all Israel may mourn for these two; only the father and brethren may not. God is jealous, lest their sorrow should seem to countenance the sin which he had punished; even the fearfullest acts of God must be applauded by the heaviest hearts of the faithful.

That which the father and brother may not do, the cousins are commanded. Dead carcases are not for the presence of God; his justice was shown sufficiently in killing them; they are now fit for the grave, not the sanctuary; neither are they carried out naked, but in their coats. It was an unusual sight for Israel to see a linen ephod upon the bier; the judgment was so much the more remarkable, because they had the badge of their calling upon their backs.

Nothing is either more pleasing unto God, or more commodious to men, than that, when he hath executed judgment, it should be seen and wondered at; for therefore he strikes some, that he may warn all.

CONTEMPLATION III.—OF AARON AND MIRIAM.

THE Israelites are stayed seven days in the station of Hazzeroth, for the punishment of Miriam. The sins of the governors are a just stop to the people: all of them smart in one; all must stay the leisure of Miriam's recovery. Whosoever seeks the land of promise, shall find many lets: Amalek, Og, Sinon, and the kings of Canaan, meet with Israel; these resisted, but hindered not their passage; their sins only stay them from removing. Afflictions are not crosses to us in the way to heaven, in comparison to our sins.

What is this I see? Is not this Aaron, that was brother in nature, and by office joint-commissioner with Moses? Is not this Aaron, that made his brother an intercessor for him to God, in the case of his idolatry? Is not this Aaron that climbed up the hill of Sinai with Moses? Is not this Aaron whom the mouth and hand of Moses consecrated a high-priest unto God? Is not this Miriam the elder sister of Moses? Is not this Miriam, that led the triumph of the women, and sung gloriously to the Lord? Is not this Miriam, which laid her brother Moses in the reeds, and fetched her mother to be his nurse? Both prophets of God; both the flesh and blood of Moses. And doth this Aaron repine at the honour of him that gave himself that honour, and saved his life? Doth this Miriam repine at the prosperity of him whose life she saved? Who would not have thought this should have been their glory, to have seen the glory of their own brother? What could have been a greater comfort to Miriam, than to think how happily doth he now sit at the stern of Israel, whom I saved from perishing in a boat of bulrushes? It is to me that Israel owes this commander; but now envy hath so blinded their eyes, that they can neither see this privilege of nature, nor the honour of God's choice. Miriam and Aaron are in mutiny against Moses. Who is so holy that sins not? What sin is so unnatural, that the best can avoid without God? But what weakness soever may plead for Miriam, who can but grieve to see Aaron at the end of so many sins? Of late I saw him carving the molten image, and consecrating an altar to a false god; now I see him seconding an unkind mutiny against his brother: both sins find him accessory; neither principal. It was not in the power of the legal priesthood to perform, or promise innocency to her ministers. It was necessary we should have another highpriest, which could not be tainted. That King of righteousness was of another order: he being without sin, hath fully satisfied for the sins of men. Whom can it now offend, to to see the blemishes of the evangelical priesthood, when God's first high priest is thus miscarried?

Who can look for love and prosperity at once, when holy and meek Moses finds enmity in his own flesh and blood? Rather than we shall want, " A man's enemies shall be those of his own house." Authority cannot fail of opposition, if it be never so mildly swayed: that common make-bate will rather raise it out of our own bosom. To do well, and hear ill, is princely.

The Midianitish wife of Moses cost him dear. Before, she hazarded his life; now, the favour of his people. Unequal matches are seldom prosperous. Although now this scandal was only taken, envy was not wise enough to choose a ground of the quarrel. Whether some secret and emulatory brawls passed between Zipporah and Miriam (as many times these sparks of private brawls grow into a perilous and common flame), or whether, now that Jethro and his family were joined with Israel, there were surmises of transporting the government to strangers; or whether this unfit choice of Moses is now raised up to disparage God's gifts in him; even in sight, the exceptions were frivolous. Emulation is curious, and, out of the best person, or act, will raise something to cavil at.

Seditions do not ever look the same way they move. Wise men can easily distinguish betwixt the vizor of actions, and the face. The wife of Moses is mentioned; his superiority is shot at. Pride is lightly the ground of all sedition. Which of their faces shined like Moses? Yea, let him but have drawn his veil, which of them durst look on his face? Which of them had fasted twice forty days? Which of them ascended up to the top of Sinai, and was hid with smoke and fire? Which of them received the law twice in two several tables, from God's own hand? And yet they dare say, " Hath God spoken only by Moses?" They do not deny Moses his honour, but they challenge a part with him; and as they were the elder in nature, so they would be equal in dignity, equal in administration. Acccording to her name, Miriam would be exalted. And yet how unfit were they! One a woman, whom her sex debarred from rule; the other a priest, whom his office sequestered from earthly government. Self-love makes men unreasonable, and teaches them to turn the glass, to see themselves bigger, others less than they are. It is a hard thing for a man, willingly and gladly to see his equals lifted over his head, in worth and opinion.

Nothing will more try a man's grace, than questions of emulation. That man hath true light, which can be content to be a candle before the sun of others.

As no wrong can escape God, so, least of all, those which are offered to princes. He that made the ear, needs no intelligence of our tongues. We have to do with a God that is light of hearing; we cannot whisper any evil so secretly, that he should not cry out of noise: and what need we any further evidence, when our judge is our witness?

Without any delation of Moses, God hears and challenges them. Because he was meek, therefore he complained not: because he was meek and complained not, therefore the Lord struck in for him the more. The less a man strives for himself, the more is God his champion. It is the honour of great persons to undertake the patronage of their clients: how much more will God revenge his elect, which cry to him day and night! He that said, " I seek not mine own glory," adds, " But there is one that seeks it, and judges." God takes his part ever that fights not for himself.

No man could have given more proofs of his courage than Moses. He slew the Egyptian; he confronted Pharaoh in his own court; he beat the Midianite shepherds; he feared not the troops of Egypt; he durst look God in the face amidst all the terrors of Sinai; and yet that Spirit which made and knew his heart, says, " He was the mildest man upon earth." Mildness and fortitude may well lodge together in one breast; to correct the misconceits of those men, that think none valiant but those that are fierce and cruel.

No sooner is the word out of Miriam's mouth, than the word of God's reproof meets it. How he bestirs him, and will be at once seen and heard, when the name of Moses is in question! Moses was zealously careful for God's glory, and now God is zealous for his. The remunerations of the Almighty are infinitely gracious. He cannot want honour and patronage that seeks the honour of his Maker. The ready way to true glory is goodness.

God might have spoken so loud, that heaven and earth should have heard it, so as they should not have needed to come forth for audience; but now, he calls them out to the bar, that they may be seen to hear. It did not content him to chide them within doors: the shame of their fault had been less in a private rebuke; but the scandal of their repining was public. Where the sin is not afraid of the light.

God loves not the reproof should be smothered.

They had depressed Moses; God advances him. They had equalled themselves to Moses; God prefers him to them. Their plea was, that God had spoken by them, as well as by Moses. God's reply is, That he hath, in a more entire fashion, spoken to Moses than them. God spake to the best of them, but either in their dream, sleeping, or in vision, waking; but to Moses he spake with more inward illumination, with more lively representation; to others as a stranger; to Moses as a friend. God had never so much magnified Moses to them, but for their envy. We cannot devise to pleasure God's servants so much as by despiting them.

God was angry when he chid them, but more angry when he departed. The withdrawing of his presence, is the presence of his wrath. While he stays to reprove, there is favour in his displeasure; but when he leaves either man or church, there is no hope but of vengeance. The final absence of God, is hell itself. When he forsakes us, though for a time, it is an introduction to his utmost judgment. It was time to look for a judgment when God departed: so soon as he is gone from the eyes of Miriam, the leprosy appears in her face: her foul tongue is punished with a foul face. Since she would acknowledge no difference betwixt herself and her brother Moses, every Israelite now sees his face glorious, her's leprous. Deformity is a fit cure of pride. Because the venom of her tongue would have eaten into the reputation of her brother, therefore a poisonous infection eats into her flesh. Now both Moses and Miriam need to wear a veil; the one to hide his glory, the other her deformity. That Midianite Zipporah, whom she scorned, was beautiful in respect of her.

Miriam was stricken, Aaron escaped, both sinned: his priesthood could not rescue him; the greatness of his dignity did but add to the heinousness of his sin; his repentance freed him. Alas! my Lord, I beseech thee lay not this sin upon us which we have foolishly committed! I wonder not to see Aaron free, while I see him penitent; this very confession saved him before from bleeding for idolatry, which now preserves him from leprosy, for his envious repining. The universal antidote for all the judgments of God, is our humble repentance.

Yea, his sad deprecation prevailed, both to clear himself and recover Miriam. The brother sues for himself and his sister, to that brother whom they both emulated, for pardon from himself, and that God which was offended in him. Where now is that equality which was pretended? Behold, he that so lately made his brother his fellow, now makes him his god. "Lay not this sin upon us; let her not be as one dead;" as if Moses had imposed this plague, and could remove it. Never any opposed the servants of God, but, one time or other, they have been constrained to confess a superiority.

Miriam would have wounded Moses with her tongue; Moses would heal her with his: "O Lord, heal her now." The wrong is the greater, because his sister did it. He doth not say, I sought not her shame, she sought mine; if God have revenged it, I have no reason to look on her as a sister, who looked at me as an adversary: but, as if her leprosy were his, he cries out for her cure. O admirable meekness of Moses! His people, the Jews, rebelled against him: God proffers revenge: he would rather die, than they should perish. His sister rebelled against him: God works his revenge; he will not give God peace till she be re-cured. Behold a worthy and noble pattern for us to follow! How far are they from this disposition, who are not only content God should revenge, but are ready to prevent God's revenge with their own!

God's love to Moses suffers him not to obtain presently his suit for Miriam; his good nature to his sister made him pray against himself. If the judgment had been at once inflicted, and removed, there had been no example of terror for others. God either denies, or defers the grant of our requests for our good. It were wide for us, if our suits should be ever heard. It was fit for all parts, Miriam should continue some while leprous. There is no policy in a sudden removal of just punishment: unless the rain so fall, that it lie and soak into the earth, it profits nothing. If the judgments of God should be only as passengers, and not sojourners at least, they would be no whit regarded.

CONTEMPLATION IV. — THE SEARCHERS OF CANAAN.

I can but wonder at the counsel of God. If the Israelites had gone on to Canaan, without inquiry, their confidence had possessed it. Now they send to espy the land; six hundred thousand never lived to see it: and yet I see God enjoining them to send; but enjoining it upon their instance.

Some things God allows in judgment: their importunity and distrust extorted from God this occasion of their overthrow. That which the Lord moves unto prospers; but that which we move him to first, seldom succeedeth. What needed they doubt of the goodness of that land, which God told them did flow with milk and honey? What needed they doubt of obtaining that which God promised to give? When we will send forth our senses to be our scouts in the matters of faith, and rather dare trust men than God, we are worthy to be deceived.

The basest sort of men are commonly held fit enough for intelligencers; but Moses, to make sure work, chooseth forth the best of Israel, such as were like to be most judicious in their inquiry, and most credible in their report. Those that ruled Israel at home, could best descry for them abroad. What should direct the body but the head? Men can judge but by appearance; it is for him only that sees the event, ere he appoint the means, not to be deceived. It had been better for Israel to have sent the offal of the multitude: by how much less the credit of their person is, by so much less is the danger of seducement. The error of the mighty is armed with authority, and in a sort commands assent: whether in good or evil, greatness hath ever a train to follow it at the heels.

Forty days they spent in this search; and this cowardly unbelief in the search shall cost them forty years' delay of the fruition. Who can abide to see the rulers of Israel so basely timorous? They commend the land, the fruit commends itself; and yet they plead difficulty: "We be not able to go up." Their shoulders are laden with the grapes, and yet their hearts are overlaid with unbelief. It is an unworthy thing to plead hardness of achieving, where the benefit will more than requite the endeavour. Our land of promise is above; we know the fruit thereof is sweet and glorious, the passage difficult. The giantly sons of Anak (the powers of darkness) stand in our way. If we sit down and complain, we shall once know, that "without shall be the fearful."

See the idle pleas of distrust! "We are not able; they are stronger." Could not God enable them? Was he not stronger than their giants? Had he not promised to displace the Canaanites, to settle them in their stead? How much more easy is it for us to spy their weakness, than for them to espy the strength of their adversaries! When we measure our spiritual success by our own power, we are vanquished before we fight. He that would overcome, must neither look upon his own arm, nor the arm of his enemy, but the mouth and hand of him that hath promised, and can perform. Who are we, flesh and blood, with our breath in our nostrils, that we should fight with principalities, powers, spiritual wickednesses in heavenly places? The match is too unequal: we are like grasshoppers to these giants; when we compare ourselves with them, how can we but despair? When we compare them with God, how can we be discouraged? He that hath brought us into this field, hath promised us victory. God knew their strength ere he offered to commit us.

Well might they have thought, were not the Amalekites stronger than we? Were not they armed, we naked? Did not the hand of Moses, only by lifting up, beat them down? Were not the Egyptians no less our masters? Did not death come running after us in their chariots? Did we not leave these buried in the sea, the other unburied in the wilderness? Whence had the Anakims their strength, but from him that bids us go up against them? Why have the bodies of our forefathers taken possession of their Hebron, but for us? But now, their fear hath not left them so much reason as to compare their adversaries with others, but only with themselves: doubtless, these giants were mighty, but their fear hath stretched them out some cubits beyond their stature. Distrust makes our dangers greater, and our helps less than they are, and forecasts ever worse than shall be; and if evils be possible, it makes them certain.

Amongst those twelve messengers whom our second Moses sent through the land of promise, there was but one Judas; but, amongst those twelve which the former Moses addressed through the same land, there is but one Caleb: and yet those were chosen out of the meanest; these out of the heads of Israel. As there is no society free from some corruption, so it is hard if in a community of men there be not some faithfulness.

We shall wrong God, if we fear lest good causes shall be quite forsaken. He knows how to serve himself of the best, if the fewest; and could as easily be attended with a multitude, if he did not seek his own glory in unlikelihoods.

Joshua was silent, and wisely spared his tongue for a further advantage; only Caleb spake. I do not hear him say, Who am I to strive with a multitude? What can

Joshua and I do against ten rulers? It is better to sit still than to rise and fall: but he resolves to swim against this stream, and will either draw friends to the truth, or enemies upon himself.

True Christian fortitude teaches us not to regard the number or quality of the opponents, but the equity of the cause, and cares not to stand alone, and challenge all comers; and if it could be opposed by as many worlds as men, it may be overborne, but it cannot be daunted: whereas popularity carries weak minds, and teaches them the safety of erring with a multitude.

Caleb saw the giantly Anakims and the walled cities as well as the rest, and yet he says, "Let us go up and possess it;" as if it were no more but to go, and see, and conquer. Faith is courageous, and makes nothing of those dangers wherewith others are quelled.

It is very material with what eyes we look upon all objects. Fear doth not more multiply evils, than faith diminisheth them; which is therefore bold, because either it sees not, or contemns that terror which fear represents to the weak. There is none so valiant as the believer.

It had been happy for Israel if Caleb's counsel had been as effectual as good: but how easily have these rulers discouraged a faint-hearted people! Instead of lifting up their ensigns, and marching towards Canaan, they sit them down, and lift up their voice, and cry. The rods of their Egyptian taskmasters had never been so fit for them, as now, for crying. They had cause, indeed, to weep for the sin of their infidelity; but now they weep for fear of those enemies they saw not. I fear, if there had been ten Calebs to persuade, and but two faint spies to discourage them, those two cowards would have prevailed against those ten solicitors: how much more, now ten oppose and but two encourage! An easy rhetoric draws us to the worst part; yea, it is hard not to run down the hill. The faction of evil is so much stronger in our nature than that of good, that every least motion prevails for the one; scarce any suit for the other.

Now is Moses in danger of losing all the cost and care that ever he bestowed upon Israel: his people are already gone back to Egypt in their hearts, and their bodies are returning. Oh! ye rebellious Hebrews, where shall God have you at last? Did ever Moses promise to bring you to a fruitful land, without inhabitants,—to give you a rich country, without resistance? Are not the graves of Canaan as good as those of Egypt? What, can ye but die at the hands of the Anakims? Can ye hope for less from the Egyptians? What madness is this to wish to die, for fear of death? Is there less hope from your enemies that shall be, when you go under strong and expert leaders, than from the enemies that were, when ye shall return masterless? Can those cruel Egyptians so soon have forgotten the blood of their fathers, children, brothers, husbands, which perished in pursuing you? Had ye rather trust the mercy of known enemies, than the promise of a faithful God? Which way will ye return? Who shall divide the sea for you? Who shall fetch you water out of the rock? Or can ye hope, that the manna of God will follow you while ye run from him? Feeble minds, when they meet with crosses they looked not for, repent of their good beginnings, and wish any difficulty rather than that they find. How many have pulled back their foot from the narrow way, for the troubles of a good profession!

It had been time for the Israelites to have fallen down on their faces before Moses and Aaron, and to have said, Ye led us through the sea; make way for us into Canaan. Those giants are strong, but not so strong as the rock of Rephidim; ye struck that, and it yielded: if they be tall, the pillar of God is higher than they: when we look on ourselves, we see cause of fear; but when we consider the miraculous power of you our leaders, we cannot but contemn those men of measures. Leave us not, therefore, but go before us in your directions; go to God for us in your prayers. But now contrarily, Moses and Aaron fall on their faces to them, and sue to them that they would be content to be conducted. Had they been suffered to depart, they had perished; Moses and his few had been victorious: and yet, as if he could not be happy without them, he falls on his face to them, that they would stay. We have never so much need to be importuned, as in those things whose benefit should make us most importunate. The sweetness of God's law, and our promised glory, is such as should draw all hearts after it; and yet, if we did not sue to men, as for life, that they would be reconciled to God, and be saved, I doubt whether they would obey; yea, it were well if our suit were sufficient to prevail.

Though Moses and Aaron entreat upon their faces, and Joshua and Caleb persuade, and rend their garments, yet they move nothing. The obstinate multitude, grown more violent with opposing, is ready to return them stones for their prayers. Such hath been ever the thanks of fidelity and truth. Crossed wickedness proves desperate, and, instead of yielding, seeks for revenge. Nothing is so hateful to a resolute sinner as good counsel. We are become enemies to the world, because we tell them truth.

That God, which was invisibly present while they sinned, when they have sinned, shows himself glorious. They might have seen him before, that they should not sin; now they cannot choose but see him in the height of their sin. They saw before the pillar of his ordinary presence; now, they see him unusually terrible, that they may, with shame and horror, confess him able to defend, able to revenge. The help of God uses to show itself in extremity. He that can prevent evils, conceals his aid till danger be ripe; and then he is as fearful as before he seemed connivent.

CONTEMPLATION V.—KORAH'S CONSPIRACY.

THE tears of Israel were scarce dry since the smart of their last mutiny, and now they begin another. The multitude is like a raging sea, full of unquiet billows of discontentment, whereof one rises in the fall of another. They saw God did but threaten, and therefore are they bold to sin. It was now high time they should know what it is for God to be angry. There was never such a revenge taken of Israel; never any better deserved. When lesser warnings will not serve, God looks into his quiver for deadly arrows. In the meantime, what a weary life did Moses lead in these continual successions of conspiracies! What did he gain by this troublesome government, but danger and despite? Who but he would not have wished himself rather with the sheep of Jethro, than with these wolves of Israel? But, as he durst not quit his hook without the calling of God, so now he dare not his sceptre, except he be dismissed of him that called him; no troubles, no oppositions, can drive him from his place: we are too weak if we suffer men to chase us from that station where God hath set us.

I see the Levites, not long since, drawing their swords, for God and Moses, against the rest of Israel; and that fact wins them both praise and blessing. Now they are the forwardest in the rebellion against Moses and Aaron, men of their own tribe. There is no assurance of a man for one act; whom one sin cannot fasten upon, another may. Yea, the same sin may find a repulse one while from the same hand, which another time gives it entertainment; and that yieldance loses the thank of all the former resistance. It is no praise to have done once well, unless we continue.

Outward privileges of blood can avail nothing against a particular calling of God. These Reubenites had the right of the natural primogeniture, yet do they vainly challenge pre-eminence, where God hath subjected them. If all civil honour flow from the king, how much more from the God of kings! His hand exalts the poor, and casts down the mighty from their throne. The man that will be lifting up himself in the pride of his heart, from under the foot of God, is justly trodden in the dust.

Moses is the prince of Israel, Aaron the priest; Moses was mild, Aaron popular; yet both are conspired against. Their places are no less brothers, than their persons. Both are opposed at once. He that is a traitor to the church, is a traitor to the king. Any superiority is a mark of envy. Had Moses and Aaron been but fellows with the Israelites, none had been better beloved; their dispositions were such, as must needs have forced favour from the indifferent; now they were advanced, their malice is not inferior to their honour. High towers must look for lightnings. We offer not to undermine but those walls which we cannot scale. Nature, in every man, is both envious and disdainful, and never loves to honour another, but where it may be an honour to itself.

There cannot be conceived an honour less worthy of emulation, than this principality of Israel; a people that could give nothing; a people that had nothing, but in hope; a people whom their leader was fain to feed with bread and water, which paid him no tribute but of ill words; whose command was nothing but a burden: and yet this dignity was an eye-sore to these Levites, and these Reubenites: "Ye take too much upon you, ye sons of Levi."

And this challenge, though thus unseasonable, hath drawn in two hundred and fifty captains of Israel. What wonder is it, that the ten rulers prevailed so much with the multitude to dissuade them from Canaan, when three traitors prevailed thus with two hundred and fifty rulers, famous in the congregation, and men of renown? One man may kindle such a fire, as all the world cannot quench. One plague-sore may infect a whole kingdom: the infection of evil is much worse than the act.

It is not like these leaders of Israel could err without followers. He is a mean man that draws not some clients after him. It hath been ever a dangerous policy of Satan to assault the best; he knows that the multitude, as we say of bees, will follow their master.

Nothing can be more pleasing to the vulgar sort, than to hear their governors taxed, and themselves flattered. "All the congregation is holy; every one of them; wherefore lift ye up yourselves?" Every word is a falsehood. For Moses dejected himself: "Who am I?" God lifted him up over Israel; and so was Israel holy, as Moses was ambitious. What holiness was there in so much infidelity, fear, idolatry, mutiny, disobedience? What could make them unclean, if this were holiness? They had scarce wiped their mouths, or washed their hands, since their last obstinacy; and yet these pickthanks say, "All Israel is holy."

I would never desire a better proof of a false teacher than flattery. True meaning need not uphold itself by soothing. There is nothing easier than to persuade men well of themselves: when a man's self-love meets with another's flattery, it is a high praise that will not be believed. It was more out of opposition than belief, that these men plead the holiness of Israel. Violent adversaries, to uphold a side, will maintain those things they believe not.

Moses argues not for himself, but appeals to God; neither speaks for his own right, but his brother Aaron's. He knew that God's immediate service was worthy to be more precious than his government; that his princedom served but to the glory of his master. Good magistrates are more tender over God's honour than their own; and more sensible of the wrongs offered to religion, than to themselves.

It is safest to trust God with his own causes. If Aaron had been chosen by Israel, Moses would have sheltered him under their authority. Now that God did immediately appoint him, his patronage is sought, whose the election was. We may easily fault in the managing of divine affairs; and so our want of success cannot want sin: he knows how to use, how to bless his own means.

As there was a difference betwixt the people and Levites, so betwixt the Levites and priests. The God of order loves to have our degrees kept. While the Levites would be looking up to the priests, Moses sends down their eyes to the people. The way not to repine at those above us, is to look at those below us. There is no better remedy for ambition, than to cast up our former receipts, and to compare them with our deservings, and to confer our own estate with inferiors, so shall we find cause to be thankful that we are above any, rather than of envy that any is above us.

Moses hath chid the sons of Levi for mutinying against Aaron; and so much the more, because they were of his own tribe. Now he sends for the Reubenites, who rose against himself. They come not, and their message is worse than their absence. Moses is accused of injustice, cruelty, falsehood, treachery, usurpation; and Egypt itself must be commended, rather than Moses shall want reproach. Innocency is no shelter from ill tongues; malice never regards how true any accusation is, but how spiteful.

Now it was time for Moses to be angry. They durst not have been thus bold if they had not seen his mildness. Lenity is ill bestowed upon stubborn natures; it is an injurious senselessness, not to feel the wounds of our reputation. It well appears he is angry, when he prays against them. He was displeased before; but, when he was most bitter against them, he still prayed for them; but now, he bends his very prayers against them: "Look not to their offering." There can be no greater revenge than the imprecation of the righteous: there can be no greater judgment, than God's rejection of their services. With us men, what more argues dislike of the person, than the turning back of his present? What will God accept from us, if not prayers?

The innocence of Moses calls for revenge on his adversaries. If he had wronged them in his government, in vain should he have looked to God's hand for right. Our sins exclude us from God's protection; whereas uprightness challenges, and finds his patronage. An ass taken, had made him incapable of favour. Corrupt governors lose the comfort of their own breast, and the tuition of God.

The same tongue that prayed against the conspirators, prays for the people. As lewd men think to carry it with number, Korah had so far prevailed, that he had drawn the multitude to his side. God, the avenger of treasons, would have consumed them all at once. Moses and Aaron pray for these rebels. Although they were worthy of death, and nothing but death could stop their mouths, yet their merciful leaders will not buy their own peace with the loss of such enemies. Oh rare and inimitable mercy! The people rise up against their governors; their governors fall on their faces to God for the people: so far are they from plotting revenge, that they will not endure God should revenge for them.

Moses knew well enough, that all those Israelites must perish in the wilderness; God had vowed it, for their former insurrection; yet how earnestly doth he sue to God, not to consume them at once! The very respite of evils is a favour next to the removal.

Korah kindled the fire; the two hundred and fifty captains brought sticks to it; all Israel warmed themselves by it; only the incendiaries perish. Now do the Israelites owe their life to them whose death they intended. God and Moses knew to distinguish betwixt the heads of the faction and the train: though neither be faultless, yet the one is plagued, the other forgiven. God's vengeance, when it is at the hottest, makes differences of men: "Get you away from about the tabernacles of Korah." Ever before common judgment, there is a separation. In the universal judgment of all the earth, the Judge himself will separate; in these particular executions, we must separate ourselves. The society of wicked men, especially in their sins, is mortally dangerous: while we will not be parted, how can we complain if we be enwrapped in their condemnation? Our very company sins with them, why should we not smart with them also?

Moses had well hoped, that when these rebels should see all the Israelites run from them as from monsters, and looking affrightedly upon their tents, and should hear that fearful proclamation of vengeance against them (howsoever they did before set a face on their conspiracy; yet now) their hearts would have misgiven. But lo! these bold traitors stand impudently staring in the door of their tents, as if they would outface the revenge of God; as if Moses had never wrought a miracle before them; as if no one Israelite had ever bled for rebelling. Those that shall perish are blinded. Pride and infidelity obdures the heart, and makes even cowards fearless.

So soon as the innocent are severed, the guilty perish; the earth cleaves and swallows up the rebels. This element was not used to such morsels. It devours the carcases of men; but bodies informed with living souls, never before. To have seen them struck dead upon the earth had been fearful; but to see the earth at once their executioner and grave, was more horrible. Neither the sea nor the earth are fit to give passage; the sea is moist and flowing, and will not be divided, for the continuity of it; the earth is dry and massy, and will neither yield naturally, nor meet again when it hath yielded: yet the waters did cleave to give way unto Israel, for their preservation; the earth did cleave to give way to the conspirators in judgment; both sea and earth did shut their jaws again upon the adversaries of God.

There was more wonder in this latter. It was a marvel that the waters opened; it was no wonder that they shut again; for the retiring and flowing was natural. It was no less marvel that the earth opened; but more marvel that it shut again; because it had no natural disposition to meet when it was divided. Now might Israel see they had to do with a God that could revenge with ease.

There were two sorts of traitors: the earth swallowed up the one, the fire the other. All the elements agree to serve the vengeance of their Maker. Nadab and Abihu brought fit persons, but unfit fire, to God; these Levites bring the right fire, but unwarranted persons, before him: fire from God consumes both. It is a dangerous thing to usurp sacred functions. The ministry will not grace the man; the man may disgrace the ministry.

The common people were not so fast gathered to Korah's flattering persuasion before, as now they ran from the sight and fear of his judgment. I marvel not if they could not trust that earth whereon they stood, while they knew their hearts had been false. It is a madness to run away from punishment, and not from sin.

BOOK VII.

CONTEMPLATION I.—AARON'S CENSER AND ROD.

WHEN shall we see an end of these murmurings, and these judgments? Because these men rose up against Moses and Aaron, therefore God consumed them; and because God consumed them, therefore the people rise up against Moses and Aaron: and now, because the people thus murmur, God hath again begun to consume them. What a circle is here of sins and judgments! Wrath is gone out from God: Moses is quicksighted, and spies it at the setting out. By how much more faithful and familiar we are with God, so much earlier do we discern his judgments; as those which are well acquainted with men know, by their looks and gestures, that which strangers understand but by their actions; as finer tempers are more sensible of the changes of the weather: hence the seers of God have ever, from their watchtower, descried the judgments of God afar off. If another man had seen from Carmel a cloud of a handbreadth, he could not have told Ahab he should be wet. It is enough for God's messengers, out of their acquaintance with their Master's proceedings, to foresee punishment: no marvel if those see it not, which are wilfully sinful. We men reveal not our secret purposes, either to enemies or strangers: all their favour is to feel the plague, ere they can espy it.

Moses, though he were great with God, yet he takes not upon him this reconciliation: he may advise Aaron what to do; himself undertakes not to act it. It is the work of the priesthood to make an atonement for the people: Aaron was first his brother's tongue to Pharaoh, now is he the people's tongue to God: he only must offer up the incense of the public prayers to God. Who would not think it a small thing to hold a censer in his hand? yet, if any other had done it, he had fallen with the dead, and not stood betwixt the living and the dead; instead of the smoke ascending, the fire had descended upon him: and shall there be less use, or less regard of the evangelical ministry, than the legal? When the world hath poured out all its contempt, we are they that must reconcile men to God, and without us they perish.

I know not whether more to marvel at the courage or mercy of Aaron: his mercy, that he would save so rebellious a people; his courage, that he would save them with so great a danger to himself. For, as one that would part a fray, he thrusts himself under the strokes of God, and puts it to the choice of the revenger, whether he will smite him, or forbear the rest; he stands boldly betwixt the living and the dead, as one that will either die with them, or have them live with him: the sight of fourteen hundred carcases dismayed him not: he that before feared the threats of the people, now fears not the strokes of God. It is not for God's ministers to stand upon their own perils in the common causes of the church: their prayers must oppose the judgments of the Almighty; when the fire of God's anger is kindled, their censers must smoke with fire from the altar. Every Christian must pray the removal of vengeance; how much more they whom God hath appointed to mediate for his people: every man's mouth is his own; but they are mouths to all.

Had Aaron thrust in himself with empty hands, I doubt whether he had prevailed; now his censer was his protection. When we come with supplications in our hands, we need not fear the strokes of God. We have leave to resist the divine judgments by our prayers, with favour and success. So soon as the incense of Aaron ascended up to God, he smelt a savour of rest; he will rather spare the offenders, than strike their intercessor. How hardly can any people miscarry, that have faithful ministers to sue for their safety! Nothing but the smoke of hearty prayers can cleanse the air from the plagues of God.

If Aaron's sacrifice were thus accepted, how much more shall the High-Priest of the New Testament, by interposing himself to the wrath of his Father, deliver the offenders from death? The plague was entered upon all the sons of men. O Saviour, thou stoodest betwixt the living and the dead, that all which believe in thee should not perish! Aaron offered and was not stricken; but thou, O Redeemer! wouldst offer and be struck, that by thy stripes we might be healed! So stoodest thou betwixt the dead and living, that thou wert both alive and dead; and all this, that we, when we were dead, might live for ever.

Nothing more troubled Israel, than a fear lest the two brethren should cunningly engross the government to themselves. If they had done so, what wise men would have envied them an office so little worth, so dearly purchased? But because this conceit was ever apt to stir them to rebellion, and to hinder the benefit of this holy sovereignty; therefore God hath endeavoured nothing more, than to let them see that these officers whom they so much envied, were of his own proper institution. They had scarce shut their eyes since they saw the confusion of those two hundred and fifty usurping sacrificers; and Aaron's effectual intercession for staying the plague of Israel.

In the one, the execution of God's vengeance upon the competitors of Aaron, for his sake; in the other, the forbearance of vengeance upon the people for Aaron's mediation, might have challenged their voluntary acknowledgment of his just calling from God. If there had been in them either awe or thankfulness, they could not have doubted of his lawful supremacy. How could they choose but argue thus? Why would God so fearfully have destroyed the rivals that durst contest with Aaron, if he would have allowed him any equal? Wherefore serve those plates of the altar, which we see made of those usurped censers, but to warn all posterity of such presumption! Why should God cease striking, while Aaron interposed betwixt the living and the dead, if he were but as one of us? Which of us, if we had stood in the plague, had not added to the heap? Incredulous minds will not be persuaded with any evidence. These two brothers had lived asunder forty years: God makes them both meet in one office of delivering Israel. One half of the miracles were wrought by Aaron; he struck with the rod, while it wrought those plagues on Egypt. The Israelites heard God call him up by name to Mount Sinai; they saw him anointed from God, and (lest they should think this a set match betwixt the brethren) they saw the earth opening, the fire issuing from God upon their emulous opposites: they saw his smoke, a sufficient antidote for the plague of God; and yet still Aaron's calling is questioned.

Nothing is more natural to every man than unbelief: but the earth never yielded a people so strongly incredulous as these; and, after so many thousand generations, their children do inherit their obstinacy: still do they oppose the true High-Priest, the anointed of God. Sixteen hundred years' desolation hath not drawn from them to confess him whom God hath chosen.

How desirous was God to give satisfaction even to the obstinate! There is nothing more material, than that men should be assured their spiritual guides have their commission and calling from God; the want whereof is a prejudice to our success. It should not be so: but the corruption of men will not receive good, but from due messengers.

Before, God wrought miracles in the rod of Moses; now, in the rod of Aaron. As Pharaoh might see himself in Moses' rod, which, of a rod of defence and protection, was turned into a venomous serpent, so Israel might see themselves in the rod of Aaron. Every tribe, and every Israelite, was, of himself, as a serestick, without life, without sap; and if any one of them had power to live and flourish, he must acknowledge it from the immediate power and gift of God.

Before God's calling, all men are alike: every name is alike written in their rod; there is no difference in the letters, in the wood; neither the characters of Aaron are fairer, nor the staff more precious. It is the choice of God that makes the distinction; so it is in our calling of Christianity: all are equally devoid of possibility of grace; all equally lifeless; by nature, we are all sons of wrath. If we be now better than others, who separated us? We are all crabstocks in this orchard of God; he may graff what fruit he pleases upon us; only the grace, and effectual calling of God, makes the difference.

These twelve heads of Israel would never have written their names in their rods, but in hope they might be chosen to this dignity. What an honour was this priesthood, whereof all the princes of Israel are ambitious! If they had not thought it a high preferment, they had never so much envied the office of Aaron. What shall we think of this change? Is the evangelical ministration of less worth than the Levitical? While the testament is better, is the service worse? How is it, that the great think themselves too good for this employment? How is it, that under the gospel, men are disparaged with that, which honoured them under the law; that their ambition and our scorn meet in one subject?

These twelve rods are not laid up in the several cabinets of their owners, but are brought forth and laid before the Lord. It is fit God should make choice of his own attendants. Even we men hold it injurious to have servants obtruded upon us by others. Never shall that man have comfort in his ministry, whom God hath not chosen. The great commander of the world hath set every man in his station: to one he hath said, Stand thou in this tower and watch; to another, Make thou good these trenches; to a third, Dig thou in this mine. He that gives, and knows our abilities, can best set us on work.

This rod was the pastoral staff of Aaron, the great shepherd of Israel. God testifies his approbation of his charge, by the fruit. That a rod cut off from the tree should blossom, it was strange; but, that in one night it should bear buds, blossoms, fruit, and that both ripe and hard, it was highly miraculous. The same power that revives the dead plants of winter in the spring, doth it here, without earth, without time, without sun, that Israel might see and grant it was no reason his choice should be limited, whose power is unlimited.

Fruitfulness is the best argument of the calling of God: not only all the plants of his setting, but the very boughs cut off from the body of them, will flourish. And that there may not want a succession of increase, here are fruit, blossoms, buds; both proof and hope, inseparably mixed.

It could not but be a great comfort unto Aaron, to see his rod thus miraculously flourishing; to see this wonderful testimony of God's favour and election: sure, he could not but think, who am I, O God, that thou shouldst thus choose me out of all the tribes of Israel? My weakness hath been more worthy of thy rod of correction, than my rod hath been worthy of these blossoms. How hast thou magnified me in the sight of all thy people! How able art thou to uphold my imbecility with the rod of thy support! How able to defend me with the rod of thy power, who hast thus brought fruit out of the sapless rod of my profession! That servant of God is worthy to faint, that holds it not a sufficient encouragement to see the evident proofs of his master's favour.

Commonly, those fruits which are soon ripe, soon wither; but these almonds of Aaron's rod are not more early than lasting; the same hand which brought them out before their time, preserved them beyond their time; and, for perpetual memory, both rod and fruit must be kept in the ark of God. The tables of Moses, the rod of Aaron, the manna of God, are monuments fit for so holy a shrine. The doctrine, sacraments, and government of God's people, are precious to him, and must be so to men. All times shall see and wonder how his ancient church was fed, taught, ruled. Moses' rod did great miracles, yet I find it not in the ark. The rod of Aaron hath this privilege, because it carried the miracle still in itself; whereas the wonders of that other rod were passed. Those monuments would God have continued in his church, which carry in them the most manifest evidences of that which they import.

The same God, which by many transient demonstrations had approved the calling of Aaron to Israel, will now have a permanent memorial of their conviction; that, whensoever they should see this relic they should be ashamed of their presumption and infidelity. The name of Aaron was not more plainly written in that rod, than the sin of Israel was in the fruit of it: and how much Israel finds their rebellion beaten with this rod, appears in their present relenting and complaint: "Behold, we are dead, we perish." God knows how to pull down the biggest stomach, and can extort glory to his own name, from the most obstinate gainsayers.

CONTEMPLATION II.—OF THE BRAZEN SERPENT.

SEVEN times already hath Israel mutinied against Moses, and seven times hath either been threatened or punished; yet now they fall to it afresh. As a testy man finds occasion to chaff at every trifle; so this discontented people either find, or make all things troublesome. One while they have no water, then bitter; one while no God, then one too many; one while no bread, then bread enough, but too light; one while they will not abide their governors, then they cannot abide their loss. Aaron and Miriam were never so grudged alive, as they are bewailed dead. Before, they wanted onions, garlic, flesh-pots; now, they want figs, vines, pomegranates, corn. And as crabbed children that cry for every thing they can think of, are whipped by their wise mother, so God justly serves these fond Israelites.

It was first their way that makes them repine: they were fain to go round about Idumea; the journey was long and troublesome. They had sent entreaties to Edom for licence of passage the nearest way, reasonably submissly: it was churlishly denied them. Esau lives still in his posterity, Jacob in Israel. The combat, which they began in Rebecca's belly, is not yet ended. Amalek, which was one limb of Esau, follows them at the heels. The Edomite, which was another, meets them in the face. So long as there is a world, there will be opposition to the chosen of God. They may come at their peril; the way had been nearer, but bloody; they dare not go it, and yet complain of length.

If they were afraid to purchase their resting-place with war, how much less would they their passage? What should God do with impatient men? They will not go the nearest way, and yet complain to go about. He that will pass to the promised land, must neither stand upon length of way, nor difficulty. Every way hath its inconveniences: the nearest hath more danger, the farthest hath more pain: either, or both, must be overcome, if ever we will enter the rest of God.

Aaron and Miriam were now past the danger of their mutinies; for want of another match, they join God with Moses, in their murmurings: though they had not mentioned him, they could not sever him in their insurrection; for, in the causes of his own servants, he challenges even when he is not challenged. What will become of thee, O Israel, when thou makest thy Maker thine enemy! Impatience is the cousin to frenzy: this causes men not to take care upon whom they run, so they may breathe out some revenge. How oft have we heard men, that have been dis-

THE BRAZEN SERPENT.

pleased by others, tear the name of their Maker in pieces? He that will judge, and can confound, is fetched into the quarrel without cause: but if to strive with a mighty man be unwise, and unsafe, what shall it be to strive with the mighty God?

As an angry child casts away that which is given him, because he hath not that he would, so do these foolish Israelites; their bread is light, and their water unsatisfying, because their way displeased them. Was ever people fed with such bread, or water? Twice hath the very rock yielded them water, and every day the heaven affords them bread. Did any one soul amongst them miscarry, either for hunger or thirst? But no bread will down with them, save that which the earth yields; no water but from the natural wells or rivers. Unless nature be allowed to be her own carver, she is never contented.

Manna had no fault, but that it was too good, and too frequent: the pulse of Egypt had been fitter for these coarse mouths. This heavenly bread was unspeakably delicious: it tasted like wafers of honey; and yet even this, angels' food, is contemned! He that is full, despiseth a honeycomb. How sweet and delicate is the gospel! Not only the fathers of the old testament, but the angels, desired to look into the glorious mysteries of it; and yet we are cloyed. This supernatural food is too light: the bread-corn of our human reason, and profound discourse, would better content us.

Moses will not revenge this wrong, God will: yet will he not deal with them himself, but he sends the fiery serpents to answer for him. How fitly! They had carried themselves like serpents to their governors. How often had they stung Moses and Aaron near to death? If the serpent bite when he is not charmed, no better is a slanderer. Now these venomous adders revenge it, which are therefore called fiery, because their poison scaldeth to death. God hath a hand in the annoyance and hurt of the basest creature; how much less can the sting of an ill tongue, or the malice of an evil spirit, strike us without him? While they were in Goshen, the frogs, lice, caterpillars, spared them, and plagued the Egyptians; now they are rebellious in the desert, the serpents find them out, and sting them to death. He that brought the quails thither to feed them, fetches these serpents thither to punish them. While we are at wars with God, we can look for no peace with his creatures. Every thing rejoices to execute the vengeance of its Maker. The stones of the field will not be in league with us, while we are not in league with God.

These men, when the spies had told them news of the giants of Canaan, a little before had wished, " Would God we were dead in this wilderness." Now God hath heard their prayers; what with the plague, what with the serpents, many thousands of them died. The ill wishes of our impatience are many times heard. As those good things are not granted us, which we pray for, without care; so those evils, which we pray for, and would not have, are often granted. The ears of God are not only open to the prayers of faith, but to the imprecations of infidelity. It is dangerous wishing evil to ourselves, or ours; it is just with God to take us at our word, and to effect that which our lips speak against our heart.

Before, God had ever consulted with Moses, and threatened ere he punished: now, he strikes and says nothing. The anger is so much more, by how much less notified. When God is not heard before he is felt (as in the hewing of wood, the blow is not heard till the axe be seen to have struck), it is a fearful sign of displeasure. It is with God, as with us men, that still revenges are ever most dangerous. Till now, all was well enough with Israel, and yet they grudged: those that will complain without a cause, shall have cause to complain for something. Discontented humours seldom escape unpunished, but receive that most justly, whereat they repined unjustly.

Now the people are glad to seek to Moses unbidden. Ever heretofore they have been wont to be sued to, and entreated for without their own entreaty; now their misery makes them importunate: there needs no solicitor where there is sense of smart. It were pity men should want affliction, since it sends them to their prayers and confessions. All the persuasions of Moses could not do that which the serpents have done for him. O God! thou seest how necessary it is we should be stung sometimes, else we should run wild, and never come to a sound humiliation. We should never seek thee, if thy hand did not find us out.

They had spoken against God and Moses, and now they humbly speak to Moses, that he would pray to God for them. He that so oft prayed for them unbidden, cannot but much more do it requested, and now obtains the means of their cure. It was equally in the power of God to remove the serpents, and to heal their stinging; to have cured the Israelites by his word, and by his sign: but he finds it best for his people (to exercise their faith) that the serpents may bite, and their bitings may envenom, and that this venom may endanger the Israelites; and that they, thus affected, may seek to him for remedy; and seeking, may find it from such means as should have no power but in signification; that while their bodies were cured by the sign, their souls might be confirmed by the matter signified. A serpent of brass could no more heal, than sting them. What remedy could their eyes give to their legs? or what could a serpent of cold brass prevail against a living and fiery serpent? In this troublesome desert, we are all stung by that fiery and old serpent. O Saviour! it is to thee we must look, and be cured: it is thou that wert their paschal lamb, their manna, their rock, their serpent. To all purposes dost thou vary thyself to thy church, that we may find thee everywhere. Thou art for our nourishment, refreshing, cure; as hereafter, so even now, all in all.

This serpent, which was appointed for cure to Israel, at last stings them to death by idolatrous abuse. What poison there is in idolatry, that makes even antidotes deadly! As Moses therefore raised this serpent, so Ezekias pulled it down. God commanded the raising of it; God approved the demolishing of it. Superstitious use can mar the very institutions of God: how much more the most wise and well-grounded devices of men!

CONTEMPLATION III.—OF BALAAM.

MOAB and Midian had been all this while standers by, and lookers on; if they had not seen the pattern of their own ruin in these neighbours, it had never troubled them to see the kings of the Amorites and Bashan to fall before Israel. Had not the Israelites camped in the plains of Moab, their victories had been no eye-sore to Balak. Wicked men never care to observe God's judgments, till themselves be touched. The fire of a neighbour's house would not so affect us, if it were not with the danger of our own. Secure minds never startle, till God come home to their very senses.

Balak and his Moabites had wit enough to fear, not wit enough to prevent judgment. They see an enemy in their borders, and yet take no right course for their safety. Who would not have looked, that they should have come to Israel with conditions of peace? Or why did they not think, either Israel's God is stronger than ours, or he is not? If he be not, why are we afraid of him? If he be, why do we not serve him? The same hand which gives them victory, can give us protection. Carnal men that are secure of the vengeance of God ere it do come, are mastered with it when it doth come; and, not knowing which way to turn them, run forth at the wrong door.

The Midianites join with the Moabites in consultation, in action, against Israel. One would have thought they should have looked for favour from Moses for Jethro's sake, which was both a prince of their country and father-in-law to Moses, and either now, or not long before, was with Israel in the wilderness. Neither is it like, but that Moses, having found forty years' harbour amongst them, would have been (what he might) inclinable to favourable treaties with them; but now they are so fast linked to Moab, that they will either sink or swim together. Entireness with wicked consorts is one of the strongest chains of hell, and binds us to a participation both of sin and punishment. An easy occasion will knit wicked hearts together in conspiracy against the church of God.

Their errand is devilish: " Come, curse Israel." That which Satan could not do by the swords of Og and Sihon, he will now try to effect by the tongue of Balaam. If either strength or policy would prevail against God's church, it could not stand. And why should not we be as industrious to promote the glory of God, and bend both our hands and heads to the causes of the Almighty? When all helps fail Moab, the magician is sought to. It is a sign of a desperate cause to make Satan either our counsellor or our refuge.

Why did they not send to Balaam to bless themselves, rather than to curse Israel? It had been more easy to be defended from the hurt of their enemies, than to have their enemies laid open to be hurt by them. Pride and malice did not care so much for safety as for conquest. It would not content them to escape Israel, if Israel may escape them. It was not thank-worthy to save their own blood, if they did not spill the blood of others; as if their own prosperity had been nothing, if Israel also prospered. If there be one project worse than another, a wicked heart will find it out. Nothing but destruction will content the malicious.

I know not whether Balaam were more famous, or Balak more confident. If the king had not been persuaded of the strength of his charm, he had not sent so far, and paid so dear for it: now he trusts more to his enchantment, than to the forces of Moab and Midian; and, as if heaven and earth were in the power of a charmer's tongue, he saith, "He that thou blessest, is blessed; and he whom thou cursest, is cursed." Magic, through the permission of God, is powerful; for whatsoever the devil can do, the magician may do; but it is madness to think either of them omnipotent. If either the curses of men, or the endeavours of the powers of darkness, should be effectual, all would be hell. No, Balak. So short is the power of thy Balaam, that neither thou, nor thy prophet himself, can avoid that curse, which thou wouldst have brought upon Israel. Had Balaam been a true prophet of God, this bold assurance had been but just. Both those ancient seers, and the prophets of the gospel, have the ratification of God in heaven to their sentences on earth. Why have we less care of the blessings, and less fear of the curses and censures of God's ministers? Who would not rather have Elisha's guard, than both the kings of Israel and Assyria? He himself, as he had the angelical chariots and horsemen about him, so was he the chariots and horsemen of Israel. Why should our faith be less strong than superstition? or why should God's agents have less virtue than Satan's?

I should wonder to hear God speak with a false prophet, if I did not know it had been no rare thing with him, as with men, to bestow words, even where he will not bestow favour. Pharaoh, Abimelech, Nebuchadnezzar, receive visions from God; neither can I think this strange, when I hear God speaking to Satan, in a question no less familiar than this of Balaam: "Whence comest thou," Satan? Not the sound of the voice of God, but the matter which he speaks, argues love. He may speak to an enemy; he speaks peace to none but his own. It is a vain brag, God hath spoken to me. So may he do to reprobates or devils. But what said he? Did he say to my soul, I am thy salvation? Hath he indented with me that he will be my God, and I shall be his? I cannot hear this voice, and not live.

God heard all the consultation and message of these Moabites; these messengers could not have moved their foot or their tongue but in him; and yet he which asked Adam where he was, asks Balaam, "What men are these?" I have ever seen that God loves to take occasion of proceeding with us from ourselves, rather than from his own immediate prescience. Hence it is, that we lay open our wants, and confess our sins to him that knows both better than our own hearts, because he will deal with us from our own mouths.

The prevention of God forbids both his journey and his curse. And what if he had been suffered to go and curse? What corn had this wind shaken, when God meant to bless them? How many bulls have bellowed out execrations against this church of God? What are we the worse? Yet I doubt if we had been so much blessed, had not those Balaamitish curses been spent upon us. He that knows what waste wind the causeless curses of wicked men are, yet will not have Balaam curse Israel; because he will not allow Balak so much encouragement in his opposition, as the conceit of this help. Or, perhaps if Balak thought this sorcerer a true prophet, God would not have his name, so much as in the opinion of the heathen, scandalized, in usurping it to a purpose which he meant not should succeed.

The hand of God is in the restraint of many evils, which we never knew to be towards us. The Israelites sat still in their tents: they little thought what mischief was brewing against them; without ever making them of counsel, God crosses the designs of their enemies. He that keepeth Israel, is both a sure and a secret friend. The reward of the divination had easily commanded the journey and curse of the covetous prophet, if God had not stayed him. How oft are wicked men curbed by a divine hand, even in those sins which their heart stands to! It is no thank to lewd men that their wickedness is not prosperous. Whence is it that the world is not overrun with evil, but from this, that men cannot be so ill as they would?

The first entertainment of this message would make a stranger think Balaam wise and honest. He will not give a sudden answer, but craves leisure to consult with God, and promises to return the answer he shall receive. Who would not say, This man is free from rashness, from partiality? Dissimulation is crafty, and able to deceive thousands. The words are good: when he comes to action, the fraud bewrays itself; for both he insinuates his own forwardness, and casts the blame of the prohibition upon God, and, which is worse, delivers but half his answer. He says indeed, "God refuses to give me leave to go." He says not, as it was, "He charges me not to curse them, for they are blessed." So did Balaam deny, as one that wished to be sent for again. Perhaps a peremptory refusal had hindered his further solicitation. Concealment of some truths is sometimes as faulty as a denial. True fidelity is not niggardly in her relations.

Where wickedness meets with power, it thinks to command all the world, and takes great scorn of any repulse. So little is Balak discouraged with one refusal, that he sends so much the stronger message: "More princes, and more honourable." O that we could be so importunate for our good, as wicked men are for the compassing of their own designs! A denial doth but whet the desires of vehement suitors. Why are we faint in spiritual things, when we are not denied, but delayed?

Those which are themselves transported with vanity and ambition, think that no heart hath power to resist these offers. Balak's princes thought they had struck it dead, when they had once mentioned promotion to great honour. Self-love makes them think they cannot be slaves, whilst others may be free; and that all the world would be glad to run on madding after their bait. Nature thinks it impossible to contemn honour and wealth; and because too many souls are thus taken, cannot believe that any would escape. But let carnal hearts know, there are those can spit the world in the face, and say, "Thy gold and silver perish with thee;" and that in comparison of a good conscience, can tread under foot his best proffers like shadows, as they are: and that can do as Balaam said.

How near truth and falsehood can lodge together! Here was piety in the lips, and covetousness in the heart. Who can any more regard good words, that hears Balaam speak so like a saint? A house full of gold and silver may not pervert his tongue; his heart is won with less: for if he had not already swallowed the reward, and found it sweet, why did he again solicit God in that which was peremptorily denied him? If his mind had not been bribed already, why did he stay the messengers? Why did he expect a change in God? Why was he willing to feed them with hope of success, which had fed him with hope of recompense? One prohibition is enough for a good man. While the delay of God doth but hold us in suspense, importunity is holy and seasonable: but when once he gives a resolute denial, it is profane sauciness to solicit him. When we ask what we are bidden, our suits are not more vehement than welcome: but when we beg prohibited favours, our presumption is troublesome and abominable. No good heart will endure to be twice forbidden.

Yet this importunity hath obtained a permission; but a permission worse than a denial. I heard God say before, "Go not, nor curse them:" now he says, "Go, but curse not." Anon he is angry that he did go. Why did he permit that which he forbade, if he be angry for doing that which he permitted? Some things God permits with an indignation; not for that he gives leave to the act, but that he gives a man over to his sin in the act. This sufferance implies not favour, but judgment. So did God bid Balaam to go as Solomon bids the young man follow the ways of his own heart. It is one thing to like, another thing to suffer. Moses never approved those legal divorces, yet he tolerated them. God never liked Balaam's journey, yet he displeasedly gives way to it; as if he said, Well, since thou art so hot-set on this journey, begone. And thus Balaam took it; else, when God after professed his displeasure for the journey, it had been a ready answer, "Thou commandedst me." But herein his confession argues his guilt. Balaam's suit, and Israel's quails, had both one fashion of grant — in anger. How much better is it to have gracious denials, than angry yieldings?

A small persuasion heartens the willing, It booted not to bid the covetous prophet hasten on his way. Now he makes himself sure of success. His corrupt heart tells him, that as God had relented in his licence to go, so he might perhaps in his licence to curse; and he saw how this curse might bless him with abundance of wealth: he rose up early, therefore, and saddled his ass. The night seemed long to his forwardness. Covetous men need neither clock nor bell to awaken them: their desires make them restless. O that we could, with as much eagerness, seek the true riches, which only can make us happy!

We, that see only the outside of Balaam, may marvel why he that permitted him to go, afterward opposes his going: but God, that saw his heart, perceived what corrupt affections carried him; he saw that his covetous desires and wicked hopes grew the stronger, the nearer he came to his end. An angel is therefore sent to withhold the hasty sorcerer. Our inward disposition is the life of our actions; according to that doth the God of spirits judge us, while men censure according to our external motions. To go at all, when God had commanded to stay, was presumptuous; but to go, with a desire to curse, made the act doubly sinful, and fetched an angel to resist it. It is one of the worthy employments of good angels, to make secret opposition to evil designs. Many a wicked act have they hindered, without the knowledge of the agent. It is all one with the Almighty to work by spirits and men. It is therefore our glory to be thus set on work. To stop the course of evil, either by dissuasion or violence, is an angelical service.

In what danger are wicked men that have God's angels their opposites? The devil moved him to go; a good angel resists him. If a heavenly spirit stand in the way of a sorcerer's sin, how much more ready are all those spiritual powers to stop the miscarriages of God's dear children! How oft had we fallen yet more, if these guardians had not upheld us, whether by removing occasions, or by casting in good instincts? As our good endeavours are oft hindered by Satan, so are our evil by good angels; else were not our protection equal to our danger, and we could neither stand nor rise.

It had been as easy for the angel to strike Balaam, as to stand in his way; and to have followed him in his starting aside, as to stop him in a narrow path. But even the good angels have their stints in their executions. God had somewhat more to do with the tongue of Balaam, and therefore he will not have him slain, but withstood; and so withstood, that he shall pass. It is not so much glory to God to take away wicked men, as to use their evil to his own holy purposes. How soon could the commander of heaven and earth rid the world of bad members! But so should he lose the praise of working good by evil instruments. It sufficeth that the angels of God resist their actions, while their persons continue.

That no man may marvel to see Balaam have visions from God, and utter prophecies from him, his very ass hath his eyes opened to see the angel, which his master could not; and his mouth opened to speak more reasonably than his master. There is no beast deserves so much wonder as this of Balaam, whose common sense is advanced above the reason of his rider; so as for the time the prophet is brutish, and the beast prophetical. Who can but stand amazed at the eye, at the tongue of this silly creature! For so dull a sight, it was much to see a bodily object that were not too apparent; but to see that spirit, which his rider discerned not, was far beyond nature. To hear a voice come from that mouth, which was used only to bray, it was strange and uncouth; but to hear a beast, whose nature is noted for incapacity, to outreason his master, a professed prophet, is in the very height of miracles. Yet can no heart stick at these, that considers the dispensation of the Almighty in both. Our eye could no more see a beast, than a beast can see an angel, if he had not given this power to it. How easy is it for him, that made the eye of man and beast, to dim or enlighten it at his pleasure! And if his power can make the very stones to speak, how much more a creature of sense! That evil spirit spake in the serpent to our first parents: why is it more, that a spirit should speak in the mouth of a beast? How ordinarily did the heathen receive their oracles out of stones and trees? Do not we ourselves teach birds to speak those sentences they understand not? We may wonder, we cannot distrust, when we compare the act with the author, which can as easily create a voice without a body, as a body without a voice. Who now can hereafter plead his simplicity and dulness of apprehending spiritual things, when he sees how God exalts the eyes of a beast to see a spirit? Who can be proud of seeing visions, since an angel appeared to a beast?— neither was his skin better after it than others of his kind. Who can complain of his own rudeness and inability to reply in a good cause, when the very beast is enabled by God to convince his master? There is no mouth into which God cannot put words; and how oft doth he choose the weak and unwise, to confound the learned and mighty!

What had it been better for the ass to see the angel, if he had rushed still upon his sword? Evils were as good not seen, as not avoided; but now he declines the way, and saves his burden. It were happy for perverse sinners, if they could learn of this beast to run away from foreseen judgment. The revenging angel stands before us; and though we know we shall as sure die as sin, yet we have not the wit or grace to give back, though it be with the hurt of a foot, to save the body; with the pain of the body, to save the soul.

I see what fury and stripes the impatient prophet bestows upon this poor beast, because he will not go on: yet if he had gone on, himself had perished. How oft do we wish those things, the not obtaining whereof is mercy! We grudge to be stayed in the way to death, and fly upon those which oppose our perdition.

I do not, as who would not expect, see Balaam's hair stand upright, nor himself alighting, and appalled at this monster of miracles; but as if no new thing had happened, he returns words to the beast, full of anger, void of admiration. Whether his trade of sorcering had so inured him to receive voices from his familiars in shape of beasts, that even this seemed not strange to him; or whether his rage and covetousness had so transported him, that he had no leisure to observe the unnatural unusualness of the event. Some men make nothing of those things, which overcome others with horror and astonishment.

I hear the angel of God taking notice of the cruelty of Balaam to his beast; his first words, to the unmerciful prophet, are in expostulation of his wrong. We little think it, but God shall call us to an account for the unkind and cruel usages of his poor mute creatures. He hath made us lords, not tyrants; owners, not tormentors; he that hath given us leave to kill them for our use, hath not given us leave to abuse them at our pleasure: they are so our drudges, that they are our fellows by creation. It was a sign the magician would easily wish to strike Israel with a curse, when he wished a sword to strike his harmless beast. It is ill falling into those hands, whom beasts find unmerciful.

Notwithstanding these rubs, Balaam goes on, and is not afraid to ride on that beast, whose voice he had heard. And now posts are sped to Balak, with the news of so welcome a guest; he that sent princes to fetch him, comes himself on the way to meet him. Although he can say, " Am not I able to promote thee?" yet he gives this high respect to him as his better, from whom he expected the promotion of himself and his people. O the honour that hath been formerly done by heathens, to them that have borne but the face of prophets! I shame and grieve to compare the times and men. Only, O God, be thou merciful to the contempt of thy servants!

As if nothing needed but the presence of Balaam, the superstitious king, out of the joy of this hope, feasts his gods, his prophet, his princes; and, on the morrow, carries him up to the high places of his idols. Who can doubt whether Balaam were a false prophet, that sees him sacrificing in the mount of Baal? Had he been from the true God, he would rather have said, " Pull me down these altars of Baal, than build me here seven others." The very place convinces him of falsehood and idolatry. And why seven altars? what needs all this pomp? When the true God never required but one at once, as himself is one, why doth the false prophet call for no less than seven? As if God stood upon numbers! as if the Almighty would have his power either divided or limited! Here is nothing but a glorious and magnificent pretence of devotion. It hath been ever seen, that the false worshippers of God have made more pompous shows, and fairer flourishes of their piety and religion, than the true.

Now, when Balaam sees his seven bullocks and seven rams smoking upon his seven altars, he goes up higher into the mount, as some counterfeit Moses, to receive the answer of God. But will God meet with a sorcerer? will he make a prophet of a magician? O man! who shall prescribe God what instruments to use? He knows how to employ, not only saints and angels, but wicked men, beasts, devils, to his own glory. He that put words into the mouth of the ass, put words into the mouth of Balaam: the words do but pass from him; they are not polluted, because they are not his: as the trunk, through which a man speaks, is not more eloquent for the speech that is uttered through it. What a notable proclamation had the infidels wanted of God's favour to his people, if Balaam's tongue had not been used! How many shall once say, " Lord, we have prophesied in thy name," that shall hear, " Verily, I know you not!"

What madness is this in Balaam? He that found himself constant in soliciting, thinks to find God not constant in denying; and, as if that infinite Deity were not the same everywhere, hopes to change success with places. Neither is that bold forehead ashamed to importune God again, in that wherein his own mouth had testified an assurance of denial. The reward was in one of his eyes; the revenging angel in the other: I know not whether (for the time) he more loved the bribe, or feared the angel. And, while he is in this distraction, his tongue blesses against his heart, and his heart curses against his tongue. It angers him that he cannot speak what he would; and now, at last, rather than lose his hopes, he resolves to speak worse than curses. The fear of God's judgment, in a worldly heart, is at length overcome with love of gain.

CONTEMPLATION IV.— OF PHINEAS.

BALAAM pretended a haste homeward, but he lingered so long, that he left his bones in Midian. How justly did he perish with the sword of Israel, whose tongue had insensibly slain so many thousands of them

As it is usually said of the devil, that he goes away in a stench, so may it be truly said of this prophet of his, according to the fashion of all hypocrites, his words were good; his actions abominable: he would not curse, but he would advise, and his counsel is worse than a curse; for his curse had hurt none but himself; his counsel cost the blood of twenty-four thousand Israelites. He that had heard God speak by Balaam, would not look for the devil in the same mouth: and if God himself had not witnessed against him, who could believe that the same tongue, which uttered so divine prophecies, should utter such villanous and cursed advice? Hypocrisy gains this of men, that 'it may do evil unsuspected: but now, he that heard what he spake in Balak's ear, hath bewrayed and condemned his counsel and himself.

This policy was fetched from the bottom of hell. It is not for lack of desire that I curse not Israel; thou dost not more wish their destruction, than I do thy wealth and honour; but so long as they hold firm with God, there is no sorcery against Jacob: withdraw God from them, and they shall fall alone, and curse themselves; draw them into sin, and thou shalt withdraw God from them. There is no sin more plausible than wantonness. One fornication shall draw in another, and both shall fetch the anger of God after them: send your fairest women into their tents; their sight shall draw them to lust, their lust to folly, their folly to idolatry; and now God shall curse them for thee unasked. Where Balaam did speak well, there was never any prophet spake more divinely; where he spake ill, there was never any devil spake more desperately. Ill counsel seldom succeedeth not: good seed falls often out of the way, and roots not; but the tares never light amiss. This project of the wicked magician was too prosperous. The daughters of Moab come into the tents of Israel, and have captivated those whom the Amorites and the Amalekites could not resist Our first mother Eve bequeathed this dowry to her daughters, that they should be our helpers to sin: the weaker sex is the stronger in this conquest. Had the Moabites sent their subtilest counsellors to persuade the Israelites to their idol sacrifices, they had been repelled with scorn; but now the beauty of their women is over-eloquent and successful. That which in the first world betrayed the sons of God, hath now ensnared God's people. It had been happy for Israel, if Balaam had used any charms but these. As it is the use of God to fetch glory to himself out of the worst actions of Satan, so it is the guise of that evil one, through the just permission of the Almighty, to raise advantage to himself from the fairest pieces of the workmanship of God. No one means hath so much enriched hell as beautiful faces.

All idols are abominable; but this of Baal-peor was, besides the superstition of it, beastly: neither did Baal ever put on a form of so much shame as this. Yet very Israelites are drawn to adore it. When lust hath blinded the eyes, it carries a man whither it lists; even beyond all differences of sin. A man besotted with filthy desires, is fit for any villany.

Sin is no less crafty than Satan himself: give him but room in the eye, and he will soon be possessed of body and soul. These Israelites first saw the faces of these Moabites and Midianites; then they grew to like their presence; from thence to take pleasure in their feasts; from their boards they are drawn to their beds, from their beds to their idols; and now they are joined to Baal-peor, and separated from God. Bodily fornication is the way, to spiritual. If we have made idols of flesh, it is just to be given up to idols of wood and stones. If we have not grace to resist the beginnings of sin, where shall we stay? If our foot slip into the mouth of hell, it is a miracle to stop ere we come to the bottom.

Well might God be angry to see his people go a-whoring in this double fornication; neither doth he smother his wrath, but himself strikes with his plague, and bids Moses strike with the sword. He strikes the body, and bids Moses strike the head. It had been as easy for him to plague the rulers, as the vulgar; and one would think these should be more properly reserved for his immediate hand; but these he leaves to the sword of human authority, that he might win awe to his own ordinances. As the sins of great men are exemplary, so are their punishments. Nothing procures so much credit to government, as strict and impartial executions of great and noble offenders. Those whom their sins have embased, deserve no favour in the punishment. As God knows no honour, no royalty in matter of sin, no more may his deputies. Contrarily, connivance at the outrages of the mighty cuts the sinews of a state; neither doth any thing make good laws more contemptible, than the making difference of offenders; that small sacrileges should be punished, when great ones ride in triumph. If good ordinations turn once to spider's webs, which are broken through by the bigger flies, no hand will fear to sweep them down.

God was angry; Moses and all good Israelites grieved: the heads hanged up, the people plagued. Yet behold, one of the princes of Israel fears not to brave God and his ministers, in that sin which he sees so grievously revenged in others. I can never wonder enough at the impudence of this Israelite. Here is fornication, an odious crime, and that of an Israelite, whose name challenges holiness; yea, of a prince of Israel, whose practice is a rule to inferiors; and that with a woman of Midian, with whom even a chaste contract had been unlawful; and that with contempt of all government; and that in the face of Moses, and all Israel; and that in a time of mourning and judgment for that same offence. Those that have once passed the bounds of modesty, soon grow shameless in their sins. While sin hides itself in corners, there is yet hope; for where there is shame, there is a possibility of grace: but when once it dare look upon the sun, and send challenges to authority, the case is desperate, and ripe for judgment. This great Simeonite thought he might sin by privilege: he goes, as if he said, Who dares control me? His nobility hath raised him above the reach of correction. Commonly the sins of the mighty are not without presumption, and therefore their vengeance is no less than their security: and their punishment is so much greater, as their conceit of impunity is greater. All Israel saw this bold lewdness of Zimri, but their hearts and eyes were so full of grief, that they had not room enough for indignation. Phineas looked on with the rest, but with other affections. When he saw this defiance bidden to God, and this insultation upon the sorrow of his people (that while they were wringing their hands, a proud miscreant durst outface their humiliation with his wicked dalliance), his heart boils with a desire of a holy revenge; and now that hand, which was used to a censer and sacrificing knife, takes up his javelin, and, with one stroke, joins these two bodies in their death, which were joined in their sin, and, in the very flagrance of their lust, makes a new way for their souls to their own place. O noble and heroical courage of Phineas! which, as it was rewarded of God, so is worthy to be admired of men. He doth not stand casting of scruples: Who am I to do this? The son of the high priest. My place is all for peace and mercy; it is for me to sacrifice, and pray for the sin of the people, not to sacrifice any of the people for their sin. My duty calls me to appease the anger of God what I may, not to revenge the sins of men; to pray for their conversion, not to work the confusion of any sinner. And who are these? Is not the one a great prince in Israel, the other a princess of Midian? Can the death of two so famous persons go unrevenged? Or, if it be safe and fit, why doth my uncle Moses rather shed his own tears than their blood? I will mourn with the rest; let them revenge, whom it concerneth. But the zeal of God hath barred out all weak deliberations; and he holds it now both his duty and his glory, to be an executioner of so shameless a pair of offenders.

God loves this heat of zeal in all the carriages of his servants: and if it transport us too far, he pardoneth the errors of our fervency, rather than the indifferences of lukewarmness. As these two were more beasts than any that ever he sacrificed, so the shedding of their blood was the acceptablest sacrifice that ever he offered unto God: for both all Israel is freed from the plague, and all his posterity have the priesthood entailed to them, so long as the Jews were a people. Next to our prayers, there is no better sacrifice than the blood of malefactors; not as it is theirs, but as it is shed by authority. Governors are faulty of those sins they punish not. There can be no better sight in any state than to see a malefactor at the gallows. It is not enough for us to stand gazing upon the wickedness of the times, yea although with tears, unless we endeavour to redress it; especially public persons carry not their javelin in their hand for nought.

Every one is ready to ask Phineas for his commission: and those that are willing to salve up the act, plead extraordinary instinct from God, who, no doubt, would not have accepted that which himself wrought not. But what need I run so far for this warrant, when I hear God say to Moses, "Hang up all the heads of Israel;" and Moses say to the under-rulers, "Every one slay his men that are joined to Baal-peor?" Every Israelite is now made a magistrate for this execution; and why not Phineas amongst the rest? Doth his priesthood exempt him from the blood of sinners? How then doth Samuel hew Agag in pieces? Even those may make a carcase, which may not touch it. And if Levi got the priesthood by shedding the blood of idolaters, why may it not stand with that priesthood to spill the blood of a fornicator and idolater? Ordinary justice will bear out Phineas in this act. It is not for every man to challenge this office, which this double proclamation allowed to Phineas. All that private persons can do, is either to lift up their hands to heaven for redress of sin; or to lift up their hands against the sin, not against the person. "Who made thee a judge?" is a lawful question, if it meet with a person unwarranted.

Now the sin is punished, the plague ceaseth. The revenge of God sets out ever after the sin; but if the revenge of men (which commonly comes later) can overtake it, God gives over the chase. How oft hath the infliction of a less punishment avoided a greater! There are none so good friends to the state, as courageous and impartial ministers of justice: these are the reconcilers of God and the people, more than the prayers of them that sit still and do nothing.

CONTEMPLATION V. — THE DEATH OF MOSES.

AFTER many painful and perilous enterprises, now is Moses drawing to his rest. He hath brought his Israelites from Egypt, through the sea and wilderness, within the sight of their promised land: and now himself must take possession of that land whereof Canaan was but a type. When we have done what we came for, it is time for us to be gone. This earth is only made for action, not for fruition. The services of God's children should be ill rewarded, if they must stay here always. Let no man think much, that those are fetched away which are faithful to God; they should not change, if it were not to their preferment. It is our folly that we would have good men live for ever, and account it a hard measure that they were. He that lends them to the world, owes them a better turn than this earth can pay them. It were injurious to wish, that goodness should hinder any man from glory. So is the death of God's saints precious, that it is certain.

Moses must go up to mount Nebo and die. The time, the place, and every circumstance of his dissolution, is determined. That one dies in the field, another in his bed, another in the water, one in a foreign nation, another in his own, is fore-decreed in heaven. And though we hear it not vocally, yet God hath called every man by his name, and saith, Die thou there. One man seems to die casually, another by unexpected violence: both fall by destiny and all is set down to us by an eternal decree. He that brought us into the world, will carry us out according to his own purposes.

Moses must ascend up the hill to die. He received his charge for Israel upon the hill of Sinai; and now he delivers up his charge on the hill of Nebo: his brother Aaron died on one hill, he on another. As Christ was transfigured on a hill, so was this excellent type of his: neither doubt I, but that these hills were types to them of that heaven whither they were aspiring. It is the goodness of our God, that he will not have his children die any where, but where they may see the land of promise before them: neither can they depart without much comfort, to have seen it: contrarily, a wicked man that looks down, and sees hell before him, how can he choose but find more horror in the end of death, than in the way!

How familiarly doth Moses hear of his end! It is no more betwixt God and Moses, but Go up and die. If he had invited him to a meal, it could not have been in a more sociable compellation: no otherways than he said to his other prophet, Up and eat. It is neither harsh, nor news to God's children, to hear or think of their departure: to them, death hath lost his horror through acquaintance. Those faces which at first sight seemed ill-favoured, by oft viewing grow out of dislike: they have so oft thought and resolved of the necessity, and of the issue of their dissolution, that they cannot hold it either strange or unwelcome. He that hath had such entire conversation with God, cannot fear to go to him. Those that know him not, or know that he will not know them, no marvel if they tremble.

This is no small favour, that God warns Moses of his end. He that had so oft made Moses of his counsel what he meant to do with Israel, would not now do aught with himself without his knowledge. Expectation of any main event is a great advantage to a wise heart. If the fiery chariot had fetched away Elias unlooked for, we should have doubted of the favour of his transportation: it is a token of judgment, to come as a thief in the night. God forewarns one by sickness, another by age, another by his secret instincts, to prepare for their end. If our hearts be not now in a readiness, we are worthy to be surprised.

But what is this I hear? displeasure mixed with love, and that to so faithful a servant as Moses. He must but see the land of promise ; he shall not tread upon it; because he once, long ago, sinned in distrusting. Death, though it were to him an entrance into glory, yet shall be also a chastisement of his infidelity. How many noble proofs had Moses given of his courage and strength of faith ! how many gracious services had he done to his master ! yet, for one act of distrust, he must be gathered to his fathers. All our obediences cannot bear out one sin against God. How vainly shall we hope to make amends to God for our former trespasses, by our better behaviour, when Moses hath this one sin laid in his dish, after so many and worthy testimonies of his fidelity ! When we have forgotten our sins, yet God remembers them, and although not in anger, yet he calls for our arrearages. Alas ! what shall become of them with whom God hath ten thousand greater quarrels, that, amongst many millions of sins, have scattered some few acts of formal services ! If Moses must die the first death for one fault, how shall they escape the second for sinning always ! Even where God loves, he will not wink at sin ; and if he do not punish, yet he will chastise. How much less can it stand with that eternal justice, to let wilful sinners escape judgment !

It might have been just with God to have reserved the cause to himself; and, in a generality, to have told Moses, that his sin must shorten his journey ; but it is more of mercy than justice, that his children shall know why they smart ; that God may, at once, both justify himself and humble them for their particular offences. Those to whom he means vengeance, have not the sight of their sins, till they be past repentance. Complain not that God upbraids thee with thy old sins, whosoever thou art : but know it is an argument of love ; whereas concealment is a fearful sign of a secret dislike from God.

But what was that noted sin which deserves this late exprobration, and shall carry so sharp a chastisement ? Israel murmured for water ; God bids Moses take the rod in his hand, and speak to the rock to give water : Moses, instead of speaking, and striking the rock with his voice, strikes it with his rod. Here was his sin ; an overreaching of his commission, a fearfulness and distrust of the effect. The rod, he knew, was approved for miracles : he knew not how powerful his voice might be ; therefore he did not speak, but strike, and he struck twice for failing ; and now, after these many years, he is stricken for it of God. It is a dangerous thing in divine matters to go beyond our warrant. Those sins, which seem trivial to men, are heinous in the account of God. Any thing that savours of infidelity, displeases him more than some other crimes of morality. Yet the moving of the rod was but a diverse thing from the moving of the tongue : it was not contrary ; he did not forbid the one, but he commanded the other : this was but across the stream, not against it. Where shall they appear, whose whole courses are quite contrary to the commandments of God ?

Upon the act done, God passed the sentence of restraining Moses, with the rest, from the promised land : now he performs it. Since that time, Moses had many favours from God ; all which could not reverse this decreed castigation. That everlasting rule is grounded upon the very essence of God : I am Jehovah ; I change not. Our purposes are as ourselves, fickle and uncertain ; his are certain and immutable. Some things which he reveals, he alters ; nothing that he hath decreed. Besides the soul of Moses, to the glory whereof God principally intended this change, I find him careful of two things ; his successor, and his body. Moses moves for the one ; the other God doth unasked. He that was so tender over the welfare of Israel, in his life, would not slacken his care in death. He takes no thought for himself, for he knew how gainful an exchange he must make. All his care is for his charge. Some envious natures desire to be missed when they must go, and wish that the weakness, or want of a successor, may be the foil of their memory and honour. Moses is in a contrary disposition ; it sufficeth him not to find contentment in his own happiness, unless he may have an assurance that Israel shall prosper after him. Carnal minds are all for themselves, and make use of government only for their own advantages. But good hearts look ever to the future good of the Church, above their own, against their own. Moses did well, to show his good affection to his people ; but, in his silence, God would have provided for his own. He that called him from the sheep of Jethro, will not want a governor for his chosen to succeed him : God hath fitted him whom he will choose. Who can be more meet than he, whose name, whose experience, whose graces might supply, yea, revive Moses to the people ? He that searched the land before, was fittest to guide Israel into it. He, that was endued with the spirit of God, was the fittest deputy for God. He, that abode still in the tabernacle of Ohel-moed, as God's attendant, was fittest to be sent forth from him, as his lieutenant. But O the unsearchable counsel of the Almighty! Aged Caleb, and all the princes of Israel, are past over, and Joshua, the servant of Moses, is chosen to succeed his master. The eye of God is not blinded either with gifts, or with blood, or with beauty, or with strength; but as in his eternal elections, so in his temporary, " He will have mercy on whom he will."

And well doth Joshua succeed Moses. The very acts of God of old were allegories. Where the law ends, there the Saviour begins. We may see the land of promise in the law: only Jesus, the Mediator of the New Testament, can bring us into it. So was he a servant of the law, that he supplies all the defects of the law to us. He hath taken possession of the promised land for us: he shall carry us from this wilderness to our rest.

It is no small happiness to any state, when their governors are chosen by worthiness; and such elections are ever from God; whereas the intrusions of bribery, and unjust favour, or violence, as they make the commonwealth miserable, so they come from him which is the author of confusion. Woe be to that state that suffers it! woe be to that person that works it! for both of them have sold themselves, the one to servitude, the other to sin.

I do not hear Moses repine at God's choice, and grudge that this sceptre of his is not hereditary; but he willingly lays hands upon his servant, to consecrate him for his successor. Joshua was a good man, yet he had some sparks of envy; for when Eldad and Medad prophesied, he stomached it: " My lord Moses, forbid them." He, that would not abide two of the elders of Israel to prophesy, how would he have allowed his servant to sit in his throne? What an example of meekness, besides all the rest, doth he here see in this last act of his master, who, without all murmuring, resigns his chair of state to his page? It is all one, to a gracious heart, whom God will please to advance. Emulation and discontentment are the affections of carnal minds. Humility goes ever with regeneration; which teaches a man to think, whatever honour be put upon others, I have more than I am worthy of.

The same God, that, by the hands of his angels, carried up the soul of Moses to his glory, doth also, by the hands of his angels, carry his body down into the valley of Moab to his sepulture. Those hands which had taken the law from him, those eyes that had seen his presence, those lips that had conferred so oft with him, that face that did so shine with the beams of his glory, may not be neglected when the soul is gone. He that took charge of his birth, and preservation in the reeds, takes charge of his carriage out of the world. The care of God ceaseth not over his own, either in death, or after it. How justly do we take care of the comely burials of our friends, when God himself gives us this example!

If the ministry of man had been used in this grave of Moses, the place might have been known to the Israelites: but God purposely conceals this treasure, both from men and devils, that so he might both cross their curiosity, and prevent their superstition. If God had loved the adoration of his servants' reliques, he could never have had a fitter opportunity for this devotion, than in the body of Moses. It is folly to place religion in those things which God hides on purpose from us: it is not the property of the Almighty to restrain us from good.

Yet that divine hand, which locked up this treasure, and kept the key of it, brought it forth afterwards glorious. In the transfiguration, this body, which was hid in the valley of Moab, appeared in the hill of Tabor, that we may know these bodies of ours are not lost, but laid up, and shall as sure be raised in glory, as they are laid down in corruption. " We know that when he shall appear we shall also appear with him in glory."

BOOK VIII.

CONTEMPLATION I.—OF RAHAB.

JOSHUA was one of those twelve searchers which were sent to view the land of Canaan; yet now he addresses two spies, for a more particular survey. Those twelve were only to inquire of the general condition of the people and land; these two to find out the best entrance into the next part of the country, and into their greatest city. Joshua himself was full of God's spirit, and had the oracle of God ready for his direction: yet now he goes not to the propitiatory for consultation, but to the spies. Except where ordinary means fail us, it is no appealing to the immediate help of God; we may not seek to the postern, but where the common gate is shut. It was promised Joshua, that he should lead Israel into the promised land; yet he knew it was unsafe to presume. The condition of his provident care was included in that assurance of success. Heaven is promised to us, but not to our carelessness, infidelity, disobedience. He that hath set this blessed inheritance before us, presupposes our wisdom, faith, holiness.

Either force or policy is fit to be used unto Canaanites. He that would be happy in this spiritual warfare, must know where the strength of his enemy lieth; and must frame his guard according to the other's assault. It is a great advantage to a Christian to know the fashion of Satan's onsets, that he may the more easily compose himself to resist. Many a soul hath miscarried through the ignorance of his enemy, which had not perished, if it had well known that the weakness of Satan stands in our faith.

The spies can find no other lodging but Rahab's house. She was a victualler by profession, and (as those persons and trades, by reason of the commonness of entertainment, were amongst the Jews infamous by name and note) she was Rahab the harlot. I will not think she professed filthiness; only her public trade, through the corruption of those times, hath cast upon her this name of reproach: yea, rather will I admire her faith, than make excuses for her calling. How many women in Israel (now Miriam was dead) have given such proofs of their knowledge and faith! How noble is that confession which she makes of the power and truth of God! Yea, I see here not only a disciple of God but a prophetess. Or, if she had once been public, as her house was, now she is a chaste and worthy convert; and so approved herself for honest and wise behaviour, that she is thought worthy to be the great grandmother of David's father: and the holy line of the Messias is not ashamed to admit her into that happy pedigree. The mercy of our God doth not measure us by what we were. It would be wide with the best of us, if the eye of God should look backward to our former estate; there he should see Abraham an idolater; Paul a persecutor; Manasses a necromancer; Mary Magdalen a courtezan; and the best vile enough to be ashamed of himself. Who can despair of mercy, that sees even Rahab fetched into the blood of Israel, and line of Christ!

If Rahab had not received these spies, but as unknown passengers, with respect to their money, and not to their errand, it had been no praise: for in such cases, the thank is rather to the guest than to the host. But now she knew their purpose; she knew that the harbour of them was the danger of her own life; and yet she hazards this entertainment. Either faith or friendship is never tried, but in extremities. To show countenance to the messengers of God, while the public face of the state smiles upon them, is but a courtesy of course; but to hide our own lives in theirs, when they are persecuted, is an act that looks for a reward. These times need not our favour; we know not what may come. Alas! how likely is it they would shelter them in danger, which respect them not in prosperity!

All intelligences of state come first to the court. It most concerns princes to hearken after the affairs of each other. If this poor inn-holder knew of the sea dried up before Israel, and of the discomfiture of Og and Sihon; surely this rumour was stale with the king of Jericho: he had heard it, and feared; and yet, instead of sending ambassadors for peace, he sends pursuivants for the spies. The spirit of Rahab melted with that same report, wherewith the king of Jericho was hardened. All make not one use of the messages of the proceedings of God.

The king sends to tell her what she knew; she had not hid them, if she had not known their errand. I know not whether first to wonder at the gracious provision of God for the spies, or at the strong faith which he wrought in the heart of a weak woman. Two strangers, Israelites, spies (and noted for all these), in a foreign, in a hostile land, have a safe harbour provided them even amongst their enemies; in Jericho, at the very court-gate, against the proclamation of a king, against the endeavours of the people. Where cannot the God of heaven either find, or raise up friends, to his own causes and servants?

Who could have hoped for such faith in Rahab? which contemned her life for the present, that she might save it for the future; neglected her own king and country, for strangers which she never saw; and more feared the destruction of that city, before it knew that it had an adversary, than the displeasure of her king, in the mortal revenge of that which he would have accounted treachery. She brings them up to the roof of her house, and hides them with stalks of flax. That plant, which was made to hide the body from nakedness and shame, now is used to hide the spies from death. Never could these stalks have been improved so well with all her housewifery after they were bruised, as now, before they were fitted to her wheel: of these she hath woven an everlasting web, both of life and propagation. And now her tongue hides them no less than her hand. Her charity was good, her excuse was not good. "Evil may not be done, that good may come of it;" we may do any thing, but sin, for promoting a good cause: and, if not in so main occasions, how shall God take it, that we are not dainty of falsehoods in trifles?

No man will look that these spies could take any sound sleep in these beds of stalks: it is enough for them that they live, though they rest not. And now, when they hear Rahab coming up the stairs, doubtless they looked for an executioner; but behold, she comes up with a message better than their sleep, adding to their protection advice for their future safety; whereto she makes way by a faithful report of God's former wonders, and the present disposition of her people; and by wise capitulations for the life and security of her family. The news of God's miraculous proceedings for Israel have made her resolve of their success, and the ruins of Jericho. Then only do we make a right use of the works of God, when, by his judgments upon others, we are warned to avoid our own. He intends his acts for precedents of justice.

The parents and brethren of Rahab take their rest; they are not troubled with the fear and care of the success of Israel, but securely go with the current of the present condition. She watches for them all; and breaks her midnight sleep, to prevent their last. One wise and faithful person does well in a house: where all are careless, there is no comfort but in perishing together. It had been an ill nature in Rahab, if she had been content to be saved alone. That her love might be a match to her faith, she covenants for all her family, and so returns life to those of whom she received it. Both the bond of nature and of grace will draw all ours to the participation of the same good with ourselves.

It had been never the better for the spies, if, after this night's lodging, they had been turned out of doors to the hazard of the way; for so the pursuers had lighted upon them, and prevented their return with their death. Rahab's counsel therefore was better than her harbour; which sent them (no doubt with victuals in their hands) to seek safety in the mountains, till the heat of that search were past. He that hath given us charge of our lives, will not suffer us to cast them upon wilful adventures. Had not these spies hid themselves in those desert hills, Israel had wanted director for their enterprises. There is nothing more expedient for the church, than that some of God's faithful messengers should withdraw themselves, and give way to persecutions. Courage, in those that must die, is not a greater advantage to the gospel, than a prudent retiring of those, which may survive, to maintain and propagate it.

It was a just and reasonable transaction betwixt them, that her life should be saved by them which had saved theirs: they owe no less to her, to whom they were not so much guests as prisoners. And now they pass not their promise only, but their oath. They were strangers to Rahab, and, for aught she knew, might have been godless; yet she dares trust her life upon their oath. So sacred and inviolable hath this bond ever been, that a heathen woman thought herself secure upon the oath of an Israelite.

Neither is she more confident of their oath taken, than they are careful both of taking and performing it. So far are they from desiring to salve up any breach of promise by equivocation, that they explain all conditions, and would prevent all possibilities of violation. All Rahab's family must be gathered into her house; and that red cord, which was an instrument of their delivery, must be a sign of hers. Behold, this is the saving colour! the destroying angel sees the door-cheeks of the Israelites sprinkled with red, and passes them over. The warriors of Israel see the window of Rahab dyed with red, and save her family from the common destruction. If our souls have this tincture of the precious blood of our Saviour upon our doors or windows, we are safe.

But if any one of the brethren of Rahab shall fly from this red flag, and rove about the city, and not contain himself under that roof which hid the spies, it is in vain for him to tell the avengers that he is Rahab's brother. That title will not save him in the street — within doors it will. If we will wander out of the limits that God hath set us, we cast ourselves out of his protection. We cannot challenge the benefit of his gracious preservation, and our most precious redemption, when we fly out into the bye-ways of our own hearts, not for innocence, but for safety and harbour. The church is that house of Rahab which is saved, when all Jericho shall perish. While we keep us in the lists thereof, we cannot miscarry through misopinion; but, when once we run out of it, let us look for judgment from God, and error in our own judgment.

CONTEMPLATION II.—JORDAN DIVIDED.

The two spies returned with news of the victory that should be. I do not hear them say, The land is unpeopled; or the people are unfurnished with arms, unskilful in the discipline of war; but, "They faint because of us, therefore their land is ours." Either success, or discomfiture, begins ever at the heart. A man's inward disposition doth more than presage the event. As a man raises up his own heart before his fall, and depresses it before his glory; so God raises it up before his exaltation, and casts it down before his ruin. It is no otherwise in our spiritual conflicts. If Satan sees us once faint, he gives himself the day. There is no way to safety, but that our hearts be the last that shall yield. That which the heathens attributed to fortune, we may justly to the hand of God, that he speedeth those that are forward. All the ground that we lose, is given to our adversaries.

This news is brought but over night; Joshua is on his way by morning, and prevents the sun for haste. Delays, whether in the business of God or our own, are hateful and prejudicial. Many a one loses the land of promise by lingering. If we neglect God's time, it is just with him to cross us in ours.

Joshua hastens till he has brought Israel to the verge of the promised land: nothing parts them now but the river of Jordan. There he stays a time, that the Israelites might feed themselves a while with the sight of that which they should afterwards enjoy. That which they had been forty years in seeking, may not be seized upon too suddenly. God loves to give us cools and heats in our desires; and will so allay our joys, that their fruition hurt us not. He knows, that as it is in meats, the long forbearance whereof causes a surfeit when we come to full feed; so it fares in the contentments of the mind: therefore he feeds us not with the dish, but with the spoon, and will have us neither cloyed nor famished. If the mercy of God have brought us within sight of heaven, let us be content to pause a while, and, upon the banks of Jordan, fit ourselves for our entrance.

Now that Israel is brought to the brim of Canaan, the cloud is vanished which led them all the way; and, as soon as they have but crossed Jordan, the manna ceaseth, which nourished them all the way. The cloud and manna were for their passage, not for their rest; for the wilderness, not for Canaan. It were as easy for God to work miracles always; but he knows that custom were the way to make them no miracles. He goes bye-ways but till he have brought us into the road, and then he refers us to his ordinary proceedings. That Israelite should have been very foolish, that would still have said, I will not stir till I see the cloud; I will not eat, unless I may have that food of angels. Wherefore serves the ark, but for their direction? wherefore serves the wheat of Canaan, but for bread? So fond is that Christian, that will still depend upon expectation of miracles, after the fulness of God's kingdom. If God bear us in his arms when we are children, yet when we are well grown, he looks we should go on our feet: it is enough that he upholds us, though he carry us not.

He, that hitherto had gone before them in the cloud, doth now go before them in the ark; the same guide in two diverse signs of his presence. The cloud was for Moses', the ark for Joshua's time. The cloud was fit for Moses; the law offered us Christ, but enwrapped in many obscurities. If he were seen in the cloud, he was heard from the cover of the ark. Why was it the ark of the testimony, but because it witnessed both his presence and love? and within it were his word the law, and his sacrament the manna. Who can wish a better guide than the God of heaven, in his word and sacraments? Who can know the way into the land of promise so well as he that owns it? and what means can better direct us thither than those of his institution?

That ark, which before was as the heart, is now as the head: it was in the midst of Israel, while they camped in the desert; now, when the cloud is removed, it is in the front of the army; that, as before they depended upon it for life, so now they should for direction. It must go before them on the shoulders of the sons of Levi: they must follow it, but within sight, not within breathing. The Levites may not touch the ark, but only the bars: the Israelites may not approach nearer than a thousand paces to it. What awful respects doth God require to be given unto the testimonies of his presence! Uzzah paid dear, for touching it; the men of Bethshemesh for looking into it. It is a dangerous thing to be too bold with the ordinances of God. Though the Israelites were sanctified, yet they might not come near either the mount of Sinai, when the law was delivered, or the ark of the covenant, wherein the law was written. How fearful shall their estate be, that come with unhallowed hearts and hands to the word of the gospel, and the true manna of the evangelical sacrament? As we use to say of the court, and of fire, so may we of these divine institutions, — We freeze, if we be far off from them; and if we be more near than befits us, we burn. Under the law, we might look at Christ aloof; now, under the gospel, we may come near him: he calls us to him; yea, he enters into us.

Neither was it only for reverence that the ark must be not stumbled at, but waited on afar; but also for convenience, both of sight and passage. Those things that are near us, though they be less, fill our eye; neither could so many thousand eyes see the same object upon a level, but by distance. It would not content God, that one Israelite should tell another. Now the ark goes, now it turns, now it stands; but he would have every one his own witness. What can be so comfortable to a good heart, as to see the pledges of God's presence and favour? To hear of the lovingkindnesses of God is pleasant; but to behold and feel the evidences of his mercy is unspeakably delectable. Hence the saints of God, not contenting themselves with faith, have still prayed for sight and fruition, and mourned when they have wanted it. What a happy prospect hath God set before us of Christ Jesus crucified for us, and offered unto us!

Ere God will work a miracle before Israel, they have charge to be sanctified. There is a holiness required, to make us either patients or beholders of the great works of God; how much more, when we should be actors in his sacred services! There is more use of sanctification when we must present something to God, than when he must do aught to us.

The same power that divided the Red Sea before Moses, divides Jordan before Joshua, that they might see the ark no less effectual than the cloud; and the hand of God as present with Joshua to bring them into Canaan, as it was with Moses to bring them out of Egypt. The bearers of the ark had need be faithful; they must first set their foot into the streams of Jordan, and believe that it will give way; the same faith that led Peter upon the water, must carry them into it. There can be no Christian without belief in God; but those that are near to God in his immediate services, must go before others, no less in believing, than they do in example.

The waters know their Maker. That Jordan, that flowed with full streams when Christ went into it to be baptized, now gives way, when the same God must pass through it in state. Then there was use of his water, now of his sand. I hear no news of any rod to strike the waters; the presence of the ark of the Lord God, the Lord of all the world, is sign enough to these waves, which now, as if a sinew were broken, run back to their issues, and dare not so much as wet the feet of the priests that bore it. " What ailed thee, O sea, that thou fleddest, and thou Jordan, that thou wert driven back? Ye mountains, that ye leaped like rams, and ye little hills, like lambs? The earth trembled at the presence of the Lord, at the presence of the God of Jacob!" How observant are all the creatures to the God that made them! How glorious a God do we serve, whom all the powers of the heavens and elements are willingly subject unto, and gladly take that nature which he pleases to give them! He could have made Jordan like some solid pavement of crystal, for the Israelites' feet to have trode upon; but this work had not been so magnificent. Every strong frost congeals the water, in a natural force, but for the river to stand still, and run on heaps, and to be made a liquid wall for the passage of God's people, is for nature to run out of itself, to do homage to her Creator. Now must the Israelites needs think, how can the Canaanites stand out against us, when the seas and rivers give us way? With what joy did they now trample upon the dry channel of Jordan, while they might see the dry deserts overcome, the promised land before them, the very waters so glad of them that they ran back to welcome them into Canaan! The passages into our promised land are troublesome and perilous, and even at last offer themselves to us the main hindrances of our salvation, which, after all our hopes, threaten to defeat us: for what will it avail us to have passed a wilderness, if the waves of Jordan should swallow us up? But the same hand that hath made the way hard, hath made it sure; he that made the wilderness comfortable, will make Jordan dry; he will master all difficulties for us; and those things which we most feared, will he make most sovereign and beneficial to us. O God! as we have trusted thee with the beginning, so will we with the finishing of our glory! Faithful art thou that hast promised, which wilt also do it!

He that led them about, in forty years' journey through the wilderness, yet now leads them the nearest cut to Jericho; he will not so much as seek for a ford for their passage, but divides the waters. What a sight was this to their heathen adversaries, to see the waters make both a lane and a wall for Israel! Their hearts could not choose but be broken, to see the streams broken off for a way to their enemies. I do not see Joshua hastening through this channel, as if he feared lest the tide of Jordan should return; but, as knowing that watery wall stronger than the walls of Jericho, he paces slowly; and, lest this miracle should pass away with themselves, he commands twelve stones to be taken out of the channel of Jordan by twelve selected men from every tribe, which shall be pitched in Gilgal: and twelve other stones to be set in the midst of Jordan, where the feet of the priests had stood with the ark; that so both land and water might testify the miraculous way of Israel: while it should be said of the one, These stones were fetched out of the pavement of Jordan; of the other, there did the ark rest, while we walked dry-shod the deeps of Jordan: of the one, Jordan was once as dry as this Gilgal; of the other, Those waves which drown these stones, had so drowned us, if the power of the Almighty had not restrained them. Many a great work had God done for Israel, which was now forgotten: Joshua therefore will have monuments of God's mercy, that future ages might be both witnesses and applauders of the great works of their God.

CONTEMPLATION III.—THE SIEGE OF JERICHO.

Joshua begins his wars with the circumcision and passover; he knew that the way to keep the blood of his people from shedding, was to let out that paganish blood of their uncircumcision. The person must be in favour, ere the work can hope to prosper. His predecessor Moses had like to have been slain for neglect of this sacrament, when he went to call the people out of Egypt: he justly fears his own safety, if now he omit it, when they are brought into Canaan. We have no right of inheritance in the spiritual Canaan, the church of God, till we have received the sacrament of our matriculation. So soon as our covenants are renewed with our Creator, we may well look for the vision of God for the assurance of victory.

What sure work did the king of Jericho think he had made! He blocked up the passages, barred up the gates, defended the walls, and did enough to keep out a common enemy. If we could do but this to our spiritual adversaries, it were as impossible for us to be surprised, as for Jericho to be safe. Methinks I see how they called their council of war, debated of all means of defence, gathered their forces, trained their soldiers, set strong guards to the gates and walls; and now would persuade one another, that, unless Israel could fly into their city, the siege was vain. Vain worldlings think their rampires and barricadoes can keep out the vengeance of God; their blindness suffers them to look no further than the means. The supreme hand of the Almighty comes not within the compass of their fears. Every carnal heart is a Jericho shut up; God sits down before it, and displays mercy and judgment in sight of the walls thereof: it hardens itself in a wilful security, and saith, " Tush, I shall never be moved."

Yet their courage and fear fight together within their walls, within their bosoms. Their courage tells them of their own strength; their fear suggests the miraculous success of this (as they could not but think) enchanted generation; and now, while they have shut out their enemy, they have shut in their own terror. The most secure heart in the world hath some flashes of fear; for it cannot but sometimes look out of itself, and see what it would not. Rahab had notified that their hearts fainted; and yet now their faces bewray nothing but resolution. I know not whether the heart or the face of a hypocrite be more false; and as each of them seeks to beguile the other, so both of them agree to deceive the beholders. In the midst of laughter, their heart is heavy. Who would not think him merry that laughs? yet their rejoicing is but in the face. Who would not think a blasphemer, or profane man, resolutely careless? If thou hadst a window into his heart, thou shouldst see him tormented with horrors of conscience.

Now the Israelites see those walled cities and towers, whose height was reported to reach to heaven, the fame whereof had so affrighted them, ere they saw them, and were ready, doubtless, to say, in their distrust, Which way shall we scale these invincible fortifications? what ladders, what engines, shall we use to so great a work? God prevents their infidelity: " Behold, I have given Jericho into thine hand." If their walls had their foundations laid in the centre of the earth; if the battlements had been so high built, that an eagle could not soar over them; this is enough, " I have given it thee." For, on whose earth have they raised these castles? out of whose treasure did they dig those piles of stone? whence had they their strength and time to build? Cannot he that gave, recall his own? O ye fools of Jericho! what if your walls be strong, your men valiant, your leaders skilful, your king wise, when God hath said, " I have given thee the city!" What can swords or spears do against the Lord of hosts! Without him means can do nothing; how much less against him! How vain and idle is that reckoning, wherein God is left out! Had the captain of the Lord's host drawn his sword for Jericho, the gates might have been opened; Israel could no more have entered, than they can now be kept from entering when the walls were fallen. What courses soever we take for our safety, it is good making God of our side. Neither men nor devils can hurt us against him; neither men nor angels can secure us from him. There was never so strange a siege as this of Jericho: here was no mount raised, no sword drawn, no engine planted, no pioneers undermining; here were trumpets sounded, but no enemy seen; here were armed men, but no stroke given: they must walk and not fight; seven several days must they pace about the walls, which they may not once look over, to see what was within. Doubtless these inhabitants of Jericho made themselves merry with this sight: when they had stood six days upon their walls, and beheld none but a walking enemy; What, say they, could Israel find no walk to breathe them with, but about our walls? Have they not travelled enough in their forty years' pilgrimage, but they must stretch their limbs in this circle? Surely if their eyes were engines, our wall could not stand: we see they are good footmen; but when shall we try their hands? What, do these vain men think Jericho will be won with looking at? or do they only come to count how may paces it is about our city? If this be their manner of siege, we shall have no great cause to fear the sword of Israel. Wicked men think God in jest, when he is preparing for their judgment. The Almighty hath ways and counsels of his own, utterly unlike to ours; which, because our reason cannot reach, we are ready to condemn as foolishness and impossibility. With us, there is no way to victory but fighting, and the strongest carries the spoil: God can give victory to the feet, as well as to the hands; and, when he will, makes weakness no disadvantage. What should we do but follow God through by-ways, and know that he will, in spite of nature, lead us to our end?

All the men of war must compass the city; yet it was not the presence of the great warriors of Israel that threw down the walls of Jericho. Those foundations were not so slightly laid, as that they could not endure either a look, or a march, or a battery. It was the ark of God whose presence demolished the walls of that wicked city. The same power that drave back the waters of Jordan before, and afterwards laid Dagon on the floor, cast down all those forts. The priests bear on their shoulders that mighty engine of God, before which those walls, if they had been of molten brass, could not stand. Those spiritual wickednesses, yea, those gates of hell, which to nature are utterly invincible, by the power of the word of God (which he hath committed to the carriage of his weak servants) are overthrown, and triumphed over. Thy ark, O God, hath been long amongst us; how is it that the walls of our corruptions stand still unruined? It hath gone before us, his priests have carried it: we have not followed it, our hearts have not attended it; and therefore, how mighty soever it is in itself, yet to us it hath not been so powerful as it would.

Seven days together they walked this round; they made this, therefore, their Sabbath-day's journey; and who knows whether the last and longest walk, which brought victory to Israel, were not on this day? Not long before, an Israelite is stoned to death, for but gathering a few sticks that day: now, all the host of Israel must walk about the walls of a large and populous city, and yet do not violate the day. God's precept is the rule of the justice and holiness of all our actions. Or was it, for that revenge upon God's enemies is a holy work, and such as God vouchsafes to privilege with his own day? or because, when we have undertaken the exploits of God, he will abide no intermission till we have fulfilled them? He allows us to breathe, not to break off, till we have finished.

It had been as easy for God to have given this success to their first day's walk; yea to their first pace, or their first sight of Jericho; yet he will not give it, until the end of their seven days' toil. It is the pleasure of God to hold us both in work, and in expectation; and though he require our continual endeavours for the subduing of our corruptions, during the six days of our life, yet we shall never find it perfectly effected till the very evening of our last day. In the meantime, it must content us that we are in our walk, and that these walls cannot stand, when we come to the measure and number of our perfection. A good heart groans under the sense of his infirmities, fain would be rid of them, and strives and prays: but when he hath all done, until the end of the seventh day it cannot be. If a stone or two moulder off from these walls, in the meantime, that is all; but the foundations will not be removed till then.

When we hear of so great a design as the miraculous winning of a mighty city, who would not look for some glorious means to work it? When we hear that the ark of God must besiege Jericho, who would not look for some royal equipage? But behold, here seven priests must go before it, with seven trumpets of ram's horns. The Israelites had trumpets of silver, which God had appointed for the use of assembling and dissolving the congregation, for war, and for peace: now I do not hear them called for; but instead thereof, trumpets of rams' horns, base for the matter, and not loud for sound; the shortness and equal measure of those instruments could not afford either shrillness of noise, or variety. How mean and homely are those means which God commonly uses in the most glorious works! No doubt the citizens of Jericho answered this dull alarm of theirs from their walls with other instruments of louder report and more martial ostentation: and the vulgar Israelites thought, we have as clear and as costly trumpets as theirs; yet no man dares offer to sound the better, when the worse are commanded. If we find the ordinances of God poor and weak, let it content us that they are of his own choosing, and such as whereby he will so much more honour himself, as they in themselves are more inglorious. Not the outside, but the efficacy, is it that God cares for.

No ram of iron could have been so forcible for battery, as these rams' horns: for when they sounded long, and were seconded with the shout of the Israelites, all the walls of Jericho fell down at once. They made the heavens ring with their shout: but the ruin of those walls drowned their voice, and gave a pleasant kind of horror to the Israelites. The earth shook under them with the fall; but the hearts of the inhabitants shook yet more. Many of them, doubtless, were slain with those walls wherein they had trusted. A man might see death in the faces of all the rest that remained, who now, being half dead with astonishment, expected the other half from the sword of their enemies. They had now neither means nor will to resist; for if only one breach had been made (as it uses in other sieges) for the entrance of the enemy, perhaps new supplies of defendants might have made it up with their carcases: but now that, at once, Jericho is turned to a plain field, every Israelite, without resistance, might run to the next booty; and the throats of their enemies seemed to invite their swords to a despatch.

If but one Israelite had knocked at the gates of Jericho, it might have been thought their hand had helped to the victory. Now, that God may have all the glory, without the show of any rival, yea, of any means, they do but walk and shout, and the walls give way. He cannot abide to part with any honour from himself. As he doth all things, so he would be acknowledged.

They shout all at once. It is the presence of God's ark, and our conjoined prayers, that are effectual to the beating down of wickedness. They may not shout till they be bidden. If we will be unseasonable in our good actions, we may hurt, and not benefit ourselves.

Every living thing in Jericho—man, woman, child, cattle—must die. Our folly would think this merciless; but there can be no mercy in injustice, and nothing but injustice in not fulfilling the charge of God.

The death of malefactors, the condemnation of wicked men, seem harsh to us; but we must learn of God, that there is a punishing mercy. Cursed be that mercy that opposes the God of mercy.

Yet was not Joshua so intent upon the slaughter, as not to be mindful of God's part and Rahab's. First, he gives charge, under a curse, of reserving all the treasure for God; then of preserving the family of Rahab. Those two spies that received life from her, now return it to her, and hers: they call at the window with the red cord, and send up news of life to her, the same way which they received theirs. Her house is no part of Jericho: neither may fire be set to any building of that city, till Rahab and her family be set safe without the host. The actions of our faith and charity will be sure to pay us; if late, yet surely. Now Rahab finds what it is to believe God; while out of an impure idolatrous city, she is transplanted into the church of God, and made a mother of a royal and holy posterity.

CONTEMPLATION IV.—OF ACHAN.

WHEN the walls of Jericho were fallen, Joshua charged the Israelites but with two precepts: of sparing Rahab's house, and of abstaining from that treasure which was anathematized to God: and one of them is broken; as in the entrance to paradise, but one tree was forbidden, and that was eaten of. God had provided for our weakness in the paucity of commands; but our innocency stands not so much in having few precepts, as in keeping those we have. So much more guilty are we in the breach of the one, as we are more favoured in the number.

They needed no command to spare no living thing in Jericho; but to spare the treasure, no command was enough. Impartiality of execution is easier to perform, than contempt of these worldly things; because we are more prone to covet for ourselves, than to pity others. Had Joshua bidden save the men, and divide the treasure, his charge had been more plausible, than now to kill the men and save the treasure; or, if they must kill, earthly minds would more gladly shed their enemies' blood for a booty, than out of obedience, for the glory of their Maker. But now it is good reason, since God threw down those walls, and not they, that both the blood of that wicked city should be spilt to him, not to their own revenge; and that the treasure should be reserved for his use, not for theirs. Who but a miscreant can grudge that God should serve himself of his own? I cannot blame the rest of Israel, if they were well pleased with their conditions; only one Achan troubles the peace, and his sin is imputed to Israel. The innocence of so many thousand Israelites is not so forcible to excuse his one sin, as his one sin is to taint all Israel.

A lewd man is a pernicious creature: that he damns his own soul, is the least part of his mischief; he commonly draws vengeance upon a thousand, either by the desert of his sin, or by the infection. Who would not have hoped that the same God, which for ten righteous men would have spared the five wicked cities, should not have been content to drown one sin in the obedience of so many righteous? But so venomous is sin, especially when it lights among God's people, that one drachm of it is able to infect the whole mass of Israel.

O righteous people of Israel, that had but one Achan! How had their late circumcision cut away the unclean foreskin of their disobedience! How had the blood of their paschal lamb scoured their souls from covetous desires! The world was well mended with them, since their stubborn murmurings in the desert. Since the death of Moses, and the government of Joshua, I do not find them in any disorder. After that the law hath brought us under the conduct of the true Jesus, our sins are more rare, and ourselves are more conscionable. While we are under the law, we do not so keep it, as when we are delivered from it: our Christian freedom is more holy than our servitude. Then have the sacraments of God their due effect, when their receipt purgeth us from our old sins, and makes our conversation clean and spiritual.

Little did Joshua know that there was any sacrilege committed by Israel. That sin is not half cunning enough that hath not learned secrecy. Joshua was a vigilant leader, yet some sins will escape him. Only that eye which is every where, finds us out in our close wickedness. It is no blame to authority that some sins are secretly committed: the holiest congregation or family may be blemished with some malefactors. It is just blame, that open sins are not punished: we shall wrong government, if we shall expect the reach of it should be infinite. He therefore, which, if he had known the offence, would have sent up prayers and tears to God, now sends spies for a further discovery of Ai; they return with news of the weakness of their adversaries; and, as contemning their paucity, persuade Joshua that a wing of Israel is enough to overshadow this city of Ai. The Israelites were so flushed with their former victory, that now they think no walls or men can stand before them. Good success lifts up the heart with too much confidence; and, while it dissuades men from doing their best, ofttimes disappoints them. With God, the mean can never be too weak; without him, never strong enough.

It is not good to contemn an impotent enemy. In this second battle the Israelites are beaten. It was not the fewness of their assailants that overthrew them, but the sin that lay lurking at home. If all the host of Israel had set upon this poor village of Ai, they had been all equally discomfited: the wedge of Achan did more fight against them, than all the swords of the Canaanites. The victories of God go not by strength, but by innocence.

Doubtless these men of Ai insulted in this foil of Israel, and said, Lo, these are the men, from whose presence the waters of Jordan ran back; now they run as fast away from ours. These are they, before whom the walls of Jericho fell down; now they are fallen as fast before us. And all their neighbours took heart from this victory. Wherein, I doubt not but, besides the punishment of Israel's sin, God intended the further obduration of the Canaanites: like as some skilful player loses on purpose at the beginning of the game, to draw on the more abetments. The news of their overthrow spread as far as the fame of their speed; and every city of Canaan could say, Why not we as well as Ai?

But good Joshua, that succeeded Moses, no less in the care of God's glory than in his government, is much dejected with this event. He rends his clothes, falls on his face, casts dust upon his head, and, as if he had learned of his master how to expostulate with God, says, "What wilt thou do to thy mighty name?"

That Joshua might see God took no pleasure to let the Israelites lie dead upon the earth before their enemies, himself is taxed for but lying all day upon his face, before the ark. All his expostulations are answered in one word: "Get thee up; Israel hath sinned." I do not hear God say, Lie still, and mourn for the sin of Israel. It is to no purpose to pray against punishment, while the sin continues. And though God loves to be sued to, yet he holds our requests unseasonable, till there be care had of satisfaction. When we have risen, and redressed sin, then may we fall down for pardon.

Victory is in the free hand of God, to dispose where he will; and no man can marvel, that the dice of war run ever with hazard on both sides: so as God needed not to have given any other reason of this discomfiture of Israel, but his own pleasure; yet Joshua must now know, that Israel, which before prevailed for their faith, is beaten for their sin. When we are crossed in just and holy quarrels, we may well think there is some secret evil, unrepented of, which God would punish in us; which, though we see not, yet he so hates, that he will rather be wanting to his own cause, than not revenge it. When we go about any enterprise of God, it is good to see that our hearts be clear from any pollution of sin; and when we are thwarted in our hopes, it is our best course to ransack ourselves, and to search for some sin hid from us in our bosom, but open to the view of God.

The oracle of God, which told him a great offence was committed, yet reveals not the person. It had been as easy for him to have named the man, as the crime. Neither doth Joshua request it; but refers that discovery to such a means, as whereby the offender, finding himself singled out by the lot, might be most convinced. Achan thought he might have lain as close in all that throng of Israel, as the wedge of gold lay in his tent. The same hope of secrecy, which moved him to sin, moved him to confidence in his sin: but now, when he saw the lot fall upon his tribe, he began to start a little; when upon his family, he began to change countenance; when upon his household, to tremble and fear; when upon his person, to be utterly confounded in himself. Foolish men think to run away with their privy sins, and say, Tush, no eye shall see me; but, when they think themselves safest, God pulls them out with shame. The man that hath escaped justice, and now is lying down in death, would think, My shame shall never be disclosed; but, before men and angels, shall he be brought on the scaffold, and find confusion as sure as late.

What needed any other evidence, when God had accused Achan? Yet Joshua will have the sin out of his mouth, in whose heart it was hatched: "My son, I beseech thee, give glory to God." Whom God had convinced as a malefactor, Joshua beseeches as a son. Some hot spirit would have said, Thou wretched traitor! how hast thou pilfered from thy God, and shed the blood of so many Israelites, and caused the host of Israel to show their backs, with dishonour, to the heathen? Now shall we fetch this sin out of thee with tortures, and plague thee with a condign death. But, like the disciple of Him whose servant he was, he meekly entreats that which he might have extorted by violence: "My son, I beseech thee." Sweetness of compellation is a great help towards the good entertainment of an admonition: roughness and rigour many times harden those hearts, which meekness would have melted to repentance. Whether we sue, or convince, or reprove, little good is gotten by bitterness. Detestation of the sin may well stand with favour to the person; and these two not distinguished, cause great wrong, either in our charity or justice; for either we uncharitably hate the creature of God or unjustly affect the evil of men. Subjects are, as they are called, sons to the magistrate. All Israel was not only of the family, but as of the loins of Joshua. Such must be the corrections, such the provisions of governors, as for their children; as again, the obedience and love of subjects must be filial.

God has glorified himself sufficiently, in finding out the wickedness of Achan; neither needs he honour from men, much less from sinners. They can dishonour him by their iniquities; but what recompense can they give him for their wrongs? Yet Joshua says, " My son, give glory to God." Israel should now see, that the tongue of Achan did justify God in his lot. The confession of our sins doth no less honour God, than his glory is blemished by their commission. Who would not be glad to redeem the honour of his Redeemer with his own shame?

The lot of God, and the mild words of Joshua, won Achan to accuse himself, ingenuously, impartially. A storm, perhaps, would not have done that which a sunshine had done. If Achan had come in uncalled, and, before any question made, out of an honest remorse, had brought in his sacrilegious booty, and cast himself and it at the foot of Joshua, doubtless Israel had prospered, and his sin had carried away pardon; now he hath gotten thus much thank, that he is not a desperate sinner. God will once wring from the conscience of wicked men their own indictments; they have not more carefully hid their sin, than they shall one day freely proclaim their own shame.

Achan's confession, though it were late, yet was it free and full: for he doth not only acknowledge the act, but the ground of his sin : " I saw, and coveted, and took." The eye betrayed the heart, and that the hand, and now all conspire in the offence. If we list not to flatter ourselves, this hath been the order of our crimes. Evil is uniform ; and, beginning at the senses, takes the inmost fort of the soul, and then arms our own outward forces against us. This shall once be the lascivious man's song, " I saw, and coveted, and took ;" this the thief's, this the idolater's, this the glutton's and drunkard's : all these receive their death by the eye. But, O foolish Achan, with what eyes didst thou look upon that spoil, which thy fellows saw and contemned ! Why couldst thou not before, as well as now, see shame hid under that gay Babylonish garment, and a heap of stones covered with those shekels of silver ? The over-prizing and over-desiring of these earthly things, carries us into all mischief, and hides from us the sight of God's judgments. Whosoever desires the glory of metals, or of gay clothes, or honour, cannot be innocent.

Well might Joshua have proceeded to the execution of him, whom God and his own mouth accused: but, as one that thought no evidence could be too strong, in a case that was capital, he sends to see whether there was as much truth in the confession, as there was falsehood in the stealth. Magistrates and judges must pace slowly and sure in the punishment of offenders. Presumptions are not ground enough for the sentence of death; no, not, in some cases, the confessions of the guilty. It is no warrant for the law to wrong a man, that he hath before wronged himself. There is less ill in sparing an offender, than in punishing the innocent.

Who would not have expected, since the confession of Achan was ingenuous, and his pillage still found entire, that his life should have been pardoned? But here was, Confess and die: he had been too long sick of this disease, to be recovered. Had his confession been speedy and free, it had saved him. How dangerous it is to suffer sin to lie fretting into the soul, which, if it were washed off betimes with our repentance, could not kill us ! In mortal offences, the course of human justice is not stayed by our penitence. It is well for our souls that we have repented ; but the laws of men take not notice of our sorrow. I know not whether the death or the tears of a malefactor, be a better sight. The censures of the church are wiped off with weeping, not the penalties of laws.

Neither is Achan alone called forth to death, but all his family, all his substance. The actor alone doth not smart with sacrilege: all that concerns him is enwrapped in the judgment. Those that defile their hands with holy goods, are enemies to their own flesh and blood. God's first revenges are so much the more fearful, because they must be exemplary.

CONTEMPLATION V. — THE GIBEONITES.

THE news of Israel's victory had flown over all the mountains and valleys of Canaan ; and yet those heathenish kings and people are mustered together against them. They might have seen themselves in Jericho and Ai, and have well perceived it was not an arm of flesh that they must resist ; yet they gather their forces and say, Tush, we shall speed better. It is madness in a man not to be warned, but to run upon the point of those judgments wherewith he sees others miscarry, and not to believe till he cannot recover. Our assent is purchased too late, when we have overstayed prevention, and trust to that experience which we cannot live to redeem.

Only the Hivites are wiser than their fellows, and will rather yield and live. Their intelligence was not diverse from the rest ; all had equally heard of the mi-

I

raculous conduct and success of Israel: but their resolution was diverse. As Rahab saved her family in the midst of Jericho, so these four cities preserved themselves in the midst of Canaan; and both of them by believing what God would do. The efficacy of God's marvellous works is not in the acts themselves, but in our apprehension: some are overcome with those motives which others have contemned for weak.

Had these Gibeonites joined with the forces of all their neighbours, they had perished in their common slaughter; if they had not gone away by themselves, death had met them. It may have more pleasure, it cannot have so much safety, to follow the multitude. If examples may lead us, the greatest part shuts out God upon earth, and is excluded from God elsewhere. Some few poor Hivites yield to the church of God, and escape the condemnation of the world. It is very like, their neighbours flouted at this base submission of the Gibeonites, and, out of their terms of honour, scorned to beg life of an enemy, while they were out of the compass of mercy; but, when the bodies of these proud Jebusites and Perizites lay strewed upon the earth, and the Gibeonites survived, whether was more worthy of scorn and insultation?

If the Gibeonites had stayed till Israel had besieged their cities, their yieldance had been fruitless: now they make an early peace, and are preserved. There is no wisdom in staying till a judgment come home to us; the only way to avoid it, is to meet it half way. These is the same remedy of war and of danger. To provoke an enemy in his own borders is the best stay of invasion; and to solicit God betimes, in a manifest danger, is the best antidote for death.

I commend their wisdom in seeking peace; I do not commend their falsehood in the manner of seeking it: who can look for any better of pagans! But as the faith of Rahab is so rewarded, that her lie is not punished, so the fraud of these Gibeonites is not an equal match of their belief, since the name of the Lord God of Israel brought them to this suit of peace.

Nothing is found fitter to deceive God's people, than a counterfeit copy of age. Here are old sacks, old bottles, old shoes, old garments, old bread. The Israelites, that had worn one suit forty years, seemed new clad in comparison of them. It is no new policy, that Satan would beguile us with a vain colour of antiquity, clothing falsehood in rags. Errors are never the older for their patching. Corruption can do the same that time would do: we may make age as well as suffer it. These Gibeonites did tear their bottles and shoes, and clothes, and made them naught, that they might seem old: so do the false patrons of new errors. If we be caught with this Gibeonite stratagem, it is a sign we have not consulted with God.

The sentence of death was gone out against all the inhabitants of Canaan. These Hivites acknowledge the truth and judgments of God, and yet seek to escape by a league with Israel. The general denunciations of the vengeance of God enwrap all sinners; yet may we not despair of mercy. If the secret counsel of the Almighty had not designed these men to live, Joshua could not have been deceived with their league. In the generality there is no hope. Let us come, in the old rags of our vileness, to the true Joshua, and make our truce with him: we may live, yea, we shall live. Some of the Israelites suspect the fraud; and, notwithstanding all their old garments and provisions, can say, " It may be, thou dwellest amongst us." If Joshua had continued this doubt, the Gibeonites had torn their bottles in vain. In cases and persons unknown, it is safe not to be too credulous. Charity itself will allow suspicion, where we have seen no cause to trust.

If these Hivites had not put on new faces with their old clothes, they had surely changed countenance when they heard this argument of the Israelites, " It may be, thou dwellest among us; how then can I make a league with thee?" They had, perhaps, hoped their submission would not have been refused, wheresoever they had dwelt: but, lest their neighbourhood might be a prejudice, they come disguised; and now hear, that their nearness of abode was an unremoveable bar of peace. It was quarrel enough that they were Canaanites: God had forbidden both the league and the life of the native inhabitants. He that calls himself the God of peace, proclaims himself the God of hosts: and not to fight where he hath commanded, is to break the peace with God, while we nourish it with men. Contention with brethren is not more hateful to him, than leagues with idolaters. The condition that he hath set to our peace, is our possibility and power: that falls not within the possibility of our power, which we cannot do lawfully.

What a smooth tale did these Gibeonites tell for themselves, of the remoteness of their country, the motives of their journey, the consultation of their elders, the ageing of their provisions by the way: that it might seem not only safe, but deserved on their parts, that they should be admitted to a peace so far sought, and purchased with so much toil and importunity. Their clothes and their tongues agreed together; and both disagree from the truth. Deceit is ever lightly wrapped up in plausibility of words; as fair faces oftentimes hide much unchastity. But this guile sped the better, because it was clad with much plainness: for who would have suspected, that clouted shoes and ragged coats could have covered so much subtilty? The case seemed so clear, that the Israelites thought it needless to consult with the mouth of the Lord. Their own eyes and ears were called only to counsel; and now their credulity hath drawn them into inconvenience.

There is no way to convince the Gibeonitish pretences of antiquity, but to have recourse to the oracle of God. Had this been advised with, none of these false rags had shamed the church of God. Whether in our practice or judgment, this direction cannot fail; whereas what we take upon the words of men, proves ever either light or false wares.

The facility of Israel had led them into a league, to an oath, for the safety of the Gibeonites: and now, within three days, they find both their neighbourhood and deceit. Those old shoes of theirs would easily hold to carry them back to their home. The march of a great army is easy; yet within three days the Israelites were before their cities. Joshua might now have taken advantage of their own words, to dissolve his league; and have said, Ye are come from a far country; these cities are near: these are not therefore the people to whom we are engaged by our promise and oath; and if these cities be yours, yet ye are not yourselves. Erewhile ye were strangers; now ye are Hivites born, and dwelling in the midst of Canaan: we will therefore destroy these cities near hand, and do you save your people afar off. It would seem very questionable, whether Joshua needed to hold himself bound to this oath; for fraudulent conventions oblige not; and Israel had put in a direct caveat of their vicinity: yet dare not Joshua and the princes trust to shifts, for the eluding their oath, but must faithfully perform what they have rashly promised.

Joshua's heart was clear from any intention of a league with a Canaanite, when he gave his oath to these disguised strangers: yet he durst neither repeal it himself, neither do I hear him sue to Eleazar the high-priest to dispense with it, but takes himself tied to the very strict words of his oath, not to his own purpose. His tongue had bound his heart and hands, so as neither might stir; lest, while he was curious of fulfilling the word of God, he should violate the oath of God. And if the Gibeonites had not known these holy bonds indissoluble, they neither had been so importunate to obtain their vow, nor durst they have trusted it, being obtained. If either dispensation with oaths, or equivocation in oaths, had been known in the world, or at least approved, these Gibeonites had not lived, and Israel had slain them without sin. Either Israel wanted skill, or our reservers honesty.

The multitude of Israel, when they came to the walls of these four exempted cities, itched to be at the spoil. Not out of a desire to fulfil God's commandment, but to enrich themselves, would they have fallen upon these Hivites: they thought all lost that fell beside their fingers. The wealthy city of Jericho was first altogether interdicted them: the walls and houses either fell or must be burnt, the men and cattle killed, the goods and treasure confiscate to God. Achan's booty shows, that that city was both rich and proud; yet Israel might be no whit the better for them, carrying away nothing but empty victory: and now four other cities must be exempted from their pillage. Many an envious look did Israel therefore cast upon these walls; and many bitter words did they cast out against their princes, the enemies of their gain, whether for swearing, or for that they would not forswear. But, howsoever, the princes might have said, in a return to their fraud, We swore indeed to you, but not to the people; yet, if any Israelite had but pulled down one stone from their walls, or shed one drop of Gibeonitish blood, he had no less plagued all Israel for perjury than Achan had before plagued them for sacrilege. The sequel shows how God would have taken it; for when, three hundred years after, Saul (perhaps forgetting the vow of his forefathers) slew some of these Gibeonites, although out of a well-meant zeal, all Israel smarted for the fact, with a three years' famine, and that in David's reign, who received this oracle from God: "It is for Saul, and for his bloody house, because he slew the Gibeonites." Neither could this wrong be expiated, but by the blood of Saul's seven sons, hanged up at the very court gates of their father.

Joshua and the princes had promised them life; they promised them not liberty: no covenant was passed against their servitude. It was just, therefore, with the rulers of Israel, to make slavery the price both of their lives and their deceit. The Israelites had themselves been drudges, if the Gibeonites had not beguiled them and lived. The old rags, therefore, wherewith they came disguised, must now be their best suits, and their life must be toilsomely spent in hewing of wood and drawing of water for all Israel. How dear is life to our nature, that men can be content to purchase it with servitude! It is the wisdom of God's children to make good use of their oversights. The rash oath of Israel proves their advantage. Even wicked men gain by the outside of good actions; good men make a benefit of their sins.

BOOK IX.

CONTEMPLATION I.—THE RESCUE OF GIBEON.

THE life of the Gibeonites must cost them servitude from Israel, and dangers from their neighbours. If Joshua will but sit still, the deceit of the Gibeonites shall be revenged by his enemies. Five kings are up in arms against them, and are ready to pay their fraud with violence. What should these poor men do? If they make not their peace, they die by strangers; if they do make their peace with foreigners, they must die by neighbours. There is no course that threatens not some danger. We have sped well, if our choice hath lighted upon the easiest inconvenience.

If these Hivites have sinned against God, against Israel; yet what have they done to their neighbours? I hear of no treachery, no secret information, no attempt. I see no sin but their league with Israel, and their life; yet, for aught we find, they were free men, no way either obliged or obnoxious. As Satan, so wicked men cannot abide to lose any of their community. If a convert come home, the angels welcome him with songs, the devils follow him with uproar and fury, his old partners with scorns and obloquy.

I find these neighbour princes half dead with fear, and yet they can find time to be sick of envy. Malice in a wicked heart is the king of passions; all other vail and bow when it comes in place. Even their own life was not so dear to them as revenge. Who would not rather have looked that these kings should have tried to have followed the copy of this league? Or, if their fingers did itch to fight, why did they not rather think of a defensive war against Israel, than an offensive against the Gibeonites? Gibeon was strong, and would not be won without blood; yet these Amorites, which at their best were too weak for Israel, would spend their forces before-hand on their neighbours. Here was a strong hatred in weak breasts: they feared, and yet began to fight; they feared Israel, yet began to fight with Gibeon. If they had sat still, their destruction had not been so sudden. The malice of the wicked hastens the pace of their own judgment. No rod is so fit for a mischievous man as his own.

Gibeon and these other cities of the Hivites, had no king; and none yielded and escaped but they. Their elders consulted before for their league; neither is there any challenge sent to the king, but to the city. And now these five kings of the Amorites have unjustly compacted against them. Sovereignty abused is a great spur to courage. The conceit of authority, in great persons, many times lies in the way of their own safety, while it will not let them stoop to the ordinary courses of inferiors. Hence it is, that heaven is peopled with so few great ones; hence it is, that true contentment seldom dwells high, while meaner men of humble spirits enjoy both earth and heaven.

The Gibeonites had well proved, that though they wanted a head, yet they wanted not wit; and now the same wit that won Joshua and Israel to their friendship and protection, teacheth them to make use of those they had won. If they had not more trusted Joshua than their walls, they had never stolen that league; and when should they have use of their new protectors, but now that they were assailed? Whither should we fly, but to our Joshua, when the powers of darkness, like mighty Amorites, have besieged us? If ever we will send up our prayers to him, it will be when we are beleaguered with evils. If we trust to our own resistance, we cannot stand; we cannot miscarry, if we trust to his. In vain shall we send to our Joshua in these straits, if we have not before come to him in our freedom.

Which of us would not have thought Joshua had a good pretence for his forbearance, and have said, You have stolen your league with me; why do you expect help from him whom ye have deceived? All that we promised you was a sufferance to live. Enjoy what we promised: we will not take your life from you. Hath your faithfulness deserved to expect more than our covenant? We never promised to hazard our lives for you; to give you life with the loss of our own. But that good man durst not construe his own covenant to such an advantage. He knew little difference betwixt killing them with his own sword, and the sword of an Amorite: whosoever should give the blow, the murder would be his. Even permission, in those things we may remedy, makes us no less actors, than consent. Some men kill as much by looking on, as others by smiting. We are guilty of all the evil we might have hindered.

The noble disposition of Joshua, besides his engagement, will not let him forsake his new vassals: their confidence in him is argument enough to draw him into the field. The greatest obligation to a good mind is another's trust; which to disappoint, were mercilessly perfidious. How much less shall our true Joshua fail the confidence of our faith! O my Saviour, if we send the messengers of our prayers to thee into thy Gilgal, thy mercy binds thee to relief. Never any soul miscarried that trusted thee. We may be wanting in our trust, our trust can never want success.

Speed in bestowing, doubles a gift; a benefit deferred, loses the thanks, and proves unprofitable. Joshua marches all night, and fights all day for the Gibeonites. They took not so much pains in coming to deceive him, as he in going to deliver them. It is the noblest victory to overcome evil with good. If his very Israelites had been in danger, he could have done no more. God and his Joshua make no difference betwixt Gibeonites Israelited, and his own natural people. All are Israelites whom he hath taken to league. We, strangers of the Gentiles, are now the true Jews. God never did more for the natural olive, than for that wild imp which he had graffed in. And as these Hivites could never be thankful enough to such a Joshua, no more can we to so gracious a Redeemer, who, forgetting our unworthiness, descended to our Gibeon, and rescued us from the powers of hell and death.

Joshua fought, but God discomfited the Amorites. The praise is to the workman, not to the instrument. Neither did God slay them only with Joshua's sword, but with his own hailstones; that now the Amorites may see both these revenges come from one hand. These bullets of God do not wound, but kill. It is no wonder than these five kings fly: they may soon run away from their hope, never from their horror. If they look behind, there is the sword of Israel, which they dare not turn upon, because God had taken their heart from them, before their life: if they look upwards, there is the hail-shot of God fighting against them out of heaven, which they can neither resist nor avoid.

If they had no enemy but Israel, they might hope to run away from death, since fear is a better footman than desire of revenge; but now, whithersoever they run, heaven will be about their heads. And now, all the reason that is left them, in this confusion of their thoughts, is to wish themselves well dead. There is no evasion, where God intends a revenge. We men have devised to imitate these instruments of death, and send forth deadly bullets out of a cloud of smoke; wherein yet as there is much danger, so much uncertainty; but this God, that discharges his ordnance from heaven, directs every shot to a head, and can as easily kill as shoot. "It is a fearful thing to fall into the hands of the living God." He hath more ways of vengeance than he hath creatures. The same heaven that sent forth water to the old world, fire to the Sodomites, lightning and thunderbolts to the Egyptians, sends out hailstones to the Amorites. It is a good care how we may not anger God; it is a vain study how we may fly from his judgments, when we have angered him: if we could run out of the world, even there shall we find his revenges far greater.

Was it not miracle enough that God did brain their adversaries from heaven, but that the sun and moon must stand still in heaven? It is not enough that the Amorites fly, but that the greatest planets of heaven must stay their own course, to witness and wonder at the discomfiture. For him, which gave them both being and motion, to bid them stand still, it seems no difficulty, although the rareness would deserve admiration; but for a man to command the chief stars of heaven (by whose influence he liveth), as the centurion would do his servant (Sun, stay in Gibeon, and moon stand still in Ajalon), it is more than a wonder. It was not Joshua, but his faith, that did this; not by way of precept, but of prayer: if I may not say, that the request of a faithful man, as we say of the great, commands. God's glory was that which Joshua aimed at: he knew that all the world must needs be witnesses of that which the eye of the world stood still to see. Had he respected but the slaughter of the Amorites, he knew the hailstones could do that alone; the sun needed not stand still to direct that cloud to persecute them: but the glory of the slaughter was sought by Joshua, that he might send up that whence those hailstones and that victory came. All the earth might see the sun and moon; all could not see the cloud of hail, which because of that heavy burden flew but low. That all nations might know the same hand commands both in earth, in the clouds, in heaven, Joshua now prays, that he, which disheartened his enemies upon earth, and smote them from the cloud, would stay the sun and moon in heaven. God never got himself so much honour by one day's work amongst the heathen: and when was it more fit than now, when five heathen kings are joined against him?

The sun and the moon were the ordinary gods of the world; and who would not but think, that their standing still but one hour should be the ruin of nature? And now all nations shall well see, that there is a higher than their highest; that their gods are but servants to the God whom themselves should serve; at whose pleasure both they and nature shall stand at once. If that God which meant to work this miracle had not raised up his thoughts to desire it, it had been a blameable presumption, which now is a faith worthy of admiration. To desire a miracle without cause, is a tempting of God. O powerful God, that can effect this! O power of faith, that can obtain it! What is there that God cannot do? and what is there which God can do, that faith cannot do?

CONTEMPLATION II. — THE ALTAR OF THE REUBENITES.

REUBEN and Gad were the first that had an inheritance assigned them, yet they must enjoy it last. So it oft falls out in the heavenly Canaan: the first in title are last in possession. They had their lot assigned them beyond Jordan; which, though it were allotted them in peace, must be purchased with their war; that must be done for their brethren, which needed not be done for themselves. They must yet still fight, and fight foremost, that, as they had the first patrimony, they might endure the first encounter. I do not hear them say, This is our share; let us sit down and enjoy it quietly; fight who will for the rest: but, when they knew their own portion, they leave wives and children to take possession, and march armed before their brethren, till they had conquered all Canaan. Whether should we more commend their courage or their charity? Others were moved to fight with hope; they only with love: they could not win more; they might lose themselves: yet they will fight, both for that they had something, and that their brethren might have. Thankfulness and love can do more with God's children, than desire to merit or necessity. No true Israelite can (if he might choose) abide to sit still beyond Jordan, when all his brethren are in the field. Now, when all this war of God was ended, and all Canaan is both won and divided, they return to their own; yet not till they were dismissed by Joshua. All the sweet attractions of their private love cannot hasten their pace. If heaven be never so sweet to us, yet may we not run from this earthly warfare, till our great Captain shall please to discharge us. If these Reubenites had departed sooner, they had been recalled, if not as cowards, surely as fugitives: now they are sent back with victory and blessing. How safe and happy it is to attend both the call and the despatch of God!

Being returned in peace to their home, their first care is not for trophies, nor for houses, but for an altar to God; an altar, not for sacrifice, which had been abominable, but for a memorial what God they served. The first care of true Israelites must be the safety of religion. The world, as it is inferior in worth, so must it be in respect. He never knew God aright, that can abide any competition with his Maker.

The rest of the tribes no sooner hear news of their new altar, but they gather to Shiloh to fight against them. They had scarce breathing from the Canaanitish war, and now they will go fight with their brethren: if their brethren will, as they suspected, turn idolaters, they cannot hold them any other than Canaanites. The Reubenites and their fellows had newly settled the rest of Israel in their possessions; and now, ere they can be warm in their seats, Israel is up in arms to thrust them out of their own. The hatred of their suspected idolatry makes them forget either their blood, or their benefits. Israel says, These men were the first in ' our battles, and shall be the first in our revenge: they fought well for us; we will try how they can fight for themselves. What if they were our champions? their revolt from God hath lost them the thank of their former labours: their idolatry shall make them, of brethren, adversaries; their

ALTAR OF THE REUBENITES.

own blood shall give handsel to their new altar. O noble and religious zeal of Israel! Who would think these men the sons of them that danced about the molten calf? that consecrated an altar to that idol? Now they are ready to die or kill, rather than endure an altar without an idol. Every overture, in matter of religion, is worthy of suspicion, worthy of our speedy opposition. God looks for an early redress of the first beginnings of impiety. As in treasons or mutinies, wise statesmen find it safest to kill the serpent in the egg; so, in motions of spiritual alterations, one spoonful of water will quench that fire at first, which afterwards whole buckets cannot abate.

Yet do not these zealous Israelites run rashly and furiously upon their brethren, nor say, What need we expostulate? the fact is clear: what care we for words, when we see their altar? What can this mean, but either service to a false god, or division in the service of the true? There can be no excuse for so manifest a crime: why do we not rather think of punishment than satisfaction? But they send ere they go, and consult ere they execute. Phineas the son of Eleazar the priest, and ten princes, for every tribe one, are addressed both to inquire and dissuade: to inquire of the purpose of the fact; to dissuade from that which they imagined was purposed. Wisdom is a good guide to zeal, and only can keep it from running out into fury. If discretion do not hold in the reins, good intentions will both break their own necks, and the rider's: yea, which is strange, without this, the zeal of God may lead us from God.

Not only wisdom, but charity, moved them to this message. For, grant they had been guilty, must they perish unwarned? Peaceable means must first be used to recall them, ere violence be sent to persecute them. The old rule of Israel hath been, still to inquire of Abel. No good shepherd sends his dog to pull out the throat of his strayed sheep, but rather fetches it on his shoulders to the fold. Sudden cruelty stands not with religion. He which will not himself break the bruised reed, how will he allow us either to bruise the whole, or to break the bruised, or to burn the broken?

Neither yet was here more charity in sending, than uncharitableness in the misconstruction. They begin with a challenge, and charge their brethren deeply with transgression, apostasy, rebellion. I know not how two contrary qualities fall into love: it is not naturally suspicious, and yet many times suggests jealous fears of those we affect. If these Israelites had not loved their brethren, they would never have sent so far to restrain them; they had never offered them part of their own patrimony: if they had not been excessively jealous, they had not censured a doubtful action so sharply. They met at Shiloh, where the tabernacle was; but if they had consulted with the ark of God, they had saved both this labour, and this challenge. This case seemed so plain, that they thought advice needless: their inconsiderateness therefore brands their brethren with crimes whereof they were innocent, and makes themselves the only offenders. In cases which are doubtful and uncertain, it is safe either to suspend the judgment, or to pass it in favour; otherwise, a plain breach of charity in us shall be worse than a questionable breach of justice in another.

Yet this little gleam of their uncharitable love began at themselves: if they had not feared their own judgments in the offence of Reuben, I know not whether they had been so vehement. The fearful revenges of their brethren's sin are still in their eye. The wickedness of Peor stretched not so far as the plague. Achan sinned, and Israel was beaten; therefore, by just induction, they argue, " Ye rebel to-day against the Lord; to-morrow will the Lord be wroth with all the congregation." They still tremble at the vengeance passed, and find it time to prevent their own punishment, in punishing their brethren. God's proceedings have then their right use, when they are both carefully remembered, and made patterns of what he may do.

Had these Reubenites been as hot in their answer, as the Israelites were in their charge, here had grown a bloody war out of misprision: but now their answer is mild and moderate, and such as well showed, that though they were further from the ark, yet no less near to God. They thought in themselves, This act of ours, though it were well meant by us, yet might well be, by interpretation, scandalous; it is reason our mildness should give satisfaction for that offence which we have not prevented. Hereupon their answer was as pleasing, as their act was dangerous. Even in those actions whereby an offence may be occasioned, though not given, charity binds us to clear both our own name, and the conscience of others.

Little did the Israelites look for so good a ground of an action so suspicious: an altar without a sacrifice; an altar and no tabernacle; an altar without a precept, and yet not against God. It is not safe to measure all men's actions by our own conceit, but rather to think there may be a further drift and warrant of their act, than we can attain to see.

By that time the Reubenites have commented upon their own work, it appears as justifiable, as before offensive. What wisdom and religion is found in that altar, which before showed nothing but idolatry! This discourse of theirs is full both of reason and piety. We are severed by the river Jordan from the other tribes; perhaps hereafter our choice may exclude us from Israel. Posterity may peradventure say, Jordan is the bounds of all natural Israelites, the streams whereof never gave way to those beyond the river: if they had been ours, either in blood or religion, they would not have been sequestered in habitation. Doubtless, therefore, these men are the offspring of some strangers, which, by vicinity of abode, have gotten some tincture of our language, manners, religion: what have we to do with them? what have they to do with the tabernacle of God? Since, therefore, we may not either remove God's altar to us, or remove our patrimony to the altar, the pattern of the altar shall go with us, not for sacrifice, but for memorial, that both the posterity of the other Israelites may know we are no less derived from them, than this altar from theirs; and that our posterity may know, they pertain to that altar whereof this is the resemblance. There was no danger of the present; but posterity might both offer and receive prejudice, if this monument were not. It is a wise and holy care to prevent the dangers of ensuing times, and to settle religion upon the succeeding generations. As we affect to leave a perpetuity of our bodily issue, so much more to traduce piety with them. Do we not see good husbands set and plant those trees whereof their grandchildren shall receive the first-fruit and shade? Why are we less thrifty in leaving true religion entire to our children's children?

CONTEMPLATION III.—EHUD AND EGLON.

As every man is guilty of his own sorrow, these Israelites bred mischief to themselves. It was their mercy that plagued them with those Canaanites, which their obedience should have rooted out. If foolish pity be a more humane sin, yet it is no less dangerous than cruelty. Cruelty kills others; unjust pity kills ourselves. They had been lords alone of the promised land, if their commiseration had not overswayed their justice; and now their enemies are too cruel to them, in the just revenge of God, because they were too merciful. That God, which in his revealed will had commanded all the Canaanites to the slaughter, yet secretly gives over Israel to a toleration of some Canaanites, for their own punishment. He hath bidden us cleanse our hearts of all our corruptions; yet he will permit some of these thorns still in our sides, for exercise, for humiliation. If we could lay violent hands upon our sins, our souls should have peace: now our indulgence costs us many stripes, and many tears. What a continued circle is here of sins, judgments, repentance, deliverances? The conversation with idolaters taints them with sin; their sin draws on judgment; the smart of the judgment moves them to repentance; upon their repentance follows speedy deliverance; upon their peace and deliverance they sin again.

Othniel, Caleb's nephew, had rescued them from idolatry and servitude; his life, and their innocence and peace, ended together. How powerful the presence of one good man is in a church or state, is best found in his loss.

A man that is at once eminent in place and goodness, is like a stake in a hedge; pull that up, and all the rest are but loose and rotten sticks easily removed: or like the pillar of a vaulted roof, which either supports or ruins the building. Who would not think idolatry an absurd and unnatural thing? which as it hath the fewest inducements, so had also the most direct inhibitions from God; and yet, after all these warnings, Israel falls into it again. Neither affliction nor repentance can secure an Israelite from redoubling the worst sin, if he be left to his own frailty. It is no censuring of the truth of our present sorrow, by the event of a following miscarriage. The former cries of Israel to God were unfeigned, yet their present wickedness is abominable: "Let him that thinks he stands, take heed lest he fall."

No sooner had he said, Israel had rest, but he adds, They committed wickedness. The security of any people is the cause of their corruption. Standing waters soon grow noisome. While they were exercised with war, how scrupulous were they of the least intimation of idolatry! The news of a bare altar beyond Jordan drew them together for a revenge: now they are at peace with their enemies, they are at variance with God. It is both hard and happy not to be the worse with liberty. The sedentary life is most subject to diseases.

Rather than Israel shall want a scourge for their sin, God himself shall raise them up an enemy. Moab had no quarrel but his own ambition; but God meant by the ambition of the one part, to punish the idolatry of the other: his justice can make one sin the execution of another, whilst neither shall look for any other measure from him but judgment. The evil of the city is so his, that the instrument is not guiltless. Before, God had stirred up the king of Syria against Israel; now, the king of Moab; afterwards, the king of Canaan. He hath more variety of judgments, than there can be offences. If we have once made him our adversary, he shall be sure to make us adversaries enough, which shall revenge his quarrel whilst they prosecute their own.

Even those were idolaters, by whose hands God plagued the idolatries of Israel. In Moab, the same wickedness prospers, which in God's own people is punished. The justice of the Almighty can least brook evil in his own. The same heathen which provoked Israel to sin, shall scourge them for sinning. Our very profession hurts us, if we be not innocent.

No less than eighteen years did the rod of Moab rest upon the inheritance of God. Israel seems as born to servitude: they came from their bondage in the land of Egypt to serve in the land of promise. They had neglected God; now they are neglected of God: their sins have made them servants, whom the choice of God had made free, yea his first-born. Worthy are they to serve those men, whose false gods they had served, and to serve them always in thraldom, whom they have once served in idolatry. We may not measure the continuance of punishment by the time of the commission of sin: one minute's sin deserves a torment beyond all time.

Doubtless Israel was not so insensible of their own misery, as not to complain sooner than the end of eighteen years. The first hour they sighed for themselves, but now they cried unto God. The very purpose of affliction is to make us importunate. He hears the secret murmurs of our grief; yet will not seem to hear us, till our cries be loud and strong. God sees it best to let the penitent dwell for the time under their sorrows: he sees us sinking all the while, yet he lets us alone, till we be at the bottom; and when once we can say, " Out of the depths have I cried to thee;" instantly follows, " The Lord heard me." A vehement suitor cannot but be heard of God, whatsoever he asks. If our prayers want success, they want heart; their blessing is according to their vigour. We live in bondage to these spiritual Moabites, our own corruptions. It discontents us: but where are our strong cries unto the God of heavens? where are our tears? If we could passionately bemoan ourselves in him, how soon should we be more than conquerors? Some good motions we have to send up to him, but they faint in the way. We may call long enough, if we cry not to him.

The same hand that raised up Eglon against Israel, raised up also Ehud for Israel against Eglon. When that tyrant hath revenged God of his people, God will revenge his people of him. It is no privilege to be an instrument of God's vengeance by evil means. Though Eglon were an usurper, yet had Ehud been a traitor if God had not sent him. It is only in the power of him that makes kings, when they are once settled, to depose them. It is no more possible for our modern butchers of princes, to show they are employed by God, than to escape the revenge of God, in offering to do this violence, not being employed.

What a strange choice doth God make of an executioner! A man wanting of his right hand: either he had but one hand, or used but one, and that the worse, and the more unready. Who would not have thought both hands too little for such a work? or, if either might have been spared, how much rather the left? " God seeth not as man seeth." It is the ordinary way of the Almighty to make choice of the unlikeliest means. The instruments of God must not be measured by their own power or aptitude, but by the will of the agent. Though Ehud had no hands, he that employed him had enabled him to this slaughter. In human things, it is good to look to the means: in divine, to the worker. No means are to be contemned, that God will use: no means to be trusted, that man will use without him.

It is good to be suspicious, where is least show of danger, and most appearance of favour. This left-handed man comes with a present in his hand, but a dagger under his skirt. The tyrant, besides service, looked for gifts; and now receives death in his bribe: neither God nor men do always give where they love. How oft doth God give extraordinary illumination, power of miracles, besides wealth and honour, where he hates! So do men too oft accompany their curses with presents; either lest an enemy should hurt us, or that we may hurt them. The intention is the favour in gifts, and not the substance.

Ehud's faith supplies the want of his hand. Where God intends success, he lifts up the heart with resolutions of courage and contempt of danger. What indifferent beholder of this project would not have condemned it, as unlikely to speed! to see a maimed man go alone to a great king, in the midst of all his troops; to single him out from all witnesses; to set upon him with one hand in his own parlour, where his courtiers might have heard the least exclamation, and have come in, if not to the rescue, yet to the revenge! Every circumstance is full of improbabilities. Faith evermore overlooks the difficulties of the way, and bends her eyes only to the certainty of the end. In this intestine slaughter of our tyrannical corruptions, when we cast our eyes upon ourselves, we might well despair. Alas! what can our left hands do against these spiritual wickednesses! But, when we see who hath both commanded and undertaken to prosper those holy designs, how can we misdoubt the success? "I can do all things through him that strengthens me."

When Ehud had obtained the convenient secrecy both of the weapon and place, now with a confident forehead he approaches the tyrant, and salutes him with a true and awful preface to so important an act: "I have a message to thee from God." Even Ehud's poniard was God's message: not only the vocal admonitions, but also the real judgments of God, are his errands to the world. He speaks to us in rain and waters, in sicknesses and famine, in unseasonable times and inundations: these are the secondary messages of God; if we will not hear the first, we must hear these to our cost.

I cannot but wonder at the devout reverence of this heathen prince. He sat in his chair of state: the unwieldiness of his fat body was such, that he could not rise with readiness and ease; yet no sooner doth he hear news of a message from God, but he rises up from his throne, and reverently attends the tenor thereof. Though he had no superior to control him, yet he cannot abide to be unmannerly in the business of God.

This man was an idolater, a tyrant; yet what outward respects doth he give to the true God? External ceremonies of piety, and compliments of devotion, may well be found with falsehood in religion. They are a good shadow of truth where it is; but where it is not, they are the very body of hypocrisy. He that had risen up in arms against God's people, and the true worship of God, now rises up in reverence to his name. God would have liked well to have had less of his courtesy, more of his obedience.

He looked to have heard the message with his ears, and he feels it in his guts; so sharp a message, that it pierced the body, and let out the soul through that unclean passage: neither did it admit of any answer but silence and death. In that part had he offended, by pampering it and making it his god; and now his bane finds the same way with his sin.

This one hard and cold morsel, which he cannot digest, pays for all those gluttonous delicates, whereof he had formerly surfeited. It is the manner of God to take fearful revenges of the professed enemies of his church.

It is a marvel, that neither any noise in his dying, nor the fall of so gross a body, called in some of his attendants: but that God, which hath intended to bring about any design, disposes of all circumstances to his own purpose. If Ehud had not come forth with a calm and settled countenance, and shut the doors after him, all his project had been in the dust. What had it been better that the king of Moab was slain, if Israel had neither had a messenger to inform, nor a captain to guide them? Now he departs peaceably, and blows a trumpet in Mount Ephraim, gathers Israel and falls upon the body of Moab, as well as he had done upon the head, and procures freedom to his people. He that would undertake great enterprises, had need of wisdom and courage; wisdom to contrive, and courage to execute; wisdom to guide his courage, and courage to second his wisdom: both which, if they meet with a good cause, cannot but succeed.

CONTEMPLATION IV.—OF JAEL AND SISERA.

It is no wonder if they, who, ere fourscore days after the law delivered, fell to idolatry alone; now, after fourscore years since the law restored, fell to idolatry among the Canaanites. Peace could in a shorter time work looseness in any people. And if, forty years after Othniel's deliverance, they relapsed, what marvel is it, that, in twice forty after Ehud, they thus miscarried? What are they the better to have killed Eglon the king of Moab, if the idolatry of Moab have killed them? The sin of Moab shall be found a worse tyrant than their Eglon. Israel is for every market: they sold themselves to idolatry, God sells them to the Canaanites: it is no marvel they are slaves, if they will be idolaters. After their longest intermission, they have now the sorest bondage. None of their tyrants were so potent as Jabin, with his nine hundred chariots of iron. The longer the reckoning is deferred, the greater is the sum. God provides on purpose mighty adversaries for his church, that their humiliation may be the greater in sustaining, and his glory may be greater in deliverance.

I do not find any prophet in Israel during their sin; but so soon as I hear news of their repentance, mention is made of a prophetess, and judge of Israel. There is no better sign of God's reconciliation, than the sending of his holy messengers to any people. He is not utterly fallen out with those whom he blesses with prophecy. Whom yet do I see raised to this honour? — not any of the princes of Israel; not Barak the captain; not Lapidoth the husband: but a woman, for the honour of her sex; a wife, for the honour of wedlock; Deborah, the wife of Lapidoth.

He, that had choice of all the millions of Israel, calls out two weak women to deliver his people: Deborah shall judge; Jael shall execute. All the palaces of Israel must yield to the palm-tree of Deborah: the weakness of the instruments redounds to the greater honour of the workman. Who shall ask God any reason of his elections, but his own pleasure? Deborah was to sentence, not to strike; to command, not to execute. This act is masculine, fit for some captain of Israel. She was the head of Israel; it was meet some other should be the hand. It is an imperfect and titular government, where there is a commanding power, without correction, without execution. The message of Deborah finds out Barak the son of Abinoam, in his obscure secrecy, and calls him from a corner of Naphtali to the honour of this exploit. He is sent for, not to get the victory, but to take it; not to overcome, but to kill; to pursue, and not to beat Sisera. Who could not have done this work, whereto not much courage, no skill, belonged? yet, even for this, will God have an instrument of his own choice. It is most fit that God should serve himself where he lists, of his own: neither is it to be inquired, whom we think meet for any employment, but whom God hath called.

Deborah had been no prophetess, if she durst have sent in her own name: her message is from him that sent herself, "Hath not the Lord God of Israel commanded?" Barak's answer is faithful, though conditional; and doth not so much intend a refusal to go without her, as a necessary bond of her presence with him. Who can blame him, that he would have a prophetess in his company? If the man had not been as holy as valiant, he would not have wished such society. How many think it a perpetual bondage to have a prophet of God at their elbow! God had never sent for him so far, if he could have been content to go up without Deborah: he knew that there was both a blessing and encouragement in that presence. It is no putting any trust in the success of those men that neglect the messengers of God.

To prescribe that to others, which we draw back from doing ourselves, is an argument of hollowness and falsity. Barak shall see that Deborah doth not offer him that cup whereof she dares not begin: without regard of her sex, she marches with him to Mount Tabor, and rejoices to be seen of the ten thousand of Israel. With what scorn did Sisera look at these gleanings of Israel! How unequal did this match seem, of ten thousand Israelites against his three hundred thousand foot, ten thousand horse, nine hundred chariots of iron! And now in bravery he calls for his troops, and means to kill this handful of Israel with the very sight of his spiked chariots, and only feared it would be no victory to cut the throats of so few. The faith of Deborah and Barak was not appalled with this world of adversaries, which from Mount Tabor they saw hiding all the valley below them: they knew whom they had believed, and how little an arm of flesh could do against the God of Hosts.

Barak went down against Sisera, but it was God that destroyed him. The Israelites did not this day wield their own swords: lest they should arrogate anything, God told them before-hand, it should be his own act. I hear not of one stroke that any Canaanite gave in this fight, as if they were called hither only to suffer. And now proud Sisera, after many curses of the heaviness of that iron carriage, is glad to quit his chariot, and betake himself to his heels. Who ever yet knew any earthly thing trusted in, without disappointment? It is wonder if God make us not at last as weary of whatsoever hath stolen our hearts from him, as ever we were fond.

Yet Sisera hopes to have sped better than his followers, in so seasonable a harbour of Jael. If Heber and Jael had not been great persons, there had been no note taken of their tents; there had been no league betwixt king Jabin and them: now their greatness makes them known, their league makes them trusted. The distress of Sisera might have made him importunate; but Jael begins the courtesy, and exceeds the desire of her guest. He asks water to drink, she gives him milk; he wishes but shelter, she makes him a bed; he desires the protection of her tent, she covers him with a mantle. And now Sisera pleases himself with this happy change, and thinks how much better it is to be here, than in that whirling of chariots, in that horror of flight, amongst those shrieks, those wounds, those carcases. While he is in these thoughts, his weariness and easy reposal hath brought him asleep. Who would have looked that in this tumult and danger, even betwixt the very jaws of death, Sisera should find time to sleep! How many worldly hearts do so in the midst of their spiritual perils!

Now, while he was dreaming, doubtless, of the clashing of armours, rattling of chariots, neighing of horses, the clamour of the conquered, the furious pursuit of Israel, Jael, seeing his temples lie so fair, as if they invited the nail and hammer, entered into the thought of this noble execution; certainly not without some checks of doubt, and pleas of fear. What if I strike him? And yet, who am I that I should dare to think of such an act? Is not this Sisera, the most famous captain of the world, whose name hath wont to be fearful to whole nations? What if my hand should swerve in the stroke? what if he should awake while I am lifting up this instrument of death? what if I should be surprised by some of his followers, while the fact is green, and yet bleeding? Can the murder of so great a leader be hid, or unrevenged? Or, if I might hope so, yet can my heart allow me to be secretly treacherous? Is there not peace betwixt my house and him? did not I invite him into my tent? doth he not trust to my friendship and hospitality? But what do these weak fears, these idle fancies of civility? If Sisera be in league with us, yet is he not at defiance with God? is he not a tyrant to Israel? Is it for nothing that God hath brought him into my tent? May I not now find means to repay unto Israel all their kindness to my grandfather Jethro? Doth not God offer me this day the honour to be the rescuer of his people? Hath God bidden me strike, and shall I hold my hand? No: Sisera, sleep now thy last, and take here this fatal reward of all thy cruelty and oppression.

He, that put this instinct into her heart, did put also strength into her hand: he that guided Sisera to her tent, guided the nail through his temples, which hath made a speedy way for his soul through those parts, and now hath fastened his ear so close to the earth, as if the body had been listening what was become of the soul. There lies now the great terror of Israel at the foot of a woman! He, that brought so many hundred thousands into the field, hath not now one page left, either to avert his death, or to accompany it or bewail it! He, that had vaunted of his iron chariots, is slain by one nail of iron, wanting only this one point of his infelicity, that he knows not by whose hand he perished!

CONTEMPLATION V —GIDEON'S CALLING.

THE judgments of God, still the further they go, the sorer they are. The bondage of Israel under Jabin was great, but it was freedom in comparison of the yoke of the Midianites. During the former tyranny, Deborah was permitted to judge Israel under a palm tree; under this, not so much as private habitations will be allowed to Israel. Then, the seat of judgment was in sight of the sun; now, their very dwellings must be secret under the earth. They that rejected the protection of God, are glad to seek to the mountains for shelter; and as they had savagely abused themselves, so they are fain to creep into dens and caves of the rocks, like wild creatures, for safeguard. God had sown spiritual seed amongst them, and they suffered their heathenish neighbours to pull it up by the roots; and now, no sooner can they sow their material seed, but Midianites and Amalekites are ready by force to destroy it. As they inwardly dealt with God, so God deals outwardly by them: their eyes may tell them what their souls have done; yet that God, whose mercy is above the worst of our sin, sends first his prophet with a message of reproof, and then his angel with a message of deliverance. The Israelites had smarted enough with their servitude, yet God sends them a sharp rebuke. It is a good sign when God chides us; his round reprehensions are ever gracious forerunners of mercy; whereas, his silent connivance at the wicked argues deep and secret displeasure: the prophet made way for the angel, reproof for deliverance, humiliation for comfort.

Gideon was thrashing wheat by the winepress. Yet Israel hath both wheat and wine, for all the incursions of their enemies. The worst estate out of hell, hath either some comfort, or, at least, some mitigation. In spite of the malice of the world, God makes secret provision for his own. How should it be, but he that owns the earth, and all creatures, should reserve ever a sufficiency from foreigners (such the wicked are) for his household? In the worst of the Midianitish tyranny, Gideon's field and barn are privileged, as his fleece was afterwards, from the shower.

Why did Gideon thrash out his corn? To hide it, not from his neighbours, but his enemies. His granary might easily be more close than his barn. As then Israelites thrashed out their corn to hide it from the Midianites, but now Midianites thrash out corn to hide it from the Israelites. These rural tyrants of our time do not more lay up corn, than curses. He that withdraweth corn, the people will curse him; yea, God will curse him, with them, and for them.

What shifts nature will make to live! O that we could be so careful to lay up spiritual food for our souls, out of the reach of those spiritual Midianites! we could not but live in despite of all adversaries.

The angels, that have ever God in their face, and in their thoughts, have him also in their mouths: " The Lord is with thee." But this which appeared unto Gideon was the Angel of the covenant, the Lord of angels. While he was with Gideon, he might well say, " The Lord is with thee." He that sent the Comforter, was also the true comforter of his church. He well knew how to lay a sure ground of consolation, and that the only remedy of sorrow, and beginning of true joy, is, " The presence of God." The grief of the apostles, for the expected loss of their Master, could never be cured by any receipt, but this of the same Angel, " Behold, I am with you to the end of the world." What is our glory, but the fruition of God's presence? The punishment of the damned is a separation from the beatifical face of God; needs must therefore his absence in this life be a great torment to a good heart: and no cross can be equivalent to this beginning of heaven in the elect, " The Lord is with thee."

Who can complain either of solitariness or opposition, that hath God with him; with him, not only as a witness, but as a party? Even wicked men and devils cannot exclude God, not the bars of hell can shut him out. He is with them by force, but to judge, to punish them; yea, God will be ever with them to their cost; but to protect, comfort, save, he is with none but his.

While he calls Gideon valiant, he makes him so. How could he be but valiant, that had God with him? The godless man may be careless, but cannot be other than cowardly. It pleases God to acknowledge his own graces in men, that he may interchange his own glory with their comfort; how much more should we confess the graces of one another? An envious nature is prejudicial to God. He is a strange man in whom there is not some visible good; yea, in the devils themselves we may easily note some commendable parts of knowledge, strength, agility. Let God have his own in the worst creature; yea, let the worst creature have that praise which God would put upon it.

Gideon cannot pass over this salutation as some fashionable compliment, but lays hold on that part which was most important, the tenure of all his comfort; and, as not regarding the praise of his valour, inquires after that which should be the ground of his valour, the presence of God. God had spoken particularly to him; he expostulates for all. It had been possible God should be present with him, not with the rest; as he promised to have been with Moses, Israel; and yet when God says, " The Lord is with thee," he answers, " Alas, Lord, if the Lord be with us," Gideon cannot conceive of himself as an exempt person; but puts himself among the throng of Israel, as one that could not be sensible of any particular comfort, while the common case of Israel laboured. The main care of a good heart is still for the public; neither can it enjoy itself, while the church of God is distressed. As faith draws home generalities, so charity diffuses generalities from itself to all.

Yet the valiant man was here weak, weak in faith, weak in discourse, whilst he argues God's absence by affliction, his presence by deliverances, and the unlikelihood of success by his own inability—all gross inconsequences. Rather should he have inferred God's presence upon their correction; for wheresoever God chastises, there he is, yea, there he is in mercy. Nothing more proves us his, than his stripes: he will not bestow whipping where he loves not. Fond nature thinks God should not suffer the wind to blow upon his dear ones, because herself makes this use of her own indulgence; but none out of the place of torment have suffered so much as his dearest children. He says not, We are idolaters; therefore the Lord hath forsaken us, because we have forsaken him. This sequel had been as good, as the other was faulty; the Lord hath delivered us unto the Midianites, therefore he hath forsaken us. Sins, not afflictions, argue God absent.

Whilst Gideon bewrayeth weakness, God both gives him might, and employs it: "Go in this thy might, and save Israel." Who would not have looked, that God should have looked angrily on him, and chid him for his unbelief? But he, whose mercy will not quench the weakest fire of grace, though it be but in flax, looks upon him with compassionate eyes; and, to make good his own word, gives him that valour he had acknowledged.

Gideon had not yet said, "Lord, deliver Israel;" much less had he said, "Lord, deliver Israel by my hand." The mercy of God prevents the desire of Gideon. If God should not begin with us, we should be ever miserable: if he should not give us till we ask, yet who should give us to ask? If his spirit did not work those holy groans and sighs in us, we should never make suit to God. He that commonly gives us power to crave, sometimes gives us without craving, that the benefit might be so much more welcome, by how much less it was expected; and we so much more thankful as he is more forward. When he bids us ask, it is not for that he needs to be entreated, but that he may make us more capable of blessings by desiring them. And where he sees fervent desires, he stays not for words; and he that gives ere we ask, how much more will he give when we ask?

He that hath might enough to deliver Israel, yet hath not might enough to keep himself from doubting. The strongest faith will ever have some touch of infidelity. And yet this was not so much a distrust of the possibility of delivering Israel, as an inquiry after the means. Whereby shall I save Israel? The salutation of the angel to Gideon was as like Gabriel's salutation of the blessed virgin, as their answers were like: both angels brought news of deliverance; both were answered with a question of the means of performance, with a report of the difficulties in performing: "Ah, my Lord, whereby shall I save Israel?" How the good man disparages himself! It is a great matter, O Lord, that thou speakest of, and great actions require mighty agents. As for me, who am I? my tribe is none of the greatest in Israel; my father's family is one of the meanest in his tribe, and I the meanest in his family. Poverty is a sufficient bar to great enterprises.

"Whereby shall I?" Humility is both a sign of following glory, and a way to it, and an occasion of it. Bragging and height of spirit will not carry it with God. None have ever been raised by him, but those which have formerly dejected themselves: none have been confounded by him that have been abased in themselves. Thereupon it is that he adds: "I will therefore be with thee;" as if he had answered, Hadst thou not been so poor in thyself, I would not have wrought by thee. How should God be magnified in his mercies, if we were not unworthy? How should he be strong, if not in our weakness?

All this while Gideon knew not it was an angel that spake with him; he saw a man stand before him like a traveller, with a staff in his hand. The unusualness of those revelations, in those corrupted times, was such, that Gideon might think of any thing rather than an angel. No marvel if so strange a promise, from an unknown messenger, found not a perfect assent: fain would he believe, but fain would he have good warrant for his faith. In matters of faith, we cannot go upon too sure grounds. As Moses, therefore, being sent upon the same errand, desired a sign whereby Israel might know that God sent him; so Gideon desires a sign from this bearer, to know that this news is from God.

Yet the very hope of so happy news, not yet ratified, stirs up in Gideon both joy and thankfulness. After all the injury of the Midianites, he was not so poor, but he could bestow a kid and cakes upon the reporter of such tidings. Those which are rightly affected with the glad news of our spiritual deliverance, study to show their loving respects to the messengers.

The angel stays for the preparing of Gideon's feast. Such pleasure doth God take in the thankful endeavours of his servants, that he patiently waits upon the leisure of our performances. Gideon intended a dinner; the angel turned it into a sacrifice. He, whose meat and drink it was to do his Father's will, calls for the broth and flesh to be poured out upon the stone; and when Gideon looked he should have blessed, and eaten, he touches the feast with his staff, and consumes it with fire from the stone, and departs. He did not strike the stone with his staff (for the attrition of two hard bodies would naturally beget fire), but he touched the meat, and brought fire from the stone. And now, while Gideon saw and wondered at the spiritual act, he lost the sight of the agent.

He, that came without entreating, would not have departed without taking leave, but that he might increase Gideon's wonder, and that his wonder might increase his faith. His salutation, therefore, was not so strange as his farewell. Moses touched the rock with his staff, and brought forth water and yet a man, and yet continued with the Israelites. This messenger touches the stone with his staff, and brings forth fire, and presently vanishes, that he may approve himself a spirit. And now, Gideon, when he had gathered up himself, must needs think, He that can raise fire out of a stone, can raise courage and power out of my dead breast: he that by this fire hath consumed the broth and flesh, can, by the feeble flame of my fortitude, consume Midian.

Gideon did not so much doubt before, as now he feared. We, that shall once live with, and be like angels, in the estate of our impotency, think we cannot see an angel and live. Gideon was acknowledged for mighty in valour, yet he trembles at the sight of an angel. Peter, that durst draw his sword upon Malchus and all the train of Judas, yet fears when he thought he had seen a spirit. Our natural courage cannot bear us out against spiritual objects. This angel was homely and familiar, taking upon him, for the time, a resemblance of that flesh whereof he would afterwards take the substance: yet even the valiant Gideon quakes to have seen him. How awful and glorious is the God of angels, when he will be seen in the state of heaven!

The angel that departed for the wonder, yet returns for the comfort of Gideon. It is not usual with God to leave his children in amaze, but he brings them out in the same mercy which led them in, and will magnify his grace in the one, no less than his power in the other.

Now Gideon grows acquainted with God, and interchanges pledges of familiarity; he builds an altar to God, and God confers with him, and (as he uses where he loves) employs him. His first task must be to destroy the god of the Midianites, then the idolaters themselves. While Baal's altar and grove stood in the hill of Ophrah, Israel should in vain hope to prevail. It is most just with God, that judgment should continue with the sin, and no less mercy if it may remove after it. Wouldst thou fain be rid of any judgment? inquire what false altars and groves thou hast in thy heart; down with them first.

First must Baal's altar be ruined, ere God's be built; both may not stand together: the true God will have no society with idols, neither will allow it us. I do not hear him say, That altar and grove, which were abused to Baal, consecrate now to me; but, as one whose holy jealousy will abide no worship till there be no idolatry, he first commands down the monuments of superstition, and then enjoins his own service; yet the wood of Baal's grove must be used to burn a sacrifice unto God. When it was once cut down, God's detestation and their danger ceased. The good creatures of God that have been profaned to idolatry, may, in a change of their use, be employed to the holy service of their Maker.

Though some Israelites were penitent under this humiliation, yet still many of them persisted in their wonted idolatry. The very household of Gideon's father were still Baalites, and his neighbours of Ophrah were in the same sin: yea, if his father had been free, what did he with Baal's grove and altar? He dares not therefore take his father's servants, though he took his bullocks, but commands his own. The master is best seen in the servants: Gideon's servants (amongst the idolatrous retinue of Joash) are religious like their master; yet the misdevotion of Joash and the Ophrathites was not obstinate. Joash is easily persuaded by his sons, and easily persuades his neighbours, how unreasonable it is to plead for such a god, as cannot speak for himself; to revenge his cause, that could not defend himself. "Let Baal plead for himself." One example of a resolute onset in a noted person, may do more good than a thousand seconds in the proceeding of an action.

Soon are all the Midianites in an uproar to lose their god; they need not now be bidden to muster themselves for revenge. He hath no religion, that can suffer an indignity offered to his God.

CONTEMPLATION VI.—GIDEON'S PREPARATION AND VICTORY.

Of all the instruments that God did use in so great a work, I find none so weak as Gideon, who yet of all others was styled valiant. Natural valour may well stand with spiritual cowardice. Before he knew that he spake with a God, he might have had just colours for his distrust; but after God had approved his presence and almighty power, by fetching fire out of the stone, then to call for a watery sign of his promised deliverance, was no other than to pour water upon the fire of the Spirit. The former trial God gave vanished; this, upon Gideon's choice and entreaty. The former miracle was strong enough to carry Gideon through his first exploit of ruinating the idolatrous grove and altar; but now, when he saw the swarm of the Midianites and Amalekites about his ears, he calls for new aid; and, not trusting to the Abiezrites, and his other thousands of Israel, he runs to God for a further assurance of victory.

The refuge was good, but the manner of seeking it savours of distrust. There is nothing more easy than to be valiant, when no peril appeareth; but when evils assail us upon equal terms, it is hard, and commendable, not to be dismayed. If God had made that proclamation now, which afterwards was commanded to be made by Gideon, "Let the timorous depart;" I doubt whether Israel had not wanted a guide: yet how willing is the Almighty to satisfy our weak desires!

What tasks is he content to be set by our infirmity! The fleece must be wet, and the ground dry; the ground must be wet, and the fleece dry: both are done, that now Gideon may see whether he would make himself hard earth, or yielding wool. God could at pleasure distinguish betwixt him and the Midianites, and pour down either mercies or judgments where he lists; and that he was set on work by that God which can command all the elements, and they obey him; fire, water, earth, serve both him and (when he will) his.

And now when Gideon had this reciprocal proof of his ensuing success, he goes on (as he well may) harnessed with resolution, and is seen at the head of his troops, and in the face of the Midianites. If we cannot make up the match with God, when we have our own asking, we are worthy to sit out.

Gideon had thirty-two thousand soldiers at his heels. The Midianites covered all the valley like grasshoppers: and now, whilst the Israelites think, we are too few, God says, "The people are too many." If the Israelites must have looked for victory from their fingers, they might have well said, the Midianites are too many for us: but that God, whose thoughts and words are unlike to men's, says, "They are too many for me to give the Midianites into their hands." If human strength were to be opposed, there should have needed an equality; but now God meant to give the victory, his care is not how to get it, but how not to lose or blemish the glory of it gotten. How jealous God is of his honour! He is willing to give deliverance to Israel; but the praise of the deliverance he will keep to himself, and will shorten the means, that he may have the full measure of the glory. And if he will not allow lawful means to stand in the light of his honour, how will he endure it to be crossed so much as indirectly? It is less danger to steal any thing from God than his glory.

As a prince, which, if we steal or clip his coin may pardon it; but if we go about to rob him of his crown, will not be appeased. There is nothing that we can give to God, of whom we receive all things: that which he is content to part with, he gives us; but he will not abide we should take ought from him which he would reserve for himself. It is all one with him to save with many as with few; but he rather chooses to save by few, that all the victory may redound to himself. O God, what art thou better for praises, to whom, because thou art infinite, nothing can be added! It is for our good that thou wouldst be magnified of us. O teach us to receive the benefit of thy merciful favours, and to return thee the thanks!

Gideon's army must be lessened. Who are so fit to be cashiered as the fearful? God bids him, therefore, proclaim licence for all faint hearts to leave the field. An ill instrument may shame a good work. God will not glorify himself by cowards. As the timorous shall be without the gates of heaven, so shall they be without the lists of God's field. Although it was not their courage that should save Israel, yet without their courage God would not serve himself of them. Christianity requires men; for if our spiritual difficulties meet not with high spirits, instead of whetting our fortitude, they quell it. David's royal band of worthies was the type of the forces of the church, all valiant men, and able to encounter with thousands.

Neither must we be strong only, but acquainted with our own resolutions, not out of any carnal presumption, but out of a faithful reliance upon the strength of God, in whom, when we are weak, then we are strong. O thou white-liver! doth but a foul word, or a frown, scare thee from Christ? doth the loss of a little land, or silver, disquiet thee? doth but the sight of the Midianites in the valley strike thee? Home, then, home to the world! thou art not then for the conquering band of Christ: if thou canst not resolve to follow him through infamy, prisons, racks, gibbets, flames, depart to thine house, and save thy life to thy loss.

Methinks now Israel should have complained of indignity, and have said, Why shouldst thou think, O Gideon, that there can be a cowardly Israelite? And if the experience of the power and mercy of God be not enough to make us fearless, yet the sense of servitude must needs have made us resolute; for who had not rather to be buried dead than quick? Are we not fain to hide our heads in the caves of the earth, and to make our graves our houses? Not so much as the very light that we can freely enjoy. The tyranny of death is but short and easy to this of Midian; and yet what danger can there be of that, since thou hast so certainly assured us of God's promise of victory, and his miraculous confirmation? No, Gideon; those hearts that have brought us hither after thy colours, can as well keep us from retiring,

But now, who can but bless himself to find, of two-and-thirty thousand Israelites, two-and-twenty thousand cowards? Yet all these in Gideon's march, made as fair a flourish of courage as the boldest. Who can trust the faces of men, that sees in the army of Israel, above two for one timorous? How many make a glorious shew in the warfaring church, which, when they shall see danger of persecution, shall shrink from the standard of God? Hope of safety, examples of neighbours, desire of praise, fear of censures, coaction of laws, fellowship of friends, draw many into the field, which, so soon as ever they see the adversary, repent of their conditions; and, if they may cleanly escape, will be gone early from mount Gilead. Can any man be offended at the number of these shrinkers, when he sees but ten thousand Israelites left of two-and-thirty thousand in a morning?

These men, that would have been ashamed to go away by day, now drop away by night: and if Gideon should have called any one of them back, and said, Wilt thou fly? would have made an excuse: the darkness is a fit veil for their paleness, or blushing; fearfulness cannot abide the light.— None of these thousands of Israel but would have been loath Gideon should have seen his face, whilst he said, I am fearful! Very shame holds some in their station, whose hearts are already fled. And if we cannot endure that men should be witnesses of that fear, which we might live to correct, how shall we abide once to show our fearful heads before that terrible Judge, when he calls us forth to the punishment of our fear? O the vanity of foolish hypocrites, that run upon the terrors of God, whilst they would avoid the shame of men!

How do we think the small remainder of Israel looked, when, in the next morning-muster, they found themselves but ten thousand left? How did they accuse their timorous countrymen, that had left but this handful to encounter the millions of Midian? And yet still God complains of too many; and, upon his trial dismisses nine thousand seven hundred more. His first trial was of the valour of their minds; his next is of the ability of their bodies. Those which, besides boldness, are not strong, patient of labour and thirst, willing to stoop, content with a little (such were those that took up water with their hands), are not for the select band of God. The Lord of Hosts will serve himself of none but able champions. If he have therefore singled us into his combat, this very choice argues, that he finds that strength in us, which we cannot confess in ourselves. How can it but comfort us in our great trials, that if the Searcher of hearts did not find us fit, he would never honour us with so hard an employment.

Now, when there is not scarce left one Israelite to every thousand of the Midianites, it is seasonable with God to join battle. When God hath stripped us of all our earthly confidence, then doth he find time to give us victory, and not till then, lest he should be a loser in our gain: likeas at last he unclothes us of our body, that he may clothe us upon with glory.

If Gideon feared when he had two-and-thirty thousand Israelites at his heels, is it any wonder if he feared when all these were shrunk unto three hundred? Though his confirmation were more, yet his means were abated. Why was not Gideon rather the leader of those two-and-twenty thousand run-aways, than of these three hundred soldiers? O infinite mercy and forbearance of God, that takes not advantage of so strong an infirmity, but instead of casting, encourages him! That wise providence hath prepared a dream in the head of one Midianite, an interpretation in the mouth of another, and hath brought Gideon to be an auditor of both; and hath made his enemies prophets of his victory, encouragers of the attempt, proclaimers of their own confusion. A Midianite dreams, a Midianite interprets. Our very dreams many times are not without God; there is a providence in our sleeping fancies. Even the enemies of God may have visions, and power to construe them aright. How usually are wicked men forewarned of their own destruction! To foreknow, and not avoid, is but an aggravation of judgment.

When Gideon heard good news, though from an enemy, he fell down and worshipped. To hear himself but a barley-cake troubled him not, when he heard withal that his rolling down the hill should break the tents of Midian. It matters not how base we be thought, so we may be victorious. The soul that hath received full confirmation from God in the assurance of his salvation, cannot but bow the knee, and by gestures of body tell how it is ravished. I would have thought Gideon should rather have found full confirmation in the promise and act of God, than in the dream of the Midianite. Dreams may be full of uncertainty; God's undertakings are infallble. Well, therefore, might the miracle of God give strength to the dream of a Midianite; but what strength could a pagan's dream give to the miraculous act of God? yet by this is Gideon throughly settled. When we are going, a little thing drives us on; when we are come near the shore, the very tide, without sails, is enough to put us into the harbour. We shall now hear no more of Gideon's doubts, but of his achievements. And though God had promised by these three hundred to chase the Midianites, yet he neglects not wise stratagems to effect it. To wait for God's performance in doing nothing, is to abuse that divine providence, which will so work, that will not allow us idle.

Now, when we would look that Gideon should give charge of whetting their swords, and sharping their spears, and fitting their armour, he only gives order for empty pitchers, and lights, and trumpets. The cracking of these pitchers shall break in pieces this Midianitish clay; the kindling of these lights shall extinguish the light of Midian; these trumpets sound no other than a soul-peal to all the host of Midian: there shall need nothing but noise and light to confound this innumerable army.

And if the pitchers, and brands, and trumpets of Gideon, did so daunt and dismay the proud troops of Midian and Amalek, who can we think shall be able to stand before the last terror, wherein the trumpet of the archangel shall sound, and the heaven shall pass away with a noise, and the elements shall be on a flame about our ears?

Any of the weakest Israelites would have served to have broken an empty pitcher, to have carried a light, and to have sounded a trumpet, and to strike a flying adversary. Not to the basest use will God employ an unworthy agent: he will not allow so much as a cowardly torch-bearer.

Those two-and-twenty thousand Israelites that slipped away for fear, when the fearful Midianites fled, can pursue and kill them, and can follow them at the heels, whom they durst not look at in the face. Our flight gives advantage to the feeblest adversary, whereas our resistance foileth the greatest. How much more, if we have once turned our backs upon a temptation, shall our spiritual enemies, which are ever strong, trample us in the dust? Resist, and they shall fly; stand still, and we shall see the salvation of the Lord.

CONTEMPLATION VII.—THE REVENGE OF SUCCOTH AND PENUEL.

GIDEON was of Manasseh: Ephraim and he were brothers, sons of Joseph. None of all the tribes of Israel fall out with their victorious leader but he. The agreement of brothers is rare: by how much nature hath more endeared them, by so much are their quarrels more frequent and dangerous. I did not hear the Ephraimites offering themselves into the front of the army before the fight, and now they are ready to fight with Gideon, because they were not called to fight with Midian; I hear them expostulating after it. After the exploit done, cowards are valiant. Their quarrel was, that they were not called. It had been a greater praise of their valour to have gone unbidden. What need was there to call them, when God complained of multitude, and sent away those which were called? None speak so big in the end of the fray, as the fearfullest.

Ephraim flies upon Gideon, whilst the Midianites fly from him; when Gideon should be pursuing his enemies, he is pursued by brethren, and now is glad to spend that wind in pacifying of his own, which should have been bestowed in the slaughter of a common adversary. It is a wonder if Satan suffer us to be quiet at home, whilst we are exercised with wars abroad. Had not Gideon learned to speak fair, as well as to smite, he had found work enough from the swords of Joseph's sons: his good words are as victorious as his sword; his pacification of friends, better than his execution of enemies.

For aught I see, the envy of Israelites was not more troublesome to Gideon, than the opposition of Midian. He hath left the envy of Ephraim behind him; before him, he finds the envy of Succoth and Penuel. The one envies that he should overcome without them; the other, that he should say he had overcome. His pursuit leads him to Succoth; there he craves relief, and is repelled. Had he said, Come forth and draw your sword with me against Zeba and Zalmunna, the motion had been but equal. A common interest challenges a universal aid. Now he says but " Give.

SUCCOTH AND PENUEL.

morsels of bread to my followers," he is turned off with a scorn; he asks bread, and they give him a stone. Could he ask a more slender recompense of their deliverance, or a less reward of his victory? " Give morsels of bread." Before this act, all their substance had been too small a hire for their freedom from Midian; now, when it is done, a morsel of bread is too much, Well might he challenge bread, where he gave liberty and life. It is hard if those which fight the wars of God may not have necessary relief; that whilst the enemy dies by them, they should die by famine. If they had laboured for God at home in peace, they had been worthy of maintenance; how much more now, that danger is added to their toil? Even very executioners look for fees; but here were not malefactors, but adversaries to be slain; the sword of power and revenge was now to be wielded, not of quiet justice. Those that fight for our souls against spiritual powers, may challenge bread from us; and it is shameless unthankfulness to deny it. When Abraham had vanquished the five kings, and delivered Lot and his family, the king of Salem met him with bread and wine; and now these sons of Abraham, after an equal victory, ask dry bread, and are denied by their brethren. Craftily yet, and under pretence of a false title, had they acknowledged the victory of Gideon; with what forehead could they have denied him bread?

Now, I know not whether their faithlessness or envy lies in their way; " Are the hands of Zeba and Zalmunna in thy hands?" There were none of these princes of Succoth and Penuel, but thought themselves better men than Gideon; that he therefore alone should do that, which all the princes of Israel durst not attempt, they hated and scorned to hear. It is never safe to measure events by the power of the instrument; nor, in the causes of God (whose calling makes the difference), to measure others by themselves. There is nothing more dangerous, than in holy businesses to stand upon comparisons, and our own reputation; since it is reason God should both choose and bless where he lists.

To have questioned so sudden a victory had been pardonable; but to deny it scornfully, was unworthy of Israelites. Carnal men think that impossible to others, which themselves cannot do: from hence are their censures, hence their exclamations.

Gideon hath vowed a fearful revenge, and now performs it; the taunts of his brethren may not stay him from the pursuit of the Midianites: common enmities must first be opposed, domestical at more leisure. The princes of Succoth feared the tyranny of the Midianitish kings, but they more feared Gideon's victory. What a condition hath their envy drawn them into, that they are sorry to see God's enemies captive, that Israel's freedom must be their death, that the Midianites and they must tremble at one and the same revenger! To see themselves prisoners to Zeba and Zalmunna had not been so fearful, as to see Zeba and Zalmunna prisoners to Gideon. Nothing is more terrible to evil minds, than to read their own condemnation in the happy success of others. Hell itself would want one piece of its torment, if the wicked did not know those, whom they contemned, glorious.

I know not whether more to commend Gideon's wisdom and moderation in the proceedings, than his resolution and justice in the execution of this business. I do not see him run furiously into the city, and kill the next; his sword had not been so drunken with blood, that it should know no difference: but he writes down the names of the princes, and singles them forth for revenge.

When the leaders of God came to Jericho, or Ai, their slaughter was unpartial; not a woman or child might live to tell the news: but now that Gideon comes to Succoth, a city of Israelites, the rulers are called forth to death; the people are frighted with the example, not hurt with the judgment. To enwrap the innocent in any vengeance, is a murderous injustice indeed; where all join in the sin, all are worthy to meet in the punishment. It is like, the citizens of Succoth could have been glad to succour Gideon, if their rulers had not forbidden. They must therefore escape, while their princes perish.

I cannot think of Gideon's revenge without horror; that the rulers of Succoth should have their flesh torn from their backs with thorns and briers, that they should be at once beaten and scratched to death. What a spectacle it was, to see their bare bones looking somewhere through the bloody rags of their flesh and skin, and every stroke worse than the last, death multiplied by torment! Justice is sometimes so severe, that a tender beholder can scarce discern it from cruelty.

I see the Midianites far less ill; the edge of the sword makes a speedy and easy passage for their lives, while these rebellious Israelites die lingering under thorns and briers, envying those in their death whom their life abhorred. Howsoever men live or die without the pale of the church, a wicked Israelite shall be sure of plagues. How many shall unwish themselves Christians, when God's revenges have found them out!

The place where Jacob wrestled with God, and prevailed, now hath wrestled against God, and takes a fall: they see God avenged, which would not believe him delivering.

It was now time for Zeba and Zalmunna to follow their troops to the grave, whom they had led in the field. Those, which the day before were attended with a hundred and thirty-five thousand followers, have not so much as a page now left to weep for their death, and have lived only to see all their friends, and some enemies, die for their sakes.

Who can regard earthly greatness, that sees one night change two of the greatest kings of the world into captives! It had been both pity and sin, that the heads of that Midianitish tyranny, into which they had drawn so many thousands, should have escaped that death.

And yet, if private revenge had not made Gideon just, I doubt whether they had died. The blood of his brothers calls for theirs, and awakes his sword to their execution. He both knew and complained of the Midianitish oppression, under which Israel groaned: yet the cruelty offered to all the thousands of his father's sons had not drawn the blood of Zeba and Zalmunna, if his own mother's sons had not bled by their hands.

He that slew the rulers of Succoth and Penuel, and spared the people, now hath slain the people of Midian, and would have spared their rulers: but that God, which will find occasions to wind wicked men into judgment, will have them slain in a private quarrel, which had more deserved it for the public; if we may not rather say, that Gideon revenged these as a magistrate, not as a brother. For governors to respect their own ends in public actions, and to wear the sword of justice in their own sheath, it is a wrongful abuse of authority. The slaughter of Gideon's brethren was not the greatest sin of the Midianitish kings: this alone shall kill them, when the rest expected an unjust remission. How many lewd men hath God paid with some one sin for all the rest!

Some, that have gone away with unnatural filthiness, and capital thefts, have clipped off their own days with their coin; others, whose bloody murders have been punished in a mutinous word; others, whose suspected felony hath paid the price of their unknown rape. O God, thy judgments are just, even when men's are unjust!

Gideon's young son is bidden to revenge the death of his uncles; his sword had not yet learned the way to blood, especially of kings, though in irons. Deadly executions require strength both of heart and face. How are those aged in evil that can draw their swords upon the lawfully anointed of God? These tyrants plead not now for continuance of life, but for the haste of death: "Fall thou upon us." Death is ever accompanied with pain, which it is no marvel if we wish short. We do not more affect protraction of an easy life, than speed in our dissolution; for here every pang, that tends towards death, renews it. To lie an hour under death is tedious, but to be dying a whole day, we think above the strength of human patience. O what shall we then conceive of that death which knows no end! As this life is no less frail than the body which it animates, so that death is no less eternal than the soul which must endure it.

For us to be dying so long as we now have leave to live, is intolerable; and yet one only minute of that other tormenting death is worse than an age of this. O the desperate infidelity of careless men, that shrink at the thought of a momentary death, and fear not eternal! This is but a killing of the body; that is a destruction of body and soul.

Who is so worthy to wear the crown of Israel, as he that won the crown from Midian? Their usurpers were gone; now they are heedless: it is a doubt whether they were better to have had no kings, or tyrants. They sue to Gideon to accept of the kingdom, and are repulsed. There is no greater example of modesty, than Gideon. When the angel spake to him, he abased himself below all Israel; when the Ephraimites contended with him, he prefers their gleanings to his vintage, and casts his honour at their feet; and now, when Israel proffers him that kingdom which he had merited, he refuses it. He that in overcoming would allow them to cry, "The sword of the Lord and of Gideon," in governing will have none but "The sword of the Lord."

That which others plot and sue, and swear, and bribe for (dignity and superiority), he seriously rejects, whether it were for that he knew God had not yet called them to a monarchy, or rather for that he saw the crown among thorns. Why do we ambitiously affect the command of these mole-hills of earth, when wise men have refused the proffers of kingdoms? Why do we not rather labour for that kingdom which is free from all cares, from all uncertainty? Yet he that refuses their crown, calls for their ear-rings, although not to enrich himself, but religion. So long had God been a stranger to Israel, that now superstition goes current for devout worship. It were pity that good intentions should make any man wicked; here they did so. Never man meant better than Gideon in his rich ephod; yet this very act set all Israel on whoring. God had chosen a place, and a service of his own. When the wit of man will be overpleasing God with better devices than his own, it turns to madness, and ends in mischief.

CONTEMPLATION VIII.—ABIMELECH'S USURPATION.

GIDEON refused the kingdom of Israel when it was offered; his seventy sons offered not to obtain that sceptre, which their father's victory had deserved to make hereditary: only Abimelech, the concubine's son, sues and ambitiously plots for it. What could Abimelech see in himself, that he should overlook all his brethren? If he looked to his father, they were his equals; if to his mother, they were his betters. Those that are most unworthy of honour are hottest in the chase of it; whilst the consciousness of better deserts bids men sit still, and stay to be either importuned or neglected. There can be no greater sign of unfitness, than vehement suit. It is hard to say, whether there be more pride or ignorance in ambition. I have noted this difference betwixt spiritual and earthly honour, and the clients of both; we cannot be worthy of the one without earnest prosecution, nor with earnest prosecution worthy of the other. The violent obtain heaven; only the meek are worthy to inherit the earth.

That which an aspiring heart hath projected, it will find both argument and means to effect: if either bribes or favour will carry it, the proud man will not sit out. The Shechemites are fit brokers for Abimelech: that city which once betrayed itself to utter depopulation, in yielding to the suit of Hamor, now betrays itself, and all Israel, in yielding to the request of Abimelech. By them hath this usurper made himself a fair way to the throne. It was an easy question, Whether will ye admit of the sons of Gideon for your rulers, or of strangers? If of the sons of Gideon, whether of all, or one? If of one, whether of your own flesh and blood, or of others unknown? To cast off the sons of Gideon for strangers, were unthankful; to admit of seventy kings in one small country, were unreasonable; to admit of any other, rather than their own kinsman, were unnatural. Gideon's sons therefore must rule amongst all Israel; one of his sons amongst those seventy: and who should be that one but Abimelech? Natural respects are the most dangerous corrupters of all elections. What hope can there be of worthy superiors in any free people, where nearness of blood carries it from fitness of disposition? Whilst they say, "He is our brother," they are enemies to themselves and Israel.

Fair words have won his brethren, they the Shechemites: the Shechemites furnish him with money, money with men: his men begin with murder, and now Abimelech reigns alone. Flattery, bribes, and blood, are the usual stairs of the ambitious. The money of Baal is a fit hire for murderers; that which idolatry hath gathered is fitly spent upon treason. One devil is ready to help another in mischief; seldom ever are ill-gotten riches better employed. It is no wonder if he, that hath Baal his idol, now make an idol of honour. There was never any man that worshipped but one idol. Woe be to them that lie in the way of the aspiring! though they be brothers, they shall bleed; yea, the nearer they are, the more sure is their ruin. Who would not now think that Abimelech should find a hell in his breast, after so barbarous and unnatural a massacre? and yet, behold, he is as senseless as the stone upon which the blood of his seventy brethren was spilt. Where ambition hath possessed itself thoroughly of the soul, it turns the heart into steel, and makes it incapable of a conscience. All sins will easily down with the man that is resolved to rise.

Only Jotham fell not at that fatal stone with his brethren. It is a hard battle where none escapes. He escapes, not to reign, nor to revenge, but to be a prophet, and a witness of the vengeance of God upon the usurper, upon the abettors; he lives to tell Abimelech that he was but a bramble, a weed, rather than a tree. A right bramble indeed, that grew out of the base hedge-row of a concubine; that could not lift up his head from the earth, unless he were supported by some bush or pale of Shechem, that had laid hold of the fleece of Israel, and had drawn blood of all his brethren; and, lastly, that had no substance in him, but the sap of vain glory, and the pricks of cruelty. It was better than a kingdom to him, out of his obscure bier, to see the fire out of this bramble to consume those trees. The view of God's revenge is so much more pleasing to a good heart, than his own, by how much it is more just and full.

There was never such a pattern of unthankfulness as these Israelites. They who lately thought a kingdom too small recompense for Gideon and his sons, now think it too much for his seed to live; and take life away from the sons of him that gave them both life and liberty. Yet if this had been some hundreds of years after, when time had worn out the memory of Jerub-baal, it might have borne a better excuse. No man can hope to hold pace with time the best names may not think scorn to be unknown to following generations. But ere their deliverer was cold in his coffin, to pay his benefits (which deserve to be everlasting) with the extirpation of his posterity, it was more than savage. What can be looked for from idolaters? If a man have cast off his God, he will easily cast off his friends. When religion is once gone, humanity will not stay long after.

That which the people were punished afterwards for but desiring, he enjoys. Now is Abimelech seated in the throne which his father refused, and no rival is seen to envy his peace. But how long will this glory last? Stay but three years, and ye shall see this bramble withered and burnt. The prosperity of the wicked is but short and fickle. A stolen crown (though it may look fair) cannot be made of any but brittle stuff. All life is uncertain; but wickedness overruns nature.

The evil spirit thrust himself into the plot of Abimelech's usurpation and murder, and wrought with the Shechemites for both; and now God sends the evil spirit betwixt Abimelech and the Shechemites to work the ruin of each other. The first could not have been without God; but, in the second, God challenges a part. Revenge is his, where the sin is ours. It had been pity that the Shechemites should have been plagued by any other hand than Abimelech's. They raised him unjustly to the throne; they are the first that feel the weight of his sceptre. The foolish bird limes herself with that which grew from her own excretion. Who wonders to see the kind peasant stung with his own snake?

The breach begins at Shechem: his own countrymen fly off from their promised allegiance. Though all Israel should have fallen off from Abimelech, yet they of Shechem should have stuck close. It was their act, they ought to have made it good. How should good princes be honoured, when even Abimelechs, once settled, cannot be opposed with safety? Now they begin to revolt to the rest of Israel. Yet, if this had been done out of repentance, it had been praiseworthy; but to be done out of a treacherous inconstancy, was unworthy of Israelites. How could Abimelech hope for fidelity, of them, whom he had made and found traitors to his father's blood? No man knows how to be sure of him that is unconscionable. He that hath been unfaithful to one, knows the way to be perfidious, and is only fit for his trust that is worthy to be deceived; whereas faithfulness, besides the present good, lays a ground of further assurance. The friendship that is begun in evil cannot stand: wickedness, both of its own nature, and through the curse of God, is ever unsteady; and though there be not a disagreement in hell (being but the place of retribution, not of action), yet on earth there is no peace among the wicked; whereas that affection which is knit in God, is indissoluble.

If the men of Shechem had abandoned their false god, with their false king, and out of a serious remorse, and desire of satisfaction for their idolatry and blood, had opposed this tyrant, and preferred Jotham to his throne, there might have been both warrant for their quarrel, and hope of success: but now, if Abimelech be a wicked usurper, yet the Shechemites are idolatrous traitors. How could they think, that God would rather revenge Abimelech's bloody intrusion by them, than their treachery and idolatry by Abimelech? When the quarrel is betwixt God and Satan, there is no doubt of the issue; but when one devil fights with another, what certainty is there of the victory? Though the cause of God had been good, yet it had been safe for them to look to themselves. The unworthiness of the agent many times curses a good enterprise.

No sooner is a secret dislike kindled in any people against their governors, than there is a gale ready to blow the coals. It were a wonder, if ever any faction should want a head; as, contrarily, never any man was so ill, as not to have some favourers: Abimelech hath a Zebul in the midst of Shechem. Lightly, all treasons are betrayed, even with some of their own: his intelligence brings the sword of Abimelech upon Shechem, who now hath demolished the city, and sown it with salt. O the just successions of the revenges of God! Gideon's ephod is punished with the blood of his sons; the blood of his sons is shed by the procurement of the Shechemites; the blood of the Shechemites is shed by Abimelech; the blood of Abimelech is spilt by a woman. The retaliations of God are sure and just, and make a more due pedigree than descent of nature.

The pursued Shechemites fly to the house of their god Berith: now they are safe; that place is at once a fort, and a sanctuary. Whither should we fly in our distress, but to our God? And now this refuge shall teach them what a god they have served. The jealous God, whom they had forsaken, hath them now where he would, and rejoices at once to be avenged of their god and them. Had they not made the house of Baal their shelter, they had not died so fearfully. Now, according to the prophecy of Jotham, a fire goes out of the bramble, and consumes these cedars, and their eternal flames begin in the house of their Berith. The confusion of wicked men rises out of the false deities which they have doted on.

Of all the conspirators against Gideon's sons, only Abimelech yet survives; and his day is now coming. His success against Shechem hath filled his heart with thoughts of victory; he hath caged up the inhabitants of Tebez within their tower also; and what remains for them, but the same end with their neighbours? And behold, while his hand is busy in putting fire to the door of their tower, which yet was not high (for then he could not have discerned a woman to be his executioner), a stone from a woman's hand strikes his head. His pain in dying was not so much, as his indignation to know by whom he died; and rather will he die twice, than a woman should kill him. If God had not known his stomach so big, he had not vexed him with the impotency of his victor. God finds a time to reckon with wicked men, for all the arrearages of their sins. Our sins are not more our debts to God, than his judgments are his debts to our sins, which at last he will be sure to pay home. There now lies the greatness of Abimelech: upon one stone had he slain his seventy brethren, and now a stone slays him: his head had stolen the crown of Israel, and now his head is smitten. And what is Abimelech better that he was a king? What difference is there between him and any of his seventy brethren whom he murdered, save only in guiltiness? They bear but their own blood; he the weight of all theirs. How happy a thing it is to live well, that our death, as it is certain, so may be comfortable! What a vanity is it to exult in the death of them whom we must follow the same way!

The tyrant hath his payment, and that time which he should have bestowed in calling for mercy to God, and washing his soul with the last tears of contrition, he vainly spends in deprecating an idle reproach: "Kill me," that it may not be said he died by a woman—a fit conclusion for such a life! The expectation of true and endless torment doth not so much vex him, as the frivolous report of a dishonour: neither is he so much troubled with Abimelech's frying in hell, as Abimelech is slain by a woman. So vain fools are niggardly of their reputation, and prodigal of their souls. Do we not see them run wilfully into the field, into the grave, into hell? and all lest it should be said, they have but as much fear as wit.

BOOK X.

CONTEMPLATION I.—JEPHTHAH.

ISRAEL, that had now long gone a whoring from God, hath been punished by the regiment of the concubine's son, and at last seeks protection from the son of a harlot. It is no small misery to be obliged unto the unworthy. The concubine's son made suit to them; they made suit to the son of the harlot. It was no fault of Jephthah that he had an ill mother; yet is he branded with the indignity of his bastardy. Neither would God conceal this blemish of nature, which Jephthah could neither avoid nor remedy. God, to show his detestation of whoredom, revenges it not only upon the actors, but upon their issue. Hence he hath shut out the base son from the congregation of Israel, to the tenth generation, that a transient evil might have a durable reproach attending it; and that after the death of the adulterer, yet his shame might live. But that God, who justly ties men to his laws, will not abide we should tie him to our laws, or his own: he can both rectify and ennoble the blood of Jephthah. That no man should be too much discouraged with the errors of his propagation, even the base son of man may be the lawfully begotten of God; and though he be cast out from the inheritance of his brethren upon earth, may be admitted to the kingdom of Israel.

I hear no praise of the lawful issue of Gilead; only this misbegotten son is commended for his valour, and set at the stern of Israel. The common gifts of God respect not the parentage or blood, but are indifferently scattered where he pleases to let them fall. The choice of the Almighty is not guided by our rules: as in spiritual, so in earthly things, it is not in him that willeth. If God would have men glory in these outward privileges, he would bestow them upon none but the worthy.

Now, who can be proud of strength or greatness, when he sees him that is not so honest, yet is more valiant, and more advanced? Had not Jephthah been base, he had not been thrust out; and if he had not been thrust out from his brethren, he had never been the captain of Israel. By contrary paces to ours, it pleaseth God to come to his own ends: and how usually doth he look the contrary way to that he moves? No man can measure the conclusion of God's act by his beginning. He that fetches good out of evil, raises the glory of men out of their ruin. Men love to go the nearest way, and often fail. God commonly goes about, and in his own time comes surely home.

The Gileadites were not so forward to expel Jephthah, as glad to recal him. No Ammonite threatened them, when they parted with such a helper: now, whom they cast out in their peace, they fetch home in their danger and misery. That God who never gave aught in vain, will find a time to make use of any gift that he hath bestowed upon men. The valour of Jephthah shall not rust in his secresy, but be employed to the common preservation of Israel. Necessity will drive us to seek up all our helps, even those whom our wantonness hath despised.

How justly are the suits of our need upbraided with the errors of our prosperity! The elders of Gilead now hear of their ancient wrong, and dare not find fault with their exprobration: "Did ye not hate me, and expel me out of my father's house? how then come ye now to me in time of tribulation?" The same expostulation that Jephthah makes with Gilead, God also at the same time makes with Israel: "Ye have forsaken me, and have served other gods; wherefore should I deliver you any more? Go, and cry unto the gods whom ye have served." As we, so God also finds it seasonable to tell his children of their faults, while he is whipping them. It is a safe and wise course, to make much of those in our peace, whom we must make use of in our extremity; else it is but just that we should be rejected of those whom we have rejected.

Can we look for any other answer from God than this? Did ye not drive me out of your houses, out of your hearts, in the time of your health and jollity? Did ye not plead the strictness of my charge, and the weight of my yoke? Did not your wilful sins expel me from your souls? What do you now, crouching and creeping to me in the evil day? Surely, O God, it is but justice, if thou be not found of those which were glad to lose thee! It is thy mercy if, after many checks and delays, thou wilt be found at last. Where an act cannot be reversed, there is no amends but confession; and if God himself take up with this satisfaction, " He that confesses shall find mercy," how much more should men hold themselves well paid, with words of humility and deprecation!

Jephthah's wisdom had not been answerable to his valour, if he had not made his match beforehand. He could not but know how treacherously Israel had dealt with Gideon. We cannot make too sure work, when we have to do with unfaithful men. It hath been an old policy to serve ourselves of men, and, after our advantage, to turn them up. He bargains, therefore, for his sovereignty, ere he win it: " Shall I be your head?" We are all naturally ambitious, and are ready to buy honour even with hazard. And if the hope of a troublesome superiority encouraged Jephthah to fight against the forces of Ammon, what heart should we take in the battles of God, against spiritual wickednesses, when the God of heaven hath said, " To him that overcomes, will I give power over nations, and to sit with me in my throne?" O that we could bend our eyes upon the recompense of our reward! how willingly should we march forward against those mighty Ammonites! Jephthah is noted for his valour, and yet he treats with Ammon, ere he fights. To make war any other than our last remedy, is not courage, but cruelty and rashness. And now, when reason will not prevail, he betakes himself to his sword.

As God began the war with Jephthah. in raising up his heart to that pitch of fortitude; so Jephthah began his war at God, in craving victory from him, and pouring out his vow to him. His hand took hold of his sword, his heart of God; therefore he, whom the Old Testament styles valiant, the New styles faithful; he who is commended for his strength, dares trust in none but the arm of God: "If thou wilt give the Ammonites into my hand." If Jephthah had not looked upward for his victory, in vain had the Gileadites looked up to him. This is the disposition of all good hearts: they look to their sword, or their bow, as servants, not as patrons; and, whilst they use them, trust to God. If we could do so in all our businesses, we should have both more joy in their success, and less discomfort in their miscarriage. It was his zeal to vow; it was his sin to vow rashly. Jacob, his forefather, of whom he learned to vow, might have taught him a better form: "If God will be with me, then shall the Lord be my God." It is well with vows, when the thing promised makes the promise good. But when Jephthah says, "Whatsoever thing cometh out of the doors of my house shall be the Lord's, and I will offer it for a burnt sacrifice;" his devotion is blind, and his good affection overruns his judgment. For what if a dog or a swine, or an ass, had met him? where had been the promise of his consecration?

Vows are as they are made, like unto scents: if they be of ill composition, nothing offends more; if well tempered, nothing is more pleasant. Either certainty of evil, or uncertainty of good, or impossibility of performance, makes vows no service to God. When we vow what we cannot, or what we ought not do, we mock God. instead of honouring him. It is a vain thing for us to go about to catch God hoodwinked. The conscience shall never find peace in any way, but that which we see before us, and which we know safe, both in the kind and circumstances. There is no comfort in, Peradventure I may please God. What good child will not take part of the parent's joy? If Jephthah return with trophies, it is no marvel if his daughter meet him with timbrels. O that we could be so affected with the glorious acts of our heavenly Father! Thou subduest thine enemies, and mightily deliverest thy people, O God: a song waiteth for thee in Sion.

Who would have suspected danger in a dutiful triumph? Well might Jephthah's daughter have thought, My sex forbade me to do any thing towards the help of my father's victory: I can do little, if I cannot applaud it. If nature have made me weak, yet not unthankful: nothing forbids my joy to be as strong as the victor's. Though I might not go out with my father to fight, yet I may meet him with gratulations. A timbrel may become these hands which were unfit for a sword: this day hath made me the daughter of the head of Israel; this day hath made both Israel free, my father a conqueror, and myself in him noble: and shall my affection make no difference? What must my father needs think, if he shall find me sitting sullenly at home, whilst all Israel strives who shall run first to bless him with their acclamations? Should I only be insensible of his and the common happiness?

And now behold, when she looks for most thanks, her father answers the measure of her feet with the knockings of his breast, and weeps at her music, and tears his clothes, to look upon her whom he best loved, and gives no answer to her timbrels, but, "Alas, my daughter, thou art of them that trouble me!" Her joy alone hath changed the day, and lost the comfort of that victory which she enjoyed to see won. It falls out often, that those times and occasions which promise most contentment, prove most doleful in the issue. The heart of this virgin was never lifted up so high as now, neither did any day of her life seem happy but this; and this only proves the day of her solemn and perpetual mourning. As contrarily, the times and events which we have most distrusted, prove most beneficial. It is good, in a fair morning, to think of the storm that may rise ere night, and to enjoy both good and evil fearfully.

Miserable is that devotion which troubles us in the performance. Nothing is more pleasant than the acts of true piety. Jephthah might well see the wrong of this religion, in the distaste of it: yet, while himself had troubled his daughter, he says, "Alas, my daughter, thou art of them that trouble me!" She did but her duty; he did what he should not: yet he would be rid of the blame, though he cannot of the smart. No man is willing to own a sin: the first man shifted it from himself to his wife; this from himself to his daughter. He was ready to accuse another, which only committed it himself. It were happy if we could be as loath to commit sin, as to acknowledge it.

The inconsideration of this vow was very tough and settled: "I have opened my mouth, and cannot go back." If there were just cause to repent, it was the weakness of his zeal to think that a vow could bind him to evil. An unlawful vow is ill made, but worse performed. It were pity this constancy should light upon any one but a holy object. No loan can make a truer debt than our vow; which if we pay not in our performance, God will pay us with judgment. We have all opened our mouths to God, in that initial and solemn vow of Christianity. O that we could not go back! So much more is our vow obligatory, by how much the thing vowed is more necessary

Why was the soul of Jephthah thus troubled, but because he saw the entail of his new honour thus suddenly cut off? he saw the hope of posterity extinguished in the virginity of his daughter. It is natural to us to affect that perpetuity in our succession, which is denied us in our persons: our very bodies would emulate the eternity of the soul. And if God have built any of us a house on earth, as well as prepared us a house in heaven, it must be confessed a favour worth our thankfulness; but as the perpetuity of our earthly houses is uncertain, so let us not rest our hearts upon that, but make sure of the house which is eternal in the heavens.

Doubtless the goodness of the daughter added to the father's sorrow: she was not more loving, than religious; neither is she less willing to be the Lord's than her father's; and, as provoking her father to that which he thought piety, though to her own wrong, she says, "If thou hast opened thy mouth unto the Lord, do with me as thou hast promised." Many a daughter would have dissuaded her father with tears, and have wished rather her father's impiety, than her own prejudice; she sues for the smart of her father's vow. How obsequious should children be to the will of their careful parents, even in their final disposition in the world, when they see this holy maid willing to abandon the world upon the rash vow of a father! They are the living goods of their parents, and must therefore wait upon the bestowing of their owners. They mistake themselves which think they are their own. If this maid had vowed herself to God, without her father, it had been in his power to abrogate it; but now that she vowed her to God without herself, it stands in force. But what shall we say to those children, whom their parents' vow and care cannot make so much as honest,—that will be no other than godless, in spite of their baptism and education? what but that they are given their parents for a curse, and shall one day find what it is to be rebellious?

All her desire is, that she may have leave to bewail that which she must be forced to keep, her virginity. If she had not held it an affliction, there had been no cause to bewail it; it had been no thank to undergo it, if she had not known it to be a cross.

Tears are no argument of impatience; we may mourn for that we repine not to bear. How comes that to be a meritorious virtue under the gospel, which was but a punishment under the law? The daughters of Israel had been too lavish of their tears, if virginity had been absolutely good. What injury should it have been, to lament that spiritual preferment which they should rather have emulated!

While Jephthah's daughter was two months in the mountains, she might have had good opportunity to escape her father's vow; but as one whom her obedience tied as close to her father, as his vow tied him to God, she returns to take up that burden which she had bewailed to foresee. If we be truly dutiful to our Father in heaven, we would not slip our necks out of the yoke, though we might, nor fly from his commands, though the door were open.

CONTEMPLATION II.—SAMSON CONCEIVED.

Of extraordinary persons, the very birth and conception is extraordinary: God begins his wonders betimes, in those whom he will make wonderful. There was never any of those which were miraculously conceived, whose lives were not notable and singular. The presages of the womb and the cradle, are commonly answered in the life: it is not the use of God to cast away strange beginnings. If Manoah's wife had not been barren, the angel had not been sent to her. Afflictions have this advantage, that they occasion God to show that mercy to us, whereof the prosperous are incapable. It would not beseem a mother to be so indulgent to a healthful child, as to a sick. It was to the woman that the angel appeared, not to the husband; whether for that the reproach of barrenness lay upon her more heavily than on the father; or for that the birth of the child should cost her more dear than her husband; or, lastly, for that the difficulty of this news was more in her conception than in his generation. As Satan lays his batteries ever to the weakest; so, contrarily God addresseth his comforts to those hearts that have most need: as, at the first, because Eve had most reason to be dejected, for that her sin had drawn man into the trangression; therefore the cordial of God most respecteth her: "The seed of the woman shall break the serpent's head."

As a physician first tells the state of the disease with its symptoms, and then prescribes; so doth the angel of God first tell the wife of Manoah her complaint, then her remedy: "Thou art barren." All our afflictions are more noted of that God which sends them, than of the patient that suffers them: how can it be but less possible to endure any thing that he knows not, than that he inflicteth it not? He saith to one, Thou art sick; to another, Thou art poor; to a third, Thou art defamed; Thou art oppressed, to another. That all-seeing eye takes notice from heaven of every man's condition, no less than if he should send an angel to tell us he knew it. His knowledge, compared with his mercy, is the just comfort of all our sufferings. O God, we are many times miserable, and feel it not! thou knowest even those sorrows which we might have; thou knowest what thou hast done: do what thou wilt.

"Thou art barren." Not that the angel would upbraid the poor woman with her affliction; but therefore he names her pain, that the mention of her cure might be much more welcome. Comfort shall come unseasonably to that heart which is not apprehensive of his own sorrow. We must first know our evils, ere we can quit them. It is the just method of every true angel of God, first to let us see that whereof either we do, or should complain, and then to apply comforts: like as a good physician first pulls down the body, and then raises it with cordials. If we cannot abide to hear of our faults, we are not capable of amendment.

If the angel had first said, "Thou shalt conceive," and not premised, "Thou art barren," I doubt whether she had conceived faith in her soul, of that infant which her body should conceive: now his knowledge of her present estate makes way for the assurance of the future. Thus ever it pleases our good God to leave a pawn of his fidelity with us; that we should not distrust him in what he will do, when we find him faithful in that which we see done.

It is good reason that he, which gives the son to the barren mother, should dispose of him, and diet him, both in the womb first, and after in the world. The mother must first be a Nazarite, that her son may be so. While she was barren, she might drink what she would; but now, that she shall conceive a Samson, her choice must be limited. There is a holy austerity that ever follows the special calling of God. The worldling may take his full scope, and deny his back and belly nothing; but he that hath once conceived that blessed burden, whereof Samson was a type, must be strict and severe to himself: neither his tongue, nor his palate, nor his hand, may run riot. Those pleasures which seemed not unseemly for the multitude, are now debarred him. We borrow more names of our Saviour than one: as we are Christians, so we are Nazarites. The consecration of our God is upon our heads, and therefore our very hair should be holy. Our appetites must be curbed, our passions moderated, and so estranged from the world, that in the loss of parents, or children, nature may not make us forget grace. What doth the looseness of vain men persuade them that God is not curious, when they see him thus precisely ordering the very diet of his Nazarites? Nature pleads for liberty, religion for restraint; not that there is more uncleanness in the grape, than in the fountain; but that wine finds more uncleanness in us, than water; and that the high feed is not so fit for devotion, as abstinence. Who sees not a ceremony in this command? which yet carries with it this substance of everlasting use, that God and the belly will not admit of one servant; that quaffing and cramming is not the way to heaven. A drunken Nazarite is a monster among men. We have now more scope than the ancients: not drinking of wine, but drunkenness with wine is forbidden to the evangelical Nazarite; wine, wherein is excess. O that ever Christians should quench the Spirit of God with a liquor of God's own making! that they should suffer their hearts to be drowned with wine, and should so live, as if the practice of the gospel were quite contrary to the rule of the law!

The mother must conceive the only giant of Israel, and yet must drink but water; neither must the child touch any other cup. Never wine made so strong a champion, as water did here. The power of nourishment is not in the creatures, but in their Maker. Daniel and his three companions kept their complexion, with the same diet wherewith Samson got his strength; he that gave that power to the grape, can give it to the stream. O God, how justly do we raise our eyes from our tables unto thee, which can make water nourish, and wine enfeeble us!

Samson had not a better mother than Manoah had a wife; she hides not the good news in her own bosom, but imparts it to her husband. That wife hath learned to make a true use of her head, which is ever ready to consult with him about the messages of God. If she were made for his helper, he is much more her's. Thus should good women make amends for their first offence; that as Eve no sooner had received an ill motion, but she delivered it to her husband; so they should no sooner receive good, than they should impart it.

Manoah (like one which in those lewd times had not lost his acquaintance with God) so soon as he hears the news, falls down upon his knees. I do not hear him call forth and address his servants to all the coasts of heaven (as the children of the prophets did in the search of Elias) to find out the messenger; but I see him rather look straight up to that God which sent him: " My Lord, I pray thee, let that man of God come again." As a straight line is the shortest, the nearest cut to any blessing is to go by heaven: as we may not sue to God, and neglect means, so we must sue to God for those means which we shall use.

When I see the strength of Manoah's faith, I marvel not that he had a Samson to his son: he saw not the messenger, he heard not the errand, he examined not the circumstances; yet now he takes thought, not whether he should have a son, but how he shall order the son which he must have; and sues to God, not for the son which as yet he had not, but for the direction of governing him when he should be. Zechariah had the same message, and, craving a sign, lost that voice wherewith he craved it. Manoah seeks no sign for the promise, but counsel for himself; and yet that angel spake to Zachary himself; this only to the wife of Manoah: that in the temple, like a glorious spirit; this in the house, or field, like some prophet or traveller: that to a priest; this to a woman. All good men have not equal measures of faith: the bodies of men have not more differences of stature, than their graces. Credulity to men is faulty and dangerous; but, in the matters of God, is the greatest virtue of a Christian. Happy are they that have not seen, yet believed. True faith takes all for granted, yea, for performed, which is once promised.

He, that before sent his angel unasked, will much more send him again upon entreaty: those heavenly messengers are ready both to obey their Maker, and to relieve his children. Never any man prayed for direction in his duties to God, and was repulsed: rather will God send an angel from heaven to instruct us, than our good desires shall be frustrate.

Manoah prayed; the angel appeared again, not to him, but to his wife. It had been the shorter way to have come first to the man, whose prayers procured his presence. But as Manoah went directly and immediately to God, so God comes immediately and about to him; and will make her the means to bear the message to her husband, who must bear him the son: both the blessing and the charge are chiefly meant to her. It was a good care of Manoah, when the angel had given order to his wife alone for the governing of the child's diet, to proffer himself to his charge: " How shall we order the child?" As both the parents have their part in the being of their children, so should they have in their education; it is both unreasonable and unnatural in husbands to cast this burden upon the weaker vessel alone: it is no reason that she, which alone hath had the pain of their birth, should have the pain of their breeding. Though the charge be renewed to the wife, yet the speech is directed to the husband; the act must be her's, his must be the oversight: " Let her observe all I commanded her." The head must overlook the body; it is the duty of the husband to be careful that the wife do her duty to God.

As yet Manoah saw nothing but the outside of a man, and therefore offers the angel an answerable entertainment, wherein there is at once hospitality and thankfulness. No man shall bring him good news from God, and go away unrecompensed How forward he is to feast him, whom he took for a prophet! Their feet should be so much more beautiful that bring us news of salvation, by how much their errand is better.

That Manoah might learn to acknowledge God in this man, he sets off the proffer of his thankfulness from himself to God, and (as the same angel which appeared to Gideon) turns his feast into a sacrifice. And now he is Manoah's solicitor to better thanks than he offered. How forward the good angels are to incite us unto piety! Either this was the Son himself, which said, " It was his meat and drink to do his Father's will," or else one of his spiritual attendants of the same diet. We can never feast the angels better, than with our hearty sacrifices to God. Why do not we learn this lesson of them, whom we propound to ourselves as patterns of our obedience? We shall be once like the angels in condition; why are we not, in the meantime, in our dispositions? If we do not provoke and exhort one another to godliness, and do care more for a feast than a sacrifice, our appetite is not angelical, but brutish.

It was an honest mind in Manoah, while he was addressing a sacrifice to God, yet not to neglect his messenger: fain would he know whom to honour. True piety is not uncivil, but, while it magnifies the author of all blessings, is thankful to the means. Secondary causes are worthy of regard; neither need it detract any thing from the praise of the agent, to honour the instrument. It is not only rudeness, but injustice in those which can be content to hear good news from God, with contempt to the bearers.

The angel will neither take nor give, but conceals his very name from Manoah. All honest motions are not fit to be yielded to; good intentions are not always sufficient grounds of condescent. If we do sometimes ask what we know not, it is no marvel if we receive not what we ask. In some cases, the angel of God tells his name unasked, as Gabriel to the virgin here, not by entreaty. If it were the angel of the covenant, he had as yet no name but Jehovah; if a created angel, he had no commission to tell his name; and a faithful messenger hath not a word beyond his charge. Besides that he saw it would be of more use for Manoah, to know him really, than by words. O the bold presumption of those men, which (as if they had long sojourned in heaven, and been acquainted with all the holy legions of spirits) discourse of their orders, of their titles, when this one angel stops the mouth of a better man than they, with " Why dost thou ask after my name, which is secret?" " Secret things belong to God; revealed, to us and our children." No word can be so significant as actions. The act of the angel tells best who he was: he did wonderfully; Wonderful, therefore, was his name. So soon as ever the flame of the sacrifice ascended, he mounted up in the smoke of it, that Manoah might see the sacrifice and the messenger belonged both to one God, and might know both whence to acknowledge the message, and whence to expect the performance.

Gideon's angel vanished at his sacrifice, but this in the sacrifice; that Manoah might at once see both the confirmation of his promise, and the acceptance of his obedience, while the angel of God vouchsafed to perfume himself with that holy smoke, and carry the scent of it up into heaven. Manoah believed before, and craved no sign to assure him; God voluntarily confirms it to him above his desire: " To him that hath, shall be given." Where there are beginnings of faith, the mercy of God will add perfection.

How do we think Manoah and his wife looked to see this spectacle? They had not spirit enough left to look one upon another; but, instead of looking up cheerfully to heaven, they fall down to the earth upon their faces; as weak eyes are dazzled with that which should comfort them. This is the infirmity of our nature, to be afflicted with the causes of our joy, to be astonished with our confirmations, to conceive death in that vision of God, wherein our life and happiness consist. If this homely sight of the angel did so confound good Manoah, what shall become of the enemies of God, when they shall be brought before the glorious tribunal of the God of angels.

I marvel not now, that the angel appeared both times rather to the wife of Manoah: her faith was the stronger of the two. It falls out sometimes, that the weaker vessel is fuller, and that of more precious liquor. That wife is no helper, which is not ready to give spiritual comfort to her husband. The reason was good and irrefragable: " If the Lord were pleased to kill us, he would not have received a burnt-offering from us." God will not accept gifts where he intends punishment, and professes hatred: " The sacrifice of the wicked is abomination to the Lord." If we can find assurance of God's acceptation of our sacrifices, we may be sure he loves our persons. If I incline to wickedness in my heart, the Lord will not hear me: but the Lord hath heard me.

CONTEMPLATION III. — SAMSON'S MARRIAGE.

Of all the deliverers of Israel, there is none of whom are reported so many weaknesses, or so many miracles, as of Samson. The news which the angel told of his conception and education was not more strange than the news of his own choice: he but sees a daughter of the Philistines, and falls in love. All this strength begins in infirmity. One maid of the Philistines overcomes that champion, which was given to overcome the Philistines. Even he that was dieted with water, found heat of unfit desires. As his body was strong, notwithstanding that fare, so were his passions; without the gift of continency, a low feed may impair nature, but not inordination. To follow nothing but the eye in the choice of his wife, was a lust unworthy of a Nazarite: this is to make the sense not a counsellor but a tyrant.

Yet was Samson in this very impotency dutiful: he did not, in the presumption of his strength, ravish her forcibly; he did not make up a clandestine match, without consulting with his parents, but he makes suit to them for consent: " Give me her to wife;" as one that could be master of his own act, though not of his passion, and as one that had learned so to be a suitor, as not to forget himself to be a son. Even in this deplored state of Israel, children durst not presume to be their own carvers: how much less is this tolerable in a well guided and Christian commonwealth? Whosoever now dispose of themselves without their parents, they do wilfully unchild themselves, and change natural affection for violent.

It is no marvel if Manoah and his wife were astonished at this unequal motion of her son. Did not the angel (thought they) tell us, that this child should be consecrated to God; and must he begin his youth in unholy wedlock? Did not the angel say, that our son should begin to save Israel from the Philistines; and is he now captivated in his affections by a daughter of the Philistines? Shall our deliverance from the Philistines begin in an alliance? Have we been so scrupulously careful that he should eat no unclean thing, and shall we now consent to a heathenish match? Now, therefore, they gravely endeavour to cool this intemperate heat of his passion with good counsel; as those which well knew the inconveniences of an unequal yoke: corruption in religion, alienation of affections, distraction of thoughts, connivance at idolatry, death of zeal, dangerous underminings, and lastly, an unholy seed. Who can blame them, if they were unwilling to call a Philistine daughter?

I wish Manoah could speak so loud, that all our Israelites might hear him: " Is there never a woman among the daughters of thy brethren, or among all God's people, that thou goest to take a wife of the uncircumcised Philistines?" If religion be any other than a cipher, how dare we not regard it in our most important choice? Is she a fair Philistine? Why is not this deformity of the soul more powerful to dissuade us than the beauty of the face or of metal to allure us? To dote upon a fair skin, when we see a Philistine under it, is sensual and brutish.

Affection is not more blind than deaf. In vain do the parents seek to alter a young man, not more strong in body than in will. Though he cannot defend his desires, yet he pursues them: " Get her, for she pleases me." And although it must needs be a weak motion that can plead no reason but appetite, yet the good parents, since they cannot bow the affection of their son with persuasion, dare not break it with violence. As it becomes not children to be forward in their choice, so parents may not be too peremptory in their denial. It is not safe for children to overrun parents in settling their affections; nor for parents (where the impediments are not very material) to come short of their children, when the affections are once settled: the one is disobedience; the other may be tyranny.

I know not whether I may excuse either Samson in making this suit, or his parents in yielding to it, by a divine dispensation in both; for, on the one side, while the Spirit of God notes that as yet his parents knew not this was of the Lord, it may seem that he knew it; and is it likely he would know and not impart it? This alone was enough to win, yea, to command his parents: it is not mine eye only, but the counsel of God that leads me to this choice. The way to quarrel with the Philistines is to match with them. If I follow mine affection, mine affection follows God in this project. Surely he that commanded his prophet afterwards to marry a harlot, may have appointed his Nazarite to marry with a Philistine. On the other side, whether it were of God's permitting, or allowing, I find not. It might so be of God, as all the evil in the city; and then the interposition of God's decree shall be no excuse of Samson's infirmity. I would rather think that God meant only to make a treacle of a viper; and rather appointed to fetch good out of Samson's evil, than to approve that for good in Samson, which in itself was evil.

When Samson went on wooing, he might have made the sluggard's excuse, " There is a lion in the way;" but he that could not be stayed by persuasion, will not by fear. A lion, young, wild, fierce, hungry, comes roaring upon him, when he had no weapon but his hand, no fence but his strength. The same providence that carried him to Timnah, brought the lion to him. It hath been ever the fashion of God to exercise his champions with some initiatory encounters: both Samson and David must first fight with lions, then with Philistines; and he, whose type they bore, meets with that roaring lion of the wilderness in the very threshold of his public charge. The same hand that prepared a lion for Samson, hath proportionable matches for every Christian: God never gives strength, but he employs it. Poverty meets one like an armed man; infamy, like some furious mastiff, comes flying in the face of another: the wild boar out of the forest, or the bloody tiger of persecution, sets upon one; the brawling curs of heretical pravity, or contentious neighbourhood, are

SAMSON'S MARRIAGE.

ready to bait another: and by all these meaner and brutish adversaries, will God fit us for greater conflicts. It is a pledge of our future victory over the spiritual Philistines, if we can say, My soul hath been among lions. Come forth now, thou weak Christian, and behold this preparatory battle of Samson. Dost thou now think God deals hardly with thee, in matching thee so hard, and calling thee forth to so many frays? What, dost thou but repine at thine own glory? How shouldst thou be victorious, without resistance?

If the parents of Samson had now stood behind the hedge, and seen this encounter, they would have taken no further care of matching their son with a Philistine; for who, that should see a strong lion ramping upon an unarmed man, would hope for his life and victory? The beast came bristling up his fearful mane, wafting his raised stern, his eyes sparkling with fury, his mouth roaring out knells of his last passage, and breathing death from his nostrils, and now rejoicing at so fair a prey. Surely, if the lion had had no other adversary than him whom he saw, he had not lost his hope; but now he could not see that his Maker was his enemy: " The spirit of the Lord came upon Samson." What is a beast in the hand of the Creator? He that struck the lions with the awe of Adam, Noah, and Daniel, subdued this rebellious beast to Samson. What marvel is it if Samson now tore him, as if it had been a young kid? If his bones had been brass, and his skin plates of iron, all had been one: " The right hand of the Lord bringeth mighty things to pass."

If that roaring lion, that goes about continually seeking whom he may devour, find us alone among the vineyards of the Philistines, where is our hope? Not in our heels; he is swifter than we: not in our weapons; we are naturally unarmed: not in our hands, which are weak and languishing: but in the Spirit of that God by whom we can do all things. If God fight in us, who can resist us? There is a stronger lion in us, than that against us.

Samson was not more valiant than modest; he made no words of this great exploit. The greatest performers ever make the least noise. He that works wonders alone could say, " See thou tell no man;" whereas those whose hands are most impotent, are busiest of their tongues. Great talkers show that they desire only to be thought eminent, whereas the deepest waters are least heard.

But, while he concealed this event from others, he pondered it in himself; and when he returned to Timnah, went out of the way to see his dead adversary, and could not but recall to himself his danger and deliverance. Here the beast met me; thus he fought; thus I slew him! The very dead lion taught Samson thankfulness; there was more honey in this thought than in the carcass. The mercies of God are ill bestowed upon us, if we cannot step aside to view the monuments of his deliverances: dangers may be at once past and forgotten. As Samson had not found his honeycomb, if he had not turned aside to see his lion; so we shall lose the comfort of God's benefits, if we do not renew our perils by meditation.

Lest any thing should befall Samson, wherein is not some wonder, his lion doth more amaze him dead than alive; for lo! that carcass is made a hive, and the bitterness of death is turned into the sweetness of honey! The bee, a nice and dainty creature, builds her cells in an unsavoury carcass; that carcass, that promised nothing but stench and annoyance, now offers comfort and refreshing, and, in a sort, pays Samson for the wrong offered. O the wonderful goodness of our God, that can change our terrors into pleasure, and can make the greatest evils beneficial! Is any man, by his humiliation under the hand of God, grown more faithful and conscionable? There is honey out of the lion. Is any man by his temptation or fall become more circumspect? There is also honey out of the lion. There is no Samson to whom every lion doth not yield honey. Every Christian is the better for his evils; yea, Satan himself, in his exercise of God's children, advantageth them.

Samson doth not disdain these sweets, because he finds them uncleanly laid: his diet was strict, and forbade him anything that savoured of legal impurity; yet he eats the honeycomb out of the belly of a dead beast. Good may not be refused, because the means are accidentally evil. Honey is honey still, though in a dead lion. Those are less wise and more scrupulous than Samson, which abhor the graces of God, because they find them in ill vessels. One cares not for the preacher's true doctrine, because his life is evil; another will not take a good receipt from the hand of a physician, because he is given to unlawful studies; a third will not receive a deserved contribution from the hands of a usurer. It is a weak neglect not to take the honey, because we hate the lion. God's children have right to their Father's blessings wheresoever they find them.

The match is now made; Samson (though a Nazarite) hath both a wedding and a feast. God never mislikes moderate solemnities in the severest life; and yet this bridal feast was long, the space of seven days. If Samson had matched with the best Israelite, this celebration had been no greater; neither had this perhaps been so long, if the custom of the place had not required it. Now I do not hear him plead his Nazaritism, for a colour of singularity. It is both lawful and fit, in things not prohibited, to conform ourselves to the manners and rites of those with whom we live.

That Samson might think it an honour to match with the Philistines, he, whom before the lion found alone, is now accompanied with thirty attendants: they called them companions, but they meant them for spies. The courtesies of the world are hollow and thankless; neither doth it ever purpose so ill, as when it shows fairest. None are so near to danger, as those whom it entertains with smiles. While it frowns, we know what to trust to; but the favours of it are worthy of nothing but fears and suspicion. Open defiance is better than false love.

Austerity had not made Samson uncivil: he knows how to entertain Philistines with a formal familiarity; and that his intellectual parts might be approved answerable to his arms, he will first try masteries of wit, and set their brains on work with harmless thoughts: his riddle shall oppose them, and a deep wager shall bind the solution; thirty shirts and thirty suits of raiment: neither their loss nor their gain could be much, besides the victory being divided into thirty partners: but Samson's must needs be both ways very large, who must give or receive thirty alone. The seven days of the feast are expiring, and yet they, which had been all this while devouring of Samson's meat, cannot tell who that eater should be from whence meat should come. In the course of nature, the strong feeder takes in meat, and sends out filthiness; but that meat and sweetness should come from a devouring stomach, was beyond their apprehension.

And as fools and dogs used to begin in jest and end in earnest, so did these Philistines; and therefore they force the bride to entice her husband to betray himself. Covetousness and pride have made them impatient of loss; and now they threat to fire her and her father's house, for recompense of their entertainment, rather than they will lose a small wager to an Israelite.

Somewhat of kin to these savage Philistines, are those choleric gamesters, which if the dice be not their friend, fall out with God, curse (that which is not) fortune, strike their fellows, and are ready to take vengeance upon themselves: those men are unfit for sport, that lose their patience together with their wager.

I do not wonder that a Philistine woman loved herself and her father's family more than an Israelitish bridegroom; and if she bestowed tears upon her husband, for the ransom of them, Samson himself taught her this difference, "I have not told it my father or my mother, and should I tell it thee?" If she had not been as she was, she had neither done this to Samson, nor heard this from him: matrimonial respects are dearer than natural. It was the law of Him that ordained marriage (before ever parents were), that parents should be forsaken for the husband or wife: but now Israelitish parents are worthy of more entireness than a wife of the Philistines; and yet whom the lion could not conquer, the tears of a woman have conquered. Samson never bewrayed infirmity but in uxoriousness. What assurance can there be of him that hath a Philistine in his bosom! Adam the most perfect man, Samson the strongest man, Solomon the wisest man, were betrayed with the flattery of their helpers. As there is no comfort comparable to a faithful yoke-fellow, so woe be to him that is matched with a Philistine!

It could not but much discontent Samson, to see that his adversaries had ploughed with his heifer, and that upon his own back; now therefore he pays his wager to their cost. Ascalon, the city of the Philistines, is his wardrobe; he fetches thence thirty suits, lined with the lives of their owners. He might with as much ease have slain these thirty companions, which were the authors of this evil; but his promise forbade him, while he was to clothe their bodies, to unclothe their souls; and that Spirit of God, which stirred him up to revenge, directed him in the choice of the subjects. If we wonder to see thirty throats cut for their suits, we may easily know, that this was but the occasion of that slaughter, whereof the cause was their oppression and tyranny. David slew two hundred Philistines for their foreskins; but the ground of this act was their hostility. It is just with God to destine what enemies he pleases to execution. It is not to be expostulated, why this man is stricken than another, when both are Philistines.

CONTEMPLATION IV.—SAMSON'S VICTORY.

I CAN no more justify Samson in the leaving of his wife, than in the choosing her: he chose her, because she pleased him; and because she despised him, he left her. Though her fear made her false to him in his riddle, yet she was true to his bed. That weak treachery was worthy of a check, not a desertion. All the passions of Samson were strong like himself; but (as vehement motions are not lasting) this vehement wind is soon allayed; and he is now returning with a kid to win her that had offended him, and to renew that feast which ended in her unkindness. Slight occasions may not break the knot of matrimonial love; and if any just offence have slackened it on either part, it must be fastened again by speedy reconciliation.

Now Samson's father-in-law shows himself a Philistine, the true parent of her that betrayed her husband; for no sooner is the bridegroom departed, than he changes his son: what pretence of friendship soever he make, a true Philistine will soon be weary of an Israelite. Samson had not so many days' liberty to enjoy his wedding, as he spent in celebrating it. Marriage hath been ever a sacred institution, and who but a Philistine would so easily violate it? One of his thirty companions enjoys his wife, together with his suit, and now laughs to be a partner of that bed whereon he was an attendant. The good nature of Samson, having forgotten the first wrong, carried him to a proffer of familiarity, and is repulsed; but with a gentle violence: "I thought thou hadst hated her." Lawful wedlock may not be dissolved by imaginations, but by proofs.

Who shall stay Samson from his own wife? He that slew the lion in the way of his wooing, and before whom thousands of the Philistines could not stand, yet suffers himself to be resisted by him that was once his father-in-law, without any return of private violence.

Great is the force of duty, once conceived, even to the most unworthy. This thought (I was a son) binds the hands of Samson; else how easily might he, that slew those thirty Philistines for their suits, have destroyed this family for his wife? How unnatural are those mouths that can curse the loins from which they are proceeded, and those hands that dare lift up themselves against the means of their life and being!

I never read that Samson slew any but by the motion and assistance of the Spirit of God: and the divine wisdom hath reserved these offenders to another revenge. Judgment must descend from others to them, since the wrong proceeded from others by them. In the very marriage, God foresaw and intended this parting, and in the parting, this punishment upon the Philistines. If the Philistines had not been as much enemies to God as to Samson—enemies to Israel in their oppression, no less than to Samson in this particular injury—that purpose and execution of revenge had been no better than wicked. Now he to whom vengeance belongs, sets him on work, and makes the act justice: when he commands, even very cruelty is obedience.

It was a busy and troublesome project of Samson, to use the foxes for his revenge; for not without great labour, and many hands, could so many wild creatures be got together; neither could the wit of Samson want other devices of hostility: but he meant to find out such a punishment as might in some sort answer the offence, and might imply as much contempt as trespass. By wiles, seconded with violence, had they wronged Samson, in extorting his secret, and taking away his wife: and what other emblems could these foxes tied together present unto them, than wiliness, combined with force, to work mischief?

These foxes destroy their corn, before he which sent them destroy the persons. Those judgments which begin in outward things, end in the owners. A stranger that had been of neither side, would have said, What pity it is to see good corn thus spoiled! If the creature be considered apart from the owners, it is good; and therefore if it be mispent, the abuse reflects upon the Maker of it; but if it be looked upon, with respect to an ill master, the best use of it is to perish. He, therefore, that slew the Egyptian cattle with murrain, and smote their fruit with hailstones; he that consumed the vines of Israel with the palmer-worm, and caterpillar, and cankerworm, sent also foxes by the hand of Samson, into the fields of the Philistines. Their corn was too good for them to enjoy, not too good for the foxes to burn up. God had rather his creatures should perish any way, than serve for the lust of the wicked.

There could not be such secresy in the catching of three hundred foxes, but it might well be known who had procured them. Rumour will swiftly fly of things not done; but of a thing so notoriously executed, it is no marvel if fame be a blab

The mention of the offence draws in the provocation; and now the wrong to Samson is scanned and revenged; because the fields of the Philistines are burned for the wrong done to Samson by the Timnite and his daughter, therefore the Philistines burn the Timnite and his daughter. The tying of the fire-brand between two foxes was not so witty a policy, as the setting a fire of dissension betwixt the Philistines. What need Samson be his own executioner, when his enemies will undertake that charge? There can be no more pleasing prospect to an Israelite, than to see the Philistines together by the ears.

If the wife of Samson had not feared the fire for herself and her father's house, she had not betrayed her husband; her husband had not thus plagued the Philistines; the Philistines had not consumed her and her father with fire: now she leaps into that flame which she meant to avoid. That evil which the wicked feared, meets them in their flight. How many, in a fear of poverty, seek to gain unconscionably, and die beggars! How many, to shun pain and danger, have yielded to evil, and in the long run have been met in the teeth with that mischief which they had hoped to have left behind them! How many, in a desire to eschew the shame of men, have fallen into the confusion of God! Both good and evil are sure paymasters at the last.

He that was so soon pacified towards his wife, could not but have thought this revenge more than enough, if he had not rather wielded God's quarrel than his own: he knew that God had raised him up on purpose to be a scourge to the Philistines, whom as yet he had angered more than punished. As if these, therefore, had been out-flourishes before the fray, he stirs up his courage, and strikes them, both hip and thigh, with a mighty plague. That God which can do nothing imperfectly, where he begins either mercy or judgment, will not leave till he have happily finished. As it is in his favours, so in his punishments, one stroke draws on another.

The Israelites were but slaves, and the Philistines were their masters; so much more indignantly, therefore, must they needs take it, to be thus affronted by one of their own vassals: yet shall we commend the moderation of these pagans. Samson, being not mortally wronged by one Philistine, falls foul upon the whole nation: the Philistines, heinously offended by Samson, do not fall upon the whole tribe of Judah, but, being mustered together, call to them for satisfaction from the person offending. The same hand of God, which wrought Samson to revenge, restrained them from it. It is no thank to themselves, that sometimes wicked men cannot be cruel.

The men of Judah are by their fear made friends to their tyrants, and traitors to their friend; it was in their cause that Samson had shed blood, and yet they conspire with the Philistines to destroy their own flesh and blood. So shall the Philistines be quit with Israel, that as Samson by Philistines revenged himself of Philistines, so they of an Israelite, by the hand of Israelites. That which open enemies dare not attempt, they work by false brethren; and these are so much more perilous, as they are more entire.

It had been no less easy for Samson to have slain those thousands of Judah that came to bind him, than those other of the Philistines that meant to kill him bound. And what if he had said, Are you turned traitors to your deliverer? your blood be upon your own heads! But the Spirit of God (without whom he could not kill either beast or man) would never stir him up to kill his brethren, though degenerated into Philistines; they have more power to bind him than he to kill them. Israelitish blood was precious to him, that made no more scruple of killing a Philistine than a lion. That bondage and usury, that was allowed to a Jew from a pagan, might not be exacted from a Jew.

The Philistines, that had before ploughed with Samson's heifer, in the case of the riddle, are now ploughing a worse furrow with a heifer more his own. I am ashamed to hear these cowardly Jews say, "Knowest thou not that the Philistines are lords over us? Why hast thou done this unto us? We are therefore come to bind thee." Whereas they should have said, We find these tyrannical Philistines to usurp dominion over us; thou hast happily begun to shake off their yoke, and now we are come to second thee with our service; the valour of such a captain shall easily lead us forth to liberty. We are ready either to die with thee, or to be freed by thee. A fearful man can never be a true friend; rather than incur danger, he will be false to his own soul. O cruel mercy of these men of Judah! "We will not kill thee, but we will bind thee, and deliver thee into the hands of the Philistines, that they may kill thee;" as if it had not been much worse to die an ignominious and tormenting death, by the hands of the Philistines, than to be at once despatched by them which wished either his life safe, or his death easy.

When Saul was pursued by the Philistines upon the mountains of Gilboa, he could say to his armour-bearer, "Draw forth thy sword, and kill me, lest the uncircumcised come and thrust me through, and mock me;" and, at last, would rather fall upon his own sword than theirs: and yet these cousins of Samson can say, "We will not kill thee, but we will bind thee, and deliver thee." It was no excuse to these Israelites, that Samson's binding had more hope than his death. It was more in the extraordinary mercy of God, than their will, that he was not tied with his last bonds. Such is the goodness of the Almighty, that he turns the cruel intentions of wicked men to an advantage.

Now these Jews, that might have let themselves loose from their own bondage, are binding their deliverer, whom yet they knew able to have resisted. In the greatest strength, there is use of patience: there was more fortitude in this suffering than in his former actions. Samson abides to be tied by his own countrymen, that he may have the glory of freeing himself victoriously. Even so, O Saviour! our better Nazarite! thou which couldst have called to thy Father, and have had twelve legions of angels for thy rescue, wouldst be bound voluntarily, that thou mightest triumph; so the blessed martyrs were racked, and would not be loosed, because they expected a better resurrection. If we be not as well ready to suffer ill, as to do good, we are not fit for the consecration of God.

To see Samson thus strongly manacled, and exposed to their full revenge, could not but be a glad spectacle to these Philistines; and their joy was so full, that it could not but fly forth of their mouths in shouting and laughter: whom they saw loose with terror, it is pleasure to see bound. It is the sport of the spiritual Philistines, to see any of God's Nazarites fettered with the cords of iniquity; and their imps are ready to say, Aha! so would we have it. But the event answers their false joy, with that clause of triumph, "Rejoice not over me, O mine enemy; though I fall, yet I shall rise again." How soon was the countenance of these Philistines changed, and their shouts turned unto shriekings! "The Spirit of the Lord came upon Samson;" and then, what are cords to the Almighty? His new bonds are as flax burnt with fire; and he rouses up himself, like that young lion whom he first encountered, and flies upon those cowardly adversaries, who, if they had not seen his cords, durst not have seen his face. If they had been so many devils as men, they could not have stood before the Spirit which lifted up the heart and hand of Samson. Wicked men never see fairer prospect, than when they are upon the very threshold of destruction. Security and ruin are so close bordering upon each other, that, where we see the face of the one, we may be sure the other is at his back. Thus didst thou, O blessed Saviour, when thou wert fastened to the cross, when thou layest bound in the grave with the cords of death—thus didst thou miraculously raise up thyself, vanquish thine enemies, and lead captivity captive! Thus do all thy holy ones, when they seem most forsaken, and laid open to the insultation of the world, find thy Spirit mighty to their deliverance, and the discomfiture of their malicious adversaries.

Those three thousand Israelites were not so ill advised, as to come up into the rock unweaponed to apprehend Samson. Samson therefore might have had his choice of swords or spears for his skirmish with the Philistines; yet he leaves all the munition of Israel, and finding the new jaw-bone of an ass, takes that up in his hand, and, with that base instrument of death, sends a thousand Philistines to their place. All the swords and shields of the armed Philistines cannot resist that contemptible engine, which hath now left a thousand bodies as dead as the carcass of that beast whose bone it was. This victory was not in the weapon, was not in the arm; it was in the Spirit of God, which moved the weapon in the arm. O God! if the means be weak, yet thou art strong! Through God we shall do great acts; yea, I can do all things through him that strengtheneth me. Seest thou a poor Christian, which by weak council hath obtained to overcome a temptation? there is the Philistine vanquished with a sorry jaw-bone.

It is no marvel, if he were thus admirably strong and victorious, whose bodily strength God meant to make a type of the spiritual power of Christ. And behold, as the three thousand of Judah stood still gazing, with their weapons in their hands, whilst Samson alone subdued the Philistines; so did men and angels stand looking upon the glorious achievements of the Son of God, who might justly say, "I have trode the wine-press alone."

Both the Samsons complained of thirst. The same God, which gave this champion victory, gave him also refreshing; and by the same means. The same bone yields him both conquest and life, and is, of a weapon of offence, turned into a well of water. He that fetched water out of the flint for Israel, fetches it out of a bone for Samson. What is not possible to the infinite power of that Almighty Creator, that made all things of nothing! He can give Samson honey from the mouth of the lion, and water from the mouth of the ass. Who would not cheerfully depend upon that God, which can fetch moisture out of dryness, and life out of death?

CONTEMPLATION V.—SAMSON'S END.

I CANNOT wonder more at Samson's strength, than his weakness. He, that began to cast away his love upon a wife of the Philistines, goes on to mispend himself upon the harlots of the Philistines: he did not so much overcome the men, as the women overcame him. His affections blinded him first, ere the Philistines could do it: would he else, after the effusion of so much of their blood, have suffered his lust to carry him within their walls, as one that cared more for his pleasure than his life? O strange debauchedness and presumption of a Nazarite! The Philistines are up in arms to kill him: he offers himself to their city, to their stews, and dares expose his life to one of their harlots whom he had slaughtered. I would have looked to have seen him betake himself to his stronger rock than that of Etam, and, by his austere devotion, to seek protection of Him of whom he received strength: but now, as if he had forgotten his consecration, I find him turned Philistine for his bed, and of a Nazarite scarce a man. In vain doth he nourish his hair, while he feeds these passions. How easily do vigour of body, and infirmity of mind, lodge under one roof! On the contrary, a weakish outside is a strong motive to mortification. Samson's victories have subdued him, and have made him first a slave to lewd desires, and then to the Philistines. I may safely say, that more vessels miscarry with a fair gale, than with a tempest.

Yet was not Samson so blinded with lust, as not at all to look before him: he foresaw the morning would be dangerous; the bed of his fornication, therefore, could hold him no longer than midnight. Then he rises, and, in a mock of those ambushes which the Azzahites laid for him, he carries away the gates wherein they thought to have engaged him. If a temptation have drawn us aside to lie down to sin, it is happy for us, if we can arise, ere we be surprised with judgment. Samson had not left his strength in the bed of a harlot, neither had that God, which gave it him, stripped him of it with his clothes, when he laid him down in uncleanness. His mercy uses not to take vantage of our unworthiness, but even, when we cast him off, holds us fast. That bountiful hand leaves us rich of common graces, when we have mispent our better store: likeas our first parents, when they had spoiled themselves of the image of their Creator, yet were left wealthy of noble faculties of the soul.

I find Samson come off from his sin with safety; he runs away lightly with a heavier weight than the gates of Azzah—the burden of an ill act. Present impunity argues not an abatement of the wickedness of his sin, or of the dislike of God. Nothing is so worthy of pity, as sinners' peace. Good is not therefore good, because it prospers, but because it is commanded. Evil is not evil because it is punished, but because it is forbidden.

If the holy parents of Samson lived to see these outrages of their Nazarite, I doubt whether they did not repent them of their joy to hear the news of a son. It is a shame to see how he, that might not drink wine, is drunk with the cup of fornications. His lust carries him from Azzah to the plain of Sorek, and now hath found a Delilah that shall pay him for all his former uncleanness. Sin is steep and slippery; and if after one fall, we have found where to stand, it is the praise, not of our footing, but of the hand of God.

The princes of the Philistines knew already where Samson's weakness lay, though not his strength; and therefore they would entice his harlot by gifts to entice him, by her dalliance, to betray himself. It is no marvel if she, which would be filthy, would be also perfidious. How could Samson choose but think, if lust had not bewitched him, She, whose body is mercenary to me, will easily sell me to others; she will be false, if she will be a harlot: a wide conscience will swallow any sin. Those that have once thralled themselves to a known evil, can make no other difference of sins, but their own loss, or advantage. A liar can steal; a thief can kill; a cruel man can be a traitor; a drunkard can falsify: wickedness, once entertained, can put on any shape. Trust him in nothing, that makes not a conscience of every thing.

Was there ever such another motion made to a reasonable man? "Tell me wherein thy great strength lieth, and wherewith thou mayest be bound to do thee hurt." Who would not have spurned such a suitor out of doors? What will not impudency ask, or stupidity receive? He that killed the thousand Philistines for coming to bind him, endures this harlot of the Philistines to consult with himself of binding him; and when, upon the trial of a false answer, he saw so apparent treachery, yet wilfully betrays his life by her to his enemies. All sins, all passions, have power to infatuate a man, but lust most of all. Never man, that had drunk flagons of wine, had less reason than this Nazarite. Many a one loses his life, but this casts it away; not in hatred of himself, but in love to a strumpet. We wonder that a man could possibly be so sottish, and yet we ourselves by temptation become no less insensate. Sinful pleasures, like a common Delilah, lodge in our bosoms; we know they aim at nothing but the death of our soul; we will yield to them, and die. Every willing sinner is a Samson; let us not inveigh against his senselessness, but our own. Nothing is so gross and unreasonable to a well-disposed mind, which temptation will not represent fit and plausible. No soul can, out of his own strength, secure himself from that sin which he most detesteth.

As a hoodwinked man sees some little glimmering of light, but not enough to guide him; so did Samson, who had reason enough left him to make trial of Delilah, by a crafty misinformation; not enough upon that trial, to distrust and hate her; he had not wit enough to deceive her thrice, not enough to keep himself from being deceived by her. It is not so great wisdom to prove them whom we distrust, as it is folly to trust them whom we have found treacherous. Thrice had he seen the Philistines in her chamber, ready to surprise him upon her bonds; and yet will needs be a slave to his traitor. Warning not taken is a certain presage of destruction; and if, once neglected, it receive pardon, yet thrice is desperate.

What man would ever play thus with his own ruin? His harlot binds him, and calls in her executioners to cut his throat; he rises to save his own life, and suffers them to carry away theirs in peace. Where is the courage of Samson? where his zeal? He that killed the Philistines for their clothes, he that slew a thousand of them in the field at once in this quarrel, now suffers them in his chamber unrevenged. Whence is this? His hands were strong, but his heart was effeminate; his harlot had diverted his affection. Whosoever slackens the reins to his sensual appetites shall soon grow unfit for the calling of God. Samson hath broke the green withes, the new ropes, the woof of his hair, and yet still suffers himself fettered with those invisible bonds of a harlot's love; and can endure her to say, " How canst thou say I love thee, when thy heart is not with me? Thou hast mocked me these three times;" whereas he should rather have said unto her, How canst thou challenge any love from me, that hast thus thrice sought my life? O, canst thou think my mocks a sufficient revenge of this treachery? But, contrarily, he melts at this fire; and by her importunate insinuations, is wrought against himself. Weariness of solicitation hath won some to those actions, which at the first motion they despised; likeas we see some suitors are despatched, not for the equity of the cause, but the trouble of the prosecution; because it is more easy to yield, not more reasonable. It is more safe to keep ourselves out of the noise of suggestions, than to stand upon our power of denial. Who can pity the loss of that strength which was so abused? Who can pity him the loss of his locks, which, after so many warnings, can sleep in the lap of Delilah? It is but just that he should rise up from thence shaven and feeble: not a Nazarite, scarce a man. If his strength had lain in his hair, it had been out of himself; it was not therefore in his locks — it was in his consecration, whereof that hair was a sign. If the razor had come sooner upon his head, he had ceased to be a Nazarite, and the gift of God had at once ceased with the calling of God; not for the want of that excretion, but for want of obedience. If God withdraw his graces, when he is too much provoked, who can complain of his mercy? He that sleeps in sin must look to wake in loss and weakness. Could Samson think, Though I tell her my strength lies in my hair, yet she will not cut it; or though she do cut my hair, yet shall I not lose my strength; that now he rises and shakes himself, in hope of his former vigour? Custom of success makes men confident in their sins, and causes them to mistake an arbitrary tenure for a perpetuity.

His eyes were the first offenders, which betrayed him to lust; and now they are first pulled out, and he is led a blind captive to Azzah, where he was first captivated to his lust. The Azzahites, which lately saw him, not without terror, running lightly away with their gates at midnight, see him now in his own perpetual night, struggling with his chains; and, that he may not want pain, together with his bondage he must grind in his prison.

As he passed the street, every boy among the Philistines could throw stones at him, every woman could laugh and shout at him; and what one Philistine doth not say, while he lashes him unto blood, There is for my brother, or my kinsman, whom thou slewest? Who can look to run away with a sin, when Samson, a Nazarite, is thus plagued? This great heart could not but have broken with indignation, if it had not pacified itself with the conscience of the just desert of all this vengeance.

It is better for Samson to be blind in prison, than to abuse his eyes in Sorek: yea, I may safely say, he was more blind when he saw licentiously, than now that he sees not; he was a greater slave when he served his affections, than now in grinding for the Philistines. The loss of his eyes shows him his sin; neither could he see how ill he had done, till he saw not.

Even yet, still the God of mercy looked upon the blindness of Samson, and in these fetters enlarged his heart from the worst prison of his sin: his hair grew, together with his repentance, and his strength with his hair. God's merciful humiliations of his own are sometimes so severe, that they seem to differ little from desertions; yet, at the worst, he loves us bleeding; and when we have smarted enough, we shall feel it.

What thankful idolaters were these Philistines! They could not but know that their bribes, and their Delilah, had delivered Samson to them, and yet they sacrifice to their Dagon; and, as those that would be liberal in casting favours upon a senseless idol (of whom they could receive none), they cry out, "Our god hath delivered our enemy into our hands." Where was their Dagon, when a thousand of his clients were slain with an ass's jaw? There was more strength in that bone, than in all the makers of this god; and yet these vain pagans say, "Our god." It is the quality of superstition to misinterpret all events, and to feed itself with the conceit of those favours, which are so far from being done, that their authors never were. Why do not we learn zeal of idolaters? and if they be so forward in acknowledgment of their deliverances to a false deity, how cheerfully should we ascribe ours to the true! O God! whatsoever be the means, thou art the author of all our success. "O that men would praise the Lord for his goodness, and tell the wonders that he doth for the sons of men!"

No musician would serve for this feast but Samson: he must now be their sport which was once their terror; that he might want no sorrow, scorn is added to his misery: every wit and hand plays upon him. Who is not ready to cast his bone and his jest at such a captive? So as doubtless he wished himself no less deaf than blind, and that his soul might have gone out with his eyes. Oppression is able to make a wise man mad; and the greater the courage is, the more painful the insultation.

Now Samson is punished, shall the Philistines escape? If the judgment of God begin at his own, what shall become of his enemies? This advantage shall Samson make of their tyranny, that now death is no punishment to him: his soul shall fly forth in this bitterness, without pain; and that his dying revenge shall be no less sweet to him, than the liberty of his former life. He could not but feel God mocked through him; and therefore, while they are scoffing, he prays: his seriousness hopes to pay them for all those jests. If he could have been thus earnest with God in his prosperity, the Philistines had wanted this laughing-stock. No devotion is so fervent, as that which arises from extremity; "O Lord God, I pray thee think upon me; O God, I beseech thee, strengthen me at this time only." Though Samson's hair was shorter, yet he knew God's hand was not. As one, therefore, that had yet eyes enough to see him that was invisible, and whose faith was recovered before his strength, he sues to that God, which was a party in this indignity, for power to revenge his wrongs, more than his own. It is zeal that moves him, and not malice. His renewed faith tells him, that he was destined to plague the Philistines; and reason tells him, that his blindness puts him out of the hope of such another opportunity. Knowing, therefore, that this play of the Philistines must end in his death, he re-collects all the forces of his soul and body, that his death may be a punishment, instead of a disport, and that his soul may be more victorious in the parting, than in the animation; and so addresses himself, both to die and kill, as one whose soul shall not feel his own dissolution, while it shall carry so many thousand Philistines with it to the pit. All the acts of Samson are for wonder, not for imitation. So didst thou, O blessed Saviour, our better Samson, conquer in dying; and triumphing upon the chariot of the cross, didst lead captivity captive: the law, sin, death, hell, had never been vanquished

CONTEMPLATION VI.—MICAH'S IDOLATRY.

The mother of Micah hath lost her silver, and now she falls to cursing. She did afterwards but change the form of her god: her silver was her god, ere it did put on the fashion of an image, else she had not so much cursed to lose it, if it had not too much possessed her in the keeping. A carnal heart cannot forego that wherein it delights, without impatience; cannot be impatient without curses; whereas the man, that hath learned to enjoy God, and use the world, smiles at a shipwreck, and pities a thief, and cannot curse, but pray.

Micah had so little grace as to steal from his mother; and that out of wantonness, not out of necessity; for if she had not been rich, so much could not have been stolen from her: and now he hath so much grace as to restore it; her curses have fetched again her treasures. He cannot so much love the money, as he fears her imprecations. Wealth seems too dear, bought with a curse. Though his fingers were false, yet his heart was tender. Many that make not conscience of committing sin, yet make conscience of facing it: it is well for them that they are but novices in evil. Those whom custom hath fleshed in sin, can either deny and forswear, or excuse and defend it: their seared heart cannot feel the gnawing of any remorse; and their forehead hath learned to be as imprudent, as their heart is senseless.

I see no argument of any holiness in the mother of Micah: her curses were sin to herself, yet Micah dares not but fear them. I know not whether the causeless curse be more worthy of pity or derision; it hurts the author, not his adversary: but the deserved curses, that fall even from unholy mouths, are worthy to be feared: how much more should a man hold himself blasted with the just imprecations of the godly! What metal are those made of, that can applaud themselves in the bitter curses which their oppressions have wrung from the poor, and rejoice in these signs of their prosperity!

Neither yet was Micah more stricken with his mother's curses, than with the conscience of sacrilege: so soon as he finds there was a purpose of devotion in this treasure, he dares not conceal it, to the prejudice (as he thought) of God, more than of his mother. What shall we say to the palate of those men, which, as they find no good relish but in stolen waters, so best in those which are stolen from the fountain of God! How soon hath the old woman changed her note! Even now she passed an indefinite curse upon her son for stealing, and now she blesses him absolutely for restoring: "Blessed be my son of the Lord." She hath forgotten the theft, when she sees the restitution: how much more shall the God of mercies be more pleased with our confession, than provoked with our sin!

I doubt not but this silver and this superstition came out of Egypt, together with the mother of Micah. This history is not so late in time, as in place: for the tribe of Dan was not yet settled in that first division of the promised land: so as this old woman had seen both the idolatry of Egypt, and the golden calf in the wilderness, and, no doubt, contributed some of her ear-rings to that deity; and after all the plagues which she saw inflicted upon her brethren for that idol of Horeb and Baal-peor, she still reserves a secret love to superstition, and now shows it. Where misreligion hath once possessed itself of the heart, it is very hardly cleansed out; but (like the plague) it will hang in the very clothes, and, after long lurking, break forth in an unexpected infection; and old wood is the aptest to take this fire. After all the airing in the desert, Micah's mother will smell of Egypt.

It had been better the silver had been stolen than thus bestowed; for now they have so employed it, that it hath stolen away their hearts from God; and yet, while it is molten into an image, they think it dedicated to the Lord. If religion might be judged according to the intention, there should scarce be any idolatry in the world. This woman loved her silver enough; and if she had not thought this costly piety worth thanks, she knew which way to have employed her stock to advantage. Even evil actions have ofttimes good meanings, and these good meanings are answered with evil recompenses. Many a one bestows their cost, their labour, their blood, and receives torment instead of thanks.

Behold a superstitious son of a superstitious mother! she makes a god, and he harbours it! Yea (as the stream is commonly broader than the head), he exceeds his mother in evil: he hath a house of gods, an ephod, teraphim; and that he might be complete in his devotion, he makes his son his priest, and entails that sin upon his son which he received from his mother! Those sins which nature conveys not to us, we have by imitation. Every action and gesture of the parents is an example to the child; and the mother, as she is more tender over her son, so, by the power of a reciprocal love, she can work most upon his inclination. Whence it is, that, in the history of the Israelitish kings, the mother's name is commonly noted; and, as civilly, so also morally, the birth follows the belly. Those sons may bless their second birth, that are delivered from the sins of their education.

Who cannot but think how far Micah overlooked all his fellow Israelites, and thought them profane and godless in comparison of himself! How did he secretly clap himself on the breast, as the man whose happiness it was to engross religion from all the tribes of Israel, and little can imagine, that the further he runs, the more out of the way. Can an Israelite be thus paganish? O Micah, how hath superstition bewitched thee, that thou canst not see rebellion in every of these actions, yea, in every circumstance rebellion! What, more gods than one! a house of gods, besides God's house! an image of silver, to the invisible God! an ephod, and no priest! a priest, besides the family of Levi! a priest of thine own begetting, of thine own consecration! What monsters doth man's imagination produce, when it is forsaken of God! It is well seen there is no king in Israel. If God had been their king, his laws had ruled them; if Moses or Joshua had been their king, their sword had awed them; if any other, the courses of Israel had not been so heedless. We are beholden to government for order, for peace, for religion. Where there is no king, every one will be a king, yea, a god to himself. We are worthy of nothing but confusion, if we bless not God for authority.

It is no marvel, if Levites wandered for maintenance, while there was no king in Israel. The tithes and offerings were their due; if these had been paid, none of the holy tribe needed to shift his station. Even where royal power seconds the claim of the Levite, the injustice of men shortens his right. What should become of the Levites, if there were no king? and what of the church, if no Levites? No king, therefore, no church. How could the impotent child live without a nurse? Kings shall be thy nursing fathers, and queens thy nurses, saith God. Nothing more argues the disorder of any church, or the decay of religion, than the forced straggling of the Levites. There is hope of growth, when Micah rides to seek a Levite; but when the Levite comes to seek a service of Micah, it is a sign of gasping devotion.

Micah was no obscure man: all Mount Ephraim could not but take notice of his domestical gods. This Levite could not but hear of his disposition, of his misdevotion; yet want of maintenance, no less than conscience, draws him on to the danger of idolatrous patronage. Holiness is not tied to any profession. Happy were it for the church, if the clergy could be a privilege from lewdness. When need meets with unconscionableness, all conditions are easily swallowed, of unlawful entrances, of wicked executions. Ten shekels, and a suit of apparel, and his diet, are good wages for a needy Levite. He that could bestow eleven hundred shekels upon his puppets, can afford but ten to his priest; so hath he at once a rich idol, and a beggarly priest. Whosoever affects to serve God cheap, shows that he makes God but a stale to Mammon.

Yet was Micah a kind patron, though not liberal. He calls the young Levite his father, and uses him as his son; and what he wants in means, supplies in affection, It were happy, if Christians could imitate the love of idolaters towards them which serve at the altar. Micah made a shift with the priesthood of his own son; yet, that his heart checks him in it, appears both by the change, and his contentment in the change: "Now I know that the Lord will be good to me, seeing I have a Levite to my priest." Therefore, while his priest was no Levite, he sees there was cause why God should not be good to him. If the Levite had not come to offer his service, Micah's son had been a lawful priest. Many times the conscience runs away smoothly with an unwarrantable action, and rests itself upon those grounds, which afterwards it sees cause to condemn. It is a sure way, therefore, to inform ourselves thoroughly ere we settle our choice, that we be not driven to reverse our acts with late shame, and unprofitable repentance.

Now did Micah begin to see some little glimpse of his own error: he saw his priesthood faulty; he saw not the faults of his ephod, of his images, of his gods: and yet (as if he had thought all had been well when he had amended one) he says, "Now I know the Lord will be good to me." The carnal heart pleases itself with an outward formality, and so delights to flatter itself, as that it thinks if one circumstance be right, nothing can be amiss.

Israel was at this time extremely corrupted; yet the spies of the Danites had taken notice even of this young Levite, and are glad to make use of his priesthood. If they had but gone up to Shiloh, they might have consulted with the ark of God; but worldly minds are not curious in their holy services. If they have a god, an ephod, a priest, it suffices them. They had rather enjoy a false worship with ease, than to take pains for the true. Those that are curious in their diet, in their purchases, in their attire, in their contracts, yet in God's business are very indifferent.

The author of lies sometimes speaks truth for an advantage; and, from his mouth, this flattering Levite speaks what he knew would please, not what he knew would fall out. The event answers his prediction, and now the spies magnify him to their fellows. Micah's idol is a god, and the Levite is his oracle. In matter of judgment, to be guided only by the event, is the way to error. Falsehood shall be truth, and Satan an angel of light, if we follow this rule. Even very conjectures sometimes happen right. A prophet, or a dreamer, may give a true sign or wonder, and yet himself say, "Let us go after other gods." A small thing can win credit with weak minds, which, where they have once sped, cannot distrust.

The idolatrous Danites are so besotted with this success, that they will rather steal than want the gods of Micah; and because the gods without the priest can do them less service than the priest without the gods, therefore they steal the priest with the gods. O miserable Israelites, that could think that a god which could be stolen!—that could look for protection from that which could not keep itself from stealing, which was won by their theft, not their devotion! Could they worship those idols more devoutly than Micah that made them? And if they could not protect their maker from robbery, how shall they protect their thieves? If it had been the holy ark of the true God, how could they think it would bless their violence, or that it would abide to be translated by rapine and extortion? Now their superstition hath made them mad upon a god, they must have him, by what means they care not, though they offend the true God by stealing a false. Sacrilege is fit to be the first service of an idol. The spies of Dan had been courteously entertained by Micah; thus they reward his hospitality. It is no trusting the honesty of idolaters; if they have once cast off the true God, whom will they respect?

It seems Levites did not more want maintenance, than Israel wanted Levites. Here was a tribe of Israel without a spiritual guide. The withdrawing of due means is the way to the utter desolation of the church: rare offerings make cold altars. There needed small force to draw this Levite to change his charge: "Hold thy peace, and come, and be our father and priest: whether is it better," &c. Here is no patience, but joy. He that was won with ten shekels, may be lost with eleven: when maintenance and honour call him, he goes undriven, and rather steals himself away, than is stolen. The Levite had too many gods, to make conscience of pleasing one. There is nothing more inconstant than a Levite that seeks nothing but himself.

Thus the wild-fire of idolatry, which lay before couched in the private hall of Micah, now flies furiously through all the tribe of Dan, who, like the thieves that have carried away plaguy clothes, have insensibly infected themselves and their posterity to death. Heresy and superstition have small beginnings, dangerous proceedings, pernicious conclusions. This contagion is like a canker, which at the first is scarce visible; afterwards it eats away the flesh, and consumes the body.

BOOK XI.

CONTEMPLATION I.—THE LEVITE'S CONCUBINE.

THERE is no complaint of a publicly disordered state, where a Levite is not at one end of it, either as an agent or a patient. In the idolatry of Micah and the Danites, a Levite was an actor: in the violent uncleanness of Gibeah, a Levite suffers. No tribe shall sooner feel the want of government than that of Levi.

The law of God allowed the Levite a wife; human connivance, a concubine: neither did the Jewish concubine differ from a wife, but in some outward compliments; both might challenge all the true essence of marriage. So little was the difference, that the father of the concubine is called the father-in-law to the Levite. She, whom ill custom had of a wife made a concubine, is now, by her lust, of a concubine made a harlot; her fornication, together with the change of her bed, hath changed her abode. Perhaps her own conscience thrust her out of doors; perhaps the just severity of her husband. Dismission was too easy a penalty for that which God had sentenced with death. She that had deserved to be abhorred of her husband, seeks shelter from her father. Why would her father suffer his house to be defiled with an adulteress, though out of his own loins? Why did he not rather say, What, dost thou think to find my house an harbour for thy sins? While thou wert a wife to thine husband, thou wert a daughter to me; now thou art neither: thou art not mine, I gave thee to thy husband; thou art not thy husband's, thou hast betrayed his bed; thy filthiness hath made thee thine own, and thine adulterer's. Go seek thine entertainment where thou hast lost thine honesty: thy lewdness hath brought a necessity of shame upon thy abettors. How can I countenance thy person, and abandon thy sin? I had rather be a just man, than a kind father. Get thee home, therefore, to thy husband, crave his forgiveness upon thy knees, redeem thy love with thy modesty and obedience: when his heart is once open to thee, my doors shall not be shut. In the mean time, know, I can be no father to an harlot. Indulgence of parents is the refuge of vanity, the bawd of wickedness, the bane of children. How easily is that thief induced to steal, that knows his receiver! When the lawlessness of youth knows where to find pity and toleration, what mischief can it forbear!

By how much better this Levite was, so much more injurious was the concubine's sin. What husband would not have said, She is gone, let shame and grief go with her! I shall find one no less pleasing, and more faithful: or, if it be not too much mercy in me to yield to a return, let her that hath offended seek me. What more direct way is there to a resolved looseness, than to let her see I cannot want her? The good nature of this Levite cast off all these terms; and now, after four months' absence, sends to seek for her that had run away from her fidelity; and now he thinks, She sinned against me; perhaps she hath repented; perhaps shame and fear have withheld her from returning; perhaps she will be more loyal for her sin. If her importunity should win me, half the thanks were lost; but now, my voluntary offer of favour shall oblige her for ever. Love procures truer servitude than necessity. Mercy becomes well the heart of any man, but most of a Levite. He that had helped to offer so many sacrifices to God, for the multitude of every Israelite's sins, saw how proportionable it was, that man should not hold one sin unpardonable. He had served at the altar to no purpose, if he, whose trade was to sue for mercy, had not at all learned to practise it.

And if the reflection of mercy wrought this in a servant, what shall we expect from him whose essence is mercy! O God! we do every day break the holy covenant of our love; we prostitute ourselves to every filthy temptation, and then run and hide ourselves in our father's house, the world! If thou didst not seek us, we should never return; if thy gracious proffer did not prevent us, we should be incapable of forgiveness. It were abundant goodness in thee to receive us, when we should entreat thee; but lo! thou entreatest us that we would receive thee! How should we now adore and imitate thy mercy, since there is more reason we should sue to each other, than that thou shouldst sue to us, because we may as well offend as be offended!

I do not see the woman's father make any means for reconciliation; but when remission came home to his doors, no man could entertain it more thankfully. The nature of many men is forward to accept, and negligent to sue for; they can spend secret wishes upon that which shall cost them no endeavour.

Great is the power of love, which can in a sort undo evils past; if not for the act, yet for the remembrance. Where true affection was once conceived, it is easily pieced again, after the strongest interruption. Here needs no tedious recapitulation of wrongs; no importunity of suit: the unkindnesses are forgotten, their love is renewed; and now the Levite is not a stranger, but a son: by how much more willingly he came, by so much more unwillingly he is dismissed. The four months' absence of his daughter is answered with four days' feasting; neither was there so much joy in the former wedding-feast, as in this; because then he delivered his daughter entire, now desperate; then he found a son; but now that son hath found his lost daughter, and he found both. The recovery of any good is far more pleasant than the continuance.

Little do we know what evil is towards us. Now did this old man and this restored couple, promise themselves all joy and contentment after this unkind storm, and said in themselves, Now we begin to live. And now this feast, which was meant for their new nuptials, proves her funeral. Even when we let ourselves loosest to our pleasures, the hand of God, though invisibly, is *writing bitter things against us. Since we are not worthy to know, it is wisdom to suspect the worst, while it is least seen.

Sometimes it falls out, that nothing is more injurious than courtesy. If this old man had thrust his son and daughter early out of doors, they had avoided this mischief; now his loving importunity detains them to their hurt, and his own repentance. Such contentment doth sincere affection find in the presence of those we love, that death itself hath no other name but departing. The greatest comfort of our life is the fruition of friendship, the dissolution whereof is the greatest pain of death. As all earthly pleasures, so this of love, is distasted with the necessity of leaving. How worthy is that only love to take up our hearts, which is not open to any danger of interruption, which shall outlive the date even of faith and hope, and is as eternal as that God, and those blessed spirits whom we love! If we hang never so importunately upon one another's sleeves, and shed floods of tears to stop their way, yet we must begone hence: no occasion, no force, shall then remove us from our father's house.

The Levite is stayed beyond his time by importunity, the motions whereof are boundless and infinite: one day draws on another; neither is there any reason of this day's stay, which may not serve still for to-morrow. His resolution at last breaks through all those kind hindrances; rather will he venture a benighting, than an unnecessary delay. It is a good hearing, that the Levite makes haste home. An honest man's heart is where his calling is; such a one, when he is abroad, is like a fish in the air, whereinto if it leap for recreation or necessity, yet it soon returns to its own element. This charge, by how much more sacred it is, so much more attendance it expecteth: even a day breaks square with the conscionable.

The sun is ready to lodge before them: his servant advises him to shorten his journey, holding it more fit to trust an early inn of the Jebusites, than to the mercy of the night. And if that counsel had been followed, perhaps they, which found Jebusites in Israel, might have found Israelites in Jebus. No wise man can hold good counsel disparaged by the meanness of the author: if we be glad to receive any treasure from our servant, why not precious admonitions?

It was the zeal of this Levite that shut him out of Jebus: "We will not lodge in the city of strangers." The Jebusites were strangers in religion, not strangers enough in their habitation. The Levite will not receive common courtesy from those which were aliens from God, though home-born in the heart of Israel. It is lawful enough, in terms of civility, to deal with infidels: the earth is the Lord's and we may enjoy it in the right of the owner, while we protest against the wrong of the usurper; yet the less communion with God's enemies, the more safety. If there were another air to breathe in from theirs, another earth to tread upon, they should have their own. Those that affect a familiar entireness with Jebusites, in conversation, in leagues of amity, in matrimonial contracts, bewray either too much boldness, or too little conscience.

He hath no blood of an Israelite, that delights to lodge in Jebus. It was the fault of Israel, that an heathenish town stood yet in the navel of the tribes, and that Jebus was no sooner turned to Jerusalem: their lenity and neglect were guilty of this neighbourhood, that now no man can pass from Bethlehem-Judah to Mount Ephraim, but by the city of the Jebusites. Seasonable justice might prevent a thousand evils, which afterwards know no remedy but patience.

The way was not long betwixt Jebus and Gibeah; for the sun was stooping when the Levite was over against the first, and is but now declined when he comes to the other. How his heart was lightened, when he entered into an Israelitish city! and can think of nothing but hospitality, rest, security. There is no perfume so sweet to a traveller as his own smoke. Both expectation and fear do commonly disappoint us: for seldom ever do we enjoy the good we look for, or smart with a feared evil. The poor Levite could have found but such entertainment with the Jebusites. Whether are the posterity of Benjamin degenerated, that their Gibeah should be no less wicked than populous! The first sign of a settled godlessness, is that a Levite is suffered to lie without doors. If God had been in any of their houses, his servant had not been excluded. Where no respect is given to God's messengers, there can be no religion.

Gibeah was a second Sodom; even there also is another Lot; which is therefore so much more hospitable to strangers, because himself was a stranger. The host, as well as the Levite, is of Mount Ephraim. Each man knows best to commiserate that evil in others, which himself hath passed through. All that profess the name of Christ are countrymen, and yet strangers here below. How cheerfully should we entertain each other, when we meet in the Gibeah of this inhospitable world!

This good old man of Gibeah came home late from his work in the fields; the sun was set ere he gave over: and now, seeing this man a stranger, an Israelite, a Levite, an Ephraimite, and that in his way to the house of God, to take up his lodging in the street, he proffers him the kindness of his house-room. Industrious spirits are the fittest receptacles of all good motions; whereas those which give themselves to idle and loose courses, do not care so much as for themselves. I hear of but one man at his work in all Gibeath; the rest were quaffing and revelling. That one man ends his work with a charitable entertainment; the other end their play in a brutish beastliness, and violence. These villains had learned both the actions and the language of the Sodomites: one unclean devil was the prompter to both; and this honest Ephraimite had learned of righteous Lot, both to entreat and to proffer. As a perplexed mariner, that in a storm must cast away something, although precious; so this good host rather will prostitute his daughter, a virgin, together with the concubine, than this prodigious villany should be offered to a man, much more to a man of God.

The detestation of a fouler sin drew him to overreach in the motion of a lesser; which, if it had been accepted, how could he have escaped the partnership of their uncleanness, and the guilt of his daughter's ravishment! No man can wash his hands of that sin to which his will hath yielded. Bodily violence may be inoffensive in the patient; voluntary inclination to evil, though out of fear, can never be excusable: yet behold, this wickedness is too little to satisfy these monsters!

Who would have looked for so extreme abomination from the loins of Jacob, the womb of Rachel, the sons of Benjamin? Could the very Jebusites, their neighbours, be ever accused of such unnatural outrage? I am ashamed to say it, even the worst pagans were saints to Israel. What avails it, that they have the ark of God in Shiloh, while they have Sodom in their streets? that the law of God is in their fringes, while the devil is in their hearts? Nothing but hell itself can yield a worse creature than a depraved Israelite; the very means of his reformation are the fuel of his wickedness.

Yet Lot sped so much better in Sodom, than this Ephraimite did in Gibeah, by how much more holy guests he entertained: there the guests were angels, here a sinful man; there the guests saved the host, here the host could not save the guest from brutish violence; those Sodomites were stricken with outward blindness, and defeated; these Benjamites are only blinded with lust, and prevail. The Levite comes forth; perhaps his coat saved his person from this villany; who now thinks himself well, that he may have leave to redeem his own dishonour with his concubine's. If he had not loved her dearly, he had never sought her so far, after so foul a sin; yet now his hate of that unnatural wickedness overcame his love to her; she is exposed to the furious lust of ruffians, and, which he misdoubteth, abused to death.

O the just and even course which the Almighty Judge of the world holds in all his retributions! This woman had shamed the bed of a Levite by her former wantonness; she had thus far gone smoothly away with her sin; her father harboured her; her husband forgave her; her own heart found no cause to complain, because she smarted not: now, when the world had forgotten her offence, God calls her to reckoning, and punishes her with her own sin. She had voluntarily exposed herself to lust, now is exposed forcibly. Adultery was her sin; adultery was her death. What smiles soever wickedness casts upon the heart, while it solicits, it will owe us a displeasure, and prove itself a faithful debitor.

The Levite looked to find her humbled with this violence, not murdered; and now indignation moves him to add horror to the fact. Had not his heart been raised up with an excess of desire to make the crime as odious as it was sinful, his action could not be excused. Those hands, that might not touch a carcase, now carve the corpse of his own dead wife into morsels, and send these tokens to all the tribes of Israel; that when they should see these gobbets of the body murdered, the more they might detest the murderers. Himself puts on cruelty to the dead, that he might draw them to a just revenge of her death. Actions notoriously villanous, may justly countenance an extraordinary means of prosecution. Every Israelite hath a part in a Levite's wrong; no tribe hath not his share in the carcase and the revenge.

CONTEMPLATION II.—THE DESOLATION OF BENJAMIN.

These morsels could not choose but cut the hearts of Israel with horror and compassion; horror of the act, and compassion of tne sufferer; and now their zeal draws them together, either for satisfaction or revenge. Who would not have looked that the hands of Benjamin should have been first upon Gibeah; and that they should have readily sent the heads of the offenders, for a second service, after the gobbets of the concubine! But now, instead of punishing the sin, they patronised the actors; and will rather die in resisting justice, than live and prosper in furthering it!

Surely, Israel had one tribe too many. All Benjamin is turned into Gibeah; the sons not of Benjamin, but of Belial. The abetting of evil is worse than the commission; this may be upon infirmity, but that must be upon resolution. Easy punishment is too much favour to sin; connivance is much worse: but the defence of it, and that unto blood, is intolerable. Had not these men been both wicked and quarrellous, they had not drawn their swords in so foul a cause. Peaceable dispositions are hardly drawn to fight for innocence; yet these Benjamites (as if they were in love with villany, and out of charity with God) will be the wilful champions of lewdness. How can Gibeah repent them of that wickedness which all Benjamin will make good, in spite of their consciences? Even where sin is suppressed, it will rise; but where it is encouraged, it insults and tyrannizes.

It was more just that Israel should rise against Benjamin, than that Benjamin should rise for Gibeah; by how much it is better to punish offenders, than to shelter the offenders from punishment: and yet the wickedness of Benjamin sped better for the time, than the honesty of Israel. Twice was the better part foiled by the less and worse: the good cause was sent back with shame; the evil returned with victory and triumph: O God, their hand was for thee in the fight, and thy hand was with them in their fall! They had not fought for thee, but by thee; neither could they have miscarried in the fight, if thou hadst not fought against them: thou art just and holy in both. The cause was thine; the sin in managing of it was their own. They fought in a holy quarrel, but with confidence in themselves; for, as presuming of victory, they ask of God, not what should be their success, but who should be their captain. Number and innocence made them too secure: it was just, therefore, with God to let them feel, that even good zeal cannot bear out presumption; and that victory lies not in the cause, but in the God that owns it.

Who cannot imagine how much the Benjamites insulted in their double field and day, and now began to think, God was on their side! Those swords, which had been taught the way into forty thousand bodies of their brethren, cannot fear a new encounter. Wicked men cannot see their prosperity a piece of their curse; neither can examine their actions, but the events. Soon after they shall find what it was to add blood unto filthiness, and that the victory of an evil cause is the way to ruin and confusion.

I should have feared lest this double discomfiture should have made Israel either distrustful, or weary of a good cause: but still I find them no less courageous, with more humility. Now they fast and weep, and sacrifice. These weapons had been victorious in their first assault. Benjamin had never been in danger of pride for overcoming, if this humiliation of Israel had prevented the fight. It is seldom seen, but that which we do with fear prospereth; whereas confidence in undertaking, lays even good endeavours in the dust.

Wickedness could never brag of any long prosperity, nor complain of the lack of payment: still God is even with it at last. Now he pays the Benjamites both that death which they had lent to the Israelites, and that wherein they stood indebted to their brotherhood of Gibeah: and now, that both are met in death, there is as much difference betwixt those Israelites, and these Benjamites, as betwixt martyrs and malefactors. To die in a sin is a fearful revenge of giving patronage to sin. The sword consumes their bodies, another fire their cities, whatsoever became of their souls.

Now might Rachel have justly wept for her children, because they were not; for behold, the men, women, and children of her wicked tribe, are cut off; only some few scattered remainders ran away from this vengeance, and lurked in caves, and rocks, both for fear and shame. There was no difference but life betwixt their brethren and them; the earth covered them both; yet unto them doth the revenge of Israel stretch itself, and vows to destroy, if not their persons, yet their succession, as holding them unworthy to receive comfort by that sex to which they had been so cruel, both in act and maintenance. If the Israelites had not held marriage and issue a very great blessing, they had not thus revenged themselves of Benjamin: now they accounted the withholding of their wives a punishment second to death. The hope of life in our posterity, is the next contentment to an enjoying of life in ourselves.

They have sworn, and now, upon cold blood, repent them. If the oath were not just, why would they take it? and if it were just, why did they recant it? If the act were justifiable, what needed these tears? Even a just oath may be rashly taken. Not only injustice, but temerity of swearing, ends in lamentation. In our very civil actions, it is a weakness to do that which we would after reverse; but in our affairs with God, to check ourselves too late, and to steep our oaths in tears, is a dangerous folly. He doth not command us to take voluntary oaths; he commands us to keep them. If we bind ourselves to inconvenience, we may justly complain of our own fetters. Oaths do not only require justice, but judgment; wise deliberation, no less than equity.

Not conscience of their fact, but commiseration of their brethren, led them to this public repentance. "O God! why is this come to pass, that this day one tribe of Israel shall want?" Even the justest revenge of men is capable of pity. Insultation, in the rigour of justice, argues cruelty; charitable minds are grieved to see that done, which they would not wish undone: the smart of the offender doth not please them, which yet are thoroughly displeased with the sin, and have given their hands to punish it. God himself takes no pleasure in the death of a sinner, yet loves the punishment of sin: as a good parent whips his child, yet weeps himself. There is a measure in victory and revenge, if never so just, which to exceed, loses mercy in the suit of justice.

If there were no fault in their severity, it needed no excuse: and if there were a fault, it will admit of no excuse: yet, as if they meant to shift off the sin, they expostulate with God: "O Lord God of Israel, why is this come to pass this day?" God gave them no command of this rigour: yea, he twice crossed them in the execution; and now, in that which they entreated of God with tears, they challenge him. It is a dangerous injustice to lay the burden of our sins upon him, which tempteth no man, nor can be tempted with evil; while we so remove our sin, we double it.

A man that knew not the power of an oath, would wonder at this contrariety in the affections of Israel: they are sorry for the slaughter of Benjamin; and yet they slay those that did not help them in the slaughter. Their oath calls them to more blood: the excess of their revenge upon Benjamin may not excuse the men of Gilead. If ever oath might look for a dispensation, this might plead it: now they dare not but kill the men of Jabesh-Gilead, lest they should have left upon themselves a greater sin of sparing than punishing. Jabesh-Gilead came not up to aid Israel, therefore all the inhabitants must die. To exempt ourselves, whether out of singularity or stubbornness, from the common actions of the church, when we are lawfully called to them, is an offence worthy of judgment. In the main quarrels of the church, neutrals are punished. This execution shall make amends for the former; of the spoil of Jabesh-Gilead shall the Benjamites be stored with wives. That no man may think these men slain for their daughters, they plainly die for their sin; and these Gileadites might not have lived without the perjury of Israel; and now, since they must die, it is good to make benefit of necessity. I inquire not into the rigour of the oath: if their solemn vow did not bind them to kill all of both sexes in Benjamin, why did they not spare their virgins? and if it did so bind them, why did they spare the virgins of Gilead? Favours must be enlarged in all these religious restrictions. Where breath may be taken in them, it is not fit nor safe they should be straitened.

Four hundred virgins of Gilead have lost parents, and brethren, and kindred, and now find husbands in lieu of them. An enforced marriage was but a miserable comfort for such a loss: like wards, or captives, they are taken, and choose not, These suffice not; their friendly adversaries consult for more upon worse conditions. Into what troublesome and dangerous straits do men thrust themselves, by either unjust or inconsiderate vows!

In the midst of all this common lawlessness of Israel, here was conscience made on both sides of matching with infidels. The Israelites can rather be content their daughters should be stolen by their own, than that the daughters of aliens should be given them. These men, which had not grace enough to detest and punish the beastliness of their Gileadites, yet are not so graceless as to choose them wives of the heathen. All but atheists, howsoever they let themselves loose, yet in some things find themselves restrained, and show to others that they have a conscience. If there were not much danger and much sin in this unequal yoke, they would never have persuaded to so heavy an inconvenience. Disparity of religion, in matrimonial contracts, hath so many mischiefs, that it is worthy to be redeemed with much prejudice.

They which might not give their own daughters to Benjamin, yet give others, while they give leave to steal them. Stolen marriages are both unnatural and full of hazard; for love, whereof marriage is the knot, cannot be forced; this was rather rape, than wedlock. What unlikeness, perhaps contrariety of disposition, what averseness of affection, may there be, in not only a sudden, but a forcible meeting! If these Benjamites had not taken liberty of giving themselves ease by divorcement, they would often have found leisure to rue this stolen booty. This act may not be drawn to example; and yet here was a kind of indefinite consent. Both deliberation and good liking, are little enough for a during estate, and that which is once done for ever.

These virgins come up to the feast of the Lord; and now, out of the midst of their dances, are carried to a double captivity. How many virgins have lost themselves in dances? And yet this sport was not immodest. These virgins danced by themselves, without the company of those which might move towards unchastity; for if any men had been with them, they had found so many rescuers as they had assaulters; now, the exposing of their weak sex to this injury proves their innocence. Our usual dances are guilty of more sin. Wanton gestures, and unchaste touches, looks, motions, draw the heart to folly. The ambushes of evil spirits carry away many a soul from dances, to a fearful desolation.

It is supposed, that the parents, thus robbed of their daughters, will take it heavily. There cannot be a greater cross than the miscarriage of children: they are not only the living goods, but pieces of their parents; that they should, therefore, be torn from them by violence, is no less injury than the dismembering of their own bodies.

CONTEMPLATION III.—NAOMI AND RUTH.

BETWIXT the reign of the judges, Israel was plagued with tyranny, and, while some of them reigned, with famine. Seldom did that rebellious people want somewhat to humble them. One rod is not enough for a stubborn child. The famine must needs be great, that makes the inhabitants to run their country. The name of home is so sweet, that we cannot leave it for a trifle. Behold, that land which had wont to flow with milk and honey, now abounds with want and penury; and Bethlehem, instead of an house of bread, is an house of famine : " A fruitful land doth God make barren, for the wickedness of them that dwell therein." The earth bears not for itself, but for us; God is not angry with it, but with men. For our sakes it was first cursed to thorns and thistles; after that, to moisture; and since that, not seldom to drought, and by all these to barrenness. We may not look always for plenty. It is a wonder, while there is such superfluity of wickedness, that our earth is no more sparing of her fruits.

The whole earth is the Lord's, and in him ours. It is lawful for the owners to change their houses at pleasure. Why should we not make free use of any part of our own possessions? Elimelech and his family remove from Bethlehem-Judah unto Moab. Nothing but necessity can dispense with a local relinquishing of God's church; not pleasure, nor profit, nor curiosity. Those which are famished out, God calls, yea, drives from thence. The Creator and Possessor of the earth hath not confined any man to his necessary destruction.

It was lawful for Elimelech to make use of pagans and idolaters, for the supply of all needful helps. There cannot be a better employment of Moabites, than to be the treasurers and purveyors of God's children. Wherefore serve they, but to gather for the true owners? It is too much niceness in them, which forbear the benefit they might make of the faculties of profane or heretical persons; they consider not that they have more right to the good such men can do, than they that do it, and challenge that good for their own.

But I cannot see how it could be lawful for his sons to match with the daughters of Moab. Had these men heard how far, and under how solemn an oath, their father Abraham sent for a wife of his own tribe, for his son Isaac? Had they heard the earnest charge of holy Isaac to the son he blessed, " Thou shalt not take a wife of the daughters of Canaan ?" Had they forgotten the plagues of Israel, for but a short conversation with the Moabitish women? If they plead remoteness from their own people, did they not remember how far Jacob walked to Padan-Aram? Was it farther from Moab to Bethlehem, than from Bethlehem to Moab? And if the care of themselves led them from Bethlehem to Moab, should not their care of obedience to God have as well carried them back from Moab to Bethlehem? Yet if their wives would have left their idolatry with their maidenhead, the match had been more safe; but now, even at the last farewell, Naomi can say of Orpah, that she is returned to her gods. These men have sinned in their choice, and it speeds with them accordingly. Where did ever one of these unequal matches prosper? The two sons of Elimelech are swept away childless in the prime of their age, and, instead of their seed, they leave their carcases in Moab, their wives widows, their mother childless and helpless amongst infidels, in that age which most needed comfort. How miserable do we find poor Naomi, which is left destitute of her country, her husband, her children, her friends, and turned loose and solitary to the mercy of the world! Yet even out of these hopeless ruins will God raise comfort to his servant. The first good news is, that God hath visited his people with bread; now, therefore, since her husband and sons were unrecoverable, she will try to recover her country and kindred. If we can have the same conditions in Judah that we have in Moab, we are no Israelites if we return not. While her husband and sons lived, I hear no motion of retiring home; now these her earthly stays are removed, she thinks presently of removing to her country. Neither can we so heartily think of our home above, while we are furnished with these worldly contentments: when God strips us of them, straightways our mind is homeward.

She that came from Bethlehem under the protection of a husband, attended with her sons, stored with substance, resolves now to measure all that way alone. Her adversity had stripped her of all but a good heart: that remains with her, and bears up her head, in the deepest of her extremity. True Christian fortitude wades through all evils; and, though we be up to the chin, yet keeps firm footing against the stream: where this is, the sex is not discerned; neither is the quantity of the evil read in the face. How well doth this courage become Israelites, when we are left comfortless in the midst of the Moab of this world, to resolve the contempt of all dangers in the way to our home! as, contrarily, nothing doth more misbeseem a Christian, than that his spirits should flag with his estate, and that any difficulty should make him despair of attaining his best ends.

Goodness is of a winning quality, wheresoever it is; and, even amongst infidels, will make itself friends. The good disposition of Naomi carries away the hearts of her daughters-in-law with her, so as they are ready to forsake their kindred, their country, yea, their own mother, for a stranger, whose affinity died with her sons. Those men are worse than infidels, and next to devils, that hate the virtues of God's saints, and could love their persons well, if they were not conscionable.

How earnestly do these two daughters of Moab plead for their continuance with Naomi; and how hardly is either of them dissuaded from partaking of the misery of her society! There are good natures even among infidels, and such as, for moral disposition and civil respects, cannot be exceeded by the best professors. Who can suffer his heart to rest in those qualities, which are common to them that are without God!

Naomi could not be so insensible of her own good, as not to know how much comfort she might reap to the solitariness, both of her voyage and her widowhood, by the society of these two younger widows, whose affections she had so well tried. Even every partnership is a mitigation of evils: yet, so earnestly doth she dissuade them from accompanying her, as that she could not have said more, if she had thought their presence irksome and burdensome. Good dispositions love not to pleasure themselves with the disadvantage of others, and had rather be miserable alone, than to draw in partners to their sorrow; for the sight of another's calamity doth rather double their own, and, if themselves were free, would affect them with compassion; as, contrarily, ill minds care not how many companions they have in misery, nor how few consorts in good: if themselves miscarry, they would be content all the world were enwrapped with them in the same distress.

I marvel not that Orpah is by this seasonable importunity persuaded to return from a mother-in-law, to a mother in nature; from a toilsome journey to rest; from strangers to her kindred; from a hopeless condition, to likelihoods of contentment. A little entreaty will serve to move nature to be good unto itself. Every one is rather a Naomi to his own soul, to persuade it to stay still, and enjoy the delights of Moab, rather than to hazard our entertainment in Bethlehem. Will religion allow me this wild liberty of my actions, this loose mirth, these carnal pleasures? Can I be a Christian, and not live sullenly? None but a regenerate heart can choose rather to suffer adversity with God's people, than to enjoy the pleasures of sin for a season.

The one sister takes an unwilling farewell, and moistens her last kisses with many tears: the other cannot be driven back, but repels one entreaty with another: "Entreat me not to leave thee; for whither thou goest I will go, where thou dwellest I will dwell, thy people shall be my people, thy God my God, where thou diest I will die, and there will I be buried." Ruth saw so much, upon ten years' trial, in Naomi, as was more worth than all Moab; and, in comparison whereof, all worldly respects deserved nothing but contempt. The next degree unto godliness is the love of goodness: he is in a fair way to grace, that can value it. If she had not been already a proselyte, she could not have set this price upon Naomi's virtue. Love cannot be separated from a desire of fruition: in vain had Ruth protested her affection to Naomi, if she could have turned her out to her journey alone. Love to the saints doth not more argue our interest in God, than society argues the truth of our love.

As some tight vessel that holds against wind and water, so did Ruth against all the powers of a mother's persuasions; the impossibility of the comfort of marriage, in following her (which drew back her sister-in-law), cannot move her. She hears her mother, like a modest matron (contrary to the fashion of these times), say, "I am too old to have a husband;" and yet she thinks not, on the contrary, I am too young to want a husband. It should seem, the Moabites had learned this fashion of Israel, to expect the brother's raising of seed to the deceased: the widowhood and age of Naomi cuts off that hope; neither could Ruth then dream of a Boaz that might advance her: it is no love that cannot make us willing to be miserable for those we affect. The hollowest heart can be content to follow one that prospereth. Adversity is the only furnace of friendship. If love will not abide both fire and anvil, it is but counterfeit; so, in our love to God, we do but crack and vaunt in vain, if we cannot be willing to suffer for him.

But if any motive might hope to speed, that which was drawn from example was most likely: "Behold, thy sister-in-law is gone back unto her people, and to her gods; return thou after her." This one artless persuasion hath prevailed more with the world, than all the pleas of reason. How many millions miscarry upon this ground! Thus did my forefathers; thus do the most; I am neither the first nor the last; "Do any of the rulers?" We straight think that either safe or pardonable, for which we can plead a precedent. This good woman hath more warrant for her resolution than another's practice. The mind can never be steady, while it stands upon others' feet, and till it be settled upon such grounds of assurance, that it will rather lead than follow; and can say with Joshua, whatsoever become of the world, "I and my house will serve the Lord."

If Naomi had not been a person of eminent note, no knowledge had been taken at Bethlehem of her return. Poverty is ever obscure; and those that have little may go and come without noise. If the streets of Bethlehem had not before used to say, "There goes Naomi," they had not now asked, "Is not this Naomi?" She that had lost all things but her name, is willing to part with that also; "Call me not Naomi, but call me Marah." Her humility cares little for a glorious name in a dejected estate. Many a one would have set faces upon their want, and, in the bitterness of their condition, have affected the name of beauty. In all forms of good, there are more that care to seem, than to be: Naomi hates this hypocrisy, and, since God hath humbled her, desires not to be respected of men. Those who are truly brought down, make it not dainty, that the world should think them so, but are ready to be the first proclaimers of their own vileness.

Naomi went full out of Bethlehem to prevent want, and now she brings that want home with her, which she desired to avoid. Our blindness ofttimes carries us into the perils we seek to eschew. God finds it best, many times, to cross the likely projects of his dearest children, and to multiply those afflictions which they feared single.

Ten years have turned Naomi into Marah. What assurance is there of these earthly things whereof one hour may strip us? What man can say of the years to come, Thus I will be? How justly do we contemn this uncertainty, and look up to those riches that cannot but endure when heaven and earth are dissolved!

M

CONTEMPLATION IV.—BOAZ AND RUTH.

While Elimelech shifted to Moab to avoid the famine, Boaz abode still at Bethlehem, and continued rich and powerful. He stayed at home, and found that which Elimelech went to seek and missed. The judgment of famine doth not lightly extend itself to all. Pestilence and the sword spare none; but dearth commonly plagueth the meaner sort, and baulketh the mighty. When Boaz's storehouse was empty, his fields were full, and maintained the name of Bethlehem. I do not hear Ruth stand upon the terms of her better education, or wealthy parentage; but now that God hath called her to want, she scorns not to lay her hand unto all homely services, and thinks it no disparagement to find her bread in other men's fields. There is no harder lesson to a generous mind, nor that more beseems it, than either to bear want or to prevent it. Base spirits give themselves over to idleness and misery, and, because they are crossed, will sullenly perish.

That good woman hath not been for nothing in the school of patience; she hath learned obedience to a poor stepmother; she was now a widow past reach of any danger of correction; besides that penury might seem to dispense with awe. Even children do easily learn to contemn the poverty of their own parents; yet hath she inured herself to obedience, that she will not so much as go forth into the field to glean without the leave of her mother-in-law, and is no less obsequious to Marah, than she was to Naomi. What shall we say to those children that, in the main actions of their life, forget they have natural parents? It is a shame to see, that, in mean families, want of substance causeth want of duty; and that children should think themselves privileged for unreverence, because the parent is poor. Little do we know, when we go forth in the morning, what God means to do with us ere night! There is a providence that attends on us in all our ways, and guides us insensibly to his own ends: that divine hand leads Ruth blindfold to the field of Boaz. That she meets with his reapers, and falls upon his land amongst all the fields of Bethlehem, it was no praise to her election, but the gracious disposition of Him in whom we move. His thoughts are above ours, and do so order our actions, as we, if we had known, should have wished. No sooner is she come into the field, but the reapers are friendly to her. No sooner is Boaz come into his field, but he invites her to more bounty than she could have desired. Now God begins to repay into her bosom her love and duty to her mother-in-law. Reverence and loving respects to parents never yet went away unrecompensed. God will surely raise up friends among strangers to those that have been officious at home.

It was worth Ruth's journey from Moab, to meet with such a man as Boaz, whom we find thrifty, religious, charitable: though he were rich, yet he was not careless; he comes into the field to oversee his reapers. Even the best estate requires careful managing of the owner: he wanted no officers to take charge of his husbandry, yet he had rather be his own witness. After all the trust of others, the master's eye feeds the horse.

The Master of the great household of the world gives us an example of this care, whose eye is in every corner of his large possession. Not civility only, but religion, binds us to good husbandry. We are all stewards; and what account can we give to our Master, if we never look after our estate? I doubt whether Boaz had been so rich, if he had not been so frugal; yet was he not more thrifty than religious. He comes not to his reapers but with a blessing in his mouth—"The Lord be with you;" as one that knew, if he were with them, and not the Lord, his presence could avail nothing. All the business of the family speeds the better for the master's benediction. Those affairs are likely to succeed, that take their beginning at God. Charity was well matched with his religion, without which, good works are but hypocrisy. No sooner doth he hear the name of the Moabitess, but he seconds the kindness of his reapers, and still he rises in his favours. First, she may glean in his field; then she may drink of his vessels; then she shall take her meal with his reapers, and part of it from his own hand; lastly, his workmen must let fall sheaves for her gathering. A small thing helps the needy. A handful of gleanings, a lapful of parched corn, a draught of the servants' bottles, a loose sheaf, was such a favour to Ruth, as she thought was above all recompense. This was not seen in the estate of Boaz, which yet makes her for the time happy. If we may refresh the soul of the poor with the very offals of our estate, and not hurt ourselves, woe be to us if we do it not! Our barns shall be as full of curses as of corn, if we grudge the scattered ears of our field to the hands of the needy.

How thankfully doth Ruth take these

small favours from Boaz! Perhaps some rich jewel in Moab would not have been so welcome. Even this was a presage of her better estate. Those which shall receive great blessings, are ever thankful for little: and if poor souls be so thankful to us for but an handful, or a sheaf, how should we be affected to our God, for whole fields full, for full barns, full garners!

Doubtless Boaz, having taken notice of the good nature, dutiful carriage, and the near affinity of Ruth, could not but purpose some greater beneficence, and higher respects to her; yet now onwards he fits his kindness to her condition, and gives her that, which to her meanness seemed much, though he thought it little. Thus doth the bounty of our God deal with us. It is not for want of love that he gives us no greater measure of grace, but for want of our fitness and capacity. He hath reserved greater preferments for us when it shall be seasonable for us to receive them.

Ruth returns home wealthy with her ephah of barley, and thankfully magnifies the liberality of Boaz, her new benefactor. Naomi repays his beneficence with her blessing: "Blessed be he of the Lord!" If the rich can exchange their alms with the poor for blessings, they have no cause to complain of an ill bargain. Our gifts cannot be worth their faithful prayers: therefore it is better to give than to receive; because he that receives, hath but a worthless alms; he that gives, receives an invaluable blessing.

I cannot but admire the modesty and silence of these two women: Naomi had not so much as talked of her kindred in Bethlehem, nor till now had she told Ruth that she had a wealthy kinsman; neither had Ruth inquired of her husband's great alliance; but both sat down meekly with their own wants, and cared not to know any thing else, save that themselves were poor. Humility is ever the way to honour.

It is a discourtesy, where we are beholden, to alter our dependency, like as men of trade take it ill, if customers, which are in their books, go for their wares to another shop. Wisely doth Naomi advise Ruth not to be seen in any other field, while the harvest lasted. The very taking of their favours, is a contentment to those that have already well deserved; and it is quarrel enough that their courtesy is not received. How shall the God of heaven take it, that while he gives and proffers large, we run to the world, that can afford us nothing but vanity and vexation?

Those that can least act, are ofttimes the best to advise. Good old Naomi sits still at home, and by her counsel pays Ruth all the love she owes her. The face of that action, to which she directs her, is the worst piece of it; the heart was sound. Perhaps the assurance, which long trial had given her, of the good government and firm chastity of her daughter-in-law, together with her persuasion of the religious gravity of Boaz, made her think that design safe, which to others had been perilous, if not desperate. But besides that, holding Boaz next of blood to Elimelech, she made account of him as the lawful husband of Ruth; so as there wanted nothing but a challenge, and consummation. Nothing was abated but some outward solemnities, which, though expedient for the satisfaction of others, yet were not essential to marriage; and if there were not these colours for a project so suspicious, it would not follow that the action was warrantable, because Naomi's. Why should her example be more safe in this, than in matching her sons with infidels, than in sending back Orpah to her father's gods? If every act of an holy person should be our rule, we should have crooked lives. Every action that is reported, is not straightways allowed. Our courses were very uncertain, if God had not given us rules, whereby we may examine the examples of the best saints, and as well censure as follow them. Let them that stumble at the boldness of Ruth, imitate the continence of Boaz.

These times were not delicate. This man, though great in Bethlehem, lays him down to rest upon a pallet, in the floor of his barn: when he awakes at midnight, no marvel if he were amazed to find himself accompanied; yet, though his heart were cheered with wine, the place solitary, the night silent, the person comely, the invitation plausible, could he not be drawn to a rash act of lust; his appetite could not get the victory of reason, though it had wine and opportunity to help it. Herein Boaz shewed himself a great master of his affections, that he was able to resist a fit temptation. It is no thank to many, that they are free of some evils; perhaps they wanted not will, but convenience. But if a man, when he is fitted with all helps to his sin, can repel the pleasure of sin out of conscience, this is true fortitude.

Instead of touching her as a woman, he blessed her as a father, encourageth her as a friend, promiseth her as a kinsman, rewards her as a patron, and sends her away laden with hopes and gifts; no less chaste, more happy, than she came. O admirable temperance, worthy the progenitor of Him, in whose lips and heart was no guile!

If Boaz had been the next kinsman, the marriage had needed no protraction, but now that his conscience told him that Ruth was the right of another, it had not been more sensuality than injustice to have touched his kinswoman. It was not any bodily impotency, but honesty and conscience, that restrained Boaz; for the very next night she conceived by him: that good man wished his marriage-bed holy, and durst not lie down in the doubt of a sin. Many a man is honest out of necessity, and affects the praise of that which he could not avoid: but that man's mind is still an adulterer, in the forced continence of his body. No action can give us true comfort, but that which we do out of the grounds of obedience.

Those which are fearful of sinning, are careful not to be thought to sin: Boaz, though he knew himself to be clear, would not have occasion of suspicion given to others: "Let no man know that a woman came into the floor." A good heart is no less afraid of a scandal, than of a sin; whereas those that are resolved not to make any scruple of sin, despise others' constructions, not caring whom they offend, so that they may please themselves. That Naomi might see her daughter-in-law was not sent back in dislike, she comes home laden with corn. Ruth had gleaned more this night, than in half the harvest. The care of Boaz was, that she should not return to her mother empty. Love, wheresoever it is, cannot be niggardly. We measure the love of God by his gifts: how shall he abide to send us away empty from those treasures of goodness!

Boaz is restless in the prosecution of this suit, and hies him from his threshing-floor to the gate, and there convenes the nearer kinsman before the elders of the city. What was it that made Boaz so ready to entertain, so forward to urge this match? Wealth she had none, not so much as bread, but what she gleaned out of the field; friends she had none, and those she had elsewhere Moabites; beauty she could not have much, after that scorching in her travel, in her gleanings. Himself tells her what drew his heart to her: "All the city of my people doth know that thou art a virtuous woman." Virtue, in whomsoever it is found, is a great dowry, and, where it meets with an heart that knows how to value it, is accounted greater riches than all that is hid in the bowels of the earth. The corn-heap of Boaz was but chaff to this, and his money dross.

As a man that had learned to square all his actions to the law of God, Boaz proceeds legally with his rival; and tells him of a parcel of Elimelech's land, which, it is like, upon his removal to Moab, he had alienated; which he, as the next kinsman, might have power to redeem; yet so, as he must purchase the wife of the deceased with the land. Every kinsman is not a Boaz: the man could listen to the land, if it had been free from the clog of a necessary marriage; but now he will rather leave the land than take the wife, lest, whilst he should preserve Elimelech's inheritance, he should destroy his own; for the next seed, which he should have by Ruth, should not be his heir, but his deceased kinsman's. How knew he whether God might not, by that wife, send heirs enough for both their estates? Rather had he, therefore, incur a manifest injustice, than hazard the danger of his inheritance. The law of God bound him to raise up seed to the next in blood; the care of his inheritance draws him to a neglect of his duty, though with infamy and reproach; and now he had rather his face should be spit upon, and his name should be called "The house of him whose shoe was pulled off," than to reserve the honour of him that did his brother right, to his own prejudice. How many are there that do so over-love their issue, as that they regard neither sin nor shame in advancing it, and that will rather endanger their soul, than lose their name! It is a woful inheritance that makes men heirs of the vengeance of God.

Boaz is glad to take the advantage of his refusal; and holds that shoe (which was the sign of his tenure) more worth than all the lands of Elimelech. And whereas other wives purchase their husbands with a large dowry, this man purchaseth his wife at a dear rate, and thinks his bargain happy. All the substance of the earth is not worth a virtuous and prudent wife; which Boaz doth now so rejoice in, as if he this day only began to be wealthy.

Now is Ruth taken into the house of Boaz; she, that before had said she was not like one of his maidens, is now become their mistress. This day she hath gleaned all the fields and barns of a rich husband; and that there might be no want in her happiness, by a gracious husband she hath gained a happy seed, and hath the honour, above all the dames of Israel, to be the great-grandmother of a king, of David, of the Messiah.

Now is Marah turned back again to

Naomi; and Orpah, if she hear of this in Moab, cannot but envy at her sister's happiness. O the sure and bountiful payments of the Almighty! Who ever came under his wing in vain? Who ever lost by trusting him? Who ever forsook the Moab of this world for the true Israel, and did not at last rejoice in the change?

CONTEMPLATION V.—HANNAH AND PENINNAH.

ILL customs, where they are once entertained, are not easily discharged: polygamy, besides carnal delight, might now plead age and example, so as even Elkanah, though a Levite, is tainted with the sin of Lamech; like as fashions of attire, which at the first were disliked as uncomely, yet, when they are once grown common, are taken up of the gravest. Yet this sin, as then current with the time, could not make Elkanah not religious. The house of God in Shiloh was duly frequented of him; oftentimes alone, in his ordinary course of attendance, with all his males thrice a-year, and once a-year with all his family. The continuance of an unknown sin cannot hinder the uprightness of a man's heart with God; as a man may have a mole upon his back, and yet think his skin clear; the least touch of knowledge or wilfulness mars his sincerity.

He, that by virtue of his place was employed about the sacrifices of others, would much less neglect his own. It is a shame for him that teaches God's people that they should not appear before the Lord empty, to bring no sacrifice for himself. If Levites be profane, who should be religious?

It was the fashion, when they sacrificed, to feast; so did Elkanah: the day of his devotion is the day of his triumph; he makes great cheer for his whole family, even for that wife which he loved less. There is nothing more comely than cheerfulness in the services of God. What is there in all the world, wherewith the heart of man should be so lift up, as with the conscience of his duty done to his Maker! While we do so, God doth to us, as our glass, smile upon us, while we smile on him.

Love will be seen by entertainment: Peninnah and her children shall not complain of want, but Hannah shall find her husband's affection in her portion; as his love to her was double, so was her part: she fared not the worse because she was childless. No good husband will dislike his wife for a fault out of the power of her redress; yea rather, that which might seem to lose the love of her husband, wins it, her barrenness. The good nature of Elkanah laboured, by his dear respects, to recompense this affliction; that so she might find no less contentment in the fruit of his hearty love, than she had grief from her own fruitlessness. It is the property of true mercy to be most favourable to the weakest; thus doth the gracious spouse of the Christian soul pity the barrenness of his servants. O Saviour, we should not find thee so indulgent to us, if we did not complain of our own unworthiness! Peninnah may have the more children, but barren Hannah hath the most love. How much rather could Elkanah have wished Peninnah barren, and Hannah fruitful! But if she should have had both issue and love, she had been proud, and her rival despised. God knows how to disperse his favours so that every one may have cause both of thankfulness and humiliation: while there is no one that hath all, no one but hath some. If envy and contempt were not thus equally tempered, some would be overhaughty, and others too miserable; but now every man sees that in himself which is worthy of contempt, and matter of emulation in others; and, contrarily, sees what to pity and dislike in the most eminent, and what to applaud in himself; and out of this contrariety arises a sweet mean of contentation.

The love of Elkanah is so unable to free Hannah from the wrongs of her rival, that it procures them rather. The unfruitfulness of Hannah had never with so much despite been laid in her dish, if her husband's heart had been as barren of love to her. Envy, though it take advantage of our weaknesses, yet is ever raised upon some grounds of happiness in them whom it emulates; it is ever an ill effect of a good cause. If Abel's sacrifice had not been accepted, and if the acceptation of his sacrifice had not been a blessing, no envy had followed upon it.

There is no evil of another, wherein it is fit to rejoice, but his envy, and this is worthy of our joy and thankfulness; because it shows us the price of that good which we had, and valued not. The malignity of envy is thus well answered, when it is made the evil cause of a good effect to us, when God and our souls may gain by another's sin. I do not find that Hannah insulted upon Peninnah, for the greater measure of her husband's love, as Peninnah did upon her for her fruitlessness. Those that are truly gracious, know how to receive the blessings of God, without contempt of them that want; and have learned to be thankful without overliness.

Envy, when it is once conceived in a malicious heart, is like fire in billets of juniper, which, they say, continues more years than one. Every year was Hannah thus vexed with her emulous partner, and troubled both in her prayers and meals. Amidst all their feastings, she fed on nothing but her tears. Some dispositions are less sensible, and more careless of the despite and injuries of others, and can turn over unkind usages with contempt. By how much more tender the heart is, so much more deeply is it ever affected with discourtesies: as wax receives and retains that impression, which in the hard clay cannot be seen; or, as the eye feels that mote, which the skin of the eye-lid could not complain of; yet the husband of Hannah, as one that knew his duty, labours, by his love, to comfort her against these discontentments: "Why weepest thou? Am I not better to thee than ten sons?" It is the weakness of good natures to give so much advantage to an enemy. What would malice rather have, than the vexation of them whom it persecutes? We cannot better please an adversary, than by hurting ourselves. This is no other than to humour envy, to serve the turn of those that malign us, and to drawn on that malice whereof we are weary; whereas carelessness puts ill-will out of countenance, and makes it withdraw itself in a rage, as that which doth but shame the author, without the hurt of the patient. In causeless wrongs, the best remedy is contempt.

She, that could not find comfort in the loving persuasions of her husband, seeks it in her prayers: she rises up hungry from the feast, and hastens to the temple; there she pours out her tears and supplications. Whatsoever the complaint be, here is the remedy. There is one universal receipt for all evils, prayer; when all helps fail us, this remains, and, while we have an heart, comforts it.

Here was not more bitterness in the soul of Hannah, than fervency; she did not only weep and pray, but vow unto God: if God will give her a son, she will give her son to God back again. Even nature itself had consecrated her son to God; for he could not but be born a Levite: but if his birth make him a Levite, her vow shall make him a Nazarite, and dedicate his minority to the tabernacle. The way to obtain any benefit, is to devote it, in our hearts, to the glory of that God of whom we ask it: by this means shall God both pleasure his servant, and honour himself; whereas, if the scope of our desires be carnal, we may be sure either to fail of our suit, or of a blessing.

CONTEMPLATION VI.—ELI AND HANNAH.

OLD Eli sits on a stool by one of the posts of the tabernacle. Where should the priests of God be, but in the temple? Whether for action or for oversight, their very presence keeps God's house in order, and the presence of God keeps their hearts in order.

It is oft found, that those which are themselves conscionable, are too forward to the censuring of others. Good Eli, because he marks the lips of Hannah to move without noise, chides her as drunken, and uncharitably misconstrues her devotion. It was a weak ground whereon to build so heavy a sentence. If she had spoken too loud and incomposedly, he might have had some just colour for this conceit; but now, to accuse her silence, notwithstanding all her tears which he saw, of drunkenness, it was a zealous breach of charity.

Some spirits would have been enraged with so rash a censure. When anger meets with grief, both turn into fury. But this good woman had been inured to reproaches, and besides, did well see the reproof arose from misprision, and the misprision from zeal; and therefore answers meekly, as one that had rather satisfy than expostulate, "Nay, my lord, but I am a woman troubled in spirit." Eli may now learn charity of Hannah. If she had been in that distemper whereof he accused her, his just reproof had not been so easily digested. Guiltiness is commonly clamorous and impatient, whereas innocence is silent, and careless of misreports. It is natural unto all men to wipe off from their name all aspersions of evil, but none do it with such violence as they which are faulty. It is a sign the horse is galled, that stirs too much when he is touched.

She that was censured for drunken, censures drunkenness more deeply than her reprover: "Count not thine handmaid for a daughter of Belial." The drunkard's style begins in lawlessness, proceeds in unprofitableness, ends in misery; and all shut up in the denomination of this pedigree, a son of Belial.

If Hannah had been tainted with this sin, she would have denied it with more fervour, and have disclaimed it with an extenuation: what if I should have been merry with wine? yet I might be devout. If I should have overjoyed in my sacrifice to God, one cup of excess had not been so heinous: now her freedom is seen in her severity. Those which have clear hearts from any sin, prosecute it with rigour, whereas the guilty are ever partial: their conscience holds their hands, and tells them that they beat themselves while they punish others.

Now Eli sees his error, and recants it; and, to make amends for his rash censure, prays for her. Even the best may err, but not persist in it. When good natures have offended, they are unquiet till they have hastened satisfaction. This was within his office, to pray for the distressed: wherefore serves the priest, but to sacrifice for the people? And the best sacrifices are the prayers of faith.

She that began her prayers with fasting and heaviness, rises up from them with cheerfulness and repast. It cannot be spoken how much ease and joy the heart of man finds in having unloaded his cares, and poured out his supplications into the ears of God; since it is well assured, that the suit which is faithfully asked, is already granted in heaven. The conscience may well rest, when it tells us, that we have neglected no means of redressing our affliction; for then it may resolve to look either for amendment, or patience.

The sacrifice is ended, and now Elkanah and his family rise up early to return unto Ramah; but they dare not set forward, till they have worshipped before the Lord. That journey cannot hope to prosper, that takes no God with it. The way to receive blessings at home, is to be devout at the temple.

She that before conceived faith in her heart, now conceives a son in her womb. God will rather work miracles, than faithful prayers shall return empty. I do not find that Peninnah asked any son of God, yet she had store; Hannah begged hard for this one, and could not till now obtain him. They which are dearest to God, do ofttimes, with great difficulty, work out those blessings, which fall into the mouths of the careless. That wise disposer of all things knows it fit to hold us short of those favours which we sue for; whether for the trial of our patience, or the exercise of our faith, or the increase of our importunity, or the doubling of our obligation.

Those children are most like to prove blessings, which the parents have begged of God, and which are no less the fruit of our supplications than of our body. As this child was the son of his mother's prayers, and was consecrated to God ere his possibility of being; so now himself shall know, both how he came, and whereto he was ordained; and, lest he should forget it, his very name shall teach him both: "She called his name Samuel." He cannot so much as hear himself named, but he must needs remember both the extraordinary mercy of God, in giving him to a barren mother, and the vow of his mother, in restoring him back to God by her zealous dedication; and by both of them earn holiness and obedience. There is no necessity of significant names; but we cannot have too many monitors to put us in mind of our duty.

It is wont to be the father's privilege to name his child; but because this was his mother's son, begotten more by her prayers than the seed of Elkanah, it was but reason that she should have the chief hand both in his name and disposing. It had been indeed in the power of Elkanah to have changed both his name and profession, and abrogate the vow of his wife; that wives might know they were not their own, and that the rib might learn to know the head; but husbands shall abuse their authority, if they shall wilfully cross the holy purposes and religious endeavours of their yoke-fellows. How much more fit is it for them to cherish all good desires in the weaker vessels, and, as we use, when we carry a small light in a wind, to hide it with our lap, or hand, that it may not go out. If the wife be a vine, the husband should be an elm, to uphold her in all worthy enterprises, else she falls to the ground, and proves fruitless.

The year is now come about; and Elkanah calls his family to their holy journey, to go up to Jerusalem, for the anniversary solemnity of their sacrifice. Hannah's heart is with them, but she hath a good excuse to stay at home—the charge of her Samuel: her success in the temple, keeps her happily from the temple, that her devotion may be doubled, because it was respited. God knows how to dispense with necessities; but if we suffer idle and needless occasions to hold us from the tabernacle of God, our hearts are but hollow to religion.

Now, at last, when the child was weaned from her hand, she goes up and pays her vow, and with it pays the interest of her intermission. Never did Hannah go up with so glad a heart to Shiloh, as now that she carries God this reasonable present, which himself gave to her, and she vowed to him; accompanied with the bounty of other sacrifices, more in number and measure than the law of God required of her: and all this is too little for her God, that so mercifully remembered her affliction, and miraculously remedied it. Those hearts which are truly thankful, do no less rejoice in repayment, than in their receipt; and do as much study how to show their humble and fervent affections for what they have, as how to compass favours when they want them; their debt is their burden, which, when they have discharged, they are at ease.

If Hannah had repented of her vow, and not presented her son to the tabernacle, Eli could not have challenged him: he had only seen her lips stir, not hearing the promise of her heart. It was enough that her own soul knew her vow, and God, which was greater than it. The obligation of a secret vow is no less, than if it had ten thousand witnesses.

Old Eli could not choose but much rejoice to see this fruit of those lips, which he thought moved with wine; and this good proof, both of the merciful audience of God, and the thankful fidelity of his handmaid: this sight calls him down to his knees: "He worshipped the Lord." We are unprofitable witnesses of the mercies of God and the graces of men, if we do not glorify him for others' sakes, no less than for our own.

Eli and Hannah grew now better acquainted; neither had he so much cause to praise God for her as she afterwards for him; for if her own prayers obtained her first child, his blessings enriched her with five more. If she had not given her first son to God, ere she had him, I doubt whether she had not been ever barren; or, if she had kept her Samuel at home, whether ever she had conceived again. Now that piety which stripped her of her only child for the service of her God, hath multiplied the fruit of her womb, and gave her five for that one, which was still no less hers because he was God's. There is no so certain way of increase as to lend or give unto the owner of all things.

CONTEMPLATION VII.—ELI AND HIS SONS.

If the conveyance of grace were natural, holy parents would not be so ill suited with children. What good man would not rather wish his loins dry, than fruitful of wickedness? Now we can neither traduce goodness, nor choose but traduce sin. If virtue were as well entailed upon us as sin, one might serve to check the other in our children; but now, since grace is derived from heaven on whomsoever it pleases the Giver, and that evil, which ours receive hereditarily from us, is multiplied by their own corruption, it can be no wonder that good men have ill children; it is rather a wonder that any children are not evil. The sons of Eli are as lewd, as himself was holy. If the goodness of examples, precepts, education, profession, could have been preservatives from extremity of sin, these sons of a holy father had not been wicked; now neither parentage, nor breeding, nor priesthood, can keep the sons of Eli from the sons of Belial. If our children be good, let us thank God for it; this was more than we could give them: if evil, they may thank us, and themselves: us for their birth-sin; themselves for the improvement of it to that height of wickedness.

If they had not been sons of Eli, yet being priests of God, who would not have hoped their very calling should have infused some holiness into them? But now, even their white ephod covers foul sins; yea, rather, if they which serve at the altar degenerate, their wickedness is so much more above others, as their place is holier. A wicked priest is the worst creature upon earth. Who are devils but they which were once angels of light? Who can stumble at the sins of the evangelical Levites, that sees such impurity even before the ark of God? That God which promised to be the Levite's portion, had set forth the portion of his ministers; he will feast them at his own altar; the breast and the right shoulder of the peace-offering was their morsel. These bold and covetous priests will rather have the flesh-hook their arbiter, than God. Whatsoever those three teeth fasten upon, shall be for their tooth; they were weary of one joint, and now their delicacy affects variety; God is not worthy to carve for these men, but their own hands; and this they do not receive, but take; and take violently, unseasonably. It had been fit God should be first served; their presumption will not stay his leisure: ere the fat be burned, ere the flesh be boiled, they snatch more than their share from the altar; as if the God of heaven should wait on their palate; as if the Israelites had come thither to sacrifice to their bellies. And, as commonly a wanton tooth is the harbinger of luxurious wantonness, they are no sooner fed, than they neigh after the dames of Israel. Holy women assemble to the door of the tabernacle; these varlets tempt them to lust, that came thither for devotion: they had wives of their own, yet their unbridled desires rove after strangers, and fear not to pollute even that holy place with abominable filthiness. O sins too shameful for men, much more for the spiritual guides of Israel! He that makes himself a servant to his tooth, shall easily become a slave to all inordinate affections. That altar, which expiated other men's sins, added to the sins of the sacrificers. Doubtless many a soul was the cleaner for the blood of the sacrifices which they shed, while their own were more impure; and as the altar cannot sanctify the priest, so the uncleanliness of the minister cannot pollute the offering; because the virtue thereof is not in the agent, but in the institution; in the representation, his sin is his own, the comfort of the sacrament is from God. Our clergy is no charter for heaven. Even those, whose trade is devotion, may at once show the way to heaven by their tongue, and by their foot lead the way to hell. It is neither a cowl, nor an ephod, that can privilege the soul.

The sin of these men was worthy of contempt, yea, perhaps their persons; but for the people therefore to abhor the offerings of the Lord, was to add their evil unto the priests, and to offend God, because he was offended. There can no offence be justly taken, even at men, much less at God for the sake of men. No man's sins should bring the service of God into dislike: this is to make holy things guilty of our profaneness. It is a dangerous ignorance, not to distinguish betwixt the work and the instrument; whereupon it oft comes to pass, that we fall out with God, because we find cause of offence from men, and give God just cause to abhor us, because we abhor his service unjustly. Although it be true, of great men especially, that they are the last to know the evils of their own house; yet either it could not be, when all Israel rung of the lewdness of Eli's sons, that he only should not know it; or, if he knew it not, his ignorance cannot be excused; for a seasonable restraint might have prevented this extremity of debauchedness. Complaints are long muttered of the great, ere they dare break forth into open contestation. Public accusations of authority argue intolerable extremities of evil. Nothing but age can plead for Eli, that he was not the first accuser of his sons. Now, when their enormities came to be the voice of the multitude, he must hear it by force; and doubtless he heard it with grief enough, but not with anger enough: he that was the judge of Israel, should have impartially judged his own flesh and blood; never could he have offered a more pleasing sacrifice, than the depraved blood of so wicked sons. In vain do we rebuke those sins abroad, which we tolerate at home. That man makes himself ridiculous, that, leaving his own house on fire, runs to quench his neighbour's.

I heard Eli sharp enough to Hannah, upon but a suspicion of sin, and now how mild I find him to the notorious crimes of his own! "Why do you so, my sons? it is no good report; my sons, do no more so." The case is altered with the persons. If nature may be allowed to speak in judgment, and to make difference, not of sins, but of offenders, the sentence must needs savour of partiality. Had these men but some little slackened their duty, or heedlessly omitted some rite of the sacrifice, this censure had not been unfit; but to punish the thefts, rapines, sacrileges, adulteries, incests of his sons, with "why do ye so?" was no other than to shave that head, which had deserved cutting off. As it is with ill humours, that a weak dose doth but stir and anger them, and drive them out, so it fareth with sins: an easy reproof doth but encourage wickedness, and makes it think itself so slight as that censure importeth. A vehement rebuke to a capital evil is but like a strong shower to a ripe field, which lays that corn which were worthy of a sickle. It is a breach of justice, not to proportionate the punishment to the offence: to whip a man for a murder, or to punish the purse for incest, or to burn treason in the hand, or to award the stocks to burglary,—it is to patronize evil, instead of avenging it. Of the two extremes, rigour is more safe for the public weal, because the over punishing of one offender frights many from sinning. It is better to live in a commonwealth where nothing is lawful, than where every thing.

Indulgent parents are cruel to themselves and their posterity. Eli could not have devised which way to have plagued himself and his house so much, as by his kindness to his children's sins. What variety of judgments doth he now hear of from the messenger of God! First, because his old age (which uses to be subject to choler) inclined now to misfavour his sons, therefore there shall not be an old man left of his house for ever; and because it vexed him not enough to see his sons enemies to God in their profession, therefore he shall see his enemy in the habitation of the Lord; and because himself forbore to take vengeance of his sons, and esteemed their life above the glory of his Master, therefore God will revenge himself, by killing them both in one day; and because he abused his sovereignty by conniving at sin, therefore shall his house be stripped of this honour, and see it translated to another; and, lastly, because he suffered his sons to please their own wanton appetite, in taking meat off from God's trencher, therefore those which remain of his house shall come to his successors to beg a piece of silver, and a morsel of bread. In a word, because he was partial to his sons, God shall execute all this severely upon him and them. I do not read of any fault Eli had, but indulgence; and which of the notorious offenders were plagued more? Parents need no other means to make them miserable, than sparing the rod.

Who should be the bearer of these fearful tidings to Eli, but young Samuel, whom himself had trained up! He was now grown past his mother's coats, fit for the message of God. Old Eli rebuked not his young sons, therefore young Samuel is sent to rebuke him. I marvel not, while the priesthood was so corrupted, if the word of God were precious, if there were no public vision. It is not the manner of God to grace the unworthy. The ordinary ministration in the temple was too much honour for those that robbed the altar, though they had no extraordinary revelations. Hereupon it was, that God lets old Eli sleep (who slept in his sin), and awakes Samuel, to tell him what he would do with his master. He which was wont to be the mouth of God to the people, must now receive the message of God from the mouth of another: as great persons will not speak to those with whom they are highly offended, but send them their checks by others.

The lights of the temple were now dim, and almost ready to give place to the morning, when God called Samuel; to signify perhaps, that those which should have been the lights of Israel, burned no less dimly, and were near their going out, and should be succeeded with one so much more lightsome than they, as the sun was more bright than the lamps. God had good leisure to have delivered this message by day, but he meant to make use of Samuel's mistaking; and therefore so speaks, that Eli may be asked for an answer, and perceive himself both omitted and censured. He that meant to use Samuel's voice to Eli, imitates the voice of Eli to Samuel: Samuel had so accustomed himself to obedience, and to answer the call of Eli, that lying in the further cells of the Levites, he is easily raised from his sleep; and even in the night runs for his message to him who was rather to receive it from him. Thrice is the old man disquieted with the diligence of his servant; and, though visions were rare in his days, yet is he not so unacquainted with God, as not to attribute that voice to him which himself heard not. Wherefore, like a better tutor than a parent, he teaches Samuel what he shall answer: "Speak, Lord, for thy servant heareth."

It might have pleased God, at the first call, to have delivered his message to Samuel, not expecting the answer of a novice unseen in the visions of God; yet doth he rather defer it till the fourth summons, and will not speak till Samuel confessed his audience. God loves ever to prepare his servants for his employments, and will not commit his errands but to those whom he addresseth, both by wonder and attention, and humility.

Eli knew well the gracious fashion of God, that, where he intended a favour, prorogation could be no hindrance; and therefore, after the call of God thrice answered with silence, he instructs Samuel to be ready for the fourth. If Samuel's silence had been wilful, I doubt whether he had been again solicited; now God doth both pity his error, and requite his diligence, by redoubling his name at the last.

Samuel had now many years ministered before the Lord, but never till now heard his voice; and now hears it with much terror, for the first word that he hears God speak is threatening, and that of vengeance to his master. What were these menaces, but so many premonitions to himself that he should succeed Eli? God begins early to season their hearts with fear, whom he means to make eminent instruments of his glory. It is his mercy to make us witnesses of the judgments of others, that we may be forewarned, ere we have the occasions of sinning.

I do not hear God bid Samuel deliver his message to Eli. He, that was but now made a prophet, knows, that the errands of God intend not silence; and that God would not have spoken to him of another, if he had meant the news should be reserved to himself: neither yet did he run with open mouth unto Eli, to tell him this vision unasked. No wise man will be hasty to bring ill tidings to the great; rather doth he stay till the importunity of his master should wring it from his unwillingness; and then, as his concealment showed his love, so his full relation shall approve his fidelity. If the heart of Eli had not told him this news, before God told it Samuel, he had never been so instant with Samuel not to conceal it: his conscience did well presage that it concerned himself. Guiltiness needs no prophet to assure it of punishment. The mind that is troubled, projecteth terrible things; and though it cannot single out the judgment allotted to it, yet it is in a confused expectation of some grievous evil. Surely Eli could not think it worse than it was: the sentence was fearful, and such as I wonder the neck or the heart of old Eli could hold out the report of: That God swears he will judge Eli's house, and that with beggary, with death, with desolation, and that the wickedness of his house shall not be purged with sacrifice or offerings for ever: and yet this, which every Israelite's ear should tingle to hear of, when it should be done, old Eli hears with an unmoved patience and humble submission: " It is the Lord, let him do what seemeth him good." O admirable faith, and more than human constancy and resolution, worthy of the aged president of Shiloh, worthy of a heart sacrificed to that God, whose justice had refused to expiate his sin by sacrifice! If Eli have been an ill father to his sons, yet he is a good son to God, and is ready to kiss the very rod he shall smart withal: " It is the Lord," whom I have ever found holy and just and gracious, and he cannot but be himself; " let him do what seemeth him good;" for whatsoever seemeth good to him, cannot but be good, howsoever it seems to me. Every man can open his hand to God while he blesses; but to expose ourselves willingly to the afflicting hand of our Maker, and to kneel to him while he scourges us, is peculiar only to the faithful.

If ever a good heart could have freed a man from temporal punishments, Eli must needs have escaped. God's anger was appeased by his humble repentance, but his justice must be satisfied. Eli's sin, and his sons', was in the eye and mouth of all Israel; his, therefore, should have been much wronged by their impunity. Who would not have made these spiritual guides an example of lawlessness, and have said, What care I how I live, if Eli's sons go away unpunished? As not the tears of Eli, so not the words of Samuel, may fall to the ground. We may not measure the displeasure of God by his stripes. Many times, after the remission of the sin, the very chastisements of the Almighty are deadly. No repentance can assure us that we shall not smart with outward afflictions, that can prevent the eternal displeasure of God, but still it may be necessary and good we should be corrected: our care and suit must be, that the evils, which shall not be averted, may be sanctified.

If the prediction of these evils were fearful, what shall the execution be? The presumption of the ill-taught Israelites shall give occasion to this judgment; for, being smitten before the Philistines, they send for the ark into the field. Who gave them authority to command the ark of God at their pleasure? Here was no consulting with the ark, which they would fetch; no inquiry of Samuel, whether they should fetch it; but a heady resolution of presumptuous elders to force God into the field, and to challenge success. If God were not with the ark, why did they send for it, and rejoice in the coming of it? If God were with it, why was not his allowance asked that it should come? How can the people be good, where the priests are wicked? When the ark of the covenant of the Lord of hosts, that dwells between the cherubims, was brought into the host, though with mean and wicked attendance, Israel doth, as it were, fill the heaven and shake the earth with shouts; as if the ark and victory were no less inseparable, than they and their sins. Even the lewdest men will be looking for favour from that God, whom they cared not to displease, contrary to the conscience of their deservings. Presumption doth the same in wicked men, which faith doth in the holiest. Those that regarded not the God of the ark, think themselves safe and happy in the ark of God. Vain men are transported with a confidence in the outside of religion, not regarding the substance and soul of it, which only can give them true peace. But rather than God will humour superstition in Israelites, he will suffer his own ark to fall into the hands of Philistines. Rather will he seem to slacken his hand of protection, than he will be thought to have his hands bound by a formal misconfidence. The slaughter of the Israelites was no plague to this; it was a greater plague rather to them that should survive and behold it. The two sons of Eli, which had helped to corrupt their brethren, die by the hands of the uncircumcised, and are now too late separated from the ark of God by Philistines, which should have been before separated by their father. They had lived formerly to bring God's altar into contempt; and now live to carry his ark into captivity: and at last, as those that had made up the measure of their wickedness, are slain in their sin.

Ill news doth ever either run or fly. The man of Benjamin, which ran from the host, hath soon filled the city with outcries, and Eli's ears with the cry of the city. The good old man, after ninety and eight years, sits in the gate, as one that never thought himself too aged to do God service, and hears the news of Israel's discomfiture, and his sons' death, though with sorrow, yet with patience: but when the messenger tells him the ark of God is taken, he can live no longer; that word strikes him down backward from his throne, and kills him in the fall. No sword of a Philistine could have slain him more painfully: neither know I whether his neck or his heart were first broken. O fearful judgment, that ever any Israelite's ear could tingle withal! The ark lost! What good man would wish to live without God? Who can choose but think he hath lived too long, that hath overlived the testimonies of God's presence with his church? Yea, the very daughter-in-law of Eli, a woman, the wife of a lewd husband, when she was at once travailing (upon that tidings), and in that travail dying, to make up the full sum of God's judgment upon that wicked house, as one insensible of the death of her father, of her husband, of herself, in comparison of this loss, calls her (then unseasonable) son Ichabod, and with her last breath says, "The glory is departed from Israel, the ark is taken." What cares she for a posterity which should want the ark? What cares she for a son come into the world of Israel, when God was gone from it? And how willingly doth she depart from them, from whom God was departed! Not outward magnificence, not state, not wealth, not favour of the mighty, but the presence of God in his ordinances, are the glory of Israel; the subduing whereof is a greater judgment than destruction.

O Israel, worse now than no people! a thousand times more miserable than Philistines! Those Pagans went away triumphing with the ark of God and victory, and leave the remnants of the chosen people to lament that they once had a God.

O cruel and wicked indulgence, that is now found guilty of the death, not only of the priests and people, but of religion! Unjust mercy can never end in less than blood: and it were well if only the body should have cause to complain of that kind cruelty.

BOOK XII.

CONTEMPLATION IV.—THE ARK AND DAGON.

If men did not mistake God, they could not arise to such height of impiety; the acts of his just judgment are imputed to impotence. That God would send his ark captive to the Philistines, is so construed by them, as if he could not keep it. The wife of Phinehas cried out, that glory was departed from Israel; the Philistines dare say in triumph that glory is departed from the God of Israel. The ark was not Israel's but God's: this victory reaches higher than to men. Dagon had never so great a day, so many sacrifices, as now that he seems to take the God of Israel prisoner. Where should the captive be bestowed, but in custody of the victor? It is not love, but insultation, that lodges the ark close beside Dagon. What a spectacle was this, to see uncircumcised Philistines laying their profane hands upon the testimony of God's presence! to see the glorious mercy-seat under the roof of an idol! to see the two cherubims spreading their wings under a false god!

O the deep and holy wisdom of the Almighty, which overreaches all the finite conceits of his creatures! who, while he seems most to neglect himself, fetches about most glory to his own name! He winks, and sits still, on purpose to see what men would do, and is content to suffer indignity from his creature for a time, that he may be everlastingly magnified in his justice and power. That honour pleaseth God and men best, which is raised out of contempt.

The ark of God was not used to such porters: the Philistines carry it unto Ashdod, that the victory of Dagon may be more glorious. What pains superstition puts men unto, for the triumph of a false cause! And if profane Philistines can think it no toil to carry the ark where they should not, what a shame is it for us, if we do not gladly attend it where we should! How justly may God's truth scorn the imparity of our zeal!

If the Israelites did put confidence in the ark, can we marvel that the Philistines did put confidence in that power, which, as they thought, had conquered the ark? The less is ever subject unto the greater; what could they now think, but that heaven and earth were theirs? Who shall stand out against them, when the God of Israel hath yielded? Security and presumption attend ever at the threshold of ruin.

God will let them sleep in this confidence: in the morning they shall find how vainly they have dreamed. Now they begin to find they have but gloried in their own plague, and overthrown nothing but their own peace. Dagon hath a house, when God hath but a tabernacle. It is no measuring of religion by outward glory. Into this house the proud Philistines come the next morning, to congratulate unto their god so great a captive, such divine spoils, and, in their early devotions, to fall down before him, under whom the God of Israel was fallen; and lo! where they find their god fallen down on the ground upon his face, before him whom they thought both his prisoner and theirs. Their god is forced to do that, which they should have done voluntarily; although God casts down that dumb rival of his for scorn, not for adoration. O ye foolish Philistines! could ye think that the same house would hold God and Dagon? could ye think a senseless stone a fit companion and guardian for the living God? Had ye laid your Dagon upon his face, prostrate before the ark, yet would not God have endured the indignity of such a lodging; but now that ye presume to set up your carved stone equal to his cherubims, go, read your folly in the floor of your temple; and know, that He, which cast your god so low, can cast you lower.

The true God owes a shame to those which will be making matches between himself and Belial.

But this perhaps was only a mischance, or a neglect of attendance. Lay to your hands, O ye Philistines, and raise up Dagon into his place. It is a miserable god that needs helping up: had ye not been more senseless than that stone, how could ye choose but think, How shall he raise us above our enemies, that cannot rise alone? how shall he establish us in the station of our peace, that cannot hold his own foot? If Dagon did give the foil unto the God of Israel, what power is it that hath cast him upon his face, in his own temple? It is just with God, that those which want grace shall want wit too. It is the power of superstition to turn men into those stocks and stones which they worship: they that make them are like unto them. Doubtless this first fall of Dagon was kept as secret, and excused as well as it might, and served rather for astonishment than conviction: there was more strangeness than horror in that accident. That whereas Dagon had wont to stand, and the Philistines fall down,—now Dagon fell down, and the Philistines stood, and must become the patrons of their own god; their god worships them upon his face, and craves more help from them than ever he could give. But if their sottishness can digest this, all is well.

Dagon is set in his place; and now those hands are lift up to him which helped to lift him up; and those faces are prostrate unto him, before whom he lay prostrate. Idolatry and superstition are not easily put out of countenance: but will the jealousy of the true God put it up thus? shall Dagon escape with a harmless fall? Surely, if they had let him lie still upon the pavement, perhaps that insensible statue had found no other revenge; but now they will be advancing it to the rood-loft again, and affront God's ark with it: the event will shame them, and let them know, how much God scorns a partner, either of his own making or theirs.

The morning is fittest for devotion; then do the Philistines flock to the temple of their god. What a shame is it for us to come late to ours! although not so much piety as curiosity did now hasten their speed, to see what rest their Dagon was allowed to get in his own roof. And now, behold, their kind god is come to meet them in the way; some pieces of him salute their eyes upon the threshold: Dagon's head and hands are overrun their fellows, to tell the Philistines how much they were mistaken in their god.

This second fall breaks the idol in pieces, and threats the same confusion to the worshippers of it. Easy warnings neglected, end ever in destruction. The head is for devising; the hand for execution: in these two powers of their God did the Philistines chiefly trust; these are therefore laid under their feet upon the threshold, that they might afar off see their vanity, and that, if they would, they might set their foot on that best piece of their god, whereon their heart was set.

There was nothing wherein that idol resembled a man but in his head and hands; the rest was but a scaly portraiture of a fish: God would therefore separate from this stone that part which had mocked man with the counterfeit of himself, that man might see what an unworthy lump he had matched with himself, and set up above himself. The just quarrel of God is bent upon those means, and that parcel, which had dared to rob him of his glory.

How can the Philistines now miss the sight of their own folly? how can they be but enough convicted of their mad idolatry, to see their god lie broken to morsels under their feet? every piece whereof proclaims the power of Him that brake it, and the stupidity of those that adored it! Who would expect any other issue of this act, but to hear the Philistines say, We now see how superstition hath blinded us! Dagon is no god for us; our hearts shall never more rest upon a broken statue; that only true God, which hath broken ours, shall challenge us by the right of conquest. But here is none of this; rather a further degree of their dotage follows upon this palpable conviction; they cannot yet suspect that god, whose head they may trample upon; but, instead of hating their Dagon, that lay broken upon their threshold, they honour the threshold on which Dagon lay, and dare not set their foot on that place, which was hallowed by the broken head and hands of their deity. O the obstinacy of idolatry, which, where it hath got hold of the heart, knows neither to blush nor yield, but rather gathers strength from that which might justly confound it! The hand of the Almighty, which moved them not in falling upon their God, falls now nearer them upon their persons, and strikes them in their bodies, which would not feel themselves stricken in their idol. Pain shall humble them whom shame cannot. Those which had entertained the secret thoughts of abominable idolatry within them, are now plagued, in the inwardest and most secret part of their bodies, with a loathsome disease; and now grow weary of themselves, instead of their idolatry. I do not hear them acknowledge it was God's hand which had stricken Dagon their god, till now they find themselves stricken. God's judgments are the rack of godless men: if one strain make them not confess, let them be stretched but one wrench higher, and they cannot be silent. The just avenger of sin will not lose the glory of his executions, but will have men know from whom they smart.

The emerods were not a disease beyond the compass of natural causes; neither was it hard for the wiser sort to give a reason of their complaint; yet they ascribe it to the hand of God. The knowledge and operation of secondary causes should be no prejudice to the first. They are worse than the Philistines, who, when they see the means, do not acknowledge the first mover, whose active just power is no less seen in employing ordinary agents, than in raising up extraordinary; neither doth he less smite by a common fever, than by a revenging angel.

They judge right of the cause: what do they resolve for the cure? "Let not the ark of the God of Israel abide with us;" where they should have said, Let us cast out Dagon, that we may pacify and retain the God of Israel: they determine to thrust out the ark of God, that they might peaceably enjoy themselves and Dagon. Wicked men are upon all occasions glad to be rid of God, but they can, with no patience, endure to part with their sins; and while they are weary of the hand that punisheth them, they hold fast the cause of their punishment.

Their first and only care is to put away him, who, as he hath corrected, so can ease them. Folly is never separated from wickedness.

Their heart told them that they had no right to the ark. A council is called of their princes and priests. If they had resolved to send it home, they had done wisely. Now they do not carry it away, but they carry it about from Ebenezer to Ashdod, from Ashdod to Gath, from Gath to Ekron. Their stomach was greater than their conscience. The ark was too sore for them; yet it was too good for Israel, and they will rather die than make Israel happy. Their conceit, that the change of the air could appease the ark, God useth to his own advantage; for by this means his power is known, and his judgment spread over all the country of the Philistines. What do these men now, but send the plague of God to their fellows? The justice of God can make the sins of men their mutual executioners. It is the fashion of wicked men to draw their neighbours into the partnership of their condemnation.

Wheresoever the ark goes, there is destruction. The best of God's ordinances, if they be not proper to us, are deadly. The Israelites did not more shout for joy, when they saw the ark come to them, than the Ekronites cry out for grief to see it brought amongst them. Spiritual things are either sovereign or hurtful, according to the disposition of the receivers. The ark doth either save or kill, as it is entertained.

At last, when the Philistines are well weary of pain and death, they are glad to be quit of their sin. The voice of the princes and people is changed to the better: " Send away the ark of the God of Israel, and let it return to his own place." God knows how to bring the stubbornest enemy upon his knees, and makes him do that out of fear, which his best child would do out of love and duty. How miserable was the estate of these Philistines! Every man was either dead or sick. Those that were left living, through their extremity of pain, envied the dead, and the cry of their whole cities went up to heaven. It is happy that God hath such store of plagues and thunderbolts for the wicked: if he had not a fire of judgment, wherewith the iron hearts of men might be made flexible, he would want obedience, and the world peace.

CONTEMPLATION II. — THE ARK'S REVENGE AND RETURN.

It had wont to be a sure rule, wheresoever God is among men, there is the church: here only it failed. The testimony of God's presence was many months amongst the Philistines, for a punishment to his own people whom he left; for a curse to those foreigners which entertained it. Israel was seven months without God. How do we think faithful Samuel took this absence? How desolate and forlorn did the tabernacle of God look without the ark! There were still the altars of God; his priests, Levites, tables, vails, censers, and all their legal accoutrements: these, without the ark, were as the sun without light in the midst of an eclipse. If all these had been taken away, and only the ark had been remaining, the loss had been nothing to this, that the ark should be gone, and they left: for what are all these without God, and how all-sufficient is God without these! There are times wherein God withdraws himself from his church, and seems to leave her without comfort, without protection. Sometimes we shall find Israel taken from the ark; other whiles the ark is taken from Israel: in either, there is a separation betwixt the ark and Israel. Heavy times to every true Israelite; yet such, as whose example may relieve us in our desertions. Still was this people Israel the seed of him that would not be left of God without a blessing; and therefore, without the testimony of his presence, was God present with them. It were wide with the faithful, if God were not oftentimes with them, when there is no witness of his presence.

One act was a mutual penance to the Israelites and Philistines; I know not to whether more. Israel grieved for the loss of that, whose presence grieved the Philistines; their pain was therefore no other than voluntary. It is strange that the Philistines would endure seven months' smart with the ark, since they saw that the presence of that prisoner would not requite, no, nor mitigate to them one hour's misery. Foolish men will be struggling with God, till they be utterly either breathless or impotent. Their hope was, that time might abate displeasure, even while they persisted to offend. The false hopes of worldly men cost them dear: they could not be so miserable, if their own hearts did not deceive them with misexpectations of impossible favour.

In matters that concern a God, who is so fit to be consulted with as the priests? The princes of the Philistines had before given their voices; yet nothing is determined, nothing is done without the direction and assent of those whom they accounted sacred. Nature itself sends us, in divine things, to those persons whose calling is divine. It is either distrust or presumption, or contempt, that carries us our own ways in spiritual matters, without advising with them whose lips God hath appointed to preserve knowledge. There cannot but arise many difficulties in us about the ark of God: whom should we consult with, but those which have the tongue of the learned?

Doubtless, this question of the ark did abide much debating. There wanted not fair probabilities on both sides. A wise Philistine might well plead, If God hath either so great care of the ark, or power to retain it, how is it become ours? A wiser than he would reply, If the God of Israel had wanted either care or power, Dagon and we had been still whole: why do we thus groan and die, all that are but within the air of the ark, if a divine hand do not attend it? Their smart pleads enough for the dismission of the ark. The next demand of their priests and soothsayers is, how it should be sent home. Affliction had made them so wise as to know, that every fashion of parting with the ark would not satisfy the owner. Oftentimes the circumstance of an action mars the substance. In divine matters we must not only look that the body of our service be sound, but the clothes be fit. Nothing hinders, but that sometimes good advice may fall from the mouth of wicked men. These superstitious priests can counsel them not to send away the ark of God empty, but to give it a sin-offering. They had not lived so far from the smoke of the Jewish altars, but that they knew God was accustomed to manifold oblations, and chiefly those of expiation. No Israelite could have said better: superstition is the ape of true devotion; and if we look not to the ground of both, many times it is hard, by the very outward acts, to distinguish them. Nature itself teacheth us, that God loves a full hand: he that hath been so bountiful to us as to give us all, looks for a return of some offering from us. If we present him with nothing but our sins, how can we look to be accepted? The sacrifices under the Gospel are spiritual; with these must we come into the presence of God, if we desire to carry away remission and favour.

The Philistines knew well that it were bootless for them to offer what they listed: their next suit is to be directed in the matter of their oblation. Pagans can teach us how unsafe it is to walk in the ways of religion without a guide; yet here their best teachers can but guess at their duty, and must devise for the people that which the people durst not impose upon themselves. The golden emerods and mice were but conjectural prescripts. With what security may we consult with them which have their directions from the mouth and hand of the Almighty!

God struck the Philistines at once in their god, in their bodies, in their land: in their god, by his ruin and dismembering; in their bodies, by the emerods; in their land, by the mice. That base vermin did God send among them, on purpose to shame their Dagon and them, that they might see how unable their god was, which they thought the victor of the ark, to subdue the least mouse which the true God did create, and command to plague them. This plague upon their fields began together with that upon their bodies; it was mentioned, not complained of, till they think of dismissing the ark. Greater crosses do commonly swallow up the less; at least, lesser evils are either silent or unheard, while the ear is filled with the clamour of greater. Their very princes were punished with the mice, as well as with the emerods. God knows no persons in the execution of judgments: the least and meanest of all God's creatures is sufficient to be the revenger of his Creator.

God sent them mice, and emerods of flesh and blood: they return him both these of gold, to imply both that these judgments came out from God, and that they did gladly give him the glory of that whereof he gave them pain and sorrow, and that they would willingly buy off their pain with the best of their substance. The proportion betwixt the complaint and satisfaction is more precious to him than the metal. There was a public confession in this resemblance, which is so pleasing unto God, that he rewards it, even in wicked men, with a relaxation of outward punishment. The number was no less significant than the form: five golden emerods and mice, for the five princes and divisions of Philistines. As God made no difference in punishing, so they make none in their oblation. The people are comprised in them in whom they are united, their several princes: they were one with their prince; their offspring is one with his; as they were ringleaders in the sin, so they must be in the satisfaction. In a multitude it is ever seen, as in a beast, that the body follows the head. Of all others, great men had need look to their ways; it is in them as in figures — one stands for a thousand. One offering serves not all; there must be five, according to the five heads of the offence. Generalities will not content God; every man must make his several peace, if not in himself, yet in his head. Nature taught them a shadow of that, the substance and perfection whereof is taught us by the grace of the Gospel. Every soul must satisfy God, if not in itself, yet in Him in whom we are both one, and absolute. We are the body, whereof Christ is the head: our sin is in ourselves; our satisfaction must be in him.

Samuel himself could not have spoken more divinely than these priests of Dagon: they do not only talk of giving glory to the God of Israel, but fall into a holy and grave expostulation: Wherefore, then, should ye harden your hearts, as the Egyptians and Pharaoh hardened their hearts, when he wrought wonderfully amongst them? &c. They confess a super-eminent and revenging hand of God over their gods; they parallel their plagues with the Egyptians'; they make use of Pharaoh's sin and judgment: what could be better said? All religions have afforded them that could speak well. These good words left them still both Philistines and superstitious. How should men be hypocrites, if they had not good tongues? Yet, as wickedness can hardly hide itself, these holy speeches are not without a tincture of that idolatry wherewith the heart was infected; for they profess care not only of the persons and lands of the Philistines, but of their gods: " That he may take his hand from you, and from your gods." Who would think that wisdom and folly could lodge so near together? that the same men should have care both of the glory of the true God, and preservation of the false? that they should be so vain as to take thought for those gods which they granted to be obnoxious unto a higher Deity? Ofttimes even one word bewrayeth a whole pack of falsehood; and though superstition be a cleanly counterfeit, yet some one slip of the tongue discovers it; as we say of devils, which, though they put on fair forms, yet are they known by their cloven feet.

What other warrant these superstitious priests had for the main substance of their advice, I know not; sure I am, the probability of the event was fair, that two kine, never used to any yoke, should run from their calves, which were newly shut up from them, to draw the ark home into a contrary way, must needs argue a hand above nature. What else should overrule brute creatures to prefer a forced carriage unto a natural burden? What should carry them from their own home towards the home of the ark? What else should guide an untamed and untaught team in as right a path towards Israel as their teachers could have gone? What else could make very beasts more wise than their masters? There is a special providence of God in the very motions of brute creatures: neither Philistines nor Israelites saw ought that drove them, yet they saw them so run as those that were led by a divine conduct. The reasonless creatures also do the will of their Maker: every act that is done either by them, or to them, makes up the decree of the Almighty: and if, in extraordinary actions and events, his hand is more visible, yet it is no less certainly present in the common.

Little did the Israelites of Beth-shemesh look for such a sight, while they were reaping their wheat in the valley, as to see the ark of God come running to them without a convoy: neither can it be said whether they were more affected with joy or with astonishment; with joy at the presence of the ark, with astonishment at the miracle of the transportation. Down went their sickles, and now every man runs to reap the comfort of this better harvest — to meet that bread of angels — to salute those cherubims — to welcome that God, whose absence had been their death. But as it is hard not to overjoy in a sudden prosperity, and to use happiness is no less difficult than to forbear it, these glad Israelites cannot see, but they must gaze: they cannot gaze on the glorious outside, but they must be, whether out of rude jollity, or curiosity, or suspicion of the purloining some of those sacred implements, prying into the secrets of God's ark. Nature is too subject to extremities, and is ever either too dull in want, or wanton in fruition: it is no easy matter to keep a mean, whether in good or evil.

Beth-shemesh was a city of priests: they should have known better how to demean themselves towards the ark; this privilege doubled their offence. There was no malice in this curious inquisition: the same eyes that looked into the ark, looked also up to heaven in their offerings; and the same hands that touched it, offered sacrifice to the God that brought it. Who could expect any thing now but acceptation? who would suspect any danger? It is not a following act of devotion that can make amends for a former sin. There was a death owing them immediately upon their offence: God will take his own time for the execution. In the meanwhile they may sacrifice, but they cannot satisfy; they cannot escape. The kine are sacrificed; the cart burns them that drew it. Here was an offering of praise, when they had more need of a trespass-offering. Many a heart is lifted up in a conceit of joy, when it hath just cause of humiliation. God lets them alone with their sacrifice; but, when that is done, he comes over them with a back-reckoning for their sin. Fifty thousand and seventy Israelites are struck dead, for this unreverence to the ark: a woful welcome for the ark of God into the borders of Israel! It killed them for looking into it, who thought it their life to see it. It dealt blows and death on both hands, to Philistines, to Israelites; to both of them for profaning it, the one with their idol, the other with their eyes. It is a fearful thing to use the holy ordinances of God with an unreverent boldness. Fear and trembling become us, in our access to the majesty of the Almighty. Neither was there more state than secrecy in God's ark. Some things the wisdom of God desires to conceal. The unreverence of the Israelites was no more faulty than their curiosity. "Secret things belong to God; things revealed, to us and to our children."

CONTEMPLATION III. — THE REMOVAL OF THE ARK.

I HEAR of the Beth-shemites' lamentation; I hear not of their repentance: they complain of their smart, they complain not of their sin; and, for aught I can perceive, speak as if God were curious, rather than they faulty: "Who is able to stand before this holy Lord God, and to whom shall he go from us?" As if none could please that God, which misliked them. It is the fashion of natural men, to justify themselves in their own courses: if they cannot charge any earthly thing with the blame of their suffering, they will cast it on heaven. That a man pleads himself guilty of his own wrong, is no common work of God's Spirit. Beth-shemesh bordered too near upon the Philistines. If these men thought the very presence of the ark hurtful, why do they send to their neighbours of Kirjath-jearim, that they might make themselves miserable? Where there is a misconceit of God, it is no marvel if there be a defect of charity. How cunningly do they send their message to their neighbours! They do not say, the ark of God is come to us of its own accord; lest the men of Kirjath-jearim should reply, It is come to you; let it stay with you. They say only, the Philistines have brought it. They tell of the presence of the ark; they do not tell of the success, lest the example of their judgment should have discouraged the forwardness of their relief. And, after all, the offer was plausible; "Come ye down, and take it up to you;" as if the honour had been too great for themselves; as if their modesty had been such, that they would not forestall and engross happiness from the rest of Israel.

It is no boot to teach nature how to tell her own tale; smart and danger will make a man witty. He is rarely constant, that will not dissemble for ease. It is good to be suspicious of the evasions of those which would put off misery. Those of Beth-shemesh were not more crafty than these of Kirjath-jearim (which was the ground of their boldness) faithful. So many thousand Beth-shemites could not be dead, and no part of the rumour fly to them. They heard how thick not only the Philistines, but the bordering Israelites, fell down dead before the ark; yet they durst adventure to come, and fetch it, even from amongst the carcases of their brethren. They had been formerly acquainted with the ark; they knew it was holy, it could not be changeable; and therefore they well conceived this slaughter to arise from the unholiness of men, not from the rigour of God, and thereupon can seek comfort in that which others found deadly. God's children cannot, by any means, be discouraged from their honour and love to his ordinances. If they see thousands struck down to hell by the sceptre of God's kingdom, yet they will kiss it upon their knees; and if their Saviour be a rock of offence, and the occasion of the fall of millions in Israel, they can feed temperately of that whereof others have surfeited to death.

Beth-shemesh was a city of priests and Levites. Kirjath-jearim a city of Judah, where we hear but of one Levite, Abinadab; yet this city was more zealous for God, more reverent and conscionable in the entertainment of the ark, than the other. We heard of the taking down of the ark by the Beth-shemites, when it came miraculously to them: we do not hear of any man sanctified for the attendance of it, as was done in this second lodging of the ark. Grace is not tied either to number or means. It is in spiritual matters, as in an estate; small helps with good thrift enrich us, when great patrimonies lose themselves in the neglect. Shiloh was wont to be the place which was honoured with the presence of the ark. Ever since the wickedness of Eli's sons, that was forlorn and desolate, and now Kirjath-jearim succeeds into this privilege. It did not stand with the royal liberty of God, no, not under the law, to tie himself unto places and persons. Unworthiness was ever a sufficient cause of exchange. It was not yet his time to stir from the Jews, yet he removed from one province to another. Less reason have we to think, that so God will reside amongst us, that none of our provocations can drive him from us.

Israel, which had found the misery of God's absence, is now resolved into tears of contrition and thankfulness upon his return. There is no mention of their lamenting after the Lord while he was gone; but when he was returned, and settled in Kirjath-jearim, the mercies of God draw more tears from his children, than his judgments do from his enemies. There is no better sign of good nature or grace, than to be won to repentance with kindness. Not to think of God, except we be beaten into it, is servile. Because God was come again to Israel, therefore Israel is returned to God: if God had not come first, they had never come. If he, that came to them, had not made them come to him, they had been ever parted. They were cloyed with God, while he was perpetually resident with them: now that his absence had made him dainty, they cleave to him fervently and penitently in his return. This was it that God meant in his departure, a better welcome at his coming back.

I heard no news of Samuel, all this while the ark was gone. Now when the ark is returned and placed in Kirjath-jearim, I hear him treat with the people. It is not like he was silent in this sad desertion of God; but now he takes full advantage of the professed contrition of Israel, to deal with them effectually, for their perfect conversion unto God. It is great wisdom, in spiritual matters, to take occasion by the forelock, and to strike while the iron is hot. We may beat long enough at the door, but till God have opened, it is no going in; and, when he hath opened, it is no delaying to enter. The trial of sincerity is the abandoning of our wonted sins. This Samuel urgeth: "If ye be come again unto the Lord with all your heart, put away the strange gods from among you, and Ashtaroth." In vain had it been to profess repentance, whilst they continued in idolatry. God will never acknowledge any convert that stays in a known sin. Graces and virtues are so linked together, that he which hath one, hath all. The partial conversion of men unto God is but hateful hypocrisy. How happily effectual is a word spoken in season! Samuel's exhortation wrought upon the hearts of Israel, and fetched water out of their eyes, suits and confessions and vows out of their lips, and their false gods out of their hands; yet it was not merely remorse, but fear also, that moved Israel to this humble submission.

The Philistines stood over them still, and threatened them with new assaults; the memory of their late slaughter and spoil was yet fresh in their minds; sorrow for the evils past, and fear of the future, fetched them down upon their knees. It is not more necessary for men to be cheered with hopes, than to be awed with dangers. Where God intends the humiliation of his servants, there shall not want means of their dejection. It was happy for Israel that they had an enemy. Is it possible that the Philistines, after those deadly plagues which they had sustained from the God of Israel, should think of invading Israel? Those that were so mated with the presence of the ark, that they never thought themselves safe till it was out of sight, do they now dare to thrust themselves upon the new revenge of the ark? It slew them while they thought to honour it; and do they think to escape whilst they resist it? It slew them in their own coasts; and do they come to it to seek death? Yet, behold, no sooner do the Philistines hear that the Israelites are gathered to Mizpeh, but the princes of the Philistines gather themselves against them. No warnings will serve obdurate hearts: wicked men are even ambitious of destruction. Judgments need not go to find them out; they run to meet their bane.

The Philistines come up, and the Israelites fear; they that had not the wit to fear, whilst they were not friends with God, have not now the grace of fearlessness, when they were reconciled to God. Boldness and fear are commonly misplaced in the best hearts: when we should tremble, we are confident; and when we should be assured, we tremble. Why should Israel have feared, since they had made their peace with the God of hosts? Nothing should affright those which are upright with God. The peace which Israel had made with God was true, but tender. They durst not trust their own innocency, so much as the prayers of Samuel: "Cease not to cry to the Lord our God for us." In temporal things, nothing hinders but we may fare better for other men's faith than for our own. It is no small happiness to be interested in them which are favourites in the court of heaven. One faithful man, in these occasions, is more worth than millions of the wavering and uncertain.

A good heart is easily won to devotion. Samuel cries, and sacrificeth to God: he had done so, though they had entreated his silence, yea, his forbearance. While he is offering, the Philistines fight with Israel, and God fights with the Philistines: "The Lord thundered with a great thunder that day, upon the Philistines, and scattered them." Samuel fought more upon his knees, than all Israel besides. The voice of God answered the voice of Samuel, and speaks confusion and death to the Philistines. How were the proud Philistines dead with fear ere they died, to hear the fearful thunder-claps of an angry God against them! to see that heaven itself fought against them! He that slew them secretly, in the revenges of his ark, now kills them with open horror in the fields. If presumption did not make wicked men mad, they would never lift their hand against the Almighty: what are they in his hands, when he is disposed to vengeance

CONTEMPLATION IV.—THE MEETING OF SAUL AND SAMUEL.

SAMUEL began his acquaintance with God early, and continued it long. He began it in his long coats, and continued to his grey hairs. He judged Israel all the days of his life. God doth not use to put off his old servants; their age endeareth them to him the more: if we be not unfaithful to him, he cannot be unconstant to us. At last, his decayed age met with ill partners; his sons for deputies, and Saul for a king. The wickedness of his sons gave the occasion of a change. Perhaps Israel had never thought of a king, if Samuel's sons had not been unlike their father. Who can promise himself holy children, when the loins of a Samuel, and the education in the temple, yielded monsters? It is not likely that good Samuel was faulty in that indulgence, for which his own mouth had denounced God's judgment against Eli: yet this holy man succeeds Eli in his cross, as well as his place, though not in his sin, and is afflicted with a wicked succession. God will let us find, that grace is by gift, not by inheritance.

I fear Samuel was too partial to nature in the surrogation of his sons: I do not hear of God's allowance to this act; if this had been God's choice, as well as his, it had been like to have received more blessing. Now all Israel had cause to rue, that these were the sons of Samuel: for now the question was not of their virtues, but of their blood; not of their worthiness, but their birth. Even the best heart may be blinded with affection. Who can marvel at these errors of parents' love, when he, that so holily judged Israel all his life, misjudged of his own sons!

It was God's ancient purpose to raise up a king to his people. How doth he take occasion to perform it, but by the unruly desires of Israel: even as we say of human proceedings, that ill manners beget good laws. That monarchy is the best form of government, there is no question: good things may be ill desired; so was this of Israel. If an itching desire of alteration had not possessed them, why did they not rather sue for a reformation of their governors, than for a change of government? Were Samuel's sons so desperately evil, that there was no possibility of amendment? or, if they were past hope, were there not some others to have succeeded the justice of Samuel, no less than these did his person? What needed Samuel to be thrust out of place? What needed the ancient form of administration to be altered? He, that raised them up judges, would have found time to raise them up kings. Their curious and inconstant newfangledness will not abide to stay it, but with an heady importunity labours to over-hasten the pace of God. Where there is a settled course of good government, howsoever blemished with some weaknesses, it is not safe to be over-forward to a change, though it should be to the better. He, by whom kings reign, says, they have cast him away, that he should not reign over them, because they desire a king to reign over them. Judges were his own institution to his people; as yet, kings were not: after that kings were settled, to desire the government of judges had been a much more seditious inconstancy. God hath not appointed, to every time and place, such forms which are simply best in themselves, but those which are best to them unto whom they are appointed; which we may neither alter till he begin, nor recall when he hath altered.

This business seemed personally to concern Samuel; yet he so deals in it, not as a party, not as a judge in his own case, but as a prophet of God, as a friend of his opposite. He prays to God for advice; he foretells the state and courses of their future king. Wilful men are blind to all dangers; are deaf to all good counsels. Israel must have a king, though they pay never so dear for their longing. The vain affectation of conformity to other nations overcomes all discouragements. There is no readier way to error, than to make others' examples the rule of our desires or actions. If every man have not grounds of his own, whereon to stand, there can be no stability in his resolutions or proceedings.

Since, then, they choose to have a king, God himself will choose and appoint the king which they shall have. The kingdom shall begin in Benjamin, which was to endure in Judah. It was no probability or reason this first king should prove well, because he was abortive: their humour of innovation deserved to be punished with their own choice. Kish, the father of Saul, was mighty in estate; Saul was mighty in person, overlooking the rest of the people in stature, no less than he should do in dignity. The senses of the Israelites could not but be well pleased for the time, howsoever their hearts were afterwards. When men are carried with outward shows, it is a sign that God means them a delusion.

How far God fetches his purposes about! The asses of Kish, Saul's father, are strayed away: what is that to the news of a kingdom? God lays these small accidents for the ground of greater designs. The asses must be lost; none but Saul must go with his father's servant to seek them: Samuel shall meet them in the search; Saul shall be premonished of his ensuing royalty. Little can we, by the beginning of any action, guess at God's intention in the conclusion.

Obedience was a fit entrance into sovereignty. The service was homely for the son of a great man; yet he refuseth not to go, as a fellow to his father's servant, upon so mean a search. The disobedient and scornful are good for nothing; they are neither fit to be subjects nor governors. Kish was a great man in his country, yet he disdained not to send his son Saul upon a thrifty errand; neither doth Saul plead his disparagement for a refusal. Pride and wantonness have marred our times. Great parents count it a disreputation to employ their sons in courses of frugality; and their pampered children think it a shame to do any thing, and so bear themselves as those that hold it the only glory to be either idle or wicked.

Neither doth Saul go fashionably to work, but does this service heartily and painfully, as a man that desires rather to effect the command, than please the commander. He passed from Ephraim to the land of Shalisha, from Shalisha to Salim, from Salim to Jemini, whence his house came, from Jemini to Zuph; not so much as staying with any of his kindred so long as to victual himself. He, that was afterward an ill king, approved himself a good son. As there is diversity of relations and offices, so there is of dispositions: those which are excellent in some, attain not to a mediocrity in others. It is no arguing from private virtues to public; from dexterity in one station, to the rest. A several grace belongs to the particular carriage of every place whereto we are called, which, if we want, the place may well want us.

There was more praise of his obedience in ceasing to seek, than in seeking. He takes care, lest his father should take for him, that, whilst he should seem officious in the less, he might not neglect the greatest. A blind obedience, in some cases, doth well; but it doth far better, when it is led with the eyes of discretion; otherwise, we may more offend in pleasing, than in disobeying.

Great is the benefit of a wise and religious attendant; such a one puts us into those duties and actions which are most expedient, and least thought of. If Saul had not had a discreet servant, he had returned but as wise as he came; now he is drawn in to consult with the man of God, and hears more than he hoped for. Saul was now a sufficient journey from his father's house; yet his religious servant, in this remoteness, takes knowledge of the place where the prophet dwells: and how honourably doth he mention him to his master! "Behold, in this city is a man of God, and he is an honourable man; all that he saith cometh to pass." God's prophets are public persons; as their function, so their notice concerns every man. There is no reason God should abate any of the respect due to his ministers under the gospel. St Paul's suit is both universal and everlasting: "I beseech you, brethren, know them that labour amongst you."

The chief praise is to be able to give good advice; the next is, to take it. Saul is easily induced to condescend. He, whose curiosity led him voluntarily at last to the witch of Endor, is now led at first, by good counsel, to the man of God: neither is his care in going, less commendable than his will to go. For, as a man that had been catechized not to go unto God empty-handed, he asks, "What shall we bring unto the man? what have we?" The case is well altered in our times. Every man thinks, what may I keep back? There is no gain so sweet, as of a robbed altar; yet God's charge is no less under the gospel: "Let him that is taught, make his teacher partaker of all." As this faithful care of Saul was a just presage of success, more than he looked for, or could expect; so the sacrilegious unthankfulness of many, bodes that ruin to their soul and estate, which they could not have grace to fear.

He that knew the prophet's abode, knew also the honour of his place; he could not but know that Samuel was a mixt person, the judge of Israel and the seer: yet both Saul and his servant purpose to present him with the fourth part of a shekel, to the value of about our fivepence. They had learned, that thankfulness was not to be measured of good men, by the weight, but by the will of the retributor. How much more will God accept the small offerings of his weak servants, when he sees them proceed from great love!

The very maids of the city can give direction to the prophet: they had listened after the holy affairs; they had heard of the sacrifice, and could tell of the necessity of Samuel's presence. Those that live within the sunshine of religion, cannot but be somewhat coloured with those beams. Where there is practice and example of piety in the better sort, there will be a reflection of it upon the meanest. It is no small benefit to live in religious and holy places. We shall be much to blame, if all goodness fall beside us. Yea, so skilful were these damsels in the fashions of their public sacrifices, that they could instruct Saul and his servant unasked, how the people would not eat, till Samuel came to bless the sacrifice. This meeting was not more a sacrifice, than it was a feast. These two agree well. We have never so much cause to rejoice in feasting, as when we have duly served our God. The sacrifice was a feast to God, the other to men. The body may eat and drink with contentment, when the soul hath been first fed, and hath first feasted the Maker of both: " Go, eat thy bread with joy, and drink thy drink with a merry heart; for God now accepteth thy works." The sacrifice was before consecrated, when it was offered to God; but it was not consecrated to them, till Samuel blessed it: his blessing made that meat holy to the guests, which was formerly hallowed to God. All creatures were made good, and took holiness from him which gave them their being. Our sin brought that curse upon them, which, unless our prayers remove it, cleaves to them still, so as we receive them not without a curse. We are not our own friends, except our prayers help to take that away which our sin hath brought, that so to the clean all may be clean. It is an unmannerly godlessness to take God's creatures without the leave of their Maker; and well may God withhold his blessing from them which have not the grace to ask it.

Those guests, which were so religious that they would not eat their sacrifice unblessed, might have blessed it themselves. Every man might pray, though every man might not sacrifice; yet would they not either eat, or bless, while they looked for the presence of a prophet. Every Christian may sanctify his own meat; but, where those are present that are peculiarly sanctified to God, this service is fittest for them. It is commendable to teach children the practice of thanksgiving, but the best is ever most meet to bless our tables, and those especially whose office it is to offer our prayers to God.

Little did Saul think, that his coming and his errand were so noted of God, as that it was fore-signified unto the prophet; and now, behold, Samuel is told a day before, of the man, the time, and the place of his meeting. The eye of God's providence is no less over all our actions, all our motions. We cannot go any whither without him; he tells all our steps. Since it pleaseth God, therefore, to take notice of us, much more should we take notice of him, and walk with him, in whom we move. Saul came, besides his expectation, to the prophet: he had no thought of any such purpose, till his servant made this sudden motion unto him of visiting Samuel; and yet God says to his prophet, " I will send thee a man out of the land of Benjamin." The overruling hand of the Almighty works us insensibly, and all our affairs, to his own secret determinations; so as, while we think to do our own wills, we do his. Our own intentions we may know; God's purposes we know not: we must go the way that we are called, let him lead us to what end he pleaseth. It is our duty to resign ourselves and our ways to the disposition of God, and patiently and thankfully to wait the issue of his decrees. The same God, that fore-showed Saul to Samuel, now points to him: " See, this is the man," and commands the prophet to anoint him governor over Israel. He, that told of Saul before he came, knew before he came into the world, what a man, what a king, he would be; yet he chooseth him out and enjoins his inunction. It is one of the greatest praises of God's wisdom, that he can turn the evil of men to his own glory. Advancement is not ever a sign of love, either to the man or to the place. It had been better for Saul, that his head had been ever dry. Some God raiseth up in judgment, that they may fall the more uneasily; there are no men so miserable as those that are great and evil.

It seems that Samuel bore no great port in his outside, for that Saul, not discerning him either by his habit or attendants, comes to him, and asks him for the seer: yet was Samuel as yet the judge of Israel; the substitution of his sons had not displaced himself. There is an affable familiarity that becometh greatness. It is not good for eminent persons to stand always upon the height of their state; but so to behave themselves, that as their sociable carriage may not breed contempt, so their over-highness may not breed a servile fearfulness in their people.

How kindly doth Samuel entertain and invite Saul: yet it was he only that should receive wrong by the future royalty of Saul! Who would not have looked, that aged Samuel should have emulated rather the glory of his young rival, and have looked churlishly upon the man that should rob him of his authority? Yet now, as if he came on purpose to gratify him, he bids him to the feast, he honours him with the chief seat, he reserves a select morsel for him, he tells him ingenuously the news of his ensuing sovereignty: " On whom is set the desire of all Israel? is it not upon thee, and thy father's house?" Wise and holy men, as they are not ambitious of their own burden, so they are not unwilling to be eased, when God pleaseth to discharge them; neither can they envy those whom God lifteth above their heads. They make an idol of honour, that are troubled with their own freedom, or grudge at the promotion of others.

Doubtless Saul was much amazed with this strange salutation, and news of the prophet: and how modestly doth he put it off, as that which was neither fit nor likely, disparaging his tribe, in respect of the rest of Israel; his father's family, in respect of the tribe; and himself, in respect of his father's family! Neither did his humility stoop below the truth; for, as Benjamin was the youngest son of Israel, so he was now by much the least tribe of Israel. They had not yet recovered that universal slaughter which they had received from the hands of their brethren, whereby a tribe was almost lost to Israel: yet even out of the remainder of Benjamin doth God choose the man that shall command Israel; out of the rubbish of Benjamin doth God raise the throne. That is not ever the best and fattest which God chooseth; but that which God chooseth is ever the fittest. The strength or weakness of means is neither spur nor bridle to the determinate choices of God; yea, rather, he holds it the greatest proof of his freedom and omnipotence, to advance the unlikeliest. It was no hollow and feigned excuse that Saul makes, to put off that which he would fain enjoy, and to cause honour to follow him the more eagerly: it was the sincere truth of his humility, that so dejected him under the hand of God's prophet. Fair beginnings are no sound proof of our proceedings and ending well. How often hath a bashful childhood ended in an impudency of youth; a strict entrance, in licentiousness; early forwardness, in atheism! There might be a civil meekness in Saul; true grace there was not in him. They that be good, bear more fruit in their age.

Saul had but fivepence in his purse to give the prophet. The prophet, after much good cheer, gives him the kingdom: he bestows the oil of royal consecration on his head, the kisses of homage upon his face, and sends him away rich in thoughts and expectation. And now, lest his astonishment should end in distrust, he settles his assurance, by forewarnings of those events which he should find in his way: he tells him whom he shall meet, what they shall say, how himself shall be affected. That all these, and himself, might be so many witnesses of his following coronation, every word confirmed him. For well might he think, He that can foretell me the motions and words of others, cannot fail in mine; especially when (as Samuel had prophesied to him) he found himself to prophesy: his prophesying did enough foretell his kingdom. No sooner did Samuel turn his back from Saul, but God gave him another heart, lifting up his thoughts and disposition to the pitch of a king. The calling of God never leaves a man unchanged: neither did God ever employ any man in his service, whom he did not enable to the work he set him; especially those whom he raiseth up to the supply of his own place, and the representation of himself. It is no marvel if princes excel the vulgar in gifts, no less than in dignity. Their crowns and their hearts are both in one and the same hand. If God did not add to their powers, as well as their honours, there would be no equality.

CONTEMPLATION V. — THE INAUGURATION OF SAUL.

God hath secretly destined Saul to the kingdom. It could not content Israel that Samuel knew this; the lots must so decide the choice as if it had not been predetermined: that God, which is ever constant to his own decrees, makes the lots to find him out whom Samuel had anointed. If once we have notice of the will of God, we may be confident of the issue. There is no chance to the Almighty: even casual things are no less necessary in their first cause, than the natural. So far did Saul trust the prediction and oil of Samuel, that he hides him among the stuff. He knew where the lots would light before they were cast; this was but a modest declination of that honour which he saw must come: his very withdrawing showed some expectation, why else should he have hid himself, rather than the other Israelites? Yet could he not hope his subduing himself could disappoint the purpose of God: he well knew, that he which found out and designed his name amongst the thousands of Israel, would easily find out his person in a tent. When once we know God's decree, in vain shall we strive against it: before we know it, it is indifferent for us to work to the likeliest.

I cannot blame Saul for hiding himself from a kingdom, especially of Israel. Honour is heavy, when it comes upon the best terms: how should it be otherwise, when all men's cares are cast upon one; but most of all in a troubled estate? No man can put to sea without danger; but he that launcheth forth in a tempest, can expect nothing but the hardest event: such was the condition of Israel. Their old enemies the Philistines were stilled with that fearful thunder of God, as finding what it was to war against the Almighty. There were adversaries enough besides in their borders: it was but a hollow truce that was betwixt Israel and their heathenish neighbours, and Nahash was now at their gates. Well did Saul know the difference between a peaceful government and the perilous and wearisome tumults of war. The quietest throne is full of cares; but the perplexed, of dangers. Cares and dangers drove Saul into this corner, to hide his head from a crown: these made him choose rather to lie obscurely among the baggage of his tent, than to sit gloriously in the throne of state. This hiding could do nothing but show, that he both suspected lest he should be chosen, and desired he should not be chosen. That God, from whom the hills and the rocks could not conceal him, brings him forth to the light, so much more longed for, as he was more unwilling to be seen, and more applauded, as he was more longed for.

Now then, when Saul is drawn forth in the midst of the eager expectation of Israel, modesty and goodliness showed themselves in his face. The crowd cannot hide him, whom the stuff had hid: as if he had been made to be seen, he overlooks all Israel in height of stature, for presage of the eminence of his state: "From the shoulders upwards, was he higher than any of the people." Israel sees their lots are fallen upon a noted man, one whose person showed he was born to be a king: and now all the people shout for joy; they have their longing, and applaud their own happiness, and their king's honour. How easy is it for us to mistake our own estates; to rejoice in that which we shall find the just cause of our humiliation! The end of a thing is better than the beginning. The safest way is to reserve our joy till we have good proof of the worthiness and fitness of the object. What are we the better for having a blessing, if we know not how to use it? The office and observance of a king was uncouth to Israel: Samuel therefore informs the people of their mutual duties, and writes them in a book, and lays it up before the Lord; otherwise, novelty might have been a warrant for their ignorance, and ignorance for neglect. There are reciprocal respects of princes and people, which, if they be not observed, government languisheth into confusion: these Samuel faithfully teacheth them. Though he may not be their judge, yet he will be their prophet; he will instruct, if he may not rule; yea, he will instruct him that shall rule. There is no king absolute, but he that is the King of all gods. Earthly monarchs must walk by a rule, which, if they transgress, they shall be accountable to him that is higher than the highest, who hath deputed them. Not out of care of civility, so much as conscience, must every Samuel labour to keep even terms betwixt kings and subjects, prescribing just moderation to the one; to the other, obedience and loyalty, which, whoever endeavours to trouble, is none of the friends of God or his church.

The most and best applaud their new king; some wicked ones despised him, and said, "How shall he save us?" It was not the might of his parents, the goodliness of his person, the privilege of his lot, the fame of his prophesying, the panegyric of Samuel, that could shield him from contempt, or win him the hearts of all. There was never yet any man, to whom some took not exception. It is not possible either to please or displease all men; while some men are in love with vice, as deeply as others with virtue, and some as ill dislike virtue, if not for itself, yet for contradiction. They well saw Saul chose not himself; they saw him worthy to have been chosen, if the election should have been carried by voices, and those voices by their eyes; they saw him unwilling to hold, or yield, when he was chosen; yet they will envy him. What fault could they find in him whom God had chosen? His parentage was equal, his person above them, his inward parts more above them than the outward. Malcontents will rather devise than want causes of flying out; and rather than fail, the universal approbation of others is ground enough of their dislike. It is a vain ambition of those that would be loved of all. The Spirit of God, when he enjoins us peace, withal he adds, "If it be possible;" and favour is more than peace. A man's comfort must be in himself, the conscience of deserving well.

The neighbouring Ammonites could not but have heard of God's fearful vengeance upon the Philistines, and yet they will be taking up the quarrel against Israel. Nahash comes up against Jabesh-Gilead. Nothing but grace can teach us to make use of others' judgments. Wicked men are not moved with aught that falls beside them: they trust nothing but their own smart. What fearful judgments doth God execute every day! Resolute sinners take no notice of them, and are grown so peremptory, as if God had never showed dislike of their ways.

The Gileadites were not more base than Nahash the Ammonite was cruel. The

Gileadites would buy their peace with servility; Nahash would sell them a servile peace for their right eyes. Jephthah the Gileadite did yet stick in the stomach of Ammon; and now they think their revenge cannot be too bloody. It is a wonder that he which would offer so merciless a condition to Israel, would yield to the motion of any delay; he meant nothing but shame and death to the Israelites, yet he condescends to a seven days' respite: perhaps his confidence made him thus careless. Howsoever, it was the restraint of God that gave this breath to Israel, and this opportunity to Saul's courage and victory. The enemies of God's church cannot be so malicious as they would, cannot approve themselves so malicious as they are. God so holds them in sometimes, that a stander-by would think them favourable. The news of Gilead's distress hath soon filled and afflicted Israel; the people think of no remedy but their pity and tears. Evils are easily grieved for; not easily redressed: only Saul is more stirred with indignation than sorrow: that God, which put into him a spirit of prophecy, now puts into him a spirit of fortitude. He was before appointed to the throne, not settled in the throne; he followed the beasts in the field, when he should have commanded men.

Now, as one that would be a king no less by merit than election, he takes upon him, and performs the rescue of Gilead; he assembles Israel, he leads them, he raiseth the siege, breaks the troops, cuts the throats of the Ammonites. When God hath any exploit to perform, he raiseth up the heart of some chosen instrument with heroical motions for the achievement. When all hearts are cold and dead, it is a sign of intended destruction.

This day hath made Saul a complete king; and now the thankful Israelites begin to inquire after those discontented mutineers, which had refused allegiance unto so worthy a commander: "Bring those men, that we may slay them." This sedition had deserved death, though Saul had been foiled at Gilead; but now his happy victory whets the people much more to a desire of this just execution. Saul, to whom the injury was done, hinders the revenge: "There shall no man die this day, for to-day the Lord hath saved Israel;" that his fortitude might not go beyond his mercy. How noble were these beginnings of Saul! His prophecy showed him miraculously wise, his battle and victory no less valiant, his pardon of his rebels as merciful. There was not more power showed in overcoming the Ammonites than in overcoming himself and the impotent malice of these mutinous Israelites. Now Israel sees they have a king, that can both shed blood and spare it; that can shed the Ammonites' blood, and spare theirs. His mercy wins those hearts whom his valour could not. As in God, so in his deputies, mercy and justice should be inseparable: wheresoever these two go asunder, government follows them into distraction, and ends in ruin. If it had been a wrong offered to Samuel, the forbearance of the revenge had not been so commendable, although, upon the day of so happy a deliverance, perhaps it had not been seasonable. A man hath reason to be most bold with himself. It is no praise of mercy, since it is a fault in justice, to remit another man's satisfaction; his own he may.

CONTEMPLATION VI.—SAMUEL'S CONTESTATION.

Every one can be a friend to him that prospereth. By this victory hath Saul as well conquered the obstinacy of his own people. Now there is no Israelite that rejoiceth not in Saul's kingdom. No sooner have they done objecting to Saul, than Samuel begins to expostulate with them. The same day wherein they began to be pleased, God shows himself angry. All the passages of their proceedings offended him; he deferred to let them know it, till now that the kingdom was settled, and their hearts lifted up. Now doth God cool their courage and joy, with a back-reckoning for their forwardness. God will not let his people run away with the arrearages of their sins; but, when they least think of it, calls them to an account. All this while was God angry with their rejection of Samuel; yet, as if there had been nothing but peace, he gives them a victory over their enemies; he gives way to their joy in their election; now he lets them know, that after their peace-offerings he hath a quarrel with them. God may be angry enough with us, while we outwardly prosper. It is the wisdom of God to take his best advantages: he suffers us to go on, till we should come to enjoy the fruit of our sin, till we seem past the danger either of conscience or punishment; then, even when we begin to be past the feeling of our sin, we shall begin to feel his displeasure for our sins: this is only where he loves, where he would both forgive and reclaim. He hath now to do with his Israel. But where he means utter vengeance, he lets men harden themselves to a reprobate senselessness, and make up their own measure without contradiction, as purposing to reckon with them but once for ever.

Samuel had dissuaded them before; he reproves them not until now. If he had thus bent himself against them, ere the settling of the election, he had troubled Israel in that which God took occasion by their sin to establish; his opposition would have savoured of respects to himself, whom the wrong of this innovation chiefly concerned. Now therefore, when they are sure of their king, and their king of them; when he hath set even terms betwixt them mutually, he lets them see how they were at odds with God. We must ever dislike sins; we may not ever show it. Discretion in the choice of seasons for reproving is no less commendable and necessary, than zeal and faithfulness in reproving. Good physicians use not to evacuate the body in extremities of heat or cold; wise mariners do not hoist sails in every wind.

First doth Samuel begin to clear his own innocence, ere he dare charge them with their sin. He that will cast a stone at an offender, must be free himself, otherwise he condemns and executes himself in another person. The conscience stops the mouth of the guilty man, and chokes him with that sin which lies in his own breast, and, having not come forth by a penitent confession, cannot find the way out in a reproof, or, if he do reprove, he doth more shame himself, than reform another. He, that was the judge of Israel, would not now judge himself, but would be judged by Israel: "Whose ox have I taken? whose ass have I taken? or to whom have I done wrong?" No doubt Samuel found himself guilty before God of many private infirmities; but for his public carriage he appeals to men. A man's heart can best judge of himself; others can best judge of his actions. As another man's conscience and approbation cannot bear us out before God, so cannot our own before men; for ofttimes that action is censured by the beholders as wrongful, wherein we applaud our own justice. Happy is that man that can be acquitted by himself in private, in public by others, by God in both. Standers-by may see more. It is very safe for a man to look into himself by others' eyes. In vain shall a man's heart absolve him that is condemned by his actions.

It was not so much the trial of his carriage that Samuel appealed for, as his justification. Not for his own comfort, so much as their conviction. His innocence hath not done him service enough, unless it shame them, and make them confess themselves faulty. In so many years, wherein Samuel judged Israel, it cannot be but many thousand causes passed his hands, wherein both parties could not possibly be pleased; yet so clear doth he find his heart and hands, that he dare make the grieved part judges of his judgment. A good conscience will make a man undauntedly confident, and dare put him upon any trial: where his own heart strikes him not, it bids him challenge all the world, and take up all comers. How happy a thing is it for man to be his own friend and patron! He needs not to fear foreign broils, that is at peace at home. Contrarily, he that hath a false and foul heart, lies at every man's mercy, lives slavishly, and is fain to daub up a rotten peace with the basest conditions. Truth is not afraid of any light; and therefore dare suffer her wares to be carried from a dim shop-board unto the street-door. Perfect gold will be but the purer with trying; whereas falsehood, being a work of darkness, loves darkness, and therefore seeks where it may work closest.

This very appellation cleared Samuel; but the people's attestation cleared him more. Innocency and uprightness become every man well, but most public persons, who shall be else obnoxious to every offender. The throne and the pulpit, of all places, call for holiness, no more for example of good, than for liberty of controlling evil. All magistrates swear to do that, which Samuel protesteth he hath done; if their oath were so verified, as Samuel's protestation, it were a shame for the state not to be happy. The sins of our teachers are the teachers of sin; the sins of governors do both command and countenance evil. This very acquitting of Samuel was the accusation of themselves; for how could it be but faulty to cast off a faultless governor? If he had not taken away an ox or an ass from them, why do they take away his authority? They could not have thus cleared Saul at the end of his reign. It was just with God, since they were weary of a just ruler, to punish them with an unjust.

He that appealed to them for his own uprightness, durst not appeal to them for their own wickedness, but appeals to heaven from them. Men are commonly flatterers of their own cases: it must be a strong evidence that will make a sinner convicted in himself. Nature hath so many shifts to cozen itself in this spiritual verdict, that unless it be taken in the manner, it will hardly yield to a truth; either she will deny the fact, or the fault, or the measure: and now, in this case, they might seem to have some fair pretences; for though Samuel was righteous, yet his sons were corrupt. To cut off all excuses, therefore, Samuel appeals to God, the highest judge, for his sentence of their sin, and dares trust to a miraculous conviction. It was now their wheat-harvest; the hot and dry air of that climate did not wont to afford, in that season, so much moist vapour as might raise a cloud, either for rain or thunder. He that knew God could and would do both these without the help of second causes, puts the trial upon this issue. Had not Samuel before consulted with his Maker, and received warrant for his act, it had been presumption and tempting of God, which was now a noble improvement of faith. Rather than Israel shall go clear away with a sin, God will accuse and arraign them from heaven. No sooner hath Samuel's voice ceased, than God's voice begins. Every crack of thunder spake judgment against the rebellious Israelites, and every drop of rain was a witness of their sin; and now they found they had displeased Him which ruleth in the heaven, by rejecting the man that ruled for him on earth. The thundering voice of God, that had lately in their sight confounded the Philistines, they now understood to speak fearful things against them. No marvel if they now fell upon their knees, not to Saul, whom they had chosen, but to Samuel, who, being thus cast off by them, is thus countenanced in heaven.

CONTEMPLATION VII.—OF SAUL'S SACRIFICE.

GOD never meant the kingdom should either stay long in the tribe of Benjamin, or remove suddenly from the person of Saul. Many years did Saul reign over Israel: yet God computes him but two years a king. That is not accounted of God to be done, which is not lawfully done. When God, which chose Saul, rejected him, he was no more a king, but a tyrant. Israel obeyed him still; but God makes no reckoning of him as his deputy, but as an usurper.

Saul was of good years when he was advanced to the kingdom. His son Jonathan, the first year of his father's reign, could lead a thousand Israelites into the field, and give a foil to the Philistines; and now Israel could not think themselves less happy in their prince than in their king. Jonathan is the heir of his father's victory, as well as of his valour and his estate. The Philistines were quiet, after those first thunderclaps, all the time of Samuel's government; now they begin to stir under Saul.

How utterly is Israel disappointed in their hopes! That security and protection which they promised themselves in the name of a king, they found in a prophet, failed of in a warrior. They were more safe under the mantle than under arms. Both enmity and safeguard are from heaven. Goodness hath been ever a stronger guard than valour. It is the surest policy always to have peace with God.

We find, by the spoils, that the Philistines had some battles with Israel which are not recorded. After the thunder had scared them into a peace, and restitution of all the bordering cities, from Ekron to Gath, they had taken new heart, and so enslaved Israel, that they had neither weapon nor smith left among them; yet, even in this miserable nakedness of Israel, have they both fought and overcome. Now might you have seen the unarmed Israelites marching with their slings and ploughstaves, and hooks and forks. and other instruments of their husbandry, against a mighty and well-furnished enemy, and returning laden both with arms and victory. No armour is of proof against the Almighty, neither is he unweaponed, that carries the revenge of God. There is the same disadvantage in our spiritual conflicts: we are turned naked to principalities and powers. Whilst we go under the conduct of the Prince of our peace, we cannot but be bold and victorious.

Vain men think to overpower God with munition and multitude: the Philistines are not any way more strong than in conceit. Thirty thousand chariots, six thousand horsemen, footmen like the sand for number, make them scorn Israel no less than Israel fears them. When I see the miraculous success which had blessed the Israelites in all their late conflicts with these very Philistines, with the Ammonites, I cannot but wonder how they could fear. They, which in the time of their sin found God to raise such trophies over their enemies, run now into caves, and rocks, and pits, to hide them from the faces of men, when they found God reconciled, and themselves penitent. No Israelite but hath some cowardly blood in him. If we had no fear, faith would have no mastery; yet these fearful Israelites shall cut the throats of these confident Philistines. Doubt and resolution are not measures of our success: a presumptuous confidence goes commonly bleeding home, when an humble fear returns in triumph. Fear drives those Israelites which dare show their heads out of the caves unto Saul, and makes them cling unto their new king. How troublesome were the beginnings of Saul's honour! Surely, if that man had not exceeded Israel no less in courage than in stature, he had now hid himself in a cave, who before hid himself in the stuff. But now, though the Israelites ran away from him, yet he ran not away from them. It was not any doubt of Saul's valour that put his people to their heels; it was the absence of Samuel. If the prophet had come up, Israel would never have run away from their king. While they had a Samuel alone, they were never well till they had a Saul; now they have a Saul, they are as far from contentment, because they want a Samuel: unless both joined together, they think there can be no safety. Where the temporal and spiritual state combine not together, there can follow nothing but distraction in the people. The prophets receive and deliver the will of God; kings execute it. The prophets are directed by God; the people are directed by their kings. Where men do not see God in his ordinances, their hearts cannot but fail them, both in their respects to their superiors, and their courage in themselves. Piety is the mother of perfect subjection. As all authority is derived from heaven, so it is thence established. Those governors that would command the hearts of men, must show them God in their faces.

No Israelite can think himself safe without a prophet. Saul had given them good proof of his fortitude, in his late victory over the Ammonites; but then proclamation was made before the fight, through all the country, that every man should come up after Saul and Samuel. If Samuel had not been with Saul, they would rather have ventured the loss of their oxen, than the hazard of themselves. How much less should we presume of any safety in our spiritual combats, when we have not a prophet to lead us! It is all one, saving that it savours of more contempt, not to have God's seers, and not to use them. He can be no true Israelite, that is not distressed with the want of a Samuel.

As one that had learned to begin his rule in obedience, Saul stays seven days in Gilgal, according to the prophet's direction; and still he looks long for Samuel, which had promised his presence: six days he expects, and part of the seventh; yet Samuel is not come. The Philistines draw near; the Israelites run away; Samuel comes not; they must fight; God must be supplicated: what should Saul do? Rather than God should want a sacrifice, and the people satisfaction, Saul will command that which he knew Samuel would, if he were present, both command and execute. It is not possible, thinks he, that God should be displeased with a sacrifice: he cannot but be displeased with indevotion. Why do the people run from me, but for want of means to make God sure? What would Samuel rather wish, than that we should be godly? The act shall be the same; the only difference shall be in the person. If Samuel be wanting to us, we will not be wanting to God; it is but an holy prevention to be devout unbidden. Upon this conceit he commands a sacrifice. Saul's sins make no great show, yet are they still heinously taken; the impiety of them was more hidden and inward from all eyes but God's. If Saul were among the prophets before, will he now be among the priests? Can there be any devotion in disobedience! O vain man! what can it avail thee to sacrifice to God against God? Hypocrites rest only in formalities; if the outward act be done, it sufficeth them, though the ground be distrust, the manner unreverence, the carriage presumption.

What, then, should Saul have done? Upon the trust of God and Samuel, he should have staid out the last hour, and have secretly sacrificed himself and his prayers unto that God which loves obedience above sacrifice. Our faith is most commendable in the last act: it is no praise to hold out until we be hard driven. Then, when we are forsaken of means, to live by faith in our God, is worthy of a crown. God will have no worship of our devising: we may only do what he bids us, not bid what he commands not. Never did any true piety arise out of the corrupt puddle of man's brain: if it flow not from heaven, it is odious to heaven. What was it that did thus taint the valour of Saul with this weakness, but distrust? He saw some Israelites go; he thought all would go: he saw the Philistines come; he saw Samuel came not: his diffidence was guilty of his misdevotion. There is no sin that hath not its ground from unbelief; this, as it was the first infection of our pure nature, so is it the true source of all corruption: man could not sin if he distrusted not.

The sacrifice is no sooner ended, than Samuel is come. And why came he no sooner? He could not be a seer, and not know how much he was looked for; how troublesome and dangerous his absence must needs be: he that could tell Saul that he should prophesy, could tell him that he would sacrifice; yet he purposely forbears to come, for the trial of him that must be the champion of God. Samuel durst not have done thus, but by direction from his Master. It is the ordinary course of God to prove us by delays, and to drive to exigents, that we may show what we are. He that anointed Saul, might lawfully from God control him. There must be discretion, there may not be partiality, in our censures of the greatest. God makes difference of sins, none of persons. If we make difference of sins according to persons, we are unfaithful both to God and man. Scarce is Saul warm in his kingdom, when he hath even lost it. Samuel's first words, after the inauguration, are of Saul's rejection, and the choice and establishment of his successor. It was ever God's purpose to settle the kingdom in Judah. He, that took occasion by the people's sin to raise up Saul in Benjamin, takes occasion by Saul's sin to establish the crown upon David. In human probability the kingdom was fixed upon Saul and his more worthy son. In God's decree it did but pass through the hands of Benjamin to Judah. Besides trouble, how fickle are these earthly glories! Saul doubtless looked upon Jonathan as the inheritor of his crown; and behold, ere his peaceable possession, he hath lost it from himself. Our sins strip us not of our hopes in heaven only, but of our earthly blessings. The way to entail a comfortable prosperity upon our seed after us, is our conscionable obedience to God.

CONTEMPLATION VIII.—JONATHAN'S VICTORY AND SAUL'S OATH.

It is no wonder if Saul's courage was much cooled with the heavy news of his rejection. After this he stays under the pomegranate-tree in Gibeah: he stirs not towards the garrison of the Philistines. As hope is the mother of fortitude, so nothing doth more breed cowardliness than despair. Every thing dismays that heart which God hath put out of protection. Worthy Jonathan, which sprung from Saul, as some sweet imp grows out of a crab-stock, is therefore full of valour, because full of faith. He well knew, that he should have nothing but discouragements from his father's fear; as rather choosing therefore to avoid all the blocks that might lie in the way, than to leap over them, he departs secretly, without the dismission of his father, or notice of the people; only God leads him, and his armour-bearer follows him. O admirable faith of Jonathan, whom neither the steepness of rocks, nor the multitude of enemies, can dissuade from so unlikely an assault! Is it possible, that two men, whereof one was weaponless, should dare to think of encountering so many thousands? O divine power of faith, that in all difficulties and attempts makes a man more than men, and regards no more armies of men than swarms of flies! There is no restraint to the Lord, saith he, to save with many, or by few. It was not so great news that Saul should be amongst the prophets, as that such a word should come from the son of Saul.

If his father had but so much divinity, he had not sacrificed. The strength of his God is the ground of his strength in God. The question is not, what Jonathan can do, but what God can do, whose power is not in the means, but in himself. That man's faith is well underlaid, that upholds itself by the omnipotency of God. Thus the father of the faithful built his assurance upon the power of the Almighty. But many things God can do, which he will not do. How knowest thou, Jonathan, that God will be as forward, as he is able, to give thee victory? For this, saith he, I have a watch-word from God out of the mouths of the Philistines: "If they say, Come up, we will go up: for God hath delivered them into our hands. If they say, Tarry till we come to you, we will stand still." Jonathan was too wise to trust unto a casual presage. There might be some far-fetched conjectures of the event from the word. We will come to you, was a threat of resolution: Come you to us, was a challenge of fear; or, perhaps, Come up to us, was a word of insultation from them that trusted to the inaccessibleness of the place, and multitudes of men. Insultation is from pride: pride argued a fall: but faith hath nothing to do with probabilities, as that which acknowledgeth no argument but demonstration. If there had not been an instinct from God of this assured warrant of success, Jonathan had presumed instead of believing, and had tempted that God whom he professed to glorify by his trust.

There can be no faith where there is no promise; and where there is a promise, there can be no presumption. Words are voluntary; the tongues of the Philistines were as free to say, Tarry, as Come. That God, in whom our very tongues move, overruled them so, as now they shall speak that word which will cut their own throats. They knew no more harm in Come, than Tarry; both were alike safe for the sound, for the sense: but he that put a signification of their slaughter in the one, not in the other, did put that word into their mouths, whereby they might invite their own destruction. The disposition of our words is from the providence of the Almighty. God and our hearts have not always the same meaning in our speeches. In those words which we speak at random, or out of affectation, God hath a further drift of his own glory, and perhaps our judgment. If wicked men say, Our tongues are our own, they could not say so but from Him whom they defy in saying so, and who makes their tongue their executioner.

No sooner doth Jonathan hear this invitation, than he answers it. He, whose hands had learned never to fail his heart, puts himself upon his hands and knees to climb up into this danger: the exploit was not more difficult than the way; the pain of the passage was equal to the peril of the enterprise, that his faith might equally triumph over both. He doth not say, How shall I get up? much less, Which way shall I get down again? But, as if the ground were level, and the action dangerless, he puts himself into the view of the Philistines. Faith is never so glorious, as when it hath most opposition, and will not see it. Reason looks ever to the means, faith to the end; and, instead of consulting how to effect, resolves what shall be effected. The way to heaven is more steep, more painful. O God, how perilous a passage hast thou appointed for thy labouring pilgrims! If difficulties will discourage us, we shall but climb to fall. When we are lifting up our foot to the last step, there are the Philistines of death, of temptations, to grapple with. Give us but faith, and turn us loose to the spite either of earth or hell.

Jonathan is now on the top of the hill; and now, as if he had an army at his heels, he flies upon the host of the Philistines: his hands, that might have been weary with climbing, are immediately commanded to fight, and deal as many death-blows to the amazed enemy. He needs not walk far for this execution; himself and his armour-bearer, in one half acre's space, have slain twenty Philistines. It is not long since Jonathan smote their garrison in the hill of Geba: perhaps from that time his name and presence carried terror in it; but sure, if the Philistines had not seen and felt more than a man in the face and hands of Jonathan, they had not so easily grovelled in death. The blows and shrieks cannot but affect the next, who, with a ghastly noise, run away from death, and affright their fellows no less than themselves are affrighted. The clamour and fear run on, like fire in a train, to the very foremost ranks: every man would fly, and thinks there is so much more cause of flight, for that his ears apprehend all, his eyes nothing. Each man thinks his fellow stands in his way: and therefore, instead of turning upon him which was the cause of their flight, they bend their swords upon those whom they imagine to be the hinderers of their flight: and now a miraculous astonishment hath made the Philistines Jonathan's champions and executioners. He follows and kills those which helped to kill others; and the more he killed, the more they feared and fled, and the more they killed each other in the flight: and, that fear itself might prevent Jonathan in killing them, the earth itself trembles under them. Thus doth God at once strike them with his own hand, with Jonathan's, with theirs, and makes them run away from life, while they would fly from an enemy. Where the Almighty purposes destruction to any people, he needs not call in foreign powers; he needs not any hands or weapons but their own; he can make vast bodies die by no other death than their own weight. We cannot be sure to be friends among ourselves, while God is our enemy.

The Philistines fly fast, but the news of their flight overruns them, even unto Saul's pomegranate-tree. The watchmen discern afar off a flight and execution. Search is made; Jonathan is found missing: Saul will consult with the ark. Hypocrites, while they have leisure, will perhaps be holy; for some fits of devotion they cannot be bettered. But when the tumult increased, Saul's piety decreases. It is now no season to talk with a priest: withdraw thine hand, Ahaiah; the ephod must give place to arms; it is more time to fight, than to pray: what needs he God's guidance, when he sees his way before him? He, that before would needs sacrifice ere he fought, will now, in the other extreme, fight in a wilful indevotion. Worldly minds regard holy duties no further than may stand with their own carnal purposes: very easy occasions shall interrupt them in their religious intentions; like unto children, which, if a bird do but fly in their way, cast their eye from their book.

But if Saul serve not God in one kind, he will serve him in another; if he honour him not by attending on the ark, he will honour him by a vow: his negligence in the one is recompensed with his zeal in the other. All Israel is adjured not to eat any food until the evening. Hypocrisy is ever masked with a blind and thankless zeal. To wait upon the ark, and to consult with God's priest, in all cases of importance, was a direct commandment of God; to eat no food in the pursuit of their enemies, was not commanded: Saul leaves that which he was bidden, and does that which he was not required. To eat no food all day was more difficult than to attend an hour upon the ark: the voluntary services of hypocrites are many times more painful than the duties enjoined by God.

In what awe did all Israel stand of the oath, even of Saul! It was not their own vow, but Saul's for them; yet, coming into the wood, where they saw the honey dropping, and found the meat as ready as their appetite, they dare not touch that sustenance, and will rather endure famine and fainting, than an indiscreet curse. Doubtless, God had brought those bees thither, on purpose to try the constancy of Israel. Israel could not but think that which Jonathan said, that the vow was unadvised and injurious; yet they will rather die than violate it. How sacred should we hold the obligation of our own vows, in things just and expedient, when the bond of another's rash vow is thus indissoluble!

There was a double mischief followed upon Saul's oath — an abatement of the victory, and eating with the blood: for, on the one side, the people were so faint, that they were more likely to die than kill; they could neither run nor strike in this emptiness: neither hands nor feet can do their office, when the stomach is neglected. On the other, an unmeet forbearance causes a ravenous repast. Hunger knows neither choice, nor order, nor measure: the one of these was a wrong to Israel: the other was a wrong done by Israel to God; Saul's zeal was guilty of both. A rash vow is seldom ever free from inconvenience. The heart that hath unnecessarily entangled itself, draws mischief either upon itself or others.

Jonathan was ignorant of his father's adjuration; he knew no reason why he should not refresh himself, in so profitable a service, with a little taste of honey upon his spear: full well had he deserved this unsought dainty. And now, behold, his honey is turned into gall: if it were sweet in the mouth, it was bitter in the soul; if the eyes of his body were enlightened, the light of God's countenance was clouded by this act. After he heard of the oath, he pleads justly against it, the loss of so fair an opportunity of revenge, and the trouble of Israel; yet neither his reasons against the oath, nor his ignorance of the oath, can excuse him from a sin of ignorance in violating that which first he knew not, and then knew unreasonable. Now, Saul's leisure would serve him to ask counsel of God: as before Saul would not inquire, so now God will not answer. Well might Saul have found sins enough of his own, whereto to impute this silence. He hath grace enough to know that God was offended, and to guess at the cause of his offence. Sooner will a hypocrite find out another man's sin than his own; and now he swears more rashly to punish with death the breach of that which he had sworn rashly. The lots were cast, and Saul prays for the decision: Jonathan is taken. Even the prayers of wicked men are sometimes heard, although in justice, not in mercy. Saul himself was punished not a little in the fall of this lot upon Jonathan. Surely Saul sinned more in making this vow, than Jonathan in breaking it unwittingly; and now the father smarts for the rashness of his double vow, by the unjust sentence of death upon so worthy a son. God had never singled out Jonathan by his lot, if he had not been displeased with his act. Vows rashly made, may not be rashly broken. If the thing we have vowed be not evil in itself, or in the effect, we cannot violate it without evil. Ignorance cannot acquit, if it can abate our sin. It is like, if Jonathan had heard his father's adjuration, he had not transgressed; his absence at the time of that oath cannot excuse him from displeasure. What shall become of those, which may know the charge of their heavenly Father, and will not? which do know his charge, and will not keep it? Affectation of ignorance, and willing disobedience, are desperate.

Death was too hard a censure for such an unknown offence. The cruel piety of Saul will revenge the breach of his own charge, so as he would be loath God should avenge on himself the breach of his divine command. If Jonathan had not found better friends than his father, so noble a victory had been recompensed with death. He, that saved Israel from the Philistines, is saved by Israel from the hand of his father. Saul hath sworn Jonathan's death; the people, contrarily, swear his preservation: his kingdom was not so absolute, that he could run away with so unmerciful a justice; their oath, that savoured of disobedience, prevailed against his oath, that savoured too strong of cruelty. Neither doubt I but Saul was secretly not displeased with this loving resistance; so long as his heart was not false to his oath, he could not be sorry that Jonathan should live.

BOOK XIII.

CONTEMPLATION I. — SAUL AND AGAG.

GOD holds it no derogation from his mercy to bear a quarrel long, where he hates. He, whose anger to the vessels of wrath is everlasting, even in temporal judgment revengeth late. The sins of his own children are no sooner done, and repented of, than forgotten; but the malicious sins of his enemies stick fast in an infinite displeasure. " I remember what Amalek did to Israel, how they laid wait for them by the way, as they came up from Egypt." Alas, Lord! (might Amalek say) they were our forefathers; we never knew their faces, no, nor their names; the fact was so far from our consent, that it is almost past the memory of our histories. It is not in the power of time to raze out any of the arrearages of God. We may lay up wrath for our posterity. Happy is that child whose progenitors are in heaven; he is left an inheritor of blessing, together with estate: whereas wicked ancestors lose the thank of a rich patrimony, by the curse that attends it. He that thinks, because punishment is deferred, that God hath forgiven or forgot his offence, is unacquainted with justice, and knows not that time makes no difference in eternity.

The Amalekites were wicked idolaters, and therefore could not want many present sins, which deserved their extirpation. That God, which had taken notice of all their offences, picks out this one noted sin of their forefathers for revenge: amongst all their indignities, this shall bear the name of their judgment; as in legal proceedings with malefactors, one indictment found gives the style of their condemnation. In the lives of those which are notoriously wicked, God cannot look beside a sin; yet when he draws to an execution, he fastens his sentence upon one evil, as principal, others as accessories, so as, at the last, one sin, which perhaps we make no account of, shall pay for all.

The paganish idolatries of the Amalekites could not but be greater sins to God, than their hard measure to Israel; yet God sets this upon the file, while the rest are not recorded: their superstitions might be of ignorance; this sin was of malice. Malicious wickednesses, of all others, as they are in greatest opposition to the goodness and mercy of God, shall be sure of the payment of greatest vengeance. The detestation of God may be measured by his revenge: " Slay both man and woman, both infant and suckling, both ox and sheep, camel and ass:" not themselves only, but every thing that drew life, either from them, or for their use, must die. When the God of mercy speaks such bloody words, the provocation must needs be vehement. Sins of infirmity do but mutter; spiteful sins cry loud for judgment in the ears of God. Prepensed malice, in courts of human justice, aggravates the murder, and sharpens the sentence of death.

What, then, was this sin of Amalek, that is called unto this late reckoning? what, but their envious and unprovoked onsets upon the back of Israel: this was it that God took so to heart, as that he not only remembers it now by Samuel, but he bids Israel ever to remember it, by Moses: " Remember how Amalek met thee by the way, and smote the hindmost of you, all that were feeble behind thee, when thou wast faint and weary." Besides this, did Amalek meet Israel in a pitched battle openly, in Rephidim; for that God paid them in the present. The hand of Moses, lifted up on the hill, slew them in the valley. He therefore repeats not that quarrel; but the cowardly and cruel attempts upon an impotent enemy, stick still in the stomach of the Almighty. Oppression and wrong, upon even terms, are not so heinous unto God, as those that are upon manifest disadvantage: in the one, there is a hazard of return; in the other, there is ever a tyrannous insultation. God takes still the weaker part and will be sure therefore to plague them which seek to put injuries on the unable to resist.

This sin of Amalek slept all the time of the judges: those governors were only for rescue and defence; now, so soon as Israel hath a king, and that king is settled in peace, God gives charge to call them to account: it was that which God had both threatened and sworn, and now he chooses out a fit season for the execution. As we use to say of winter, the judgments of God do never rot in the sky, but shall fall, if late, yet surely, yet seasonably. There is small comfort in the delay of vengeance, while we are sure it shall lose nothing in the way by length of protraction.

The Kenites were the offspring of Hobab or Jethro, father-in-law to Moses: the affinity of him, to whom Israel owed their deliverance and being, was worthy of respect; but it was the mercy of that good and wise Midianite showed unto Israel in the wilderness, by his grave advice, cheerful gratulation and aid, which won this grateful forbearance of his posterity. He that is not less in mercy than in justice, as he challenged Amalek's sin of their succeeding generations, so he derives the recompense of Jethro's kindness unto his far descended issue. Those that were unborn many ages after Jethro's death, receive life from his dust, and favour from his hospitality: the name of their dead grandfather saves them from the common destruction of their neighbours. The services of our love to God's children are never thankless. When we are dead and rotten, they shall live, and procure blessings to those which never knew, perhaps, nor heard of their progenitors. If we sow good works, succession shall reap them, and we shall be happy in making them so.

The Kenites dwelt in the borders of Amalek, but in tents, as did their issue the Rechabites, so as they might remove with ease. They are warned to shift their habitation, lest they should perish with ill neighbours. It is the manner of God, first to separate before he judge, as a good husbandman weeds his corn ere it be ripe for the sickle, and goes to the fan ere he go to the fire. When the Kenites pack up their fardels, it is time to expect judgment. Why should not we imitate God, and separate ourselves, that we may not be judged; separate not one Kenite from another, but every Kenite from among the Amalekites; else, if we will needs live with Amalek, we cannot think much to die with him.

The Kenites are no sooner removed, than Saul falls upon the Amalekites. he destroys all the people, but spares their king. The charge of God was universal, for man and beast. In the corruption of partiality, lightly the greatest escape. Covetousness or misaffection are commonly guilty of the impunity of those which are at once more eminent in dignity and in offence. It is a shameful hypocrisy, to make our commodity the measure and rule of our execution of God's command, and, under pretence of godliness, to intend gain. The unprofitable vulgar must die: Agag may yield a rich ransom. The lean and feeble cattle, that would but spend stover, and die, alone shall perish by the sword of Israel; the best may stock the grounds, and furnish the markets. O hypocrites! did God send you for gain, or for revenge? Went you to be purveyors, or executioners? If you plead that all those wealthy herds had been but lost in a speedy death, think ye that he knew not this which commanded it? Can that be lost, which is devoted to the will of the Owner and Creator? or can ye think to gain anything by disobedience? That man can never either do well, or fare well, which thinks there can be more profit in anything than in his obedience to his Maker. Because Saul spared the best of the men, the people spared the best of the cattle: each is willing to favour the other in the sin. The sins of the great command imitation, and do as seldom go without attendants as their persons.

Saul knew well how much he had done amiss, and yet dare meet Samuel, and can say, "Blessed be thou of the Lord! I have fulfilled the commandment of the Lord." His heart knew that his tongue was as false as his hands had been; and if his heart had not been more false than either of them, neither of them had been so gross in their falsehood. If hypocrisy were not either foolish or impudent, she durst not show her head to a seer of God. Could Saul think that Samuel knew of the asses that were lost, and did not know of the oxen and sheep that were spared? could he foretell his thoughts, when it was, and now not know of his open actions? Much less, when we have to do with God himself, should dissimulation presume either of safety or secrecy. Can the God, that made the heart, not know it? can He, that comprehends all things, be shut out of our close corners? Saul was otherwise crafty enough, yet herein his simplicity is palpable. Sin can besot even the wisest man; and there was never but folly in wickedness.

No man brags so much of holiness as he that wants it. True obedience is joined ever with humility, and fear of unknown errors. Falsehood is bold, and can say, "I have fulfilled the commandment of the Lord." If Saul had been truly obsequious and holy, he had made no noise of it. A gracious heart is not a blab of his tongue, but rests and rejoiceth silently in the conscience of a secret goodness. Those vessels yield most sound, that have the least liquor. Samuel had reason to believe the sheep and oxen above Saul; their bleating and lowing was a sufficient conviction of a denied and outfaced disobedience. God opened their mouths to accuse Saul of their life, and his falsehood: but as sin is crafty, and never wanted a cloak wherewith both to hide and deck itself, even this very rebellion is holy. First, the act, if it were evil, was not mine, but the people's. And, secondly, their intention makes it good; for these flocks and herds were preserved, not for gain, but for devotion. What needs this quarrel? If any gain by this act, it is the Lord thy God: his altars shall smoke with these sacrifices; ye, that serve at them, shall fare so much the better. This godly thriftiness looks for thanks rather than censure. If Saul had been in Samuel's clothes, perhaps this answer would have satisfied him; surely himself stands out in it, as that whereto he dares trust; and after he hears of God's angry reproof, he avows, and doubles his hold of his innocency: as if the commanders should not answer for the known sins of the people; as if our intentions could justify us to God, against God. How much ado is it to bring sinners upon their knees, and to make their tongues accuse their hands! But there is no halting with the Maker of the heart: he knew it was covetousness, and not piety, which was accessory to this forbearance; and if it had been as was pretended, he knew it was an odious impiety to raise devotion out of disobedience. Saul shall hear and find, that he hath dealt no less wickedly in sparing an Agag, than in killing an innocent Israelite; in sparing these beasts for sacrifice, than in sacrificing beasts that had been unclean. Why was sacrifice itself good, but because it was commanded? What difference was there betwixt slaughter and sacrifice, but obedience? To sacrifice disobediently, is wilfully to mock God in honouring him.

CONTEMPLATION II. — THE REJECTION OF SAUL, AND CHOICE OF DAVID.

EVEN when Saul had abandoned God in disobedience, he would not forego Samuel, yea, though he reproved him; when he had forsaken the substance, yet he would maintain the formality. If he cannot hold the man, he will keep the pledge of his garment: such was the violence of Saul's desire, that he will rather rend Samuel's coat than part with his person. Little did Saul think, that he had in his hand the pawn of his own rejection; that this act of kind importunity should carry in it a presage of his judgment: yet so it did. This very rending of the coat was a real prophecy, and did bode no less than the rending of the kingdom from him and his posterity. Wicked men, while they think by carnal means to make their peace, plunge themselves deeper into misery.

Any stander-by would have said, What a good king is this! how dear is God's prophet unto him! how happy is Israel in such a prince, as thus loves the messengers of God! Samuel, that saw the bottom of his hollow affection, rejects him whom God hath rejected. He was taught to look upon Saul, not as a king, but as an offender, and therefore refuses with no less vehemency than Saul entreated. It was one thing, what he might do as a subject; another, what he must do as a prophet. Now, he knows not Saul any otherwise, than as so much the greater trespasser as his place was higher; and therefore he doth no more spare his greatness, than the God against whom he sinned; neither doth he countenance that man with his presence, on whom he sees God to frown.

There needs no other character of hypocrisy, than Saul, in the carriage of this one business with Agag and Samuel: first he obeys God, where there is no gain in disobedience; then he serves God by halves, and disobeys where the obedience might be loss. He gives God of the worst; he doth that in a colour, which might seem answerable to the charge of God; he respects persons in the execution; he gives good words when his deeds were evil; he protests his obedience against his conscience; he faces out his protestation against a reproof: when he sees no remedy, he acknowledges the fact, denies the sin; yea, he justifies the act by a profitable intention: when he can no longer maintain his innocence, he casts the blame from himself, upon the people. He confesseth not, till the sin be wrung from his mouth: he seeks his peace out of himself, and relies more upon another's virtue than his own penitency; he would cloak his guiltiness with the holiness of another's presence: he is more tormented with the danger and damage of his sin, than with the offence: he cares to hold in with men, in what terms soever he stands with God: he fashionably serves that God whom he hath not cared to reconcile by his repentance. No marvel if God cast him off, whose best was dissimulation.

Old Samuel is forced to do a double

execution, and that upon no less than two kings: the one upon Saul, in dividing the kingdom from him, who had divided himself from God; the other upon Agag, in dividing him in pieces, whom Saul should have divided. Those holy hands were not used to such sacrifices; yet did he never spill blood more acceptably. If Saul had been truly penitent, he had, in a desire of satisfaction, prevented the hand of Samuel in this slaughter: now, he coldly stands still, and suffers the weak hands of an aged prophet to be imbrued with that blood, which he was commanded to shed. If Saul might not sacrifice in the absence of Samuel, yet Samuel might kill in the presence of Saul. He was yet a judge of Israel, although he suspended the execution: in Saul's neglect, this charge reverted to him. God loves just executions so well, that he will hardly take them ill at any hand.

I do not find that the slaughter of Agag troubled Samuel: that other act of his severity upon Saul, though it drew no blood, yet struck him in the striking, and fetched tears from his eyes. Good Samuel mourned for him, that had not grace to mourn for himself. No man in all Israel might seem to have so much reason to rejoice in Saul's ruin as Samuel, since that he knew him raised up in despite of his government; yet he mourns more for him than he did for his sons, for himself. It grieved him to see the plant, which he had set in the garden of Israel, thus soon withered. It is an unnatural senselessness not to be affected with the dangers, with the sins, of our governors. God did not blame this sorrow, but moderated it: "How long wilt thou mourn for Saul?" It was not the affection he forbade, but the measure. In this is the difference betwixt good men and evil; that evil men mourn not for their own sins; good men do so mourn for the sins of others, that they will hardly be taken off.

If Samuel mourn because Saul hath cast away God by his sin, he must cease to mourn, because God hath cast away Saul from reigning over Israel in his just punishment. A good heart hath learned to rest itself upon the justice of God's decree, and forgets all earthly respects when it looks up to heaven. So did God mean to show his displeasure against the person of Saul, that he would show favour to Israel; he will not therefore bereave them of a king, but change him for a better. Either Saul had slandered his people, or else they were partners with him in disobedience; yet, because it was their ruler's fault that they were not overruled, we do not hear of their smarting any otherwise than in the subjection to such a king as was not loyal to God. The loss of Saul is their gain: the government of their first king was abortive; no marvel if it held not. Now was the maturity of that state; and therefore God will bring them forth a kindly monarchy, settled where it should. Kings are of God's providing. It is good reason he should make choice of his own deputies; but where goodness meets with sovereignty, both his right and his gift are doubled. If kings were merely from the earth, what needs a prophet to be seen in the choice, or inauguration? The hand of Samuel doth not now bear the sceptre to rule Israel, but it bears the horn for the anointing of him that must rule. Saul was sent to him, when the time was, to be anointed; but now he is sent to anoint David; then Israel sought a king for themselves; now God seeks a king for Israel. The prophet is therefore directed to the house of Jesse the Bethlehemite, the grandchild of Ruth: now is the faithful love of that good Moabitess crowned with the honour of a kingdom in the succeeding generation. God fetched her out of Moab, to bring a king unto Israel. While Orpah wants bread in her own country, Ruth is grown a great lady in Bethlehem, and is advanced to be great grandmother to the king of Israel. The retributions of God are bountiful: never any man forsook aught for his sake, and complained of a hard bargain.

Even the best of God's saints want not their infirmities. He, that never replied when he was sent to reprove the king, moveth doubts, when he is bidden to go and anoint his successor: "How can I go? If Saul hear it, he will kill me." Perhaps desire of full direction drew from him this question, but not without a mixture of diffidence; for the manner of doing it doth not so much trouble him, as the success. It is not to be expected that the most faithful hearts should be always in an equal height of resolution: God doth not chide Samuel, but instruct him. He, which is wisdom itself, teacheth him to hide his counsels in an honest policy: " Take an heifer with thee, and say, I am come to do sacrifice to the Lord." This was to say true, not to say all. Truth may not be crossed by denials or equivocations: it may be concealed in a discreet silence. Except in the case of an oath, no man is bound to speak all he knows: we are not only allowed, but commanded, to be innocently serpentine. There were, doubtless, heifers enough in Bethlehem:

Jesse had both wealth and devotion enough to have bestowed a sacrifice upon God and his prophet. But, to give a more perfect colour to his intention, Samuel must take a heifer with him: the act itself was serious and necessary. There was no place, no time, wherein it was not fit for Samuel to offer peace-offerings unto God; but when a king should be anointed, there was no less than necessity in this service. Those which must represent God to the world, ought to be consecrated to that Majesty whom they resemble, by public devotions. Every important action requires a sacrifice to bless it, much more that act which imports the whole church or commonwealth.

It was great news to see Samuel at Bethlehem: he was no gadder abroad; none but necessary occasions could make him stir from Ramah. The elders of the city therefore welcome him with trembling; not for that they were afraid of him, but of themselves: they knew that guest would not come to them for familiarity: straight do they suspect it was the purpose of some judgment that drew him thither: "Comest thou peaceably?" It is a good thing to stand in awe of God's messengers, and to hold good terms with them upon all occasions. The Bethlehemites are glad to hear of no other errand but a sacrifice; and now must they sanctify themselves for so sacred a business. We may not presume to sacrifice unto God unsanctified; this were to mar an holy act, and make ourselves more profane, by profaning that which should be holy.

All the citizens sanctify themselves; but Jesse and his sons were, in a special fashion, sanctified by Samuel. This business was most theirs, and all Israel in them. The more God hath to do with us, the more holy should we be. With what desire did Samuel look upon the sons of Jesse, that he might see the face of the man whom God had chosen! And now, when Eliab, the eldest son, came forth, a man of a goodly presence, whose person seemed fit to succeed Saul, he thinks with himself, This choice is soon made; I have already espied the head on which I must spend this holy oil; this is the man which hath both the privilege of nature in his primogeniture, and of outward goodliness in proportion: surely the Lord's anointed is before me. Even the holiest prophet, when he goes without God, runs into error; the best judgment is subject to deceit: it is no trusting to any mortal man, when he speaks of himself. Our eyes can be led by nothing but signs and appearances, and those have commonly in them either a true falsehood, or uncertain truth.

That which would have forewarned Samuel, deceived him: he had seen the proof of a goodly stature unanswerable to their hopes, and yet his eye errs in the shape. He that judgeth by the inside, both of our hearts and actions, checks Samuel in his misconceit: "Look not on his countenance, nor on the height of his stature, because I have refused him; for God seeth not as man seeth." The king with whom God meant to satisfy the untimely desires of Israel was chosen by his stature; but the king with whom God meant to please himself, is chosen by the heart. All the seven sons of Jesse are presented to the prophet; no one is omitted whom their father thought capable of any respect. If either Samuel or Jesse should have chosen, David should never have been king. His father thought him fit to keep sheep; his brethren fit to rule men: yet even David, the youngest son, is fetched from the fold, and, by the choice of God, destined to the throne. Nature, which is commonly partial to her own, could not suggest ought to Jesse, to make him think David worthy to be remembered in any competition of honour; yet him hath God singled out to rule.

God will have his wisdom magnified in the unlikelihoods of his election. David's countenance was ingenuous and beautiful; but if it had promised so much as Eliab's or Aminadab's, he had not been in the fields while his brethren were at the sacrifice. If we do altogether follow our eye, and suffer ourselves to be guided by outward respects in our choice for God or ourselves, we cannot but go amiss. What do we think the brethren of David thought, when they saw the oil poured upon his head? Surely, as they were envious enough, they had too much repined, if they had either fully apprehended the purpose of the prophet, or else had not thought of some improbability in the success; either they understood not, or believed not, what God would do with their brother; they saw him graced with God's spirit above his wont, but perhaps foresaw not whither it tended. David, as no whit changed in his condition, returns to his sheep again, and, with an humble admiration of God's gracious respect to him, casts himself upon the wise and holy decree of the Almighty, resigning himself to the disposition of those hands which had chosen him; when suddenly a messenger is sent from Saul, to call him in all haste to that court whereof he shall once be-master. The occasion is no less from God than the event.

CONTEMPLATION III. — DAVID CALLED TO THE COURT.

That the kingdom is, in the appointment of God, departed from Saul, it is his least loss; now the Spirit of God is also departed from him: one spirit is no sooner gone, but another is come; both are from God. Even the worst spirits have not only permission, but commission from heaven for the infliction of judgment. He that at first could hide himself among the stuff, that he might not be king, is now so transported with this glory, that he grows passionate with the thought of foregoing it. Satan takes advantage of his melancholic dejection, and turns this passion into frenzy. God will have even evil spirits work by means: a distempered body, and an unquiet mind, are fit grounds for Satan's vexation. Saul's courtiers, as men that were more witty than religious, advise him to music: they knew the strength of that skill in allaying the fury of passions, in cheering up the dejected spirits of their master. This was done like some fond chirurgeon, that, when the bone is out of joint, lays some suppling poultices to the part, for the assuaging of the ache, in the meantime not caring to remedy the luxation.

If they had said, Sir, you know this evil comes from that God whom you have offended; there can be no hope but in reconcilement: how easy is it for the God of spirits to take off Satan! labour your peace with him by a serious humiliation; make means to Samuel to further the atonement! they had been wise counsellors, divine physicians: whereas now, they do but skin over the sore, and leave it rankled at the bottom. The cure must ever proceed in the same steps with the disease, else in vain shall we seem to heal: there is no safety in the redress of evils, but to strike at the root. Yet, since it is no better with Saul and his courtiers, it is well it is no worse: I do not hear either the master or servants say, This is an ill spirit; send for some magician that may countermand him: there are forcible enchantments for these spiritual vexations; if Samuel will not, there are witches that may give ease. But as one that would rather be ill than do worse, he contents himself to do that which was lawful, if unsufficient. It is a shame to say, that he, whom God had rejected for his sin, was yet a saint to some that should be Christians, who care not how much they are beholden to the devil in their distresses, affecting to cast out devils by Beelzebub. In cases of loss, or sickness, they make hell their refuge, and seek for patronage from an enemy. Here is a fearful agreement: Satan seeks to them in his temptations; they, in their consultations, seek to him: and now that they have mutually found each other, if ever they part it is a miracle.

David had lived obscurely in his father's house: his only care and ambition was the welfare of the flock he tended; and now, while his father and his brothers neglected him, as fit for nothing but the field, he is talked of at the court. Some of Saul's followers had been at Jesse's house, and taken notice of David's skill; and now that harp, which he practised for his private recreation, shall make him of a shepherd a courtier. The music that he meant only to himself and his sheep, brings him before kings. The wisdom of God thought fit to take this occasion of acquainting David with that court which he shall once govern. It is good that education should perfect our children in all those commendable qualities whereto they are disposed. Little do we know what use God means to make of those faculties which we know not how to employ! Where the Almighty purposes an advancement, obscurity can be no prejudice: small means shall set forward that which God hath decreed.

Doubtless, old Jesse noted, not without admiration, the wonderful accordance of God's proceedings, that he, which was sent for out of the field to be anointed, should now be sent for out of the country into the court; and now he perceived God was making way for the execution of that which he purposed: he attends the issue in silence, neither shall his hand fail to give furtherance to the project of God; he therefore sends his son laden with a present to Saul. The same God which called David to the court, welcomes him thither: his comeliness, valour, and skill, have soon won him favour in the eyes of Saul. The Giver of all graces hath so placed his favours, that the greatest enemies of goodness shall see somewhat in the holiest men, which they shall affect, and for which they shall honour the persons of them whose virtues they dislike; as, contrarily, the saints on earth see somewhat to love even in the worst creatures.

No doubt David sung to his harp: his harp was not more sweet than his song was holy. Those Psalms alone had been more powerful to chase the evil spirit, than the music was to calm passions: both together gave ease to Saul; and God gave this effect to both, because he would have Saul train up his successor. This sacred music did not more dispel Satan, than wanton music invites him, and more cheers him than us. He plays and dances at a filthy song; he sings at an obscene dance. Our sin is his best pastime; whereas psalms and hymns, and spiritual songs, are torment unto the tempter, and music to the angels in heaven, whose trade is to sing Hallelujahs in the choir of glory.

CONTEMPLATION IV.—DAVID AND GOLIAH.

After the news of the Philistines' army, I hear no more mention of Saul's frenzy: whether the noise of war diverted those thoughtful passions, or whether God, for his people's sake, took off that evil spirit, lest Israel might miscarry under a frantic governor. Now David hath leisure to return to Bethlehem: the glory of the court cannot transport him to ambitious vanity; he had rather be his father's shepherd than Saul's armour-bearer. All the magnificence and state which he saw could not put his mouth out of the taste of retired simplicity; yea, rather, he loves his hook the better, since he saw the court; and now his brethren serve Saul in his stead. A good heart hath learned to frame itself unto all conditions, and can change estates without change of disposition, rising and falling according to occasion. The worldly mind can rise easily, but, when it is once up, knows not how to descend either with patience or safety.

Forty days together had the Philistines and the Israelites faced each other: they pitched on two hills, one in sight of the other; nothing but a valley was betwixt them. Both stand upon defence and advantage: if they had not meant to fight, they had never drawn so near; and if they had been eager to fight, a valley could not have parted them. Actions of hazard require deliberation; not fury, but discretion, must be the guide of war.

So had Joshua destroyed the giantly Anakims out of the land of Israel, that yet some were left in Azzah, Gath, and Ashdod; both to show Israel what adversaries their forefathers found in Canaan, and whom they mastered; as also, that God might win glory to himself by these subsequent executions. Of that race was Goliah, whose heart was as high as his head: his strength was answerable to his stature; his weapons answerable to his strength; his pride exceeded all: because he saw his head higher, his arms stronger, his sword and spear bigger, his shield heavier than any Israelite's, he defies the whole host; and, walking between the two armies, braves all Israel with a challenge: "Why are ye come out to set your battle in array? Am not I a Philistine, and you servants to Saul? Choose you a man for you, and let him come down to me. Give me a man, that we may fight together." Carnal hearts are carried away with presumption of their own abilities, and, not finding matches to themselves in outward appearance, insult over the impotency of inferiors, and as those that can see no invisible opposition, promise themselves certainty of success. Insolence and self-confidence argue the heart to be nothing but a lump of proud flesh.

The first challenge of a duel, that ever we find, came out of the mouth of an uncircumcised Philistine; yet was that in open war, and tended to the saving of many lives, by adventuring one or two; and whosoever imitateth, nay, surpasseth him in challenge to private duels, in the attempt partaketh of his uncircumcision, though he should overcome, and of his manner of punishment, if in such private combats he cast away his life. For of all such desperate prodigals we may say, that their heads are cut off by their own sword, if not by their own hand. We cannot challenge men, and not challenge God, who justly challengeth to himself both to take vengeance and to give success. The more Goliah challenges, and is unanswered, the more he is puffed up in the pride of his own power. And is there none of all Israel that will answer this champion otherwise than with his heels? Where is the courage of him that that was higher than all Israel from the shoulders upward? The time was, when Nahash the Ammonite had made that tyrannous demand of the right eyes of the Gileadites, that Saul could say, unasked, "What aileth the people to weep?" and could hew his oxen in pieces to raise the spirits of Israel; and now he stands still, and sees the host turn their back, and never so much as asks, What aileth the people to flee? The time was, when Saul slew forty thousand Philistines in one day, and perhaps Goliah was in that discomfiture; and now one Philistine is suffered by him to brave all Israel forty days. Whence is this difference? The Spirit of God, the spirit of fortitude, was now departed from him. Saul was not more above himself when God was with him, than he is below others now that he is left of God. Valour is not merely of nature; nature is ever like itself: by this rule, he that is once valiant should never turn coward. But now we see the greatest spirits inconstant, and those, which have given good proofs of magnanimity at other times, have bewrayed white livers unto their own reproach. He, that is the God of hosts, gives and takes away men's hearts at his pleasure. Neither is it otherwise in our spiritual combats: sometimes the same soul dare challenge all the powers of darkness, which other times gives ground to a temptation. We have no strength but what is given us; and if the Author of all good gifts remit his hand for our humiliation, either we fight not, or are foiled.

David hath now lain long enough close among his flock in the fields of Bethlehem; God sees a time to send him to the pitched field of Israel. Good old Jesse, that was doubtless joyful to think that he had afforded three sons to the wars of his king, is no less careful of their welfare and provision; and who, amongst all the rest of his seven sons, shall be picked out for this service, but his youngest son David, whose former and almost worn-out acquaintance in court, and employment under Saul, seemed to fit him best for this errand? Early in the morning is David upon his way, yet not so early as to leave his flock unprovided. If his father's command dismiss him, yet will he stay till he have trusted his sheep with a careful keeper. We cannot be faithful shepherds if our spiritual charge be less dear unto us; if, when necessity calls us from our flocks, we depute not those who are vigilant and conscionable.

Ere David's speed can bring him to the valley of Elah, both the armies are on foot ready to join: he takes not this excuse to stay without, as a man daunted with the horror of war; but, leaving his present with his servant, he thrusts himself into the thickest of the host, and salutes his brethren, who were now thinking of killing or dying. When the proud champion of the Philistines comes stalking forth before all the troops, and renews this insolent challenge against Israel, David sees the man, and hears his defiance, and looks about him, to see what answer would be given; and when he spies nothing but pale faces, and backs turned, he wonders, not so much that one man should dare all Israel, as that all Israel should run from one man. Even when they fly from Goliah, they talk of the reward that should be given to that encounter and victory, which they dare not undertake; so those, who have not grace to believe, can yet say, there is glory laid up for the faithful. Ever since his anointing, was David possessed of God's Spirit, and thereby filled both with courage and wisdom: the more strange doth it seem to him, that all Israel should be thus dastardly. Those that are themselves eminent in any grace, cannot but wonder at the miserable defects of others: and the more shame they see in others' imperfections, the more is their zeal in avoiding those errors in themselves.

While base hearts are moved by example, the want of example is encouragement enough for an heroical mind; therefore is David ready to undertake the quarrel, because no man else dare do it. His eyes sparkled with holy anger, and his heart rose up to his mouth, when he heard this proud challenge: "Who is this uncircumcised Philistine, that he should revile the host of the living God?" Even so, O Saviour, when all the generations of men run away affrighted from the powers of death and darkness, thou alone hast undertaken, and confounded them!

Who should offer to daunt the holy courage of David, but his own brethren? The envious heart of Eliab construes this forwardness as his own disgrace. Shall I, thinks he, be put down by this puisne? shall my father's youngest son dare to attempt that, which my stomach will not serve me to adventure? Now, therefore, he rates David for his presumption; and instead of answering to the recompense of the victory which others were ready to give, he recompenseth the very inquiry of David with a check. It was for his brethren's sake that David came thither; and yet his very journey is cast upon him, by them, for a reproach: "Wherefore camest thou down hither?" and, when their bitterness can meet with nothing else to shame him, his sheep are cast in his teeth. Is it for thee, an idle proud boy, to be meddling with our martial matters? Doth not yonder champion look as if he were a fit match for thee? What makest thou of thyself? or what dost thou think of us? I think it were fitter for thee to be looking to thy sheep, than looking at Goliah. The wilderness would become thee better than the field. Wherein art thou equal to any man thou seest, but in arrogancy and presumption? The pastures of Bethlehem could not hold thee; but thou thoughtest it a goodly matter to see the wars. I know thee, as if I were in thy bosom: this was thy thought, There is no glory to be got among fleeces, I will go seek it in arms: now are my brethren winning honour in the troops of Israel, while I am basely tending on sheep; why should not I be as forward as the best of them? This vanity would make thee straight of a shepherd a soldier, and of a soldier a champion. Get thee home, foolish stripling, to thy hook and thy harp; let swords and spears alone to those that know how to use them.

It is quarrel enough, amongst many, to a good action, that it is not their own. There is no enemy so ready, or so spiteful, as the domestical. The hatred of brethren is so much more, as their blood is nearer. The malice of strangers is simple, but of a brother is mixt with envy. The more unnatural any quality is, the more extreme it is: a cold wind from the south is intolerable. David's first victory is of himself, next of his brother. He overcomes himself, in a patient forbearance of his brother; he overcomes the malicious rage of his brother, with the mildness of his answer. If David had wanted spirit, he had not been troubled with the insultation of a Philistine. If he had a spirit to match Goliah, how doth he so calmly receive the affront of a brother? " What have I now done? is there not a cause?" That which would have stirred the choler of another, allayeth his. It was a brother that wronged him, and that his eldest. Neither was it time to quarrel with a brother, while the Philistines' swords were drawn, and Goliah was challenging. O that these two motives could induce us to peace! If we have injury in our person, in our cause, it is from brethren, and the Philistines look on: I am deceived, if this conquest were less glorious than the following; he is fit to be God's champion, that hath learned to be victor of himself.

It is not this sprinkling of cold water that can quench the fire of David's zeal, but still his courage sends up flames of desire; still he goes on to inquire, and to proffer. He, whom the regard of others' envy can dismay, shall never do aught worthy of envy. Never man undertook any exploit of worth, and received not some discouragement in the way. This courageous motion of David was not more scorned by his brother, than by the other Israelites applauded. The rumour flies to the ears of the king, that there is a young man desirous to encounter the giant. David is brought forth. Saul, when he heard of a champion that durst go into the lists with Goliah, looked for one as much higher than himself, as he was taller than the rest; he expected some stern face, and brawny arm; young and ruddy David is so far below his thoughts, that he receives rather contempt than thanks. His words were stout; his person was weak. Saul doth not more like his resolution, than distrust his ability: " Thou art not able to go against this Philistine, to fight with him; for thou art a boy, and he is a man of war from his youth." Even Saul seconds Eliab in the conceit of this disparity; and if Eliab spake out of envy, Saul speaks out of judgment: both judge, as they were judged of, by the stature. All this cannot weaken that heart, which receives his strength from faith. David's greatest conflict is with his friends; the overcoming of their dissuasions, that he might fight, was more work than to overcome his enemy in fighting. He must first justify his strength to Saul, ere he may prove it upon Goliah. Valour is never made good but by trial. He pleads the trial of his puissance upon the bear and the lion, that he may have leave to prove it upon a worst beast than they: " Thy servant slew both the lion and the bear, therefore this uncircumcised Philistine shall be as one of them." Experience of good success is no small comfort to the heart; this gives possibility and hope, but no certainty. Two things there were on which David built his confidence: on Goliah's sin, and God's deliverance: " Seeing he hath railed on the host of the living God: the Lord, that delivered me out of the paws of the lion and the bear, he will deliver me out of the hand of this Philistine." Well did David know, that if this Philistine's skin had been as hard as the brass of his shield, his sin would make it penetrable by every stroke. After all brags of manhood, he is impotent that hath provoked God. While others labour for outward fortification, happy and safe were we, if we could labour for innocence. He that hath found God present in one extremity, may trust him in the next. Every sensible favour of the Almighty invites both his gifts and our trust.

Resolution, thus grounded, makes even Saul himself confident: David shall have both his leave and his blessing. If David came to Saul as a shepherd, he shall go toward Goliah as a warrior. The attire of the king is not too rich for him that shall fight for his king and country. Little did Saul think, that his helmet was now on that head, which should once wear his crown. Now, that David was arrayed in the warlike habit of a king, and girded with his sword, he looked upon himself, and thought this outside glorious: but when he offered to walk, and found that the attire was not so strong as unwieldy, and that it might be more for show than use, he lays down these accoutrements of honour, and, as caring rather to be a homely victor, than a glorious spoil, he craves pardon to go in no clothes but his own: he takes his staff instead of the spear, his shepherd's scrip instead of his brigandine, and instead of his sword he takes his sling, and instead of darts and javelins, he takes five smooth stones out of the brook. Let Saul's coat be never so rich, and his armour never so strong, what is David the better, if they fit him not? It is not to be inquired, how excellent any thing is, but how proper. Those things which are helps to some, may be encumbrances to others. An unmeet good may be as inconvenient as an accustomed evil. If we could wish another man's honour, when we feel the weight of his cares we should be glad to be in our own coat.

Those that depend upon the strength of faith, though they neglect not means, yet they are not curious in the proportion of outward means to the effect desired. — Where the heart is armed with an assured confidence, a sling and a stone are weapons enough; to the unbelieving, no helps are sufficient. Goliah, though he were presumptuous enough, yet had one shield carried before him; another he carried on his shoulder: neither will his sword alone content him, but he takes his spear too. David's armour is his plain shepherd's russet, and the brook yields him his artillery; and he knows there is more safety in his cloth, than in the other's brass; and more danger in his pebbles, than in the other's spear. Faith gives both heart and arms. The inward munition is so much more noble, because it is of proof for both soul and body: if we be furnished with this, how boldly shall we meet with the powers of darkness, and go away more than conquerors!

Neither did the quality of David's weapons bewray more confidence than the number. If he will put his life and victory upon the stones of the brook, why doth he not fill his scrip full of them? why will he content himself with five? Had he been furnished with store, the advantage of his nimbleness might have given him hope, if one fail, that yet another might speed; but now this paucity puts the despatch to a sudden hazard, and he hath but five stones-cast either to death or victory: still the fewer helps, the stronger faith. David had an instinct from God that he should overcome; he had not a particular direction how he should overcome. For had he been at first resolved upon the sling and stone, he had saved the labour of girding his sword. It seems while they were addressing him to the combat, he made account of hand blows; now he is purposed rather to send, than bring death to his adversary: in either, or both, he durst trust God with the success, and beforehand (through the conflict) saw the victory: it is sufficient, that we know the issue of our fight. If our weapons and wards vary, according to the occasion given by God, that is nothing to the event: sure we are, that if we resist, we shall overcome; and if we overcome, we shall be crowned.

When David appeared in the lists to so unequal an adversary, as many eyes were upon him, so in those eyes diverse affections. The Israelites looked upon him with pity and fear, and each man thought, Alas! why is this comely stripling suffered to cast away himself upon such a monster? why will they let him go unarmed to such an affray? Why will Saul hazard the honour of Israel on so unlikely a head? The Philistines, especially their great champion, looked upon him with scorn, disdaining so base a combatant: "Am I a dog, that thou comest to me with staves?" What could be said more fitly? Hadst thou been any other than a dog, O Goliah, thou hadst never opened thy foul mouth to bark against the host of God, and the God of hosts. If David had thought thee any other than a very dog, he had never come to thee with a staff and a stone.

The last words that ever the Philistine shall speak, are curses and brags: "Come to me, and I will give thy flesh unto the fowls of the heaven, and the beasts of the field." Seldom ever was there a good end of ostentation. Presumption is at once the presage and cause of ruin. He is a weak adversary that can be killed with words. That man which could not fear the giant's hand, cannot fear his tongue. If words shall first encounter, the Philistine receives the first foil, and shall first let in death unto his ear, ere it enter into his forehead. "Thou comest to me with a sword, and a spear, and a shield; but I come to thee in the name of the Lord of hosts, the God of the host of Israel, whom thou hast railed upon. This day shall the Lord close thee in my hand, and I shall smite thee, and take thine head from thee." Here is another style, not of a boaster, but of a prophet. Now shall Goliah know whence to expect his bane, even from the hands of a revenging God, that shall smite him by David, and now shall learn, too late, what it is to meddle with an enemy that goes under the invisible protection of the Almighty. No sooner hath David spoken, than his foot and hand second his tongue; he runs to fight with the Philistine. It is a cold courage that stands only upon defence: as a man that saw no cause of fear, and was full of the ambition of victory, he flies upon that monster, and, with a stone out of his bag, smites him in the forehead. There was no part of Goliah that was capable of that danger, but the face, and that piece of the face; the rest was defended with a brazen wall, which a weak sling would have tried to batter in vain. What could Goliah fear, to see an adversary come to him without edge or point! And, behold, that one part hath God found out for the entrance of death. He, that could have caused the stone to pass through the shield and breast-plate of Goliah, rather directs the stone to that part whose nakedness gave advantage. Where there is power or possibility of nature, God uses not to work miracles, but chooses the way that lies most open to his purposes.

The vast forehead was a fair mark; but how easily might the sling have missed it, if there had not been another hand in this cast besides David's! He that guided David into this field, and raised his courage to this combat, guides the stone to his end, and lodges it in that seat of impudence. There now lieth the great defier of Israel, grovelling and grinning in death, and is not suffered to deal one blow for his life, and bites the unwelcome earth, for indignation that he dies by the hand of a shepherd! Earth and hell share him betwixt them. Such is the end of insolence and presumption. O God, what is flesh and blood to thee, who canst make a little pebble-stone stronger than a giant, and, when thou wilt, by the weakest means, canst strew thine enemies in the dust! Where now are the two shields of Goliah, that they did not bear off this stroke of death? or wherefore serves that weaver's beam, but to strike the earth in falling? or that sword, but to behead his master? What needed David load himself with an unnecessary weapon! one sword can serve both Goliah and him. If Goliah had a man to bear his shield, David had Goliah to bear his sword, wherewith that proud blasphemous head is severed from his shoulders. Nothing more honours God, than the turning of wicked men's forces against themselves. There are none of his enemies but carry with them their own destruction. Thus didst thou, O son of David, foil Satan with his own weapon; that whereby he meant destruction to thee and us, vanquished him through thy mighty power, and raised thee to that glorious triumph and super-exaltation wherein thou art, wherein we shall be with thee.

CONTEMPLATION V.—JONATHAN'S LOVE, AND SAUL'S ENVY.

BESIDES the discomfiture of the Philistines, David's victory had a double issue: Jonathan's love, and Saul's envy, which God so mixed, that the one was a remedy of the other. A good son makes amends for a wayward father. How precious was that stone that killed such an enemy as Goliah, and purchased such a friend as Jonathan! All Saul's courtiers looked upon David: none so affected him, none did match him but Jonathan; that true correspondence, that was both in their faith and valour, hath knit their hearts. If David did set upon a bear, a lion, a giant; Jonathan had set upon a whole host, and prevailed: the same spirit animated both; the same faith incited both; the same hand prospered both. All Israel was not worth this pair of friends, so zealously confident, so happily victorious. Similitude of dispositions and estates ties the fastest knots of affection. A wise soul hath piercing eyes, and hath quickly discerned the likeness of itself in another; as we do no sooner look into the glass of water, but face answers to face, and, where it sees a perfect resemblance of itself, cannot choose but love it with the same affection that it reflects upon itself.

No man saw David that day, which had so much cause to disaffect him; none in Israel should be a loser by David's success, but Jonathan. Saul was sure enough settled for his time: only his successor should forego all that which David should gain; so as none but David stands in Jonathan's light; and yet all this cannot abate one jot or dram of his love. Where God uniteth hearts, carnal respects are too weak to dissever them, since that, which breaks off affection, must needs be stronger than that which conjoineth it.

Jonathan doth not desire to smother his love by concealment, but professes it in his carriage and actions; he puts off the robe that was upon him, and all his garments, even to his sword, and bow and girdle, and gives them unto his new friend. It was perhaps not without a mystery, that Saul's clothes fitted not David, but Jonathan's fitted him; and these he is as glad to wear, as he was to be disburdened of the other: that there might be a perfect resemblance, their bodies are suited as well as their hearts. Now the beholders can say, There goes Jonathan's other self; if there be another body under those clothes, there is the same soul. Now David hath cast off his russet coat, and his scrip, and is a shepherd no more; he is suddenly become both a courtier and a captain, and a companion to the prince; yet himself is not changed with his habit, with his condition; yea, rather, as if his wisdom had reserved itself for his exaltation, he so manageth a sudden greatness, as that he winneth all hearts. Honour shows the man; and if there be any blemishes of imperfection, they will be seen in the man that is unexpectedly lifted above his fellows: he is out of the danger of folly, whom a speedy advancement leaveth wise.

Jonathan loved David, the soldiers honoured him, the court favoured him, the people applauded him; only Saul stomached him, and therefore hated him, because he was so happy in all besides himself. It had been a shame for all Israel, if they had not magnified their champion. Saul's own heart could not but tell him, that they did owe the glory of that day, and the safety of himself and Israel, unto the sling of David, who, in one man, slew all those thousands at a blow. It was enough for the puissant king of Israel to follow the chase, and to kill them whom David had put to flight; yet he, that could lend his clothes and his armour to this exploit, cannot abide to part with the honour of it to him that had earned it so dearly. The holy songs of David had not more quieted his spirits before, than now the thankful song of the Israelitish women vexes him. One little ditty, of " Saul hath slain his thousands, and David his ten thousands," sung unto the timbrels of Israel, fetched again that evil spirit, which David's music had expelled. Saul needed not the torment of a worse spirit than envy. O the unreasonableness of this wicked passion! The women gave Saul more, and David less, than he deserved; for Saul alone could not kill a thousand, and David, in that one act of killing Goliah, slew in effect all the Philistines that were slain that day: and yet, because they gave more to David than to himself, he that should have indited, and begun that song of thankfulness, repines, and grows now as mad with envy, as he was before with grief. Truth and justice are no protection against malice. Envy is blind to all objects, save other men's happiness. If the eyes of men could be contained within their own bounds, and not rove forth into comparisons, there could be no place for this vicious affection; but, when they have once taken this lawless scope to themselves, they lose the knowledge of home, and care only to be employed abroad in their own torment.

Never was Saul's breast so fit a lodging for the evil spirit, as now that it is dressed up with envy. It is as impossible that hell should be free from devils, as a malicious heart. Now doth the frantic king of Israel renew his old fits, and walks and talks distractedly: he was mad with David, and who but David must be called to allay his madness? Such was David's wisdom, he could not but know the terms wherein he stood with Saul; yet, in lieu of the harsh and discordant notes of his master's envy, he returns pleasing music unto him. He can never be a good courtier, nor a good man, that hath not learned to repay, if not injuries with thanks, yet evil with good. While there was a harp in David's hand, there was a spear in Saul's, wherewith he threatens death, as the recompense of that sweet melody. He said, "I will smite David through to the wall. It is well for the innocent, that wicked men cannot keep their own counsel. God fetcheth their thoughts out of their mouths, or their countenance, for a seasonable prevention, which else might proceed to secret execution. It was time for David to withdraw himself; his obedience did not tie him to be the mark of a furious master; he might ease Saul with his music, with his blood he might not: twice, therefore, doth he avoid the presence, not the court, nor the service of Saul.

One would have thought rather, that David should have been afraid of Saul, because the devil was so strong with him, than that Saul should be afraid of David, because the Lord was with him; yet we find all the fear in Saul of David, none in David of Saul. Hatred and fear are ordinary companions. David had wisdom and faith to dispel his fears; Saul had nothing but infidelity, and dejected, self-condemned, distempered thoughts, which must needs nourish them; yet Saul could not fear any hurt from David, whom he found so loyal and serviceable: he fears only too much good unto David; and the envious fear is much more than the distrustful. Now David's presence begins to be more displeasing, than his music was sweet: despite itself had rather prefer him to a remote dignity, than endure him a nearer attendant. This promotion increaseth David's honour and love; and his love and honour aggravate Saul's hatred and fear.

Saul's madness hath not bereaved him of his craft; for, perceiving how great David was grown in the reputation of Israel, he dares not offer any personal or direct violence to him, but hires him into the jaws of a supposed death, by no less price than his eldest daughter: " Behold my eldest daughter Merab, her will I give thee to wife; only be a valiant son to me, and fight the Lord's battles." Could ever man speak more graciously, more holily? What could be more graciously offered by a king than his eldest daughter? what care could be more holy than of the Lord's battles? Yet never did Saul intend so much mischief to David, or so much unfaithfulness to God, as when he spake thus. There is never so much danger of the falsehearted, as when they make the fairest weather. Saul's spear bade David be gone, but his plausible words invite him to danger. This honour was due to David before, upon the compact of his victory; yet he, that twice inquired into the reward of that enterprise before he undertook it, never demanded it after that achievement; neither had Saul the justice to offer it as a recompense of so noble an exploit, but as a snare to envied victory. Charity suspects not: David construes that as an effect and argument of his master's love, which was no other but a child of envy, but a plot of mischief; and though he knew his own desert, and the justice of his claim to Merab, yet he, in a sincere humility, disparageth himself, his birth and parentage, with a " Who am I?"

As it was not the purpose of this modesty in David to reject, but to solicit the proffered favour of Saul, so was it not in the power of this bashful humiliation to turn back the edge of so keen an envy. It helps not that David makes himself mean, while others magnify his worth: whatsoever the colour was, Saul meant nothing to David but danger and death; and since all those battles will not effect that which he desired, himself will not effect that which he promised. If he cannot kill David, he will disgrace him. David's honour was Saul's disease: it was not likely, therefore, that Saul would add unto that honour whereof he was so sick already. Merab was given unto another; neither do I hear David complain of so manifest an injustice: he knew, that the God whose battles he fought had provided a due reward of his patience. If Merab fail, God hath a Michal in store for him: she is in love with David; his comeliness and valour hath so won her heart, that she now emulates the affection of her brother Jonathan. If she be the younger sister, yet she is more affectionate. Saul is glad of the news: his daughter could never live to do him better service, than to be a new snare to his adversary. She shall be therefore sacrificed to his envy; and her honest and sincere love shall be made a bait for her worthy and innocent husband: " I will give him her, that she may be a snare unto him, that the hand of the Philistines may be against him." The purpose of any favour is more than the value of it. Even the greatest honours may be given with an intent of destruction. Many a man is raised up for a fall. So forward is Saul in the match, that he sends spokesmen to solicit David to that honour, which he hopes will prove the highway to death. The dowry is set: a hundred foreskins of the Philistines; not their heads, but their foreskins, that this victory might be more ignominious: still thinking, Why may not one David miscarry, as well as a hundred Philistines? And what doth Saul's envy all this while, but enhance David's zeal, and valour, and glory? That good captain, little imagining that himself was the Philistine whom Saul maligned, supererogates of his master, and brings two hundred for one, and returns home safe and renowned. Neither can Saul now fly off for shame: there is no remedy, but David must be a son, where he was a rival; and Saul must feed upon his own heart, since he cannot see David's. God's blessing graces equally together with men's malice; neither can they devise which way to make us more happy, than by wishing us evil.

CONTEMPLATION VI. — MICHAL'S WILE.

THIS advantage can Saul yet make of David's promotion, that as his adversary is raised higher, so he is drawn nearer to the opportunity of death. Now hath his envy cast off all shame; and, since those crafty plots succeed not, he directly suborns murderers of his rival. There is none in all the court that is not set on to be an executioner. Jonathan himself is solicited to embrue his hand in the blood of his friend, of his brother. Saul could not but see Jonathan's clothes on David's back; he could not but know the league of their love; yet, because he knew withal how much the prosperity of David would prejudice Jonathan, he hoped to have found him his son in malice. Those that have the jaundice see all things yellow:

those which are overgrown with malicious passions, think all men like themselves.

I do not hear of any reply that Jonathan made to his father, when he gave him that bloody charge; but he waits for a fit time to dissuade him from so cruel an injustice. Wisdom had taught him to give way to rage, and, in so hard an adventure, to crave aid of opportunity. If we be not careful to observe good moods when we deal with the passionate, we may exasperate, instead of reforming. Thus did Jonathan, who, knowing how much better it is to be a good friend, than an ill son, had not only disclosed that ill counsel, but, when he found his father in the fields in a calmer temper, laboured to divert it. And so far doth the seasonable and pithy oratory of Jonathan prevail, that Saul is convinced of his wrong, and swears, " As God lives, David shall not die." Indeed, how could it be otherwise, upon the plea of David's innocence and well-deservings? How could Saul say, he should die, whom he could accuse of nothing but faithfulness? why should he design him to death, which had given life to all Israel? Ofttimes wicked men's judgments are forced to yield unto that truth against which their affections maintain a rebellion. Even the foulest hearts do sometimes entertain good motions: likeas, on the contrary, the holiest souls give way sometimes to the suggestions of evil. The flashes of lightning may be discerned in the darkest prisons. But if good thoughts look into a wicked heart, they stay not there; as those that like not their lodging, they are soon gone: hardly any thing distinguishes betwixt good and evil, but continuance. The light that shines into a holy heart is constant, like that of the sun, which keeps due times, and varies not his course for any of these sublunary occasions.

The Philistines' wars renew David's victories, and David's victory renews Saul's envy, and Saul's envy renews the plots of David's death. Vows and oaths are forgotten. That evil spirit which vexes Saul hath found so much favour with him, as to win him to these bloody machinations against an innocent: his own hands shall first be employed in this execution; the spear, which hath twice before threatened death to David, shall now once again go upon that message. Wise David, that knew the danger of a hollow friend, and reconciled enemy, and that found more cause to mind Saul's earnest, than his own play, gives way by his nimbleness to that deadly weapon, and, resigning that stroke unto the wall, flies for his life. No man knows how to be sure of an unconscionable man. If either goodness or merit, or affinity, or reasons, or oaths, could secure a man, David had been safe; now, if his heels do no more befriend him than all these, he is a dead man. No sooner is he gone, than messengers are sped after him. It hath been seldom seen that wickedness wanted executioners: David's house is beset with murderers, which watch at all his doors for the opportunity of blood. Who can but wonder to see how God hath fetched from the loins of Saul a remedy for the malice of Saul's heart? His own children are the only means to cross him in the sin, and to preserve his guiltless adversary. Michal hath more than notice of the plot, and with her subtle wit countermines her father, for the rescue of a husband; she taking the benefit of the night, lets David down through a window: he is gone, and disappoints the ambushes of Saul. The messengers begin to be impatient of this delay, and now think it time to inquire after their prisoner: she puts them off with the excuse of David's sickness, so as now her husband had good leisure for his escape, and lays a statue in his bed. Saul likes the news of any evil befallen to David; but, fearing he is not sick enough, sends to aid his disease. The messengers return, and rushing into the house with their swords drawn, after some harsh words to their imagined charge, surprise a sick statue lying with a pillow under his head; and now blush to see they have spent all their threats upon a senseless stock, and made themselves ridiculous, while they would be serviceable.

But how shall Michal answer this mockage unto her furious father? Hitherto she hath done like David's wife; now she begins to be Saul's daughter: " He said to me, Let me go, or else I will kill thee." She, whose wit had delivered her husband from the sword of her father, now turns the edge of her father's wrath from herself to her husband. His absence made her presume of his safety. If Michal had not been of Saul's plot, he had never expostulated with her in those terms: " Why hast thou let mine enemy escape?" Neither had she framed that answer, " He said, Let me go." I do not find any great store of religion in Michal: for, both she had an image in the house, and afterward mocked David for his devotion; yet nature hath taught her to prefer a husband to a father: to elude a father, from whom she could not fly; to save a husband, who durst not but fly from her. The bonds of matrimonial love are, and should be, stronger than those of.

nature. Those respects are mutual which God appointed in the first institution of wedlock, that husband and wife should leave father and mother for each other's sake. Treason is ever odious; but so much more in the marriage-bed, by how much the obligations are deeper.

As she loved her husband better than her father, so she loved herself better than her husband: she saved her husband by a wile; and now she saves herself by a lie, and loses half the thank of her deliverance by an officious slander. Her act was good, but she wants courage to maintain it; and therefore seeks to the weak shelter of untruth. Those that do good offices, not out of conscience, but good nature or civility, if they meet an affront of danger, seldom come off cleanly, but are ready to catch at all excuses, though base, though injurious; because their grounds are not strong enough to bear them out in suffering for that which they have well done.

Whither doth David fly, but to the sanctuary of Samuel? He doth not (though he knew himself gracious with the soldiers) raise forces, or take some strong fort, and there stand upon his own defence, and at defiance with his king: but he gets him to the college of the prophets, as a man that would seek the peaceable protection of the King of heaven, against the unjust fury of a king on earth: only the wing of God shall hide him from that violence.

God intended to make David not a warrior and a king only, but a prophet too. As the field fitted him for the first, and the court for the second, so Najoth shall fit him for the third. Doubtless, such was David's delight in holy meditations, he never spent his time so contentedly, as when he was retired to that divine academy, and had so full freedom to enjoy God, and to satiate himself with heavenly exercises. The only doubt is, how Samuel can give harbour to a man fled from the anger of his prince; wherein the very persons of both give abundant satisfaction; for both Samuel knew the counsel of God, and durst do nothing without it; and David was by Samuel anointed from God. This unction was a mutual bond. Good reason had David to sue to him which had poured the oil on his head, for the hiding of that head which he had anointed: and good reason had Samuel to hide him, whom God by his means had chosen, from him whom God by his sentence had rejected: besides that, the cause deserved commiseration. Here was not a malefactor running away from justice, but an innocent avoiding murder; not a traitor countenanced against his sovereign, but the deliverer of Israel harboured in a sanctuary of prophets till his peace might be made.

Even thither doth Saul send to apprehend David. All his rage did not incense him against Samuel as the abettor of his adversary: such an impression of reverence had the person and calling of the prophet left in the mind of Saul, that he cannot think of lifting up his hand against him. The same God who did at the first put an awe of man in the fiercest creatures, hath stamped in the cruellest hearts a reverend respect to his own image in his ministers; so as even they that hate them, do yet honour them.

Saul's messengers came to lay hold on David: God lays hold on them. No sooner do they see a company of prophets busy in these divine exercises, under the moderation of Samuel, than they are turned from executioners to prophets. It is good going up to Najoth, into the holy assemblies: who knows how we may be changed, beside our intentions? Many a one hath come into God's house to carp, or scoff, or sleep, or gaze, that hath returned a convert.

The same heart, that was thus disquieted with David's happy success, is now vexed with the holiness of his other servants. It angers him that God's Spirit could find no other time to seize upon his agents, than when he had sent them to kill; and now, out of an indignation at this disappointment, himself will go, and be his own servant; his guilty soul finds itself out of the danger of being thus surprised; and behold, Saul is no sooner come within the smell of the smoke of Najoth, than he also prophesies: the same spirit that, when he went first from Samuel, enabled him to prophesy, returns in the same effect, now that he was going his last unto Samuel. This was such a grace as might well stand with rejection; an extraordinary gift of the Spirit, but not sanctifying. Many men have had their mouths opened to prophesy unto others, whose hearts have been deaf to God. But this, such as it was, was far from Saul's purpose, who, instead of expostulating with Samuel, falls down before him; and laying aside his weapons and his robes, of a tyrant proves for the time a disciple. All hearts are in the hands of their Maker: how easy is it for him that gave them their being, to frame them to his own bent! Who can be afraid of malice, that knows what hooks God hath in the nostrils of men and devils? what charms he hath for the most serpentine hearts?

CONTEMPLATION VII. — DAVID AND AHIMELECH.

Who can ever judge of the children by the parents, that knows Jonathan was the son of Saul! There was never a falser heart than Saul's: there was never a truer friend than Jonathan: neither the hope of a kingdom, nor the frowns of a father, nor the fear of death, can remove him from his vowed amity. No son could be more officious and dutiful to a good father; yet he lays down nature at the foot of grace, and, for the preservation of his innocent rival for the kingdom, crosses the bloody designs of his own parent. David needs no other counsellor, no other advocate, no other intelligencer, than he. It is not in the power of Saul's unnatural reproaches, or of his spear, to make Jonathan any other than a friend and patron of innocence. Even, after all these difficulties, doth Jonathan shoot beyond David, that Saul may shoot short of him. In vain are those professions of love, which are not answered with action. He is no true friend, that, besides talk, is not ready both to do and suffer.

Saul is no whit the better for his prophesying: he no sooner rises up from before Samuel, than he pursues David. Wicked men are rather the worse for those transitory good motions they have received. If the swine be never so clean washed, she will wallow again. That we have good thoughts, it is no thank to us; that we answer them not, it is both our sin and judgment.

David hath learned not to trust these fits of devotion, but flies from Samuel to Jonathan, from Jonathan to Ahimelech: when he was hunted from the prophet, he flies to the priest, as one that knew justice and compassion should dwell in those breasts which are consecrated unto God.

The ark and the tabernacle were then separated; the ark was at Kirjath-jearim, the tabernacle at Nob; God was present with both. Whither should David flee for succour, but to the house of that God which had anointed him?

Ahimelech was wont to see David attended with the troops of Israel, or with the gallants of the court; it seems strange therefore to him, to see so great a peer and champion of Israel come alone. These are the alterations to which earthly greatness is subject. Not many days are passed, since no man was honoured at court but Jonathan and David: now they are both for the time in disgrace; now dare not the king's son-in-law, brother to the prince both in love and in marriage, show his head at the court; nor any of those that bowed to him dare stir a foot with him. Princes are as the sun, and great subjects are like to dials: if the sun shine not on the dial, no man will look at it.

Even he that overcame the bear, the lion, the giant, is overcome with fear. He that had cut off two hundred foreskins of the Philistines, had not circumcised his own heart of the weak passions that follow distrust: now that he is hard driven, he practises to help himself with an unwarrantable shift. Who can look to pass this pilgrimage without infirmities, when David dissembleth to Ahimelech? A weak man's rules may be better than the best man's actions. God lets us see some blemishes in his holiest servants, that we may neither be too highly conceited of flesh and blood, nor too much dejected when we have been miscarried into sin. Hitherto hath David gone upright; now he begins to halt with the priest of God, and under pretence of Saul's employment, draws that favour from Ahimelech, which shall afterwards cost him his head.

What could Ahimelech have thought too dear for God's anointed, God's champion? It is not like but that, if David had sincerely opened himself to the priest as he had done to the prophet, Ahimelech would have seconded Samuel in some secret and safe succour of so unjust a distress, whereas he is now, by a false colour, led to that kindness which shall be prejudicial to his life. Extremities of evil are commonly inconsiderate; either for that we have not leisure to our thoughts, or perhaps (so we may be perplexed) not thoughts to our leisure. What would David have given afterwards to have redeemed this oversight!

Under this pretence, he craves a double favour of Ahimelech; the one of bread for his sustenance, the other of a sword for his defence. There was no bread under the hands of the priest, but that which was consecrated to God, and whereof none might taste but the devoted servants of the altar; even that which was, with solemn dedication, set upon the holy tables before the face of God; a sacramental bread presented to God with incense, figuring that true bread that came down from heaven: yet even this bread might, in case of necessity, become common, and be given by Ahimelech, and received by David and his followers. Our Saviour himself justifies the act of both. Ceremonies must give place to substance. God will have mercy and not sacrifice. Charity is the sum and the end of the law, that must be aimed at in all our actions, wherein it may fall out, that the way to keep the law may be to break it; the intention may be kept, and the letter violated; and it may be a dangerous transgression of the law to observe the words, and neglect the scope of God. That which would have dispensed with David for the substance of the act, would have much more dispensed with him for the circumstance: the touch of their lawful wives had contracted a legal impurity, not a moral: that could have been no sufficient reason, why in an urgent necessity they might not have partaken of the holy bread. Ahimelech was no perfect casuist: these men might not famish, if they were ceremonially impure. But this question bewrayed the care of Ahimelech in distributing the holy bread. There might be in these men a double incapacity; the one as they were seculars, the other as unclean: he saw the one must be, he feared lest the other should be; as one that wished as little indisposition as possible might be, in those which should be fed from God's table.

It is strange that David should come to the priest of God for a sword: who in all Israel was so unlikely to furnish him with weapons, as a man of peace, whose armour was only spiritual? Doubtless David knew well where Goliah's sword lay, as the noble relic of God's victorious deliverance, dedicated to the same God which won it; at this did that suit aim. None could be so fit for David, none could be so fit for it as David. Who could have so much right to that sword, as he against whom it was drawn, and by whom it was taken? There was more in that sword than metal and form: David could never cast his eye upon it, but he saw an undoubted monument of the merciful protection of the Almighty; there was therefore more strength in that sword, than sharpness: neither was David's arm so much strengthened by it, as his faith; nothing can overcome him, while he carries with him that assured sign of victory. It is good to take all occasions of renewing the remembrance of God's mercies to us, and our obligations to him.

Doeg, the master of Saul's herdmen (for he, that went to seek his father's asses before he was king, hath herds and droves now that he is a king), was now in the court of the tabernacle, upon some occasion of devotion: though an Israelite in profession, he was an Edomite no less in heart than in blood; yet he hath some vow upon him, and not only comes up to God's house, but abides before the Lord. Hypocrites have equal access to the public places and means of God's service. Even he that knows the heart, yet shuts his door upon none: how much less should we dare to exclude any, which can only judge of the heart by the face!

Doeg may set his foot as far within the tabernacle as David; he sees the passages betwixt him and Ahimelech, and lays them up for an advantage: while he should have edified himself by those holy services, he carps at the priest of God, and, after a lewd misinterpretation of his actions, of an attendant, proves an accuser. To incur favour with an unjust master, he informs against innocent Ahimelech, and makes that his act, which was drawn from him by a cunning circumvention. When we see our auditors before us, little do we know with what hearts they are there, or what use they will make of their pretended devotion. If many come in simplicity of heart to serve their God, some others may perhaps come to observe their teachers, and to pick quarrels where none are: only God, and the issue, can distinguish betwixt a David and a Doeg, when they are both in the tabernacle. Honest Ahimelech could little suspect, that he now offered a sacrifice for his executioner, yea, for the murderer of all his family. O the wise and deep judgments of the Almighty! God owed a revenge to the house of Eli, and now, by the delation of Doeg, he takes occasion to pay it. It was just in God, which in Doeg was most unjust. Saul's cruelty, and the treachery of Doeg, do not lose one dram of their guilt by the counsel of God; neither doth the holy counsel of God gather any blemish by their wickedness. If it had pleased God to inflict death upon them sooner, without any pretence of occasion, his justice had been clear from all imputations; now, if Saul and Doeg be instead of a pestilence or fever, who can cavil? The judgments of God are not open, but are always just: he knows how by one man's sin to punish the sin of another, and, by both their sins and punishments, to glorify himself. If his word sleep, it shall not die, but after long intermissions break forth in those effects which we had forgotten to look for, and ceased to fear. O Lord! thou art sure when thou threatenest, and just when thou judgest! Keep thou us from the sentence of death, else in vain we shall labour to keep ourselves from the execution!

BOOK XIV.

CONTEMPLATION I. — SAUL IN DAVID'S CAVE.

It was the strange lot of David, that those whom he pursued, preserved him from those whom he had preserved. The Philistines, whom David had newly smitten in Keilah, call off Saul from smiting David in the wilderness, when there was but a hillock betwixt him and death. Wicked purposes are easily checked, not easily broken off. Saul's sword is scarce dry from the blood of the Philistines, when it thirsts anew for the blood of David,' and now, in a renewed chace, hunts him dry-foot through every wilderness. The very desert is too fair a refuge for innocence. The hills and rocks are searched in an angry jealousy; the very wild goats of the mountains were not allowed to be companions for him, who had no fault but his virtue. O the seemingly unequal distribution of these earthly things! Cruelty and oppression reign in a palace, while goodness lurks among the rocks and caves, and thinks it happiness enough to steal a life.

Like a dead man, David is fain to be hid under the earth, and seeks the comfort of protection in darkness: and now the wise providence of God leads Saul to his enemy without blood. He, which before brought them within a hill's distance without interview, brings them now both within one roof; so as that, while Saul seeks David and finds him not, he is found of David unsought. If Saul had known his own opportunities, how David and his men had interred themselves, he had saved a treble labour of chace, of execution, and burial; for had he but stopt the mouth of that cave, his enemies had laid themselves down in their own graves. The wisdom of God thinks fit to hide from evil men and spirits, those means and seasons, which might be, if they had been taken, most prejudicial to his own. We had been oft foiled, if Satan could but have known our hearts. Sometimes we lie open to evils, and happy it is for us, that he only knows it, who pities instead of tempting us.

It is not long since Saul said of David, lodged then in Keilah, God hath delivered him into mine hands, for he is shut in, seeing he is come into a city that hath gates and bars; but now contrarily God delivers Saul, ere he was aware, into the hands of David, and without the help of gates and bars, hath inclosed him within the valley of death. How just is it with God, that those who seek mischief to others, find it to themselves, and, even while they are spreading nets, are ensnared, their deliberate plotting of evil is surprised with a sudden judgment.

How amazedly must David needs look, when he saw Saul enter into the cave where himself was! What is this, thinks he, which God hath done? is this presence purposed or casual? is Saul here to pursue or to tempt me? where suddenly the action bewrays the intent, and tells David, that Saul sought secrecy and not him. The superfluity of his maliciousness brought him into the wilderness; the necessity of nature led him into the cave. Even those actions, wherein we place shame, are not exempted from a providence. The fingers of David's followers itched to seize upon their master's enemy; and that they might not seem led so much by faction as by faith, they urge David with a promise from God: The day is come, whereof the Lord saith unto thee, Behold, I will deliver thine enemy into thine hand, and thou shalt do unto him as it shall seem good to thee. This argument seemed to carry such command with it, as that David not only may, but must imbrue his hands in blood, unless he will be found wanting to God and himself. Those temptations are most powerful, which fetch their force from the pretence of a religious obedience: whereas those which are raised from arbitrary and private respects, admit of an easy dispensation.

If there was such a prediction, one clause of it was ambiguous, and they take it at the worst: Thou shalt do to him as shall seem good to thee. That might not seem good to him, which seemed evil unto God. There is nothing more dangerous than to make construction of God's purposes out of eventual appearance. If carnal probabilities might be the rule of our judgment, what could God seem to intend other than Saul's death, in offering him naked into the hands of those whom he unjustly persecuted? How could David's soldiers think that God hath sent Saul thither on any other errand, than to fetch his bane? And if Saul could have seen his own danger, he had given himself for dead: for his heart, guilty to his own bloody desire, could not but have expected the same measure which it meant. But wise and holy David, not transported either with misconceit of the event, or fury of passion, or solicitation of his followers, dares make no other use of this accident than the trial of his loyalty, and the inducement of his peace. It had been as easy for him to cut the throat of Saul as his garment; but now his coat only shall be the worse, not his person; neither doth he in this maiming of a cloak seek his own revenge, but a monument of his innocence. Before Saul rent Samuel's garment: now David cutteth Saul's; both were significant: the rending of the one, signified the kingdom torn out of those unworthy hands; the cutting of the other, that the life of Saul might have been as easily cut off.

Saul needs no other monitor of his own danger than what he wears. The upper garment of Saul was laid aside while he went to cover his feet, so as the cut of the garment did not threaten any touch of the body; yet even the violence offered to a remote garment strikes the heart of David, which finds a present remorse for harmfully touching that which once touched the person of his master. Tender consciences are moved to regret at those actions, which strong hearts pass over with a careless ease. It troubled not Saul to seek after the blood of a righteous servant. There is no less difference of consciences than stomachs: some stomachs will digest the hardest meats, and turn over substances, not in their nature edible, while others surfeit of the lightest food, and complain even of dainties. Every gracious heart is in some measure scrupulous, and finds more safety in fear than in presumption: and if it be so straight as to curb itself in from the liberty which it might take in things which are not unlawful, how much less will it dare to take scope unto evil! By how much that state is better, where nothing is allowed, than where all things, by so much is the strict and timorous conscience better than the lawless. There is good likelihood of that man who is any ways scrupulous of his ways: but he, who makes no bones of his actions, is apparently hopeless.

Since David's followers pleaded God's testimony to him as a motive to blood, David appeals to the same God for his preservation from blood: The Lord keep me from doing that thing to my master, the Lord's anointed. And now the good man hath work enough to defend both himself and his persecutor: himself from the importunate necessity of doing violence, and his master from suffering it. It was not more easy to rule his own hands, than difficult to rule a multitude. David's troops consisted of malcontents; all that were in distress, in bitterness of soul, were gathered to him. Many, if never so well ordered, are hard to command; a few, if disorderly, more hard; many and disorderly must needs be so much the hardest of all, that David never achieved any victory like unto this, wherein he first overcame himself, then his soldiers.

And what was the charm wherewith David allayed those raging spirits of his followers? No other but this, He is the anointed of the Lord. That holy oil was the antidote for his blood: Saul did not lend David so impierceable an armour, when he should encounter Goliah, as David now lent him in this plea of his unction. Which of all the discontented outlaws that lurked in that cave durst put forth his hand against Saul, when they once heard, He is the Lord's anointed? Such an impression of awe hath the divine Providence caused his image to make in the hearts of men, as that it makes traitors cowards, so as instead of striking they tremble; how much more lawless, than the outlaws of Israel, are those professed ring-leaders of Christianity, which teach, and practise, and encourage, and reward, and canonize the violation of majesty! It is not enough for those, who are commanders of others, to refrain their own hands from doing evil, but they must carefully prevent the iniquity of their heels, else they shall be justly reputed to do that by others, which, in their own persons, they avoided. The laws both of God and man pre-suppose us in some sort answerable for our charge; as taking it for granted, that we should not undertake those reins which we cannot manage.

There was no reason David should lose the thanks of so noble a demonstration of his loyalty, whereto he trusts so much, that he dares call back the man by whom he was pursued, and make him judge, whether that fact had not deserved a life. As his act, so his word and gesture, imported nothing but humble obedience; neither was there more meekness than force in that seasonable persuasion, wherein he lets Saul see the error of his credulity; the unjust slanders of maliciousness, the opportunity of his revenge, the proof of his forbearance, the undeniable evidence of his innocence; and, after a lowly disparagement of himself, appeals to God for judgment, for protection.

So lively and feeling oratory did Saul find in the lap of his garment, and the lips of David, that it is not in the power of his envy, or ill nature, to hold out any longer. "Is this thy voice, my son David? And Saul lift up his voice and wept, and said, Thou art more righteous than I." He whose harp was wont to quiet the frenzy of Saul, hath now by his words calmed his fury: so that now he sheds tears instead of blood, and confesses his own wrong, and David's integrity; and, as if he were now again entered into the bounds of Najoth in Ramah, he prays and prophesies good to him, whom he maliced for good: "The Lord render thee good for that thou hast done to me this day; for now, behold, I know that thou shalt be king."

There is no heart made of flesh, that some time or other relents not; even flint and marble will, in some weather, stand on drops. I cannot think these tears and protestations feigned. Doubtless Saul meant as he said, and passed through sensible fits of good and evil. Let no man think himself the better for good motions. The praise and benefit of those guests is not in the receipt but the retention.

Who, that had seen this meeting, could but have thought that all had been sure on David's side? What can secure us, if not tears, and prayers, and oaths? Doubtless David's men, which knew themselves obnoxious to laws and creditors, began to think of some new refuge, as making account this new-pieced league would be everlasting: they looked when Saul would take David home to the court, and dissolve his army, and recompense that unjust persecution with just honour; when, behold, in the loose, Saul goes home, but David and his men go up unto the hold. Wise David knows Saul not to be more kind than untrusty; and therefore had rather seek safety in his hold, than in the hold of a hollow and unsteady friendship. Here are good words, but no security; which therefore an experienced man gives the hearing, but stands the while upon his guard. No charity binds us to a trust of those whom we have found faithless. Credulity upon weak grounds, after palpable disappointments, is the daughter of folly. A man that is weatherwise, though he find an abatement of the storm, yet will not stir from under his shelter, while he sees it thick in the wind. Distrust is the just gain of unfaithfulness.

CONTEMPLATION II. — NABAL AND ABIGAIL.

IF innocency could have secured from Saul's malice, David had not been persecuted; and yet, under that wicked king, aged Samuel dies in his bed. That there might be no place for envy, the good prophet had retired himself to the schools. Yet he, that hated David for what he should be, did no less hate Samuel for what he had been. Even in the midst of Saul's malignity, there remained in his heart impressions of awfulness unto Samuel; he feared where he loved not. The restraint of God curbeth the rage of his most violent enemies, so as they cannot do their worst. As good husbands do not put all their corn to the oven, but save some for seed, so doth God ever in the worst of persecutions.

Samuel is dead, David banished, Saul tyrannizeth: Israel hath good cause to mourn. It is no marvel if this lamentation be universal: there is no Israelite that feeleth not the loss of a Samuel. A good prophet is the common treasure, wherein every gracious soul hath a share. That man hath a dry heart, which can part with God's prophet without tears.

Nabal was, according to his name, foolish, yet rich and mighty. Earthly possessions are not always accompanied with wit and grace. Even the line of faithful Caleb will afford an ill-conditioned Nabal. Virtue is not, like unto lands, inheritable. All that is traduced with the seed, is either evil or not good. Let no man brag with the Jews, that he hath Abraham to his father: God hath raised up of this stone a son to Caleb.

Abigail (which signifies her father's joy) had sorrow enough, to be matched with so unworthy an husband. If her father had meant she should have had joy in herself, or in her life, he had not disposed her to an husband, though rich, yet fond and wicked: it is like he married her to the wealth, not to the man. Many a child is cast away upon riches. Wealth, in our matches, should be as some grains or scruples in the balance, superadded to the gold of virtuous qualities, to weigh down the scales: when it is made the substance of the weight, and good qualities the appendance, there is but one earth poised with another; which, wheresoever it is done, it is a wonder if either the children prove not the parents' sorrow, or the parents theirs.

Nabal's sheep-shearing was famous: three thousand fleeces must needs require many hands; neither is any thing more plentiful, commonly, than a churl's feast. What a world was this, that the noble champion and rescuer of Israel, God's anointed, is driven to send to a base carle for victuals! It is no measuring of men by the depth of the purse, by outward prosperity. Servants are ofttimes set on horseback, while princes go on foot. Our estimation must be led by their inward worth, which is not alterable by time, nor diminished with external conditions.

One rag of a David is more worth than

the wardrobes of a thousand Nabals. Even the best deservings may want. No man should be contemned for his necessity; perhaps he may be so much richer in grace, as he is poorer in estate: neither hath violence or casualty more impoverished a David, than his poverty hath enriched him. He, whose folly hath made himself miserable, is justly rewarded with neglect; but he that suffers for good, deserves so much more honour from others, as his distress is more. Our compassion or respect must be ruled according to the cause of another's misery.

One good turn requires another. In some cases, not hurting is meritorious. He that should examine the qualities of David's followers, must needs grant it worthy of a fee, that Nabal's flocks lay untouched in Carmel; but more, that David's soldiers were Nabal's shepherds; yea, the keepers of his shepherds gave them a just interest in that sheep-shearing feast; justly should they have been set at the upper end of the table. That Nabal's sheep were safe, he might thank his shepherds; that his shepherds were safe, he might thank David's soldiers. It is no small benefit that we receive in a safe protection: well may we think our substance due, where we owe ourselves. Yet this churlish Nabal doth not only give nothing to David's messengers, but, which is worse than good words, ill words: "Who is David, or who is the son of Jesse? There be many servants now-a-days that break away from their masters." David asked him bread, he giveth him stones. All Israel knew and honoured their deliverer; yet this clown, to save his victuals, will needs make him a man either of no merits or ill, either an obscure man or a fugitive. Nothing is more cheap than good words: these Nabal might have given, and been never the poorer. If he had been resolved to shut his hands, in a fear of Saul's revenge, he might have so tempered his denial, that the repulse might have been free from offence; but now his foul mouth doth not only deny, but revile. It should have been Nabal's glory, that his tribe yielded such a successor to the throne of Israel: now, in all likelihood, his envy stirs him up to disgrace that man who surpassed him in honour and virtue, more than he was surpassed by him in wealth and ease. Many a one speaks fair, that means ill; but when the mouth speaks foul, it argues a corrupt heart. If, with St. James's verbal benefactors, we say only, Depart in peace, warm yourselves, fill your bellies, we shall answer for hypocritical uncharitableness; but if we rate and curse those needy souls whom we ought to relieve, we shall give a more fearful account of a savage cruelty, in trampling on those whom God hath humbled. If healing with good words be justly punishable, what torment is there for those that wound with evil?

David, which had all this while been in the school of patience, hath now his lesson to seek: he, who hath happily digested all the railings and persecutions of a wicked master, cannot put up this affront of a Nabal: nothing can assuage his choler, but blood. How subject are the best of God's saints to weak passions; and if we have the grace to ward an expected blow of temptation, how easily are we surprised with a sudden foil!

Wherefore serve these recorded weaknesses of holy men, but to strengthen us against the conscience of our infirmities? Not that we should take courage to imitate them in the evil whereunto they have been miscarried; but we should take heart to ourselves against the discouragement of our own evils.

The wisdom of God hath so contrived it, that commonly, in societies, good is mixed with evil: wicked Nabal hath in his house a wise and good servant, a prudent and worthy wife; that wise servant is careful to advertise his mistress of the danger; his prudent mistress is careful to prevent it.

The lives of all his family were now in hazard. She dares not commit this business to the fidelity of a messenger, but, forgetting her sex, puts herself into the errand. Her foot is not slow, her hand is not empty; according to the offence, she frames her satisfaction. Her husband refused to give, she brings a bountiful gift; her husband gave ill words, she sweetens them with a meek and humble deprecation; her husband could say, "Who is David?" she falls at his feet; her husband dismisses David's men empty, she brings her servants laden with provisions, as if it had been only meant to ease the repelled messengers of the carriage, not to scant them of the required benevolence: no wit, no art, could devise a more pithy and powerful oratory. As all satisfaction, so hers, begins with a confession, wherein she deeply blameth the folly of her husband; she could not have been a good wife, if she had not honoured her unworthy head. If a stranger should have termed him fool in her hearing, he could not have gone away in peace; now, to save his life, she is bold to acknowledge his folly. It is a good disparagement that preserveth. There is the same way to our peace in heaven. The only means to escape judgment, is to complain of our own vileness: she pleadeth her ignorance of the fact, and therein their freedom from the offence; she humbly craveth acceptation of her present, with pardon of the fault; she professeth David's honourable acts and merits; she foretells his future success and glory; she lays before him the happy peace of his soul, in refraining from innocent blood. David's breast, which could not, through the seeds of grace, grow to a stubbornness in ill resolutions, cannot but relent with these powerful and seasonable persuasions; and now, instead of revenge, he blesseth God for sending Abigail to meet him; he blesseth Abigail for her counsel; he blesseth the counsel for so wholesome efficacy; and now rejoiceth more in being overcome with a wise and gracious advice, than he would have rejoiced in a revengeful victory.

A good heart is easily stayed from sinning, and is glad when it finds occasion to be crossed in ill purposes. Those secret checks, which are raised within itself, do readily conspire with all outward retentives: it never yielded to a wicked motion, without much reluctation; and when it is overcome, it is but with half a consent: whereas perverse and obdurate sinners, by reason they take full delight in evil, and have already in their conceit swallowed the pleasure of sin, abide not to be resisted, running on headily in those wicked courses they have propounded, in spite of opposition; and, if they be forcibly stopped in their way, they grow sullen and mutinous. David had not only vowed, but deeply sworn, the death of Nabal, and all his family, to the very dog that lay at his door; yet now he praiseth God, that hath given the occasion and grace to violate it. Wicked vows are ill made, but worse kept. Our tongue cannot tie us to commit sin. Good men think themselves happy, that since they had not the grace to deny sin, yet they had not the opportunity to accomplish it. If Abigail had sat still at home, David had sinned, and she had died. Now her discreet admonition hath preserved her from the sword, and diverted him from bloodshed. And now, what thanks, what benedictions, hath she for this seasonable counsel? How should it encourage us to admonish our brethren, to see that, if we prevail, we have blessings from them; if we prevail not, we have yet blessings from God, and thanks of our own hearts!

How near was Nabal to a mischief, and perceives it not! David was coming to the foot of the hill to cut his throat, while he was feasting in his house without fear. Little do sinners know how near their jollity is to perdition. Many times judgment is at the threshold, while drunkenness and surfeit are at the board. Had he been any other than a Nabal, he had not sat down to feast, till he had been sure of his peace with David. Either not to expect danger, or not to clear it, was sottish; so foolish are carnal men, that give themselves over to their pleasures, while there are deadly quarrels depending against them in heaven. There is nothing wherein wisdom is more seen, than in the temperate use of prosperity. A Nabal cannot abound but he must be drunk and surfeit. Excess is a true argument of folly. We use to say, that when drink is in, wit is out; but if wit were not out, drink would not be in.

It was no time to advise Nabal, while his reason was drowned in a deluge of wine. A beast, or a stone, is as capable of good counsel as a drunkard. O that the noblest creature should so far abase himself, as, for a little liquor, to lose the use of those faculties whereby he is a man! Those, that have to do with drink or frenzy, must be glad to watch times; so did Abigail, who, the next morning, presents to her husband the view of his faults, of his danger; he then sees how near he was to death, and felt it not. That worldly mind is so apprehensive of the death that should have been, as that he dies to think that he had like to have died. Who would think a man could be so affected with a danger past, and yet so senseless of a future, yea, imminent? He that was yesternight as a beast, is now as a stone: he was then overmerry, now dead and lumpish. Carnal hearts are ever in extremities: if they be once down, their dejection is desperate, because they have no inward comfort to mitigate their sorrow. What difference there was betwixt the dispositions of David and Nabal! How oft had David been in the valley of the shadow of death, and feared no evil! Nabal is but once put in mind of a death that might have been, and is stricken dead.

It is just with God, that they who live without grace, should die without comfort; neither can we expect better, while we go on in our sins. The speech of Abigail smote Nabal into a qualm: that tongue hath doubtless oft advised him well, and prevailed not; now it occasions his death, whose reformation it could not effect: she meant nothing but his amendment; God meant to make that loving instrument the means of his revenge. She speaks, and God strikes; and within ten days, that swoon ends in death. And now Nabal pays dear for his uncharitable reproach, for his riotous excess. That God, which would not suffer David to right himself by his own sword, takes the quarrel of his servant into his own hand: David hath now his ends without sin, rejoicing in the just executions of God, who would neither suffer him to sin in revenging, nor suffer his adversaries to sin unrevenged.

Our loving God is more angry with the wrongs done to his servants than themselves can be, and knows how to punish that justly, which we could not undertake without wronging God more than men have wronged us. He that saith, "Vengeance is mine, I will repay," repays ofttimes when we have forgiven, when we have forgotten; and calls to reckoning after our discharges. It is dangerous offending any favourite of him whose displeasure and revenge is everlasting.

How far God looks beyond our purposes! Abigail came only to plead for an ill husband, and now God makes this journey a preparation for a better: so that, in one act, she preserved an ill husband, and won a good one for the future. David well remembers her comely person, her wise speeches, her graceful carriage; and now, when modesty found it seasonable, he sends to sue her who had been his suppliant. She entreated for her husband; David treats with her for his wife. Her request was to escape his sword; he wisheth her to his bed. It was a fair suit to change a David for a Nabal; to become David's queen, instead of Nabal's drudge. She that learned humility under so hard a tutor, abaseth herself no less when David offers to advance her: "Let thine handmaid be a servant, to wash the feet of the servants of my lord." None are so fit to be great, as those that can stoop lowest. How could David be more happy in a wife? he finds at once piety, wisdom, humility, faithfulness, wealth, beauty. How could Abigail be more happy in a husband, than in the prophet, the champion, the anointed of God? Those marriages are well made, wherein virtues are matched, and happiness is mutual.

CONTEMPLATION III.—DAVID AND ACHISH.

Good motions that fall into wicked hearts are like some sparks that fall from the flint and steel into wet tinder, lightsome for the time, but soon out. After Saul's tears and protestations, yet he is now again in the wilderness, with three thousand men, to hunt after innocent David. How invincible is the charity and loyalty of an honest heart! The same hand that spared Saul in the cave, spares him sleeping in the field: the same hand that cut away the lap of his master's garment, carries away his spear; that spear, which might as well have carried away the life of the owner, is only borne away for the proof of the fidelity of the bearer. Still Saul is strong, but David victorious, and triumphs over the malice of his persecutor: yet still the victor flieth from him whom he hath overcome. A man that sees how far Saul was transported with his rancorous envy, cannot but say, that he was never more mad than when he was sober. For, even after he had said, "Blessed art thou, my son David, thou shalt do great things, and also prevail;" yet still he pursues him whom he grants assured to prevail. What is this, but to resolve to lose his labour in sinning, and in spite of himself to offend? How shameful is our inequality of disposition to good! We know we cannot miss of the reward of well-doing, and yet do it not. While wicked men cast away their endeavours upon evil projects, whereof they are sure to fail, sin blinds the eyes and hardens the heart, and thrusts men into wilful mischiefs, however dangerous, however impossible, and never leaves them till it have brought them to utter confusion.

The over-long continuance of a temptation may easily weary the best patience, and may attain that by protraction which it could never do by violence. David himself at last begins to bend under this trial, and resolves so to fly from Saul, as he runs from the church of God; and, while he will avoid the malice of his master, joins himself with God's enemies. The greatest saints upon earth are not always upon the same pitch of spiritual strength: he that sometimes said, "I will not be afraid of ten thousands," now says, "I shall perish one day by the hand of Saul." He had wont to consult with God; now he says thus in his own heart. How many evident experiments had David of God's deliverances! how certain and clear predictions of his future kingdom! how infallible an earnest was the holy oil wherewith he was anointed to the crown of Israel! And yet David said in his heart, "I shall now perish one day by the hand of Saul." The best faith is but like the twilight, mixed with some degrees of darkness and infidelity. We do utterly misreckon the greatest earthly holiness, if we exempt it from infirmities. It is not long since David told Saul, that those wicked enemies of his, which cast

DAVID AND ACHISH.

him out from abiding in the inheritance of the Lord, did as good bid him, Go serve other gods; yet now is he gone from the inheritance of God into the land of the Philistines. That Saul might seek him no more, he hides himself out of the list of the church, where a good man would not look for him. Once before had David fled to this Achish, when he was glad to scrabble on the doors, and let his spittle fall upon his beard, in a semblance of madness, that he might escape: yet now, in 'a semblance of friendship, is he returned to save that life which he was in danger to have lost in Israel. Goliah, the champion of the Philistines, whom David slew, was of Gath: yet David dwells with Achish, king of the Philistines, in Gath; even amongst them whose foreskins he had presented to Saul, by two hundreds at once, doth David choose to reside for safety. Howsoever it was weakness in David, thus, by his league of amity, to strengthen the enemies of God; yet doth not God take advantage of it for his overthrow, but gives him protection even where his presence offended, and gives him favour where himself bore just hatred. O the infinite patience and mercy of our God, who doth good to us for our evil, and, in the very act of our provocation, upholdeth, yea blesseth us with preservation!

Could Saul have rightly considered it, he had found it no small loss and impairing to his kingdom, that so valiant a captain, attended with six hundred able soldiers and their families, should forsake his land, and join with his enemies: yet he is not quiet till he have abandoned his own strength. The world hath none so great an enemy to a wicked man as himself: his hands cannot be held from his own mischief: he will needs make his friends enemies, his enemies victors, himself miserable.

David was too wise to cast himself into the hands of a Philistine king, without assurance: what assurance could he have but promises? Those David had from Saul abundantly, and trusted them not: he dares trust the fidelity of a pagan; he dares not trust the vows of a king of Israel. There may be fidelity without the church, and falsehood within. It need not be any news to find some Turks true, and some Christians faithless.

Even unwise men are taught by experience: how much more they who have wit to learn without it! David had well found what it was to live in a court; he, therefore, whom envy drove from the court of Israel, voluntarily declines the Philistine court, and sues for a country habitation.

It had not been possible for so noted a stranger, after so much Philistine bloodshed, to live long in such an eminency amongst the press of those, whose sons, or brothers, or fathers, or allies, he had slaughtered, without some perilous machination of his ruin; therefore he makes suit for an early remove: "For why should thy servant dwell in the chief city of the kingdom with thee?" Those that would stand sure, must not affect too much height, or conspicuity: the tall cedars are most subject to winds and lightnings, while the shrubs of the valleys stand unmoved. Much greatness doth but make a fairer mark for evil. There is true firmness and safety in mediocrity.

How rarely is it seen that a man loseth by his modesty! The change fell out well to David, of Ziklag for Gath: now he hath a city of his own; all Israel, where he was anointed, afforded him not so much possession. Now the city, which was anciently assigned to Judah, returns to the just owner, and is, by this means, entailed to the crown of David's successors. Besides that, now might David live out of the sight and hearing of the Philistine idolatries, and enjoy God no less in the walls of a Philistine city than in an Israelitish wilderness: withal, a happy opportunity was now opened to his friends of Israel to resort unto his aid: the heads of the thousands that were of Manasseh, and many valiant captains of the other tribes, fell daily to him, and raised his six hundred followers to an army like the host of God. The deserts of Israel could never have yielded David so great an advantage. That God, whose the earth is, makes room for his own everywhere, and ofttimes provideth them a foreign home more kindly than the native. It is no matter for change of our soil, so we change not our God: if we can everywhere acknowledge him, he will nowhere be wanting to us.

It was not for God's champion to be idle: no sooner is he free from Saul's sword, than he begins an offensive war against the Amalekites, Gerizites, Geshurites; he knew these nations branded by God to destruction, neither could his increasing army be maintained with a little; by one act therefore he both revenges for God, and provides for his host. Had it not been for that old quarrel, which God had with this people, David could not be excused for a bloody cruelty, in killing whole countries, only for the benefit of the spoil; now his soldiers were at once God's executioners, and their own foragers. The intervention of a command from the Almighty alters the state of any act, and makes that worthy of praise, which else were no better than damnable. It is now justice, which were otherwise murder. The will of God is the rule of good: what need we inquire into other reasons of any act or determination, when we hear it comes from heaven?

How many hundred years had this brood of Canaanites lived securely in their country, since God commanded them to be rooted out, and now promised themselves the certainest peace! The Philistines were their friends, if not their lords: the Israelites had their hands full, neither did they know any grudge betwixt them and their neighbours, when suddenly the sword of David cuts them off, and leaves none alive to tell the news.

There is no safety in protraction: with men, delay causeth forgetfulness, or abates the force of anger, as all violent motions are weakest at the furthest; but with Him, to whom all times are present, what can be gained by prorogation? Alas! what can it avail any of the cursed seed of Canaan, that they have made a truce with heaven, and a league with hell? Their day is coming, and is not the further off, because they expect it not.

Miserable were the straits of David, while he was driven not only to maintain his army by spoil, but to colour his spoil by a sinful dissimulation: he tells Achish, that he had been roving against the south of Judah, and the south of the Jerahmeelites, and the south of the Kenites, either falsely or doubtfully, so as he meant to deceive him under whom he lived, and by whom he was trusted. If Achish were a Philistine, yet he was David's friend, yea his patron; and if he had been neither, it had not become David to be false. The infirmities of God's children never appear but in their extremities. It is hard for the best man to say how far he will be tempted. If a man will put himself among Philistines, he cannot promise to come forth innocent.

How easily do we believe that which we wish! The more credit Achish gives unto David, the more sin it was to deceive him. And now the conceit of this engagement procures him a further service. The Philistines are assembled to fight with Israel; Achish dares trust David on his side, yea, to keep his head for ever; neither can David do any less than promise his aid against his own flesh. Never was David, in all his life, driven to so hard an exigent; never was he so extremely perplexed: for what should he do now? To fight with Achish, he was tied by promise, by merit; not to fight against Israel, he was tied by his calling, by his unction: not to fight for Achish were to be unthankful; to fight against Israel, were to be unnatural. O what an inward battle must David needs have in his breast, when he thinks of this battle of Israel and the Philistines! How doth he wish now, that he had rather stood to the hazard of Saul's persecution, than to have put himself upon the favour of Achish: he must fight on one side, and on whether side soever he should fight, he could not avoid to be treacherous; a condition worse than death to an honest heart. Which way he would have resolved, if it had come to the execution, who can know, since himself was doubtful? Either course had been no better than desperate. How could the Israelites ever have received him for their king, who, in the open field, had fought against them? And, contrarily, if he would have fought against his friend for his enemy, against Achish for Saul, he was now environed with jealous Philistines, and might rather look for the punishment of his treason, than the glory of a victory.

His heart had led him into these straits; the Lord finds a way to lead him out: the suggestions of his enemies do herein befriend him; the princes of the Philistines, whether of envy or suspicion, plead for David's dismission: "Send this fellow back, that he may go again to his place which thou hast appointed him; and let him not go down to the battle, lest he be an adversary to us." No advocate could have said more; himself durst not have said so much. O the wisdom and goodness of our God, that can raise up an adversary to deliver out of those evils, which our friends cannot! that, by the sword of an enemy, can let out that apostume, which no physician could tell how to cure! It would be wide with us sometimes, if it were not for others' malice.

There could not be a more just question, than this of the Philistine princes: "What do these Hebrews here?" An Israelite is out of his element, when he is in an army of Philistines. The true servants of God are in their due places, when they are in opposition to his enemies. Profession of hostility becomes them better than leagues of amity.

Yet Achish likes David's conversation and presence so well, that he professeth himself pleased with him, as with an angel of God. How strange it is to hear, that a Philistine should delight in that holy man whom an Israelite abhors, and should be loath to be quit of David whom Saul hath expelled! Terms of civility are equally open to all religions, to all professions: the common graces of God's children are able to attract love from the most obstinate enemies of goodness: If we affect them for by-respects of valour, wisdom, discourse, wit, it is their praise, not ours; but if for divine grace and religion, it is our praise with theirs.

Such now was David's condition, that he must plead for that he feared, and argue against that which he desired: "What have I done, and what hast thou found in thy servant, that I may not go and fight against the enemies of my lord the king?" Never any news could be more cordial to him than this of his dismission; yet must he seem to strive against it, with an importunate profession of his forwardness to that act which he most detested.

One degree of dissimulation draws on another; those which have once given way to a faulty course, cannot easily either stop or turn back, but are, in a sort, forced to second their ill beginnings with worse proceedings. It is a dangerous and miserable thing to cast ourselves into those actions, which draw with them a necessity either of offending or miscarriage.

CONTEMPLATION IV.—SAUL AND THE WITCH OF ENDOR.

Even the worst men may sometimes make head against some sins. Saul hath expelled the sorcerers out of the land of Israel, and hath forbidden magic upon pain of death. He that had no care to expel Satan out of his own heart, yet will seem to drive him out of his kingdom. That we see wicked men oppose themselves to some sins, there is neither marvel nor comfort in it. No doubt Satan made sport at this edict of Saul: what cares he to be banished in sorcery, while he is entertained in malice? He knew and found Saul his, while he resisted; and smiled to yield thus far unto his vassal. If we quit not all sins, he will be content we should either abandon or persecute some.

Where there is no place for holy fear, there will be place for the servile. The graceless heart of Saul was astonished at the Philistines; yet was never moved at the frowns of that God whose anger sent them, nor of those sins of his which procured them. Those that cannot fear for love, shall tremble for fear; and how much better is awe than terror, prevention than confusion! There is nothing more lamentable than to see a man laugh when he should fear: God shall laugh when such a one's fear cometh.

Extremity of distress will send even the profanest man to God; likeas the drowning man reacheth out his hand to that bough, which he contemned while he stood safe on the bank. Saul now asketh counsel of the Lord, whose prophet he hated, whose priests he slew, whose anointed he persecutes. Had Saul consulted with God when he should, this evil had not been; but now, if this evil had not been, he had not consulted with God: the thank of this act is due, not to him, but to his affliction. A forced piety is thankless and unprofitable; God will not answer him, neither by dreams, nor by Urim, nor by prophets. Why should God answer that man by dreams, who had resisted him waking? Why should he answer him by Urim, that had slain his priests? Why should he answer him by prophets, who hated the Father of the prophets, and rebelled against the word of the prophets?

It is an unreasonable inequality to hope to find God at our command, when we would not be at his; to look that God should regard our voice in trouble, when we would not regard his in peace.

Unto what mad shifts are men driven by despair! If God will not answer, Satan shall. Saul said to his servants, "Seek me a woman that hath a familiar spirit." If Saul had not known this course devilish, why did he decree to banish it, to mulct it with death? yet now, against the stream of his conscience, he will seek to those whom he had condemned: there needs no other judge of Saul's act than himself; had he not before opposed this sin, he had not so heinously sinned in committing it. There cannot be a more fearful sign of a heart given up to a reprobate sense, than to cast itself wilfully into those sins which it hath proclaimed to detest. The declinations to evil are many times insensible; but when it breaks forth into such apparent effects, even other eyes may discern it. What was Saul the better to foreknow the issue of his approaching battle? If this consultation could have strengthened him against his enemies, or promoted his victory, there might have been some colour for so foul an act: now, what could he gain, but the satisfying of his bootless curiosity, in foreseeing that which he should not be able to avoid?

Foolish men give away their souls for nothing. The itch of impertinent and unprofitable knowledge hath been the hereditary disease of the sons of Adam and Eve. How many have perished, to know that which hath procured their perishing! How ambitious should we be to know these things, the knowledge whereof is eternal life!

Many a lewd office are they put to, who serve wicked masters. One while, Saul's servants are sent to kill innocent David; another while, to shed the blood of God's priests; and now they must go seek for a witch. It is no small happiness to attend them, from whom we may receive precepts and examples of virtue.

Had Saul been good, he had needed no disguise: honest actions never shame the doers. Now that he goeth about a sinful business, he changeth himself; he seeks the shelter of the night; he takes but two followers with him: it is true, that if Saul had come in the port of a king, the witch had as much dissembled her condition, as now he dissembleth his; yet it was not only desire to speed, but guiltiness, that thus altered his habit. Such is the power of conscience, that even those who are most affected to evil, yet are ashamed to be thought such as they desire to be.

Saul needed another face to fit that tongue, which should say, "Conjure to me by the familiar spirit, and bring me up whom I shall name unto thee." An obdurate heart can give way to any thing.

Notwithstanding the peremptory edict of Saul, there are still witches in Israel. Neither good laws, nor careful executions, can purge the church from malefactors; there will still be some that will jeopard their heads upon the grossest sins. No garden can be so curiously tended, that there should not be one weed left in it. Yet so far can good statutes, and due inflictions of punishment upon offenders, prevail, that mischievous persons are glad to pull in their heads, and dare not do ill, but in disguise and darkness. It is no small advantage of justice that it affrights sin, if it cannot be expelled; as, contrarily, woful is the condition of that place, where is a public profession of wickedness.

The witch was no less crafty than wicked: she had before, as is like, bribed officers to escape indictment, to lurk in secrecy; and now she will not work her feats without security. Her suspicion projects the worst: "Wherefore seekest thou to take me in a snare, to cause me to die?" O vain sorceress, that could be wary to avoid the punishment of Saul, careless to avoid the judgment of God! Could we forethink what our sin would cost us, we durst not but be innocent. This is a good and seasonable answer for us to make unto Satan when he solicits us to evil: "Wherefore seekest thou to take me in a snare, to cause me to die?" Nothing is more sure than this intention in the tempter, than this event in the issue. O that we could but so much fear the eternal pains, as we do the temporary; and be but so careful to save our souls from torment, as our bodies!

No sooner hath Saul sworn her safety, than she addresseth herself to her sorcery: hope of impunity draws on sin with boldness. Were it not for the delusions of false promises, Satan should have no clients. Could Saul be so ignorant as to think that magic had power over God's deceased saints, to raise them up, yea, to call them down from their rest? Time was, when Saul was among the prophets. And yet now, that he is the impure lodge of devils, how senseless he is to say, "Bring me up Samuel!" It is no rare thing to lose even our wit and judgment, together with graces: how justly are they given to sottishness, that have given themselves over to sin!

The sorceress, it seems, exercising her conjurations in a room apart, is informed by her familiar, who it was that set her on work; she can therefore find time, in the midst of her exorcisms, to bind the assurance of her own safety by expostulation: "She cried with a loud voice, why hast thou deceived me? for thou art Saul." The very name of Saul was an accusation: yet is he so far from striking his breast, that, doubting lest this fear of the witch should interrupt the desired work, he encourages her whom he should have condemned: "Be not afraid;" he that had more cause to fear, for his own sake, in an expectation of just judgment, cheers up her that feared nothing but himself. How ill doth it become us to give that counsel to others, whereof we have more need and use in our own persons!

As one that had more care to satisfy his own curiosity, than her suspicion, he asks, "What sawest thou?" Who would not have looked, that Saul's hair should have started on his head, to hear of a spirit raised? His sin hath so hardened him, that he rather pleases himself in that which hath nothing in it but horror: so far is Satan content to descend to the service of his servants, that he will approve his feigned obedience to their very outward senses: what form is so glorious, that he either cannot or dare not undertake? Here gods ascend out of the earth; elsewhere Satan transforms him into an angel of light: what wonder is it, that his wicked instruments appear like saints in their hypocritical dissimulation! If we will be judging by the appearance, we shall be sure to err. No eye could distinguish betwixt the true Samuel and a false spirit. Saul, who was well worthy to be deceived, seeing those grey hairs, and that mantle, inclines himself to the ground, and bows himself. He that would not worship God in Samuel alive, now worships Samuel in Satan; and no marvel: Satan was now become his refuge instead of God; his Urim was darkness, his prophet a ghost. Every one that consults with Satan worships him, though he bow not, neither doth that evil spirit desire any other reverence, than to be sought unto.

How cunningly doth Satan resemble not only the habit and gesture, but the language of Samuel! "Wherefore hast thou disquieted me, and wherefore dost thou ask of me, seeing the Lord is gone from thee, and is thine enemy?" Nothing is more pleasing to that evil one, than to be solicited; yet, in the person of Samuel, he can say, "Why hast thou disquieted me?" Had not the Lord been gone from Saul, he had never come to the devilish oracle of Endor; and yet the counterfeiting spirit can say, "Why dost thou ask of me, seeing the Lord is gone from thee?" Satan cares not how little he is known to be himself: he loves to pass under any form, rather than his own.

The more holy the person is, the more carefully doth Satan act him, that by his stale he may ensnare us. In every motion, it is good to try the spirits, whether they be of God. Good words are no means to distinguish a prophet from a devil. Samuel himself, while he was alive, could not have spoken more gravely, more severely, more divinely, than this evil ghost: "For the Lord will rend thy kingdom out of thy hand, and give it to thy neighbour David, because thou obeyedst not the voice of the Lord, nor executedst his fierce wrath upon the Amalekites, therefore hath the Lord done this unto thee this day." When the devil himself puts on gravity and religion, who can marvel at the hypocrisy of men? Well may lewd men be good preachers, when Satan himself can play the prophet. Where are those ignorants, that think charitably of charms and spells, because they find nothing in them but good words? What prophet could speak better words than this devil in Samuel's mantle? Neither is there at any time so much danger of that evil spirit, as when he speaks best.

I could wonder to hear Satan preach thus prophetically, if I did not know, that as he was once a good angel, so he can still act what he was. While Saul was in consultation of sparing Agag, we shall never find that Satan would lay any block in his way: yea, then he was a prompt orator to induce him into that sin; now that it is past and gone, he can lade Saul with fearful denunciations of judgment. Till we have sinned, Satan is a parasite; when we have sinned, he is a tyrant. What cares he to flatter any more, when he hath what he would? Now, his only work is to terrify and confound, that he may enjoy what he hath won: how much better it is serving that master, who, when we are most dejected with the conscience of evil, heartens us with inward comfort, and speaks peace to the soul in the midst of tumult!

CONTEMPLATION V. — ZIKLAG SPOILED AND REVENGED.

HAD not the king of the Philistines sent David away early, his wives and his people and substance, which he left at Ziklag, had been utterly lost: now Achish did not more pleasure David in his entertainment, than in his dismission. Saul was not David's enemy more in the persecution of his person, than in the forbearance of God's enemies: behold, thus late doth David feel the smart of Saul's sin in sparing the Amalekites, who, if God's sentence had been duly executed, had not now survived, to annoy this parcel of Israel.

As in spiritual respects our sins are always hurtful to ourselves, so in temporal, ofttimes prejudicial to posterity. A wicked man deserves ill of those he never lived to see.

I cannot marvel at the Amalekites' assault made upon the Israelites of Ziklag; I cannot but marvel at their clemency: how just was it, that while David would give aid to the enemies of the church against Israel, the enemies of the church should rise against David, in his peculiar charge of Israel? But while David's roving against the Amalekites, not many days before, left neither man nor woman alive, how strange is it, that the Amalekites, invading and surprising Ziklag, in revenge, kill neither man nor woman! Shall we say that mercy is fled from the breasts of Israelites, and rests in heathens? Or shall we rather ascribe this to the gracious restraint of God, who, having designed Amalek to the slaughter of Israel, and not Israel to the slaughter of Amalek, moved the hands of Israel, and held the hands of Amalek? This was that alone which made the heathens take up with an unbloody revenge, burning only the walls, and leading away the persons. Israel crossed the revealed will of God in sparing

Amalek; Amalek fulfils the secret will of God in sparing Israel.

It was still the lot of Amalek to take Israel at all advantages. Upon their first coming out of Egypt, when they were weary, weak, and unarmed, then did Amalek assault them: and now, when one part of Israel was in the field against the Philistines, another was gone with the Philistines against Israel, the Amalekites set upon the coasts of both, and go away loaded with the spoil. No other is to be expected of our spiritual adversaries, who are ever readiest to assail, when we are the unreadiest to defend.

It was a woful spectacle for David and his soldiers, upon their return, to find ruins and ashes instead of houses; and instead of their families, solitude: their city was vanished into smoke, their households into captivity; neither could they know whom to accuse, or where to inquire for redress. While they made account that their home should recompense their tedious journey with comfort, the miserable desolation of their home doubles the discomfort of their journey: what remained there but tears and lamentations? They lifted up their voices, and wept till they could weep no more. Here was plenty of nothing but misery and sorrow. The heart of every Israelite was brimful of grief: David's ran over; for besides that his cross was the same with theirs, all theirs was his alone: each man looked on his fellow as a partner of affliction; but every one looked upon David as the cause of all their affliction; and, as common displeasure is never but fruitful of revenge, they all agree to stone him as the author of their undoing, whom they followed all this while as the hopeful means of their advancement.

Now David's loss is his least grief; neither, as if every thing had conspired to torment him, can he look besides the aggravation of his sorrow and danger. Saul and his soldiers had hunted him out of Israel; the Philistine courtiers had hunted him from the favour of Achish; the Amalekites spoiled him in Ziklag: yet all these are easy adversaries in comparison of his own; his own followers are so far from pitying his participation of the loss, that they are ready to kill him, because they are miserable with him. O the many and grievous perplexities of the man after God's own heart! If all his train had joined their best helps for the mitigation of his grief, their cordials had been too weak; but now the vexation that arises from their fury and malice, drowneth the sense of their loss, and were enough to distract the most resolute heart. Why should it be strange to us that we meet with hard trials, when we see the dear anointed of God thus plunged in evils?

What should the distressed son of Jesse now do? whither should he think to turn him? To go back to Israel he durst not; to go to Achish he might not; to abide among those waste heaps he could not; or, if there might have been harbour in those burnt walls, yet there could have been no safety to remain with those mutinous spirits. But David comforted himself in the Lord his God. O happy and sure refuge of a faithful soul! The earth yielded him nothing but matter of disconsolation and heaviness; he lifts his eyes above the hills, whence cometh his salvation. It is no marvel that God remembereth David in all his troubles, since David in all his troubles did thus remember his God: he knew, that though no mortal eye of reason or sense could discern any evasion from these intricate evils, yet that the eye of Divine Providence had descried it long before; and that, though no human power could make way for his safety, yet that the over-ruling hand of his God could do it with ease. His experience had assured him of the fidelity of his guardian in heaven; and therefore he comforted himself in the Lord his God.

In vain is comfort expected from God, if we consult not with him. Abiathar the priest is called for: David was not in the court of Achish, without the priest by his side; nor the priest without the ephod: had these been left behind in Ziklag, they had been miscarried with the rest, and David had now been hopeless. How well it succeeds to the great, when they take God with them in his ministers, in his ordinances! As, contrarily, when these are laid by, as superfluous, there can be nothing but uncertainty of success, or certainty of mischief. The presence of the priest and ephod would have little availed him, without their use: by them he asks counsel of the Lord in these straits. The mouth and ears of God, which were shut unto Saul, are open unto David: no sooner can he ask, than he receives answer; and the answer that he receives is full of courage and comfort: "Follow, for thou shalt surely overtake them, and recover all." That God of truth never disappointed any man's trust. David now finds, that the eye, which waited upon God, was not sent away weeping.

David, therefore, and his men, are now upon their march after the Amalekites. It is no lingering when God bids us go. They who had promised rest to their weary limbs, after their return from Achish, in their harbour of Ziklag, are glad to forget their hopes, and to put their stiff joints upon a new task of motion. It is no marvel if two hundred of them were so over-tired with their former toil, that they were not able to pass over the river Besor. David was a true type of Christ: we follow him in these holy wars, against the spiritual Amalekites. All of us are not of an equal strength: some are carried by the vigour of their faith through all difficulties; others, after long pressure, are ready to languish in the way. Our leader is not more strong than pitiful; neither doth he scornfully cashier those whose desires are hearty, while their abilities are unanswerable. How much more should our charity pardon the infirmities of our brethren, and allow them to sit by the stuff, who cannot endure the march?

The same Providence which appointed David to follow the Amalekites, had also ordered an Egyptian to be cast behind them. This cast servant, whom his cruel master had left to faintness and famine, shall be used as the means of the recovery of the Israelites' loss, and of the revenge of the Amalekites. Had not his master neglected him, all these rovers of Amalek had gone away with their life and booty: it is not safe to despise the meanest vassal upon earth. There is a mercy and care due to the most despicable piece of all humanity, wherein we cannot be wanting without the offence, without the punishment of God.

Charity distinguisheth an Israelite from an Amalekite. David's followers are strangers to this Egyptian; an Amalekite was his master: his master leaves him to die in the field of sickness and hunger; these strangers relieved him: and ere they know whether they might, by him, receive any light in their pursuit, they refresh his dying spirits with bread and water, with figs and raisins; neither can the haste of their way be any hinderance to their compassion. He hath no Israelitish blood in him, that is utterly merciless: perhaps yet David's followers might also, in the hope of some intelligence, show kindness to this forlorn Egyptian. Worldly wisdom teacheth us to sow small courtesies, where we may reap large harvests of recompense. No sooner are his spirits recalled, than he requites his food with information. I cannot blame the Egyptian, that he was so easily induced to descry these unkind Amalekites to merciful Israelites; those that gave him over unto death, to the restorers of his life; much less that, ere he would descry them, he requires an oath of security from so bad a master. Well doth he match death with such a servitude! Wonderful is the providence of God, even over those that are not in the nearest bonds his own! Three days and three nights had this poor Egyptian slave lain sick and hunger-starved in the fields, and looks for nothing but death, when God sends him succour from the hands of those Israelites whom he had helped to spoil; though not so much for his sake, as for Israel's, is this heathenish straggler preserved.

It pleases God to extend his common favours to all his creatures; but, in miraculous preservations, he hath still wont to have respect to his own. By this means therefore are the Israelites brought to the sight of their late spoilers, whom they find scattered abroad, upon all the earth, eating and drinking, and dancing in triumph, for the great prey they had taken.

It was three days at least since this gainful foraging of Amalek: and now, seeing no fear of any pursuer, and promising themselves safety, in so great and untraced a distance, they make themselves merry with so rich and easy a victory; and now suddenly, when they began to think of enjoying the booty and wealth they had gotten, the sword of David was upon their throats. Destruction is never nearer, than when security hath chased away fear. With how sad faces and hearts had the wives of David, and the other captives of Israel, looked upon the triumphant revels of Amalek! and what a change do we think appeared in them, when they saw their happy and valiant rescuers flying in upon their insolent victors, and making the death of the Amalekites the ransom of their captivity! They mourned even now at the dances of Amalek; now in the shrieks and death of Amalek, they shout and rejoice. The mercy of our God forgets not to interchange our sorrows with joy, and the joy of the wicked with sorrow.

The Amalekites have paid a dear loan for the goods of Israel, which they now restore with their own lives: and now their spoil hath made David richer than he expected: that booty, which they had swept from all other parts, accrued to him.

Those Israelites, that could not go on to fight for their share, are come to meet their brethren with gratulation. How partial are we wont to be to our own causes! Even very Israelites will be ready to fall out for matter of profit. Where self-love hath bred a quarrel, every man is subject to flatter his own case. It seemed plausible, and but just to the actors in this rescue, that those which had taken no part in the pain and hazard of the journey, should receive no part of the commodity. It was favour enough for them to recover their wives and children, though they shared not in the goods. Wise and holy David, whose praise was no less to overcome his own in time of peace, than his enemies in war, calls his contending followers from law to equity, and so orders the matter, that, since the plaintiffs were detained, not by will, but by necessity, and since their forced stay was useful in guarding the stuff, they should partake equally of the prey with their fellows : a sentence well beseeming the justice of God's anointed. Those that represent God upon earth, should resemble him in their proceedings. It is the just mercy of our God to measure us by our wills, not by our abilities ; to recompense us graciously, according to the truth of our desires and endeavours ; and to account that performed by us, which he only letteth us from performing. It were wide with us, if sometimes purpose did not supply actions. While our heart faulteth not, we that, through spiritual sickness, are fain to bide by the stuff, shall share both in grace and glory with the victors.

CONTEMPLATION VI.—THE DEATH OF SAUL.

THE witch of Endor had half slain Saul before the battle : it is just that they who consult with devils should go away with discomfort. He hath eaten his last bread at the hand of a sorceress ; and now necessity draws him into that field, where he sees nothing but despair. Had not Saul believed the ill news of the counterfeit Samuel, he had not been struck down on the ground with words : now his belief made him desperate. Those actions, which are not sustained by hope, must needs languish, and are only promoted by outward compulsion : while the mind is uncertain of success, it relieves itself with the possibilities of good. In doubts there is a comfortable mixture ; but when it is assured of the worst event, it is utterly discouraged and dejected. It hath therefore pleased the wisdom of God to hide from wicked men his determination of their final estate, that the remainders of hope may hearten them to good.

In all likelihood, one self-same day saw David a victor over the Amalekites, and Saul discomfited by the Philistines : how should it be otherwise ? David consulted with God, and prevailed : Saul with the witch of Endor, and perisheth. The end is commonly answerable to the way : it is an idle injustice, when we do ill, to look to speed well. The slaughter of Saul and his sons was not in the first scene of this tragical field : that was rather reserved by God for the last act, that Saul's measure might be full. God is long ere he strikes, but when he doth, it is to purpose. First, Israel flies, and falls down wounded in mount Gilboa : they had their part in Saul's sin ; they were actors in David's persecution ; justly, therefore, do they suffer with him whom they had seconded in offence. As it is hard to be good under an evil prince, so it is as rare not to be enwrapped in his judgments. It was no small addition to the anguish of Saul's death, to see his sons dead, to see his people flying, and slain before him : they had sinned in their king, and in them is their king punished. The rest were not so worthy of pity ; but whose heart would it not touch to see Jonathan, the good son of a wicked father, involved in the common destruction ? Death is not partial : all dispositions, all merits, are alike to it. If valour, if holiness, if sincerity of heart, could have been any defence against mortality, Jonathan had survived. Now, by their wounds and death, no man can discern which is Jonathan : the soul only finds the difference which the body admitteth not. Death is the common gate both to heaven and hell ; we all pass that, ere our turning to either hand. The sword of the Philistines fetcheth Jonathan through it with his fellows ; no sooner is his foot over that threshold, than God conducteth him to glory. The best cannot be happy but through their dissolution ; now, therefore, hath Jonathan no cause of complaint : he is, by the rude and cruel hand of a Philistine, but removed to a better kingdom than he leaves to his brother ; and at once is his death both a temporal affliction to the son of Saul, and an entrance of glory to the friend of David.

The Philistine archers shot at random : God directs their arrows into the body of Saul. Lest the discomfiture of his people, and the slaughter of his sons, should not be grief enough to him, he feels himself wounded, and sees nothing before him but horror and death ; and now, as a man forsaken of all hopes, he begs of his armour-bearer that death's blow, which else he must, to the doubling of his indignation, receive from a Philistine. He begs this bloody favour of his servant, and is denied. Such an awfulness hath God placed in sovereignty, that no entreaty, no extremity, can move the hand against it. What metal are those men made of, that can suggest or resolve, and attempt the violation of majesty? Wicked men care more for the shame of the world than the danger of their souls. Desperate Saul will now supply his armour-bearer; and as a man that bore arms against himself, he falls upon his own sword. What if he had died by the weapon of a Philistine? so did his son Jonathan, and lost no glory: these conceits of disreputation prevail with carnal hearts above all spiritual respects. There is no greater murderer than vain-glory. Nothing more argues a heart void of grace, than to be transported by idle popularity into actions prejudicial to the soul.

Evil examples, especially of the great, never escape imitation: the armour-bearer of Saul follows his master, and dares do that to himself which to his king he durst not; as if their own swords had been more familiar executioners, they yielded unto them what they grudged to their pursuers. From the beginning was Saul ever his own enemy; neither did any hands hurt him but his own: and now his death is suitable to his life; his own hand pays him the reward of all his wickedness. The end of hypocrites and envious men is commonly fearful. Now is the blood of God's priests, which Saul shed, and of David, which he would have shed, required and requited. The evil spirit had said, the evening before, "To-morrow thou shalt be with me;" and now Saul hasteth to make the devil no liar: rather than fail, he gives himself his own mittimus. O the woful extremities of a despairing soul, plunging him ever into a greater mischief, to avoid the less! He might have been a patient in another's violence, and faultless; now, while he will needs act the Philistine's part upon himself, he lived and died a murderer: the case is deadly, when the prisoner breaks the jail, and will not stay for his delivery; and though we may not pass sentence upon such a soul, yet upon the fact we may: the soul may possibly repent in the parting; the act is heinous, and such as, without repentance, kills the soul.

It was the next day ere the Philistines knew how much they were victors; then, finding the dead corpse of Saul and his sons, they begin their triumphs. The head of king Saul is cut off in lieu of Goliah's, and now all their idol temples ring of their success. Foolish Philistines! if they had not been more beholden to Saul's sins than their gods, they had never carried away the honour of those trophies; instead of magnifying the justice of the true God, who punished Saul with deserved death, they magnify the power of the false. Superstition is extremely injurious to God: it is no better than theft to ascribe unto the second causes, that honour which is due unto the first; but to give God's glory to those things which neither act, nor are, it is the highest degree of spiritual robbery.

Saul was none of the best kings; yet so impatient are his subjects of the indignity offered to his dead corpse, that they will rather leave their own bones amongst the Philistines, than the carcase of Saul. Such a close relation there is betwixt a prince and subject, that the dishonour of either is inseparable from both. How willing should we be to hazard our bodies or substance for the vindication either of the person or name of a good king, while he lives to the benefit of our protection! It is an unjust ingratitude in those men which can endure the disgrace of them under whose shelter they live; but how unnatural is the villany of those miscreants that can be content to be actors in the capital wrongs offered to sovereign authority!

It were a wonder, if, after the death of a prince, there should want some pickthank to insinuate himself into his successor. An Amalekite young man rides post to Ziklag to find out David, whom even common rumour had notified for the anointed heir to the kingdom of Israel, to be the first messenger of that news, which he thought could be no other than acceptable, the death of Saul; and, that the tidings might be so much more meritorious, he adds to the report what he thinks might carry the greatest retribution. In hope of reward or honour, the man is content to belie himself to David: it was not the spear, but the sword of Saul, that was the instrument of his death; neither could this stranger find Saul, but dying, since the armour-bearer of Saul saw him dead ere he offered that violence to himself: the hand of this Amalekite, therefore, was not guilty; his tongue was. Had not this messenger measured David's foot by his own last, he had forborne this piece of the news, and not hoped to advantage himself by this falsehood. Now he thinks the tidings of a kingdom cannot but please; none but Saul and Jonathan stood in David's way: he cannot choose but like to hear of their removal, especially since Saul did so tyrannously persecute his innocence. If I shall only report the fact done by another, I shall go away with but the recompense of a lucky post; whereas, if I take upon me the action, I am the man to whom David is beholden for the kingdom; he cannot but honour and requite me as the author of his deliverance and happiness. Worldly minds think no man can be of any other than of their own diet; and because they find the respects of self-love and private profit so strongly prevailing with themselves, they cannot conceive how these should be capable of a repulse from others.

How much was this Amalekite mocked of his hopes! While he imagined that David would now triumph and feast in the assured expectation of the kingdom, and possession of the crown of Israel, he finds him rending his clothes, and wringing his hands, and weeping and mourning as if all his comfort had been dead with Saul and Jonathan: and yet perhaps he thought, this sorrow of David is but fashionable, such as great heirs make show of in the fatal day they have longed for: these tears will be soon dry; the sight of a crown will soon breed a succession of other passions. But this error is soon corrected; for when David had entertained this bearer with a sad fast all the day, he calls him forth in the evening to execution: "How, wast thou not afraid," saith he, "to put forth thy hand to destroy the anointed of the Lord?" Doubtless the Amalekite made many fair pleas for himself, out of the grounds of his own report. Alas! Saul was before fallen upon his own spear; it was but mercy to kill him that was half dead, that he might die the shorter: besides, his entreaty and importunate prayers moved me to hasten him through those painful gates of death: had I stricken him as an enemy, I had deserved the blow I had given; now I lent him the hand of a friend; why am I punished for obeying the voice of a king, and for perfecting what himself had begun, and could not finish? And if neither his own wound, nor mine, had despatched him, the Philistines were at his heels, ready to do this same act with insultation, which I did in favour; and if my hand had not prevented him, where had been the crown of Israel, which I now have here presented to thee? I could have delivered that to king Achish, and have been rewarded with honour: let me not die for an act well meant to thee, however construed by thee. But no pretence can make his own tale not deadly: " Thy blood be upon thine own head, for thine own mouth hath testified against thee, saying, I have slain the Lord's anointed." It is a just supposition, that every man is so great a favourer of himself, that he will not misreport his own actions, nor say the worst of himself. In matter of confession, men may, without injury, be taken at their words: if he did it, his fact was capital; if he did it not, his lie. It is pity any other recompense should befall those false flatterers, that can be content to father a sin to get thanks. Every drop of royal blood is sacred; for a man to say that he hath shed it, is mortal. O how far different spirits from this of David, are those men which suborn the death of princes, and celebrate and canonize the murderers! " Into their secret, let not my soul come; my glory, be not thou joined to their assembly."

CONTEMPLATION VII.—ABNER AND JOAB.

How merciful and seasonable are the provisions of God! Ziklag was now nothing but ruins and ashes: David might return to the soil where it stood, to the roofs and walls he could not; no sooner is he disappointed of that harbour, than God provides him cities of Hebron: Saul shall die to give him elbow-room. Now doth David find the comfort that his extremity sought in the Lord his God; now are his clouds for a time passed over, and the sun breaks gloriously forth: David shall reign after his sufferings. So shall we, if we endure to the end, find a crown of righteousness, which the Lord, the righteous Judge, shall give us at that day. But though David well knew that his head was long before anointed, and had heard Saul himself confidently avouching his succession, yet he will not stir from the heaps of Ziklag, till he has consulted with the Lord. It did not content him, that he had God's warrant for the kingdom, but he must have his instructions for the taking possession of it. How safe and happy is the man that is resolved to do nothing without God! Neither will generalities of direction be sufficient; even particular circumstances must look for a word; still is God a pillar of fire and cloud to the eye of every Israelite: neither may there be any motion or stay but from him; that action cannot but succeed, which proceeds upon so sure a warrant.

God sends him to Hebron, a city of Judah; neither will David go up thither alone, but he takes with him all his men, with their whole households: they shall take such part as himself; as they had shared with him in his misery, so they shall now

ABNER AND JOAB.

in his prosperity: neither doth he take advantage of their late mutiny, which was yet fresh and green, to cashier those unthankful and ungracious followers; but pardoning their secret rebellions, he makes them partakers of his good success. Thus doth our heavenly leader, whom David prefigured, take us to reign with him, who have suffered with him. Passing by our manifold infirmities, as if they had not been, he removeth us from the land of our banishment, and the ashes of our forlorn Ziklag, to the Hebron of our peace and glory: the expectation of this day must, as it did with David's soldiers, digest all our sorrows.

Never any calling of God was so conspicuous, as not to find some opposites. What Israelite did not know David appointed by God to the succession of the kingdom? Even the Amalekite could carry the crown to him as the true owner: yet there wants not an Abner to resist him, and the title of an Ishbosheth to colour his resistance. If any of Saul's house could have made challenge to the crown, it should have been Mephibosheth, the son of Jonathan, who, it seems, had too much of his father's blood to be a competitor with David: the question is not, who may claim the most right, but who may best serve the faction: neither was Ishbosheth any other than Abner's stale. Saul could not have a fitter courtier: whether in the imitation of his master's envy, or the ambition of ruling under a borrowed name, he strongly opposed David. There are those who strive against their own hearts, to make a side with whom conscience is oppressed by affection. An ill quarrel, once undertaken, shall be maintained, although with blood: now, not so much the blood of Saul, as the engagement of Abner, makes the war. The sons of Zeruiah stand fast to David. It is much how a man placeth his first interest: if Abner had been in Joab's room, when Saul's displeasure drove David from the court, or Joab in Abner's, these actions, these events, had been changed with the persons: it was the only happiness of Joab that he fell on the better side.

Both the commanders under David and Ishbosheth were equally cruel: both are so inured to blood, that they make but a sport of killing. Custom makes sin so familiar, that the horror of it is to some turned into pleasure. "Come, let the young men play before us." Abner is the challenger, and speeds thereafter; for though, in the matches of duel, both sides miscarried, yet, in the following conflict, Abner and his men are beaten. By the success of those single combats no man knows the better of the cause: both sides perish, to show how little God liked either the offer or the acceptation of such a trial; but when both did their best, God punisheth the wrong part with discomfiture.

O the misery of civil dissension! Israel and Judah were brethren; one carried the name of the father, the other of the son. Judah was but a branch of Israel; Israel was the root of Judah: yet Israel and Judah must fight, and kill each other, only upon the quarrel of an ill leader's ambition. The speed of Asahel was not greater than his courage. It was a mind fit for one of David's worthies, to strike at the head, to match himself with the best. He was both swift and strong; but " the race is not to the swift, nor the battle to the strong." If he had gone never so slowly, he might have overtaken death: now he runs to fetch it. So little lust had Abner to shed the blood of a son of Zeruiah, that he twice advises him to retreat from pursuing his own peril. Asahel's cause was so much better as Abner's success. Many a one miscarries in the rash prosecution of a good quarrel, when the abettors of the worst part go away with victory. Heat of zeal sometimes, in the indiscreet pursuit of a just adversary, proves mortal to the agent, prejudicial to the service.

Abner, while he kills, yet he flies; and runs away from his own death, while he inflicts it upon another. David's followers had the better of the field and day. The sun, as unwilling to see any more Israelitish blood shed by brethren, hath withdrawn himself: and now both parties, having got the advantage of a hill under them, have safe convenience of parley. Abner begins, and persuades Joab to surcease the fight: " Shall the sword devour for ever? Knowest thou not, that it will be bitterness in the end? How long shall it be ere thou bid the people return from following their brethren?" It was his fault that the sword devoured at all; and why was not the beginning of a civil war bitterness? why did he call forth the people to skirmish, and invite them to death? Had Abner been on the winning hand, this motion had been thank-worthy. It was a noble disposition in a victor, to call for a cessation of arms; whereas necessity wrings this suit from the over-mastered. There cannot be a greater praise to a valiant and wise commander, than a propension to all just terms of peace; for war, as it is sometimes necessary, so it is always evil; and if fighting have any other end proposed besides peace, it proves murder. Abner shall find himself no less overcome by Joab in clemency, than power: he says not, I will not so easily leave the advantage of my victory; since the dice of war run on my side, I will follow the chance of my good success: thou shouldest have considered of this before thy provocation; it is now too late to move unto forbearance. But, as a man that meant to approve himself equally free from cowardice in the beginning of the conflict, and from cruelty in the end, he professeth his forwardness to entertain any pretence of sheathing up the swords of Israel; and swears to Abner, that if it had not been for his proud irritation, the people had in the morning before ceased from that bloody pursuit of their brethren. As it becomes public persons to be lovers of peace, so they must show it upon all good occasions; letting pass no opportunity of making spare of blood.

Ishbosheth was, it seems, a man of no great spirits; for being no less than forty years old when his father went into his last field against the Philistines, he was content to stay at home. Abner hath put ambition into him, and hath easily raised him to the head of a faction, against the anointed prince of God's people. If this usurped crown of Saul's son had any worth or glory in it, he cannot but acknowledge to owe it all unto Abner; yet how forward is unthankful Ishbosheth to receive a false suggestion against his chief abettor! "Wherefore hast thou gone into my father's concubine?" He that made no conscience of an unjust claim to the crown, and a maintenance of it with blood, yet seems scrupulous of a less sin, that carried in it the colour of a disgrace: the touch of her, who had been honoured by his father's bed, seemed an intolerable presumption, and such as could not be severed from his own dishonour. Self-love sometimes borrows the face of honest zeal. Those who, out of true grounds, dislike sins, do hate them all indifferently, according to their heinousness; hypocrites are partial in their detestation, bewraying ever most bitterness against those offences, which may most prejudice their persons and reputations.

It is as dangerous as unjust for princes to give both their ears and their heart to misgrounded rumours of their innocent followers. This wrong hath stripped Ishbosheth of the kingdom. Abner, in the meantime, cannot be excused from a treacherous inconstancy: if Saul's son had no true title to the crown, why did he maintain it? if he had, why did he forsake the cause and person. Had Abner, out of remorse for furthering a false claim, taken off his hand, I know not wherein he could be blamed, except for not doing it sooner; but now to withdraw his professed allegiance, upon a private revenge, was to take a lewd leave of an ill action. If Ishbosheth were his lawful prince, no injury could warrant a revolt. Even betwixt private persons, a return of wrongs is both uncharitable and unjust, however this go current for the common justice of the world: how much more should we learn, from a supreme hand, to take hard measures with thanks! It had been Abner's duty to have given his king a peaceable and humble satisfaction, and not to fly out in a snuff: "If the spirit of the ruler rise up against thee, leave not thy place; for yielding pacifieth great offences." Now, his impatient falling, although to the right side, makes him no better than traitorously honest.

So soon as Abner hath entertained a resolution of his rebellion, he persuades the elders of Israel to accompany him in the change; and whence doth he fetch his main motive, but from the oracle of God? "The Lord hath spoken of David, saying, By the hand of my servant David will I save my people Israel out of the hand of the Philistines, and out of the hand of all their enemies." Abner knew this full well before, yet then was well content to smother a known truth for his own turn; and now, that the publication of it may serve for his advantage, he wins the heart of Israel, by showing God's charter for him whom he had so long opposed. Hypocrites make use of God for their own purposes, and care only to make divine authority a colour for their own designs. No man ever heard Abner godly till now; neither had be been so at this time, if he had not intended a revengeful departure from Ishbosheth. Nothing is more odious, than to make religion a stalking-horse to policy.

Who can but glorify God in his justice, when he sees the bitter end of this treacherous dissimulation? David may, upon considerations of state, entertain his new guest with a feast; and well might he seem to deserve a welcome, that undertakes to bring all Israel to the league and homage of David; but God never meant to use so unworthy means for so good a work. Joab returns from pursuing a troop, and finding Abner dismissed in peace, and expectation of a beneficial return, follows him; and, whether out of envy at a new rival of honour, or out of the revenge of Asahel, he repays him both dissimulation and death. God doth most justly by Joab, that which

Joab did for himself most unjustly. I know not, setting the quarrel aside, whether we can worthily blame Abner for the death of Asahel, who would needs, after fair warnings, run himself upon Abner's spear; yet this fact shall procure his payment for the worse. Now is Ishbosheth's wrong revenged by an enemy. We may not always measure the justice of God's proceedings by present occasions: he needs not make us acquainted, or ask us leave, when he will call for the arrearages of forgotten sins.

BOOK XV.

CONTEMPLATION I.— UZZAH, AND THE ARK REMOVED.

The house of Saul is quiet, the Philistines beaten: victory cannot end better than in devotion. David is no sooner settled in his house at Jerusalem, that he fetcheth God to be his guest there: the thousands of Israel go now, in a holy march, to bring up the ark of God to the place of his rest. The tumults of war afforded no opportunity of this service: only peace is a friend to religion; neither is peace ever our friend, but when it is a servant of piety. The use of war is not more pernicious to the body, than the abuse of peace is to the soul. Alas! the riot, bred of our long ease, rather drives the ark of God from us; so the still sedentary life is subject to diseases, and standing waters putrefy. It may be just with God to take away the blessing, which we do so much abuse, and to scour off our rust with bloody war.

The ark of God had now many years rested in the obscure lodge of Abinadab, without the honour of a tabernacle. David will not endure himself glorious, and the ark of God contemptible: his first care is to provide a fit room for God, in the head of the tribes, in his own city. The chief care of good princes must be the advancement of religion: what should the deputies of God rather do, than honour him whom they represent! It was no good that Israel could learn of Philistines; those pagans had sent the ark back in a new cart; the Israelites saw that God blessed that conduct, and now they practise it at home: but that which God will take from Philistines, he will not brook from Israel: aliens from God are no fit patterns for children. Divine institution had made this a carriage for the Levites, not for oxen; neither should those sons of Abinadab have driven the cart, but carried that sacred burden. God's businesses must be done after his own forms, which if we do, with the best intentions, alter, we presume.

It is long since Israel saw so fair a day as this, wherein they went, in this holy triumph, to fetch the ark of God. Now their warlike trumpets are turned into harps and timbrels; and their hands, instead of wielding the sword and spear, strike upon those musical strings, whereby they might express the joy of their hearts: here was no noise but of mirth, no motion but pleasant. O happy Israel, that had a God to rejoice in! that had this occasion of rejoicing in their God, and a heart that embraced this occasion! There is nothing but this wherein we may not joy immoderately, unseasonably; this spiritual joy can never be either out of time, or out of measure: " Let him that rejoiceth, rejoice in the Lord." But now, when the Israelites were in the midst of this angel-like jollity, their hearts lifted up, their hands playing, their feet moving, their tongues singing and shouting, God sees good to strike them into a sudden damp by the death of Uzzah. They are scarce set into the tune, when God mars their music by a fearful judgment, and changes their mirth into astonishment and confusion. There could not be a more excellent work than this they were about; there could not be more cheerful hearts in the performing of it; yet will the most holy God rather damn all this solemn service, than endure an act of presumption or infidelity. Abinadab had been the faithful host of God's ark for the space of twenty years: even in the midst of the terrors of Israel, who were justly affrighted with the vengeance inflicted upon Bethshemesh, did he give harbour unto it; yet even the son of Abinadab is stricken dead, in the first departing of that blessed guest. The sanctity of the parent cannot bear out the sin of his son. The Holy One of Israel will be sanctified in all that come near him: he will be served like himself.

What, then, was the sin of Uzzah? what was the capital crime for which he so fearfully perished? That the ark of God was committed to the cart, it was not his device only, but the common act of many; that it was not carried on the shoulders of the Levites, was no less the fault of Ahio, and the rest of their brethren. Only Uzzah is stricken: the rest sinned in negligence; he in presumption: the ark of God shakes with the agitation of that carriage; he puts forth his hand to hold it steady. Human judgment would have found herein nothing heinous. God sees not with the eyes of men: none but the priests should have dared to touch the ark; it was enough for the Levites to touch the bars that carried it; an unwarranted hand cannot so lightly touch the ark, but he strikes the God that dwells in it. No marvel if God strike that man with death, that strikes him with presumption: there was well near the same quarrel against the thousands of Bethshemesh, and against Uzzah; they died for looking into the ark, he for touching it: lest Israel should grow into a contemptuous familiarity with this testimony of God's presence, he will hold them in awe with judgments. The revenging hand of the Almighty, that, upon the return of the ark, staid at the house of Abinadab, upon the remove of the ark, begins there again. Where are those that think God will take up with a careless and slubbered service? He whose infinite mercy uses to pass by our sins of infirmity, punisheth yet severely our bold faults. If we cannot do any thing in the degrees that he requireth, yet we must learn to do all things in the form that he requireth: doubtless Uzzah meant no otherwise than well, in putting forth his hand to stay the ark; he knew the sacred utensils that were in it, the pot of manna, the tables of the law, the rod of Aaron which might be wronged by that over-rough motion; to these he offers his aid, and is stricken dead: the best intention cannot excuse, much less warrant us in unlawful actions. Where we do aught in faith, it pleases our good God to wink at and pity our weaknesses; but if we dare to present God with the well-meant services of our own making, we run into the indignation of God. There is nothing more dangerous than to be our own carvers in matters of devotion.

I marvel not if the countenance of David were suddenly changed, to see the pale face of death in one of the chief actors in this holy procession. He, that had found God so favourable to him in actions of less worth, is troubled to see this success of a business so heartily directed unto his God: and now he begins to look through Uzzah at himself, and to say, "How shall the ark of the Lord come to me?" Then only shall we make a right use of the judgments of God upon others, when we shall fear them in ourselves, and, finding our sins at least equal, shall tremble in the expectation of the same deserved punishments. God intends not only revenge in his execution, but reformation; as good princes regard not so much the smart of the evil past, as the prevention of the future, which is never attained, but when we make applications of God's hand, and draw common causes out of God's particular proceedings.

I do not hear David say, Surely this man is guilty of some secret sin that the world knows not; God hath met with him, there is no danger to us; why should I be discouraged to see God just? We may go on safely and prosper. But here his foot stays, and his hand falls from his instrument, and his tongue is ready to tax his own unworthiness: "How shall the ark of the Lord come unto me?" That heart is carnal and proud that thinks any man worse than himself. David's fear stays his progress: perhaps he might have proceeded with good success, but he dares not venture, where he sees such a deadly check. It is better to be too fearful than too forward, in those affairs which do immediately concern God. As it is not good to refrain from holy businesses, so it is worse to do them ill: awfulness is a safe interpreter of God's secret actions, and a wise guide of ours.

This event hath holpen Obed-Edom to a guest he looked not for: God shall now sojourn in the house of him, in whose heart he dwelt before by a strong faith, else the man durst not have undertaken to receive that dreadful ark, which David himself feared to harbour. O the courage of an honest and faithful heart! Obed-Edom knew well enough what slaughter the ark had made among the Philistines, and after that among the Bethshemites, and now he saw Uzzah lie dead before him: yet doth he not make any scruple of entertaining it; neither doth he say, My neighbour Abinadab was a careful and religious host to the ark, and is now paid with the blood of his son; how shall I hope to speed better? But he opens his doors with a bold cheerfulness, and, notwithstanding all those terrors, bids God welcome. Nothing can make God not amiable to his own; even his very justice is lovely. Holy men know how to rejoice in the Lord with trembling, and can fear without discouragement.

The God of heaven will not receive any thing from men on free cost: he will pay liberally for his lodging; a plentiful blessing upon Obed-Edom, and all his household. It was an honour to that zealous Gittite, that the ark should come under his roof; yet God rewards that honour with benediction: never man was a loser by true godliness. The house of Obed-Edom cannot this while want observation; the eyes of David and all Israel were never off from it, to see how it fared with this entertainment. And now, when they find nothing but a gracious acceptation and sensible blessing, the good king of Israel takes new heart, and hastens to fetch the ark into his royal city. The view of God's favours upon the godly is no small encouragement to confidence and obedience. Doubtless, Obed-Edom was not free from some weaknesses: if the Lord should have taken the advantage of judgment against him, what Israelites had not been disheartened from attending the ark? Now David and Israel were not more affrighted with the vengeance upon Uzzah, than encouraged by the blessing of Obed-Edom. The wise God doth so order his just and merciful proceedings, that the awfulness of men may be tempered with love. Now the sweet singer of Israel revives his holy music, and adds both more spirit and more pomp to so devout a business. I did not before hear of trumpets, nor dancing, nor shouting, nor sacrifice, nor the linen ephod. The sense of God's past displeasure doubles our care to please him, and our joy in his recovered approbation; we never make so much of our health as after sickness, nor ever are so officious to our friend as after an unkindness. In the first setting out of the ark, David's fear was at least an equal match to his joy; therefore, after the first six paces, he offered a sacrifice, both to pacify God and thank him: but now, when they saw no sign of dislike, they did more freely let themselves loose to a fearless joy, and the body strove to express the holy affection of the soul: there was no limb, no part, that did not profess their mirth by motion; no noise of voice or instrument wanted to assist their spiritual jollity: David led the way, dancing with all his might in his linen ephod. Uzzah was still in his eye: he durst not usurp upon a garment of the priests', but will borrow their colour to grace the solemnity, though he dare not the fashion. White was ever the colour of joy, and linen was light for use: therefore he covers his princely robes with white linen, and means to honour himself by his conformity to God's ministers. Those that think there is disgrace in the ephod, are far from the spirit of the man after God's own heart: neither can there be a greater argument of a foul soul, than a dislike of the glorious calling of God. Barren Michal hath too many sons that scorn the holy habit and exercises. She looks through her window, and seeing the attire and gestures of her devout husband, despiseth him in her heart: neither can she conceal her contempt, but, like Saul's daughter, casts it proudly in his face: "O how glorious was the king of Israel this day, which was uncovered this day in the eyes of the maidens of his servants, as a fool uncovereth himself!" Worldly hearts can see nothing in actions of zeal, but folly and madness. Piety hath no relish to their palate, but distasteful.

David's heart did never swell so much at any reproach, as this of his wife: his love was for the time lost in his anger; and, as a man impatient of no affront so much as in the way of his devotion, he returns a bitter check to his Michal: "It was before the Lord, which chose me, rather than thy father, and all his house," &c. Had not Michal twitted her husband with the shame of his zeal, she had not heard of the shameful rejection of her father: now, since she will be forgetting whose wife she was, she shall be put in mind whose daughter she was. Contumelies, that are cast upon us in the causes of God, may safely be repaid. If we be meal-mouthed in the scorns of religion, we are not patient, but zealless: here we may not forbear her that lies in our bosom. If David had not loved Michal dearly, he had never stood upon those points with Abner: he knew, that if Abner came to him, the kingdom of Israel would accompany him; and yet he sends him the charge of not seeing his face, except he brought Michal, Saul's daughter, with him; as if he would not regard the crown of Israel, while he wanted that wife of his: yet here he takes her up roundly, as if she had been an enemy, not a partner of his bed. All relations are aloof off, in comparison of that betwixt God and the soul: "He that loves father, or mother, or wife, or child, better than me (saith our Saviour), is not worthy of me." Even the highest delights of our hearts must be trampled upon, when they will stand out in rivalry with God. O happy resolution of the royal prophet and prophetical king of Israel! "I will be yet more vile than thus, and will be low in mine own sight." He knew this very abasement heroical; and that the only way to true glory, is not to be ashamed of our lowest humiliation unto God. Well might he promise himself honour, from those whose contempt she had threatened. The hearts of men are not their own: he that made them overrules them, and inclines them to an honourable conceit of those that honour their Maker; so as holy men have ofttimes inward reverence, even where they have outward indignities. David came to bless his house; Michal brings a curse upon herself; her scorns shall make her childless to the day of her death. Barrenness was held in those times none of the least judgments. God doth so revenge David's quarrel upon Michal, that her sudden disgrace shall be recompensed with perpetual: she shall not be held worthy to bear a son to him whom she unjustly contemned. How just is it with God to provide whips for the backs of scorners! It is no marvel if those that mock at goodness be plagued with continual fruitlessness.

CONTEMPLATION II.—MEPHIBOSHETH AND ZIBA.

So soon as ever David can but breathe himself from the public cares, he casts back his thoughts to the dear remembrance of his Jonathan. Saul's servant is likely to give him the best intelligence of Saul's sons: the question is therefore moved to Ziba, "Remaineth there none of the house of Saul?" And, lest suspicion might conceal the remainders of an emulous line, in fear of revenge intended, he adds, "On whom I may show the mercy of God for Jonathan's sake?" O friendship worthy of the monuments of eternity! fit only to requite him whose love was more than the love of women! He doth not say, Is there any of the house of Jonathan?—but of Saul?—that, for his friend's sake, he may show favour to the posterity of his persecutor. Jonathan's love could not be greater than Saul's malice, which also survived long in his issue, from whom David found a busy and stubborn rivality for the crown of Israel: yet, as one that gladly buried all the hostility of Saul's house in Jonathan's grave, he asks, "Is there any man left of Saul's house, that I may show him mercy for Jonathan's sake?" It is true love, that, overliving the person of a friend, will be inherited of his seed; but to love the posterity of an enemy in a friend, it is a miracle of friendship. The formal amity of the world is confined to a face, or to the possibility of recompense, languishing in the disability, and dying in the decease of the party affected. That love was ever false that is not ever constant, and the most operative when it cannot be either known or requited.

To cut off all unquiet competition for the kingdom of Israel, the providence of God had so ordered, that there is none left of the house of Saul, besides the sons of his concubines, save only young and lame Mephibosheth: so young, that he was but five years of age when David entered upon the government of Israel; so lame, that, if his age had fitted, his impotency had made him unfit for the throne. Mephibosheth was not born a cripple; it was a heedless nurse that made him so. She, hearing of the death of Saul and Jonathan, made such haste to fly, that her young master was lamed with the fall. Certainly there needed no such speed to run away from David, whose love pursues the hidden son of his brother Jonathan. How often doth our ignorant mistaking, cause us to run from our best friends, and to catch knocks and maims of them that profess our protection!

Mephibosheth could not come otherwise than fearfully into the presence of David, whom he knew so long, so spitefully opposed by the house of Saul. He could not be ignorant that the fashion of the world is to build their own security upon the blood of the opposite faction; neither to think themselves safe, while any branch remains springing out of that root of their emulation. Seasonably doth David therefore first expel all those unjust doubts, ere he administer his further cordials: "Fear not, for I will surely show thee kindness for Jonathan thy father's sake, and will restore thee all the fields of Saul thy father, and thou shalt eat bread at my table continually."

David can see neither Saul's blood, nor lame legs in Mephibosheth, while he sees in him the features of his friend Jonathan: how much less shall the God of mercies regard our infirmities, or the corrupt blood of our sinful progenitors, while he beholds us in the face of his Son, in whom he is well pleased!

Favours are wont so much more to affect us, as they are less expected by us. Mephibosheth, as overjoyed with so comfortable a word, and confounded in himself at the remembrance of the contrary deservings of his family, bows himself to the earth, and says, "What is thy servant, that thou shouldst look upon such a dead dog as I am?" I find no defect of wit, though of limbs, in Mephibosheth: he knew himself the grandchild of the king of Israel, the son of Jonathan, the lawful heir of both; yet in regard of his own impotency, and the trespass and rejection of his house, he thus abaseth himself unto David. Humiliation is a right use of God's affliction. What if he was born great? If the sin of his grandfather hath lost his estate, and the hand of his nurse hath deformed and disabled his person, he now forgets what he was, and calls himself worse than he is, "a dog." Yet, "a living dog is better than a dead lion." There is dignity and comfort in life;

MEPHIBOSHETH AND ZIBA.

Mephibosheth is therefore a dead dog unto David. It is not for us to nourish the same spirits in our adverse estate, that we found in our highest prosperity. What use have we made of God's hand, if we be not the lower with our fall? God intends we should carry our cross, not make a fire of it to warm us: it is no bearing up our sails in a tempest. Good David cannot disesteem Mephibosheth ever the more for disparaging himself; he loves and honours this humility in the son of Jonathan. There is no more certain way to glory and advancement, than a lowly dejection of ourselves. He that made himself a dog, and therefore fit only to lie under the table, yea a dead dog, and therefore fit only for the ditch, is raised up to the table of a king; his seat shall be honourable, yea royal; his fare delicious, his attendance noble. How much more will our gracious God lift up our heads unto true honour before men and angels, if we can be sincerely humbled in his sight! If we miscall ourselves in the meanness of our conceits to him, he gives us a new name, and sets us at the table of his glory. It is contrary with God and men: if they reckon of us as we set ourselves, he values us according to our abasements. Like a prince truly munificent and faithful, David promises and performs at once. Ziba, Saul's servant, hath the charge given him of the execution of that royal word: "He shall be the bailiff of this great husbandry of his master Mephibosheth." The land of Saul, however forfeited, shall know no other master than Saul's grandchild. As yet, Saul's servant had sped better than his son. I read of twenty servants of Ziba, none of Mephibosheth. Earthly possessions do not always admit of equal divisions. The wheel is now turned up: Mephibosheth is a prince; Ziba is his officer. I cannot but pity the condition of this good son of Jonathan: into ill hands did honest Mephibosheth fall; first of a careless nurse, then of a treacherous servant: she maimed his body; he would have overthrown his estate. After some years of eyeservice to Mephibosheth, wicked Ziba intends to give him a worse fall than his nurse. Never any court was free from detractors, from delators, who, if they see a man to be a cripple, that he cannot go to speak for himself, will be telling tales of him in the ears of the great. Such a one was this perfidious Ziba, who, taking the opportunity of David's flight from his son Absalom, follows him with a fair present, and a false tale, accusing his impotent master of a foul and traitorous ingratitude, labouring to tread upon his lame lord. to raise himself to honour. True-hearted Mephibosheth had as good a will as the best: if he could have commanded legs, he had not been left behind David. Now, that he cannot go with him, he will not be well without him, and therefore puts himself to a wilful and sullen penance for the absence and danger of his king; he will not so much as put on clean clothes for the time, as he that could not have any joy in himself for the want of his lord David. Unconscionable miscreants care not how they collogue, whom they slander, for a private advantage. Lewd Ziba comes with a gift in his hand, and a smooth tale in his mouth: O, sir, you thought you had a Jonathan at home, but you will find a Saul: it were pity but he should be set at your table, that would sit in your throne! You thought Saul's land would have contented Mephibosheth, but he would have all yours; though he be lame, yet he would be climbing: would you have thought that this cripple could be plotting for your kingdom, now that you are gone aside? Ishbosheth will never die while Mephibosheth lives. How did he now forget his impotence, and raised up his spirits in hope of a day; and durst say, that now the time was come, wherein the crown should revert to Saul's true heir. O viper! if a serpent bite in secret when he is not charmed, no better is a slanderer. Honest Mephibosheth, in good manners, made a dead dog of himself, when David offered him the favour of his board; but Ziba would make him a very dog indeed, an ill-natured cur, that when David did thus kindly feed him at his own table, would not only bite his fingers, but fly at his throat.

But what shall we say to this? Neither earthly sovereignty, nor holiness, can exempt men from human infirmity. Wise and good David hath now but one ear, and that misled with credulity. His charity in believing Ziba, makes him uncharitable in distrusting, in censuring Mephibosheth. The detractor hath not only sudden credit given him, but Saul's land. Jonathan's son hath lost (unheard) that inheritance which was given him unsought. Hearsay is no safe ground of any judgment; Ziba slanders, David believes, Mephibosheth suffers.

Lies shall not always prosper: God will not abide the truth to be ever oppressed. At last Jonathan's lame son shall be found as sound in heart, as lame in his body; he, whose soul was like his father Jonathan's soul, whose body was like to his grandfather Saul's soul, meets David, as it was high time, upon his return; bestirs his tongue to discharge himself of so foul a slander: the more horrible the crime had been, the more villanous was the unjust suggestion of it, and the more necessary was a just apology: sweetly, therefore, and yet passionately, doth he labour to greaten David's favours to him, his own obligations and vileness; showing himself more affected with his wrong, than with his loss; welcoming David home with a thankful neglect of himself, as not caring that Ziba had his substance, now that he had his king. David is satisfied; Mephibosheth restored to favour and lands: here are two kind hearts well met. David is full of satisfaction from Mephibosheth; Mephibosheth runs over with joy in David: David, like a gracious king, gives Mephibosheth, as before, Saul's lands to halves with Ziba; Mephibosheth, like a king, gives all to Ziba, for joy that God had given him David: all had been well, if Ziba had fared worse. Pardon me, O holy and glorious soul of a prophet, of a king, after God's own heart! I must needs blame thee for mercy; a fault that the best and most generous natures are most subject to: it is a pity that so good a thing should do hurt; yet we find that the best, misused, is most dangerous. Who should be the pattern of kings, but the King of God? Mercy is the goodliest flower in his crown; much more in theirs, but with a difference: God's mercy is infinite, theirs limited: he says, " I will have mercy on whom I will;" they must say, I will have mercy on whom I should: and yet he, for all his infinite mercy, hath vessels of wrath, so must they; of whom his justice hath said, " Thine eye shall not spare them." A good man is pitiful to his beast; shall he therefore make much of toads and snakes? O that Ziba should go away with any possession, save of shame and sorrow! that he should be coupled with a Mephibosheth in a partnership of estates! O that David had changed the word a little!

A division was due here indeed — but of Ziba's ears from his head, or his head from his shoulders, for going about so maliciously to divide David from the sons of Jonathan: an eye for an eye was God's rule. If that had been true which Ziba suggested against Mephibosheth, he had been worthy to lose his head with his lands; being false, it had been but reason Ziba should have changed heads with Mephibosheth. Had not holy David himself been so stung with venomous tongues, that he cries out, in the bitterness of his soul, " What reward shall be given thee; O thou false tongue? even sharp arrows, with hot burning coals." He that was so sensible of himself in Doeg's wrong, doth he feel so little of Mephibosheth in Ziba's? Are these the arrows of David's quiver? Are these his hot burning coals? " Thou and Ziba divide." He that had said, Their tongue is a sharp sword; now that the sword of just revenge is in his hand, is this the blow he gives? " Divide the possession." I know not whether excess or want of mercy may prove most dangerous in the great: the one discourages good intentions with fear; the other may encourage wicked practices through presumption: those that are in eminent place must learn the mid-way betwixt both; so pardoning faults, that they may not provoke them; so punishing them, that they may not dishearten virtuous and wellmeant actions: they must learn to sing that absolute ditty, whereof David had here forgotten one part, of mercy and judgment.

CONTEMPLATION III.—HANUN AND DAVID'S AMBASSADORS.

It is not the meaning of religion to make men uncivil. If the king of Ammon were heathenish, yet his kindness may be acknowledged, may be returned, by the king of Israel. I say not but that perhaps David might maintain too strait a league with that forbidden nation. A little friendship is enough to an idolater; but even the savage cannibals may receive an answer of outward courtesy. If a very dog fawn upon us, we stroke him on the head, and clap him on the side; much less is the common band of humanity untied by grace. Disparity, in spiritual professions, is no warrant for ingratitude. He therefore, whose good nature proclaimed to show mercy to any branch of Saul's house for Jonathan's sake, will now also show kindness to Hanun, for the sake of Nahash his father.

It was the same Nahash that offered the cruel condition to the men of Jabesh-Gilead, of thrusting out their right eyes for the admission into his covenant. He that was thus bloody in his designs against Israel, yet was kind to David, perhaps for no cause so much as Saul's opposition; and yet even this favour is held worthy both of memory and retribution. Where we have the acts of courtesy, it is not necessary we should enter into a strict examination of the grounds of it; while the benefit is ours, let the intention be their own. Whatever the hearts of men are, we must look at their hands, and repay, not what they meant, but what they did.

Nahash is dead; David sends ambassadors to condole his loss, and to comfort his son Hanun. No Ammonite but is sadly affected with the death of a father, though it gain him a kingdom. Even Esau could say, " The days of mourning for my father will come :" no earthly advantage can fill up the gap of nature. Those children are worse than Ammonites, that can think either gain or liberty worthy to countervail a parent's loss.

Carnal men are wont to measure another's foot by their own last; their own falsehood makes them unjustly suspicious of others. The princes of Ammon, because they are guilty to their own hollowness and doubleness of heart, are ready so to judge of David and his messengers: " Thinkest thou that David doth honour thy father, that he hath sent comforters unto thee? Hath not David rather sent his own servants to thee to search the city, and to spy it out, to overthrow it ?" It is hard for a wicked heart to think well of any other; because it can think none better than itself, and knows itself evil. The freer a man is from vice himself, the more charitable he uses to be unto others.

Whatsoever David was, particularly in his own person, it was ground enough of prejudice that he was an Israelite. It was an hereditary and deep-settled hatred that the Ammonites had conceived against their brethren of Israel; neither can they forget that shameful and fearful foil which they received from the rescuers of Jabesh-Gilead: and now still do they stomach at the name of Israel. Malice once conceived in worldly hearts, is not easily extinguished, but, upon all occasions, is ready to break forth into a flame of revengeful actions.

Nothing can be more dangerous, than for young princes to meet with ill counsel in the entrance of their government; for both then are they most prone to take it, and most difficultly recovered from it. If we be set out of our way in the beginning of our journey, we wander all the day. How happy is that state, where both the counsellors are faithful to give only good advice, and the king wise to discern good advice from evil. The young king of Ammon is easily drawn to believe his peers, and to mistrust the messengers: and having now, in his conceit, turned them into spies, entertains them with a scornful disgrace; he shaves off one half off their beards, and cuts off one half of their garments, exposing them to the derision of all beholders. The Israelites were forbidden either a shaven beard or a short garment. In despite, perhaps, of their law, these ambassadors are sent away with both; certainly in a despite of their master, and a scorn of their persons.

King David is not a little sensible of the abuse of his messengers, and of himself in them: first, therefore, he desires to hide their shame; then to revenge it. Man hath but a double ornament of body; the one of nature, the other of art; the natural ornament is the hair, the artificial is apparel. David's messengers are deformed in both: the one is easily supplied by a new suit; the other can only be supplied out of the wardrobe of time: " Tarry at Jericho till your beards be grown." How easily had this deformity been removed, if, as Hanun had shaven one side of their faces, so they had shaven the other ! What had this been but to resemble their younger age, or that other sex, in neither of which do we use to place any imagination of unbeseeming? Neither did there want some of their neighbour nations, whose faces age itself had not wont to cover with this shade of hair. But so respective is good David, and his wise senators, of their country's forms, that they shall, by appointment, rather tarry abroad till time have wrought their conformity, than vary from the received fashions of their own people. Alas ! into what a licentious variety of strange disguises are we fallen! The glory of attire is sought in novelty, in misshapenness, in monstrousness : there is much latitude, much liberty, in the use of these indifferent things ; but, because we are free, we may not run wild, and never think we have scope enough unless we outrun modesty.

It is lawful for public persons to feel their own indignities, and to endeavour their revenge. Now David sends all the host of the mighty men to punish Ammon for so foul an abuse. Those that received the messengers of his love with scorn and insolency, shall now be severely saluted with the messengers of his wrath. It is just both with God and men, that they who know not how to take favours aright, should smart with judgments. Kindness repulsed, breaks forth into indignation; how much more when it is repaid with an injurious affront?

David cannot but feel his own cheeks shaven, and his own coat cut in his ambassadors': they did but carry his person to Hanun; neither can he therefore but appropriate to himself the kindness or injury offered unto them. He that did so take to heart the cutting off but the lap of king Saul's garment, when it was laid aside from him, how must he needs be affected with this disdainful halving of his hair and robes in the person of his deputies ! The name of ambassadors hath ever been sacred, and, by the universal law of nations, hath carried in it sufficient protection from all public wrongs: neither hath it been violated without a revenge. O God, what shall we say to those notorious contempts, which are daily cast upon thy spiritual messengers? Is it possible thou shouldst not feel them, thou shouldst not avenge them? We are made a gazing-stock to the world, to angels, and to men: we are despised and trodden down in the dust: "Who hath believed our report, and to whom is the arm of the Lord revealed?"

How obstinate are wicked men in their perverse resolutions! Those foolish Ammonites had rather hire Syrians to maintain a war against Israel in so foul a quarrel, besides the hazard of their own lives, than confess the error of their jealous misconstruction.

It is one of the mad principles of wickedness, that it is a weakness to relent, and rather to die than yield. Even ill causes, once undertaken, must be upheld, although with blood; whereas the gracious heart, finding his own mistaking, doth not only remit of an ungrounded displeasure, but studies to be revenged of itself, and to give satisfaction to the offended.

The mercenary Syrians are drawn to venture their lives for a fee: twenty thousand of them are hired into the field against Israel. Fond pagans, that know not the value of a man! their blood cost them nothing, and they care not to sell it good-cheap. How can we think those men have souls, that esteem a little white earth above themselves? that never inquire into the justice of the quarrel, but the rate of the pay? that can rifle for drachms of silver in the bowels of their own flesh, and either kill or die for a day's wages?

Joab, the wise general of Israel, soon finds where the strength of the battle lay, and so marshals his troops, that the choice of his men shall encounter the vanguard of the Syrians. His brother Abishai leads the rest against the children of Ammon, with this covenant of mutual assistance, "If the Syrians be too strong for me, then thou shalt help me; but if the children of Ammon be too strong for thee, then will I come and help thee." It is a happy thing when the captains of God's people join together as brethren, and lend their hand to the aid of each other against the common adversary. Concord in defence, or assault, is the way to victory; as, contrarily, the division of the leaders is the overthrow of the army.

Set aside some particular actions, Joab was a worthy captain, both for wisdom and valour. Who could either exhort or resolve better than he? "Be of good courage, and let us play the men, for our people, and for the cities of our God; and the Lord do that which seemeth him good!" It is not either private glory or profit that whets his fortitude, but the respect to the cause of God and his people. That soldier can never answer it to God, that strikes not more as a justiciar, than as an enemy; neither doth he content himself with his own courage, but he animates others. The tongue of a commander fights more than his hand. It is enough for private men to exercise what life and limbs they have: a good leader must, out of his own abundance, put life and spirits into all others: if a lion lead sheep into the field, there is hope of victory. Lastly, when he hath done his best, he resolves to depend upon God for the issue, not trusting to his sword, or his bow, but to the providence of the Almighty, for success, as a man religiously awful, and awfully confident, while there should be no want in their own endeavours. He knew well that the race was not to the swift, nor the battle to the strong; therefore he looks up above the hills whence cometh his salvation. All valour is cowardice to that which is built upon religion.

I marvel not to see Joab victorious, while he is thus godly. The Syrians fly before him like flocks of sheep; the Ammonites follow them; the two sons of Zeruiah have nothing to do but to pursue and execute The throats of the Ammonites are cut, for cutting the beards and coats of the Israelitish messengers: neither doth this revenge end in the field: Rabbah, the royal city of Ammon, is strongly beleaguered by Joab the City of Waters (after well-near a year's siege) yieldeth; the rest can no longer hold out. Now Joab, as one that desireth more to approve himself a loyal and a careful subject, than a happy general, sends to his master David, that he should come personally, and encamp against the city, and take it: "Lest (saith he) I take it, and it be called after my name." O noble and admirable fidelity of a dutiful servant, that prefers his lord to himself, and is so far from stealing honour from his master's deserts, that he willingly remits of his own to add unto his! The war was not his; he was only employed by his sovereign: the same person, that was wronged in the ambassadors, revengeth by his soldiers. The praise of the act shall, like fountain water, return to the sea, whence it originally came. To seek a man's own glory, is not glory. Alas! how many are there, who being sent to sue for God, woo for themselves! O

God, it is a fearful thing to rob thee of that which is dearest to thee, glory, which, as thou wilt not give to any creature, so much less wilt thou endure that any creature should filch it from thee, and give it to himself! Have thou the honour of all our actions, who givest a being to our actions and us, and in both hast most justly regarded thine own praise!

CONTEMPLATION IV.— DAVID WITH BATHSHEBA AND URIAH.

With what unwillingness, with what fear, do I still look upon the miscarriage of the man after God's own heart! O holy prophet, who can promise himself always to stand, when he sees thee fallen and maimed with the fall? Who can assure himself of an immunity from the foulest sins, when he sees thee offending so heinously, so bloodily? Let profane eyes behold thee contentedly, as a pattern, as an excuse of sinning; I shall never look upon thee but through tears, as a woful spectacle of human infirmity.

While Joab and all Israel were busy in the war against Ammon, in the siege of Rabbah, Satan finds time to lay siege to the secure heart of David. Who ever found David thus tempted, thus foiled, in the days of his busy wars? Now only do I see the king of Israel rising from his bed in the evening: the time was, when he rose up in the morning to his early devotions; when he brake his nightly rest with public cares, with the business of the state: all that while, he was innocent, he was holy; but now that he wallows in the bed of idleness, he is fit to invite temptation. The industrious man hath no leisure to sin; the idle hath neither leisure nor power to avoid sin. Exercise is not more wholesome for the body than for the soul, the remission whereof breeds matter of disease in both. The water that hath been heated soonest freezeth. The most active spirit soonest tireth with slackening. The earth stands still, and is all dregs: the heavens ever move, and are pure. We have no reason to complain of the assiduity of the work: the toil of action is answered by the benefit; if we did less we should suffer more. Satan, like an idle companion, if he finds us busy, flies back, and sees it no time to entertain vain purposes with us: we cannot please him better, than by casting away our work, to hold chat with him; we cannot yield so far, and be guiltless.

Even David's eyes have no sooner the sleep rubbed out of them, than they rove to wanton prospects: he walks upon his roof, and sees Bathsheba washing herself; inquires after her, sends for her, solicits her to uncleanness. The same spirit, that shut up his eyes in unseasonable sleep, opens them upon an enticing object: while sin hath such a solicitor, it cannot want either means or opportunity. I cannot think Bathsheba could be so immodest, as to wash herself openly, especially from her natural uncleanness. Lust is quick-sighted. David hath espied her, where she could espy no beholder. His eyes recoil upon his heart, and have smitten him with sinful desire.

There can be no safety to that soul, where the senses are let loose. He can never keep his covenant with God, that makes not a covenant with his eyes. It is an idle presumption to think the outward man may be free, while the inward is safe. He is more than a man whose heart is not led by his eyes; he is no regenerate man, whose eyes are not restrained by his heart.

O Bathsheba, how wert thou washed from thine uncleanness, when thou yieldedst to go into an adulterous bed! never wert thou so foul, as now when thou wert new washed. The worst of nature is cleanliness to the best of sin. Thou hadst been clean, if thou hadst not washed; yet for thee, I know how to plead infirmity of sex, and the importunity of a king. But what shall I say for thee, O thou royal prophet, and prophetical king of Israel? Where shall I find ought to extenuate that crime, for which God himself hath noted thee? Did not thine holy profession teach thee to abhor such a sin more than death? Was not thy justice wont to punish this sin with no less than death? Did not thy very calling call thee to a protection and preservation of justice, of chastity in thy subjects? Didst thou want store of wives of thine own? Wert thou restrained from taking more? Was there no beauty in Israel, but in a subject's marriage bed? Wert thou overcome by the vehement solicitations of an adulteress? Wert thou not the tempter, the prosecutor of this uncleanness? I should accuse thee deeply, if thou hadst not accused thyself; nothing wanted to greaten thy sin, or our wonder and fear. O God, whither do we go, if thou stay us not? Who ever amongst the millions of thy servants could find himself furnished with stronger preservatives against sin? Against whom could such a sin find less pretence of prevailing? O keep thou us, that presumptuous sins prevail not over us; so only shall we be free from great offences.

The suits of kings are imperative: ambition did now prove a bawd to lust. Bathsheba yielded to offend God, to dishonour her husband, to clog and wound her own soul, to abuse her body. Dishonesty grows bold, when it is countenanced with greatness. Eminent persons had need be careful of their demands: they sin by authority, that are solicited by the mighty.

Had Bathsheba been mindful of her matrimonial fidelity, perhaps David had been soon checked in his inordinate desire; her facility furthers the sin. The first motioner of evil is most faulty; but as in quarrels, so in offences, the second blow (which is the consent) makes the fray. Good Joseph was moved to folly by his great and beautiful mistress; this fire fell upon wet tinder, and therefore soon went out.

Sin is not acted alone; if but one party be wise, both escape. It is no excuse to say, I was tempted, though by the great, though by the holy and learned: almost all sinners are misled by that transformed angel of light. The action is that we must regard, not the person. Let the mover be never so glorious, if he stir us to evil, he must be entertained with defiance.

The God, that knows how to raise good out of evil, blesses an adulterous copulation with that increase, which he denies to the chaste embracements of honest wedlock. Bathsheba hath conceived by David; and now at once conceives a sorrow and care how to smother the shame of her conception: he that did the fact, must hide it.

O David, where is thy repentance? where is thy tenderness and compunction of heart? where are those holy meditations, which had wont to take up thy soul? Alas, instead of clearing thy sin, thou labourest to cloak it, and spendest those thoughts in the concealing of thy wickedness, which thou shouldst rather have bestowed in preventing it. The best of God's children may not only be drenched in the waves of sin, but lie in them for the time, and perhaps sink twice to the bottom: what hypocrite could have done worse, than study how to cover the face of his sin from the eyes of men, while he regarded not the sting of sin in his soul?

As there are some acts wherein the hypocrite is a saint, so there are some wherein the greatest saint upon earth may be a hypocrite. Saul did thus go about to colour his sin, and is cursed. The vessels of mercy and wrath are not ever distinguishable by their actions: he makes the difference, that will have mercy on whom he will, and whom he will he hardeneth.

It is rare and hard to commit a single sin. David hath abused the wife of Uriah: now he would abuse his person, in causing him to father a false seed. That worthy Hittite is sent for from the wars: and now, after some cunning and far-fetched questions, is dismissed to his house, not without a present of favour. David could not but imagine, that the beauty of his Bathsheba must needs be attractive enough to a husband, whom long absence in wars had withheld all that while from so pleasing a bed; neither could he think, that since that face and those breasts had power to allure himself to an unlawful lust, it could be possible that Uriah should not be invited by them to an allowed and warrantable fruition.

That David's heart might now the rather strike him, in comparing the chaste resolutions of his servant with his own light incontinence, good Uriah sleeps at the door of the king's palace, making choice of a stony pillow, under the canopy of heaven, rather than the delicate bed of her whom he thought as honest as he knew fair. "The ark (saith he), and Israel, and Judah, dwell in tents, and my lord Joab, and the servants of my lord, abide in the open fields; shall I then go into my house to eat and drink, and lie with my wife? By thy life, and by the life of thy soul, I will not do this thing."

Who can but be astonished at this change, to see a soldier austere, and a prophet wanton? And how doth that soldier's austerity shame the prophet's wantonness? O zealous and mortified soul, worthy of a more faithful wife, of a more just master, how didst thou overlook all base sensuality, and hatedst to be happy alone! War and lust had wont to be reputed friends: thy breast is not more full of courage than chastity, and is so far from wandering after forbidden pleasures, that it refuseth lawful.

"There is a time to laugh, and a time to mourn; a time to embrace, and a time to be far from embracing." Even the best actions are not always seasonable, much less the indifferent. He, that ever takes liberty to do what he may, shall offend no less, than he that sometimes takes liberty to do what he may not.

If any thing, the ark of God is fittest to lead our tunes; according as that is either distressed, or prospereth, should we frame our mirth or mourning. To dwell in ceiled houses, while the temple lies waste, is the ground of God's just quarrel.

"How shall we sing a song of the Lord in a strange land? If I forget thee, O Jerusalem, let my right hand forget her cunning; if I do not remember thee, let my tongue cleave to the roof of my mouth; yea, if I prefer not Jerusalem to my chief joy."

As every man is a limb of the community, so must he be affected with the estate of the universal body, whether healthful or languishing: it did not more aggravate David's sin, that while the ark and Israel were in hazard and distress, he could find time to loose the reins to wanton desires and actions, than it magnifies the religious zeal of Uriah, that he abandons comfort, till he see the ark and Israel victorious.

Common dangers or calamities must (like the rapt motion) carry our hearts contrary to the ways of our private occasions. He, that cannot be moved with words, shall be tried with wine. Uriah had equally protested against feasting at home, and society with his wife: to the one, the authority of a king forceth him abroad, in hope that the excess thereof shall force him to the other. It is like, that holy captain intended only to yield so much obedience as might consist with his course of austerity. But wine is a mocker: when it goes plausibly in, no man can imagine how it will rage and tyrannize; he, that receives that traitor within his gates, shall too late complain of surprisal. Like unto that ill spirit, it insinuates sweetly, but in the end it bites like a serpent, and hurts like a cockatrice. Even good Uriah is made drunk: the holiest soul may be overtaken; it is hard gainsaying, where a king begins a health to a subject: where, O where will this wickedness end? David will now procure the sin of another to hide his own. Uriah's drunkenness is more David's offence than his. It is weakly yielded to of the one, which was wilfully intended of the other. The one was as the sinner, the other as the tempter.

Had not David known that wine was an inducement to lust, he had spared those superfluous cups. Experience had taught him, that the eye, debauched with wine, will look upon strange women. The drunkard may be anything save good. Yet in this the aim failed; grace is stronger than wine ; while that withholds, in vain shall the fury of the grape attempt to carry Uriah to his own bed. Sober David is now worse than drunken Uriah. Had not the king of Israel been more intoxicate with sin, than Uriah with drink, he had not, in a sober intemperance, climbed up into that bed, which the drunken temperance of Uriah refused.

If David had been but himself, how had he loved, how had he honoured this honest and religious zeal, in his so faithful servant, whom now he cruelly seeks to reward with death! That fact, which wine cannot hide, the sword shall. Uriah shall bear his own mittimus unto Joab: "Put ye Uriah in the forefront of the strength of the battle, and retire back from him, that he may be smitten and die." What is become of thee, O thou good Spirit, that hadst wont to guide thy chosen servant in his former ways? Is not this the man, whom we lately saw so heart-smitten, for but cutting off the lap of the garment of a wicked master, that is now thus lavish of the blood of a gracious and well-deserving servant? Could it be likely, that so worthy a captain could fall alone? Could David have expiated this sin with his own blood, it had been but well spent; but to cover his sin with the innocent blood of others, was a crime above astonishment.

O the deep deceitfulness of sin! If the devil should have come to David, in the most lovely form of Bathsheba herself, and at the first should have directly, and in plain terms, solicited him to murder his best servant, I doubt not but he would have spit scorn in that face, on which he should otherways have doated; now, by many cunning windings, Satan rises up to that temptation, and prevails; that shall be done for a colour of guiltiness, whereof the soul would have hated to be immediately guilty: even those, that find a just horror in leaping down from some high tower, yet may be persuaded to descend by stairs to the bottom. He knows not where he shall stay, that hath willingly slipt into a known wickedness.

How many doth an eminent offender draw with him into evil? It could not be, but that divers of the attendants, both of David and Bathsheba, must be conscious to that adultery: great men's sins are seldom secret; and now Joab must be fetched in, as accessory to the murder. How must this example needs harden Joab against the conscience of Abner's blood! while he cannot but think, David cannot avenge that in me, which he acteth himself.

Honour is pretended to poor Uriah; death is meant. This man was one of the worthies of David; their courage sought glory in the difficultest exploits. That reputation had never been purchased, without attempts of equal danger. Had not the leader and followers of Uriah been more treacherous than his enemies were strong, he had come off with victory. Now, he was not the first or last that perished by his friends. David hath forgotten, that himself was in like sort betrayed in his master's intention, upon the dowry of the Philistines' foreskins. I fear to ask, who ever noted so foul a plot in David's rejected predecessor? Uriah must be the messenger of his own death, Joab must be a traitor to his friend, the host of God must shamefully turn their backs upon the Ammonites, all that Israelitish blood must be shed, that murder must be seconded with dissimulation: and all this to hide one adultery. O God, thou hadst never suffered so dear a favourite of thine to fall so fearfully, if thou hadst not meant to make him an universal example to mankind, of not presuming, of not despairing. How can we presume of not sinning, or despair for sinning, when we find so great a saint thus fallen, thus risen!

CONTEMPLATION V. — NATHAN AND DAVID.

YET Bathsheba mourned for the death of that husband, whom she had been drawn to dishonour. How could she bestow tears enough upon that funeral, whereof her sin was the cause! If she had but a suspicion of the plot of his death, the fountains of her eyes could not yield water enough to wash off her husband's blood; her sin was more worthy of sorrow than her loss. If this grief had been right placed, the hope of hiding her shame, and the ambition to be a queen, had not so soon mitigated it; neither had she, upon any terms, been drawn into the bed of her husband's murderer. Every gleam of earthly comfort can dry up the tears of worldly sorrow. Bathsheba hath soon lost her grief at the court; the remembrance of a husband is buried in the jollity and state of a princess. David securely enjoys his ill-purchased love, and is content to exchange the conscience of his sin, for the sense of his pleasures. But the just and holy God will not put it up so; he that hates sin so much the more, as the offender is more dear to him, will let David feel the bruise of his fall. If God's best children have been sometimes suffered to sleep in a sin, at last he hath awakened them in a fright.

David was a prophet of God, yet he hath not only stept into these foul sins, but sojourns in them. If any profession or state of life could have privileged from sin, the angels had not sinned in heaven, nor man in paradise. Nathan the prophet is sent to the prophet David, for reproof, for conviction: had it been any other man's case, none could have been more quick-sighted than the princely prophet; in his own he is so blind, that God is fain to lend him others' eyes. Even the physician himself, when he is sick, sends for the counsel of those whom his health did mutually aid with advice. Let no man think himself too good to learn; teachers themselves may be taught that, in their own particular, which in a generality they have often taught others · it is not only ignorance that is to be re moved, but misaffection.

Who can prescribe a just period to the best man's repentance? About ten months are passed since David's sin; in all which time I find no news of any serious compunction; it could not be but some glances of remorse must needs have passed through his soul long ere this; but a due and solemn contrition was not heard of till Nathan's message, and, perhaps, had been further adjourned, if that monitor had been longer deferred. Alas! what long and dead sleeps may the holiest soul take in fearful sins! Were it not for thy mercy, O God, the best of us should end our spiritual lethargy in sleep of death.

It might have pleased God as easily to have sent Nathan to check David in his first purpose of sinning; so had his eyes been restrained, Bathsheba honest, Uriah alive with honour: now the wisdom of the Almighty knew how to win more glory by the permission of so foul an evil, than by the prevention; yea, he knew how, by the permission of one sin, to prevent millions. How many thousands had sinned, in a vain presumption on their own strength, if David had not thus offended! how many thousands had despaired, in the conscience of their own weaknesses, if these horrible sins had not received forgiveness! It is happy for all times, that we have so holy a sinner, so sinful a penitent: it matters not how bitter the pill is, but how well wrapped; so cunningly hath Nathan conveyed this dose, that it begins to work ere it be tasted. There is no one thing wherein is more use of wisdom, than the due contriving of a reprehension, which, in a discreet delivery, helps the disease; in an unwise, destroys nature.

Had not Nathan been used to the possession of David's ear, this complaint had been suspected. It well beseems a king to take information by a prophet. While wise Nathan was querulously discoursing of the cruel rich man, that had forcibly taken away the only lamb of his poor neighbour, how willingly doth David listen to the story, and how sharply, even above law, doth he censure the fact! "As the Lord liveth, the man that hath done this thing shall surely die." Full little did he think that he had pronounced sentence against himself: it had not been so heavy, if he had known on whom it should have lighted. We have open ears and quick tongues to the vices of others: how severe justicers we can be to our very own crimes in others! how flattering parasites to another's crime in ourselves! The life of doctrine is in application. Nathan might have been long enough in his narration, in his invective, ere David would have been touched with his own guiltiness; but now, that the prophet brings the word home to his bosom, he cannot but be affected. We may take pleasure to hear men speak in the clouds; we never take profit till we find a propriety in the exhortation or reproof. There was not more cunning in the parable, than courage in the application: "Thou art the man." If David be a king, he may not look not to hear of his faults: God's messages may be no other than impartial. It is a treacherous flattery, in divine errands, to regard greatness. If prophets must be mannerly in the form, yet in the matter of reproof resolute: the words are not their own; they are but the heralds of the King of heaven: "Thus saith the Lord God of Israel."

How thunder-stricken do we think David did now stand! how did the change of his colour bewray the confusion in his soul, while his conscience said the same within, which the prophet sounded in his ear! And now, lest aught should be wanting to his humiliation, all God's former favours shall be laid before his eyes, by way of exprobration. He is worthy to be upbraided with mercies, that hath abused mercies unto wantonness. While we do well, God gives and says nothing; when we do ill, he lays his benefits in our dish, and casts them in our teeth, that our shame may be so much the more, by how much our obligations have been greater. The blessings of God, in our unworthy carriage, prove but the aggravations of sin, and additions to judgment.

I see all God's children falling into sin; some of them lying in sin, none of them maintaining their sin: David cannot have the heart, or the face, to stand out against the message of God; but now, as a man confounded and condemned in himself, he cries out, in the bitterness of a wounded soul, "I have sinned against the Lord." It was but a short word, but passionate; and such as came from the bottom of a contrite heart. The greatest griefs are not most verbal. Saul confessed his sin more largely, less effectually. God cares not for phrases, but for affections. The first piece of our amends to God for sinning is the acknowledgment of sin: he can do little, that in a just offence cannot accuse himself. If we cannot be so good as we would, it is reason we should do God so much right, as to say how evil we are. And why was not this done sooner? It is strange to see how easily sin gets into the heart; how hardly it gets out of the mouth: is it because sin, like unto Satan, where it hath got possession, is desirous to hold it, and knows that it is fully ejected by a free confession? or because, in a guiltiness of deformity, it hides itself in the breast where it is once entertained, and hates the light? or because the tongue is so feed with self-love, that it is loath to be drawn unto any verdict against the heart or hands? or is it out of an idle misprision of shame, which, while it should be placed in offending, is misplaced in disclosing of our offence?

However, sure I am, that God hath need even of racks to draw out confessions, and scarce in death itself are we wrought to a discovery of our errors.

There is no one thing wherein our folly shows itself more than in these hurtful concealments. Contrary to the proceedings of human justice, it is with God, "Confess and live." No sooner can David say, "I have sinned," than Nathan infers, "The Lord also hath put away thy sin." "He that hides his sins, shall not prosper; but he that confesseth and forsaketh them shall find mercy." Who would not accuse himself to be acquitted of God? O God, who would not tell his wickedness to thee, that knowest it better than his own heart, that his heart may be eased of that wickedness, which being not told, killeth? Since we have sinned, why should we be niggardly of that action, wherein we may at once give glory to thee, and relief to our souls?

David had sworn, in a zeal of justice, that the rich oppressor, for but taking his poor neighbour's lamb, should die the death; God, by Nathan, is more favourable to David, than to take him at his word: "Thou shalt not die." O the marvellous power of repentance! Besides adultery, David had shed the blood of innocent Uriah. The strict law was, "Eye for eye, tooth for tooth. He that smiteth with the sword shall perish with the sword;" yet, as if a penitent confession had dispensed with the rigour of justice, now God says, "Thou shalt not die." David was the voice of the law, awarding death unto sin: Nathan was the voice of the gospel, awarding life unto the repentance for sin. Whatsoever the sore be, never any soul applied this remedy and died; never any soul escaped death, that applied it not.

David himself shall not die for this fact; but his misbegotten child shall die for him. He that said, "The Lord hath put away thy sin," yet said also, "The sword shall not depart from thine house."

The same mouth, with one breath, pronounces the sentence both of absolution and death: absolution to the person, death to the issue. Pardon may well stand with temporal afflictions. Where God hath forgiven, though he doth not punish, yet he may chastise, and that unto blood: neither doth he always bear correction, where he remits revenge. So long as he smites us not as an angry judge, we may endure to smart from him as a loving father.

Yet even this rod did David deprecate with tears: how fain would he shake off so easy a load! The child is stricken: the father fasts, and prays, and weeps, and lies all night upon the earth, and abhors the noise of comfort; that child, which was the fruit and monument of his odious adultery, whom he could never have looked upon without recognition of his sin, in whose face he could but have still read the records of his own shame, is thus mourned for, thus sued for. It is easy to observe that good man over-passionately affected to his children. Who would not have thought, that David might have held himself well appaid that his soul escaped an eternal death, his body a violent, though God should punish his sin in that child in whom he sinned? Yet even against this cross he bends his prayers, as if nothing had been forgiven him. There is no child that would be scourged, if he might escape for crying: no affliction is for the time other than grievous; neither is therefore yielded unto, without some kind of reluctation. Far yet was it from the heart of David to make any opposition to the will of God: he sued, he struggled not: there is no impatience in entreaties: he well knew that the threats of temporal evils ran commonly with a secret condition, and therefore might perhaps be avoided by humble importunity: if any means under heaven can avert judgments, it is our prayers.

God could not choose but like well the boldness of David's faith, who, after the apprehension of so heavy a displeasure, is so far from doubting of the forgiveness of his sin, that he dares become a suitor unto God for his sick child. Sin doth not make us more strange, than faith confident.

But it is not in the power of the strongest faith to preserve us from all afflictions: after all David's prayers and tears, the child must die. The careful servants dare not whisper this sad news: they who had found their master so averse from the motion of comfort in the sickness of the child, feared him incapable of comfort in his death.

Suspicion is quick-witted. Every occasion makes us misdoubt that event which we fear. This secrecy proclaims that which they were so loath to utter. David perceives his child dead, and now he rises up from the earth whereon he lay, and washeth himself, and changeth his apparel, and goes first into God's house to worship, and into his own to eat: now he refuses no comfort, who before would take none. The issue of things doth more fully show the will of God than the prediction: God never did any thing but what he would; he hath sometimes foretold that for trial, which his secret will intended not: he would foretell it: he would not effect it; because he would therefore foretell it, that he might not effect it. His predictions of outward evils are not always absolute; his actions are. David well sees, by the event, what the decree of God was concerning his child, which now he could not strive against without a vain impatience. Till we know the determination of the Almighty, it is free for us to strive in our prayers; to strive with him, not against him: when once we know them, it is our duty to sit down in a silent contentation.

"While the child was yet alive, I fasted and wept; for I said, who can tell whether the Lord will be gracious to me, that the child may live; but now he is dead, wherefore should I fast? Can I bring him back again?"

The grief that goes before an evil for remedy, can hardly be too much; but that which follows an evil past remedy, cannot be too little. Even in the saddest accident, death, we may yield something to nature, nothing to impatience: immoderation of sorrow, for losses past hope of recovery, is more sullen than useful; our stomach may be bewrayed by it, not our wisdom.

CONTEMPLATION VI. — AMNON AND TAMAR.

IT is not possible that any word of God should fall to the ground. David is not more sure of forgiveness than smart. Three main sins passed him in this business of Uriah; adultery, murder, dissimulation; for all which he receives present payment: for adultery, in the deflowering of his daughter

Tamar; for murder, in the killing of his son Amnon; for dissimulation, in the contriving of both: yet all this was but the beginning of evils. Where the father of the family brings sin home to the house, it is not easily swept out. Unlawful lust propagates itself by example. How justly is David scourged by the sin of his sons, whom his act taught to offend!

Maacha was the daughter of a heathenish king: by her had David that beautiful, but unhappy issue, Absalom, and his no less fair sister Tamar. Perhaps thus late doth David feel the punishment of that unfit choice. I should have marvelled, if so holy a man had not found crosses in so unequal a match, either in his person, or at least in his seed.

Beauty, if it be not well disciplined, proves not a friend, but a traitor: three of David's children are undone by it at once. What else was guilty of Amnon's incestuous love, Tamar's ravishment, Absalom's pride? It is a blessing to be fair, yet such a blessing, as, if the soul answer not to the face, may lead to a curse. How commonly have we seen the foulest soul dwell fairest? It was no fault of Tamar's that she was beautiful: the candle offends not in burning; the foolish fly offends in scorching itself in the flame; yet it is no small misery to become a temptation unto another, and to be made but the occasion of other's ruin. Amnon is love-sick of his sister Tamar, and languishes of that unnatural heat. Whither will not wanton lust carry the inordinate minds of pampered and ungoverned youths? None but this half-sister will please the eyes of the young prince of Israel. Ordinary pleasures will not content those whom the conceit of greatness, youth, and ease, have let loose to their appetite.

Perhaps yet this unkindly flame might in time have gone out alone, had not there been a Jonadab to blow these coals with ill counsel. It were strange, if great princes should want some parasitical followers, that are ready to feed their ill humours. " Why art thou, the king's son, so lean from day to day?" as if it were unworthy the heir of a king to suffer either law or conscience to stand in the way of his desires: whereas wise princes know well, that their places give them no privilege of sinning, but call them in rather to so much more strictness, as their example may be more prejudicial.

Jonadab was the cousin-german of Amnon. Ill advice is so much more dangerous, as the interest of the giver is more. Had he been a true friend, he had bent all the forces of his dissuasion against the wicked motions of that sinful lust; and had showed the prince of Israel how much those lewd desires provoked God, and blemished himself, and had lent his hand to strangle them in their first conception. There cannot be a more worthy improvement of friendship, than in a fervent opposition to the sins of them whom we profess to love. No enemy can be so mortal to great princes, as those officious clients, whose flattery soothes them up in wickedness: these are traitors to the soul, and by a pleasing violence, kill the best part eternally.

How ready at hand is an evil suggestion! Good counsel is like unto well-water, that must be drawn up with a pump or bucket: ill counsel is like to conduit-water, which, if the cock be but turned, runs out alone. Jonadab hath soon projected how Amnon shall accomplish his lawless purpose. The way must be to feign himself sick in body, whose mind was sick of lust; and under this pretence, to procure the presence of her who had wounded, and only might cure him.

The daily increasing languor and leanness and paleness of love-sick Amnon, might well give colour to a kerchief and a pallet. Now is it soon told David that his eldest son is cast upon his sick-bed: there needs no suit for his visitation. The careful father hastens to his bed-side, not without doubts and fears. He that was lately so afflicted with the sickness of a child that scarce lived to see the light, how sensible must we needs think he would be of the indisposition of his first-born son, in the prime of his age and hopes! It is not given to any prophet to foresee all things. Happy had it been for David, if Amnon had been truly sick, and sick unto death; yet who could have persuaded this passionate father to have been content with this succession of losses, this early loss of his successor! How glad is he to hear, that his daughter Tamar's skill might be likely to fit the diet of so dear a patient! Conceit is wont to rule much, both in sickness and in the cure. Tamar is sent by her father to the house of Amnon: her hand only must dress that dish which may please the nice palate of her sick brother. Even the children of kings, in those homlier times, did not scorn to put their fingers to some works of housewifery: " She took flour and did knead it, and did make cakes in his sight, and did bake the cakes, and took a pan, and poured them out before him." Had she not been sometimes used to such domestic employments, she had been now to seek; neither had this been required of her, but upon the knowledge of her skill. She doth not plead the impairing of her beauty by the scorching of the fire, nor thinks her hand too dainty for such mean services, but settles to the work, as one that had rather regard the necessities of her brother, than her own state. Only pride and idleness have banished honest and thrifty diligence out of the houses of the great.

This was not yet the dish that Amnon longed for: it was the cook, and not the cakes, which that wanton eye affected. Unlawful acts seek for secrecy: the company is dismissed; Tamar only stays. Good meaning suspects nothing: while she presents the meat she had prepared to her sick brother, herself is made a prey to his outrageous lust. The modest virgin entreats and persuades in vain: she lays before him the sin, the shame, the danger of the fact; and, since none of these can prevail, fain would win time by the suggestion of impossible hopes. Nothing but violence can stay a resolved sinner; what he cannot by entreaty, he will have by force. If the devil were not more strong in men than nature, they would never seek pleasure in violence. Amnon hath no sooner fulfilled his beastly desires, than he hates Tamar more than he loved her. Inordinate lust never ends but in discontentment; loss of spirits, and the remorse of soul, make the remembrance of that act tedious, whose expectation promised delight. If we could see the back of sinful pleasures, ere we behold their face, our hearts could not but be forestalled with a just detestation. Brutish Amnon, it was thyself whom thou shouldst have hated for this villany, not thine innocent sister! Both of you lay together; only one committed incest. What was she but a patient in that impotent fury of lust? How unjustly do carnal men misplace their affections! No man can say, whether that love or this hatred were more unreasonable. Fraud drew Tamar into the house of Amnon; force entertained her within, and drove her out. Fain would she have hid her shame where it was wrought, and may not be allowed it. That roof, under which she came with honour, and in obedience and love, may not be lent her, for the time, as a shelter for her ignominy. Never any savage could be more barbarous. Shechem had ravished Dinah; his offence did not make her odious; his affection so continued, that he is willing rather to draw blood of himself and his people, than forego her whom he had abused; Amnon, in one hour, is in the excess of love and hate, and is sick of her for whom he was sick: she that lately kept the keys of his heart, is now locked out of his doors. Unruly passions run ever into extremities, and are then best appaid, when they are furthest off from reason and moderation.

What could Amnon think would be the event of so foul a fact, which, as he had not the grace to prevent, so he hath not the care to conceal? If he looked not so high as heaven, what could he imagine would follow hereupon, but the displeasure of a father, the danger of law, the indignation of a brother, the shame and outcries of the world; all which he might have hoped to avoid by secrecy and plausible courses of satisfaction. It is the just judgment of God upon presumptuous offenders, that they lose their wit, together with their honesty; and are either so blinded, that they cannot foresee the issue of their actions, or so besotted, that they do not regard it.

Poor Tamar can but bewail that which she could not keep, her virginity, not lost, but torn from her, by a cruel violence. She rends her princely robe, and lays ashes on her head, and laments the shame of another's sin, and lives more desolate than a widow, in the house of her brother Absalom.

In the meantime, what a corrosive must this news needs be to the heart of good David, whose fatherly command had, out of love, cast his daughter into the jaws of this lion! What an insolent affront must he needs construe this to be offered by a son to a father, that the father should be made the pander of his own daughter to his son! He that lay upon the ground weeping for but the sickness of an infant, how vexed do we think he was with the villany of his heir, with the ravishment of his daughter, both of them worse than many deaths! What revenge can he think of for so heinous a crime, less than death? and what less than death is it to him, to think of a revenge? Rape was, by the law of God, capital; how much more when it is seconded with incest! Anger was not punishment enough for so high an offence; yet this is all that I hear of from so indulgent a father, saving that he makes up the rest with sorrow, punishing his son's outrage in himself. The better natured and more gracious a man is, the more subject he is to the danger of an over-remissness, and the excess of favour and mercy. The mild injustice is no less perilous to the commonwealth, than the cruel.

If David, perhaps out of the conscience of his own late offence, will not punish this fact, his son Absalom shall; not out of any care of justice, but in a desire of revenge;

Two whole years hath this sly courtier smothered his indignation, and feigned kindness, else his invitation of Amnon, in special, had been suspected. Even gallant Absalom was a great sheep-master. The bravery and magnificence of a courtier must be built upon the grounds of frugality. David himself is bidden to this bloody sheep-shearing: it was no otherwise meant, but that the father's eyes should be the witnesses of the tragical execution of one son by another; only David's love kept him from that horrible spectacle. He is careful not to be chargeable to that son who cares not to overcharge his father's stomach with a feast of blood.

Amnon hath so quite forgot his sin, that he dares go to feast in that house where Tamar was mourning, and suspects not the kindness of him, whom he had deserved, of a brother, to make an enemy. Nothing is more unsafe to be trusted, than the fair looks of a festered heart. Where true charity or just satisfaction have not wrought a sound reconciliation, malice doth but lurk for the opportunity of an advantage.

It was not for nothing that Absalom deferred his revenge, which is now so much more exquisite, as it is longer protracted. What could be more fearful than, when Amnon's heart was merry with wine, to be suddenly stricken with death? as if this execution had been no less intended to the soul than to the body. How wickedly soever this was done by Absalom, yet how just was it with God, that he, who in two years' impunity would find no leisure of repentance, should now receive a punishment without possibility of repentance!

O God, thou art righteous to reckon for those sins which human partiality or negligence hath omitted; and while thou punishest sin with sin, to punish sin with death. If either David had called Amnon to account for this villany, or Amnon had called himself, the revenge had not been so desperate. Happy is the man, that by an unfeigned repentance acquits his soul from his known evils, and improves the days of his peace to the prevention of future vengeance, which, if it be not done, the hand of God shall as surely overtake us in judgment, as the hand of Satan hath overtaken us in miscarriage unto sin.

CONTEMPLATION VII.—ABSALOM'S RETURN AND CONSPIRACY.

ONE act of injustice draws on another: the injustice of David, in not punishing the rape of Amnon, procures the injustice of Absalom, in punishing Amnon with murder. That which the father should have justly revenged, and did not, the son revenges unjustly. The rape of a sister was no less worthy of death, than the murder of a brother; yea, this latter sin was therefore the less, because that brother was worthy of death, though by another hand; whereas that sister was guilty of nothing but modest beauty: yet he that knew this rape passed over a whole two years with impunity; dares not trust the mercy of a father in the pardon of his murder; but for three years hides his head in the court of his grandfather, the king of Geshur. Doubtless that heathenish prince gave him a kind welcome, for so meritorious a revenge of the dishonour done to his own loins.

No man can tell how Absalom should have sped from the hands of his otherwise over-indulgent father, if he had been apprehended in the heat of the fact. Even the largest love may be over-strained, and may give a fall in the breaking: these fearful effects of lenity might perhaps have whetted the severity of David, to shut up these outrages in blood. Now this displeasure was weakened with age. Time and thoughts have digested this hard morsel. David's heart told him, that his hands had a share in this offence; that Absalom did but give that stroke which himself had wrongfully forborne; that the unrecoverable loss of one son would be but wofully relieved with the loss of another; he therefore, that in the news of the deceased infant could change his clothes, and wash himself, and cheer up his spirits, with the resolution of, "I shall go to him, he shall not return to me," comforts himself concerning Amnon; and begins to long for Absalom.

Those three years' banishment seemed not so much a punishment to the son, as to the father. Now David begins to forgive himself: yet, out of his wisdom, he inclines to favour, that he conceals it; and yet so conceals it, that it may be descried by a cunning eye. If he had cast out no glances of affection, there had been no hopes for his Absalom; if he had made profession of love after so foul an act, there had been no safety for others: now, he lets fall so much secret grace as may both hold up Absalom in the life of his hopes, and not hearten the presumption of others.

Good eyes see light through the smallest chink. The wit of Joab hath soon discerned David's reserved affection, and knows how to serve him in that which he would and would not accomplish; and now devises how to bring into the light that birth of desire, whereof he knew David was both big and ashamed. A woman of Tekoah (that sex hath been ever held more apt for wiles) is suborned to personate a mourner, and to say that by way of parable, which in plain terms would have sounded too harshly; and now, while she lamentably lays forth the loss and danger of her son, she shows David his own; and, while she moves compassion to her pretended issue, she wins David to a pity of himself, and a favourable sentence for Absalom. We love ourselves better than others, but we see others better than ourselves: whoso would perfectly know his own case, let him view it in another's person.

Parables sped well with David: one drew him to repent of his own sin, another to remit Absalom's punishment: and now, as glad to hear this plea, and willing to be persuaded unto that which, if he durst, he would have sought for, he gratifies Joab with the grant of that suit, which Joab more gratified him in suing for: " Go, bring again the young man Absalom."

How glad is Joab that he hath lighted upon one act, for which the sun, both setting and rising, should shine upon him! and now he speeds to Geshur, to fetch back Absalom to Jerusalem. He may bring the long-banished prince to the city, but to the court he may not bring him: " Let him turn to his own house, and let him not see my face."

The good king hath so smarted with mercy, that now he is resolved upon austerity, and will relent but by degrees: it is enough for Absalom that he lives, and may now breathe in his native air; David's face is no object for the eyes of murderers. What a darling this son was to his father appears in that, after an unnatural and barbarous rebellion, passionate David wishes to have changed lives with him; yet now, while his bowels yearned, his brow frowned: the face may not be seen where the heart is set.

The best of God's saints may be blinded with affection; but when they shall once see their errors, they are careful to correct them. Wherefore serves the power of grace, but to subdue the insolencies of nature? It is the wisdom of parents, as to hide their hearts from their best children, so to hide their countenances from the ungracious: fleshly respects may not abate their rigour to the ill-deserving. For the child to see all his father's love, it is enough to make him wanton, and of wanton, wicked. For a wicked child to see any of his father's love, it emboldens him in evil, and draws on others.

Absalom's house is made his prison: justly is he confined to the place which he had stained with blood. Two years doth he live in Jerusalem without the happiness of his father's sight: it was enough for David and him to see the smoke of each other's chimneys. In the meantime, how impatient is Absalom of this absence! He sends for Joab, the solicitor of his return: so hard a hand doth wise and holy David carry over his reduced son, that his friendly intercessor Joab dares not visit him.

He that afterwards kindled that seditious fire over all Israel, sets fire now on the field of Joab: whom love cannot draw to him, fear and anger shall. Continued displeasure hath made Absalom desperate. Five years are passed since he saw the face of his father, and now he is no less weary of his life than of this delay: " Wherefore am I come down from Geshur? It had been better for me to have been there still. Now, therefore, let me see the king's face; and if there be any iniquity in me, let him kill me." Either banishment or death seemed as tolerable to him, as the debarring of his father's sight.

What a torment shall it be to the wicked, to be shut out for ever from the presence of a God, without all possible hopes of recovery! This was but a father of the flesh, by whom, if Absalom lived at first, yet in him he lived not; yea, not without him only, but against him, that son found he could live. God is the Father of spirits, in whom we so live, that without him can be no life, no being: to be ever excluded from Him in whom we live and are, what can it be but an eternal dying, an eternal perishing? If in thy presence, O God, be the fulness of joy, in thine absence must needs be the fulness of horror and torment: " Hide not thy face from us, O Lord, but show us the light of thy countenance, that we may live and praise thee."

Even the fire of Joab's field warmed the heart of David, while it gave him proof of the heat of Absalom's filial affection. As a man, therefore, inwardly weary of so long displeasure, at last he receives Absalom to his sight, to his favour, and seals his pardon with a kiss. Natural parents know not how to retain an everlasting anger towards the fruit of their loins: how much less shall the God of mercies be unreconcileably displeased with his own, and suffer his wrath to burn like fire that cannot be quenched! " He will not always chide, neither will he keep his anger for ever; his wrath endureth but a moment; in his favour is life: weeping may endure for a night, but joy cometh in the morning."

Absalom is now as great as fair: beauty and greatness make him proud; pride works his ruin: great spirits will not rest content with a moderate prosperity. Ere two years be run out, Absalom runs out into a desperate plot of rebellion: none but his own father was above him in Israel; none was so likely, in human expectation, to succeed his father. If his ambition could but have contained itself for a few years, as David was now near his period, dutiful carriage might have procured that by succession, which now he sought by force. An aspiring mind is ever impatient, and holds time itself an enemy, if it thrust itself importunately betwixt the hopes and fruition. Ambition is never but in travail, and can find no intermission of painful throes, till she have brought forth her abortive desires. How happy were we, if our affection could be so eager of spiritual and heavenly promotions! O that my soul could find itself so restless, till it feel the weight of that crown of glory!

Outward pomp, and unwonted shows of magnificence, are wont much to affect the light minds of the vulgar. Absalom, therefore, to the incomparable comeliness of his person, adds the unusual state of a more than princely equipage. His chariots rattle, and his horses trample proudly in the streets; fifty footmen run before their glittering master; Jerusalem rings of their glorious prince, and is ready to adore these continual triumphs of peace. Excess and novelty of expensive bravery and ostentation in public persons, gives just cause to suspect either vanity, or a plot. True-hearted David can misdoubt nothing in him, to whom he had both given life, and forgiven this. Love construed all this as meant to the honour of a father's court, to the expression of joy and thankfulness for his reconcilement. The eyes and tongues of men are thus taken up; now hath Absalom laid snares for their hearts also: " He rises early, and stands beside the way of the gate." Ambition is no niggard of her pains; seldom ever is good meaning so industrious. The more he shined in beauty and royal attendance, so much more glory it was to neglect himself, and to prefer the care of justice to his own case. Neither is Absalom more painful than plausible: his ear is open to all plaintiffs, all petitioners; there is no cause which he flatters not: " See thy matters are good and right:" his hand flatters every comer with a salutation, his lips with a kiss. All men, all matters, are soothed, saving the state and government; the censure of that is no less deep, than the applause of all others: " There is none deputed of the king to hear thee." What insinuations could be more powerful? No music can be so sweet to the ears of the unstable multitude, as to near well of themselves, ill of their governors. Absalom needs not to wish himself upon the bench; every man says, O what a courteous prince is Absalom! what a just and careful ruler would Absalom be! how happy were we, if we might be judged by Absalom! Those qualities, which are wont single to grace others, have conspired to meet in Absalom: goodliness of person, magnificence of state, gracious affability, unwearied diligence, humility in greatness, feeling pity, love of justice, care of the commonwealth! The world hath not so complete a prince as Absalom! Thus the hearts of the people are not won, but stolen, by a close traitor, from their lawfully anointed sovereign. Over-fair shows are a just argument of unsoundness; no natural face hath so clear a white and red as the painted. Nothing wants now but a cloak of religion, to perfect the treachery of that ungracious son, who carried peace in his name, war in his heart: and how easily is that put on! Absalom hath a holy vow to be paid in Hebron: the devout man had made it long since, while he was exiled in Syria, and now he hastes to perform it: " If the Lord shall bring me back again to Jerusalem, then I will serve the Lord." Wicked hypocrites care not to play with God, that they may mock men. The more deformed any act is, the fairer vizard it still seeketh.

How glad is the good old king, that he is blessed with so godly a son, whom he dismisseth laden with his causeless blessings! What trust is there in flesh and blood, when David is not safe from his own loins? The conspiracy is now fully formed: there lacked nothing but this gilding of piety to win favour and value in all eyes; and now it is a wonder, that but two hundred honest citizens go up with Absalom from Jerusalem: the true-hearted lie most open to credulity: how easy is it to beguile harmless intentions! The name of David's son carries them against the father of Absalom; and now these simple Israelites are unwittingly made loyal rebels. Their hearts are free from a plot, and they mean nothing but fidelity in the attendance of a traitor. How many thousands are thus ignorantly misled into the train of error! Their simplicity is as worthy of pity, as their misguidance of indignation. Those that will suffer themselves to be carried with semblances of truth and faithfulness, must needs be as far from safety as innocence.

BOOK XVI.

CONTEMPLATION I.—SHIMEI CURSING.

WITH a heavy heart and a covered head, and a weeping eye and bare feet, is David gone away from Jerusalem; never did he with more joy come up to this city, than now he left it with sorrow: how could he do otherwise, whom the insurrection of his own son drove out from his house, from his throne, from the ark of God? And now, when the depth of this grief deserved nothing but compassion, the foul mouth of Shimei entertains David with curses!— There is no small cruelty in the picking out of a time for mischief; that word would scarce gall at one season, which at another killeth. The same shaft flying with the wind pierces deep, which against it can hardly find strength to stick upright. The valour and justice of children condemn it for injuriously cowardly, to strike their adversary when he is once down. It is the murder of the tongue to insult upon those whom God hath humbled, and to draw blood of that back which is yet blue from the hand of the Almighty. If Shimei had not presumed upon David's dejection, he durst not have been thus bold; now he, that perhaps durst not have looked at one of these worthies single, defies them all at once, and doth both cast and speak stones against David and all his army. The malice of base spirits sometimes carries them further than the courage of the valiant.

In all the time of David's prosperity, we heard no news of Shimei: his silence and colourable obedience made him pass for a good subject; yet all that while was his heart unsound and traitorous. Peace and good success hide many a false heart, likeas the snow-drift covers a heap of dung, which once melting away, descries the rottenness that lay within. Honour and welfare are but flattering glasses of men's affections. Adversity will not deceive us, but will make a true report, as of our own powers, so of the disposition of others.

He that smiled on David in his throne, curseth him in his flight. If there be any quarrels, any exceptions to be taken against a man, let him look to have them laid in his dish when he fares the hardest. This practice have wicked men learned of their master, to take the utmost advantages of our afflictions. He that suffers had need to be double armed, both against pain and censure.

Every word of Shimei was a slander. He that took Saul's spear from his head, and repented to have but cut the lap of his garment, is reproached as a man of blood. The man after God's own heart is branded for a man of Belial. He, that was sent for out of the fields to be anointed, is taxed for an usurper. If David's hands were stained with blood, yet not of Saul's house; it was his servant, not his master, that bled by him; yet is the blood of the Lord's anointed cast in David's teeth, by the spite of a false tongue. Did we not see David, after all the proofs of his humble loyalty, shedding the blood of that Amalekite, who did but say he shed Saul's? Did we not hear him lament passionately for the death of so ill a master, chiding the mountains of Gilboa on which he fell; and angrily wishing, that no dew might fall where that blood was poured out; and charging the daughters of Israel to weep over Saul, who had clothed them in scarlet? Did we not hear and see him inquiring for any remainder of the house of Saul, that he might show him the kindness of God? Did we not see him honouring lame Mephibosheth with a princely seat at his own table? Did we not see him revenging the blood of his rival Ishbosheth, upon the heads of Rechab and Baanah? What could any living man have done more to wipe off these bloody aspersions? Yet is not a Shimei ashamed to charge innocent David with all the blood of the house of Saul.

How is it likely this clamorous wretch had secretly traduced the name of David, all the time of his government, that dares thus accuse him to his face, before all the mighty men of Israel, who were witnesses of the contrary? The greater the person is, the more open do his actions lie to misinterpretation and censure. Every tongue speaks partially, according to the interest he hath in the cause, or the patient. It is not possible that eminent persons should be free from imputations: innocence can no more protect them than power.

If the patience of David can digest this indignity, his train cannot; their fingers could not but itch to return iron for stones. If Shimei rail on David, Abishai rails on Shimei; Shimei is of Saul's family, Abishai of David's; each speaks for his own. Abishai most justly bends his tongue against Shimei, as Shimei against David most unjustly. Had Shimei been any other than a dog, he had never so rudely barked at a harmless passenger; neither could he deserve less than the loss of that head which had uttered such blasphemies against God's anointed. The zeal of Abishai doth but plead for justice, and is checked: "What have I to do with you, ye sons of Zeruiah?" David said not so much to his reviler, as to his abettor: he well saw that a revenge was just, but not seasonable; he found the present a fit time time to suffer wrongs, not to right them: he therefore gives way rather meekly to his own humiliation, than to the punishment of another. There are seasons wherein lawful motions are not fit to be cherished: anger doth not become a mourner; one passion at once is enough for the soul. Unadvised zeal may be more prejudicial than a cold remissness.

What if the Lord, for the correction of his servant, had said unto Shimei, Curse David; yet is Shimei's curse no less worthy of Abishai's sword: the sin of Shimei's curse was his own; the smart of the curse was God's. God wills that, as David's chastisement, which he hates as Shimei's wickedness: that lewd tongue moved from God, it moved lewdly from Satan. Wicked men are never the freer from guilt or punishment, for that hand which the holy God hath in their offensive actions: yet David can say, "Let him alone, and let him curse, for the Lord hath bidden him;" as meaning to give a reason of his own patience, rather than Shimei's impunity. The issue showed, how well David could distinguish betwixt the act of God and of a traitor; how he could both kiss the rod and burn it. There can be none so strong motive of our meek submission to evils, as the acknowledgment of their original. He that can see the hand of God striking him by the hand or tongue of an enemy, shall more awe the first mover of his arm, than malign the instrument. Even while David laments the rebellion of his son, he gains by it, and makes that the argument of his patience, which was the exercise of it: "Behold my son, which came forth of my bowels, seeketh my life; how much more now may this Benjamite do it?" The wickedness of an Absalom may rob his father of comfort, but shall help to add to his father's goodness. It is the advantage of great crosses, that they swallow up the less. One man's sin cannot be excused by another's, the lesser by the greater. If Absalom be a traitor, Shimei may not curse and rebel: but the passion conceived from the indignity of a stranger, may be abated by the harder measure of our own; if we can therefore suffer, because we have suffered, we have profited by our affliction. A weak heart faints with every addition of succeeding trouble; the strong recollects itself, and is grown so skilful, that it bears off one mischief with another.

It is not either the unnatural insurrection of Absalom, nor the unjust curses of Shimei, that can put David quite out of heart: "It may be that the Lord will look on mine affliction, and will requite good for his cursing, this day." So well was David acquainted with the proceedings of God, that he knew cherishing was ever wont to follow stripes; after vehement evacuation, cordials; after a dark night, the clear light of the morning. Hope, therefore, doth not only uphold, but cheer up his heart, in the midst of his sorrow. If we can look beyond the cloud of our affliction, and see the sunshine of comfort on the other side of it, we cannot be so discouraged with the presence of evil, as heartened with the issue: as, on the contrary, let a man be never so merry within, and see pain and misery waiting for him at the door, his expectation of evil shall easily daunt all the sense of his pleasure. The retributions of temporal favours go but by peradventures: "It may be, the Lord will look on mine affliction;"—of eternal, are certain and infallible; if we suffer, we shall reign: why should not the assurance of reigning make us triumph in suffering?

David's patience draws on the insolence of Shimei. Evil natures grow presumptuous upon forbearance. In good dispositions, injury unanswered grows weary of itself, and dies in a voluntary remorse; but in those dogged stomachs, which are only capable of the restraints of fear, the silent digestion of a former wrong provokes a second. Mercy had need to be guided with wisdom, lest it prove cruel to itself.

O the base minds of inconstant timeservers! Stay but a while, till the wheel be a little turned, you shall see humble Shimei fall down on his face before David, in his return over Jordan: now his submission shall equal his former rudeness; his prayers shall requite his curses, his tears makes amends for his stones: "Let not my lord impute iniquity unto me: neither do thou remember that which thy servant did perversely, the day that my lord the king went out of Jerusalem, that the king should take it to his heart; for thy servant doth know that I have sinned." False-hearted Shimei! had Absalom prospered, thou hadst not sinned, thou hadst not repented; then hadst thou bragged of thine insultation over his miseries, whose pardon thou now beggest with tears. The changes of worldly minds are thankless, since they are neither wrought out of conscience nor love, but only by slavish fear of just punishment.

David could say no more, to testify his sorrow for his heinous sin against God, to Nathan, than Shimei says of himself to David; whereto may be added the advantage of a voluntary confession in this offender, which in David was extorted by the reproof of a prophet; yet is David's confession seriously penitent, Shimei's craftily hypocritical. Those alterations are justly suspected, which are shaped according to the times and outward occasions. The true penitent looks only at God and his sin, and is changed when all other things are themselves.

Great offences had need of answerable satisfaction. As Shimei was the only man, of the house of Benjamin, that came forth and cursed David in his flight, so is he the first man (even before those of the house of Joseph, though nearer in situation) that comes to meet David in his return with prayers and gratulations. Notorious offenders may not think to sit down with the task of ordinary services: the retributions of their obedience must be proportionable to their crimes.

CONTEMPLATION II.—AHITHOPHEL.

So soon as David heard of Ahithophel's hand in that conspiracy, he falls to his prayers: " O Lord, I pray thee, turn the counsel of Ahithophel into foolishness." The known wisdom of his revolted counsellor made him a dangerous and dreadful adversary. Great parts misemployed cannot but prove most mischievous. When wickedness is armed with wit and power, none but a God can defeat it; when we are matched with a strong and subtle enemy, it is high time, if ever, to be devout. If the bounty of God have thought good to furnish his creatures with powers to war against himself, his wisdom knows how to turn the abuse of those powers to the shame of the owners, and the glory of the giver.

O the policy of this Machiavel of Israel, no less deep than hell itself! " Go into thy father's concubines, which he hath left to keep the house: and when all Israel shall hear that thou art abhorred of thy father, the hands of all that are with thee shall be strong." The first care must be to secure the faction. There can be no safety in siding with a doubtful rebel. If Absalom be a traitor, yet he is a son. Nature may return to itself; Absalom may relent; David may remit: Where then are we that have helped to promote the conspiracy? The danger is ours, while this breach may be pieced. There is no way but to engage Absalom in some further act, uncapable of forgiveness: besides the throne, let him violate the bed of his father; unto his treason, let him add an incest no less unnatural; now shall the world see that Absalom neither hopes nor cares for the reconciliation of a father. Our quarrel can never have any safe end but victory; the hope whereof depends upon the resolution of our followers: they cannot be resolute, but upon the unpardonable wickedness of their leader; neither can this villany be shameful enough, if it be secret. The closeness of evil argues fear, or modesty; neither of which can beseem him that would be a successful traitor. Set up a tent on the top of the house, and let all Israel be witnesses of thy sin, and thy father's shame. Ordinary crimes are for vulgar offenders; let Absalom sin eminently, and do that which may make the world at once to blush and wonder.

Who would ever have thought that Ahithophel had lived at court, at the council-table of a David? who would think that mouth had ever spoken well? Yet had he been no other than as the oracle of God to the religious court of Israel, even while he was not wise enough to be good. Policy and grace are not always lodged under one roof. This man, while he was one of David's deep counsellors, was one of David's fools, that said in their hearts, "There is no God;" else he could not have hoped to make good an evil with worse, to build the success of treason upon incest.

Profane hearts do so contrive the plots of their wickedness, as if there were no overruling power to cross their designs, or to revenge them. He that sits in heaven laughs them to scorn, and so far gives way to their sins, as their sins may prove plagues unto themselves.

These two sons of David met with pestilent counsel: Amnon is advised to incest with his sister; Absalom is advised to incest with his father's concubines; that by Jonadab, this by Ahithophel: both prevail. It is as easy at least to take ill counsel as to give it. Proneness to villany in the great cannot want either projectors to devise, or parasites to execute the most odious sins.

The tent is spread, lest it should not be conspicuous enough, on the top of the house. The act is done in the sight of all Israel. The filthiness of the sin was not so great as the impudency of the manner.

When the prophet Nathan came with that heavy message of reproof and menace to David, after his sin with Bathsheba, he could say from God, "Behold, I will raise up evil against thee, out of thine own house, and will take thy wives before thine eyes, and give them to thy neighbour, and he shall lie with thy wives in the sight of this sun: for thou didst it secretly, but I will do this thing before all Israel, and before this sun." The counsel of Ahithophel, and the lust of Absalom, have fulfilled the judgment of God. O the wisdom of the Almighty, that can use the worst evils well, and most justly make the sins of men his executioners!

It was the sin of Reuben that he defiled his father's bed; yet not in the same height of lewdness. What Reuben did in a youthful wantonness, Absalom did in a malicious despite: Reuben sinned with one, Absalom with ten; Reuben secretly, Absalom in the open eyes of heaven and earth: yet old Jacob could say of Reuben, "Thou shalt not excel; thy dignity is gone;" while Ahithophel says to Absalom, "Thy dignity shall arise from incest: climb up to thy father's bed, if thou wilt sit in his throne. Ahithophel was a politician; Jacob was a prophet: if the one spake from carnal sense, the other from divine revelation. Certainly, to sin is not the way to prosper: whatever vain fools promise to themselves, there is no wisdom, nor understanding, nor counsel, against the Lord.

After the rebellion is secured for continuance, the next care is, that it may end in victory: this also hath the working head of Ahithophel projected. Wit and experience told him, that in these cases of assault, celerity uses to bring forth the happiest despatch; whereas protraction is no small advantage to the defendant: "Let me (saith he) choose out now twelve thousand men, and I will up, and follow after David this night; and I will come upon him when he is weary and weak-handed." No advice could be more pernicious; for, besides the weariness and unreadiness of David and his army, the spirits of that worthy leader were daunted, and dejected with sorrow, and offered way to the violence of a sudden assault. The field had been half won, ere any blow stricken. Ahithophel could not have been reputed so wise, if he had not learned the due proportion betwixt actions and times. He that observeth every wind, shall never sow; but he that observes no wind at all, shall never reap.

The likeliest devices do not always succeed. The God that had appointed to establish David's throne, and determined Solomon to his succession, finds means to cross the plot of Ahithophel by a less probable advice. Hushai was not sent back for nothing. Where God hath, in his secret will, decreed any event, he inclines the wills of men to approve that which may promote his own purposes. Neither had Hushai so deep a head, neither was his counsel so sure as that of Ahithophel; yet his tongue shall refel Ahithophel, and divert Absalom. The pretences were fairer, though the grounds were unsound: first, to sweeten his opposition, he yields the praise of wisdom to his adversary in all other counsels, that he may have leave to deny it in this; his very contradiction in the present, insinuates a general allowance. Then he suggests certain apparent truths concerning David's valour and skill, to give countenance to the inferences of his improbabilities. Lastly, he cunningly feeds the proud humour of Absalom, in magnifying the power and extent of his commands, and ends in the glorious boasts of his forepromised victory. As it is with faces, so with counsel: that is fair that pleaseth. He that gives the utterance to words, gives also their speed. Favour, both of speech and men, is not ever according to desert, but according to foreordination. The tongue of Hushai, and the heart of Absalom, are guided by a power above their own: Hushai shall therefore prevail with Absalom, that the treason of Absalom may not prevail. He that worketh all in all things, so disposeth of wicked men and spirits, that while they do most oppose his revealed will, they execute his secret; and while they think most to please, they overthrow themselves.

When Absalom first met Hushai returned to Jerusalem, he upbraided him pleasantly with the scoff of his professed friendship to David: "Is this thy kindness to thy friend?" Sometimes there is more truth in the mouth than in the heart; more in jest than in earnest. Hushai was a friend; his stay was his kindness: and now he hath done that for which he was left at Jerusalem, disappointed Ahithophel, preserved David: neither did his kindness to his friend rest here, but, as one that was justly jealous of him with whom he was allowed to temporize, he mistrusts the approbation of Absalom; and not daring to put the life of his master upon such a hazard, he gives charge to Zadok and Abiathar of this intelligence unto David. We cannot be too suspicious, when we have to do with those that are faithless. We cannot be too curious of the safety of good princes.

Hushai fears not to descry the secrets of Absalom's counsel: to betray a traitor, is no other than a commendable work. Zadok and Abiathar are fast within the gates of Jerusalem; their sons lay purposely abroad in the fields: this message, that concerned no less than the life of David, and the whole kingdom of Israel, must be trusted with a maid. Sometimes it pleaseth the wisdom of God, who hath the variety of heaven and earth before him, to single out weak instruments for great services; and they shall serve his turn, as well as the best. No counsellor of state could have made this despatch more effectual: Jonathan and Ahimaaz are sent, descried, pursued, preserved. The fidelity of a maid instructed them in their message, the subtilty of a woman saved their lives. At the well of Rogel they received their message; in the well of Bahurim was their life saved: the sudden wit of a woman hath choked the mouth of her well with dried corn, that it might not bewray the messengers: and now David hears safely of his danger, and prevents it; and though weary with travel, and laden with sorrow, he must spend the night in his remove. God's promises of his deliverance, and the confirmation of his kingdom, may not make him neglect the means of his safety. If he be faithful, we may not be careless, since our diligence and care are appointed for the factors of that divine Providence. The acts of God must abate nothing of ours; rather must we labour, by doing that which he requireth, to further that which he decreeth.

There are those that have great wits for the public; none for themselves. Such was Ahithophel, who, while he had power to govern a state, could not tell how to rule his own passions: never till now do we find his counsel baulked; neither was it now rejected as ill, only Hushai's was allowed for better: he can live no longer now, that he is beaten at his own weapon; this alone is cause enough to saddle his ass, and to go home, and put the halter about his own neck. Pride causes men both to misinterpret disgraces, and to overrate them. Now is David's prayer heard: " Ahithophel's counsel is turned into foolishness." Desperate Ahithophel! what if thou be not the wisest man of all Israel? even those that have not attained to the highest pitch of wisdom have found contentment in a mediocrity: what if thy counsel were despised? a wise man knows to live happily, in spite of an unjust contempt: what madness is this, to revenge another man's reputation upon thyself! and, while thou strivest for the highest room of wisdom, to run into the grossest extremity of folly! Wordly wisdom is no protection from shame and ruin. How easily may a man, though naturally wise, be made weary of life. A little pain, a little shame, a little loss, a small affront, can soon rob a man of all comfort, and cause his own hands to rob him of himself. If there be not higher respects than the world can yield, to maintain us in being, it should be a miracle if indignation did not kill more than disease. Now, that God, by whose appointment we live here, for his most wise and holy purposes, hath found means to make life sweet, and death terrible.

What a mixture do we find here of wisdom and madness! Ahithophel will needs hang himself; there is madness: he will yet set his house in order; there is an act of wisdom. And could it be possible that he, who was so wise as to set his house in order, should be so mad as to hang himself? that he should be careful to order his house, who regarded not to order his impotent passions? that he should care for his house, who cared not for either body or soul? How vain it is for a man to be wise, if he be not wise in God! How preposterous are the cares of idle worldlings, that prefer all other things to themselves, and, while they look at what they have in their coffers, forget what they have in their breasts!

CONTEMPLATION III.—THE DEATH OF ABSALOM.

THE same God that raised enmity to David from his own loins, procured him favour from foreigners; strangers shall relieve him, whom his own son persecutes: here is not a loss, but an exchange of love. Had Absalom been a son of Ammon, and Shobi a son of David, David had found no cause of complaint. If God takes with one hand, he gives with another; while that divine bounty serves us in good meat, though not in our own dishes, we have good reason to be thankful. No sooner is David come to Mahanaim, than Barzillai, Machir, and Shobi, refresh him with provisions. Who ever saw any child of God left utterly destitute? Whosoever be the messenger of our aid, we know whence he comes: heaven shall want power, and earth means, before any of the household of faith shall want maintenance.

He, that formerly was forced to employ his arms for his defence against a tyrannous father-in-law, must now buckle them on

DEATH OF ABSALOM.

against an unnatural son: now, therefore, he musters his men and ordains his commanders, and marshals his troops; and since their loyal importunity will not allow the hazard of his person, he at once encourages them by his eye, and restrains them with his tongue: "Deal gently with the young man Absalom for my sake." How unreasonably favourable are the wars of a father! O holy David, what means this ill-placed love, this unjust mercy? Deal gently with a traitor! but of all traitors with a son! of all sons with an Absalom, the graceless darling of so good a father! and all this for my sake, whose crown, whose blood, he hunts after! For whose sake should Absalom be pursued, if he must be forborne for thine? He was still courteous to thy followers, affable to suitors, plausible to all Israel; only to thee he is cruel. Wherefore are those arms, if the cause of the quarrel must be a motive of mercy? Yet thou sayest, "Deal gently with the young man Absalom for my sake." Even in the holiest parents, nature may be guilty of an injurious tenderness, of a bloody indulgence.

Or, whether shall we not rather think this was done in type of that unmeasurable mercy of the true King and Redeemer of Israel, who prayed for his persecutors, for his murderers? and even while they were at once scorning and killing him, could say, "Father, forgive them, for they know not what they do?" If we be sons, we are ungracious, we are rebellious; yet still is our heavenly Father compassionately regardful of us. David was not sure of his success: there was great inequality in the number; Absalom's forces were more than double to his: it might have come to the contrary issue, that David should have been forced to say, "Deal gently with the father of Absalom;" but in a supposition of that victory, which only the goodness of his cause bade him hope for, he saith, "Deal gently with the young man Absalom." As for us, we are never but under mercy: our God needs no advantages to sweep us from the earth any moment; yet he continues that life and those powers to us, whereby we provoke him, and bids his angels deal kindly with us, and bear us in their arms, while we lift up our hands, and bend our tongues against heaven. O mercy past the comprehension of all finite spirits, and only to be conceived by him whose it is! never more resembled by any earthly affection, than by this of his deputy and type! "Deal gently with the young man Absalom for my sake."

The battle is joined. David's followers are but a handful to Absalom's. How easily may the fickle multitude be transported to the wrong side! What they wanted in abettors, is supplied in the cause. Unnatural ambition draws the sword of Absalom; David's, a necessary and just defence. They, that in simplicity of heart followed Absalom, cannot in malice of heart persecute the father of Absalom. With what courage could any Israelite draw his sword against a David? or, on the other side, who can want courage to fight for a righteous sovereign and father, against the conspiracy of a wicked son? The God of hosts, with whom it is all one to save with many or with few, takes part with justice, and lets Israel feel what it is to bear arms for a traitorous usurper. The sword devours twenty thousand of them, and the wood devours more than the sword: it must needs be a very universal rebellion, wherein so many perished. What virtue or merits can assure the hearts of the vulgar, when so gracious a prince finds so many revolters? Let no man look to prosper by rebellion: the very thickets, and stakes, and pits, and wild beasts of the wood, shall conspire to the punishment of traitors. Amongst the rest, see how a fatal oak hath singled out the ringleader of this hateful insurrection, and will at once serve for his hangman and gallows, by one of those spreading arms snatching him away to speedy execution. Absalom was comely, and he knew it well enough: his hair was no small piece of his beauty, nor matter of his pride; it was his wont to cut it once a year, not for that it was too long, but too heavy; his heart would have borne it longer, if his neck had not complained: and now the justice of God hath plaited a halter of those locks. Those tresses had formerly hanged loosely dishevelled on his shoulders; now he hangs by them: he had wont to weigh his hair, and was proud to find it so heavy; now his hair poiseth the weight of his body, and makes his burden his torment. It is no marvel if his own hair turned traitor to him who durst rise up against his father. That part, which is misused by man to sin, is commonly employed by God to revenge: the revenge that it worketh for God, makes amends for the offence whereto it is drawn against God. The very beast whereon Absalom sat, as weary to bear so unnatural a burden, resigns over his load to the tree of justice: there hangs Absalom between heaven and earth, as one that was hated and abandoned both of earth and heaven; as if God meant to prescribe this punishment for traitors: Absalom, Ahithophel, and Judas, die all one death: so let them perish, that dare lift up their hand against God's anointed!

The honest soldier sees Absalom hanging in the oak, and dares not touch him; his hands were held with the charge of David: "Beware that none touch the young man Absalom." Joab, upon that intelligence, sees him, and smites him, with no less than three darts. What the soldier forebore in obedience, the captain doth in zeal; not fearing to prefer his sovereign's safety to his command, and more tendering the life of a king, and the peace of his country, than the weak affection of a father. I dare not sit judge betwixt his zeal and that obedience; betwixt the captain and the soldier: the one was a good subject, the other a good patriot; the one loved the king, the other loved David, and out of love disobeyed; the one meant as well as the other sped. As if God meant to fulfil the charge of his anointed, without any blame of his subjects, it pleased him to execute that immediate revenge upon the rebel, which would have despatched him without hand or dart: only the mule and the oak conspired to this execution; but that death would have required more leisure, than it was safe for Israel to give, and still life would give hope of rescue: to cut off all fears, Joab lends the oak three darts to help forward so needful a work of justice. All Israel did not afford so firm a friend to Absalom as Joab had been: who but Joab had suborned the witty widow of Tekoah to sue for the recalling of Absalom from his three years exile? who but he went to fetch him from Geshur to Jerusalem? who but he went to fetch him from his house at Jerusalem, whereto he had been two years confined, to the face, to the lips of David? Yet now he, that was his solicitor for the king's favour, is his executioner against the king's charge. With honest hearts, all respects, either of blood or friendship, cease in the case of treason: well hath Joab forgotten himself to be a friend to him, who had forgotten himself to be a son. Even, civilly, the king is our common father, our country our common mother; nature hath no private relations, which should not gladly give place to these: he is neither father, nor son, nor brother, nor friend, that conspires against the common parent. Well doth he, who spake parables for his master's son, now speak darts to his king's enemy, and pierces that heart which was false to so great a father. Those darts are seconded by Joab's followers; each man tries his weapon upon so fair a mark. One death is not enough for Absalom; he is at once hanged, shot, mangled, stoned. Justly was he lift up to the oak, who had lift up himself against his father and sovereign; justly is he pierced with darts, who had pierced his father's heart with so many sorrows; justly is he mangled, who hath dismembered and divided all Israel; justly is he stoned, who not only cursed, but pursued his own parent.

Now Joab sounds the retreat, and calls off his eager troops from execution, however he knew what his rebellious countrymen had deserved in following an Absalom Wise commanders know how to put a difference betwixt the heads of a faction and the misguided multitude; and can pity the one, while they take revenge on the other.

So did Absalom esteem himself, that he thought it would be a wrong to the world to want the memorial of so goodly a person. God had denied him sons; how just it was that he should want a son, who had robbed his father of a son, who would have robbed himself of a father, his father of a kingdom! It had been pity so poisonous a plant should have been fruitful: his pride shall supply nature; he rears up a stately pillar in the king's dale, and calls it by his own name, that he might live in dead stones, who could not survive in living issue; and now behold this curious pile ends in a rude heap, which speaks no language but the shame of that carcass which it covers. Hear this, ye glorious fools, that care not to perpetuate any memory of yourselves to the world, but of ill-deserving greatness; the best of this affectation is vanity; the worst, infamy and dishonour; whereas the memorial of the just shall be blessed: and if his humility shall refuse an epitaph, and choose to hide himself under the bare earth, God himself shall engrave his name upon the pillar of eternity.

There now lies Absalom in the pit, under a thousand grave-stones, in every of which is written his everlasting reproach. Well might this heap overlive that pillar; for when that ceased to be a pillar, it began to be a heap; neither will it cease to be a monument of Absalom's shame, while there are stones to be found upon earth. Even at this day, very pagans and pilgrims that pass that way, cast each man a stone into that heap, and are wont to say in a solemn execration, Cursed be the parricide Absalom, and cursed be all unjust persecutors of their parents, for ever. Fasten your eyes upon this woful spectacle, O all ye rebellious and ungracious children, which rise up against the loins and thighs from which ye fell; and know, that it is the least part of your punishment, that your carcasses rot in the earth, and your name in ignominy: these do but shadow out those eternal sufferings of your souls, for your foul and unnatural disobedience.

Absalom is dead: who shall report it to his father? Surely Joab was not so much afraid of the fact as of the message. There are busy spirits that love to carry news, though thankless, though purposeless: such was Ahimaaz, the son of Zadok, who importunately thrust himself into this service. Wise Joab, who well saw how unwelcome tidings must be the burden of the first post, dissuades him in vain: he knew David too well to employ a friend to that errand. An Ethiopian servant was a fitter bearer of such a message, than the son of the priest. The entertainment of the person doth so follow the quality of the news, that David could argue afar off, " He is a good man, he cometh with good tidings." O how welcome deserve those messengers to be, that bring us the glad tidings of salvation, that assure us of the foil of all spiritual enemies, and tell us of nothing but victories, and crowns, and kingdoms! If we think not their feet beautiful, our hearts are foul with infidelity and secure worldliness.

So wise is Ahimaaz grown by Joab's intimation, that though he out-went Cushi in his pace, he suffers Cushi to out-go him in his tale, cunningly suppressing that part which he knew must be both necessarily delivered, and unpleasingly received.

As our care is wont to be where our love is, David's first word is not, How fares the host? but, " How fares the young man Absalom?" Like a wise and faithful messenger, Cushi answers by an honest insinuation, " The enemies of my Lord the king, and all that rise against thee to do thee hurt, be as that young man is;" implying both what was done, and why David should approve it being done. How is the good king thunder-struck with that word of his blackamoor; who, as if he were at once bereaved of all comfort, and cared not to live but in the name of Absalom, goes, and weeps, and cries out, " O my son Absalom! my son, my son Absalom! would God I had died for thee! O Absalom, my son, my son!" What is this we hear? that he, whose life Israel valued at ten thousand of theirs, should be exchanged with a traitor's: that a good king, whose life was sought, should wish to lay it down for the preservation of his murderer. The best men have not wont to be the least passionate. But what shall we say to that love of thine, O Saviour, who hast said of us wretched traitors, not " Would God I had died for you!" but, I will die, I do die, I have died for you. O love, like thyself, infinite, incomprehensible, whereat the angels of heaven stand yet amazed, wherewith thy saints are ravished! " Turn away thine eyes from me, for they overcome me. O thou that dwellest in the gardens, the companions hearken to thy voice; cause us to hear it;" that we may in our measure answer thy love, and enjoy it for ever.

CONTEMPLATION IV.—SHEBA'S REBELLION.

It was the doom which God passed upon the man after his own heart, by the mouth of Nathan, that the sword should never depart from his house, for the blood of Uriah: after that wound healed by remission, yet this scar remains. Absalom is no sooner cast down into the pit, than Sheba, the son of Bichri, is up in arms. If David be not plagued, yet he shall be corrected; first by the rod of a son, then of a subject. He had lifted up his hands against a faithful subject; now a faithless dares to lift up his hand against him. Malice, like some hereditary sickness, runs in the blood: Saul and Shimei, and Sheba, were all of an house: that ancient grudge was not yet dead; the fire of the house of Jemini was but raked up, never thoroughly out; and now that, which did but smoke in Shimei, flames in Sheba; although, even through this chastisement, it is not hard to discern a type of that perpetual succession of enmity which should be raised against the true King of Israel. O son of David, when didst thou ever want enemies? How wert thou designed by thine eternal Father, for a sign that should be spoken against! " How did the Gentiles rage, and the people imagine vain things! The kings of the earth assembled, and the rulers came together against thee." Yea, how do the subjects of thine own kingdom daily conspire against thee! Even now, while thou enjoyest peace and glory at thy Father's right hand, as soon shalt thou want friends as enemies upon earth.

No eye of any traitor could espy a just quarrel in the government of David; yet Sheba blows the trumpet of rebellion; and while Israel and Judah are striving who should have the greatest part in their re-established sovereign, he sticks not to say, " We have no part in David, neither have we inheritance in the son of Jesse;" and while he says, " Every man to his tents, O Israel," he calls every man to his own: so, in proclaiming a liberty from a just and loyal subjection, he invites Israel to the bondage of an usurper.

That a lewd conspirator should breathe treason, it is no wonder: but is it not wonder and shame, that, upon every mutinous blast, Israel should turn traitor to God's anointed? It was their late expostulation with David, why their brethren, the men of Judah, should have stolen him from them. Now might David more justly expostulate, why a rebel of their brethren should have stolen them from him. As nothing is more unstable than the multitude, so nothing is more subject to distates than sovereignty; for, as weak minds seek pleasure in change, so every light conceit of irritation seems sufficient colour of change: such the false dispositions of the vulgar are! Love cannot be security enough for princes without the awfulness of power. What hold can there be of popularity, when the same hands that even now fought for David to be all theirs, now fight against him, under the son of Bichri, as none of theirs? As bees, when they are once up in a swarm, are ready to light upon every bough, so the Israelites, being stirred by the late commotion of Absalom, are apt to follow every Sheba. It is unsafe for any state, that the multitude should once know the way to an insurrection: the least track in this kind is easily made a path. Yet, if Israel rebel, Judah continues faithful; neither shall the son of David ever be left destitute of some true subjects in the worst of apostasies. He, that could command all hearts, will ever be followed by some: God had rather glorify himself by a remnant.

Great commanders must have active thoughts: David is not so taken up with the embroiled affairs of his state, as not to intend domestic justice. His ten concubines, which were shamelessly defiled by his incestuous son, are condemned to ward and widowhood. Had not that constupration been partly violent, their punishment had not been so easy; had it not also been partly voluntarily, they had not been so much punished: but how much soever the act did partake of either force or will, justly are they sequestered from David's bed. Absalom was not more unnatural in his rebellion than in his lust: if now David should have returned to his own bed, he had seconded the incest. How much more worthy of separation are they, who have stained the marriage-bed with their wilful sin!

Amasa was one of the witnesses and abettors of Absalom's filthiness; yet is he, out of policy, received to favour and employment, while the concubines suffer. Great men yield many times to those things, out of reasons of state, which, if they were private persons, could not be easily put over. It is no small wisdom to engage a new reconciled friend, that he may be confirmed by his own act; therefore is Amasa commanded to levy the forces of Judah. Joab, after many great merits and achievements, lies rusting in neglect: he, that was so entire with David, as to be of his counsel for Uriah's blood, and so firm to David, as to lead all his battles against the house of Saul, the Ammonites, the Aramites, Absalom, is now cashiered, and must yield his place to a stranger, late an enemy. Who knows not that this son of Zeruiah had shed the blood of war in peace? But if the blood of Absalom had not been louder than the blood of Abner, I fear this change had not been. Now Joab smarteth for a loyal disobedience. How slippery are the stations of earthly honours, and subject to continual mutability! Happy are they who are in favour with him, in whom there is no shadow of change!

Where men are commonly most ambitious to please with their first employments. Amasa slackens his pace. The least delay in matters of rebellion is perilous, may be irrecoverable. The sons of Zeruiah are not sullen: Abishai is sent, Joab goes unsent, to the pursuit of Sheba. Amasa was in their way, whom no quarrel but their envy had made of a brother an enemy. Had the heart of Amasa been privy to any cause of grudge, he had suspected the kiss of Joab; now his innocent eyes look to the lips, not to the hand of his secret enemy; the lips were smooth: "Art thou in health, my brother?" The hand was bloody, which smote him under the fifth rib; that unhappy hand knew well this way unto death, which with one wound hath let out the souls of two great captains, Abner and Amasa: both they were smitten by Joab, both under the fifth rib, both under a pretence of friendship. There is no enmity so dangerous as that which comes masked with love. Open hostility calls us to our guard; but there is no fence against a trusted treachery. We need not be bidden to avoid an enemy; but who would run away from a friend? Thus spiritually deals the world with our souls: it kisses us and stabs us at once; if it did not embrace us with one hand, it could not murder us with the other: only God deliver us from the danger of our trust, and we shall be safe.

Joab is gone, and leaves Amasa wallowing in blood, That spectacle cannot but stay all passengers: the death of great persons draws ever many eyes. Each man says,

SHEBA'S REBELLION.

"Is not this my lord Amasa?" Wherefore do we go to fight, while our general lies in the dust? What a sad presage is this of our own miscarriage! The wit of Joab's followers hath therefore soon both removed Amasa out of the way, and covered him, not regarding so much the loss, as the eyesore of Israel. Thus wicked politics care not so much for the commission of villany, as for the notice. Smothered evils are as not done: if oppressions, if murder, if treasons, may be hid from view, the obdured heart of the offender complains not of remorse.

Bloody Joab, with what face, with what heart, canst thou pursue a traitor to thy king, while thou thyself art so foul a traitor to thy friend, to thy cousin-german, and, in so unseasonable a slaughter, to thy sovereign, whose cause thou professest to revenge? If Amasa were now, in an act of loyalty, justly, on God's part, paid for the arrearages of his late rebellion; yet that it should be done by thy hand, then and thus, it was flagitiously cruel: yet behold, Joab runs away securely with the fact, hasting to plague that, in another, whereof himself was no less guilty. So vast are the gorges of some consciences, that they can swallow the greatest crimes, and find no strain in the passage.

It is possible for a man to be faithful to some one person, and perfidious to all others. I do not find Joab other than firm and loyal to David, in the midst of all his private falsehoods, whose just quarrel he pursues against Sheba, through all the tribes of Israel. None of all the strong forts of revolted Israel can hide the rebel from the zeal of his revenge. The city of Abel lends harbour to that conspirator, whom all Israel would, and cannot protect. Joab casts up a mound against it, and having environed it with a siege, begins to work upon the wall; and now, after long chase, is in hand to dig out that vermin, which had earthed himself in this borough of Bethmaachah. Had not the city been strong and populous, Sheba had not cast himself for succour within those walls; yet of all the inhabitants, I see not any one man move for the preservation of their whole body: only a woman undertakes to treat with Joab for their safety. Those men, whose spirits were great enough to maintain a traitor against a mighty king, scorn not to give way to the wisdom of a matron: there is no reason that sex should disparage, where the virtue and merit are no less than masculine. Surely the soul acknowledgeth no sex, neither is varied according to the outward frame. How oft have we known female hearts in the breasts of men, and, contrarily, manly powers in the weaker vessels! It is injurious to measure the act by the person, and not rather to esteem the person for the act.

She, with no less prudence than courage, challengeth Joab for the violence of his assault, and lays to him that law, which he could not be an Israelite and disavow—the law of the God of peace, whose charge it was, that, when they should come near to a city to fight against it, they should offer it peace: and if this tender must be made to foreigners, how much more to brethren? So as they must inquire of Abel ere they battered it. War is the extreme act of vindictive justice; neither doth God ever approve it for any other than a desperate remedy; and, if it hath any other end than peace, it turns into public murder. It is therefore an inhuman cruelty to shed blood, where we have not proffered fair conditions of peace, the refusal whereof is justly punished with the sword of revenge.

Joab was a man of blood; yet, when the wise woman of Abel charged him with going about to destroy a mother in Israel, and swallowing up the inheritance of the Lord, with what vehemence doth he deprecate that challenge! "God forbid, God forbid it me, that I should devour or destroy it." Although that city, with the rest, had engaged itself in Sheba's sedition, yet how zealously doth Joab remove from himself the suspicion of an intended vastation! How fearful shall their answer be, who, upon the quarrel of their own ambition, have not spared to waste whole tribes of the Israel of God! It was not the fashion of David's captains to assault any city ere they summoned it: here they did. There be some things that in the very fact carry their own conviction; so did Abel in the entertaining and abetting a known conspirator: Joab challenges them for the offence, and requires no other satisfaction than the head of Sheba. This matron had not deserved the name of wise and faithful in Israel, if she had not both apprehended the justice of the condition, and commended it to her citizens, whom she had easily persuaded to spare their own heads in not sparing a traitor's. It had been pity those walls should have stood, if they had been too high to throw a traitor's head over.

Spiritually the case is ours: every man's breast is as a city inclosed; every sin is as a traitor that lurks within those walls: God calls to us for Sheba's head; neither hath he any quarrel to our person, but for our sin. If we love the head of our traitor above the life of our soul, we shall justly perish in the vengeance. We cannot be more willing to part with our sin, than our merciful God is to withdraw his judgments.

Now is Joab returned with success, and hopes, by Sheba's head, to pay the price of Amasa's blood; David hates the murder, entertains the man, defers the revenge; Joab had made himself so great, so necessary, that David may neither miss nor punish him. Policy led the king to connive at that which his heart abhorred. I dare not commend that wisdom which holds the hands of princes from doing justice. Great men have ever held it a point of worldly state, not always to pay where they have been conscious to a debt of either favour or punishment; but to make time their servant for both. Solomon shall once defray the arrearages of his father. In the mean time, Joab commands and prospers, and David is fain to smile on that face, whereon he hath, in his secret destination, written characters of death.

CONTEMPLATION V. — THE GIBEONITES REVENGED.

The reign of David was most troublesome towards the shutting up, wherein both war and famine conspire to afflict him: almost forty years had he sat in the throne of Israel with competency, if not abundance, of all things; now at last are his people visited with a long dearth. We are not at first sensible of common evils: three years' drought and scarcity are gone over, ere David consults with God, concerning the occasion of the judgment; now he found it high time to seek the face of the Lord. The continuance of an affliction sends us to God, and calls upon us to ask for a reckoning; whereas, like men stricken in their sleep, a sudden blow cannot make us to find ourselves, but rather astonisheth than teacheth us.

David was himself a prophet of God; yet had not the Lord, all this while, acquainted him with the grounds of his proceedings against Israel; this secret was hid from him, till he consulted with the Urim: ordinary means shall reveal that to him which no vision had descried; and if God will have prophets to have recourse unto the priests for the notice of his will, how much more must the people? Even those that are inwardest with God must have the use of the ephod.

Justly it is presupposed by David, that there was never judgment from God, where hath not been a provocation from men; therefore, when he sees the plague, he inquires for the sin. Never man smarted causelessly from the hand of divine justice. O that, when we suffer, we could ask what we have done, and could guide our repentance to the root of our evils!

That God, whose counsels are secret, even where his actions are open, will not be close to his prophet, to his priest: without inquiry, we shall know nothing; upon inquiry, nothing shall be concealed from us, that is fit for us to know.

Who can choose but wonder at once, both at David's slackness in consulting with God, and God's speed in answering so slow a demand? He, that so well knew the way to God's oracle, suffers Israel to be three years pinched with famine, ere he asks why they suffer. Even the best hearts may be overtaken with dulness in holy duties; but O the marvellous mercy of God, that takes not the advantage of our weaknesses! David's question is not more slow, than his answer is speedy: "It is for Saul, and for his bloody house, because he slew the Gibeonites." Israel was full of sins, besides those of Saul's house; Saul's house was full of sins, besides those of blood: much blood was shed by them, besides that of the Gibeonites; yet the justice of God singles out this one sin of violence offered to the Gibeonites, contrary to the league made by Joshua, some four hundred years before, for the occasion of this late vengeance. Where the causes of offence are infinite, it is just with God to pitch upon some; it is merciful not to punish for all: well near forty years are past betwixt the commission of the sin, and the reckoning for it. It is a vain hope that is raised from the delay of judgment: no time can be any prejudice to the Ancient of days: when we have forgotten our sins, when the world hath forgotten us, he sues us afresh for our arrearages. The slaughter of the Gibeonites was the sin, not of the present, but rather of the former generation; and now posterity pays for their forefathers. Even we men hold it not unjust to sue the heirs and executors of our debtors: eternal payments God uses only to require of the persons, temporary ofttimes of succession.

As Saul was higher by the head and shoulders than the rest of Israel, both in stature and dignity, so were his sins more conspicuous than those of the vulgar. The eminence of the person makes the offence more remarkable to the eyes both of God and men.

Neither Saul nor Israel were faultless in

other kinds; yet God fixes the eye of his revenge upon the massacre of the Gibeonites. Every sin hath a tongue, but that of blood overcries and drowns the rest. He, who is mercy itself, abhors cruelty in his creature above all other inordinateness: that holy soul, which was heavy pressed with the weight of a heinous adultery, yet cries out, "Deliver me from blood, O God, the God of my salvation, and my tongue shall joyfully sing of thy righteousness."

If God would take account of blood, he might have entered the action upon the blood of Uriah spilt by David; or, if he would rather insist in Saul's house, upon the blood of Abimelech the priest, and fourscore and five persons that did wear a linen ephod: but it pleased the wisdom and justice of the Almighty rather to call for the blood of the Gibeonites, though drudges of Israel, and a remnant of Amorites. Why this? There was a perjury attending upon this slaughter: it was an ancient oath, wherein the princes of the congregation had bound themselves, upon Joshua's league, to the Gibeonites, that they would suffer them to live — an oath extorted by fraud, but solemn, by no less name than the Lord God of Israel. Saul will now, thus late, either not acknowledge it, or not keep it; out of his zeal, therefore, to the children of Israel and Judah, he roots out some of the Gibeonites, whether in a zeal of revenge of their first imposture, or in a zeal of enlarging the possessions of Israel, or in a zeal of executing God's charge upon the brood of Canaanites: he that spared Agag, whom he should have smitten, smites the Gibeonites, whom he should have spared. Zeal and good intention is no excuse, much less a warrant for evil: God holds it a high indignity, that his name should be sworn by, and violated. Length of time cannot dispense with our oaths, with our vows: the vows and oaths of others may bind us; how much more our own?

There was a famine in Israel: a natural man would have ascribed it unto the drought, and that drought, perhaps, to some constellations: David knows to look higher, and sees a divine hand scourging Israel for some great offence, and overruling those second causes to his most just executions. Even the most quick-sighted worldling is purblind to spiritual objects; and the weakest eyes of the regenerate pierce the heavens, and espy God in all earthly occurrences.

So well was David acquainted with God's proceedings, that he knew the removal of the judgment must begin at the satisfaction of the wronged. At once, therefore, doth he pray unto God, and treat with the Gibeonites: "What shall I do for you, and wherewith shall I make the atonement, that ye may bless the inheritance of the Lord?" In vain should David, though a prophet, bless Israel, if the Gibeonites did not bless them. Injuries done us on earth, give us power in heaven: the oppressor is in no man's mercy, but his whom he hath trampled upon.

Little did the Gibeonites think that God had so taken to heart their wrongs, that for their sakes all Israel should suffer. Even when we think not of it, is the righteous Judge avenging our unrighteous vexations. Our hard measures cannot be hid from him; his returns are hid from us. It is sufficient for us, that God can be no more neglective than ignorant of our sufferings. It is now in the power of these despised Hivites to make their own terms with Israel; neither silver nor gold will savour with them towards their satisfaction: nothing can expiate the blood of their fathers, but the blood of seven sons of their deceased persecutor. Here was no other than a just retaliation: Saul had punished in them the offence of their predecessors; they will now revenge Saul's sin in his children. The measure we mete unto others, is, with much equity, remeasured unto ourselves. Every death would not content them of Saul's sons, but a cursed and ignominious hanging on the tree; neither would that death content them, unless their own hands might be the executioners; neither would any place serve for the execution but Gibeah, the court of Saul; neither would they do any of this for the wrecking of their own fury, but for the appeasing of God's wrath: "We will hang them up unto the Lord in Gibeah of Saul."

David might not refuse the condition: he must deliver, they must execute. He chooses out seven of the sons and grandchildren of Saul. That house had raised long an unjust persecution against David; now God pays it upon another's score. David's love and oath to Jonathan preserve lame Mephibosheth: how much more shall the Father of all mercies do good unto the children of the faithful, for the covenant made with their parents?

The five sons of Adriel the Meholathite, David's ancient rival in his first love, which were born to him by Merab, Saul's daughter, and brought up by her barren sister Michal, the wife of David, are yielded up to death. Merab was, after a promise of marriage to David, unjustly given away by Saul to Adriel: Michal seems to abet the match, in breeding the children. Now, in one act,

S

not of David's seeking, the wrong is thus late avenged upon Saul, Adriel, Merab, Michal, the children. It is a dangerous matter to offer injury to any of God's faithful ones: if their meekness have easily remitted it, their God will not pass it over without a severe retribution.

These five, together with two sons of Rizpah, Saul's concubine, are hanged up at once before the Lord, yea, and before the eyes of the world; no place but a hill will serve for this execution. The acts of justice, as they are intended for example, so they should be done in that eminent fashion, that may make them both most instructive and most terrifying. Unwarrantable courses of private revenge seek to hide their heads in secrecy; the beautiful face of justice both affects the light, and becomes it.

It was the general charge of God's law, that no corpse should remain all night upon the gibbet: the Almighty hath power to dispense with his own command, so, doubtless, he did in this extraordinary case; these carcases did not defile, but expiate. Sorrowful Rizpah spreads her a tent of sackcloth upon the rock, for a sad attendance upon those sons of her womb: death might bereave her of them, not them of her love. This spectacle was not more grievous to her, than pleasing to God, and happy to Israel. Now the clouds drop fatness, and the earth runs forth into plenty. The Gibeonites are satisfied, God reconciled, Israel relieved.

How blessed a thing it is for any nation, that justice is unpartially executed, even upon the mighty! A few drops of blood have procured large showers from heaven. A few carcases are a rich compost to the earth; the drought and dearth remove away with the breath of those pledges of the offender. Judgment cannot tyrannize where justice reigns; as, contrarily, there can be no peace where blood cries unheard, unregarded.

CONTEMPLATION VI. — THE NUMBERING OF THE PEOPLE.

ISRAEL was grown wanton and mutinous: God pulls them down; first by the sword, then by famine, now by pestilence. O the wondrous, and yet just ways of the Almighty! Because Israel hath sinned, therefore David shall sin, that Israel may be punished; because God is angry with Israel, therefore David shall anger him more, and strike himself in Israel, and Israel through himself.

The Spirit of God elsewhere ascribes this motion to Satan, which here it attributes to God: both had their hand in the work; God by permission, Satan by suggestion; God as a judge, Satan as an enemy; God as in a just punishment for sin, Satan as in an act of sin; God in a wise ordination of it to good, Satan in a malicious intent of confusion. Thus at once God moved, and Satan moved; neither is it any excuse to Satan or David that God moved; neither is it any blemish to God that Satan moved, the ruler's sin is a punishment to a wicked people: though they had many sins of their own, whereon God might have grounded a judgment; yet as before he had punished them with dearth for Saul's sin, so now he will not punish them with plagues but for David's sin. If God were not angry with a people, he would not give up their governors to such evils, as whereby he is provoked to vengeance; and if their governors be thus given up, the people cannot be safe. The body drowns not while the head is above the water; when that once sinks, death is near: justly, therefore, are we charged to make prayers and supplications, as for all, so especially for those that are in eminent authority: when we pray for ourselves, we pray not always for them; but we cannot pray for them, and not pray for ourselves: the public weal is not comprised in the private, but the private in the public.

What, then, was David's sin? He will needs have Israel and Judah numbered. Surely there is no malignity in numbers; neither is it unfit for a prince to know his own strength: this is not the first time that Israel had gone under a reckoning. The act offends not, but the misaffection; the same thing had been commendably done out of a princely providence, which now, through the curiosity, pride, misconfidence of the doer, proves heinously vicious. Those actions, which are in themselves indifferent, receive either their life or their bane from the intentions of the agent. Moses numbereth the people with thanks; David with displeasure. Those sins, which carry the smoothest foreheads, and have the most honest appearances, may more provoke the wrath of God, than those which bear the most abomination in their faces. How many thousand wickednesses passed through the hands of Israel, which we men would rather have branded out for judgment, than this of David's! The righteous judge of the world censures sins, not by their ill looks, but by their foul hearts.

Who can but wonder to see Joab the saint, and David the trespasser? No prophet could speak better than that man of

NUMBERING OF THE PEOPLE.

blood: "The Lord thy God increase the people a hundred-fold more than they be, and that the eyes of my lord the king may see it; but why doth my lord the king desire this thing?" There is no man so lewd as not to be sometimes in good moods, as not to dislike some evil; contrarily, no man on earth can be so holy, as not sometimes to overlash. It were pity that either Joab or David should be tried by every act. How commonly have we seen those men ready to give good advice to others, for the avoiding of some sins, who, in more gross outrages, have not had grace to counsel their own hearts! The same man, that had deserved death from David for his treacherous cruelty, dissuades David from an act that carried but a suspicion of evil: it is not so much to be regarded who it is that admonisheth us, as what he brings. Good counsel is never the worse for the foul carriage. There are some dishes that we may eat even from sluttish hands.

The purpose of sin in a faithful man is odious, much more the resolution. Notwithstanding Joab's discreet admonition, David will hold on his course, and will know the number of the people, only that he may know it. Joab and the captains address themselves to the work. In things which are not in themselves evil, it is not for subjects to dispute, but to obey. That which authority may sin in commanding, is done of the inferior, not with safety only, but with praise. Nine months and twenty days is this general muster in hand; at last the number is brought in: Israel is found eight hundred thousand strong; Judah five hundred thousand; the ordinary companies, which served by course for the royal guard, four and twenty thousand each month, needed not be reckoned; the addition of them, with their several captains, raises the sum of Israel to the rate of eleven hundred thousand—a power able to puff up a carnal heart: but how can a heart that is more than flesh, trust to an arm of flesh? O holy David, whither hath a glorious vanity transported thee!—thou which once didst sing so sweetly, "Put not your trust in princes, nor in the son of man, for there is no help in him. His breath departeth, and he returneth to his earth, then his thoughts perish. Blessed is he that hath the God of Jacob for his help, whose hope is in the Lord his God." How canst thou now stoop to so unsafe and unworthy a confidence?

As some stomachful horse that will not be stopt in his career with the sharpest bit, but runs on headly, til he come to some wall or ditch, and there stands still, and trembles; so did David: all the dissuasions of Joab could not restrain him from his intended course; almost ten months doth he run on impetuously in a way of his own, rough and dangerous: at last his heart smites him; the conscience of his offence, and the fear of judgment, have fetched him upon his knees: "O Lord, I have sinned exceedingly in that I have done; therefore now, Lord, I beseech thee, take away the trespass of thy servant, for I have done very foolishly." It is possible for a sin not to bait only, but to sojourn in the holiest soul: but, though it sojourn there as a stranger, it shall not dwell there as an owner. The renewed heart, after some rovings of error, will once, ere over-long, return home to itself, and fall out with that ill guide wherewith it was misled, and with itself for being misled; and now it is resolved into tears, and breathes forth nothing but sighs, and confessions, and deprecations.

Here needed no Nathan, by a parabolical circumlocution, to fetch in David to a sight and acknowledgment of his sin: the heart of the penitent supplied the prophet; no other tongue could smite him so deep as his own thoughts: but though his reins chastised him in the night, yet his seer scourges him in the morning; "Thus saith the Lord, I offer thee three things, choose thee which of them I shall do unto thee." But what shall we say to this? When, upon the prophet's reproof for an adultery cloaked with murder, David did but say, "I have sinned," it was presently returned, "God hath put away thy sin;" neither did any smart follow, but the death of a misbegotten infant; and now, when he voluntarily reproved himself for but a needless muster, and sought for pardon unbidden, with great humiliation, God sends him three terrible scourges; famine, sword, or pestilence; that he may choose with which of them he had rather to bleed, he shall have the favour of an election, not of a remission. God is more angered with a spiritual and immediate affront offered to his majesty, in our pride and false confidence in earthly things, than with a fleshly crime, though heinously seconded.

It was a hard and woful choice, of three years' famine added to three fore-past; or of three months' flight from the sword of an enemy, or three days' pestilence: the Almighty, that had fore-determined his judgment, refers it to David's will as fully as if it were utterly undetermined. God had resolved, yet David may choose: that infinite wisdom hath foreseen the very will of his creature; which, while it freely inclines itself to what it had rather, unwittingly wills that which was fore-appointed in heaven.

We do well believe thee, O David, that thou wert in a wonderful strait: this very liberty is no other than fetters: thou needest not have famine, thou needest not have the sword, thou needest not have pestilence; one of them thou must have: there is misery in all; there is misery in any: thou and thy people can die but once; and once they must die, either by famine, war, or pestilence. O God, how vainly do we hope to pass over our sins with impunity, when all the favour that David and Israel can receive, is to choose their bane!

Yet behold, neither sins, nor threats, nor fears, can bereave a true penitent of his faith: "Let us fall now into the hands of the Lord, for his mercies are great." There can be no evil of punishment wherein God hath not a hand; there could be no famine, no sword, without him: but some evils are more immediate from a divine stroke; such was that plague into which David is unwillingly willing to fall. He had his choice of days, months, years, in the same number; and though the shortness of time, prefixed to the threatened pestilence, might seem to offer some advantage for the leading of his election; yet God meant, and David knew it, herein to proportion the difference of time to the violence of the plague: neither should any fewer perish by so few days' pestilence, than by so many years' famine. The wealthiest might avoid the dearth; the swiftest might run away from the sword: no man could promise himself safety from that pestilence. In likelihood, God's angel would rather strike the most guilty: however, therefore, David might well look to be enwrapped in the common destruction, yet he rather chooseth to fall into that mercy which he had abused, and to suffer from that justice which he had provoked: "Let us now fall into the hands of the Lord."

Humble confessions and devout penance cannot always avert temporal judgments: God's angel is abroad, and, within that short compass of time, sweeps away seventy thousand Israelites. David was proud of the number of his subjects; now they are abated, that he may see cause of humiliation in the matter of his glory. In what we have offended, we commonly smart. These thousands of Israel were not so innocent, that they should only perish for David's sin; their sins were the motives both of this sin and punishment: besides the respect of David's offence, they die for themselves.

It was no ordinary pestilence that was thus suddenly and universally mortal. Common eyes saw the botch and the marks, but not the angel: David's clearer sight hath espied him, after that killing peragration throughout the tribes of Israel, shaking his sword over Jerusalem, and hovering over Mount Sion; and now he, who doubtless had spent those three dismal days in the saddest contrition, humbly casts himself down at the feet of the avenger, and lays himself ready for the fatal stroke of justice: it was more terror that God intended in the visible shape of his angel, and deeper humiliation; and what he meant, he wrought. Never soul could be more dejected, more anguished with the sense of a judgment, in the bitterness whereof he cries out, "Behold, I have sinned, yea, I have done wickedly; but these sheep, what have they done? Let thine hand, I pray thee, be against me, and against my father's house." The better any man is, the more sensible he is of his own wretchedness. Many of those sheep were wolves to David. What had they done? They had done that which was the occasion of David's sin, and the cause of their own punishment: but that gracious penitent knew his own sin; he knew not theirs; and therefore can say, " I have sinned, what have they done?" It is safe accusing ourselves, where we may be boldest, and are best acquainted.

O the admirable charity of David, that would have engrossed the plague to himself, and his house, from the rest of Israel, and sues to interpose himself betwixt his people and the vengeance! He that had put himself upon the paws of the bear and lion, for the rescue of his sheep, will now cast himself upon the sword of the angel, for the preservation of Israel. There was hope in those conflicts; in this yieldance there could be nothing but death. Thus didst thou, O Son of David, the true and great Shepherd of thy church, offer thyself to death for them who had their hands in thy blood, who both procured thy death, and deserved their own. Here he offered himself, that had sinned, for those whom he professed to have not done evil; thou that didst no sin, vouchsafedst to offer thyself for us that were all sin: he offered and escaped; thou offeredst and diedst, and by thy death we live, and are freed from everlasting destruction.

But, O Father of all mercies, how little pleasure dost thou take in the blood of sinners! It was thine own pity that inhibited the destroyer. Ere David could see the angel, thou hadst restrained him. " It is sufficient, hold now thy hand." If thy compassion did not both withhold and abridge thy judgments, what place were there for us out of hell?

How easy and just had it been for God, to have made the shutting up of that third evening red with blood! His goodness repents of the slaughter, and calls for that sacrifice wherewith he will be appeased. An altar must be built in the threshing-floor of Araunah the Jebusite: lo, in that very hill, where the angel held the sword of Abraham from killing his son, doth God now hold the sword of the angel from killing his people! Upon this very ground shall the temple after stand: here shall be the holy altar, which shall send up the acceptable oblations of God's people in succeeding generations.

O God, what was the threshing-floor of a Jebusite to thee above all other soils? what virtue, what merit was in this earth? As in places, so in persons, it is not to be heeded what they are, but what thou wilt; that is worthiest, which thou pleasest to accept.

Rich and bountiful Araunah is ready to meet David in so holy a motion, and munificently offers his Sion for the place, his oxen for the sacrifice, his carts and ploughs, and other utensils of his husbandry, for the wood. Two frank hearts are well met: David would buy, Araunah would give: the Jebusite would not sell, David will not take. Since it was for God, and to David, Araunah is loath to bargain: since it was for God, David wisheth to pay dear: " I will not offer burnt-offerings to the Lord my God, of that which doth cost me nothing." Heroical spirits do well become eminent persons. He that knew it was better to give than to receive, would not receive, but give. There can be no devotion in a niggardly heart: as unto dainty palates, so to the godly soul, that tastes sweetest that costs most: nothing is dear enough for the Creator of all things. It is a heartless piety of those base-minded Christians that care only to serve God good-cheap.

BOOK XVII.

CONTEMPLATION I.—ADONIJAH DEFEATED.

DAVID had not so carefully husbanded his years, as to maintain a vigorous age; he was therefore, what through wars, what with sorrows, what with sickness, decrepit betimes. By that time he was seventy years old; his natural heat was so wasted, that his clothes could not warm him: how many have we known of more strength at more age? The holiest soul dwells not in an impregnable fort. If the revenging angel spared David, yet age and death will not spare him; neither his new altar, nor his costly sacrifice, can be of force against decay of nature; nothing but death can prevent the weaknesses of age.

None can blame a people, if, when they have a good king, they are desirous to hold him. David's servants and subjects have commended unto his bed a fair young virgin; not for the heat of lust, but of life, that by this means they might make an outward supply of fuel for that vital fire which was well near extinguished with age.

As it is in the market, or the stage, so it is in our life; one goes out, another comes in. When David was withering, Adonijah was in his bosom: that son, as he was next to Absalom, both in the beauty of his body, and the time of his birth, so was he, too, like him in practice: he also, taking advantage of his father's infirmity, will be carving himself of the kingdom of Israel; that he might no whit vary from his pattern, he gets him also chariots and horsemen, and fifty men to run before him. These two, Absalom and Adonijah, were the darlings of their father: their father had not displeased them from their childhood; therefore they both displeased him in his age: those children had need to be very gracious that are not marred with pampering. It is more than God owes us, if we receive comfort in those children whom we have overloved: the indulgence of parents at last pays them home in crosses.

It is true that Adonijah was David's eldest son now remaining, and therefore might seem to challenge the justest title to the crown; but the kingdom of Israel, in so late an erection, had not yet known the right of succession. God himself, that had ordained the government, was as yet the immediate elector: he fetched Saul from amongst the stuff, and David from the sheepfold, and had now appointed Solomon from the ferule to the sceptre.

And if Adonijah, which is unlike, had not known this, yet it had been his part to have taken his father with him in this claim of his succession; and not so to prevent a brother, that he should shoulder out a father; and not so violently to preoccupate the throne, that he should rather be a rebel, than an heir.

As Absalom, so Adonijah wants not furtherers in this usurpation, whether spiritual or temporal; Joab the general, and Abiathar the priest, give both counsel and aid to so unseasonable a challenge: these two had been firm to David in all his troubles, in all insurrections; yet now, finding him fastened to the bed of age and death, they show themselves thus slippery in the loose. Outward happiness and friendship are not known till our last act. In the impotency of either our revenge or recompense, it will easily appear who loved us for ourselves, who for their own ends.

Had not Adonijah known that Solomon was designed to the kingdom, both by God and David, he had never invited all the rest of the king's sons, his brethren, and left out Solomon, who was otherwise the most unlikely to have been his rival in this honour; all the rest were elder than he, and might therefore have had more pretence for their competition. Doubtless the court of Israel could not but know that, immediately upon the birth of Solomon, God sent him, by Nathan the prophet, a name and message of love; neither was it for nothing that God called him Jedidiah, and forepromised him the honour of building a house to his name; and, in return of so glorious a service, the establishment of the throne of his kingdom over Israel for ever. Notwithstanding all which, Adonijah, backed by the strength of a Joab, and the gravity of an Abiathar, will underwork Solomon, and justle into the not-yet-vacant seat of his father David. Vain men, while like proud, and yet brittle clay, they will be knocking their sides against the solid and eternal decree of God, break themselves in pieces.

I do not find that Adonijah sent any message of threats or unkindness to Zadok the priest, or Nathan the prophet, or Benaiah the son of Jehoiada, and the other worthies; only he invited them not to his feast with the king's sons and servants: sometimes a very omission is an affront and a menace. They well knew, that since they were not called as guests, they were counted as enemies. Ceremonies of courtesy, though they be in themselves slight and arbitrary, yet the neglect of them, in some cases, may undergo a dangerous construction.

Nathan was the man by whom God had sent that errand of grace to David concerning Solomon, assuring him both to reign and prosper; yet now, when Adonijah's plot was thus on foot, he doth not sit still, and depend upon the issue of God's decree, but he bestirs him in the business, and consults with Bathsheba, how at once to save their lives, and to advance Solomon, and defeat Adonijah. God's predetermination includes the means, as well as the end; the same Providence that had ordained a crown to Solomon, a repulse to Adonijah, preservation to Bathsheba and Nathan, had fore-appointed the wise and industrious endeavours of the prophet to bring about his just and holy purposes. If we would not have God wanting to us, we must not be wanting to ourselves; even when we know what God hath meant to us, we may not be negligent.

The prophets of God did not look for revelation in all their affairs; in some things they were left to the counsel of their own hearts. The policy of Nathan was of use, as well as his prophecy: that alone hath turned the stream into the right channel. Nothing could be more wisely contrived, than the sending in of Bathsheba to David, with so seasonable and forcible an expostulation, and the seconding of hers with his own.

Though lust were dead in David, yet the respects of his old matrimonial love lived still; the very presence of Bathsheba pleaded strongly, but her speech more: the time was, when his affection offended in excess towards her, being then another's; he cannot now neglect her, being his own; and if either his age, or the remorse of his old offence, should have set him off, yet she knew his oath was sure: " My lord, thou swarest by the Lord thy God unto thine handmaid, saying, Assuredly, Solomon thy son shall reign after me, and he shall sit upon my throne." His word had been firm, but his oath was inviolable: we are engaged if we have promised; but if we have sworn, we are bound.

Neither heaven nor earth have any gyves for that man that can shake off the fetters of an oath; for he cares not for that God whom he dares invoke to a falsehood; and he that cares not for God, will not care for man.

Ere Bathsheba can be over the threshold, Nathan, upon compact, is knocking at the door. God's prophet was never but welcome to the bed-chamber of king David; in a seeming strangeness he falls upon the same suit, upon the same complaint, with Bathsheba: honest policies do not misbecome the holiest prophets; she might seem to speak as a woman, as a mother out of passion; the word of a prophet could not be misdoubted. He, therefore, that had formerly brought to David that chiding and bloody message concerning Bathsheba, comes now to David to sue for the life and honour of Bathsheba: and he that was sent from God to David to bring the news of a gracious promise of favour unto Solomon, comes now to challenge the execution of it from the hands of a father; and he, whose place freed him from suspicion of a faction, complains of the insolent demeanour and proclamation of Adonijah; what he began with an humble obeisance, shutting up in a lowly and loving expostulation: " Is this thing done by my lord the king, and thou hast not showed thy servant who should sit on the throne of my lord the king after him?" As Nathan was of God's council unto David, so was he of David's council both to God and the state. As God, therefore, upon all occasions, told Nathan what he meant to do with David, so had David wont to tell Nathan what he meant to do in his holy and most important civil affairs. There are cases wherein it is not unfit for God's prophets to meddle with matters of state: it is no disparagement to religious princes to impart their counsels unto them who can requite them with the counsels of God.

That wood which a single iron could not rive, is soon splitted with a double wedge: the seasonable importunity of Bathsheba and Nathan, thus seconding each other, hath so wrought upon David, that now his love to Adonijah gives place to indignation, nature to a holy fidelity; and now he renews his ancient oath to Bathsheba with a passionate solemnity: " As the Lord liveth, who hath redeemed my soul out of all adversity, even as I sware unto thee by the Lord God of Israel, saying, Assuredly Solomon thy son shall reign after me, and he shall sit upon my throne in my stead; so will I certainly do this day." In the decay of David's body, I find not his intellectual powers any whit impaired: as one, therefore, that from his bed could, with a perfect, if weak hand, steer the government of Israel, he gives wise and full directions for the inauguration of Solomon: Zadok the priest, and Nathan the prophet, and Benaiah the captain, receive his grave and princely charge for the carriage of that so weighty a business. They are commanded to take with them the royal guard, to set Solomon upon his father's mule, to carry him down in state to Gihon, to anoint him with the holy oil of the tabernacle, to sound the trumpets, and proclaim him in the streets, to bring him back with triumph and magnificence to the court, and set him in the royal throne, with all the due ceremonies of coronation.

How pleasing was this command to them, who, in Solomon's glory, saw their own safety! Benaiah applauds it, and not fearing a father's envy, in David's presence wishes Solomon's throne exalted above his; the people are ravished with the joy of so hopeful a succession, and break the earth, and fill the heaven, with the noise of their music and shouting.

Solomon's guests had now at last better cheer than Adonijah's, whose feast, as all wicked men's, ended in horror: no sooner are their bellies full of meat, than their ears are full of the sound of those trumpets which at once proclaim Solomon's triumph, and their confusion: ever after the meal is ended, comes the reckoning. God could as easily have prevented this jolity, as marred it; but he willingly suffers vain men to please themselves for a time in the conceited success of their own projects, that afterwards their disappointment may be so much the more grievous. No doubt, at this feast there was many a health drunken to Adonijah, many a confident boast of their prospering design, many a scorn of the despised faction of Solomon; and now, for their last dish, is served up astonishment, and fearful expectation of a just revenge. Jonathan, the son of Abiathar the priest, brings the news of Solomon's solemn and joyful enthronization: now all hearts are cold, all faces pale, and every man hath but life enough to run away. How suddenly is this braving troop dispersed! Adonijah, their new prince, flies to the horns of the altar, as distrusting all hopes of life, save the sanctity of the place, and the mercy of his rival.

So doth the wise and just God befool proud and insolent sinners, in those secret plots wherein they hope to undermine the true Son of David, the Prince of peace; he suffers them to lay their heads together, and to feast themselves in jocund security, and promise of success; at last, when they are at the height of their joys and hopes, he confounds all their devices, and lays them open to the scorn of the world, and to the anguish of their own guilty hearts.

CONTEMPLATION II. — DAVID'S END, AND SOLOMON'S BEGINNING.

It well became Solomon to begin his reign in peace. Adonijah receives pardon upon his good behaviour, and finds the throne of Solomon as safe as the altar. David lives to see a wise son warm in his seat; and now he, that yielded to succession, yields to nature. Many good counsels had David given his heir; now he sums them up in his end. Dying words are wont to be weightiest; the soul, when it is entering into glory, breathes nothing but divine: "I go the way of all the earth." How well is that princely heart content to subscribe to the conditions of human mortality! as one that knew sovereignty doth not reach to the affairs of nature. Though a king, he neither expects nor desires an immunity from dissolution, making no account to go in any other than the common tract, to the universal home of mankind, the house of age. Whither should earth, but to earth? and why should we grudge to do that which all do? "Be thou strong, therefore, and show thyself a man." Even when his spirit was going out, he puts spirit into his son: age puts life into youth, and the dying animates the vigorous. He had well found, that strength was requisite to government; that he had need to be no less than a man, that should rule over men. If greatness should never receive any opposition, yet those worlds of cares and businesses that attend the chair of state are able to overlay any mean powers. A weak man may obey; none but the strong can govern. Graceless courage were but the whetstone of tyranny: "Take heed therefore to the charge of the Lord thy God, to walk in his ways, and to keep his statutes." The best legacy that David bequeaths to his heir, is the care of piety: himself had found the sweetness of a good conscience, and now he commends it to his successor. If there be any thing that, in our desires of the prosperous condition of our children, takes place of goodness, our hearts are not upright. Here was the father of a king, charging the king's son to keep the statutes of the King of kings; as one that knew greatness could neither exempt from obedience, nor privilege sin; as one that knew the least deviation in the greatest and highest orb, is both most sensible, and most dangerous. Neither would he have his son to look for any prosperity, save only from well-doing. That happiness is built upon sand or ice, which is raised upon any foundation besides virtue. If Solomon was wise, David was good; and if old Solomon had well remembered the counsel of old David, he had not so foully miscarried.

After the precepts of piety, follow those of justice, distributing in a due recompense, as revenge to Joab and Shimei, so favour to the house of Barzillai. The bloodiness of Joab had lain long upon David's heart: the hideous noise of those treacherous murders, as it had pierced heaven, so it still filled the ears of David: he could abhor the villany, though he could not revenge it; what he cannot pay, he will owe, and approve himself at last a faithful debitor: now he will defray it by the hand of Solomon. The slaughter was of Abner and Amasa. David appropriates it: "Thou knowest what Joab did to me." The sovereign is smitten in the subject; neither is it other than just, that the arraignment of mean malefactors runs in the style of wrong to the king's crown and dignity. How much more dost thou, O Son of David, take to thyself those insolencies which are done to thy poorest subjects, servants, sons, members, here upon earth! No Saul can touch a Christian here below, but thou feelest it in heaven, and complainest.

But what shall we think of this? David was a man of war, Solomon a king of peace; yet David refers this revenge to Solomon. How just it was that he who shed the blood of war in peace, and put the blood of war upon his girdle that was about his loins, should have his blood shed in peace, by a prince of peace! Peace is fittest to rectify the outrages of war: or whether is not this done in type of that divine administration, wherein thou, O Father of heaven, hast committed all judgment unto thine eternal Son? Thou, who couldst immediately either plague or absolve sinners, wilt do neither, but by the hand of a Mediator.

Solomon learned betimes what his ripeness taught afterwards: "Take away the wicked from the king, and his throne shall be established in righteousness." Cruel Joab and malicious Shimei must be therefore upon the first opportunity removed: the one lay open to present justice, for abetting the conspiracy of Adonijah, neither needs the help of time for a new advantage; the other went under the protection of an oath from David, and therefore must be fetched in upon a new challenge. The hoary head of both must be brought to the grave with blood, else David's head could not be brought to his grave in peace. Due punishment of malefactors is the debt of authority: if that holy king has run into arrearages, yet, as one that hates and fears to break the bank, he gives order to his paymaster; it shall be defrayed, if not by him, yet for him.

Generous natures cannot be unthankful. Barzillai had showed David some kindness in his extremity; and now the good man will have posterity to inherit the thanks. How much more bountiful is the Father of mercies, in the remuneration of our poor unworthy services! Even successions of generations shall fare the better for one good parent.

DAVID'S END, AND SOLOMON'S BEGINNING.

The dying words and thoughts of the man after God's own heart did not confine themselves to the straits of these particular charges, but enlarged themselves to the care of God's public service. As good men are best at last, David did never so busily and carefully marshal the affairs of God, as when he was fixed to the bed of his age and death. Then did he load his son Solomon with the charge of building the house of God ; then did he lay before the eyes of his son the model and pattern of that whole sacred work, whereof if Solomon bear the name, yet David no less merits it. He now gives the platform of the courts and buildings ; he gives the gold and silver for that holy use, a hundred thousand talents of gold, a thousand thousand talents of silver, besides brass and iron passing weight; he weighs out those precious metals for their several designments : every future vessel is laid out already in his poise, if not in his form. He excites the princes of Israel to their assistance, in so high a work ; he takes notice of their bountiful offerings ; he numbers up the Levites for the public service, and sets them their tasks. He appoints the singers and other musicians to their stations ; the porters to the gates that should be : and now, when he hath set all things in a desired order and forwardness, he shuts up with a zealous blessing of his Solomon, and his people, and sleeps with his fathers. O blessed soul, how quiet a possession hast thou now taken, after so many tumults, of a better crown! Thou that hast prepared all things for the house of thy God, how happily art thou now welcomed to that house of his, not made with hands, eternal in the heavens ! Who now shall envy unto good princes the honour of overseeing the businesses of God and his church, when David was thus punctual in these divine provisions ? What fear can be of usurpation, where they have so glorious a precedent ?

Now is Solomon the second time crowned king of Israel ; and now in his own right, as formerly in his father's, sits peaceably upon the throne of the Lord : his awe and power come on faster than his years. Envy and ambition, where it is once kindled, may sooner be hid in the ashes than quite put out. Adonijah yet hangs after his old hopes : he remembers how sweet he found the name of a king; and now hath laid a new plot for the setting up of his cracked title. He would make the bed a step to the throne ; his old complices are sure enough ; his part would gather much strength, if he might enjoy Abishag, the relict of his father, to wife. If it were not the Jewish fashion, as is pretended, that a king's widow should marry none but a king ; yet certainly the power both of the alliance and friendship of a queen, must needs not a little advance his purpose. The crafty rival dare not either move the suit to Solomon, or effect the marriage without him ; but would cunningly undermine the son by the suit of that mother, whose suit had undermined him. The weaker vessels are commonly used in the most dangerous suggestions of evil.

Bathsheba was so wise a woman, that some of her counsels are canonized for divine ; yet she saw not the depth of this drift of Adonijah : therefore she both entertains the suit, and moves it. But whatever were the intent of the suitor, could she choose but see the unlawfulness of so incestuous a match ? It is not long since she saw her late husband David abominating the bed of those his concubines that had been touched by his son Absalom ; and can she hold it lawful that his son Adonijah should climb up to the bed of his father's wife ? Sometimes even the best eyes are dim, and discern not those things which are obvious to weaker sights : or whether did not Bathsheba well see the foulness of the suit ; and yet, in compassion of Adonijah's late repulse, wherein she was the chief agent, and in a desire to make him amends for the loss of the kingdom, she yields even thus to gratify him. It is an injurious weakness to be drawn upon any by-respects, to the furtherance of faulty suits of unlawful actions.

No sooner doth Bathsheba come in place, than Solomon, her son, rises from his chair of state, and meets her, and bows to her, and sets her on his right hand, as not so remembering himself to be a king, that he should forget he was a son. No outward dignity can take away the rights and obligations of nature. Had Bathsheba been as mean as Solomon was mighty, she had carried away this honour from a gracious son ; yet, for all these due compliments, Bathsheba goes away with a denial : reverence she shall have ; she shall not have a condescent.

In the acts of magistracy, all regards of natural relations must give way. That which she propounded as a small request, is now, after a general and confused engagement, rejected as unreasonable. It were pity we should be heard in all our suits. Bathsheba makes a petition against herself, and knows it not : her safety and life depend upon Solomon's reign, yet she unwittingly moves for the advancement of Adonijah.

Solomon was too dutiful to check his

mother, and too wise to yield to her. In unfit supplications, we are most heard when we are repelled. Thus doth our God many times answer our prayers with merciful denials; and most blesseth us in crossing our desires.

Wise Solomon doth not find himself perplexed with the scruple of his promise: he that had said, "Ask on, for I will not say thee nay," can now swear, " God do so to me, and more also, if Adonijah hath not spoken this word against his own life." His promise was according to his supposition; his supposition was of no other than of a suit—honest, reasonable, expedient; now, he holds himself free from that grant, wherein there was at once both sin and danger. No man can be entangled with general words against his own just and honest intentions.

The policies of wicked men befool them at last: this intercession hath undone Adonijah, and, instead of the throne, hastens his grave. The sword of Benaiah puts an end to that dangerous rivalry. Joab and Abiathar still held champerty with Adonijah: their hand was both in the claim of his kingdom, and in the suit of Abishag. There are crimes wherein there are no accessaries: such is this of treason. Abiathar may thank his burden that he lives: had he not borne the ark of the Lord before David, he had not now carried his head upon his shoulders: had he not been afflicted with David, he had perished with Adonijah: now, though he were, in his own merit, a man of death, yet he shall survive his partners: " Get thee to Anathoth, unto thine own fields." The priesthood of Abiathar, as it aggravated his crime, so it shall preserve his life. Such honour have good princes given to the ministers of the sanctuary, that their very coat hath been defence enough against the sword of justice: how much more should it be of proof against the contempt of base persons!

Besides his function, respect is had to his sufferings; the father and brethren of Abiathar were slain for David's sake, therefore for David's sake Abiathar, though worthy of death, shall live: he had been now a dead man, if he had not been formerly afflicted. Thus doth our good God deal with us: by the rod he prevents the sword, and therefore will not condemn us for our sins, because we have suffered. If Abiathar do not forfeit his life, yet his office he shall; he must change Jerusalem for Anathoth, and the priesthood for a retired privacy. It was fourscore years ago since the sentence of judgment was denounced against the house of Eli; now doth it come to execution. This just quarrel against Abiathar, the last of that line shall make good the threatened judgment. The wickedness of Eli's house was neither purged by sacrifice, nor obliterated by time. If God pay slowly, yet he pays sure. Delay of most certain punishment is neither any hinderance to his justice, nor any comfort to our miseries.

CONTEMPLATION III.—THE EXECUTION OF JOAB AND SHIMEI.

ABIATHAR shall live, though he serve not. It is in the power of princes to remit, at least, those punishments which attend the breach of human laws: good reason they should have power to dispense with the wrongs done to their own persons. The news of Adonijah's death, and Abiathar's removal, cannot but affright Joab, who now runs to Gibeon, and takes sanctuary in the tabernacle of God: all his hope of defence is in the horns of the altar. Fond Joab, hadst thou formerly sought for counsel from the tabernacle, thou hadst not now needed to seek to it for refuge; if thy devotions had not been wanting to that altar, thou hadst not needed it for a shelter. It is the fashion of our foolish presumption to look for protection where we have not cared to yield obedience.

Even a Joab clings fast to God's altar in his extremity, which in his prosperity he regarded not. The worst men would be glad to make use of God's ordinances for their advantage. Necessity will drive the most profane and lawless man to God: but what do these bloody hands touching the holy altar of God? Miserable Joab! what help canst thou expect from that sacred pile? Those horns, that were besprinkled with the blood of beasts, abhor to be touched by the blood of men; that altar was for the expiation of sin by blood, not for the protection of the sin of blood. If Adonijah fled thither and escaped, it is murder that pursues thee more than conspiracy. God hath no sanctuary for a wilful homicide.

Yet such respect doth Benaiah give to that holy place, that his sword is unwilling to touch him that touches the altar. Those horns shall put off death for the time, and give protraction of the execution, though not preservation of life. How sweet is life, even to those who have been prodigal of the blood of others, that Joab shifts thus to hold it but some few hours! Benaiah returns with Joab's answer, instead of his head, " Nay, but I will die here ." as not daring to unsheath his sword against a man sheltered in God's tabernacle, without a new commission. Young Solomon is so well acquainted with the law of God, in such a case, that he sticks not at the sentence: he knew that God had enacted, "If a man come presumptuously upon his neighbour, to slay him with guile, thou shalt take him from mine altar, that he may die." He knew Joab's murders had not been more presumptuous than guileful; and therefore he sends Benaiah to take away the offender both from God and men, from the altar and the world.

No subject had merited more than Joab. When proclamation was made in Israel, that whoever should smite the Jebusites first, he should be the chief and captain, Joab was the man: when David built some part of Jerusalem, Joab built the rest; so that Jerusalem owes itself to Joab, both for recovery and reparation. No man held so close to David; no man was more intent to the weal of Israel; none so successful in victories; yet now is he called to reckon for his old sins, and must repay blood to Amasa and Abner. It is not in the power of all our deserts to buy off one sin, either with God or man: where life is so deeply forfeited, it admits of no redemption.

The honest simplicity of those times knew not of any infamy in the execution of justice. Benaiah, who was the great marshal under Solomon, thinks not his fingers defiled with that fatal stroke. It is a foolish niceness to put more shame in the doing of justice, than in the violating of it.

In one act Solomon hath approved himself both a good magistrate and a good son, fulfilling at once the will of a father and the charge of God; concluding upon this just execution, that, "Upon David, and upon his seed, and upon his house, and upon his throne, there shall be peace for ever from the Lord;" and inferring, that without this there could have been no peace.

Blood is a restless suitor, and will not leave clamouring for judgment, till the mouth be stopped with revenge. In this case favour to the offender is cruelty to the favourer.

Now hath Joab paid all his arrearages by the sword of Benaiah; there is no suit against his corpse, that hath the honour of a burial fit for a peer of Israel, for the near cousin to the king. Death puts an end to all quarrels: Solomon strikes off the score when God is satisfied: the revenge that survives death, and will not be shut up in the coffin, is barbarous, and unbeseeming true Israelites.

Only Shimei remains upon the file; his course is next, yet so, as that it shall be in his own liberty to hasten his end. Upon David's remission, Shimei dwells securely in Bahurim, a town of the tribe of Benjamin: doubtless, when he saw so round justice done upon Adonijah and Joab, his guilty heart could not think Solomon's message portended aught but his execution; and now he cannot but be well pleased with so easy conditions of dwelling at Jerusalem, and not passing over the brook Kidron: what more delightful place could he choose to live in than that city, which was the glory of the whole earth? what more pleasant bounds could he wish than the sweet banks of Kidron? Jerusalem could be no prison to him, while it was a paradise to his betters; and, if he had a desire to take fresh air, he had the space of six furlongs to walk from the city to the brook; he could not complain to be so delectably confined; and besides, thrice every year, he might be sure to see all his friends, without stirring his foot.

Wise Solomon, while he cared to seem not too severe an exactor of that which his father had remitted, prudently lays insensible twigs for so foul an offender: besides the old grudge, no doubt, Solomon saw cause to suspect the fidelity of Shimei, as a man who was ever known to be hollow to the house of David; the obscurity of a country life would easily afford him more safe opportunities of secret mischief: many eyes shall watch him in the city; he cannot look out unseen, he cannot whisper unheard; upon no other terms shall he enjoy his life, which the least straying shall forfeit.

Shimei feels no pain in this restraint. how many nobles of Israel do that for pleasure, which he doth upon command? Three years hath he lived within compass, limited both by Solomon's charge and his own oath; it was still in his power, notwithstanding David's caveat, to have laid down his hoary head in the grave, without blood: the just God infatuates those whom he means to plague. Two of Shimei's servants are fled to Gath; and now he saddles his ass, and is gone to fetch them back: either he thinks this word of Solomon is forgotten, or in the multitude of greater affairs, not heeded, or this so small an occurence will not come to his ears. Covetousness, and presumption of impunity, are the destruction of many a soul; Shimei seeks his servants, and loses himself. How many are there who cry out of this folly, and yet imitate it! These earthly things either are our servants, or should be: how commonly do we see men run out of the bounds set by God's law, to hunt after them, till their souls incur a fearful judgment!

Princes have thousands of eyes and ears: if Shimei will for more secrecy saddle his own ass, and take, as is like, the benefit of night for his passage, his journey cannot be hid from Solomon. How wary had those men need to be which are obnoxious! Without delay is Shimei complained of, convented, charged with violation both of the oath of God, and the injunction of Solomon: and that all these might appear to be but on occasion of that punishment, whose cause was more remote, now is all that old venom laid before him, which his malice had long since spit at God's anointed: "Thou knowest all the wickedness whereto thine heart is privy, that thou didst to David my father."

Had this old tally been stricken off, yet could not Shimei have pleaded aught for his life; for had he said, Let not my lord the king be thus mortally displeased for so small an offence: who ever died for passing over Kidron? what man is the worse for my harmless journey? — it had soon been returned, If the act be small, yet the circumstances are deadly: the commands of sovereign authority make the slightest duties weighty: if the journey be harmless, yet not the disobedience: it is not for subjects to poise the prince's charge in the scales of their weak constructions, but they must suppose it ever to be of such importance as is pretended by the commander. Besides, the precept here was a mutual adjuration: Shimei swore not to go; Solomon swore his death if he went: the one oath must be revenged; the other must be kept: if Shimei were false in offending, Solomon will be just in punishing. Now, therefore, that which Abishai, the son of Zeruiah, wished to have done in the greenness of the wound, and was repelled, after long festering, Benaiah is commanded to do. The stones that Shimei threw at David, struck not so deep as Benaiah's sword: the tongue that cursed the Lord's anointed hath paid the head to boot. Vengeance against rebels may sleep; it cannot die: a sure, though late judgment, attends those that dare lift up either their hand or tongue against the sacred persons of God's vicegerents. How much less will the God of heaven suffer unrevenged the insolencies and blasphemies against his own divine Majesty! It is a fearful word, He should not be just, if he should hold these guiltless.

CONTEMPLATION IV. — SOLOMON'S CHOICE, WITH HIS JUDGMENT UPON THE TWO HARLOTS.

AFTER so many messages and proofs of grace, Solomon begins doubtfully, both for his match, and for his devotion. If Pharaoh's daughter were not a proselyte, his early choice was besides unwarrantable, dangerous. The high places not only stood, but were frequented, both by the people and king. I do not find David climbing up those mishallowed hills, in an affection of the variety of altars: Solomon doth so, and yet loves the Lord, and is loved of God again. Such is the mercy of our God, that he will not suffer our well-meant weaknesses to bereave us of his favours: he rather pities than plagues us for the infirmities of upright hearts.

Gibeon was well worthy to be the chief, yea, the only high place: there was the hallowed altar of God; there was the tabernacle, though, as then, severed from the ark: thither did young Solomon go up; and, as desiring to begin his reign with God, there he offers no less than a thousand sacrifices.

Solomon worships God by day: God appears to Solomon by night. Well may we look to enjoy God when we have served him; the night cannot but be happy, whose day hath been holy.

It was no unusual course with God, to reveal himself unto his servants by dreams; so did he here to Solomon, who saw more with his eyes shut, than ever they could see open, even him that was invisible. The good king offereth unto God a thousand burnt-sacrifices; and now God offereth him his option: "Ask what I shall give thee." He, whose the beasts are on a thousand mountains, graciously accepts a small return of his own. It stands not with the munificence of a bountiful God to be indebted to his creature: we cannot give him aught unrecompensed: there is no way wherein we can be so liberal to ourselves, as by giving to the Possessor of all things. And art thou still, O God, less free unto us thy meaner servants under the gospel? Hast thou not said, "Whatsoever ye shall ask the Father in my name, it shall be given you?" Only give us grace not to be wanting unto thee, and we know thou canst not suffer any thing to be wanting unto us.

The night follows the temper of the day; and the heart so useth to sleep as it wakes. Had not the thoughts of Solomon been intent upon wisdom by day, he had not made it his suit in his dream. There needs no leisure of deliberation: the heart was so forestalled with the love and admiration of wisdom, that, not abiding the least motion of a competition, it fastens on that grace it had longed for: " Give unto thy servant an understanding heart to judge thy people." Had not Solomon been wise before, he had not known the worth of wisdom; he had not preferred it in his desires. The dunghill cocks of the world cannot know the price of this pearl: those that have it, know that all other excellencies are but trash and rubbish unto it. Solomon was a great king, and saw that he had power enough; but withal, he found that royalty, without wisdom, was no other than eminent dishonour. There is no trade of life whereto there belongs not a peculiar wisdom, without which there is nothing but a tedious unprofitableness; much more to the highest and busiest vocation, the regiment of men. As God hath no reason to give his best favours unasked, so hath he no will to withhold them where they are asked.

He, that in his cradle had the title of " Beloved of God," is now beloved more in the throne for the love and desire of wisdom: this soil could never have borne this fruit alone: Solomon could not so much as have dreamed of wisdom, if God had not put it into him: and now God takes the suit so well, as if he were beholden to his creature for wishing the best to itself; and because Solomon hath asked what he should, he shall now receive both what he asked, and what he asked not: riches and honour shall be given him into the match. So doth God love a good choice, that he recompenses it with overgiving. " Could we but first seek the kingdom of God, and his righteousness, all these earthly things should be superadded to us." Had Solomon made wealth his boon, he had failed both of riches and wisdom: now he asks the best, and speeds of all. They are in a fair way of happiness that can pray well. It was no discomfort to Solomon, that he awaked, and found it a dream; for he knew this dream was divine and oracular; and he already found, in his first waking, the real performance of what was promised him sleeping: such illumination did he sensibly find in all the rooms of his heart, as if God had now given him a new soul. No marvel if Solomon, now returning from the tabernacle to the ark, testified his joy and thankfulness by burnt-offerings, and peace-offerings, and public feastings: the heart that hath found in itself the lively testimonies of God's presence and favour cannot contain itself from outward expressions.

God likes not to have his gifts lie dead where he hath conferred them: Israel shall soon witness, that they have a king enlightened from heaven, in whom wisdom did not stay for heirs, did not admit of any parallel in his predecessors: the all-wise God will find occasions to draw forth those graces to use and light which he hath bestowed on man. Two harlots come before young Solomon with a difficult plea. It is not like, the prince's ear was the first that heard this complaint; there was a subordinate course of justice for the determination of these meaner incidences: the hardness of this decision brought the matter, through all the benches of inferior judicature, to the tribunal of Solomon. The very Israelitish harlots were not so unnatural, as some now-a-days that counterfeit honesty: these strive for the fruit of their womb; ours to put them off. One son is yet alive; two mothers contend for them. The children were alike for features, for age; the mothers were alike for reputation: here can be no evidence from others' eyes, whether's now is the living child, and whether's is the dead. Had Solomon gone about to wring forth the truth by tortures, he had perhaps plagued the innocent, and added pain to the misery of her loss: the weaker had been guilty, and the more able to bear had carried away both the child and the victory. The countenance of either of the mothers bewrayed an equality of passion: sorrow possessed the one for the son she had lost, and the other for the son she was in danger to lose, both were equally peremptory and importunate in their claim. It is in vain to think that the true part can be discerned by the vehemence of their challenge: falsehood is ofttimes more clamorous than truth. No witnesses can be produced: they two dwelt apart under one roof; and if some neighbours have seen the children at their birth and circumcision, yet how little difference, how much change is there in the favour of infants! how doth death alter more confirmed lines!

The impossibility of proof makes the guilty more confident, more impudent: the true mother pleads that her child was taken away at midnight by the other, but in her sleep, she saw it not, she felt it not; and if all her senses could have witnessed it, yet here was but the affirmation of the one against the denial of the other, which, in persons alike credible, do but counterpoise. What is there now to lead the judge, since there is nothing either in the act, or circumstances, or persons, or plea, or evidence that might sway the sentence? Solomon well saw, that when all outward proof failed, there was an inward affection, which, if it could be fetched out, would certainly betray the true mother; he knew sorrow might more easily be dissembled than natural love: both sorrowed for their own; both could not love one as theirs. To draw forth, then, this true proof of motherhood, Solomon calls for a sword. Doubtless, some of the wiser hearers smiled upon each other, and thought in themselves, What, will the young king cut these knotty causes in pieces? will he divide justice with edge-tools? will he smite at hazard, before conviction? The actions of wise princes are riddles to vulgar constructions; neither is it for the shallow capacities of the multitude to fathom the deep projects of sovereign authority. That sword which had served for execution, shall now serve for trial: " Divide ye the living child in twain, and give the one half to the one, and the other half to the other!" O divine oracle of justice, commanding that which it would not have done, that it might find out that which could not be discovered!. neither God, nor his deputies, may be so taken at their words, as if they always intended their commands for action, and not sometimes for probation.

This sword hath already pierced the breast of the true mother, and divided her heart with fear and grief at so killing a sentence: there needs no other rack to discover nature; and now she thinks, Woe is me, that came for justice, and am answered with cruelty! " Divide ye the living child!" Alas! what hath that poor infant offended, that it survives, and is sued for? How much less miserable had I been, that my child had been smothered in my sleep, than mangled before mine eyes! If a dead carcass could have satisfied me, I needed not to have complained! What a woful condition am I fallen into, who am accused to have been the death of my supposed child already, and now shall be the death of my own! If there were no loss of my child, yet how can I endure this torment of mine own bowels! How can I live to see this part of myself sprawling under that bloody sword! And while she thinks thus, she sues to that suspected mercy of her just judge: " Oh, my lord, give her the living child, and slay him not!" as thinking, if he live, he shall but change a mother; if he die, his mother loseth a son: while he lives, it shall be my comfort that I have a son, though I may not call him so; dying, he perisheth to both: it is better he should live to a wrong mother, than to neither. Contrarily, her envious competitor, as holding herself well satisfied that her neighbour should be as childless as herself, can say, " Let it be neither mine nor thine, but divide it." Well might Solomon, and every hearer, conclude, that either she was no mother, or a monster, that could be content with the murder of her child; and that, if she could have been the true mother, and yet have desired the blood of her infant, she had been as worthy to have been stripped of her child for so foul unnaturalness, as the other had been worthy to enjoy him for her honest compassion. Not more justly than wisely, therefore, doth Solomon trace the true mother by the footsteps of love and pity; and adjudgeth the child to those bowels that had yearned at his danger.

Even in morality it is thus also: truth, as it is one, so it loves entireness; falsehood, division. Satan, that hath no right to the heart, would be content with a piece of it: God, that made it all, will have either the whole or none. The erroneous church strives with the true for the living child of saving doctrine; each claims it for her own: heresy, conscious of her own injustice, would be content to go away with a leg or an arm of sound principles, as hoping to make up the rest with her own mixtures: truth cannot abide to part with a joint; and will rather endure to lose all by violence, than a piece through a willing connivancy.

CONTEMPLATION V.—THE TEMPLE.

It is a weak and injurious censure that taxeth Solomon's slackness in founding the house of God: great bodies must have but slow motions. He was wise that said, " The matters must all be prepared without, ere we build within;" and if David have laid ready a great part of the metals and timber, yet many a tree must be felled and squared, and many a stone hewn and polished, ere this foundation could be laid: neither could those large cedars be cut, sawn, seasoned in one year; four years are soon gone in so vast a preparation. David had not been so entire a friend to Hiram, if Hiram had not been a friend to God. Solomon's wisdom had taught him to make use of so good a neighbour, of a father's friend: he knew that the Tyrians' skill was not given them for nothing: not Jews only, but Gentiles, must have their hand in building the temple of God: only Jews meddled with the tabernacle, but the temple is not built without the aid of Gentiles; they, together with us, make up the church of God.

Even Pagans have their arts from heaven; how justly may we improve their graces to the service of the God of heaven! If there be a Tyrian that can work more curiously in gold, in silver, in brass, in iron, in purple, and blue silk, than an Israelite, why should not he be employed about the temple? Their heathenism is their own; their skill is their Maker's: many a one works for the church of God, that yet hath no part in it.

Solomon raises a tribute for the work, not of money, but of men: thirty thousand Israelites are levied for the service; yet not continuedly, but with intermission; their labour is more generous, and less pressing. it is enough if they keep their courses one month in Lebanon, two at home; so as ever ten thousand work, while twenty thousand breathe. So favourable is God to his creature, that he requires us not to be overtoiled in the works of his own service. Due respirations are requisite in the holiest acts. The main stress of the work lies upon proselytes; whose both number and pains were herein more than the natives: a hundred and fifty thousand of them are employed in bearing burdens, in hewing stones; besides their three thousand three hundred overseers. Now were the despised Gibeonites of good use; and in vain doth Israel wish that the zeal of Saul had not robbed them of so serviceable drudges.

There is no man so mean but may be some way useful to the house of God: those that cannot work in gold, and silver, and silk, yet may cut and hew; and those that can do neither, yet may carry burdens. Even the services that are more homely, are not less necessary. Who can dishearten himself in the conscience of his own insufficiency, when he sees God can as well serve himself of his labour, as of his skill?

The temple is framed in Lebanon, and set upon Zion: neither hammer nor axe was heard in that holy structure; there was nothing but noise in Lebanon, nothing in Sion but silence and peace. Whatever tumults are abroad, it is fit there should be all quietness and sweet concord in the church. O God, that the axes of schism, or the hammers of furious contentions, should be heard within thy sanctuary! Thine house is not built with blows; with blows it is beaten down. O knit the hearts of thy servants together in the unity of the spirit, and the bond of peace, that we may mind and speak the same things; that thou, who art the God of peace, mayest take pleasure to dwell under the quiet roof of our hearts!

Now is the foundation laid, and the walls rising of that glorious fabric, which all nations admired, and all times have celebrated; even those stones which were laid in the base of the building were not ragged and rude, but hewn and costly: the part that lies covered with earth from the eyes of all beholders, is no less precious, than those that are more conspicuous. God is not all for the eye; he pleaseth himself with the hidden value of the living stones of his spiritual temple. How many noble graces of his servants have been buried by obscurity! not discerned so much as by their own eyes! which yet as he gave, so he crowneth. Hypocrites regard nothing but show; God nothing but truth.

The matter of so goodly a frame strives with the proportion, whether shall more excel: here was nothing but white marble without, nothing but cedar and gold within. Upon the hill of Sion stands that glittering and snowy pile, which both inviteth and dazzleth the eyes of passengers afar off; so much more precious within, as cedar is better than stone, gold than cedar. No base thing goes to the making up of God's house. If Satan may have a dwelling, he cares not though he patch it up of the rubbish of stone, or rotten sticks, or dross of metals: God will admit of nothing that is not pure and exquisite; his church consists of none but the faithful; his habitation is in no heart but the gracious.

The fashion was no other than that of the tabernacle; only this was more costly, more large, more fixed: God was the same that dwelt in both; he varied not: the same mystery was in both; only it was fit there should be a proportion betwixt the work and the builder. The tabernacle was erected in a popular estate; the temple in a monarchy: it was fit this should savour of the munificence of a king, as that of the zeal of a multitude: that was erected in the flitting condition of Israel in the desert; this, in their settled residence in the promised land: it was fit therefore that should be framed for motion, this for rest. Both of them were distinguished into three remarkable divisions, whereof each was more noble, more reserved, than other.

But what do we bend our eyes upon?—stone, wood, and metals? God would never have taken pleasure in these dead materials for their own sakes, if they had not had a further intendment. Methinks I see four temples in this one: it is but one in matter, as the God that dwells in it is but one; three yet more in resemblance, according to the division of them in whom it pleases

God to inhabit; for wherever God dwells, there is his temple. O God! thou vouchsafest to dwell in the believing heart. As we, thy silly creatures, have our being in thee, so thou, the Creator of heaven and earth, hast thy dwelling in us. The heaven of heavens is not able to contain thee, and yet thou disdainest not to dwell in the strait lodgings of our renewed souls. So then, because God's children are many, and those many divided in respect of themselves, though united in their head, therefore this temple, which is but one in collection, as God is one, is manifold in the distribution, as the saints are many; each man bearing about with him a little shrine of this Infinite Majesty: and for that the most general division of the saints is in their place and estate, some struggling and toiling in this earthly warfare, others triumphing in heavenly glory: therefore hath God two other, more universal temples; one the church of his saints on earth; the other, the highest heaven of his saints glorified. In all these, O God, thou dwellest for ever: and this material house of thine is a clear representation of these three spiritual: else what were a temple made with hands unto the God of spirits? And though one of these was a true type of all, yet how are they all exceeded each by other! This of stone, though most rich and costly; yet what is it to the living temple of the Holy Ghost, which is our body? What is the temple of this body of ours to the temple of Christ's body, which is his church? And what is the temple of God's church on earth, to that which triumpheth gloriously in heaven?

How easily do we see all these in this one visible temple! which, as it had three distinctions of rooms, the porch, the holy place, the holy of holies, so is each of them answered spiritually. In the porch we find the regenerate soul entering into the blessed society of the church: in the holy place, the communion of the true visible church on earth, selected from the world: in the holy of holies, whereinto the high priest entered once a-year, the glorious heaven, into which our true High Priest, Christ Jesus, entered once for all, to make an atonement betwixt God and man. In all these, what a meet correspondence there is in proportion, matter, situation!

In proportion; the same rule that skilful carvers observe in the cutting out of the perfect statue of a man, that the height be thrice the breadth, and the breadth one third of the height, was likewise duly observed in the fabric of the temple, whose length was double to the height, and treble to the breadth, as being sixty cubits long, thirty-high, and twenty broad. How exquisite a symmetry hast thou ordained, O God, betwixt the faithful heart, and thy church on earth, with that in heaven! how accurate in each of these, in all their powers and parts, compared with other! So hath God ordered the believing soul, that it hath neither too much shortness of grace, nor too much height of conceit, nor too much breadth of passion: so hath he ordered his visible church, that there is a necessary inequality, without any disproportion; a height of government, a length of extent, a breadth of jurisdiction, duly answerable to each other: so hath he ordered his triumphant church above, that it hath a length of eternity, answered with a height of perfection, and a breadth of incomprehensible glory.

In matter; all was here of the best: the wood was precious, sweet, lasting; the stones beautiful, costly, insensible of age; the gold: pure and glittering: so are the graces of God's children, excellent in their nature, dear in their acceptation, eternal in their use; so are the ordinances of God in his church, holy, comfortable, irrefragable; so is the perfection of his glorified saints, incomparable, unconceivable.

In situation; the outer parts were here more common; the inner more holy and peculiarly reserved. I find one court of the temple open to the unclean, to the uncircumcised; within that, another open only to the Israelites, and of them, to the clean; within that, yet another, proper only to the priests and Levites, where was the brazen altar for sacrifice, and the brazen sea for washing: the eyes of the laity might follow their oblations in hither; their feet might not.

Yet more, in the covered rooms of the temple, there is, whither the priests only may enter, not the Levites; there is, whither the high priest only may enter, not his brethren.

It is thus in every renewed man, the individual temple of God: the outward parts are allowed common to God and the world; the inwardest and secretest, which is the heart, is reserved only for the God that made it. It is thus in the church visible: the false and foul-hearted hypocrite hath access to the holy ordinances of God, and treads in his courts; only the true Christian hath entire and private conversation with the Holy One of Israel; he only is admitted into the holy of holies, and enters within the glorious vail of heaven.

If, from the walls, we look into the furniture; what is the altar, whereon our sacrifices of prayer and praises are offered to the Almighty, but a contrite heart? what the golden candlesticks, but the illumined understanding, wherein the light of the knowledge of God, and his divine will, shineth for ever? what the tables of shewbread, but the sanctified memory, which keepeth the bread of life continually? Yea, if we shall presume so far as to enter into the very closet of God's oracle, even there, O God, do we find our unworthy hearts so honoured by thee, that they are made thy very ark, wherein thy royal law, and the pot of thy heavenly manna, are kept for ever; and from whose Propitiatory, shaded with the wings of thy glorious angels, thou givest the gracious testimonies of thy good Spirit, witnessing with ours, that we are the children of the living God.

Behold, if Solomon built a temple unto thee, thou hast built a temple unto thyself in us: we are not only, through thy grace, living stones in thy temple, but living temples in thy Sion. O do thou ever dwell in this thine house, and in this thy house let us ever serve thee! Wherefore else hast thou a temple, but for thy presence with us, and for our worshipping of thee? The time was, when, as thy people, so thyself didst lodge in flitting tents, ever shifting, ever moving; thence thou thoughtest best to sojourn both in Shiloh, and the roof of Obed-Edom; after that, thou condescendedst to settle thine abode with men, and wouldst dwell in a house of thine own at thy Jerusalem. So didst thou, in the beginning, lodge with our first parents in a tent, sojourn with Israel under the law, and now makest a constant residence under the Gospel, in the hearts of thy chosen children, from whence thou wilt remove no more: they shall remove from the world, from themselves; thou shalt not remove from them.

Wheresoever thou art, O God, thou art worthy of adoration! since thou ever wilt dwell in us, be thou ever worshipped in us! Let the altars of our clean hearts send up ever to thee the sweetest perfumed smokes of our holy meditations and faithful prayers, and cheerful thanksgivings! Let the pure lights of our faith and godly conversation, shine ever before thee and men, and never be put out! Let the bread of life stand ever ready upon the pure and precious tables of our hearts! Lock up thy law and thy manna within us, and speak comfortably to us from thy mercy-seat! Suffer nothing to enter in hither that is unclean! sanctify us unto thyself, and be thou sanctified in us.

CONTEMPLATION VI.—SOLOMON AND THE QUEEN OF SHEBA.

God hath no use of the dark lanterns of secret and reserved perfections; we ourselves do not light up candles to put them under bushels. The great lights, whether of heaven or earth, are not intended to obscurity; but as to give light unto others, so to be seen themselves. Dan and Beersheba were too strait bounds for the fame of Solomon, which now hath flown over all lands and seas, and raised the world to an admiration of his more than human wisdom. Even so, O thou everlasting King of peace! thy name is great among the Gentiles: there is no speech nor language, where the report of thee is not heard: " The sound of thee is gone forth through all the earth; thy name is an ointment poured out, therefore the virgins love thee."

No doubt many, from all coasts, came to learn and wonder; none with so much note as this noble daughter of Cham, who herself deserves the next wonder to him whom she came to hear and admire: that a woman, a princess, a rich and great queen, should travel from the remotest South, from Sheba, a region famous for the greatest delicacies of nature, to learn wisdom, is a matchless example. We know merchants that venture to either Indies for wealth; others we know daily to cross the seas for wanton curiosity: some few philosophers we have known to have gone far for learning; and, amongst princes, it is no unusual thing to send their ambassadors to far distant kingdoms, for transaction of businesses either of state or commerce: but that a royal lady should in person undertake and overcome so tedious a journey, only to observe and inquire into the mysteries of nature, art, religion, is a thing past both parallel and limitation. Why do we think any labour great, or any way long, to hear a greater than Solomon? How justly shall the queen of the South rise up in judgment, and condemn us, who may hear wisdom crying in our streets, and neglect her!

Certainly so wealthy a queen, and so great a lover of wisdom, could not want great scholars at home; them she had first opposed with her enigmatical demands; and now, finding herself unsatisfied, she betakes herself to this oracle of God. It is a good thing to doubt; better to be resolved: the mind that never doubts, shall learn nothing; the mind that ever doubts, shall never profit by learning. Our doubts only serve to stir us up to seek truth: our resolutions settle us in the truth we have found. There were no pleasure in resolutions, if we had not been formerly troubled with doubts; there were nothing but discomfort and disquietness in doubts, if it were not for the hope of resolution: it is not safe to suffer doubts to dwell too long upon the heart; there may be good use of them as passengers, dangerous as inmates: happy are we, if we can find a Solomon to remove them.

Fame, as it is always a blab, so ofttimes a liar. The wise princess found cause to distrust so uncertain an informer, whose reports are still either doubtful or fabulous; and, like winds or streams, increase in passing. If very great things were not spoken of Solomon, fame should have wronged him; and, if but just rumours were spread of his wisdom, there needed much credulity to believe them. This great queen would not suffer herself to be led by the ears, but comes in person to examine the truth of foreign relations. How much more unsafe is it, in the most important businesses of our souls, to trust the opinions and reports of others! Those ears and eyes are ill bestowed, that do not serve to choose and judge for their owners.

When we come to a rich treasure, we need not be bidden to carry away what we are able. This wise lady, as she came far for knowledge, so, finding the plenty of this vein, she would not depart without her full load: there was nothing wherein she would leave herself unsatisfied. She knew that she could not every day meet with a Solomon; and therefore she makes her best use of so learned a master: now she empties her heart of all her doubts, and fills it with instruction. It is not good neglecting the opportunities of furnishing our souls with profitable, with saving knowledge. There is much wisdom in moving a question well, though there be more in assoiling it: what use do we make of Solomon's teacher, if, sitting at the feet of Christ, we leave our hearts either ignorant or perplexed?

As if the errand of this wealthy queen had been to buy wisdom, she came with her camels laden with gold, and precious stones, and rich odours: though to a mighty king, she will not come to school empty-handed: if she came to fetch an invaluable treasure, she finds reason to give thanks unto him that kept it. As he is a fool that hath a price in his hand to get wisdom, and wants a heart; so is he unthankful, that hath a heart to get wisdom, and hath no price in his hand: a price not countervailable to what he seeks, but retributory to him of whom he seeks. How shameful is it to come always with close hands to them that teach us the great mysteries of salvation!

Expectation is no better than a kind enemy to good deserts. We lose those objects which we overlook. Many had been admired, if they had not been overmuch befriended by fame, who now, in our judgment, are cast as much below their rank, as they were fore-imagined above it. This disadvantage had wise Solomon with this stranger, whom rumour had bid to look for incredible excellencies; yet so wonderful were the graces of Solomon, that they overcame the highest expectation, and the most liberal belief: so, as when she saw the architecture of his buildings, the provisions of his tables, the order of his attendants, the religion of his sacrifices, she confessed both her unjust incredulity, in not believing the report of his wisdom, and the injury of report in underrating it: "I believed not the words till I came, and mine eyes had seen it, and lo, the one half·was not told me." Her eyes were more sure informers than her ears. She did not so much hear, as see, Solomon's wisdom in these real effects: his answers did not so much demonstrate it, as his prudent government. There are some whose speeches are witty, while their carriage is weak; whose deeds are incongruities, while their words are apophthegms. It is not worth the name of wisdom, that may be heard only, and not seen. Good discourse is but the froth of wisdom; the pure and solid substance of it is in well-framed actions: "If we know these things, happy are we if we do them."

And if this great person admired the wisdom, the buildings, the domestic order, of Solomon, and chiefly his stately ascent into the house of the Lord, how should our souls be taken up with wonder at thee, O thou true Son of David, and Prince of everlasting Peace, who receivedst the Spirit not by measure! who hast built this glorious house not made with hands, even the heaven of heavens! whose infinite providence hath sweetly disposed of all the family of thy creatures, both in heaven and earth; and who, lastly, didst " ascend up on high, and leddest captivity captive, and gavest gifts to men!"

So well had this studious lady profited by the lectures of that exquisite master, that now she envies, she magnifies none but them who may live within the air of Solomon's wisdom: "Happy are thy men, and happy are thy servants, which stand continually before thee, and that hear th wisdom!" as if she could have been content to have changed her throne for the footstool of Solomon. It is not easy to conceive, how great a blessing it is to live under those lips, which do both preserve knowledge and utter it. If we were not glutted with good counsel, we should find no relish in any worldly contentment, in comparison hereof: but he that is full despiseth an honey-comb.

She, whom her own experience had taught how happy a thing it is to have a skilful pilot sitting at the stern of the state, blesseth Israel for Solomon, blesseth God for Israel, blesseth Solomon and Israel mutually in each other: " Blessed be the Lord thy God which delighteth in thee, to set thee on the throne of Israel. Because the Lord loved Israel for ever, therefore made he thee king to do judgment and justice." It was not more Solomon's advancement to be king of Israel, than it was the advancement of Israel to be governed by a Solomon. There is no earthly proof of God's love to any nation, comparable to the substitution of a wise and pious governor: to him we owe our peace, our life, and, which is deservedly dearer, the life of our souls, the gospel. But, O God, how much hast thou loved thine Israel for ever, in that thou hast set over it that righteous Branch of Jesse, whose name is " Wonderful, Counsellor, the Mighty God, the Everlasting Father, the Prince of Peace; in whose days Judah shall be saved, and Israel shall dwell safely! Sing, O heaven, and rejoice, O earth, and break forth into singing, O mountains; for God hath comforted his people, and will have everlasting mercy upon his afflicted."

The queen of Sheba did not bring her gold and precious stones to look on, or to re-carry, but to give to a wealthier than herself. She gives therefore to Solomon a hundred and twenty talents of gold, besides costly stones and odours. He, that hath made silver in Jerusalem as stones, is yet richly presented on all hands. The rivers still run into the sea; to him that hath shall be given. How should we bring unto thee, O thou King of heaven, the purest gold of thine own graces, the sweetest odours of our obediences! Was not this withal a type of that homage which should be done unto thee, O Saviour, by the heads of the nations? " The kings of Tarshish and the isles bring presents; the kings of Sheba and Seba bring gifts; yea, all kings shall worship thee, all nations shall serve thee!" They cannot enrich themselves, but by giving unto thee.

It could not stand with Solomon's magnificence to receive rich courtesies without a return; the greater the person was, the greater was the obligation of requital. The gifts of mean persons are taken but as tributes of duty. It is dishonourable to take from equals, and not to retribute: there was not therefore more freedom in her gift, than in her receipt; her own will was the measure of both: she gave what she would, she received whatsoever she would ask; and she had little profited by Solomon's school, if she had not learned to ask the best. She returns, therefore, more richly laden than she came: she gave to Solomon as a thankful client of wisdom; Solomon returns to her, as a munificent patron, according to the liberality of a king. We shall be sure to be gainers by whatsoever we give unto thee, O thou God of wisdom and peace! O that we could come, from the remote regions of our infidelity and worldliness, to learn wisdom of thee, who both teachest and givest it abundantly, without upbraiding, without grudging, and could bring with us the poor presents of our faithful desires and sincere services! how wouldst thou receive us with a gracious acceptation, and send us away laden with present comfort, with eternal glory!

CONTEMPLATION VII. — SOLOMON'S DEFECTION.

SINCE the first man Adam, the world hath not yielded either so great an example of wisdom, or so fearful an example of apostasy, as Solomon. What human knowledge Adam had in the perfection of nature by creation, Solomon had by infusion: both fully; both from one fountain. If Adam called all creatures by their names, Solomon spake from the cedars of Lebanon, to the moss that springs out of the wall; and, besides these vegetables, there was no beast, nor fowl, nor fish, nor creeping thing, that escaped his discourse. Both fell; both fell by one means: as Adam, so might Solomon have said, " The woman deceived me." It is true, indeed, that Adam fell as all, Solomon as one, yet so as that this one is the pattern of the frailty of all. If knowledge could have given an immunity from sin, both had stood. Affections are those feet of the soul on which it either stands or falls: " Solomon loved many outlandish women." I wonder not if the wise king miscarried; every word hath bane enough for a man. Women, many women, outlandish, idolatrous, and those not only had, but doated on; sex, multitude, nation, condition, all conspired to the ruin of a Solomon. If one woman undid all mankind, what marvel is it if many women undid one? Yet, had those many been the daughters of Israel, they had tempted him only to lust, not to misdevotion: now they were of those nations, whereof the Lord had said to the children of Israel, "Go not ye into them, nor let them come into you, for surely they will turn your hearts after their gods." To them did Solomon join in love: who can marvel, if they disjoined his heart from God? Satan hath found this bait to take so well, that he never changed it since he crept into Paradise. How many have we known whose heads have been broken with their own rib!

In the first world, the sons of God saw the daughters of men, and took them wives of all they liked; they multiplied not children, but iniquities. Balaam knew well, if the dames of Moab could make the Israelites wanton, they should soon make them idolaters. All lies open, where the covenant is not both made with the eye, and kept.

It was the charge of God to the kings of Israel, before they were, that they should not multiply wives. Solomon hath gone beyond the stakes of the law, and now is ready to lose himself amongst a thousand bedfellows. Whoso lays the reins in the neck of his carnal appetite, cannot promise where he will rest. O Solomon! where was thy wisdom, while thine affections run away with thee into so wild a voluptuousness? What boots it thee to discourse of all things, while thou misknowest thyself? The perfections of speculation do not argue the inward power of self-government: the eye may be clear, while the hand is palsied. It is not so much to be heeded, how the soul is informed, as how it is disciplined; the light of knowledge doth well, but the due order of the affections doth better. Never any mere man, since the first, knew so much as Solomon; many that have known less, have had more command of themselves. A competent estate, well husbanded, is better than a vast patrimony neglected.

There can be no safety to that soul, where is not a strait curb upon our desires. If our lusts be not held under as slaves, they will rule as tyrants. Nothing can prevent the extremity of our miscarriage, but early and strong denials of our concupiscence: had Solomon done this, delicacy and lawless greatness had not led him into these bogs of intemperance.

The ways of youth are steep and slippery, wherein as it is easy to fall, so it is commonly relieved with pity; but the wanton inordinations of age are not more unseasonable than odious; yet behold, Solomon's younger years were studious and innocent; his over-hastened age was licentious and misgoverned: "For when Solomon was old, his wives turned away his heart after other gods." If any age can secure us from the danger of a spiritual fall, it is our last; and if any man's old age might secure him, it was Solomon's, the beloved of God, the oracle, the miracle of wisdom: who would have looked but that the blossoms of so hopeful a spring should have yielded a goodly and pleasant fruit in the autumn of age? Yet behold even Solomon's old age vicious. There is no time wherein we can be safe, while we carry this body of sin about us: youth is impetuous, mid age stubborn, old age weak, all dangerous: say not now, "The fury of my youthful flashes is over, I shall henceforth find my heart calm and impregnable," while thou seest old Solomon doating upon his concubines, yea, upon their idolatry.

It is no presuming upon time, or means, or strength. How many have begun and proceeded well, who have yet shamed themselves in their last stage! If God uphold us not, we cannot stand: if God uphold us, we cannot fall. When we are at the strongest, it is the best to be weak in ourselves; and when at our weakest, strong in him, in whom we can do all things.

I cannot yet think so hard of Solomon, that he would project his person to Ashtaroth, the goddess of the Sidonians; or Milchom, the idol of the Ammonites; or Chemosh, the abomination of Moab. He that knew all things from the shrub to the cedar, could not be ignorant that these statues were but stocks, or stones, or metals, and the powers resembled by them devils. It is not like he could be so insensate to adore such deities; but so far was the uxorious king blinded with affection, that he gave not passage only to the idolatry of his heathenish wives, but furtherance.

So did he doat upon their persons, that he humoured them in their sins; their act is therefore his, because his eyes winked at it, his hand advanced it. He that built a temple to the living God, for himself and Israel, in Sion, built a temple to Chemosh in the Mount of Scandal, for his mistresses of Moab, in the very face of God's house. No hill about Jerusalem was free from a chapel of devils: each of his dames had their puppets, their altars, their incense: because Solomon feeds them in their superstition, he draws the sin home to himself, and is branded for what he should have forbidden. Even our very permission appropriates crimes to us. We need no more guiltiness of any sin than our willing toleration.

Who can but yearn, and fear, to see the woful wreck of so rich and goodly a vessel? O Solomon! wert not thou he, whose younger years God honoured with a message and style of love? to whom God twice appeared, and in a gracious vision renewed the covenant of his favour? whom he singled out from all the generation of men, to be the founder of that glorious temple, which was no less clearly the type of heaven, than thou wert of Christ, the son of the ever-living God? wert not thou that deep sea of wisdom, which God ordained to send forth rivers and fountains of all divine and human knowledge to all nations, to all ages? wert not thou one of those select secretaries, whose hand it pleased the Almighty to employ in three pieces of the divine monuments of sacred scriptures? Which of us dares ever hope to aspire unto thy graces? which of us can promise to secure ourselves from thy ruins? We fall, O God, we fall to the lowest hell, if thou prevent us not, if thou sustain us not! " Uphold thou me, according to thy word, that I may live, and let me not be ashamed of my hope. Order my steps in thy word, and let not any iniquity have dominion over me." All our weakness is in ourselves; all our strength is in thee. O God! be thou strong in our weakness, that our weak knees may be ever steady in thy strength.

But, in the midst of the horror of this spectacle, able to affright all the sons of men, behold some glimpse of comfort. Was it of Solomon that David his father prophesied, " Though he fall, he shall not be utterly cast down, for the Lord upholdeth him with his hand?" If sensible grace, yet final mercy, was not taken from that beloved of God: in the hardest of this winter, the sap was gone down to the root, though it showed not in the branches. Even while Solomon removed, that word stood fast, " He shall be my son, and I will be his father." He that foresaw his sin, threatened and limited his correction: " If he break my statutes, and keep not my commandments, then will I visit his transgression with a rod, and his iniquity with stripes; nevertheless, my loving-kindness will I not utterly take from him, nor suffer my faithfulness to fail; my covenant will I not break, nor alter the thing that is gone out of my mouth." Behold, the favour of God doth not depend upon Solomon's obedience: if Solomon shall suffer his faithfulness to fail towards his God, God will not requite him with the failing of his faithfulness to Solomon; if Solomon break his covenant with God, God will not break his covenant with the father of Solomon, with the son of David: he shall smart, he shall not perish. O gracious word of the God of all mercies, able to give strength to the languishing, comfort to the despairing, to the dying, life ! Whatsoever we are, thou wilt be still thyself, O Holy One of Israel, true to thy covenant, constant to thy decree; the sins of thy chosen can neither frustrate thy counsel, nor outstrip thy mercies.

Now I see Solomon, of a wanton lover, a grave preacher of mortification: I see him quenching those inordinate flames with the tears of his repentance. Methinks I hear him sighing deeply, betwixt every word of that his solemn penance, which he would needs enjoin himself before all the world: " I have applied my heart to know the wickedness of folly, even the foolishness of madness; and I find more bitter than death the woman whose heart is as nets and snares, and her hands as bands: whoso pleaseth God shall be delivered from her, but the sinner shall be taken by her."

Solomon was taken as a sinner, delivered as a penitent. His soul escaped as a bird out of the snare of the fowlers; the snare was broken, and he delivered. It is good for us that he was both taken and delivered: taken, that we might not presume; and, that we might not despair, delivered. He sinned, that we might not sin; he recovered, that we may not sink under our sin.

But O the justice of God, inseparable from his mercy! Solomon's sin shall not escape the rod of men: rather than so wise an offender shall want enemies, God shall raise up three adversaries unto Solomon— Hadad, the Edomite, Rezon, the king of Aram, Jeroboam, the son of Nebat; whereof two were foreign, one domestical. Nothing but love and peace sounded in the name of Solomon; nothing else was found in his reign, while he held in good terms with his God; but when once he fell foul with his Maker, all things began to be troubled. There are whips laid up against the time of Solomon's foreseen offence, which are now brought forth for his correction. On purpose was Hadad, the son of the king of Edom, hid in a corner of Egypt from the sword of David and Joab, that he might be reserved for a scourge to the exorbitant son of David. God would have us make account that our peace ends with our innocence. The same sin that sets debate betwixt God and us, arms the creatures against us: it were pity we should be at any quiet, while we are fallen out with the God of peace.

BOOK XVIII.

CONTEMPLATION I.—REHOBOAM.

Who would not but have looked, that seven hundred wives, and three hundred concubines, should have furnished Solomon's palace with choice of heirs, and have peopled Israel with royal issue? and now, behold, Solomon has by all these but one son, and him by an Ammonitess! Many a poor man hath an houseful of children by one wife, while this great king has but one son by many housefuls of wives. Fertility is not from the means, but from the author. It was for Solomon that David sung of old, " Lo, children are an heritage of the Lord, and the fruit of the womb is his reward!" How oft doth God deny this heritage of heirs, where he gives the largest heritage of lands, and gives most of these living possessions, where he gives least of the dead, that his blessings may be acknowledged free unto both, entailed upon neither!

As the greatest persons cannot give themselves children, so the wisest cannot give their children wisdom. Was it not of Rehoboam that Solomon said, " I hated all my labour which I had taken under the sun, because I should leave it to the man that shall be after me; and who knoweth whether he shall be a wise man or a fool: yet shall he rule over all my labour, wherein I have laboured, and showed myself wise under the sun." All Israel found that Solomon's wit was not propagated; many a fool hath had a wiser son than this wisest father: amongst many sons, it is no news to find some one defective; Solomon hath but one son, and he no miracle of wisdom. God gives purposely so eminent an instance, to teach men to look up to heaven, both for heirs and graces.

Solomon was both the king of Israel, and the father of Rehoboam, when he was scarce out of his childhood: Rehoboam enters into the kingdom at a ripe age; yet Solomon was the man, and Rehoboam the child. Age is no just measure of wisdom; there are beardless sages, and grey-headed children; not the ancient are wise, but the wise are ancient. Israel wanted not for thousands that were wiser than Rehoboam; yet, because they knew him to be the son of Solomon, no man makes question of his government. In the case of succession into kingdoms, we may not look into the qualities of the person, but into the right. So secure is Solomon of the people's fidelity to David's seed, that he follows not his father's example, in setting his son by him in his own throne; here was no danger of a rivalry to enforce it, no eminency in the son to merit it: it sufficeth him to know, that no bond can be surer than the natural allegiance of subjects. I do not find that the following kings stood upon the confirmation of their people; but, as those that knew the way to the throne, ascended their steps without aid. As yet the sovereignty of David's house was green and unsettled: Israel, therefore, doth not now come to attend Rehoboam, but Rehoboam goes up to meet Israel; they come not to his Jerusalem, but he goes to their Shechem: " To Shechem were all Israel come to make him king." If loyalty drew them together, why not rather to Jerusalem? There, the majesty of his father's temple, the magnificence of his palace, the very stones in those walls, besides the strength of his guards, had pleaded strongly for their subjection. Shechem had been many ways fatal, was every way incommodious. It is an infinite help or disadvantage that arises from circumstances. The very place puts Israel in mind of a rebellion: there Abimelech had raised up his treacherous usurpation over and against his brethren; there Gaal against Abimelech; there was Joseph sold by his brethren; as if the very soil had been stained with perfidiousness. The time is no less ill chosen: Rehoboam had ill counsel ere he bewrayed it; for had he speedily called up Israel, before Jeroboam could have been sent for out of Egypt, he had found the way clear: a little delay may lose a great deal of opportunity; what shall we say of both, but that misery is led in by infatuation?

Had not Israel been somewhat predisposed to a mutiny, they had never sent into Egypt for such a spokesman as Jeroboam, a fugitive, a traitor to Solomon; long had that crafty conspirator lurked in a foreign court. The alliances of princes are not ever necessary bonds of friendship: the brother-in-law of Solomon harbours this snake in his bosom, and gives that heat, which is repaid with a sting to the posterity of so near an ally. And now Solomon's death calls him back to his native soil. That

REHOBOAM.

Israel would entertain a rebel, it was an ill sign; worse yet, that they would countenance him; worst of all, that they would employ him. Nothing doth more bewray evil intentions, than the choice of vicious agents. Those that mean well, will not hazard either the success or credit of their actions upon offensive instruments: none but the sluttish will wipe their faces with foul cloths. Upright hearts would have said, as David did to God, so to his anointed, " Do not I hate them that hate thee? yea, I hate them with a perfect hatred." Jeroboam's head had been a fit present to have been tendered unto their new king; and now, instead thereof, they tender themselves to Jeroboam, as the head of their faction.

Had not Rehoboam wanted spirits, he had first, after Solomon's example, done justice to his father's traitor, and then have treated of mercy towards his subjects; the people soon found the weakness of their new sovereign, else they durst not have spoken to him by so obnoxious a tongue: " Thy father made our yoke grievous, make thou it lighter, and we will serve thee." Doubtless the crafty head of Jeroboam was in this suit which his mouth uttered in the name of Israel: nothing could have been more subtile; it seemed a promise, but it was a threat; that which seemed a supplication, was a complaint: humility was but a vail for discontentment; one hand held a paper, the other a sword. Had they said, Free us from tributes, the capitulation had been gross, and strongly savouring of sedition; now they say, " Ease us;" they profess his power to impose, and their willingness to yield; only craving favour in the weight of the imposition. If Rehoboam yield, he blemishes his father; if he deny, he endangers his kingdom; his wilfulness shall seem worthily to abandon his sceptre, if he stick at so unreasonable a suit: surely Israel came with a purpose to cavil; Jeroboam had secretly troubled these waters, that he might fish more gainfully. One malcontent is enough to embroil a whole kingdom.

How harshly must it needs sound in the ears of Rehoboam, that the first word he hears from his people is a querulous challenge of his father's government! " Thy father made our yoke grievous." For aught I see, the suggestion was not more spiteful than unjust. Where was the weight of this yoke, the toil of these services? Here were none of the turmoils of war; no trainings, marchings, encampings, entrenchings, watchings, minings, sieges, fortifications; none of that tedious world of work that attends hostility. Solomon had not his name for nought: all was calm, during that long reign; and if they had paid dear for their peace, they had no cause to complain of a hard match: the warlike times of Saul and David had exhausted their blood, together with their substance; what ingratitude was this to cry out of ease! Yea, but that peace brought forth costly and laborious buildings; God's house, and the king's, the walls of Jerusalem, Hazor, Megiddo, and Gezer, the cities of store, the cities of defence, could not rise without many a shoulder: true, but not of any Israelites; the remainders of Amorites, Hittites, Perizzites, Hivites, and Jebusites, were put to all the drudgery of these great works: the tasks of Israel were easy and ingenuous, free from servility, free from painfulness. " But the charge was theirs, whosoever's was the labour. The diet of so endless a retinue, the attendance of his seraglio, the purveyance for his forty thousand stables, the cost of his sacrifices, must needs weigh heavy." Certainly, if it had lain on none but his own. But wherefore went Solomon's navy every three years to Ophir? to what use served the six hundred threescore and six talents of gold, that came in one year to his exchequer? wherefore served the large tributes of foreign nations? how did he make silver to be in Jerusalem as stones, if the exactions were so pressive? The multitude is ever prone to pick quarrels with their governors; and whom they feared alive, to censure dead. The benefits of so quiet and happy a reign are passed over in silence; the grievances are recounted with clamour. Who can hope that merit or greatness can shield him from obloquy, when Solomon is traduced to his own loins?

The proposition of Israel puts Rehoboam to a deliberation: " Depart ye for three days, then come again to me." I hear no other word of his that argued wisdom: not to give sudden resolutions, in cases of importance, was a point that well might beseem the son of Solomon. I wonder that he, who had so much wit as to call for leisure in his answer, should show so little wit in the improving of that leisure, in the return of that answer. Who cannot but hope well to see the grey heads of Solomon's secret council called to Rehoboam's cabinet? As counsellors, as ancient as Solomon's, they cannot choose but see the best, the safest course for their new sovereign: they had learned of their old master, that " A soft answer appeaseth wrath;" wisely, therefore, do they advise him, " If thou wilt be a servant to this people this day, and speak good words to them, they will be thy servants for ever." It was an easy condition, with one mouthful of breath to purchase an everlasting homage; with one gentle motion of his tongue, to bind all people's hearts to his allegiance for ever. Yet, as if the motion had been unfit, a new council-table is called. Well might this people say, "What will not Rehoboam grudge us, if he think much to give us good words for a kingdom?" There is not more wisdom in taking variety of advice, where the matter is doubtful, than folly when it is plain. The young heads are consulted; this very change argues weakness: some reason might be pleaded for passing from the younger council to the aged; none for the contrary. Age brings experience; and it is a shame, if with the ancient be not wisdom. Youth is commonly rash, heady, insolent, ungoverned, wedded to will, led by humour, a rebel to reason, a subject to passion, fitter to execute than advise. Green wood is ever shrinking and warping, whereas the well-seasoned holds a constant firmness. Many a life, many a soul, many a flourishing state, hath been ruined by undisciplined monitors: such were these of Rehoboam, whose great stomach tells them, that this conditionating of subjects was no other than an affront to their new master, and suggests to them, how unfit it is for majesty to brook so saucy a treaty; how requisite and princely to crush this presumption in the egg. As scorning, therefore, to be braved by the base vulgar, they put words of greatness and terror in their new prince: "My little finger shall be thicker than my father's loins; my father made your yoke heavy, I will add to your yoke. My father hath chastised you with whips, I will chastise you with scorpions." The very words have stings: now must Israel needs think, How cruel will this man's hands be, when he thus draws blood with his tongue! Men are not wont to speak out their worst: who can endure the hopes of him that promiseth tyranny? There can be no good use of an indefinite profession of rigour and severity; fear is an unsafe guardian of any state, much less of an unsettled: which was yet worse, not the sins of Israel were threatened, nor their purses, but their persons; neither had they desired a remission of justice, but of exactions: and now they hear of nothing but burdens, and scourges, and scorpions.

Here was a prince and, people well met: I do not find them sensible of aught, save their own profit: they do not say, Religion was corrupted in the shutting up of thy father's days; idolatry found the free favour of priests, and temples, and sacrifices. Begin thy reign with God: purge the church, demolish those piles of abomination, abandon those idol-mongers, restore devotion to her purity. They are all for their penny; for their ease. He, on the other side, is all for his will; for an imperious sovereignty, without any regard, either of their reformation or satisfaction: they were worthy of load that cared for nothing but their backs; and he worthy of such subjects, who professed to affect their misery and torment.

Who would not but have looked any whither for the cause of this evil, rather than to heaven? yet the holy God challenges it to himself: the cause was from the Lord, that he might perform this saying by Abijah, the Shilonite, to Jeroboam. As sin is a punishment of sin, it is a part of justice: the Holy One of Israel doth not abhor to use even the grossest sin to his own just purposes. While our wills are free to our own choice, his decrees are as necessary as just: Israel had forsaken the Lord, and worshipped Ashtaroth, the goddess of the Sidonians, and Chemosh, and Milcom: God owes them and Solomon a whipping; the frowardness of Rehoboam shall pay it them. I see Jeroboam's plot, the people's insolence, the young men's misadvice, the prince's unreasonable austerity, meeting together through the wise Providence of the Almighty, unwittingly to accomplish his most just decree. All these might have done otherwise, for any force that was offered to their will; all would no more do otherwise than if there had been no predetermination in heaven; that God may be magnified in his wisdom and justice, while man wittingly perisheth in his folly.

That three days' expectation had warmed these smoking Israelites, and made them ready for a combustion: upon so peremptory a resolution of rigour, the flame bursts out, which all the waters of the well of Bethlehem could never quench. The furious multitude flies out into a desperate revolt: "What portion have we in David? neither have we inheritance in the son of Jesse. To your tents, O Israel; now, see to thine own house, David."

How durst these seditious mouths mention David in defiance? One would have thought that very name had been able to have tempered their fury, and to have contained them within the limits of obedience. It was the father of Rehoboam, and the son of David, that had led Israel into idolatry: Solomon hath drawn contempt upon his father, and upon his son. If Israel have cast off their God, is it marvel that they shake off his anointed? Irreligion is the way to disobedience; there can be no true subjection, but out of conscience: they cannot make conscience of civil duties who make none of divine.

In vain shall Rehoboam hope to prevail by his officer, when himself is rejected. The persons of princes carry in them characters of majesty: when their presence works not, how should their message? If Adoram solicit the people too late with good words, they answer him with stones. Nothing is more untractable and violent than an enraged multitude. It was time for Rehoboam to betake himself to his chariot: he saw those stones were thrown at him in his Adoram. As the messenger suffers for the master, so the master suffers in his messenger. Had Rehoboam been in Adoram's clothes, this death had been his: only flight can deliver him from those that might have been subjects: Jerusalem must be his refuge against the conspiracy of Shechem.

Blessed be God for lawful government: even a mutinous body cannot want a head. If the rebellious Israelites have cast off their true sovereign, they must choose a false: Jeroboam, the son of Nebat, must be the man. He had need be skilful, and sit sure, that shall back the horse which hath cast his rider. Israel could not have anywhere met with more craft and courage than they found in this leader.

Rehoboam returns to Jerusalem lighter by a crown than he went forth; Judah and Benjamin still stick fast to their loyalty; the example of a general rebellion cannot make them unfaithful to the house of David. God will ever reserve a remnant free from the common contagion. Those tribes, to approve their valour no less than their fidelity, will fight against their brethren for their prince, and will hazard their lives to reduce the crown to the son of Solomon. A hundred and fourscore thousand of them are up in arms, ready to force Israel to their denied subjection. No noise sounded on both parts but military; no man thought of any thing but blood: when suddenly God sends his prophet to forbid the battle. Shemaiah comes with a message of cessation, " Ye shall not go up, nor fight against your brethren the children of Israel; return every man to his house; for this thing is from me, saith the Lord." The word of one silly prophet dismisses these mighty armies: he, that would not lay down the threats of his rigour, upon the advice of his ancient counsellors, will lay down his sword upon the word of a seer. Shall we envy, or shame, to see how much the prophets of the Old Testament could do? how little those of the New? If our commission be no less from the same God, the difference of success cannot go away unrevenged.

There was yet some grace in Rehoboam, that he would not spurn against that which God challenged as his own work. Some godless ruffian would have said, Whosoever is the author, I will be revenged on the instruments. Rehoboam hath learned this lesson of his grandfather: " I held my peace, because thou, Lord, hadst done it." If he might strive with the multitude, he knew it was no striving with his Maker: quietly therefore doth he lay down his arms, not daring, after that prohibition, to seek the recovery of his kingdom by blood.

Where God's purposes are hid from us, we must take the fairest ways of all lawful remedies: but where God hath revealed his determination, we must sit down in an humble submission: our struggling may aggravate, cannot redress, our miseries.

CONTEMPLATION II.—JEROBOAM.

As there was no public and universal conflict betwixt the ten tribes and the two, so no peace. Either king found reason to fortify the borders of his own territories. Shechem was worthy to be dear to Jeroboam; a city, as of old, seasoned with many treasons, so, now, auspicious to his new usurpation. The civil defection was soon followed by the spiritual. As there are near respects betwixt God and his anointed, so there is great affinity betwixt treason and idolatry; there is a connexion betwixt " Fear God, and honour the king;" and no less betwixt the neglects of both. In vain shall a man look for faith in an irreligious heart.

Next to Ahitophel, I do not find that Israel yielded a craftier head than Jeroboam's: so hath he plotted this conspiracy, that, whatever fall, there is no place for a challenge; not his own intrusion, but Israel's election, hath raised him to their throne: neither is his cunning less in holding a stolen sceptre. Thus he thinks in himself, If Israel have made me their king, it is but a pang of discontentment; these violent thoughts will not last always; sudden fits have commonly sudden recoveries: their return to their loyalty shall forfeit my head, together with my crown; they cannot return to God and hold off from their lawful sovereign; they cannot return to Jerusalem, and keep off from God, from their loyalty:

thrice a-year will their devotion call them up thither, besides the exigence of their frequent vows: how can they be mine, while that glorious temple is in their eye? while the magnificence of the royal palace of David and Solomon shall admonish them of their native allegiance? while, besides the solicitation of their brethren, the priests and Levites shall preach to them the necessity of their due obedience, and the abomination of their sacrifices in their wilful disobedience? while they shall, by their presence, put themselves upon the mercy or justice of their lawful and forsaken prince? Either, therefore, I must divert them from Jerusalem, or else I cannot live and reign : it is no diverting them by a direct restraint ; such prohibition would both endanger their utter distaste, and whet their desire to more eagerness : I may change religion, I may not inhibit it. So the people have a God, it sufficeth them: they shall have so much formality as may content them: their zeal is not so sharp but they can be well pleased with ease. I will proffer them both a more compendious and more plausible worship: Jerusalem shall be supplied within mine own borders. Naturally men love to see the objects of their devotion ; I will therefore feed their eyes with two golden representations of their god, nearer home; and what can be more proper, than those which Aaron devised of old to humour Israel?

Upon this pestilent ground, Jeroboam sets up two calves in Dan and Bethel, and persuades the people: "It is too much for you to go up to Jerusalem; behold thy gods, O Israel, which brought thee out of the land of Egypt." Oh the mischief that comes of wicked infidelity! It was God's prophet that had rent Jeroboam's garment into twelve pieces, and had given ten of them to him, in token of his sharing the ten tribes ; who, with the same breath also, told him, that the cause of this distraction was their idolatry. Yet now will he institute an idolatrous service for the holding together of them, whom their idolatry had rent from their true sovereign to him. He says not, God hath promised me this kingdom ; God hath conferred it ; God shall find means to maintain his own act ; I will obey him, let him dispose of me. The God of Israel is wise and powerful enough to fetch about his own designs ; but, as if the devices of men were stronger than God's providence and ordination, he will be working out his own ends by profane policies. Jeroboam, being born an Israelite, and bred in the court of a Solomon, could not but know the express charge of God against the making of images, against the erecting of any rival altars to that of Jerusalem ; yet now, that he sees both these may avail much to the advancing of his ambitious project, he sets up those images, those altars. Wicked men care not to make bold with God, in cases of their own commodity. If the laws of their Maker lie in the way of their profit or promotion, they either spurn them out, or tread upon them at pleasure. Aspiring minds will know no God but honour. Israel sojourned in Egypt, and brought home a golden calf; Jeroboam sojourns there, and brought home two: it is hard to dwell in Egypt untainted. Not to savour of the sins of the place we live in, is no less strange, than for wholesome liquor, tunned up in a musty vessel, not to smell of the cask. The best body may be infected in a contagious air. Let him beware of Egypt, that would be free from idolatry.

No sooner are Jeroboam's calves up, than Israel is down on their knees: their worship follows immediately upon the erection. How easily is the unstable vulgar carried into whatsoever religion of authority! The weathercock will look which way soever the wind blows : it is no marvel if his subjects be brutish, who hath made a calf his god.

Every accessory to sin is filthy, but the first authors of sin are abominable. How is Jeroboam branded in every of these sacred leaves! how do all ages ring of his fact, with the accent of dishonour and indignation! "Jeroboam, the son of Nebat, that made Israel to sin." It was a shame for Israel that it could be made to sin, by a Jeroboam: but O cursed name of Jeroboam, that would draw Israel to sin ! The followers and abettors of evil are worthy of torment, but no hell is too deep for the leaders of public wickedness.

Religion is clothed with many requisite circumstances. As a new king would have a new god, so that new god must have new temples, altars, services, priests, solemnities ; all these hath Jeroboam instituted; all these hath he cast in the same mould with his golden calves. False devotion doth not more cross than imitate the true. Satan is no less a counterfeit than an enemy of God; he knows it is more easy to adulterate religion, than to abolish it.

That which God ordained, for the avoidance of idolatry, is made the occasion of it: a limitation of his holy services to Jerusalem. How mischievously do wicked men pervert the wholesome institutions of God to their sin, to their bane !

Jeroboam could not be ignorant how fearfully this very act was revenged upon Israel in the wilderness; yet he dares renew it in Dan and Bethel. No example of judgment can affright wilful offenders.

It is not the metal that makes their gods, but the worship, the sacrifices. What sacrifices could there be without priests? No religion could ever want sacred masters of divine ceremonies: God's clergy was select and honourable, branches of the holy stem of Aaron; Jeroboam rakes up his priests out of the channel of the multitude; all tribes, all persons, were good enough to his spurious devotion. Leaden priests are well fitted for golden deities. Religion receives either much honour or blemish, by the quality of those that serve at her altars. We are not worthy to profess ourselves servants of the true God, if we do not hold his service worthy of the best.

Jeroboam's calves must have sacrifices, must have solemn festivities, though in a day and month of his own devising. In vain shall we pretend to worship a god, if we grudge him the just days and rites of his worship.

It is strange that he, who thought the dregs of the vulgar good enough for that priesthood, would grace those gods by acting their priest himself; and yet, behold where the new king of Israel stands before his new altar, with a sceptre in one hand, and a censer in the other, ready to sacrifice to his new gods, when the man of God comes from Judah with a message of judgment! O desperate condition of Israel, that was so far gone with impiety, that it yielded not one faithful monitor to Jeroboam! The time was, that the erecting of but a new altar, for memory, for monument, on the other side of Jordan, bred a challenge to the tribes of Reuben, Gad, and Manasses; and had cost much Israelitish blood, if the quarrelled tribes had not given a seasonable and pious satisfaction: and now, lo, how the stronger stomach of degenerated Israel can digest new altars, new temples, new gods! What a difference there is betwixt a church and kingdom newly breathing from affliction, and settled upon the lees of a misused peace!

But O the patience and mercy of our long-suffering God, that will not strike a very Jeroboam unwarned! Judgment hovers over the heads of sinners, ere it light. If Israel afford not a bold reprover of Jeroboam, Judah shall. When the king of Israel is in all the height both of his state and superstition, honouring his solemn day with his richest devotion, steps forth a prophet of God, and interrupts that glorious service with a loud inclamation of judgment. Doubtless the man wanted not wit to know what displeasure, what danger, must needs follow so unwelcome a message; yet dares he, upon the commission of God, do this affront to an idolatrous king, in the midst of all his awful magnificence. The prophets of God go upon many a thankless errand. He is no messenger for God, that either knows or fears the faces of men.

It was the altar, not the person of Jeroboam, which the prophet thus threatens; yet not the stones are stricken, but the founder, in both their apprehensions: so dear are the devices of our own brain to us, as if they were incorporated into ourselves. There is no opposition whereof we are so sensible as that of religion.

That the royal altar should be thus polluted by dead men's bones, and the blood of the priests, was not more unpleasing, than that all this should be done by a child of the house of David; for Jeroboam well saw, that the throne and the altar must stand or fall together; that a son of David could not have such power over the altar, without an utter subversion of the government, of the succession; therefore is he thus galled with this comminatory prediction. The rebellious people who had said, "What portion have we in David?" hear now, that David will perforce have a portion in them; and might well see what beasts they had made themselves in worshipping the image of a beast, and sacrificing to such a god, as could not preserve his own altar from violation and ruin.

All this while, I do not see this zealous prophet laying his hand to the demolition of this idolatrous altar, or threatening a knife to the author of this depravation of religion; only his tongue smites both, not with foul, but sharp words of menace, not of reproach. It was for Josias, a king, to shed the blood of those sacrificers, to deface those altars: prophets are for the tongue, princes for the hand; prophets must only denounce judgment, princes execute.

Future things are present to the Eternal. It was some two hundred and sixty years ere this prophecy should be fulfilled; yet the man of God speaks of it as now acting. What are some centuries of years to the Ancient of days? How slow, and yet how sure, is the pace of God's revenge! It is not in the power of time to frustrate God's determinations; there is no less justice, nor severity in a delayed punishment.

What a perfect record there is of all names in the roll of heaven, before they be, after they are past! Whatever seeming contingency there is in their imposition, yet they fall under the certainty of a decree, and are better known in heaven ere they be, than on earth while they are. He, that knows what names we shall have, before we or the world have a being, doth not oft reveal this piece of his knowledge to his creature; here he doth, naming the man that should be two hundred years after; for more assurance of the event, that Israel may say, this man speaks from a God who knows what shall be. There cannot be a more sure evidence of a true godhead, than the foreknowledge of those things, whose causes have yet no hope of being; but because the proof of this prediction was no more certain than remote, a present demonstration shall convince the future: — " The altar shall rend in pieces, the ashes shall be scattered." How amazedly must the seduced Israelites needs look upon this miracle! and why do they not think with themselves, While these stones rend, why are our hearts whole? Of what an over-ruling power is the God whom we have forsaken, that can thus tear the altars of his corrivals! How shall we stand before his vengeance, when the very stones break at the word of his prophet? Perhaps some beholders were thus affected; but Jeroboam, whom it most concerned, instead of bowing his knees for humiliation, stretched forth his hand for revenge, and cries, Lay hold on him! Resolute wickedness is impatient of a reproof, and, instead of yielding to the voice of God, rebelleth. Just and discreet reprehension doth not more reform some sinners than exasperate others.

How easy is it for God to cool the courage of proud Jeroboam! The hand which his rage stretches out, dries up, and cannot be pulled back again; and now stands the king of Israel, like some antique statue, in a posture of impotent endeavour, so disabled to the hurt of the prophet, that he cannot command that piece of himself. What are the great potentates of the world, in the powerful hand of the Almighty? Tyrants cannot be so harmful, as they are malicious.

The strongest heart may be brought down with affliction. Now the stout stomach of Jeroboam is fallen to an humble deprecation: " Entreat now the face of the Lord thy God, and pray for me, that my hand may be restored me again." It must needs be a great strait that could drive a proud heart to beg mercy, where he bent his persecution; so doth Jeroboam, holding it no scorn to be beholden to an enemy. In extremities, the worst men can be content to sue for favour where they have spent their malice.

It well becomes the prophets of God to be merciful. I do not see this seer to stand upon terms of exprobration, and overly contestations with Jeroboam, to say, Thine intentions to me were cruel: had thine hand prevailed, I should have sued to thee in vain; continue ever a spectacle of the fearful justice of thy Maker, whom thou hast provoked by thine idolatry, whom thou wouldst have smitten in my persecution: but he meekly sues for Jeroboam's release, and, that God might abundantly magnify both his power and mercy, is heard, and answered with success. We do not win favour of heaven, if we have not learned to do good for evil.

When both wind and sun, the blasts of judgment and the beams of favour, met together to work upon Jeroboam, who would not look that he should have cast off his cumberous and misbeseeming cloak of his idolatry, and have said, Lord, thou hast stricken me in justice, thou hast healed me in mercy; I will provoke thee no more. This hand, which thou hast restored, shall be consecrated to thee in pulling down these bold abominations: yet now, behold, he goes on in his old courses, and as if God had neither done him good nor evil, lives and dies idolatrous. No stone is more hard or insensate, than a sinful heart; the changes of judgment and mercy do but obdure it, instead of melting.

CONTEMPLATION III. — THE SEDUCED PROPHET.

JEROBOAM's hand is amended, his soul is not; that continues still dry and inflexible: yet, while he is unthankful to the author of his recovery, he is thankful to the instrument: he kindly invites the prophet whom he had threatened, and will remunerate him whom he endeavoured to punish. The worst men may be sensible of bodily favours. Civil respects may well stand with gracelessness. Many a one would be liberal of their purses, if they might be allowed to be niggardly of their obedience.

As God, so his prophet, cares not for these waste courtesies, where he sees main duties neglected. More piety would have done well with less compliment. The man of God returns a blunt and peremptory denial to so bounteous an offer: " If thou wilt give me half thine house, I will not go in with thee; neither will I eat bread, nor drink water in this place." Kindness is more safely done to an idolater, than taken from him: that which is done to him obligeth him; that which is taken from him obligeth us: this obligation to us may be occasion of his good; our obligation to him may occasion our hurt; the surest way is to keep aloof from the infectiously wicked.

The prophet is not uncivil, to reject the favour of a prince without some reason; he yields no reason of his refusal, but the command of his God. God hath charged him, "Eat no bread, nor drink water, nor turn again by the same way that thou camest." It is not for a prophet to plead human or carnal grounds for the actions of his function: he may not move but upon a divine warrant. Would this seer have looked with the eyes of flesh and blood, he might have found many arguments for his yielding: He is a king that invites me; his reward, by enriching me, may benefit many; and who knows how much my further conversation may prevail to reform him? How can he be but well prepared for good counsel by a miraculous cure! How gainfully should my receipt of a temporal courtesy be exchanged with a spiritual to him! All Israel will follow him either in idolatry or reformation: which way can be devised of doing so great service to God and the church, as by reclaiming him? What can yield so great likelihood of his reclamation, as the opportunity of my further entireness with him? But the prophet dares not argue cases where he had a command; whatever become of Jeroboam and Israel, God must be obeyed; neither profit nor hopes may carry us cross to the word of our Maker. How safe had this seer been, if he had kept him ever upon this sure guard, which he no sooner leaves, than he miscarries!

So deeply doth God detest idolatry, that he forbids his prophet to eat the bread, to drink the water, of a people infected with this sin; yea, to tread in those very steps which their feet have touched. If this inhibition were personal, yet the grounds of it are common. No pestilence should be more shunned than the conversation of the misreligious or openly scandalous. It is no thank to us, if their familiarity do not infect us with their wickedness.

I know not what to think of an old prophet that dwells in Bethel, within the air of Jeroboam's idol, within the noise of his sacrifices; that lives where the man of God dares not eat; that permitted his sons to be present at that idolatrous service. If he were a prophet of God, what did he now in Bethel? why did he wink at the sin of Jeroboam? what needed a seer to come out of Judah for the reproof of that sin which was acted under his nose? why did he lie? why did his family partake with idolaters? If he were not a prophet of God, how had he true visions? how had he true messages from God? why did he second the menacing word of that prophet whom he seduced? why did he desire that his own bones might be honoured with his sepulchre? Doubtless he was a prophet of God, but corrupt, resty, vicious. Prophecy doth not always presuppose sanctification: many a one hath had visions from God, who shall never enjoy the vision of God. A very Balaam, in his ecstasies, hath so clear revelation of the Messiah to come, as scarce ever any of the holiest prophets; yea, his very ass hath both her mouth miraculously opened, and her eyes, to see and notify that angel, which was hid from her master; yea, Satan himself sometimes receives notice from God of his future actions, which else that evil spirit could neither foretell nor foresee. These kinds of graces are both rare and common: rare, in that they are seldom given to any; common, in that they are indifferently given to the evil and to the good. A little holiness is worth much illumination.

Whether out of envy to hear that said by the seer of Judah, which he either knew not or smothered; to hear that done by another, which he could not have effected, and could not choose but admire; or whether out of desire to make trial of the fidelity of so powerful a messenger, the old prophet hastens to overtake, to recall that man of God, who had so defied his Bethel; whom he finds sitting faint and weary under an oak in the way, taking the benefit of that shade which he hated to receive from those contagious groves that he had left behind him. His habit easily bewrayed him to a man of his own trade; neither doth his tongue spare to profess himself. The old prophet of Bethel invites him to return to a repast; and is answered with the same words wherewith Jeroboam's offer was repelled: the man of God varies not a syllable from his message. It concerns us to take good heed of our charge, when we go on God's errand. A denial doth but invite the importunate: what he cannot do by entreaty the old man tries to do by persuasion: "I am a prophet as thou also art, and an angel spake to me by the word of the Lord, saying, Bring him back with thee into thine house, that he may eat bread and drink water." There is no temptation so dangerous, as that which comes shrouded under a vail of holiness, and pretends authority from God himself. Jeroboam threatens, the prophet stands undaunted; Jeroboam fawns and promises, the prophet holds constant: now comes a grey-headed seer, and pleads a counter-message from God: the prophet yields and transgresses. Satan may affright us as a fiend, but he seduces us as an angel of light.

Who would have looked for a liar under hoary hairs, and a holy mantle? who would not have trusted that gravity, when there was no colour of any gain in the untruth? Nothing is so apt to deceive as the fairest semblances, as the sweetest words. We cannot err, if we believe not the speech for the person, but the person for the speech. Well might this man of God think, an aged man, a prophet, an old prophet, will not, sure, belie God unto a prophet; no man will forge a lie, but for an advantage. What can this man gain by this match, but the entertainment of an unprofitable guest? Perhaps, though God would not allow me to feast with Jeroboam, yet pitying my faintness, he may allow me to eat with a prophet. Perhaps now that I have approved my fidelity in refusing the bread of Bethel, God thinks good to send me a gracious release of that strict charge. Why should I think, that God's revelations are not as free to others, as to me? and if this prophet hath received a countermand from an angel of God, how shall I not disobey God, if I do not follow him!

Upon this ground he returns with this deceitful host; and, when the meat was now in his mouth, receives the true message of death, from the same lips that brought him the false message of his invitation: thus saith the Lord, " Forasmuch, as thou hast disobeyed the mouth of the Lord, and hast not kept the commandment of the Lord thy God, but camest back, and hast eaten bread and drunk water in the place forbidden thee, thy carcass shall not come to the sepulchre of thy fathers." O woful prophet! when he looks on his host, he sees his executioner; while he is feeding of his body, he hears of his carcass; at the table he hears of his denied sepulchre; and all this for eating and drinking where he was forbidden by God, though bidden as from God. The violation of the least charge of God is mortal: no pretences can warrant the transgression of a divine command. A word from God is pleaded on both sides: the one was received immediately from God; the other related mediately by man: one the prophet was sure of; the other was questionable. A sure word of God may not be left for an uncertain: an express charge of the Almighty admitteth not of any check: his will is but one, as himself is; and therefore it is out of the danger of contradiction.

Methinks I see the man of God change countenance at this sharp sauce of his pleasing morsels; his face beforehand is dyed with the paleness of death. Methinks I hear him urging many unkind expostulations with his injurious host, who yet dismisses him better provided for the ease of his journey than he found him. Perhaps this officiousness was out of desire to make some amends for this late seducement. It is a poor recompense, when he hath betrayed his life, and wronged the soul, to cast some courtesies upon the body.

This old Bethelite, that had taken pains to come and fetch the man of God into sin, will not now go back with him to accompany his departure. Doubtless he was afraid to be enwrapped in the judgment which he saw hanged over that obnoxious head. Thus the mischievous guides of wickedness leave a man, when they have led him to his bane; as familiar devils forsake their witches, when they have brought them once into fetters.

The man of God returns alone, careful, no doubt, and pensive for his offence, when a lion out of the wood meets, assaults, and kills him. O the just and severe judgments of the Almighty, who hath brought this fierce beast out of his wild ranges into the highway, to be the executioner of his offending servant! Doubtless this prophet was a man of great holiness, of singular fidelity, else he durst not have been God's herald to carry a message of defiance to Jeroboam, king of Israel, in the midst of all his royal magnificence; yet now, for varying from but a circumstance of God's command, though upon the suggestion of a divine warrant, is given for a prey to the lion. Our interest in God is so far from excusing our sin, that it aggravates it: of all others, the sin of a prophet shall not pass unrevenged.

The very wild beasts are led by a providence; their wise and powerful Creator knows how to serve himself of them. The lions guard one prophet, kill another, according to the commission received from their Maker. What sinner can hope to escape unpunished, when every creature of God is ready to be an avenger of evil? The beasts of the field were made to serve us; we to serve our Creator. When we forsake our homage to him that made us, it is no marvel if the beasts forget their duty to us, and deal with us not as masters, but as rebels. When a holy man buys so dearly such a slight frailty, of a credulous mistaking, what shall become of our heinous and presumptuous sins?

I cannot think but this prophet died in the favour of God: though by the teeth of the lion, his life was forfeited for example, his soul was safe; yea, his very carcass was left, though torn, yet fair, after those deadly grasps; as if God had said, I will only take thy breath from thee, as the penalty of thy disobedience: a lion shall do that which an apoplexy or fever might do. I owe thee no further revenge than may be satisfied with thy blood.

Violent events do not always argue the anger of God; even death itself is to his servants a fatherly castigation.

But, O the unsearchable ways of the Almighty! The man of God sins, and dies speedily: the lying prophet that seduced him survives; yea, wicked Jeroboam enjoys his idolatry, and treads upon the grave of his reprover. There is neither favour in the delay of stripes, nor displeasure in the haste; rather whom God loves he chastises, as sharply, so speedily, while the rest prospers to condemnation: even the rod of a loving father may draw blood. How much happier is it for us, that we die now, to live for ever, than that we live a while, to die for ever!

Had this lion set upon the prophet for hunger, why did he not devour, as well as kill him? why did he not rather kill the beast than the man? since we know the nature of the lion such, that he is not wont to assail man, save in the extreme want of other prey. Certainly the same power that employed those fangs restrained them, that the world might see it was not appetite that provoked the beast to this violence, but the overruling command of God. Even so, O Lord! thy powerful hand is over that roaring lion, that goes about continually seeking whom he may devour: thine hand withholds him, that though he may shed the blood of thine elect, yet he cannot hurt their souls; and while he doth those things which thou permittest and orderest, to thy just ends, yet he cannot do lesser things which he desireth, and thou permittest not.

The fierce beast stands by the carcass, as to avow his own act, and to tell who sent him, so to preserve that body which he had slain. O wonderful work of God! the executioner is turned guardian; and, as the officer of the Highest, commands all other creatures to stand aloof from his charge, and commands the fearful ass that brought this burden thither, not to stir thence, but to stand ready prest, to carry it to the sepulchre: and now, when he hath sufficiently witnessed to all passengers that this act was not done upon his own hunger, but upon the quarrel of his Maker, he delivers up his charge to that old prophet, who was no less guilty of this blood than himself.

This old seducer had so much truth, as both to give a right commentary upon God's intention in this act, for the terror of the disobedient, and to give his voice to the certainty of that future judgment which his late guest had threatened to Israel: sometimes it pleaseth the wisdom of God to express and justify himself, even by the tongues of faulty instruments. Withal, he hath so much faith and courage, as to fetch that carcass from the lion; so much pity and compassion, as to weep for the man of God, to inter him in his own sepulchre; so much love, as to wish himself joined in death to that body which he had hastened unto death. It is hard to find a man absolutely wicked: some grace will bewray itself in the most forsaken breasts.

It is a cruel courtesy to kill a man, and then to help him to his grave; to betray a man with our breath, and then to bedew him with our tears. The prophet had needed no such friend, if he had not met with such an enemy: " The mercies of the wicked are cruel."

CONTEMPLATION IV. — JEROBOAM'S WIFE.

IT is no measuring of God's favour by the line of outward welfare: Jeroboam, the idolatrous usurper of Israel, prospers better than the true heirs of David; he lives to see three successions in the throne of Judah: thus the ivy lives, when the oak is dead. Yet could not that misgotten crown of his keep his head always from aching: he hath his crosses too. God whips sometimes more than his own: his enemies smart from him as well as his children; his children in love, his enemies in judgment. Not simply the rod argues love, but the temper of the hand that wields it, and the back that feels it. First, Jeroboam's hand was stricken, now his son; Abijah, the eldest, the best son of Jeroboam, is smitten with sickness. As children are but the pieces of their parents in another skin, so parents are no less stricken in their children, than in their natural limbs; Jeroboam doth not more feel his arm, than his son: not wicked men only, but beasts, may have natural affections. It is no thank to any creature to love his own.

Nature wrought in Jeroboam, not grace: he is enough troubled with his son's disease, no whit bettered. I would have heard him say, God follows me with his afflictions; it is for mine impiety: what other measure can I expect from his justice? while mine idols stand, how can I look that my house should prosper? I will turn from my wickedness; O God, turn thou from thy wrath. These thoughts were too good for that obdurate heart: his son is sick, he is sorrowful; but, as an amazed man seeks to go forth at the wrong door, his distraction sends him to a false help: he thinks not of God, he thinks of his prophet; he thinks of the prophet that had foretold him he should be a king; he thinks not of the God of that prophet who made him a king. It is the property of a carnal heart to confine both his obligations and his hopes to the means, neglecting the Author of good. Vain is the respect that is given to the servant, where the master is contemned.

Extremity draws Jeroboam's thoughts to the prophet, whom else he had not cared to remember. The king of Israel had divines enow of his own, else he must needs have thought them miserable gods that were not worth a prophet: and, besides, there was an old prophet, if he yet survived, dwelling within the smoke of his palace, whose visions had been too well approved: why should Jeroboam send so far, to an Abijah?

Certainly his heart despised those base priests of his high places; neither could he trust either to the gods or the clergy of his own making: his conscience rests upon the fidelity of that man whose doctrine he had forsaken. How did this idolater strive against his own heart, whilst he inwardly despised those whom he professed to honour, and inwardly honoured them whom he professed to despise! Wicked breasts are false to themselves, neither trusting to their own choice, nor making choice of that which they may dare to trust. They will set a good face upon their secretly unpleasing sins, and had rather be self-condemned than wise and penitent. As for that old seer, it is like Jeroboam knew his skill, but doubted of his sincerity: that man was too much his neighbour to be good; Abijah's truth had been tried in a case of his own. He, whose word was found just in the prediction of his kingdom, was well worthy of credit in the news of his son. Experience is a great encouragement of our trust. It is a good matter to be faithful: this loadstone of our fidelity shall draw to us even hearts of iron, and hold them to our reliance; as, contrarily, deceit doth both argue and make a bankrupt. Who can trust where he is disappointed? O God! so oft, so ever have we found thee true in all thy promises, in all thy performances, that, if we do not seek thee, if we do not trust thee in the sequel, we are worthy of our loss, worthy of thy desertions.

Yet I do not see that Jeroboam sends to the prophet for his aid, but for intelligence. Curiosity is guilty of this message, and not devotion; he calls not for the prayers, nor for the benediction of that holy man, but for mere information of the event. He well saw what the prayers of a prophet could do: that which cured his hand, might it not have cured his son? yet he that said to a man of God, "Entreat the face of the Lord thy God, that he may restore my hand," says not now, in his message to Abijah, Entreat thy God to restore my son. Sin makes such a strangeness betwixt God and man, that the guilty heart either thinks not of suing to God, or fears it. What a poor contentment it was to foreknow that evil which he could not avoid, and whose notice could but hasten his misery! Yet thus fond is our restless curiosity, that it seeks ease in the drawing on of torment: he is worthy of sorrow, that will not stay till it comes to him, but goes to fetch it.

Whom doth Jeroboam send on this message but his wife? and how, but disguised? why her, and why thus? Neither durst he trust this errand with another, nor with her in her own form: it was a secret that Jeroboam sends to a prophet of God; none might know it but his own bosom, and she that lay in it: if this had been noised in Israel, the example had been dangerous: who would not have said, The king is glad to leave his counterfeit deities, and seek to the true? why should we adhere to them whom he forsakes? As the message must not be known to the people, so she that bears it must not be known to the prophet: her name, her habit, must be changed; she must put off her robes, and put on a russet coat; she must put off the queen, and put on the peasant; instead of a sceptre, she must take up a basket, and go a masked pilgrimage to Shiloh. O the fondness of vain men, that think to juggle with the Almighty, and to hide their counsels from that all-seeing eye! If this change of habit were necessary at Bethel, yet what needs it at Shiloh? though she would hide her face from her subjects, yet why should she not pull off her muffler, and show herself to the prophet? Certainly, what policy began, guiltiness must continue. Well might she think, there can be no good answer expected of the wife of Jeroboam; my presence will do no less than solicit a reproof: no prophet can speak well to the consort of a founder of idolatry; I may perhaps hear good as another, though, as for myself, I can look for nothing but tidings of evil. Wicked hearts know they deserve ill at God's hands, and therefore they do all they can to avoid the eyes of his displeased justice, and if they cannot do it by colours of dissimulation, they will do it by imploration of shelter; they shall say to the rocks, " Fall on us, and cover us."

But O the gross folly mixt with the craft of wickedness! Could Jeroboam think that the prophet could know the event of his son's disease, and did he think he could not know the disguise of his wife? The one was present, the other future: this was but wrapt in a clout; that event was wrapt in the counsel of God: yet this politic head presumes that the greater shall be revealed, where the lesser shall be hid. There was never a wicked man that was not infatuate, and in nothing more than in those things wherein he hoped most to transcend the reach of others.

Abijah, shunning the iniquity of the times, was retired to a solitary corner of Shiloh. No place could be too private for an honest prophet, in so extreme depravedness; yet even there doth the king of Israel take notice of his seclusion, and sends his wife to that poor cell laden with presents, presents that dissembled their bearer: had she offered jewels, or gold, her greatness had been suspected; now she brings loaves, and cracknels, and honey; her hand answers her back; she gives as she seems, not as she is. Something she must give, even when she acts the poorest client.

The prophets of God were not wont to have empty visitations; they who hated bribes, yet refused not tokens of gratitude. Yea, the God of heaven, who neither needs our goods, nor is capable of our gratifications, yet would have no man to come to come to him giftless. Woe to those sacrilegious hands, that instead of bringing to the prophets, carry from them!

Jeroboam was a bad man, yet, as he had a towardly son, so he had an obedient wife, else she had not wanted excuses to turn off both the journey and the disguise: against the disguise, she had pleaded the unbeseemingness of her person and state; against the journey, the perils of so long and solitary a walk. Perhaps a lion might be in the way, the lion that tore the prophet in pieces; perhaps robbers; or, if not they, perhaps her chastity might be in danger: an unguarded solitariness in the weaker sex might be a provocation to some forced uncleanness. She casts off all these shifting projections of fear; according to the will of her husband, she changes her raiment, she sets upon the journey, and overcomes it. What needed this disguise to an old prophet, whose dim eyes were set with age? all clothes, all faces, were alike to a blind seer. The visions of Abijah were inward, neither was his bodily sight more dusky, than the eyes of his mind were clear and piercing. It was not the common light of men whereby he saw; but divine illumination: things absent, things future, were no less obvious to those spiritual beams, than present things are to us. Ere the quick eyes of that great lady can discern him, he hath espied her; and, so soon as he hears the sound of her feet, she hears from him the sound of her name: " Come in, thou wife of Jeroboam." How God laughs in heaven at the frivolous fetches of crafty politicians, and, when they think themselves most sure, shames them with a detection, with a defeat! What an idleness it is for foolish hypocrites to hope they can dance in a net, unseen of heaven!

Never before was this queen troubled to hear of herself, now she is; her very name strikes her with astonishment, and prepares her for the assured horror of following judgments: " I am sent to thee with heavy tidings; go, tell Jeroboam, thus saith the Lord God of Israel." Could this lady less wonder at the mercy of this style of God, than tremble at the sequel of his justice? Lo, Israel hath forsaken God, yet God still owns Israel. Israel hath gone a-whoring, yet God hath not divorced her. O the infinite goodness of our long-suffering God, whom our foulest sins cannot rob of his compassions!

By how much dearer Israel was to God, so much more odious is Jeroboam that hath marred Israel. Terrible is that vengeance which God thunders against him by his prophet, whose passionate message upbraids him with his promotions, chargeth him with his sins, and, lastly, denounceth his judgments. No mouth was fitter to cast this royalty in the teeth of Jeroboam, than that by which it was foretold, fore-promised: every circumstance of the advancement aggravates the sin: " I exalted thee;" thou couldst not rise to honour alone. " I exalted thee from among the people," not from the peers; thy rank was but common before this rise. " I exalted thee from among the people to be a prince:" subordinate height was not enough for thee; no seat would serve thee but a throne; "yea, to be a prince of my people Israel." No nation was for thee but my chosen one; none but my royal inheritance: neither did I raise thee into a vacant throne: a forlorn and forsaken principality might be thankless, but " I rent the kingdom away from another for thy sake." Yea, from what other but the grandchild of David? Out of his hands did I wrest the sceptre, to give it into thine. O what high favours doth God sometimes cast away upon unworthy subjects! How do his abused bounties double both their sin and judgment!

The sins of this prince were no less eminent than his obligations; therefore his judgments shall be no less eminent than his sins. How bitterly doth God express that, which shall be more bitter in the execution! "Behold, I will bring evil upon the house of Jeroboam, and will cut off from Jeroboam him that pisseth against the wall, and him that is shut up and left in Israel, and will take away the remnant of the house of Jeroboam, as a man taketh away dung, till it be all gone. Him that dieth of Jeroboam in the city shall the dogs eat, and him that dieth in the field shall the fowls of the air eat." O heavy load that this disguised princess must carry to her husband! But because these evils, though grievous, yet might be remote, therefore, for a present hansel of vengeance, she is dismissed with the sad tidings of the death of her son: "When thy feet enter into the city, the child shall die." It is heavy news for a mother, that she must lose her son; but worse yet, that she may not see him. In these cases of our final departures, our presence gives some mitigation to our grief. Might she but have closed the eyes, and have received the last breath of her dying son, the loss been more tolerable. I know not how our personal farewell eases our heart, even while it increases our passion; but now she shall no more see, nor be seen of, her Abijah: she shall no sooner be in the city, than he shall be out of the world. Yet more, to perfect her sorrow, she hears, that in him alone there is found some good; the rest of her issue are graceless: she must lose the good, and hold the graceless: he shall die to afflict her, they shall live to afflict her.

Yet what a mixture is here of severity and favour in one act! favour to the son, severity to the father: severity to the father, that he must lose such a son; favour to the son, that he shall be taken from such a father. Jeroboam is wicked, and therefore he shall not enjoy an Abijah: Abijah hath some good things, therefore he shall be removed from the danger of the depravation of Jeroboam. Sometimes God strikes in favour, but more often forbears out of severity. The best are fittest for heaven, the earth is fittest for the worst; this is the region of sin and misery, that of immortality. It is no argument of disfavour to be taken early from a well-led life, as not of approbation to age in sin.

As the soul of Abijah is favoured in the removal, so is his body with a burial. He shall have alone both tears and tomb; all the rest of his brethren shall have no grave but dogs and fowls, no sorrow but for their life. Though the carcass be insensible of any position, yet honest sepulture is a blessing. It is fit the body should be duly respected on earth, whose soul is glorious in heaven.

CONTEMPLATION V.—OF ASA.

THE two houses of Judah and Israel grow up now together in an ambitious rivalry: this splitted plant branches out so severally, as if it had forgotten that ever it was joined in the root. The throne of David oft changeth the possessors, and more complaineth of their iniquity than their remove. Abijam inherits the sins of his father Rehoboam, no less than his crown; and so spends his three years, as if he had been no whit of kin to his grandfather's virtues. It is no news that grace is not traduced, while vice is; therefore is his reign short, because it was wicked. It was a sad case, when both the kings of Judah and Israel, though enemies, yet conspired in sin. Rehoboam, like his father Solomon, began graciously, but fell to idolatry; as he followed his father, so his son, so his people, followed him. O what a face of a church was here, when Israel worshipped Jeroboam's calves, when Judah built them high places, and images and groves on every high hill, and under every green tree! On both hands God is forsaken, his temple neglected, his worship adulterate; and this not for some short brunt, but during the succession of two kings; for, after the first three years, Rehoboam changed his father's religion, as his shields, from gold to brass; the rest of his seventeen years were led in impiety. His son Abijam trode in the same miry steps, and Judah with them both. If there were any (and doubtless there were some) faithful hearts yet remaining in both kingdoms during these heavy times, what a corrosive it must needs have been to them, to see so deplored and miserable a depravation!

There was no visible church upon earth but here; and this, what a one! O God, how low dost thou sometimes suffer thine own flock to be driven! what woful wanes and eclipses hast thou ordained for this heavenly body! Yet, at last, an Asa shall rise from the loins, from the grave of Abijam; he shall revive David and reform Judah. The gloomy times of corruption shall not last always; the light of truth and peace shall at length break out, and bless the sad hearts of the righteous.

It is a wonder how Asa should be good, of the seed of Abijam, of the soil of Maachah, both wicked, both idolatrous. God would have us see that grace is from heaven; neither needs the help of these earthly conveyances. Should not the children of good parents sometimes be evil, and the children of evil parents good, virtue would seem natural, and the giver would lose his thanks. Thus we have seen a fair flower spring out of dung, and a well-fruited tree rise out of a sour stock: education hath no less power to corrupt, than nature. It is therefore the just praise of Asa, that, being trained up under an idolatrous Maachah, he maintained his piety; as, contrarily, it is a shame for those that have been bred up in the precepts and examples of virtue and godliness, to fall off to lewdness or superstition. There are four principal monuments of Asa's virtue, as so many rich stones in his diadem: he took away sodomy and idols out of Judah. Who cannot wonder more that he found them there, than that he removed them? What a strange incongruity is this! Sodom in Jerusalem! idols in Judah! Surely debauched profession proves desperate: admit the idols; ye cannot doubt of the sodomy. If they have changed the glory of the uncorruptible God into an image made like to corruptible man, and to birds, and four-footed beasts, and creeping things, it is no marvel if God give them up to uncleanness, through the lusts of their own hearts, to dishonour their own bodies between themselves. If they changed the truth of God into a lie, and worshipped and served the creature more than the Creator, who is blessed for ever, no marvel if God give them to vile affections, to change the natural use into that which is against nature, burning in lust one towards another, men with men working that which is unseemly.

Contrarily, admit the sodomy, ye cannot doubt of the idols: unnatural beastliness in manners is punished justly with a sottish dotage in religion; bodily pollution with spiritual. How should the soul care to be chaste, that keeps a stew in the body? Asa begins with the banishment of both, scouring Judah of this double uncleanness. In vain should he have hoped to restore God to his kingdom, while these abominations inhabited it. It is justly the main care of worthy and religious princes to clear their coasts of the foulest sins. O the impartial zeal of Asa! There were idols that challenged a prerogative of favour, the idols that his father had made; all these he defaces: the name of a father cannot protect an idol; the duty to his parent cannot win him to a liking, to a forbearance, of his misdevotion: yea, so much the more doth the heart of Asa rise against these puppets, for that they were the sin, the shame of his father. Did there want, think we, some courtier of his father's retinue, to say, Sir, favour the memory of him that begot you; you cannot demolish these statues, without the dishonour of their erector; hide your dislike at the least; it will be your glory to lay your finger upon this blot of your father's reputation; if you list not to allow his act, yet wink at it. The godly zeal of Asa turns the deaf ear to these monitors, and lets them see, that he doth not more honour a father, than hate an idol: no dearness of person should take off the edge of our detestation of the sin. Nature is worthy of forgetfulness and contempt, in opposition to the God of nature; upon the same ground as he removed the idols of his father Abijam, so for idols he removed his grandmother Maachah: she would not be removed from her obscene idols; she is therefore removed from the station of her honour. That princess had aged, both in her regency and superstition. Under her rod was Asa brought up, and schooled in the rudiments of her idolatry: whom she could not infect, she hoped to overawe; so as if Asa will not follow her gods, yet she presumes that she may retain her own. Doubtless, no means were neglected for her reclamation; none would prevail. Religious Asa gathers up himself, and begins to remember that he is a king, though a son; that she, though a mother, yet is a subject; that her eminence could not but countenance idolatry; that her greatness suppressed religion, which he should in vain hope to reform while her superstition swayed: forgetting, therefore, the challenges of nature, the awe of infancy, the custom of reverence, he strips her of that command which he saw prejudicial to his Maker. All respects of flesh and blood must be trampled on for God. Could that long settled idolatry want abettors? Questionless, some or other would say, This was the religion of your father Abijam, this of your grandfather Rehoboam, this of the latter days of your wise and great-grandfather Solomon, this of your grandmother Maachah, this of your great-grandmother Naamah; why should it not be yours? why should you suspect either the wisdom, or piety, or salvation of so many predecessors? Good Asa had learned to contemn prescription against a direct law; he had the grace to know it was no measuring truth by so modern antiquity: his eyes scorning to look so low, raise up themselves to the uncorrupt times of Solomon, to David, to Samuel, to the Judges; to Joshua, to Moses, to the patriarchs, to Noah, to the religious founders of the first world, to the first father of mankind, to paradise, to heaven. In comparison of these, Maachah's god cannot overlook yesterday,: the ancientest error is but as a novice to truth; and if never any example could be pleaded for purity of religion, it is enough that the precept is express. He knew what God said in Sinai, and wrote in the tables: " Thou shalt not make to thyself any graven image, nor any similitude; thou shalt not bow down to them, nor worship them." If all the world had been an idolater, ever since that word was given, he knew how little that precedent could avail for disobedience. Practice must be corrected by law, and not the law yield to practice: Maachah, therefore, goes down from her seat, her idols from their grove; she to retiredness, they to the fire, and from thence to the water: woful deities, that could both burn and drown!

Neither doth the zeal of Asa more magnify itself in these private weedings out of the corruptions of religion, than in the positive acts of a holy plantation. In the falling down of those idolatrous shrines, the temple of God flourishes; that doth he furnish with those sacred treasures which were dedicated by himself, by his progenitors: like the true son of David, he would not serve God cost free: Rehoboam turned Solomon's gold into brass; Asa turns Rehoboam's brass into gold. Some of these vessels, it seems, Abijam, Asa's father, had dedicated to God; but, after his vow, inquired, yea, withheld them. Asa, like a good son, pays his father's debts, and his own. It is a good sign of a well-meant devotion, when we can abide it chargeable; as, contrarily, in the affairs of God, a niggardly hand argues a cold and hollow heart.

All these were noble and excellent acts: the extirpation of sodomy, the demolition of idols, the removal of Maachah, the bounteous contribution to the temple; but that which gives true life unto all these, is a sound root: " Asa's heart was perfect with the Lord all his days." No less laudable works than these have proceeded from hypocrisy, which, while they have carried away applause from men, have lost their thanks with God. All Asa's gold was but dross to his pure intentions.

But O what great and many infirmities may consist with uprightness! what alloys of imperfection will there be found in the most refined soul! Four no small faults are found in true-hearted Asa: First, the high places stood still, unremoved; what high places? There were some dedicated to the worship of false gods; these Asa took away: there were some misdevoted to the worship of the true God; these he lets stand. There was gross idolatry in the former; there was a weak will-worship in the latter: while he opposes impiety, he winks at mistakings: yet even the variety of altars was forbidden by an express charge from God, who had confined his service to the temple. With one breath doth God report both these: " The high places were not removed, yet, nevertheless, Asa's heart was perfect." God will not see weaknesses where he sees truth, How pleasing a thing is sincerity, that, in favour thereof, the mercy of our just God digests many an error! O God, let our hearts go upright, though our feet slide; the fall cannot, through thy grace, be deadly, however it may shame or pain us.

Besides, to confront his rival of Israel, Baasha, this religious king of Judah fetches in Benhadad, the king of Syria, into God's inheritance, upon too dear a rate, — the breach of his league, the expilation of the temple. All the wealth wherewith Asa had endowed the house of the Lord, was little enough to hire an Edomite to betray his fidelity, and to invade Israel. Leagues may be made with infidels; not at such a price, upon such terms: there can be no warrant for a wilful subornation of perfidiousness. In these cases of outward things, the mercy of God dispenseth with our true necessities, not with the affected. O Asa! where was thy piety, while thou robbedst God, to corrupt an infidel, for the slaughter of Israelites? O princes' where is your piety, while ye hire Turks to the slaughter of Christians, to the spoil of God's church?

Yet, which was worse, Asa doth not only employ the Syrian, but relies on him; relies not on God: a confidence less sinful cost his grandfather David dear; and when Ha nani, God's seer, the herald of heaven, came to denounce war against him for these sins, Asa, instead of penitence, breaks into choler: fury sparkles in those eyes which should have gushed out with water; those lips that should have called for mercy, command revenge. How ill do those two agree, the heart of David, the tongue of Jeroboam! That holy grandfather of his would not have done so: when God's messenger reproved him for sin, he condemned it, and himself for it: I see his tears; I do not hear his threats. It ill becomes a faithful heart to rage where it should sorrow, and, instead of submission, to persecute. Sometimes no difference appears betwixt a son of David and the son of Nebat. Any man may do ill; but to defend it, to outface it, is for rebels; yet even upright Asa imprisons the prophet, and crusheth his gainsayers. It were pity that the best man should be judged by every of his actions, and not by all: the course of our life must either allow or condemn us, not these sudden eruptions.

As the life, so the death-bed of Asa wanted not infirmities: long and prosperous had his reign been; now, after forty years' health and happiness, he, that imprisoned the prophet, is imprisoned in his bed.— There is more pain in those fetters which God put upon Asa, than those which Asa puts upon Hanani; and now behold, he that in his war seeks to Benhadad, not to God, in his sickness seeks not to God, but to physicians. We cannot easily put upon God a greater wrong, than the alienation of our trust. Earthly means are for use, not for confidence: we may, we must employ them, we may not rely on them. Well may God challenge our trust as his peculiar, which, if we cast upon any creature, we deify it. Whence have herbs, and drugs, and physicians, their being and efficacy, but from that divine hand? No marvel, then, if Asa's gout struck to his heart, and his feet carried him to his grave, since his heart was miscarried, for the cure of his feet, to an injurious misconfidence in the means, with neglect of his Maker.

CONTEMPLATION VI.— ELIJAH WITH THE SAREPTAN.

Who should be matched with Moses in the hill of Tabor, but Elijah? Surely, next after Moses, there was never any prophet of the Old Testament more glorious than he; none more glorious, none more obscure: the other prophets are not mentioned without the name of their parent, for the mutual honour both of the father and the son; Elijah, as if he had been a son of the earth, comes forth with the bare mention of the place of his birth. Meanness of descent is no block in God's way to the most honourable vocations; it matters not whose son he be, whom God will grace with his service. In the greatest honours that human nature is capable of, God forgets our parents; as, when we shall be raised up to a glorious life, there shall be no respect had to the loins whence we came; so it is, proportionally, in these spiritual advancements.

These times were fit for an Elijah; an Elijah was fit for them: the eminentest prophet is reserved for the corruptest age. Israel had never such a king as Ahab for impiety; never so miraculous a prophet as Elijah. This Elijah is addressed to this Ahab: the God of spirits knows how to proportion men to the occasions, and to raise up to himself such witnesses as may be most able to convince the world. A mild Moses was for the low estate of afflicted Israel; mild in spirit, but mighty in wonders; mild of spirit, because he had to do with a persecuted, and yet a touchy and perverse people; mighty in wonders, because he had to do with a Pharaoh. A grave and holy Samuel was for the quiet consistence of Israel; a fiery-spirited Elijah was for the desperatest declination of Israel. And if, in the late times of the depraved condition of his church, God have raised up some spirits, that have been more warm and stirring than those of common mould, we cannot censure the choice, when we see the service.

The first word that we hear from Elijah is an oath, and a threat to Ahab, to Israel; "As the Lord God of Israel liveth, before whom I stand, there shall not be dew nor rain, these years, but according to my word." He comes in like a tempest, who went out in a whirlwind: doubtless he had spoken fair and peaceable invitations to Israel, though we hear them not; this was but the storm which followed his repulse, their obstinacy. After many solicitations and warnings, Israel is stricken by the same tongue that had prayed for it; Elijah dares avouch these judgments to their head, to Ahab. I do not so much wonder at the boldness of Elijah, as at his power; yea, whoso sees his power, can no whit wonder at his boldness: how could he but be bold to the face of a man, who was thus powerful with God? As if God had lent him the keys of heaven to shut it up, and open it at pleasure, he can say, "There shall be neither dew nor rain these years, but according to my word." O God, how far it hath pleased thee to communicate thyself to a weak man! what angel could ever say thus? Thy hand, O Lord, is not shortened; why art thou not thus marvellous in the ministers of thy gospel? Is it for that their miracles were ours? is it for that thou wouldst have us live by faith, not by sense? is it for that our task is spiritual, and therefore more abstracted from bodily helps? We cannot command the sun with Joshua, nor the thunder with Samuel, nor the rain with Elijah: it shall content us, if we can fix the Sun of Righteousness in the soul, if we can thunder out the judgments of God against sin, if we can water the earthen hearts of men with the former and latter rain of heavenly doctrine.

Elijah's mantle cannot make him forget his flesh; while he knows himself a prophet, he remembers to be a man; he doth not therefore arrogate his power, as his own, but publisheth it as his master's: this restraint must be according to his word, and that word was from a higher mouth than his. He spake from him by whom he sware, whose word was as sure as his life; and therefore he durst say, "As the Lord liveth, there shall be no rain." Man only can denounce what God will execute, which, when it is once revealed, can no more fail than the Almighty himself.

He that had this interest and power in heaven, what needed he fly from an earthly pursuit? Could his prayers restrain the clouds, and not hold the hands of flesh and blood? yet, behold, Elijah must fly from Ahab, and hide him by the brook Cherith. The wisdom of God doth not think fit so to make a beaten path of miracles, as that he will not walk beside it: he will have our own endeavours concur to our preservation. Elijah wanted neither courage of heart, nor strength of hand, and yet he must trust to his feet for safety. How much more lawful is it, for our impotence, to fly from persecution! Even that God sends him to hide his head, who could as easily have protected as nourished him. He that wilfully stands still to catch dangers, tempteth God, instead of trusting him.

The prophet must be gone, not without order taken for his purveyance: O the strange caterers for Elijah! "I have commanded the ravens to feed thee there." I know not whether it had been more miraculous, to preserve him without meat, or to provide meat by such mouths. The raven, a devouring and ravenous fowl, that uses to snatch away meat from others, brings it to him. He, that could have fed Elijah by angels, will feed him by ravens. There was then in Israel a hospitable Obadiah, that kept a secret table, in two several caves, for a hundred prophets of God. There were seven thousand faithful Israelites, in spite of the devil, who had never bowed knee to Baal: doubtless, any of these would have had a trencher ready for Elijah, and have thought himself happy to have defrauded his own belly for so noble a prophet: God rather chooses to make use of the most unlikely fowls of the air, than their bounty, that he might give both to his prophet, as a pregnant proof of his absolute command over all his creatures, and win our trust in all extremities. Who can make question of the provisions of God, when he sees the very ravens shall forget their own hunger, and purvey for Elijah? O God! thou that providest meat for the fowls of the air, wilt make the fowls of the air provide meat for man, rather than his dependence on thee shall be disappointed: O let not our faith be wanting to thee; thy care can never be wanting to us.

Elijah might have lived for the time with bread and water; neither had his fare been worse than his fellows in the caves of Obadiah; but the munificence of God will have his meals better furnished. The ravens shall bring him both bread and flesh twice in the day. It is not for a persecuted prophet to long after delicates: God gives order for competency, not for wantonness; not out of the dainty compositions in Jezebel's kitchen, not out of the pleasant wines in her cellar, would God provide for Elijah; but the ravens shall bring him plain and homely victuals, and the river shall afford him drink: if we have wherewith to sustain nature, though not to pamper it, we owe thanks to the giver. Those of God's family may not be curious, not disdainful. Ill doth it become a servant of the Highest to be a slave to his palate. Doubtless, one bit from the mouth of the raven was more pleasing to Elijah, than a whole tableful of Ahab's. Nothing is more comfortable to God's children, than to see the sensible demonstrations of the divine care and providence.

The brook Cherith cannot last always; that stream shall not, for Elijah's sake, be exempted from the universal exsiccation: yea, the prophet himself feels the smart of this drought, which he had denounced. It is no unusual thing with God to suffer his own dear children to be inwrapped in the common calamities of offenders. He makes difference in the use and issue of their stripes, not in the infliction The corn is cut down with the weeds, but to a better purpose.

When the brook fails, God hath a Sarepta for Elijah; instead of the ravens, a widow shall there feed him, yea, herself by him. Who can enough wonder at the pitch of this selective providence of the Almighty? Sarepta was a town of Sidon, and therefore without the pale of the church: poverty was the best of this widow; she was a pagan by birth, heathenishly superstitious by institution. Many widows were in Israel in the days of Elijah, when the heaven was shut up three years and six months, when great famine was throughout all the land; but unto none of them was Elijah sent, save unto this Sarepta, a city of Sidon, unto a woman that was a widow. He, that first fed the prophet by the mouth of unclean fowls, will now feed him by the hand of a heathenish hostess; his only command sanctifies those creatures, which, by a general charge, were legally impure.

There were other birds besides ravens, other widows beside this Sareptan; none but the ravens, none but the Sareptan, shall nourish Elijah. God's choice is not led in the string of human reasons; his holy will is the guide and the ground of all his elections: "It is not in him that wills, nor in him that runs, but in God that shows mercy."

The prophet follows the call of his God: the same hand that brought him to the gate of Sarepta, led also this poor widow out of her doors; she shall then go to seek her sticks, when she shall be found of Elijah: she thought of her hearth, she thought not of a prophet, when the man of God calls to her, "Fetch me a little water, I pray thee, in a vessel, that I may drink." It was no easy suit in so droughty a season; and yet at the first sight, the prophet dares second it with a greater, "Bring me a morsel of bread in thine hand." That long drought had made every drop, every crumb, precious; yet the prophet is emboldened by the charge of God to call for both water and bread: he had found the ravens so officious, that he cannot make doubt of the Sareptan. She sticks not at the water; she would not stick at the bread, if necessity had not pressed her: "As the Lord thy God liveth, I have not a cake, but a handful of meal in a barrel. and a little oil in a cruse; and behold I am gathering two sticks, that I may go in and dress it for me and my son, that we may eat and die."

If she knew not the man, how did she know his God? and if she knew not the God of Elijah, how did she swear by him?

Certainly, though she were without the bounds of Israel, yet she was within the borders: so much she had gained by her neighbourhood to know an Israelite, a prophet, by his habit; to know the only living God was the God of the prophet, the God of Israel; and if this had not been, yet it is no marvel if the widow knew Elijah, since the ravens knew him. It was high time for the prophet to visit the Sareptan: poor soul, she was now making her last meal; after one mean morsel she was yielding herself over to death. How opportunely hath God provided succours to our distresses! It is his glory to help at a pinch, to begin where we have given over; that our relief might be so much the more welcome, by how much it is less looked for.

But O what a trial is this of the faith of a weak proselyte, if she were so much! "Fear not, go, do as thou hast said; but make me thereof a little cake first, and bring it to me; and after, make for thee and thy son: for thus saith the God of Israel, the barrel of meal shall not waste, nor the cruse of oil fail, till the day that God send rain upon the earth." She must go spend upon a stranger part of that little she hath, in hope of more which she hath not, which she may have; she must part with her present food which she saw, in trust of future which she could not see; she must rob her sense in the exercise of her belief, and shorten her life in being, upon the hope of a protraction of it in promise; she must believe God will miraculously increase what she hath yielded to consume; she must first feed the stranger with her last victuals, and then, after, herself and her son. Some sharp dame would have taken up the prophet, and have sent him away with an angry repulse: "Bold Israelite, there is no reason in this request; wert thou a friend or a brother, with what face couldst thou require to pull my last bite out of my mouth? Had I superfluity of provision, thou mightest hope for this effect of my charity; now, that I have but one morsel for myself and my son, this is an injurious importunity. What can induce thee to think thy life, an unknown traveller, should be more dear to me than my son's, than my own? How uncivil is this motion, that I should first make provision for thee in this dying extremity! it had been too much to have begged my last scraps. Thou tellest me, the meal shall not waste, nor the oil fail; how shall I believe thee? let me see that done before thou eatest; in vain should I challenge thee, when the remainder of my poor store is consumed.

If thou canst so easily multiply victuals, how is it that thou wantest? Do that beforehand, which thou promisest shall be afterwards performed, there will be no need of my little." But this good Sareptan was wrought on by God not to mistrust a prophet: she will do what he bids, and hope for what he promises; she will live by faith rather than by sense, and give away the present, in the confidence of a future remuneration. First she bakes Elijah's cake, then her own, not grudging to see her last morsels go down another's throat, while herself was famishing. How hard precepts doth God lay, where he intends bounty! Had not God meant her preservation, he had suffered her to eat her last cake alone, without any interpellation; now the mercy of the Almighty, purposing as well this miraculous favour to her as to his prophet, requires of her this task, which flesh and blood would have thought unreasonable. So we are wont to put hard questions to those scholars whom we would promote to higher forms. So in all achievements, the difficulty of the enterprise makes way for the glory of the actor.

Happy was it for this widow, that she did not shut her hand to the man of God, that she was no niggard of her last handful: never corn or oil did so increase in growing, as here in consuming. This barrel, this cruse of hers, had no bottom; the barrel of meal wasted not, the cruse of oil failed not: behold, not getting, not saving, is the way to abundance, but giving. The mercy of God crowns our beneficence with the blessing of store; who can fear want by a merciful liberality, when he sees the Sareptan had famished, if she had not given, and, by giving, abounded? With what thankful devotion must this woman every day needs look upon her barrel and cruse, wherein she saw the mercy of God renewed to her continually? Doubtless her soul was no less fed by faith, than her body with this supernatural provision. How welcome a guest must Elijah needs be to this widow, that gave her life and her son's to her for this board! yea that, in that woful famine, gave her and her son their board for his houseroom.

The dearth thus overcome, the mother looks hopefully upon her only son, promising herself much joy in his life and prosperity, when an unexpected sickness surpriseth him, and doth that which the famine but threatened. When can we hold ourselves secure from evils? no sooner is one of these sergeants compounded withal, than we are arrested by another.

How ready are we to mistake the grounds of our afflictions, and to cast them upon false causes. The passionate mother cannot find whether to impute the death of her son but to the presence of Elijah, to whom she comes distracted with perplexity, not without an unkind challenge of him, from whom she had received both that life she had lost, and that she had: "What have I to do with thee, O thou man of God? art thou come to me to call my sin to remembrance, and to slay my son?" as if her son could not have died, if Elijah had not been her guest; whereas her son had died but for him. Why should she think that the prophet had saved him from the famine, to kill him with sickness? as if God had not been free in his actions, and must needs strike by the same hands by which he preserved. She had the grace to know that her affliction was for her sin; yet was so unwise to imagine the arrearages of her iniquities had not been called for, if Elijah had not been the remembrancer: he, who had appeased God towards her, is suspected to have incensed him: this wrongful misconstruction was enough to move any patience. Elijah was of a hot spirit; yet his holiness kept him from fury: this challenge rather increased the zeal of his prayer, than stirred his choler to the offender. He takes the dead child out of his mother's bosom, and lays him upon his own bed, and cries unto the Lord, "O Lord my God, hast thou brought evil also upon the widow, with whom I sojourn, by slaying her son?" Instead of chiding the Sareptan, out of the fervency of his soul, he humbly expostulates with his God: his only remedy is in his prayer; that which shut heaven for rain, must open it for life. Every word enforceth: first, he pleads his interest in God, "O Lord my God;" then the quality of the patient, "a widow," and therefore both most distressed with the loss, and most peculiar to the charge of the Almighty; then his interest, as in God, so in this patient, "with whom I sojourn;" as if the stroke were given to himself, through her, sides; and lastly, the quality of the punishment, "by slaying her son," the only comfort of her life: and in all these, implying the scandal that must needs arise from this event, wherever it should be noised, to the name of his God, to his own; when it should be said, Lo! how Elijah's entertainment is rewarded: surely the prophet is either impotent, or unthankful.

Neither doth his tongue move thus only: thrice doth he stretch himself upon the dead body, as if he could wish to infuse of his own life into the child, and so often calls to his God for the restitution of his soul. What can Elijah ask to be denied? The Lord heard the voice of the prophet; the soul of the child came into him again, and he revived. What miracle is impossible to faithful prayers? There cannot be more difference betwixt Elijah's devotion and ours, than betwixt supernatural and ordinary acts; if he therefore obtained miraculous favours by his prayers, do we doubt of those which are within the sphere of nature and use? What could we want, if we did not slack to ply heaven with our prayers?

Certainly Elijah had not been premonished of this sudden sickness and death of the child; he, who knew the remote affairs of the world, might not know what God would do within his own roof. The greatest prophet must content himself with so much of God's counsel as he will please to reveal; and he will sometimes reveal the greater secrets, and conceal the less, to make good both his own liberty, and man's humiliation. So much more unexpected as the stroke was, so much more welcome is the cure. How joyfully doth the man of God take the revived child into his arms, and present him to his mother! How doth his heart leap within him, at this proof of God's favour to him, mercy to the widow, power to the child!

What life and joy did now show itself in the face of that amazed mother, when she saw again the eyes of her son fixed upon her's! when she felt his flesh warm, his motions vital! Now she can say to Elijah, "By this I know that thou art a man of God, and that the word of the Lord in thy mouth is truth." Did she not till now know this? had she not said before, "What have I to do with thee, O thou man of God?" Were not her cruse and her barrel sufficient proofs of his divine commission? Doubtless, what her meal and oil had assured her of, the death of her son made her to doubt; and now the reviving did reascertain. Even the strongest faith sometimes staggereth, and needeth new acts of heavenly supportation: the end of miracles is confirmation of truth. It seems, had this widow's son continued dead, her belief had been buried in his grave: notwithstanding her meal and her oil, her soul had languished. The mercy of God is fain to provide new helps for our infirmities, and graciously condescends to our own terms, that he may work out our faith and salvation.

CONTEMPLATION VII.— ELIJAH WITH THE BAALITES.

THREE years and a half did Israel lie gasping under a parching drought and miserable famine. No creature was so odious to them as Elijah, to whom they ascribed all their misery. Methinks I hear how they railed on, and cursed the prophet: how much envy must the servants of God undergo for their master! Nothing but the tongue was Elijah's, the hand was God's; the prophet did but say what God would do. I do not see them fall out with their sins, that had deserved the judgment, but with the messenger, that denounced it. Baal had no fewer servants, than if there had been both rain and plenty. Elijah safely spends this storm under the lee of Sarepta; some three years had he lain close in that obscure corner, and lived upon the barrel and cruse which he had multiplied: at last God calls him forth, "Go, shew thyself to Ahab, and I will send rain upon the earth." No rain must fall till Elijah was seen of Ahab: he carried away the clouds with him; he must bring them again. The king, the people of Israel, shall be witnesses that God will make good the word, the oath of his prophet. Should the rain have fallen in Elijah's absence, who could have known it was by his procurement? God holds the credit of his messengers precious, and neglects nothing that may grace them in the eyes of the world; not the necessity of seven thousand religious Israelites could crack the word of one Elijah. There is nothing wherein God is more tender, than in approving the veracity of himself in his ministers.

Lewd Ahab hath a holy steward; as his name was, so was he a servant of God, while his master was a slave to Baal. He, that reserved seven thousand in the kingdom of Israel, hath reserved an Obadiah in the court of Israel, and by him hath reserved them. Neither is it likely there had been so many free hearts in the country, if religion had not been secretly backed in the court: it is a great happiness when God gives favour and honour to the virtuous. Elijah did not lie more close in Sarepta, than Obadiah did in the court; he could not have done so much service to the church, if he had not been as secret as good. Policy and religion do as well together, as they do ill asunder. The dove, without the serpent, is easily caught; the serpent, without the dove, stings deadly. Religion, without policy, is too simple to be safe; policy, without religion, is too subtile to be good: their match makes themselves secure, and many happy.

O degenerated estate of Israel! any thing was now lawful there, saving piety. It is well if God's prophets can find an hole to hide their heads in; they must needs be hard driven, when fifty of them are fain to crowd together into one cave: there they had both shade and repast. Good Obadiah hazards his own life to preserve theirs, and spends himself in that extreme dearth, upon their necessary diet: bread and water was more now, than other whiles wine and delicates. Whether shall we wonder more at the mercy of God in reserving a hundred prophets, or in thus sustaining them, being reserved? When did God ever leave his Israel unfurnished of some prophets? when did he leave his prophets unprovided of some Obadiah? How worthy art thou, O Lord, to be trusted with thine own charge! While there are men upon earth, or birds in the air, or angels in heaven, thy messengers cannot want provision.

Goodness carries away trust, where it cannot have imitation. Ahab divides with Obadiah the survey of the whole land; they two set their own eyes on work, for the search of water, of pasture, to preserve the horses and mules alive. O the poor and vain cares of Ahab! he casts to kill the prophet, to save the cattle; he never seeks to save his own soul, to destroy idolatry; he takes thought for grass, none for mercy. Carnal hearts are ever either grovelling on the earth, or delving into it; no more regarding God or their souls, than if they either were not, or were worthless.

Elijah hears of the progress, and offers himself to the view of them both. Here was wisdom in this courage: first, he presents himself to Obadiah, ere he will be seen of Ahab, that Ahab might, upon the report of so discreet an informer, digest the expectation of his meeting; then he takes the opportunity of Ahab's presence, when he might be sure Jezebel was away.

Obadiah meets the prophet, knows him, and, as if he had seen God in him, falls on his face to him, whom he knew his master persecuted: though a great peer, he had learned to honour a prophet. No respect was too much for the president of that sacred college. To the poor boarder of the Sareptan, here was no less than a prostration, and "My lord Elijah," from the great high steward of Israel. Those that are truly gracious cannot be niggardly of their observances to the messengers of God.

Elijah receives the reverence, returns a charge: "Go, tell thy lord, Behold, Elijah is here." Obadiah finds this load too heavy; neither is he more stricken with the boldness than with the unkindness of this command; boldness in respect of Elijah, unkindness in respect of himself; for thus he thinks: "If Elijah do come to Ahab, he dies; if he do not come, I die: if it be known that I met him, and brought him not, it is death; if I say that he will come voluntarily, and God shall alter his intentions, it is death. How unhappy a man am I, that must be either Elijah's executioner, or my own! Were Ahab's displeasure but smoking, I might hope to quench it; but now that the flame of it hath broken forth to the notice, to the search, of all the kingdoms and nations round about, it may consume me; I cannot extinguish it. This message was for an enemy of Elijah, for a client of Baal. As for me, I have well approved my true devotion to God, my love to his prophets: what have I done, that I should be singled out either to kill Elijah, or to be killed for him?" Many a hard plunge must that man needs be driven to, who would hold his conscience together with the service and favour of a tyrant. It is a happy thing to serve a just master; there is no danger, no stain, in such obedience.

But when the prophet binds his resolution with an oath, and clears the heart of Obadiah from all fears, from all suspicions, the good man dares be the messenger of that which he saw was decreed in heaven. Doubtless Ahab startled to hear of Elijah coming to meet him, as one that did not more hate, than fear, the prophet. Well might he think, "Thus long, thus far have I sought Elijah; Elijah would not come to seek me, but under a sure guard, and with some strange commission: his coarse mantle hath the advantage of my robe and sceptre; if I can command a piece of the earth, I see he can command heaven." The edge of his revenge is taken off with a doubtful expectation of the issue; and now, when Elijah offers himself to the eyes of Ahab, he, who durst not strike, yet durst challenge the prophet: "Art thou he that troubleth Israel?" Jeroboam's hand was still in Ahab's thoughts; he holds it not so safe to smite, as to expostulate. He, that was the head of Israel, speaks out that which was in the heart of all his people, that Elijah was the cause of all their sorrow. Alas! what hath the righteous prophet done? he taxed their sin, he foretold the judgment, he deserved it not, he inflicted it not: yet he smarts, and they are guilty: as if some fond people should accuse the herald or the trumpet as the cause of their war; or as if some ignorant peasant, when he sees his fowls bathing in his pond, should cry out of them as the causes of foul weather.

O the heroical spirit of Elijah! he stands alone amidst all the train of Ahab, and dares not only repel this charge, but retort it: "I have not troubled Israel, but thou and thy father's house, in that ye have forsaken the commandments of the Lord, and thou hast followed Baalim." No earthly glory can daunt him, who hath the clear and heartening visions of God: this holy seer discerns the true cause of our sufferings to be our sins; foolish men are plagued for their offences; and it is no small part of their plague, that they see it not. The only common disturber of men, families, cities, kingdoms, worlds, is sin: there is no such traitor to any state, as the wilfully wicked; the quietest and most plausible offender is secretly seditious, and stirreth quarrels in heaven.

The true messengers of God carry authority even where they are maligned: Elijah doth at once reprove the king, and require of him the improvement of his power, in gathering all Israel to Carmel, in fetching thither all the prophets of Baal. Baal was rich in Israel, while God was poor; while God hath but one hundred prophets hid closely in Obadiah's caves, Baal hath eight hundred and fifty; four hundred and fifty dispersed over the villages and towns of Israel, four hundred at the court. God's prophets are glad of bread and water, while the four hundred trencher-prophets of Jezebel feed on her dainties: they lurk in caves, while these lord it in the pleasantest groves. Outward prosperity is a false note of truth. All these, with all Israel, doth Elijah require Ahab to summon unto Carmel. It is in the power of kings to command the assembly of the prophets; the prophet sues to the prince for the indiction of this synod. They are injurious to sovereignty, who arrogate this power to none but spiritual hands. How is it that Ahab is as ready to perform this charge, as Elijah to move it? I dare answer for his heart, that it was not drawn with love. Was it out of the sense of one judgment, and fear of another? He smarted with the dearth and drought, and well thinks Elijah would not be so round with him for nothing. Was it out of an expectation of some miraculous exploit which the prophet would do in the sight of all Israel? or, was it out of the overruling power of the Almighty? "The heart of kings is in the hands of God, and he turns it which way soever he pleaseth."

Israel is met together. Elijah rates them, not so much for their superstition, as for their unsettledness and irresolution. One Israelite serves God, another Baal; yea, the same Israelite, perhaps, serves both God and Baal: "How long halt ye between two opinions? If the Lord be God, follow him; but if Baal, then follow him." Nothing is more odious to God, than a profane neutrality in main oppositions of religion: to go upright in a wrong way, is a less eye-sore to God, than to halt betwixt right and wrong. The Spirit wished that the Loadicean were either hot or cold; either temper would be better borne than neither, than both. In reconcileable differences, nothing is more safe than indifferency both of practice and opinion; but in cases of so necessarily hostility, as betwixt God and Baal, he that is on neither side is the deadliest enemy to both: less hateful are they to God that serve him not at all, than they that serve him with a rival.

Whether out of guiltiness, or fear, or uncertainty, Israel is silent; yet, while their mouth was shut, their eyes were open. It was a fair motion of Elijah: "I am only remaining a prophet of the Lord: Baal's prophets are four hundred and fifty: let them choose one bullock, let me choose another; their devotion shall be combined, mine single; the God that consumes the sacrifice by fire from heaven, let him be God." Israel cannot but approve it; the prophets of Baal cannot refuse it: they had the appearance of the advantage, in their number, in the favour of king and people. O strange disputation, wherein the argument, which must be used is fire; the place whence it must be fetched, heaven; the mood and figure, devotion; the conclusion, death to be overcome!

Had not Elijah, by divine instinct, been assured of the event, he durst not have put religion upon such hazard: that God commanded him this trial, who meant confusion to the authors of idolatry, victory to the truth. His terror shall be approved both by fire and by water: first by fire, then by water: there was no less terror in the fire, than mercy in the rain. It was fit they should be first humbled by his terrors, that they might be made capable of his mercy; and, by both, might be won to repentance. Thus, still the fears of the law make way for the influences of grace; neither do those sweet and heavenly dews descend upon the soul, till way be made for them by the terrible flashes of the law.

Justly doth Elijah urge this trial. God's sacrifices were used to none but heavenly fires; whereas the base and earthly religion of the heathen contented itself with gross and natural flames.

The prophets of Baal durst not, though with faint and guilty hearts, but embrace the condition: they dress their bullock, and lay it ready upon the wood, and send out their cries to Baal from morning until midday: " O Baal, hear us!" What a yelling was here of four hundred and fifty throats tearing the skies for an answer! What leaping was here upon the altar, as if they would have climbed up to fetch that fire, which would not come down alone! Mount Carmel might give an echo to their voice, heaven gave none: in vain do they roar out, and weary themselves, in imploring a dumb and deaf deity. Grave and austere Elijah holds it not too light to flout their zealous devotion; he laughs at their tears, and plays upon their earnest: " Cry aloud, for he is a god; either he is talking, or he is pursuing, or he is travelling, or he is sleeping, and must be awaked."

Scorns and taunts are the best answers for serious idolatry: holiness will bear us out in disdainful scoffs and bitterness against wilful superstition. No less in the indignation at these insulting frumps, than zeal of their own safety and reputation, do these idolatrous prophets now rend their throats with acclamations; and that they may assure the beholders they were not in jest, they cut and slash themselves with knives and lancets, and solicit the fire with their blood. How much painfulness is there in misreligion! I do not find that the true God ever required or accepted the self-tortures of his servants; he loves true inward mortification of our corruptions; he loves the subduing of our spiritual insurrections, by due exercises of severe restraint; he takes no pleasure in our blood, in our carcasses: they mistake God, that think to please him by destroying that nature which he hath made, and measure truth by rigour of outward extremities: Elijah drew no blood of himself, the priests of Baal did. How fain would the devil, whom these idolaters adored, have answered the suit of his suppliants! What would that ambitious spirit have given, that, as he was cast down from heaven like lightning, so now he might have fallen down in that form upon his altar!

God forbids it: all the powers of darkness can no more show one flash of fire in the air, than avoid the unquenchable fire in hell. How easy were it for the power of the Almighty to cut short all the tyrannical usurpations of that wicked one, if his wisdom and justice did not find the permission thereof useful to his holy purposes.

These idolaters, now towards evening, grew so much more vehement, as they were more hopeless; and at last, when neither their shrieks, nor their wounds, nor their mad motions, could prevail, they sit down hoarse and weary, tormenting themselves afresh with their despairs, and with the fears of better success of their adversary; when Elijah calls the people to him, the witnesses of his sincere proceedings, and taking the opportunity, both of the time, just the hour of the evening sacrifice, and of the place (a ruined altar of God, now by him repaired), convinces Israel with his miracle, and more cuts these Baalites with envy, than they had cut themselves with their lancets.

O holy prophet, why didst thou not save this labour? What needed these unseasonable reparations? was there not an altar, was there not a sacrifice ready prepared to thine hand? That, which the prophets of Baal had addressed, stood still waiting for that fire from thee, which the founders threatened in vain: the stones were not more impure, either for their touch or for their intentions. Yet such was thy detestation of idolatry, that thou abhorredst to meddle with aught which their wickedness had defiled: even that altar whose ruins thou didst thus repair, was misereected, though to the name of the true God; yet didst thou find it better to make up the breaches of that altar which was misconsecrated to the service of thy God, than to make use of that pile which was idolatrously devoted to a false god. It cannot be but safe to keep aloof from participation with idolaters, even in those things, which, not only in nature, but in use, are unclean.

Elijah lays twelve stones in his repaired altar, according to the number of the tribes of the sons of Jacob. Alas! ten of these were perverted to Baal. The prophet regards not their present apostasy; he regards the ancient covenant that was made with their father Israel; he regards their first station, to which he would reduce them: he knew, that the unworthiness of Israel could not make God forgetful; he would, by this monument, put Israel in mind of their own degeneration and forgetfulness. He employs those many hands for the making a large trench round about the altar, and causes it to be filled with those precious remainders of water which the people would have grudged to their own mouths, neither would easily have parted with, but as those that pour down a pailful into a dry pump, in the hope of fetching more. The altar, the trench is full. A barrelful is poured out for each of the tribes, that every tribe might be afterwards replenished. Ahab and Israel are no less full of expectation; and now, when God's appointed hour of the evening sacrifice was come, Elijah comes confidently to his altar, and, looking up into heaven, says, " Lord God of Abraham, Isaac, and Israel, let it be known this day, that thou art God in Israel, and that I am thy servant, and that I have done all these things at thy word! Hear me, O Lord, hear me, that this people may know that thou art the Lord God, and that thou hast turned their hearts back again !"

The Baalites' prayers were not more tedious than Elijah's was short, and yet more pithy than short, charging God with the care of his covenant, of his truth, of his glory. It was Elijah that spake loud. O strong cries of faith, that pierce the heavens, and irresistibly make their way to the throne of grace! Israel shall well see, that Elijah's God, whom they have forsaken, is neither talking, nor pursuing, nor travelling, nor sleeping. Instantly the fire of the Lord falls from heaven and consumes the burnt sacrifice, the wood, the stones, the dust, and licks up the water that was in the trench. With what terror must Ahab and Israel needs see this fire rolling down out of the sky, and alighting with such fury so near their heads, heads no less fit for this flame, than the sacrifice of Elijah! Well might they have thought, how easily might this fire have dilated itself, and have consumed our bodies, as well as the wood and stone, and have licked up our blood as well as that water! I know not whether they had the grace to acknowledge the mercy of God; they could do no less than confess his power: " The Lord is God, the Lord is God."

The iron was now hot with this heavenly fire; Elijah stays not till it cool again, but strikes immediately : " Take the prophets of Baal; let not one of them escape." This wager was for life: had they prevailed in procuring this fire, and Elijah failed of effect, his head had been forfeited to them: now, in the contrary success, theirs are lost to him. Let no man complain that those holy hands were bloody: this sacrifice was no less pleasing to God than that other. Both the man and the act were extraordinary, and led by a peculiar instinct; neither doth the prophet this without the assent of the supreme magistrate, who was now so affected with this miraculous work, that he could not, in the heat of that conviction, but allow the justice of such a sentence. Far be it from us to accuse God's commands or executions of cruelty. It was the ancient and peremptory charge of God, that the authors of idolatry and seduction should die the death; no eye, no hand, might spare them. The prophet doth but move the performance of that law, which Israel could not without sin have omitted. It is a merciful and thankworthy severity, to rid the world of the ringleaders of wickedness.

CONTEMPLATION VIII. — ELIJAH RUNNING BEFORE AHAB, FLEEING FROM JEZEBEL.

I HEAR no news of the four hundred prophets of the groves: they lie close under the wing of Jezebel, under their pleasing shades; neither will be suffered to undergo the danger of this trial: the carcasses of their fellows help to fill up the half-dry channel of Kishon. Justice is no sooner done, than Ahab hears news of mercy from Elijah: " Get thee up, eat and drink; for there is a sound of abundance of rain." Their meeting was not more harsh than their parting was friendly. It seems Ahab had spent all that day fasting, in an eager attendance of those conflicting prophets. It must needs be late ere the execution could be done: Elijah's part began not till the evening. So far must the king of Israel be from taking thought of the massacre of those four hundred and fifty Baalites, that now " he may go eat his bread with joy, and drink his wine with a cheerful heart;" for God accepteth this work, and testifies it in the noise of much rain. Every drop of that idolatrous blood was answered with a shower of rain, with a stream of water, and plenty poured down in every shower. A sensible blessing follows the impartial strokes of severe justice: nothing is more cruel than an unjust pity.

No ears but Elijah's could as yet perceive a sound of rain; the clouds were not yet gathered, the vapours were not yet risen, yet Elijah hears that which shall be. Those that are of God's counsel can discern either favours or judgments afar off. The slack apprehensions of carnal hearts make them hard to believe that as future, which the quick and refined senses of the faithful perceive as present.

Ahab goes up to his repast; Elijah goes up to his prayers. That day had been painful to him; the vehemency of his spirit draws him to a neglect of his body. The holy man climbs up to the top of Carmel.

that now he may talk with his God alone; neither is he sooner ascended, than he casts himself down upon the earth. He bows his knees to God, and bows his face down to his knees; by this humble posture, acknowledging his awful respects to that Majesty which he implored. We cannot prostrate our bodies or souls too low to that infinitely glorious Deity who is the Creator of both.

His thoughts were more high than his body was low. What he said we know not; we know that what he said opened the heavens, that for three years and a half had been shut up. God had said before, "I will send rain upon the earth; yet Elijah must pray for what God did promise. The promises of the Almighty do not discharge our prayers, but suppose them: he will do what he undertakes; but we must sue for that which we would have him do. Our petitions are included in the decrees, in the engagements of God.

The prophet had newly seen, and caused the fire to descend immediately out of heaven: he doth not look the water should do so; he knew that the rain must come from the clouds, and that the clouds must arise from vapours, and those vapours from the sea, thence doth he expect them: but as not willing that the thoughts of his fixed devotion should be distracted, he doth not go himself, only sends his servant to bring him the news of his success. At the first sight, nothing appears; seven times must he walk to that prospect, and not till his last view can discern aught.

All that while is the prophet in his prayers, neither is any whit undaunted with that delay. Hope holds up the head of our holy desires, and perseverance crowns it. If we receive not an answer to our suits at the sixth motion, we may not be out of countenance, but must try the seventh. At last a little cloud arises out of the sea, of a handbreadth. So many, so fervent prayers cannot but pull water out of heaven as well as fire: those sighs reflect upon the earth, and from the earth reflect upon heaven, from heaven rebound upon the sea, and raise vapours up thence to heaven again. If we find that our prayers are heard for the substance, we may not cavil at the quantity. Even a hand-broad cloud contents Elijah, and fills his heart full of joy and thankfulness. He knew well this meteor was not at the biggest; it was newly born of the womb of the waters, and in some minutes of age must grow to a large stature: stay but awhile, and heaven is covered with it. From how small beginnings have great matters arisen! It is no otherwise in all the gracious proceedings of God with the soul; scarce sensible are those first works of his spirit in the heart, which grow up at last to the wonder of men, and applause of angels.

Well did Elijah know that God, who is perfection itself, would not defile his hand with an imperfect and scanted favour; as one, therefore, that foresaw the face of heaven overspread with this cloudy spot, he sends to Ahab to hasten his chariot, that the rain stop him not. It is long since Ahab feared this let; never was the news of a danger more welcome. Doubtless the king of Israel, while he was at his diet, looked long for Elijah's promised showers. "Where is the rain whose sound the prophet heard? how is it that his ears were so much quicker than our eyes? We saw his fire to our terror; how gladly would we see his waters!" When now the servant of Elijah brings him news from heaven, that the clouds were setting forward, and if he hastened not, would be before him; the wind arises, the clouds gather, the sky thickens; Ahab betakes him to his chariot; Elijah girds up his loins, and runs before him. Surely the prophet could not want the offer of more ease in his passage; but he will be for the time Ahab's lackey, that the king and all Israel may see his humility no less than his power, and may confess that the glory of those miracles hath not made him insolent. He knew that his very sight was monitory; neither could Ahab's mind be beside the miraculous works of God, while his eye was upon Elijah; neither could the king's heart be otherwise than well affected towards the prophet, while he saw that himself and all Israel had received a new life by his procurement. But what news was here for Jezebel! Certainly Ahab minced nothing of the report of all those astonishing accidents: if but to salve up his own honour, in the death of those Baalites, he made the best of Elijah's merits; he told of his challenge, conflict, victory; of the fire that fell down from heaven, of the conviction of Israel, of the unavoidable execution of the prophets, of the prediction and fall of those happy showers, and lastly, of Elijah's officious attendance. Who would not have suspected that Jezebel should have said, It is no striving, no dallying with the Almighty? No reasonable creature can doubt, after so prodigious a decision: God hath won us to heaven; he must possess us. Justly are our seducers perished: none but the God that can command fire and water shall be ours; there is no prophet but his. But she, contrarily, instead of relenting, rageth; and sends a message of death to Elijah: "So let the gods do to me, and more also, if I make not thy life as the life of one of them, by to-morrow about this time." Neither scourges nor favours can work any thing with the obstinately wicked. All evil hearts are not equally disaffected to good: Ahab and Jezebel were both bad enough, yet Ahab yields to that work of God, which Jezebel stubbornly opposeth: Ahab melts with that water, with that fire, wherewith Jezebel is hardened: Ahab was bashfully, Jezebel audaciously impious. The weaker sex is ever commonly stronger in passion, and more vehemently carried with the sway of their desires, whether to good or evil: she swears and stamps at that whereat she should have trembled; she swears by those gods of hers, which were not able to save their prophets, that she will kill the prophet of God, who had scorned her gods, and slain her prophets.

It is well that Jezebel could not keep counsel: her threat preserved him whom she had meant to kill. The wisdom and power of God could have found evasions for his prophet, in her greatest secrecy; but now, he needs no other means of rescue but her own lips. She is no less vain than the gods she swears by. In spite of her fury, and her oath, and her gods, Elijah shall live: at once shall she find herself frustrate and forsworn: she is now ready to bite her tongue, to eat her heart, for anger, at the disappointment of her cruel vow. It were no living for godly men, if the hands of tyrants were allowed to be as bloody as their hearts. Men and devils are under the restraint of the Almighty; neither are their designs more lavish, than their executions short.

Holy Elijah flies for his life: We hear not of the command of God, but we would willingly presuppose it: so divine a prophet should do nothing without God. His heels were no new refuge: as nowhere safe within the ten tribes, he flies to Beersheba, in the territories of Judah; as not there safe from the machinations of Jezebel, he flies alone, one day's journey, into the wilderness; there he sits him down under a juniper tree, and, as weary of life, no less than of his way, wishes to rise no more: "It is enough now, O Lord, take away my life, for I am not better than my fathers." O strange and uncouth mutation! What is this we hear? Elijah fainting and giving up! that heroical spirit dejected and prostrate! He that durst say to Ahab's face, "It is thou and thy father's house that troubleth Israel;" he that could raise the dead, open and shut the heavens, fetch down both fire and water with his prayers; he that durst chide and contest with all Israel; that durst kill the four hundred and fifty Baalites with the sword,—doth he shrink at the frowns and threats of a woman? doth he wish to be rid of his life, because he feared to lose it? Who can expect an undaunted constancy from flesh and blood, when Elijah fails? The strongest and holiest saint upon earth is subject to some qualms of fear and infirmity: to be always and unchangeably good, is proper only to the glorious spirits in heaven. Thus the wise and holy God will have his power perfected in our weakness. It is in vain for us, while we carry this flesh about us, to hope for so exact health, as not to be cast down sometimes with fits of spiritual distemper. It is no new thing for holy men to wish for death: who can either marvel at, or blame the desire of advantage? For the weary traveller to long for rest, the prisoner for liberty, the banished for home, it is so natural, that the contrary disposition were monstrous. The benefit of the change is a just motive to our appetition; but to call for death out of a satiety of life, out of an impatience of suffering, is a weakness unbeseeming a saint. It is not enough, O Elijah! God hath more work yet for thee: thy God hath more honoured thee than thy fathers, and thou shalt live to honour him.

Toil and sorrow have lulled the prophet asleep under this juniper-tree; that wholesome shade was well chosen for his repose. While death was called for, the cozen of death comes unbidden; the angel of God waits on him in that hard lodging. No wilderness is too solitary for the attendance of those blessed spirits. As he is guarded, so is he awaked by that messenger of God, and stirred up from his rest to his repast; while he slept, his breakfast is made ready for him by those spiritual hands: "There was a cake baked on the coals, and a cruse of water at his head." O the never-ceasing care and providence of the Almighty, not to be barred by any place, by any condition! When means are wanting to us, when we are wanting to ourselves, when to God, even then doth he follow us with his mercy, and cast favour upon us, beyond, against expectation! What variety of purveyance doth he make for his servant! One while the ravens, then the Sareptan, now the angel, shall be his caterer; none of them without a miracle: those other provided for him waking, this sleeping. O God! the eye of thy providence is not dimmer, the hand of thy power is not shorter;

only teach thou us to serve thee, to trust thee.

Needs must the prophet eat, and drink, and sleep, with much comfort, while he saw that he had such a guardian, attendance, purveyor; and now the second time is he raised, by that happy touch, to his meal, and his way: " Arise, and eat, because the journey is too great for thee." What needed he to travel farther, since that divine power could as well protect him in the wilderness, as in Horeb? what needed he to eat, since he, that meant to sustain him forty days with one meal, might as well have sustained him without it? God is a most free agent; neither will he be tied to the terms of human regularities: it is enough that he knows and approves the reasons of his own choice and commands. Once in forty days and nights shall Elijah eat, to teach us what God can do with little means; and but once, to teach us what he can do without means. Once shall the prophet eat —" Man lives by bread;" and but once —" Man lives not by bread only, but by every word that proceeds out of the mouth of God." Moses, Elijah, our Saviour, fasted each of them forty days and forty nights: the three great fasters met gloriously in Tabor. I find not where God ever honoured any man for feasting: it is abstinence, not fulness, that makes a man capable of heavenly visions of divine glory.

The journey was not of itself so long: the prophet took those ways, those hours, which his heart gave him. In the very same mount where Moses first saw God, shall Elijah see him: one and the same cave, as is very probable, was the receptacle to both. It could not but be a great confirmation of Elijah, to renew the sight of those sensible monuments of God's favour and protection to his faithful predecessor. Moses came to see God in the bush of Horeb; God came to find Elijah in the cave of Horeb. What dost thou here, Elijah? The place was directed by a providence, not by a command. He is hid sure enough from Jezebel; he cannot be hid from the all-seeing eye of God: " Whither shall I go from thy Spirit? or whither shall I fly from thy presence? If I ascend up into heaven, thou art there; if I make my bed in hell, behold, thou art there. If I take the wings of the morning, and dwell in the utmost parts of the sea, even there shall thine hand find me, and thy right hand shall hold me." Twice had God propounded the same question to Elijah: once in the heart, once in the mouth of the cave. Twice doth the prophet answer in the same words. Had the first answer satisfied, the question had not been re-demanded. Now, that sullen answer, which Elijah gave in the darkness of the cave, is challenged into the light, not without an awful preface. The Lord first passeth by him with the terrible demonstrations of his power: a great and strong wind rent the mountains, and brake the rocks in pieces: that tearing blast was from God — God was not in it; so was he in it, as in his other extraordinary works; not so in it, as by it to impart himself to Elijah: it was the usher, not the carriage of God. After the wind came an earthquake, more fearful than it; that did but move the air, this the earth; that beat upon some prominences of earth, this shook it from the centre. After the earthquake came a fire, more fearful than either. The other affected the ear, the feeling; but this lets in horror into the soul by the eye, the quickest and most apprehensive of the senses. Elijah shall see God's mighty power in the earth, air, fire, before he hear him in the soft voice: all these are but boisterous harbingers of a meek and still word. In that God was! behold, in that gentle and mild breath there was omnipotency; there was but powerfulness in those fierce representations: there is not always the greatest efficacy, where is the greatest noise. God loves to make way for himself by terror; but he conveys himself to us in sweetness. It is happy for us, if, after the gusts and flashes of the law, we have heard the soft voice of evangelical mercy.

In this very mount, with the same horror, God had delivered his law to Moses and Israel. It is no marvel if Elijah wrapt his face in his mantle: his obedience draws him forth to the mouth of the cave; his fear still hides his head. Had there not been much courage in the prophet's faith, he had not stood out these affrightful forerunners of the divine presence, though with his face covered. The very angels do no less, before that all-glorious Majesty, than veil themselves with their wings. Far be it from us, once to think of that infinite and omnipotent Deity, without an humble awfulness!

Fear changes not the tenor of Elijah's answer: he hath not left one word behind him in the cave: " I have been very jealous for the Lord God of Hosts, because the children of Israel have forsaken thy covenant, thrown down thine altars, and slain thy prophets with the sword, and I, even I only, am left, and they seek my life to take it away." I hear not a direct answer from the prophet to the demand of God: then he had said, I run away from the threats of Jezebel, and here I hide my head from her malicious pursuit. His guiltiness would not let him speak out all: he had rather say, " I have been more jealous for the Lord God of Hosts, than I was fearful of Jezebel." We are all willing to make the best of our own case; but what he wants of his own accusation, he spends upon the complaint of Israel. Neither doth he more bemoan himself than exclaim against them, as apostates from God's covenant, violaters of his altars, murderers of his prophets. It must needs be a desperate condition of Israel, that drives Elijah to indict them before the throne of God. That tongue of his was used to plead for them, to sue for their pardon: it could not be but a forcible wickedness that makes it their accuser. Those idolatrous Israelites were well forward to reformation : the fire and rain from heaven, at the prayers of Elijah, had won them to a scorn of Baal: only the violence of Jezebel turned the stream, and now they are re-settled in impiety, and persecute him for an enemy, whom they almost adored for a benefactor, otherwise Elijah had not complained of what they had been. Who would think it? Jezebel can do more than Elijah. No miracle is so prevalent with the vulgar as the sway of authority, whether to good or evil.

Thou art deceived, O Elijah! thou art not left alone; neither is all Israel tainted. God hath children and prophets in Israel, though thou see them not: those clear eyes of the seer discern not the secret store of God; they looked not into Obadiah's caves, they looked not into the closets of the religious Israelites. He that sees the heart, can say, " I have left me seven thousand in Israel;" all the knees which have not bowed to Baal, and every mouth which hath not kissed him. According to the fashion of the wealthy, God pleaseth himself in hidden treasures: it is enough that his own eyes behold his riches Never did he, never will he, leave himself unfurnished with holy clients, in the midst of the foulest depravations of his church. The sight of his faithful ones hath sometimes been lost, never the being. Do your worst, O ye gates of hell! God will have his own. He, that could have more, will have some: that foundation is sure, " God knoweth who are his."

It was a true cordial for Elijah's solitariness, that he had seven thousand invisible abettors: neither is it a small comfort to our weakness, to have companions in good. For the wickedness of Israel God hath another receipt, the oil of royal and prophetical unction: Elijah must anoint Hazael king of Syria, Jehu king of Israel, Elisha for his successor. All these shall revenge the quarrels of God and him; one shall begin, the other shall prosecute, the third shall perfect the vengeance upon Israel.

A prophet shall avenge the wrongs done to a prophet. Elisha is found, not in his study, but in the field; not with a book in his hand, but a plough. His father Shaphat was a rich farmer in Abel-meholah; himself was a good husbandman, trained up, not in the schools of the prophets, but in the thrifty trade of tillage; and, behold, this is the man whom God will pick out of all Israel for a prophet. God seeth not as man seeth; neither doth he choose men because they are fit, but therefore fits them, because he hath chosen them: his call is above all earthly institution.

I hear not of aught that Elijah said; only he casts his cloak upon Elisha in the passage: that mantle, that act, was vocal. Together with this sign, God's instinct teacheth this amazed son of Shaphat, that he was designed to a higher work, to break up the fallow-ground of Israel by his prophetical function. He finds a strange virtue in that robe; and, as if his heart were changed with that habit, forgets his team, and runs after Elijah, and sues for the leave of a farewell to his parents, ere he had any but a dumb command to follow. The secret call of God offers an inward force to the heart, and insensibly draws us beyond the power of our resistance. Grace is no enemy to good nature: well may the respects to our earthly parents stand with our duties to our Father in heaven. I do not see Elisha wring his hands, and deplore his condition, that he shall leave the world and follow a prophet, but for the joy of that change he makes a feast; those oxen, those utensils of husbandry, whereon his former labours had been bestowed, shall now be gladly devoted to the celebration of that happy day, wherein he is honoured with so blessed an employment. If with desire, if with cheerfulness, we do not enter into the works of our heavenly Master, they are not like to prosper in our hands. He is not worthy of this spiritual station, who holds not the service of God his highest, his richest preferment.

BOOK XIX.

CONTEMPLATION I.—AHAB AND BENHADAD.

THERE is nothing more dangerous for any state, than to call in foreign powers, for the suppressing of a home-bred enemy; the remedy hath often, in this case, proved worse than the disease. Asa, king of Judah, implores the aid of Benhadad the Syrian, against Baasha, king of Israel. That stranger hath good colour to set his foot in some outskirt towns of Israel; and now these serve him but for the handsel of more. Such sweetness doth that Edomite find in the soil of Israel, that his ambition will not take up with less than all; he, that entered as a friend, will proceed as a conqueror; and now aims at no less than Samaria itself, the heart, the head, of the ten tribes. There was no cause to hope for better success of so perfidious a league with an infidel; who can look for other than war, when he sees Ahab and Jezebel in the throne, Israel in the groves and temples of Baalim? The ambition of Benhadad was not so much guilty of this war, as the idolatry of that wicked nation. How can they expect peace from earth, who do wilfully fight against heaven? Rather will the God of hosts arm the brute, the senseless creatures, against Israel, than he will suffer their defiance unrevenged. Ahab and Benhadad are well matched; an idolatrous Israelite with a paganish Idumean: well may God plague each with other, who means vengeance to them both. Ahab finds himself hard pressed with the siege, and therefore is glad to enter into treaties of peace. Benhadad knows his own strength, and offers insolent conditions: "Thy silver and thy gold is mine; thy wives also and thy children, even the goodliest are mine." It is a fearful thing to be in the mercy of an enemy: in case of hostility, might will carve for itself. Ahab now, after the division of Judah, was but half a king. Benhadad had two-and-thirty kings to attend him: what equality was in this opposition? Wisely doth Ahab, therefore, as a reed in a tempest, stoop to this violent charge of so potent an enemy: — "My lord, O king, according to thy saying, I am thine, and all that I have." It is not for the overpowered to capitulate. Weakness may not argue, but yield. Tyranny is but drawn on by submission; and where it finds fear and dejection, insulteth. Benhadad, not content with the sovereignty of Ahab's goods, calls for the possession: Ahab had offered the dominion, with reservation of his subordinate interest; he will be a tributary, so he may be an owner. Benhadad imperiously, besides the command, calls for the property, and suffers not the king of Israel to enjoy those things at all, which he would enjoy but under the favour of that predominancy. Overstrained subjection turns desperate. If conditions be imposed worse than death, there needs no long disputation of the remedy. The elders of Israel, whose share was proportional in this danger, hearten Ahab to a denial; which yet comes out so fearfully, as that it appears rather extorted by the peremptory indignation of the people, than proceeding out of any generosity of his spirit; neither doth he say, I will not, but, I may not. The proud Syrian, who would have taken it in foul scorn to be denied, though he had sent for all the heads of Israel, snuffs up the wind like the wild ass in the wilderness, and brags, and threats, and swears: "The gods do so to me, and more also, if the dust of Samaria shall suffice for handfuls for all the people that follow me." Not the men, not the goods only, of Samaria, shall be carried away captive, but the very earth whereon it stands; and this, with how much ease! No soldier shall need to be charged with more than an handful, to make a valley where the mother city of Israel once stood. O vain boaster! in whom I know not whether pride or folly be more eminent. Victory is to be achieved, not to be sworn: future events are no matter of an oath; thy gods, if they had been, might have been called as witnesses of thy intentions, not of that success whereof thou wouldst be the author without them. Thy gods can do nothing to thee, nothing for thee, nothing for themselves! All thine Aramites shall not carry away one corn of sand out of Israel, except it be upon the soles of their feet, in their shameful flight: it is well if they can carry back those skins that they brought thither. "Let not him that girdeth on his harness, boast himself as he that putteth it off." There is no cause to fear that man that trusts in himself. Man may cast the dice of war, but the disposition of them is of the Lord.

Ahab was lewd, but Benhadad was insolent: if, therefore, Ahab shall be scourged with the rod of Benhadad's fear, Benhadad shall be smitten with the sword of Ahab's revenge. Of all things, God will not endure a presumptuous and self-confident vaunter. After Elijah's flight and complaint, yet a prophet is addressed to Ahab: "Thus saith the Lord, hast thou seen all this great multitude? behold, I will deliver it into thine hand this day, and thou shalt know that I am the Lord." Who can wonder enough at this unweariable mercy of God? After the fire and rain fetched miraculously from heaven, Ahab had promised much, performed nothing; yet again will God bless and solicit him with victory: one of those prophets, whom he persecuted to death, shall comfort his dejection with the news of his deliverance and triumph. Had this great work been wrought without premonition, either chance, or Baal, or the golden calves, had carried away the thanks. Beforehand, therefore, shall Ahab know both the author and the means of his victory: God for the author; the two hundred and thirty-two young men of the princes for the means. What are these for the vanguard, and seven thousand Israelites for the main battle, against the troops of three and thirty kings, and as many centuries of Syrians as Israel had single soldiers? An equality of number had taken away the wonder of the event; but now the God of Hosts will be confessed in this issue, not the valour of men. How indifferent is it with thee, O Lord, to save by many or by few, to destroy many or few! A world is no more to thee than a man: how easy is it for thee to enable us to be more than conquerors over principalities and powers! to subdue spiritual wickedness to flesh and blood! Through thee we can do great things; yea, we can do all things through thee that strengthenest us. Let us not want faith: we are sure there can be no want in thy power or mercy.

There was nothing in Benhadad's pavilions but drink, and surfeit, and jollity, as if wine should make way for blood. Security is the certain usher of destruction. We never have so much cause to fear, as when we fear nothing. This handful of Israel dares look out, upon the prophet's assurance, to the vast host of Benhadad. It is enough for that proud pagan to sit still and command amongst his cups. To defile their fingers with the blood of so few, seemed no mastery; that act would be inglorious on the part of the victors: more easily might they bring in three heads of dead enemies, than one alive. Imperiously enough, therefore, doth this boaster, out of his chair of state and ease, command, "Whether they be come out for peace, take them alive; or whether they be come out for war, take them alive:" there needs no more, but, "take them;" this field is won with a word. O the vain and ignorant presumptions of wretched men, that will be reckoning without, against their Maker!

Every Israelite kills his man; the Syrians fly, and cannot run away from death: Benhadad and his kings are more beholden to their horses, than to their gods or themselves, for life and safety, else they had been either taken or slain by those whom they commanded to be taken.

How easy is it for him that made the heart, to fill it with terror and consternation, even where no fear is! Those whom God hath destined to slaughter, he will smite; neither needs he any other enemy or executioner, than what he finds in their own bosom. We are not the masters of our own courage or fears: both are put into us by that overruling power that created us. Stay now, O stay, thou great king of Syria, and take with thee those forgotten handfuls of the dust of Israel; thy gods will do so to thee, and more also, if thy followers return without their vowed burden. Learn now of the despised king of Israel, from henceforth, not to sound the triumph before the battle, not to boast thyself in the girding on of thine harness, as in the putting off.

I hear not of either the public thanksgiving or amendment of Ahab. Neither danger nor victory can change him from himself. Benhadad and he, though enemies, agree in unrepentance; the one is no more moved with mercy, than the other with judgment: neither is God any changeling in his proceedings towards both; his judgment shall still follow the Syrian, his mercy Israel; mercy both in forewarning and re-delivering Ahab; judgment in overthrowing Benhadad. The prophet of God comes again, and both foretels the intended re-encounter of the Syrian, and advises the care and preparation of Israel: "Go, strengthen thyself, and mark, and see what thou dost; for at the return of the year, the king of Syria will come up against thee." God purposeth the deliverance of Israel, yet may not they neglect their fortifications: the merciful intentions of God towards them may not make them careless; the industry and courage of the Israelites fall within the decree of their victory. Security is the bane of good success. It is no contemning of a foiled enemy: the shame of a former disgrace and miscarriage whets his valour, and sharpens it to revenge. No power is so dreadful as that which is recollected from an overthrow.

The hostility against the Israel of God may sleep, but will hardly die. If the Aramites sit still, it is but till they be fully ready for an assault; time will show that their cessation was only for their advantage. Neither is it otherwise with our spiritual adversaries: sometime their onsets are intermitted; they tempt not always, they always hate us; their forbearance is not out of favour, but attendance of opportunity. Happy are we, if, out of a suspicion of their silence, we can as busily prepare for their resistance, as they do for our impugnation.

As it is a shame to be beaten, so yet the shame is less by how much the victor is greater. To mitigate the grief and indignation of Benhadad's foil, his parasites ascribe it to gods, not to men: a human power could no more have vanquished him, than a divine power could by him be resisted: "Their gods are gods of the hills." Ignorant Syrians, that name gods and confine them, varying their deities according to situations: they saw that Samaria, whence they were repelled, stood upon the hill of Shemer; they saw the temple of Jerusalem stood upon Mount Sion; they knew it usual with the Israelites to sacrifice in their high places, and perhaps they had heard of Elijah's altar upon mount Carmel; and now they sottishly measure the effects of the power by the place of the worship, as if he, that was omnipotent on the hill, was impotent in the valley. What doltish conceits doth blind paganism frame to itself of a godhead! As they have many gods, so finite; every region, every hill, every dale, every stream, hath their several gods, and each so knows his own bounds, that he dares not offer to encroach upon the other, or, if he do, buys it with loss. Who would think that so gross blockishness should find harbour in a reasonable soul? A man doth not alter with his station: he that wrestled strongly upon the hill, loseth not his force in the plain; all places find him alike active, alike valorous: yet these barbarous Aramites shame not to imagine that of God, which they would blush to affirm of their own champions. Superstition infatuates the heart out of measure; neither is there any fancy so absurd or monstrous, which credulous infidelity is not ready to entertain with applause.

In how high scorn doth God take it, to be thus basely undervalued by rude heathens! This very misopinion concerning the God of Israel shall cost the Syrians a shameful and perfect destruction. They may call a council of war, and lay their heads together, and change their kings into captains, and the hills into valleys; but they shall find more graves in the plains than in the mountains. This very misprision of God shall make Ahab, though he were more lewd, victorious: an hundred thousand Syrians shall fall in one day by those few hands of Israel; and a dead wall in Aphek, to whose shelter they fled, shall revenge God upon the rest that remained. The stones in the wall shall rather turn executioners, than a blasphemous Aramite shall escape unrevenged! So much doth the jealous God hate to be robbed of his glory, even by ignorant pagans, whose tongues might seem no slander. That proud head of Benhadad, that spoke such big words of the dust of Israel, and swore by his gods that he would kill and conquer, is now glad to hide itself in a blind hole of Aphek; and now, instead of questioning the power of the God of Israel, is glad to hear the mercy of the kings of Israel: "Behold now, we have heard that the kings of the house of Israel are merciful kings; let us, I pray thee, put sackcloth on our loins, and ropes on our heads, and go out to the king of Israel; peradventure he will save thy life."

There can be no more powerful attractive of humble submission, than the intimation and conceit of mercy; we do at once fear and hate the inexorable. This is it, O Lord, that allures us to thy throne of grace, the knowledge of the grace of that throne: with thee is mercy and plenteous redemption; thine hand is open before our mouths, before our hearts. If we did not see thee smile upon suitors, we durst not press to thy footstool. Behold now, we know that the king of heaven, the God of Israel, is a merciful God; let us put sackcloth upon our loins, and strew ashes upon our heads, and go meet the Lord God of Israel, that he may save our souls.

How well doth this habit become insolent and blasphemous Benhadad and his followers! a rope and sackcloth! a rope for a crown, sackcloth for a robe! Neither is there less change in the tongue: "Thy servant Benhadad saith, I pray thee let me live;" even now the king of Israel said to Benhadad, "My Lord, O king, I am thine; tell my lord the king, all that thou didst send for to thy servant, I will do:" now Benhadad sends to the king of Israel— "Thy servant Benhadad saith, I pray thee, let me live." He that was erewhile a lord and king, is now a servant; and he that was a servant to the king of Syria, is now his lord: he that would blow away all Israel in dust, is now glad to beg for his own life at the door of a despised enemy. No courage is so haughty, which the God of hosts cannot easily bring under: what are men or devils in those Almighty hands?

The greater the dejection was, the stronger was the motive of commiseration; that halter pleaded for life, and that plea, but for a life, stirred the bowels for favour. How readily did Ahab see, in Benhadad's sudden misery, the image of the instability of all human things, and relents at the view of so deep and passionate a submission! Had not Benhadad said, "Thy servant," Ahab had never said, "My brother." Seldom ever was there loss in humility. How much less can we fear disparagement in the annihilating of ourselves before that infinite Majesty! The drowning man snatches at every twig: it is no marvel if the messengers of Benhadad catch hastily at that last of grace, and hold it fast, " Thy brother Benhadad." Favours are wont to draw on each other; kindnesses breed on themselves; neither need we any other persuasions to beneficence, than from our own acts. Ahab calls for the king of Syria, sets him in his own chariot, treats with him of an easy yet firm league, gives him both his life and his kingdom. Neither is the crown of Syria sooner lost than recovered; only he, that came a free prince, returns tributary; only his train is clipped too short for his wings; a hundred and twenty-seven thousand Syrians are abated of his guard homeward. Blasphemy hath escaped too well. Ahab hath at once peace with Benhadad, war with God: God proclaims it by his herald, one of the sons of the prophets; not yet in his own form, but disguised, both in fashion and complaint. It was a strange suit of a prophet, " Smite me, I pray thee:" many a prophet was smitten and would not; never any but this wished to be smitten. The rest of his fellows were glad to say, " Save me;" this only says, " Smite me." His honest neighbour, out of love and reverence, forbears to strike: there are too many, thinks he, that smite the prophets, though I refrain; what wrong hast thou done, that I should repay with blows? Hadst thou sued for a favour, I could not have denied thee: now thou suest for thine hurt, the denial is a favour. Thus he thought, but charity cannot excuse disobedience. Had the man of God called for blows upon his own head, the refusal had been just and thankworthy; but now that he says, " In the word of the Lord, smite me," this kindness is deadly: " Because thou hast not obeyed the voice of the Lord, behold, as soon as thou art departed from me, a lion shall slay thee." It is not for us to examine the charges of the Almighty: be they never so harsh or improbable, if they be once known for his, there is no way but obedience or death. Not to smite a prophet, when God commands, is no less sin than to smite a prophet when God forbids. It is the divine precept or prohibition that either makes or aggravates an evil; and if the Israelite be thus revenged that smote not a prophet, what shall become of Ahab that smote not Benhadad! Every man is not thus indulgent: an easy request will gain blows to a prophet from the next hand, yea, and a wound in smiting. I know not whether it were an harder task for the prophet to require a wound, than for a well-meaning Israelite to give it: both must be done. The prophet hath what he would, what he must will, a sight of his own blood; and now disguised herewith, and with ashes upon his face, he waylays the king of Israel, and sadly complains of himself in a real parable, for dismissing a Syrian prisoner delivered to his hands, upon no less charge than his life, and soon receives sentence of death from his own mouth. Well was that wound bestowed, that struck Ahab's soul through the flesh of the prophet: the disguise is removed; the king sees not a soldier but a seer; and now finds that he hath unawares passed sentence upon himself. There needs no other doom than from the lips of the offender: " Thus saith the Lord, Because thou hast let go out of thy hand a man whom I appointed to utter destruction, therefore thy life shall go for his life, and thy people for his people." Had not Ahab known the will of God concerning Benhadad, that had been mercy to an enemy, which was now cruelty to himself, to Israel. His ears had heard of the blasphemies of that wicked tongue. His eyes had seen God go before him, in the example of that revenge. No prince can strike so deep into his state, as in not striking: in private favour there may be public unmercifulness.

CONTEMPLATION II.—AHAB AND NABOTH.

NABOTH had a fair vineyard: it had been better for him to have had none: his vineyard yielded him the bitter grapes of death. Many a one hath been sold to death by his lands and goods: wealth hath been a snare, as to the soul, so to the life. Why do we call those goods, which are many times the bane of the owner? Naboth's vineyard lay near to the court of Jezebel: it had been better for him had it been planted in the wilderness. Doubtless this vicinity made it more commodious to the possessor, but more envious and unsafe. It was now the perpetual object of an evil eye, and stirred those desires which could neither be well denied, nor satisfied: eminency is still joined with peril, obscurity with peace. There can be no worse annoyance to an inheritance, than the greatness of an evil neighbourhood. Naboth's vines stood too near the smoke of Jezebel's chimneys, too much within the prospect of Ahab's window. Now, lately, had the king of Israel been twice victorious over the Syrians; no sooner is he returned home, than he is overcome with evil desires: the foil he gave was not worse than that he took. There is more true glory in the conquest of our lusts, than in all bloody trophies. In vain shall Ahab boast of subduing a foreign enemy, while he is subdued by a domestic enemy within his own breast. Opportunity and convenience are guilty of many a theft: had not this ground lain so fair, Ahab had not been tempted; his eye lets in this evil guest into the soul, which now dares come forth at the mouth: " Give me thy vineyard, that I may have it for a garden of herbs, because it is near to my house, and I will give thee a better vineyard for it; or, if it seem good to thee, I will give thee the worth of it in money." Yet had Ahab so much civility and justice, that he would not wring Naboth's patrimony out of his hands by force, but requires it upon a fair composition, whether of price or of exchange. His government was vicious, not tyrannical; propriety of goods was inviolably maintained by him: no less was Naboth allowed to claim a right in his vineyard, than Ahab in his palace. This we owe to lawful sovereignty to call aught our own; and well worthy is this privilege to be repaid with all humble and loyal respects. The motion of Ahab, had it been to any other than an Israelite, had been as just, equal, reasonable, as the repulse had been rude, churlish, inhumane. It is fit that princes should receive due satisfaction in the just demands, not only of their necessities, but convenience and pleasure: well may they challenge this retribution to the benefit of our common peace and protection. If there be any sweetness in our vineyards, any strength in our fields, we may thank their sceptres: justly may they expect from us the commodity, the delight of their habitation; and if we gladly yield not to their full elbow-room, both of their site and provision, we can be no other than ungrateful. Yet dares not Naboth give any other answer to so plausible a motion, than, " The Lord forbid it me, that I should give thee the inheritance of my fathers." The honest Israelite saw violence in this ingenuity: there are no stronger commands than the requests of the great. It is well that Ahab will not wrest away this patrimony; it is not well that he desired it: the land was not so much stood upon as the law. One earth might be as good as another, and money equivalent to either; the Lord had forbidden to alien their inheritance. Naboth doth not fear loss, but sin: what Naboth might not lawfully do, Ahab might not lawfully require. It pleased God to be very punctual and cautelous, both in the distinction and preservation of the entireness of these Jewish inheritances. Nothing but extreme necessity might warrant a sale of land, and that but for a time; if not sooner, yet, at the jubilee, it must revert to the first owner. It was not without a comfortable signification, that whosoever had once his part in the land of promise, could never lose it. Certainly Ahab could not but know this divine restriction, yet doubts not to say, " Give me thy vineyard." The unconscionable will know no other law, but their profit, their pleasure. A lawless greatness hates all limitations, and abides not to hear men should need any other warrant but will.

Naboth dares not be thus tractable. How gladly would he be quit of his inheritance, if God would acquit him from the sin! not out of wilfulness, but obedience, doth this faithful Israelite hold off from this demand of his sovereign; not daring to please an earthly king, with offending the heavenly. When princes command lawful things, God commands by them; when unlawful, they command against God. Passive obedience we must give; active we may not: we follow them as subordinate, not as opposite, to the Highest.

Who cannot but see and pity the straits of honest Naboth? Ahab requires what God forbids; he must fall out either with his God or his king. Conscience carries him against policy; and he resolved not to sin, that he might be gracious: for a world he may not give his vineyard. Those who are themselves godless, think the holy care of others but idly scrupulous. The king of Israel could not choose but see, that only God's prohibition lay in the way of his designs, not the stomach of a froward subject; yet he goes away into his house heavy and displeased, and casts himself down upon his bed, turns away his face, and refuses his meat: he hath taken a surfeit of Naboth's grapes, which mars his appetite, and threats his life. How ill can great hearts endure to be crossed, though upon the most reasonable and just grounds! Ahab's place called him to the guardianship of God's law; and now his heart is ready to break, that this parcel of that law may not be broken. No marvel if he made not dainty to transgress a local statute of God, who did so shamefully violate the eternal law of both tables.

I know not whether the spleen or the gall of Ahab be more affected; whether more of anger or grief, I cannot say; but sick he is, and keeps his bed, and baulks his meat, as if he should die of no other death, than the salads that he would have nad. O the impotent passion and insatiable desires of covetousness! Ahab is lord and king of all the territories of Israel: Naboth is the owner of one poor vineyard. Ahab cannot enjoy Israel, if Naboth enjoy his vineyard. Besides Samaria, Ahab was the great lord paramount of Damascus and all Syria, the victor of him that was attended with two-and-thirty kings. Naboth was a plain townsman of Jezreel, the good husband of a little vineyard. Whether is the wealthier? I do not hear Naboth wish for any thing of Ahab's: I hear Ahab wishing, not without indignation of a repulse, for somewhat from Naboth. Riches and poverty are no more in the heart, than in the hand: he is wealthy, that is contented; he is poor, that wanteth more. O rich Naboth, that carest not for all the large possessions of Ahab, so thou mayest be the lord of thine own vineyard! O miserable Ahab, that carest not for thine own possessions, while thou mayest not be the lord of Naboth's vineyard!

He that caused the disease sends him a physician. Satan knew of old how to make use of such helpers. Jezebel comes to Ahab's bedside, and casts cold water in his face, and puts into him spirits of her own extracting: " Dost thou now govern the kingdom of Israel? Arise, eat bread, and let thine heart be merry; I will give thee the vineyard of Naboth." Ahab wanted neither wit nor wickedness; yet is he in both a very novice to this Sidonian dame. There needs no other devil than Jezebel, whether to project evil, or to work it. She chides the pusillanimity of her dejected husband, and persuades him his rule cannot be free, unless it be licentious; that there should be no bounds for sovereignty, but will. Already hath she contrived to have by fraud and force, what was denied to entreaty. Nothing needs but the name, but the seal, of Ahab: let her alone with the rest. How present are the wits of the weaker sex for the devising of wickedness! She frames a letter in Ahab's name to the senators of Jezreel, wherein she requires them to proclaim a fast, to suborn two false witnesses against Naboth, to charge him with blasphemy against God and the king, to stone him to death: a ready payment for a rich vineyard. Whose indignation riseth not, to hear Jezebel name a fast? The great contemners of the most important laws of God, yet can be content to make use of some divine, both statutes and customs, for their own advantage. She knew the Israelites had so much remainder of grace, as to hold blasphemy worthy of death; she knew their manner was to expiate those crying sins with public humiliation; she knew that two witnesses at least must cast the offender: all these she urges to her own purpose. There is no mischief so devilish, as that which is cloaked with piety. Simulation of holiness doubleth a villany. This murder had not been half so foul, if it had not been thus masked with a religious observation. Besides devotion, what a fair pretence of legality is here! Blasphemy against God and his anointed may not pass unrevenged. The offender is convented before the sad and severe bench of magistracy. The justice of Israel allows not to condemn an absent, an unheard malefactor: witnesses come forth and agree in the intentation of the crime; the judges rend their garments, and strike their breasts as grieved, not more for the sin than the punishment: their very countenance must say, Naboth should not die if his offence did not force our justice; and now he is no good subject, no true Israelite, that hath not a stone for Naboth.

Jezebel knew well to whom she wrote. Had not those letters fallen upon the times of a woful degeneration of Israel, they had received no less strong denials from the elders, than Ahab had from Naboth: "God forbid, that the senate of Jezreel should forge a perjury, belie truth, condemn innocency, brook corruption." Command just things, we are ready to die in the zeal of our obedience; we dare not imbrue our hands in the blood of an innocent.

But she knew whom she had engaged, whom she had marred, by making conscious. It were strange if they, who can countenance evil with greatness, should want factors for the unjustest designs. Miserable is that people whose rulers, instead of punishing, plot and encourage wickedness; when a distillation of evil falls from the head, upon the lungs of any state, there must needs follow a deadly consumption.

Yet perhaps there wanted not some colour of pretence for this proceeding: they could not but hear, that some words had passed betwixt the king and Naboth; haply it was suggested, that Naboth had secretly overlashed into saucy and contemptuous terms to his sovereign, such as neither might be well borne, nor yet, by reason of their privacy, legally convinced. The bench of Jezreel should but supply a form to the just matter and desert of condemnation: what was it for them to give their hand to this obscure midwifery of justice? It is enough that their king is an accuser and witness of that wrong which only their sentence can formally revenge. All this cannot wash their hands from the guilt of blood: if justice be blind, in respect of partiality, she may not be blind in respect of the grounds of execution. Had Naboth been a blasphemer, or a traitor, yet these men were no better than murderers. What difference is there betwixt the stroke of magistracy, and of man-slaughter, but due conviction?

Wickedness never spake out of a throne, and complained of the defect of instruments. Naboth was, it seems, strictly conscionable, his fellow-citizens loose and lawless; they are glad to have gotten such an opportunity of despatch. No clause of Ahab's letter is not observed: a fast is warned, the city is assembled, Naboth is convented, accused, confronted, sentenced, stoned. His vineyard is escheated to the crown; Ahab takes speedy and quiet possession. How still doth God sit in heaven, and look upon the complots of treachery and villanies, as if they did not concern him! The success so answers their desires, as if both heaven and earth were their friends. It is the plague, which seems the felicity of sinners, to speed well in their lewd enterprises; no reckoning is brought in the midst of the meal; the end pays for all. While Ahab is rejoicing in his new garden-plot, and promising himself contentment in this commodious enlargement, in comes Elijah, sent from God, with an errand of vengeance. Methinks I see how the king's countenance changed, with what aghast eyes and pale cheeks he looked upon that unwelcome prophet. Little pleasure took he in his prospect, while it was clogged with such a guest; yet his tongue begins first, "Hast thou found me, O mine enemy?" Great is the power of conscience. Upon the last meeting, for aught we know, Ahab and Elijah parted friends. The prophet had lackeyed his coach, and took a peaceable leave at this town's end; now Ahab's heart told him (neither needed any other messenger) that God and his prophet were fallen out with him: his continuing idolatry, now seconded with blood, bids him look for nothing but frowns from heaven. A guilty heart can never be at peace. Had not Ahab known how ill he had deserved of God, he had never saluted his prophet by the name of an enemy; he had never been troubled to be found by Elijah, if his own breast had not found him out for an enemy to God. Much good may thy vineyard do thee. O thou king of Israel! many fair flowers, and savoury herbs, may thy new garden yield thee! please thyself with thy Jezebel, in the triumph over the carcass of a scrupulous subject: let me rather die with Naboth, than rejoice with thee; his turn is over, thine is to come. The stones that overwhelmed innocent Naboth, were nothing to those that smite thee: "Hast thou killed, and also taken possession? Thus saith the Lord, In the place where dogs licked the blood of Naboth, shall dogs lick thy blood, even thine." What meanest thou, O Elijah, to charge this murder upon Ahab? he kept his chamber, Jezebel wrote, the elders condemned, the people stoned; yet thou sayest, "Hast thou killed?" Well did Ahab know, that Jezebel could not give this vineyard with dry hands; yet was he content to wink at what she would do: he but sits still while Jezebel works, only his signet is suffered to walk for the sealing of this unknown purchase. Those that are trusted with authority, may offend no less in connivancy or neglect, than others in act, in participation; not only command, consent, countenance, but very permission, feoffs public persons in those sins which they might and will not prevent. God loves to punish by retaliation: Naboth and Ahab shall both bleed; Naboth by the stones of the Jezreelites, Ahab by the shafts of the Aramites; the dogs shall taste of the blood of both. What Ahab hath done in cruelty, he shall suffer in justice: the case and the end make the difference happy on Naboth's side: on Ahab's, woful: Naboth bleeds as a martyr, Ahab as a murderer. Whatever is Ahab's condition, Naboth changes a vineyard on earth, for a kingdom in heaven. Never any wicked man gained by the persecution of an innocent; never any innocent man was a loser by suffering from the wicked.

Neither was this judgment personal, but hereditary: "I will take away thy posterity, and will make thine house like the house of Jeroboam." Him that dieth of Ahab in the city, "the dogs shall eat;" and him that dieth in the field, "shall the fowls of the air eat." Ahab shall not need to take thought for the traducing of this ill-gotten inheritance; God hath taken order for his heirs, whom his sin hath made no less the heirs of his curse, than of his body. Their father's cruelty to Naboth hath made them, together with their mother Jezebel, dog's meat. The revenge of God doth at last make amends for the delay. Whether now is Naboth's vineyard paid for?

The man that had sold himself to work wickedness, yet rues the bargain. I do not hear Ahab, as bad as he was, revile or threaten the prophet, but he rends his clothes, and wears and lies in sackcloth, and fasts, and walks softly. Who that had seen Ahab, would not have deemed him a true penitent? All this was the vizard of sorrow, not the face; or if the face, not the heart; or if the sorrow of the heart, yet not the repentance: a sorrow for the judgment, not a repentance for the sin. The very devils howl to be tormented. Grief is not ever a sign of grace. Ahab rends his clothes, he did not rend his heart; he puts on sackcloth, not amendment; he lies in sackcloth, but he lies in his idolatry; he walks softly, he walks not sincerely. Wordly sorrow causeth death; happy is that grief for which the soul is the holier.

Yet what is this I see? this very shadow of penitence carries away mercy. It is no small mercy to defer an evil; even Ahab's humiliation shall prorogue the judgment: such as the penitence was, such shall be the reward; a temporary reward of a temporary penitence. As Ahab might be thus sorrowful, and never the better, so he may be thus favoured, and never the happier. O God, how graciously art thou ready to reward a sound and holy repenfance, who art thus indulgent to a carnal and servile dejection!

CONTEMPLATION III.—AHAB AND MICAIAH; OR, THE DEATH OF AHAB.

Who would have looked to have heard any more of the wars of the Syrians with Israel, after so great a slaughter, after so firm a league; a league not of peace only, but of brotherhood: the halters, the sackcloth of Benhadad's followers, were worn out, as of use, so of memory, and now they are changed for iron and steel. It is but three years that t' is peace lasts; and now that war begins which shall make an end of Ahab. The king of Israel rues his unjust mercy: according to the word of the prophet, that gift of a life was but an exchange; because Ahab gave Benhadad his life, Benhadad shall take Ahab's: he must forfeit in himself what he hath given to another. There can be no better fruit of too much kindness to infidels. It was one article of the league betwixt Ahab and his brother Benhadad, that there should be a speedy restitution of all the Israelitish cities: the rest are yielded; only Ramoth-Gilead is held back, unthankfully, injuriously. He that begged but his life, receives his kingdom, and now rests not content with his own bounds. Justly doth Ahab challenge his own, justly doth he move a war to recover his own from a perfidious tributary: the lawfulness of actions may not be judged by the events, but by the grounds. The wise and holy Arbiter of the world knows why, many times, the better cause hath the worst success. Many a just business is crossed, for a punishment to the agent.

Yet Israel and Judah were now pierced in friendship. Jehoshaphat, the good king of Judah, had made affinity with Ahab, the idolatrous king of Israel; and, besides a personal visitation, joins his forces with his new kinsman, against an old confederate. Judah had called in Syria against Israel; and now Israel calls in Judah against Syria: Thus rather should it be: it is fit that the more pure church should join with the more corrupt, against a common paganish enemy.

Jehoshaphat hath matched with Ahab; not with a divorce of his devotion. He will fight, not without God: " Inquire, I pray thee, at the word of the Lord to-day." Had he done thus sooner, I fear Athaliah had never called him father: this motion was news in Israel. It was wont to be said, " Inquire of Baal." The good king of Judah will bring religion into fashion in the court of Israel. Ahab had inquired of his counsellor: what needed he be so devout as to inquire of his prophets? Only Jehoshaphat's presence made him thus godly. It is an happy thing to converse with the virtuous; their counsel and example cannot but leave some tincture behind them of a good profession, if not of piety. Those that are truly religious dare not but take God with them in all their affairs; with him they can be as valiant, as timorous without him.

Ahab had clergy enough, such as it was. Four hundred prophets of the groves were reserved from appearing to Elijah's challenge: these are now consulted by Ahab; they live to betray the life of him who saved theirs. These care not so much to inquire about what God would say, as what Ahab would have them say: they saw which way the king's heart was bent; that way they bent their tongues: " Go up, for the Lord shall deliver it into the hands of the king." False prophets care only to please: a plausible falsehood passes with them above a harsh truth. Had they seen Ahab fearful, they had said, " Peace, peace;" now they see him resolute, " War and victory." It is a fearful presage of ruin, when the prophets conspire in assentation.

Their number consent: confidence hath

easily won credit with Ahab; we do all willingly believe what we wish. Jehoshaphat is not so soon satisfied: these prophets were, it is like, obtruded to him (a stranger) for the true prophets of the true God. The judicious king sees cause to suspect them, and now, perceiving at what altars they served, hates to rest in their testimony: " Is there not here a prophet of the Lord besides, that we might inquire of him?" One single prophet, speaking from the oracles of God, is more worth than four hundred Baalites: truth may not ever be measured by the poll. It is not number, but weight, that must carry it in a council of prophets. A solid verity in one mouth is worthy to preponderate light falsehood in a thousand.

Even king Ahab, as bad as he was, kept tale of his prophets, and could give account of one that was missing: " There is yet one man, Micaiah, the son of Imlah, by whom they may inquire of the Lord; but I hate him, for he doth not prophesy good concerning me, but evil. It is very probable, that Micaiah was that disguised prophet, who brought to Ahab the fearful message of displeasure and death, for dismissing Benhadad, for which he was ever since fast in prison, deep in disgrace. O corrupt heart of self-condemned Ahab! If Micaiah spake true to thee, how was it evil? If others said false, how was it good? And if Micaiah spake from the Lord, why dost thou hate him? This hath wont to be the ancient lot of truth, censure and hatred: censure of the message; hatred of the bearer. To carnal ears, the message is evil, if unpleasing; and, if plausible, good: if it be sweet, it cannot be poison; if bitter, it cannot be wholesome. The distemper of the receiver is guilty of this misconceit: in itself, every truth, as it is good, so amiable; every falsehood, loathsome, as evil. A sick palate cries out of the taste of those liquors which are well allowed of the healthful. It is a sign of a good state of the soul, when every verdure can receive his proper judgment.

Wise and good Jehoshaphat dissuades Ahab from so hard an opinion, and sees cause so much more to urge the consultation of Micaiah, by how much he finds him more unpleasing. The king of Israel, to satisfy the importunity of so great and dear an ally, sends an officer for Micaiah: he knew well, belike, where to find him; within those four walls, where unjust cruelty had disposed of that innocent seer. Out of the obscurity of the prison is the poor prophet fetched in the light of so glorious a confession of two kings, who thought this convocation of prophets not unworthy of their greatest representation of state and majesty: there he finds Zedekiah, the leader of that false crew, not speaking only, but acting his prediction. Signs were no less used by the prophets than words: this arch flatterer hath made him horns of iron; the horn is forcible, the iron irresistible: by an irresistible force shall Ahab push the Syrians, as if there were more certainty in this man's hands, than in his tongue. If this son of Chenaanah had not had a forehead of brass for impudency, and a heart of lead for flexibleness to humours and times, he had never devised these horns of iron wherewith his king was gored unto blood. However, it is enough for him that he is believed, that he is seconded. All this great inquest of these prophets gave up their verdict to this foreman; not one of four hundred dissented. Unanimity of opinion in the greatest ecclesiastical assemblies, is not ever an argument of truth; there may be as common, and as firm, agreement in error.

The messenger that came from Micaiah, like a carnal friend, sets him in a way of favour; tells him what the rest had said; how they pleased; how unsafe it would be for him to vary, how beneficial to assent. Those that adore earthly greatness, think every man should doat upon their idols, and hold no terms too high for their ambitious purchases. Faithful Micaiah scorns the motion; he knows the price of the word, and contemns it: " As the Lord liveth, what the Lord saith unto me, that will I speak." Neither fears, nor favours, can tempt the holily resolute; they can trample upon dangers or honours with a careless foot; and, whether they be smiled or frowned on by the great, dare not either alter or conceal their errand.

The question is moved to Micaiah: he at first yields, then he contradicts; yields in words, contradicts in pronunciation: the syllables are for them, the sound against them: ironies deny strongest in affirming. And now, being pressed home, he tells them, that God had showed him those sheep of Israel should, ere long, by this means, want their shepherd. The very resemblance, to a good prince, had been effective: the sheep is a helpless creature, not able either to guard or guide itself; all the safety, all the direction of it, is from the keeper, without whom every cur chases and worries it, every tract seduceth it: such shall Israel soon be, if Ahab be ruled by his prophets. The king of Israel doth not believe, but quarrel; not at himself, who had deserved evil, but at the prophet, who foresignified it; and is more careful that the king of Judah should mark how true he had foretold concerning the prophet, than how the prophet had foretold concerning him.

Bold Micaiah, as no whit discouraged with the unjust checks of greatness, doubles his prediction, and, by a second vision, particularizeth the means of this dangerous error. While the two kings sat majestically on their thrones, he tells them of a more glorious throne than theirs, whereon he saw the King of gods sitting: while they were compassed with some hundreds of prophets, and thousands of subjects and soldiers, he tells them of all the host of heaven attending that other throne: while they were deliberating of a war, he tells them of a God of heaven justly decreeing the judgment of a deadly deception to Ahab. The decree of the Highest is not more plainly revealed, than expressed parabolically. The wise and holy God is represented, after the manner of men, consulting of that ruin which he intended to the wicked king of Israel. That uncreated and infinite Wisdom needs not the advice of any finite and created powers to direct him, needs not the assent or aid of any spirit for his execution, much less of an evil one; yet here an evil spirit is brought in, by way of vision mixt with parable, proffering the service of his lie, accepted, employed, successful. These figures are not void of truth: the action and event are reduced to a decree; the decree is shadowed out by the resemblance of human proceedings. All evil motions and counsels are originally from that malignant spirit: that evil spirit could have no power over men, but by the permission, by the decree, of the Almighty. That Almighty, as he is no author of sin, so he ordains all evil to good: it is good that is just; it is just that one sin should be punished by another: Satan is herein no other than the executioner of that God, who is as far from infusing evil, as from not revenging it. Now Ahab sees the ground of that applauded consent of his rabble of prophets; one evil spirit hath no less deceived them, than they their master: he is one, therefore he agrees with himself; he is evil, therefore both he and they agree in deceit.

O the noble and undaunted spirit of Micaiah! Neither the thrones of the kings, nor the number of the prophets, could abate one word of his true, though displeasing message: the king of Israel shall hear that he is misled by liars, they by a devil. Surely, Jehoshophat cannot but wonder at so unequal a contention, to see one silly prophet affronting four hundred; with whom, lest confidence should carry it, behold Zedekiah, more bold, more zealous: if Micaiah have given him, with his fellows, the lie, he gives Micaiah the fist. Before these two great guardians of peace and justice, swaggering Zedekiah smites Micaiah on the face; and with the blow expostulates: "Which way went the Spirit of the Lord from me, to speak unto thee?" For a prophet to smite a prophet, in the face of two kings, was intolerably insolent; the act was much unbeseeming the person, more the presence: prophets may reprove, they may not strike. It was enough for Ahab to punish with the hand; no weapon was for Zedekiah, but his tongue: neither could this rude presumption have been well taken, if malice had not made magistracy insensible of this usurpation. Ahab was well content to see that hated mouth beaten by any hand. It is no new condition of God's faithful messengers to smart for saying truth. Falsehood doth not more bewray itself in any thing than in blows: truth suffers, while error persecutes. None are more ready to boast of the Spirit of God, than those that have the least; as in vessels, the full are silent.

Innocent Micaiah neither defends nor complains. It would have well beseemed the religious king of Judah to have spoken in the cause of the dumb, to have checked insolent Zedekiah. He is content to give way to this tide of peremptory and general opposition. The helpless prophet stands alone, yet lays about him with his tongue: "Behold, thou shalt see, in that day when thou shalt go into an inner chamber to hide thyself." Now the proud Baalite showed himself too much; ere long, he shall be glad to lurk unseen; his horns of iron cannot bear off his danger. The son of Ahab cannot choose but, in the zeal of revenging his father's deadly seducement, call for that false head of Zedekiah. In vain shall that impostor seek to hide himself from justice; but, in the meanwhile, he goes away with honour, Micaiah with censure: "Take Micaiah, and carry him back to Amon, the governor of the city, and to Joash the king's son, and say, Thus saith the king, put this fellow in prison, and feed him with bread of affliction, and with water of affliction, until I come in peace."

A hard doom of truth! the jail for his lodging, coarse bread and water for his food, shall but reserve Micaiah for a further revenge: the return of Ahab shall be the bane of the prophet. Was not this he that advised Benhadad not to boast in the putting on his armour, as in the ungirding it; and doth he now promise himself peace and victory, before he buckle it on? No warning will dissuade the wilful: so assured doth Ahab make himself of success, that he threatens, ere he go, what he will do when he returns in peace. How justly doth God deride the misreckonings of proud and foolish men! If Ahab had no other sins, his very confidence shall defeat him; yet the prophet cannot be overcome in his resolution; he knows his grounds cannot deceive him, and dares, therefore, cast the credit of his function upon this issue: "If thou return at all in peace, the Lord hath not spoken by me;" and he said, "Hearken, O people, every one of you." Let him never be called a prophet, that dare not trust his God. This was no adventure, therefore, of reputation or life: since he knew whom he believed, the event was no less sure, than if it had been past. He is no God, that is not constant to himself: hath he spoken, and shall he not perform? What hold have we for our souls, but his eternal word? The being of God is not more sure than his promises, than his sentences of judgment. Well may we appeal to the testimony of the world in both: if there be not plagues for the wicked, if there be not rewards for the righteous, God hath not spoken by us.

Not Ahab only, but good Jehoshaphat, is carried with the multitude: their forces are joined against Ramoth. The king of Israel doth not so trust his prophets, that he dares trust himself in his own clothes; thus shall he elude Micaiah's threat: I wist the judgment of God, the Syrian shafts, cannot find him out in this unsuspected disguise. How fondly do vain men imagine to shift off the just revenges of the Almighty!

The king of Syria gives charge to his captains to fight against none but the king of Israel. Thus doth the unthankful infidel repay the mercy of his late victor; ill was the snake saved, that requites the favour of his life with a sting: thus, still the greatest are the fairest mark to envious eyes. By how much more eminent any man is in the Israel of God, so many more and more dangerous enemies must he expect: both earth and hell conspire in their opposition to the worthiest. Those who are advanced above others, have so much more need of the guard, both of their own vigilancy, and others' prayers. Jehoshaphat had like to have paid dear for his love: he is pursued for him, in whose amity he offended; his cries deliver him—his cries, not to his pursuers, but to his God; whose mercy takes not advantage of our infirmity, but rescues us from those evils which we wilfully provoke. It is Ahab against whom, not the Syrians only, but God himself, intends this quarrel; the enemy is taken off from Jehoshaphat. O the just and mighty hand of that divine Providence, which directeth all our actions to his own ends, which takes order where every shaft shall light, and guides the arrow of the strong archer into the joints of Ahab's harness! It was shot at a venture, falls by a destiny; and that falls, where it may carry death to a hidden debtor. In all actions, both voluntary and casual, thy will, O God, shall be done by us, with whatever intentions. Little did the Syrian know whom he had stricken, no more than the arrow wherewith he struck: an invisible hand disposeth of both, to the punishment of Ahab, to the vindication of Micaiah. How worthily, O God, art thou to be adored in thy justice and wisdom! to be feared in thy judgments! Too late doth Ahab now think of the fair warnings of Micaiah, which he unwisely contemned; of the painful flatteries of Zedekiah, which he stubbornly believed: that guilty blood of his runs down out of his wound into the midst of his chariot, and pays Naboth his arrearages. O Ahab, what art thou the better for thine ivory house, while thou hast a black soul? what comfort hast thou now in those flattering prophets, which tickled thine ears, and secured thee of victories? what joy is it to thee now, that thou wast great? Who had not rather be Micaiah in the jail, than Ahab in the chariot? Wicked men have the advantage of the way; godly men of the end. The chariot is washed in the pool of Samaria; the dogs come to claim their due; they lick up the blood of the great king of Israel. The tongues of those brute creatures shall make good the tongue of God's prophet. Micaiah is justified, Naboth is revenged, the Baalites confounded, Ahab judged. "Righteous art thou, O God, in all thy ways, and holy in all thy works!"

CONTEMPLATION IV.—AHAZIAH SICK, AND ELIJAH REVENGED.

AHAZIAH succeeded his father Ahab, both in his throne and in his sin. Who could look for better issue of those loins, of those examples? God follows him with a double judgment—of the revolt of Moab, and of his own sickness. All the reign of

Ahab, had Moab been a quiet tributary, and furnished Israel with rich flocks and fleeces; now their subjection dies with that warlike king, and will not be inherited. This rebellion took advantage, as from the weaker spirits, so from the sickly body of Ahaziah, whose disease was not natural, but casual: walking in his palace of Samaria, some grate in the floor of his chamber breaks under him, and gives way to that fall, whereby he is bruised, and languisheth. The same hand that guided Ahab's shaft, cracks Ahaziah's lattice. How infinite variety of plagues hath the just God for obstinate sinners! whether in the field or in the chamber, he knows to find them out. How fearlessly did Ahaziah walk on his wonted pavement! The Lord hath laid a trap for him, whereinto, while he thinks least, he falls irrecoverably. No place is safe for the man that is at variance with God.

The body of Ahaziah was not more sick, than his soul was graceless: none but chance was his enemy, none but the god of Ekron must be his friend. He looks not up to the omnipotent hand of Divine Justice for the disease, or of mercy for the remedy; an idol is his refuge, whether for cure or intelligence. We hear not till now of Baal-zebub: this new god of flies is, perhaps, of his making, who now is a suitor to his own erection. All these heathen deities were but a devil, with change of appellations; the influence of that evil spirit deluded those miserable clients; else, there was no fly so impotent as that outside of the god of Ekron. Who would think that any Israelite could so far doat upon a stock or a fiend? Time gathered much credit to this idol: insomuch as the Jews afterwards styled Beel-zebub the prince of all the regions of darkness. Ahaziah is the first that brings his oracle in request, and pays him the tribute of his devotion: he sends messengers, and says, "Go, inquire of Baal-zebub, the god of Ekron, whether I shall recover of this disease." The message was either idle or wicked: idle, if he sent it to a stock; if to a devil, both idle and wicked. What can the most intelligent spirits know of future things, but what they see either in their causes, or in the light of participation? What a madness was it in Ahaziah to seek to the postern, while the fore-gate stood open! Could those evil spirits truly foretell events no way pre-existent, yet they might not, without sin, be consulted: the evil of their nature debars all the benefits of their information; if not as intelligencers, much less may they be sought to as gods. Who cannot blush to hear and see that even the very evangelical Israel should yield pilgrims to the shrines of darkness! How many, after this clear light of the gospel, in their losses, in their sicknesses, send to these infernal oracles, and damn themselves wilfully in a vain curiosity! The message of the jealous God intercepts them with a just disdain, as here by Elijah: "Is it not because there is not a God in Israel, that ye go to inquire of Baal-zebub the god of Ekron?" What can be a greater disparagement to the true God than to be neglected, than to stand aside, and see us make love to a hellish rival? Were there no God in Israel, in heaven, what could we do other, what worse? This affront, of whatever kind, Ahaziah cannot escape without a revenge: "Therefore thus saith the Lord, Thou shalt not come down from that bed on which thou art gone up, but shalt surely die." It is a high indignity to the true God, not to be sought to in our necessities; but so to be cashiered from our devotions, as to have a false God thrust in his room, is such a scorn, as it is well if it can escape with one death: let now the famous god of Ekron take off that brand of feared mortality which the living God hath set upon Ahaziah; let Baal-zebub make good some better news to his distressed supplicant: rather the king of Israel is himself, without his repentance, hasting to Baal-zebub. This errand is soon done: the messengers are returned, ere they go. Not a little were they amazed to hear their secret message from another's mouth. neither could choose but think, he that can tell what Ahaziah said, what he thought, can foretell how he shall speed. We have met with a greater God than we went to seek; what need we inquire for another answer? With this conceit, with this report, they return to their sick lord, and astonish him with so short, so sad a relation. No marvel, if the king inquired curiously of the habit and fashion of the man that could know this, that durst say this. They describe him a man, whether of a hairy skin, or of rough, coarse, careless attire; thus drest, thus girded. Ahaziah readily apprehends it to be Elijah, the old friend of his father Ahab, of his mother Jezebel: more than once had he seen him, an unwelcome guest, in the court of Israel. The times had been such, that the prophet could not at once speak true, and please: nothing but reproofs and menaces sounded from the mouth of Elijah. Micaiah and he were still as welcome to the eyes of that guilty prince, as the Syrian arrow was into his flesh. Too well, therefore, had Ahaziah noted that querulous seer, and now is not a little troubled to see himself, in succession, haunted with that bold and ill-boding spirit.

Behold the true son of Jezebel! The anguish of his disease, the expectation of death, cannot take off his persecution of Elijah: it is against his will that his deathbed is not bloody. Had Ahaziah meant any other than a cruel violence to Elijah, he had sent a peaceable messenger to call him to the court; he had not sent a captain, with a band of soldiers, to fetch him: the instruments which he useth, carry revenge in their face. If he had not thought Elijah more than a man, what needed a band of fifty men to apprehend one? and if he did think him such, why would he send to apprehend him by fifty? Surely Ahaziah knew of old, how miraculous a prophet Elijah was; what power that man had over all their base deities, what command of the elements, of the heavens; and yet he sends to attack him. It is a strange thing to see how wilfully godless men strive against the stream of their own hearts, hating that which they know good, fighting against that which they know divine. What a gross disagreement is in the message of this Israelitish captain! "Thou man of God, the king hath said, come down." If he were a man of God, how hath he offended? and if he hath justly offended the anointed of God, how is he a man of God? and if he be a man of God, and have not offended, why should he come down to punishment? Here is a kind confession, with a false heart, with bloody hands. The world is full of these windy courtesies, real cruelties. Deadly malice lurks under fair compliments, and, while it flatters, killeth. The prophet hides not himself from the pursuit of Ahaziah: rather he sits where he may be most conspicuous, on the top of a hill. This band knows well where to find him, and climbs up, in the sight of Elijah, for his arrest. The steepness of the ascent, when they drew near to the highest reach, yielded a convenience both of respiration and parley: thence doth the captain imperiously call down the prophet. Who would not tremble at the dreadful answer of Elijah? "If I be a man of God, then let fire come down from heaven, and consume thee and thy fifty." What shall we say? that a prophet is revengeful? that soldiers suffer while a prophet strikes? that a prince's command is answered with imprecation—words with fire? that an unarmed seer should kill one and fifty at a blow? There are few tracks of Elijah that are ordinary, and fit for common feet: his actions are more for wonder than for precedent. Not in his own defence would the prophet have been the death of so many, if God had not, by a peculiar instinct, made him an instrument of this just vengeance. The divine justice finds it meet to do this for the terror of Israel, that he might teach them what it was to contemn, to persecute a prophet, that they might learn to fear him whom they had forsaken, and confess that heaven was sensible of their insolences and impieties. If not as visibly, yet as certainly, doth God punish the violations of his ordinances; the affronts offered to his messengers, still and ever, not ever with the same speed; sometimes the punishment overtakes the act, sometimes dogs it afar off, and seizeth upon the offender, when his crime is forgotten. Here, no sooner is the word out of Elijah's mouth, than the fire is out of heaven. O the wonderful power of a prophet! There sits Elijah in his coarse mantle, on the top of the hill, and commands the heavens, and they obey him: "Let fire fall down from heaven." He needs no more but say what he would have done: the fire falls down, as before upon the sacrifice in Carmel, so now upon the soldiers of Ahaziah. What is man in the hands of his Maker! One flash of lightning hath consumed these one and fifty: and if all the hosts of Israel, yea of the world, had been in their rooms, there had needed no other force. What madness is it for him whose breath is in his nostrils, to contend with the Almighty! The time was, when two zealous disciples would fain have imitated this fiery revenge of Elijah, and were repelled with a check: the very place puts them in mind of the judgment; not far from Samaria was this done by Elijah, and wished to be done by the disciples. So churlish a rejection of a Saviour seemed no less heinous, than the endeavour of apprehending a prophet: "Lord, wilt thou that we command fire to come down from heaven, and consume them, as Elias did?" The world yielded but one Elias; that, which was zeal in him, might be fury in another: the least variation of circumstance may make an example dangerous; presently, therefore, do they hear, "Ye know not of what spirit ye are." It is the calling that varies the spirit: Elijah was God's minister for the execution of so severe a judgment; they were but the servants of their own impotent anger; there was fire in their breasts which God never kindled. Far was it from the Saviour of men to second their earthly fire with this heavenly. He came indeed to send fire upon earth, but to warm, not to burn; and if to burn, not the persons of men, but their corruptions. How much more safe is it for us to follow the meek prophet of the New Testament, than that fervent prophet of the Old! Let the matter of our prayers be the sweet dews of mercy, not the fires of vengeance.

Would not any man have thought Ahaziah sufficiently warned by so terrible a judgment? Could he choose but say, It is no meddling with a man that can speak lightning and death? What he hath said concerning me is too well approved, by what he hath done to my messengers: God's hand is with him; mine shall not be against him. Yet now behold, the rage of Ahaziah is so much the more kindled by this fire from heaven; and a more resolute captain, with a second band, is sent to fetch Elijah to death. This man is in haste, and commands not only his descent, but his speed: " Come down quickly." The charge implies a threat; Elijah must look for force, if he yield not. There needs no other weapon for defence, for offence, than the same tongue, the same breath. God hath fire enough for all the troops of Ahaziah. Immediately doth a sudden flame break out of heaven, and consume this forward leader, and his bold followers. It is a just presage and desert of ruin, not to be warned. Worthily are they made examples, that will not take them.

What marble or flint is harder than a wicked heart? As if Ahaziah would despitefully spit in the face of Heaven, and wrestle a fall with the Almighty, he will needs yet again set a third captain upon so desperate an employment. How hot a service must this commander needs think himself put upon! who can but pity his straits? There is death before him, death behind him: if he go not, the king's wrath is the messenger of death; if he go, the prophet's tongue is the executioner of death. Many a hard task will follow the service of a prince wedded to his passion, divorced from God. Unwillingly, doubtless, and fearfully, doth this captain climb up the hill to scale that impregnable fort; but now, when he comes near to the assault, the battery that he lays to it is his prayers; his surest fight is upon his knees: " He went up, and came and fell upon his knees before Elijah, and besought him, and said unto him, O man of God, I pray thee, let my life, and the life of these fifty thy servants, be precious in thy sight." He confesses the judgment that befel his predecessors; the monuments of their destruction were in his eye, and the terror of it in his heart: of an enemy, therefore, he is become a supplicant, and sues, not so much for the prophet's yieldance, as for his own life. This was the way to offer violence to the prophet of God, to the God of that prophet, even humble supplications. We must deprecate that evil which we would avoid; if we would force blessings, we must entreat them. There is nothing to be gotten from God by strong hand; anything by suit. The life of the captain is preserved: Elijah is by the angel commanded to go down with him speedily, fearlessly. The prophet casts not with himself, What safety can there be in this journey? I shall put myself into the hands of rude soldiers, and, by them, into the hands of an enraged king: if he did not eagerly thirst after my blood, he had never sought it with so much loss. But so soon as he had a charge from the angel, he walks down resolutely, and, as it were, dares the dangers of so great a hostility. He knew that the same God, who had fought for him upon the hill, would not leave him in the valley: he knew the angel, which bade him go, was guard enough against a world of enemies. Faith knows not how to fear, and can as easily contemn the suggestion of perils, as infidelity can raise them.

The prophet looks boldly upon the court, which doubtless was not a little disaffected to him, and comes confidently into the bedchamber of Ahaziah, and sticks not to speak over the same words to his head, which he had sent him, not long since, by his first messengers. Not one syllable will the prophet abate of his errand. It is not for a herald of heaven to be out of countenance, or to mince aught of the most killing messages of his God.

Whether the unexpected confidence, both of the man and of the speech, amazed the sick king of Israel; or whether the fear of some present judgment (wherewith he might suspect Elijah to come armed, upon any act of violence that should be offered) overawed him; or whether now, at last, upon the sight and hearing of this man of God, the king's heart began to relent, and check itself for that sin for which he was justly reproved, I know not; but sure I am, the prophet goes away untouched: neither the furious purposes of Ahaziah, nor the exasperations of a Jezebel, can hurt that prophet, whom God hath intended to a fiery chariot. The hearts of kings are not their own; subjects are not so much in their hands, as they are in their Maker's. How easily can God tame the fierceness of any creature, and, in the midst of their most heady career, stop them on the sudden, and fetch them upon the knees of their humble submission! It is good trusting God with the events of his own commands, who can, at pleasure, either avert evils, or improve them to good.

According to the word of the prophet, Ahaziah dies: not two whole years doth he sit in the throne of Israel, which he now must yield, in the want of children, to his brother. Wickedness shortens his reign: he had too much of Ahab and Jezebel, to expect the blessing, either of length or prosperity of government. As always in the other, so ofttimes in this world, doth God testify his anger to wicked men. Some live long, that they may aggravate their judgment; others die soon, that they may hasten it.

CONTEMPLATION V. — THE RAPTURE OF ELIJAH.

Long and happily hath Elijah fought the wars of his God; and now, after his noble and glorious victories, God will send him a chariot of triumph: not suddenly would God snatch away his prophet without warning, without expectation; but acquaints him, before-hand, with the determination of his glory. How full of heavenly joy was the soul of Elijah, while he foreknew, and looked for this instant happiness! with what contempt did he cast his eyes upon that earth, which he was now presently to leave! with what ravishment of an inward pleasure did he look upon that heaven which he was to enjoy! For a meet farewell to the earth, Elijah will go visit the schools of the prophets before his departure: these were in his way; of any part of the earth, they were nearest unto heaven. In a holy progress, therefore, he walks his last round, from Gilgal, near Jordan, to Bethel, from Bethel to Jericho, from Jericho to Jordan again. In all these sacred colleges of divines, he meant to leave the legacy of his love, counsel, confirmation, blessing. How happy a thing it is, while we are upon earth, to improve our time and gifts to the best behoof of God's church; and, after the assurance of our own blessedness, to help others to the same heaven! But, O God, who can but wonder at the course of thy wise and powerful administrations! Even in the midst of the degeneration and idolatries of Israel, hast thou reserved to thyself whole societies of holy prophets; and, out of those sinful and revolted tribes, hast raised the two great miracles of prophets, Elijah and Elisha, in an immediate succession. Judah itself, under a religious Jehoshaphat, yielded not so eminent and clearly illuminated spirits. The mercy of our provident God will neither be confined nor excluded; neither confined to the places of public profession, nor excluded from the depraved congregations of his own people: where he hath loved, he cannot easily be estranged; rather, where sin abounds, his grace aboundeth much more, and raiseth so much stronger helps as he sees the dangers greater.

Happy was Elisha in the attendance of so gracious a master, and the more happy that he knows it. Fain would Elijah shake him off at Gilgal; if not there, at Bethel; if not yet there, at Jericho. A private message, on which Elijah must go alone, is pretended from the Lord. Whether shall we say the prophet did this for the trial of the constant affection of his careful and diligent servant; or, that it was concealed from Elijah, that his departure was revealed to Elisha? Perhaps he, that knew of his own reception into heaven, did not know what witnesses would be allowed to that miraculous act; and now his humble modesty affected a silent and unnoted passage: even Elisha knew something that was hid from his master, now upon the threshold of heaven. No mere creature was ever made of the whole counsel of the Highest: some things have been disclosed to babes and novices, that have been closed up to the most wise and judicious. In natural speculations, the greater wit and deeper judgment still carries it; but, in the revelations of God, the favour of his choice sways all, not the power of our apprehension. The master may both command and entreat his servant's stay in vain. Elisha must be pardoned this holy and zealous disobedience: " As the Lord liveth, and as thy soul liveth, I will not leave thee." His master may be withdrawn from him; he will not be withdrawn from his master. He knew that the blessing was at the parting; and if he had diligently attended all his life, and now slacked in the last act, he had lost the reward of his service. The evening praises the day, and the chief grace of the theatre is in the last scene: " Be faithful to the death, and I will give thee a crown of life."

That Elijah should be translated, and what day he should be translated, God would have no secret: the sons of the prophets at Bethel, at Jericho, both know it, and ask Elisha if he knew it not: " Knowest thou that the Lord will take away thy master from thy head this day?" and he answered, " Yea, I know it, hold ye your peace." How familiarly do these prophets interknow one another! how kindly do they communicate their visions! Seldom ever was any knowledge given to keep, but to impart: the grace of this rich jewel is lost in concealment. The removal of an Elijah is so important a business, that it is not fit to be done without noise. Many shall have their share in his loss; he must be missed on the sudden: it was meet, therefore, that the world should know his rapture should be divine and glorious. I do not find where the day of any natural death is notified to so many; by how much more wonder there was in this assumption, by so much more shall it be fore-revealed. It is enough for ordinary occurrents to be known by their event: supernatural things have need of premonition, that men's hearts may both be prepared for their receipt, and confirmed in their certainty. Thrice was Elisha entreated, thrice hath he denied to stay behind his now departing master; on whom both his eyes and his thoughts are so fixed, that he cannot give allowance so much as to the interpellation of a question of his fellow-prophets: together, therefore, are this wonderful pair come to the last stage of their separation, the banks of Jordan. Those, that were not admitted to be attendants of the journey, yet will not be debarred from being spectators of so marvellous an issue. Fifty men of the sons of the prophets went and stood to view afar off. I marvel there were no more: how could any son of the prophets stay within the college walls that day, when he knew what was meant to Elijah? Perhaps, though they knew that to be the prophet's last day, yet they might think his disparition should be sudden and insensible; besides, they found how much he affected secresy in this intended departure: yet the fifty prophets of Jericho will make proof of their eyes, and with much intention essay who shall have the last sight of Elijah. Miracles are not purposed to silence and obscurity: God will not work wonders without witnesses; since he doth them on purpose to win glory to his name, his end were frustrate without their notice. Even so, O Saviour, when thou hadst raised thyself from the dead, thou wouldst be seen of more than five hundred brethren at once; and when thou wouldst raise up thy glorified body from earth into heaven, thou didst not ascend from some close valley, but from the mount of Olives; not in the night, not alone, but in the clear day, in the view of many eyes, which were so fixed upon that point of thine heaven, that they could scarce be removed by the check of angels.

Jordan must be crossed by Elijah in his way to heaven. There must be a meet parallel betwixt the two great prophets, that shall meet Christ upon Tabor, Moses and Elias: both received visions on Horeb; to both God appeared there in fire, and other forms of terror: both were sent to kings; one to Pharaoh, the other to Ahab: both prepared miraculous tables; the one of quails and manna in the desert, the other of meal and oil in Sarepta: both opened heaven; the one for that nourishing dew, the other for those refreshing showers: both revenged idolatries with the sword; the one upon the worshippers of the golden calf, the other upon the four hundred Baalites: both quenched the drought of Israel; the one out of the rock, the other out of the cloud: both divided the waters, the one of the Red Sea, the other of Jordan: both of them are forewarned of their departure; both must be fetched away beyond Jordan: the body of Elijah is translated; the body of Moses is hid: what Moses doth by his rod, Elijah doth by his mantle; with that he smites the waters, and they, as fearing the Divine Power which wrought with the prophet, run away from him, and stand on heaps, leaving their dry channel for the passage of those awful feet: it is not long since he mulcted them with a general exsiccation; now he only bids them stand aside, and give way to his last walk, that he might with dry feet mount up into the celestial chariot.

The waters do not now first obey him: they know that mantle of old, which hath oft given laws to their falling, rising, standing: they are past over, and now, when Elijah finds himself treading on his last earth, he proffers a munificent boon to his faithful servant: " Ask what I shall do for thee, before I am taken from thee." I do not hear him say, Ask of me when I am gone: in my glorified condition, I shall be more able to bestead thee; but, Ask before I go. We have a communion with the saints departed, not a commerce: when they are enabled to do more for us, they are less apt to be solicited by us: it is safe suing where we are sure to be heard. Had not Elijah received a peculiar instinct for this proffer, he had not been thus liberal: it were presumption to be bountiful on another's cost, without leave of the owner. The mercy of our good God allows his favourites not only to receive, but to give; not only to receive for themselves, but to convey blessings to others: what can that man want, that is befriended of the faithful?

Elisha needs not go far to seek for a suit;

it was in his heart, his mouth: "Let a double portion of thy spirit be upon me." Every prophet must be a son to Elijah; but Elisha would be his heir, and craves the happy right of his primogeniture, the double share to his brethren. It was not wealth, nor safety, nor ease, nor honour, that Elisha cares for: the world lies open before him; he may take his choice; the rest he contemneth; nothing will serve him but a large measure of his master's spirit. No carnal thought was guilty of this sacred ambition. Affectation of eminence was too base a conceit to fall into that man of God. He saw that the times needed strong convictions; he saw that he could not otherwise wield the succession to such a master; therefore he sues for a double portion of spirit; the spirit of prophecy to foreknow, the spirit of power to work. We cannot be too covetous, too ambitious, of spiritual gifts, such especially as may enable us to win most advantage to God in our vocations. Our wishes are the true touchstone of our estate: such as we wish to be, we are. Worldly hearts affect earthly things; spiritual, divine. We cannot better know what we are indeed, than by what we would be.

Elijah acknowledges the difficulty, and promises the grant of so great a request, suspended yet upon the condition of Elisha's eye-sight: "If thou see me when I am taken from thee, it shall be so unto thee; but if not, it shall not be." What are the eyes to the furniture of the soul? what power is there in those visive beams to draw down a double portion of Elijah's spirit? God doth not always look at efficacy and merit in the conditions of our actions, but at the freedom of his own appointments. The eye was only to be employed as the servant of the heart, that the desires might be so much more intended with the sight. Vehemence is the way to speed, both in earth and in heaven. If but the eyelids of Elisha fall, if his thoughts slacken, his hopes are dashed. There must be fixedness and vigilance in those that desire double graces.

Elijah was going on and talking, when the chariot of heaven came to fetch him: surely, had not that conference been needful and divine, it had given way to meditation, and Elijah had been taken up rather from his knees, than from his feet. There can be no better posture or state, for the messenger of our dissolution to find us in, than in a diligent prosecution of our calling. The busy attendance of our holy vocation is no less pleasing to God, than an immediate devotion. Happy is the servant whom the master, when he comes, shall find so doing.

O the singular glory of Elijah! What mortal creature ever had this honour, to be visibly fetched by the angels of God to his heaven? Every soul of the elect is attended and carried to blessedness by those invisible messengers; but what flesh and blood was ever graced with such a convoy? There are three bodily inhabitants of heaven: Enoch, Elijah, our Saviour Christ; the first before the law, the second under the law, the third under the Gospel; all three in a several form of translation. Our blessed Saviour raised himself to and above the heavens, by his own immediate power: he ascended as the Son, they as servants: he as God, they as creatures. Elijah ascended by the visible ministry of angels; Enoch insensibly. Wherefore, O God, hast thou done this, but to give us a taste of what shall be? to let us see that heaven was never shut to the faithful? to give us assurance of the future glorification of this mortal and corruptible part?

Even thus, O Saviour, when thou shalt descend from heaven with a shout, with the voice of an archangel, and with the trumpet of God, we that are alive and remain shall be caught up, together with the raised bodies of thy saints, into the clouds, to meet thee in the air, to dwell with thee in glory.

Many forms have those celestial spirits taken to themselves, in their apparitions to men: but, of all other, most often hath the Almighty made his messengers "a flame of fire;" never more properly than here. How had the Spirit of God kindled the hot fires of zeal in the breast of Elijah! How had this prophet thrice commanded fire from heaven to earth! How fitly now at last do these seraphical fires carry him from earth to heaven!

What do we see in this rapture of Elijah, but violence and terror, whirlwind and fire? two of those fearful representations which the prophet had in the rock of Horeb. Never any man entered into glory with ease; even the most favourable change hath some equivalency to a natural dissolution. Although, doubtless, to Elijah this fire had a lightsomeness and resplendence, not terror; this whirlwind had speed, not violence. — Thus hast thou, O Saviour, bidden us, when the elements shall be dissolved, and the heavens shall be flaming about our ears, to lift up our heads with joy, because our redemption draweth nigh. Come death! come fire! come whirlwind! they are worthy to be welcome, that shall carry us to immortality!

This arreption was sudden; yet Elisha sees both the chariot, and the horses, and the ascent; and cries to his now changed master, between heaven and earth, " My father, my father, the chariot of Israel, and the horsemen thereof." Shaphat of Abelmeholah hath yielded this title to Elijah, the natural father of Elisha, to the spiritual: neither of them may be neglected; but, after the yoke of oxen killed at the farewell, we hear of no more greetings, no more bewailings of his bodily parent; and now, that Elijah is taken from him, he cries out, like a distressed orphan, " My father! my father!" and, when he hath lost the sight of him, he rends his clothes in pieces, according to the fashion of the most passionate mourners: that Elisha sees his master half way in heaven, cannot take away the sorrow of his loss. The departure of a faithful prophet of God is worthy of our lamentation: neither is it private affection that must sway our grief, but respects to the public. Elisha says not only, " My father," but, " the chariot and horsemen of Israel." That we have foregone a father, should not so much trouble us, as that Israel hath lost his guard. Certainly the view of this heavenly chariot and horses, that came for Elijah, puts Elisha in mind of that chariot and horsemen which Elijah was to Israel. These were God's chariots, Elijah was theirs: God's chariot and theirs are, upon the same wheels, mounted into heaven. No forces are so strong as the spiritual; the prayers of an Elijah are more powerful than all the armies of flesh. The first thing that this seer discerns, after the separation of his master, is the nakedness of Israel in his loss. If we muster soldiers, and lose zealous prophets, it is but a woful exchange.

Elijah's mantle falls from him in the rising: there was no use of that whither he was going; there was, whence he was taken. Elisha justly takes up this dear monument of his glorified master: a good supply for his rent garments. This was it which, in presage of his future right, Elijah invested him withal upon the first sight, when he was ploughing with the twelve yoke of oxen; now it falls from heaven to his possession. I do not see him adore so precious a relic: I see him take it up, and cast it about him. Pensive and masterless doth he now come back to the banks of Jordan, whose stream he must pass in his return to the schools of the prophets. Erewhile he saw what way that river gave to the mantle of Elijah; he knew that power was not in the cloth, but in the spirit of him that wore it. To try, therefore, whether he were no less the heir of that spirit, than of that garment, he took the mantle of Elijah, and smote the waters, and said, " Where is the Lord God of Elijah?" Elisha doth not expostulate and challenge, but pray; as if he had said, " Lord God, it was thy promise to me by my departed master, that if I should see him in his last passage, a double portion of his spirit should be upon me: I followed him with my eyes in that fire and whirlwind: now therefore, O God, make good thy gracious word to thy servant; show some token unto me for good: make this the first proof of the miraculous power wherewith thou shalt endue me; let Jordan give the same way to me that it gave to my master." Immediately the stream, as acknowledging the same mantle, though in another hand, divides itself, and yields passage to the successor of Elijah.

The fifty sons of the prophets, having been afar off witnesses of these admirable events, do well see that Elijah, though translated in body, hath yet left his spirit behind him: they meet Elisha, and bow themselves to the ground before him. It was not the outside of Elijah which they had wont to stoop unto with so much veneration; it was his spirit, which, since they now find in another subject, they entertain with equal reverence: no envy, no emulation, raiseth up their stomachs against Elijah's servant, but, where they see eminent graces, they are willingly prostrate. Those that are truly gracious, do no less rejoice in the riches of other's gifts, than humbly undervalue their own. These men were trained up in the schools of the prophets, Elisha at the plough and cart; yet, now they stand not upon terms of their worth, and his meanness, but meekly fall down before him whom God had honoured: it is not to be regarded who the man is, but whom God would make him. The more unlikely the means are, the more is the glory of the workman: it is the praise of a holy ingenuity to magnify the graces of God wherever it finds them.

These young prophets are no less full of zeal than reverence; zeal to Elijah, reverence to Elisha. They see Elijah carried up in the air; they knew this was not the first time of his supernatural removal: imagining it therefore possible, that the Spirit of God had cast him upon some remote mountain, or valley, they proffer the labour of their servants to seek him. In some things, even professed seers are blind: could they think God would send such a chariot and horses for a less voyage than heaven?

Elisha, knowing his master beyond all

the sphere of mortality, forbids them; good-will makes them unmannerly; their importunity urges him till he is ashamed: not his approbation, but their vehemence, carries at last a condescent, else he might perhaps have seemed enviously unwilling to fetch back so admired a master, and loath to forego that mantle. Some things may be yielded for the redeeming of our own vexation, and avoidance of others' misconstruction, which, out of true judgment, we see no cause to affect.

The messengers, tired with three days' search, turn back as wise as they went. Some men are best satisfied when they have wearied themselves in their own ways: nothing will teach them wit but disappointments. Their painful error leads them to a right conceit of Elijah's happier transportation. Those that would find Elijah, let them aspire to the heavenly paradise; let them follow the high steps of his sincere faithfulness, strong patience, undaunted courage, fervent zeal: shortly, let them walk in the way of his holy and constant obedience; at last, God shall send the fiery chariot of death to fetch them up to that heaven of heavens, where they shall triumph in everlasting joys.

CONTEMPLATION VI.—ELISHA HEALING THE WATERS,—CURSING THE CHILDREN,—RELIEVING THE KINGS.

It is good making use of a prophet while we have him. Elisha staid somewhile at Jericho; the citizens resort to him with a common suit: their structure was not more pleasant than their waters unwholesome, and their soil by those corrupt waters: they sue to Elisha for the remedy. Why had they not all this while made their moan to Elijah? Was it that they were more awed with his greater austerity? or was it, that they met not with so fit an opportunity of his commoration amongst them? It was told them what power Elisha had exercised upon the waters of Jordan, and now they ply him for theirs. Examples of beneficence easily move us to a request and expectation of favours.

What ailed the waters of Jericho? Surely, originally they were not ill affected: no men could be so foolish as to build a city where neither earth nor water were useful: mere prospect could not carry men to the neglect of health and profit. Hiel the Bethelite would never have re-edified it with the danger of a curse, so lately as in the days of Ahab, if it had been of old notorious for so foul an annoyance: not therefore the ancient malediction of Joshua, not the neighbourhood of that noisome lake of Sodom, was guilty of this disease of the soil and the waters, but the late sins of the inhabitants: "He turneth the rivers into a wilderness, and water-springs into a dry ground; a fruitful land into barrenness, for the wickedness of them that dwell therein." How oft have we seen the same field both full and famishing! how oft the same waters both safe, and, by some eruption, or new tincture, hurtful! Howsoever natural causes may concur, heaven and earth, and air and waters, follow the temper of our souls, of our lives, and are therefore indisposed because we are so. Jericho began now to make itself capable of a better state, since it was now become a receptacle of prophets. Elisha is willing to gratify his hosts; it is reason that any place should fare the better for the presence of divines. The medicine is more strange than the disease: "Bring me a new cruse, and put salt therein." Why a cruse? why new? why salt in that new cruse? How should salt make water potable? or, if there were any such virtue in it, what could a cruseful do to a whole current? or, if that measure were sufficient, what was the age of the cruse to the force of the salt? Yet Elisha calls for salt in a new cruse. God, who wrought this by his prophet, is a free agent; as he will not bind his power to means, so will he, by his power, bind unlikely means to perform his will.

Natural properties have no place in miraculous works: no less easy is it for God to work by contrary, than subordinate powers.

The prophet doth not cast the salt into the channel, but into the spring of the waters. If the fountain be redressed, the stream cannot be faulty; as, contrarily, the purity and soundness of the stream avail nothing to the redress of the fountain. Reformation must begin at the well-head of the abuse. The order of being is a good guide to the method of amending. Virtue doth not run backward. Had Elisha cast the salt into the brooks and ditches, the remedy must have striven against the stream to reach up to the spring; now it is but one labour to cure the fountain. Our heart is a well of bitter and venomous water; our actions are the streams: in vain shall we cleanse our hands, while our hearts are evil.

The cruse and the salt must be their own; the act must be his, the power God's. "He cast the salt into the spring," and said, "Thus saith the Lord, I have healed these waters; there shall not be from thence any more death or barrenness." Far was it from Elisha to challenge aught to himself. Before, when he should divide the waters of Jordan, he did not say, Where is the power of Elisha, but, Where is the Lord God of Elijah? And now, when he should cure the waters of Jericho, he says not, Thus saith Elisha, but, Thus saith the Lord, " I have healed these waters." How careful is the man of God that no part of God's glory should stick to his own fingers! Jericho shall know to whom they owe the blessing, that they may duly return the thanks. Elisha professes he can do no more of himself than that salt, than that cruse: only God shall work by him, by it; and whatever that Almighty hand undertakes, cannot fail, yea, is already done: neither doth he say, I will heal, but, " I have healed." Even so, O God, if thou cast into the fountain of our hearts but one cruseful of the salt of thy Spirit, we are whole; no thought can pass between the receipt and the remedy.

As the general visitor of the schools of the prophets, Elisha passeth from Jericho to that other college at Bethel. Bethel was a place of strange composition: there were at once the golden calf of Jeroboam, and the school of God; true religion and idolatry found a free harbour within those walls. I do not marvel that God's prophets would plant there; there was the most need of their presence, where they found the springhead of corruption: physicians are of most use where diseases do abound. " As he was going up by the way, there came forth little children out of the city, and mocked him, and said to him, Go up, thou baldhead; Go up, thou bald-head." Even the very boys of Bethel have learned to scoff at a prophet; the spite of their idolatrous parents is easily propagated: children are such as their institution; infancy is led altogether by imitation; it hath neither words nor actions, but infused by others; if it have good or ill language, it is but borrowed, and the shame or thank is due to those that lent it them.

What was it that these ill-taught children upbraided to the prophet, but a slight natural defect, not worthy the name of a blemish, the want of a little hair; at the best a comely excrement, no part of the body. Had there been deformity in that smoothness of the head, which some great wits have honoured with praises, a faultless and remediless eye-sore had been no fit matter for a taunt. How small occasions will be taken to disgrace a prophet! If they could have said aught worse, Elisha had not heard of this: God had crowned that head with honour, which the Bethelitish children loaded with scorn. Who would have thought the rude terms of waggish boys worthy of any thing but neglect! Elisha looks at them with severe brows, and, like the heir of him that called down fire upon the two captains and their fifties, curses them in the name of the Lord. Two she-bears out of the wood, hasten to be his executioners, and tear two-and-forty of them in pieces. O fearful example of Divine justice! This was not the revenge of an angry prophet, it was the punishment of a righteous judge. God and his seer looked through these children at the parents, at all Israel; he would punish the parents' misnurturing their children, to the contemptuous usage of a prophet, with the death of those children which they had mistaught. He would teach Israel what it was to misuse a prophet; and, if he would not endure these contumelies unrevenged in the mouths of children, what vengeance was enough for aged persecutors?

Doubtless some of the children escaped to tell the news of their fellows. What lamentation do we think there was in the streets of Bethel! how did the distressed mothers wring their hands for this woful orbation! and now, when they came forth to fetch the remnants of their own flesh, what a sad spectacle it was to find the fields strewed with those mangled carcasses! It is an unprofitable sorrow that follows a judgment. Had these parents been as careful to train up their children in good discipline, and to correct their disorders, as they are now passionate in bemoaning their loss, this slaughter had never been. In vain do we look for good of those children, whose education we have neglected. In vain do we grieve for those miscarriages which our care might have prevented.

Elisha knew the success, yet doth he not baulk the city of Bethel. Do we not wonder that the furious impatience of those parents whom the curse of Elisha robbed of their children, did not break forth to some malicious practice against the prophet? Would we not think the prophet might misdoubt some hard measure from those exasperated citizens! There lay his way; he follows God without fear of men, as well knowing that either they durst not, or they could not act violence. They knew there were bears in the wood, and fires in heaven, and if their malice would have ventured above their courage, they could have no more power over Elisha in the streets, than those hungry beasts had in the way.

Whither dare not a prophet go when God calls him? Having visited the schools of the prophets, Elisha retires to Mount Carmel, and, after some holy solitariness, returns to the city of Samaria. He can never be a profitable seer, that is either always or never alone. Carmel shall fit him for Samaria; contemplation for action: that mother city of Israel must needs afford him most work; yet is the throne of Ahaziah succeeded by a brother less ill than himself, than the parents of both. Ahab's impiety hath not a perfect heir of Jehoram: that son of his hates his Baal, though he keeps his calves. Even into the most wicked families it pleaseth God to cast his powerful restraints, that all are not equally vicious. It is no news to see lewd men make scruple of some sins; the world were not to live in, if all sins were affected by all: it is no thank to Ahab and Jezebel that their son is no Baalite. As no good is traduced from parents, so not all evil: there is an Almighty hand that stops the foul current of nature at his pleasure; no idolater can say that his child shall not be a convert.

The affinity betwixt the houses of Israel and Judah holds good in succession: Jehoram inherits the friendship, the aid of Jehoshaphat; whose counsel, as is most likely, had cured him of that Baalism. It was a good war whereto he solicits the good king of Judah. The king of Moab, who had been an ancient tributary from the days of David, falls now from his homage, and refuses to pay his hundred thousand lambs, and hundred thousand rams with fleeces, to the king of Israel: the backs of Israel can ill miss the wool of Moab; they will put on iron to recover their cloth. Jehoshaphat had been once well chid, well frighted, for joining with Ahab against Aram; yet doth he not stick now again to come into the field with Jehoram, against Moab: the cause is more favourable, less dangerous: Baal is cast down; the images of the false gods are gone, though the false images of the true God stand still; besides, this rebellious Moab had joined with the Syrians formerly against Judah, so as Jehoshaphat is interested in the revenge.

After resolution of the end, wisely do these kings deliberate of the way. It is agreed to pass through Edom: that kingdom was annexed to the crown of Judah; well might Jehoshaphat make bold with his own. It was, it seems, a march far about in the measure of the way, but nearest to their purpose: the assault would be more easy, if the passage were more tedious. The three kings of Israel, Judah, Edom, together with their armies, are upon foot: they are no sooner come into the parching wilds of Edom, than they are ready to die for thirst. If the channels were far off, yet the waters were farther: the scorching beams of the sun have dried them up, and have left those rivers more fit for walk than entertainment. What are the greatest monarchs of the world, if they want but water to their mouths? What can their crowns, and plumes, and rich arms, avail them, when they are abridged but of that which is the drink of beasts? With dry tongues and lips, do they now confer of their common misery. Jehoram deplores the calamity into which they were fallen, but Jehoshaphat asks for a prophet. Every man can bewail a misery; every man cannot find the way out of it: still yet I hear good Jehoshaphat speak too late; he should have inquired for a prophet ere he had gone forth: so had he avoided these straits. Not to consult at all with God, is Jehoram's sin; to consult late, is Jehoshaphat's: the former is atheous carelessness, the latter forgetful oversight. The best man may slacken good duties; the worst contemns them.

Not without some specialty from God, doth Elisha follow the camp; else, that had been no element for a prophet. Little did the good king of Judah think that God was so near him; purposely was this holy seer sent for the succour of Jehoshaphat and his faithful followers, when they were so far from dreaming of their delivery, that they knew not of a danger. It would be wide with the best men, if the eye of Divine Providence were not open upon them, when the eye of their care is shut towards it. How well did Elisha in the wars! The strongest squadron of Israel was within that breast: all their armour of proof had not so much safety and protection as his mantle. Though the king of Israel would take no notice of the prophet, yet one of his courtiers did: "Here is Elisha, the son of Shaphat, which poured water on the hands of Elijah." This follower of Jehoram knows Elisha by his own name, by his father's, by his master's. The court of Israel was profane and idolatrous enough; yet even there God's prophet had both knowledge and honour; his very service to Elijah was enough to win him reverence. It is better to be an attendant of some man, than be attended by many: that he had poured water on Elijah's hands was insinuation enough that he could pour out water for those three kings. The three kings walked down by the motion of Jehoshaphat, to the man of God: it was news to see three kings going down to the servant of him who ran before the chariot of Ahab. Religion and necessity have both of them much power of humiliation; I know not whether more: either zeal, or need, will make a prophet honoured.

How sharply dares the man of God to chide his sovereign, the king of Israel! The liberty of the prophets was no less singular than their calling; he that would borrow their tongue, must show their commission. As God reproved kings for their sakes, so did not they stick to reprove kings for his sake. Thus much freedom they must leave to their successors, that we might not spare the vices of them, whose persons we must spare.

Justly is Jehoram turned off to the prophets of his father, and the prophets of his mother. It is but right and equal, that those, which we have made the comfort and stay of our peace, should be the refuge of our extremity. If our prosperity have made the world our god, how worthily shall our deathbed be choked with this exprobration! Neither would the case bear an apology, nor the time an expostulation; Jehoram cannot excuse; he can complain: he finds that now three kings, three kingdoms, are at the mercy of one prophet; it was time for him to speak fair. Nothing sounds from him but lamentations and entreaties: " Nay, for the Lord hath called these three kings together to deliver them into the hand of Moab." Jehoram hath so much grace as to confess the impotency of those he had trusted, and the power of that God whom he had neglected: every sinner cannot see and acknowledge the hand of God in his sufferings. Already hath the distressed prince gained something by his misery: none complain so much as he, none feel so much as he; all the rest suffer for him, and therefore he suffers in them all.

The man of God, who well sees the insufficiency of Jehoram's humiliation, lays on yet more load: " As the Lord liveth before whom I stand, surely, were it not that I regard the presence of Jehoshaphat the king of Judah, I would not look toward thee, nor see thee." Behold the double spirit of Elijah! The master was not more bold with the father, than the servant was with the son. Elisha was a subject and a prophet; he must say that as a prophet, which he might not as a subject; as a prophet he would not have looked at him, whom as a subject he would have bowed to. It is one thing when God speaks by him; another when he speaks of himself. That it might well appear his dislike of sin stood with his honour of sovereignty, Jehoshaphat goes away with that respect which Jehoram missed: no less doth God and his prophet regard religious sincerity, than they abhor idolatry and profaneness. What shall not be done for a Jehoshaphat? for his sake shall those two other princes, and their vast armies, live and prevail. Edom and Israel, whether single or conjoined, had perished by the drought of the desert, by the sword of Moab: one Jehoshaphat gives them both life and victory. It is in the power of one good man to oblige a world: we receive true, though insensible favours, from the presence of the righteous. Next to being good, it is happy to converse with them that are so: if we be not bettered by their example, we are blest by their protection.

Who wonders not to hear a prophet call for a minstrel in the midst of that mournful distress of Israel and Judah? who would not have expected his charge of tears and prayers, rather than of music? How unreasonable are songs to a heavy heart! It was not for their ears, it was for his own bosom, that Elisha called for music; that his spirits, after their zealous agitation, might be sweetly composed, and put into a meet temper for receiving the calm visions of God. Perhaps it was some holy Levite that followed the camp of Jehoshaphat, whose minstrelsy was required for so sacred a purpose. None but a quiet breast is capable of Divine revelations; nothing is more powerful to settle a troubled heart than a melodious harmony: the spirit of prophecy was not the more invited, the prophet's spirit was the better disposed, by pleasing sounds. The same God, that will reveal his will to the prophet, suggests this demand, " Bring me a minstrel." How many say thus, when they would get God from them! Profane mirth, wanton music, debauches the soul, and makes no less room for the unclean spirit, than spiritual melody doth for the divine.

No prophet had ever the spirit at command. The hand of the minstrel can do nothing without the hand of the Lord: while the music sounds in the ear, God speaks to the heart of Elisha: " Thus saith the Lord, Make this valley full of ditches; ye shall not see wind, neither shall ye see rain, yet that valley shall be full of water," &c. To see wind and rain, in the height of that drought, would have seemed as wonderful as pleasing; but to see abundance of water, without wind or rain, was yet more miraculous. I know not how the sight of the means abates our admiration of the effect: where no causes can be found out, we are forced to confess omnipotency. Elijah relieved Israel with water, but it was out of the clouds, and those clouds rose from the sea; but whence Elisha shall fetch it, is not more marvellous than secret.

All that evening, all that night, must the faith of Israel and Judah be exercised with expectation. At the hour of the morning sacrifice, no sooner did the blood of that oblation gush forth, than the streams of water gushed forth into their new channels, and filled the country with a refreshing moisture: Elijah fetched down his fire at the hour of the evening sacrifice; Elisha fetched up his water at the hour of the morning sacrifice. God gives respect to his own hours, for the encouragement of our observation: if his wisdom hath set us any peculiar times, we cannot keep them without a blessing: the devotions of all true Jews, all the world over, were in that hour combined. How seasonably doth the wisdom of God pick out that instant, wherein he might at once answer both Elisha's prophecy, and his people's prayers?

The prophet hath assured the kings, not of water only, but of victory. Moab hears of enemies, and is addressed to war: their own error shall cut their throats. They rise soon enough to beguile themselves: the beams of the rising sun, glistening upon those vaporous and unexpected waters, carried, in the eyes of some Moabites, a semblance of blood. A few eyes were enough to fill all ears with a false noise; the deceived sense miscarries the imagination: "This is blood; the kings are surely slain, and they have smitten one another; now therefore, Moab, to the spoil." Civil broils give just advantage to a common enemy; therefore must the camps be spoiled, because the kings have smitten each other. Those that shall be deceived are given over to credulity: the Moabites do not examine either the conceit or the report, but fly in confusedly upon the camp of Israel, whom they find, too late, to have no enemies but themselves. As if death would not have hastened enough to them, they come to fetch it, they come to challenge it: it seizeth upon them unavoidably; they are smitten, their cities razed, their lands marred, their wells stopped, their trees felled, as if God meant to waste them but once.

No onsets are so furious as the last assaults of the desperate. The king of Moab, now hopeless of recovery, would be glad to shut up with a pleasing revenge: with seven hundred resolute followers, he rushes into the battle towards the king of Edom, as if he would bid death welcome, might he but carry with him that despited neighbour; and now, mad with repulse, he returns; and, whether as angry with his destiny, or as barbarously affecting to win his cruel gods with so dear a sacrifice, he offers them, with his own hands, the blood of his eldest son in the sight of Israel, and sends him up in the smoke to those hellish deities. O prodigious act, whether of rage or of devotion! What a hand hath Satan over his miserable vassals! What marvel is it to see men sacrifice their souls in an unfelt oblation, to these plausible tempters, when their own flesh and blood have not been spared? There is no tyrant like to the prince of darkness.

CONTEMPLATION VII.—ELISHA WITH THE SHUNAMITE.

The holy prophets under the Old Testament did not abhor the marriage-bed: they did not think themselves too pure for an institution of their Maker. The distressed widow of one of the sons of the prophets comes to Elisha to bemoan her condition. Her husband is dead, and dead in debt: death hath no sooner seized on him, than her two sons, the remaining comfort of her life, are to be seized on by his creditors, for bondmen. How thick did the miseries of this poor afflicted woman light upon her! Her husband is lost, her estate clogged with debts, her children ready to be taken for slaves. Her husband was a religious and worthy man; he paid his debts to nature, he could not to his creditors: they are cruel, and rake in the scarce closed wound of her sorrow, passing an arrest worse than death upon her sons: widowhood, poverty, servitude, have conspired to make her perfectly miserable. Virtue and goodness can pay no debts. The holiest man may be deep in arrearages, and break the bank; not through lavishness, and riot of expense (religion teaches us to moderate our hands, to spend within the proportion of our estate), but through either iniquity of times, or evil casualties. Ahab and Jezebel were lately in the throne: who can marvel that a prophet was in debt? It was well that any good man might have his breath free, though his estate were not: wilfully to overlash our ability, cannot stand with wisdom and good government; but no providence can guard us from crosses. Holiness is no more defence against debt, than against death. Grace can keep us from unthriftiness, not from want. Whither doth the prophet's widow come to bewail her case but to Elisha? Every one would not be sensible of her affliction, or if they would pity, yet could not relieve her: Elisha could do both; into his ear doth she unload her griefs. It is no small point of wisdom to know where to plant our lamentation; otherwise, instead of comfort, we may meet with scorn and insultation.

None can so feelingly compassionate the hard terms of a prophet as an Elisha; he finds that she is not querulously impatient, expressing her sorrow without murmuring and discontentment, making a loving and honourable mention of that husband who had left her distressed; readily, therefore, doth he incline to her succour: "What shall I do for thee? Tell me what hast thou in thine house?" Elisha, when he hears of her debts, asks of her substance. Had her house been furnished with any valuable commodity, the prophet implies the necessity of selling it for satisfaction. Our own abundance can ill stand with our engagement to others: it is great injustice for us to be full of others' purses. It is not our own which we owe to another: what is it other than a plausible stealth, to feed our riot with the want of the owner? He that could multiply our substance, could know it: God and his prophet love to hear our necessities out of our own mouths. "Thine handmaid hath not any thing in the house save a pot of oil." It is neither news nor shame for a prophet to be poor: grief and want perhaps hastened his end; both of them are left for the dowry of his careful widow. She had not complained, if there had been any possibility of remedy at home; bashfulness had stopt her mouth thus long, and should have done yet longer, if the exigence of her children's servitude had not opened it. No want is so worthy of relief, as that which is loathest to come forth. "Then he said, Go borrow thee vessels abroad of all thy neighbours, even empty vessels, borrow not a few; and when thou art come in, thou shalt shut the door upon thee, and upon thy sons, and shalt pour out into all those vessels, and thou shalt set aside that which is full."

She that owed much, and had nothing, yet must borrow more, that she may pay all. Poverty had not so discredited her with her neighbours, that they should doubt to lend her those vessels empty, which they had grudged full. Her want was too well known: it could not but seem strange to the neighbours, to see this poor widow so busily pestering her house with empty tubs, which they knew she had nothing to fill; they knew well enough, she had neither field, nor vineyard, nor orchard, and therefore must needs marvel at such unprofitable diligence. If their curiosity would be inquiring after her intentions, she is commanded secresy. The doors must be shut upon herself, and her sons, while the oil is increasing. No eye shall see the miracle in working; enough shall see it, once wrought. This act was no less a proof of her faith, than an improvement of her estate; it was an exercise of her devotion, as well as of her diligence; it was fit her doors should be shut, while her heart and lips were opened in an holy invocation. Out of one small jar was poured out so much oil, as by a miraculous multiplication filled all these empty casks. Scarce had that pot any bottom, at least the bottom that it had was to be measured by the brims of all those vessels; this was so deep, as they were high; could they have held more, this pot had not been empty. Even so the bounty of our God gives grace and glory, according to the capacity of the receiver: when he ceaseth to infuse, it is for want of room in the heart that takes it in. Could we hold more, O God, thou wouldst give more: if there be any defect, it is in our vessels, not in thy beneficence. How did the heart of this poor widow run over, as with wonder, so with joy and thankfulness, to see such a river of oil rise out of so small a spring! to see all her vessels swimming full with so beneficial a liquor! Justly is she affected with this sight; she is not transported from her duty. I do not see her run forth into the street, and proclaim her store, nor calling in her neighbours, whether to admire or bargain: I see her running to the prophet's door, and gratefully acknowledging the favour, and humbly depending on his directions, as not daring to dispose of that which was so wonderfully given her, without the advice of him, by whose powerful means she had received it. Her own reason might have sufficiently suggested what to do: she dares not trust it, but consults with the oracle of God. If we would walk surely, we must do nothing without a word; every action, every motion must have a warrant: we can no more err with this guide, than not err without him.

The prophet sets her in a right way: "Go sell the oil, and pay thy debts, and live, thou and thy children, on the rest." The first care is of her debts; the next of her maintenance. It should be gross injustice to raise means for herself, and her charge, ere she have discharged the arrearages of her husband. None of the oil was hers, till her creditors were satisfied; all was hers that remained. It is but stealth to enjoy a borrowed substance: while she had nothing, it was no sin to owe; but, when once her vessels were full, she could not have been guiltless, if she had not paid, before she stored. God and his prophets were bountiful: after the debts paid, they provide not only against the thraldom of her charge, but against the want. It is the just care of a religious heart to defend the widow and children of a prophet from distress and penury.

Behold the true servant, and successor of Elijah: what he did to the Sareptan widow, this did to the widow of a prophet. That increase of oil was by degrees, this at once; both equally miraculous; this so much more charitable, as it less concerned himself.

He that gives kindnesses, doth by turns receive them. Elisha hath relieved a poor woman, is relieved by a rich. The Shunamite, a religious and wealthy matron, invites him to her house; and now, after the first entertainment, finding his occasions to call him to a frequent passage that way, moves her husband to fit up, and furnish a lodging for the man of God. It was his holiness that made her desirous of such a guest: well might she hope that such an inmate would pay a blessing for his house-rent. O happy Shunamite, that might make herself the hostess of Elisha! As no less dutiful than godly, she imparts her desire to her husband, whom her suit hath drawn into a partnership in this holy hospitality: blessed of God is that man, whose bed yields him an help to heaven! The good Shunamite desires not to harbour Elisha in one of her wonted lodgings; she solicits her husband to build him a chamber on the wall apart; she knew the tumult of a large family unfit for the quiet meditations of a prophet: retiredness is most meet for the thoughts of a seer. Neither would she bring the prophet to bare walls, but sets ready for him a bed, a table, a stool, and a candlestick, and whatever necessary utensils for his entertainment. The prophet doth not affect delicacy; she takes care to provide for his convenience. Those that are truly pious and devout, think their houses and their hands cannot be too open to the messengers of God, and are most glad to exchange their earthly commodities for the others' spiritual. Superfluity should not fall within the care of a prophet, necessity must: he, that could provide oil for the widow, could have provided all needful helps for himself. What room had there been for the charity and beneficence of others, if the prophet should have always maintained himself out of power?

The holy man is so far sociable, as not to neglect the friendly offer of so kind a benefactor: gladly does he take up his new lodging, and, as well pleased with so quiet a repose, and careful attendance, he sends his servant Gehazi with the message of his thanks, with a treaty of retribution: "Behold, thou hast been careful for us, with all this care: what is to be done for thee? wouldst thou be spoken for to the king, or to the captain of the host?" An ingenuous disposition cannot receive favours without thoughts of return. A wise debtor is desirous to retribute in such kind as may be most acceptable to his obligers. Without this discretion, we may offer such requitals as may seem goodly to us — to our friends, worthless. Every one can choose best for himself; Elisha, therefore, who had never been wanting in spiritual duties to so hospitable a friend, gives the Shunamite the election of her suit, for temporal recompense also: no man can be a loser by his favour to a prophet. It is good hearing that an Elisha is in such grace at the court; that he can promise himself access to the king in a friend's suit. It was not ever thus: the time was, when his master heard, "Hast thou found me, O mine enemy?" Now the late miracle which Elisha wrought, in gratifying the three kings with water and victory, hath endeared him to the king of Israel: and now, who but Elisha? Even that rough mantle finds respect amongst those silks and tissues. As bad as Jehoram was, yet he honoured the man of God. He that could not prevail with an idolatrous king in a spiritual reformation, yet can carry a civil suit. Neither doth the prophet, in a sullen discontentment, fly off from the court, because he found his labours unprofitable, but still holds good terms with that prince, whom he cannot reclaim, and will make use, notwithstanding, of his countenance, in matters whether of courtesy or justice. We may not cast off our due respects even to faulty authority, but must still submit and persist, where we are repelled. Not to his own advancement doth Elisha desire to improve the king's favour, but to the behoof, to the relief, of others. If the Shunamite have business at the court, she need no other solicitor. There cannot be a better office, nor more beseeming a prophet, than to speak in the cause of the dumb; to befriend the oppressed, to win greatness unto the protection of innocence.

The good matron needs no shelter of the great: "I dwell among mine own people;" as if she said, The courtesy is not small in itself, but not useful to me: I live here quietly, in a contented obscurity, out of the reach either of the glories or cares of a court; free from wrongs, free from envies. Not so high as to provoke an evil eye, not so low as to be trodden on: I have neither fears nor ambitions: my neighbours are my friends, my friends are my protectors, and, if I should be so unhappy as to be the subject of main injuries, would not stick to be mine advocates: this favour is for those that either affect greatness, or groan under oppression; I do neither, for "I live among my own people." O Shunamite, thou shalt not escape envy! Who can hear of thine happy condition, and not say, why am I not thus? If the world afford any perfect contentment, it is in a middle estate, equally distant from penury, from excess: it is in a calm freedom, a secure tranquillity, a sweet fruition of ourselves, of ours. But what hold is there of these earthly things? how long is the Shunamite thus blessed with peace? Stay but a while, you shall see her come on her knees to the king of Israel, pitifully complaining that she was stripped of house and land; and now Gehazi is fain to do that good office for her, which was not accepted from his master. Those that stand safest upon earth have but slippery footing; no man can say that he shall not need friends.

Modesty sealed up the lips of the good Shunamite; she was ashamed to confess her longing. Gehazi easily guessed that her barrenness could not but be her affliction: she was childless, her husband old. Elisha gratifies her with the news of a son: "About this season, according to the time of life, thou shalt embrace a son." How liberal is God, by his prophet, in giving beyond her requests: not seldom doth his bounty over-reach our thoughts, and meet us with those benefits which we thought too good for us to ask. Greatness and inexpectation make the blessing seem incredible: "Nay, my lord, thou man of God, do not lie to thine handmaid." We are never sure enough of what we desire; we are not more hard to believe, than loath to distrust beneficial events. She well knew the prophet's holiness could not stand with wilful falsehood: perhaps she might think it spoken by way of trial, not of serious affirmation. As unwilling, therefore, that it should not be, and willing to hear that pleasing word seconded, she says, "Do not lie to thine handmaid." Promises are made good, not by iteration, but by the effect: the Shunamite conceives, and bears a son at the set season. How glad a mother she was, those know best that have mourned under the discomfort of a sad sterility. The child grows up, and is now able to find out his father in the field, amongst his reapers: his father now grew young again with the pleasure of this sight, and more joyed in this spring of his hopes, than in all the crops of his harvest. But what stability is there in these earthly delights? The hot beams of the sun beat upon that head which too much care had made tender and delicate; the child complains to his father of his pain. O that grace could teach us, what nature teaches infants, in all our troubles to bemoan ourselves to our heavenly Father! He sends him to his mother: upon her lap, about noon, the child dies, as if he would return his soul into that bosom from which it was derived to him. The good Shunamite hath lost her son; her faith she had not lost. Passion hath not robbed her of her wisdom: as not distracted with an accident so sudden, so sorrowful, she lays the dead child upon the prophet's bed, she locks the door, she hides her grief, lest that consternation might hinder her design. She hastens to her husband, and, as not daring to be other than officious in so distressful an occasion, acquaints him with her journey, though not with the cause, requires of him both attendance and conveyance; she posts to Mount Carmel. She cannot so soon find out the man of God as he hath found her: he sees her afar off, and, like a faithful guest, sends his servant hastily to meet her, to inquire of the health of herself, her husband, her child. Her errand was not to Gehazi; it was to Elisha: no messenger shall interrupt her, no ear shall receive her complaint but the prophet's. Down she falls passionately at his feet, and, forgetting the fashion of her bashful strangeness, lays hold of them, whether in an humble veneration of his person, or in a fervent desire of satisfaction. Gehazi, who well knew how uncouth, how unfit this gesture of salutation was for his master, offers to remove her, and admonisheth her of her distance. The merciful prophet easily apprehends that no ordinary occasion could so transport a grave and well-governed matron; as, therefore, pitying her unknown passion, he bids "Let her alone, for her soul is vexed within her, and the Lord hath hid it from me, and hath not told me." If extremity of grief have made her unmannerly, wise and holy Elisha knows how to pardon it: he dares not add sorrow to the afflicted; he can better bear an unseemliness in her greetings, than cruelty in her molestation. Great was the familiarity that the prophet had with his God; and as friends are wont mutually to impart their counsels to each other, so had the Lord done to him. Elisha was not idle on mount Carmel: what was it that he saw not from thence? not heaven only, but the world, was before him. Yet the Shunamite's loss is concealed from him, neither doth he shame to confess it. Ofttimes those that know greater matters may yet be ignorant of the less: it is no disparagement to any finite creature not to know something. By her mouth will God tell the prophet, what by vision he had not: "Then she said, Did I desire a son of my lord? did I not say, do not deceive me?" Deep sorrow is sparing of words: the expostulation could not be more short, more quick, more pithy. Had I begged a son, perhaps my importunity might have been yielded to in anger: too much desire is justly punished with loss: it is no marvel if what we wring from God prosper not. This favour to me was of thine own motion; thy suit, O Elisha, made me a mother: couldst thou intend to torment me with a blessing? How much more easy had the want of a son been, than the miscarriage! barrenness than abortion! Was there no other end of my having a son, than that I might lose him? O man of God, let me not complain of a cruel kindness! Thy prayers gave me a son, let thy prayers restore him; let not my dutiful respects to thee be repaid with an aggravation of misery: give not thine handmaid cause to wish that I were but so unhappy as thou foundest me: O woful fruitfulness, if I must now say that I had a son!

I know not whether the mother or the prophet were more afflicted; the prophet for the mother's sake, or the mother for her own. Not a word of reply do we hear from the mouth of Elisha; his breath is only spent in the remedy: he sends his servant with all speed to lay his staff upon the face of the child, charging him to avoid all the delays of the way. Had not the prophet supposed that staff of his able to beat away death, why did he send it? and if upon that supposition he send it, how was it that it failed of effect? Was this act done out of human conceit, not out of instinct from God? or did the want of the mother's faith hinder the success of that cure? She, not regarding the staff, or the man, holds fast to Elisha; no hopes of his message can loose her fingers: "As the Lord liveth, and as thy soul liveth, I will not leave thee."

She imagined that the servant, the staff, might be severed from Elisha; she knew, that wherever the prophet was, there was power. It is good relying upon those helps that cannot fail us.

Merit and importunity have drawn Elisha from Carmel to Shunem. He finds his lodging taken up by that pale carcass: he shuts his door, and falls to his prayers. This staff of his, whatever became of the other, was long enough, he knew, to reach up to heaven, to knock at those gates, yea, to wrench them open. He applies his body to those cold and senseless limbs: by the fervour of his soul, he reduces that soul; by the heat of his body, he educeth warmth out of that corpse: the child sneezeth seven times, and, as if his spirit had been but hid for the time, not departed, it falls to work afresh; the eyes look up, the lips and hands move. The mother is called in to receive a new life in her twice-given son: she comes in, full of joy, full of wonder, and bows herself to the ground, and falls down before those feet which she had so boldly laid hold of in Carmel. O strong faith of the Shunamite, that could not be discouraged with the seizure and continuance of death; raising up her heart still in an expectation of that life, which to the eyes of nature had been impossible, irrevocable! O infinite goodness of the Almighty, that would not suffer such faith to be frustrated, that would rather reverse the laws of nature, in returning a guest from heaven, and raising a corpse from death, than the confidence of a believing heart should be disappointed!

How true an heir is Elisha of his master, not in his graces only, but in his actions! Both of them divided the waters of Jordan; the one as his last act, the other as his first: Elijah's curse was the death of the captains and their troops; Elisha's curse was the death of the children: Elijah rebuked Ahab to his face; Elisha, Jehoram: Elijah supplied the drought of Israel, by rain from heaven; Elisha supplied the drought of the three kings, by waters gushing out of the earth; Elijah increased the oil of the Sareptan; Elisha increased the oil of the prophet's widow: Elijah raised from death the Sareptan's son; Elisha, the Shunamite's: both of them had one mantle, one spirit; both of them climbed up one Carmel, one heaven.

CONTEMPLATION VIII. — ELISHA WITH NAAMAN.

Of the full showers of grace which fell upon Israel and Judah, yet some drops did light upon their neighbours. If Israel be the worse for her nearness to Syria, Syria is better for the vicinity of Israel. Amongst the worst of God's enemies, some are singled out for mercy. Naaman was a great warrior, an honourable courtier, yet a leper. No disease incident to the body is so nasty, so loathsome, as leprosy. Greatness can secure no man from the most odious and wearisome condition. How little pleasure did this Syrian peer take to be stooped to by others, while he hated to see himself! Even those that honoured him, avoided him; neither was he other than abhorred of those that flattered him; yea, his hand could not move to his mouth, without his own detestation; the basest slave of Syria would not change skins with him, if he might have his honour to boot. Thus hath the wise God thought meet to sauce the valour, dignity, renown, victories of the famous general of the Syrians. Seldom ever was any man served with simple favours: these compositions make both our crosses tolerable, and our blessings wholesome.

The body of Naaman was not more tainted with his leprosy, than his soul was tainted with Rimmon; and besides his idolatry, he was a professed enemy to Israel, and successful in his enmity. How far doth God fetch about his purposes! The leprosy, the hostility of Naaman, shall be the occasions of his salvation: that leprosy shall make his soul sound; that hostility shall adopt him a son of God. In some prosperous inroads that the Syrians, under Naaman's conduct, have made into the land of Israel, a little maid is taken captive: she shall attend on Naaman's wife, and shall suggest to her mistress the miraculous cures of Elisha. A small chink may serve to let in much light: her report finds credit in the court, and begets both a letter from the king, and a journey of his peer. While the Syrians thought of nothing but their booty, they bring happiness to the house of Naaman: the captivity of a poor Hebrew girl is a means to make the greatest lord of Syria a subject to God. It is good to acquaint our children with the works of God, with the praises of his prophets. Little do we know how they may improve this knowledge, and whither they may carry it: perhaps the remotest nations may light their candle at their coal. Even the weakest intimations may not be neglected; a child, a servant, a stranger, may say that which we may bless God to have heard. How well did it become the mouth of an Israelite to extol a prophet, to wish the cure of her master, though an Aramite, to advise that journey unto the man of God, by whom both body and soul might be cured! True religion teacheth us pious and charitable respects to our governors, though aliens from the commonwealth of God.

No man that I hear blames the credulity of Naaman. Upon no other ground doth the king of Syria send his chief peer, with his letters to the king of Israel, from his hands requiring the cure: the Syrian supposed, that whatever a subject could do, a sovereign might command; that such a prophet could neither be out of the knowledge, nor out of the obedience to his prince. Never did he dream of any exemption, but imagining Jehoram to be no less a king of prophets than of people, and Elisha no less a subject than a seer, he writes: " Now when this letter is come to thee, behold, I have herewith sent Naaman my servant to thee, that thou mayest recover him of his leprosy." Great is the power of princes; every man's hand is their's, whether for skill, or for strength; besides the eminency of their own gifts, all the subordinate excellencies of their subjects are no less at their service, than if they were inherent in their persons. Great men are wanting to their own perfections, if they do not both know and exercise the graces of their inferiors.

The king of Israel cannot read the letter without amazement of heart, without rending of garments, and says, " Am I a god, to kill and to make alive, that this man sends to me, to recover a man of his leprosy? Wherefore consider, and see, I pray you, how he seeketh a quarrel against me!" If God have vouchsafed to call kings gods, it well becomes kings to call themselves men, and to confess the distance wherein they stand to their Maker. Man may kill; man cannot kill and make alive; yea, of himself, he can do neither: with God, a worm, or a fly, may kill a man; without God, no potentate can do it; much less can any created power both kill and revive; since to restore life is more than to bereave it, more than to continue it, more than to give it: and if leprosy be a death, what human power can either inflict or cure it? It is a trouble to a well affected heart to receive impossible commands: to require that of an inferior which is proper to the Highest, is a derogation from that supreme power whose property it is. Had Jehoram been truly religious, the injury done to his Maker, in this motion, as he took it, had more afflicted him, than the danger of his own quarrel. Belike, Elisha was not in the thoughts of the king of Israel; he might have heard that this prophet had made alive one whom he killed not. Himself, with the two other kings, had been eye-witnesses of what Elisha could do; yet now the calves of Dan and Bethel have so often taken up his heart, that there is no room for the memory of Elisha: whom he sued to in his extremity, now his prosperity hath forgotten. Carnal hearts, when need drives them, can think of God and his prophet; when their turn is served, can as utterly neglect them, as if they were not.

Yet cannot good Elisha repay neglect and forgetfulness. He listens to what is done at the court; and finding the distress of his sovereign, proffers that service which should have been required: " Wherefore hast thou rent thy clothes? Let him come now to me, and he shall know that there is a prophet in Israel." It was no small fright from which Elisha delivers his king. Jehoram was in awe of the Syrians, ever since their last victory, wherein his father Ahab was slain, Israel and Judah discomfited: nothing was more dreadful to him than the frowns of these Aramites. The quarrel, which he suspected to be hatched by them, is cleared by Elisha; their leper shall be healed; both they and Israel shall know, they have neglected a God, whose prophet can do wonders. Many eyes, doubtless, are fastened upon the issue of this message. But what state is this that Elisha takes upon him? He doth not say, " I will come to him;" but, " Let him come now to me." The three kings came down once to his tent: it is no marvel if he prevent not the journey of a Syrian courtier. It well beseems him that will be a suitor for favour, to be obsequious: we may not stand upon terms of our labour or dignity, where we expect a benefit. Naaman comes richly attended with his troops of servants and horses, and waits in his chariot at the door of a prophet. I do not hear Elisha call him in; for though he were great, yet he was leprous; neither do I see Elisha come forth to him, and receive him with such outward courtesies, as might be fit for an honourable stranger: for in those rich clothes the prophet saw an Aramite, and perhaps some tincture of the late-shed blood of Israel. Rather that he might make a perfect trial of the humility of that man, whom he means to gratify and honour, after some short attendance at his door, he sends his servant with a message to that peer, who could not but think the meanest of his retinue a better man than Gehazi's master.

What could the prophet have done other to the lacquey of Naaman's man? He, that would be a meet subject of mercy, must be thoroughly abased in his own conceit, and must be willingly pliable to all the conditions of his humiliation. Yet, had the message carried in it either respect to the person, or probability of effect, it could not have been unwelcome; but now it sounded of nothing but sullenness and unlikelihood: " Go and wash in Jordan seven times, and thy flesh shall come again to thee, and thou shalt be clean." What wise man could take this for any other than a mere scorn and mockery? " Go, wash." Alas! what can water do? it can cleanse from filthiness, not from leprosy. And why in Jordan? what differs that from other streams? And why just seven times? what virtue is either in that channel, or in that number? Naaman can no more put off nature than leprosy. In what a chafe did he fling away from the prophet's door, and says, Am I come thus far to fetch a flout from an Israelite? Is this the issue both of my journey, and the letters of my king? could this prophet find no man to play upon but Naaman? Had he meant seriously, why did he think himself too good to come forth unto me? why did he not touch me with his hand, and bless me with his prayers, and cure me with his blessing? Is my misery fit for his derision? If water could do it, what needed I to come so far for this remedy? Have I not oft done thus in vain? have we not better streams at home, than any Israel can afford? " Are not Abana and Pharpar, rivers of Damascus, better than all the waters of Israel?" Folly and pride strive for place in a natural heart, and it is hard to say whether is more predominant—folly in measuring the power of God's ordinances by the rule of human discourse and ordinary event; pride, in a scornful valuation of the institutions of God, in comparison of our own devices. Abana and Pharpar, two for one; rivers, not waters, of Damascus, a stately city, and incomparable; are they not? who dares deny it? better, not as good, than the waters, not the rivers, all the waters, Jordan, and all the rest of Israel, a beggarly region to Damascus. Nowhere shall we find a truer pattern of the disposition of nature: how she is altogether led by sense and reason, how she fondly judges of all objects by the appearance, how she acquaints herself only with the common road of God's proceedings, how she sticks to her own principles, how she misconstrues the intentions of God, how she over-conceits her own, how she disdains the mean conditions of others, how she upbraids her opposites with the proud comparison of her own privileges.

Nature is never but like herself. No marvel if carnal minds despise the foolishness of preaching, the simplicity of sacraments, the homeliness of ceremonies, the seeming inefficacy of censures. These men look upon Jordan with Syrian eyes, one drop of whose water, set apart by divine ordination, hath more virtue than all the streams of Abana and Pharpar.

It is a good matter for a man to be attended with wise and faithful followers. Many a one hath had better counsel from his heels, than from his elbows. Naaman's servants were his best friends; they came to him, and spake to him, and said, " My father, if the prophet had bid thee do some great thing, wouldst thou not have done it? how much rather then, when he saith to thee, Wash, and be clean." These men were servants, not of the humour, but of the profit of their master. Some servile spirits would have cared only to soothe up, not to benefit their governor, and would have encouraged his rage by their own: Sir, will you take this at the hand of a base fellow? was ever man thus flouted? will you let him carry it away thus? is any harmless anger sufficient revenge for such an insolence? Give us leave at least to pull him out by the ears, and force him to do that by violence, which he would not do out of good manners: let our fingers teach this saucy prophet, what it is to offer an affront to a prince of Syria. But these men loved more their master's health than his passion; and had rather therefore to advise, than flatter; to draw him to good, than follow him to evil: since it was a prophet from whom he received this prescription, they persuade him not to despise it; intimating, there could be no fault in the slightness of the receipt, so long as there was no defect of power in the commander; that the virtue of the cure should be in his obedience, not in the nature of the remedy. They persuade and prevail. Next to the prophet, Naaman may thank his servants, that he is not a leper. He goes down, upon their entreaty, and dips seven times in Jordan: his flesh riseth, his leprosy vanisheth. Not the unjust fury and tetchiness of the patient shall cross the cure; lest, while God is severe, the prophet should be discredited. Long enough might Naaman have washed there in vain, if Elisha had not sent him. Many a leper hath bathed in that stream, and hath come forth no less impure. It is the word, the ordinance of the Almighty, which puts efficacy into those means, which of themselves are both impotent and improbable. What can our font do to the washing away of sin? If God's institution shall put virtue into our Jordan, it shall scour off the spiritual leprosies of our hearts, and shall more cure the soul than cleanse the face.

How joyful is Naaman to see this change of his skin, this renovation of his flesh, of his life! Never did his heart find such warmth of inward gladness, as in this stream.

Upon the sight of his recovery, he doth not post home to the court, or to his family, to call for witnesses, for partners of his joy, but thankfully returns to the prophet, by whose means he received this mercy: he comes back with more contentment, than he departed with rage. Now will the man of God be seen of that recovered Syrian, whom he would not see leprous: his presence shall be yielded to the gratulation, which was not yielded to the suit. Purposely did Elisha forbear before, that he might share no part of the praise of this work with his Maker; that God might be so much more magnified, as the means were more weak and despicable. The miracle hath its due work. First doth Naaman acknowledge the God that wrought it, then the prophet by whom he wrought it: " Behold, now I know there is no God in all the earth, but in Israel." O happy Syrian, that was at once cured of his leprosy, and his misprision of God! Naaman was too wise to think that either the water had cured him, or the man: he saw a Divine power working in both, such as he vainly sought from his heathen deities; with the heart, therefore, he believes, with the mouth he confesses.

While he is thus thankful to the Author of his cure, he is not unmindful of the instrument: " Now, therefore, I pray thee, take a blessing of thy servant." Naaman came richly furnished with ten talents of silver, six thousand pieces of gold, ten changes of raiment: all these, and many more, would the Syrian peer have gladly given to be delivered from so noisome a disease: no marvel if he importunately offer some part of them to the prophet, now that he is delivered; some testimony of thankfulness did well, where all earthly recompense was too short. The hands of this man were no less full of thanks than his mouth. Dry and barren professions of our obligations, where is power to requite, are unfit for noble and ingenuous spirits.

Naaman is not more frank in offering his gratuity, than Elisha vehement in refusing it: " As the Lord liveth, before whom I stand, I will receive none." Not that he thought the Syrian gold impure; not that he thought it unlawful to take up a gift, where he hath laid down a benefit: but the prophet will remit of Naaman's purse, that he may win of his soul. The man of God would have his new convert see cause to be more enamoured of true piety, which teacheth her clients to contemn those worldly riches and glories which base worldliness adore; and would have him think, that these miraculous powers are so far transcending the valuation of all earthly pelf, that those glittering treasures are worthy of nothing but contempt in respect thereof. Hence it is that he, who refused not the Shunamite's table, and stool, and candlestick, will not take Naaman's present. There is much use of godly discretion in directing us when to open, when to shut our hands.

He, that will not be allowed to give, desires yet to take: " Shall there not, I pray thee, be given to thy servant two mules' load of earth? for thy servant will henceforth offer neither burnt-offering nor sacrifice to other gods, but unto the Lord." Israelitish mould lay open to his carriage, without leave of Elisha; but Naaman regards not to take it, unless it may be given him, and given him by the prophet's hand. Well did this Syrian find that the man of God had given a supernatural virtue to the water of Israel; and therefore supposed he might give the like to his earth: neither would any earth serve him but Elisha's, else the mould of Israel had been more properly craved of the king, than the prophet of Israel.

Doubtless it was devotion that moved this suit. The Syrian saw God had a propriety in Israel, and imagines that he will be best pleased with his own. On the sudden was Naaman half a proselyte: still here was a weak knowledge with strong intentions. He will sacrifice to the Lord; but where? in Syria, not in Jerusalem: not the mould, but the altar, is what God respects, which he hath allowed nowhere but in his chosen Sion. This honest Syrian will be removing God home to his country; he should have resolved to remove his home to God: and though he vows to offer no sacrifice to any other god, yet he craves leave to offer an outward courtesy to Rimmon, though not for the idol's sake, yet for his master's: " In this thing the Lord pardon thy servant, that when my master goeth into the house of Rimmon to worship there, and he leaneth on my hand, and I bow myself in the house of Rimmon, the Lord pardon thy servant in this thing." Naaman goes away resolute to profess himself an Israelite for religion: all the Syrian court shall know that he sacrifices upon Israelitish earth to the God of Israel; they shall hear him protest to have neither heart nor knee for Rimmon. If he must go into the house of that idol, it shall be as a servant, not as a supplicant; his duty to his master shall carry him, not his devotion to his master's god; if his master go to worship there, not he. Neither doth he say, " When I bow myself to the image of Rimmon," but, " in the house:" he shall bow to be leaned upon, not to adore. yet had not Naaman thought this a fault, he had not craved a pardon; his heart told him, that a perfect convert should not have abided the roof, the sight, the air of Rimmon; that his observance of an earthly master should not draw him to the semblance of an act of outward observance to the rival of his Master in heaven; that a sincere detestation of idolatry could not stand with so unseasonable a courtesy.

Far, therefore, is Naaman from being a pattern, save of weakness; since he is yet more than half a Syrian; since he willingly accuses himself, and, instead of defending, deprecates his offence. As nature, so grace, rises by many degrees to perfection. It is not for us to expect a full stature in the cradle of conversion. Leprosy was in Naaman cured at once, not corruption.

The prophet, as glad to see him but thus forward, dismisses him with a civil valediction. Had an Israelite made this suit, he had been answered with a check. Thus much from a Syrian was worthy of a kind farewell; they are parted.

Gehazi cannot thus take his leave: his heart is mauled up in the rich chests of Naaman, and now he goes to fetch it. The prophet and his man had not looked with the same eyes upon the Syrian treasure; the one with the eye of contempt, the other with the eye of admiration and covetous desire. The disposition of the master may not be measured by the mind, by the act of his servant. Holy Elisha may be attended by a false Gehazi: no examples, no counsels, will prevail with some hearts. Who would not have thought that the follower of Elisha could be no other than a saint ? yet, after the view of all those miracles, this man is a mirror of worldliness. He thinks his master either too simple, or too kind, to refuse so just a present from a Syrian; himself will be more wise, more frugal. Desire hastens his pace; he doth not go, but run after his booty: Naaman sees him, and, as true nobleness is ever courteous, alights from his chariot to meet him. The great lord of Syria comes forth of his coach to salute a prophet's servant; not fearing that he can humble himself overmuch to one of Elisha's family. He greets Gehazi with the same word wherewith he was lately demitted by his master: "Is it peace?" So sudden a messenger might seem to argue some change. He soon receives from the breathless bearer, news of his master's health and request: " All is well; my master hath sent me, saying, Behold, even now there be come to me, from mount Ephraim, two young men of the sons of the prophets: give me, I pray thee, a talent of silver, and two changes of garments." Had Gehazi craved a reward in his own name, calling for the fee of the prophet's servant, as the gain, so the offence had been the less; now, reaching at a greater sum, he belies his master, robs Naaman, burdens his own soul. What a round tale hath the craft of Gehazi devised, of the number, the place, the quality, the age, of his master's guests, that he might set a fair colour upon that pretended request, so proportioning the value of his demand, as might both enrich himself, and yet well stand with the moderation of his master! Love of money can never keep good quarter with honesty, with innocence. Covetousness never lodged in the heart alone; if it find not, it will breed, wickedness. What a mint of fraud there is in a worldly breast! how readily can it coin subtile falsehood for an advantage!

How thankfully liberal was this noble Syrian! Gehazi could not be more eager in taking, than he was in giving: as glad of so happy an occasion of leaving any piece of his treasure behind him, he forces two talents upon the servant of Elisha, and binds them in two bags, and lays them upon two of his own servants: his own train shall yield porters to Gehazi. Cheerfulness is the just praise of our beneficence. Bountiful minds are as zealous in over-paying good turns, as the niggardly are in scanting retributions.

What projects do we think Gehazi had all the way? How did he please himself with the waking dreams of purchases, of traffic, of jollity! and now, when they are come to the tower, he gladly disburdens and dismisses his two Syrian attendants, and hides their load, and wipes his mouth, and stands boldly before that master whom he had so foully abused. O Gehazi, where didst thou think God was this while? Couldst thou thus long pour water upon the hands of Elisha, and be either ignorant or regardless of that undeceivable eye of Providence, which was ever fixed upon thy hands, thy tongue, thy heart? couldst thou thus hope to blind the eyes of a seer? Hear then thy indictment, thy sentence, from him whom thou thoughtst to have mocked with thy concealment: " Whence comest thou, Gehazi?" Thy servant went no whither. He, that had begun a lie to Naaman, ends it to his master: whoso lets his tongue once loose to a wilful untruth, soon grows impudent in multiplying falsehoods. Of what metal is the forehead of that man, that dares lie to a prophet? what is this but to outface the senses? " Went not my heart with thee, when the man turned again from his chariot to meet thee?" Didst thou not, till now, know, O Gehazi, that prophets have spiritual eyes, which are not confined to bodily prospects? didst thou not know, that their hearts were often where they were not? didst thou not know that thy secretest ways were overlooked by invisible witnesses? Hear then, and be convinced: hither thou wentst, thus thou saidst, thus thou didst, thus thou spedst. What answer was now here but confusion? Miserable Gehazi! how didst thou stand pale and trembling before the dreadful tribunal of thy severe master, looking for the woful sentence of some grievous judgment for so heinous an offence! " Is this a time to receive money, and to receive garments, and (which thou hadst already purchased in thy conceit) oliveyards, and vineyards, and sheep, and oxen, and men-servants, and maid-servants?" Did my mouth refuse, that thy hands might take?

Was I so careful to win honour to my God, and credit to my profession, by denying these Syrian presents, that thou mightest dash both in receiving them? was there no way to enrich thyself, but by belying thy master, by disparaging this holy function in the eyes of a new convert? Since thou wouldst needs therefore take part of Naaman's treasure, take part with him in his leprosy: " The leprosy of Naaman shall cleave unto thee, and unto thy seed for ever." O heavy talents of Gehazi! O the horror of this one unchangeable suit, which shall never be but loathsomely white, not somely unclean! How much better had been a light purse and a homely coat, with a sound body, a clear soul! Too late doth that wretched man now find, that he hath loaded himself with a curse, that he hath clad himself with shame: his sin shall be read ever in his face, in his seed: all passengers, all posterities, shall now say, Behold the characters of Gehazi's covetousness, fraud, sacrilege! The act overtakes the word: " He went out of his presence a leper as white as snow." It is a woful exchange that Gehazi hath made with Naaman: Naaman came a leper; returned a disciple: Gehazi came a disciple; returned a leper: Naaman left behind both his disease and his money; Gehazi takes up both his money and his disease. Now shall Gehazi never look upon himself, but he shall think of Naaman, whose skin is transferred upon him with those talents, and shall wear out the rest of his days in shame, in pain, and sorrow. His tears may wash off the guilt of his sin, but shall not, like another Jordan, wash off his leprosy; that shall ever remain as a hereditary monument of divine severity. This son of the prophet shall more loudly and lively preach the justice of God by his face, than others by their tongue. Happy was it for him, if, while his skin was snow-white with leprosy, his humbled soul was washed white as snow with the water of true repentance.

CONTEMPLATION IX.— ELISHA RAISING THE IRON; BLINDING THE ASSYRIANS.

THERE was no loss of Gehazi: when he was gone, the prophets increased. An ill man in the church is but like some shrubby tree in a garden, whose shade keeps better plants from growing: a blank doth better in a room, than an ill filling. The view of God's just judgments doth rather draw clients unto him, than alienate them. The kings of Israel had succeeded in idolatry and hate of sincere religion, yet the prophets multiply: persecution enlargeth the bounds of the church. These very tempestuous showers bring up flowers and herbs in abundance: there would have been neither so many, nor so zealous prophets, in the languishment of peace. Besides, what marvel is it if the immediate succession of two such noble leaders, as Elijah and Elisha, established and augmented religion, and bred multitudes of prophets? Rather who can marvel, upon the knowledge of all their miracles, that all Israel did not prophesy? It is a good hearing that the prophets want elbow-room out of their store, not out of the envy of neighbours, or incompetency of provision: where vision fails, the people perish; they are blessed where it abounds.

When they found themselves straitened, they did not presume to carve for themselves, but they craved the leave, the counsel of Elisha: "Let us go, we pray thee, unto Jordan, and take thence every man a beam, and let us make us a place where we may dwell: and he said, Go ye."

It well becomes the sons of the prophets to enterprise nothing without the allowance of their superiors. Here was a building towards none of the curiousest. I do not see them making means for the procurement of some cunning artificers, nor for the conquisition of some costly marbles and cedars; but every man shall hew, and square, and frame his own beam. No nice terms were stood upon by these sons of the prophets; their thoughts were fixed upon the perfection of a spiritual building: as a homely roof may serve them, so their own hands shall raise it. The fingers of these contemplative men did not scorn the axe, and mallet, and chisel: it was better being there than in Obadiah's cave; and they that dwell now contentedly under rude sticks, will not refuse the squared stones and polished contignations of better times. They shall be ill teachers of others, that have not learnt both to want and to abound.

The master of this sacred society, Elisha, is not stately, nor austere: he gives not only passage to this motion of his collegiates, but assistance. It was fit the sons of the prophets should have convenience of dwelling, though not pomp, not costliness. They fall to their work: no man goes slackly about the building of his own house. One of them, more regarding the tree than the tool, lets fall the head of the axe into the river. Poor men are sensible of small losses: he makes his moan to Elisha, "Alas, master, for it was borrowed." Had the axe been his own, the trouble had been the less to forego it; therefore doth the miscarriage afflict him, because it was of a borrowed axe. Honest minds are more careful of what they have by loan than by propriety. In lending there is a trust, which a good heart cannot disappoint without vexation. Alas! poor novices of the prophet, they would be building, and were not worth their axes; if they would give their labour, they must borrow their instruments.

Their wealth was spiritual; outward poverty may well stand with inward riches: he is rich, not that hath the world, but that can contemn it.

Elisha loves and cherishes this just simplicity: rather will he work a miracle, than a borrowed axe shall not be restored. It might easily be imagined, he that could raise up the iron out of the bottom of the water, could tell where it fell in: yet even that powerful hand calls for direction. . In this one point the son of the prophet knows more than Elisha. The notice of particularities is neither fit for a creature, nor communicable: a mean man may best know his own case: this novice better knows where his axe fell, than his master; his master knows better how to get it out than he. There is no reason to be given of supernatural actions: the prophet borrows an axe to cut a helve for the lost axe, why did he not make use of that handle which had cast the head? Did he hold it unworthy of respect, for that it had abandoned the metal wherewith it was trusted? or did he make choice of a new stick, that the miracle might be the more clear and unquestionable? Divine power goes a contrary way to art: we first would have procured the head of the axe, and then would have fitted it with an helve: Elisha fits the head to the helve, and causeth the wood, which was light, and knew not how to sink, to fetch up the iron, which was heavy, and naturally incapable of supernatation. Whether the metal were stripped of the natural weight, by the same power which gave it being, or whether, retaining the wonted poise, it was raised by some spiritual operation, I inquire not: only, I see it swim like cork upon the stream of Jordan, and move towards the hand that lost it. What creature is not willing to put off the properties of nature, at the command of the God of nature! O God, how easy is it for thee, when this hard and heavy heart of mine is sunk down into the mud of the world, to fetch it up again by thy mighty word, and cause it to float upon the streams of life, and to see the face of heaven again!

Yet still do the sides of Israel complain of the thorns of Aram: the children of Ahab rue their father's unjust mercy. From an enemy, it is no making question whether of strength or wile. The king of Syria consults with his servants, where to encamp for his greatest advantage: their opinion is not more required than their secrecy. Elisha is a thousand scouts: he sends word to the king of Israel of the projects, of the removes of his enemy. More than once had Jehoram saved both his life and his host by these close admonitions: it is well, that in something yet a prophet may be obeyed. What strange state-service was this which Elisha did, besides the spiritual! The king, the people of Israel, owe themselves and their safety to a despised prophet. The man of God knew and felt them idolaters; yet how careful and vigilant is he for their rescue! If they were bad, yet they were his own: if they were bad, yet not all; God had his number amongst their worst: if they were bad, yet the Syrians were worse. The Israelites mis-worshipped the true God; the Syrians worshipped a false; that, if it were possible, he might win them, he will preserve them; and, if they will needs be wanting to God, yet Elisha will not be wanting to them. Their impiety shall not make him undutiful.

There cannot be a juster cause of displeasure, than the disclosing of those secret counsels which are laid up in our ear, in our breast. The king of Syria, not without reason, stomachs this supposed treachery. What prince can bear that an adverse power should have a party, a pensionary, in his own court? How famous was Elisha, even in foreign regions! Besides Naaman, others of the Syrian nobility take notice of the miraculous faculties of this prophet of Israel. He is accused for this secret intelligence: no words can escape him, though spoken in the bed-chamber. O Syrian! whosoever thou wert, thou saidst not enough: if thy master do but whisper in thine ear, if he smother his words within his own lips, if he do but speak within his own bosom, Elisha knows it from an infallible information. What counsel is it, O God, that can be hid from thee! what counsel is it that thou wilt hide from thy seer! Even this very word, that accuseth the prophet, is known to the accused. He hears this tale while it is in telling; he hears the plot for his apprehension. How ill do the projects of wicked men hang together! They that confess Elisha knows their secretest words, do yet confer to take him. There are spies upon him, whose espials have moved their anger and admiration. He is described to be in Dothan, a small town of Manasseh. A whole army is sent hither to surprise him: the opportunity of the night is chosen for the exploit. There shall be no want either in the number, or valour, or secrecy of these conspired troops: and now, when they have fully girt in the village with a strong and exquisite siege, they make themselves sure of Elisha, and please themselves to think how they have encaged the miserable prophet; how they should take him at unawares in his bed, in the midst of a secure dream; how they should carry him fettered to their king; what thanks they should have for so welcome a prisoner.

The successor of Gehazi riseth early in the morning, and seeth all the city encompassed with a fearful host of foot, horse, chariots: his eyes could meet with nothing but woods of pikes, and walls of harness, and lustre of metals; and now he runs in affrighted to his master: "Alas, my master, what shall we do?" He had day enough to see they were enemies that environed them; to see himself helpless and desperate; and hath only so much life left in him, as to lament himself to the partner of his misery. He cannot flee from his new master, if he would; he runs to him with a woful clamour: "Alas, my master, what shall we do?"

O the undaunted courage of faith! Elisha sees all this, and sits in his chamber so secure, as if these had only been the guard of Israel, for his safe protection. It is a hard precept that he gives his servant: "Fear not." As well might he have bid him not to see when he saw, as not to fear when he saw so dreadful a spectacle. The operations of the senses are no less certain than those of the affections, where the objects are no less proper. But the task is easy, if the next word may find belief: "For there are more with us than with them." Multitude, and other outward probabilities, do both lead the confidence of natural hearts, and fix it. It is for none but David to say, "I will not be afraid of ten thousands of people, that have set themselves against me round about." Flesh and blood riseth and falleth, according to the proportion of the strength or weakness of apparent means.

Elisha's man looked about him; yet his master prays, "Lord, open his eyes, that he may see." Naturally we see not while we do see; every thing is so seen as it is: bodily eyes discern bodily objects; only spiritual can see the things of God. Some men want both eyes and light: Elisha's servant had eyes, wanted illumination; no sooner were his eyes open, than he saw the mountain full of horses and chariots of fire round about Elisha. They were there before; neither doth Elisha pray that those troops may be gathered, but that they may be seen: not till now were they descried. Invisible armies guard the servants of God, while they seem most forsaken of earthly aid, most exposed to certain dangers. If the eyes of our faith be as open as those of our sense, to see angels as well as Syrians, we cannot be appalled with the most unequal terms of hostility. Those blessed spirits are ready either to rescue our bodies, or to carry up our souls to blessedness; whichsoever shall be enjoined by their Maker, there is just comfort in both, in either.

Both these chariots that came to fetch Elijah, and those that came to defend Elisha, were fiery. God is not less lovely to his own in the midst of his judgments, than he is terrible to his enemies in the demonstration of his mercies. Thus guarded, it is no marvel if Elisha dare walk forth into the midst of the Syrians. Not one of those heavenly presidiaries struck a stroke for the prophet, neither doth he require their blows; only he turns his prayer to his God, and and says, " Smite this people, I pray thee, with blindness." With no other than deadly intentions did those Aramites come down to Elisha, yet doth he not say, Smite them with the sword, but, " Smite them with blindness." All the evil he wisheth to them is their repentance: there was no way to see their error, but by blindness. He that prayed for the opening of his servant's eyes to see his safeguard, prays for the blinding of his enemies, that they might not see to do hurt.

As the eyes of Elisha's servant were so shut, that they saw not the angels when they saw the Syrians; so the eyes of the Syrians shall be likewise shut, that, when they see the man, they shall not see the prophet. To all other objects their eyes are clear, only to Elisha they shall be blind; blind, not through darkness, but through misknowledge: they shall see and mistake both the person and place. He that made the senses, can either hold or delude them at pleasure: how easily can he offer to the sight other representations than those which arise from the visible matter, and make the heart to believe them!

Justly now might Elisha say, "This is not the way, neither is this the city," wherein Elisha shall be descried. He was in Dothan, but not as Elisha; he shall not be found but in Samaria; neither can they have any guide to him but himself. No sooner are they come into the streets of Samaria, than their eyes have leave to know both the place and the prophet. The first sight they have of themselves is in the trap of Israel, in the jaws of death. Those stately palaces, which they now wonder at unwillingly, carry no resemblance to them but of their graves. Every Israelite seems an executioner, every house a jail, every beam a gibbet: and now they look upon Elisha, transformed from their guide to their common murderer, with horror and paleness. It is most just with God to entangle the plotters of wickedness in their own snare.

How glad is a mortal enemy to snatch at all advantages of revenge! Never did the king of Israel see a more pleasing sight, than so many Syrian throats at his mercy; and, as loath to lose so fair a day, as if his fingers itched to be dipt in blood, he says, " My father, shall I smite them, shall I smite them?" The repetition argued desire, the compellation reverence. Not without allowance of a prophet, would the king of

Israel lay his hand upon an enemy, so miraculously trained home. His heart was still foul with idolatry, yet would he not taint his hand with forbidden blood. Hypocrisy will be still scrupulous in something; and in some awful restraints, is a perfect counterfeit of conscience.

The charitable prophet soon gives an angry prohibition of slaughter: "Thou shalt not smite them : wouldst thou smite those whom thou hast taken captive with thy sword and with thy bow?" as if he had said, These are God's captives, not thine; and if they were thine own, their blood could not be shed without cruelty. Though in the hot chases of war, executions may be justifiable ; yet in the coolness of deliberation, it can be no other than inhuman, to take those lives which have been yielded to mercy. But here, thy bow and thy sword are guiltless of the success; only a strange providence of the Almighty hath cast them into thine hands, whom neither thy force nor thy fraud could have compassed. If it be victory thou aimest at, overcome them with kindness ; " Set bread and water before them, that they may eat and drink." O noble revenge of Elisha, to feast his persecutors! to provide a table for those who had provided a grave for him! These Syrians came to Dothan full of bloody purposes, to Elisha : he sends them from Samaria full of good cheer and jollity. Thus, thus should a prophet punish his pursuers. No vengeance but this is heroical, and fit for Christian imitation. " If thine enemy hunger, give him bread to eat ; if he thirst, give him water to drink ; for thou shalt heap coals of fire upon his head ; and the Lord shall reward thee. Be not overcome with evil, but overcome evil with good."

The king of Israel hath done that by his feast, which he could not have done by his sword. The bands of Syria will no more come by way of ambush or incursion into the bounds of Israel. Never did a charitable act go away without the retribution of a blessing. In doing some good to our enemies, we do most good to ourselves. God cannot but love in us this imitation of his mercy, who bids his sun shine and his rain fall where he is most provoked; and that love is never fruitless.

CONTEMPLATION X. — THE FAMINE OF SAMARIA RELIEVED.

Not many good turns are written in marble : soon have these Syrians forgotten the merciful beneficence of Israel. After the forbearance of some hostile inroad, all the forces of Syria are mustered against Jehoram. That very Samaria, which had relieved the distressed Aramites, is by the Aramites besieged, and is famished by those whom it had fed. The famine within the walls was more terrible than the sword without. Their worst enemy was shut within, and could not be dislodged of their own bowels. Whither hath the idolatry of Israel brought them! Before they had been scourged with war, with drought, with dearth, as with a single cord; they remain incorrigible : and now God twists two of these bloody lashes together, and galls them even to death : there needs no other executioners than their own maws. Those things, which in their nature were not edible, at least to an Israelite, were now both dear and dainty. The ass was, besides the untoothsomeness, an impure creature. That which the law of ceremonies had made unclean, the law of necessity had made delicate and precious: the bones of so carrion a head could not be picked for less than four hundred pieces of silver. Neither was this scarcity of victuals only, but of all other necessaries for human use: that the belly might not complain alone, the whole man was equally pinched.

The king of Israel is neither exempted from the judgment, nor yet yields under it. He walks upon the walls of his Samaria, to oversee the watches set, the engines ready, the guards changed, together with the posture of the enemy; when a woman cries to him out of the city, " Help, my lord, O king." Next to God, what refuge have we in all our necessities, but his anointed ? Earthly sovereignty can aid us in the case of the injustice of men, but what can it do against the judgments of God ? " If the Lord do not help thee, whence shall I help thee? out of the barn-floor, or out of the wine press?" Even the greatest powers must stoop to afflictions in themselves : how should they be able to prevent them in others ? To sue for aid, where is an utter impotence of redress, is but to upbraid the weakness, and aggravate the misery, of those whom we implore. Jehoram mistakes the suit : the supplicant calls to him for a woful piece of justice. Two mothers have agreed to eat their sons : the one hath yielded hers to be boiled and eaten ; the other, after she had taken her part of so prodigious a banquet, withdraws her child, and hides him from the knife. Hunger and envy make the plaintiff importunate; and now she craves the benefit of royal justice. She that made the first motion, withholds her part of the bargain, and flies from that promise, whose trust had made this mother childless. O the direful effects of famine, that turns off all respects of nature, and gives no place to horror, causing the tender mother to lay her hands, yea her teeth, upon the fruit of her own body, and to receive that into her stomach, which she hath brought forth of her womb! What should Jehoram do? The match was monstrous; the challenge was just, yet unnatural. This complainant had purchased one half of the living child, by the one half of hers dead. The mother of the surviving infant is pressed by covenant, by hunger; restrained by nature. To force a mother to deliver up her child to voluntary slaughter, had been cruel; to force a debitor to pay a confessed arrearage, seemed but equal. If the remaining child be not dressed for food, this mother of the devoured child is both robbed and famished: if he be, innocent blood is shed by authority. It is no marvel if the question astonished the judge; not so much for the difficulty of the demand, as the horror of the occasion. To what lamentable distress did Jehoram find his people driven! Not without cause did the king of Israel rend his garments, and show his sackcloth; well might he see his people branded with that ancient curse, which God had denounced against the rebellious: "The Lord shall bring a nation against thee of a fierce countenance, which shall not regard the person of the old, nor show favour to the young; and he shall besiege thee in all thy gates; and thou shalt eat the fruit of thine own body, the flesh of thy sons, and of thy daughters. The tender and delicate woman, her eyes shall be evil towards her young one that cometh out between her feet, and toward the children which she shall bear, for she shall eat them for want of all things, secretly in the siege and straitness." He mourns for the plague; he mourns not for the cause of this plague, his sin, and theirs: I find his sorrow, I find not his repentance. The worst man may grieve for his smart; only the good heart grieves for his offence. Instead of being penitent, Jehoram is furious, and turns his rage from his sins, against the prophet: "God do so to me, and more also, if the head of Elisha, the son of Shaphat, shall stand on him this day." Alas! what hath the righteous done? Perhaps Elisha, that we may imagine some colours of this displeasure, forethreatened this judgment, but they deserved it: perhaps he might have averted it by his prayers; their unrepentance disabled him: perhaps he persuaded Jehoram to hold out the siege, though through much hardness he foresaw the deliverance. In all this, how hath Elisha forfeited his head? All Israel did not afford a head so guiltless, as this that was destined to slaughter. This is the fashion of the world: the lewd blame the innocent, and will revenge their own sins upon others' uprightness.

In the midst of all this sad estate of Samaria, and those storms of Jehoram, the prophet sits quietly in his own house, amongst his holy consorts, bewailing, no doubt, both the sins and misery of their people, and prophetically conferring of the issue; when suddenly God reveals to him the bloody intent and message of Jehoram, and he at once reveals it to his fellows: "See ye how this son of a murderer hath sent to take away mine head?" O the inimitable liberty of a prophet! The same God that showed him his danger, suggested his words: he may be bold, where we must be awful. Still is Naboth's blood laid in Jehoram's dish; the foul act of Ahab blemisheth his posterity; and now, when the son threatens violence to the innocent, murder is objected to him as hereditary.

He, that foresaw his own peril, provides for his safety: " Shut the door, and hold him fast at the door." No man is bound to tender his throat to an unjust stroke: this bloody commission was prevented by a prophetical foresight. The same eye that saw the executioner coming to smite him, saw also the king hastening after him to stay the blow: the prophet had been no other than guilty of his own blood, if he had not reserved himself awhile, for the rescue of authority. O the inconstancy of carnal hearts! It was not long since Jehoram could say to Elisha, " My father, shall I smite them?" now he is ready to smite him as an enemy, whom he honoured as a father; yet again his lips had no sooner given sentence of death against the prophet, than his feet stir to recal it.

It should seem that Elisha, upon the challenges and expostulations of Jehoram's messenger, had sent a persuasive message to the king of Israel, yet awhile to wait patiently upon God for his deliverance. The discontented prince flies off in an impotent anger: " Behold, this evil is of the Lord, what should I wait for the Lord any longer?" O the desperate resolutions of impatient minds! They have stinted God both for his time and his measure: if he exceed either, they either turn their backs upon him, or fly in his face. The position was true; the inference deadly. All that evil was of the Lord: they deserved it; he sent it. What then? It should have been therefore argued, He that sent it can remove it: I will wait upon his mercy, under whose justice I suffer. Impatience and distrust shall but aggravate my judgment: "It is the Lord, let him do what he will." But now to despair because God is just, to defy mercy because it lingers, to reject God for correction, it is a presumptuous madness, an impious pettishness.

Yet, in spite of all these provocations, both of king and people, Elisha hath good news for Jehoram: "Thus saith the Lord, To-morrow, about this time, shall a measure of fine flour be sold for a shekel, and two measures of barley for a shekel, in the gate of Samaria." Miserable Israel now sees an end of this hard trial; one day's patience shall free them both of the siege and famine. God's deliverances may overstay our expectation, not the due period of his own counsels. O infinite mercy! when man says, No longer, God says, "To-morrow," as if he would condescend where he might judge, and would please them who deserve nothing but punishment. The word seemed not more comfortable than incredible: "A lord, on whose hand the king leaned, answered the man of God, and said, Behold, if the Lord would make windows in heaven, might this thing be." Prophecies, before they be fulfilled, are riddles; no spirit can read them, but that by which they are delivered. It is a foolish and injurious infidelity, to question a possibility, where we know the message is God's: how easy is it for that Omnipotent hand to effect those things which surpass all the reach of human conceit! Had God intended a miraculous multiplication, was it not as easy for him to increase the corn or meal of Samaria, as the widow's oil? was it not as easy for him to give plenty of victuals, without opening the windows of heaven, as to give plenty of water, without wind or rain? The Almighty hates to be distrusted. This peer of Israel shall rue his unbelief: "Behold, thou shalt see it with thine eyes, but shalt not eat thereof." The sight shall be yielded for conviction; the fruition shall be denied for punishment. Well is that man worthy to want the benefit which he would not believe: who can pity to see infidelity excluded from the blessings of earth, from the glory of heaven?

How strange a choice doth God make of the intelligencers of so happy a change! Four lepers sit at the entering of the gate: they see nothing but death before them; famine within the walls, the enemy without. The election is woful: at last they resolve upon the lesser evil; famine is worse than the Syrian: in the famine there is certainty of perishing, amongst the Syrians hazard; perhaps the enemy may have some pity, hunger hath none; and, were the death equally certain, it were more easy to die by the sword, than by famine. Upon this deliberation they come down into the Syrian camp, to find either speed of mercy or despatch. Their hunger would not give them respite till morning: by twilight are they fallen upon the uttermost tents: "Behold, there was no man." They marvel at the silence and solitude: they look and listen; the noise of their own feet affrighted them; their guilty hearts supplied the Syrians, and expected fearfully, those which were as fearfully fled. How easily can the Almighty confound the power of the strong, the policy of the wise! God puts a panic terror into the hearts of the proud Syrians; he makes them hear a noise of chariots, and a noise of horses, even the noise of a great host. They say one to another, "Lo, the king of Israel hath hired against us the kings of the Hittites and the kings of the Egyptians to come upon us!" They rise therefore in a confused rout, and, leaving all their substance behind them, flee for their lives. Not long before, Elisha's servant saw chariots and horses, but heard none: now, these Syrians hear chariots and horses, but see none: that sight comforted his heart, this sound dismayed theirs. The Israelites heard no noise within the walls; the lepers heard no noise without the gates; only the Syrians heard this noise in their camp. What a scorn doth God put upon these presumptuous Aramites! he will not vouchsafe to use any substantial stratagem against them; nothing but an empty sound shall scatter them, and send them home empty of substance, laden with shame, half dead with fear: the very horses, that might have hastened their flight, are left tied in their tents; their very garments are a burden; all is left behind, save their bodies, and those breathless for speed.

Doubtless these Syrians knew well to what miserable exigents the inclosed Israelites were brought, by their siege; and now made full account to sack and ransack their Samaria; already had they divided, and swallowed the prey; when suddenly God puts them into a ridiculous confusion, and sends them to seek safety in their heels: no booty is now in price with them but their life, and happy is he that can run fastest.

Thus the Almighty laughs at the designs of insolent men, and shuts up their counsels in shame.

The fear of the four lepers began now to give way to security: they fill their bellies, and hide their treasures, and pass from one tent to another, in a fastidious choice of the best commodities; they, who erewhile would have held it happiness enough to have been blessed with a crust, now wantonly rove for dainties, and from necessity leap into excess.

How far self-love carries us in all our actions, even to the neglect of the public! Not till their own bellies, and hands, and eyes, were filled, did these lepers think of imparting this news to Israel. At last, when themselves are glutted, they begin to remember the hunger of their brethen, and now they find room for remorse: " We do not well; this day is a day of good tidings, and we hold our peace." Nature teaches us, that it is an injury to engross blessings, and so to mind the private, as if we had no relation to a community. We are worthy to be shut out of the city gates for lepers, if the respects to the public good do not oversway with us in all our desires, in all our demeanour; and well may we, with these covetous lepers, fear a mischief upon ourselves, if we shall wilfully conceal blessings from others.

The conscience of this wrong and danger sends back the lepers into the city; they call to the porters, and soon transmit the news to the king's household. The king of Israel complains not to have his sleep broken with such intelligence; he ariseth in the night, and not contemning good news, though brought by lepers, consults with his servants of the business.

We cannot be too jealous of the intentions of an enemy. Jehoram wisely suspects this flight of the Syrians to be but simulatory and politic, only to draw Israel out of their city for the spoil of both. There may be more peril in the back of an enemy than in his face: the cruelest slaughters have been in retiring. Easily therefore is the king persuaded to adventure some few forlorn scouts for further assurance. The word of Elisha is out of his head, out of his heart, else there had been no place for this doubt. Timorous hearts never think themselves sure; those that have no faith, had need of much sense.

Those few horses that remain are sent forth for discovery; they find nothing but monuments of frightfulness, pledges of security. Now Israel dares issue forth to the prey: there, as if the Syrians had come thither to enrich them, they find granaries, wardrobes, treasures, and whatever may serve either for use or ostentation. Every Israelite goes away filled, laden, wearied with the wealthy spoil.

As scarcity breeds dearth, so plenty cheapness. To-day a measure of fine flour is lower rated, than yesterday of dung.

The distrustful peer of Israel sees this abundance, according to the word of the prophet, but enjoys it not. He sees this plenty can come in at the gate, though the windows of heaven be not open. The gate is his charge: the famished Israelites press in upon him, and bear him down in the throng. Extreme hunger hath no respect to greatness. Not their rudeness, but his own unbelief, hath trampled him under feet. He that abased the power of God by his distrust, is abased worthily to the heels of the multitude. Faith exalts a man above his own sphere; infidelity depresses him into the dust, into hell: " He that believes not, is condemned already."

BOOK XX.

CONTEMPLATION I.—THE SHUNAMITE SUING TO JEHORAM; ELISHA CONFERRING WITH HAZAEL.

How royally hath Elisha paid the Shunamite for his lodging! To him already she owes the life of her son, both given and restored; and now again, after so many years, as might well have worn out the memory of so small a courtesy, herself, her son, her family, owe their lives to so thankful a guest. That table and bed, and stool and candlestick, were well bestowed. That candlestick repaid her the light of her future life and condition, that table the means of maintenance, that stool a seat of safe abode, that bed a quiet rest from the common calamities of her nation. He is a niggard to himself that scants his beneficence to a prophet, whose very cold water shall not go unrewarded. Elijah preserved the Sareptan from famine; Elisha the Shunamite: he, by provision of oil and meal; this, by premonition: " Arise, and go, thou and thine household, and sojourn wheresoever thou canst sojourn." The Sareptan was poor, and driven to extremes; therefore the prophet provides for her from hand to mouth; the Shunamite was wealthy; and therefore the prophet sends her to provide for herself. The same goodness, that relieves our necessity, leaves our competency to the hand of our own counsel; in the one he will make use of his own power, in the other of our providence.

The very prophet advises this holy client to leave the bounds of the church, and to seek life, where she should not find religion. Extremity is for the time a just dispensation, with some common rules of our outward demeanour and motions, even from better to worse. All Israel and Judah shall be famished: the body can be preserved nowhere, but where the soul shall want. Sometimes the conveniences of the soul must yield to bodily necessities. Wantonness and curiosity can find no advantage from that which is done out of the power of need.

It is a long famine that shall afflict Israel. He, upon whom the spirit of Elijah was doubled, doubled the judgment inflicted by his master. Three years and a half did Israel gasp under the drought of Elijah: seven years' dearth shall it suffer under Elisha. The trials of God are many times not more grievous for their sharpness, than for their continuance.

This scarcity shall not come alone: God shall call for it: whatever be the second cause, he is the first. The executioners of the Almighty (such are his judgments) stand ready waiting upon his just throne; and do no sooner receive the watch-word, than they fly upon the world, and plague it for sin. Only the cry of our sins moves God to call for vengeance; and, if God once call, it must come. How oft, how earnestly, are we called to repentance, and stir not! The messengers of God's wrath fly forth at the least beck, and fulfil the will of his revenge upon those whose obedience would not fulfil the will of his command.

After so many proofs of fidelity, the Shunamite cannot distrust the prophet; not staying, therefore, to be convicted by the event, she removes her family into the land of the Philistines. No nation was more opposite to Israel, none more worthily odious; yet there doth the Shunamite seek and find shelter: even the shade of those trees that are unwholesome may keep us from a storm. Everywhere will God find room for his own. The fields of the Philistines flourish, while the soil of Israel yields nothing but weeds and barrenness. Not that Israel was more sinful, but that the sin of Israel was more intolerable. The offers of grace are so many aggravations of wickedness. In equal offences, those do justly smart more, who are more obliged. No pestilence is so contagious as that which hath taken the purest air.

These Philistine neighbours would never have endured themselves to be pestered with foreigners, especially Israelites, whom they hated, besides religion, for their usurpation: neither were they, in all likelihood, pressed with multitude. The rest of Israel were led on with hopes, presuming upon the amends of the next harvest, till their want grew desperate and irremediable; only the forewarned Shunamite prevents the mischief: now she finds what it is to have a prophet her friend. Happy are those souls, that upon all occasions consult with God's seers: they shall be freed from the plagues wherein the secure blindness of others is heedlessly overtaken.

Seven years had this Shunamite sojourned in Palestine; now she returns to her own, and is excluded. She, that found harbour among Philistines, finds oppression and violence among Israelites: those of her kindred, taking advantage of her absence, had shared her possessions. How oft doth it fall out, that the worst enemies of a man are those of his own house! All went by contraries with this Shunamite: in the famine she had enough, in the common plenty she was scanted: Philistines were kind unto her, Israelites cruel. Both our fears and our hopes do not seldom disappoint us. It is safe trusting to that stay which can never fail us, who can easily provide us both of friendship in Palestine, and of justice in Israel. We may not judge of the religion by particular actions: a very Philistine may be merciful, when an Israelite is unjust; the person may be faulty, when the profession is holy.

It was not long since the prophet made that friendly offer to the Shunamite, out of the desire of a thankful requital: "What is to be done for thee? wouldst thou be spoken for to the king, or to the captain of the host?" and she answered, "I dwell among my brethren." Little did she then think of this injurious measure, else she might have said, I dwell among my enemies, I dwell among robbers. It is like they were then friendly, who were now cruel and oppressive. There is no trust to be reposed in flesh and blood. How should their favours be constant, who are, in their nature and disposition, variable? It is the surest way to rely on Him who is ever like himself, the measure of whose love is eternity.

Whither should the Shunamite go to complain of her wrong, but to the court? There is no other refuge of the oppressed, but public authority. All justice is derived from sovereignty: kings are not called gods for nothing; they do both sentence and execute for the Almighty.

Doubtless now the poor Shunamite thought of the courteous proffer of Elisha, and, missing a friend at the court, is glad to be the presenter of her own petition.

How happily doth God contrive all events for the good of his! This supplicant shall fall upon that instant for her suit, when the king shall be talking with Gehazi, when Gehazi shall be talking of her to the king: the words of Gehazi, the thoughts of the king, the desires of the Shunamite, shall be all drawn together, by the wise providence of God, into the centre of one moment, that his oppressed servant might receive a speedy justice. O the infinite wisdom, power, mercy of our God, that insensibly orders all our ways, as to his own holy purposes, so to our best advantage!

What doth Jehoram, the king, talking with Gehazi the leper? That very presence was an eye-sore.

But if the cohabitation with the infectious were forbidden, yet not the conference. Certainly I begin to think of some goodness in both these. Had there not been some goodness in Jehoram, he had not taken pleasure to hear, even from a leprous mouth, the miraculous acts and praises of God's prophet. Had there not been some goodness in Gehazi, he had not, after so fearful an infliction of judgment, thus ingenuously recounted the praises of his severe master. He, that told that dear-bought lie to the prophet, tells now all truths of the prophet to the king. Perhaps his leprosy had made him clean; if so, happy was it for him that his forehead was white with the disease, if his soul became hereupon white with repentance: but we may well know that the desire or report of historical truths doth not always argue grace. Still Jehoram, after the inquiry of the prophet's miracles, continues in idolatry. He, that was curious to hearken after the wonders of Elisha, is not careful to follow his doctrine: therefore are Gehazi and the Shunamite met before him, that he may be convicted, who will not be reformed. Why was it else, that the presence of the persons should thus unexpectedly make good the relation, if God had not meant the inexcusableness of Jehoram, while he must needs say within himself, Thus potent is the prophet of that God whom I obey not. Were not Elisha's the true God, how could he work such wonders? and if he be the true God, why is he not mine? But what—shall I change Ahab's god for Jehoshaphat's? No; I cannot deny the miracles, I will not admit of the author: let Elisha be powerful, I will be constant. O wretched Jehoram! how much better had it been for thee never to have seen the face of Gehazi, and the son of the Shunamite, than to go away unmoved with the vengeance of leprosy in the one, with the merciful resuscitation of the other! Therefore is thy judgment fearfully aggravated, because thou wouldst not yield to what thou couldst not oppose. Had not Ahab's obdurateness been propagated to his son, so powerful demonstrations of divine power could not have been uneffectual. Wicked hearts are so much worse, by how much God is better: this anvil is the harder by being continually beaten upon, whether with judgments or mercy.

Yet this good use will God have made of this report, and this presence, that the poor Shunamite shall have justice. That son, whose life was restored, shall have his inheritance revived: his estate shall fare the better for Elisha's miracles. How much more will our merciful God second his own blessings, when the favours of unjust men are therefore drawn to us, because we have been the subjects of divine beneficence!

It was a large and full award, that this occurrence drew from the king: "Restore all that was hers, and all the fruits of the field, since the day that she left the land, even until now." Not the present possession only is given her, but the arrearages.

Nothing hinders but that outward justice may stand with gross idolatry. The widow may thank Elisha for this: his miracle wrought still, and puts this new life in her dead estate; his absence did that for the preservation of life, which his presence did for the restoring it from death. She that was so ready to expostulate with the man of God upon the loss of her son, might, perhaps, have been as ready to impute the loss of her estate to his advice. Now, that for his sake she is enriched with her own, how doth she bless God for so happy a guest! When we have forgotten our own good turns, God remembers and crowns them. Let us do good to all while we have time, but especially to the household of faith.

Could Israel have been sensible of their own condition, it was no small unhappiness to lose the presence of Elisha. Whether for the idolatries, or for the famine of Israel, the prophet is gone into Syria, no doubt Naaman welcomed him thither, and now would force upon him thanks for his cure, which the man of God would not receive at home.

How famous is he now grown that was taken from the team! His name is not confined to his own nation: foreign countries take notice of it, and kings are glad to listen after him, and woo him with presents. Benhadad, the king of Syria, whose counsels he had detected, rejoiceth to hear of his presence; and now, as having forgotten that he had sent a whole host to besiege the prophet in Dothan, sends an honourable messenger to him, laden with the burden of forty camels, to consult with this oracle concerning his sickness and recovery.

This Syrian, belike, in his distress, dares not trust to his own gods; but, having had good proof of the power of the God of Israel, both in Naaman's cure, and in the miraculous defeats of his greatest forces, is glad to send to that servant of God whom he had persecuted. Wicked men are not the same in health and in sickness: their affliction is worthy of the thanks, if they be well-minded, not themselves.

Doubtless the errand of Benhadad was not only to inquire of the issue of his disease, but to require the prayers of the prophet for a good issue. Even the worst man doth so love himself, that he can be content to make a beneficial use of those instruments whose goodness he hateth.

Hazael, the chief peer of Syria, is designed to this message: the wealth of his present strives with the humility of his carriage and speech: "Thy son, Benhadad, king of Syria, hath sent me to thee, saying, Shall I recover of this disease?" Not long since, Jehoram, king of Israel, had said to Elisha, "My father, shall I smite them?" and now Benhadad, king of Syria, says, "My father, shall I recover?" Lo, how this poor Meholathite hath kings to his sons! How great is the honour of God's prophets with pagans, with princes! Who can be but confounded to see evangelical prophets despised by the meanest Christians?

It is more than a single answer that the prophet returns to this message: one answer he gives to Benhadad that sent it, another he gives to Hazael that brings it: that to Benhadad is, "Thou mayest surely recover;" that to Hazael, "The Lord hath showed me that he shall surely die." What shall we say then? Is there a lie, or an equivocation in the holy mouth of the prophet? God forbid. It is one thing, what shall be the nature and issue of the disease; another thing, what may outwardly befall the person of Benhadad: the question is moved of the former, whereto the answer is direct, The disease is not mortal; but, withal, an intimation is given to the bearer, of an event beyond the reach of his demand, which he may know, but either need not, or may not return: "The Lord hath showed me that he shall surely die," by another means, though not by the disease.

The seer of God descries more in Hazael, than he could see in himself; he fixes his eyes, therefore, stedfastly in the Syrian's face, as one that in those lines read the bloody story of his life.

Hazael blushes; Elisha weeps. The intention of those eyes did not so much amaze Hazael, as the tears: as yet, he was not guilty to himself of any wrong that might strain out this juice of sorrow: "Why weepeth my lord?"

The prophet fears not to foretell Hazael all the villanies which he should once do to Israel; how he should fire their forts, and kill their young men, and rip the mothers, and dash their children. I marvel not now at the tears of those eyes, which foresaw this miserable vastation of the inheritance of God; the very mention whereof is abhorred of the future author: "What, is thy servant a dog, that I should do this great thing?" They are savage cruelties whereof thou speakest: it were more fit for me to weep, that thou shouldst repute me so brutish: I should no less condemn myself for a beast, if I could suspect my own degeneration so far. Wicked men are carried into those heights of impiety, which they could not, in their good mood, have possibly believed: nature is subject to favourable opinions of herself, and will rather mistrust a prophet of God, than her own good disposition. How many, from honest beginnings, have risen to incredible licentiousness! whose lives are now such, that it were as hard for a man to believe they had ever been good, as to have persuaded them once they should prove so desperately ill.

To give some overture unto Hazael of the opportunity of this ensuing mischief, the prophet foretells him, from God, that he shall be the king of Syria.

He that shows the event, doth not appoint the means. Far was it from the spirit of God's prophet to set or encourage a treason: while he said, therefore, "Thou shalt be king of Syria," he said not, Go home and kill thy master. The wicked ambition of Hazael draws this damnable conclusion out of holy premises; and now, having fed the hopes of his sovereign with the expectation of recovery, the next day he smothers his master. The impotent desire of rule brooks no delay. Had not Hazael been gracelessly cruel, after he had received this prediction of the seer, he should have patiently waited for the crown of Syria, till lawful means had set it upon his head: now he will, by a close execution, make way to the throne. A wet cloth hath stopt the mouth of his sick sovereign: no noise is heard; the carcass is fair; who can complain of any thing but the disease?

O Hazael, thou shalt not thus easily stop the mouth of thine own conscience: that shall call thee traitor, even in thy chair of state, and shall check all thy royal triumphs with—" Thou hast founded thy throne in blood!" I am deceived if this wet cloth shall not wipe thy lips in thy jolliest feasts, and make thy best morsels unsavoury. Sovereignty is painful upon the fairest terms; but, upon treachery and murder, tormenting. Woful is the case of that man, whose public cares are aggravated with private guiltiness; and happy is he that can enjoy a little with the peace of an honest heart.

CONTEMPLATION II.—JEHU WITH JEHORAM AND JEZEBEL.

YET Hazael began his cruelty with loss. Ramoth-Gilead is won from him: Jehoram the son hath recovered that which Ahab his father attempted in vain. That city was dear-bought of Israel; it cost the life of Ahab, the blood of Jehoram: those wounds were healed with victory. The king tends his health at Jezreel, while the captains were enjoying and seconding their success at Ramoth.

Old Elisha hath neither cottage nor foot of land, yet, sitting in an obscure corner, he gives order for kingdoms; not by way of authority (this usurpation had been no less proud than unjust), but by way of message from the God of kings: even a mean herald may go on a great errand. The prophets of the gospel have nothing to do but with spiritual kingdoms; to beat down the kingdoms of sin and Satan, to translate souls to the kingdom of heaven.

He that renewed the life of the Shunamite's son, must stoop to age; that block lies in his way to Jehu. The aged prophet employs a speedier messenger, who must also gird up his loins for haste. No common pace will serve us, when we go on God's message: the very loss of minutes may be unrecoverable. This great seer of God well saw a present concurrence of all opportunities. The captains of the host were then readily combined for this exploit; the army was on foot, Jehoram absent: a small delay might have troubled the work: the dispersion of the captains and host, or the presence of the king, might either have defeated or slacked the dispatch. He is prodigal of his success, that is slow in his execution.

The directions of Elisha to the young prophet are full and punctual, whither to go, what to carry, what to do, where to do it, what to say, what speed to make, in his act, in his return. In the businesses of God, it matters not how little is left to our discretion: there is no important business of the Almighty, wherein his precepts are not strict and express: look how much more specialty there is in the charge of God, so much more danger is in the violation.

The young prophet is curiously obedient, in his haste, in his observation and carriage; and finding Jehu, according to Elisha's prediction, set amongst the captains of the host, he singles him forth by a reverent compellation: " I have an errand to thee, O captain." Might not the prophet have stayed till the table had risen, and then have followed Jehu to his lodging? Surely the wisdom of God hath purposely pitched upon this season, that the public view of a sacred messenger, and the hasty evocation of so noted a person to such a secresy, might prepare the hearts of those commanders of Israel to the expectation of some great design.

The inmost room is but close enough for this act. Ere many hours, all Israel shall know that, which yet may not be trusted with one eye: the goodness of God makes wise provision for the safety of his messengers, and, while he employs their service, prevents their dangers.

But how is it that, of all the kings of the ten tribes, none was ever anointed but Jehu? Is it for that the God, who would not countenance the erection of that usurped throne, would countenance the alteration? or is it, that by this visible testimony of divine ordination, the courage of the Israelitish captains might be raised up to second the high and bold attempt of him whom they saw destined from heaven to rule?

Together with the oil of this unction, here was a charge of revenge; a revenge of the blood of the prophets upon Jezebel, of wickedness and idolatry upon Ahab: neither was the extirpation of this lewd family fore-prophesied only to Jehu, but enjoined.

Elijah foretold, and the world expected, some fearful account of the abominable cruelty and impiety of that accursed house; now it is called for, when it seemed forgotten. Ahab shall have no posterity; Jezebel shall have no tomb but the dogs. This woful doom is committed to Jehu's execution.

O the sure, though patient justice of the Almighty! Not only Ahab and Jezebel had been bloody and idolatrous, but Israel was drawn into the partnership of their crimes: all these shall share in the judgment. Elijah's complaint in the cave now receives this late answer: Hazael shall plague Israel, Jehu shall plague the house of Ahab and Jezebel. Elisha's servant thus seconds Elisha's master. When wickedness is ripe in the field, God will not let it shed to grow again, but cuts it up, by a just and seasonable vengeance. Ahab's drooping under the threat, hath put off the judgment from his own days; now it comes, and sweeps away his wife, his issue, and falls heavy upon his subjects. Please yourselves, O ye vain sinners, in the slow pace of vengeance; it will be neither less certain, nor more easy, for the delay; rather it were to pay for that leisure in the extremity.

The prophet hath done his errand, and is gone. Jehu returns to his fellows, with his head not more wet with oil, than busied with thoughts: no doubt, his face bewrayed some inward tumults and distractions of imagination; neither seemed he to return the same he went out. They ask, therefore, "Is all well? Wherefore came this mad fellow to thee?" The prophets of God were to these idolatrous Israelites like comets, who were never seen without the portendment of a mischief. When the priests of their Baal were quietly sacrificing, all was well; but now, when a prophet of God comes in sight, their guiltiness asks, "Is all well?" All would be well but for their sins: they fear not these; they fear the reprover.

Israel was come to a good pass, when the prophets of God went with them for madmen. O ye Baalitish ruffians, whither hath your impiety and profaneness carried you, that ye should thus blaspheme the servants of the living God? Ye, that run on madding after vain idols, tax the sober guides of true worship for madness. Thus it becomes the godless enemies of truth, the heralds of our patience, to miscall our innocence, to revile our most holy profession. What wonder is it that God's messengers are madmen unto those to whom the wisdom of God is foolishness?

The message was not delivered to Jehu for a concealment, but for publication. Silence could not effect the word that was told him, common notice must: "Ye know the man, and his communication." The habit shows you the man, the calling shows you his errand. Even prophets were distinguished by their clothes: their mantle was not the common wear. Why should not this sacred vocation be known by a peculiar attire? These captains had not called him a madman, if they had not known him a prophet: by the man, therefore, they might guess at his message. Prophets do not use to appear, but upon serious errands, whether of reproof, or of prediction.

Nice civilities of denials were not then known to the world: they said, "It is false, tell us now." Amongst these captains, no combat, no unkindness, follows upon a word so rudely familiar.

Jehu needs not tell them that the man was a prophet; he tells them the prophecy of the man, what he had said, what he had done.

Their eyes had no sooner seen the oil, their ears had no sooner heard, "Thus saith the Lord, I have anointed thee king over Israel," than they rise from their seats, as rapt with a tempest, and are hurled into arms: so do they haste to proclaim Jehu, that they scarce stay to snatch up their garments, which they had perhaps left behind them for speed, had they not meant, with these rich habiliments, to garnish a state for their new sovereign, to whom, having now erected an extemporal throne, they do, by the sound of trumpets, give the style of royalty, "Jehu is king."

So much credit hath that mad fellow with these gallants of Israel, that upon his word they will presently adventure their lives, and change the crown. God gives a secret authority to his despised servants, so as they which hate their person, yet reverence their truth: even very scorners cannot but believe them. If, when the prophets of the gospel tell us of a spiritual kingdom, they be distrusted of those which profess to observe them, how shameful is the disproportion! how just shall their judgment be!

Yet I cannot say whether mere obedience to the prophet, or personal dislikes of Jehoram, or partial respects to Jehu, drew the captains of Israel. The will of God may be done thanklessly, when, fulfilling the substance, we fail of the intention, and err in circumstance.

Only Ramoth is conscious of this sudden inauguration: this new princedom yet reaches no further than the sound of the trumpet. Jehu is no less subtile than valiant: he knew, that the notice of this unexpected change might work a busy and dangerous resistance; he therefore gives order, that no messenger of the news may prevent his personal execution, that so he might surprise Jehoram in his palace of Jezreel, whether tending his late wounds, or securely feasting his friends, and dreaming of nothing less than danger; and might be seen and felt at once. Secresy is the safest guard of any design; disclosed projects are either frustrated, or made needlessly difficult.

Neither is Jehu more close than swift: that very trumpet, with the same wind, sounds his march; from the top of the stairs, he steps down into his chariot. That man means to speed, who can be at once reserved in his own counsels, and resolute and quick in his performances.

Who could but pity the unhappy and unseasonable visitation of the grandchild of Jehoshaphat, were it not that he was degenerated into the family of Ahab? Ahaziah king of Judah is come to visit Jehoram king of Israel; the knowledge of his late received wounds hath drawn thither this kind, ill-matched ally. He, who was partner of the war, cannot but be a visitor of the wounds.

The two kings are in the height of their compliment and entertainments, when the watchman of the tower of Jezreel espies a troop afar off. For ought was known, there was nothing but peace in all the land of Israel; and Judah was now so combined with it, that both their kings were feasting under one roof; yet, in the midst of their supposed safety, the watch-tower is not unfurnished with heedy eyes. No security of peace can free wise governors from a careful suspicion of what may come, and a providence against the worst. Even while we know of no enemies, the watch-tower of due intelligence may not be empty.

In vain are dangers foreseen, if they be not premonished; it is all one to have a blind and a mute watchman: this speaks what he sees, "I see a company."

Doubtless Jehoram's head was now full of thoughts; neither knew he what construction to put upon this approaching troop. Perhaps the Syrians, he thinks, may have recovered Ramoth, and chased the garrison of Israel: neither can he imagine whether these should be hostile victors, or vanquished subjects, or conspiring rebels. Every main this rout was dreadful. O Jehoram! thou beginnest thy fears too late: hadst thou been afraid to provoke the God of Israel, thine innocency had yielded no room to these terrors.

A horseman is despatched, to discover the meaning of this descried concourse. He meets them, and inquires of peace; but receives a short answer: "What hast thou to do with peace? turn thee behind me." A second is addressed with the same success. Both attend the train of Jehu, instead of returning. Indeed, it is not for private persons to hope to rectify the public affairs, when they are grown to a height of disorder, and from thence to a ripeness of miscarriage. Sooner may a well-meaning man hurt himself, than redress the common danger.

These messengers were now within the mercy of a multitude: had they but endeavoured to retire, they had perished as wilfully as vainly. Whosoever will be striving against the torrent of a just judgment, must needs be carried down in the stream. Sometimes there is as much wisdom in yielding, as courage in resistance.

Had this troop been far off, the watchman could not have descried the arrival of the messengers, their turning behind, the manner of the march. Jehu was a noted captain; his carriage and motion were observed more full of fire than his fellows: "The driving is like Jehu's, for he driveth furiously." God makes choice of fit instruments, as of mercy, so of revenge. These spirits were needful for so tragical a scene as was now preparing in Israel.

Jehoram and Ahaziah, as nettled with this forced patience of expectation, can no longer keep their seats, but will needs hasten their chariots, and fetch that costly satisfaction, which would not be sent, but given.

They are infatuated which shall perish, otherwise Jehoram had been warned enough by the forcible retention of his messengers, to expect nothing but an enemy. A friend or a subject could not have been unwilling to be known, to be looked for. Now, forgetting his wounds, he will go to fetch death.

Yet when he sees Jehu, whom he left a subject, hopes strive with his doubts: "Is it peace, Jehu?" What may be the reason of this sudden journey? is the army foiled by the Syrians? is Ramoth recovered? or hath the flight of the enemy left thee no further work? or is some other ill news guilty of thy haste? What means this unwished presence and return?

There needs no stay for an answer: the very face of Jehu, and those sparkling eyes of his, speak fury and death to Jehoram, which yet his tongue angrily seconds: "What peace, so long as the whoredoms of thy mother Jezebel, and her witchcrafts, are so many?"

Wicked tyrant! what speakest thou of peace with men, when thou hast thus long waged war with the Almighty? that cursed mother of thine hath nursed thee with blood, and trained thee up in abominable idolatries.

Thou art not more hers, than her sin is thine; thou art polluted with her spiritual whoredoms, and enchanted with her hellish witchcrafts: now that just God, whom thou and thy parents have so heinously despised, sends thee by me this last message of his vengeance; which, while he spake, his hand is drawing up that deadly arrow, which shall cure the former wounds with a worse.

Too late now doth wretched Jehoram turn his chariot and flee, and cry, Treason, O Ahaziah! There was treason before, O Jehoram! Thy treason against the majesty of God is now revenged by the treason of Jehu against thee.

That fatal shaft, notwithstanding the swift pace of both the chariots, is directed to the heart of Jehoram: there is no erring of those feathers which are guided by the hand of destiny.

How just are the judgments of God! It was in the field of Naboth, wherein Jehoram met with Jehu; that very ground called to him for blood. And now this new avenger remembers that prophecy which he heard out of the mouth of Elijah, in that very place, following the heels of Ahab, and is careful to perform it. Little did Jehu think, when he heard that message of Elijah, that his hands should act it. Now, as zealous of accomplishing the word of a prophet, he gives charge to Bidkar his captain, that the bleeding carcass of Jehoram should be cast upon that very plat of Naboth. O Naboth's blood well paid for! Ahab's blood is licked by dogs in the very place where those dogs licked Naboth's; Jehoram's blood shall manure that ground, which was wrung from Naboth; and Jezebel shall add to this compost. O garden of herbs dearly bought, royally dunged!

What a resemblance there is betwixt the death of the father and the son, Ahab and Jehoram! Both are slain in their chariots, both with an arrow, both repay their blood to Naboth. And how perfect is this retaliation! Not only Naboth miscarried in that cruel injustice, but his sons also; else the inheritance of the vineyard had descended to his heirs, notwithstanding his pretended offence. And now, not only Ahab forfeits his blood to this field, but his son Jehoram also. Face doth not more answer to face, than punishment to sin.

It was time for Ahaziah, king of Judah, to flee. Nay, it had been time long before to have fled from the sins, yea, from the house of Ahab. That brand is fearful which God sets upon him: "He did evil in the sight of the Lord, as did the house of Ahab;" for he was the son-in-law of the house of Ahab. Affinity is too often guilty of corruption: the son of good Jehoshaphat is lost in Ahab's daughter.

Now he pays for his kind alliance, accompanying the son of Ahab in his death, whom he consorted with in his idolatry. Young Ahaziah was scarce warm in his throne, when the mismatched blood of Athaliah is required from him. Nothing is more dangerous than to be imped in a wicked family; this relation too often draws in a share both of sin and punishment.

Who would not have looked that Jezebel, hearing of this bloody end of her son and pursuit of her ally, and the fearful proceedings of this prosperous conspiracy, should have put herself into sackcloth and ashes; and now, finding no means either of defence or escape, should have cast herself into such a posture of humiliation as might have moved the compassion of Jehu? Her proud heart could not suddenly learn to stoop; rather she recollects her high spirits, and, instead of humbling her soul by repentance, and addressing herself for an imminent death, she pranks up her old carcass, and paints her wrinkled face, and, as one that vainly hopes to daunt the courage of an usurper by the sudden beams of majesty, she looks out, and thinks to fright him with the challenge of a traitor, whose either mercy or justice could not be avoided. Extremity finds us such as our peace leaves us. Our last thoughts are spent upon that we most care for. Those, that have regarded their face more than their soul, in their latter end are more taken up with desire of seeming fair, than being happy. It is no marvel if a heart, obdured with the custom of sin, shut up gracelessly. Counterfeit beauty agrees well with inward uncleanness.

Jehu's resolution was too strongly settled to be removed with a painted face, or an opprobrious tongue. He looks up to the window, and says, "Who is on my side, who?" There want not those everywhere, which will be ready to observe prevailing greatness. Two or three eunuchs look out; he bids them "throw her down:" They instantly lay hold on their lately adored mistress, and, notwithstanding all her shrieks and prayers, cast her down headlong into the street.

What heed is to be taken of the deep professed services of hollow-hearted followers? All this while they have humbly, with smiles and officious devotions, fawned upon their great queen; now, upon the call of a prosperous enemy, they forget their respects, her royalty; and cast her down, as willing executioners, into the jaws of a fearful death. It is hard for greatness to know them whom it may trust: perhaps the fairest semblance is from the falsest heart. It was a just plague of God upon wicked Jezebel, that she was inwardly hated of her own. He, whose servants she persecuted, raised up enemies to her from her own elbow.

Thus must pride fall; insolent, idolatrous, cruel Jezebel, besprinkles the walls and pavement with her blood; and now those brains, that devised mischief against the servants of God, are strewed upon the stones; and she, that insulted upon the prophets, is trampled upon by the horses' heels: " The wicked is kept for the day of destruction, and shall be brought forth to the day of wrath."

Death puts an end commonly to the highest displeasure. He, that was severe in the execution of the living, is merciful in the sepulture of the dead: " Go, see now this cursed woman, and bury her, for she is a king's daughter." She, that upbraided Jehu with the name of Zimri, shall be interred by Jehu as Omri's daughter-in-law, as a Sidonian princess; somewhat must be yielded to humanity, somewhat to state.

The dogs have prevented Jehu in this purpose, and have given her a living tomb, more ignoble than the worst of the earth; only the scull, hands, and feet of that vanished carcass, yet remain; the scull which was the roof of all her wicked devices, the hands and feet which were the executioners, these shall remain as the monuments of those shameful exequies; that future times, seeing these fragments of a body, might say, " The dogs were worthy of the rest: thus Jezebel is turned to dung and dog's meat; Elijah is verified, Naboth is revenged, Jezreel is purged, Jehu is zealous, and, in all, God is just."

CONTEMPLATION III.— JEHU KILLING THE SONS OF AHAB, AND THE PRIESTS OF BAAL.

THERE were two prime cities of the ten tribes, which were the set courts of the kingdom of Israel— Samaria and Jezreel. The chief palace of the kingdom was Jezreel, the mother city of the kingdom was Samaria. Jehu is possessed of the one, without any sword drawn against him; Jezreel willingly changes the master, yielding itself to the victor of two kings, to the avenger of Jezebel: the next care is Samaria; either policy or force shall fetch in that head of the tribes.

The plentiful issue of princes is no small assurance to the people. Ahab had sons enough to furnish the thrones of all the neighbour nations, to maintain the hopes of succession to all times. How secure did he think the perpetuation of his posterity, when he saw seventy sons from his own loins! Neither was this royal issue trusted either to weak walls or to one roof; but to the strong bulwarks of Samaria, and therein to the several guards of the chief peers: it was the wise care of their parents not to have them obnoxious to the danger of a common miscarriage, or of those emulations which wait upon the cloyedness of an undivided conversation, but to order their separation, so as one may rescue other from the peril of assault, as one may respect other out of a familiar strangeness. Had Ahab and Jezebel been as wise for their souls, as they were for their seed, both had prospered.

Jehu is yet but in his first act: if all the sons of Ahab bleed not, the prophecy is unanswered; there shall be no need of his sword, his pen shall work all this slaughter. He writes a challenge to Samaria, and therein to the guardians of the sons of Ahab, daring them, out of the confidence in their defenced city, in their chariots and horses, in their associates and arms, to set up the best of their master's sons on his father's throne, and to fight for his succession.

All the governors of Ahab's children conspire in one common fear. No doubt there wanted not in that numerous brood of kings, some great spirits, that, if at least they attained to the notice of this design, longed for a revenge, and suggested counsels of resolution to their cowardly guardians. Shall an audacious usurper run thus away with the crown of Israel? Shall the blood of Jezebel be thus traitorously spilt, thus wilfully forgotten? O Israelites, can you be so base, as to be ruled by my father's servant? Where are the merits of Ahab and Jehoram? What is become of the loyal courage of Israel? Doubtless ye shall not want able seconds to your valour. Do ye think the royal and potent alliances of our mother Jezebel, and the remaining heirs of Judah, can draw back their hands from your aid? will they endure to swallow so cruel an indignity? Stir up your astonished fortitude, O ye nobles of Israel! redeem your bleeding honour, revenge this treacherous conspirator, and establish the right of the undoubted heirs of your sovereign. But as warm clothes to a dead man, so are the motions of valour to a fearful heart: " Behold, two kings stood not before him, how then shall we stand?"

Fear affrights itself, rather than it will want bugs of terror. It is true, two kings fell before Jehu, but two kings unarmed, unguarded. Had not the surprisal of Jehu taken advantage of the unsuspicious nakedness of these two princes, his victory had not been thus successful, thus easy. One of those two kings, upon advertisement and preparation, had abated the fury of that hot leader. It is the fashion of fear to represent unto us always the worst, in every event, not looking at the inequality of the advantages, but the misery of the success: as, contrarily, it is the guise of faith and valour, by the good issue of one enterprise, to raise up the heart to an expectation and assurance of more.

These men's hearts are dead with their king's: neither dare entertain the hope of a safe and prosperous resistance, but basely return, " We are thy servants, and will do all that thou shalt bid us: we will not make any king; do thou that which is good in thine eyes."

Well may Jehu think, These men, which are thus disloyal to their charge, cannot be faithful to me: it is their fear that draws them to this observation; were they not cowards, they would not be traitors to their princes, subjects to me: I may use their hands, but I will not trust them. It is a thankless obedience that is grounded upon fear: there can be no true fidelity without love and reverence. Neither is it other betwixt God and us; if out of a dread of hell we be officious, who shall thank us for these respects to ourselves?

As one that had tasted already the sweetness of a resolute expedition, Jehu writes back instantly, " If ye be mine, and if ye will hearken unto my voice, take ye the heads of the men, your master's sons, and come to me to Jezreel to-morrow this time." Valiant Jehu was so well acquainted with the nature of fear, that he well knew this passion, once grown desperate, would be ready to swallow all conditions: so far, therefore, doth his wisdom improve it, as to make these peers his executioners, who presently, upon the receipt of his charge, turn cruel, and by a joint consent fetch off the seventy heads of those princes, whom they undertook to guard, whom they had flattered with the hopes of greater honour.

No doubt but amongst so many sons of Ahab, some had so demeaned themselves, that they had won zealous professions of love from their guardians. Except, perhaps, death stole upon them in sleep, what tears, what entreaties, what conjurations, must here needs have been!

What have we done, O ye peers of Israel, that might deserve this bloody measure? We are the sons of Ahab, therefore have ye hitherto professed to observe us. What change is this? why should that which hath hitherto kept you loyal, now make you cruel? Is this the reward of the long peaceable government of our father? are these the trophies of Ahab's victories against Benhadad, Jehoram's against Hazael? If we may not reign, yet at least let us live: or, if we must die, why will your hands be imbrued in that blood which ye had wont to term royal and sacred? why will ye of tutors turn murderers? All pleas are in vain to them that are deafened with their own fears. Perhaps these expostulations might have fetched some dews of pity from the eyes, and kisses from the lips of these unfaithful tutors, but cannot prevent the stroke of death. These crocodiles weep upon those whom they must kill; and if their own sons had been in the place of Ahab's, doubtless they had been sacrificed to the will of an usurper, to the parent's safety. It is ill relying upon timorous natures: upon every occasion, those crazy reeds will break and run into our hands. How worthy were Ahab and Jezebel of such friends! They had been ever false to God, how should men be true to them? They had sold themselves to work wickedness, and now they are requited with a mercenary fidelity: for a few lines have these men sold all the heads of Ahab's posterity. Could ever the policy of Jezebel have reached so far, as to suspect the possibility of the extirpation of so ample an issue, in one night, by the hands of her trustiest subjects?

Now she, that by her letters sent to the elders of Jezreel, shed the blood of Naboth and his sons, hath the blood of all her sons shed, by a letter sent from Jezreel to the elders of Samaria. At last, God will be sure to come out of the debt of wicked sinners, and will pay them with that coin, which is both most proper, and least looked for.

Early in the morning, in that gate of Jezreel, where Ahab had passed many an unjust sentence, is presented unto Jehu the fearful pledge of his sovereignty, seventy ghastly heads of the sons of Ahab.

Some carnal eye, that had seen so many young and smooth faces besmeared with blood, would have melted into compassion, bemoaning their harmless age, their untimely end. It is not for the justice of God to stand at the bar of our corrupted judgment. Except we include some grandchildren of Ahab within this number, none of these died before they were seasoned with horrible idolatry; or, if they had, they were in the loins of Ahab, when he sold himself to work wickedness; and now it is just with God to punish Ahab's wickedness in this fruit of his loins. The holy severity of God, in the revenge of sin, sometimes goes so far, that our ignorance is ready to mistake it for cruelty.

The wonder and horror of those two heaps hath easily drawn together the people of Jezreel. Jehu meets them in that seat of public judgment, and, finding much amazedness and passionate confusion in their faces, he clears them, and sends them to the true original of these sudden and astonishing massacres.

However his own conspiracy, and the cowardly treachery of the princes of Israel, had been, not without their heinous sin, the visible means of this judgment, yet he directs their eyes to a higher authority, the just decree of the Almighty, manifested by his servant Elijah, who, even by the willing sins of men, can most wisely, most holily fetch about his most righteous and blessed purposes.

If the peers of Samaria, out of a base fear, if Jehu, out of an ambition of reigning, shed the foul blood of Ahab's posterity, the sin is their own; but, in the meantime, the act is no other than what the infinite justice of God would justly work by their misintentions. Let these Israelites but look up from earth to heaven, these tragical changes cannot trouble them: thither Jehu sends them, wiping off the envy of all this blood, by the warrant of the divine pre-ordination. In obedience whereunto, he sends after these heirs of Ahab all his kinsfolk, favourites, priests, that remained in Jezreel. And now, having cleared these coasts, he hastens to Samaria: whom should he meet with in the way, but the brethren of Ahaziah king of Judah? They are going to visit their cousins the sons of Ahab. This young troop was thinking of nothing but jollity and courtly entertainment, when they meet with death. So suddenly, so secretly, had Jehu despatched these bold executions, that these princes could imagine no cause of suspicion. How could they think it might be dangerous to be known for the brethren of Ahaziah, or friends to the brethren of Jehoram? The just providence of the Almighty hath brought all this covey under one net. Jehu thinks it not safe to let go so many avengers of Ahaziah's blood, so many co-rivals of his sovereignty. The unhappy affinity of Jehoshaphat with Ahab is no less guilty of this slaughter than Jehu's ambition: this match, by the inoculation of one bud, hath tainted all the sap of the house of Judah. The two and forty brethren of Ahaziah are therefore sent after the seventy sons of Ahab, that they may overtake them in death, whom they came to visit: God will much less brook idolatry from the loins of a Jehoshaphat. Our entireness with wicked men feoffs us both in their sins and judgments.

Doubtless, many Israelites, that were devoted to the family and allies of Ahab, looked (what they durst) awry at this common effusion of royal blood; yet, in the worst of the depravedness of Israel, there were some which both drooped under the deplored idolatry of the times, and congratulated to Jehu this severe vindication of God's inheritance: amongst the rest, Jonadab the son of Rechab was most eminent. That man was by descent derived from Jethro, a Midianite by nation, but incorporated into Israel; a man whose piety and strict conversation did both teach and shame those twelve tribes to which he was joined. He was the author of an austere rule of civility to his posterity, to whom he debarred the use of wine, cities, possessions. This old and rough friend of Jehu, out of his moving habitations, meets him, and applauds his success. He that allowed not wine to his seed, allows the blood of Ahab's seed poured out by the hand of Jehu: he, that shunned the city, is carried in Jehu's chariot to the palace of Samaria.

How easily might Jehu have been deceived! Many a one professes uprightness, who yet is all guile. Jonadab's carriage hath been such, that his word merits trust. It is a blessing upon the plain-hearted, that they can be believed. Honest Jonadab is admitted to the honour of Jehu's seat, and called, instead of many, to witness the zeal of the new anointed king of Israel.

While Jehu had to do with kings, his cunning and his courage held equal pace together; but now, that he is to deal with idolatrous priests, his wile goes alone, and prevails: he calls the people together, and, dissembling his intentions, says, "Ahab served Baal a little, but Jehu shall serve him much; now therefore call unto me all the prophets of Baal, all his servants, and all his priests, let none be wanting; for I have a great sacrifice to do to Baal; whosoever shall be wanting, he shall not live."

What a dead paleness was there now in the faces of those few true-hearted Israelites, that looked for a happy restoration of the religion of God! How could they choose but think, Alas! how are we fallen from our hopes! is this the change we looked for? was it only ambition that hath set this edge upon the sword of Jehu? It was not the person of Ahab that we disliked, but the sins: if those must still succeed, what have we gained? Woe be to us, if only the author of our misery be changed, not the condition, not the cause of our misery.

On the other side, what insultations and triumphs sounded everywhere of the joyful Baalites! what glorying of the truth of their profession, because of their success! what scorns of their dejected opposites! what exprobrations of the disappointed hopes and predictions of their adverse prophets! what promises to themselves of a perpetuity of Baalism! How did the dispersed priests of Baal now flock together, and applaud each other's happiness, and magnify the devotion of their new sovereign! Never had that idol so glorious a day as this for the pomp of his service: before, he was adored singly in corners; now solemn sacrifices shall be offered to him by all his clients, in the great temple of the mother city of Israel. I can commend the zeal of Jehu; I cannot commend the fraud of Jehu. We may come to our end, even by crooked ways. He that bade him to smite for him, did not bid him to lie for him. Falsehood, though it be but tentative, is neither needed nor approved by the God of truth. If policy have allowed officious untruths, religion never.

By this device the house of Baal is well furnished, well filled; not one of his Chemarim either might or would be absent; not one of those which were present might be unrobed. False gods have ever affected to imitate the true: even Baal hath temples, altars, priests, vestments: all religions have allotted peculiar habits to their highest devotions. These vestments, which they miscalled sacred, are brought forth and put on, for the glory of this service.

Jehu and Jonadab are first careful that this separation be exact: they search and see that no servant of the Lord be crept into that throng. What should a religious Israelite do in the temple of Baal? Were any such there, he had deserved their smart, who would partake with their worship; but if curiosity had drawn any thither, the mercy of Jehu seeks his rescue. How much more favourable is the God of mercies, in not taking advantage of our infirmities!

Well might this search have bred suspicion, were it not, that in all those idolatrous sacrifices, the first care was to avoid the profane: even Baal would admit no mixture; how should the true God abide it?

Nothing wanted now, but the sacrifice. No doubt whole herds and flocks were ready for a pretence of some royal hecatombs, whereof some had now already smoked on their altars. O Jehu, what means this dilation? If thou abhorrest Baal, why didst thou give way to this last sacrifice? why didst not thou cut off these idolaters, before this upshot of their wickedness? Was it, that thou mightest be sure of their guiltiness? was it, that their number, together with their sin, might be complete? What acclamations were here to Baal! what joy in the freedom of their revived worship! when all on the sudden, those that had sacrificed, are sacrificed. The soldiers of Jehu, by his appointment, rush in with their swords drawn, and turn the temple into a slaughter-house. How is the tune now changed! what shrieking was here! what outcries! what running from one sword to the edge of another! what scrambling up the walls and pillars! what climbing into the windows! what vain endeavours to escape that death which would not be shunned! Whether running, or kneeling, or prostrate, they must die.

The first part of the sacrifice was Baal's; the latter is God's: the blood of beasts was offered in the one; of men in the other. The shedding of this was so much the more acceptable to God, by how much these men were more beasts than those they sacrificed. O happy obedience! God was pleased with a sacrifice from the house of Baal: the idolaters are slain, the idols burnt, the house of Baal turned to a draught, though even thus less unclean, less noisome, than in the former perfumes; and, in one word, Baal is destroyed out of Israel.

Who, that had seen all this zeal for God, would not have said, Jehu is a true Israelite? Yet he, that rooted out Ahab, would not be rid of Jeroboam: he, that destroyed Baal, maintained the two calves of Dan and Bethel. That idolatry was of a lower rank, as being a mis-worship of the true God: whereas, the other was a worship of the false. Even the easier of both is heinous, and shall rob Jehu of the praise of his uprightness.

A false heart may laudably quit itself of some one gross sin, and in the meantime hug some lesser evil that may condemn it; as a man recovered of a fever may die of jaundice or a dropsy: we lose the thank of all, if we wilfully fail in one.

It is an entire goodness that God cares for: perhaps such is the bounty of our God, a partial obedience may be rewarded with a temporal blessing, as Jehu's severity to

Ahab shall carry the crown to his seed for four generations; but we can never have any comfortable assurance of an eternal retribution, if our hearts and ways be not perfect with God. Woe be to us, O God, if we be not all thine! we cannot but everlastingly depart from thee, if we depart not from every sin. Thou hast purged our hearts from the Baal of our gross idolatries; O clear us from the golden calves of our petty corruptions also, that thou mayest take pleasure in our uprightness, and we may reap the sweet comforts of thy glorious remuneration!

CONTEMPLATION IV.—ATHALIAH AND JOASH.

Oh the woful ruins of the house of good Jehoshaphat! Jehu hath slain two and forty of his issue; Athaliah hopes to root out the rest. This daughter of Ahab was not like to be other than fatal to that holy line; one drop of that wicked blood was enough, both to impure and spill all the rest, which affinity had mixed with it.

It is not unlike that Ahaziah, betaking himself to the society of Jehoram's wars, committed the sway of his sceptre to his mother Athaliah. The daughter of Jezebel cannot but be plotting: when she hears of the death of Ahaziah and his brethren, inflicted by the heavy hand of Jehu, she straight casts for the kingdom of Judah. The true heirs are infants: their minority gives her both colour of rule, and opportunity of an easy extirpation. Perhaps her ambition was not more guilty than her zeal of Baalism: she saw Jehu, out of a detestation of idolatry, trampling on the blood of Jehoram, Jezebel, Ahaziah, the sons of Ahab, the brethren of Ahaziah, the priests and prophets of Baal, and, in one word, triumphing in the destruction both of Ahab and his gods out of Israel; and now she thinks, Why should not I destroy Jehoshaphat and his God out of Judah?

Who ever saw an idolater that was not cruel? Athaliah must needs let out some of her own blood out of the throat of Ahaziah's sons; yet she spares not to shed it out of a thirst of sovereignty. O God, how worthy of wonder are thy just and merciful dispensations! in that thou sufferest the seed of good Jehoshaphat to be destroyed by her hand, in whose affinity he offended, and yet savest one branch of this stock of Jehoshaphat, for the sake of so faithful a progenitor!

Wicked Athaliah, couldst thou think God would so far forget his servant David, though no other of those loins had seconded his virtues, as to suffer all his seed to be rooted out of the earth? This vengeance was for thy father Ahab. The man according to God's own heart shall have a lineal heir to succeed in his throne, when thou and thy father's house shall have vanished into forgetfulness.

For this purpose hath the wise providence of God ordained a Jehosheba, and matched her in the priestly tribe. Such reverence did Jehoram king of Judah, though degenerated into the idolatry of his father-in-law Ahab, bear to this sacred function, that he marries his daughter to Jehoiada the priest. Even princesses did not then scorn the bed of those that served at God's altar. Why should the Gospel pour contempt upon that which the law honoured?

The good lady had too much of Jehoshaphat in her, to suffer the utter extirpation of that royal seed; she could not, doubtless, without the extreme danger of her own life, save the life of her nephew Joash: with what a loving boldness doth she adventure to steal him from amongst those bleeding carcasses in the chamber of death! Her match gave her opportunity to effect that, which both nature and religion moved her to attempt: neither know I whether more to wonder at the cunning of the device, or the courage of the enterprise or the secresy of the concealment, or the happiness of the success. Certainly Athaliah was too cruelly careful to forget this so late born son of Ahaziah; of all the rest, his age would not suffer him to be out of her eye. In all likelihood, therefore, she must needs have missed so noted a corpse, had there not been a substitution of some other dead child in his room: in that age, the favour is not so distinguishable, especially of a dead face. Without some pious deceit, this work could never have been effected: else had the child been secretly subduced, and missed by his bloody grandmother: her perpetual jealousy had both expected a surviving heir, and continued a curious and unavoidable search; both which were now shunned at once, whilst Athaliah reckons him for dead, whom Jehosheba hath preserved. Mischief sometimes fails of those appointments, wherein it thinks to have made the surest work: God laughs in heaven at the plots of tyrants, and befools them in their deepest projects. He had said to David, " Of the fruit of thy body will I set upon thy seat;" in vain shall earth and hell conspire to frustrate it.

Six years hath Joash and his nurse been hid in a close cell of the temple. Those rooms were destined only to the holy tribe, yet now rejoice to harbour such a guest. The rigour of the ordinary law must yield to cases of so important necessity.

All this could not possibly be done, and continued, without the privity of many faithful priests and Levites, who were as careful to keep this counsel, as hopeful of the issue of it. It is not hard for many honest hearts to agree in a religious secresy; needs must those lips be shut, which God hath sealed up.

Judah hath not been used to such a yoke: long had it groaned under the tyranny, not of a woman only, but of an idolatrous Sidonian: if any of that sex might have claimed that sceptre, none had so much right to it as Jehosheba herself. But good Jehoiada the priest, who had rather be a loyal guardian to the king, than a husband to a queen, now finds time to set on foot the just title of Joash, and to put him into the misusurped throne of his father Ahaziah.

In the seventh year, therefore, he sends for the captains, and the guard; and, having sworn them to secresy, by undoubted witnesses, makes faith unto them of the truth of their native prince, thus happily rescued from the bloody knife of his merciless grandmother, marshals the great business of his inauguration, gives every one his charge, sets every one his station, and so disposes of his holy forces, as was most needful for the safety of the king, the revenge of the usurper, the prevention of tumults, the establishment of the crown upon the owner's head in peace and joy.

There was none of all these agents, who did not hold the business to be his own: every true subject of Judah was feelingly interested in this service; neither was there any of them, who was not secretly heart-burned, all this while, with the hateful government of this idolatrous tyranness: and now this inward fire is glad to find a vent. How gladly do they address themselves to this welcome employment! The greatest part of this sacred band were Levites, who might therefore both meet together with least suspicion, and be more securely trusted by Jehoiada, under whom they served. Even that holy priest of God, instead of teaching the law, sets the guard, orders the captains, ranges the troops of Judah; and, instead of a censer, brings forth the spears and shields of David: the temple is for the present a field, or an artillery-yard, and the ephods are turned into harness. That house, in the rearing whereof not the noise of a hammer might be heard, now admits of the clashing of armour, and the secret murmurs of some military achievement. No circumstances, either of place or calling, are so punctual, as that public necessity may not dispense with their alteration.

All things are now ready for this solemnity: each man rejoices to fix upon his own footing, and longs to see the face of their long-concealed sovereign, and vows his blood to the vindication of the common liberty, to the punishment of a cruel intruder. Now Jehoiada brings forth unto them the king's son, and presents him to the peers and people: hardly can the multitude contain itself from shouting out too soon: one sees in his countenance the features of his father Ahaziah, another of his grandfather Jehoram; a third professes to discern in him some lines and fashion of his great-grandfather Jehoshaphat: all find in his face the natural impressions of majesty, and read in it the hopes, yea, the prophecies, of their future happiness. Not with more joy than speed doth Jehoiada accomplish all the rites of the coronation. Before that young king could know what was done to him, he is anointed, crowned, presented with the book of the law. Those ceremonies were instructive, and no doubt Jehoiada failed not to comment upon them in due time to that royal pupil.

The oil wherewith he was anointed, signified his designation to that high service; and those endowments from heaven that might enable him to so great a function.

The crown wherewith he was adorned, signified that glory and majesty which should both encourage and attend his princely cares.

The book of the testimony signified the divine rules and directions, whereto he must frame his heart and actions, in the wielding of that crown, in the improvement of that oil.

These three, the oil, the crown, the testimony, that is, inward powers, outward magnificence, true piety and justice, make up a perfect prince: none of these may be wanting: if there be not a due calling of God, and abilities meet for that greatness, the oil faileth; if there be not a majestic grace and royalty, that may command reverence, the crown is missing; if there be not a careful respect to the law of God, as the absolute guide of all counsels and determinations, the testimony is neglected: all of them concurring, make both king and people happy.

Now it is time for the people to clap their hands, and, by their loud acclamations, to witness their joy, which must needs break forth with so much more force, by how much it was longer, upon fears and policy, suppressed.

The court and temple were near together: however it was with Athaliah, and the late revolted princes of Judah, according to the common word, the nearer to the church, the farther from God: their religious predecessors held it the greatest commodity of their house, that it neighboured upon the house of God. From her palace might Athaliah easily hear the joyful shouts of the multitude, the loud noise of the trumpets, and, as astonished with this new tumult of public gratulations, she comes running into the temple. Never had her foot trod upon that holy pavement till now, that she came to fetch a just revenge from that God whose worship she had contemned.

It fell out well, that her sudden amazedness called her forth, without the attendance of any strong guard, whose side-taking might have made that quarrel mutually bloody. She soon hears and sees what she likes not: her ear meets with, God save the king; her eye meets with the unlooked-for heir of the kingdom, sitting on his throne, crowned and robed in the royal fashion, guarded with the captains and soldiers, proclaimed by the trumpeters, acclaimed and applauded by the people.

Who can say whether this sight drove her more near to frenzy or death? How could it be otherwise, when those great spirits of hers, that had been so long used to an uncontrolled sovereignty, find themselves so unexpectedly suppressed?

She now rends her clothes, and cries, Treason! treason! as if that voice of hers could still command all hearts, all hands; as if one breath of hers were powerful enough to blow away all these new designs. O Athaliah! to whom dost thou complain thyself? They are thy just executioners wherewith thou art encompassed: if it be treason to set up the true heir of Ahaziah, thou appealest to thy traitors: the treason was thine; theirs is justice. The time is now come of thy reckonings for all the royal blood of Judah, which thy ambition shed; wonder rather at the patience of this long forbearance, than the rigour of this execution.

There needs no formal seat of justice in so apparent offence. Jehoiada passes the sentence of death upon her: "Have her forth of the ranges, let her not be slain in the house of the Lord; and him that followeth her, kill with the sword."

Had not this usurpation been palpable, Jehoiada would not have presumed to intermeddle. Now, being both the priest of God, and uncle and protector to the lawful king, he doth that out of the necessity of the state, which his infant sovereign, if he could have been capable of those thoughts, would have desired.

Violent hands are laid upon Athaliah, whom, no doubt, a proud and furious disdain of so quick a charge, and of so rough a usage, made miserably impatient. Now she frowns and calls, and shrieks and commands, and threatens and reviles, and entreats in vain, and dies with as much ill-will from herself, as she lived with the ill-will of her repining subjects.

I see not any one man, of all her late flatterers, that follows her, either for pity or rescue. Every man willingly gives her up to justice; not one sword is drawn in her defence, not one eye laments her. Such is the issue of a tyrannical misgovernment; that which is obeyed not without secret hate, is lost not without public joy.

How like is Athaliah to her mother Jezebel! as in conditions and carriage, so even in death: both killed violently, both killed under their own walls, both slain with treason in their mouths, both slain in the entrance of a changed government; one trode on by the horses, the other slain in the horse-gate; both paid their own blood for the innocent blood of others.

How suddenly, how easily, is Judah restored to itself, after so long and so fearful a deprivation! The people scarce believe their own eyes, for the wonder of this happy change: neither know I whether they be more joyed in the sight of their new king thus strangely preserved, or in the sight of Jehoiada that had preserved him.

No man can envy the protection of the young king unto him by whose means he lives and reigns. That holy man cares only to improve his authority to the common good: "He makes a covenant between the Lord, and the king, and the people;" and, after so long and dangerous a disjunction, re-unites them to each other. Their revived zeal bestirs itself, and breaks down the temples, and altars, and images of Baal, and sacrifices his idolatrous priests. Shortly both Ahab and Baal are destroyed out of Judah.

The sceptre of Judah is changed from a woman to a child; but a child trained up and tutored by Jehoiada. This minority, so guided, was not inferior to the mature age of many predecessors. Happy is that land, the nonage of whose princes falls into holy and just hands; yet, even these holy and just hands came short of what they might have done. The high places remained still; those altars were erected to the true God, but in a wrong place. It is marvel if there be not some blemishes found in the best government: I doubt Jehoiada shall once buy it dear, that he did not his utmost.

But for the main, all was well with Judah, in all the days of Jehoiada, even after that Joash was grown past his pupilage. He that was the tutor to his infancy, was the counsellor of his ripe age, and was equally happy in both. How pleasing was it to that good high priest, to be commanded by that charge of his in the business of God! The young king gives order to the priests, for the collection of large sums, to the repairing of the breaches of God's house. It becomes him well to take care of that which was the nursery of his infancy: and now, after three and twenty years, he expostulates with his late guardian, Jehoiada, and the rest of his court, "Why repair ye not the breaches?"

O gracious and happy vicissitude! Jehoiada the priest had ruled the infancy of king Joash in matters of state, and now Joash the king commands aged Jehoiada the priest in matters of devotion. In the affairs of God, the action is the priest's, the oversight and coaction is the prince's: by the careful endeavour of both, God's house is repaired, his service flourisheth.

But alas! that it may too well appear, that the ground of this devotion was not altogether inward, no sooner doth the life of Jehoiada cease, than the devotion of Joash begins to languish; and, after some languor, dies.

The benefit of a truly religious prelate, or statesman, is not known till his loss.

Now, some idolatrous peers of Judah have soon miscarried the king, from the house of the Lord God of their fathers, to serve groves, and idols. Yea, whither go we wretched men, if we be left by our Maker? King Joash is turned, not idolater only, but persecutor; yea, which is yet more horrible to consider, persecutor of the son of that Jehoiada to whom he owes his own life. Zechariah, his cousin-german, his foster-brother, the holy issue of those parents by whom Joash lives and reigns, for the conscionable rebuke of the idolatry of prince and people, is unjustly and cruelly murdered by that unthankful hand. How possible is it for fair and saint-like beginnings to shut up in monstrous impieties! Let him that thinks he stands, take heed lest he fall. When did God ever put up so foul ingratitude to himself, to his servants? O Joash! what eyes can pity the fearful destruction of thee and thy Judah?

If ye have forgotten the kindness of Jehoiada, your unkindness to Jehoiada shall not be forgotten: "An army of Syrians shall come up against Judah and Jerusalem, and destroy all the princes of the people, and send all the spoil of them to Damascus." Now Hazael revenges this quarrel of God and his anointed, and plagues that people which made themselves unworthy to be the Lord's inheritance.

And what becomes of Joash? He is left in great diseases, when his own servants conspired against him "for the blood of the sons of Jehoiada, and slew him on his bed, and he died; and they buried him not in the sepulchre of the kings." Dying Zechariah had said, in the bitterness of his departing soul, "The Lord look upon it, and require it." I confess, I had rather to have heard him say, " The Lord pass it over, and remit it." So said Stephen: such difference there is between a martyr of the law and of the Gospel; although I will hope the zeal of justice, not the uncharitable heat of revenge, drew forth this word: God hears it, and now gives an account of his notice. Thus doth the Lord require the blood of Jehoiada's son, even by the like unthankful hand of the obliged servants of Joash. He that was guilty of abominable idolatry, yet, as if God meant to wave that challenge, is called to reckoning for his cruel unthankfulness to Jehoiada: this crime shall make him odious alive, and shall abandon him dead from the sepulchre of his fathers; as if this last royalty were too good for him, who had forgotten the law of humanity. Some vices are such, as nature smiles upon, though frowned at by divine justice. Others are such, as even nature itself abhors; such is this of ingratitude, which, therefore carries so much more detestation from God, as it is more odious even to them that have blotted out the image of God.

CONTEMPLATION V. — JOASH WITH ELISHA DYING.

The two kingdoms of Judah and Israel, however divided both in government and affection, yet loved to interchange the names of their kings: even Israel had their Joash, no better than that of Judah; he was not more the father of the latter Jeroboam, than, in respect of misworship, he was the son of the first Jeroboam, who made Israel to sin. Those calves of Dan, and Bethel, out of a politic misdevotion, besotted all the succession of the ten usurped tribes. Yet even this idolatrous king of Israel comes down to visit the sick bed of Elisha, and weeps upon his face.

That holy prophet was never any flatterer of princes, neither spared he invectives against their most plausible sins: yet king Joash, that was beaten by his reproofs, washes that face with the tears of love and sorrow, which had often frowned upon his wickedness.

How much difference there was betwixt the Joash of Israel, and the Joash of Judah! That of Judah, having been preserved and nurtured by Jehoiada the priest, after all professions of dearness, shuts up in the unkind murder of his son, and that merely for the just reproof of his own idolatry; this of Israel, having been estranged from the prophet Elisha, and sharply rebuked for the like offence, makes love to his dying reprover, and bedews his pale face with his tears. Both were bad enough; but this of Israel was, however vicious, yet good-natured: that of Judah added to his wickedness an ill disposition, a dogged humour. There are varieties even of evil men: some are worse at the root, others at the branch; some more civilly harmless, others fouler in morality. According to the exercise of the restraining grace, natural men do either rise or fall in their ill.

The longest day must have its evening. Good Elisha, that had lived some ninety years, a wonder of prophets, and had outworn many successions in the thrones of Israel and Judah, is now cast upon the bed of his sickness, yea, of his death. That very age might seem a disease, which yet is seconded with a languishing distemper. It is not in the power of any holiness to privilege us from infirmity of body, from final dissolution. He that stretched himself upon his bed, over the dead carcass of the Shunamite's son, and revived it, must now stretch out his own limbs upon his sick bed, and die. He saw his master Elijah rapt up suddenly from the earth, and fetched by a fiery chariot from this vale of mortality; himself must leisurely wait for his last pangs, in a lingering passage to the same glory. There is not one way appointed to us by the divine Providence, unto one common blessedness: one hath more pain, another hath more speed: violence snatcheth away one; another, by an insensible pace, draws every day nearer to his term: the wisdom and goodness of God magnifies itself in both. Happy is he, that, after due preparation, is passed through the gates of death, ere he be aware! Happy is he, that, by the holy use of long sickness, is taught to see the gates of death afar off, and addressed for a resolute passage: the one dies like Elijah, the other like Elisha, both blessedly.

The time was when a great king sent to Elisha, to know if he should recover: now the king of Israel, as knowing that Elisha shall not recover, so had his consumption spent him, comes to visit the dying prophet; and, when his tears would give him leave, breaks forth into a passionate exclamation: "O my father! my father! the chariots of Israel, and the horsemen thereof!" Yet the calves of Dan and Bethel have left some goodness in Joash: as the best man hath something in him worthy of reproof, so the faultiest hath something commendable. Had not the Spirit of God himself told us, that Joash did that which was evil in the sight of the Lord, we had admired this piety, this reverent respect to the prophet: the holiest man could not have said more. It is possible for the clients of a false worship to honour, out of another regard, the professors of truth. From the hand of Elisha had Jehu, the grandfather of Joash, received his unction to the kingdom; this favour might not be forgotten.

Visitation of the sick is a duty required both by the law of humanity, and of religion. Bodily infirmity is sad and comfortless; and therefore needs the presence and counsel of friends to relieve it; although, when we draw the curtains of those that are eminently gracious, we do rather fetch, with Joash, than bring, a blessing.

How sensible should we be of the loss of holy men, when a Joash spends his tears upon Elisha! If we be more affected with the foregoing of a natural friend, or kinsman, than of a noted and useful prophet, it argues more love to ourselves, than to the church of God, than to God himself.

What use there was of chariots and horsemen in those wars of the ancients, all histories can tell us; all the strength of the battle stood in these; there could be neither defence nor offence but by them: such was Elisha unto Israel. The greatest safeguard to any nation is the sanctity and faithfulness of their prophets, without which the church and state lie open to utter desolation.

The same words that Elisha said of his master Elijah, when he saw him taken up from the earth, doth Joash now speak of Elisha, near his dissolution: "O my father! my father! the chariots of Israel, and the horsemen thereof!" The words were good, the tears were pious; but where are the actions? O Joash! if the prophet were thy father, where was thy filial obedience? he cried down thy calves, thou upheldest them; he counselled thee to good, thou didst evil in the sight of the Lord.

If the prophet was the chariot and horsemen of Israel, why didst thou fight against his holy doctrine? if thou weepedst for his loss, why didst thou not weep for those sins of thine that procured it?

Had thine hand answered thy tongue, Israel had been happy in Elisha, Elisha had been happy in Israel and thee. Words are no good trial of profession: the worst men may speak well. Actions have only the power to descry hypocrites.

Yet even a Joash, thus complying, shall not go away unblessed. This outward kindness shall receive an outward retribution. These few drops of warm water, shed upon the face of a prophet, shall not lose their reward. The spirit of prophecy forsakes not the deathbed of Elisha: he calls for bow and arrows, and puts them into the hand of Joash, and, putting his hands upon the king's hand, he bids to shoot eastward, and while the shaft flies, and lights, he says, " The arrow of the Lord's deliverance from Syria; for thou shalt smite the Syrians in Aphek, till thou have consumed them." If the weak and withered hand of the prophet had not been upon the youthful and vigorous hand of the king, this bow had been drawn in vain: the strength was from the hand of the king, the blessing from the hand of the prophet. He, whose real parable hath made the earth to be Syria, the arrow revenge, the archer Joash, hath obtained for his last boon from God to Israel, that this archer shall shoot this arrow of revenge into the heart of Syria, and wound it to death. When, then, the hand of the king and of the prophet draw together, there cannot choose but success must follow.

How readily doth Elisha now make good the words of Joash! how truly is he the chariots and horsemen of Israel! Israel had not fought without him, much less had been victorious; if theirs be the endeavour, the success is his. Even the dying prophet puts life and speed into the forces of Israel; and, while he is digging his own grave, is raising trophies to God's people.

He had received kindness from the Syrians: amongst them was he harboured in the dearth, and from some of their nobles was presented with rich gifts; but their enmity to Israel drowns all his private respects. He cannot but profess hostility to the public enemies of the church, neither can he content himself with a single prediction of their ruin. He bids Joash to take the arrows, and smite upon the ground; he sets no number of those strokes, as supposing the frequence of those blows, which Joash might well, upon this former parabolical act, understand to be significant. The slack hand of the king smites but thrice: so apt we are to be wanting to ourselves; so coldly do we execute the commands of God. The sick prophet is not more grieved than angry at this dull negligence. Doubtless, God had revealed to him, for his last gratification, that, upon his fervent prayers, so often as Joash should voluntarily, after his general charge, smite the earth, so oft should Israel smite Syria. Elisha's zeal doth not languish with his body: with a fatherly authority, he chides him who had styled him father, not fearing to spend some of his last breath in a mild reproof: " Thou shouldst have smitten five or six times, then thou hadst smitten Syria till thou hadst consumed it; whereas now thou shalt smite Syria but thrice." Not that the unchangeable decree of the Almighty meant to suspend itself upon the uncertain issue of Joash's will; but he, that puts this word into the mouth of his prophet, puts this motion into the hand of the king, which did not more willingly stay, than necessarily obey the providence whereby it was stirred. Even while we have the freest choice, we fall upon those actions and circumstances, whereby the just and holy will of our God is brought about. Our very neglects, our ignorances, shall fulfil his eternal counsels.

Elisha dies, and is buried: his miracles do not cease with his life. Who can marvel that his living prayers raised the son of the Shunamite, when his dead bones raise the carcass that touched them! God will be free in his works; he that must die himself, yet shall revive another: the same power might have continued life to him, that gave it by his bones. Israel shall well see that he lives, by whose virtue Elisha was both in life and death miraculous. While the prophet was alive, the impetration might seem to be his, though the power were God's. Now that he is dead, the bones can challenge nothing, but send the wandering Israelite to that Almighty agent, to whom it is all one to work by the quick or dead. Were not the men of Israel more dead than the carcass thus buried, how could they choose but see, in this revived corpse, an emblem of their own condition? how could they choose but think, If we adhere to the God of Elisha, he shall raise our decayed estates, and restore our nation to the former glory?

The Sadducees had as yet no being in Israel. With what face could that heresy ever after look into the world, when before the birth of it, it was so palpably convinced, with an example of the resurrection? Intermission of time, and degrees of corruption, add nothing to the impossibility of our rising. The body that is once cold in death, hath no more aptitude to a re-animation, than that which is mouldered into dust; only the divine power of the Maker must restore either, can restore both. When we are dead, and buried in the grave of our sin, it is only the touch of God's prophets, applying unto us the death and resurrection of the Son of God, that can put new life into us. No less true, though spiritual, is the miracle of our rising up from an estate of inward corruption, to a life of grace.

Yet all this prevails not with Israel. No bones of Elisha could raise them from their wicked idolatry; and, notwithstanding their gross sins, Joash their king prospers. Whether it were for the sake of Jehu, whose grandchild he was, or for the sake of Elisha, whose face he wept upon, his hand is notably successful, not only against the son of Hazael king of Syria, whom he beats out of the cities of Israel, but against Amaziah king of Judah, whom he took prisoner, beating down the very walls of Jerusalem, and returning laden with the sacred and rich spoil, both of the temple and court, to his Samaria.

O the depth of Divine justice and wisdom in these outward administrations! The best cause, the best man, doth not ever fare best. Amaziah did that which was right in the sight of the Lord, Joash evil; Amaziah follows David, though not with equal paces; Joash follows Jeroboam; yet is Amaziah shamefully foiled by Joash. Whether God yet meant to visit, upon this king of Judah, the still odious unthankfulness of his father Jehoiada, or to plague Judah for their share in the blood of Zechariah, and their late revolt to idolatry; or, whether Amaziah's too much confidence in his own strength, which moved his bold challenge to Joash, were thought fit to be thus taken down; or whatever other secret ground of God's judgment there might be, it is not for our presumption to inquire. Whoso by the event shall judge of love or hatred, shall be sure to run upon that woe, which belongs to them that call good evil, and evil good.

What a savage piece of justice it is, to put the right, whether of inheritance or honour, to the decision of the sword, when it is no news for the better to miscarry by the hand of the worse!

The race is not to the swift, the battle is not to the strong, no, not to the good. Perhaps God will correct his own by a foil; perhaps he will plague his enemy by a victory. They are only our spiritual combats wherein our faithful courage is sure of a crown.

CONTEMPLATION VI.—UZZIAH LEPROUS.

EVEN the throne of David passed many changes of good and evil. Good Jehoshaphat was followed with three successions of wicked princes, and those three were again succeeded with three others godly and virtuous. Amaziah for a long time shone fair, but at the last, shut up in a cloud: the gods of the Edomites marred him. His rebellion against God stirred up his people's rebellion against him. The same hands that slew him, crowned his son Uzziah; so as the young king might imagine, it was not their spite that drew violence upon his father, but his own wickedness. Both early did this prince reign, and late: he began at sixteen, and sat fifty-two years in the throne of Judah. They, that mutinied in the declining age of Amaziah the father, are obsequious to the childhood of the son, as if they professed to adore sovereignty, while they hated lewdness. The unchanged government of good princes is the happiness no less of the subjects, than of themselves. The hand knows best to guide those reins to which it hath been inured; and even mean hackneys go on cheerfully in their wonted road. Custom, as it makes evils more supportable, so, where it meets with constant minds, makes good things the more pleasing and beneficial.

The wise and holy Zechariah was a happy tutor to the minority of king Uzziah. That vessel can hardly miscarry, where a skilful steersman sits at the helm. The first praise of a good prince is to be judicious and just, and pious in himself: the next is, to give ear and way to them that are such. While Zechariah hath the visions of God, and Uzziah takes the counsels of Zechariah, it is hard to say, whether the prophet, or the king, or the state, be happier.

God will be in no man's debt. So long as Uzziah sought the Lord, "God made him to prosper." Even what we do out of duty, cannot want a reward. Godliness never disappointed any man's hopes, oft hath exceeded them. If Uzziah fight against the Philistines, if against the Arabians, and Mehunims (according to his names), the strength, the help of the Almighty is with him. The Ammonites come in with presents, and all the neighbour nations ring of the greatness, of the happiness of Uzziah: his bounty and care make Jerusalem both strong and proud of her new towers; yea, the very desert must taste of his munificence.

The outward munificence of princes cannot stand firm, unless it be built upon the foundations of providence and frugality. Uzziah had not been so great a king, if he had not been so great a husband; he had his flocks in the deserts, and his herds in the plains; his ploughs in the fields, his vine-dressers upon the mountains, and in Carmel; neither was this more out of profit than delight, for he loved husbandry. Who can contemn those callings for meanness, which have been the pleasures of princes?

Hence was Uzziah so potent at home, so dreadful to his neighbours. His wars had better sinew than theirs. Which of his predecessors was able to maintain so settled an army, of more than three hundred and ten thousand trained soldiers, well furnished, well fitted for the suddenest occasions? Thrift is the strongest prop of power.

The greatness of Uzziah, and the rare devices of his artificial engines for war, have not more raised his fame than his heart: so is he swollen up with the admiration of his own strength and glory, that he breaks again. How easy it is for the best man to doat upon himself, and to be lifted up so high, as to lose the sight both of the ground whence he rises, and of the hand that advanced him! How hard it is for him that hath invented strange engines for the battering his enemies, to find out any means to beat down his own proud thoughts! Wise Solomon knew what he did, when he prayed to be delivered from too much: "Lest," said he, "I be full, and deny thee, and say, Who is the Lord?" Upon this rock did the son of Solomon run, and split himself. His full sails of prosperity carried him into presumption and ruin. What may he not do? what may he not be? Because he found his power otherwise unlimited, overruling in the court, the cities, the fields, the deserts, the armies, and magazines, therefore he thinks he may do so in the temple too. As things royal, civil, husbandry, military, passed his hands: so why should not, thinks he, sacred also? It is a dangerous indiscretion for a man not to know the bounds of his own calling. What confusion doth not follow upon this breaking of the ranks!

Upon a solemn day, king Uzziah clothes himself in pontifical robes, and, in the view of that populous assembly, walks up in state into the temple of God, and boldly approaching to the altar of incense, offers to burn sweet odours upon it to the God of heaven. Azariah the priest is sensible of so perilous an encroachment; he therefore, attended with fourscore valiant assistants of that holy tribe, hastens after the king, and finding him with the censer in his hand, ready addressed to that sinful devotion, stays him with a free and grave expostulation. There is no place wherein I could be sorry to see thee, O king, but where thou art; neither is there any act that we should grudge thee so much, as this which is the most sacred. Is it possible that so great an oversight should fall into such wisdom? can a religious prince, trained up under a holy Zechariah, after so many years' zealous profession of piety, be either ignorant or regardless of those limits, which God hath set to his own services?

O! what means this uncouth attempt? Consider, O dear sovereign, for God's sake, for thy soul's sake, consider where thou art, what thou dost! it is God's house wherein thou standest, not thine own! Look about thee, and see, whether these vails, these tables, these pillars, these walls, these pavements, have any resemblance of earth:— there is no place in all the world, whence thy God hath excluded thee, but only this: this he hath reserved for his own use; and canst thou think much to allow one room as proper to him, who hath not grudged all the rest to thee? But if it be thy zeal of a personal service to God that hath carried thee thither, alas! how canst thou hope to please the Almighty with a forbidden sacrifice? which of thine holy progenitors ever dared to tread where thy foot now standeth? which of them ever put forth their hand to touch this sacred altar? Thou knowest that God hath set apart, and sanctified his own attendants. Wherefore serves the priesthood, if this be the right of kings? Were it not for the strict prohibition of our God, it could seem no other than an honour to our profession, that a king should think to dignify himself by our employment. But now, knowing the severe charge of the great King of heaven, we cannot but tremble to see that censer in thine hand: who ever, out of the holy tribe, hath wielded it unrevenged? This affront is not to us, it is to the God whom we serve. In awe of that terrible Majesty, as thou wouldst avoid some exemplary judgment, O king, withdraw thyself, not without humble deprecations, from this presence, and lay down that interdicted handful, with fear and trembling. Be thou ever a king; let us he priests: the sceptre is thine, let censers be ours.

What religious heart could do other, than relent at so faithful and just an admonition? but how hard is it for great persons to yield they have offended! Uzziah must not be faulty: what is done rashly, shall be borne out with power; he was wroth, and thus expresseth it: "What means this saucy expostulation, O ye sons of Levi? how dare ye thus malapertly control the well-meant actions of your sovereign? If ye be priests, remember that ye are subjects; or if ye will needs forget it, how easy is it for this hand to awake your memory. What such offence can it be for me to come into that house, and to touch that altar, which my royal progenitors have made, beautified, consecrated? Is the God of this place only yours? Why do ye thus ambitiously engross religion? If princes have not intermeddled with these holy affairs, it was because they would not—not because they might not. When those laws were made for the sanctuary, there were no kings to grace these divine ceremonies; yet even then, Moses was privileged. The persons of princes, if ye know not, are no less sacred than your own. It is your presumption to account the Lord's anointed profane. Contest with those, whose dry and unhallowed heads are subject to your power; for me, I will not ask your leave to be devout. Look ye to your own censers, presume not to meddle with mine: in the meantime, can ye think this insolence of yours shall escape unrevenged? Can it stand with the honour of my sovereignty, to be thus proudly checked by subjects? 'God do so to me, and more also, if"——While Uzziah yet speaks, God strikes: ere the words of fury can come forth of his mouth, the leprosy appears in his forehead. Leprosy was a most loathsome disease: the forehead is the most conspicuous part. Had this shameful scurf broken forth upon his hand, or foot, or breast, it might have been hid from the eyes of men: now the forehead is smitten with this judgment, that God may proclaim to all beholders. Thus shall it be done to the man, whose arrogance hath thrust him upon a sacred charge. Public offences must have open shame.

It is a dangerous thing to put ourselves into the affairs, into the presence of God, unwarranted. There cannot be a more foolish misprision, than, because we are great on earth, to think we may be bold with Heaven. When God's messengers cannot prevail by counsels, entreaties, threats, it is time for God to show his immediate judgments. Wilful offenders can expect nothing but a fearful revenge.

Now begins Uzziah to be confounded in himself; and shame strives with leprosy for a place in his forehead: the hand of God hath done that in an instant, which all the tongues of men had attempted in vain. There needs no farther solicitor of his egress; the sense of his plague sends him forth alone. And now he thinks, Wretched man that I am, how have I angered God, and undone myself! I would needs come in like a priest, and now go forth a leper: the pride of my heart made me think myself worthy the presence of a God; God's just displeasure hath now made me unworthy of the presence of men: while I affected the altar, I have lost my throne; while I scornfully rejected the advice and censures of God's ministers, I am now become a spectacle of horror and deformity to my own servants; I, that would be sending up perfumes to heaven, have made my nastiness hateful to my own senses. What do I under this sacred roof? neither is God's house now for me, nor mine own: what cell, what dungeon is close enough for me, wherein to wear out the residue of mine unhappy and uncomfortable days? O God, thou art just, and I am miserable!

Thus, with a dejected countenance, and sad heart, doth Uzziah hasten to retire himself; and wishes that he could be no less hid from himself, than from others. How easy is it for the God of heaven to bring down the highest pitch of earthly greatness, and to humble the stubbornest pride!

Upon the leisure of second thoughts, Uzziah cannot but acknowledge much favour in this correction, and confess to have escaped well: others, he knew, had been struck dead, or swallowed up quick, for so presumptuous an intrusion. It is happy for him, if his forehead may excuse his soul.

Uzziah ceased not to be a king, when he began to be a leper; the disease of his forehead did not remove his crown: his son Jotham reigned for him, under him; and while he was not seen, yet he was obeyed. The character of sovereignty is indelible, whether by bodily infirmity, or by spiritual censure. Neither is it otherwise, O God, betwixt thee and us; if we be once a royal generation unto thee, our leprosies may deform us, they shall not dethrone us; still shall we have the right, still the possession of that glorious kingdom, wherein we are invested from eternity.

CONTEMPLATION VII.—AHAZ WITH HIS NEW ALTAR.

AFTER many unhappy changes of the two thrones, Ahaz succeeds Jotham in the kingdom of Judah, an ill son of a good father; not more the heir of David's seat, than of Jeroboam's sin. Though Israel play the harlot, yet who can abide that Judah should sin? It is hard not to be infected with a contagious neighbourhood: who ever read that the kingdom of Israel was seasoned with the vicinity of the true religion of Judah? Goodness, such our nature is, is not so apt to spread. A tainted air doth more easily affect a sound body, than a wholesome air can clear the sick. Superstition hath ever been more successful than truth: the young years of Ahaz are soon misled to a plausible misdevotion.

A man that is once fallen from truth, knows not where he shall stay. From the calves of Jeroboam is Ahaz drawn to the gods of the heathen; yea, now bulls and goats are too little for those new deities; his own flesh and blood is but dear enough: "He made his son to pass through their fire." Where do we find any religious Israelite thus zealous for God! Neither doth the holiness and mercy of our God require so cruel a sacrifice; neither is our dull and niggardly hand ready to gratify him with more easy obediences. O God, how gladly should we offer unto thee our souls and bodies, which we may enjoy so much the more, when they are thine; since zealous pagans stick not to lose their own flesh and blood in an idol's fire!

He, that hath thus shamefully cast off the God of his fathers, cannot be long without a fearful revenge. The king of Israel galls him on the one side, the king of Syria on the other. To avoid the shock of both, Ahaz doth not betake himself to the God whom he had offended, who was able to make his enemies at peace with him, but to Tiglath-pileser king of Ashur: him doth he woo with suits, with gifts, and robs God of those presents, which may endear so strong a helper. He that thought not his son too dear for an idol, thinks not God's silver and gold too dear for an idolatrous abettor.

O the infinite patience of the Almighty! God gives success awhile to so offensive a rivality. This Assyrian king prevails against the king of Syria, kills him, and takes his chief city Damascus. The quarrel of the king of Judah hath enlarged the territories of his assistant beyond hope: and now, while this Assyrian victor is enjoying the possession of his new-won Damascus, Ahaz goes up thither to meet him, to congratulate the victor, to add unto those triumphs, which were drawn on by his solicitation. There he sees a new-fashioned altar, that pleases his eye; that old form of Solomon's, which was made by the pattern showed to Moses in the mount, is now grown stale and despicable: a model of this more exquisite frame is sent to Urijah the priest, and must be sampled in Jerusalem.

It is a dangerous presumption to make innovations, if but in the circumstances of God's worship. Those human additions, which would seem to grace the institution of God, deprave it: that infinite wisdom knows best what will please itself, and prescribes accordingly. The foolishness of God is wiser than the wisdom of men. Idolatry and falsehood are commonly more gaudy and plausible than truth. That heart which can, for the outward homeliness, despise the ordinances of God, is already alienated from true religion, and lies open to the grossest superstition.

Never any prince was so foully idolatrous, as that he wanted a priest to second him: An Urijah is fit to humour an Ahaz. Greatness could never command any thing, which some servile wits were not ready both to applaud and justify.

Ere the king can be returned from Damascus, the altar is finished. It were happy if true godliness could be so forward in the prosecutions of good. Neither is this strange pile reared only, but thrust up betwixt God's altar and the temple, in an apparent precedency, as if he had said, Let the God of Judah come behind the deities of Syria.

And now, to make up the full measure of his impiety, this idolatrous king will himself be sacrificing upon his new altar, to his new gods, the gods of Damascus. An usurped priesthood well becomes a false deity: "Because," saith he, "the gods of the kings of Syria help them, therefore will I sacrifice to them, that they may help me."

O blind superstition! How did the gods of Syria help their kings, when both those kings and their gods were vanquished and taken by the king of Assyria? Even this Damascus and this altar were the spoil of a foreign enemy: how then did the gods of

Syria help their kings, any other than to their ruin? What dotage is this, to make choice of a foiled protection? But had the Syrians prospered, must their gods have the thanks? Are there no authors of good but blocks or devils? or is an outward prosperity the only argument of truth, the only motive of devotion? O foolish Ahaz! it is the God thou hast forsaken that plagues thee, under whose only arm thou mightst have prevailed. His power beats those pagan stocks one against another, so as, one while, one seems victorious, another vanquished; and at last he confounds both together with their proudest clients. Thyself shall be the best instance.

Of all the kings of Judah hitherto, there is none so dreadful an example, either of sin or judgment, as this son of good Jotham. I abhor to think that such a monster should descend from the loins of David. Where should be the period of this wickedness? He began with the high places; thence he descends to the calves of Dan and Bethel; from thence he falls to a Syrian altar, to the Syrian god; then, from a partnership, he falls to an utter exclusion of the true God, and blocking up his temple; and then to the sacrifice of his own son; and, at last, as if hell were broken loose upon God's inheritance, every several city, every high place of Judah, hath a new god. No marvel if he be branded by the Spirit of God, with, "This is that king Ahaz."

What a fearful plague did this noisome deluge of sin leave behind it in the land of Judah! Who can express the horror of God's revenge upon a people that should have been his? Pekah the king of Israel slew a hundred and twenty thousand of them in one day, amongst whom was Maaseiah the son of Ahaz. O just judgment of the Almighty! Ahaz sheds the blood of one son to an idol: the true God sheds the blood of another of his sons in revenge.

Yet the hand of the Lord is stretched out still. Two hundred thousand of them were carried away, by the Israelites, captive to Samaria. The Edomites came, and carried away another part of them for bond slaves to their country. The Philistines came up and shared the cities of the south of Judah, and the villages thereof: shortly, what other is miserable Judah, than the prey and spoil of all the neighbouring nations! "For the Lord brought Judah low because of Ahaz king of Israel; for he made Judah naked, and transgressed sore against the Lord." As for the great king of Ashur, whom Ahaz purchased with the sacrilegious pillage of the house of God, instead of an aid, he proves a burden: however he sped in his first onsets, now "he distressed Judah, but strengthened it not." The charge was as great as the benefit small; sooner shall he eat them out, than rescue them. No arm of flesh can shelter Ahaz from a vengeance.

"Be wise, O ye kings; be instructed, O ye judges of the earth: serve the Lord with fear, and rejoice with trembling. Kiss the son, lest he be angry, and ye perish from the way, when his wrath is kindled but a little."

His subjects complain, that he died so late; and, as repenting that he ever was, denying him a room in the sepulchres of kings; as if they had said, The common earth of Jerusalem is too good for him that degenerated from his progenitors, spoiled his kingdom, depraved his people, forsook his God.

CONTEMPLATION VIII.—THE UTTER DESTRUCTION OF THE KINGDOM OF ISRAEL.

Judah was at a sore heave; yet Israel shall miscarry before it; such are the sins of both, that they strive whether shall fall first; but this lot must light upon the ten tribes. Though the late king of Judah were personally worse than the most of Jeroboam's successors, yet the people were generally less evil, upon whom the encroachments of idolatry were more by obtrusion, than by consent: besides that the thrones of Judah had some interchanges of good princes; Israel none at all. The same justice, therefore, that made Israel a scourge to Judah, made Assyria a scorpion to Israel.

It was the quarrel of Judah that first engaged the king of Ashur in this war against Israel: now he is not so easily fetched off. So we have seen some eager mastiff, that hath been set on by the least clap of the hand, but could not be loosened by the force of staves.

Salmaneser king of Assyria comes up against Hoshea king of Israel, and subdues him, and puts him to his tribute. This yoke was uncouth and unpleasing: the vanquished prince was neither able to resist, nor willing to yield: secretly, therefore, he treats with the king of Egypt for assistance; as desiring rather to hazard his liberty by the hand of an equal, than to enjoy a quiet subjection under the hand of an overruling power. We cannot blame princes to be jealous of their sovereignties. The detain-

DESTRUCTION OF ISRAEL.

ing of his yearly tribute, and the whisperings with new confederates, have drawn up the king of Ashur to perfect his own victories. He returns, therefore, with a strong power, and, after three years' siege, takes Samaria, imprisons Hoshea, and, in the exchange of a woful captivity, he peoples Israel with Assyrians, and Assyria with Israelites. Now that abused soil hath, upon a surfeit of wickedness, cast out her perfidious owners, and will try how it can fare with heathenish strangers. Now the Assyrian gallants triumph in the palaces of Samaria and Jezreel, while the peers and captains of Israel are driven manacled through the Assyrian streets, and billeted to the several places of their perpetual servitude. Shortly now the flourishing kingdom of the ten tribes is come to a final and shameful end, and so vanished in this last dissipation, that, since that day, no man could ever say, this was Israel.

O terrible example of vengeance, upon that peculiar people, whom God hath chosen for himself out of all the world! All the world were witnesses of the favours of their miraculous deliverances and protections; all the world shall be witnesses of their just confusion.

It is not in the power of slight errors to set off that infinite mercy. What was it, O God, what was it that caused thee to cast off thine own inheritance? what but the same that made thee to cast the angels out of heaven, even their rebellious sins? Those sins dared to emulate the greatness of thy mercies, no less than they forced the severity of thy judgments: " They left all the commandments of the Lord their God; and made them molten images, even two calves; and made a grove, and worshipped all the host of heaven, and served Baal, and caused their sons and daughters to pass through the fire, and used divinations and enchantments, and sold themselves to do evil in the sight of the Lord, to provoke him to anger."

Neither were these slips of frailty, or ignorant mistakings, but wilful crimes, obstinate impieties, in spite of the doctrines, reproofs, menaces, miraculous convictions of the holy prophets, which God sent amongst them. Thy destruction is of thyself, O Israel! What could the just hand of the Almighty do less than consume a nation so incorrigibly flagitious—a nation so unthankful for mercies, so impatient of remedies, so incapable of repentance—so obliged, so warned, so shamelessly, so lawlessly wicked?

What nation under heaven can now challenge an indefeasible interest in God, when Israel itself is cast off? what church in the world can show such dear love-tokens from the Almighty, as this now abhorred and adulterous spouse? He, that spared not the natural olive, shall he spare the wild? It is not for us sinners of the Gentiles to be high-minded, but awful.

The Israelites are carried captive into Assyria. These goodly cities of the ten tribes may not lie waste and unpeopled; the wisdom of the victor finds it fit to transplant his own colonies thither, that so he may raise profit thence, with security. From Babylon, therefore, and Cuthah, and Ava, and Hamath, and Sepharvaim, doth he send of his own subjects, to possess and inhabit the cities of Samaria. The land doth not brook her new tenants; " They feared not the Lord:" how should they? they knew him not; " Therefore the Lord sent lions amongst them, which slew some of them." Not the veriest pagan can be excused for his ignorance of God: even the most depraved nature might teach us to tremble at a Deity. It is just with the Almighty not to put up with neglect, where he hath bestowed reason.

The brute creatures are sent to revenge the quarrel of their Maker, upon worse beasts than themselves. Still hath God left himself champions in Israel: lions tear the Assyrians in pieces, and put them in mind, that, had it not been for wickedness, that land needed not to have changed masters. The great Lord of the world cannot want means to plague offenders: if the men be gone, yet the beasts are there; and if the beasts had been gone, yet, so long as there were stones in the walls, in the quarries, God would be sure of avengers. There is no security but in being at peace with God.

The king of Assyria is sued to for remedy. Even these pagans have learned to know that these lions were sent from a God; that this punishment is for sin: " They know not the manner of the God of the land; therefore he hath sent lions among them." These blind heathens, that think every land hath a several god, yet hold that god worthy of his own worship; yet hold, that worship must be grounded upon knowledge, the want of that knowledge punishable, the punishment of that want just and divine. How much worse than Assyrians are they that are ready to ascribe all calamities to nature, to chance! that, acknowledging but one God of all the world, are yet careless to know him, to serve him?

One of the priests of Israel is appointed

to be carried back to Samaria, to teach the Assyrian colony the fashions of the god of the land; not for devotion, but for impunity. Vain politicians think to satisfy God by patching up religions: any forms are good enough for an unknown deity. The Assyrian priests teach and practise the worship of their own gods. The Israelitish priest prescribes the worship of the true God. The people will follow both; the one out of liking, the other out of fear. What a prodigious mixture was here of religions! true with false, Jewish with paganish—divine with devilish! Every division of these transplanted Assyrians had their several deities, high places, sacrifices. This high priest of Israel intercommunes with every one of them: so that now these fathers of Samaritanism are in at all: " They fear the Lord, and serve their idols." No beggar's cloak is more pieced, than the religion of these new inhabitants of Israel. I know not how their bodies sped for the lions; I am sure their souls fared the worse for this medley. Above all things, God hates a mongrel devotion: if we be not all Israel, it were better to be all Ashur. It cannot so much displease God to be unknown or neglected, as to be consorted with idols.

CONTEMPLATION IX. — HEZEKIAH AND SENNACHERIB.

ISRAEL is gone, Judah is left standing; or rather, some few sprigs of those two tribes. So we have seen, in the shredding of some large timber-tree, one or two boughs left at the top to hold up the sap. Who can but lament the poor remainders of that languishing kingdom of David!

Take out of the two tribes of Judah and Benjamin one hundred and twenty thousand, whom Pekah the king of Israel slew in one day; take out two hundred thousand that were carried away captive to Samaria; take out those that were transported into the bondage of the Edomites, and those that were subdued in the south parts by the Philistines: alas! what a handful was left to the king of Judah! scarce worth the name of a dominion! Yet, even now, out of the gleeds of Judah, doth God raise up a glorious light to his forlorn church; yea, from the wretched loins of Ahaz, doth God fetch a holy Hezekiah. It had been hard to conceive the state of Judah worse than it was; neither was it more miserable than sinful, and, in regard of both, desperate. When beyond hope, God revives this dying stock of David, and, out of very ruins, builds up his own house. Ahaz was not more the ill son of a good father, than he was the ill father of a good son; he was the ill son of good Jotham, the ill father of good Hezekiah. Good Hezekian makes amends for his father's impiety, and puts a new life into the heartless remnant of God's people.

The wisdom of our good God knows when his aid will be most seasonable, most welcome, which he then loves to give, when he finds us left of our hopes. That merciful hand is reserved for a dead lift; then he fails us not.

Now ye might have seen this pious prince busily bestirring himself, in so late and needful a reformation; removing the high places, battering and burning the idols, demolishing their temples, cutting down their groves, opening the temple, purging the altars and vessels, sanctifying the priests, rekindling the lamps, renewing the incense, re-instituting the sacrifices, establishing the order of God's service, appointing the courses, settling the maintenance of the ministers, publishing the decrees of the long-neglected passover, celebrating it and the other feasts with due solemnity, encouraging the people, contributing bountifully to the offerings; and, in one word, so ordering all the affairs of God as if he had been sent down from heaven to restore religion, as if David himself had been alive again in this blessed heir, not so much of his crown, as of his piety. O Judah! happy in thy Hezekiah! O Hezekiah! happy in the gracious restoration of thy Judah! Ahaz shall have no thanks for such a son: the God, that is able of the very stones to raise children to Abraham, raises a true seed of David, out of the corrupt loins of an idolater. That infinite mercy is not tied to the terms of an immediate propagation: for the space of three hundred years, the man after God's own heart had no perfect heir till now. Till now did the high places stand: the devotions of the best princes of Judah were blemished with some weak omissions. Now, the zeal of good Hezekiah clears all those defects, and works an entire change.

How seasonably hath the providence of God kept the best man for the worst times! When God hath a great work to do, he knows to fit himself with instruments.

No marvel if the paganish idols go to wreck, when even the brazen serpent, that Moses had made by God's own appointment, is broken in pieces. The Israelites were stung with fiery serpents; this brazen serpent healed them, which they did no sooner see than they recovered. But now, such was the venom of the Israelitish idolatry, that this serpent of brass stung worse than the fiery; that which first cured by the eye, now by the eye poisoned the soul; that which was at first the type of a Saviour, is now the deadly engine of the enemy: while it helped, it stood; it stood while it hurt not: but when once wicked abuse had turned it into an idol, what was it but Nehushtan?

The holiness of the first institution cannot privilege aught from the danger of a future profanation; nor, as the case may stand, from an utter abolition. What antiquity, what authority, what primary service, might this serpent have pleaded? All that cannot keep it out of the dust. Those things which are necessary in their being, beneficial in their continuance, may still remain when their abuse is purged: but those things whose use is but temporary, and whose duration is needless and unprofitable, may cease with the occasion, and much more perish with an inseparable abuse. Hezekiah willingly forgets who made the serpent, when he sees the Israelites make it an idol. It is no less intolerable for God to have a rival of his own making.

Since Hezekiah was thus, above all his ancestors, upright with the Lord, it is no marvel if the Lord were with him, if he prospered whithersoever he went: the same God, that would have his justice magnified in the confusion of the wicked princes of Israel and Judah, would have his mercy no less acknowledged in the blessings of faithful Hezekiah.

The great king of Assyria had, in a sort, swallowed up both the kingdoms of Judah and Israel; yet not with an equal cruelty: he made Israel captive; Judah, upon a willing composition, tributary. Israel is vanished in a transportation; Judah continues under the homage wherein Ahaz left it. Hezekiah had reigned but six years, when he saw his neighbours of Israel packing into a miserable captivity, and the proud Assyrians lording in their cities; yet, even then, when he stood alone, in a corner of Judah, durst Hezekiah draw his neck out of the yoke of the great and victorious monarch of Assyria; and, as if one enemy had not been enough, at the same time he falls upon the encroaching Philistines, and prevails. It is not to be asked what powers a man can make, but in what terms he stands with Heaven. The unworthy father of Hezekiah had clogged Judah with this servile fealty to the Assyrian; what the conditions of that subjection were, it is too late, and needless for us to inquire. If this payment were limited to a period of time, the expiration acquitted him; if upon covenants of aid, the cessation therefore acquitted him; if the reforming of religion, and banishment of idolatry, ran under the censure of rebellion, the quarrel on Hezekiah's part was holy, on Sennacherib's unjust: but if the re-stipulation were absolute, and the withdrawing of this homage upon none but civil grounds, I cannot excuse the good king from a just offence. It was a human frailty in an obliged prince, by force to effect a free and independent sovereignty.

What! do we mince that fact, which holy Hezekiah himself censures? " I have offended, return from me; what thou puttest on me will I bear." The comfort of liberty may not be had with an unwarranted violence. Holiness cannot free us from infirmity. It was a weakness to do that act, which must be soon undone with much repentance, and more loss; this revolt shall cost Hezekiah, besides much humiliation, three hundred yearly talents of silver, thirty talents of gold. How much better had it been for the cities of Judah to have purchased their peace with an easy tribute, than war with intolerable taxation.

Fourteen years had good Hezekiah fed upon a sweet peace, sauced only with a set pension; now he must prepare his palate for the bitter morsels of war. The king of Assyria has come up against all the defenced cities of Judah, and hath taken them. Hezekiah is fain to buy him out with too many talents; the poor kingdom of Judah is exhausted with so deep a payment, insomuch that the king is forced to borrow of God himself, for "Hezekiah gave him all the silver that was found in the house of the Lord; yea, at that time did Hezekiah cut off the gold from the doors of the temple of the Lord, and from the pillars which he had overlaid, and gave it to the king of Assyria." How hard was good Hezekiah driven, ere he would be thus bold with his God! Surely if the mines or coffers of Judah could have yielded any supply, this shift had been hateful; to fetch back for an enemy that which he had given to his Maker. Only necessity excuses that from sacrilege in the son, which will make sacrilege in the father: that which is once devoted to a sacred use, may not be called back to a profane. But He, whose the earth is, and the fulness of it, is not so taken with our metals, that he should more regard our gold than our welfare: his goodness cannot grudge any outward thing for the price of our peace. To rob God, out of covetousness, or wantonness, or neglect, is justly damnable; we cannot rob him out

2 B

of our need; for then he gives us all we take, and bids us ransom our lives, our liberties. The treasures of God's house were precious, for his sake, to whom they were consecrated; but more precious in the sight of the Lord was the life of any one of his saints.

Every true Israelite was the spiritual house of God. Why should not the door of the material temple be willingly stripped, to save the whole frame of the spiritual temple? Take therefore, O Hezekiah, what thou hast given; no gold is too holy to redeem thy vexation. It matters not so much how bare the doors of the temple be, in a case of necessity, as how well the insides be furnished with sincere devotion. O the cruel hard-heartedness of those men, which will rather suffer the living temples of God to be ruined, than they will ransom their lives with farthings.

It could not be, but that the store of needy Judah must soon be drawn dry with so deep an exaction. That sum cannot be sent, because it cannot be raised. The cruel tyrant calls for his bricks, while he allows no straw: his anger is kindled, because Hezekiah's coffers have a bottom. With a mighty host doth he come up against Jerusalem; therefore shall that city be destroyed by him, because by him it hath been impoverished: the inhabitants must be slaves, because they are beggars.

O lamentable, and, in sight, desperate condition, of distressed Jerusalem! Wealth it had none; strength it had but a little: all the country round about was subdued to the Assyrian; that proud victor hath begirt the walls of it with an innumerable army, scorning that such a shovelful of earth should stand out but one day. Poor Jerusalem stands alone, blocked up with a world of enemies, helpless, friendless, comfortless, looking for the worst of a hostile fury, when Tartan, and Rabsaris, and Rabshakeh, the great captains of the Assyrians, call to a parley. Hezekiah sends to them three of his prime officers, his steward, his secretary, his recorder. Lord! what insolent blasphemies doth that foul mouth of Rabshakeh belch out against the living God, against his anointed servant!

How plausibly doth he discourage the subjects of Hezekiah! how proudly doth he insult upon their impotency! how doth he brave them with base offers of advantage! and, lastly, how cunningly doth he forelay their confidence, which was only left them, in the Almighty, protesting not to be come up thither without the Lord! " The Lord said to me, Go up to this land and destroy it." How fearful a word was this! the rest were but vain cracks; this was a thunderbolt to strike dead the heart of Hezekiah. If Rabshakeh could have been believed, Jerusalem could not but have flown open; how could it think to stand out no less against God than men? Even thus doth the great enemy of mankind: if he can dishearten the soul from a dependence upon the God of mercies, the day is his. Lewd miscreants care not how they belie God, for their own purposes.

Eliakim, the steward of Hezekiah, well knew how much the people must needs be affected with this pernicious suggestion; and fain would, therefore, if not stop that wicked mouth, yet divert these blasphemies into a foreign expression. I wonder that any wise man should look for favour from an enemy: " Speak, I pray thee, to thy servants in the Syrian language." What was this, but to teach an adversary how to do mischief? Wherefore came Rabshakeh thither, but to gall Hezekiah, to withdraw his subjects? That tongue is most proper for him which may hurt most. Deprecations of evil, to a malicious man, are no better than advices. An unknown idiom is fit to keep counsel: they are familiar words that must convey aught to the understanding. Lewd men are the worse for admonitions.

Rabshakeh had not so strained his throat, to corrupt the citizens of Jerusalem, had it not been for the humble obtestation of Eliakim. Now he rears up his voice, and holds his sides, and roars out his double blasphemies: one while affrighting the people with the great power of the mighty king of Assyria; another while debasing the contemptible force of Hezekiah: now smoothly alluring them with the assurances of a safe and successful yieldance; then discouraging them with the impossibility of their deliverance; laying before them the fearful examples of greater nations vanquished by that sword, which was now shaken over them, triumphing in the impotency and miscarriage of their gods: " Who are they, among all the gods of the countries, that have delivered their country out of mine hand, that the Lord should deliver Jerusalem out of mine hand? where are the gods of Arpad and of Hamath?" Where, but in that hellish darkness that is ordained both for them and for thee, barbarous Assyrian, that darest thus open thy mouth against thy Maker. And can those atheous eyes of thine see no difference of gods? is there no distance betwixt a stock, or stone, and that infinite Deity that made heaven and earth? It is enough that thou now feelest it; thy torments have taught thee too late, that thou affrontest a living God.

How did the fingers and tongues of those Jewish peers and people itch to be at Rabshakeh, in a revengeful answer to those impieties! All is hushed; not a word sounds from those walls. I do not more wonder at Hezekiah's wisdom, in commanding silence, than at the subjects' obedience in keeping it. This railer could not be more spited, than with no answer; and if he might be exasperated, he could not be reformed: besides, the rebounding of those multiplied blasphemies might leave some ill impressions in the multitude; this sulphurous flash, therefore, dies in its own smoke, only leaving a hateful stench behind it.

Good Hezekiah cannot easily pass over this devilish oratory: no sooner doth he hear of it, than he rends his clothes, and covers himself with sackcloth, and betakes himself to the house of the Lord, and sends his officers, and the gravest of the priests, clad in sackcloth, to Isaiah, the prophet of God, with a doleful and querulous message.

O the noble piety of Hezekiah! Notwithstanding all the straits of the siege, and the danger of so powerful an enemy, I find not the garments of this good king, any otherwise than whole, and unchanged: but now, so soon as ever a blasphemy is uttered against the majesty of his God, though by a pagan dog, his clothes are torn, and turned into sackcloth. There can be no better argument of an upright heart, than to be more sensible of the indignities offered to God, than of our own dangers. Even these desperate reproaches send Hezekiah to the temple. The more we see God's name profaned, the more shall we, if we be truly religious, love and honour it.

Whither should Hezekiah run, but to the temple, to the prophet? There, there is the refuge of all faithful ones, where they may speak with God, where they may be spoken to from God, and fetch comfort from both. It is not possible that a believing heart should be disappointed. Isaiah sends that message to the good king, that may dry up his tears, and cheer his countenance, and change his suit: " Thus saith the Lord, Be not afraid of the words which thou hast heard, with which the servants of the king of Assyria have blasphemed me: Behold, I will send a blast upon him, and he shall hear a rumour, and shall return to his own land; and I will cause him to fall by the sword, in his own land."

Lo! even while Sennacherib was in the height of his jollity and assurance, God's prophet foresees his ruin, and gives him for dead, while that tyrant thought of nothing but life and victory. Proud and secure worldlings little dream of the near approach of their judgments: while they are plotting their deepest designs, the overruling justice of the Almighty hath contrived their sudden confusion, and sees and sets them their day.

Rabshakeh returns, and finding the king of Assyria warring against Libnah, reports to him the silent, and therein contemptuous answer, and firm resolutions of Hezekiah: in the meantime God pulls Sennacherib by the ear, with the news of the approaching arm of Tirhakah, king of Ethiopia, which was coming up to raise the siege, and to succour his confederates. That dreadful power will not allow the Assyrian king, in person, to lead his other forces up against Jerusalem, nor to continue his former leaguer long before those walls. But now he writes big words to Hezekiah, and thinks, with his thundering menaces, to beat open the gates, and level the bulwarks of Jerusalem. Like the true master of Rabshakeh, he reviles the God of heaven, and basely parallels him with the dunghill deities of the heathen.

Good Hezekiah gets him into his sanctuary. There he spreads the letter before the Lord; and calls to the God that dwells between the cherubims, to revenge the blasphemies of Sennacherib, to protect and rescue himself and his people. Every one of those words pierced heaven, which was no less open to mercy unto Hezekiah, than vengeance to Sennacherib. Now is Isaiah addressed with a second message of comfort to him, who doubtless distrusted not the first: only the reiteration of that furious blasphemy made him take faster hold, by his faithful devotion. Now the jealous God, in a disdain of so blasphemous a contestation, rises up in a style of majesty, and gloriously tramples upon this saucy insolency: " Because thy rage against me, and thy tumult, is come up into mine ears, therefore I will put my hook into thy nose, and my bridle into thy lips, and will turn thee back by the way thou camest." Lo, Sennacherib, the God of heaven makes a beast of thee, who hast so brutishly spurned at his name. If thou be a ravenous bear, he hath a hook for thy nostrils; if thou be a resty horse, he hath a bridle for thy mouth: in spite of thee, thou shalt follow his hook, or his bridle, and shalt be led to thy just shame by either.

It is not for us to be the lords of our own actions: " Thus saith the Lord concerning the king of Assyria, He shall not come into this city, nor shoot an arrow there, nor come before it with a shield, nor cast a bank against it; by the way that he came, shall he return," &c. Impotent men! what are we in the hands of the Almighty? We purpose, he overrules; we talk of great matters, and think to do wonders; he blows upon our projects, and they vanish with ourselves. He that hath set bounds to the sea, hath appointed limits to the rage of the proudest enemies; yea, even the devils themselves are confined. Why boast ye yourselves, O ye tyrants, that ye can do mischief? ye are stinted, and even within those lists is confusion.

O the trophies of Divine justice! "That very night the angel of the Lord went out, and smote in the camp of the Assyrians? an hundred fourscore and five thousand, and when they arose early in the morning, behold they were all dead corpses."

How speedy an execution was this! how miraculous! No human arm shall have the glory of this victory: it was God that was defied by that presumptuous Assyrian; it is God that shall right his own wrongs. Had the Egyptian or Ethiopian forces been come up, though the same God had done this work by them, yet some praise of this slaughter had, perhaps, cleaved to their fingers: now an invisible hand sheds all this blood, that his very enemies may clear him from all partnership of revenge. Go now, wicked Sennacherib, and tell of the gods of Hamath, and Arpad, and Sepharvaim, and Hena, and Ivah, which thou hast destroyed, and say, that Hezekiah's God is but as one of these. Go, and add this deity to the number of thy conquests; now say, that Hezekiah's God, in whom he trusted, hath deceived him, and graced thy triumphs.

With shame and grief enough is that sheeped tyrant returned to his Nineveh, having left behind him all the pride and strength of Assyria, for compost to Jewish fields. Well were it for thee, O Sennacherib! if thou couldst escape thus: vengeance waits for thee at home, and welcomes thee into thy place: while thou art worshipping in the house of Nisroch thy god, two of thine own sons shall be thine executioners. See now if that false deity of thine can preserve thee from that stroke, which the true God sends thee by the hand of thine own flesh. He, that slew thine host by his angels, slays thee by thy sons: the same angel, that killed all those thousands, could as easily have smitten thee; but he rather reserves thee for the further torment of an unnatural stroke, that thou mayest see, too late, how easy it is for him, in spite of thy god, to arm thine own loins against thee.

Thou art avenged, O God! thou art avenged plentifully of thine enemies! Whosoever strives with thee, is sure to gain nothing but loss, but shame, but death, but hell. The Assyrians are slain; Sennacherib is rewarded for his blasphemy: Jerusalem is rescued; Hezekiah rejoices: the nations wonder and tremble. "O love the Lord, all ye saints; for the Lord preserveth the faithful, and plenteously rewardeth the proud doer."

CONTEMPLATION X. — HEZEKIAH SICK, RECOVERED, VISITED.

HEZEKIAH was freed from the siege of the Assyrians, but he is surprised with a disease. He, that delivered him from the hand of his enemies, smites him with sickness. God doth not let us loose from all afflictions, when he redeems us from one.

To think that Hezekiah was either not thankful enough for his deliverance, or too much lifted up with glory of so miraculous a favour, were an injurious misconstruction of the hand of God, and an uncharitable censure of a holy prince: for though no flesh and blood can avoid the just desert of bodily punishment, yet God doth not always strike with an intuition of sin: sometimes he regards the benefit of our trial, sometimes the glory of his mercy in our cure.

It was no slight distemper that seized upon Hezekiah, but a disease both painful and fierce, and in nature deadly. O God, how thou lashest even those whom thou lovest! Hadst thou ever any such darling in the throne of Judah, as Hezekiah? yet he no sooner breatheth from a miserable siege, than he panteth under a mortal sickness, when as yet he had not so much as the comfort of a child to succeed him. Thy prophet is sent to him with a heavy message of his death: "Set thine house in order, for thou shalt die and not live." It is no small mercy of God that he gives us warning of our end: we shall make an ill use of so gracious a premonition, if we make not a meet preparation for our passage. Even those that have not a house, yet have a soul. No soul can want important affairs to be ordered for a final dissolution: the neglect of this best thrift is desperate. Set thy soul in order, O man, for thou shalt die and not live.

If God had given Hezekiah a son, nature had bequeathed his estate: now, he must study to find heirs. Even these outward things, though in themselves worthless, require our careful disposition to those we leave behind us; and, if we have delayed these thoughts till then, our sickbeds may not complain of their importunity. We cannot leave to our families a better legacy than peace.

Never was the prophet Isaiah unwelcome to this good king, until now. Even sad tidings must be carried by those messengers which would be faithful: neither may we regard so much how they will be taken, as by whom they are sent.

It was a bold and harsh word, to say to a king, "Thou shalt die and not live." I do not hear Hezekiah rage, and fret at the message, or threaten the bearer; but he meekly turns his face to the wall, and weeps, and prays. Why to the wall? Was it for the greater secresy of his devotion? was it for the more freedom from distraction? was it that all the passion, which accompanied his prayer, might have no witnesses? or, was it for that this wall looked towards the temple, which his heart and eyes still moved unto, though his feet could not?

Howsoever, the patient soul of good Hezekiah turns itself to that holy God, from whom he smarts and bleeds, and pours out itself into a fervent deprecation: "I beseech thee, O Lord, remember now how I have walked before thee in truth, and with a perfect heart; and have done that which is good in thy sight."

Couldst thou fear, O Hezekiah, that God had forgotten thine integrity? the grace that was in thee was his own work; could he in thee neglect himself? or dost thou therefore doubt of his remembrance of thy faithfulness, because he summons thee to receive the crown of thy faithfulness, glory and immortality? Wherein canst thou be remembered, if this be to forget thee? What challenge is this? Is God a debitor to thy perfection? hath thine holy carriage merited anything from that infinite justice? Far, far were these presumptuous conceits from that humble and mortified soul: thou hadst hated thine own breast, if it could once have harboured so proud a thought. This perfection of thine was no other than an honest fondness of heart and life, which thou knewest God had promised to reward. It was the mercy of the covenant that thou pleadedst not the merit of thine obedience.

Every one of these words was steeped in tears: but what meant these words, these tears? I hear not of any suit moved by Hezekiah;—only he wishes to be remembered in that which never could be forgotten, though he should have entreated for an oblivion.

Speak out, Hezekiah: what is it that thy tears crave, while thy lips express not? "O let me live, and I shall praise thee, O God."

In a natural man, none could wonder at this passionate request: who can but wonder at it in a saint, whose happiness doth but then begin when his life ceaseth; whose misery doth but then end when his death enters? The word of faith is, "O let me die, that I may enjoy thee." How, then, doth the good king cry at the news of that death, which some resolute pagans have entertained with smiles? Certainly the best man cannot strip himself of some flesh; and while nature hath an undeniable share in him, he cannot but retain some smatch of the sweetness of life, of the horror of dissolution: both these were in Hezekiah; neither of them could transport him into this passion: they were higher respects that swayed with so holy a prince; a tender care of the glory of God, a careful pity of the church of God. His very tears said, O God, thou knowest that the eyes of the world are bent upon me, as one that hath abandoned their idolatry, and restored thy sincere worship; I stand alone in the midst of a wicked and idolatrous generation, that looks through all my actions, all my events: if now they shall see me snatched away in the midst of my days, what will these heathens say? how can thy great name but suffer in this mine untimely extinction? Besides, what will become of thy poor church, which I shall leave feebly religious, and as yet scarce warm in the course of a pious reformation? How soon shall it be miserably overgrown with superstition and heathenism! how soon shall the wild boar of Assyria root up this little vineyard of thine! What need I beseech thee, O Lord, to regard thy name, to regard thine inheritance?

What one tear of Hezekiah can run waste? what can that good king pray for, unheard, unanswered? Sennacherib came, in a proud confidence, to swallow up his city and people: prayers and tears send him away confounded. Death comes to swallow up his person, and that not without authority: prayers and tears send him away disappointed. Before Isaiah was gone out into the middle court, the word of the Lord came to him, saying, "Turn again, and tell Hezekiah, the captain of my people, Thus saith the Lord, the God of David thy father, I have heard thy prayer, I have seen thy tears; behold, I will heal thee: on the third day thou shalt go up to the house of the Lord, and I will add to thy days fifteen years."

What shall we say, then? O God! hast thou thus soon changed thy purpose? Was it not thy true message which thy prophet, even now, delivered to Hezekiah? Is somewhat fallen out that thou foresawest not? or dost thou now decree somewhat thou meantest not? The very thought of any of these were no better than blasphemous impiety. Certainly, Hezekiah could not live one day longer than was eternally decreed: the decree of God's eternal counsel had from everlasting determined him fifteen years yet longer. Why then doth God say by his prophet, " Thou shalt die, and not live?" He is not as man, that he should repent; the message is changed, the will is not changed; yea, rather the message is explicated, not changed: for the signified will of God, though it sound absolutely, yet must be understood with condition; that tells Hezekiah what he must expect from the nature of his disease, what would befall him without his deprecations. There was nothing but death in the second causes, whatever secret purpose there was in the first; and that purpose shall lie hid for a time, under a reserved condition. The same decree that says, Nineveh shall be destroyed, means, If Nineveh repent, it shall not be destroyed. He, that finds good reason to say Hezekiah shall die, yet still means, If the quickened devotion of Hezekiah shall importune me for life, it shall be protracted. And the same God, that hath decreed this addition of fifteen years, had decreed to stir up the spirit of Hezekiah to that vehement and weeping importunity which should obtain it. O God! thou workest thy good pleasure in us, and with us; and, by thy revealed will, movest us in those ways, whereby thou effectest thy secret will.

How wonderful is this mercy! Hezekiah's tears are not dry upon his cheeks, yea, his breath is not passed his lips, when God sends him a comfortable answer. How careful is the God of compassions, that his holy servant should not languish one hour, in the expectation of his denounced death! What speed was here, as in the errand, so in the act of recovery! Within three days shall Hezekiah be upon his feet; yea, his feet shall stand in the courts of God's house: he that now in his bed sighs and groans, and weeps out a petition, shall then sing out a thanksgiving in the temple. "O thou that hearest prayer! unto thee shall all flesh come." With what cheerful assurance should we approach to the throne of that grace, which never failed any suppliant.

Neither was this grant more speedy than bountiful. We are wont to reckon seven years for the life of a man; and now, behold, more than two lives hath God added to the age of Hezekiah. How unexampled a favour is this! Who ever but Hezekiah knew his period so long before? The fixedness of his term is no less merciful than the protraction: we must be content to live or die at uncertainties: we are not worthy to calculate the date of our times: "Teach us, O Lord, so to number our days, that we may apply our hearts to wisdom."

There is little joy in many days, if they be evil. Hezekiah shall not be blessed only with life, but with peace. The proud Assyrian threatens an invasion; his late foil still sticks in his stomach, and stirs him to revenge: the hook is in his nostrils; he cannot move whither he list. The God of heaven will maintain his own quarrel: "I will defend this city for mine own sake, and for my servant David's sake." Lo! for his life, Hezekiah is beholden, next under the infinite goodness of God, to his prayers; for his protection, to the dear memory of his father David. Surely, for aught we find, Hezekiah was no less upright, and less offensive than David; yet both Hezekiah and Jerusalem shall fare the better for David's sake, above three hundred years after.

To that man after his own heart, had God engaged himself, by his gracious promise, to preserve his throne, his seed. God loves to remember his ancient mercies. How happy a thing is it to be faithful with God! This is the way to oblige those which are yet unborn, and to entail blessings upon the successions of future generations.

It seems it was some pestilent ulcer that thus endangered the life of Hezekiah.— Isaiah is not a prophet only, but a physician: "And Isaiah said, Take a lump of figs." He that gave an assurance of recovery, gives a receipt for the recovery. The decree of God includes the means: neither can the medicine work without a word; neither will the word work without the medicine; both of them must meet in the cure. If we so trust the promise, that we neglect the prescript, we presume to no purpose. Happy is that soul, that so regards the promise of God's prophets, as that withal he receives their counsels.

Nothing could be more proper for the ripening of hard and purulent tumours, than dry figs. Herein Isaiah's direction was according to nature. Wherefore should we baulk the ordinary road, where it is both fair and near?

The sudden contradiction of the message causes a just difficulty in the assent. Hezekiah therefore craves a sign; not for that he distrusted, but that he might trust the more: we can never take too fast hold of those promises of God, which have not more comfort in the application, than natural impossibility in the performance. "We believe: Lord, help our unbelief!"

The sick king hath his option: his father was offered a sign, and refused it; he sues for one, and obtains it: "Shall the shadow go forward ten degrees, or back ten degrees?" as if heaven itself lay open to his choice, and were ready either to mend his pace, or retire for his confirmation. What creature is not cheerfully forward to obey the faith of God's servants?

Hezekiah fastens rather upon that sign which is more hard, more disagreeing from the course of nature: not without good reason; every proof must be clearer than the thing to be proved, neither may there want a meet proportion betwixt both: now the going forward of the shadow was a motion, no other than natural; the recovery of that pestilent disease was against the stream of nature: the more difficult sign, therefore, the surer evidence.

Whether shall we more wonder at the measure of the love of God to Hezekiah, or at the power of Isaiah's faith in God? Out of both, either the sun goes back in heaven, that his shadow may go back on earth, or the shadow no less miraculously goes back on earth, while the sun goes forward in heaven. It is true that the prophet speaks of the shadow, not of the sun; except perhaps because the motion of the sun is best discerned by the shadow, and the motion of the shadow is led by the course of the sun; besides that the demonstration of this miracle is reported to be local in the dial of Ahaz, not universal in the sensible length of the day: withal, the retreat of the sun had made a public and noted change in the frame of nature. This particular alteration of the shadow, in places limited, might satisfy no less without a confusive mutation in the face of the world. Whethersoever, to draw the sun back together with the shadow, or to draw the shadow back without the sun, was the proof of a divine omnipotence, able therefore to draw back the life of Hezekiah fifteen degrees from the night of death, towards which it was hastening.

O God! thou wilt rather alter the course of heaven and earth, than the faith of thy children shall sink for want of supportation.

It should seem, the Babylonians, finding the Assyrian power abated by the revengeful hand of God's angel, and their own discord, took this advantage of a revolt; and now, to strengthen their part, fall in with Hezekiah king of Judah, whom they found the old enemy to the Assyrians, and the great favourite of heaven: him they woo with gifts, him they congratulate with embassages. The fame of Hezekiah's sickness, recovery, form, and assurance of cure, have drawn thither messengers and presents from Berodach-baladan, king of Babylon.

The Chaldees were curious searchers into the secrets of nature, especially into the motions of the celestial bodies: though there had been no politic relations, this very astronomical miracle had been enough to fetch them to Jerusalem, that they might see the man, for whose sake the sun forsook his place, or the shadow forsook the sun.

How easily have we seen those holy men miscarried by prosperity, against whom no miseries could prevail! He that stood out stoutly against all the Assyrian onsets, clinging the faster to his God, by how much he was harder assaulted by Sennacherib, melted now with these Babylonian favours, and runs abroad into offensive weaknesses.

The Babylonian ambassadors are too welcome to Hezekiah: as a man transported with the honour of their respective and costly visitations, he forgets his tears, and his turning to the wall; he forgets their incompatible idolatry, so hugging them in his bosom, as if there had been no cause of strangeness, all his doors fly open to them, and, in a vain-glorious ostentation, all his new-gathered treasures, all his strong armories, entertain their eyes: nothing in his house, nothing in his dominion, is hid from them.

O Hezekiah! what means this impotent ambition? It is not long since thou tearedst off the very plates of the temple-doors, to give unto Sennacherib; and can thy treasures be suddenly so multiplied, that they can be so worthy to astonish foreign beholders? or, if thy store-house were as rich as the earth, can thy heart be so vain as to be lifted up with these heavy metals? Didst thou not see, that heaven itself was at thy beck, whilst thou wert humbled? and shall a little earthly dross have power over thy soul? Can the flattering applause of strangers let thee loose into a proud joy, whom the late message of God's prophet resolved into tears? O God! if thou do not keep us, as well in our sunshine as in our storm, we are sure to perish: as in all time of our tribulation, so in all time of our wealth, good Lord, deliver us!

Alas! how slight doth this weakness seem in our eyes, to rejoice in the abundance of

God's blessings, to call in foreign friends to be witnesses of our plenty; to raise our conceits some little, upon the acclamations of others, upon the value of our own abilities!

Lay thy hand upon thy mouth, O foolish flesh and blood, when thou seest the censure of thy Maker.

Isaiah the prophet is sent speedily to Hezekiah, with a sharp and heart-breaking message: "Behold, the days come that all that is in thine house, and that which thy fathers have laid up in store unto this day, shall be carried into Babylon; nothing shall be left, saith the Lord; and of thy sons, that shall issue from thee, which thou shalt beget, shall they take away, and they shall be eunuchs in the palace of the king of Babylon."

No sin can be light in Hezekiah: the holiness of the person adds to the unholiness of the act; eminency of profession doubles both the offence and the judgment. This glory shall end in an ignominious loss.

The great and holy God will not digest pride in any, much less in his own. That which was the subject of Hezekiah's sin, shall be the matter of his punishment; those with whom he sinned, shall be his avengers. It was his treasure and munition, wherein he prides himself to these men of Babylon: the men of Babylon shall carry away his treasure and munition. What now doth Hezekiah, but tempt them with a glorious booty, as some fond traveller that would show his gold to a thief?

These worldly things are furthest off from the heart: perhaps Hezekiah might not be much troubled with their loss. Lo! God comes closer to him yet.

As yet was Hezekiah childless. how much better had it been to continue so still, than to be plagued in his issue! He shall now beget children to servitude, his loins shall yield pages to the court of Babylon: while he sees them born princes, he shall foresee them made eunuchs in a foreign palace. What comfort can he take in the wishes and hopes of sons, when, ere they be born, he hears them destined to captivity and bondage!

This rod was smart, yet good Hezekiah kisses it: his heart struck him no less, than the mouth of the prophet; meekly, therefore, doth he yield to this divine correction: "Good is the word of the Lord which thou hast spoken." Thou hast spoken this word, but from the Lord: it is not thine, but his; and, being his, it must needs be, like himself, good: good, because it is just; for I have deserved more, and worse: good, because merciful; for I suffer not according to my deserts. "Is it not good, if there be peace and truth in my days?" I have deserved a present payment; O God! thou deferrest it: I have deserved it in person; thou reservest it for those whom I cannot yet so feel, because they are not. I have deserved war and tumult; thou favourest me with peace: I have deserved to be overrun with superstition and idolatry; thou blessest me with truth: shouldst thou continue truth unto me, though upon the most unquiet terms, the blessing were too good for me; but now thou hast promised, and will not reverse it, that both truth and peace shall be in my days. Lord! I adore thy justice, I bless thy mercy.

God's children are neither waspish nor sullen, when they are chid or beaten, but patiently hold their backs to the stripes of a displeased mercy; knowing how much more God is to be magnified for what he might have done, than repined at for what he hath done; resigning themselves over into the hand of that gracious justice, which, in their smart, seeks their reformation and glory.

CONTEMPLATION XI.—MANASSEH.

At last, some three years after his recovery, Hezekiah hath a son: but such a one as, if he could have foreseen, orbity had been a blessing.

Still in the throne of Judah there is a succession and interchange of good and evil: good Jotham is succeeded by wicked Ahaz; wicked Ahaz is succeeded by good Hezekiah; good Hezekiah is succeeded by wicked Manasseh. Evil princes succeed to good, for the exercise of the church; and good succeed to evil, for the comfort of the church.

The young years of Manasseh gave advantage to his miscarriage; even while he might have been under the ferule, he swayed the sceptre. Whither may not a child be drawn, especially to a garish and puppet-like superstition? As infancy is capable of all impressions, so most of the worst.

Neither did Manasseh begin more early than he held out long: he reigned more years than his good father lived, notwithstanding the miraculous addition to his age; more than ever any king of Judah besides could reach. Length of days is no true rule of God's favour: as plants last longer than sensitive creatures, and brute creatures outlive the reasonable; so amongst the reasonable, it is no news for the wickedly great to inherit these earthly glories, longer than the best.

There wants not apparent reason for this

difference. Good princes are fetched away to a better crown: they cannot be losers, that exchange a weak and fading honour for a perfection and eternity of blessedness. Wicked men live long, to their own disadvantage; they do but carry so many more brands to their hell. If, therefore, there be a just man that perisheth in his righteousness, and there be a wicked man that prolongs his life in his wickedness, far be it from us, either to pity the removal of the just, or to envy the continuance of the wicked. This continues to his loss; that departs to a happy advancement.

It is very like that Hezekiah marrying so late, in the vigour both of his age and holiness, made a careful choice of a wife suitable to his own piety: neither had his delight been so much in her, according to her name, if her delight had not been, as his, in God: their issue swerves from both, so fully inheriting the vices of his grandfather Ahaz, as if there had been no intervention of a Hezekiah. So we have seen the kernel of a well fruited plant degenerate into that crab, or willow, which gave the original to his stock; yet can I not say, that Hezekiah was as free from traducing evil to his son Manasseh, as Ahaz was free from traducing good to his son Hezekiah. Evil is incorporated in the best nature, whereas even the least good descends from above.

We may not measure grace by means. Was it possible that Manasseh, having been trained up in the religious court of his father Hezekiah, under the eye of so holy prophets and priests, under the shadow of the temple of God, after a childhood seasoned with so gracious precepts, with so frequent exercise of devotion, should run thus wild into all heathenish abominations; as if there had been nothing but idolatry in the seed of his conception, in the milk of his nourishment, in the rules of his institution, in the practice of his examples? How vain are all outward helps without the influence of God's Spirit, and that spirit that breathes where he listeth! Good education raiseth great hopes; but the proof of them is in the divine benediction.

I fear to look at the outrages of this wicked son of Hezekiah. What havoc doth he make in the church of God! as if he had been born to ruin religion; as if his only felicity had been to untwist, or tear, in one day, that holy web which his father had been weaving, nine and twenty years; and contrarily, in one hour, to set up that offensive pile which had been above three hundred years in pulling down: so long had the high places stood. The zeal of Hezekiah in demolishing them, honoured him above all his predecessors; and now the first act of this green head was their re-edifying. That mischief may be done in a day, which many ages cannot redress.

Fearful were the presages of these bold beginnings. From the misbuilding of those chapels of the hills to the true God, Manasseh proceeds to erecting of altars to a false, even to Baal, the god of Ahab, the stale idol of the heathen: Yet further, not content with so few deities, he worships all the host of heaven; and, that he might despite God yet more, he sets up altars to these abused rivals of their Maker, in the very house of the Lord: that holy place doth he not fear to defile with the graven image of the grove that he had made. Never Amorite did so wickedly as Manasseh; and, which was yet worse, it sufficed not to be thus wicked himself, but he seduced God's people to these abominations; and, that his example might move the more, he spares not his own son from the fire of the idol-sacrifice. Neither were his witcheries less enormous than his idolatry: he observed times, he used enchantments, he dealt with familiar spirits, and with wizards. Neither were either of these worse than his cruelty: he shed innocent blood, till he had filled Jerusalem from one end to another.

O Manasseh, how no less cruel wert thou to thine own soul, than to thy Judah! What a hideous lift of monstrous impieties is here! any one of which were enough to draw judgment upon a world; but what hell is sufficient for all together!

What brows are not now lifted up to an attentive expectation of some present and fearful vengeance from God, upon such flagitious wickedness! "Therefore, thus saith the Lord, Behold, I am bringing such evil upon Jerusalem and Judah, that whosoever heareth of it, both his ears shall tingle."— The person of Manasseh is not capable of revenge enough: as his sin dilated itself by an infectious diffusion to his people, so shall the punishment. We are sensible of the least touch of our own miseries: how rarely are we affected with other men's calamities! Yet this evil shall be such, as that the rumour of it shall beat no ear, that shall not glow with an astonishing commiseration. What then, O God, what shall that plague be, which thou threatenest with so much preface of horror? "I will stretch over Jerusalem the line of Samaria, and the plummet of the house of Ahab; and I will wipe Jerusalem as a man wipeth a dish, wiping it, and turning it upside down: and I will forsake the remnant of mine inheritance; and I will deliver them into the hand of their enemies, and they shall become a prey and a spoil unto all their enemies."

It is enough, O God! it is enough. What ear can but tingle, what eye can but weep, what hair can but start up, what heart can be but confounded at the mention of so dreadful a revenge? Can there be a worse judgment than desolation, captivity, desertion, spoil, and torture of prevailing enemies? But however other cities and nations have undergone these disasters, without wonder, that all this should befall to thy Jerusalem, the place which thou hast chosen to thyself out of the whole earth, the lot of thine inheritance, the seat of thine abode, whereof thou hast said, "Here shall be my rest for ever," it is able to amaze all eyes, all ears.

No city could fare worse than Samaria, whose inhabitants, after a woful siege, were driven, like cattle, into a wretched servitude. Jerusalem shall fare no better from Nebuchadnezzar the king of Babylon; Jerusalem, the glory of the earth, the darling of heaven. See, O ye vain men, that boast of the privileges of chairs and churches, see and tremble. There is no place under heaven, to which the presence of God is so wedded, as that the sins thereof shall not procure a disdainful and final divorce: the height of former favours shall be but an aggravation of vengeance.

This total vastation of Jerusalem shall take time. Onwards, God begins with the person of wicked Manasseh, against whom he stirs up the captains of the host of the late friend, and old enemy of Judah. Those thorns, amongst which he had shrouded his guilty head, cannot shelter him from their violence: they take him and bind him with fetters of iron, and carry him to Babylon. There he lies, loaded with chains, in an uncomfortable dungeon, exercised with variety of tortures, fed with such coarse pittances of bread, and sips of water, as might maintain an unwilling life to the punishment of the owner. What eye can now pity the deepest miseries of Manasseh? what but bondage can befit him, that hath so lawlessly abused his liberty? what but an utter abdication can befit him, that hath cast off his God, and doted upon devils? what but a dying life, and a tormenting death, can be fit for a man of blood?

Who now would not have given this man for lost, and have looked when hell should claim her own? But, O the height, O the depth, of Divine mercy! After all these prodigies of sin, Manasseh is a convert: "When he was in affliction, he besought the Lord his God; and humbled himself greatly before the God of his fathers." How true is that word of the prophet, "Vexation gives understanding!" The viper, when he is lashed, casts up his poison. The traitor, when he is racked, tells that truth which he had else never uttered. If the cross bear us not to heaven, nothing can. What use were there of the grain, but for the edge of the sickle wherewith it is cut down, the stroke of the flail wherewith it is beaten, the weight and attrition of the mill wherewith it is crushed, the fire of the oven wherewith it is baked? Say now, Manasseh, with that grandfather of thine, who was, till now, too good for thee, "It was good for me that I was afflicted." Even thine iron was more precious to thee than thy gold; thy gaol was a more happy lodging to thee than thy palace; Babylon was a better school to thee than Jerusalem. What fools are we, to frown upon our afflictions! These, how crabbed soever, are our best friends. They are not indeed for our pleasure; they are for our profit: their issue makes them worthy of a welcome. What do we care how bitter that potion be, which brings health?

How far a man may go, and yet turn! Could there be fouler sins than these? Lo! here was idolatry in the height, violation of God's house, sorceries of all kinds, bloody cruelty to his own flesh, to the saints of God, and all these against the stream of a religious institution, of the zealous counsels of God's prophets, of the checks of his own heart.

Who can complain, that the way of heaven is blocked up against him, when he sees such a sinner enter? Say the worst against thyself, O thou clamorous soul! here is one that murdered men, defied God, worshipped devils, and yet finds the way to repentance. If thou be worse than he, deny, if thou canst, that to thyself, which God hath not denied to thee, capacity of grace: in the meantime know, that it is not thy sin, but thine impenitence, that bars heaven against thee.

Presume not yet, O man, whosoever thou art, of the liberty of thy conversion, as if thou couldst run on lawlessly in a course of sinning, till thou come to the brim of hell, and then couldst suddenly stop, and return at leisure. The mercy of God never set period to a wilful sinner; neither yet did his own corrupt desires, so as, when he is gone the furthest, he could yet stay himself from another step. No man that truly repents is refused: but many a one sins so long, that he cannot repent; his custom of wickedness hath obdured his heart, and made it flint to all good impressions. There were Jeroboams, and Abijams, and Ahabs, and Joashes, and Ahazes, in these sacred thrones; there was but one Manasseh. God hath not left in any man's hand the reins of his own heart, to pace, and turn, and stop as he lists: this privilege is reserved to him that made it. "It is not of him that wills, nor of him that runs, but of God that shows mercy;" and that mercy neglected, justly binds over to judgment.

I wonder not at Manasseh either sinning or repenting; I wonder at thy goodness, O Lord, who, after thy just permission of his sin, callest him thus graciously to repent, and so receivest him repenting: so as Manasseh was not a more loathsome and monstrous spectacle of wickedness, than he is now a pleasing and useful pattern of conversion. Who can now despair of thy mercy, O God, that sees the tears of a Manasseh accepted? When we have debauched our worst, our evil cannot match with thy goodness; rather it is the praise of thy infinite store, that where sin abounds, grace abounds much more. O keep us from a presumption of grace, that we may repent; and raise us from a distrust of grace, when we have repented.

No sooner is Manasseh penitent, than he is free: his prayers have at once loosed him from his sins and from his chains, and of a captive have made him a king; and, from the dungeon of Babylon, have restored him to the palace of Jerusalem. How easy is it for the same hand that wounds to cure! What cannot fervent prayers do, either for our rescuing from evil, or for our investing with good!

"Then Manasseh knew that the Lord he was God;" then, and not before. Could his younger years escape the knowledge of God's miraculous deliverance of Jerusalem from the Assyrians? could he but know the slaughter that God's angel made in one night, of a hundred fourscore and five thousand? could he but have heard the just revenge upon Sennacherib? could he be ignorant of his father's supernatural recovery? could he but see that everlasting monument of the noted degrees in the dial of Ahaz? could he avoid the sense of those fifteen years which were superadded to his father's age? What one of these proofs doth not evince a Deity? Yet, till his own smart and cure, Manasseh knew not that the Lord was God.

Foolish sinners pay dear for their knowledge; neither will endure to be taught good cheap. So we have seen resty horses, that will not move, till they bleed with the spur; so we have seen dull and careless children, that will learn nothing but what is put into them with the rod.

The Almighty will be sure to be known for what he is, if not by fair means, yet by foul. If our prosperity and peace, and sweet experience of his mercy, can win us to acknowledge him, it is more for our ease; but if we will needs be taught by stripes, it is no less for his glory.

Manasseh now returns another man to Jerusalem. With what indignation doth he look upon his old follies! And now, all the amends he can make is to undo what he did, to do that which he undid: "He took away the strange gods, and the idol out of the house of the Lord, and all the altars that he had built in the mount of the house of the Lord, and in Jerusalem, and cast them out of the city." True repentance begins to decline at the ablative, destroying those monuments of shame which former error had reared. The thorns must first be stubbed up, ere the ground can be capable of seed. The true method of grace is, first, "Cease to do evil," then "Learn to do good."

In vain had Manasseh professed a repentance, if the strange gods had still held possession of Jerusalem, if the idol had still harboured in God's temple, if foreign altars had still smoked upon the holy mountain. Away with all this trash, when once Manasseh comes to a true sense of piety!

There is nothing but hypocrisy in that penitent, who, after all vows and tears, retains his old abominations. It is that poor piece of satisfaction which we can give to the Divine justice, in a hearty indignation to fling down that cup of wickedness wherewith we have been bewitched, and to trample upon the sherds; without which, confession is but wind, and the drops of contrition, water.

The living God loves to dwell clean: he will not come under the roof of idols, nor admit idols to come under his. First, therefore, Manasseh casts out the strange gods, and idols, and altars, and then "he repairs the altars of the Lord, and sacrifices thereon peace-offerings and thank-offerings." Not till he had pulled down, might he build; and when he had pulled down, he must build. True repentance is no less active of good. What is it the better, if, when the idolatrous altars are defaced, the true God hath not an altar erected to his name? In many altars was superstition, in no altars atheism.

Neither doth penitent Manasseh build God a new altar, but he repairs the old, which, by long disuse, lay waste, and was mossy and mouldered with age and neglect.

God loves well his own institutions; neither can he abide innovations, so much as in the outsides of his services. It is a happy work to vindicate any ordinance of God from the injuries of times, and to restore it to the original glory.

What have our pious governors done other in religion? Had we gone about to lay a new foundation, the work had been accursed: now we have only scraped off some superfluous moss, that was grown upon these holy stones; we have cemented some broken pieces, we have pointed some crazy corners with wholesome mortar, instead of base clay wherewith it was disgracefully patched up. The altar is old; it is God's altar; it is not new, not ours: if we have laid one new stone in this sacred building, let it fly in our faces, and beat out our eyes.

On this repaired altar doth Manasseh send up the sacrifices of his peace, of his thankfulness; and doubtless the God of heaven smells a sweet savour of rest. No perfume is so pleasing to God, as that which is cast in by a penitent hand.

It had not served the turn that Manasseh had approached alone to this renewed altar: as his lewd example had drawn the people from their God, so now " he commands Judah to serve the Lord God of Israel:" had he been silent, he could not have been unfollowed. Every act of greatness is preceptive; but now, that religion is made law, what Israelite will not be devout?

The true God hath now no competitor in Judah: all the idols are pulled down, the high places will not be pulled down. An ill guise is easily taken up, it is not so easily left. After a common depravation of religion, it is hard to return unto the first purity: as when a garment is deeply soiled, it cannot, without many lavers, recover the former cleanness.

CONTEMPLATION XII.—JOSIAH'S REFORMATION.

YET, if we must alter from ourselves, it is better to be a Manasseh than a Joash: Joash began well, and ended ill; Manasseh began ill, and ended well. His age varied from his youth, no less than one man's condition can vary from another's; his posterity succeeded in both. Amon his son succeeded in the sins of Manasseh's youth; Josiah his grandchild succeeded in the virtues of his age. What a vast difference doth grace make in the same age! Manasseh began his reign at twelve years; Josiah at eight: Manasseh was religiously bred under Hezekiah; Josiah was misnurtured under Amon: and yet Manasseh runs into absurd idolatries; Josiah is holy and devout. The Spirit of God breathes freely, not confining itself to times or means.

No rules can bind the hands of the Almighty. It is an ordinary proof, too true a word, that was said of old, " Woe be to thee, O land, whose king is a child!" The goodness of God makes his own exceptions: Judah never fared better than in the green years of a Josiah. If we may not rather measure youth and age by government and disposition, than by years, surely thus Josiah was older with smooth cheeks, than Manasseh with grey hairs. Happy is the infancy of princes, when it falls into the hands of counsellors.

A good pattern is no small help for young beginners. Josiah sets his father David before him — not Amon, not Manasseh. Examples are the best rules for the unexperienced: where their choice is good, the directions are easiest. The laws of God are the ways of David: those laws were the rule, those ways were the practice. Good Josiah walks in all the ways of his father David.

Even the minority of Josiah was not idle: we cannot be good too early. At eight years, it was enough to have his ear open to hear good counsel, to have his eyes and heart open to seek after God; at twelve, he begins to act, and shows well that he hath found the God he sought. Then he addresses himself to purge Judah and Jerusalem from the high places, groves, images, altars, wherewith it was defiled; burning the bones of the idolatrous priests upon their altars; strewing the ashes of the idols upon the graves of them that had sacrificed to them; striving, by those fires and mattocks, to testify his zealous detestation of all idolatry.

The house must be first cleansed, ere it can be garnished: no man will cast away his cost upon unclean heaps. So soon as the temple was purged, Josiah bends his thoughts upon the repairing and beautifying of the house of the Lord.

What stir was there in Judah, wherein God's temple suffered not? Six several times was it pillaged, whether out of force, or will. First, Joash king of Judah is fain, by the spoil of it, to stop the mouth of Hazael; then Joash king of Israel fills his own hands with that sacred spoil, in the days of Amaziah; after this, Ahaz rifles it for Tiglath-pileser king of Assyria; then Hezekiah is forced to ransack the treasures of it for Sennacherib; yet, after, the sacrilege of Manasseh makes that booty of it, which his latter times endeavour to restore; and now, lastly, Amon his son neglects the frame, embezzles the furniture of this holy place: the very pile began to complain of age and unrespect. Now comes good Josiah, and in his eighteenth year (when other young gallants would have thought of nothing but pleasure and jollity) takes up the latest care of his father David, and gives order for the repairing of the temple.

The keepers of the door have received the contribution of all faithful Jews for this pious use. The king sends Shaphan the scribe to Hilkiah the priest, to sum it up, and to deliver it unto carpenters and masons for so holy a work.

How well doth it beseem the care of a religious prince, to set the priests and scribes in hand with re-edifying the temple! The command is the king's, the charge is the high priest's, the execution is the workmen's. When the labourers are faithful in doing the work, and the high priest in the directing it, and the king in enjoining it, God's house cannot fail of a happy perfection; but when any of these slackens, the business must needs languish.

How God blesses the devout endeavours of his servants! While Hilkiah was diligently surveying the breaches and reparation of the temple, he lights upon the book of the law. The authentic and original book of God's law, was, by a special charge, appointed to be carefully kept within a safe shrine in the sanctuary. In the depraved times of idolatry, some faithful priest, to make sure work, had locked it fast up, in some corner of the temple, from the reach of all hands, of all eyes, as knowing how impossible it was that divine monument could otherwise escape the fury of profane guiltiness. Some few transcripts there were, doubtless, parcels of this sacred book in other hands: neither doubt I, but, as Hilkiah had been formerly well acquainted with this holy volume, now of a long time hid, so the ears of good Josiah had been inured to some passages thereof. But the whole body of these awful records, since the late night of idolatrous confusion and persecution, saw no light till now. This precious treasure doth Hilkiah find, while he digs for the temple. Never man laboured to the reparation of God's church, but he met with a blessing more than he looked for.

Hilkiah the priest, and Shaphan the scribe, do not engross this invaluable wealth into their own hands, nor suppress these more than sacred rolls for their own advantage; but transmit them first to the ears of the king, then by him to the people. It is not the praise of a good scribe to lay up, but to bring forth, both old and new. And if the priest's lips shall keep knowledge, they keep it to impart, not to smother: " The people shall seek the law at his mouth; for he is the messenger of the Lord of hosts."

So soon as the good king hears the words of the book of the law, and in special, those dreadful threats of judgment denounced against the idolatries of his Judah, he rends his clothes, to show his heart rent with sorrow and fearful expectation of those plagues, and washes his bosom with tears. O gracious tenderness of Josiah! he doth but once hear the law read, and is thus humbled; humbled for his father's sins, for the sins of his people. How many of us, after a thousand hammerings of the menaces of God's law upon our guilty souls, continue yet insensible of our danger! The very reading of this law doth thus affect him; the preaching of it stirs not us: the sins of others struck thus deep with him; our own are slighted by us. A soft heart is the best tempered for God. So physicians are wont to like those bodies best, which are easiest to work upon. O God! make our clay wax, and our wax pliable to thine hand, so shall we be sure to be free either from sin, or from the hurt of sin.

It is no holy sorrow that sends us not to God. Josiah is not moped with a distractive grief, or an astonishing fear, but, in the height of his passion, sends five choice messengers to Huldah the prophetess, to inquire of the Lord, for himself, for Judah. It is a happy trouble that drives us to this refuge. I do not hear any of these courtiers reply, to this godly motion of their young king, Alas, sir, what means this deep perplexity? what needs all this busy inquisition? If your father were idolatrous, what is that to you who have abandoned his sins? if your people were once idolatrous, what is that to you, yea, to them, who have expiated these crimes by their repentance? Have you not carefully reformed all those abuses? hath not your happy reformation made an abundant amends for those wrongs? Spare your tears, and save the labour of your messengers: all is well, all shall be well. These judgments are for the obstinate: had we been still guilty, these fears had been just: were we still in danger, what had we gained by our conversion? Rather as glad to second the religious cares of their young king, they feed his holy anxieties with a just aggravation of peril; and by their good counsel whet these his zealous desires of a speedy resolution. That state cannot but be happy, whose priests and peers are ready, as to suggest, so to cherish and execute the devout projects of their sovereigns.

The grave priest, the learned scribe, the honourable courtiers, do not disdain to knock at the door of a prophetess: neither doth any of them say, It were hard if we should not have as much acquaintance with God, as a woman: but, in an humble acknowledgment of her graces, they come to learn the will of God from her mouth. True piety is modest, and stands not upon terms of reputation in the businesses of God, but willingly honours his gifts in any subject, least of all in itself.

The sex is not more noted in Huldah, than the condition. As she was a woman, so a wife, the wife of Shallum. Holy matrimony was no hindrance to her divine revelations: she was at once a prophetess in her college, a housewife in her family. It was never the practice of God to confine his graces to virginity. At this very time, the famous prophet Jeremiah flourished: some years had he already spent in this public service; why was not he rather consulted by Josiah? It is not unlike, that some prophetical employments called him away at this time from Jerusalem: his presence could not have been baulked. Purposely, doubtless, doth God cast his message upon the point of that absence, that he might honour the weaker vessel with his divine oracle, and exercise the humility of so great clients. In the answers of God, it is not to be regarded who speaks, but from whom. The injury redounds to God, if the weaknesses of the person cause us to undervalue the authority of the function.

As Josiah and his messengers do not despise Huldah because she was a woman, so Huldah doth not flatter Josiah, because a king: " Go, tell the man that sent you, thus saith the Lord, Behold, I will bring evil upon this place." Lo! he that was as God to his subjects, is but as man to the prophetess: neither is the message ever the sweeter, because it is required by a prince. No circumstance may vary the form of divine truth.

Evil must befall Jerusalem and Judah, yea, all the words of that book must alight upon the inhabitants of both. In how bad a case we may be, and yet think ourselves not safe only, but happy! These Jews had forgotten their old revolts; and now, having framed themselves to holy courses, promised themselves nothing but peace, when the prophetess foresees and foretells their approaching ruin. Even their old score must be paid, after the opinion of a clear agreement. In vain shall we hope to quit our arrearages by prorogation. This prophetess had immediate visions from God, yet she must speak out of the book. There was never any revelation from the Lord that crossed his writings: his hand and his tongue agree eternally. If that book have cursed Judah, she may not absolve it.

Yet, what a gracious mixture was here of mercy with severity!—severity to Judah, mercy to Josiah: Judah shall be plagued, and shall become a desolation and a curse; Josiah shall be quietly housed in his grave, before this storm fall upon Judah: his eye shall not see what his people shall feel. It is enough that the expectation of these evils afflicts him, the sense shall not.

Whence is this indulgence? " Because thine heart was tender, and thou hast humbled thyself before the Lord." How happy a thing it is to be a reed unto God's judgments, rather than an oak! the meek and gentle reed stoops, and therefore stands; the oak stands stiffly out against the strongest gust, and therefore is turned up by the roots. At least, let us lament those sins we have not avoided; and mourn for the sins of others, while we hate our own.

He that found himself exempted from this vengeance by his repentance and deep humiliation, would fain find the same way for the deliverance of his people. The same words of the law, therefore, that had wrought upon his heart, are by him caused to be publicly read in the ears of Judah and Jerusalem. The assembly is universal, of priests, prophets, people both small and great; because the sin was such, the danger was such; that no man may complain to want information, the law of God sounds in every ear. If our ears be shut to the law, the sin is ours; but if the law be shut to our ears, the sin is of our governors. Woe be to them that hide God's book from the people, as they would do ratsbane from the eyes of children! Ignorant souls cannot perish without their murder. There is no fear of knowing too much; there is too much fear of practising too little. Now, if the people do not imitate their king in relenting, they are not worthy to partake with him in his impunity. Howsoever, they shall not want a great example, as of sorrow, so of amendment. Good Josiah stands by the pillar, and solemnly renews his covenant with his God; the people cannot for shame refuse to second him: even they that looked for a destruction, yet do not withdraw their obedience. God's children may not be sullen under his corrections, but whether they expect or feel smart, are no other than dutiful to his awful hand. As a man that finds he hath done something that might endanger the forfeit of his favour, puts himself into some deserving action, whereby he may hope to re-endear himself, so doth Josiah here. No endeavour is enough to testify his zeal to that name of God which was so profaned by his people's idolatry: whatever monuments were yet remaining of wicked paganism, he defaces with indignation: he burns the vessels of Baal, and puts down his Chemarim, destroys the houses of the Sodomites, strews the powder of their idols in the brook Kedron, defiles Tophet, takes away the horses of the sun, burns the chariots of the sun with fire, and omits nothing that might reconcile God, clear Judah, perfect a reformation.

Neither is this care confined to Jerusalem and the neighbouring towns, but stretches itself to the utmost coasts of Josiah's kingdom. Bethel was the infamous seat of the pollution of Israel: it seems the heirs of Jeroboam, who set up his golden calf there, enjoyed it not long; the kings of Judah recovered it to their crown, but it had not yet recovered itself from that ancient infection. Thither doth good Josiah send the unhallowed ashes of Baal's relics, to stain that altar first, which he will soon after deface.

The time was, and it was no less than three hundred and fifty years since, that the man of God, out of Judah, cried against Jeroboam's altar: — " O altar, altar! thus saith the Lord: Behold, a child shall be born unto the house of David, Josiah by name, and upon thee shall he offer the priests of the high places, that burn incense upon thee, and men's bones shall be burnt upon thee." And now is the hour come, wherein every of those words shall be accomplished. It could not but be a great confirmation to Josiah, to see, that God so long ago foremarked him for his own, and forenamed him so to zealous a service.

All our names are equally foreknown of that divine Providence, though not forespoken; neither can any act pass from us, which was not predetermined in that eternal counsel of the Almighty; neither can any act, that is predetermined, be unfulfilled upon earth. Intervention of time breaks no square in the divine decrees: our purblind eyes see nothing but that which toucheth their lids; the quick sight of God's prescience sees that, as present, which is a world off. According to the prediction, the stench of dead men's bones is a fit perfume to send up from this altar to heaven, whose best sacrifices savoured worse in the nostrils of God: and the blood of the idolatrous sacrifices was a meet oblation to that God, who had been dishonoured by their burnt-offerings to his base corrivals.

Even that prophet, who foretold this, had his tomb in Bethel, and that tomb had his inscription; his weakness might not rob him of the honour of his sepulchre. How palpably do these Israelites condemn themselves, while they reserve so famous a monument of their own conviction! It was no prejudice to this holy prophet, that his bones lay amongst the sepulchres of idolaters. His epitaph preserved those bones from burning upon that altar, which he had accursed: as the lion might not tear his carcass when he died, so now the fury of the multitude may not violate the very bones in his grave. I do not see Josiah save them for relics; I hear him command they shall rest in peace. It is fit the dead bodies of God's saints should be as free from contempt, as from superstition.

After the removal of these rites of false worship, it is time to bring in the true. Now a solemn passover shall be kept unto the Lord, by the charge of Josiah: that book of the law sets him the time, place, circumstances, of this sacrament; his zeal so carefully follows it, that since the days of Samuel, this feast was never so gloriously, so punctually celebrated. Jerusalem is the place, the fourteenth day of the first month is the time, the Levites are the actors, a yearly and spotless lamb is the provision: no bone of it is broken; the blood is sprinkled upon the door-posts; it is roasted whole; eaten with sour herbs, with bread unleavened; the remainder is consumed by fire. The law, the sacrifices, had been in vain, if the passover had been neglected. No true Israelite might want, whether this monument of their deliverance past, or this type of the Messiah to come. Rather than fail, Josiah's bounty shall supply to Judah lambs for their paschal devotion. No alms is so acceptable, as that whereby the soul is furthered.

CONTEMPLATION XIII. — JOSIAH S DEATH, WITH THE DESOLATION OF THE TEMPLE AND JERUSALEM.

Josiah hath now happily settled the affairs, both of God, and the state; and now hath sweet leisure to enjoy himself and his people: his conscience doth not more cheer him at home, than his subjects abroad: never king reigned with more officious piety to God, with more love and applause of men. But what stability is there in these earthly things? how seldom is excellency in any kind long-lived! In the very strength of his age, in the height of his strength, is Josiah withdrawn from the earth; as not without a merciful intention of his glory on God's behalf, so not without some weakness on his own. Pharaoh Necho, king of Egypt, comes up to fight against the king of Assyria. What is that to Josiah? Perhaps the Egyptians attempted to pass through the land of Judah towards Carchemish, the seat of his war; but as a neighbour, not as an enemy: Josiah resists him, as neither holding it safe to admit a foreign power into the bosom of his country, nor daring to give so fair an occasion of provoking the Assyrian hostility against him.

The king of Egypt mildly deprecates this enmity: he sends ambassadors to Josiah, saying, "What have I to do with thee, thou king of Judah? I come not against thee this day, but against the house wherewith I have war; for God commanded me to make haste: forbear thee from meddling with God, who is with me, that he destroy thee not."

What friend could have said more? what prophet could have advised more holily? why doth not good Josiah say with himself, There may be truth in this suggestion; God may have sent this man to be a scourge of mine old enemy, of Ashur? If the hand of the Almighty be in this design, why do I oppose it? The quarrel is not mine; why do I thrust my finger into this flame unbidden? wherefore should I hazard the effusion of blood upon a harmless passage? Can I hear him plead a command from God, and not inquire into it? How easy is it for me to know the certainty of this pretended commission! have not I the priests and prophets of God about me? Let me first go and consult his oracle: if God have sent him, and forbidden me, why should my courage carry me against my piety?

It is strange that the good heart of Josiah could escape these thoughts, these resolutions: yet he that, upon the general threats of God's law against Judah, sends messengers to inquire of a prophetess, now, upon these particular threats of danger to himself, speaks not, stirs not. The famous prophet Jeremiah was then living, and Zephaniah, besides a whole college of seers: Josiah doth not so much as send out of doors to ask, "Shall I go up against the king of Egypt?" Sometimes both grace and wit are asleep in the holiest and wariest breast: the best of all God's saints may be sometimes miscarried by their passions to their cost.

The wise providence of God hath mercifully determined to leave Josiah to his own counsels, that, by the weakness of his servant, he might take occasion to perfect his glory. Even that, wherein Josiah was wanting unto God, shall concur to the making up of God's promise to Josiah: when we are the most blindfolded, we run on the ways of God's hidden decrees; and whatever our intents be, cannot, if we would, go out of that unknown path.

Needs will Josiah put himself into arms against an unwilling enemy; and, to be less noted, disguises himself. The fatal arrow of an Egyptian archer finds him out in the throng, and gives him his death's-wound: now too late he calls to a retreat; his changed chariot is turned to a bier to carry his bleeding corpse to his grave in Jerusalem.

What eye doth not now pity and lament the untimely end of a Josiah? whom can it choose but affect, to see a religious, just, virtuous prince, snatched away in the vigour of his age? After all our foolish moan, the Providence that directed that shaft to his lighting place, intends that wound for a stroke of mercy. The God whom Josiah serves, looks through his death at his glory, and by this sudden violence will deliver him from the view and participation of the miseries of Judah, which had been many deaths, and fetches him to the participation of that happiness, which could countervail more deaths than could be incident to a Josiah. O the wonderful goodness of the Almighty, whose very judgments are merciful! O the safe condition of God's children, whom very pain easeth, whom death revives, whom dissolution unites, whom, lastly, their very sin and temptation glorifies!

How happily hath Josiah gained by this change! instead of a froward people, he now is sorted with saints and angels: instead of a fading and corruptible crown, he now enjoys an eternal. The orphan subjects are ready to weep out their eyes for sorrow; their loss cannot be so great as his gain: he is glorious; they, as their sins had deserved, miserable. If the separated soul could be capable of passion—could Josiah have seen, after his departure, the calamities of his sons, of his people—it could not but have laid siege to his peace.

The sad subjects proclaim his son Jehoahaz king, instead of so lamented a father.

He both doth ill, and fares ill. By the time he hath sat but three months on the throne, Pharaoh Necho, king of Egypt, seconds the father's death with the son's captivity. This enemy puts down the wicked son of Josiah, and lades him with chains at Riblath, in the land at Hamath ; and lades his people with a tribute of a hundred talents of silver, and a talent of gold : yet, as if he that was unwilling to fight with Josiah, were no less unwilling to root out his posterity, this Egyptian sets Eliakim, the second son of Josiah, upon the seat of his father; and, that he might be all his, changes his name to Jehoiakim. O the woful and unworthy succession of Josiah! one son is a prisoner, the other is a tributary, both are wicked. After that Jehoiakim hath been some years Pharaoh's bailiff, to gather and rack the dear rents of Judah, Nebuchadnezzar, the great king of Babylon, comes up, and sweeps away both the lord and his feodary, Pharaoh and Jehoiakim.

So far was the ambitious Egyptian from maintaining his encroachment upon the territories of Judah, that he could not now hold his own. From Nilus to Euphrates, all is lost : so subject are the lesser powers still to be swallowed up of the greater ; so just it is with God, that they which will be affecting undue enlargement of their estates, should fall short of what they had.

Jehoiakim is carried in fetters to Babylon; and now, in that dungeon of his captivity, hath more leisure than grace, to bethink himself of all his abominations; and, while he inherits the sad lodging of his great-grandfather Manasseh, inherits not his success.

While he is rotting in this gaol, his young son Jehoiakim starts up in his throne, like to a mushroom that rises up in a night, and withers in a day. Within three months and ten days is that young prince, the meet son of such a father, fetched up in irons to his father's prison : neither shall he go alone (his attendance shall add to his misery); his mother, his wives, his officers, his peers, his craftsmen, his warriors, accompany him, manacled and chained, to their perpetual bondage.

Now, according to Isaiah's word, it would have been great preferment for the fruit of Hezekiah's loins to be pages in the court of Babylon.

Only one branch yet remains of the unhappy stock of holy Josiah : Mattaniah, the brother of Jehoiakim, whom Nebuchadnezzar, changing his name to Zedekiah, sets up in that forlorn and tributary throne : there might he have lived, though an underling, yet peaceable. This man, to make up the measure of God's judgments, as he was ever a rebel to God, so proves rebellious to his sovereign master the king of Babylon. The prophet Jeremiah hath forewarned him in vain : nothing could teach this man but smart.

Who can look for other than fury from Nebuchadnezzar against Jerusalem, which now had affronted him with three several successions of revolts and conspiracies against his government ; and thrice abused his bounty and indulgence? With a mighty army doth he therefore come up against his seditious deputy, and besieges Jerusalem, and blocks it up with forts round about. After two years' siege. the Chaldees without, and the famine within, have prevailed : king Zedekiah and his soldiers are fled away by night, as thinking themselves happy if they might abandon their walls and save their lives.

The Chaldees, as caring more for the birds than for the nest, pursue them, and overtake Zedekiah, forsaken of all his forces, in the plain of Jericho, and bring him to Nebuchadnezzar king of Babylon. What can so unthankful and perfidious a vassal expect, but the worst of revenge? The sentence is fearful : first, the sons of Zedekiah are slain before his eyes; then those eyes of his, as if they had seen enough, when they had seen him childless, are put out. His eyes are only lent him so long, as to torment him with the sight of his own utmost discomfort: had his sons but overlided his eyes, the grief had been so much the less, as the apprehension of it had been less lively and piercing: now this woful object shall shut up his sight, that even when his bodily eyes are gone, yet the eyes of his mind might ever see what he last saw ; that thus his sons might be ever dying before him, and himself in their death ever miserable.

Who doth not now wish that the blood of Hezekiah and Josiah could have been severed from these impure dregs of their lewd issue? No man could pity the offenders, were it not for the mixture of the interest of so holy progenitors.

No more sorrow can come in at the windows of Zedekiah ; more shall come in at his doors : his ears shall receive what more to rue for, his Jerusalem. Nebuzaradan. the great marshal of the king of Babylon, comes up against that deplored city. and breaks down the walls of it round about, and burns the temple of the Lord, and the king's house, and every fair palace of Jerusalem, with fire; drives away the remainder of her inhabitants into captivity, carries away the last spoils of the glorious temple. O Jerusalem, Jerusalem, the wonder of all times, the paragon of nations, the glory of the earth, the favourite of heaven, how art thou now become heaps of ashes, hills of rubbish, a spectacle of desolation, a monument of ruin! If later, yet no less deep hast thou now pledged that bitter cup of God's vengeance to thy sister Samaria: how careful had thy God forewarned thee! Though Israel play the harlot, yet let not Judah sin: lo now, as thine iniquities, so thy judgments have overtaken her. Both lie together in the dust; both were made a curse to all posterities. O God, what place shall thy justice spare, if Jerusalem have perished? If that delight of thine were cut off for her wickedness, " Let us not be high-minded, but fear."

What pity it was to see those goodly cedars of the temple flaming up higher than they stood in Lebanon! to see those curious marbles, which never felt the dint of the pick-axe or hammer in the laying, wounded with mattocks, and wounding the earth in their fall! to see the holy of holies, whereunto none might enter but the high priest once a-year, thronged with pagans! the vails rent, the sacred ark of God violated and defaced, the tables overturned, the altars broken down, the pillars demolished, the pavements digged up, yea, the very ground where that famous pile stood, deformed! O God, thou wouldst rather have no visible house upon earth, than endure it defiled with idolatries.

Four hundred thirty and six years had that temple stood, and beautified the earth, and honoured heaven: now, it is turned into rude heaps. There is no prescription to be pleaded for the favour of the Almighty: only that temple, not made with hands, is eternal in the heavens. Thither he graciously brings us, that hath ordained us thither, for the sake of that glorious High Priest, that hath once for all entered into that holy of holies.— Amen.

BOOK XXI.

CONTEMPLATION I.— ZERUBBABEL AND EZRA.

THE first transportation into Babylon, under Jehoiakim, wherein Daniel, Ezekiel, and many others of the best note, were driven into captivity, was, some eleven years after, followed with a second, under Zedekiah, wherein the remnant of the now ruined Jerusalem and Judah were swept away. Seventy years was the period of their longest servitude: while Babylon was a queen, Judah was her vassal; when that proud tyranness fell, God's people began to rise again. The Babylonian monarchy was no sooner swallowed up of the Persian, than the Jews felt the comfort of liberty; for Cyrus conquering Babylon, and finding the Jews groaning under that captivity, straight releases them, and sends them, under the conduct of their captain Zerubbabel, back to their almost forgotten country.

The world stands upon vicissitudes: every nation hath her turn, and must make up her measure. Threescore and ten years ago, it was the curse of Judah: the iniquity of that rebellious people was full. Some hundred and thirty years before that, was the turn of Samaria, and her Israelites: now the staff is come to the doors of Babylon, even that wherewith Judah was beaten; and those Persians, which are now victorious, must have their term also. It is in vain for any earthly state to promise to itself an immutable condition. At last, the rod that scourged God's children is cast into the fire: " Thou hast remembered, O Lord, the children of Edom, in the day of Jerusalem, how they said, Down with it, down with it, even to the ground. O daughter of Babylon, wasted with misery, how happy is he that rewardeth thee as thou hast served them!" It is Cyrus that hath wrought this revenge, this rescue.

Doubtless, it did not a little move Cyrus to this favour, that he found himself honourably forenamed in these Jewish prophecies, and foreappointed to this glorious service, no less than a hundred and seventy years before he was. Who would not be glad to make good so noble and happy a destiny? O God, if we hear that thou hast ordained us to life, how gladly, how carefully, should we work out our salvation! if to good works, how should we abound!

In the first year of his monarchy, doth Cyrus both make proclamations, and publish them in writing, through all his kingdom, wherein he both professeth his zealous resolutions, and desires to build up God's house in Jerusalem, and enjoins and encourages all the Jews, through his dominions, to address themselves to that sacred work; and incites all his subjects to aid them with silver and gold, and goods and beasts. How gracious was the command of that, whereof the very allowance was a favour!

Was it Cyrus that did this? was it not thou, O God, in whose hands are the hearts of kings, that stirredst up the spirit of that

Persian, as if he had been more than a son of thy church — a father? How easy is it for thee to make very pagans protectors to thy church, enemies benefactors!

Not with an empty grace doth this great king dismiss the Jews, but with a royal bounty: " He brings forth the vessels of the house of the Lord, which Nebuchadnezzar had brought forth out of Jerusalem, and had put them in the house of his gods, and causes them to be numbered by his treasurer to the hands of Sheshbazzar, the prince of Judah, for the use of the temple; no fewer than five thousand and four hundred vessels of gold and silver."

Certainly this great monarch wanted not wit to think, It is a rich booty that I find in the temples of Babylon: by the law of conquest it is mine; having vanquished their gods, I may well challenge their spoil: how seasonably doth it now fall into my hands, upon this victory, to reward my soldiers, to settle my new empire! What if this treasure came from Jerusalem; the propriety is now altered: the very place, according to the conceit of the Jews, hath profaned it. The true God, I have heard, is curious; neither will abide those vessels, which have been polluted with idolatrous uses: it shall be enough if I loose the bonds of this miserable people; if I give liberty, let the next give wealth. They will think themselves happy in bare walls, in their native earth: to what purpose should I pamper their penury with a sudden store? But the princely heart of Cyrus would admit of no such base sacrilegious thoughts. Those vessels that he finds stamped with God's mark, he will return to their owner; neither his own occasions, nor their abuse, shall be any colour of their detention. O Cyrus, how many close-handed, gripple-minded Christians, shall once be choked in judgment with the example of thy just munificence! Thou restoredst that which we purloin. Woe be to those houses that are stored with the spoils of God's temple; woe be to those fingers that are tainted with holy treasures.

Kings can hardly do good alone: their laws are not more followed, than their examples. No sooner do the chief of the fathers of Judah and Benjamin, and the priests and Levites, set their faces towards Jerusalem for the building of the temple, than the liberal hands of their pagan neighbours furnish them with gold and silver, and precious things. Every Persian is glad to be at the charge of laying a stone in God's house. The same God, that had given them these metals out of his coffers of the earth, gives it out of their coffers to his temple.

He that took away by the Chaldees, gives by the Persians. Where the Almighty intends a work, there cannot be any want of means.

Thus heartened, thus laded, do the joyful families of Judah return to their old home. How many thousands of them were worn out and lost in that seventy years' servitude! how few of them yet survived, that could know the place of their birth and habitation, or say, Here stood the temple, here the palace! Amongst those forty and two thousand three hundred and threescore Jews that returned in this first expedition, there were whom the confusion of their long captivity had robbed of their pedigree; they knew themselves Jews, but could not derive their line: these were yet admitted without difficulty; but those of the priestly tribe, which could not deduce their genealogy from the register, are cashiered as unclean: then, God would be served in blood; now, in a due succession. If we could not fetch the line of our pedigree from Christ and his apostles, we were not fit for the evangelical altars. Their calling was by nature, ours by grace — the grace of inward abilities, of outward ordination: if we cannot approve both these, we are justly abandoned. Now had the children of Israel taken down their harps from the willows which grew by the waters of Babylon, and could, unbidden, sing the true songs of their recovered Sion: they are newly settled in their old mansions, when, upon the first public feast, in the autumn immediately following their return, they flock up to Jerusalem: their first care is their public sacrifice; that school of their captivity, wherein they have been long trained, hath taught them to begin with God. A forced discontinuance makes devotion more savoury, more sweet, to religious hearts; whereas, in an open freedom, piety doth too often languish.

Joshua the priest, and Zerubbabel the prince, are fitly joined in the building of the altar: neither of their hands may be out of that sacred work. No sooner is that set upon the basis, than it is employed to the daily burnt-offerings: the altar may not stay the leisure of the temple; God's church may not want her oblations. He can be none of the sons of Israel, that doth not every day renew his acknowledgments of God.

How feelingly do these Jews keep their feast of tabernacles, while their sojourning in Babylon was still in their thoughts, while as yet their tents must supply their ruined houses! The first motions of zeal are commonly strong and fervent: how carefully do these governors and priests make preparation for God's temple! Carpenters and masons are hired; Tyrian workmen are again called for, and Lebanon is now anew olicited for cedar trees. The materials are ready: every Israelite with such courage addresses himself to this service, as if his life lay in those stones; and now, while the foundation of the temple was laying, the priests stand in their habits, with trumpets, the Levites with cymbals, interchanging their holy music, and melodiously singing praises to the God of Israel, who had turned their captivity as the streams in the south, and honoured their eyes and their hands with the first stones of his house. The people second their songs with shouts: the earth sounds, and heaven rings with the joyful acclamations of the multitude. It is no small comfort, in a good action, to have begun well. The entrance of any holy enterprise is commonly encountered with many discouragements, which, if we have once overcome, the passage is smooth.

How would these men have shouted at the laying on of the last stone of the battlements, who are thus joyed with laying the first stones of the foundation! The end of any thing is better than the beginning; that hath certainty, this danger; this labour, that rest: little did these men think, that, for all this, few of them should live to see the roof.

What different affections shall we see produced in men by the same occasion! the younger Jews shouted at this sight, the elder wept: the younger shouted to see a new foundation, the elder wept to remember the old: they who had seen no better, thought this goodly; they who had seen the former, thought this mean and homely; more sorrowing for what they had lost, than rejoicing in so unequal a reparation.

As it may fall out, it is some piece of misery to have been happier: every abatement of the degrees of our former height lays siege to' our thankfulness for lesser mercies. Sometimes it proves an advantage to have known no better: he shall more comfortably enjoy present benefits, who takes them as they are, without any other comparisons than of the weakness of his own deservings. It is nothing to me what myself or others have been, so I be now well. Neither is it otherwise in particular churches: if one be more gloriously built than another, yet if the foundation be rightly laid in both, one may not insult, the other, may not repine; each must congratulate the truth to other, each must thankfully enjoy itself.

The noise was not more loud than confused; here was a discordant mixture of lamentation and shouting; it was hard to say whether drowned the other.

This assembly of Jews was a true image of God's church on earth: one sings, another cries; never doth it all either laugh or mourn at once. It shall be in our triumph, that all tears shall be wiped from our eyes; till then, our passions must be mixed, according to the occasions.

The Jews are busy at work, not more full of joy than hopes; and now that the walls begin to overlook the earth, their thoughts seem to overlook the walls. But what great enterprise was ever set on foot for God, which found not some crosses?

There was a mongrel brood of Samarit-Assyrians, which, ever since the days of Sennacherib, dwelt in the land of Israel, whose religion was a patched coat of several shreds: some little part Jewish, the rest pagan, not without much variety of idolatry. These hollow neighbours proffer their assistance to the children of the captivity; "Let us build with you, for we seek your God, as ye do, and do sacrifice to him." Might men be their own judges, there would be no heresy in the world, no misworship. It is true, these men did sacrifice to the true God; the lions taught them to seek, and the Israelitish priests taught them to find, the fashions of the God of the land. Some of these Jews knew their devotion of old; they served Israel's God, but with their own: as good no God as too many. In a just indignation, therefore, do these Jewish governors repel the partnership of such helpers: "You have nothing to do with us, to build an house to our God; but we ourselves together will build unto the Lord God of Israel." The hand of an idolater is contagious; yet had it been to the building of some fortress, or common hall, perhaps their aid had not been refused; but when the walls of God's house are to be raised, this society had been piacular.

Those, that may not be allowed to help the work, will ask no leave to hinder it; their malicious suggestions weaken the hands of the people of Judah, and stir up authority to suppress them.

Cyrus was afar off; neither lived he long after that gracious commission, and, besides, was so taken up the while with his wars, that he could not have leisure to sift those querulous accusations. Now, therefore, during the last years of Cyrus, and the reign of his son Cambyses, and the long government of Darius Hystaspides, and of his son Xerxes, or Ahasuerus, and lastly, of his son Artaxerxes, until the days of Darius Nothus (which was no less than five successions of kings besides Cyrus), do the walls of the temple stand still, yea, lie waste, subject to the wrongs of time and weather, the fit matter of sorrow to the Jews, insultation to the enemies, derision to passengers.

What a wide gap of time was here, betwixt the foundation of God's house and the battlements! How large a trial doth God now secondly take of the faith, of the patience of his people! how large a proof doth he give of his own long-suffering! O God, when thou hadst but one house upon earth, thou wert content to put up with delays, yea, affronts, in the building of it: now thou hast many, it is no marvel if thy longanimity and justice abide some of them to lie desolate. They are not stones, or metals, or men, that can make thee more glorious: thou best knowest when to serve thyself of all these, when to honour these with thy service.

A small matter hinders the worthiest action; as a little fish, they say, stays the greatest ship. Before, the Jews were discouraged with words, but now they are stopped by commands.

These envious Samaritans have corrupted the governors which the Persian kings set over those parts, and from their hands have obtained letters of deep calumniation, to Ahasuerus the king, and after him to his son Artaxerxes, wherein Jerusalem is charged with old rebellion to kings; and for proof, appellation is made to the records; from which evidence is spitefully inferred, that if these walls be once built, the king shall receive no tribute on this side the river. Never was God's church but subject to reproaches.

Princes have reason to be jealous of their rights. The records are searched: it soon appears, that, within one century of years, Jerusalem had rebelled against Nebuchadnezzar, and held out two years' siege of that great Babylonian. The scandal of disloyalty is perpetual; although indeed they held him rather a prevailing enemy, than a lawful sovereign: one act disparages either place or person, to all posterities. Therefore shall the walls of Jerusalem lie waste, because it had once been treacherous; after a hundred years doth that city rue one perfidious act of Zedekiah. Fidelity to our governors is ever both safe and honourable.

Command is now sent out from Artaxerxes, even the son of queen Esther, to restrain tne work. All respects must cease with carnal minds, when their honours and profits are in question. Rehum the chancellor, and Shimshai the scribe, come now armed with authority: the sword hath easily prevailed against the trowel. Still do the Jews find themselves, as it were, captives at home; and, in silence and sorrow, cense from their labours, until the days of the next successor, Darius Nothus.

As those that had learned to sow after a bad crop, these Jews, upon the change of the prince, by the encouragement of the prophets of God, Haggai and Zechariah, take new heart to build again. If others' power hinder us in the work of God, our will may not be guilty.

Their new governors come, as before, to expostulate: " Who hath commanded you to build this house, and to make up this wall? and what are your names?" They wisely and modestly plead the service of the God of heaven, the decree of Cyrus; still persisting to build, as if the prohibition of Artaxerxes had died with the author. The impartial governors do neither claw nor exasperate, but, relating the humble and just answer of the Jews, move the king, that search may be made in the rolls of Babylon, whether such an edict were made by Cyrus, and require his royal pleasure concerning the validity of such a pretended decree.—Darius searches, finds, ratifies, enlargeth it; not only charging his officers not to hinder the work, but commanding to levy sums of his own tribute, beyond the river, for the expenses of the building, for the furnishing of sacrifices; threatening utter ruin to the house of that man, and death to his person, who should offer to impeach this bounty; and shutting up with a zealous imprecation, " The God of heaven, that hath caused his name to dwell there, destroy all kings and people that shall put to their hand to alter and to destroy this house of God which is at Jerusalem: I Darius have made a decree; let it be done with speed."

Who could have looked for such an edict from a Persian? No Solomon, no David, could have said more. The ruler of all hearts makes choice of his own instruments, and, when he pleaseth, can glorify himself by those means which are least expected. That sacred work, which the husband and son of an Esther crossed, shall be happily accomplished by a Darius. In the sixth year of his reign is the temple of God fully finished; and now the dedication of it is celebrated by a joyful feast: an hundred bullocks, two hundred rams, four hundred lambs, in a meet proportion, smoke upon their altars. And now the children of the captivity think this day a sufficient payment for all their sorrows. We have reason to think it the fairest day that ever shone forth to us, wherein the spiritual building of God's house is raised up in our souls. How should we shout at the laying of this foundation, and feast at the laying on of the roof! What other, what better sacrifice can we offer up to God in the sense of our joy, than ourselves? Let our hearts be at once the temple, the altar, the sacrifice. O God, be thou glorified in all these, who hast graciously honoured all these with thyself.

Every holy feast is now duly kept: the priests know their divisions, the Levites their courses, and the whole service of God is put into a settled order. But, as there can be no new beginnings without imperfection, nor long continuance without corruption, reformation is no less necessary than good institutions. Artaxerxes Mnemon had learned of his father Darius to befriend God's people, and strives to inherit his beneficence: under his government is Ezra the priest and learned scribe sent with a large commission from Babylon to Jerusalem, to inquire into the wants, and redress the disorders of the Jews, with full power, not only to carry with him all the voluntaries of his nation, and the treasures contributed in all the province of Babylon, but to raise such sums out of the king's revenues as should be found requisite; and, withal, to ordain magistrates and judges, and to crown the laws with due execution, whether to death, or banishment, or confiscation; and, lastly, with a large exemption of the priests and Levites, and all the inferior officers of the temple, from all tolls, tributes, customs. Nothing wanted here, whether for direction or encouragement. It is a sign of God's great favour to any nation, when the hearts of sovereign governors are raised up, both to the choice of worthy agents, and to the commanding of pious and restorative actions.

Holy and careful Ezra gathers a new colony of Jews, takes view of them at the river of Ahava; and finding a miss of the sons of Levi (without whom no company, no plantation, can be complete), sends for their supply; and, now fully furnished, he proclaims a fast in the way.

I do not hear him say, The journey is long and dangerous; the people have need of all their strength. I could well wish us all afflicted with a religious fast, were it not that the abatement of the courage and vigour of the multitude, may endanger our success; but, without all these carnal consultations, he begins with this solemn act of humiliation. It is better to have God strong in our weakness, than to have flesh and blood strong in his neglect.

Artaxerxes was a patron of the Jews, yet a pagan by profession. Wise Ezra was afraid of quenching those sparks of piety, which he descried in his semi-proselyte: rather, therefore, than he will seem to imply a distrust in the providence of that God, in whose service he went, by seeking a convoy of soldiers from the king, Ezra chooses to put himself upon the hazard of the way, and the immediate protection of the Almighty. Any death were better than to hear Artaxerxes say, Is this the man that so confidently told me, " The hand of our God is upon all them for good that seek him; but his power and his wrath is against all them that forsake him?" Doth he believe himself, that he thus doubts ere he begin? Dare he not trust his God with his own businesses?

The resolutions of faithful hearts are heroical. No heathen man shall stumble at Ezra's fear: he can find more assurance in his fast, than in a Persian band. With a courageous reliance upon the hand of his God, he puts himself into the journey, and finds nothing but safety and success. The fidelity of the Almighty never disappointed the confidence of his servants. All the army of Artaxerxes could not have been so strong a guard to the Jews, as their invisible protection.

In the space of four months is Ezra and his company happily arrived at Jerusalem, where he joys to see the new temple, and his old colleagues: and now, having delivered up the charge of his treasure, by weight, in the chambers of the house of the Lord, he applies himself to his work, and delivers the king's commissions to the lieutenants and governors, for their utmost assistance.

The princes of Judah do not, for aught I hear, repine at the large patent granted to this priest, nor say, What doth a man of this robe meddle with placing or displacing magistrates, with executions of judgments, to death, bonds, banishments? but rather, as congratulating this power to sacred hands, gladly present unto him all their grievances. Truly religious hearts cannot grudge any honour to their spiritual guides.

This holy commissioner is soon welcomed with a sad bill of complaint from some good peers of Israel; wherein they charge divers of the priests, Levites, people, not to have separated themselves from the idolatrous inhabitants of the lands, nor therefore from their abominations, even from Canaanites, Hittites, Perizzites, and the rest of those branded nations; that they have taken of their daughters for themselves, and for their sons, so that the holy seed have mingled themselves with those forbidden people; and, which made the matter so much more heinous, less remediable, that the "hand of the princes and rulers hath been chief in this trespass."

O hypocritical Jews! did ye refuse to suffer your Samaritan neighbours to join with you in building a lifeless house unto God, and do ye now join affinity with a more accursed generation, for the building of living houses unto posterity, for the pulling down of the lively house of God?

How could Ezra hear this with his clothes, his hair, his beard untorn? What grief, what astonishment, must this news needs bring to a zealous heart! And were it not that the conscience of his sincere respect of God's glory relieved him, how could Ezra choose but repent him of his journey, and say, "Am I come from Babylon to find paganism in Judah? did I leave Persians to meet with Canaanites? What do I here, if Jerusalem be removed? how much better were a clear captivity than an idolatrous freedom? Woe is me, that, having left many Jewish hearts in Babylon, I now am forced to find heathen blood in Jerusalem!"

As a man distracted with sorrow, Ezra sits down upon the earth with his garments rent, with the hair of his head and beard plucked off, wringing his hands, knocking his breast, not moving from his place until the evening sacrifice. It is hard to be too much affected with the public sins of God's people. Those who find themselves in the ship of God's church, cannot but be much troubled with every dangerous leak that it takes. Common cases are not more neglected by the careless, than taken to heart by the wise and godly.

There, and thus, Ezra sits astonished until the evening sacrifice: others resorted to him the while, even all that trembled at the words of the God of Israel; but to help on his sorrow, not to relieve; neither doth any man wish a mitigation of his own or others' grief. At last he rises up from his heaviness, and casts himself upon his knees, and spreads out his hands unto the Lord his God. Wherefore was all that pensiveness, fasting, silence, tearing of hair and clothes, but to serve as a meet preface to his prayers? wherein he so freely pours out his heart, as if it had been all dissolved into devotion; professing his shame to lift up his face towards the throne of God; confessing the iniquities of his people, which were increased over their heads, and grown up unto heaven; fetching their trespass far, and charging them deep; feelingly acknowledging the just hand that had followed them in all their judgments, and the just confusion wherein they now stand before the face of their God.

Tears, and sighs, and grovellings, accompanied his prayers; the example and noise whereof drew Israel into a participation of this public mourning; "for the people wept very sore." How can they choose but think, If he thus lament for us, how should we grieve for ourselves!

All Judah went away merrily with their sin, till this check of Ezra: now they are afflicted. Had not the hands of the peers been in this trespass, the people had not been guilty; had not the cheeks of Ezra been first drenched with tears, the people had not been penitent. It cannot be spoken what power there is in a great example, whether to evil or good.

Prayers and tears are nothing without endeavours. Shecaniah, the son of Jehiel, puts the first life into this business. Having seconded the complaint of Ezra, he now adds, "Yet there is hope in Israel concerning this thing; now therefore let us make a covenant with our God to put away all the wives, and such as are born of them: arise, for this matter belongeth to thee, we also will be with thee; be of good courage, and do it."

When mischief is once done, the chief care is, how to redress it. The best way of redress is the deliberate undoing of that which we have rashly committed. The surest obligation to the undoing of an evil act, is an oath or covenant made with God, for the performance.

There is no man so wise, but he may make use of good counsel; there is no man so forward, but he may abide incitation. It is no small encouragement to see a hearty assistance in an envious and difficult service. "Then arose Ezra, and made the chief priests, the Levites, and all Israel, to swear that they should do according to this word."

It is half done that is thus assured. There was need of a strong power to dissolve a matrimonial, though inordinate love. Doubtless these men had married out of affection: their hearts were no less set upon these wives, though heathenish, than if they had been of their own tribes; neither were their children, thus begotten, less dear unto them, than if they had lain in Jewish wombs. Nothing less than an oath of God, therefore, could quiet these passions: that is both required and taken.

Now begins Ezra to conceive some hope of present redress; the comfort whereof yet cannot turn off his sorrow for the offence passed. He neither eats bread nor drinks water, willingly punishing himself, because Israel had sinned. Now shall his countrymen easily read in his face their own penance, and just humiliation, and say, This man takes no joy in our sufferings; he would not smart thus for us, if he did not descry more danger towards us than we can apprehend.

Proclamation is made through Judah and Jerusalem, under pain of forfeiture of substance, and excommunication from God's people, that all the children of the captivity should gather themselves together unto Jerusalem. They are met accordingly: the courts of God's house are thronged with penitents; and now, as if the heavens would teach them what to do, the clouds rain down abundance of tears. What with those sad showers, what with their inward remorse, the people sit trembling in the open courts, and humbly wait for the reproof, for the sentence of Ezra. He rises up, and with a severe countenance lays before them their sin, their amends; the sin of their strange wives, the amends of their confession, of their separation; not sparing to search their wound, nor neglecting the meet plaster for their cure.

The people, as willing to be healed, yield themselves patiently to that rough hand, not shrinking at the pain, nor favouring the sore: "As thou hast said, so must we do;" only craving a fit proportion of time, and a due assistance for the despatch of so long and important a work. Ezra gladly hearkens to this not so much request, as counsel of Israel. The charge is divided to men and days; for two months space, the commissioners sit close, and within that compass finish this business, not more thankless than necessary. Doubtless much variety of passion met with them in this busy service. Here you should have seen an affectionate husband bitterly weeping at the dismission of a loving wife, and drowning his last farewell in sobs: there you might have seen a passionate wife hanging upon the arms of her beloved husband, and on her knees conjuring him by his former vows, and the dear pledges of their loves, and proffering, with many tears, to redeem the loss of her husband with the change of her religion. Here you might have seen the kindred and parents of the dismissed, shutting up their denied suits with rage and threats: there the abandoned children kneeling to their seemingly cruel father, beseeching him not to cast off the fruit of his own loins, and expostulating what they have offended in being his. The resolved Israelites must be deaf or blind to these moving objects, and so far forget nature as to put off part of themselves. Personal inconveniences have reason to yield to public mischiefs: long entertainment makes that sin hard to be ejected, whose first motions might have been repelled with ease.

Had not the prohibition of these marriages been express, and their danger and mischief palpable, the care of their separation had not bred so much tumult in Israel. He, that ordained matrimony, had, upon fearful curses, forbidden an unequal yoke with infidels. Besides the marring of the church by the mixture of an unholy seed, religion suffered for the present, and all good hearts with it. Many tears, many sacrifices, need to expiate so foul an offence, and to set Israel straight again.

All this while, even these mis-line Jews were yet forward to build the temple. The worst sinners may yield an outward conformity to actions of piety. Ezra hath done more service in pulling down, than the Jews in building: without this act, the temple might have stood, religion must needs have fallen: Babel had been translated to Jerusalem, Jews had turned Gentiles. O happy endeavours of devout and holy Ezra, that hath at once restored Judah to God and to itself!

CONTEMPLATION II.—NEHEMIAH BUILDING THE WALLS OF JERUSALEM.

THIRTEEN years were now passed since Ezra's going up to Jerusalem, when Nehemiah, the religious courtier of Artaxerxes, inquires of the estate of his country, and brethren of Judea: he might well find that holy scribe had not been idle. The commission of Artaxerxes had been improved by him to the utmost. Disorders were reformed, but the walls lay waste: the temple was built, but the city was ruinous; and if some streets were repaired, yet they stood unguarded, open to the mercy of an enemy, to the infestation of ill neighbourhood.— Great bodies must have slow motions: as Jerusalem, so the church of God, whose type it was, must be finished by leisure.

Nehemiah sat warm in the court at Shushan, favoured by the great king Artaxerxes: nothing could be wanting to him, whether for pleasure or state. What needed he to trouble his head with thoughts for Jerusalem? What if those remote walls lay on heaps, while himself dwelt fair? what if his far distant countrymen be despised, while himself is honoured by the great monarch of the world?

It is not so easy for gracious dispositions to turn off the public calamities of God's church: neither can they do other than lose their private felicities, in the common distresses of the universal body: "If I forget thee, O Jerusalem, let my right hand forget her cunning: if I do not remember thee, let my tongue cleave to the roof of my mouth."

Many Jews went up from Babylon and Shushan to Jerusalem; few ever returned voluntarily from their native home to the region of their captivity. Some occasion drew Hanani, with certain others of Judah, to this voyage. Of them doth Nehemiah carefully inquire the present condition of Jerusalem. It was no news that the people were afflicted and reproached, the walls broken down, the gates burnt with fire. Ever since the furious devastation of Nebuzaradan, that city knew not better terms. Seldom doth the spiritual Jerusalem fare otherwise, in respect of outward estate. External glory and magnificence is an unsure note of the church.

Well had Nehemiah hoped, that the gracious edict and beneficence of Darius, and the successive patronage of his lord Artaxerxes, had, by the continuance of twenty years' favour, advanced the strength and glory of Jerusalem; but now, finding the holy city to lie still in the dust of her confusion, neglected of God, despised of men, he sits down and weeps, and mourns, and fasts, and prays to the God of heaven. How many saw those ruins, and were little affected! he hears of them afar off, and is thus passionate. How many were, upon this sight, affected with a fruitless sorrow! his mourning is joined with the endeavours of redress. In vain is that grief, which hath no other end than itself.

Nehemiah is resolved to kneel to the king his master, for the repair of his Jerusalem: he dares not attempt the suit till he have begun with God. This good courtier knew well, that the hearts of these earthly kings are in the overruling hand of the King of heaven, to incline whither he pleaseth. Our prayers are the only true means to make way for our success. If in all our occasions we do not begin with the first mover, the course is preposterous, and commonly speeds accordingly.

Who dares censure the piety of courtiers, when he finds Nehemiah standing before Artaxerxes? Even the Persian palace is not incapable of a saint. No man that waits on the altar at Jerusalem, can compare for zeal with him that waits on the cup of a pagan monarch. The mercies of God are unlimited to places, to callings.

Thus armed with devotions, doth Nehemiah put himself into the presence of his master Artaxerxes. His face was overclouded with a deep sadness, neither was he willing to clear it. The king easily notes the disparity of the countenance of the bearer, and the wine that he bears; and, in a gracious familiarity, asks the reason of such unwonted change. How well it becomes the great to stoop unto a courteous affability, and to exchange words of respect, even with their humble vassals!

Nehemiah had not been so long in the court, but he knew that princes like no other than cheerful attendants; neither was he wont to bring any other face into that presence, than smooth and smiling.

Greatness uses to be full of suspicion, and, where it sees a dejection and sourness of the brows, is ready to apprehend some sullen thoughts of discontentment, or, at the least, construes it for a disrepect to that sovereignty, whose beams should be of power to disperse all our inward mists. Even good manners forbid a man to press into the presence of a prince, except he can either lay by these unpleasing passions, or hide them: so had Nehemiah hitherto done. Now, he purposely suffers his sorrow to look through his eyes, that it may work both inquiry and compassion from his master; neither doth he fail of his hopes in either: "Why is thy countenance sad, seeing thou art not sick?" How sensible do we think the Father of mercies is of all our pensive thoughts, when a heathen master is so tender of a servant's grief! How ready should our tongues be to lay open our cares to the God of all comfort, when we see Nehemiah so quick in the expressions of his sorrow to an uncertain ear! "Let the king live for ever! Why should not my countenance be sad, when the city, the place of my fathers' sepulchres, lieth waste, and the gates thereof burnt with fire?" Not without an humble preface doth Nehemiah lay forth his grievance: complaints have ever an unpleasing harshness in them, which must be taken off by some discreet insinuation; although it could not but sound well in the generous ear of Artaxerxes, that his servant was so careful for the honour of his country. As nature hath made us all members of a community, and hath given us common interests, so it is most pleasing to us, to see these public cares divide us from our own.

The king easily descries a secret supplication wrapped up in this moanful answer, which the modest suitor was afraid to disclose; and therefore he helps that bashful motion into the light: "For what dost thou make request?" It is the praise of bounty to draw on the just petitions of fearful supplicants.

Nehemiah dares not open his mouth to the king, till his heart hath opened itself by a sudden ejaculation to his God : no business can be so hasty, but our prayer may prevent it; the wings whereof are so nimble, that it can fly up to heaven, and solicit God, and bring down an answer, before ever our words need to come forth of our lips. In vain shall we hope that any design of ours can prosper, if we have not first sent this messenger on our errand.

After this silent and insensible preparation, Nehemiah moves his suit to the king, yet not at once, but by meet degrees: first he craves leave for his journey, and for building; then he craves aid for both : both are granted. Nehemiah departs, furnished with letters to the governors for a convoy, with letters to the keeper of the king's forest for timber, not more full of desire than hope.

Who ever put his hand to any great work for the behoof of God's church, without opposition? As the walls of the temple found busy enemies, so shall the walls of the city; and these so much more, as they promise more security and strength to Jerusalem. Sanballat, the deputy-lieutenant of the Moabites, and Tobiah, the like officer to the Amorites, and Geshem to the Arabians, are galled with envy at the arrival of a man authorised to seek the welfare of the children of Israel. There cannot be a greater vexation to wicked hearts, than to see the spiritual Jerusalem in any likelihood of prosperity. Evil spirits and men need no other torment than their own despite.

This wise courtier hath learned, that secresy is the surest way of any important despatch. His errand could not but be known to the governors : their furtherance was enjoined for the provision of materials, else the walls of Jerusalem had overlooked the first notice of their heathen neighbours. Without any noise doth Nehemiah arise in the dead of night, and taking some few into his company, none into his council, he secretly rounds the decayed walls of Jerusalem, and views the breaches, and observes the gates, and returns home in silence, joying in himself to foresee those preparations, which none of the inhabitants did once dream of. At last, when he had fully digested this great work in his own breast, he calls the rulers and citizens together; and having condoled with them the common distress and reproach, he tells them of the hand of his God, which was good upon him; he shows them the gracious commission o the king, his master, for that good work. They answer him with a zealous encouragement of each other: "Let us rise up and build." Such a hearty invitation, countenanced by authority, hath easily strengthened the hands of the multitude. With what observance and dearness do they now look upon their unexpected patron! how do they honour him as a man sent from heaven, for the welfare of Jerusalem! Every man flies to his hod and trowel, and rejoices to second so noble a leader, in laying a stone in that wall of their common defence.

Those emulous neighbours of theirs, Sanballat, Tobiah, Geshem — the chief commanders of Moab, Ammon, Arabia — have soon espied the first mortar that is laid upon that old foundation. Envy is usually more quick-sighted than love: and now they scornfully apply themselves to these despised Jews, and think to scoff them out of their work. The favourablest persecution of any good cause is the lash of lewd tongues, whether by bitter taunts or by scurrilous invectives; which it is as impossible to avoid, as necessary to contemn. The barking of these dogs doth not hinder Nehemiah from walking on his way, professing his confidence in the God of heaven, whose work that was; he shakes off their impotent malice, and goes on cheerfully to build. Every Israelite knows his station : Eliashib the high priest, and the rest of that sacred tribe, put the first hand to this work ; they build the sheep-gate, and sanctify it, and in it all the rest. As the first fruits of the field, so the first stones of the wall, are hallowed to God, by the consecration of those devout agents. That business is like to prosper which begins with God.

No man was idle, no part was intermitted: all Jerusalem was at once encompassed with busy labourers. It cannot be, but the joint endeavours of faithful hearts must raise the walls of the church.

Now Sanballat, and his brethren, find some matter to spend their scoffs upon : "What do these feeble Jews? Will they fortify themselves? will they sacrifice? will they make an end in a day? will they revive the stones out of the heaps of rubbish which are burnt?"

How basely do carnal minds think of the projects and actions of God's children! therefore vilifying them, because they measure them by no other line than outward probability. O foolish Moabites! this work is God's, and therefore, in despite of all your tongues and hands, it shall prosper. He hears you whom ye have blasphemed, and shall turn your reproach upon your own heads. And thou, proud Ammonite, that couldst say, "If a fox go upon their stone-wall, he shall break it down," shalt well find, that all the wolvish troops of your confederates shall not be able to remove one stone of this sure fortification: while Moab and Ammon repine and bluster in vain, this wall shall rise; and when Moab and Ammon shall lie in the dust, this wall shall stand. The mortar that hath been tempered with so many prayers, cannot but outlast all the flints and marbles of human confidence.

Now the growth of this wall hath turned the mirth of the adversaries into rage: these Moabites, Ammonites, Arabians, Ashdodites, conspire all together to fight against Jerusalem, and, while the mortar is yet green, to demolish those envied heaps.

What hath this city offended, in desiring to be defenced? what wrong could it be to wish a freedom from wrongs? Were this people so mighty, that there could be danger in overpowering their neighbours, or in resisting a common sovereign, there might have appeared some colour for this hostile opposition: but alas! what could a despised handful do to the prejudice of either? It is quarrel enough to Jerusalem, that it would not be miserable.

Neither is it otherwise with the head of these hellish complices: there needs no other cause of his utmost fury, than to see a poor soul struggling to get out of the reach of his tyranny. So do savage beasts bristle up themselves, and make the most fierce assaults, when they are in danger of losing the prey which they had once seized on.

In the meanwhile, what doth Nehemiah with his Jews for their common safety? They pray and watch: they pray unto God; they watch against the enemy. Thus, thus shall we happily prevail against those spiritual wickednesses which war against our souls. No evil can surprise us, if we watch; no evil can hurt us, if we pray. " This is the victory that overcomes the world, even our faith."

There was need of a continued vigilancy: the enemy was not more malicious than subtile, and had said, "They shall not know, neither see, till we come in the midst amongst them, and slay them." Open force is not so dangerous as close dissimulation: they meant to seem Jews, while they were Moabites and Ammonites, and in the clothes of brethren purposed to hide murderers.

Never is Satan so prevalent as when he comes transformed into an angel of light.

It was a merciful providence of God that made these men's tongues the blabs of their own counsel. Many a fearful design had prospered, if wickedness could have been silent. Warning is a lawful guard to a wise adversary: now doth Nehemiah arm his people, and, for the time, changes their trowels into swords, and spears, and bows, raising up their courage with a vehement exhortation to remember the Lord, which is "great and terrible, and to fight for their brethren, their sons, their daughters, their wives, and their houses." Nothing can so hearten us to the encountering of an evil, as the remembrance of that infinite Power and Wisdom, which can either avert, or mitigate, or sanctify it. We could not faint, if we did not forget God.

Necessity urges a man to fight for himself; love enables his hand to fight for those which challenge a part in him. Where love meets with necessity, there can want no endeavour of victory. Necessity can make even cowards valiant; love makes the valiant unresistible. Nehemiah doth not therefore persuade these Jews to fight for themselves, but for theirs. The judgment of the interest, and danger, cannot but quicken the dullest spirits.

Discovered counsels are already prevented. These serpents die by being first seen: " When the enemies heard that it was known unto us," they let fall their plot. Could we descry the enterprises of Satan, that tempter would return ashamed.

It is a safe point of wisdom to carry a jealous eye over those whom we have once found hollow, and hostile. From that time forth, Nehemiah divided the task betwixt the trowel and the sword, so disposing of every Israelite, that while one hand was a mason, the other was a soldier; one is for work, the other for defence. O lively image of the church militant! wherein every one labours weaponed; wherein there is neither an idle soldier, nor a secure workman. every one so builds, that he is ready to ward temptations; every one so wields the sword of the spirit for defence, that withal he builds up himself in his most holy faith: here is neither a fruitless valour, nor an unsafe diligence.

But what can our weapons avail us, if there be not means to warn us of an enemy? without a trumpet, we are armed in vain : " The work is great and large, and we are separated upon the wall, one far from another." Yea, so far as the utmost bounds of the earth, are we separated one from another, upon the walls of the spiritual Jerusalem; only the sacred trumpets of God call us, who are distant in place, to a combination in profession. And who are those trumpets but the public messengers of God, of whom God hath said, " If the watchman see the sword come, and blow not the trumpet, and the people be not warned; if the sword come, and take any person from among them, he is taken away in his iniquity, but his blood will I require at the watchman's hand." Woe be to us, if we sound not, if the sound we give be uncertain! woe be to our people, if, when we premonish them of enemies, of judgments, they sit still unmoved, not buckling themselves to a resistance, to a prevention!

It is a mutual aid to which these trumpets invite us; we might fight apart, without the signals of war: " In what place ye hear the sound of the trumpet, resort ye thither unto us." There can be no safety to the church, but where every man thinks his life and welfare consists in his fellows. Conjoined forces may prosper; single oppositions are desperate. All hearts and hands must meet in the common quarrel.

CONTEMPLATION III.—NEHEMIAH REDRESSING THE EXTORTION OF THE JEWS.

With what difficulty do these miserable Jews settle in their Jerusalem! The fear of foreign enemies doth not more afflict them than the extortion of their own. Dearth is added unto war. Miseries do not stay for a mannerly succession to each other, but, in a rude importunity, throng in at once. Babel may be built with ease; but whosoever goes about to raise the walls of God's city, shall have his hands full. The incursion of public enemies may be prevented by vigilancy and power; but there is no defence against the secret gripes of oppression.

There is no remedy: the Jews are so taken up with their trowel and sword for the time, that they cannot attend their trades; so as, while the wall did rise, their estates must needs impair. Even in the cheapest season they must needs be poor, that earned nothing but the public safety; how much more in common scarcity? Their houses, lands, vineyards, are therefore mortgaged, yea, their very skins are sold, for corn to their brethren; necessity forces them to sell that, which it was cruelty to buy. What will we not, what must we not, part with for life? The covetous rulers did not consider the occasions of this want, but the advantage. Sometimes a bargain may be as unmerciful as a robbery. Charity must be the rule of all contracts; the violation whereof, whether in the matter or the price, cannot but be sinful.

There could not be a juster ground of expostulation, than this of the oppressed Jews: " Our flesh is as the flesh of our brethren, our children as their children; and lo, we bring into bondage our sons and our daughters." While there is no difference in nature, why should there be such an injurious disproportion in condition? Even the same flesh may bear a just inequality: some may be rulers, while others are subjects; some wealthy, others poor: but why those wealthy rulers should tyrannize over those poor inferiors, and turn brotherhood into bondage, no reason can be given but lawless ambition. If there were one flesh of peers, another of peasants, there should be some colour for the proud impositions of the great, as, because the flesh of beasts is in a lower rank than ours, we kill, we devour it at pleasure; but now, since the large body of mankind consists of the same flesh, why should the hand strike the foot? and if one flesh may challenge meet respects from us, how much more one spirit? The spirit is more noble than the flesh is base: the flesh is dead without the spirit; the spirit, without the flesh, active and immortal. Our soul, though shapeless and immaterial, is more apparently one than the flesh; and if the unity of our human spirit calls us to a mutual care and tenderness, in our carriage each to other, how much more of the divine? By that we are men, by this we are Christians. As the soul animates us to a natural life, so doth God's spirit animate the soul to a heavenly, which is so one, that it cannot be divided. How should then one spirit cause us so far to forget all natural and civil differences, as not to contemn, not to oppress any whom it informeth? They are not Christians, not men, that can enjoy the miseries of their brethren, whether in the flesh or spirit.

Good Nehemiah cannot choose but be much moved at the barbarous extortion of the people: and now, like an impartial governor, he rebukes the rulers and nobles, whose hand was thus bloody with oppression. As of fishes, so of men, the lesser are a prey to the great. It is an ill use made of power, when the weight of it only serves to crush the weak. There were no living amongst men, had not God ordained higher than the highest; and yet higher than they. Eminency of place cannot be better improved, than by taking down mighty offenders.

If nobility do embase itself to any foul sin, it is so much more worthy of coercion, by how much more the person is of greater mark.

The justice of this reproof could not but shame impudence itself: "We, after our ability, have redeemed our brethren the Jews which were sold to the heathen; and will you sell your brethren, or shall they be sold to us?" Shall they find at home that yoke of bondage which they had put off abroad? while they are still Jews, shall we turn Assyrians? if they must be slaves, why not rather to enemies than to brethren? how much more tolerable were a foreign servitude, than a domestical! Be ashamed, O ye nobles of Israel, to renew Babylon in Jerusalem! I marvel not if the offenders be stricken dumb with so unanswerable an expostulation. Guiltiness and confusion have stopped their mouths.

Many of those who have not had grace enough to refrain sin, yet are not so utterly void of grace as to maintain sin. Our afterwits are able to discern a kind of unreasonableness in those wicked actions, which the first appearance represents unto us as plausible. Gain leads in sin, but shame follows it out. There are those that are bold and witty to bear out commodious or pleasant evils: neither could these Jewish enormities have wanted some colours of defence: their stock was their own, which might have been otherwise improved to no less profit. The offer, the suit of these bargains, was from the sellers: these escheats fell into their hands unsought; neither did their contract cause the need of their brethren, but relieve it: but their conscience will not bear this plea. I know not whether the maintenance of the least evil be not worse than the commission of the greatest: this may be of frailty, that argues obstinacy. There is hope of that man that can blush and be silent.

After the conviction of the fact, it is seasonable for Nehemiah to persuade reformation. No oratory is so powerful as that of mildness, especially when we have to do with those, who, either through stomach, or greatness, may not endure a rough reproof. The drops that fall easily upon the corn, ripen and fill the ear; but the stormy showers, that fall with violence, beat down the stalks flat to the earth, and lay whole fields without hope of recovery. Who can resist this sweet and sovereign reprehension: "Ought ye not to walk in the fear of our God, because of the reproach of the heathen, our enemies?" Did we dwell alone in the midst of the earth, yet the fear of our God should overawe our ways; but now, that we dwell in the midst of our enemies, whose eyes are bent upon all our actions, whose tongues are as ready to blaspheme God, as we to offend him, how carefully should we avoid those sins which may draw shame upon our profession!

Now the scandal is worse than the fact. Thus shall religion suffer more from the heathen, than our brethren do from us. If justice, if charity, cannot sway with us, yet let the scornful insultations of the profane Gentiles fright us from these pressures. No ingenuous disposition can be so tender of his own disgrace, as the true Israelite is of the reproach of his God: what is it that he will not rather refrain, do, suffer, than that glorious name shall hazard a blemish? They cannot want outward retentives from sin, that live either among friends or enemies: if friends, they may not be grieved; if enemies, they may not be provoked. Those that would live well, must stand in awe of all eyes; even those that are without the church, yet may not be without regard. No person can be so contemptible, as that his censure should be contemned.

In dissuading from sin, reason itself cannot prevail more than example: " I likewise, and my brethren, and my servants, might exact of them money and corn; but from the time that I was appointed to the charge of Judah, I and my brethren have not eaten the bread of the governor." He shall never rule well, that doth all that he may: it is not safe for either part, that a prince should live at the height of his power; and if the greatest abate of their right, is it for inferiors to extort? Had Nehemiah aimed at his own greatness, no man could have had fairer pretences for his gain. —" The former governors, that were before me, were chargeable unto the people, and had taken of them bread and wine, besides forty shekels of silver." His foot had not first trod in this commodious path: it was beaten by the steps of his predecessors; neither did any of them walk beside it. However it might be envious to raise new taxations, yet to continue those he found unrepined at, had been out of the reach of exception. A good governor looks not so much what hath been done, as what should be: precedents are not the rule whereby he rules, but justice, but piety: " So did not I, because of the fear of the Lord." Laws are not a straiter curb to subjects, than conscience is to good princes. They dare not do what they cannot do charitably. What advantage can they think it, to be from under the controlment of men, when the God of heaven notes, and punishes their offences? Whoso walketh by this rule, can neither err nor miscarry. It is no trusting to the external remedies of sin; either they are not always present, or, if present, not powerful enough: but if the fear of God have once taken up the heart, it goes ever with us, and is strong enough to overmaster the most forcible temptation.

Therefore must these Jews follow this example of Nehemiah, because he followed not the example of his predecessors: because he left their evil, they must imitate his good. In vain shall rulers advise against their own practice: when they lead the way, they may well challenge to be followed. Seldom hath it been ever seen, that great persons have not been seconded in evil: why should not their power serve to make partners of their virtues.

Thus well did it speed with Nehemiah: his merciful carriage, and zealous suit, have drawn the rulers to a promise of restitution: "We will restore them, and will require nothing of them, so will we do as thou sayest."

It is no small advantage that these nobles must forego in their releases: there cannot be a better sign of a sound amendment, than that we can be content to be losers by our repentance. Many formal penitents have yielded to part with so much of their sin as may abate nothing of their profit: as if these rulers should have been willing to restore the persons, but withal should have stood stiffly to require their sums: this whining and partial satisfaction had been thankless. True remorse enlargeth the heart, and openeth the hand, to a bountiful redemption of our errors.

Good purposes do too often cool in time, and vanish into a careless forgetfulness. Nehemiah feared this issue of these holy resolutions, and therefore he prosecutes them in their first heat; not leaving these promises, till he had secured them with an oath: the priests are called for, that in their mouths the adjuration may be more solemn and sacred. It is the best point of wisdom to take the first opportunity of fixing good motions, which otherwise are of themselves light and flighty. To make all yet more sure, their oaths are cross-barred with his execration: "Also I shook my lap, and said, So God shake out every man from his house, and from his labour, that performeth not this promise, even thus be he shaken out, and emptied; and all the congregation said, Amen." A promise, an oath, a curse, are passed upon this act: now, no Israelite dares falter in the execution. When we have a sin in chase, it is good to follow it home, not slackening our pursuit, till we have fully prevailed; and when it is once fallen under our hands, we cannot kill it too much.

Now, Nehemiah having thus happily delivered his people from a domestical captivity, commends his service to the gracious remuneration of the Almighty: "Think upon me, my God, for good, according to all that I have done for this people:" therefore doth he refuse the bread of the governor, that he may receive the reward of the Governor of heaven. Had he taken a temporary recompense, both he and it had been forgotten; now he hath made a happy change for eternity. Not that he pleads his merit, but sues for mercy; neither doth he pray to be remembered for his work, but according to his work.

Our good deeds, as they are well accepted of God, so they shall not go unrewarded; and what God will give, why may not we crave? Doubtless, as we may offer up our honest obedience unto God, so we may expect and beg his promised retributions; not out of a proud conceit of the worth of our earnings, which, at the best, are no other than unprofitable servants, but out of a faithful dependence upon his pact of bounty, who cannot be less than his word. O God, if we do aught that is good, it is thine act, and not ours! crown thine own work in us, and take thou the glory of thine own mercies.

While Nehemiah is busy in reforming abuses at home, the enemy is plotting against him abroad: Sanballat, and Tobiah, and Geshem the Arabian, conspire against his life, and, in him, against the peace of Jerusalem. What open hostility could not do, they hope to effect by pretence of treaties: four several messages call Nehemiah to a friendly meeting. Distrust is a sure guard. The wise governor hath learned to suspect the hollow favours of an enemy, and to return them with safe and just excuses: "I cannot come down: why should the work cease, while I leave it, and come down to you?" I do not hear him say, You intend mischief to me, I will not come forth to you, though this were the proper cause of his forbearance; but he turns them off with an answer, that had as much truth as reservedness. Fraud is the fittiest answered with subtlety: even innocency is allowed a lawful craft. That man is in an ill case, that conceals no truth from an adversary.

What entreaties cannot do, shall be attempted by threats. Sanballat's servant comes now the fifth time with an open letter, importing dangerous intimations, wherein it is written, "It is reported among the heathen, and Gashmu saith it, that the Jews think to rebel; for which cause thou buildest the wall, that thou mayest be their king." "It is reported:" and what falsehood may not plead this warrant? what can be more lying than report? "Among the heathen:" and who is more ethnic than Sanballat? what pagan can be worse than a mongrel idolater? "And Gashmu saith it," ask my fellow else: this Arabian was one of those three heads of all the hostile combination against Jerusalem, against Nehemiah. It would be wide with innocence, if enemies might be allowed to accuse. "That the Jews think to rebel:" a stale suggestion, but once powerful: malice hath learned to miscal all actions; where the hands cannot be taxed, the very thoughts are prejudged: "For which cause thou buildest the wall, that thou mayest be their king." He was never a true Israelite, that hath not passed spiteful slanders and misconstructions. Artaxerxes knew his servant too well, to believe any rumour that should have been so shameless. The ambition of Nehemiah was well known to reach only to the cup, not to the sceptre of his sovereign; and yet, to make up a sound tale, "Prophets are suborned to preach, There is a king in Judah;" as if that loyal governor had corrupted the pulpits also, and had taught them the language of treason.

But what of all this? what if some false tongue have whispered such idle tales? It is not safe for thee, O Nehemiah, to contemn report: perhaps this news shall fly to the court, and work thee a deadly displeasure, ere thou canst know thyself traduced; come, therefore, and let us take counsel together. Surely that man cannot be sparing of any thing, that is prodigal of his reputation. If aught under heaven can fetch Nehemiah out of his hold, it is the care of his fame. But that wary governor sees a net spread near unto this stall, and therefore keeps aloof, not without contempt of those sly devices: "There are no such things done as thou sayest, but thou feignest them out of thine own heart." Some imputations are best answered with a neglective denial. It falls out often, that plain dealing puts craft out of countenance.

Since neither force nor fraud can kill Nehemiah, they will now try to draw him into a sin, and thereby into a reproach: O God! that any prophet's tongue should be mercenary! Shemaiah the seer is hired by Tobiah and Sanballat, to affright the governor with the noise of his intended murder, and to advise him, for shelter, to fly to the forbidden refuge of the temple. The colour was fair. Violence is meant to thy person; no place but one can promise thee safety; the city hath as yet no gates; come, therefore, and shut thyself up in the temple: there only shalt thou be free from all assault.

And what if Nehemiah had hearkened to this counsel? sin and shame had followed: that holy place was for none but persons sacred, such as were privileged by blood and function; others should presume and offend in entering: and now, what would the people say? What shall become of us, while our governor hides his head for fear? Where shall we find a temple to secure us? What do we depending upon a cowardly leader?

Well did Nehemiah forecast these circumstances, both of act and event; and therefore, resolving to distrust a prophet that persuaded him to the violation of a law, he rejects the motion with scorn: "Should such a man as I flee? should I go into the temple to save my life? I will not go." It is fit for great persons to stand upon the honour of their places: their very stations should put those spirits into them, that should make them hate to stoop unto base conditions.

Had God sent this message, we know he hath power to dispense with his own laws; but well might the contradiction of a law argue the message not sent of God: God, as he is one, so doth he perfectly agree with himself. If any private spirit cross a written word, let him be accursed.

CONTEMPLATION IV.—AHASUERUS FEASTING —VASHTI CAST OFF—ESTHER CHOSEN.

WHAT bounds can be set to human ambition? Ahasuerus, that is, Xerxes, the son of Darius, is already the king of a hundred and seven and twenty provinces, and now is ready to fight for more. He hath newly subdued Egypt, and is now addressing himself for the conquest of Greece. He cannot hope ever to see all the land that he possesseth, and yet he cannot be quiet while he hears of more. Less than two ells of earth shall ere long serve him, whom, for the time, a whole world shall scarce satisfy. In vain shall a man strive to have that which he cannot enjoy, and to enjoy aught by mere relation: it is a windy happiness that is sought in the exaggeration of these titles which are taken upon others' credit, without the sense of the owner.

Nothing can fill the heart of man, but he that made it.

This great monarch, partly in triumph of the great victories that he had lately won in Egypt, and partly for the animation of his princes and soldiers to his future exploits, makes a feast, like himself, royal and magnificent.

What is greatness if it be not showed? and wherein can greatness be better shown than in the achievements of war, and the entertainments of peace?

All other feasts were but hunger to this of Ahasuerus, whether we regard the number of guests, or the largeness of preparation, or continuance of time. During the space of a whole half year, all the tables were sumptuously furnished for all comers, from India to Ethiopia; a world of meat; every meal was so set on, as if it should have been the last: yet all this long feast hath an end, and all this glory is shut up in forgetfulness. What is Ahasuerus the better, that his peers then said he was incomparably great? what are his peers the better, that they were feasted? Happy is he that eats bread, and drinks new wine, in the kingdom of God; this banquet is for eternity, without intermission, without satiety!

What variety of habits, of languages, of manners, met at the boards of Ahasuerus? What confluence of strange guests was there now to Shushan? And, lest the glory of this great king might seem, like some coarse picture, only fair afar off, after the princes and nobles of the remote provinces, all the people of Shushan are entertained for seven days, with equal pomp and state. The spacious court of the palace is turned into a royal hall, the walls are of rich hangings, the pillars of marble, the beds of silver and gold, the pavement of porphyry, curiously checkered: the wine and the vessels strove whether should be the richer; no men drunk in worse than gold: and while the metal was the same, the form of each cup was diverse. The attendance was answerable to the cheer, and the freedom matched both: here was no compulsion, either to the measure or quality of the draught; every man's rule was his own choice. Who can but blush to see forced healths in Christian banquets, when the civility of very pagans commands liberty?

I cannot but envy the modesty of heathen dames: Vashti the queen, and her ladies, with all the several ranks of that sex, feast apart, entertaining each other with a bashful courtesy, without wantonness, without that wild scurrility which useth to haunt promiscuous meetings. O shameful unchastity of those loose Christians, who must feed their lust while they fill their bellies, and think the feast imperfect, where they may not satiate their eye no less than palate!

The last day of this pompous feast is now come: king Ahasuerus is so much more cheerful, by how much his guests are nearer to their dismission. Every one is wont to close up his courtesy with so much more passion, as the last acts use to make the deeper impression. And now, that he might at once amaze and endear the beholders, Vashti the queen, in all her royalty, is called for: her sight shall shut up the feast, that the princes and people may say, How happy is king Ahasuerus, not so much in this greatness, as in that beauty!

Seven officers of the chamber are sent to carry the message, to attend her entrance, and are returned with a denial. Perhaps Vashti thought, What means this uncouth motion? More than six months hath this feast continued; and, all this while, we have enjoyed the wonted liberty of our sex. Were the king still himself, this command could not be sent; it is the wine, and not he, that is guilty of this errand is it for me to humour him in so vain a desire? will it agree with our modest reservedness, to offer ourselves to be gazed at by millions of eyes? Who knows what wanton attempts may follow upon this ungoverned excess? This very message argues, that wit and reason have yielded their places to that besotting liquor. Nothing but absence can secure us from some unbeseeming proffer: neither doubt I but the king, when he returns to himself, will give me thanks for so wise a forbearance.

Thus, upon the conceit, as is likely, that her presence would be either needless or unsafe, Vashti refuseth to come; although, perhaps, her great spirit thought much to receive a command from the hand of officers.

The blood, that is once inflamed with wine, is apt to boil with rage; Ahasuerus is very wroth with this indign repulse. It was the ostentation of his glory and might that he affected before these princes, peers, people; and now that seems eclipsed, in the shutting up of all his magnificence, with the disgraceful affront of a woman. It vexes him to think that those nobles, whom he meant to send away astonished with the admiration of his power and majesty, should now say, What boots it Ahasuerus to rule afar off, when he cannot command at home? In vain doth he boast to govern kings, while he is checked by a woman.

Whatever were the intentions of Vashti,

VASHTI CAST OFF.

surely her disobedience was inexcusable. It is not for a good wife to judge of her husband's will, but to execute it; neither wit nor stomach may carry her into a curious inquisition into the reasons of an enjoined charge, much less to a resistance; but in a hood-winked simplicity, she must follow whither she is led, as one that holds her chief praise to consist in subjection.

Where should the perfection of wisdom dwell, if not in the courts of great princes? or what can the treasures of monarchs purchase more invaluably precious, than learned and judicious attendance? or who can be so fit for honour, as the wisest?

I doubt how Ahasuerus could have been so great, if his throne had not been still compassed with them that knew the times, and understood the law and judgment. These were his oracles in all his doubts; these are now consulted in this difficulty: neither must their advice be secretly whispered in the king's ear, but publicly delivered in the audience of all the princes. It is a perilous way that these sages are called to go, betwixt a husband and wife, especially of such power and eminency: yet Memucan fears not to pass a heavy sentence against queen Vashti: "Vashti the queen hath not done wrong to the king only, but also to all the princes, and all the people, that are in all the provinces of the king Ahasuerus." A deep and sore crimination. Injuries are so much more intolerable, as they are dilated unto more: those offences, which are of narrow extent, may receive an easy satisfaction; the amends are not possible, where the wrong is universal: "For this deed of the queen shall come abroad to all women, so that they shall despise their husbands in their eyes." Indeed, so public a fact must needs fly; that concourse gave fit opportunity to diffuse it all the world over. The examples of the great are easily drawn into rules. Bad lessons are apt to be taken out; as honour, so contempt, falls down from the head to the skirts, never ascends from the skirts to the head.

These wise men are so much the more sensible of this danger, as they saw it more likely the case might prove their own: "Likewise shall the ladies of Persia and Media say this day unto all the kings and princes." The first precedents of evil must be carefully avoided. If we care to keep a constant order in good, prudence cannot better bestir itself than in keeping mischief from home.

The foundation of this doom of Memucan is not laid so deep for nothing: "If it please the king, let there go a royal commandment from him, and let it be written among the laws of the Persians and Medians, that it be not altered, that Vashti come no more before Ahasuerus; and let the king give her royal estate to another that is better than she." How bold a word was this, and how hazardous! Had Ahasuerus more loved the beauty of Vashti than his honour, Memucan had spoken against his own life. Howsoever, a queen of so great a spirit could not want strength of favour and faction in the Persian court, which could not but take fire at so desperate a motion. Faithful statesmen, overlooking private respects, must bend their eyes upon public dangers, labouring to prevent a common mischief, though with the adventure of their own. Nature had taught these pagans the necessity of a female subjection, and the hate and scorn of a proud disobedience. They have unlearned the very dictates of nature, that can abide the head to be set below the rib.

I cannot say but Vashti was worthy of a sharp censure; I cannot say she was worthy a repudiation. This plaster drew too hard: it was but heathen justice to punish the wife's disobedience, in one indifferent act, with a divorce. Nothing but the violation of the marriage-bed can either break or untie the knot of marriage. Had she not been a queen, had not that contemptuous act been public, the sentence had not been so hard: now the punishment must be exemplary, lest the sin should be so. Many a one had smarted less, if their persons, if their place, had been meaner.

The king, the princes, approve this heavy judgment of Memucan: it is not in the power of the fair face of Vashti to warrant her stomach. No doubt, many messages passed ere the rigour of this execution. That great heart knows not to relent, but will rather break, than yield to an humble deprecation. When the stone and the steel meet, fire is stricken: it is a soft answer that appeaseth wrath. Vashti is cast off. Letters are sent from the king, into all his provinces, to command that every man should rule at home: the court affords them an awful pattern of authority. Had not Ahasuerus doted much upon Vashti's beauty, he had not called her forth at the feast to be wondered at by his peers and people; yet now he so feels the wound of his reputation, that he forgets he ever felt any wound of his affection. Even the greatest love may be overstrained: it is not safe presuming upon the deepest assurances of dearness. There is no heart that may not be estranged. It is not possible that great princes should want soothing up in all their inclinations, in all their actions. While Ahasuerus is following the chase of his ambition in the wars of Greece, his followers are providing for his lust at home. Nothing could sound more pleasing to a carnal ear, than that all the fair young virgins, throughout all his dominions, should be gathered into his palace at Shushan, for his assay and choice. The decree is soon published: the charge is committed to Hege, the king's chamberlain, both of their purification and ornaments.

What strife, what emulation, was now amongst all the Persian damsels, that either were, or thought themselves fair! Every one hopes to be a queen, and sees no reason why any other should be thought more excellent. How happy were we, if we could be so ambitious of our espousals to the King of heaven!

Amongst all this throng of virgins, God hath provided a wife for Ahasuerus, having determined his choice, where most advantage shall rise to his forlorn people.

The Jews were miserably scattered over the world, in that woful deportation under Jeconiah; scarce a handful of them returned to Jerusalem; the rest remain still dispersed, where they may but have leave to live. There are many thousands of them turned over, with the Babylonian monarchy, to the Persian: amongst the rest was Mordecai the son of Jair, of the tribe of Benjamin — a man of no mean note or ability, who, living in Shushan, had brought up Hadassah, or Esther, his uncle's daughter, in a liberal fashion. It was happy for this orphan, that, in a region of captivity, she lighted into such good hands. Her wise kinsman finds it fit, that her breeding and habit should be Persian-like: in outward and civil forms, there was no need to vary from the heathen; her religion must be her own; the rest was so altogether theirs, that her very nation was not discerned.

The same God, that had given incomparable beauty to this Jewess, gave her also favour in the eyes of Hege, the keeper of the women: she is not only taken into the Persian court, as one of the selected virgins, but observed with more than ordinary respect: all necessaries for her speedy purification are brought to her; seven maids are allowed for her attendance, and the best and most honourable place in that seraglio is allotted to her; as if this great officer had designed her for a queen, before the choice of his master.

What strange preparation was here for the impure bed of a heathen! Every virgin must be six months purified with the oil of myrrh, and six other months perfumed with sweet odours, besides those special receipts that were allowed to each upon their own election. O God, what care, what cost is requisite to that soul which should be addressed a fit bride for thine own holy and glorious Majesty! When we have scoured ourselves with the most cleansing oil of our repentance, and have perfumed ourselves with thy best graces, and our perfectest obedience, it is the only praise of thy mercy that we may be accepted.

The other virgins passed their probation unregarded. When Esther's turn came, though she required nothing, but took what was given her; though she affected nothing, but brought that face, that demeanour which nature had cast upon her, no eye sees her without admiration: the king takes such pleasure in her beauty, that, contemning all the other vulgar forms, his choice is fully fixed upon her. All things must prosper, where God hath intended the success. The most wise providence of the Almighty fetches his projects from far: the preservation and advantage of his own people is in hand; for the contriving of this, Vashti shall be abandoned, the virgins shall be chosen; Esther only shall please Ahasuerus; Mordecai shall displease Haman; Haman's ruin shall raise Mordecai. The purposes of God cannot be judged by his remote actions; only the accomplishment shows his designs: in the meantime, it pleaseth him to look another way than he moves, and to work his own ends by arbitrary and unlikely accidents.

None but Esther shall succeed Vashti; she only carries the heart of Ahasuerus from all her sex; the royal crown is set upon her head; and as Vashti was cast off at a feast, so with a solemn feast shall Esther be espoused. Here wanted no triumph to express the joy of this great bridegroom, and, that the world might witness he could be no less loving than severe, all his provinces shall feel the pleasure of this happy match, in their immunities, in their rich gifts.

With what envious eyes do we think Vashti looked upon her glorious rival! how does she now, though too late, secretly chide her peevish will, that had thus stript her of her royal crown, and made way for a more happy successor! Little did she think her refusal could have had so heinous a construction; little did she fear, that one word, perhaps not ill-meant, should have forfeited her husband, her crown, and all that she was. Whoso is not wise enough to forecast the danger of an offence or indiscretion, may have leisure enough of an unseasonable repentance.

That mind is truly great and noble that is not changed with the highest prosperity. Queen Esther cannot forget her cousin Mordecai; no pomp can make her slight the charge of so dear a kinsman: in all her royalty she casts her eye upon him amongst the throng of beholders; but she must not know him; her obedience keeps her in awe, and will not suffer her to draw him up with her to the participation of her honour. It troubles her not a little to forbear this duty, but she must: it is enough for her that Mordecai hath commanded her not to be known, who, or whose she was.

Perhaps the wise Jew feared, that while her honour was yet green and unsettled, the notice of her nation, and the name of a despised captive, might be some blemish to her in that proud court, whereas, afterwards, upon the merit of her carriage, and the full possession of all hearts, her name might dignify her nation, and countermand all reproaches.

Mordecai was an officer in the court of Ahasuerus; his service called him daily to attend in the king's gate: much better might he, being a Jew, serve a pagan master, than his foster-daughter might ascend to a pagan's bed.

If the necessity or convenience of his occasions called him to serve, his piety and religion called him to faithfulness in his service: two of the king's chamberlains, Bigthan and Teresh, conspire against the life of their sovereign. No greatness can secure from treachery or violence: he that ruled over millions of men, through a hundred and seven and twenty provinces, cannot assure himself from the hand of a villain; he that had the power of other men's lives, is in danger of his own. Happy is that man that is once possessed of a crown incorruptible, unfadeable, reserved for him in heaven: no force, no treason can reach thither; there can be no peril of either violence or forfeiture there.

The likeliest defence of the person of any prince, is the fidelity of his attendants: Mordecai overhears the whispering of these wicked conspirators, and reveals it to Esther; she (as glad of such an opportunity to commend unto Ahasuerus the loyalty of him whom she durst but secretly honour), reveals it to the king. The circumstances are examined, the plot is discovered, the traitors executed, the service recorded in the Persian annals. A good foundation is thus laid for Mordecai's advancement, which yet is not over hastened on either part: worthy dispositions labour only to deserve well, leaving the care of their remuneration to them whom it concerns; it is fit that God's leisure should be attended in all his designments. The hour is set, when Mordecai shall be raised: if in the meantime there be an intervention, not only of neglect, but of fears and dangers, all these shall make his honours so much more sweet, more precious.

CONTEMPLATION V. — HAMAN DISRESPECTED BY MORDECAI — MORDECAI'S MESSAGE TO ESTHER.

BESIDES the charge of his office, the care of Esther's prosperity calls Mordecai to the king's gate, and fixes him there. With what inward contentment did he think of his so royal pupil! Here I sit among my fellows; little doth the world think that mine adopted child sits in the throne of Persia, that the great empress of the world owes herself to me: I might have more honour, I could not have so much secret comfort, if all Shushan knew what interest I have in queen Esther.

While his heart is taken up with these thoughts, who should come ruffling by him, but the new-raised favourite of king Ahasuerus, Haman, the son of Hammedatha the Agagite: him hath the great king unexpectedly advanced, and set his seat above all the princes that were with him. The gracious respects of princes are not always led by merit, but by their own will, which is ever affected to be so much the freer as themselves would be held more great.

When the sun shines upon the dial, every passenger will be looking at it: there needed no command of reverence, where Ahasuerus was pleased to countenance: all knees will bow alone, even to forbidden idols of honour, how much more where royal authority enjoins obeisance! All the servants, all the subjects of king Ahasuerus, are willingly prostrate before this great minion of their sovereign; only Mordecai stands stiff, as if he saw nothing more than a man in that proud Agagite.

They are not observed that do as the most, but if any one man shall vary from the multitude, all eyes are turned upon him. Mordecai's fellow-officers note this palpable irreverence, and expostulate it: "Why transgressest thou the king's commandment?" Considerest thou not how far this affront reacheth? It is not the person of Haman whom thou refusest to adore, but the king in him: neither do we regard so much the man, as the command; let him be never so vile whom the king bids to be honoured, with what safety can a subject examine the charge, or resist it? His unworthiness cannot dispense with our loyalty. What a dangerous wilfulness should it be to incur the forfeiture of thy place, of thy life, for a courtesy? If thou wilt not bow with others, expect to suffer alone; perhaps they thought this omission was unheedy, in a case of ignorance or incogitancy; it was a friendly office to admonish; the sight of the error had been the remedy.

Mordecai hears their challenge, their advice, and thinks good to answer both with silence, as willing they should imagine his inflexibleness proceeded from a resolution, and that resolution upon some secret grounds, which he needed not impart: at last, yet he imparts thus much, Let it suffice that I am a Jew, and Haman an Amalekite.

After a private expostulation, the continuance of that open neglect is construed for a sullen obstinacy; and now the monitors themselves grow sensible of the contempt: men are commonly impatient to lose the thank of their endeavours, and are prone to hate whom they cannot reform. Partly, therefore, to pick a thank, and partly to revenge this contumacy, these officers turn informers against Mordecai; neither meant to make the matter fairer than it was: they tell Haman, how proud and stubborn a Jew sat amongst them; how ill they could brook so saucy an affront to be offered to his greatness: how seriously they had expostulated, how stomachfully the offender persisted; and beseech him that he would be pleased, in his next passage, to cast some glances that way, and but observe the fashion of that intolerable insolency. The proud Agagite cannot long endure the very expectation of such an indignity: on purpose doth he stalk thither, with higher than his ordinary steps, snuffing up the air as he goes, and would see the man that durst deny reverence to the greatest prince of Persia.

Mordecai holds his old posture, only he is so much more careless, as he sees Haman more disdainful and imperious. Neither of them goes about to hide his passion: one looked, as if he had said, I hate the pride of Haman; the other looked, as if he had said, I will plague the contempt of Mordecai. How did the eyes of Haman sparkle with fury, and, as it were, dart out deadly beams in the face of that despiteful Jew: how did he swell with indignation, and then again wax pale with anger! shortly, his very brow and his motion bade Mordecai look for the utmost of revenge.

Mordecai foresees his danger, and contemns it; no frowns, no threats, can supple those joints: he may break, he will not bow.

What shall we say then to this confirmed resolution of Mordecai? What is it, what can it be, that so stiffens the knees of Mordecai, that death is more easy to him than their incurvation? Certainly, if mere civility were in question, this wilful irreverence to so great a peer could not pass without the just censure of a rude perverseness. It is religion that forbids this obeisance, and tells him, that such courtesy could not be free from sin: whether it were, that more than human honour was required to this new erected image of the great king, as the Persians were ever wont to be noted for too much lavishness in these courtly devotions, or whether it were, that the ancient curse wherewith God had branded the blood and stock of Haman, made it unlawful for an Israelite to give him any observance; for the Amalekites, of whose royal line Haman was descended, were the nation, with which God had sworn perpetual hostility, and whose memory he had straitly charged his people to root out from under heaven. How may I, thinks he, adore where God commands me to detest? how may I profess respect, where God professeth enmity? how may I contribute to the establishment of that seed upon earth, which God hath charged to be pulled up from under heaven? Outward actions of indifferency, when once they are felt to trench upon the conscience, lay deep obligations upon the soul, even while they are most slighted by careless hearts.

In what a flame of wrath doth Haman live this while! wherewith he could not but have consumed his own heart, had he not given vent to that rage in his assured purposes of revenge. Great men's anger is like to themselves, strong, fierce, ambitious of an excessive satisfaction. Haman scorns to take up with the blood of Mordecai: this were but a vulgar amends. Poor men can kill where they hate, and expiate their own wrong with the life of a single enemy Haman's fury shall fly a higher pitch: millions of throats are few enough to bleed for this offence: it is a Jew that hath despited him; the whole nation of the Jews shall perish for the stomach of this one. The monarchy of the world was now in the hand of the Persian; as Judea was within this compass, so there was scarce a Jew upon earth without the verge of the Persian dominions: the generation, the name, shall now die at once; neither shall there be any memory of them but this, There was a people, which having been famous through the world for three thousand four hundred and fourscore years, were, in a moment, extinct by the power of Haman, for default of a courtesy.

Perhaps that hereditary grudge and old antipathy, that was betwixt Israel and Amalek, stuck still in the heart of this Agagite; he might know that God had commanded Israel to root out Amalek from under heaven; and now therefore an Amalekite shall be ready to take this advantage against Israel. It is extreme injustice to dilate the punishment beyond the offence, and to enwrap thousands of innocents within the trespass of one. How many that were yet unborn, when Haman was unsaluted, must rue the fact they lived not to know! How many millions of Jews were then living, that knew not there was a Mordecai! All of them are fetched into one condition, and must suffer, ere they can know their offence. O the infinite distance betwixt the unjust cruelty of men, and the just mercies of the Almighty! Even Caiaphas himself could say, "It is better that one man die, than that all the people should perish;" and here Haman can say, "It is better that all the people should perish, than that one man should die." Thy mercy, O God, by the willing death of one that had not sinned, hath defrayed the just death of a world of sinners; while the injurious rigour of a man, for the supposed fault of one, would destroy a whole nation that had not offended. It is true, that, by the sin of one, death reigned over all; but it was because all sinned in that one: had not all men been in Adam, all had not fallen in him, all had not died in him; it was not the man, but mankind, that fell into sin, and by sin into death. No man can complain of punishment, while no man can exempt himself from the transgression. Unmerciful Haman would have imbrued his hands in that blood, which he could not but confess innocent.

It is a rare thing, if the height of favour cause not presumption. Such is Haman's greatness, that he takes his design for granted, ere it can receive a motion: the fittest days for this great massacre are determined by the lots of their common divination; according whereunto, Haman chooseth the hour of this bloody suit; and now, waited on by opportunity, he addresseth himself to king Ahasuerus: "There is a certain people scattered abroad, and dispersed among the people, in all the provinces of the kingdom, and their laws are diverse from all people; neither keep they the king's laws, therefore it is not for the king's profit to suffer them: if it please the king, let it be written that they may be destroyed, and I will pay ten thousand talents of silver into the hands of the officers." With what cunning hath this man couched his malice! He doth not say, There is a Jew that hath affronted me, let me be avenged of his nation: this rancour was too monstrous to be confessed; perhaps this suggestion might have bred in the mind of Ahasuerus a conceit of Haman's ill nature, and intolerable immanity: but his pretences are plausible, and such as drive at no other than the public good. Every word hath its insinuation: "It is a scattered people:" were the nation entire, their maintenance could not but stand with the king's honour; but now, since they are but stragglers, as their loss would be insensible, so their continuance and mixture cannot but be prejudicial: it was not the fault, it was the misery of these poor Jews, that they were dispersed, and now their dispersion is made an argument of their extirpation; therefore must they be destroyed from the earth, because they were scattered over the earth. As good, so evils, draw on each other: that which should plead for pity in the well-affected is a motive to cruelty in savage minds. Seldom ever hath extremity of mischief seized, where easier afflictions have not been billeted before.

All faithful Jews had wont to say unto God, "Have mercy upon us, O God, and save us, for our soul is full of contempt, and we are scattered amongst the heathen!" And here this enemy can say of them to Ahasuerus, "Destroy them, for they are scattered;" root them out, for they are contemned. How much better is it to fall into the hands of God, than of men, since that which whets the sword of men, works commiseration in the Almighty! Besides the dissipation of the persons, "Their laws are diverse from all people." All other people live by thy laws, they only by their own; and how can this singularity of their fashions but breed disorder and inconvenience? Did they live in some corner of the earth apart, the difference in religion and government could not import much; now that they are dispersed amongst all thy subjects, what do these uncouth forms of theirs but teach all the world to be irregular? why should they live under thy protection, that will not be governed by thy laws? Wicked Haman! what were the laws of Israel, but the laws of

God? if this be a quarrel, what shall the death of the Jews be other than martyrdom?

The diversity of judgment and practice from the rest of the world hath been an old and envious imputation cast upon God's church. What if we be singled from others, while we walk with God? In matters lawful, arbitrary, indifferent, wisdom teacheth us to conform ourselves to all others; but where God hath laid a special imposition upon us, we must either vary or sin. The greatest glory of Israel was their laws, wherein they as far exceeded all other nations, as heaven is above earth; yet here their laws are quarreled, and are made the inducements of their destruction. It is not possible that the church of God should escape persecution, while that which it hath good is maligned, while that offends which makes it happy.

Yet that they have laws of their own were not so unsufferable, if withal they did observe thine, O king! but these Jews, as they are unconformable, so they are seditious: " They keep not the king's laws." Thou slanderest, Haman! they could not keep their own laws, if they kept not the king's; for their laws call them to obedience unto their sovereigns, and adjudge hell to the rebellious. In all those hundred and seven and twenty provinces, king Ahasuerus hath no subjects but them; they obey out of conscience, others out of fear: why are they charged with that, which they do most abhor? what can be the ground of this crimination? Ahasuerus commanded all knees to bow to Haman; a Jew only refuses. Malicious Haman! he that refused to bow unto thee, had sufficiently approved his loyalty to Ahasuerus; Ahasuerus had not been, if Mordecai had not been a good subject. Hath the king no laws, but what concern thine adoration? Set aside religion (wherein the Jew is ready to present, if not active, yet passive obedience) and name that Persian law which a Jew dares break. As I never yet read or heard of a conscionable Israelite, that hath not passed under this calumniation, so I cannot yield him a true Israelite that deserves it. In vain doth he profess to acknowledge a God in heaven, that denies homage to his deputy on earth.

" It is not for the king's profit to suffer them." Worldly hearts are not led by good or evil, but by profit or loss; neither have they grace to know, that nothing is profitable but what is honest, nothing so desperately incommodious as wickedness; they must needs offend by rule, that measure all things by profit, and measure profit by their imagination. How easy is it to suggest strange untruths when there is nobody to make answer! False Haman! how is it not for the king's profit to suffer the Jews? if thou construe this profit for honour, the king's honour is in the multitude of subjects; and what people more numerous than they? if for gain, the king's profit is in the largeness of his tributes; and what people are more deep in their payments? if for service, what people are more officious? How can it stand with the king's profit to bereave himself of subjects, his subjects of their lives, his exchequer of their tributes, his state of their defence? He is a weak politician that knows not to gild over the worst project with a pretence of public utility. No name under heaven hath made so many fools, so many villains, as this of profit.

Lastly, as Ahasuerus reaps nothing but disprofit by the lives of the Jews, so he shall reap no small profit by their deaths: " I will pay ten thousand talents of silver to the king's treasury for this execution." If revenge were not very sweet to the malicious man, he could not be content to purchase it at so high a rate. How do we see daily, that the thirst hereof carries men to a riotous prodigality of estate, body, soul!

Cruel Haman! if thou couldst have swimmed in a whole sea of Jewish blood, if thou couldst have raised mountains of their carcasses, if thou couldst have made all Persia thy shambles, who would have given thee one farthing for all those piles of flesh, for all those streams of blood? yea, who would not rather have been at charge for the avoiding of the annoyances of those slaughtered bodies, which thou offerest to buy at ten thousand talents? It were a happy thing, if charity could enlarge itself but so much as malice: if the preservation of mankind could be so much beholden to our bounty, as the destruction.

Now when all these are laid together— the baseness and dispersedness of the people, the diversity of the laws, the irregularity of their government, the rebellion of their practice, the inconvenience of their toleration, the gain of their extirpation; what could the wit or art of man devise more insinuative, more likely to persuade? How could it be but Ahasuerus must needs think (since he could not suspect the ground of this suit), What a zealous patriot have I raised, that can be content to buy off the incommodity of the state at his own charge! how worthy is he rather of the aid both of my power and purse! Why should I be fee'd to ease my kingdoms of rebels? " The silver is given to thee, the people also, to do with them as seemeth good to thee." Without all delay,

HAMAN AND MORDECAI.

the secretaries are called to write the warrants; the king's ring is given to seal them; the posts are sent out to carry them into all the provinces: the day is set wherein all Jews, of all ages, of both sexes, through the hundred and seven and twenty provinces of the king, shall be sacrificed to the wrath of Haman.

In all the carriage of Ahasuerus, who sees not too much headiness of passion? Vashti is cast off for a trifle; the Jews are given to the slaughter for nothing: his rage in the one, his favour in the other, is too impotent. He is not a worse husband than a king: the bare word of Haman is enough to kill so many subjects. No disposition can be more dangerous in great persons, than violence of affection mixed with credulity. O the seeming inequality of human conditions! "The king and Haman sat down to drink, but the city of Shushan was perplexed." It is a woful thing to see great ones quaff the tears of the oppressed, and to hear them make music of shrieks.

With what lamentation do we think all the synagogues of Jews, through the world, received this fatal message of their proclaimed destruction! How do they bemoan themselves each to other! how do their conjoined cries fill heaven and earth! But above all, what sackcloth and ashes could suffice woful Mordecai, that found in himself the occasion of all this slaughter! what soul could be capable of more bitterness than he felt! While he could not but think, "Wretched man that I am! it is I that have brought all this calamity upon my nation; it is I that have been the ruin of my people! Woe is me that I ever put myself into the court, into the service of a pagan! How unhappy was I to cast myself into these straits, that I must either honour an Agagite, or draw vengeance upon Israel! Yet how could I imagine, that the flame of Haman's rage would have broken out so far? Might that revenge have determined in my blood, how happy should I have been! Now I have brought death upon many thousands of innocents, that cannot know wherefore they die. Why did I not hide myself rather from the place of that proud Amalekite? why did I stand out in contestation with so over-powerful an enemy! Alas! no man of Israel shall so much as live to curse me: only mine enemies shall record my name with ignominy, and say, Mordecai was the bane of his nation! O that my zeal should have reserved me for so heavy a service! Where now are those vain ambitions, wherewith I pleased myself in this great match of Esther? How fondly did I hope, by this undue means, to raise myself and my people! yea, is not this carnal presumption the quarrel that God had against me? do I not therefore smart from these pagans, for that I secretly affected this uncircumcised alliance? Howsoever it be, yet, O God! what have thy people done? O let it be thy just mercy that I may perish alone!"

In these sad thoughts did Mordecai spend his heart, while he walked mournfully in sackcloth before that gate wherein he was wont to sit: now his habit bars his approach; no sackcloth might come within the court. Lo! that which is welcomest in the court of heaven, is here excluded from the presence of this earthly royalty: "A broken and a contrite heart, O God thou wilt not despise."

Neither did it a little add to the sorrow of Mordecai, to hear the bitter insultations of his former monitors: "Did we not advise thee better? did we not fore-admonish thee of thy danger? see now the issue of thine obstinacy:" now see, what it is for thine earthen pitcher to knock with brass. Now, where is the man that would needs contest with Haman? Hast thou not now brought thy matters to a fair pass? Thy stomach had long owed thee a spite, and now it hath paid thee: who can pity thy wilfulness? Since thou wouldst needs deride our counsel, we will take leave to laugh at thy sackcloth. Nothing but scorns, and griefs, and terrors, present themselves to miserable Mordecai. All the external buffets of adversaries were slight to the wounds that he hath made, and felt in his own heart.

The perpetual intelligences that were closely held betwixt Esther and Mordecai, could not suffer his public sorrow to be long concealed from her. The news of his sackcloth afflicts her, ere she can suspect the cause; her crown doth but clog her head, while she hears of his ashes. True friendship transforms us into the condition of those we love; and, if it cannot raise them to our cheerfulness, draws us down to their dejection. Fain would she uncase her foster-father of these mournful weeds, and change his sackcloth for tissue; that yet, at least, his clothes might not hinder his access to her presence, for the free opening of his griefs.

It is but a slight sorrow that abides to take in outward comforts: Mordecai refuses that kind offer, and would have Esther see that his affliction was such, as that he might well resolve to put off his sackcloth and his skin at once; that he must mourn to death, rather than see her face to live.

The good queen is astonished with this constant humiliation of so dear a friend; and now she sends Hatach, a trusty, though a pagan attendant, to inquire into the occasion of this so irremediable heaviness. It should seem Esther inquired not greatly into matters of state; that which perplexed all Shushan, was not yet known to her: her followers, not knowing her to be a Jewess, conceived not how the news might concern her, and therefore had forborne the relation. Mordecai first informs her, by her messenger, of the decree that was gone out against all her nation, of the day wherein they must all prepare to bleed, of the sum which Haman had proffered for their heads, and delivers the copy of that bloody edict, charging her now, if ever, to bestir herself, and to improve all her love, all her power, with king Ahasuerus, in a speedy and humble supplication for the saving of the life, not of himself, so much as of her people.

It was tidings able to confound a weak heart; and hers so much the more, as she could apprehend nothing but impossibility of redress. She needs but to put Mordecai in mind of that which all the king's servants and subjects knew well enough, that the Persian law made it no less than death, for whomsoever, man or woman, that should press into the inner court of the king uncalled: nothing but the royal sceptre extended, could keep that presumptuous offender from the grave. For her, thirty days were now passed, since she was called in to the king; an intermission, that might be justly suspicious, whether the heat of his first affection were thus soon of itself allayed towards her; or whether some suggestions of a secret enemy, perhaps this Agagite, might have set him off; or whether some more pleasing object may have laid hold on his eyes. Whatever it might be, this absence could not but argue some strangeness, and this strangeness must needs imply a danger in her bold intrusion. She could bewail, therefore, she could not hope to remedy, this dismal day of her people. This answer in the ears of Mordecai sounded truth, but weakness; neither can he take up with so feeble a return: these occasions require other spirits, other resolutions, which must be quickened by a more stirring reply: "Think not with thyself, that thou shalt escape in the king's house, more than all the Jews; for, if thou altogether holdest thy peace at this time, then shall there enlargement and deliverance arise to the Jews from another place, but thou and thy father's house shall be destroyed; and who knoweth whether thou art come to the kingdom for such a time as this?"

The expectation of death had not quelled the strong heart of faithful Mordecai: even while he mourns, his zeal droops not; there could have been no life in that breast, which this message could not have roused.

What then? is it death that thou fearest in this attempt of thy supplication? what other than death awaits thee in the neglect of it? There is but this difference: sue, and thou mayest die; sue not, and thou must die. What blood hast thou but Jewish? and if these unalterable edicts exempt no living soul, what shall become of thine? And canst thou be so vainly timorous, as to die for fear of death? to prefer certainty of danger before a possibility of hope? Away with this weak cowardice, unworthy of an Israelite, unworthy of a queen! But if faint-heartedness or private respects shall seal up thy lips, or withhold thine hand from the aid of thy people; if thou canst so far neglect God's church, know thou that God will not neglect it: it shall not be in the power of tyrants to root out his chosen seed; that Holy One of Israel shall rather work miracles from heaven, than his inheritance shall perish upon earth: and how just shall it then be for that jealous God to take vengeance upon thee and thy father's house, for this cold unhelpfulness to his distressed church? Suffer me, therefore, to adjure thee, by all that tenderness of love wherewith I have trained up thine orphan infancy, by all those dear and thankful respects which thou hast vowed to me again, by the name of the God of Israel whom we serve, that thou awaken and stir up thine holy courage, and dare to adventure thy life for the saving of many! It hath pleased the Almighty to raise thee up to that height of honour, which our progenitors could little expect: why shouldst thou be wanting to him, that hath been so bountiful to thee? yea, why should I not think that God hath put this very act into the intendment of thine exaltation, having on purpose thus seasonably raised thee to the throne, that thou mayest rescue his poor church from an utter ruin?

O the admirable faith of Mordecai, that shines through all these clouds, and, in the thickest of these fogs, descries a cheerful glimpse of deliverance! He saw the day of their common destruction enacted; he knew the Persian decrees to be unalterable; but, withal, he knew there was a Messiah to come: he was so well acquainted with God's covenanted assurances to his church, that he can, through the midst of those bloody resolutions, foresee indemnity to Israel, rather trusting the promises of God, than the threats of men. This is the victory that overcomes all the fears and fury of the world, even our faith.

It is quarrel enough against any person, or community, not to have been aidful to the distresses of God's people. Not to ward the blow, if we may, is construed for little better than striking. Till we have tried our utmost, we know not whether we have done what we came for.

Mordecai hath said enough: these words have so put a new life into Esther, that she is resolute to hazard the old: "Go, gather together all the Jews that are present in Shushan, and fast ye for me, and neither eat nor drink three days, night or day; I also and my maidens will fast likewise, and so will I go in unto the king, which is not according to the law; and if I perish I perish." Heroical thoughts do well befit great actions. Life can never be better adventured, than where it shall be gain to lose it.

There can be no law against the humble deprecation of evils: where the necessity of God's church calls to us, no danger should withhold us from all honest means of relief. Deep humiliations must make way for the success of great enterprises: we are most capable of mercy, when we are thoroughly empty. A short hunger doth but whet the appetite; but so long an abstinence meets death half-way, to prevent it. Well may they enjoin sharp penances unto others, who practise it upon themselves.

It was the face of Esther that must hope to win Ahasuerus; yet that shall be macerated with fasting, that she may prevail. A carnal heart would have pampered the flesh, that it might allure those wanton eyes: she pines it, that she may please. God, and not she, must work the heart of the king. Faith teaches her rather to trust her devotions, than her beauty.

CONTEMPLATION VI.—ESTHER SUING TO AHASUERUS.

THE Jews are easily entreated to fast, who had received in themselves the sentence of death: what pleasure can they take in meat, that knew what day they must eat their last? The three days of abstinence are expired: now Esther changes her spirits, no less than her clothes: who, that sees that face, and that habit, can say she had mourned, she had fasted? Never did her royal apparel become her so well. That God, before whom she had humbled herself, made her so much more beautiful, as she had been more dejected; and now, with a winning confidence, she walks into the inner court of the king, and puts herself into that forbidden presence; as if she said, " Here I am, with my life in my hand: if it please the king to take it, it is ready for him. Vashti, my predecessor, forfeited her place for not coming when she was called: Esther shall now hazard the forfeiture of her life, for coming when she is not called. It is necessity, not disobedience, that hath put me upon this bold approach; according to thy construction, O king, I do either live or die; either shall be welcome." The unexpectedness of pleasing objects makes them many times the more acceptable: the beautiful countenance, the graceful demeanour and goodly presence of Esther, have no sooner taken the eyes, than they have ravished the heart of king Ahasuerus: love hath soon banished all dreadfulness: "And the king held out to Esther the golden sceptre that was in his hand." Moderate intermission is so far from cooling the affection, that it inflames it. Had Esther been seen every day, perhaps that satiety had abated of the height of her welcome; now, three and thirty days' retiredness hath endeared her more to the surfeited eyes of Ahasuerus.

Had not the golden sceptre been held out, where had queen Esther been? The Persian kings affected a stern awfulness to their subjects: it was death to solicit them uncalled. How safe, how easy, how happy a thing it is, to have to do with the King of heaven, who is so pleased with our access, that he solicits suitors! who, as he is unweariable with our requests, so he is infinite in his beneficences!

How gladly doth Esther touch the top of that sceptre by which she holds her life! and now, while she thinks it well that she may live, she receives, besides pardon, favour: " What wilt thou, queen Esther, and what is thy request? it shall be given thee, even to the half of the kingdom." Commonly, when we fear most, we speed best; God then most of all magnifies his bounty to us, when we have most afflicted ourselves. Over-confident expectations are seldom but disappointed, while humble suspicions go laughing away. It was the benefit and safety of but one piece of the kingdom, that Esther comes to sue for; and, behold, Ahasuerus offers her the free power of the half: he, that gave Haman, at the first word, the lives of all his Jewish subjects, is ready to give Esther half his kingdom, ere she ask. Now she is no less amazed at the loving munificence of Ahasuerus, than she was before afraid of his austerity: "The king's heart is in the hand of the Lord; as the rivers of water, he turneth it whithersoever he will." It is not good to swallow favours too greedily, lest they either choke us in the passage, or prove hard of digestion. The wise queen, however she might seem to have a fair opportunity offered to her suit, finds it not good to apprehend it too suddenly, as desiring, by this small dilation, to prepare the ear and heart of the king for so important a request.

Now all her petition ends in a banquet: "If it seem good unto the king, let the king and Haman come this day unto the banquet that I have prepared for him." It is an easy favour to receive a small courtesy, where we offer to give great. Haman is called; the king comes to Esther's table: and now, highly pleased with his entertainment, he himself solicits her to propound that suit, for which her modesty would, but durst not solicit him. Bashfulness shall lose nothing at the hand of well-governed greatness. Yet still Esther's suit sticks in her teeth, and dares not come forth without a further preface of time and expectation; another banquet must pass, ere this reckoning can be given in. Other suitors wait long for the delivery of their petition, longer for the receipt of their answer: here the king is fain to wait for her suit. Whether Esther's heart would not yet serve her to contest with so strong an adversary as Haman, without fuller recollection; or whether she desired to get better hold of the king, by endearing him with so pleasing entertainments; or whether she would thus ripen her hopes, by working in the mind of king Ahasuerus a foreconceit of the greatness and difficulty of that suit, which was so loath to come forth; or whether she meant thus to give scope to the pride and malice of Haman, for his more certain ruin; howsoever it were, to-morrow is a new day set for Esther's second banquet, and third petition.

The king is not invited without Haman. Favours are sometimes done to men with a purpose of displeasure: doubtless Haman tasteth of the same cates with his master; neither could he, in the forehead of Esther, read any other characters, than of respect and kind applause, yet had she then in her hopes designed him to a just revenge. Little do we know, by outward carriages, in what terms we stand with either God or man.

Every little wind raiseth up a bubble. How is Haman now exalted in himself with the singular graces of queen Esther! and begins to value himself, so much more, as he sees himself higher in the rate of other's opinion!

Only surly and sullen Mordecai is an alloy to his happiness: no edict of death can bow the knees of that stout Jew; yea, the notice of that bloody cruelty of this Agagite hath stiffened them so much the more. Before, he looked at Haman as an Amalekite, now as a persecutor. Disdain and anger look out at those eyes, and bid that proud enemy do his worst. No doubt Mordecai had been listening after the speed of queen Esther: how she came in to the king; how she was welcomed with the golden sceptre, and with the more precious words of Ahasuerus; how she had entertained the king, how she pleased: the news had made him quit his sackcloth, and raised his courage to a more scornful neglect of his professed adversary.

Haman comes home, I know not whether more full of pride or of rage; calls an inward counsel of his choice friends, together with his wife; makes a glorious report of all his wealth, magnificence, height of favour, both with the king and queen; and, at last, after all his sunshine, sets in this cloudy epilogue: "Yet all this availeth me nothing, so long as I see Mordecai the Jew sitting at the king's gate." It is seldom seen that God allows, even to the greatest darlings of the world, a perfect contentment: something they must have to complain of, that shall give an unsavoury verdure to their sweetest morsels, and make their very felicity miserable.

The wit of women hath wont to be noted for more sudden, and more sharp. Zeresh, the wife of Haman, sets on foot that motion of speedy revenge, which is applauded by the rest: "Let a gallows be made of fifty cubits high, and to-morrow speak thou to the king, that Mordecai may be hanged thereon; then go thou in merrily with the king unto the banquet." I do not hear them say, Be patient a while: thou hast already set Mordecai his last day, the month Adar will not be long in coming; the determination of his death hath made him desperate, let him in the meantime eat his own heart in envy at thy greatness. But they rather advise of a quick despatch. Malice is a thing full of impatience, and hates delay of execution, next unto mercy. While any grudge lies at the heart, it cannot be freely cheerful. Forced smiles are but the hypocrisy of mirth. How happy were it for us, if we would be zealously careful to remove the hinderances of our true spiritual joy, those stubborn corruptions that will not stoop to the power of grace!

CONTEMPLATION VII.—MORDECAI HONOURED BY HAMAN.

THE wit of Zeresh had like to have gone beyond the wit of Esther: had not the working Providence of the Almighty contrived these events beyond all hopes, all conceits, Mordecai had been dispatched ere Esther's second banquet. To-morrow was the day pitched for both their designs; had not the stream been unexpectedly turned, in vain had the queen blamed her delays: Mordecai's breakfast had prevented Esther's dinner; for certainly he that had given to Haman so many thousand lives, would never have made dainty upon the same suit to anticipate one of those whom he had condemned to the slaughter. But God meant better things to his church, and fetches about all his holy purposes, after a wonderful fashion, in the very instant of opportunity: " He that keepeth Israel, and neither slumbereth nor sleepeth," causeth sleep that night to depart from him that had decreed to root out Israel. Great Ahasuerus, that commanded a hundred and seven and twenty provinces, cannot command an hour's sleep. Poverty is rather blessed with the freedom of rest, than wealth and power. Cares and surfeit withhold that from the great, which presseth upon the spare diet and labour of the meanest. Nothing is more tedious than an eager pursuit of denied sleep, which, like to a shadow, flies away so much faster as it is more followed. Experience tells us, that this benefit is best solicited by neglect, and soonest found when we have forgotten to seek it.

Whether to deceive the time, or to bestow it well, Ahasuerus shall spend his restless hours in the chronicles of his time. Nothing is more requisite for princes, than to look back upon their own actions and events, and those of their predecessors; the examination of fore-past actions makes them wise — of events, thankful and cautelous.

Amongst those voluminous registers of acts and monuments, which so many scores of provinces must needs yield, the book shall open upon Mordecai's discovery of the late treason of the two eunuchs: the reader is turned thither by an insensible sway of Providence. Our most arbitrary or casual actions are overruled by a hand in heaven.

The king now feels afresh the danger of that conspiracy; and as great spirits abide not to smother or bury good offices, inquires into the recompense of so royal a service: " What honour and dignity hath been done to Mordecai for this?" Surely Mordecai did but his duty; he had heinously sinned, if he had not revealed this wicked treachery: yet Ahasuerus takes thought for his remuneration. How much more careful art thou, O God of all mercies, to reward the weak obedience of thine (at the best) unprofitable servants!

That which was intended to procure rest, sets it off: king Ahasuerus is unquiet in himself, to think that so great a merit should lie but so long neglected; neither can he find any peace in himself, till he have given order for a speedy retribution. Hearing, therefore, by his servants, that Haman was below in the court, he sends for him up to consult with him, " What should be done to the man whom the king delighteth to honour?" O marvellous concurrence of circumstances, drawn together by the infinite wisdom and power of the Almighty! Who but Haman should be the man? and when should Haman be called to advise of Mordecai's honour, but in the very instant when he came to sue for Mordecai's hanging? Had Ahasuerus but slept that night, Mordecai had been that morning advanced fifty cubits higher than the earth, ere the king could have remembered to whom he was beholden.

What shall we say, then, to reconcile these cross-passions in Ahasuerus? Before he signed that decree of killing all the Jews, he could not but know that a Jew had saved his life; and now, after that he had enacted the slaughter of all Jews as rebels, he is giving order to honour a Jew as his preserver. It were strange, if great persons, in the multitude of their distractions, should not let fall some incongruities.

Yet who can but think that king Ahasuerus meant, upon some second thoughts, to make amends to Mordecai? neither can he choose but put these two together: the Jews are appointed to death at the suit of Haman; this Mordecai is a Jew: how then can I do more grace to him that hath saved my life, than to command him to be honoured by that man who would spill his?

When Haman heard himself called up to the bed-chamber of his master, he thinks himself too happy in so early an opportunity of presenting his suit; but yet more in the pleasing question of Ahasuerus, wherein he could not but imagine that favour forced itself upon him with strange importunity for how could he conceive that any intention of more than ordinary honour could fall besides himself? Self-love, like to a good stomach, draws to itself what nourishment it likes, and casts off that which offends it. Haman will be sure to be no niggard in advising those ceremonies of honour, which he thinks meant to his own person. Could he have once dreamed that this grace had been purposed to any under heaven besides himself, he had not been so lavish in counselling so pompous a show of excessive magnificence. Now the king's own royal apparel, and his own steed, is not sufficient, except the royal crown also make up the glory of him who shall thus triumph in the king's favour; yet all this were nothing in base hands. The actor shall be the best part of this great pageant: "Let this apparel, and this horse, be delivered to one of the king's most noble princes, that they may array the man withal whom the king delighteth to honour, and bring him on horseback through the streets of the city, and proclaim before him, Thus shall it be done to the man whom the king delighteth to honour." Honour is more in him that gives, than in him that receives it. To be honoured by the unworthy is little better than disgrace: no meaner person will serve to attend this Agagite, in his supposed greatness, than one of the noblest princes. The ambition is too high-flown, that seeks glory in the servility of equals.

The place adds much to the act; there is small heart in a concealed honour: it is nothing, unless the streets of the city of Shushan be witnesses of this pomp, and ring with that gracious acclamation.

The vain hearts of proud men can easily devise those means whereby they may best set out themselves. O that we would equally affect the means of true and immortal glory! The heart of man is never so cold within him, as when, from the height of the expectation of good, it falls into a sudden sense of evil: so did this Agagite: "Then the king said to Haman, Make haste, and take the apparel, and the horse, as thou hast said, and do even so to Mordecai the Jew, that sitteth at the king's gate; let nothing fail of all that thou hast said." How was Haman thunderstricken with this killing word! "Do thou so to Mordecai." I dare say, all the honours that Ahasuerus had heaped upon Haman cannot countervail this one vexation. Doubtless, at first, he distrusts his ear, and then muses whether the king be in earnest; at last, when he hears the charge so seriously doubled, and finds himself forced to believe it, he begins to think, What means this unconceivable alteration? Is there no man in all the court of Persia to be picked out for this extraordinary honour but Mordecai. Is there no man to be picked out for the performance of this honour to him, but Haman? Have I but one proud enemy in all the world, and am I singled out to grace him? did it gall me to the heart, and make all my happiness tedious to me, to see that this Jew would not bow to me, and must I now bow to him? That which he would rather die, and forfeit the life of all his nation, than do to me, notwithstanding the king's command, shall I be forced, by the king's command, to do unto him? Yea, did he refuse to give but a cap and a knee to my greatness, and must I lackey so base a fellow through the streets? must I be his herald, to proclaim his honour through all Shushan? Why do I not let the king know the insolent affronts that he hath offered me? why do I not signify to my sovereign, that my errand now was for another kind of advancement to Mordecai? If I obtain not my desired revenge, yet, at least, I shall prevail so far as to exempt myself from this officious attendance upon so unequal an enemy. And yet that motion cannot be now safe: I see the king's heart is, upon what ground soever, bent upon this action; should I fly off never so little, after my word so directly passed, perhaps my coldness or opposition might be construed as some wayward contestation with my master; especially since the service that Mordecai hath done to the king is of a higher nature than the despite which he hath done to me. I will, I must give way for the time; mine humble yieldance, when all the carriage of this business shall be understood, shall, I doubt not, make way for mine intended revenge. Mordecai, I will honour thee now, that by these steps I may ere long raise thee many cubits higher. I will obey the command of my sovereign in observing thee, that he may reward the merit of my loyalty in thine execution.

Thus resolved, Haman goes forth with a face and heart full of distraction, full of confusion; and addresses himself to the attiring, to the attending of his old adversary, and new master, Mordecai. What looks, do we now think, were cast upon each other at their first greeting? Their eyes had not forgotten their old language: certainly, when Mordecai saw Haman come into the room where he was, he could not but think, This man hath long thirsted for my blood, and now he comes to fetch it; I shall not live to see the success of Esther, or the fatal day of my nation. It was known that morning in the court, what a lofty gibbet Haman had provided for Mordecai; and why might it not have come to Mordecai's ear? what could he therefore now imagine other than that he was called out to that execution? But, when he saw the royal robe that Haman brought to him, he thinks, Is it not enough for this man to kill me, but he must mock me too: what an addition is this to the former cruelty, thus to insult and play upon my last distress! But, when he yet saw the royal crown ready to be set on his head, and the king's own horse richly furnished at his gate, and found himself raised by princely hands into the royal seat, he thinks, What may all this mean? Is it the purpose of mine adversary that I shall die in state? would he have me hanged in triumph? At last, when he sees such a train of Persian peers attending him, with a grave reverence, and hears Haman proclaim before him, "Thus shall it be done to the man whom the king delighteth to honour!" finding this pomp to be serious and well meant, he imagines, in all likelihood, that this unexpected change proceeds from the suit of his Esther; now he begins to lift up his head and to hope well of himself and his people, and could not but say within himself, that he had not fasted for nothing. O the wondrous alteration that one morning hath made in the court of Persia! He that was yesternight despised by Haman's footmen, is now waited on by Haman, and all his fellow princes: he, that yesternight had the homage of all knees but one, and was ready to burst for the lack of that, now doth obeisance to that one by whom he was wilfully neglected! It was not Ahasuerus that wrought this strange mutation; it was the overruling power of the Almighty, whose immediate hand would thus prevent Esther's suit, that he might challenge all the thank to himself: while princes have their own wills, they must do his; and shall either exalt or depress according to divine appointment.

I should commend Haman's obedience, in his humble condescent to so unpleasing and harsh a command of his master, were it not, that either he durst do no other, or that he thus stooped for an advantage. It is a thankless respect that is either forced, or for ends. True subjection is free and absolute, out of the conscience of duty, not out of fears or hopes.

All Shushan is in amaze at this sudden glory of Mordecai, and studies how to reconcile this day with the thirteenth of Adar. Mordecai had reason to hope well: it could not stand with the honour of the king to kill him whom he saw cause to advance; neither could this be any other than the beginning of a durable promotion: otherwise, what recompense had an hour's riding been to so great a service?

On the other side, Haman droops, and hath changed passions with Mordecai: neither was that Jew ever more deeply afflicted with the decree of his own death, than this Agagite was with that Jew's honour. How heavy doth it lie at Haman's heart, that no tongue but his might serve to proclaim Mordecai happy! Even the greatest minions of the world must have their turns of sorrow.

With a covered head, and a dejected countenance, doth he hasten home, and longs to impart his grief, where he had received his advice. It was but cold comfort that he finds from his wife Zeresh, and his friends: "If Mordecai be of the seed of the Jews, before whom thou hast begun to fall, thou shalt not prevail against him, but shalt surely fall before him." Out of the mouth of pagans, O God, thou hast ordained strength, that thou mayest still the enemy and avenger. What credit hath thy great name won with these barbarous nations, that they can out of all experience make maxims of thine undoubted protection of thy people, and the certain ruin of thine adversaries? Men find no difference in themselves: the face of a Jew looks so like other men's, that Esther and Mordecai were not, of long, taken for what they were; he that made them, makes the distinction betwixt them: so as a Jew may fall before a Persian, and get up and prevail; but if a Persian, or whosoever of the Gentiles, begin to fall before a Jew, he can neither stay nor rise. There is an invisible hand of omnipotency that strikes in for his own and confounds their opposites. O God, neither is thine hand shortened, nor thy bowels straitened in thee: thou art still and ever thyself. If we be thy true spiritual Israel, neither earth nor hell shall prevail against us; we shall either stand sure, or surely rise, while our enemies shall lick the dust.

CONTEMPLATION VIII.—HAMAN HANGED, MORDECAI ADVANCED.

Haman's day is now come: that vengeance which hath hitherto slept is now awake, and rouseth up itself to a just execution; that heavy mourning was but the preface to his last sorrow, and the sad presage of friends is verified in the speaking; while the word was in their mouths, the messengers were at the door to fetch Haman to his funeral banquet.

How little do we know what is towards us! As the fishes that are taken in an evil net, and as the birds that are caught in the snare, so are the sons of men snared in an evil time, when it falleth suddenly upon them.

It was, as Haman conceived, the only privilege of his dearness, and the comfort of his present heaviness, that he only was called with the king to Esther's banquet, when this was only meant for his bane. The face of this invitation is fair, and promiseth much; and now the ingenious man begins to set good constructions upon all events. Surely, thinks he, the king was tied in his honour to give some public gratification to Mordecai: so good an office could deserve no less than an hour's glory. But little doth my master know what terms there are betwixt me and Mordecai: had he fully understood the insolencies of this Jew, and should, notwithstanding, have enjoined me to honour him, I might have had just cause to complain of disgrace and disparagement; but now, since all this business hath been carried in ignorance and casualty, why do I wrong myself in being too much affected with that which was not ill meant? Had either the king or the queen abated aught of their favour to me, I might have dined at home: now this renewed invitation argues me to stand right in the grace of both; and why may not I hope this day to meet with a good occasion of my desired revenge? how just will it seem to the king, that the same man whom he hath publicly rewarded for his loyalty, should now be publicly punished for his disobedience.

With suchlike thoughts Haman cheers up himself, and addresseth himself to the royal banquet, with a countenance that would fain seem to forget his morning's task: Esther works her face to an unwilling smile upon that hateful guest; and the king, as not unguilty of any dignity that he hath put upon his favourite, frames himself to as much cheerfulness as his want of rest would permit. The table is royally furnished with all delicate confections, with all pleasing liquors. King Ahasuerus so eats, as one that both knew he was, and meant to make himself welcome: Haman so pours in, as one that meant to drown his cares. And now, in this fulness of cheer, the king hungers for that long-delayed suit of queen Esther: thrice hath he graciously called for it, and, as a man constant to his own favours, thrice hath he, in the same words, vowed the performance of it, though to the half of his kingdom. It falls out oftentimes, that, when large promises fall suddenly from great persons, they abate by leisure, and shrink upon cold thoughts here Ahasuerus is not more liberal in his offer than firm in his resolutions, as if his first word had been, like his law, unalterable. I am ashamed to miss that steadiness in Christians which I find in a pagan. It was a great word that he had said; yet he eats it not, as over lavishly spoken, but doubles and triples it with hearty assurances of a real prosecution; while those tongues, which profess the name of the true God, say and unsay at pleasure, recanting their good purposes, contradicting their own just engagements, upon no cause but their own changeableness.

It is not for queen Esther to drive off any longer; the same wisdom that taught her to defer her suit, now teaches her to propound it: a well chosen season, is the greatest advantage of any action, which, as it is seldom found in haste, so is too often lost in delay. Now, therefore, with an humble and graceful obeisance, and with a countenance full of modest fear and sad gravity, she so delivers her petition, that the king might see it was necessity that both forced it upon her, and wrung it from her: "If I have found favour in thy sight, O king, and if it please the king, let my life be given me at my petition, and my people at my request." Expectation is either a friend or an enemy, according to the occasion: Ahasuerus looked for some high and difficult boon; now that he hears his queen beg for her life, it could not be but that the surplusage of his love to her must be turned into fury against her adversary; and his zeal must be so much more to her, as her suit was more meek and humble: "For we are sold, I and my people, to be destroyed, to be slain, and to perish; but if we had been sold for bondmen and bondwomen, I had held my tongue, although the enemy could not countervail the king's damage." Crafty men are sometimes choked with their own plots. It was the proffer of ten thousand talents wherewith Haman hoped both to purchase his intended revenge, and the reputation of a worthy patriot: that sum is now laid in his dish, for a just argument of malicious corruption; for well might Esther plead, If we Jews deserved death, what needed our slaughter to be bought out? and if we deserved it not, what horrible cruelty was it to set a price upon innocent blood? It is not any offence of ours, it is only the despite of an enemy, that hath wrought our destruction.

Besides, now it appears the king was

abused by misinformation: the adversary suggested, that the life of the Jews could not stand with the king's profit, whereas their very bondage should be more damage to the state, than all Haman's worth could countervail. Truth may be smothered, but it cannot die; it may be disguised, but it will be known; 'it may be suppressed, but it will triumph.

But what shall we say to so harsh an aggravation? Could Esther have been silent in a case of decreed bondage, who is now so vehement in a case of death? Certainly, to a generous nature, death is far more easy than bondage: why would she have endured the greater, and yet so abhors the less? Was it for that the Jews were already too well inured to captivity, and those evils are more tolerable wherewith we are acquainted? or was it for that there may be hopes in bondage, none in death? Surely either of them were lamentable, and such as might deserve her humblest deprecation.

The queen was going on to have said, But, alas! nothing will satisfy our bloody enemy, save the utter extirpation of me and my nation: when the impatient rage of the king interrupts her sentence in the midst, and, as if he had heard too much already, and could easily supply the residue of her complaint, snatches the word out of her mouth with a furious demand: " Who is he, and where is he, that durst presume in his heart to do so?" It was the interest of queen Esther's person that raised this storm in Ahasuerus: set that aside, how quietly, how merrily, was the determined massacre of the Jews formerly digested! Actions have not the same face, when we look upon them with contrary affections.

Now queen Esther musters up her inward forces, and, with an undaunted courage, fixing her angry eyes upon that hated Agagite, she says, "The adversary and enemy is this wicked Haman." The word was loath to come forth, but it strikes home at the last. Never till now did Haman hear his true title; before, some had styled him noble, others great, some magnificent, and some, perhaps, virtuous; only Esther gave him his own, "Wicked Haman." Illdeserving greatness doth in vain promise to itself a perpetuity of applause. If our ways be foul, the time shall come, when after all vain flattery, after all our momentary glory, our sins shall be ripped up, and our iniquities laid before us, to our utter confusion. With what consternation did Haman now stand! how do we think he looked to hear himself thus enstyled, thus accused, yea thus condemned! Certainly, death was in his face, and horror in every of his joints; no sense, no limb knows his office: fain would he speak; but his tongue falters, and his lips tremble: fain would he make apologies upon his knees; but his heart fails him, and tells him the evidence is too great, and the offence above all pardon: only guiltiness and fear look through his eyes upon the enraged countenance of his master, which now bodes nothing to him but revenge and death.

In what a passionate distemper doth this banquet shut up! King Ahasuerus flies from the table, as if he had been hurried away with a tempest. His wrath is too great to come forth at his mouth; only his eyes tell Haman that he hates to see him, and vows to see his despatch. For solitarinesss, and not for pleasure, doth he now walk into his garden, and thinks with himself, "What a monster have I favoured? is it possible that so much cruelty and presumption should harbour in a breast that I thought ingenuous? Could I be so bewitched as to pass so bloody a decree? is my credulity thus abused by the treacherous subtilty of a miscreant whom I trusted? I confess it was my weak rashness to yield unto so prodigious a motion, but it was the villany of this Agagite to circumvent me by false suggestions: he shall pay for my error; the world shall see, that as I exceeded in grace, so I will not come short in justice. Haman, thy guilty blood shall expiate that innocent blood which thy malice might have shed."

In the meantime, Haman, so soon as ever he could recover the qualm of his astonishment, finding himself left alone with queen Esther, loseth no time, spareth no breath, to mitigate her anger, which had made way to his destruction. Doubtless, with many vows and tears, and solemn oaths, he labours to clear his intentions to her person, bewailing his danger, imploring her mercy, confessing the unjust extent of his malice, proffering endeavours of satisfaction. "Wretched man that I am! I am condemned before I speak; and when I have spoken, I am condemned. Upon thy sentence, O queen, I see death waits for me: in vain shall I seek to avoid it: it is thy will that I should perish; but let that little breath I have left, acquit me so far with thee, as to call heaven and earth to record, that in regard of thee, I die innocent. It is true, that mine impetuous malice miscarried me against the nation of the Jews, for the sake of one stubborn offender; but did I know there was the least drop of Israelitish blood in thy sacred person? could I suspect that Mordecai, or that people, did aught concern thee? Let not one death be enough for me, if I would ever have entertained any thought of evil against nation or man, that should have cost but a frown from thee. All the court of Persia can sufficiently witness how I have magnified and adored thee, ever since the royal crown was set on thy head; neither did I ever fail to do thee all good offices unto that my sovereign master, whom thou hast now mortally incensed against me. O queen, no hand can save my life but thine, that hath as good as bereaved it: show mercy to him, that never meant but loyalty to thee. As ever thou wouldst oblige an humble and faithful vassal to thee, as ever thou wouldst honour thy name and sex with the praise of tender compassion, take pity upon me, and spare that life which shall be vowed to thy service: and whereas thy displeasure may justly allege against me that rancorous plot for the extirpation of that people, whom I, too late, know to be thine, let it suffice that I hate, I curse mine own cruelty, and only upon that condition shall beg the reprieval of my life, that I shall work and procure, by thy gracious aid, a full defeasance of that unjust execution. O let fall upon thy despairing servant one word of favour to my displeased master, that I may yet live."

While he was speaking to this purpose, having prostrate himself, for the more humility, before the queen, and spread his arms in a vehement imploration up to her bed, the king comes in, and, as not unwilling to misconstrue the posture of him whom he now hated, says, "What, will he force the queen also before me in the house?" That which Haman meant as an humble supplicant, is interpreted as from a presumptuous offender. How oft might he have done so, and more, while he was in favour, uncensured! Actions are not the same when the man alters. As charity makes a good sense of doubtful occurrents, so prejudice and displeasure take all things, though well meant, at the worst. It is an easy thing to pick a quarrel where we intend a mischief.

The wrath of the king is as a messenger of death. While these words were yet in the mouth of Ahasuerus, Haman, in turning his head towards the king, is suddenly muffled for his execution: he shall no more see either face or sun; he shall be seen no more but as a spectacle of shame and horror: and now he thinks, "Woe is me, whose eyes serve me only to foresee the approach of a dishonourable and painful death! What am I the better to have been great? O that I had never been! O that I could not be! How too truly have Zeresh, and my friends, foretold me of this heavy destiny! Now am I ready to feel what it is that I meant to thousands of innocents; I shall die with pain and ignominy. O that the conscience of mine intended murder could die with me." It is no marvel if wicked men find nothing but utter discomforts in their end: rather than fail, their former happiness shall join with their imminent miseries to torment them. It is the just judgment of God, that presumptuous sinners should be swallowed up of those evils, which they would not fear. Happy is that man who hath grace to foresee and avoid those ways which will lead him to a perfect confusion! Happy is he that hath so lived, that he can either welcome death as a friend, or defy it as an enemy!

Who was ever the better for favours past? Those, that had before kissed the feet and smiled in the face of Haman, are now as ready to cover his head, and help him to the gallows. Harbonah, one of the chamberlains, seasonably tells the king how stately a gibbet Haman had newly set up for well-deserving Mordecai within his own palace.

I hear not one man open his mouth to intercede for the offender, to pacify the king, to excuse or lessen the fact. Every one is ready to pull him down that is falling, to trample on him that is down: yet, no doubt, there were some of these courtiers whom Haman had obliged. Had the cause been better, thus it would have been: every cur is ready to fall upon the dog that he sees worried; but here, it was the just hand of God to set off all hearts from a man that had been so unreasonably merciless, and to raise up enemies, even among friends, to him that had professed enmity to God's church. So let thine enemies perish, O Lord, unsuccoured, unpitied! "Then the king said, Hang him thereon." There can be no truer justice than in retaliation: who can complain of his own measure? "Behold, the wicked travaileth with iniquity, and hath conceived mischief, and brought forth falsehood. He made a pit and digged it, and is fallen into the ditch that he made; his mischief shall return upon his own head, and his violent dealing shall come down upon his own pate."

There hangs Haman, in more reproach than ever he stood in honour; and Mordecai, who is now first known for what he was, succeeds his favour and changes inheritances with his enemy: for while Haman inherits the gibbet of Mordecai, Mordecai inherits the house and honour of Haman. "O Lord, let the malice of the wicked come to an end, but establish thou the just."

One hour hath changed the face of the Persian court. What stability is there in earthly greatness? He, whom in the morning all knees bowed unto, as more than a man, now hangs up like a despised vermin, for a prey to the ravens; he, who this morning was destined to the gallows, now rules over princes. Neither was it for nothing that he this day rode in triumph: the king's ring, that was taken from Haman, is now given to Mordecai as the pledge of his authority; and he, that even now sat in the gate, is called up next to the throne. Wickedness and honest innocence have now paid their debts to both their clients.

Little joy would it yet have been to Esther, that her enemy was dead, her kinsman advanced, if still her people must for all this expect their fatal day: her next suit, therefore, is for the safety of her nation, in the countermand of that bloody decree which Haman had obtained against them: that which was surreptitiously gotten, and rashly given, is so much more gladly reversed, by how much mercy is more pleasing to a good nature than cruel injustice. Mordecai hath power to indite, seal, send out letters of favour to the Jews, which were causelessly sentenced to the slaughter. If a Persian law might not be reversed, yet it might be counterchanged. Mordecai may not write, "Let no Jew be slain;" he may write, "Let the Jews meet, and stand for their lives against those that would slay them." This command flies after the former so fast, as if it would overtake that which it cannot recall. The Jews are revived with these happy tidings, that they may have protection as well as enmity, that authority will not be their executioner, that their own hands are allowed to be their avengers.

Who would imagine, that after public notice of this alteration at the court, when the world could not choose but know the malicious ground of that wrongful edict, the shameful death of the procurer, the power of the party opposite, any one should be found, throughout all the provinces, that would once lift up his hand against a Jew, that with his own danger would endeavour to execute a controlled decree? The church of God should cease to be itself, if it wanted malicious persecution: there needs no other quarrel than the name, the religion of Israel.

Notwithstanding the known favour of the king, and the patronage of Mordecai, the thirteenth of Adar is meant to be a bloody day. Haman hath too many abettors in the Persian dominions: these join together to perform that sentence, whereof the author repented. The Jews take heart to defend themselves, to kill their murderers. All the provinces are turned into a field of civil war, wherein innocence vanquisheth malice. The Jews are victors, and not only are alive, but are feared; the most resist them not, many assist them, and some become theirs. The countenance of the great leads the world at pleasure; fear of authority sways thousands that are not guilty of a conscience.

Yea, besides the liberty of defence, the Jews are now made their own justices: that there may be none left from the loins of that accursed Agagite, who would have left none of the Jewish seed, they slay the ten sons of Haman, and obtain new days of further executions: neither can death satisfy their revenge; those ten sons of Haman shall, in their very carcasses, bear the reproach of their father, and hang aloft upon his gallows.

Finally, no man doth, no man dares frown upon a Jew; they are now become lords in the midst of their captivity: no marvel if they ordain and celebrate their joyful Purim, for a perpetual memory, to all posterities, of their happy deliverance. It were pity that the church of God should not have sunshines as well as storms, and should not meet with interchanges of joy in their warfare, before they enter upon the unchangeable joy of their endless triumph.

CONTEMPLATIONS

ON THE

HISTORICAL PASSAGES OF THE NEW TESTAMENT.

BOOK I.

CONTEMPLATION I.—THE ANGEL AND ZACHARY.

When things are at the worst, then God begins a change: the state of the Jewish church was extremely corrupted immediately before the news of the gospel; yet, as bad as it was, not only the priesthood, but the courses of attendance, continued even from David's time till Christ's. It is a desperately depraved condition of a church, where no good orders are left.

Judea passed many troubles, many alterations, yet this orderly combination endured about eleven hundred years. A settled good will not easily be defeated, but, in the change of persons, will remain unchanged, and, if it be forced to give way, leaves memorable footsteps behind it. If David foresaw the perpetuation of this holy ordinance, how much did he rejoice in the knowledge of it! Who would not be glad to do good, on condition that it may so long outlive him!

The successive turns of the legal ministration held on in a line never interrupted: even in a forlorn and miserable church, there may be a personal succession. How little were the Jews better for this, when they had lost the Urim and Thummim, sincerity of doctrine and manners! This stayed with them, even while they and their sons crucified Christ. What is more ordinary than wicked sons of holy parents? It is the succession of truth and holiness that makes or institutes a church, whatever become of the persons. Never times were so barren, as not to yield some good. The greatest dearth affords some few good ears to the gleaners. Christ would not have come into the world, but he would have some faithful to entertain him. He, that had the disposing of all times and men, would cast some holy ones into his own times. There had been no equality, that all should either overrun or follow him, and none attend him. Zachary and Elizabeth are just; both of Aaron's blood, and John Baptist of theirs: whence should a holy seed spring, if not of the loins of Levi? It is not in the power of parents to traduce holiness to their children; it is the blessing of God that feoffs them in the virtues of their parents, as they feoff them in their sins. There is no certainty, but there is likelihood of a holy generation, when the parents are such. Elizabeth was just, as well as Zachary, that the forerunner of a Saviour might be holy on both sides. If the stock and the graff be not both good, there is much danger of the fruit. It is a happy match, when the husband and the wife are one, not only in themselves but in God; not more in flesh, than in the spirit. Grace makes no difference of sexes; rather the weaker carries away the more honour, because it hath had less helps. It is easy to observe, that the New Testament affordeth more store of good women than the Old: Elizabeth led the ring of this mercy, whose barrenness ended in a miraculous fruit, both of her body, and of her time.

This religious pair made no less progress in virtue than in age; and yet their virtue could not make their best age fruitful "Elizabeth was barren." A just soul, and a barren womb, may well agree together. Among the Jews, barrenness was not a defect only, but a reproach: yet, while this good woman was fruitful of holy obedience, she was barren of children: as John, which was miraculously conceived by man, was a fit forerunner of him that was conceived by the Holy Ghost, so a barren matron was meet to make way for a virgin.

None but a son of Aaron might offer incense to God in the temple; and not every son of Aaron, and not any one at all seasons. God is a God of order, and hates confusion no less than irreligion. Albeit he hath not so straitened himself under the gospel, as to tie his service to persons or places; yet his choice is now no less curious, because it is more large: he allows none but the authorized; he authorizeth none but the worthy. The incense doth ever smell of the hand that offers it: I doubt not but that perfume was sweeter, which ascended up from the hand of a just Zachary. "The sacrifice of the wicked is abomination to God." There were courses of ministration in the legal services: God never purposed to burden any of his creatures with devotion. How vain is the ambition of any soul, that would load itself with the universal charge of all men! How thankless is their labour, that do wilfully overspend themselves in their ordinary avocations! As Zachary had a course in God's house, so he carefully observed it: one favour of these respites doubled his diligence. The more high and sacred our calling is, the more dangerous is neglect. It is our honour, that we may be allowed to wait upon the God of heaven in these immediate services. Woe be to us, if we slacken those duties, wherein God honours us more than we can honour him!

Many sons of Aaron, yea of the same family, served at once in the temple, according to the variety of employments. To avoid all difference, they agreed by lot to assign themselves to the several offices of each day: the lot of this day called Zachary to offer incense in the outer temple. I do not find any prescription they had from God, of this particular manner of designment. Matters of good order, in holy affairs, may be ruled by the wise institution of men, according to reason and expediency.

It fell out well, that Zachary was chosen by lot to this ministration, that God's immediate hand might be seen in all the passages that concerned his great prophet; that as the person, so the occasion, might be of God's own choosing. In lots, and their seeming casual disposition, God can give a reason, though we can give none. Morning and evening, twice a-day, their law called them to offer incense to God, that both parts of the day might be consecrate to the Maker of time. The outer temple was the figure of the whole church upon earth, like as the holy of holies represented heaven. Nothing can better resemble our faithful prayers than sweet perfume: these God looks that we should (all his church over) send up unto him morning and evening. The elevations of our hearts should be perpetual; but if, twice in the day, we do not present God with our solemn invocations, we make the gospel less officious than the law.

That the resemblance of prayers and incense might be apparent, while the priest sends up his incense within the temple, the people must send up their prayers without: their breath, and that incense, though remote in the first rising, met ere they went up to heaven. The people might no more go into the holy place to offer up the incense of prayers unto God, than Zachary might go into the holy of holies. While the partition-wall stood betwixt Jews and Gentiles, there were also partitions betwixt the Jews and themselves. Now every man is a priest unto God; every man, since the veil was rent, prays within the temple. — What are we the better for our greater freedom of access to God, under the gospel, if we do not make use of our privilege?

While they were praying to God, he sees an angel of God: as Gideon's angel went up in the smoke of the sacrifice, so did Zachary's angel, as it were, come down in the fragrant smoke of his incense. It was ever great news to see an angel of God, but now more, because God had long withdrawn from them all the means of his supernatural revelations. As this wicked people were strangers to their God in their conversation, so was God grown a stranger to them in his apparitions; yet now, that the season of the gospel approached, he visited them with his angels, before he visited them by his son. He sends his angel to men in the form of man, before he sends his Son to take human form. The presence of angels is no novelty, but their apparition; they are always with us, but rarely seen, that we may awfully respect their messages when they are seen: in the meantime, our faith may see them, though our senses do not; their assumed shapes do not make them more present, but visible.

There is an order in that heavenly hierarchy, though we know it not. This angel, that appeared to Zachary, was not with him in the ordinary course of his attendances, but was purposely sent from God with this message. Why was an angel sent? and why this angel? It had been easy for him to have raised up the prophetical spirit of some Simeon to this prediction; the same Holy Ghost, which revealed to that just man, that he should not see death ere he had seen the Messiah, might have as easily revealed unto him the birth of the fore-runner of Christ, and by him to Zachary: but God would have this voice, which should go before his Son, come with a noise; he would have it appear to the world, that the harbinger of the Messiah should be conceived by the marvellous power of that God whose coming he proclaimed. It was fit the first herald of the gospel should begin in wonder. The same angel, that came to the blessed virgin with the news of Christ's conception, came to Zachary with the news of John's, for the honour of him that was the greatest of them which were born of women, and for his better resemblance to him which was the seed of the woman: both had the gospel for their errand; one as the messenger of it, the other as the author; both are foretold by the same mouth.

When could it be more fit for the angel to appear unto Zachary, than when prayers and incense were offered by him? where could he more fitly appear than in the temple? in what part of the temple more fitly than at the altar of incense? and whereabouts rather than on the right side of the altar? Those glorious spirits, as they are always with us, so most in our devotions; and as in all places, so most of all in God's house: they rejoice to be with us, while we are with God; as, contrarily, they turn their faces from us when we go about our sins.

He, that had wont to live and serve in the presence of the master, was now astonished at the presence of the servant: so much difference there is betwixt our faith and our senses, that the apprehension of the presence of the God of spirits by faith goes down sweetly with us, whereas the sensible apprehension of an angel dismays us. Holy Zachary, that had wont to live by faith, thought he should die, when his sense began to be set on work: it was the weakness of him that served at the altar without horror, to be daunted with the face of his fellow-servant. In vain do we look for such ministers of God as are without infirmities, when just Zachary was troubled in his devotions with that wherewith he should have been comforted. It was partly the suddenness, and partly the glory, of the apparition that affrighted him. The good angel was both apprehensive and compassionate of Zachary's weakness, and presently encourages him with a cheerful excitation: "Fear not, Zacharias." The blessed spirits, though they do not vocally express it, do pity our human frailties, and secretly suggest comfort unto us, when we perceive it not. Good and evil angels, as they are contrary in estate, so also in disposition: the good desire to take away fear, the evil to bring it. It is a fruit of that deadly enmity which is betwixt Satan and us, that he would, if he might, kill us with terror; whereas the good spirits, affecting our relief and happiness, take no pleasure in terrifying us, but labour altogether for our tranquillity and cheerfulness.

There was not more fear in the face, than comfort in the speech: "Thy prayer is heard." No angel could have told him better news: our desires are uttered in our prayers. What can we wish, but to have what we would? Many good suits had Zachary made, and amongst the rest, for a son. Doubtless it was now some space of years since he made that request; for he was now stricken in age, and had ceased to hope: yet had God laid it up all the while, and, while he thinks not of it, brings it forth to effect. Thus doth the mercy of our God deal with his patient and faithful suppliants. In the fervour of their expectation, he many times holds them off, and, when they least think of it, and have forgotten their own suits, he graciously condescends. Delay of effect may not discourage our faith: it may be, God hath long granted, ere we shall know of his grant. Many a father repents him of his fruitfulness, and hath such sons as he wishes unborn: but to have so gracious and happy a son as the angel foretold, could not be less comfort than honour to the age of Zachary. The proof of children makes them either the blessings or crosses of their parents: to hear what his son should be before he was; to hear that he should have such a son, a son whose birth should concern the joy of many, a son that should be great in the sight of the Lord, a son that should be sacred to God, filled with God, beneficial to man, a harbinger to him that was God and man, was news enough to prevent the angel, and to take away that tongue with amazement, which was after lost with incredulity!

The speech was so good, that it found not a sudden belief. This good news surprised Zachary. If the intelligence had taken leisure, that his thoughts might have had time to debate the matter, he had easily apprehended the infinite power of him that had promised, the pattern of Abraham and Sarah, and would soon have concluded the appearance of the angel more miraculous than his prediction: whereas now, like a man masked with the strangeness of that he saw and heard, he misdoubts the message, and asks, " How shall I know?" Nature was on his side, and alleged the impossibility of the event, both from age and barrenness. Supernatural tidings, at the first hearing, astonish the heart, and are entertained with doubts by those, which upon further acquaintance give them best welcome.

The weak apprehensions of our imperfect faith are not so much to be censured, as pitied. It is a sure way for the heart, to be prevented with the assurance of the omnipotent power of God, to whom nothing is impossible; so shall the hardest points of faith go down easily with us: if the eye of our mind look upward, it shall meet with nothing to avert or interrupt it; but if right forward, or downward, or round about, every thing is a block in our way.

There is a difference betwixt desire of assurance, and unbelief. We cannot be too careful to raise up to ourselves arguments to settle our faith; although it should be no faith, if it had no feet to stand upon but discursive. In matters of faith, if reasons may be brought for the conviction of gainsayers, it is well; if they be helps, they cannot be grounds of our belief. In the most faithful heart there are some sparks of infidelity: so to believe, that we should have no doubt at all, is scarce incident unto flesh and blood; it is a great perfection, if we have attained to overcome our doubts. What did mislead Zachary, but that which uses to guide others, reason? " I am old, and my wife is of great age:" as if years and dry loins could be any let to him, which is able, of very stones, to raise up children unto Abraham. Faith and reason have their limits: where reason ends, faith begins; and if reason will be encroaching upon the bounds of faith, she is strait taken captive by infidelity. We are not fit to follow Christ, if we have not denied ourselves; and the chief piece of ourselves is our reason: we must yield God able to do that, which we cannot comprehend; and we must comprehend that by our faith, which is disclaimed by reason: Hagar must be driven out of doors, that Sarah may rule alone.

The authority of the reporter makes way for belief, in things which are otherwise hard to pass; although, in the matters of God, we should not so much care who speaks, as what is spoken, and from whom. The angel tells his name, place, office, unasked, that Zachary might not think any news impossible that was brought him by a heavenly messenger. Even where there is no use of language, the spirits are distinguished by names, and each knows his own appellation, and others'. He that gave leave unto man, his image, to give names to all his visible and inferior creatures, did himself put names unto the spiritual; and as their name is, so are they mighty and glorious. But lest Zachary should no less doubt of the style of the messenger, than of the errand itself, he is at once both confirmed and punished with dumbness. That tongue, which moved the doubt, must be tied up: he shall ask no more questions for forty weeks, because he asked this one distrustfully.

Neither did Zachary lose his tongue for the time, but his ears also: he was not only mute, but deaf; for otherwise, when they came to ask his allowance for the name of his son, they needed not to have demanded it by signs, but by words. God will not pass over slight offences, and those which may plead the most colourable pretences, in his best children, without a sensible check. It is not our holy entireness with God, that can bear us out in the least sin; yea rather, the more acquaintance we have with his Majesty, the more sure we are of correction when we offend. This may procure us more favour in our well doing, not less justice in evil.

Zachary stayed, and the people waited: whether some longer discourse betwixt the angel and him than needed to be recorded, or whether astonishment at the apparition and news, withheld him, I inquire not. The multitude thought him long: yet they could but see afar off; they would not depart till he returned to bless them. Their patient attendance without shames us, that are hardly persuaded to attend within, while both our senses are employed in our divine services, and we are admitted to be co-agents with our ministers.

At last Zachary comes out speechless, and more amazes them with his presence than with his delay. The eyes of the multitude, that were not worthy to see his vision, yet see the signs of his vision, that the world may be put into the expectation of some extraordinary sequel. God makes way for his voice by silence: his speech could not have said so much as his dumbness. Zachary would fain have spoken, and could not: with us too many are dumb, and need not. Negligence, fear, partiality, stop the mouths of many, which shall once say, Woe to me, because I held my peace. His hand speaks that which he cannot with his tongue, and he makes them by signs to understand that which they might read in his face. Those powers we have, we must use. But though he has ceased to speak, yet he ceased not to minister: he takes not this dumbness for a dismission, but stays out the eight days of his course, as one that knew the eyes, and hands, and heart, would be accepted of that God which had bereaved him of his tongue. We may not take slight occasions of withdrawing ourselves from the public services of our God, much less under the gospel. The law which stood much upon bodily perfection, dispensed with age for attendance. The gospel, which is all for the soul, regards those inward powers, which, while they are vigorous, exclude all excuses of our ministration.

CONTEMPLATION II.— THE ANNUNCIATION OF CHRIST.

The Spirit of God was never so accurate in any description, as that which concerns the incarnation of God. It was fit no circumstance should be omitted in that story, whereon the faith and salvation of all the world dependeth: we cannot so much as doubt of this truth, and be saved. No, not the number of the month, not the name of the angel, is concealed: every particle imports not more certainty than excellency. The time is the sixth month after John's conception, the prime of the spring. Christ was conceived in the spring, born in the solstice. He, in whom the world received a new life, receives life in the same season wherein the world received his first life from him; and he, which stretches out the days of his church, and lengthens them to eternity, appears after all the short and dim light of the law, and enlightens the world with his glory. The messenger is an angel: a man was too mean to carry the news of the conception of God. Never any business was conceived in heaven, that did so much concern the earth, as the conception of the God of heaven in the womb of the earth. No less than an archangel was worthy to bear these tidings, and never any angel received a greater honour than of this embassage.

It was fit our reparation should answer our fall: an evil angel was the first motioner of the one to Eve, a virgin, then espoused to Adam in the garden of Eden; a good angel is the first reporter of the other to Mary, a virgin espoused to Joseph, in that place, which (as the garden of Galilee) had a name from flourishing. No good angel could be the author of our restoration, as that evil angel was of our ruin; but that which those glorious spirits could not do themselves, they are glad to report as done by the God of spirits. Good news rejoice the bearer. With what joy did this holy angel bring the news of that Saviour, in whom we are redeemed to life, himself established in life and glory! The first preacher of the gospel was an angel: that office must needs be glorious, that derives itself from such a predecessor. God appointed his angel to be the first preacher, and hath since called his preachers angels. The message is well suited: an angel comes to a virgin, Gabriel to Mary; he that was by signification the strength of God, to her that was by signification exalted by God, to the conceiving of him that was the God of strength; to a maid, but espoused—a maid, for the honour of virginity—espoused, for the honour of marriage. The marriage was in a sort made, not consummate, through the instinct of him that meant to make her not an example, but a miracle of women. In this whole work, God would have nothing ordinary: it was fit that she should be a married virgin, which should be a virgin mother. He, that meant to take man's nature without man's corruption, would be the son of the man without man's seed, would be the seed of the woman without man; and amongst all women, of a pure virgin; but, amongst virgins, of one espoused, that there might be at once a witness and a guardian of her fruitful virginity. If the same God had not been the author of virginity and marriage, he had never countenanced virginity by marriage.

Whither doth this glorious angel come to find the mother of him that was God, but to obscure Galilee—a part which even the Jews themselves despised, as forsaken of their privileges? "Out of Galilee ariseth no prophet." Behold, an angel comes to that Galilee out of which no prophet comes, and the God of prophets and angels descends to be conceived in that Galilee out of which no prophet ariseth! He, that filleth all places, makes no difference of places: it is the person which gives honour and privilege to the place, not the place to the person; as the presence of God makes the heaven, the heaven doth not make the honour glorious. No blind corner of Nazareth can hide the blessed Virgin from the angel. The favours of God will find out his children, wheresoever they are withdrawn.

It is the fashion of God to seek out the most despised, on whom to bestow his honours: we cannot run away, as from the judgments, so not from the mercies of our God. The cottages of Galilee are preferred by God to the famous places of Jerusalem: he cares not how homely he converses with his own. Why should we be transported with the outward glory of places, while our God regards it not? We are not of the angels' diet, if we had not rather be with the blessed Virgin at Nazareth, than with the proud dames in the court of Jerusalem. It is a great vanity to respect any thing above goodness, and to disesteem goodness for any want. The angel salutes the Virgin; he prays not to her: he salutes her as a saint; he prays not to her as a goddess. For us to salute her, as he did, were gross presumption: for neither are we as he was, neither is she as she was. If he that was a spirit, saluted her that was flesh and blood here on earth, it is not for us, that are flesh and blood, to salute her who is a glorious spirit in heaven. For us to pray to her, in the angel's salutation, were to abuse the Virgin, the angel, the salutation.

But how gladly do we second the angel in the praise of her, which was more ours than his! How justly do we bless her, whom the angel pronounceth blessed! How worthily is she honoured of men, whom the angel proclaimeth beloved of God! O blessed Mary, he cannot bless thee, he cannot honour thee too much, that deifies thee not! That which the angel said of thee, thou hast prophesied of thyself; we believe the angel and thee. All generations shall call thee blessed, by the fruit of whose womb all generations are blessed. If Zachary was amazed with the sight of this angel, much more the Virgin. That very sex hath more disadvantage of fear: if it had been but a man that had come to her in that secresy and suddenness, she could not but have been troubled: how much more, when the shining glory of the person doubled the astonishment!

The troubles of holy minds end ever in comfort. Joy was the errand of the angel, and not terror. Fear, as all passions, disquiets the heart, and makes it, for the time, unfit to receive the messages of God. Soon hath the angel cleared these troublesome mists of passions, and sent out the beams of heavenly consolation in the remotest corner of her soul, by the glad news of her Saviour. How can joy but enter into her heart, out of whose womb shall come salvation! What room can fear find in that breast, that is assured of favour? " Fear not, Mary, for thou hast found favour with God." Let those fear, who know they are in displeasure, or know not they are gracious. Thine happy estate calls for confidence, and that confidence for joy. What should, what can they fear, who are favoured of Him, at whom the devils tremble? Not the presence of the good angels, but the temptations of the evil, strike many terrors into our weakness; we could not be dismayed with them, if we did not forget our condition. " We have not received the spirit of bondage again to fear, but the spirit of adoption, whereby we cry, Abba, Father." If that spirit, O God, witness with our spirits, that we are thine, how can we fear any of those spiritual wickednesses! Give us assurance of thy favour, and let the powers of hell do their worst.

It was no ordinary favour that the Virgin found in heaven. No mortal creature was ever thus graced, that he should take part of her nature, that was the God of Nature; that he, which made all things, should make his human body of hers; that her womb should yield that flesh which was personally united to the Godhead; that she should bear him that upholds the world: "Lo, thou shalt conceive and bear a son, and shalt call his name Jesus." It is a question, whether there be more wonder in the conception, or in the fruit; the conception of the virgin, or Jesus conceived. Both are marvellous; but the former doth not more exceed all other wonders, than the latter exceedeth it. For the child of a virgin is the reimprovement of that power which created the world: but that God should be incarnate of a virgin was an abasement of his Majesty, and an exaltation of the creature beyond all example. Well was that child worthy to make the mother blessed. Here was a double conception; one in the womb of her body, the other of the soul: if that were more miraculous, this was more beneficial; that was her privilege, this was her happiness; if that were singular to her, this is common to all his chosen. There is no renewed heart, wherein thou, O Saviour, art not formed again. Blessed be thou, that hast herein made us blessed. For what womb can conceive thee, and not partake of thee? who can partake of thee, and not be happy?

Doubtless, the Virgin understood the angel, as he meant, of a present conception, which made her so much more inquisitive into the manner and means of this event: " How shall this be, since I know not a man?" That she should conceive a son by the knowledge of man, after marriage consummate, could have been no wonder; but how then should that son of her's be the Son of God? This demand was higher: how her present virginity should be instantly fruitful, might be well worthy of admiration, of inquiry. Here was desire of information, not doubts of infidelity; yea, rather, this question argues faith; it takes for granted that which an unbelieving heart would have stuck at. She says not, Who and whence art thou? what kingdom is this? where and when shall it be erected? But smoothly supposing all those strange things would be done, she insists only on that which did necessarily require a further intimation, and doth not distrust, but demand. Neither doth she say, This cannot be, nor, How can this be? but, How shall this be? So doth the angel answer, as one that knew he needed not to satisfy curiosity, but to inform judgment and uphold faith. He doth not therefore tell her of the manner, but of the author of this act: " The Holy Ghost shall come upon thee, and the power of the Most High shall overshadow thee." It is enough to know who is the undertaker, and what he will do. O God, what do we seek? a clear light, where thou wilt have a shadow! No mother knows the manner of her natural conception: what presumption shall it be for flesh and blood to search how the Son of God took flesh and blood of his creature! It is for none but the Almighty, to know those works which he doth immediately concerning himself; those that concern us, he hath revealed: " Secrets to God, things revealed to us."

The answer was not so full, but that a thousand difficulties might arise out of the particulars of so strange a message; yet after the angel's solution, we hear of no more objections, no more interrogations. The faithful heart, when it once understands the good pleasure of God, argues no more, but sweetly rests itself in a quiet expectation: " Behold the servant of the Lord; be it to me according to thy word." There is not a more noble proof of our faith, than to captivate all the powers of our understanding and will to our Creator, and without all sciscitations to go blindfold whither he will lead us. All disputations with God, after his will known, arise from infidelity. "Great is the mystery of godliness:" and if we will give nature leave to cavil, we cannot be Christians. O God, thou art faithful, thou art powerful: it is enough that thou hast said it: in the humility of our obedience, we resign ourselves over to thee: " Behold the servants of the Lord; be it unto us according to thy word."

How fit was her womb to conceive the flesh of the Son of God, by the power of the Spirit of God, whose breast had so soon, by the power of the same Spirit, conceived an assent to the will of God! and now, of a handmaid of God, she is advanced to the mother of God. No sooner hath she said, " Be it done," than it is done; the Holy Ghost overshadows her, and forms her Saviour in her own body. This very angel, that talks with the blessed Virgin, could scarce have been able to express the joy of her heart in the sense of this divine burden. Never any mortal creature had so much cause of exultation. How could she, that was full of God, be other than full of joy in that God? Grief grows greater by concealing; joy by expression. The holy Virgin had understood by the angel, how her cousin Elizabeth was no less of kin to her in condition; the fruitfulness of whose age did somewhat suit the fruitfulness of her virginity. Happiness communicated, doubles itself. Here is no straining of courtesy. The blessed maid, whom vigour of age had more fitted for the way, hastens her journey into the hill country, to visit that gracious matron whom God had made a sign of her miraculous conception. Only the meeting of saints in heaven can parallel the meeting of these two cousins: the two wonders of the world are met under one roof, and congratulate their mutual happiness. When we have Christ spiritually conceived in us, we cannot be quiet till we have imparted our joy. Elizabeth, that holy matron, did no sooner welcome her blessed cousin, than her babe welcomes his Saviour. Both, in the retired closets of their mother's wombs, are sensible of each other's presence; the one by his omniscience, the other by instinct. He did not more forerun Christ than overrun nature. How should our hearts leap within us, when the Son of God vouchsafes to come into the secret of our souls, not to visit us, but to dwell with us, to dwell in us!

CONTEMPLATION III. — THE BIRTH OF CHRIST.

As all the actions of men, so especially the public actions of public men, are ordered by God to other ends than their own. This edict went not so much out from Augustus, as from the court of heaven. What, did Cæsar know Joseph and Mary? His charge was universal to a world of subjects through all the Roman empire. God intended this cension only for the blessed Virgin and her Son, that Christ might be born where he should. Cæsar meant to fill his coffers;

God meant to fulfil his prophecies; and so to fulfil them, that those whom it concerned might not feel the accomplishment. If God had directly commanded the Virgin to go up to Bethlehem, she had seen the intention, and expected the issue: but that wise Moderator of all things, that works his will in us, loves so to do it, as may be least with our foresight and acquaintance, and would have us fall under his decrees unawares, that we may so much the more adore the depths of his providence. Every creature walks blindfold: only he that dwells in light sees whither they go.

Doubtless, blessed Mary meant to have been delivered of her divine burden at home, and little thought of changing the place of conception for another of her birth. That house was honoured by the angel, yea, by the overshadowing of the Holy Ghost; none could equally satisfy her hopes or desires: it was fit that he, which made choice of the womb wherein his Son should be conceived, should make choice of the place where his Son should be born. As the work is all his, so will he alone contrive all the circumstances to his own ends. O the infinite wisdom of God in casting all his designs! There needs no other proof of Christ than Cæsar and Bethlehem; and of Cæsars than Augustus. His government, his edict, pleads the truth of the Messiah. His government: now was the deep peace of all the world, under that quiet sceptre which made way for him who was the Prince of Peace. If wars be a sign of the time of his second coming, peace was a sign of his first. His edict: now was the sceptre departed from Judah. It was the time for Shiloh to come. No power was left in the Jews, but to obey. Augustus is the emperor of the world; under him Herod is the king of Judea, Cyrenius is president of Syria; Jewry hath nothing of her own. For Herod, if he were a king, yet he was no Jew; and if he had been a Jew, yet he was no otherways a king than tributary and titular. The edict came out from Augustus, was executed by Cyrenius; Herod is no actor in this service. Gain and glory are the ends of this taxation: each man professed himself a subject, and paid for the privilege of his servitude. Now their very heads were not their own, but must be paid for to the head of a foreign state. They, which before stood upon the terms of their immunity, stoop at the last. The proud suggestions of Judas the Galilean might shed their blood and swell their stomachs, but could not ease their yoke: neither was it the meaning of God, that holiness (if they had been as they pretended) should shelter them from subjection. A tribute is imposed upon God's free people. This act of bondage brings them liberty. Now, when they seem most neglected of God, they are blessed with a Redeemer; when they are most pressed with foreign sovereignty, God sends them a king of their own, to whom Cæsar himself must be a subject. The goodness of our God picks out the most needful times of our relief and comfort: our extremities give him the most glory. Whither must Joseph and Mary come to be taxed, but unto Bethlehem, David's city? The very place proves their descent: he, that succeeded David in his throne, must succeed him in the place of his birth. So clearly was Bethlehem designed to this honour by the prophets, that even the priests and the scribes could point Herod unto it, and assured him the King of the Jews could be no where else born. Bethlehem, justly, The house of bread; the bread that came down from heaven is there given to the world: whence should we have the bread of life, but from the house of bread? O holy David, was this the well of Bethlehem, whereof thou didst so thirst to drink of old, when thou saidst, "O that one would give me drink of the water of the well of Bethlehem?" Surely that other water, when it was brought thee by thy worthies, thou pouredst it on the ground, and wouldst not drink of it. This was that living water for which thy soul longed, whereof thou saidst elsewhere, "As the hart panteth after the water-brooks, so longeth my soul after thee, O God: my soul thirsteth for God, for the living God."

It was no less than four days' journey from Nazareth to Bethlehem: how just an excuse might the blessed Virgin have pleaded for her absence! What woman did ever undertake such a journey, so near her delivery? And, doubtless, Joseph, which was now taught of God to love and honour her, was loath to draw forth a dear wife, in so unwieldy a case, into so manifest hazard. But the charge was peremptory, exemplary. The desire of an inoffensive observance even of heathenish authority, digests all difficulties. We may not take easy occasions to withdraw our obedience to supreme commands. Yea, how didst thou, O Saviour, by whom Augustus reigned, in the womb of thy mother yield this homage to Augustus! The first lesson that ever thy example taught us was obedience.

After many steps, are Joseph and Mary come to Bethlehem. The plight wherein she was would not allow any speed, and the forced leisure of the journey causeth disappointment: the end was worse than the way; there was no rest in the way, there was no room in the inn. It could not be but that there were many of the kindred of Joseph and Mary at that time in Bethlehem; for both there were their ancestors born, if not themselves, and thither came up all the cousins of their blood; yet there and then doth the holy Virgin want room to lay either her head or her burden! If the house of David had not lost all mercy and good nature, a daughter of David could not, so near the time of her travail, have been destitute of lodging in the city of David. Little did the Bethlehemites think what a guest they refused, else they would gladly have opened their doors to him, which was able to open the gates of heaven to them. Now their inhospitality is punishment enough to itself: they have lost the honour and happiness of being host to their God. Even still, O blessed Saviour! thou standest at our doors and knockest; every motion of thy good Spirit tells us thou art there; now thou comest in thine own name, and there thou standest, while thy head is full of dew, and thy locks wet with the drops of the night. If we suffer carnal desires and worldly thoughts to take up the lodging of our heart, and revel within us, while thou waitest upon our admission, surely our judgment shall be so much the greater, by how much better we know whom we have excluded. What, do we cry shame on the Bethlehemites, whilst we are wilfully more churlish, more unthankful? There is no room in my heart for the wonder at this humility. He, for whom heaven is too strait, whom the heaven of heavens cannot contain, lies in the strait cabin of the womb; and when he would enlarge himself for the world, is not allowed the room of an inn. The many mansions of heaven were at his disposing; the earth was his, and the fulness of it; yet he suffers himself to be refused of a base cottage, and complaineth not. What measure should discontent us wretched men, when thou, O God, farest thus from thy creatures? How should we learn, both to want and abound, from thee, which, abounding with the glory and riches of heaven, wouldst want a lodging in thy first welcome to the earth! "Thou camest to thine own, and thine own received thee not." How can it trouble us to be rejected of the world, which is not ours? What wonder is it if thy servants wandered abroad in sheep's skins and goat's skins, destitute and afflicted, when their Lord is denied harbour? How should all the world blush at this indignity of Bethlehem! He that came to save men, is sent, for his first lodging, to the beasts: the stable is become his inn, the crib his bed. O strange cradle of that great King, which heaven itself may envy! O Saviour, thou that wert both the Maker and Owner of heaven, of earth, couldst have made thee a palace without hands, couldst have commanded thee an empty room in those houses which thy creatures had made. When thou didst but bid the angels void their first place, they fell down from heaven like lightning; and when, in thy humbled estate, thou didst but say, "I am he," who was able to stand before thee? How easy had it been for thee to have made place for thyself in the throngs of the stateliest courts! Why wouldst thou be thus homely, but that, by contemning worldly glories, thou mightst teach us to contemn them, that thou mightst sanctify poverty to them whom thou calledst unto want! that since thou, which hadst the choice of all earthly conditions, wouldst be born poor and despised, those which must want out of necessity might not think their poverty grievous! Here was neither friend to entertain, nor servant to attend, nor place wherein to be attended, only the poor beasts gave way to the God of all the world. It is the great mystery of godliness, that God was manifested in the flesh, and seen of angels; but here, which was the top of all wonders, the very beasts might see their Maker. For those spirits to see God in the flesh, it was not so strange, as for the brute creatures to see him which was the God of spirits. He that would be led into the wilderness amongst wild beasts to be tempted, would come into the house of beasts to be born, that from the height of his divine glory his humiliation might be the greater. How can we be abased low enough for thee, O Saviour, that hast thus neglected thyself for us! That the visitation might be answerable to the homeliness of the place, attendants, provision, who shall come to congratulate his birth but poor shepherds? The kings of the earth rest at home, and have no summons to attend him by whom they reign. "God hath chosen the weak things of the world to confound the mighty." In an obscure time, the night, unto obscure men, shepherds, doth God manifest the light of his Son, by glorious angels. It is not our meanness, O God, that can exclude us from the best of thy mercies; yea, thus far dost thou respect persons, that thou hast put down the mighty, and exalted them of low degree. If these shepherds had been snoring in their beds, they had no more seen angels, nor heard the news of their Saviour, than their neighbours; their vigilancy is honoured with this heavenly vision. Those who are industrious in any calling, are capable of further blessings; whereas the idle are fit for nothing but temptation. No less than a whole choir of angels are worthy to sing the hymn of "Glory to God," for the incarnation of his Son! What joy is enough for us, whose nature he took, and whom he came to restore by his incarnation! If we had the tongues of angels, we could not raise this note high enough to the praise of our glorious Redeemer.

No sooner do the shepherds hear the news of a Saviour, than they run to Bethlehem to seek him. Those that left their beds to tend their flocks, leave their flocks to enquire after their Saviour. No earthly thing is too dear to be forsaken for Christ. If we suffer any worldly occasion to stay us from Bethlehem, we care more for our sheep than our souls. It is not possible, that a faithful heart should hear where Christ is, and not labour to the sight, to the fruition of him. Where art thou, O Saviour, but at home in thine own house, in the assembly of thy saints? Where art thou to be found, but in thy word and sacraments? Yea, there thou seekest for us: if there we haste not to seek for thee, we are worthy to want thee — worthy that our want of thee here should make us want the presence of thy face for ever.

CONTEMPLATION IV.— THE SAGES AND THE STAR.

THE shepherds and the crib accorded well; yet even they saw nothing which they might not contemn: neither was there any of those shepherds that seemed not more like a king, than that king whom they came to see. But, O the divine majesty that shined in this baseness! There lies the Babe in the stable, crying in the manger, whom the angels come down from heaven to proclaim, whom the sages come from the east to adore, whom a heavenly star notifies to the world; that now men might see, that heaven and earth serves him, that neglected himself. Those lights that hang low are not far seen, but those which are high-placed are equally seen in the remotest distances. Thy light, O Saviour, was no less than heavenly. The east saw that which Bethlehem might have seen: ofttimes those which are nearest in place are farthest off in affection. Large objects, when they are too close to the eye, do so overfill the sense, that they are not discerned. What a shame is this to Bethlehem! The sages came out of the east to worship him whom the village refused. The Bethlehemites were Jews; the wise men Gentiles. This first entertainment of Christ was a presage of the sequel: the Gentiles shall come from far to adore Christ, while the Jews reject him. Those easterlings were great searchers of the depths of nature, professed philosophers; them hath God singled out to the honour of the manifestation of Christ. Human learning well improved makes us capable of divine. There is no knowledge whereof God is not the author: he would never have bestowed any gift, that should lead us away from himself. It is an ignorant conceit, that inquiry into nature should make men atheistical. No man is so apt to see the star of Christ, as a diligent disciple of philosophy. Doubtless this light was visible unto more; only they followed it, who knew it had more than nature. He is truly wise that is wise for his own soul. If these wise men had been acquainted with all the other stars of heaven, and had not seen the star of Christ, they had had but light enough to lead them into utter darkness. Philosophy, without this star, is but the wisp of error. These sages were in a mean between the angels and the shepherds. God would, in all the ranks of intelligent creatures, have some to be witnesses of his Son. The angels direct the shepherds; the star guides the sages. The duller capacity hath the more clear and powerful helps. The wisdom of our God proportions the means unto the disposition of the persons. Their astronomy had taught them this star was not ordinary, whether in sight, or in brightness, or in motion. The eyes of nature might well see that some strange news was portended to the world by it: but that this star designed the birth of the Messias, there needed yet another light. If the star had not besides had the commentary of a revelation from God, it could have led the wise men only into a fruitless wonder. Grant them to be the offspring of Balaam, yet the true prediction of that false prophet was not warrant enough. If he told them the Messias should arise as a star out of Jacob, he did not tell them that a star should arise from the posterity of Jacob at the birth of the Messias. He, that did put that prophecy into the mouth of Balaam, did also put this illumination into the heart of the sages. The Spirit of God is free to breathe where he listeth. "Many shall come from the east and the west to seek Christ, when the children of the kingdom shall be shut out." Even then God did not so confine his election to the pale of the church, as that he did not sometimes look out for special instruments of his glory. Whither do these sages come, but to Jerusalem? Where should they hope to hear of the new king, but in the mother city of the kingdom? The conduct of the star was first only general to Judea; the rest is for a time left to inquiry. They were not brought thither for their own sakes, but for Jewry's, for the world's; that they might help to make the Jews inexcusable, and the world faithful. That their tongues therefore might blazon the birth of Christ, they are brought to the head city of Judea, to report and inquire. Their wisdom could not teach them to imagine, that a king could be born to Judea, of that note and magnificence, that a star from heaven should publish him to the earth, and that his subjects should not know it: and therefore, as presupposing a common notice, they say, "Where is he that is born king of the Jews?" There is much deceit in probabilities, especially when we meddle with spiritual matters: for God uses still to go a way by himself.

If we judge according to reason and appearance, who is so likely to understand heavenly truths as the profound doctors of the world? These God passes over, and reveals his will to babes. Had these sages met with the shepherds of the villages near Bethlehem, they had received that intelligence of Christ which they did vainly seek from the learned scribes of Jerusalem. The greatest clerks are not always the wisest in the affairs of God; these things go not by discourse, but by revelation.

No sooner hath the star brought them within the noise of Jerusalem, than it is vanished out of sight. God would have their eyes lead them so far, as till their tongues might be set on work, to win the vocal attestation of the chief priests and scribes, to the fore-appointed place of our Saviour's nativity. If the star had carried them directly to Bethlehem, the learned Jews had never searched the truth of those prophecies, wherewith they are since justly convinced. God never withdraws our helps, but for a further advantage. However our hopes seem crossed, where his name may gain, we cannot complain of loss.

Little did the sages think this question would have troubled Herod They had, I fear, concealed their message, if they had suspected this event. Sure they thought it might be some son or grandchild of him which then held the throne, so as this might win favour from Herod, rather than an unwelcome fear of rivality. Doubtless, they went first to the court: where else should they ask for a king? The more pleasing this news had been, if it had fallen upon Herod's own loins, the more grievous it was, to light upon a stranger. If Herod had not overmuch affected greatness, he had not, upon those indirect terms, aspired to the crown of Jewry: so much the more, therefore, did it trouble him to hear the rumour of a successor, and that not of his own. Settled greatness cannot abide either change or partnership. If any of his subjects had moved this question, I fear his head had answered it. It is well that the name of foreigners could excuse these sages. Herod could not be brought up among the Jews, and not have heard many and confident reports of a Messias that should ere long arise out of Israel; and now, when he hears the fame of a king born, whom a star from heaven signifies and attends, he is nettled with the news. Everything affrights the guilty. Usurpation is full of jealousies and fears, no less full of projects and imaginations: it makes us think every bush a man, and every man a thief.

Why art thou troubled, O Herod? A King is born; but such a King as whose sceptre may ever concur with lawful sovereignty; yea, such a King, as by whom kings do hold their sceptres, not lose them. If the wise men tell thee of a King, the star tells thee he is heavenly. Here is good cause of security, none of fear. The most general enmities, and oppositions to good, arise from mistakings. If men could but know how much safety and sweetness there is in all divine truth, it could receive nothing from them but welcomes and gratulations. Misconceits have been still guilty of all wrongs and persecutions. But if Herod were troubled, as tyranny is still suspicious, why was all Jerusalem troubled with him? Jerusalem, which now might hope for a relaxation of her bonds, for a recovery of her liberty and right! Jerusalem, which now only had cause to lift up her drooping head, in the joy and happiness of a Redeemer! Yet not Herod's court, but even Jerusalem, was troubled. So had this miserable city been over-toiled with change, that now they were settled in a condition quietly evil, they are troubled with the news of better. They had now got a habit of servility, and now they are so acquainted with the yoke, that the very noise of liberty, which they supposed would not come with ease, began to be unwelcome.

To turn the causes of joy into sorrow

argues extreme dejectedness, and a distemper of judgment no less than desperate. Fear puts on a vizard of devotion. Herod calls his learned counsel, and, as not doubting whether the Messiah should be born, he asks where he shall be born. In the disparition of that other light, there is a perpetually fixed star, shining in the writings of the prophets, that guides the chief priests and scribes directly unto Bethlehem. As yet envy and prejudice had not blinded the eyes, and perverted the hearts of the Jewish teachers, so as now they clearly justify that Christ, whom they afterwards condemned; and by thus justifying him, condemn themselves in rejecting him. The water that is untroubled yields the visage perfectly. If God had no more witness but from his enemies, we have ground enough of our faith.

Herod feared, but dissembled his fear, as thinking it a shame that strangers should see there could any power arise, under him, worthy of his respect or awe. Out of an unwillingness therefore to discover the impotency of his passion, he makes little ado of the matter, but only, after a privy inquisition into the time, employs the informers in the search of the person: "Go and search diligently for the Babe," &c. It was no great journey from Jerusalem to Bethlehem: how easily might Herod's cruelty have secretly suborned some of his bloody courtiers to this inquiry and execution. If God had not meant to mock him, before he found himself mocked of the wise men, he had rather sent before their journey than after their disappointment. But that God, in whose hands all hearts are, did purposely besot him, that he might not find the way to so horrible a mischief.

There is no villany so great, but it will mask itself under a show of piety. Herod will also worship the Babe. The courtesy of a false tyrant is death. A crafty hypocrite never means so ill, as when he speaketh fairest. The wise men are upon their way full of expectation, full of desire: I see no man either of the city or court to accompany them. Whether distrust or fear hindered them, I inquire not: but, of so many thousand Jews, no one stirs his foot to see that King of theirs, which strangers came so far to visit. Yet were not these resolute sages discouraged with this solitariness and small respect, nor drawn to repent of their journey, as thinking, What, do we come so far to honour a King whom no man will acknowledge? what mean we to travel so many hundred miles to see that which the inhabitants will not look out to behold? but cheerfully renew their journey to that place which the ancient light of prophecy had designed. And now behold, God encourages their holy forwardness from heaven, by sending them their first guide; as if he had said, What need ye care for the neglect of men, when ye see heaven honours the King whom ye seek? What joy these sages conceived, when their eyes first beheld the re-appearance of that happy star, they only can tell, that, after a long and sad night of temptation, have seen the loving countenance of God shining forth upon their souls. If with obedience and courage we can follow the calling of God, in difficult enterprises, we shall not want supplies of comfort. Let not us be wanting to God, we shall be sure he cannot be wanting to us.

He, that led Israel by a pillar of fire into the land of promise, leads the wise men by a star to the promised seed. All his directions partake of that light which is in him: for God is light. This star moves both slowly and low, as might be fittest for the pace, for the purpose of these pilgrims. It is the goodness of God, that, in those means wherein we cannot reach him, he descends unto us. Surely when the wise men saw the star stand still, they looked about to see what palace there might be near unto that station, fit for the birth of a king; neither could they think that sorry shed was it which the star meant to point out; but finding their guide settled over that base roof, they go in to see what guest it held. They enter, and, O God, what a king do they find! how poor! how contemptible! wrapt in clouts, laid in straw, cradled in the manger, attended with beasts! What a sight was this, after all the glorious promises of that star, after the predictions of prophets, after the magnificence of their expectations! All their way afforded nothing so despicable as that Babe whom they came to worship. But as those which could not have been wise men, unless they had known that the greatest glories have arisen from mean beginnings, they fall down and worship that hidden Majesty. This baseness hath bred wonder in them, not contempt: they well knew the star could not lie. They, which saw his star afar off in the east, when he lay swaddled in Bethlehem, do also see his royalty further off, in the despised state of his infancy; a royalty more than human. They well knew, that stars did not use to attend earthly kings; and if their aim had not been higher, what was a Jewish king to Persian strangers? Answerable therefore hereunto was their adoration.

Neither did they lift up empty hands to him whom they worshipped, but presented him with the most precious commodities of their country, gold, incense, myrrh; not as thinking to enrich him with these, but, by way of homage, acknowledging him the Lord of these. If these sages had been kings, and had offered a princely weight of gold, the blessed Virgin had not needed, in her purification, to have offered two young pigeons, as the sign of her penury. As God loves not empty hands, so he measures fulness by the affection. Let it be gold, or incense, or myrrh, that we offer him, it cannot but please him, who doth not use to ask how much, but how good.

CONTEMPLATION V.—THE PURIFICATION.

THERE could be no impurity in the Son of God; and if the best substance of a pure virgin carried in it any taint of Adam, that was scoured away by sanctification in the womb; and yet the Son would be circumcised, and the mother purified. He, that came to be sin for us, would, in our persons, be legally unclean, that, by satisfying the law, he might take away our uncleanness. Though he were exempted from the common condition of our birth, yet he would not deliver himself from those ordinary rites that implied the weakness and blemishes of humanity. He would fulfil one law to abrogate it, another to satisfy it. He, that was above the law, would come under the law to free us from the law. Not a day would be changed, either in the circumcision of Christ, or the purification of Mary. Here was neither convenience of place, nor of necessaries, for so painful a work, in the stable of Bethlehem; yet, he that made and gave the law, will rather keep it with difficulty, than transgress it with ease.

Why wouldest thou, O blessed Saviour, suffer that sacred foreskin to be cut off, but that, by the power of thy circumcision, the same might be done to our souls that was done to thy body? We cannot be therefore thine, if our hearts be uncircumcised. Do thou that in us, which was done to thee for us; cut off the superfluity of our maliciousness, that we may be holy in and by thee, which for us wert content to be legally impure.

There was shame in thy birth, there was pain in thy circumcision. After a contemptible welcome into the world, that a sharp razor should pass through thy skin for our sakes, which can hardly endure to bleed for our own, it was the praise of thy wonderful mercy in so early humiliation. What pain or contempt should we refuse for thee, that hast no spare of thyself for us! Now is Bethlehem left with too much honour; there is Christ born, adored, circumcised. No sooner is the blessed Virgin either able or allowed to walk, than she travels to Jerusalem, to perform her holy rites for herself, for her son; to purify herself, to present her son. She goes not to her own house at Nazareth, she goes to God's house at Jerusalem. If purifying were a shadow, yet thanksgiving is a substance. Those whom God hath blessed with fruit of body and safety of deliverance, if they make not their first journey to the temple of God, they partake more of the unthankfulness of Eve, than Mary's devotion.

Her forty days, therefore, were no sooner out than Mary comes up to the holy city. The rumour of a new king, born at Bethlehem, was yet fresh at Jerusalem, since the report of the wise men: and what good news had this been for any pickthank to carry to the court? Here is the Babe whom the star signified, whom the sages inquired for, whom the angels proclaimed, whom the shepherds talked of, whom the scribes and high-priests notified, whom Herod seeks after. Yet, unto that Jerusalem, which was troubled at the report of his birth, is Christ come; and all tongues are so locked up that he, which sent from Jerusalem to Bethlehem to seek him, finds him not, who, as to countermine Herod, is come from Bethlehem to Jerusalem. Dangers that are aloof off, and but possible, may not hinder us from the duty of our devotion. God saw it not yet time to let loose the fury of his adversaries, whom he holds up like some eager mastiffs, and then only lets go, when they shall most shame themselves, and glorify him.

Well might the blessed Virgin have wrangled with the law, and challenged an immunity from all ceremonies of purification. What, should I need purging, which did not conceive in sin? This is for those mothers whose births are unclean; mine is from God, which is purity itself. The law of Moses reaches only to those women which have conceived seed; I conceived not this seed, but the Holy Ghost in me. The law extends to the mothers of those sons which are under the law; mine is above it. But as one that cared more for her peace than her privilege, and more desired to be free from offence than from labour and charge, she dutifully fulfils the law of that God whom she carried in her womb, and in her arms, like the mother of him, who, though he knew the children of the kingdom free, yet would pay tribute unto Cæsar; like the mother of him whom it behoved to fulfil all righteousness. And if she were so officious in ceremonies, as not to admit of any excuse in the very circumstance of her obedience, how much more strict was she in the main duties of morality! That soul is fit for the spiritual conception of Christ, that is conscionably scrupulous in observing all God's commandments; whereas he hates all alliance to a negligent or froward heart.

The law of purification proclaims our uncleanness. The mother is not allowed, after her child-birth, to come unto the sanctuary, or to touch any hallowed thing, till her set time be expired. What are we, whose very birth infects the mother that bears us! At last she comes to the temple: but with sacrifices, either a lamb and a pigeon, or turtle, or (in the meaner estate) two turtle-doves, or young pigeons, whereof one is for a burnt-offering, the other for a sin-offering: the one for thanksgiving, the other for expiation: for expiation of a double sin — of the mother that conceived, of the child that was conceived. We are all born sinners; and it is a just question, whether we do more infect the world, or the world us. They are gross flatterers of nature that tell her she is clean. If our lives had no sin, we bring enough with us: the very infant that lives not to sin as Adam, yet he sinned in Adam, and is sinful in himself. But, O the unspeakable mercy of our God! we provide the sin, he provides the remedy. Behold an expiation well nigh as early as our sin; the blood of a young lamb, or dove, yea, rather the blood of him whose innocence was represented by both, cleanseth us presently from our filthiness. First went circumcision, then came the sacrifice; that, by two holy acts, that which was naturally unholy might be hallowed unto God. Under the gospel, our baptism hath the force of both: it does away our corruption by the water of the Spirit; it applies to us the sacrifice of Christ's blood, whereby we are cleansed. O that we could magnify this goodness of our God, which hath not left our very infancy without redress, but hath provided helps whereby we may be delivered from the danger of our hereditary evils!

Such is the favourable respect of our wise God, that he would not have us undo ourselves with devotion: the service he requires of us is ruled by our abilities. Every poor mother was not able to bring a lamb for her offering: there was no one so poor, but might procure a pair of turtles or pigeons. These doth God both prescribe and accept from poorer hands, no less than the beasts of a thousand mountains. He looks for somewhat of every one, not of every one alike. Since it is he that makes differences of abilities, to whom it were as easy to make all rich, his mercy will make no difference in the acceptation. The truth and heartiness of obedience is that which he will crown in his meanest servants. A mite, from the poor widow, is more worth to him than the talents of the wealthy.

After all the presents of those eastern worshippers, who intended rather homage than ditation, the blessed Virgin comes, in the form of poverty, with her two doves unto God: she could not without some charge lie all this while at Bethlehem; she could not without charge travel from Bethlehem to Jerusalem. Her offering confesseth her penury. The best are not ever the wealthiest. Who can despise any one for want, when the mother of Christ was not rich enough to bring a lamb for her purification? We may be as happy in russet as in tissue.

While the blessed Virgin brought her son into the temple with that pair of doves, here were more doves than a pair. They, for whose sake that offering was brought, were more doves than the doves that were brought for that offering. Her son, for whom she brought that dove to be sacrificed, was that sacrifice which the dove represented. There was nothing in him but perfection of innocence: and the oblation of him is that whereby all mothers and sons are fully purified. Since in ourselves we cannot be innocent, happy are we, if we can have the spotless dove sacrificed for us, to make us innocent in him!

The blessed Virgin had more business in the temple than her own; she came, as to purify herself, so as to present her son. Every male that first opened the womb was holy unto the Lord. He, that was the Son of God, by eternal generation before time, and by miraculous conception in time, was also, by common course of nature, consecrate unto God. It is fit the holy mother should present God with his own. Her first-born was the first-born of all creatures. It was he whose temple it was that he was presented in, to whom all the first-born of all creatures were consecrated, by whom they were accepted; and now is he brought in his mother's arms to his own house, and, as man, is presented to himself as God. If Moses had never written law of God's special propriety in the first-born, this Son of God's essence and love had taken possession of the temple: his right had been a perfect law to himself. Now his obedience to that law, which himself had given, doth no less call him thither, than the challenge of his peculiar interest.

He, that was the Lord of all creatures, ever since he struck the first-born of the Egyptians, requires the first male of all creatures, both man and beast, to be dedicated to him; wherein God caused a miraculous event to second nature, which seems to challenge the first and best for the Maker. By this rule God should have had his service done only by the heirs of Israel. But since God, for the honour and remuneration of Levi, had chosen out that tribe to minister unto him, now the first-born of all Israel must be presented to God as his due, but by allowance redeemed to their parents. As for beasts, the first male of the clean beasts must be sacrificed; of unclean, exchanged for a price. So much morality is there in this constitution of God, that the best of all kinds is fit to be consecrated to the Lord of all. Every thing we have is too good for us, if we think any thing we have too good for him.

How glorious did the temple now seem, that the Owner was within the walls of it! Now was the hour and guest come, in regard whereof the second temple should surpass the first. This was his house, built for him, dedicated to him: there had he dwelt long in his spiritual presence, in his typical. There was nothing either placed, or done within those walls, whereby he was not resembled: and now the body of those shadows is come, and presents himself where he had been ever represented. Jerusalem is now everywhere. There is no church, no Christian heart, which is not a temple of the living God: there is no temple of God wherein Christ is not presented to his Father. Look upon him, O God, in whom thou art well pleased, and in him and for him be well pleased with us!

Under the gospel, we are all first-born, all heirs; every soul is to be holy unto the Lord: we are a royal generation, a holy priesthood. Our baptism, as it is our circumcision, and our sacrifice of purification, so it is also our presentation unto God. Nothing can become us but holiness. O God, to whom we are devoted, serve thyself of us, glorify thyself by us, till we shall by thee be glorified with thee.

CONTEMPLATION VI.—HEROD AND THE INFANTS.

WELL might these wise men have suspected Herod's secresy. If he had meant well, what needed that whispering? That which they published in the streets, he asks in his privy chamber: yet they, not misdoubting his intention, purpose to fulfil his charge. It could not, in their apprehension, but be much honour to them to make their success known, that now both king and people might see it was not fancy that led them, but an assured revelation. That God, which brought them thither, diverted them, and caused their eyes to shut, to guide them the best way home.

These sages made a happy voyage; for now they grew into further acquaintance with God. They are honoured with a second messenger from heaven. They saw the star in the way, the angel in their bed: the star guided their journey unto Christ, the angel directed their return. They saw the star by day, a vision by night. God spake to their eyes by the star, he speaks to their heart by a dream. No doubt they had left much noise of Christ behind them. They, that did so publish his birth at Jerusalem, could not be silent when they found him at Bethlehem. If they had returned by Herod, I fear they had come short home. He, that meant death to the babe for the name of a king, could mean no other to those that honoured and proclaimed a new king, and erected a throne besides his. They had done what they came for: and now that God, whose business they came about, takes order at once for his Son's safety and for theirs. God, who is perfection itself, never begins any business but he makes an end, and ends happily. When our ways are his, there is no danger of miscarriage.

Well did these wise men know the difference, as of stars, so of dreams: they had learned to distinguish between the natural and divine; and once apprehending God in their sleep, they follow him waking, and return another way. They were no subjects to Herod; his commands pressed them so much the less: or, if the being within his dominions had been no less bond than native subjection, yet, where God did countermand Herod, there could be no question whom to obey. They say not, " We are in a strange country; Herod may meet with us, it can be no less than death to mock him in his own territories;" but cheerfully put themselves upon the way, and trust

God with the success. Where men command with God, we must obey men for God, and God in men; when against him, the best obedience is to deny obedience, and to turn our backs upon Herod.

The wise men are safely arrived in the east, and fill the world full of expectation, as themselves are full of wonder. Joseph and Mary are returned with the babe to that Jerusalem, where the wise men had inquired for his birth. The city was doubtless full of that rumour, and little thinks that he whom they talk of was so near them. From thence, they are, at least, in their way to Nazareth, where they purpose their abode. God prevents them by his angel, and sends them for safety into Egypt. Joseph was not wont to be so full of visions: it was not long since the angel appeared unto him, to justify the innocency of the mother, and the deity of the son: now he appears for the preservation of both, and a preservation by flight. Could Joseph now choose but think, " Is this the king that must save Israel, that needs to be saved by me? If he be the Son of God, how is he subject to the violence of men? How is he Almighty, that must save himself by flight? or how must he fly, to save himself, out of that land which he comes to save?" But faithful Joseph, having been once tutored by the angel, and having heard what the wise men said of the star, what Simeon and Anna said in the temple, labours not so much to reconcile his thoughts as to subject them; and, as one that knew it safer to suppress doubts than to confute them, can believe what he understands not, and can wonder where he cannot comprehend.

O strange condition of the king of all the world! He could not be born in a baser estate; yet even this he cannot enjoy with safety. There was no room for him in Bethlehem; there will be no room for him in Judea. He is no sooner come to his own, than he must fly from them; that he may save them, he must avoid them. Had it not been easy for thee, O Saviour, to have acquitted thyself from Herod a thousand ways! What could an arm of flesh have done against the God of spirits! what had it been for thee to have sent Herod five years sooner unto his place! what to have commanded fire from heaven on those that should have come to apprehend thee, or to have bidden the earth to receive them alive, whom she meant to swallow dead! We suffer misery, because we must; thou, because thou wouldst. The same will that brought thee from heaven unto earth, sends thee from Jewry into Egypt. As thou wouldst be born mean and miserable, so thou wouldst live subject to human vexations; that thou, who hast taught us how good it is to bear the yoke even in our youth, might sanctify to us early afflictions. Or whether, O Father, since it was the purpose of thy wisdom to manifest thy Son by degrees unto the world, was it thy will thus to hide him for a time under our infirmity! And what other is our condition? We are no sooner born thine, than we are persecuted. If the church travail, and bring forth a male, she is in danger of the dragon's streams. What, do the members complain of the same measure which was offered to the Head? Both our births are accompanied with tears.

Even of those whose mature age is full of trouble, yet the infancy is commonly quiet: but here life and toil began together. O blessed Virgin! even already did the sword begin to pierce thy soul. Thou, who wert forced to bear thy son in thy womb from Nazareth to Bethlehem, must now bear him in thy arms from Jewry into Egypt: yet couldst thou not complain of the way, whilst thy Saviour was with thee. His presence alone was able to make the stable a temple, Egypt a paradise, the way more pleasing than rest. But whither, then, oh whither dost thou carry that blessed burthen, by which thyself and the world are upholden? To Egypt, the slaughterhouse of God's people, the furnace of Israel's ancient affliction, the sink of the world. " Out of Egypt have I called my Son," saith the Lord. That thou calledst thy Son out of Egypt, O God, is no marvel. It is a marvel that thou calledst him into Egypt, but that we know all earths are thine, and all places and men in, like figures upon a table, such as thy disposition makes them. What a change is here! Israel, the first-born of God, flies out of Egypt into the promised land of Judea; Christ, the first-born of all creatures, flies from Judea into Egypt. Egypt is become the sanctuary, Judea the inquisition-house of the Son of God. He, that is everywhere the same, makes all places alike to his: he makes the fiery furnace a gallery of pleasure, the lion's den a house of defence, the whale's belly a lodging chamber, Egypt a harbour.

He flies, that was able to preserve himself from danger, to teach us how lawfully we may fly from those dangers we cannot avoid otherwise. It is a thankless fortitude to offer our throat unto the knife. He that came to die for us, fled for his own preservation, and hath bid us follow him.

"When they persecute you in one city, flee into another." We have but the use of our lives, and we are bound to husband them to the best advantage of God and his church. God hath made us, not as butts, to be perpetually shot at, but, as the marks of rovers, moveable, as the wind and the sun may best serve.

It was warrant enough for Joseph and Mary, that God commands them to flee: yet so familiar is God grown with his approved servants, that he gives them the reason of his commanded flight: "For Herod will seek the young child to destroy him." What wicked men will do, what they would do, is known unto God beforehand. He that is so infinitely wise to know the designs of his enemies before they are, could as easily prevent them, that they might not be: but he lets them run on in their own courses, that he may fetch glory to himself out of their wickedness.

Good Joseph, having this charge in the night, stays not till the morning. No sooner had God said, Arise, than he starts up and sets forward. It was not diffidence, but obedience, that did so hasten his departure. The charge was direct, the business important. He dares not linger for the light, but breaks his rest for the journey, and, taking advantage of the dark, departs toward Egypt. How knew he this occasion would abide any delay? We cannot be too speedy in the execution of God's commands; we may be too late. Here was no treasure to hide, no hangings to take down, no lands to secure: the poor carpenter needs do no more but lock the doors, and away. He goes lightly that wants a load. If there be more pleasure in abundance, there is more security in a mean estate. The bustard, or the ostrich, when he is pursued, can hardly get upon his wings; whereas the lark mounts with ease. The rich hath not so much advantage of the poor in enjoying, as the poor hath of the rich in leaving.

Now is Joseph come down into Egypt. Egypt was beholden to the name, as that whereto it did owe no less than their universal preservation. Well might it repay this act of hospitality to that name and blood. The going down into Egypt had not so much difficulty as the staying there: their absence from their country was little better than a banishment. But what was this other, than to serve an apprenticeship in the house of bondage? To be any where, save at home, was irksome; but to be in Egypt so many years, amongst idolatrous pagans, must needs be painful to religious hearts. The command of their God, and the presence of Christ, makes amends for all. How long should they have thought it to see the temple of God, if they had not had the God of the temple with them! how long to present their sacrifices at the altar of God, if they had not had him with them which made all sacrifices accepted, and which did accept the sacrifice of their hearts!

Herod was subtle in mocking the wise men, while he promised to worship him whom he meant to kill: now God makes the wise men to mock him, in disappointing his expectation. It is just with God to punish those which would beguile others with illusion. Great spirits are so much more impatient of disgrace. How did Herod now rage and fret, and vainly wish to have met with those false spies, and tells with what torments he would revenge their treachery, and curses himself for trusting strangers in so important a business!

The tyrant's suspicion would not let him rest long. Ere many days he sends to inquire of them whom he sent to inquire of Christ. The notice of their secret departure increaseth his jealousy; and now his anger runs mad, and his fear proves desperate. All the infants of Bethlehem shall bleed for this one; and, that he may make sure work, he cuts out to himself large measures both of time and place. It was but very lately that the star appeared, that the wise men reappeared not. They asked for him that was born, they did not name when he was born. Herod, for more security, over-reaches their time, and fetches into the slaughter all the children of two years of age. The priests and scribes had told him the town of Bethlehem must be the place of the Messiah's nativity. He fetches in all the children of the coast adjoining; yea, his own shall for the time be a Bethlehemite. A tyrannous guiltiness never thinks itself safe, but ever seeks to assure itself in the excess of cruelty. Doubtless he, which so privily inquired for Christ, did as secretly brew this massacre. The mothers were set with their children on their laps, feeding them with the breast, or talking to them in the familiar language of their love; when suddenly the executioner rushes in, and snatches them from their arms, and, at once pulling forth his commission and his knife, without regard to shrieks or tears, murders the innocent babe, and leaves the passionate mother in a mean between madness and death. What cursing of Herod! what wringing of hands! what condoling! what exclaiming! was now in the streets of Bethlehem!

O bloody Herod, that could sacrifice so many harmless lives to thine ambition! What could those infants have done? If it were thy person whereof thou wert afraid, what likelihood was it thou couldst live till those sucklings might endanger thee? This news might affect thy successors; it could not concern thee, if the heat of an impotent and furious envy had not made thee thirsty of blood. It is not long that thou shalt enjoy this cruelty: after a few hateful years, thy soul shall feel the weight of so many innocents, of so many just curses.

He, for whose sake thou killedst so many, shall strike thee with death; and then what wouldst thou have given to have been as one of those infants whom thou murderedst? In the meantime, when thine executioners returned and told thee of their impartial dispatch, thou smiledst to think how thou hadst defeated thy rival, and beguiled the star, and deluded the prophecies; while God in heaven, and his Son on earth, laugh thee to scorn, and make thy rage an occasion of further glory to him whom thou didst mean to suppress.

He, that could take away the lives of others, cannot protract his own. Herod is now sent home. The coast is clear for the return of that holy family; now God calls them from their exile. Christ and his mother had not stayed so long out of the confines of the reputed visible church, but to teach us continuance under the cross. Sometimes God sees it good for us not to sip of the cup of affliction, but to make a diet-drink of it, for constant and common use. If he allow us no other liquor for many years, we must take it off cheerfully, and know that it is but the measure of our betters.

Joseph and Mary stir not without a command: their departure, stay, removal, is ordered by the voice of God. If Egypt had been more tedious unto them, they durst not move their foot till they were bidden. It is good, in our own business, to follow reason or custom; but in God's business, if we have any other guide but himself, we presume, and cannot expect a blessing.

O the wonderful dispensation of God, in concealing of himself from men! Christ was now some five years old: he bears himself as an infant, and, knowing all things, neither takes nor gives notice of aught concerning his removal and disposing, but appoints that to be done by his angel, which the angel could not have done but by him. Since he would take our nature, he would be a perfect child, suppressing the manifestation and exercise of that Godhead whereto that infant nature was conjoined. Even so,

O Saviour, the humility of thine infancy was answerable to that of thy birth. The more thou hidest and abasest thyself for us, the more should we magnify thee, the more should we deject ourselves for thee. Unto thee, with the Father, and the Holy Ghost, be all honour and glory now and for ever. Amen.

BOOK II.

CONTEMPLATION I.—CHRIST AMONG THE DOCTORS.

EVEN the spring shews us what we may hope for of the tree in summer. In his nonage, therefore, would our Saviour give us a taste of his future proof; lest if his perfection should have shewed itself without warning to the world, it should have been entertained with more wonder than belief. Now this act of his childhood shall prepare the faith of men by fore-expectation. Notwithstanding all this early demonstration of his divine graces, the incredulous Jews could afterwards say, "Whence hath this man his wisdom and great works?" What would they have said, if he had suddenly leapt forth into the clear light of the world! The sun would dazzle all eyes, if he should break forth at his first rising into his full strength: now he hath both the day-star to go before him, and to bid men look for that glorious body, and the lively colours of the day to publish his approach; the eye is comforted, not hurt by his appearance.

The parents of Christ went up yearly to Jerusalem, at the feast of the passover: the law was only for the males. I do not find the blessed Virgin bound to this voyage; the weaker sex received indulgence from God. Yet she, knowing the spiritual profit of that journey, takes pains voluntarily to measure that long way every year. Piety regards not any distinction of sexes or degrees; neither yet doth God's acceptation: rather doth it please the mercy of the Highest, more to reward that service, which though he like in all, yet out of favour he will not impose upon all. It could not be but that she, whom the Holy Ghost overshadowed, should be zealous of God's service. Those that will go no farther than they are dragged in their religious exercises, are no whit of kin to her whom all generations shall call blessed.

The child Jesus, in the minority of his age, went up with his parents to the holy solemnity; not this year only, but in all likelihood, others also: he, in the power of whose Godhead, and by the motion of whose Spirit, all others ascended thither, would not himself stay at home. In all his examples he meant our instruction. This pious act of his nonage intended to lead our first years into timely devotion. The first liquor seasons the vessel for a long time after. It is every way good for a man to bear God's yoke, even from his infancy; it is the policy of the devil to discourage early holiness. He, that goes out betimes in the morning, is more like to despatch his journey, than he that lingers till the day be spent. This blessed family came not to look at the feast and be gone; but they duly staid out the appointed days of unleavened bread. They, and the rest of Israel, could not want household business at home: those secular affairs could not either keep them from repairing to Jerusalem, or send them away immaturely. Worldly cares must give place to the sacred. Except we will depart unblest, we must attend God's services, till we may receive his dismission.

It was the fashion of those times and places, that they went up, and so returned by troops, to those set meetings of their holy festivals. The whole parish of Nazareth went and came together. Good fellowship doth no way so well as in the passage to heaven: much comfort is added by society to that journey which is of itself pleasant. It is a happy word, " Come, let us go up to the house of the Lord." Mutual encouragement is none of the least benefits of our holy assemblies. Many sticks laid together make a good fire, which, if they lie single, lose both their light and heat.

The feast ended, what should they do but return to Nazareth? God's services may not be so attended, as that we should neglect our particular callings. Himself calls us from his own house to ours, and takes pleasure to see a painful client. They are foully mistaken, that think God cares for no other trade but devotion; piety and diligence must keep meet changes with each other. Neither doth God less accept of our return to Nazareth, than our going up to Jerusalem.

I cannot think that the blessed Virgin, or good Joseph, could be so negligent of their divine charge, as not to call the child Jesus to their setting forth from Jerusalem. But their back was no sooner turned upon the temple, than his face was towards it. He had business in that place when theirs was ended: there he was both worshipped and represented. He, in whom the Godhead dwelt bodily, could do nothing without God: his true Father led him away from his supposed. Sometimes the affairs of our ordinary vocation may not grudge to yield unto spiritual occasions. The parents of Christ knew him well to be of a disposition not strange, nor sullen and stoical, but sweet and sociable; and therefore they supposed he had spent the time and the way in company of their friends and neighbours. They do not suspect him wandered into the solitary fields, but, when evening came, they go to seek him among their kinsfolk and acquaintance. If he had not wonted to converse formerly with them, he had not now been sought amongst them. Neither as God nor man doth he take pleasure in a stern froward austerity, and wild retiredness; but in a mild affableness, and amiable conversation.

But, O blessed Virgin, who can express the sorrows of thy perplexed soul, when all that evening search could afford thee no news of thy son Jesus? Was not this one of those swords of Simeon, which should pierce through thy tender breast? How didst thou chide thy credulous neglect, in not observing so precious a charge, and blame thine eyes for once looking beside this object of thy love! How didst thou, with thy careful husband, spend that restless night in mutual expostulations and bemoanings of your loss! How many suspicious imaginations did that while rack thy grieved spirit! Perhaps thou mightest doubt, lest they which laid wait for him, by Herod's command, at his birth, had now, by the secret instigation of Archelaus, surprised him in his childhood: or, it may be, thou thoughtst thy divine Son had now withdrawn himself from the earth, and returned to his heavenly glory, without warning: or, peradventure, thou studiedst with thyself, whether any carelessness on thy behalf, had not given occasion to this absence.

O dear Saviour, who can miss, and not mourn for thee? never any soul conceived thee by faith, that was less afflicted with the sense of thy desertion, than comforted with the joy of thy presence. Just is that sorrow, and those tears seasonable, that are bestowed upon thy loss. What comfort are we capable of, while we want thee? What relish is there in these earthly delights without thee? What is there to mitigate our passionate discomforts, if not from thee? Let thyself loose, O my soul, to the fulness of sorrow, when thou findest thyself bereaved of him, in whose presence is fulness of joy; and deny to receive comfort from any thing, save from his return.

In vain is Christ sought among his kindred according to the flesh: so far are they still from giving us their aid to find the true Messias, that they lead us from him. Back again, therefore, are Joseph and Mary gone to seek him at Jerusalem. She goes about in the city, by the streets, and by the open places, and seeks him whom her soul loveth: she sought him for the time, and found him not. Do we think she spared her search? The evening of her return she hastes to the inn where she had left him, where, missing him, she inquires of every one she met, "Have you not seen him whom my soul loveth?" At last, the third day, she finds him in the temple. One day was spent in the journey towards Galilee; another in the return to Jerusalem; the third day recovers him. He, who would rise again the third day, and be found amongst the living, now also would the third day be found of his parents, after the sorrow of his absence. But where wert thou, O blessed Jesus, for the space of these three days? where didst thou bestow thyself, or who attended thee, while thou wert thus alone at Jerusalem? I know, if Jerusalem should have been as unkind to thee as Bethlehem, thou couldst have commanded the heavens to harbour thee; and if men did not minister to thee, thou couldst have commanded the service of angels. But since the form of a servant called thee to a voluntary homeliness, whether it pleased thee to exercise thyself thus early with the difficulties of a stranger, or to provide miraculously for thyself, I inquire not, since thou revealedst not: only this I know, that hereby thou intendest to teach thy parents, that thou couldst live without them, and that, not of any indigency, but out of a gracious dispensation, thou wouldst ordinarily depend upon their care.

In the meantime thy divine wisdom could not but foreknow all these corroding thoughts, wherewith the heart of thy dear mother must needs bleed, through this sudden dereliction; yet wouldst thou leave her for the time to her sorrow. Even so, O Saviour! thou thoughtst fit to visit her that bore thee with this early affliction. Never any loved thee, whom thou dost not sometimes excercise with the grief of missing thee, that both we may be more careful to hold thee, and more joyful in recovering thee. Thou hast said, and canst not lie, "I am with you to the end of the world;" but even while thou art really present, thou thinkest good to be absent unto our apprehensions. Yet, if thou leave us, thou wilt not forsake us; if thou leave us for our humiliation, thou wilt not forsake us to our final discomfort. Thou mayest for three days hide thyself, but then we shall find thee in the temple. None ever sought thee with a sincere desire, of whom thou wert not found. Thou wilt not be either so little absent as not to whet our appetites, nor so long as to fainten the heart. After three days we shall find thee: and where should we rather hope to find thee than in the temple? There is the habitation for the God of Israel, there is thy resting place for ever. O all ye that are grieved with the want of your Saviour, see where you must seek him! In vain shall ye hope to find him in the streets, in the taverns, in the theatres: seek him in his holy temple, seek him with piety, seek him with faith; there shall ye meet him, there shall ye recover him. While children of that age were playing in the streets, Christ was found sitting in the temple; not to gaze on the outward glory of that house, or on the golden candlesticks or tables, but to hear and oppose the doctors. He who, as God, gave them all the wisdom they had, as the Son of man hearkens to the wisdom he had given them. He, who sat in their hearts as the Author of all learning and knowledge, sits in the midst of their school as an humble disciple: that by learning of them, he might teach all the younger sort humility, and due attendance upon their instructors. He could, at the first, have taught the great Rabbins of Israel the deep mysteries of God: but because he was not yet called by his Father to the public function of a teacher, he contents himself to hear with diligence, and to ask with modesty, and to teach only by insinuation. Let those consider this, which will needs run as soon as they can go; and, when they find ability, think they need not stay for a further vocation of God or men. Open your eyes, ye rather ripe invaders of God's chair, and see your Saviour, in his younger years, not sitting in the eminent pulpits of the doctors, but in the lowly floors of the auditors. See him, that could have taught the angels, listening in his minority to the voice of men. Who can think much to learn of the ancients, when he looks upon the Son of God sitting at the feet of the doctors of Israel? First he hears, then he asks. How much more doth it concern us to be hearers, ere we offer to be teachers of others! He gathers that hears; he spends that teacheth: if we spend before we gather, we shall soon prove bankrupts.

When he hath heard, he asks, and after that he answers: doubtless, those very questions were instructions, and meant to teach, more than to learn: never had these great

Rabbins heard the voice of such a Tutor: in whom they might see the wisdom of God so concealing itself, that yet it would be known to be there: no marvel then, if they all wondered at his understanding and answers. Their eyes saw nothing but human weakness, their ears heard divine sublimity of matter; betwixt what they saw, and what they heard, they could not but be distracted with a doubting admiration. And why did ye not, O ye Jewish teachers, remember, " That to us a child is born, and unto us a son is given, and the government is upon his shoulders; and his name shall be called Wonderful, Counsellor, the Mighty God, the Everlasting Father, the Prince of Peace?" Why did ye not now bethink yourselves, what the star, the sages, the angels, the shepherds, Zachary, Simeon, Anna, had premonished you? Fruitless is the wonder that endeth not in faith; no light is sufficient where the eyes are held through unbelief or prejudice.

The doctors were not more amazed to hear so profound a childhood, than the parents of Christ were to see him among the doctors; the joy of finding him did strive with the astonishment of finding him thus: and now, not Joseph (he knew how little right he had to that divine Son) but Mary breaks forth into a loving expostulation: " Son, why hast thou dealt so with us?" That she might not seem to take upon her as an imperious mother, it is like she reserved this question till she had him alone; wherein she meant rather to express grief, than to chide: only herein the blessed Virgin offended, that her consideration did not suppose, as it was, that some higher respects than could be due to flesh and blood called away the Son of God from her that was the daughter of man. She, that was but the mother of humanity, should not have thought that the business of God must, for her sake, be neglected. We are all partial to ourselves naturally, and prone to the regard of our own rights. Questionless, this gracious saint would not, for all the world, have willingly preferred her own attendance to that of her God: through heedlessness she does so. Her Son and Saviour is her monitor, out of his divine love reforming her natural: " How is it that ye sought me? Know ye not that I must go about my Father's business?" Immediately before, the blessed Virgin had said, " Thy father and I sought thee with heavy hearts." Wherein, both according to the supposition of the world, she calls Joseph the father of Christ, and, according to the fashion of a dutiful wife, she names Joseph before herself. She well knew that Joseph had nothing but a name in this business; she knew how God had dignified her beyond him; yet she says, " Thy father and I sought thee." The Son of God stands not upon contradiction to his mother, but leading her thoughts from his supposed father to his true, from earth to heaven, he answers, " Know ye not that I must go about my Father's business?" It was honour enough to her, that he had vouchsafed to take flesh of her: it was his eternal honour that he was God of God, the everlasting Son of the heavenly Father. Good reason therefore was it, that the respects to flesh should give place to the God of spirits. How well contented was holy Mary with so just an answer! How doth she now again, in her heart, renew her answer to the angel, " Behold the servant of the Lord; be it according to thy word!"

We are all the sons of God in another kind. Nature and the world thinks we should attend them. We are not worthy to say, we have a Father in heaven, if we cannot steal away from these earthly distractions, and employ ourselves in the services of our God.

CONTEMPLATION II.—CHRIST'S BAPTISM.

JOHN did every way forerun Christ, not so much in the time of his birth, as in his office. Neither was there more unlikeliness in their disposition and carriage, than similitude in their function. Both did preach and baptize: only John baptized by himself, our Saviour by his disciples: our Saviour wrought miracles by himself, by his disciples: John wrought none by either. Wherein Christ meant to show himself a Lord, and John a servant; and John meant to approve himself a true servant to him whose harbinger he was. He that leapt in the womb of his mother, when his Saviour (then newly conceived) came in presence, bestirred himself when he was brought forth into the light of the church, to the honour and service of his Saviour: he did the same before Christ, which Christ charged his disciples to do after him,— " Preach and baptize." The gospel ran always in one tenor, and was never but like itself. So it became the Word of him, in whom there is no shadow of turning, and whose word it is, " I am Jehovah, I change not."

It was fit that he which had the prophets, the star, the angel, to foretell his coming into the world, should have his usher to go before him, when he would notify himself to the world. John was the voice of a crier; Christ was the Word of his Father: it was fit this voice should make a noise to the world, ere the Word of the Father should speak to it. John's note was still repentance, The axe to the root, the fan to the floor, the chaff to the fire. As his raiment was rough, so was his tongue; and if his food were wild honey, his speech was stinging locusts. Thus must the way be made for Christ in every heart. Plausibility is no fit preface to regeneration. If the heart of man had continued upright, God might have been entertained without contradiction; but now violence must be offered to our corruption, ere we can have room for grace. If the great way-maker do not cast down hills, and raise up valleys, in the bosoms of men, there is no passage for Christ. Never will Christ come into that soul, where the herald of repentance hath not been before him.

That Saviour of ours, who from eternity lay hid in the counsel of God, who in the fulness of time so came that he lay hid in the womb of his mother for the space of forty weeks, after he was come, thought fit to lie hid in Nazareth for the space of thirty years, now at last begins to shew himself to the world, and comes from Galilee to Jordan. He that was God always, and might have been perfect man in an instant, would by degrees rise to the perfection, both of his manhood and execution of his Mediatorship, to teach us the necessity of leisure in spiritual proceedings: that many suns and successions of seasons and means must be stayed for, ere we can attain our maturity; and that, when we are ripe for the employments of God, we should no less willingly leave our obscurity, than we took the benefit of it for our preparation. He, that was formerly circumcised, would now be baptized. What is baptism but an evangelical circumcision? what was circumcision but a legal baptism? One both supplied and succeeded the other; yet the author of both will undergo both. He would be circumcised, to sanctify his church that was; and baptized, to sanctify his church that should be; that so, in both testaments, he might open a way into heaven. There was in him neither filthiness nor foreskin of corruption, that should need either knife or water. He came not to be a Saviour for himself, but for us. We are all uncleanness and uncircumcision; he would, therefore, have that done to his most pure body, which should be of force to clear our impure souls. thus making himself sin for us, that we might be made the righteousness of God in him.

His baptism gives virtue to ours. His last action, or rather passion, was his baptizing with blood; his first was his baptization with water: both of them wash the world from their sins. Yea, this latter did not only wash the souls of men, but washeth that very water by which we are washed: from hence is that made both clean and holy, and can both cleanse and hallow us. And if the very handkerchief which touched his apostles had power of cure, how much more that water, which the sacred body of Christ touched! Christ comes far to seek his baptism, to teach us, for whose sake he was baptized, to wait upon the ordinances of God, and to sue for the favour of spiritual blessings. They are worthless commodities that are not worth seeking for. It is rarely seen that God is found of any man unsought for. That desire, which only makes us capable of good things, cannot stand with neglect.

John durst not baptize unbidden: his Master sent him to this service; and, behold, the Master comes to his servant, to call for the participation of that privilege, which he himself had instituted and enjoined. How willingly should we come to our spiritual superiors, for our part in those mysteries which God hath left in their keeping! Yea, how gladly should we come to that Christ who gives us these blessings, who is given to us in them!

This seemed too great an honour for the modesty of John to receive. If his mother could say, when her blessed cousin, the virgin Mary, came to visit her, " Whence is this to me, that the mother of my Lord should come to me?" how much more might he say so, when the divine Son of that mother came to call for a favour from him! " I have need to be baptized of thee, and comest thou to me?" O holy Baptist! if there were not a greater born of woman than thou, yet thou couldst not be born of a woman, and not need to be baptized of thy Saviour. He baptized with fire, thou with water. Little would thy water have availed thee without his fire. If he had not baptized thee, how wert thou sanctified from the womb? There can be no flesh without filthiness: neither thy supernatural conception, nor thy austere life, could exempt thee from the need of baptism. Even those that have not lived to sin after the similitude of Adam, yet are they so tainted with Adam, that unless the second Adam cleanse them by his baptism, they are hopeless. There is no less use of baptism unto all, than there is certainty of the need of baptism. John baptized without, Christ within. The more holy a man is, the more sensible he is of his unholiness. No carnal man could have said, " I have need to be baptized of thee ;" neither can he find what he is the better for a little font-water. The sense of our wretchedness, and the valuation of our spiritual helps, is the best trial of our regeneration. Our Saviour doth not deny, that either John hath need to be baptized of him, or that it is strange that he should come to be baptized of John; but he will need thus far both honour John, and disparage himself, to be baptized of his messenger. He, that would take flesh of the virgin, education from his parents, sustenance from his creatures, will take baptism from John. It is the praise of his mercy, that he will stoop so low as to be beholden to his creatures, which from him receive their being, and power both to take and give.

Yet not so much respect to John, as obedience to his Father, drew him to this point of humiliation : " Thus it behoves us to fulfil all righteousness." The counsels and appointments of God are righteousness itself: there needs no other motive, either to the servant or the son, than the knowledge of those righteous purposes. This was enough to lead a faithful man through all difficulties and inconveniences; neither will it admit of any reply, or any demur. John yieldeth to this honour which his Saviour puts upon him, in giving baptism to the author of it. He baptized others to the remission of their sins: now he baptizes him, by whom they were remitted, both to the baptizer and to others.

No sooner is Christ baptized, than he comes forth of the water. The element is of force but during the use: it turns common when that is past: neither is the water sooner poured on his head, than the heavens are opened, and the Holy Ghost descendeth upon that head which was baptized. The heavens are never shut while either of the sacraments is duly administered and received; neither do the heavens ever thus open without the descent of the Holy Ghost. But now that the God of heaven is baptized, they open unto him, which are opened to all the faithful by him: and that Holy Ghost which proceeded from him, together with the Father, joins with the Father in a sensible testimony of him; that now the world might see what interest he had in the heavens, in the Father, in the Holy Spirit, and might expect nothing but divine from the entrance of such a Mediator.

CONTEMPLATION III. — CHRIST TEMPTED.

No sooner is Christ come out of the water of baptism, than he enters into the fire of temptation. No sooner is the Holy Spirit descended upon his head in the form of a dove, than he is led by the Spirit to be tempted. No sooner doth God say, "This is my Son," than Satan says, " If thou be the Son of God." It is not in the power either of the gift or seals of grace to deliver us from the assaults of Satan; they may have the force to repel evil suggestions, they have none to prevent them; yea, the more we are engaged unto God by our public vows and his pledges of favour, so much more busy and violent is the rage of that evil one to encounter us. We are no sooner stept forth into the field of God, than he labours to wrest our weapons out of our hands, or to turn them against us.

The voice from heaven acknowledged Christ to be the Son of God. This divine testimony did not allay the malice of Satan, but exasperate it: now that venomous serpent swells with inward poison, and hastes to assail him whom God hath honoured from heaven. O God, how should I look to escape the suggestions of that wicked one, when the Son of thy love cannot be free! When even grace itself draws on enmity, that enmity that spared not to strike at the Head, will he forbear the weakest and remotest limb? Arm thou me, therefore, with an expectation of that evil I cannot avoid. Make thou me as strong as he is malicious. Say to my soul also, " Thou art my son," and let Satan do his worst.

All the time of our Saviour's obscurity, I do not find him set upon: now that he looks forth to the public execution of his divine office, Satan bends his forces against him. Our privacy, perhaps, may sit down in peace; but never man did endeavour a common good without opposition. It is a sign that both the work is holy, and the agent faithful, when we meet with strong affronts.

We have reason to be comforted with nothing so much as with resistance. If we were not in a way to do good, we should find no rubs: Satan hath no cause to molest his own, and that while they go about his own service. He desires nothing more, than to make us smooth paths to sin: but when we would turn our feet to holiness, he blocks up the way with temptations.

Who can wonder enough at the sauciness of that bold spirit, that dares to set upon the Son of the ever-living God? who can wonder enough at thy meekness and patience, O Saviour, that wouldst be tempted? He wanted not malice and presumption to assault thee; thou wantedst not humility to endure those assaults. I should stand amazed at this voluntary dispensation of thine, but that I see that the susception of our human nature lays thee open to this condition. It is necessarily incident to manhood to be liable to temptations. Thou wouldst not have put on flesh, if thou hadst meant utterly to put off this consequence of our infirmity. If the state of innocence could have been any defence against evil motions, the first Adam had not been tempted, much less the second. It is not the presenting of temptations that can hurt us, but their entertainment. Ill counsel is the fault of the giver, not of the refuser. We cannot forbid lewd eyes to look in at our windows, we may shut our doors against their entrance. It is no less our praise to have resisted, than Satan's blame to suggest evil. Yea, O blessed Saviour, how glorious was it for thee, how happy for us, that thou wert tempted! Had not Satan tempted thee, how shouldst thou have overcome? Without blows, there can be no victory, no triumph: how had thy power been manifested, if no adversary had tried thee? The first Adam was tempted and vanquished: the second Adam, to repay and repair that foil, doth vanquish in being tempted. Now have we not a Saviour and Highpriest that cannot be touched with a feeling of our infirmities, but such a one as was in all things tempted in like sort, yet without sin! How boldly, therefore, may we go unto the throne of grace, that we may receive mercy, and find grace to help in time of need! Yea, this duel was for us. Now we see, by this conflict of our Almighty Champion, what manner of adversary we have, how he fights, how he is resisted, how overcome. Now our very temptation affords us comfort, in that we see, the dearer we are unto God, the more obnoxious we are to this trial; neither can we be discouraged by the heinousness of those evils whereto we are moved, since we see the Son of God solicited to infidelity, covetousness, idolatry. How glorious, therefore, was it for thee, O Saviour, how happy for us, that thou wert tempted!

Where, then, wast thou tempted, O blessed Jesu? or whither wentst thou to meet our great adversary? I do not see thee led into the market-place, or any other part of the city, or thy homestead of Nazareth, but into the vast wilderness, the habitation of beasts, a place that carrieth in it both horror and opportunity! Why wouldst thou thus retire thyself from men? But as confident champions are wont to give advantage of ground or weapon to their antagonist, that the glory of their victory may be greater; so wouldst thou, O Saviour, in this conflict with our common enemy, yield him his own terms for circumstances, that thine honour and his foil may be the more. Solitariness is no small help to the speed of a temptation: "Woe to him that is alone, for if he fall, there is not a second to lift him up." Those that, out of an affectation of holiness, seek for solitude in rocks and caves of the deserts, do no other than run into the mouth of the danger of temptation, while they think to avoid it. It was enough for thee, to whose divine power the gates of hell were weakness, thus to challenge the prince of darkness: our care must be always to eschew all occasions of spiritual danger, and, what we may, to get us out of the reach of temptation.

But, O the depth of the wisdom of God: How camest thou, O Saviour, to be thus tempted? That Spirit, whereby thou wast conceived as man, and which was one with thee and the Father as God, led thee into the wilderness, to be tempted of Satan. While thou taughtest us to pray to thy Father, "Lead us not into temptation," thou didst mean to instruct us, that if the same Spirit led us not into this perilous way, we go not into it. We have still the same conduct. Let the path be what it will, how can we miscarry in the hand of a Father? Now may we say to Satan, as thou didst unto Pilate, "Thou couldst have no power over me, except it were given thee from above." The Spirit led thee; it did not drive thee: here was a sweet invitation, no compulsion of violence. So absolutely conformable was thy will to thy Deity, as if both thy natures had but one volition. In this first draught of thy bitter potion, thy soul said, in a real subjection, "Not my will, but thy will be done." We imitate thee, O Saviour, though we cannot reach to thee. All thine are led by thy Spirit: O teach us to forget that we have wills of our own. The Spirit led thee; thine invincible strength did not animate thee into this combat uncalled. What do we, weaklings, so far presume upon our abilities or success, as that we dare thrust ourselves upon temptations unbidden, unwarranted? Who can pity the shipwreck of those mariners, which will needs put forth and hoist sails in a tempest?

Forty days did our Saviour spend in the

wilderness, fasting and solitary, all which time was worn out in temptation; however the last brunt, because it was most violent, is only expressed. Now could not the adversary complain of disadvantage, while he had the full scope both of time and place to do his worst. And why did it please thee, O Saviour, to fast forty days and forty nights, unless, as Moses fasted forty days at the delivery of the law, and Elias at the restitution of the law, so thou thoughtest fit, at the accomplishment of the law, and the promulgation of the gospel, to fulfil the time of both these types of thine, wherein thou intendedst our wonder, not our imitation — not our imitation of the time, though of the act? Here were no faulty desires of the flesh in thee to be tamed, no possibility of a freer and more easy assent of the soul to God, that could be affected of thee who wast perfectly united unto God; but as for us thou wouldst suffer death, so for us thou wouldst suffer hunger, that we might learn by fasting to prepare ourselves for temptations. In fasting so long, thou intendedst the manifestation of thy power; in fasting no longer, the truth of thy manhood. Moses and Elias, through the miraculous sustentation of God, fasted so long, without any question made of the truth of their bodies; so long, therefore, thou thoughtest good to fast, as by the reason of these precedents might be without prejudice of thine humanity; which, if it should have pleased thee to support, as thou couldst, without means, thy very power might have opened the mouth of cavillers against the verity of thy human nature. That thou mightst therefore well approve that there was no difference betwixt thee and us but sin, thou that couldst have fasted without hunger, and lived without meat, wouldst both feed, and fast, and hunger.

Who can be discouraged with the scantness of friends or bodily provisions, when he sees his Saviour thus long destitute of all earthly comforts, both of society and sustenance? O the policy and malice of that old serpent! When he sees Christ bewray some infirmity of nature in being hungry, then he lays sorest at him by temptations. His eye was never off from our Saviour all the time of his sequestration; and now, that he thinks he espies any one part to lie open, he drives at it with all his might. We have to do with an adversary no less vigilant than malicious, who will be sure to watch all opportunities of our mischief, and, where he sees any advantage of weakness, will not neglect it. How should we stand upon our guard for prevention, that both we may not give him occasions of our hurt, nor take hurt by those we have given!

When our Saviour was hungry, Satan tempts him in matter of food, not then of wealth or glory. He well knows both what baits to fish withal, and when and how to lay them. How safe and happy shall we be, if we shall bend our greatest care, where we discern the most danger!

In every temptation there is an appearance of good, whether of the body, of mind or estate. The first is, the "lust of the flesh," in any carnal desire; the second, the "pride of heart and life;" the third, "the lust of the eyes." To all these the first Adam is tempted, and in all miscarried; the second Adam is tempted to them all, and overcometh. The first man was tempted to carnal appetite by the forbidden fruit; to pride, by the suggestion of being as God; to covetousness, in the ambitious desire of knowing good and evil. Satan, having found all the motions so successful with the first Adam in his innocent estate, will now tread the same steps in his temptations of the second. The stones must be made bread; there is the motion to a carnal appetite: the guard and attendance of angels must be presumed on; there is a motion to pride: the kingdoms of the earth, and the glory of them, must be offered; there to covetousness and ambition.

Satan could not but have heard God say, "This is my well-beloved Son." He had heard the message and the carol of the angels; he saw the star and the journey, and offerings of the sages; he could not but take notice of the gratulations of Zachary, Simeon, Anna; he well knew the predictions of the prophets: yet now that he saw Christ fainting with hunger, as not comprehending how infirmities could consist with a Godhead, he can say, "If thou be the Son of God." Had not Satan known that the Son of God was to come into the world, he had never said, "If thou be the Son of God." His very supposition convinces him: the ground of his temptation answers itself. If, therefore, Christ seemed to be a mere man, because after forty days he was hungry, why was he not confessed more than a man, in that for forty days he hungered not? The motive of the temptation is worse than the motion: "If thou be the son of God." Satan could not choose another suggestion of so great importance. All the work of our redemption, of our salvation, depends upon this one truth, Christ is the Son of God. How should he else have ransomed the world? how should he have done, how should he have suffered, that which was satisfactory to his Father's wrath? how should his actions or passion have been valuable to the sins of all the world? What marvel is it, if we, that are sons by adoption, be assaulted with the doubts of our interest in God, when the natural Son, the Son of his essence, is thus tempted? Since all our comfort consists in this point, here must needs be laid the chief battery, and here must be placed our strongest defence.

To turn stones into bread, had been no more faulty in itself than to turn water into wine: but to do this in a distrust of his Father's providence, to abuse his power and liberty in doing it, to work a miracle of Satan's choice, had been disagreeable to the Son of God. There is nothing more ordinary with our spiritual enemy, than by occasion of want to move us to unwarrantable courses: thou art poor, steal; thou canst not rise by honest means, use indirect. How easy had it been for our Saviour to have confounded Satan by the power of his Godhead! but he rather chooses to vanquish him by the sword of the Spirit, that he might teach us how to resist and overcome the powers of darkness. If he had subdued Satan by the almighty power of the Deity, we might have had what to wonder at, not what to imitate: now he useth that weapon which may be familiar unto us, that he may teach our weakness how to be victorious. Nothing in heaven or earth can beat the forces of hell, but the word of God. How carefully should we furnish ourselves with this powerful munition! how should our hearts and mouths be full of it! "Teach me, O Lord, the way of thy statutes: O take not from me the words of truth! let them be my songs in the house of my pilgrimage; so shall I make answer to my blasphemers." What needed Christ to have answered Satan at all, *if it had not been to teach us that temptations must not have their way, but must be answered by resistance, and resisted by the word?*

I do not hear our Saviour aver himself to be a God, against the blasphemous insinuation of Satan; neither do I see him working this miraculous conversion, to prove himself the Son of God: but most wisely he takes away the ground of the temptation. Satan had taken it for granted, that man cannot be sustained without bread; and therefore infers the necessity of making bread of stones. Our Saviour shows him, from an infallible word, that he had mislaid his suggestion; that man lives not by usual food only, "but by every word that proceeded from the mouth of God." He can either sustain without bread, as he did Moses and Elias; or with a miraculous bread, as the Israelites with manna; or send ordinary means miraculously, as food to his prophet by the ravens; or miraculously multiply ordinary means, as the meal and oil to the Sareptan widow. All things are sustained by his Almighty word. Indeed, we live by food, but not by any virtue that is without God; without the concurrence of whose providence, bread would rather choke than nourish us. Let him withdraw his hand from his creatures in their greatest abundance, we perish. Why do we therefore bend our eyes on the means, and not look up to the hand that gives the blessing?

What so necessary dependence hath the blessing upon the creature, if our prayers hold them not together? As we may not neglect the means, so we may not neglect the procurement of a blessing upon the means, nor be unthankful to the hand that hath given the blessing.

In the first assault, Satan moves Christ to doubt of his Father's providence, and to use unlawful means to help himself: in the next, he moves him to presume upon his Father's protection, and the service of his blessed angels. He grounds the first upon a conceit of want, the next of abundance. If he be in extremes, it is all to one end, to mislead unto evil: if we cannot be driven down to despair, he labours to lift us up to presumption. It is not one foil that can put this bold spirit out of countenance. Temptations, like waves, break one in the neck of another. While we are in this warfare, we must make account, that the repulse of one temptation doth but invite to another.

That blessed Saviour of ours, that was content to be led from Jordan into the wilderness, for the advantage of the first temptation, yields to be led from the wilderness to Jerusalem, for the advantage of the second. The place doth not a little avail to the act. The wilderness was fit for a temptation arising from want, it was not fit for a temptation moving to vain-glory; the populous city was the fittest for such a motion. Jerusalem was the glory of the world, the temple was the glory of Jerusalem, the pinnacle the highest piece of the temple: there is Christ content to be set for the opportunity of temptation. O Saviour of men, how can we wonder enough at this humility of thine, that thou wouldst so far abase thyself as to suffer thy pure and sacred body to be transported by the presumptuous and malicious hand of that unclean spirit! It was not his power, it was thy patience, that deserves our admiration. Neither can this seem over strange to us, when we consider, that if Satan be the head of wicked men, wicked men are the members of Satan. What was Pilate, or the Jews, that persecuted thine innocence, but limbs of the devil? And why are we then amazed to see thee touched and locally transported by the head, when we see thee yielding thyself over to be crucified by the members? If Satan did the worse and greater mediately by their hands, no marvel if he do the less and easier immediately by his own; yet neither of them without thy voluntary dispensation. He could not have looked at thee without thee. And if the Son of God did thus suffer his own holy and precious body to be carried by Satan, what wonder is it, if that enemy have sometimes power given him over the sinful bodies of the adopted sons of God? It is not the strength of faith that can secure us from the outward violences of that evil one. This difference I find betwixt his spiritual and bodily assaults: those are beaten back by the shield of faith, these admit not of such repulse. As the best man may be lame, blind, diseased, so, through the permission of God, he may be bodily vexed by an old man-slayer. Grace was never given us for a target against external afflictions.

Methinks I see Christ hoised upon the highest battlements of the temple, whose very roof was an hundred and thirty cubits high, and Satan standing by him with this speech in his mouth: "Well, then, since in the matter of nourishment thou wilt needs depend upon thy Father's providence, that he can without means sustain thee, take now further trial of that providence in thy miraculous preservation: cast thyself down from this height. Behold, thou art here in Jerusalem, the famous and holy city of the world: here thou art, on the top of the pinnacle of that temple which is dedicated to thy Father, and, if thou be God, to thyself. The eyes of all men are now fixed upon thee: there cannot be devised a more ready way to spread thy glory, and to proclaim thy deity, than by casting thyself headlong to the earth. All the world will say there is more in thee than a man. And for danger, there can be none. What can hurt him that is the Son of God? and wherefore serves that glorious guard of angels, which have by divine commission taken upon them the charge of thy humanity? Since, therefore, in one act thou mayest be both safe and celebrated, trust thy Father, and those thy serviceable spirits, with thine assured preservation: Cast thyself down." And why didst thou not, O thou malignant spirit, endeavour to cast down my Saviour by those same presumptuous hands that brought him up, since the descent is more easy than the raising up? Was it for that it had not been so great an advantage to thee, that he should fall by thy means as by his own? Falling into sin was more than to fall from the pinnacle. Still thy care and suit is to make us authors to ourselves of evil? thou gainest nothing by our bodily hurt, if the soul be safe. Or was it rather for that thou couldst not? I doubt not but thy malice could as well have served to have offered this measure to himself, as to his holy apostle soon after. But he that bounded thy power, tethers thee shorter. Thou couldst not, thou canst not do what thou wouldst. He that would permit thee to carry him up, binds thy hands from casting him down. And woe were it for us, if thou wert not ever stinted.

Why did Satan carry up Christ so high, but on purpose that his fall might be the more deadly? So deals he still with us. he exalts us, that we may be dangerously abased; he puffs men up with swelling thoughts of their own worthiness, that they may be vile in the eyes of God, and fall into condemnation.

It is the manner of God to cast down that he may raise, to abase that he may exalt. Contrarily, Satan raises up that he may throw down, and intends nothing but our dejection in our advancement.

Height of place gives opportunity of temptation. Thus busy is that wicked one in working against the members of Christ. If any of them be in eminence above others, those he labours most to ruinate. They had need to stand fast, that stand high. There is both more danger of their falling, and more hurt in their fall.

He that had presumed thus far to tempt the Lord of life, would fain now dare him also to presume upon his deity: "If thou be the son of God, cast thyself down." There is not a more tried shaft in all his quiver than this: a persuasion to men, to bear themselves too bold upon the favour of God. "Thou art the elect and redeemed of God; sin, because grace hath abounded; sin, that it may abound. Thou art safe enough, though thou offend; be not too much an adversary to thine own liberty." False spirit! it is no liberty to sin, but servitude rather; there is liberty, but in the freedom from sin. Every one of us that hath the hope of sons, must "purge himself, even as He is pure" that hath redeemed us. "We are bought with a price, therefore must we glorify God in our bodies and spirits;" for they are God's. Our sonship teaches us awe and obedience: and therefore, because we are sons, we will not cast ourselves down into sin.

How idly do Satan and wicked men measure God by the crooked line of their own misconceit! I wis Christ cannot be the Son of God, unless he cast himself down from the pinnacle, unless he come down from the cross. God is not merciful, unless he honour them in all their desires; not just, unless he take speedy vengeance where they require it. But when they have spent their folly upon these vain imaginations, Christ is the Son of God, though he stay on the top of the temple: God will be merciful, though we miscarry; and just, though sinners seem lawless: neither will he be any other than he is, or measured by any rule but himself.

But what is this I see? Satan himself with a Bible under his arm, with a text in his mouth: " It is written, He shall give his angels charge over thee!" How still in that wicked one doth subtilty strive with presumption! Who could not but overwonder at this, if he did not consider, that since the devil dared to touch the sacred body of Christ with his hand, he may well touch the scriptures of God with his tongue? Let no man henceforth marvel to hear heretics or hypocrites quote scriptures, when Satan himself hath not spared to cite them. What are they worse for this, more than that holy body which is transported? Some have been poisoned by their meats and drinks; yet either these nourish us, or nothing. It is not the letter of the scripture that can carry it, but the sense; if we divide these two, we profane and abuse that word we allege. And wherefore doth this foul spirit urge a text, but for imitation, for prevention, and for success? Christ had alleged a scripture unto him, he re-alleges scripture unto Christ; at leastwise, he will counterfeit an imitation of the Son of God. Neither is it in this alone: what one act ever passed the hand of God, which Satan did not apishly attempt to second? If we follow Christ in the outward action, with contrary intentions, we follow Satan in following Christ. Or, perhaps, Satan meant to make Christ hereby weary of this weapon, as we see fashions, when they are taken up of the unworthy, are cast off by the great. It was, doubtless, one cause why Christ afterward forbade the devil even to confess the truth, because his mouth was a slander. But chiefly doth he this, for a better colour of his temptation: he gilds over this false metal with scripture, that it may pass current. Even now is Satan transformed into an angel of light, and will seem godly for a mischief. If hypocrites make a fair show, to deceive with a glorious lustre of holiness, we see whence they borrowed it. How many thousand souls are betrayed by the abuse of that word, whose use is sovereign and saving! No devil is so dangerous as the religious devil. If good meat turn to the nourishment, not of nature, but of the disease, we may not forbear to feed, but endeavour to purge the body of those evil humours which cause the stomach to work against itself. O God, thou that hast given us light, give us clear and sound eyes, that we may take comfort of that light thou hast given us. Thy word is holy, make our hearts so; and then shall they find that word not more true than cordial. Let not this divine table of thine be made a snare to our souls.

What can be a better act than to speak scripture? It were a wonder if Satan should do a good thing well. He cites scripture then, but with mutilation and distortion; it comes not out of his mouth but maimed and perverted; one piece is left, all misapplied. Those that wrest or mangle scripture for their own turn, it is easy to see from what school they come. Let us take the word from the author, not from the usurper. David would not doubt to eat that sheep which he pulled out of the mouth of the bear or lion. "He shall give his angels charge over thee." O comfortable assurance of our protection! God's children never go unattended. Like unto great princes, we walk ever in the midst of our guard, though invisible, yet true, careful, powerful. What creatures are so glorious as the angels of heaven! yet their Maker hath set them to serve us. Our adoption makes us at once great and safe. We may be contemptible and ignominious in the eyes of the world: but the angels of God observe us the while, and scorn not to wait upon us in our homeliest occasions. The sun or the light may we keep out of our houses, the air we cannot; much less these spirits that are more simple and immaterial. No walls, no bolts, can sever them from our sides; they accompany us in dungeons, they go with us into our exile. How can we either fear danger, or complain of solitariness, while we have so inseparable, so glorious companions?

Is our Saviour distasted with scripture, because Satan mislays it in his dish? doth he not rather snatch this sword out of that impure hand, and beat Satan with the weapon which he abuseth? "It is written, Thou shalt not tempt the Lord thy God." The scripture is one, as that God whose it is; where it carries an appearance of difficulty or inconvenience, it needs no light to clear it, but that which it hath in itself. All doubts that may arise from it are fully answered by collation. It is true, that God hath taken this care, and given this charge of his own; he will have them kept, not in their sins; they may trust him, they may not tempt him; he meant to encourage their faith, not their presumption. To cast ourselves upon any immediate Providence, when means fail not, is to disobey, instead of believing God. We may challenge God on his word, we may not strain him beyond it; we may make account of what he promised, we may not subject his promises to unjust examinations, and where no need is, make trial of his power, justice, mercy, by devices of our own. All the devils in hell could not elude the force of this divine answer; and now Satan sees how vainly he tempteth Christ to tempt God.

Yet again, for all this, do I see him setting upon the Son of God. Satan is not foiled when he is resisted. Neither diffidence nor presumption can fasten upon Christ; he shall be tried with honour. As some expert fencer that challenges at all weapons, so doth his great enemy. In vain shall we plead our skill in some, if we fail in any. It must be our wisdom to be prepared for all kinds of assaults: as those that hold towns and forts do not only defend themselves from incursions, but from the cannon and the pioneer. Still doth that subtile serpent traverse his ground for an advantage. The temple is not high enough for his next temptation; he therefore carries up Christ to the top of an exceeding high mountain. All enemies, in pitched fields, strive for the benefit of the hill or river, or wind or sun. That which his servant Balak did, by his instigation, himself doth now immediately, change places, in hope of prevailing. If the obscure country will not move us, he tries what the court can do: if not our home, the tavern; if not the field, our closet. As no place is left free by his malice, so no place must be made prejudicial by our carelessness: and as we should always watch over ourselves, so then most, when the opportunity carries cause of suspicion.

Wherefore is Christ carried up so high, but for prospect? If the kingdoms of the earth, and their glory, were only to be presented to his imagination, the valley would have served; if to the outward sense, no hill could suffice. Circular bodies, though small, cannot be seen at once. This show was made to both; divers kingdoms lying round about Judea were represented to the eye, the glory of them to the imagination. Satan meant the eye could tempt the fancy, no less than the fancy could tempt the will. How many thousand souls have died of the wound of the eye! If we do not let in sin at the window of the eye, or the door of the ear, it cannot enter into our hearts.

If there be any pomp, majesty, pleasure, bravery, in the world, where should it be but in the courts of princes, whom God hath made his images, his deputies on earth? There are soft raiment, sumptuous feasts, rich jewels, honourable attendance, glorious triumphs, royal state: these Satan lays out for the fairest show. But, O the craft of that old serpent! many a care attends greatness: no crown is without thorns; high seats are never but uneasy. All those infinite discontentments, which are the shadow of earthly sovereignty, he hides out of the way; nothing may be seen but what may both please and allure. Satan is still and ever like himself. If temptations might be but turned about, and shown on both sides, the kingdom of darkness would not be so populous. Now, whensoever the tempter sets upon any poor soul, all sting of conscience, wrath, judgment, torment, is concealed, as if they were not: nothing may appear to the eye, but pleasure, profit, and a seeming happiness in the enjoying our desires. Those woful objects are reserved for the farewell of sin, that our misery may be seen and felt at once. When we are once sure, Satan is a tyrant; till then, he is a parasite. There can be no safety, if we do not view as well the back, as the face of temptations.

But, O presumption and impudence that hell itself may be ashamed of! the devil dare say to Christ, "All these will I give thee, if thou wilt fall down and worship me." That beggarly spirit, that hath not an inch of earth, can offer the whole world to the Maker, to the Owner of it: the slave of God would be adored of his Creator. How can we hope he should be sparing of false boasts, and of unreasonable promises unto us, when he dares offer kingdoms to Him by whom kings reign?

Temptations on the right hand are most dangerous. How many, that have been hardened with fear, have melted with honour. There is no doubt of that soul that will not bite at the golden hook.

False liars, and vain-glorious boasters,

see the top of their pedigree; if I may not rather say that Satan doth borrow the use of their tongues for a time: whereas, faithful is He that hath promised, who will also do it. Fidelity and truth are the issue of heaven.

If idolatry were not a dear sin to Satan, he would not be so importunate to compass it. It is miserable to see how he draws the world insensibly into this sin, which they profess to detest. Those that would rather hazard the furnace, than worship gold in a statue, yet do adore it in the stamp, and find no fault with themselves. If our hearts be drawn to stoop unto an over high respect of any creature, we are idolaters. O God, it is no marvel if thy jealousy be kindled at the admission of any of thine own works into a competition of honour with their Creator.

Never did our Saviour say, "Avoid Satan," till now. It is a just indignation that is conceived at the motion of a rivality with God. Neither yet did Christ exercise his divine power in this command, but, by the necessary force of Scripture, drives away that impure tempter: "It is written, Thou shalt worship the Lord thy God, and him only shalt thou serve." The rest of our Saviour's answers were more full and direct than that they could admit of a reply; but this was so flat and absolute, that it utterly daunted the courage of Satan, and put him to a shameful flight, and made him for the time weary of his trade.

The way to be rid of the troublesome solicitations of that wicked one is continued resistance. He that forcibly drove the tempter from himself, takes him off from us, and will not abide his assaults perpetually. It is our exercise and trial that he intends, not our confusion.

CONTEMPLATION IV.—SIMON CALLED.

As the sun, in his first rising, draws all eyes to it, so did this Sun of righteousness, when he first shone forth into the world. His miraculous cures drew patients, his divine doctrine drew auditors, both together drew the admiring multitude by troops after him. And why do we not still follow thee, O Saviour, through deserts and mountains, over land and seas, that we may be both healed and taught? It was thy word, that when thou wert lift up, thou wouldst draw all men unto thee. Behold, thou art lift up long since, both to the tree of shame, and to the throne of heavenly glory!— " Draw us, and we shall run after thee."

Thy word is still the same, though proclaimed by men; thy virtue is still the same, though exercised upon the spirits of men. O give us to hunger after both, that by both our souls may be satisfied!

I see the people not only following Christ, but pressing upon him: even very unmannerliness finds here both excuse and acceptation. They did not keep their distances in an awe to the majesty of the speaker, while they were ravished with the power of the speech; yet did not our Saviour check their unreverend thronging, but rather encourages their forwardness. We cannot offend thee, O God, with the importunity of our desires. It likes thee well, that the kingdom of heaven should suffer violence. Our slackness doth ever displease thee, never our vehemency.

The throng of auditors forced Christ to leave the shore, and to make Peter's ship his pulpit. Never were there such nets cast out of that fisher-boat before. While he was upon the land, he healed the sick bodies by his touch; now, that he was upon the sea, he cured the sick souls by his doctrine; and is purposely severed from the multitude, that he may unite them to him. He that made both sea and land, causeth both of them to conspire to the opportunities of doing good.

Simon was busy washing his nets. Even those nets that caught nothing must be washed, no less than if they had sped well. The night's toil doth not excuse his day's work. Little did Simon think of leaving those nets which he so carefully washed; and now Christ interrupts him with the favour and blessing of his gracious presence. Labour in our calling, how homely soever, makes us capable of divine benediction. The honest fisherman, when he saw the people flock after Christ, and heard him speak with such power, could not but conceive a general and confused apprehension of some excellent worth in such a teacher, and therefore is glad to honour his ship with such a guest; and is first Christ's host by sea, ere he is his disciple by land. An humble and serviceable entertainment of a prophet of God was a good foundation of his future honour. He, that would so easily lend Christ his hand and his ship, was likely, soon after, to bestow himself upon his Saviour.

Simon hath no sooner done this service to Christ, than Christ is preparing for his reward: when the sermon is ended, the ship-room shall be paid for abundantly; neither shall the host expect any other paymaster than himself. "Launch forth into the deep, and let down your nets to make a draught." That ship, which lent Christ an opportunity of catching men upon the shore, shall be requited with a plentiful draught of fish in the deep. It had been as easy for our Saviour to have brought the fish to Peter's ship, close to the shore; yet as choosing rather to have the ship carried to the shoal of fish, he bids, "Launch forth into the deep." In his miracles he loves ever to meet nature in her bounds; and, when she hath done her best, to supply the rest by his overruling power. The same power, therefore, that could have caused the fishes to leap upon dry land, or to leave themselves forsaken of the waters upon the sands of the lake, will rather find them in a place natural to their abiding: "Launch out into the deep."

Rather in a desire to gratify and obey his guest, than to pleasure himself, will Simon bestow one cast of his net. Had Christ enjoined him a harder task, he had not refused; yet not without an allegation of the unlikelihood of success: "Master, we have toiled all night, and caught nothing; yet at thy word I will let down the net." The night was the fittest time for the hopes of their trade: not unjustly might Simon misdoubt his speed by day, when he had worn out the night in unprofitable labour. Sometimes God crosseth the fairest of our expectations, and gives a blessing to those times and means whereof we despair. That pains cannot be cast away, which we resolve to lose for Christ. O God, how many do I see casting out their nets in the great lake of the world, which in the whole night of their life have caught nothing! "They conceive mischief, and bring forth iniquity; they hatch cockatrices' eggs, and weave the spider's web: he that eateth of their eggs dieth, and that which is trodden upon breaketh out into a serpent: their webs shall be no garment, neither shall they cover themselves with their labours."

"O ye sons of men, how long will ye love vanity, and follow after lies?" Yet if we have thus vainly misspent the time of our darkness, let us, at the command of Christ, cast out our new-washen nets, our humble and penitent obedience shall come home laden with blessings: "And when they had so done they enclosed a great multitude of fishes, so that their net brake." What a difference there is betwixt our own voluntary acts, and those that are done upon command; not more in the grounds of them, than in the issue! those are ofttimes fruitless, these ever successful. Never man threw out his net at the word of his Saviour, and drew it back empty. Who would not obey thee, O Christ, since thou dost so bountifully requite our weakest services! It was not mere retribution that was intended in this event, but instruction also: this act was not without a mystery. He that should be made a fisher of men, shall, in this draught, foresee his success. "The kingdom of heaven is like a draw-net cast into the sea, which, when it is full, men draw to land." The very first draught that Peter made, after the complement of his apostleship, enclosed no less than three thousand souls. O powerful gospel, that can fetch sinful men from out of the depths of natural corruption! O happy souls, that, from the blind and muddy cells of our wicked nature, are drawn forth to the glorious liberty of the sons of God! Simon's net breaks with the store. Abundance is sometimes no less troublesome than want. The net should have held, if Christ had not meant to overcharge Simon, both with blessing and admiration. How happily is that net broken, whose rupture draws the fisher to Christ! Though the net brake, yet the fish escaped not: he that brought them thither to be taken, held them there till they were taken. "They beckoned to their partners in the other ship, that they should come and help them." There are other ships in partnership with Peter; he doth not fish all the lake alone. There cannot be a better improvement of society than to help us in gain, to relieve us in our profitable labours, to draw up the spiritual draught into the vessel of Christ and his church. Wherefore hath God given us partners, but that we should beckon to them for their aid in our necessary occasions? Neither doth Simon slacken his hand, because he had assistants. What shall we say to those lazy fishers, who can set others to the drag, while themselves look on at ease, caring only to feed themselves with the fish, not willing to wet their hands with the net? what shall we say to this excess of gain? The nets break, the ships sink with their burden. O happy complaint of too large a capture! O Saviour, if those apostolic vessels of the first rigging were thus overlaid, our's float and totter with a ballasted lightness. Thou, who art no less present in these bottoms of ours, lade them with an equal fraught of converted souls, and let us praise thee for thus sinking!

Simon was a skilful fisher, and knew well the depth of his trade; and now, perceiving more than art or nature in this draught, he falls down at the knees of Jesus, saying, "Lord, go from me, for I am a sinful man." Himself is caught in this net. He doth not greedily fall upon so unexpected and profitable a booty, but he turns his eyes from the draught to himself, from the act to the author, acknowledging vileness in the one, in the other majesty: "Go from me, Lord, for I am a sinful man."

It had been pity the honest fisherman should have been taken at his word. O Simon, thy Saviour is come into thine own ship to call thee, to call others by thee unto blessedness; and dost thou say, "Lord, go from me?" As if the patient should say to the physician, Depart from me, for I am sick. It was the voice of astonishment, not of dislike; the voice of humility, not of discontentment; yea, because thou art a sinful man, therefore hath thy Saviour need to come to thee, to stay with thee; and because thou art humble in the acknowledgment of thy sinfulness, therefore Christ delights to abide with thee, and will call thee to abide with him. No man ever fared the worse for abasing himself to his God. Christ hath left many a soul for froward and unkind usage; never any for the disparagement of itself, and entreaties of humility. Simon could not devise how to hold Christ faster, than by thus suing to him to be gone, than by thus pleading his unworthiness.

O my soul, be not weary of complaining of thine own wretchedness; disgrace thyself to him that knows thy vileness; be astonished at those mercies which have shamed thine ill deservings. Thy Saviour hath no power to go away from a prostrate heart. He that resists the proud, heartens the lowly: "Fear not, for I will make thee henceforth a fisher of men." Lo, this humility is rewarded with an apostleship. What had the earth ever more glorious, than a legacy from heaven? He that bade Christ go from him, shall have the honour to go first on this happy errand. This was a trade that Simon had no skill of: it could not but be enough to him that Christ said, " I will make thee;" the miracle showed him able to make good his word. He that hath power to command the fishes to be taken, can easily enable the hands to take them.

What is this divine trade of ours, then, but a spiritual piscation? The world is a sea; souls, like fishes, swim at liberty in this deep; the nets of wholesome doctrine draw up some to the shore of grace and glory. How much skill, and toil, and patience, is requisite in this art! "Who is sufficient for these things?" This sea, these nets, the fishers, the fish, the vessels, are all thine, O God; do what thou wilt in us and by us. Give us ability and grace to take; give men will and grace to be taken, and take thou glory by that which thou hast given.

CONTEMPLATION V.—THE MARRIAGE IN CANA.

WAS this, then, thy first miracle, O Saviour, that thou wroughtst in Cana of Galilee? and could there be a greater miracle than this, that having been thirty years upon earth, thou didst no miracle till now? that thy Divinity did hide itself thus long in flesh, that so long thou wouldst lie obscure in a corner of Galilee, unknown to that world thou camest to redeem; that so long thou wouldst strain the patient expectation of those, who ever since thy star waited upon the revelation of a Messiah? We silly wretches, if we have but a dram of virtue, are ready to set it out to the best show: thou, who "receivedst not the Spirit by measure," wouldst content thyself with a willing obscurity, and concealedst that power that made the world, in the roof of a human breast, in a cottage of Nazareth! O Saviour, none of thy miracles is more worthy of astonishment, than thy not doing of miracles! What thou didst in private, thy wisdom thought fit for secrecy: but if thy blessed mother had not been acquainted with some domestical wonders, she had not now expected a miracle abroad. The stars are not seen by day; the sun itself is not seen by night. As it is no small art to hide art, so it is no small glory to conceal glory. Thy first public miracle graceth a marriage. It is an ancient and laudable institution, that the rites of matrimony should not want a solemn celebration. When are feasts in season, if not at the recovery of our lost rib? if not at this main change of our estate, wherein the joy of obtaining, meets with the hope of further comforts? The Son of the Virgin, and the mother of that Son, are both at a wedding. It was in all likelihood some of their kindred, to whose nuptial feast they were invited so far; yet was it more the honour of the act than of the person that Christ intended. He that made the first marriage in Paradise, bestows his first miracle upon a Galilean marriage: he that was the author of matrimony, and sanctified it, doth, by his holy presence, honour the resemblance of his eternal union with his church. How boldly may we spit in the faces of all the impure adversaries of wedlock, when the Son of God pleases to honour it!

The glorious Bridegroom of the church knew well how ready men would be to place shame, even in the most lawful conjunctions; and therefore his first work shall be, to countenance his own ordinance. Happy is that wedding where Christ is a guest! O Saviour, those that marry in thee, cannot marry without thee. There is no holy marriage whereat thou art not; however invisible, yet truly present by thy Spirit, by thy gracious benediction. Thou makest marriages in heaven, thou blessest them from heaven. O thou that hast betrothed us to thyself in truth and righteousness, do thou consummate that happy marriage of ours in the highest heavens! It was no rich or sumptuous bridal to which Christ, with his mother and disciples, vouchsafed to come from the farther parts of Galilee. I find him not at the magnificent feasts or triumphs of the great. The proud pomp of the world did not agree with the state of a servant. This poor needy bridegroom wants drink for his guests. The blessed Virgin, though a stranger to the house, out of a charitable compassion, and a friendly desire to maintain the decency of an hospitable entertainment, inquires into the wants of her host, pities them, bemoans them, where there was power of redress. "When the wine failed, the mother of Jesus said unto him, They have no wine." How well doth it beseem the eyes of piety and Christian love, to look into the necessities of others! She that conceived the God of mercies both in her heart and in her womb, doth not fix her eyes upon her own teacher, but searcheth into the penury of a poor Israelite, and feels those wants whereof he complains not. They are made for themselves, whose thoughts are only taken up with their own store or indigence.

There was wine enough for a meal, though not for a feast; and if there were not wine enough, there was enough of water: yet the holy Virgin complains of the want of wine, and is troubled with the very lack of superfluity. The bounty of our God reaches not to our life only, but to our contentment: neither hath he thought good to allow us only the bread of sufficiency, but sometimes of pleasure. One while that is but necessary, which some other time were superfluous. It is a scrupulous injustice to scant ourselves where God hath been liberal.

To whom should we complain of any want, but to the Maker and Giver of all things? The blessed Virgin knew to whom she sued: she had good reason to know the Divine nature and power of her Son. Perhaps the bridegroom was not so needy, but if not by his purse, yet by his credit, he might have supplied that want; or it were hard, if some of the neighbour guests, had they been duly solicited, might not have furnished him with so much wine as might suffice for the last service of a dinner. But blessed Mary knew a nearer way: she did not think best to lade at the shallow channel, but runs rather to the well-head, where she may dip and fill the firkins at once with ease. It may be, she saw that the train of Christ, which, unbidden, followed unto that feast, and unexpectedly added to the number of the guests, might help forward that defect, and therefore she justly solicits her Son Jesus for a supply. Whether we want bread, or water, or wine, necessaries or comforts, whither should we run, O Saviour, but to that infinite munificence of thine, which neither denieth nor upbraideth any thing? We cannot want, we cannot abound, but from thee. Give us what thou wilt, so thou give us contentment with what thou givest.

But what is this I hear? a sharp answer to the suit of a mother: " O woman, what have I to do with thee?" He whose sweet mildness and mercy never sent away any supplicant discontented, doth he only frown upon her that bare him? He that commands us to honour father and mother, doth he disdain her whose flesh he took? God forbid! Love and duty doth not exempt parents from due admonition. She solicited Christ as a mother; he answers her as a woman. If she were the mother of his flesh, his deity was eternal. She might not so remember herself to be a mother, that she should forget she was a woman; nor so look upon him as a son, that she should not regard him as a God. He was so obedient to her as a mother, that withal she must obey him as her God. That part which he took from her shall observe her; she must observe that nature which came from above, and made her both a woman and a mother. Matter of miracle concerned the Godhead only; supernatural things were above the sphere of fleshly relation. If now the blessed Virgin will be prescribing either time or form unto divine acts, " O woman, what have I to do with thee? my hour is not come." In all bodily actions, his style was, " O mother:" in spiritual and heavenly, " O woman." Neither is it for us, in the holy affairs of God, to know any faces; yea, " If we have known Christ heretofore according to the flesh, henceforth know we him so no more."

O blessed Virgin, if, in that heavenly

glory wherein thou art, thou canst take notice of these earthly things, with what indignation dost thou look down upon the presumptuous superstition of vain men, whose suits make thee more than a solicitor of divine favours! thy humanity is not lost in thy motherhood, nor in thy glory: the respects of nature reach not so high as heaven. It is far from thee to abide that honour which is stolen from thy Redeemer.

There is a marriage whereto we are invited; yea, wherein we are already interested, not as the guests only, but as the bride, in which there shall be no want of the wine of gladness. It is marvel, if in these earthly banquets there be not some lack. "In thy presence, O Saviour, there is fulness of joy, and at thy right hand are pleasures for evermore." Blessed are they that are called to the marriage-supper of the Lamb.

Even in that rough answer doth the blessed Virgin descry cause of hope. If his hour was not yet come, it was therefore coming: when the expectation of the guests, and the necessity of the occasion, had made fit room for the miracle, it shall come forth and challenge their wonder. Faithfully, therefore, and observantly, doth she turn her speech from her son to the waiters: "Whatsoever he saith unto thee, do it." How well doth it beseem the mother of Christ to agree with his Father in heaven, whose voice from heaven said, "This is my well-beloved Son, hear him!" She that said of herself, "Be it unto me according to thy word," says unto others, "Whatsoever he saith to you, do it." This is the way to have miracles wrought in us, obedience to his word. The power of Christ did not stand upon their officiousness: he could have wrought wonders in spite of them; but their perverse refusal of his commands might have made them incapable of the favour of a miraculous action. He that can, when he will, convince the obstinate, will not grace the disobedient. He that could work without us, or against us, will not work for us, but by us.

This very poor house was furnished with many and large vessels for outward purification; as if sin had dwelt upon the skin, that superstitious people sought holiness in frequent washings. Even this rinsing fouled them with the uncleanness of a traditional will-worship. It is the soul which needs scouring; and nothing can wash that but the blood which they desperately wished upon themselves and their children, for guilt, not for expiation. "Purge thou us, O Lord, with hyssop, and we shall be clean; wash us, and we shall be whiter than snow."

The waiters could not but think strange of so unseasonable a command, "Fill the water-pots." It is wine that we want; what do we go to fetch water? doth this holy man mean thus to quench our feast, and cool our stomachs? If there be no remedy, we could have sought this supply unbidden. Yet so far hath the charge of Christ's mother prevailed, that, instead of carrying flagons of wine to the table, they go to fetch pailfuls of water from the cisterns. It is no pleading of unlikelihoods against the command of an Almighty power.

He that could have created wine immediately in those vessels, will rather turn water into wine. In all the course of his miracles, I do never find him making aught of nothing; all his great works are grounded upon former existences. He multiplied the bread, he changed the water, he restored the withered limbs, he raised the dead, and still wrought upon that which was, and did not make that which was not. What doth he in the ordinary way of nature, but turn the watery juice that arises up from the root into wine? he will only do this now suddenly and at once, which he doth usually by sensible degrees. It is ever duly observed by the Son of God, not to do more miracle than he needs.

How liberal are the provisions of Christ! If he had turned but one of these vessels, it had been a just proof of his power, and perhaps that quantity had served the present necessity: now he furnisheth them with so much wine as would have served a hundred and fifty guests for an entire feast. Even the measure magnifies at once both his power and mercy. The munificent hand of God regards not our need only, but our honest affluence. It is our sin and our shame if we turn his favour into wantonness. There must be first a filling, ere there be a drawing out. Thus, in our vessels, the first care must be of our receipt; the next of our expense. God would have us cisterns, not channels. Our Saviour would not be his own taster, but he sends the first draught to the governor of the feast. He knew his own power, they did not: neither would he bear witness of himself, but fetch it out of others' mouths. They that knew not the original of that wine yet praised the taste, "Every man at the beginning doth set forth good wine, and when men have well drunk, then that which is worse: but thou hast kept the good wine until now." The same bounty that expressed itself in the quantity of the wine, shows itself no less in the excellence. Nothing can fall from that divine hand not exquisite: that liberality hated to provide crab-wine for his guests. It was fit that the miraculous effects of Christ, which came from his immediate hand, should be more perfect than the natural. O blessed Saviour, how delicate is that new wine which we shall one day drink with thee in thy Father's kingdom! Thou shalt turn this water of our earthly affliction into that wine of gladness, wherewith our souls shall be satiated for ever. "Make haste, O my beloved, and be thou like to a roe, or to a young hart upon the mountains of spices."

CONTEMPLATION VI.—THE GOOD CENTURION.

EVEN the bloody trade of war yielded worthy clients to Christ. This Roman captain had learned to believe in that Jesus whom many Jews despised. No nation, no trade, can shut out a good heart from God. If he were a foreigner for birth, yet he was a domestic in heart. He could not change his blood, he could overrule his affections. He loved that nation which was chosen of God; and if he were not of the synagogue, yet he built a synagogue; where he might not be a party, he would be a benefactor. Next to being good, is a favouring of goodness. We could not love religion, if we utterly want it. How many true Jews were not so zealous! either will or ability lacked in them, whom duty more obliged. Good affections do many times more than supply nature. Neither doth God regard whence, but what, we are. I do not see this centurion come to Christ as the Israelitish captain came to Elias in Carmel, but with his cap in his hand, with much suit, much submission, by others, by himself: he sends first the elders of the Jews, whom he might hope that their nation and place might make gracious; then, lest the employment of others might argue neglect, he seconds them in person. Cold and fruitless are the motions of friends, where we do wilfully shut up our own lips. Importunity cannot but speed well in both. Could we but speak for ourselves, as this captain did for his servant, what could we possibly want? What marvel is it, if God be not forward to give, where we care not to ask, or ask as if we cared not to receive? Shall we yet call this a suit, or a complaint? I hear no one word of entreaty. The less is said, the more is concealed: it is enough to lay open his want. He knew well that he had to deal with so wise and merciful a physician, as that the opening of the malady was a craving of cure. If our spiritual miseries be but confessed, they cannot fail of redress.

Great variety of suitors resorted to Christ: one comes to him for a son, another for a daughter, a third for himself: I see none come for his servant but this one centurion. Neither was he a better man than a master. His servant is sick: he doth not drive him out of doors, but lays him at home; neither doth he stand gazing by his bedside, but seeks forth: he seeks forth, not to witches or charmers, but to Christ: he seeks to Christ, not with a fashionable relation, but with a vehement aggravation of the disease. Had the master been sick, the faithfullest servant could have done no more. He is unworthy to be well served, that will not sometimes wait upon his followers. Conceits of inferiority may not breed in us a neglect of charitable offices. So must we look down upon our servants here on earth, as that we must still look up to our Master which is in heaven.

But why didst thou not, O centurion, rather bring thy servant to Christ for cure, than sue for him absent? There was a paralytic, whom faith and charity brought to our Saviour, and let down through the uncovered roof in his bed: why was not thine so carried, so presented? was it out of the strength of thy faith, which assured thee thou needest not show thy servant to him that saw all things? One and the same grace may yield contrary effects. They, because they believed, brought the patient to Christ; thou broughtst not thine to him, because thou believedst: their act argues no less desire, than more confidence; thy labour was less, because thy faith was more. O that I could come thus to my Saviour, and make such moan to him for myself, Lord, my soul is sick of unbelief, sick of self-love, sick of inordinate desires: I should not need to say more. Thy mercy, O Saviour, would not then stay by for my suit, but would prevent me, as here, with a gracious engagement: "I will come and heal thee." I did not hear the centurion say either Come, or, Heal him: the one he meant, though he said not; the other he neither said nor meant. Christ over-gives both his words and intentions. It is the manner of that divine munificence, where he meets with a faithful suitor, to give more than is requested; to give when he is not requested. The very insinuations of our necessities are no less violent than successful. We think the measure of human bounty runs over, when we obtain but what we ask with importunity: that infinite goodness keeps within bounds, when it overflows the desires of our hearts.

As he said, so he did. The word of Christ

either is his act, or concurs with it. He did not stand still when he said, "I will come;" but he went as he spake. When the ruler entreated him for his son, "Come down ere he die," our Saviour stirred not a foot: the centurion did but complain of the sickness of his servant, and Christ, unasked, says, "I will come and heal him." That he might be far from so much as seeming to honour wealth and despise meanness, he, that came in the shape of a servant, would go down to the sick servant's pallet, would not go to the bed of the rich ruler's son. It is the basest motive of respect, that ariseth merely from outward greatness. Either more grace or more need may justly challenge our favourable regards, no less than private obligations.

Even so, O Saviour, that which thou offeredst to do for the centurion's servant, hast thou done for us. We were sick unto death; so far had the dead palsy of sin overtaken us, that there was no life of grace left in us: when thou wert not content to sit still in heaven, and say, "I will cure them;" but addest also, "I will come and cure them." Thyself came down accordingly to this miserable world, and hast personally healed us; so as now we shall not die, but live, and declare thy works, O Lord. And O that we could enough praise that love and mercy, which hath so graciously abased thee, and could be but so low dejected before thee, as thou hast stooped low unto us! that we could be but as lowly subjects of thy goodness, as we are unworthy!

O admirable return of humility! Christ will go down to visit the sick servant. The master of that servant says, "Lord, I am not worthy that thou shouldst come under my roof:" the Jewish elders that went before to mediate for him, could say, He is worthy that thou shouldst do this for him; but the centurion, when he comes to speak for himself, "I am not worthy." They said, he was worthy of Christ's miracle; he says, he is unworthy of Christ's presence. There is great difference betwixt others' valuations and our own. Sometimes the world underrates him that finds reason to set a high price upon himself: sometimes again, it overvalues a man that knows just cause of his own humiliation. If others mistake us, this can be no warrant of our error. We cannot be wise, unless we receive the knowledge of ourselves by direct beams, not by reflection; unless we have learned to contemn unjust applauses, and, scorning the flattery of the world, to frown upon our own vileness: "Lord, I am not worthy."

Many a one, if he had been in the centurion's coat, would have thought well of it; a captain, a man of good ability and command, a founder of a synagogue, a patron of religion: yet he overlooks all these, and when he casts his eye upon the divine worth of Christ and his own weakness, he says, "I am not worthy." Alas, Lord, I am a Gentile, an alien, a man of blood; thou art holy, thou art omnipotent. True humility will teach us to find out the best of another, and the worst piece of ourselves: pride, contrarily, shows us nothing but matter of admiration in ourselves, in others of contempt. While he confest himself unworthy of any favour, he approved himself worthy of all. Had not Christ been before in his heart, he could not have thought himself unworthy to entertain that guest within his house. Under the low roof of an humble breast doth God ever delight to dwell: the state of his palace may not be measured by the height, but by the depth. Brags and bold faces do ofttimes carry it away with men; nothing prevails with God but our voluntary dejections.

It is fit the foundations should be laid deep, where the building is high. The centurion's humility was not more low than his faith was lofty: that reaches up into heaven, and, in the face of human weakness, descries omnipotence: "Only say the word, and my servant shall be whole."

Had the centurion's roof been heaven itself, it could not have been worthy to be come under of Him whose word was almighty, and who was the Almighty Word of his Father. Such is Christ confessed by him that says, "Only say the word." None but a divine power is unlimited: neither hath faith any other bounds than God himself. There needs no footing to remove mountains or devils, but a word. Do but say the word, O Saviour, my sin shall be remitted, my soul shall be healed, my body shall be raised from dust, both soul and body shall be glorious.

Whereupon, then, was the steady confidence of the good centurion? He saw how powerful his own word was with those that were under his command, though himself were under the command of another, the force whereof extended even to absent performances: well, therefore, might he argue, that a free and unbounded power might give infallible commands, and that the most obstinate discase must therefore needs yield to the beck of the God of nature. Weakness may show us what is in strength; by one drop of water we may see what is in the main ocean I marvel not if the centurion were kind to his servants, for they were dutiful to him; he can but say, Do this, and it is done. These mutual respects draw on each other: cheerful and diligent service in the one, calls for a due and favourable care in the other: they that neglect to please, cannot complain to be neglected. O that I could be but such a servant to mine heavenly Master! Alas! every of his commands says, Do this, and I do it not: every of his inhibitions says, Do it not, and I do it. He says, Go from the world, I run to it: he says, Come to me, I run from him. Woe is me! this is not service, but enmity. How can I look for favour, while I return rebellion? It is a gracious Master whom we serve; there can be no duty of ours that he sees not, that he acknowledges not, that he crowns not. We could not but be happy, if we could be officious.

What can be more marvellous than to see Christ marvel? All marvelling supposes an ignorance going before, and a knowledge following some accident unexpected. Now, who wrought this faith in the centurion, but he that wondered at it? He knew well what he wrought, because he wrought what he would; yet he wondered at what he both wrought and knew, to teach us much more to admire that which he at once knows and holds admirable.

He wrought this faith as God; he wondered at it as man: God wrought, and man admired: he that was both, did both, to teach us where to bestow our wonder. I never find Christ wondering at gold or silver, at the costly and curious works of human skill or industry: yea, when the disciples wondered at the magnificence of the temple, he rebuked them rather. I find him not wondering at the frame of heaven and earth, nor at the orderly disposition of all creatures and events; the familiarity of these things intercepts the admiration. But when he sees the grace or acts of faith, he so approves them, that he is ravished with wonder. He that rejoiced in the view of his creation, to see that of nothing he had made all things good, rejoices no less in the reformation of his creature, to see that he had made good of evil: " Behold, thou art fair, my love, behold, thou art fair, and there is no spot in thee. My sister, my spouse, thou hast wounded my heart, thou hast wounded my heart with one of thine eyes."

Our wealth, beauty, wit, learning, honour, may make us accepted of men, but it is our faith only that shall make God in love with us. And why are we of any other save God's diet, to be more affected with the least measure of grace in any man, than with all the outward glories of the world? There are great men whom we justly pity; we can admire none but the gracious.

Neither was that plant more worthy of wonder in itself, than that it grew in such a soil, with so little help of rain and sun. The weakness of means adds to the praise and acceptance of our proficiency. To do good upon a little is the commendation of thrift: it is small thank to be full-handed in a large estate; as, contrarily, the strength of means doubles the revenge of our neglect. It is not more the shame of Israel, than the glory of the centurion, that our Saviour says, "I have not found so great faith in Israel." Had Israel yielded any equal faith, it could not have been unespied of these all-seeing eyes: yet were their helps so much greater than their faith was less; and God never gives more than he requires. Where we have laid our tillage, and compost, and seed, who would not look for a crop? but if the uncultured fallow yield more, how unjustly is that unanswerable ground near to a curse!

Our Saviour did not mutter this censorious testimony to himself, nor whisper it to his disciples; but he turned him about to the people, and spake it in their ears, that he might at once work their shame and emulation. In all other things except spiritual, our self-love makes us impatient of equals; much less can we endure to be outstripped by those who are our professed inferiors. It is well if any thing can kindle in us holy ambitions. Dull and base are the spirits of that man, that can abide to see another overtake him in the way, and out run him to heaven.

He that both wrought this faith, and wondered at it, doth now reward it: " Go thy ways, and as thou hast believed, so be it unto thee." Never was any faith unseen of Christ, never was any seen without allowance, never was any allowed without remuneration. The measure of our receipts, in the matter of favour, is the proportion of our belief. The infinite mercy of God, which is ever like itself, follows but one rule in his gift to us, the faith that he gives us. Give us, O God, to believe, and be it to us as thou wilt, it shall be to us above that we will.

The centurion sues for his servant, and Christ says, "So be it unto thee." The servant's health is the benefit of the master, and the master's faith is the health of the servant. And if the prayers of an earthly master prevailed so much with the Son of God for the recovery of a servant, how shall the intercession of the Son of God prevail with his Father in heaven, for us that are his impotent children and servants upon earth! What can we want, O Saviour, while thou suest for us? He that hath given thee for us can deny thee nothing for us, can deny us nothing for thee. In thee we are happy, and shall be glorious. To thee, O thou mighty Redeemer of Israel, with thine eternal Father, together with thy blessed Spirit, one God infinite and incomprehensible, be given all praise, honour, and glory, for ever and ever. Amen.

BOOK III.

CONTEMPLATION I.—THE WIDOW'S SON RAISED.

The favours of our beneficent Saviour were at the least contiguous. No sooner hath he raised the centurion's servant from his bed, than he raises the widow's son from his bier.

The fruitful clouds are not ordained to fall all in one field. Nain must partake of the bounty of Christ, as well as Cana or Capernaum. And if this sun were fixed in one orb, yet it diffuseth heat and light to all the world. It is not for any place to engross the messengers of the gospel, whose errand is universal. This immortal seed may not fall all in one furrow.

The little city of Nain stood under the hill of Hermon, near unto Tabor; but now it is watered with better dews from above, the doctrine and miracles of a Saviour.

Not for state, but for the more evidence of the work, is our Saviour attended with a large train, so entering into the gate of that walled city, as if he meant to besiege their faith by his power, and to take it. His providence hath so contrived his journey, that he meets with the sad pomp of a funeral. A woful widow, attended with her weeping neighbours, is following her only son to the grave. There was nothing in this spectacle that did not command compassion: A young man, in the flower, in the strength of his age, swallowed up by death. Our decrepit age both expects death, and solicits it; but vigorous youth looks strangely upon that grim serjeant of God. Those mellow apples that fall alone from the tree we gather up with contentment: we chide to have the unripe unseasonably beaten down with cudgels.

But more: a young man, the only son, the only child, of his mother. No condition can make it other than grievous for a well-natured mother to part with her own bowels: yet surely store is some mitigation of loss. Amongst many children, one may be more easily missed; for still we hope the surviving may supply the comforts of the dead: but when all our hopes and joys must either live or die in one, the loss of that one admits of no consolation.

When God would describe the most passionate expression of sorrow that can fall unto the miserable, he can but say, " O daughter of my people, gird thee with sackcloth, and wallow thyself in the ashes, make lamentation and bitter mourning as for thine only son." Such was the loss, such was the sorrow, of this disconsolate mother: neither words nor tears can suffice to discover it.

Yet more: had she been aided by the counsel and supportation of a loving yokefellow, this burden might have seemed less intolerable. A good husband may make amends for the loss of a son; had the root been left to her entire, she might better have spared the branch: now both are cut up; all the stay of her life is gone, and she seems abandoned to a perfect misery. And now, when she gave up herself for a forlorn mourner, past all capacity of redress, the God of comfort meets her, pities her, relieves her. Here was no solicitor but his own compassion. In other occasions he was sought and sued to. The centurion comes to him for a servant, the ruler for a son, Jairus for a daughter, the neighbours for the paralytic; here he seeks up the patient, and offers the cure unrequested. While we have to do with the Father of mercies, our afflictions are the most powerful suitors. No tears, no prayers, can move him so much as his own commiseration. O God, none of our secret sorrows can be either hid from thine eyes or kept from thine heart; and when we are past all our hopes, or possibilities of help, then art thou nearest to us for deliverance.

Here was a conspiration of all parts to mercy: the heart had compassion; the mouth said, " Weep not;". the feet went to the bier, the hand touched the coffin, the power of the Deity raised the dead. What the heart felt was secret to itself; the tongue therefore expresses it in words of comfort, " Weep not." Alas! what are words to so strong and just passions? To bid her not to weep, that had lost her only son, was to persuade her to be miserable, and not feel it; to feel, and not regard it;

to regard, and yet to smother it. Concealment doth not remedy, but aggravate sorrow. That with the council of not weeping, therefore, she might see cause of not weeping, his hand seconds his tongue. He arrests the coffin, and frees the prisoner: " Young man, I say unto thee, arise." The Lord of life and death speaks with command. No finite power could have said so without presumption, or with success. That is the voice that shall one day call up our vanished bodies from those elements into which they are resolved, and raise them out of their dust. Neither sea, nor death, nor hell, can offer to detain their dead, when he charges them to be delivered. Incredulous nature! what, dost thou shrink at the possibility of a resurrection, when the God of nature undertakes it! It is no more hard for that Almighty word, which gave being unto all things, to say, " Let them be repaired," than, " Let them be made."

I do not see our Saviour stretching himself upon the dead corpse, as Elias and Elisha upon the sons of the Shunamite and Sareptan, nor kneeling down and praying by the bier, as Peter did to Dorcas; but I hear him so speaking to the dead as if he were alive, and so speaking to the dead, that by the word he makes him alive: " I say unto thee, arise." Death hath no power to bid that man lie still, whom the Son of God bids arise: immediately he that was dead sat up. So, at the sound of the last trumpet, by the power of the same voice, we shall arise out of the dust, and stand up glorious: " This mortal shall put on immortality, this corruptible incorruption." This body shall not be buried but sown, and at our day shall therefore spring up with a plentiful increase of glory. How comfortless, how desperate, should be our lying down, if it were not for this assurance of rising! And now, behold, lest our weak faith should stagger at the assent to so great a difficulty, he hath already, by what he hath done, given us tastes of what he will do. The Power that can raise one man can raise a thousand, a million, a world: no power can raise one man but that which is infinite, and that which is infinite admits of no limitation. Under the Old Testament, God raised one by Elias, another by Elisha living, a third by Elisha dead: by the hand of the Mediator of the New Testament, he raised here the son of the widow, the daughter of Jairus, Lazarus; and, in attendance of his own resurrection, he made a gaol-delivery of holy prisoners at Jerusalem. He raises the daughter of Jairus from her bed, this widow's son from his coffin, Lazarus from his grave, the dead saints of Jerusalem from their rottenness; that it might appear no degree of death can hinder the efficacy of his overruling command. He that keeps the keys of death, can not only make way for himself through the common hall and outer-rooms, but through the inwardest and most reserved closets of darkness.

Methinks I see this young man, who was thus miraculously awaked from his deadly sleep, wiping and rubbing those eyes that had been shut up in death, and descending from the bier, wrapping his winding-sheet about his loins, cast himself down in a passionate thankfulness at the feet of his Almighty Restorer, adoring that divine power which had commanded his soul back again to her forsaken lodging! and though I hear not what he said, yet, I dare say, they were words of praise and wonder, which his returned soul first uttered. It was the mother whom our Saviour first pitied in this act, not the son, who now, forced from his quiet rest, must twice pass through the gates of death. As for her sake, therefore, he was raised, so to her hands was he delivered, that she might acknowledge that soul given to her, not to the possessor. Who cannot feel the amazement and ecstasy of joy that was in this revived mother, when her son now salutes her from out of another world, and both receives and gives gratulations of his new life! How suddenly were all the tears of that mournful train dried up with a joyful astonishment! how soon is that funeral banquet turned into a new birth-day feast! what striving was here to salute the late carcass of their returned neighbour! what awful and admiring looks were cast upon that Lord of life, who, seeming homely, was approved omnipotent! how gladly did every tongue celebrate both the work and the Author! " A great prophet is raised up amongst us, and God hath visited his people." A prophet was the highest name they could find for him, whom they saw like themselves in shape, above themselves in power. They were not yet acquainted with God manifested in the flesh. This miracle might well have assured them of more than a prophet; but he that raised the dead man from the bier, would not suddenly raise these dead hearts from the grave of infidelity. They shall see reason enough to know, that the Prophet who was raised up to them, was the God that now visited them, and at last should do as much for them, as he had done for the young man, raise them from death to life, from dust to glory.

CONTEMPLATION II.— THE RULER'S SON CURED.

The bounty of God so exceedeth man's, that there is a contrariety in the exercise of it: we shut our hands, because we opened them: God therefore opens his, because he hath opened them. God's mercies are as comfortable in their issue as in themselves. Seldom ever do blessings go alone: where our Saviour supplied the bridegroom's wine, there he heals the ruler's son. He had not, in all these coasts of Galilee, done any miracle but here. " To him that hath shall be given."

We do not find Christ oft attended with nobility; here he is. It was some great peer, or some noted courtier, that was now a suitor to him for his dying son. Earthly greatness is no defence against afflictions. We men forbear the mighty; disease and death know no faces of lords or monarchs: could these be bribed, they would be too rich. Why should we grudge not to be privileged, when we see there is no spare of the greatest?

This noble ruler listens after Christ's return into Galilee. The most eminent amongst men will be glad to hearken after Christ in their necessity. Happy was it for him that his son was sick: he had not else been acquainted with his Saviour; his soul had continued sick of ignorance and unbelief. Why else doth our good God send us pain, losses, opposition, but that he may be sought to? Are we afflicted? whither should we go but to Cana, to seek Christ? whither but to the Cana of heaven, where our water of sorrow is turned to the wine of gladness? to that omnipotent Physician who healeth all our infirmities, that we may once say, " It is good for me that I was afflicted?"

It was but a day's journey from Capernaum to Cana; thence hither did this courtier come for the cure of his son's fever. What pains even the greatest can be content to take for bodily health! no way is long, no labour tedious to the desirous. Our souls are sick of a spiritual fever, labouring under the cold fit of infidelity, and the hot fit of self-love, and we sit still at home, and see them languish unto death.

This ruler was neither faithless nor faithful: had he been quite faithless, he had not taken such pains to come to Christ; had he been faithful, he had not made this suit to Christ when he was come: " Come down, and heal my son, ere he die."

" Come down," as if Christ could not have cured him absent; "ere he die," as if that power could not have raised him, being dead. How much difference was here betwixt the centurion and the ruler! that came for his servant, this for his son. This son was not more above the servant, than the faith which sued for the servant surpassed that which sued for the son. The one can say, " Master, come not under my roof, for I am not worthy; only speak the word, and my servant shall be whole." The other can say, Master, either come under my roof, or my son cannot be whole. "Heal my son" had been a good suit, for Christ is the only Physician for all diseases; but, " Come down, and heal him," was to teach God how to work.

It is good reason that he should challenge the right of prescribing to us, who are every way his own: it is presumption in us to stint him unto our forms. An expert workman cannot abide to be taught by a novice; how much less shall the all-wise God endure to be directed by his creature! This is more than if the patient should take upon him to give a recipe to the physician. That God would give us grace, is a beseeming suit; but to say, Give it me by prosperity, is a saucy motive.

As there is faithfulness in desiring the end, so modesty and patience in referring the means to the author. In spiritual things God hath acquainted us with the means whereby he will work, even his own sacred ordinances: upon these, because they have his own promise, we may call absolutely for a blessing; in all others, there is no reason that beggars should be choosers. He who doth whatsoever he will, must do it how he will: it is for us to receive, not to appoint.

He, who came to complain of his son's sickness, hears of his own: " Except ye see signs and wonders, ye will not believe." This nobleman was, as is like, of Capernaum: there had Christ often preached; there was one of his chief residences. Either this man had heard our Saviour oft, or might have done: yet because Christ's miracles came to him only by hearsay, (for as yet we find none at all wrought where he preached most) therefore the man believes not enough, but so speaks to Christ as to some ordinary physician: " Come down, and heal." It was the common disease of the Jews, incredulity, which no receipt could heal but wonders: " A wicked and adulterous generation seeks signs." Had they not been wilfully graceless, there was already proof enough of the Messias: the miraculous conception and life of the forerunner, Zechariah's dumb ness, the attestation of angels, the apparition of the star, the journey of the sages, the vision of the shepherds, the testimonies of Anna and Simeon, the prophecies fulfilled, the voice from heaven at his baptism, the divine words that he spake, and yet they must have all made up with miracles; which, though he be not unwilling to give at his own times, yet he thinks much to be tied unto theirs. Not to believe without signs, was a sign of stubborn hearts.

It was a foul fault and a dangerous one. "Ye will not believe." What is it that shall condemn the world but unbelief? what can condemn us without it? No sin can condemn the repentant. Repentance is a fruit of faith: where true faith is, then, there can be no condemnation, as there can be nothing but condemnation without it. How much more foul in a noble Capernaite, that had heard the sermons of so divine a teacher! The greater light we have, the more shame it is for us to stumble.

O what shall become of us that reel and fall in the clearest sunshine that ever looked forth upon any church! Be merciful to our sins, O God, and say any thing of us, rather than "Ye will not believe!"

Our Saviour tells him of his unbelief. He feels not himself sick of that disease: all his mind is on his dying son. As easily do we complain of bodily griefs, as we are hardly affected with spiritual. O the meekness and mercy of this Lamb of God! When we would have looked that he should have punished this suitor for not believing, he condescends to him, that he may believe: "Go thy way, thy son liveth." If we should measure our hopes by our own worthiness, there were no expectation of blessings; but if we shall measure them by his bounty and compasion, there can be no doubt of prevailing. As some tender mother, that gives the breast to her unquiet child instead of the rod, so deals he with our perversenesses.

How God differences men, according to no other conditions than of their faith! The centurion's servant was sick, the ruler's son. The centurion doth not sue unto Christ to come; only says, "My servant is sick of a palsy:" Christ answers him, "I will come and heal him." The ruler sues unto Christ, that he would come and heal his son: Christ will not go; only says, "Go thy way, thy son lives." Outward things carry no respect with God. The image of that Divine Majesty shining inwardly in the graces of the soul, is that which wins love from him in the meanest estate. The centurion's faith, therefore, could do more than the ruler's greatness; and that faithful man's servant hath more regard than this great man's son.

The ruler's request was, "Come and heal:" Christ's answer was, "Go thy way thy son lives." Our merciful Saviour meets those in the end whom he crosses in the way. How sweetly doth he correct our prayers, and, while he doth not give us what we ask, gives us better than we asked.

Justly doth he forbear to go down with this ruler, lest he should confirm him in an opinion of measuring his power by conceits of locality and distance: but he doth that in absence, for which his presence was required, with a repulse: "Thy son liveth," giving a greater demonstration of his omnipotency than was craved. How oft doth he not hear to our will, that he may hear us to our advantage! The chosen vessel would be rid of temptations; he hears of a supply of grace: the sick man asks release, receives patience; life, and receives glory. Let us ask what we think best; let him give what he knows best.

With one word doth Christ heal two patients, the son and the father; the son's fever, the father's unbelief. That operative word of our Saviour was not without the intention of a trial. Had not the ruler gone home satisfied with that intimation of his son's life and recovery, neither of them had been blessed with success. Now the news of performance meets him one half of the way: and he that believed somewhat ere he came, and more when he went, grew to more faith in the way; and, when he came home, enlarged his faith to all the skirts of his family. A weak faith may be true, but a true faith is growing: he that boasts of a full stature in the first moment of his assent, may presume, but doth not believe.

Great men cannot want clients: their example sways some, their authority more; they cannot go to either of the other worlds alone. In vain do they pretend power over others, who labour not to draw their families unto God.

CONTEMPLATION III.—THE DUMB DEVIL EJECTED.

That the Prince of our Peace might approve his victories perfect, wheresoever he met with the prince of darkness he foiled him, he ejected him. He found him in heaven: thence did he throw him headlong; and verified his prophet, "I have cast thee out of mine holy mountain." And if the devils left their first habitation, it was because, being devils, they could not keep it. Their estate indeed they might have kept, and did not; their habitation they would have kept, and might not. "How art thou fallen from heaven, O Lucifer!" He found him in the heart of man; for in that closet of God did the evil spirit, after his exile from heaven, shroud himself: sin gave him possession, which he kept with a willing violence: thence he casts him by his word and Spirit. He found him tyrannizing in the bodies of some possessed men, and, with power, commands the unclean spirits to depart.

This act is for no hand but his. When a strong man keeps possession, none but a stronger can remove him. In voluntary things, the strongest may yield to the weakest, Samson to a Delilah; but in violent, ever the mightiest carries it. A spiritual nature must needs be in rank above a bodily; neither can any power be above a spirit, but the God of spirits.

No otherways is it in the mental possession. Wherever sin is, there Satan is: as, on the contrary, "whosoever is born of God, the seed of God remains in him." That evil one not only is, but rules in the sons of disobedience: in vain shall we try to eject him, but by the divine power of the Redeemer: "For this cause the Son of God was manifested, that he might destroy the works of the devil." Do we find ourselves haunted with the familiar devils of pride, self-love, sensual desires, unbelief? None but thou, O Son of the everliving God, can free our bosoms of these hellish guests: "O cleanse thou me from my secret sins, and keep me, that presumptuous sins prevail not over me." O Saviour, it is no paradox to say, that thou castest out more devils now, than thou didst while thou wert upon earth. It was thy word, "When I am lifted up, I will draw all men unto me." Satan weighs down at the feet; thou pullest at the head, yea, at the heart. In every conversion which thou workest, there is a dispossession. Convert me, O Lord, and I shall be converted. I know thy means are now no other than ordinary. If we expect to be dispossessed by miracle, it would be a miracle if ever we were dispossessed. O let thy gospel have the perfect work in me; so only shall I be delivered from the powers of darkness.

Nothing can be said to be dumb, but what naturally speaks; nothing can speak naturally, but what hath the instruments of speech: which, because spirits want, they can no other ways speak vocally, than as they take voices to themselves, in taking bodies. This devil was not therefore dumb in his nature, but in his effect. The man was dumb by the operation of that devil which possessed him; and now the action is attributed to the spirit, which was subjectively in the man: "It is not you that speak," saith our Saviour, "but the spirit of your Father that speaketh in you."

As it is in bodily diseases, that they do not infect us alike; some seize upon the humours, others upon the spirits; some assault the brain, others the heart or lungs; so, in bodily and spiritual possessions, in some the evil spirits take away their senses, in some their limbs, in some their inward faculties; like as, spiritually, they affect to move us unto several sins: one to lust, another to covetousness or ambition, another to cruelty; and their names have distinguished them according to these various effects.

This was a dumb devil, which yet had possessed not the tongue only of this man, but his ear; not that only, but, as it seems, his eyes too.

O subtile and tyrannous spirit, that obstructs all ways to the soul, that keeps out all means of grace, both from the door and windows of the heart; yea, that stops up all passages, whether of ingress or egress; of ingress at the eye or ear, of egress at the mouth, that there might be no capacity of redress!

What holy use is there of our tongue, but to praise our Maker, to confess our sins, to inform our brethren? How rife is this dumb devil everywhere, while he stops the mouths of Christians from these useful and necessary duties!

For what end hath man those two privileges above his fellow-creatures, reason and speech; but that, as by the one he may conceive of the great works of his Maker, which the rest cannot, so by the other he may express what he conceives to the honour of the Creator, both of them and himself? And why are all other creatures said to praise God, and bidden to praise him, but because they do it by the apprehension, by the expression of man? "If the heavens declare the glory of God," how do they it, but to the eyes, and by the tongue of that man for whom they were made? It is no small honour whereof the envious spirit shall rob his Maker, if he can close up the mouth of his only rational and vocal creature, and turn the best of his workmanship into a dumb idol, that hath a mouth and speaks not. "Lord, open thou my lips, and my mouth shall show forth thy praise."

Praise is not more necessary than complaint; praise of God, than complaint of ourselves, whether to God or men. The only amends we can make to God, when we have not had the grace to avoid sin, is to confess the sin we have not avoided. This is the sponge that wipes out all the blots and blurs of our lives. " If we confess our sins, He is faithful and just to forgive us our sins, and to cleanse us from all unrighteousness."

That cunning manslayer knows there is no way to purge the sick soul but upward, by casting out the vicious humour wherewith it is clogged; and therefore holds the lips close, that the heart may not disburden itself by so wholesome evacuation. " When I kept silence, my bones consumed: for day and night thy hand, O Lord, was heavy upon me; my moisture is turned into the drought of summer. O let me confess against myself my wickedness unto thee, that thou mayest forgive the punishment of my sin."

We have a tongue for God, when we praise him; for ourselves, when we pray and confess; for our brethren, when we speak the truth for their information, which, if we hold back in unrighteourness, we yield unto that dumb devil. Where do we not see that accursed spirit? he is on the bench, when the mute or partial judge speaks not for truth and innocence; he is in the pulpit, when the prophets of God smother, or halve, or adulterate the message of their Master; he is at the bar, when irreligious jurors dare lend an oath to fear, to hope, to gain; he is in the market, when godless chapmen, for their penny, sell the truth and their soul; he is in the common conversation of men, when the tongue belies the heart, flatters the guilty, baulketh reproofs even in the foulest crimes. O Thou, who only art stronger than that strong one, cast him out of the hearts and mouths of men! " It is time for thee, Lord, to work, for they have destroyed thy law.

That it might well appear this impediment was not natural, so soon as the man is freed from the spirit, his tongue is free to his speech. The effects of spirits, as they are wrought, so they cease at once. If the son of God do but remove our spiritual possession, we shall presently break forth into the praise of God, into the confession of our vileness, into the profession of truth.

But what strange variety do I see in the spectators of his miracle! some wondering, others censuring, a third sort tempting, a fourth applauding! There was never man or action but was subject to variety of constructions. What man could be so holy as he that was of God? what act could be more worthy, than the dispossessing of an evil spirit? Yet this man, this act, passeth these differences of interpretation. — What can we do, to undergo but one opinion? If we give alms and fast, some will magnify our charity and devotion, others will tax our hypocrisy; if we give not, some will condemn our hard-heartedness, others will allow our care of justice. If we preach plainly, to some it will savour of a careless slubbering, to others of a mortified sincerity; elaborately, some will tax our affectation, others will applaud our diligence in dressing the delicate viands of God. What marvel is it if it be thus with our imperfection, when it fared not otherwise with him that was purity and righteousness itself? The austere forerunner of Christ " came neither eating nor drinking; they say, He hath a devil. The Son of man came eating and drinking; they say, This man is a glutton, a friend of publicans and sinners:" and here one of his holy acts carries away at once wonder, censure, doubt, celebration. There is no way safe for a man, but to square his actions by the right rule of justice, or charity; and then let the world have leave to spend their glosses at pleasure. It was a heroical resolution of the chosen vessel, " I pass very little to be judged of you, or of man's day."

I marvel not if the people marvelled; for here were four wonders in one: the blind saw, the deaf heard, the dumb spake, the demoniac is delivered. Wonder was due to so rare and powerful a work, and, if not this, nothing. We can cast away admiration upon the poor devices or activities of men: how much more upon the extraordinary works of omnipotency! Whoso knows the frame of heaven and earth, shall not much be affected with the imperfect effects of frail humanity, but shall, with no less ravishment of soul, acknowledge the miraculous works of the same Almighty hand. Neither is the spiritual ejection worthy of any meaner entertainment. Rarity and difficulty are wont to cause wonder. There are many things which have wonder in their worth, and lose it in their frequence; there are some which have it in their strangeness, and lose it in their facility; both meet in this. To see men haunted, yea, possessed with a dumb devil, is so frequent that it is a just wonder to find a man free: but to find the dumb spirit cast out of a man, and to hear him praising God, confessing his sins, teaching others the sweet experiments of mercy, deserves just admiration. If the cynic sought in the market for a man amongst men, well may we seek amongst men for a convert. Neither is the difficulty less than the rareness: the strong man hath the possession, all passages are blocked up, all helps barred, by the treachery of our nature. If any soul be rescued from these spiritual wickednesses, it is the praise of Him that doth wonders alone.

But whom do I see wondering? The multitude. The unlearned beholders follow that act with wonder, which the learned scribes entertain with obloquy. God hath revealed those things to babes, which he hath hid from the wise and prudent. With what scorn did those great rabbins speak of these sons of the earth! "This people that knows not the law is accursed." Yet the mercy of God makes an advantage of their simplicity, in that they are therefore less subject to cavillation and incredulity; as, contrarily, his justice causes the proud knowledge of others to lie as a block in their way, to the ready assent under the divine power of the Messias. Let the pride of glorious adversaries disdain the poverty of the clients of the gospel: it shall not repent us to go to heaven with the vulgar, while their great ones go in state to perdition.

The multitude wondered. Who censured but scribes, great doctors of the law, of the divinity of the Jews? what scribes, but those of Jerusalem, the most eminent academy of Judea? These were the men who, out of their deep reputed judgment, cast these foul aspersions upon Christ. — Great wits ofttimes mislead both the owners and followers. How many shall once wish they had been born dullards, yea, idiots, when they shall find their wit to have barred them out of heaven! "Where is the scribe? where is the disputer of this world?" Hath not God made the wisdom of the world foolishness? Say the world what it will, a dram of holiness is worth a pound of wit. Let others censure with the scribes; let me wonder with the multitude.

What could malice say worse? "He casteth out devils through Beelzebub the prince of devils." The Jews well knew, that the gods of the heathen were no other than devils; amongst whom, for that the Lord of flies (so called, whether for the concourse of flies to the abundance of his sacrifices, or for his aid implored against the infestation of those swarms), was held the chief, therefore they style him "the prince of devils." There is a subordination of spirits; some higher in degree, some inferior to others. Our Saviour himself tells us of the devil and his angels. Messengers are inferior to those that send them. The seven devils, that entered into the swept and garnished house, were worse than the former. Neither can principalities, and powers, and governors, and princes of the darkness of this world, design other than several ranks of evil angels. There can be no being without some kind of order; there can be no order in parity. If we look up into heaven, there is the King of gods, the Lord of lords, higher than the highest. If to the earth, there are monarchs, kings, princes, peers, people. If we look down to hell, there is the prince of devils. They labour for confusion that call for parity. What should the church do with such a form, as is not exemplified in heaven, in earth, in hell?

One devil, according to their supposition, may be used to cast out another. How far the command of one spirit over another may extend, it is a secret of infernal state, too deep for the inquiry of men. The thing itself is apparent, upon compact and pre-contracted composition, one gives way to other for the common advantage. As we see in the commonwealth of cheaters and cut-purses, one doth the fact, another is fee'd to bring it out, and to procure restitution: both are of the trade, both conspire to the fraud; the actor falls not out with the revealer, but divides with him that cunning spoil.

One malicious miscreant sets the devil on work to the inflicting of disease or death; another upon agreement, for a further spiritual gain, takes him off: there is a devil in both. And if there seem more bodily favour, there is no less spiritual danger in the latter; in the one, Satan wins the agent, the suitor in the other. It will be no cause of discord in hell, that one devil gives ease to the body which another tormented, that both may triumph in the gain of a soul. O God, that any creature which bears thine image should not abhor to be beholden to the powers of hell for aid, for advice! "Is it not because there is not a God in Israel that men go to inquire of the god of Ekron?" Can men be so sottish to think, that the vowed enemy of their souls can offer them a bait without a hook? "What evil is there in the city, which the Lord hath not done?" what is there which he cannot as easily redress? He wounds, he heals again; and if he will not, "It is the Lord, let him do what seems good in his eyes." If he do not deliver us, he will crown our faithfulness in a patient perseverance. The wounds of God are better than the salves of Satan.

Was it possible, that the wit of envy could devise so high a slander? Beelzebub was a god of the heathen; therefore herein they accuse him for an idolater: Beelzebub was a devil to the Jews; therefore they accuse him for a conjurer: Beelzebub was the chief of devils; therefore they accuse him for an arch-exorcist, for the worst kind of magician. Some professors of this black art, though their work be devilish, yet they pretend to do it in the name of Jesus, and will presumptuously seem to do that by command, which is secretly transacted by agreement. The scribes accuse Christ of a direct compact with the devil, and suppose both a league and familiarity, which, by the law of Moses, in the very hand of Saul, was no other than deadly. Yea, so deep doth this wound reach, that our Saviour searching it to the bottom, finds no less in it than the sin against the Holy Ghost, inferring hereupon that dreadful sentence of the irremissibleness of that sin unto death. And if this horrible crimination were cast upon thee, O Saviour, in whom the prince of this world found nothing, what wonder is it if we, thy sinful servants, be branded on all sides with evil tongues?

Yea, which is yet more, how plain is it that these men forced their tongue to speak this slander against their own heart! else this blasphemy had been only against the Son of man, not against the Holy Ghost: but now that the searcher of hearts finds it to be no less than against the blessed Spirit of God, the spite must needs be obstinate: their malice doth wilfully cross their conscience. Envy never regards how true, but how mischievous: so it may gall or kill, it cares little whether with truth or falsehood. For us, " blessed are we when men revile us, and say all manner of evil of us, for the name of Christ:" for them, " what reward shall be given to thee, thou false tongue? even sharp arrows with hot burning coals," yea, those very coals of hell from which thou wert enkindled.

There was yet a third sort, that went a mid way betwixt wonder and censure.— These were not so malicious as to impute the miracle to a satanical operation: they confess it good, but not enough, and therefore urge Christ to a further proof: Though thou hast cast out this dumb devil, yet this is no sufficient argument of thy divine power. We have yet seen nothing from thee like those ancient miracles of the times of our forefathers. Joshua caused the sun to stand still; Elias brought fire down from heaven; Samuel astonished the people with thunder and rain in the midst of harvest: if thou wouldst command our belief, do somewhat like to these. The casting out of a devil shows thee to have some power over hell; show us now that thou hast no less power over heaven." There is a kind of unreasonableness of desire, and insatiableness of infidelity: it never knows when it hath evidence enough. This, which the Jews overlooked, was a more irrefragable demonstration of divinity than •that which they desired. A devil was more than a meteor, or a parcel of an element; to cast out a devil by command, more than to command fire from heaven. Infidelity ever loves to be her own carver.

No son can be more like a father than these Jews to their progenitors in the desert: that there might be no fear of degenerating into good, they also of old tempted God in the wilderness. First, they are weary of the Egyptian bondage, and are ready to fall out with God and Moses for their stay in those furnaces. By ten miraculous plagues they are freed; and, going out of those confines, the Egyptians follow them, the sea is before them; now they are more afflicted with their liberty than their servitude: the sea yields way, the Egyptians are drowned; and now that they are safe on the other shore, they tempt the Providence of God for water; the rock yields it them; then, no less for bread and meat. God sends them manna and quails; they cry out of the food of angels. Their present enemies in the way are vanished; they whine at the men of measures in the heart of Canaan. Nothing from God but mercy, nothing from them but temptations.

Their true brood, both in nature and in sin, had abundant proofs of the Messiah: if curing the blind, lame, diseased, deaf, dumb, ejecting devils, overruling the elements, raising the dead, could have been sufficient, yet still they must have a sign from heaven, and shut up in the style of the tempter, " If thou be the Christ." The gracious heart is credulous; even where it sees not, it believes, and where it sees but a little, it believes a great deal. Neither doth it presume to prescribe unto God, what and how he shall work; but takes what it finds, and unmoveably rests in what it takes. Any miracle, no miracle, serves enough for their assent, who have built their faith upon the gospel of the Lord Jesus.

CONTEMPLATION IV.—MATTHEW CALLED.

The number of the apostles was not yet full; one room is left void for a future occupant. Who can but expect, that it is reserved for some eminent person? and, behold, Matthew the publican is the man. O the strange election of Christ! Those other disciples, whose calling is recorded, were from the fisher-boat; this from the tolbooth: they were unlettered, this infamous. The condition was not itself sinful: but as the taxes which the Romans imposed on God's free people were odious, so the collectors, the farmers of them, abominable. Besides, that it was hard to hold that seat without oppression, without exaction. One, that best knew it, branded it with polling and sycophancy. And now behold a griping publican called to the family, to the apostleship, to the secretaryship of God. Who can despair in the conscience of his unworthiness, when he sees this pattern of the free bounty of him that calleth us? Merits do not carry it in the gracious election of God, but his mere favour. There sat Matthew the publican, busy in his counting-house, reckoning up the sums of his rentals, taking up his arrearages, and wrangling for denied duties, and did so little think of a Saviour, that he did not so much as look at his passage; but "Jesus, as he passed by, saw a man sitting at the receipt of custom, named Matthew." As if this prospect had been sudden and casual, Jesus saw him in passing by. O Saviour, before the world was, thou sawest that man sitting there, thou sawest thine own passage, thou sawest his call in thy passage; and now thou goest purposely that way, that thou mightst see and call. Nothing can be hid from that piercing eye, one glance whereof hath discerned a disciple in the clothes of a publican. That habit, that shop of extortion cannot conceal from thee a vessel of election. In all forms thou knowest thine own; and, in thine own time, shalt fetch them out of the disguises of their foul sins or unfit conditions. What sawest thou, O Saviour, in that publican, that might either allure thine eye, or not offend it? what but a hateful trade, an evil eye, a gripple hand, bloody tables, heaps of spoil? yet now thou saidst, "Follow me." Thou that saidst once to Jerusalem, "Thy birth and nativity is of the land of Canaan; thy father was an Amorite, thy mother an Hittite; thy navel was not cut, neither wert thou washed in water to supple thee: thou wast not salted at all: Thou wast not swaddled at all: none eye pitied thee, but thou wast cast out in the open fields, to the loathing of thy person, in the day that thou wast born: and when I passed by thee, and saw thee polluted in thine own blood, I said unto thee, Live; yea, I said unto thee, when thou wast in thy blood, Live." Now also, when thou passedst by, and sawest Matthew sitting at the receipt of custom, thou saidst to him, " Follow me." The life of this publican was so much worse than the birth of that forlorn Amorite, as Follow me was more than Live. What canst thou see in us, O God, but ugly deformities, horrible sins, despicable miseries? yet doth it please thy mercy to say unto us, both 'Live' and 'Follow me.'

The just man is the first accuser of himself: whom do we hear to blazon the shame of Matthew but his own mouth? Matthew the Evangelist tells us of Matthew the publican? his fellows call him Levi, as willing to lay their finger upon the spot of his unpleasing profession; himself will not smother nor blanch it a whit, but publishes it to all the world, in a thankful recognition of the mercy that called him, as liking well that his baseness should serve for a fit foil to set off the glorious lustre of his grace by whom he was elected. What matters it how vile we are, O God, so thy glory may arise in our abasement?

That word was enough, "Follow me;" spoken by the same tongue that said to the corpse at Nain, "Young man, I say to thee, arise." He that said at first, " Let there be light," says now, "Follow me." That power sweetly inclines which could forcibly command: the force is not more unresistible than the inclination. When the sun shines upon the icicles, can they choose but melt and fall? when it looks into a dungeon, can the place choose but to be enlightened? Do we see the jet drawing up straws to it, the loadstone iron, and do we marvel if the omnipotent Saviour, by the influence of his grace, attract the heart of a publican? "He arose and followed him." We are all naturally averse from thee, O God; do thou but bid us follow thee, draw us by thy powerful word, and we shall run after thee. Alas! thou speakest and we sit still; thou speakest by thine outward word to our ear, and we stir not. Speak thou by the secret and effectual word of thy Spirit to our heart, the world cannot hold us down, Satan cannot stop our way, we shall arise and follow thee.

It was not a more busy than gainful trade that Matthew abandoned, to follow Christ into poverty; and now he cast away his counters, and struck his tallies, and crossed his books, and contemned his heaps of cash, in comparison of that better treasure which he foresaw lie open in that happy attendance. If any commodity be valued of us too dear to be parted with for Christ, we are more fit to be publicans than disciples. Our Saviour invites Matthew to a discipleship, Matthew invites him to a feast; the joy of his call makes him begin his abdication of the world in a banquet.

Here was not a more cheerful thankfulness in the inviter, than a gracious humility in the guest: the new servant bids his Master, the publican his Saviour, and is honoured with so blessed a presence. I do not find where Jesus was ever bidden to any table, and refused. If a Pharisee, if a publican invited him, he made not dainty to go. Not for the pleasure of the dishes; what was that to him who began his work in a whole Lent of days? but, as it was his meat and drink to do the will of his Father, for the benefit of so winning a conversation. If he sat with sinners, he converted them; if with converts, he confirmed and instructed them; if with the poor, he fed them; if with the rich in substance, he made them richer in grace. At whose board did he ever sit, and left not his host a gainer? The poor bridegroom entertains him, and hath his water-pots filled with wine. Simon the Pharisee entertains him, and hath his table honoured with the public remission of a penitent sinner, with the heavenly doctrine of remission. Zaccheus entertains him, salvation came that day to his house with the author of it. That presence made the publican a son of Abraham. Matthew is recompensed for his feast with an apostleship. Martha and Mary entertain him, and, besides divine instruction, receive their brother from the dead. O Saviour, whether thou feast us, or we feast thee, in both of them is blessedness!

Where a publican is the feast-master, it is no marvel if the guests be publicans and sinners. Whether they came alone out of the hope of that mercy which they saw their fellow had found, or whether Matthew invited them to be partners of that plentiful grace whereof he had tasted, I inquire not. Publicans and sinners will flock together, the one hateful for their trade, the other for their vicious life. Common contempt hath wrought them to an unanimity, and sends them to seek mutual comfort in that society which all others held loathsome and contagious. Moderate correction humbleth and shameth the offender, whereas a cruel severity makes men desperate, and drives them to those courses whereby they are more dangerously infected. How many have gone into the prison faulty, and returned flagitious! If publicans were not sinners, they were no whit beholden to their neighbours.

What a table-full was here! The Son of God beset with publicans and sinners. O happy publicans and sinners, that had found out their Saviour! O merciful Saviour, that disdained not publicans and sinners.

What sinner can fear to kneel before thee, when he sees publicans and sinners sit with thee? who can fear to be despised of thy meekness and mercy, which did not abhor to converse with the outcasts of men? Thou didst not despise the thief confessing upon the cross, nor the sinner weeping upon thy feet, nor the Canaanite crying to thee in the way, nor the blushing adulteress, nor the odious publican, nor the forswearing disciple, nor the persecutor of disciples, nor thine own executioners: how can we be unwelcome to thee, if we come with tears in our eyes, faith in our hearts, restitution in our hands? O Saviour, our breasts are too oft shut upon thee, thy bosom is ever open to us. We are as great sinners as the consorts of these publicans, why should we despair of a room at thy table?

The squint-eyed Pharisees look across at all the actions of Christ; where they should have admired his mercy, they cavil at his holiness; "They said to his disciples, Why eateth your Master with publicans and sinners?" They durst not say this to the Master, whose answer they knew would soon have convinced them: this wind, they hoped, might shake the weak faith of the disciples. They speak where they may be most likely to hurt. All the crew of satanical instruments have learned this craft of their old tutor in paradise. We cannot reverence that man whom we think unholy. Christ had lost the hearts of his followers, if they had entertained the least suspicion of his impurity, which the murmur of these envious Pharisees would fain insinuate; he cannot be worthy to be followed that is unclean: he cannot but be unclean that eateth with publicans and sinners. Proud and foolish Pharisees! ye fast while Christ eateth; ye fast in your houses, while Christ eateth in other men's; ye fast with your own, while Christ feasts with sinners: but if ye fast in pride, while Christ eats in humility—if ye fast at home for merit or popularity, while Christ feasts with sinners for compassion, for edification, for conversion, your fast is unclean, his feast is holy; ye shall have your portion with hypocrites, when those publicans and sinners shall be glorious.

When these censurers thought the disciples had offended, they speak not to them, but to their Master, "Why do thy disciples that which is not lawful?" now when they thought Christ offended, they speak not to him, but to the disciples. Thus, like true makebates, they go about to make a breach in the family of Christ, by setting off the one from the other. The quick eye of our Saviour hath soon espied the pack of their fraud, and therefore, he takes the words out of the mouths of his disciples into his own. They had spoke of Christ to the disciples, Christ answers for the disciples concerning himself, "The whole need not the physician, but the sick." According to the two qualities of pride, scorn and overweening, these insolent Pharisees overrated their own holiness, contemned the noted unholiness of others; as if themselves were not tainted with secret sins, as if others could not be cleansed by repentance. The Searcher of hearts meets with their arrogance, and finds those justiciaries sinful, those sinners just. The spiritual Physician finds the sickness of those sinners wholesome, the health of those Pharisees desperate: that wholesome, because it calls for the help of the physician; this desperate, because it needs not. Every soul is sick: those most that feel it not; those that feel it complain; those that complain, have cure; those that feel it not, shall find themselves dying ere they can wish to recover. O blessed Physician, by whose stripes we are healed, by whose death we live! Happy are they that are under thy hands, sick, as of sin, so of sorrow for sin. It is as impossible they should die, as it is impossible for thee to want either skill, or power, or mercy. Sin hath made us sick unto death: make thou us but as sick of our sins, we are as safe as thou art gracious.

CONTEMPLATION V. — CHRIST AMONG THE GERGESENES; OR LEGION AND THE GADARENE HERD.

I DO not any where find so furious a demoniac as amongst the Gergesenes: Satan is most tyrannous where he is obeyed most. Christ no sooner sailed over the lake, than he was met with two possessed Gadarenes: the extreme rage of the one hath drowned the mention of the other. Yet in the midst of all that cruelty of the evil spirit, there was sometimes a remission, if not an intermission of vexation. If ofttimes Satan caught him, then sometimes in the same violence he caught him not It was no thanks to that malignant one, who, as he was indefatigable in his executions, so unmeasurable in his malice; but to the merciful overruling of God, who, in a gracious respect to the weakness of his poor creatures, limits the spiteful attempts of that immortal enemy, and takes off this mastiff, while we may take breath. He who in his justice gives way to some onsets of Satan, in his mercy restrains them; so regarding our deservings, that withal he regards our strength. If way should be given to that malicious spirit, we could not subsist: no violent thing can endure; and, if Satan might have his will, we should no moment be free. He can be no more weary of doing evil to us, than God is of doing good. Are we therefore preserved from the malignity of these powers of darkness? " Blessed be our strong helper, that hath not given us over to be a prey unto their teeth:" or, if some scope have been given to that envious one to afflict us, hath it been with favourable limitations? it is thine only mercy, O God, that hath chained and muzzled up this ban-dog, so as that he may scratch us with his paws, but cannot pierce us with his fangs. Far, far is this from our deserts, who had too well merited a just abdication from thy favour and protection, and an interminable seizure by Satan, both in soul and body.

Neither do I here see more matter of thanks to our God, for our immunity from the external injuries of Satan, than occasion of serious inquiry into his power over us for the spiritual. I see some that think themselves safe from this ghostly tyranny, because they sometimes find themselves in good moods, free from the suggestions of gross sins, much more from the commission. Vain men, that feed themselves with so false and frivolous comforts! will they not see Satan, through the just permission of God, the same to the soul in mental possessions that he is to the body in corporal? The worst demoniac hath his lightsome respites, not ever tortured, not ever furious; betwixt whiles he might look soberly, talk sensibly, move regularly. It is a woful comfort, that we sin not always. There is no master so barbarous, as to require of his slave a perpetual unintermitted toil; yet, though he sometimes eat, sleep, rest, he is a vassal still. If that wicked one have drawn us to a customary perpetration of evil, and have wrought us to a frequent iteration of the same sin, this is gauge enough for our servitude, matter enough for his tyranny and insultation. He that would be our tormentor always, cares only to be sometimes our tempter.

The possessed is bound, as with the invisible fetters of Satan, so with the material chains of the inhabitants. What can bodily force prevail against a spirit? yet they endeavour this restraint of the man, whether out of charity or justice: charity, that he might not hurt himself; justice, that he might not hurt others. None do so much befriend the demoniac as those that bind him. Neither may the spiritually possessed be otherwise handled: for, though this act of the enemy be plausible, and to appearance pleasant, yet there is more danger in this dear and smiling tyranny. Two sorts of chains are fit for outrageous sinners: good laws, impartial executions; that they may not hurt, that they may not be hurt to eternal death.

These iron chains are no sooner fast than broken. There was more than a human power in this disruption. It is not hard to conceive the utmost of nature in this kind of actions. Samson doth not break the cords and ropes like a thread of tow, but God by Samson. The man doth not break these chains, but the Spirit. How strong is the arm of these evil angels! how far transcending the ordinary course of nature! They are not called powers for nothing. What flesh and blood could but tremble at the palpable inequality of this match, if herein the merciful protection of our God did not the rather magnify itself, that so much strength, met with so much malice, hath not prevailed against us! In spite of both, we are in safe hands. He that so easily brake the iron fetters can never break the adamantine chain of our faith. In vain do the chafing billows of hell beat upon that Rock whereon we are built; and though these brittle chains of earthly metal be easily broken by him, yet the sure-tempered chain of God's eternal decree he can never break. That Almighty Arbiter of heaven, and earth, and hell, hath chained him up in the bottomless pit, and hath so restrained his malice, that, but for our good, we cannot be tempted; we cannot be foiled, but for a glorious victory. Alas! it is no otherwise with the spiritually possessed. The chains of restraint are commonly broken by the fury of wickedness. What are the respects of civility, fear of God, fear of men, wholesome laws, careful executions, to the desperately licentious, but as cobwebs to a hornet? Let these wild demoniacs know, that God hath provided chains for them that will hold, even "everlasting chains under darkness." These are such as must hold the devils themselves, their masters, unto the judgment of the great day; how much more these impotent vassals! O that men would suffer themselves to be bound to their good behaviour, by the sweet and easy recognizances of their duty to their God, and the care of their own souls, that so they might rather be bound up in the bundle of life.

It was not for rest, that these chains were torn off, but for more motion. This prisoner runs away from his friends, he cannot run away from his jailer. He is now carried into the wilderness, not by mere external force, but by internal impulsion; carried by the same power that unbound him, for the opportunity of his tyranny, for the horror of the place, for the affamishment of his body, for the avoidance of all means of resistance. Solitary deserts are the delights of Satan. It is an unwise zeal that moves us to do that to ourselves in an opinion of merit and holiness, which the devil wishes to do to us for a punishment, and conveniency of temptation. The evil spirit is for solitariness; God is for society: "He dwells in the assembly of his saints, yea, there he hath a delight to dwell." Why should not we account it our happiness, that we may have leave to dwell where the Author of all happiness loves to dwell?

There cannot be any misery incident unto us, whereof our gracious Redeemer is not both conscious and sensible. Without any entreaty therefore of the miserable demoniac, or suit of any friend, the God of spirits takes pity of his distress; and, from no motion but his own, commands the evil spirit to come out of the man. O admirable precedent of mercy! preventing our requests, exceeding our thoughts, forcing favours upon our impotence, doing that for us which we should, and yet cannot desire! If men, upon our instant solicitations, would give us their best aid, it were a just praise of their bounty; but it well became thee, O God of mercy, to go without force, to give without suit: and do we think thy goodness is impaired by thy glory? If thou wert thus commiserative upon earth, art thou less in heaven? how dost thou now take notice of all our complaints, of all our infirmities? how doth thine infinite pity take order to redress them! what evil can befal us which thou knowest not, feelest not, relievest not? how safe are we that have such a guardian, such a Mediator in heaven!

Not long before, had our Saviour commanded the winds and waters, and they could not but obey him. Now he speaks in the same language to the evil spirit: he entreats not, he persuades not, he commands. Command argues superiority. He only is infinitely stronger than the strong one in possession; else, where powers are matched, though with some inequality, they tug for the victory, and, without a resistance, yield nothing. There are no fewer sorts of dealing with Satan than with men. Some have dealt with him by suit, as the old Satanian hereticks, and the present Indian savages, sacrificing to him that he hurt not; others by covenant, conditioning their service upon his assistance, as witches and magicians; others by insinuation of implicit compact, as charmers and figure-casters; others by adjuration, as the sons of Sceva and modern exorcists, unwarrantably charging him by a higher name than their own. None ever offered to deal with Satan by a direct and primary command, but the God of spirits. The great Archangel, when the strife was about the body of Moses, commanded not, but imprecated rather; "The Lord rebuke thee, Satan." It is only the God that made this spirit an angel of light, that can command him, now that he hath made himself the prince of darkness. If any created power dare to usurp a word of command, he laughs at their presumption, and knows them his vassals whom he dissembles to fear as his lords. It is thou only, O Saviour, at whose beck those stubborn principalities of hell yield and tremble. No wicked man can be so much a slave to Satan, as Satan is to thee. The interposition of thy grace may defeat that dominion of Satan: thy rule is absolute, and capable of no let. What need we to fear while we are under so omnipotent a commander! The waves of the deep rage horribly; yet the Lord is stronger than they. Let those principalities and powers do their worst: those mighty adversaries are under the command of him who loved us so well as to bleed for us. What can we now doubt of his power, or his will! how can we profess him a God, and doubt of his power! how can we profess him a Saviour, and doubt of his will! he both can and will command those infernal powers. We are no less safe than they are malicious.

The devil saw Jesus by the eyes of the demoniac; for the same saw that spake: but it was the ill spirit that said, "I beseech thee, torment me not." It was sore against his will that he saw so dreadful an object. The overruling power of Christ dragged the foul spirit into his presence. Guiltiness would fain keep out of sight. The limbs of so woful a head shall once call on the hills and rocks to hide them from the face of the Lamb: such lion-like terror is in that mild face, when it looks upon wickedness. Neither shall it be one day the least part of the torment of the damned, to see the most lovely spectacle that heaven can afford. He, from whom fled in his offers of grace, shall be so much more terrible, as he was, and is more gracious. I marvel not, therefore, that the devil, when he saw Jesus, cried out; I could marvel that he fell down, that he worshipped him. That which the proud spirit would have had Christ to have done to him in his great duel, the same he now doth unto Christ, fearfully, servilely, forcedly. Who shall henceforth brag of the external homage he performs to the Son of God, when he sees Satan himself fall down and worship? what comfort can there be in that which is common to us with devils, who, as they believe and tremble, so they tremble and worship? The outward bowing is the body of the action, the disposition of the soul is the soul of it; therein lies the difference from the counterfeit stoopings of wicked men and spirits. The religious heart "serves the Lord in fear, and rejoices in him with trembling:" what it doth is in way of service, in service to his Lord, whose sovereignty is his comfort and protection, in the fear of a son, not of a slave; in fear tempered with joy; in a joy, but allayed with trembling: whereas the prostration of wicked men and devils is only an act of form, or of force, as to their judge, as to their tormentor, not as to their Lord; in mere servility, not in reverence; in an uncomfortable dulness, without all delight; in a perfect horror, without capacity of joy,: these worship without thanks, because they fall down without the true affections of worship.

Whoso marvels to see the devil upon his knees, would much more marvel to hear what came from his mouth: "Jesu, the Son of the Most High God;" a confession, which, if we should hear without the name of the author, we should ask from what saint it came. Behold the same name given to Christ by the devil, which was formerly given him by the angel, "thou shalt call his name Jesus." That awful name, whereat every knee shall bow, in heaven, in earth, and under the earth, is called upon by this prostrate devil; and lest that should not import enough, since others have been honoured by this name, in type, he adds for full distinction, "The Son of the Most High God." The good Syrophenician, and blind Bartimeus, could say, "The Son of David,"

It was well to acknowledge the true descent of his pedigree according to the flesh: but this infernal spirit looks aloft, and fetcheth his line out of the highest heavens, "The Son of the Most High God." The famous confession of the prime apostle, which honoured him with a new name to immortality, was no other than, "Thou art the Christ, the Son of the living God:" and what other do I hear from the lips of a fiend? None more divine words could fall from the highest saint. Nothing hinders but that the veriest miscreant on earth, yea, the foulest devil in hell, may speak holily. It is no passing of judgment upon loose sentences. So Peter should have been cast for a Satan, in denying, forswearing, cursing; and the devil should have been set up for a saint, in confessing, "Jesus, the Son of the Most High God." Fond hypocrite, that pleasest thyself in talking well, hear this devil; and, when thou canst speak better than he, look to fare better: but in the meantime know, that a smooth tongue and a foul heart carry away double judgments.

Let curious heads dispute whether the devil knew Christ to be God. In this I dare believe himself, though in nothing else: he knew what he believed; what he believed that he confessed, "Jesus the Son of the Most High God:" to the confusion of those semi-christians, that have either held doubtfully, or ignorantly misknown, or blasphemously denied what the very devils have professed. How little can a bare speculation avail us in these cases of divinity! So far this devil hath attained to no ease, no comfort. Knowledge alone doth but puff up: it is our love that edifies. If there be not a sense of our sure interest in this Jesus, a power to apply his merits and obedience, we are no whit the safer, no whit the better; only we are so much the wiser, to understand who shall condemn us.

This piece of the clause was spoken like a saint, "Jesus, the Son of the Most High God!" the other piece like a devil, "What have I to do with thee?" If the disclamation were universal, the latter words would impugn the former: for, while he confesses Jesus to be the Son of the Most High God, he withal confesses his own inevitable subjection. Wherefore would he beseech, if he were not obnoxious? He cannot, he dare not say, What hast thou to do with me? but, "What have I to do with thee?" Others indeed I have vexed, thee I fear. In respect, then, of any violence, of any personal provocation, "What have I to do with thee?" And dost thou ask, O thou evil spirit, what hast thou to do with Christ, while thou vexest a servant of Christ? Hast thou thy name from knowledge, and yet so mistakest him whom thou confessest, as if nothing could be done to him, but what immediately concerns his own person? Hear that great and just Judge sentencing upon his dreadful tribunal, "Inasmuch as thou didst it unto one of these little ones, thou didst it unto me." It is an idle misprision, to sever the sense of an injury, done to any of the members, from the head.

He that had humility enough to kneel to the Son of God, hath boldness enough to expostulate, "Art thou come to torment us before our time?" Whether it were, that Satan, who useth to enjoy the torment of sinners, whose music it is to hear our shrieks and gnashings, held it no small piece of his torment to be restrained in the exercise of his tyranny; or whether the very presence of Christ were his wreck, (for the guilty spirit projecteth terrible things, and cannot behold the judge or the executioner without a renovation of horror;) or whether that, as himself professeth, he were now in a fearful expectation of being commanded down into the deep, for a further degree of actual torment, which he thus deprecates.

There are tortures appointed to the very spiritual natures of evil angels. Men that are led by sense, have easily granted the body subject to torment, who yet have not so readily conceived this incident to a spiritual substance. The Holy Ghost hath not thought it fit to acquaint us with the particular manner of these invisible acts, rather willing that we should herein fear than inquire. But as all matters of faith, though they cannot be proved by reason, for that they are in a higher sphere, yet afford an answer able to stop the mouth of all reason that dares bark against them, since truth cannot be opposite to itself; so this of the sufferings of spirits. There is therefore both an intentional torment incident to spirits, and a real: for, as in blessedness the good spirits find themselves joined unto the chief good, and hereupon feel a perfect love of God, and unspeakable joy in him, and rest in themselves; so contrarily, the evil spirits perceive themselves eternally excluded from the presence of God, and see themselves settled in a woful darkness; and from the sense of this separation arises a horror not to be expressed, not to be conceived. How many men have we known to torment themselves with their own thoughts! There needs no other gibbet than that which their troubled spirit hath erected in their own heart. And if some pains begin at the body, and from thence afflict the soul in a copartnership of grief, yet others arise immediately from the soul, and draw the body into a participation of misery. Why may we not, therefore, conceive mere and separate spirits capable of such an inward excruciation?

Besides which, I hear the judge of men and angels say, "Go, ye cursed, into everlasting fire, prepared for the devil and his angels." I hear the prophet say, "Tophet is prepared of old." If with fear, and without curiosity, we may look upon those flames, why may we not attribute a spiritual nature to that more than natural fire? In the end of the world the elements shall be dissolved by fire; and if the pure quintessential matter of the sky, and the element of fire itself, shall be dissolved by fire, then that last fire shall be of another nature than that which it consumeth. What hinders then, but that the omnipotent God hath from eternity created a fire of another nature, proportionable even to spiritual essences? or why may we not distinguish of fire, as it is itself a bodily creature, and as it is an instrument of God's justice, so working not by any material virtue or power of its own, but by a certain height of supernatural efficacy, to which it is exalted by the omnipotence of that supreme and righteous Judge? Or, lastly, why may we not conceive, that though spirits have nothing material in their nature, which that fire should work upon, yet by the judgment of the almighty Arbiter of the world, justly willing their torment, they may be made most sensible of pain, and by the obedible submission of their created nature, wrought upon immediately by their appointed tortures; besides the very horror which ariseth from the place whereto they are everlastingly confined: for, if the incorporeal spirits of living men may be held in a loathed or painful body, and conceive sorrow to be so imprisoned, why may we not as easily yield, that the evil spirits of angels or men may be held in those direful flames, and much more abhor therein to continue for ever? Tremble rather, O my soul, at the thought of this woful condition of the evil angels, who, for one only act of apostacy from God, are thus perpetually tormented; whereas we sinful wretches multiply many and presumptuous offences against the majesty of our God. And withal admire and magnify that infinite mercy to the miserable generation of man, which, after this holy severity of justice to the revolted angels, so graciously forbears our heinous iniquities, and both suffers us to be free for the time from these hellish torments, and gives us opportunity of a perfect freedom from them for ever. "Praise the Lord, O my soul, and all that is within me praise his holy name, who forgiveth all thy sins, and healeth all thine infirmities; who redeemeth thy life from destruction, and crowneth thee with mercy and compassions."

There is no time wherein the evil spirits are not tormented; there is a time wherein they expect to be tormented yet more: "Art thou come to torment us before our time?" They knew that the last assizes are the prefixed term of their full execution, which they also understood to be not yet come; for though they knew not when the day of judgment should be, a point concealed from the glorious angels of heaven, yet they knew when it should not be; and therefore they say, "Before the time." Even the very evil spirits confess, and fearfully attend a set day of universal sessions. They believe less than devils, that either doubt of, or deny that day of final retribution.

O the wonderful mercy of our God, that both to wicked men and spirits respites the utmost of their torment! He might, upon the first instant of the fall of angels, have inflicted on them the highest extremity of his vengeance; he might, upon the first sins of our youth, yea of our nature, have swept us away, and given us our portion in that fiery lake. He stays a time for both: though with this difference of mercy to us men, that here not only is a delay, but may be an utter prevention of punishment, which to the evil spirits is altogether impossible. They do suffer, they must suffer; and though they have now deserved to suffer all they must, yet they must once suffer more than they do.

Yet so doth this evil spirit expostulate, that he sues: "I beseech thee, torment me not." The world is well changed since Satan's first onset upon Christ. Then he could say, "If thou be the Son of God;" now, "Jesus, the Son of the Most High God;" then, "All these will I give thee, if thou wilt fall down and worship me;" now, "I beseech thee, torment me not." The same power, when he lifts, can change the note of the tempter to us. How happy are we that have such a Redeemer, as can command the devils to their chains! O consider this, ye lawless sinners, that have said, "Let us break his bands, and cast his cords from us." However the Almighty suffers you, for a judgment, to have free scope to evil, and he can now impotently resist the revealed will of your Creator: yet the time shall come, when ye shall see the very masters whom ye served, the powers of darkness, unable to avoid the revenges of God.

How much less shall man strive with his Maker? man, whose breath is in his nostrils, whose house is clay, whose foundation is the dust.

Nature teaches every creature to wish a freedom from pain. The foulest spirits cannot but love themselves, and this love must needs produce a deprecation of evil: yet what a thing is this, to hear the devil at his prayers! "I beseech thee torment me not." Devotion is not guilty of this, but fear. There is no grace in the suit of devils, but nature; no respect of glory to their Creator, but their own ease. They cannot pray against sin, but against torment for sin. What news is it now to hear the profanest mouth, in extremity, imploring the sacred name of God, when the devils do so? The worst of all creatures hates punishment, and can say, Lead me not into pain: only the good heart can say, "Lead me not into temptation." If we can as heartily pray against sin, for the avoiding of displeasure, as against punishment when we have displeased, there is true grace in the soul. Indeed, if we could fervently pray against sin, we should not need to pray against punishment, which is no other than the inseparable shadow of that body; but if we have not laboured against our sins, in vain do we pray against punishment. God must be just; and "the wages of sin is death."

It pleased our holy Saviour, not only to let fall words of command upon this spirit, but to interchange some speeches with him. All Christ's actions are not for example. It was the error of our grandmother to hold chat with Satan. That God, who knows the craft of that old serpent, and our weak simplicity, hath charged us not to inquire of an evil spirit. Surely, if the disciples, returning to Jacob's well, wondered to see Christ talk with a woman, well may we wonder to see him talking with an unclean spirit. Let it be no presumption, O Saviour, to ask upon what grounds thou didst this, wherein we may not follow thee. We know that sin was excepted, in thy conformity of thyself to us; we know there was no guile found in thy mouth, no possibility of taint in thy nature, in thine actions; neither is it hard to conceive, how the same thing may be done by thee without sin, which we cannot but sin in doing. There is a vast difference in the intention, in the agent; for, on the one side, thou didst not ask the name of the spirit, as one that knew not, and would learn by inquiring; but that, by the confession of that mischief which thou pleasedst to suffer, the grace of the cure might be the more conspicuous, the more glorious: so on the other, God and man might do that safely, which mere man cannot without danger. Thou mightst touch the leprosy, and not be legally unclean, because thou touchedst it to heal it, didst not touch it with possibility of infection. So mightst thou (who, by reason of the perfection of thy divine nature, wert incapable of any stain by the interlocution with Satan) safely confer with him, whom corrupt man, predisposed to the danger of such a parley, may not meddle with, without sin, because not without peril. It is for none but God to hold discourse with Satan. Our surest way is to have as little to do with that evil one as we may; and if he shall offer to maintain conference with us by his secret temptations, to turn our speech unto our God with the archangel, "The Lord rebuke thee, Satan."

It was the presupposition of him that knew it, that not only men but spirits have names. This then he asks, not out of an ignorance or curiosity (nothing could be hid from him, who calleth the stars and all the hosts of heaven by their names), but out of a just respect to the glory of the miracle he was working, whereto the notice of the name would not a little avail. For if, without inquiry or confession, our Saviour had ejected this evil spirit, it had passed for the single dispossession of one only devil; whereas now it appears, there was a combination and hellish champerty in these powers of darkness, which were all forced to vail unto that Almighty command.

Before, the devil had spoken singularly of himself, "What have I to do with thee," and "I beseech thee torment me not." Our Saviour, yet knowing that there was a multitude of devils lurking in that breast, who dissembled their presence, wrests it out of the spirit by this interrogation, "What is thy name?" Now can these wicked ones no longer hide themselves: he that asked the question forced the answer; "My name is Legion." The author of discord hath borrowed a name of war: from that military order of discipline, by which the Jews were subdued, doth the devil fetch his denomination. They were many, yet they say, My name, not Our name; though many, they speak as one, they act as one in this possession. There is a marvellous accordance even betwixt evil spirits. That kingdom is not divided, for then it could not stand. I wonder not that wicked men do so conspire in evil, that there is such unanimity in the broachers and abettors of errors, when I see those devils, which are many in substance, are one in name, action, habitation. Who can too much brag of unity, when it is incident unto wicked spirits? all the praise of concord is in the subject: if that be holy, the consent is angelical; if sinful, devilish.

What a fearful advantage have our spiritual enemies against us! If armed troops come against single stragglers, what hope is there of life, or victory? How much doth it concern us to band our hearts together in a communion of saints! Our enemies come upon us like a torrent: O let us not run asunder like drops in the dust! All our united forces will be little enough to make head against this league of destruction.

Legion imports order, number, conflict. Order, in that there is a distinction of regiment, a subordination of officers. Though in hell there be confusion of faces, yet not confusion of degrees. Number: Those that have reckoned a legion, at the lowest, have counted it six thousand, others have more than doubled it. Though here it is not strict, but figurative, yet the letter of it implies multitude. How fearful is the consideration of the number of apostate angels! and if a legion can attend one man, how many must we needs think are they, who, all the world over, are at hand to the punishment of the wicked, the exercise of the good, the temptation of both! It cannot be hoped there can be any place or time wherein we may be secure from the onsets of these enemies. Be sure, ye lewd men, ye shall want no furtherance to evil, no torment for evil. Be sure, ye godly, ye shall not want combatants to try your strength and skill. Awaken your courage to resist, and stir up your hearts; make sure the means of your safety. There are more with us than against us. The God of heaven is with us, if we be with him: and our angels behold the face of God. If every devil were a legion, we are safe. "Though we walk through the valley of the shadow of death, we shall fear no evil." Thou, O Lord, shalt stretch forth thine hand against the wrath of our enemies, and thy right hand shall save us.

Conflict: All this number is not for sight, for rest; but for motion, for action. Neither was there ever hour, since the first blow given to our first parents, wherein there was so much as a truce betwixt these adversaries. As, therefore, strong frontier towns, when there is a peace concluded on both parts, break up their garrisons, open their gates, neglect their bulwarks; but when they hear of the enemy mustering his forces in great and unequal numbers, then they double their guard, keep sentinel, repair their sconces: so must we, upon the certain knowledge of our numerous and deadly enemies in continual array against us, address ourselves always to a wary and strong resistance. I do not observe the most to think of this ghostly hostility. Either they do not find there are temptations, or those temptations hurtful: they see no worse than themselves; and if they feel motions of evil arising in them, they impute it to fancy, or unreasonable appetite, to no power but nature's; and those motions they follow without sensible hurt; neither see they what harm it is to sin. Is it any marvel that carnal eyes cannot discern spiritual objects? that the world, who is the friend, the vassal of Satan, is in no war with him? Elisha's servant, when his eyes were opened, saw troops of spiritual soldiers which before he discerned not. If the eyes of our souls be once enlightened by supernatural knowledge and the clear beams of faith, we shall as plainly descry the invisible powers of wickedness, as now our bodily eyes see heaven and earth. They are, though we see them not: we cannot be safe from them, if we do not acknowledge, nor oppose them.

The devils are now become great suitors to Christ, that he would not command them into the deep, that he would permit their entrance into the swine. What is this deep but hell, both for the utter separation from the face of God, and for the impossibility of passage to the region of rest and glory? The very evil spirits then fear, and expect a further degree of torment; they know themselves reserved in those chains of darkness for the judgment of the great day. There is the same wages due to their sins and to ours; neither are the wages paid till the work be done. They tempting men to sin, must needs sin grievously in tempting: as with us men, those that mislead into sin offend more than the actors. Not till the upshot, therefore, of their wickedness, shall they receive the full measure of their condemnation. This day, this deep, they tremble at: what shall I say of those men that fear it not? It is hard for men to believe their own unbelief. If they were persuaded of this fiery dungeon, this bottomless deep, wherein every sin shall receive a horrible portion with the damned, durst they stretch forth their hands to wickedness? No man will put his hand into a fiery crucible to fetch gold thence, because he knows it will burn him. Did we as truly believe the everlasting burning of that infernal fire, we durst not offer to fetch pleasures or profits out of the midst of those flames.

This degree of torment they grant in Christ's power to command; they knew his power irresistible: had he therefore but said, Back to hell, whence ye came! they could no more have staid upon earth, than they can now climb into heaven. O the wonderful dispensations of the Almighty! who, though he could command all the evil spirits down to their dungeons in an instant, so as they should have no more opportunity of temptation, yet thinks fit to retain them upon earth! It is not out of weakness or improvidence of that divine hand, that wicked spirits tyrannize here upon earth; but out of the most wise and most holy ordination of God, who knows how to turn evil into good, how to fetch good out of evil, and by the worst instruments to bring about his most just decrees. O that we could adore that awful and infinite Power, and cheerfully cast ourselves upon that Providence, which keeps the keys even of hell itself, and either lets out or returns the devils to their places!

Their other suit hath some marvel in moving it, more in the grant: " That they might be suffered to enter into the herd of swine." It was their ambition of some mischief that brought forth this desire; that since they might not vex the body of man, they might yet afflict men in their goods. The malice of these envious spirits reacheth from us to ours: it is sore against their wills, if we be not every way miserable. If the swine were legally unclean for the use of the table, yet they were naturally good. Had not Satan known them useful for man, he had never desired their ruin. But as fencers will seem to fetch a blow at the leg, when they intend it at the head, so doth this devil: while he drives at the swine, he aims at the souls of these Gadarenes: by this means he hoped well, and his hope was not vain, to work in these Gergesenes a discontentment at Christ, an unwillingness to entertain him, a desire of his absence; he meant to turn them into swine, by the loss of their swine. It was not the rafters or stones of the house of Job's children that he bore the grudge to, but to the owners; nor to the lives of the children, so much as to the soul of their father. There is no affliction wherein he doth not strike at the heart; which, while it holds free, all other damages are light: but "a wounded spirit (whether with sin or sorrow) who can bear?" Whatever becomes of goods or limbs, happy are we, if, like wise soldiers, we guard the vital parts. While the soul is kept sound from impatience, from distrust, our enemy may afflict us, he cannot hurt us.

They sue for a sufferance, not daring other than to grant, that, without the permission of Christ, they could not hurt a very swine. If it be fearful to think how great things evil spirits can do with permission, it is comfortable to think how nothing they can do without permission. We know they want not malice to destroy the whole frame of God's work, but of all, man; of all men, Christians: but if without leave they cannot set upon a hog, what can they do to the living images of their Creator? They cannot offer us so much as a suggestion, without the permission of our Saviour. And can he, that would give his own most precious blood for us, to save us from evil, wilfully give us over to evil?

It is no news that wicked spirits wish to do mischief; it is news that they are allowed it. If the owner of all things should stand upon his absolute command, who can challenge him for what he thinks fit to do with his creatures? The first foal of the ass is commanded under the law to have his neck broken. What is that to us? The creatures do that they were made for, if they may serve any way to the glory of their Maker. But seldom ever doth God leave his actions unfurnished with such reasons as our weakness may reach unto. There were sects amongst the Jews that denied spirits: they could not be more evidently, more powerfully convinced, than by this event. Now shall the Gadarenes see from what a multitude of devils they were delivered; and how easy it had been for the same power to have allowed these spirits to seize upon their persons as well as their swine. Neither did God this without a just purpose of their castigation. His judgments are righteous, where they are most secret. Though we cannot accuse these inhabitants of aught, yet he could, and thought good thus to mulct them. And if they had not wanted grace to acknowledge it, it was no small favour of God that he would punish them in their swine for that which he might have avenged upon their bodies and souls. Our goods are farthest off us: if but in these we smart, we must confess to find mercy.

Sometimes it pleaseth God to grant the suits of wicked men and spirits, in no favour to the suitors. He grants an ill suit, and withholds a good; he grants an ill suit in judgment, and holds back a good one in mercy. The Israelites ask meat; he gives quails to their mouths, and leanness to their souls.

The chosen vessel wishes Satan taken off, and hears only, " My grace is sufficient for thee." We may not evermore measure favours by condescent. These devils doubtless receive more punishment for that harmful act wherein they are heard. If we ask what is either unfit to receive, or unlawful to beg, it is a great favour of our God to be denied.

Those spirits, which would go into the swine by permission, go out of the man by command; they had staid long, and are ejected suddenly. The immediate works of God are perfect in an instant, and do not require the aid of time for their maturation. No sooner are they cast out of the man, than they are in the swine. They will lose no time, but pass without intermission from one mischief to another. If they hold it a pain not to be doing evil, why is it not our delight to be ever doing good? The impetuousness was no less than the speed: " The herd was carried with violence from a steep place down into the lake, and was choked." It is no small force that could do this: but if the swine had been so many mountains, these spirits, upon God's permission, had thus transported them. How easily can they carry those souls, which are under their power, to destruction? Unclean beasts, that wallow in the mire of sensuality; brutish drunkards, transforming themselves by excess; even they are the swine whom the Legion carries headlong to the pit of perdition.

The wicked spirits have their wish: the swine are choked in the waves. What ease is this to them? Good God! that there should be any creature that seeks contentment in destroying, in tormenting, the good creatures of his Maker! This is the diet of hell. Those fiends feed upon spite towards man, so much more as he doth more resemble his Creator; towards all other living substances, so much more as they may be more useful to man. The swine ran down violently: what marvel is it if their keepers fled? That miraculous work, which should have drawn them to Christ, drives them from him. They run with the news; the country comes in with the clamour : " The whole multitude of the country about besought him to depart." The multitude is a beast of many heads; every head hath a several mouth, and every mouth a several tongue, and every tongue a several accent; every head hath a several brain, and every brain thoughts of their own ; so as it is hard to find a multitude without some division ; at least, seldom ever hath a good motion found a perfect accordance: it is not so infrequent for a multitude to conspire in evil. Generality of assent is no warrant for any act. Common error carries away many, who inquire not into the reason of aught, but the practice. The way to hell is a beaten road, through the many feet that tread it. When vice grows into fashion, singularity is a virtue.

There was not a Gadarene found that either dehorted his fellows, or opposed the motion. It is a sign of a people given up to judgment, when no man makes head against projects of evil. Alas! what can one strong man do against a whole throng of wickedness? Yet this good comes of an unprevailing resistance, that God forbears to plague, where he finds but a sprinkling of faith. Happy are they, who, like unto the celestial bodies (which being carried about with the sway of the highest sphere, yet creep on their own ways), keep on the courses of their own holiness, against the swing of common corruptions; they shall both deliver their own souls, and help to withhold judgment from others.

The Gadarenes sue to Christ for his departure. It is too much favour to attribute this to their modesty, as if they held themselves unworthy of so divine a guest. Why then did they fall upon this suit in a time of their loss? why did they not tax themselves, and intimate a secret desire of that which they durst not beg? It is too much rigour to attribute it to the love of their hogs, and anger at their loss; then they had not entreated, but expelled him. It was their fear that moved this rash suit; a servile fear of danger to their persons, to their goods; lest he that could so absolutely command the devils, should have set these tormentors upon them; lest their other demoniacs should be dispossessed with like loss. I cannot blame these Gadarenes, that they feared. This power was worthy of trembling at; their fear was unjust: they should have argued, This man hath power over men, beasts, devils: it is good having him to our friend; his presence is our safety and protection. Now they contrarily misinfer, Thus powerful is he: it is good he were further off. What miserable and pernicious misconstructions do men make of God, of divine attributes and actions! God is omnipotent, able to take infinite vengeance of sin; O that he were not! he is provident, I may be careless; he is merciful, I may sin; he is holy, let him depart from me, for I am a sinful man. How witty sophisters are natural men, to deceive their own souls, to rob themselves of a God! O Saviour, how worthy are they to want thee, that wish to be rid of thee! Thou hast just cause to be weary of us, even while we sue to hold thee: but when once our wretched unthankfulness grows weary of thee, who can pity us to be punished with thy departure? who can say it is other than righteous, that thou shouldest retort one day upon us, "Depart from me, ye wicked?"

BOOK IV.

CONTEMPLATION I.—THE FAITHFUL CANAANITE.

It was our Saviour's trade to do good; therefore he came down from heaven to earth, therefore he changed one station of earth for another. Nothing more commends goodness than generality and diffusion; whereas, reservedness and close-handed restraint blemishes the glory of it. The sun stands not still in one point of heaven, but walks his daily round, that all the inferior world may share of his influences both in heat and light. Thy bounty, O Saviour, did not affect the praise of fixedness, but motion: one while I find thee at Jerusalem, then at Capernaum, soon after in the utmost verge of Galilee; never but doing good.

But as the sun, though he daily compass the world, yet never walks from under his line, never goes beyond the turning points of the longest and shortest day; so neither didst thou, O Saviour, pass the bounds of thine own peculiar people. Thou wouldst move, but not wildly; not out of thine own sphere, wherein thy glorified estate exceeds thine humbled, as far as heaven is above earth. Now thou art lift up, thou drawest all men unto thee: there are now no lists, no limits of thy gracious visitations; but as the whole earth is equidistant from heaven, so all the motions of the world lie equally open to thy bounty.

Neither yet did thou want outward occasions of thy removal. Perhaps the very importunity of the Scribes and Pharisees, in obtruding their traditions, drove thee thence; perhaps their unjust offence at thy doctrine. There is no readier way to lose Christ, than to clog him with human ordinances, than to spurn at his heavenly instructions. He doth not always subdue his spirit with his visible presence; but his very outward withdrawing is worthy of our sighs, worthy of our tears. Many a one may say, "Lord, if thou hadst been here, my soul had not died." Thou art now with us, O Saviour, thou art with us in a free and plentiful fashion: how long, thou knowest; we know our deservings, and fear. O teach us how happy we are in such a guest, and give us grace to keep thee! Hadst thou walked within the Phœnician borders, we could have told how to have made glad constructions of thy mercy in turning to the Gentiles: thou, that couldst touch the lepers without uncleanness, couldst not be defiled with aliens; but we know the partition-wall was not yet broken down, and that thou who didst charge thy disciples not to walk into the way of the Gentiles, wouldst not trangress thine own rule. Once we are sure thou camest to the utmost point of the bounds of Galilee; as not ever confined to the heart of Jewry, thou wouldst sometimes bless the outer skirts with thy presence. No angle is too obscure for the gospel: "The land of Zabulun, and the land of Naphthali, by the way of the sea beyond Jordan, Galilee of the Gentiles, the people which sat in darkness, saw great light." The sun is not scornful, but looks with the same face upon every plot of earth: not only the stately palaces and pleasant gardens are visited by his beams, but mean cottages, but neglected bogs and moors. God's word is, like himself, no excepter of persons; the wild Kern, the rude Scythian, the savage Indian, are alike to it. The mercy of God will be sure to find out those that belong to his election in the most secret corners of the world, likeas his judgments will fetch his enemies from under the hills and rocks. The good Shepherd walks the wilderness to seek one sheep strayed from many. If there be but one Syro-Phœnician soul to be gained to the church, Christ goes to the coasts of Tyre and Sidon to fetch her. Why are we weary to do good, when our Saviour underwent this perpetual toil in healing bodies and winning souls? There is no life happy, but that which is spent in a continual drudging for edification.

It is long since we heard of the name or nation of Canaanites: all the country was once so styled; that people are now forgotten; yet, because this woman was of the blood of those Phœnicians, which were anciently ejected out of Canaan, that title is revived to her. God keeps account of pedigrees, after our oblivion, that he may magnify his mercies by continuing them to thousands of the generations of the just, and by renewing favours upon the unjust. No nation carried such brands and scars of a curse, as Canaan. To the shame of those careless Jews, even a faithful Canaanite is a suppliant to Christ, while they neglect

THE FAITHFUL CANAANITE.

so great salvation. She doth not speak, but cry: need and desire have raised her voice to an importunate clamour. The God of mercy is light of hearing, yet he loves a loud and vehement solicitation; not to make himself inclinable to grant, but to make us capable to receive blessings. They are words and not prayers, which fall from careless lips. If we felt our want, or wanted not desire, we could speak to God in no tune but cries. If we would prevail with God, we must wrestle; and, if we would wrestle happily with God, we must wrestle first with our own dulness: nothing but cries can pierce heaven. Neither doth her vehemence so much argue her faith, as doth her compellation, "O Lord, thou Son of David." What proselyte, what disciple, could have said more? O blessed Syro-Phœnician, who taught thee this abstract of divinity? What can we Christians confess more than the deity and the humanity, the Messiahship of our glorious Saviour? his deity as Lord, his humanity as a Son, his Messiahship as the Son of David? Of all the famous progenitors of Christ, two are singled out by an eminence, David and Abraham, a king, a patriarch; and though the patriarch was first in time, yet the king is first in place; not so much for the dignity of the person, as the excellence of the promise, which, as it was both later and fresher in memory, so more honourable. To Abraham was promised multitude and blessing of seed, to David perpetuity of dominion. So as, when God promiseth not to destroy his people, it is for Abraham's sake; when not to extinguish the kingdom, it is for David's sake. Had she said, "The Son of Abraham," she had not come home to this acknowledgment. Abraham is the father of the faithful, David of the kings of Judah and Israel; there are many faithful, there is but one king; so as in this title she doth proclaim him the perpetual king of his church, the rod or flower which should come from the root of Jesse, the true and only Saviour of the world. Whoso would come unto Christ to purpose, must come in the right style; apprehending a true God, a true man, a true God and man: any of these severed from other, makes Christ an idol, and our prayers sin. Being thus acknowledged, what suit is so fit for him as mercy? "Have mercy on me." It was her daughter that was tormented, yet she says, " Have mercy on me." Perhaps her possessed child was senseless of her misery; the parent feels both her sorrow and her own. As she was a good woman, so a good mother. Grace and good nature have taught her to appropriate the afflictions of this divided part of her own flesh. It is not in the power of another skin to sever the interest of our own loins or womb. We find some fowls that burn themselves, while they endeavour to blow out the fire from their young; and even serpents can receive their brood into their mouth, to shield them from danger. No creature is so unnatural, as the reasonable that hath put off affection.

On me, therefore, in mine; "For my daughter is grievously vexed with a devil." It was this that sent her to Christ; it was this that must incline Christ to her. I doubt whether she had inquired after Christ, if she had not been vexed with her daughter's spirit. Our afflictions are as Benhadad's best counsellors, that sent him with a cord about his neck to the merciful king of Israel. These are the files and whetstones that set an edge on our devotions, without which they grow dull and ineffectual; neither are they stronger motives to our suit than to Christ's mercy. We cannot have a better spokesman unto God than our own misery; that alone sues, and pleads, and importunes for us. This, which sets off men, whose compassion is finite, attracts God to us. Who can plead discouragements in his access to the throne of grace, when our wants are our forcible advocates? All our worthiness is in a capable misery.

All Israel could not example the faith of this Canaanite; yet she was thus tormented in her daughter. It is not the truth or strength of our faith that can secure us from the outward and bodily vexations of Satan, against the inward and spiritual, that can and will prevail: it is no more antidote against the other, than against fevers and dropsies. How should it, when as it may fall out, that these sufferings may be profitable? and why should we expect that the love of our God shall yield to forelay any benefit to the soul? He is an ill patient that cannot distinguish betwixt an affliction, and the evil of affliction. When the messenger of Satan buffets us, it is enough that God hath said, "My grace is sufficient for thee."

Millions were in Tyre and Sidon, whose persons, whose children, were untouched with that tormenting hand: I hear none but this faithful woman say, "My daughter is grievously vexed of the devil." The worst of bodily afflictions are an insufficient proof of divine displeasure. She that hath most grace, complains of most discomfort.

Who would now expect any other than a kind answer to so pious and faithful a petition? and, behold, he answered her not a word. O holy Saviour! we have oft found cause to wonder at thy words, never till now at thy silence. A miserable suppliant cries and sues, while the God of mercies is speechless. He that comforts the afflicted, adds affliction to the comfortless by a willing disrespect. What shall we say then? Is the fountain of mercy dried up? O Saviour, couldst thou but hear! she did not murmur, nor whisper, but cry out: couldst thou but pity, but regard her, that was as good as she was miserable! If thy ears were open, could thy bowels be shut? Certainly it was thou that didst put it into the heart, into the mouth of this woman to ask, and to ask thus of thyself. She could never have said, "O Lord, thou Son of David," but from thee; but by thee. "None calleth Jesus the Lord, but by the Holy Ghost." Much more, therefore, didst thou hear the words of thine own making; and well wert thou pleased to hear what thou thoughtst good to forbear to answer. It was thine own grace that sealed up thy lips.

Whether for the trial of her patience and perseverance, for silence carried a semblance of neglect, and a willing neglect lays strong siege to the best fort of the soul; even calm tempers, when they have been stirred, have bewrayed impetuousness of passion: if there be any dregs in the bottom of the glass, when the water is shaken, they will be soon seen. Or whether for the more sharpening of her desires, and raising of her zealous importunity: our holy longings are increased with delays; it whets our appetite to be held fasting. Or whether for the more sweetening of the blessing, by the difficulty or stay of obtaining: the benefit that comes with ease is easily contemned; long and eager pursuits endear any favour. Or whether for the engaging of his disciples in so charitable a suit. Or whether for the wise avoidance of exception from the captious Jews. Or, lastly, for the drawing on of an holy and imitable pattern of faithful perseverance; and to teach us not to measure God's hearing of our suit by his present answer, or his present answer by our own sense. While our weakness expects thy words, thy wisdom resolves upon thy silence. Never wert thou better pleased to hear the acclamation of angels, than to hear this woman say, "O Lord, thou son of David;" yet silence is thy answer. When we have made our prayers, it is a happy thing to hear the report of them back from heaven; but if we always do not so, it is not for us to be dejected, and to accuse either our infidelity or thy neglect, since we find here a faithful suitor met with a gracious Saviour, and yet he answered her not a word. If we be poor in spirit, God is rich in mercy: he cannot send us away empty, yet he will not always let us feel his condescent, crossing us in our will, that he may advance our benefit.

It was no small fruit of Christ's silence, that the disciples were hereupon moved to pray for her; not for a mere dismission (it had been no favour to have required this, but a punishment; for if to be held in suspense be miserable, to be sent away with a repulse is more), but for a merciful grant. They saw much passion in the woman; much cause of passion: they saw great discouragement on Christ's part; great constancy on hers. Upon all these they feel her misery, and become suitors for her, unrequested. It is our duty, in case of necessity, to intercede for each other; and by how much more familiar we are with Christ, so much more to improve our interest for the relief of the distressed. We are bidden to say, Our Father, not mine; yea, being members of one body, we pray for ourselves in others. If the foot be pricked, the back bends, the head bows down, the eyes look, the hands stir, the tongue calls for aid; the whole man is in pain, and labours for redress. He cannot pray or be heard for himself, that is no man's friend but his own. No prayer without faith, no faith without charity, no charity without mutual intercession.

That which urged them to speak for her, is urged to Christ by them for her obtaining: "She cries after us." Prayer is as an arrow; if it be drawn up but a little, it goes not far; but if it be pulled up to the head, flies strongly, and pierces deep: if it be but dribbled forth of careless lips, it falls down at our foot; the strength of our ejaculation sends it up into heaven, and fetches down a blessing. The child hath escaped many a stripe by his loud crying; and the very unjust judge cannot endure the widow's clamour. Heartless motions do but teach us to deny; fervent suits offer violence, both to earth and heaven.

Christ would not answer the woman, but doth answer the disciples. Those that have a familiarity with God shall receive answers, when strangers shall stand out. Yea, even of domestics, some are more entire. He that lay in Jesus' bosom could receive that intelligence which was concealed from the rest. But who can tell whether that silence or this answer be more grievous? "I am not sent but to the lost sheep of the house of Israel." What is this answer, but a defence of that silence and seeming neglect? While he said nothing, his forbearance might have been supposed to proceed from the necessity of some greater thoughts; but now his answer professeth that silence to have proceeded from a willing resolution not to answer; and therefore he does not vouchsafe so much as to give to her the answer, but to her solicitors, that they might return his denial from him to her, who had undertaken to derive her suit to him: "I am not sent but to the lost sheep of the house of Israel." Like a faithful ambassador, Christ hath an eye to his commission. That may not be violated, though to an apparent advantage: whither he is not sent, he may not go. As he, so all his, have their fixed marks set; at these they aim, and think it not safe to shoot at rovers. In matter of morality, is not for us to stand only upon inhibitions, avoiding what is forbidden, but upon commands, endeavouring only what is enjoined. We need no other rule of our life than the intention of our several stations: and if he that was God, would take no further scope to himself than the limits of his commission, how much doth it concern us frail men to keep within compass? or what shall become of our lawlessness, that live in a direct contrariety to the will of him that sent us?

Israel was Jacob's name; from him derived to his posterity: till the division of the tribes under Jeroboam, all that nation was Israel; then the father's name went to the most, which were ten tribes; the name of the son, Judah, to the best, which were two. Christ takes no notice of this unhappy division; he remembers the ancient name which he gave to that faithful wrestler. It was this Christ with whom Jacob strove; it was he that wrenched his hip, and changed his name, and dismissed him with a blessing: and now he cannot forget his old mercy to the house of Israel, to that only doth he profess himself sent. Their first brood were shepherds, now they are sheep; and those not guarded, not impastured, but strayed and lost. O Saviour, we see thy charge, the house of Israel, not of Esau; sheep, not goats, not wolves; lost sheep, not securely impaled in the confidence of their safe condition. Woe were to us if thou wert not sent to us. He is not a Jew which is one without. Every Israelite is not a true one. We are not of thy fold, if we be not sheep, thou wilt not reduce us to thy fold, if we be not lost in our own apprehensions. O Lord, thou hast put a fleece upon our backs; we have lost ourselves enough: make us so sensible of our own wanderings, that we may find thee sent unto us, and may be happily found of thee.

Hath not this poor woman yet done? can neither the silence of Christ, nor his denial, silence her? is it possible she should have any glimpse of hope after so resolute repulses? Yet still, as if she saw no argument of discouragement, comes and worships, and cries, "Lord, help me!" She which could not in the house get a word of Christ, she that saw her solicitors, though Christ's own disciples, repelled, yet she comes. Before she followed, now she overtakes him; before she sued aloof, now she comes close to him: no contempt can cast her off. Faith is undaunted grace; it hath a strong heart, and a bold forehead: even very denials cannot dismay it, much less delays. She came not to face, not to expostulate, but to prostrate herself at his feet: her tongue worshipped him before, now her knee. The eye of her faith saw that divinity in Christ which bowed her to his earth. There cannot be a fitter gesture of man to God than adoration.

Her first suit was for mercy, now for help. There is no use of mercy but in helpfulness. To be pitied without aid, is but an addition to misery. Who can blame us, if we care not for an unprofitable compassion?

The very suit was gracious. She saith not, "Lord, if thou canst, help me," as the father of the lunatic; but professes the power, while she begs the act, and gives glory where she would have relief.

Who now can expect other than a fair and yielding answer to so humble, so faithful, so patient a suppliant? what can speed well, if a prayer of faith from the knees of humility succeeds not? and yet, behold, the further she goes, the worse she fares: her discouragement is doubled with her suit. "It is not good to take the children's bread, and to cast it to dogs." First, his silence implied a contempt, then his answer defended his silence, now his speech expresses and defends his contempt. Lo! he hath turned her from a woman to a dog, and, as it were, spurns her from his feet with a harsh repulse. What shall we say? Is the Lamb of God turned lion? doth that clear fountain of mercy run blood? O Saviour, did ever so hard a word fall from those mild lips? Thou calledst Herod fox most worthily; he was crafty and wicked: the Scribes and Pharisees a generation of vipers; they were venomous and cruel: Judas a devil; he was both covetous and treacherous. But here was a woman in distress, and distress challenges mercy; a good woman, a faithful suppliant, a Canaanitish disciple, a Christian Canaanite, yet rated and whipt out for a dog by thee, who wert all goodness and mercy! How different are thy ways from ours! Even thy severity argues favour. The trial had not been so sharp, if thou hadst not found the faith so strong, if thou hadst not meant the issue so happy. Thou hadst not driven her away as a dog, if thou hadst not intended to admit her for a saint; and to advance her as much for a pattern of faith, as thou depressedst her for a spectacle of contempt.

The time was when the Jews were children, and the Gentiles dogs; now the case is happily altered. The Jews are the dogs, (so their dear and divine countryman calls the concision); we Gentiles are the children. What certainty is there in an external profession, that gives us only to seem, not to be; at least, the being that it gives is doubtful and temporary. We may be children to-day, and dogs to-morrow. The true assurance of our condition is in the decree and covenant of God on his part; in our faith and obedience on ours. How they of children became dogs, it is not hard to say: their presumption, their unbelief transformed them; and, to perfect their brutishness, they set their fangs upon the Lord of life. How we of dogs become children, I know no reason. But, " O the depth!" That which at the first singled them out from the nations of the world, hath at last singled us out from the world and them. " It is not in him that willeth, nor in him that runneth, but in God that hath mercy." Lord, how should we bless thy goodness, that we of dogs are children! how should we fear thy justice, since they of children are dogs! O let us not be high-minded, but tremble. If they were cut off who crucified thee in thine humbled state, what may we expect who crucify thee daily in thy glory?

Now, what ordinary patience would not have been overstrained with so contemptuous a repulse? how few but would have fallen into intemperate passions, into passionate expostulations? Art thou the prophet of God, that so disdainfully entertainest poor suppliants? Is this the comfort that thou dealest to the distressed? is this the fruit of my humble adoration, of my faithful profession? Did I snarl or bark at thee, when I called thee the " Son of David?" did I fly upon thee otherwise than with my prayers and tears? And if this term were fit for my vileness, yet doth it become thy lips? Is it not sorrow enough to me, that I am afflicted with my daughter's misery, but that thou, of whom I hoped for relief, must add to mine affliction an unkind reproach? But here is none of all this. Contrarily, her humility grants all, her patience overcomes all, and she meekly answers, " Truth, Lord; yet the dogs eat of the crumbs which fall from their master's table." The reply is not more witty than faithful. O Lord, thou art truth itself; thy words can be no other than truth: thou hast called me a dog, and a dog I am; give me therefore the favour and privilege of a dog, that I may gather up some crumbs of mercy from under that table whereat thy children sit. This blessing, though great to me, yet to the infiniteness of thy power and mercy, is but as a crumb to a feast. I presume not to press to the board, but to creep under it. Deny me not those small offals, which else would be swept away in the dust. After this stripe, give me but a crumb, and I shall fawn upon thee, and depart satisfied. O woman, say I, great is thine humility, great is thy patience: but, " O woman," saith my Saviour, " great is thy faith." He seeth the root, we the stock. Nothing but faith could thus temper the heart, thus strengthen the soul, thus charm the tongue. O precious faith! O acceptable perseverance! It is no marvel if that chiding end in favour: " Be it to thee even as thou wilt." Never did such grace go away uncrowned. The beneficence had been strait, if thou hadst not carried away more than thou suedst for. Lo! thou that camest a dog, goest away a child! thou that wouldst but creep under the children's feet, art set at their elbow! thou, that wouldst have taken up with a crumb, art feasted with full dishes! The way to speed well at God's hand, is to be humbled in his eyes and in our own. It is quite otherwise with God and with men. With men we are so accounted of, as we account of ourselves. He shall be sure to be accounted vile in the sight of others, which is vile in his own. With God nothing is got by vain ostentation, nothing is lost by abasement. O God, when we look down to our own weakness, and cast up our eyes to thy infiniteness, thine omnipotence, what poor things we are! but when we look down upon our sins and wickedness, how shall we express our shame! None of all thy creatures, except devils, are capable of so foul a quality. As we have thus made ourselves worse than beasts, so let us, in a sincere humbleness of mind, acknowledge it to thee, who canst pity, forgive, and redress it; so setting ourselves down at the lower end of the table of thy creatures, thou the great Master of the feast mayst be pleased to advance us to the height of glory.

CONTEMPLATION II.—THE DEAF AND DUMB MAN CURED.

Our Saviour's entrance into the coasts of Tyre and Sidon was not without a miracle, neither was his egress; as the sun neither rises nor sets without light. In his entrance he delivers the daughter of the faithful Syro-Phœnician, in his egress he cures the deaf and dumb. He can no more want work, than that work can want success. Whether the patient were naturally deaf and perfectly dumb, or imperfectly dumb, and accidentally deaf, I labour not: sure I am, that he was so deaf that he could not hear of Christ; so dumb that he could not speak for himself. Good neighbours supply his ears, his tongue; they bring him to Christ. Behold a miracle led in by charity, acted by power, led out by modesty!

It was a true office of love to speak thus in the cause of the dumb, to lend senses to him that wanted. Poor man! he had nothing to entreat for him but his impotence; here was neither ear to inform, nor tongue to crave. His friends are sensible of his infirmity, and, unasked, bring him to cure: this spiritual service we owe to each other. It is true, we should be quick of hearing of the things of God and of our peace, quick of tongue to call for our helps; but, alas! we are naturally deaf and dumb to good. We have ear and tongue enough for the world: if that do but whisper, we hear it; if that do but draw back, we cry after it; we have neither ear for God: ever since our ear was lent to the serpent in Paradise, it hath been spiritually deaf; ever since we set our tooth in the forbidden fruit, our tongue hath been speechless to God: and that which was faulty in the root, is worse in the branches. Every soul is more deafened and bedumbed by increasing corruptions, by actual sins. Some ears the infinite mercy of God hath bored, some tongues he hath untied, by the power of regeneration: these are wanting to their holy faculties, if they do not improve themselves in bringing the deaf and dumb unto Christ.

There are some deaf and dumb upon necessity, some others upon affectation: those, such as live either out of the pale of the church, or under a spiritual tyranny within the church; we have no help for them but our prayers; our pity can reach further than our aid: these, such as may hear of a Christ and sue to him, but will not; a condition so much more fearful, as it is more voluntary. This kind is full of woful variety: while some are deaf by an outward obturation, whether by the prejudice of the teacher, or by secular occasions and distractions; others by the inwardly aposthuming tumours of pride, by the ill vapours of carnal affections, of froward resolutions: all of them, like the deaf adder, have their ears shut to the divine Charmer. O miserable condition of foolish men, so peevishly averse from their own salvation, so much more worthy of our commiseration, as it is more incapable of their own! These are the men whose cure we must labour, whom we must bring to Christ by admonitions, by threats, by authority, and, if need be, by wholesome compulsions.

They do not only lend their hand to the deaf and dumb, but their tongue also; they say for him that which he could not but wish to say for himself. Doubtless they had made signs to him of what they intended, and, finding him forward in his desires, now they speak to Christ for him. Every man lightly hath a tongue to speak for himself; happy is he that keeps a tongue for other men. We are charged not with supplications only, but with intercessions: herein is both the largest improvement of our love, and most effectual. No distance can hinder this fruit of our devotion. Thus we may oblige those that we shall never see, those that can never thank us. This beneficence cannot impoverish us; the more we give, we have still the more. It is a safe and happy store, that cannot be impaired by our bounty. What was their suit, but that Christ would put his hand upon the patient? not that they would prescribe the means, or imply a necessity of his touch; but for that they saw this was the ordinary course both of Christ and his disciples, by touching to heal. Our prayers must be directed to the usual proceedings of God: his actions must be the rule of our prayers; our prayers may not prescribe his actions.

That gracious Saviour, who is wont to exceed our desires, does more than they sue for: not only doth he touch the party, but takes him by the hand, and leads him from the multitude.

He that would be healed of his spiritual infirmities, must be sequestered from the throng of the world. There is a good use, in due times, of solitariness; that soul can never enjoy God, that is not sometimes retired. The modest Bridegroom of the church will not impart himself to his spouse before company. Or perhaps this secession was for our example, of a willing and careful avoidance of vain glory in our actions. Whence also it is, that our Saviour gives an aftercharge of secrecy. He that could say, "He that doeth evil hateth the light," escheweth the light even in good. To seek our own glory, is not glory. Although, besides this bashful desire of obscurity, here is a meet regard of opportunity in the carriage of our actions. The envy of the Scribes and Pharisees might trouble the passage of his divine ministry; their exasperation is wisely declined by this retiring. He in whose hands time is, knows how to make his best choice of seasons: neither was it our Saviour's meaning to have this miracle buried, but hid. Wisdom hath no better improvement than in distinguishing times, and discreetly marshalling the circumstances of our actions; which, whosoever neglects, shall be sure to shame his work, and mar his hopes.

Is there a spiritual patient to be cured? aside with him: to undertake him before the face of the multitude, is to wound, not to heal him.

Reproof and good counsel must be like our alms, in secret; so as, if possible, one ear or hand might not be conscious to other: as, in some cases, confession, so our reprehension must be auricular. The discreet chirurgeon that would cure a modest patient, whose secret complaint hath in it more shame than pain, shuts out all eyes save his own. It is enough for the God of justice to say, "Thou didst it secretly, but I will do it before all Israel, and before this sun." Our limited and imperfect wisdom must teach us to apply private redresses to private maladies: it is the best remedy that is least seen, and most felt.

What means this variety of ceremony. O Saviour, how many parts of thee are here active? Thy finger is put into the ear, thy spittle toucheth the tongue, thine eyes look up, thy lungs sigh, thy lips move to an Ephphatha: thy word alone, thy beck alone, thy wish alone, yea, the least act of velleity from thee, might have wrought this cure. Why wouldst thou employ so much of thyself in this work? Was it to show thy liberty, in not always equally exercising the power of thy deity? in that one while thine only command shall raise the dead, and eject devils; another while thou wouldst accommodate thyself to the mean and homely fashions of natural agents, and, condescending to our senses and customs, take those ways which may carry some more near respect to the cure intended? Or was it to teach us how well thou likest that there should be a ceremonious carriage of thy solemn actions, which thou pleasest to produce clothed with such circumstantial forms?

It did not content thee to put one finger into one ear, but into either ear wouldst thou put a finger: both ears equally needed cure; thou wouldst apply the means of cure to both. The Spirit of God is the finger of God: then dost thou, O Saviour, put thy finger into our ear, when thy Spirit enables us to hear effectually. If we thrust our own fingers into our ears, using such human persuasions to ourselves as arise from worldly grounds, we labour in vain: yea, these stopples must needs hinder our hearing the voice of God. Hence the great philosophers of the ancient world, the learned Rabbins of the synagogue, the great doctors of a false faith, are deaf to spiritual things. It is only that finger of thy Spirit, O blessed Jesus, that can open our ears, and make passage through our ears into our hearts. Let that finger of thine be put into our ears; so shall our deafness be removed, and we shall hear, not the loud thunders of the law, but the gentle whisperings of thy gracious motions to our souls.

We hear for ourselves, but we speak for others. Our Saviour was not content to open the ears only, but to untie the tongue. With the ear we hear, with the mouth we confess: the same hand is applied to the tongue, not with a dry touch, but with spittle: in allusion, doubtless, to the removal of the natural impediment of speech. Moisture, we know, glibs the tongue, and makes it apt to motion; how much more from that sacred mouth!

There are those whose ears are open, but their mouths are still shut to God; they understand, but do not utter the wonderful things of God. There is but half a cure wrought upon these men; their ear is but open to hear their own judgment, except their mouth be open to confess their Maker and Redeemer. O God, do thou so moisten my tongue with thy graces, that it may run smoothly, "as the pen of a ready writer," to the praise of thy name. While the finger of our Saviour was on the tongue, in the ear of the patient, his eye was in heaven. Never man had so much cause to look up to heaven as he: there was his home, there was his throne; He only was "from heaven, heavenly." Each of us hath a good mind homeward, though we meet with better sights abroad: how much more when our home is so glorious, above the region of our peregrination? But thou, O Saviour, hadst not only thy dwelling there, but thy seat of majesty; there the greatest angels adore thee; it is a wonder that thine eye could be ever any where but there. What doth thine eye in this, but teach ours where to be fixed? Every good gift, and every perfect gift, coming down from above, how can we look off from that place whence we receive all good? Thou didst not teach us to say, O infinite God, which art everywhere; but, "O our Father, which art in heaven." There let us look up to thee. O let not our eyes, our hearts, grovel upon this earth, but let us fasten them " above the hills, whence cometh our salvation:" thence let us acknowledge all the good we receive; thence let us expect all the good we want.

Why our Saviour looked up to heaven, though he had heaven in himself, we can see reason enough. But why did he sigh? Surely not for need: the least motion of a thought was in him impetratory: how could he choose but be heard by his Father, who was one with the Father? not for any fear of distrust, but partly for compassion, partly for example, for compassion of those manifold infirmities into which sin had plunged mankind, a pitiful instance whereof was here presented unto him: for example, to fetch sighs from us for the miseries of others, sighs of sorrow for them, sighs of desire for their redress. This is not the first time that our Saviour spent sighs, yea tears, upon human distresses. We are not bone of his bone, and flesh of his flesh, if we so feel not the smart of our brethren, that the fire of our passion break forth into the smoke of sighs. "Who is weak, and I am not weak? who is offended, and I burn not?"

Christ was not silent while he cured the dumb; his Ephphatha gave life to all these his other actions. His sighing, his spitting, his looking up to heaven, were the acts of a man; but his command of the ear and mouth to open, was the act of God. He could not command that which he made not; his word is imperative, ours supplicatory. He doth what he will with us; we do by him what he thinks good to impart.

In this mouth the word cannot be severed from the success. Our Saviour's lips are no sooner opened in his Ephphatha, than the mouth of the dumb and the ears of the deaf are opened. At once behold here celerity and perfection. Natural agents work by leisure, by degrees: nothing is done in an instant; by many steps is every thing carried from the entrance to the consummation. Omnipotence knows no rules: no imperfect work can proceed from a cause absolutely perfect. The man hears now more lightly, than if he had never been deaf; and speaks more plainly, than if he had never been tongue-tied: and can we blame him, if he bestowed the handsel of his speech upon the Power that restored it? if the first improvement of his tongue were the praise of the Giver, of the Maker of it? or can we expect other than that our Saviour should say, Thy tongue is free, use it to the praise of Him that made it so; thy ears are open, hear him that bids thee proclaim thy cure upon the house-top? But now, behold, contrarily, he that opens this man's mouth by his powerful word, by the same word shuts it again, charging silence by the same breath wherewith he gave speech: " Tell no man."

Those tongues, which interceded for his cure, are charged for the concealment of it. O Saviour, thou knowest the grounds of thine own commands; it is not for us to enquire, but to obey; we may not honour thee with a forbidden celebration. Good meanings have ofttimes proved injurious; those men, whose charity employed their tongues to speak for the dumb man, do now employ the same tongues to speak of his cure, when they should have been dumb. This charge, they imagine, proceeds from an humble modesty in Christ, which the respect to his honour bids them violate. I know not how we itch after those forbidden acts, which, if left to our liberty, we willingly neglect. This prohibition increaseth the rumour; every tongue is busied about this one: what can we make of this, but a well-meant disobedience? O God, I should more gladly publish thy name at thy command. I know thou canst not bid me to dishonour thee; there is no danger of such an injunction: but if thou shouldst bid me to hide the profession of thy name and wondrous works, I should fulfil thy words, and not examine thine intentions. Thou knowest how to win more honour by our silence, than by our promulgation. A forbidden good differs little from evil. What makes our actions to be sin, but thy prohibitions? our judgment avails nothing. If thou forbid us that which we think good, it becomes as faulty to theeward, as that which is originally evil. Take thou charge of thy glory; give me grace to take charge of thy precepts.

CONTEMPLATION III.—ZACCHEUS.

Now was our Saviour walking towards his passion. His last journey had most wonders. Jericho was in his way from Galilee to Jerusalem; he baulks it not, though it were outwardly cursed; but, as the first Joshua saved a Rahab there, so there the second saves a Zaccheus; that an harlot, this a publican. The traveller was wounded as he was going from Jerusalem to Jericho; this man was taken from his Jericho to the true Jerusalem, and was healed. Not as a passenger did Christ walk this way, but as a visitor; not to punish, but to heal. With us, the sick man is glad to send far for the physician; here the physician comes to seek patients, and calls at our door for work. Had not this good shepherd left the ninety-nine, and searched the desert, the lost sheep had never recovered the fold; had not his gracious frugality sought the lost groat, it had been swept up with the rushes, and thrown out in the dust. Still, O Saviour, dost thou walk through our Jericho: what would become of us, if thou shouldst stay till we seek thee alone? Even when thou hast found us, how hardly do we follow thee? The work must be all thine: we shall not seek thee, if thou find us not; we shall not follow thee, if thou draw us not.

Never didst thou, O Saviour, set one step in vain: wheresoever thou art walking, there is some Zaccheus to be won. As in a drought, when we see some weighty cloud hovering over us, we say there is rain for some grounds, wheresoever it falls: the ordinances of God bode good to some souls, and happy are they on whom it lights.

How justly is Zaccheus brought in with a note of wonder! It is both great and good news to hear of a convert. To see men perverted from God to the world, from truth to heresy, from piety to profaneness, is as common as lamentable; every night such stars fall: but to see a sinner come home to God, is both happy and wondrous to men and angels. I cannot blame that philosopher, who undertaking to write of the hidden miracles of nature, spends most of his discourse upon the generation and formation of man: surely we are "fearfully and wonderfully made!" But how much greater is the miracle of our spiritual regeneration, that a son of wrath, a child of Satan, should be transformed into the son and heir of the ever-living God! O God, thou workest both: but in the one, our spirit animates us; in the other, thine own.

Yet some things, which have wonder in them for their worth, lose it for their frequence; this hath no less rarity in it than excellence. How many painful Peters have complained to fish all night, and catch nothing! Many professors, and few converts, hath been ever the lot of the gospel God's house, as the streets of Jericho, may be thronged, and yet but one Zaccneus. As, therefore, in the lottery, when the great prize comes, the trumpet sounds before it; so the news of a convert is proclaimed with "Behold Zaccheus!" Any penitent had been worthy of a shout; but this man, by an eminence, a publican, a chief of the publicans, rich.

No name under heaven was so odious as this of a publican; especially to this nation, that stood so high upon their freedom, that every impeachment of it seemed no less than damnable; insomuch as they ask not, Is it fit, or needful? but, "Is it lawful to pay tribute unto Cæsar?" Any office of exaction must needs be heinous to a people so impatient of the yoke; and yet not so much the trade, as the extortion, drew hatred upon this profession: out of both they are deeply infamous. One while they are matched with heathens, another while with harlots, always with sinners: "And behold Zaccheus, a publican." We are all naturally strangers from God; the best is indisposed to grace: yet some there are, whose very calling gives them better advantages. But this catchpollship of Zaccheus carried extortion in the face, and, in a sort, bade defiance to his conversion; yet, behold, from this tolbooth is called both Zaccheus to be a disciple, and Matthew to be an apostle. We are in the hand of a cunning workman, that, of the knottiest and crookedest timber can make rafters and ceiling for his own house; that can square the marble or flint, as well as the freest stone. Who can now plead the disadvantage of his place, when he sees a publican come to Christ? No calling can prejudice God's gracious election.

To excel in evil must needs be worse: If to be a publican be ill, surely to be an arch-publican is more. What talk we of the chief of publicans, when he that professed himself the chief of sinners, is now among the chief of saints? who can despair of mercy, when he sees one Jericho send both an harlot and a publican to heaven?

The trade of Zaccheus was not a greater rub in his way, than his wealth. He that sent word to John for great news, that "The poor receive the gospel," said also, "How hard is it for a rich man to enter into heaven!" This bunch of the camel keeps him from passing the needle's eye; although not by any malignity that is in the creature itself—(riches are the gift of God), but by reason of these three pernicious hang-byes, cares, pleasures, pride, which too commonly attend upon wealth:

separate these, riches are a blessing. If we can so possess them, that they possess not us, there can be no danger, much benefit, in abundance: all the good or ill of wealth or poverty, is in the mind, in the use. He that hath a free and lowly heart in riches is poor; he that hath a proud heart under rags, is rich. If the rich man do good and distribute, and the poor man steal, the rich hath put off his woe to the poor. Zaccheus had never been so famous a convert, if he had been poor; nor so liberal a convert, if he had not been rich. If more difficulty, yet more glory, was in the conversion of rich Zaccheus.

It is well that rich Zaccheus was desirous to see Christ. Little do too many rich men care to see that sight; the face of Cæsar on their coin is more pleasing. This man leaves his bags, to bless his eyes with this prospect. Yet can I not praise him for this too much; it was not, I fear, out of faith, but curiosity: he that had heard great fame of the man, of his miracles, would gladly see his face; even a Herod longed for this, and was never the better. Only this I find, that this curiosity of the eye, through the mercy of God, gave occasion to the belief of the heart. He that desires to see Jesus, is in the way to enjoy him; there is not so much as a remote possibility in the man that cares not to behold him. The eye were ill bestowed, if it were only to betray our souls; there are no less beneficial glances of it. We are not worthy of this useful casement of the heart, if we do not thence send forth beams of holy desires, and thereby re-convey profitable and saving objects.

I cannot marvel if Zaccheus were desirous to see Jesus; all the world was not worth this sight. Old Simeon thought it best to have his eyes closed up with this spectacle, as if he held it pity and disparagement to see aught after it. The father of the faithful rejoiced to see him, though at nineteen hundred years' distance; and the great doctor of the Gentiles stands upon this as his highest stair: "Have I not seen the Lord Jesus?" And yet, O Saviour, many a one saw thee here, that shall never see thy face above; yea, that shall call to the hills to hide them from thy sight: and, " If we had once known thee according to the flesh, henceforth know we thee so no more." What a happiness shall it be, so to see thee glorious, that in seeing thee we shall partake of thy glory! O blessed vision, to which all others are but penal and despicable! Let me go into the mint-house, and see heaps of gold, I am never the richer; let me go to the pictures, and see goodly faces, I am never the fairer; let me go to the court, I see state and magnificence, and am never the greater: but, O Saviour, I cannot see thee, and not be blessed. I can see thee here, though in a glass; if the eye of my faith be dim, yet it is sure. O let me be unquiet, till I do now see thee through the veil of heaven, ere I shall see thee as I am seen!

Fain would Zaccheus see Jesus, but he could not: it were strange, if a man should not find some let in good desires; somewhat will be still in the way betwixt us and Christ. Here are two hinderances met, the one internal, the other external; the stature of the man, the press of the multitude; the greatness of the press, the smallness of the stature. There was great thronging in the streets of Jericho to see Jesus; the doors, the windows, the bulks, were all full. Here are many beholders, few disciples. If gazing, if profession, were godliness, Christ would not want clients; now, amongst all these wonderers, there is but one Zaccheus. In vain should we boast of our forwardness to see and hear Christ in our streets, if we receive him not into our hearts.

This crowd hides Christ from Zaccheus. Alas! how common a thing it is, by the interposition of the throng of the world, to be kept from the sight of our Jesus! Here a carnal fashionist says, Away with this austere scrupulousness! let me do as the most: the throng keeps this man from Christ. There a superstitious misbeliever says, What tell ye me of an handful of reformed? the whole world is ours: this man is kept from Christ by the throng. The covetous mammonist says, Let them that have leisure, be devout; my employments are many, my affairs great: this man cannot see Christ for the throng. There is no perfect view of Christ but in a holy secession. The spouse found not her beloved, till she was passed the company; then she found him whom her soul loved. Whoso never seeks Christ but in the crowd, shall never find comfort in finding him; the benefit of our public view must be enjoyed in retiredness. If in a press, we see a man's face, that is all; when we have him alone, every limb may be viewed. O Saviour, I would be loath not to see thee in thine assemblies; but I would be more loath not to see thee in my closet. Yet, had Zaccheus been but of the common pitch, he might perhaps have seen Christ's face over his fellow's shoulders; now his stature adds to the disadvantage: his body did not an swer to his mind; his desires were high, while his body was low. The best is, however smallness of stature was disadvantageous in a level, yet it is not so at a height. A little man, if his eye be clear, may look as high, though not as far, as the tallest: the least pigmy may, from the lowest valley, see the sun or stars as fully as a giant upon the highest mountain. O Saviour, thou art now in heaven: the smallness of our person, or of our condition, cannot let us from beholding thee. The soul hath no stature, neither is heaven to be had with reaching: only clear thou the eyes of my faith, and I am high enough.

I regard not the body; the soul is the man. It is to small purpose that the body is a giant, if the soul be a dwarf. We have to do with a God that measures us by our desires, not by our statures. All the streets of Jericho, however he seemed to the eye, had not so tall a man as Zaccheus.

The witty publican easily finds both his hinderances and the ways of their redress. His remedy for the press is to run before the multitude; his remedy for his stature is to climb up into the sycamore: he employs his feet in the one, his hands and feet in the other. In vain shall he hope to see Christ, that doth not outgo the common throng of the world. The multitude is clustered together, and moves too close to move fast: we must be nimbler than they, if ever we desire or expect to see Christ. It is the charge of God, "Thou shalt not follow a multitude to do evil:" we do evil if we lag in good. It is held commonly both wit and state for a man to keep his pace; and that man escapes not censure, who would be forwarder than his fellows. Indeed, for a man to run alone in ways of indifferency, or to set a hypocritical face in outrunning all others in a zealous profession, when the heart lingers behind, both these are justly hateful: but in a holy emulation, to strive truly and really to outstrip others in degrees of grace, and a conscionable care of obedience, this is truly Christian, and worthy of him that would hope to be blessed with the sight of a Saviour.

Tell me, ye fashionable Christians, that stand upon terms of equality, and will not go a foot before your neighbours in holy zeal and aidful charity, in conscionable sincerity, tell me, who hath made other men's progress a measure of yours? Which of you says, I will be no richer, no greater, no fairer, no wiser, no happier than my fellows? Why should you then say, I will be no holier? Our life is but a race; every good end that a man proposes to himself is a several goal: did ever any man that ran for a prize say, I will keep up with the rest; doth he not know that if he be not foremost, he loseth? We had as good to have sat still, as not "so to run that we may obtain." We obtain not, if we outrun not the multitude.

So far did Zaccheus overrun the stream of the people, that he might have space to climb the sycamore ere Jesus could pass by. I examine not the kind, the nature, the quality of this plant: what tree soever it had been, Zaccheus would have tried to scale it, for the advantage of this prospect; he hath found out this help for his stature, and takes pains to use it. It is the best improvement of our wit, to seek out the aptest furtherances for our souls. Do you see a weak and studious Christian, that being unable to inform himself in the matters of God, goes to the cabinet of heaven, "the priest's lips, which shall preserve knowledge;" there is Zaccheus in the sycamore: it is the truest wisdom that helps forward our salvation. How witty we are to supply all the deficiencies of nature! If we be low, we can add cubits to our stature; if ill coloured, we can borrow complexion; if hairless, perukes; if dim-sighted, glasses; if lame, crutches: and shall we be conscious of our spiritual wants, and be wilfully regardless of the remedy? Surely, had Zaccheus stood still on the ground, he had never seen Christ; had he not climbed the sycamore, he had never climbed into heaven. O Saviour, I have not height enough of my own to see thee; give me what sycamore thou wilt, give me grace to use it, give me a happy use of that grace.

The more I look at the mercy of Christ, the more cause I see of astonishment. Zaccheus climbs up into the sycamore to see Jesus; Jesus first sees him, preventing his eyes with a former view. Little did Zaccheus look that Jesus would have cast up his eyes to him. Well might he think, the boys in the street would spy him out, and shout at his stature, trade, ambition; but that Jesus should throw up his eyes into the sycamore, and take notice of that small despised morsel of flesh, ere Zaccheus could find space to distinguish his face from the rest, was utterly beyond his thought or expectation; all his hope is to see, and now he is seen: to be seen and acknowledged, is much more than to see. Upon any solemn occasion, many thousands see the prince, whom he sees not; and, if he please to single out any one, whether by his eye or by his tongue, amongst the press, it passes for a high favour. Zaccheus would have thought it too much boldness to have asked what was given him. As Jonathan did to David, so doth God to us; he shoots beyond us: did he not prevent us with mercy, we might climb into the sycamore in vain. If he give grace to him that doth his best, it is the praise of the giver, not the earning of the receiver. How can we do or will without him? If he sees us first, we live; and if we desire to see him, we shall be seen of him. Who ever took pains to climb the sycamore, and came down disappointed? O Lord, what was there in Zaccheus, that thou shouldst look up at him? a publican, a sinner, an arch extortioner; a dwarf in stature, but a giant in oppression; a little man, but a great sycophant; if rich in coin, more rich in sins and treasures of wrath: yet it is enough that he desires to see thee; all these disadvantages cannot hide him from thee. Be we never so sinful, if our desires towards thee be hearty and fervent, all the broad leaves of the sycamore cannot keep off thine eye from us. If we look at thee with the eye of faith, thou wilt look at us with the eye of mercy: "The eye of the Lord is upon the just," and he is just that would be so; if not in himself, yet in thee. O Saviour, when Zaccheus was above, and thou wert below, thou didst look up at him; now thou art above and we below, thou lookest down upon us; thy mercy turns thine eyes every way towards our necessities. Look down upon us that are not worthy to look up unto thee, and find us out, that we may seek thee.

It was much to note Zaccheus; it was more to name him. Methinks I see how Zaccheus startled at this, to hear the sound of his own name from the mouth of Christ; neither can he but think, Doth Jesus know me? is it his voice, or some others in the throng? Lo, this is the first sight that ever I had of him. I have heard the fame of his wonderful works, and held it happiness enough in me to have seen his face; and doth he take notice of my person, of my name? Surely, the more that Zaccheus knew himself, the more doth he wonder that Christ should know him. It was slander enough for a man to be a friend to a publican; yet Christ gives this friendly compellation to the chief of publicans, and honours him with this argument of a sudden entireness. The favour is great, but not singular; every elect of God is thus graced: the Father knows the child's name: as he calls the stars of heaven by their names, so doth he his saints, the stars on earth; and it is his own rule to his Israel,

"I have called thee by thy name; thou art mine." As God's children do not content themselves with a confused knowledge of him, but aspire to a particular apprehension and sensible application, so doth God again to them: it is not enough that he knows them, as in the crowd (wherein we see many persons, none distinctly), but he takes single and several knowledge of their qualities, conditions, motions, events. What care we that our names are obscure or contemned amongst men, while they are regarded by God; that they are raked up in the dust of earth, while they are recorded in heaven.

Had our Saviour said no more but, Zaccheus, "come down," the poor man would have thought himself taxed for his boldness and curiosity: it were better to be unknown, than noted for miscarriage. But now the next words comfort him: "For I must this day abide at thine house." What a sweet familiarity was here! as if Christ had been many years acquainted with Zaccheus, whom he now first saw. Besides our use, the host is invited by the guest, and called to an unexpected entertainment. Well did our Saviour hear Zaccheus' heart inviting him, though his mouth did not: desires are the language of the soul; those are heard by Him that is the God of spirits.

We dare not do thus to each other, save where we have eaten much salt; we scarce go where we are invited: though the face be friendly, and the entertainment great, yet the heart may be hollow. But here, He, that saw the heart, and foreknew his welcome, can boldly say, "I must this day abide at thine house." What a pleasant kind of entire familiarity there is betwixt Christ and a good heart! "If any man open, I will come in and sup with him." It is much for the King of Glory to come into a cottage, and sup there; yet thus he may do, and take some state upon him in sitting alone. No, "I will so sup with him, that he shall sup with me." Earthly state consists in strangeness, and affects a stern kind of majesty aloof. Betwixt God and us, though there be infinite more distance, yet there is a gracious affability, and a familiar entireness of conversation. O Saviour, what dost thou else every day, but invite thyself to us in thy word, in thy sacrament! Who are we, that we should entertain thee, or thou us! dwarfs in grace, great in nothing but unworthiness! Thy praise is worthy to be so much the more, as our worth is less. Thou that biddest thyself to us, bid us be fit to receive thee, and, in receiving thee, happy.

How graciously doth Jesus still prevent the publican, as in his sight, notice, compellation, so in his invitation too! That other publican, Levi, bade Christ to his house, but it was after Christ had bidden him to his discipleship. Christ had never been called to his feast, if Levi had not been called into his family. He loved us first, he must first call us; for he calls us out of love. As in the general calling of Christianity, if he did not say, "Seek ye my face," we could never say, "Thy face, Lord, will I seek:" so, in the specialities of our main benefits or employments, Christ must begin to us. If we invite ourselves to him, before he invite himself to us, the undertaking is presumptuous, the success unhappy.

If Nathanael, when Christ named him, and gave him the memorial-token of his being under the fig-tree, could say, "Thou art the son of God;" how could Zaccheus do less in hearing himself upon this wild fig-tree named by the same lips? How must he needs think, if he knew not all things, he could not know me; and if he knew not the hearts of men, he could not have known my secret desires to entertain him? He is a God that knows me, and a merciful God that invites himself to me: no marvel, therefore, if, upon this thought, Zaccheus came down in haste. Our Saviour said not, Take thy leisure, Zaccheus, but, "I will abide at thine own house to-day." Neither did Zaccheus, upon this intimation, sit still and say, When the press is over, when I have done some errands of my office; but he hastes down to receive Jesus. The notice of such a guest would have quickened his speed without a command: God loves not slack and lazy executions. The angels of God are described with wings, and we pray to do his will with their forwardness: yea, even to Judas, Christ saith, "What thou dost, do quickly." O Saviour, there is no day wherein thou dost not call us by the voice of thy gospel. What do we still lingering in the sycamore? How unkindly must thou needs take the delays of our conversion! Certainly, had Zaccheus staid still in the tree, thou hadst baulked his house as unworthy of thee. What construction canst thou make of our wilful dilations, but as a stubborn contempt? how canst thou but come to us in vengeance, if we come not down to entertain thee in a thankful obedience?

Yet do I not hear thee say, Zaccheus, cast thyself down for haste (this was the counsel of the tempter to thee), but, "Come down in haste," and he did accordingly. There must be no more haste than good speed in our performances: we may offend as well in our heady acceleration, as in our delay. Moses ran so fast down the hill, that he stumbled spiritually, and brake the tables of God: we may so fast follow after justice, that we outrun charity. It is an unsafe obedience that is not discreetly and leisurely speedful.

The speed of his descent was not more than the alacrity of his entertainment: "He made haste, and came down, and received him joyfully." The life of hospitality is cheerfulness: let our cheer be never so great, if we do not read our welcome in our friend's face, as well as in his dishes, we take no pleasure in it.

Can we marvel that Zaccheus received Christ joyfully? Who would not have been glad to have his house, yea, himself, made happy with such a guest? Had we been in the stead of this publican, how would our hearts have leaped within us for joy of such a presence? How many thousand miles are measured by some devout Christians, only to see the place where his feet stood? how much happier must he needs think himself, that owns the roof that receives him? But, O the incomparable happiness, then, of that man whose heart receives him, not for a day, not for years of days, not for millions of years, but for eternity! This may be our condition, if we be not straitened in our own bowels. O Saviour, do thou welcome thyself to these houses of clay, that we may receive a joyful welcome to thee in those everlasting habitations.

Zaccheus was not more glad of Christ, than the Jews were discontented. Four vices met here at once; envy, scrupulousness, ignorance, pride: their eye was evil, because Christ's was good. I do not hear any of them invite Christ to his home, yet they snarl at the honour of this unworthy host: they thought it too much happiness for a sinner, which themselves willingly neglected to sue for. Wretched men! they cannot see the mercy of Christ, for being bleared with the happiness of Zaccheus; yea, that very mercy which they see torments them. If that viper be the deadliest which feeds the sweetest, how poisonous must this disposition needs be, that feeds upon grace!

What a contrariety there is betwixt good angels and evil men! the angels rejoice at that whereat men pout and stomach; men are ready to cry and burst for anger, at that which makes music in heaven. O wicked and foolish elder brother, that feeds on hunger and his own heart without doors, because his younger brother is feasting on the fat calf within!

Besides envy, they stand scrupulously upon the terms of traditions. These sons of the earth might not be conversed with; their threshold was unclean : "Touch me not, for I am holier than thou." That he, therefore, who went for a prophet, should go to the house of a publican and sinner, must needs be a great eyesore. They that might not go in to a sinner, cared not what sins entered into themselves; the true cousins of those hypocrites, who held it a pollution to go into the judgment hall, no pollution to murder the Lord of life. There cannot be a greater argument of a false heart, than to stumble at these straws, and to leap over the blocks of gross impiety. Well did our Saviour know how heinously offensive it would be to turn in to this publican ; he knows, and regards it not : a soul is to be won; what cares he for idle misconstruction? Morally good actions must not be suspended upon danger of causeless scandal. In things indifferent and arbitrary, it is fit to be overruled by fear of offence; but if men will stumble on the plain ground of good, let them fall without our regard, not without their own peril. I know not if it were not David's weakness to "abstain from good words while the wicked were in place." Let justice be done in spite of the world, and, in spite of hell, mercy.

Ignorance was in part guilty of these scruples: they thought Christ either too holy to go to a sinner, or in going made unholy. Foolish men! to whom came he? to you righteous? let himself speak : " I came not to call the righteous, but sinners to repentance." Whether should the physician go but to the sick; "the whole need him not." Love is the best attractive of us; and "he to whom much is forgiven loves much."

O Saviour, the glittering palaces of proud justiciaries are not for thee; thou lovest the lowly and ragged cottage of a contrite heart. Neither could here be any danger of thy pollution: thy sun could cast his beams upon the impurest dunghill, and not be tainted. It was free and safe for the leper and bloody-fluxed to touch thee: thou couldst heal them; they could not infect thee. Neither is it otherwise in this moral contagion. We, who are obnoxious to evil, may be insensibly defiled: thy purity was enough to remedy that which might mar a world: thou canst help us; we cannot hurt thee. O let thy presence ever bless us, and let us ever bless thee for thy presence!

Pride was an attendant of this ignorance: so did they note Zaccheus for a sinner, as if themselves had been none; his sins were written in his forehead, theirs in their breast: the presumption of their secrecy makes them insult upon his notoriousness. The smoke of pride still flies upward, and, in the mounting, vanisheth : contrition beats it down, and fetches tears from the tender eyes. There are stage sins, and there are closet sins : these may not upbraid the other; they may be more heinous, though less manifest. It is a dangerous vanity to look outward at other men's sins with scorn, when we have more need to cast our eyes inward to see our own with humiliation.

Thus they stumbled, and fell ; but Zaccheus stood: all their malicious murmur could not dishearten his piety and joy in the entertaining of Christ. Before, Zaccheus lay down as a sinner; now, he stands up as a convert. Sinning is falling, continuance in sin is lying down, repentance is rising and standing up : yet perhaps this standing was not so much the sight of his constancy or of his conversion, as of his reverence. Christ's affability hath not made him unmannerly : Zaccheus stood ; and what if the desire of more audibleness raised him to his feet ? In that smallness of stature it was not fit he should lose aught of his height : it was meet so noble a proclamation should want no advantage of hearing. Never was our Saviour better welcomed : the penitent publican makes his will, and makes Christ his supervisor : his will consists of legacies given, of debts paid, gifts to the poor, payments to the injured. There is liberality in the former, in the latter justice : in both, the proportions are large : " Half to the poor, four-fold to the wronged."

This hand sowed not sparingly : here must needs be much of his own that was well gotten, whether left by patrimony, or saved by parsimony, or gained by honest improvement; for when he had restored four-fold to every one whom he had oppressed, yet there remained a whole half for pious uses; and this he so distributes, that every word commends his bounty : "I give;" and what is more free than gift? In alms we may neither sell, nor return, nor cast away. We sell, if we part with them for importunity, for vain glory, for retribution; we return them, if we give with respect to former offices; this is to pay, not to bestow : we cast away, if in our beneficence we neither regard order nor discretion. Zaccheus did neither cast away, nor return, nor sell, but give : " I do give ;" not I will. The prorogation of good makes it thankless ; the alms that smell of the hand lose the praise; it is twice given, that is given quickly. Those that defer their gifts till their deathbed, do as good as say, Lord, I will give thee something, when I can keep it no longer. Happy is the man that is his own executor: " I give my goods," not another's. It is a thankless vanity to be liberal of another man's purse: whoso gives of that which he hath taken away from the owner, doth more wrong in giving than in stealing: God expects our gifts, not our spoils. I fear there is too many a school and hospital, every stone whereof may be challenged. Had Zaccheus meant to give of his extortions, he had not been so careful of his restitution: now he restores to others, that he may give of his own: " I give half my goods." The publican's heart was as large as his estate; he was not more rich in goods than in bounty. Were this example binding, who should be rich to give? who should be poor to receive? In the strait beginnings of the church, those beneficences were requisite, which afterwards, in the larger elbow-room thereof, would have caused much confusion. If the first Christians laid down all at the apostle's feet, yet ere long it was enough for the believing Corinthians, every first day of the week, to lay aside some pittance for charitable purposes. We are no disciples, if we do not imitate Zaccheus so far as to give liberally, according to the proportion of our estate.

Giving is sowing; the larger seeding, the greater crop: giving to the poor is feneration to God: the greater bank, the more interest. Who can fear to be too wealthy? Time was when men faulted in excess. Proclamations were fain to restrain the Jews; statutes were fain to restrain our ancestors: now there needs none of this; men know how to shut their hands alone: charity is in more danger of freezing than of burning. How happy were it for the church, if men were only close-handed to hold, and not lime-fingered to take. " To the poor," not to rich heirs: God gives to him that hath, we to him that wants. Some want because they would, whether out of prodigality or idleness: some want because they must; these are the fit subjects of our beneficence, not those other. A poverty of our own making deserves no pity: he that sustains the lewd, feeds not his belly, but his vice. So then this living legacy of Zaccheus is free, " I give;" present, " I do give;" just, " my goods;" large, " half my goods;" fit, " to the poor."

Neither is he more bountiful in his gift, than just in his restitution: " If I have taken aught from any man by false accusation, I restore it four-fold."

It was proper for a publican to pill and poll the subject, by devising complaints and raising causeless vexations, that his mouth might be stopt with fees, either for silence or composition: this had Zaccheus often done. Neither is this "if" a note of doubt, but of assertion: he is sure of the fact, he is not sure of the persons; their challenge must help to further his justice. The true penitence of this holy convert expresses itself in confession, in satisfaction: his confession is free, full, open. What cares he to shame himself, that he may give glory to God? Woe be to that bashfulness that ends in confusion of face! O God, let me blush before men, rather than be confounded before thee, thy saints and angels!

His satisfaction is no less liberal than his gift. Had not Zaccheus been careful to pay the debts of his fraud, all had gone to the poor: he would have done that voluntarily, which the young man in the gospel was bidden to do, and refusing went away sorrowful. Now he knew that his misgotten gain was not for God's Corban; therefore he spares half, not to keep, but to restore: this was the best dish in Zaccheus's good cheer. In vain had he feasted Christ, given to the poor, confessed his extortions, if he had not made restitution. Woe is me for the paucity of true converts! there is much stolen goods, little brought home. Men's hands are like the fisher's flew; yea, like hell itself, which admits of no return. O God! we can never satisfy thee; our score is too great, our abilities too little; but if we make not even with men, in vain shall we look for mercy from thee. To each his own, had been well; but four for one was munificent. In our transactions of commerce, we do well to beat the bargain to the lowest; but in cases of moral or spiritual payments to God or men now, there must be a measure pressed, shaken, running over. In good offices and due retributions, we may not be pinching and niggardly. It argues an earthly and ignoble mind, where we have apparently wronged, to higgle and dodge in the amends.

O mercy and justice well repaid! " This day is salvation come to thine house." Lo, Zaccheus, that which thou givest to the poor, is nothing to that which thy Saviour gives to thee. If thou restorest four for one, here is more than thousands of millions for nothing: were every of thy pence a world, they could hold no comparison with this bounty. It is but dross that thou givest, it is salvation that thou receivest.

Thou gavest in present, thou dost not receive in hope; but, "This day is salvation come to thine house." Thine ill-gotten metals were a strong bar to bolt heaven gates against thee; now that they are dissolved by a seasonable beneficence and restitution, those gates of glory fly open to thy soul. Where is that man that can challenge God to be in his debt? who can ever say, Lord, this favour I did to the least of thine, unrequited? Thrice-happy publican, that has climbed from thy sycamore to heaven, and by a few worthless bags of unrighteous mammon, hast purchased to thyself a kingdom incorruptible, undefiled, and that fadeth not away!

CONTEMPLATION IV.— JOHN BAPTIST BEHEADED.

Three of the evangelists have (with one pen) recorded the death of the great harbinger of Christ as most remarkable and useful. He was the forerunner of Christ, as into the world, so out of it; yea, he that made way for Christ into the world, made way for the name of Christ into the court of Herod. This Herod Antipas was son to that Herod who was, and is, ever infamous for the massacre at Bethlehem. Cruelty runs in a blood. The murderer of John, the forerunner of Christ, is well descended of him who would have murdered Christ, and, for his sake, murdered the infants. It was late ere this Herod heard the fame of Jesus; not till he had taken off the head of John Baptist. The father of this Herod inquired for Christ too soon, this too late. Great men should have the best intelligence. If they improve it to all other uses of either frivolous or civil affairs, with neglect of spiritual, their judgment shall be so much more, as their helps and means were greater. Whether this Herod was taken up with his Arabian wars against Arethas his father-in-law; or whether he was employed in his journey to Rome, I inquire not: but if he was at home, I must wonder how he could be so long without the noise of Christ. Certainly, it was a sign he had a very irreligious court, that none of his followers did so much as report to him the miracles of our Saviour; who doubtless told him many a vain tale the while. One tells him of his brother Philip's discontentment; another relates the news of the Roman court; another the angry threats of Arethas; another flatters him with the admiration of his new mistress, and disparagement of the old: no man so much as says, Sir, there is a prophet in your kingdom that doth wonders. There was not a man in his country that had not been astonished with the fame of Jesus; yea, all Syria, and the adjoining regions, rung of it; only Herod's court hears nothing. Miserable is that greatness which keeps men from the notice of Christ. How plain is it from thence, that our Saviour kept aloof from the court! The austere and eremetical harbinger of Christ, it seems, preached there oft, and was heard gladly, though at last, to his cost; while our Saviour, who was more sociable, came not there. He sent a message to that fox, whose den he would not approach. Whether it were that he purposely forbore, lest he should give that tyrant occasion to revive and pursue his father's suspicion; or whether for that he would not so much honour a place so infamously graceless and disordered; or whether, by his example, to teach us the avoidance of outward pomp and glory; surely Herod saw him not till his death, heard not of him till the death of John Baptist. And now his unintelligence was not more strange than his misconstruction: "This is John Baptist, whom I beheaded." First he doubted, then he resolved; he doubted upon other suggestions, upon his own apprehensions he resolved thus. And though he thought good to set a face on it to strangers, unto whom it was not safe to bewray his fear, yet to his domestics he freely discovered his thoughts: "This is John Baptist." The troubled conscience will many a time open that to familiars, which it hides from the eyes of others. Shame and fear meet together in guiltiness. How could he imagine this to be John? That common conceit of transanimation could have no place here: there could be no transmigration of souls into a grown and well-statured body. That received fancy of the Jews held only in the case of conception and birth, not of full age. What need we scan this point, when Herod himself professes, "He is risen from the dead?" He that was a Jew by profession, and knew the story of Elisha's bones, of the Sareptan's and Shunamite's son, and, in all likelihood, had now heard of our Saviour's miraculous resuscitation of others, might think this power reflected upon himself.— Even Herod, as bad as he was, believed a resurrection. Lewdness of life and practice may stand with orthodoxy in some main points of religion. Who can doubt of this when "the devils believe and tremble?" Where shall those men appear, whose faces are Christian, but their hearts Sadducees?

O the terrors and tortures of a guilty heart! Herod's conscience told him he had offered an unjust and cruel violence to an innocent; and now he thinks that John's ghost haunts him. Had it not been for this guilt of his bosom, why might he not as well have thought that the same God, whose hand is not shortened, had conferred this power of miracles upon some other? Now it could be nobody but John that doth these wonders. And how can it be, thinks he, but that this revived prophet, who doth these strange things, will be revenged on me for his head? he, that could give himself life, can more easily take mine; how can I escape the hands of a now immortal and impassable avenger?

A wicked man needs no other tormentor, especially for the sins of blood, than his own heart. Revel, O Herod, and feast, and frolic, and please thyself with dances, and triumphs, and pastimes: thy sin shall be as some fury that shall invisibly follow thee, and scourge thy guilty heart with secret lashes, and upon all occasions shall begin thine hell within thee. He wanted not other sins, that yet cried, " Deliver me from blood-guiltiness, O God!"

What an honour was done to John in this misprision! While that man lived, the world was apt to think that John was the Christ: now, that John is dead, Herod thinks Christ to be John. God gives to his poor conscionable servants a kind of reverence and high respect, even from those men that malign them most; so as they cannot but venerate whom they hate. Contrarily, no wit or power can shield a lewd man from contempt.

John did no miracle in his life, yet now Herod thinks he did miracles in his resurrection; as supposing that a new supernatural life brought with it a supernatural power. Who can but wonder at the stupid partiality of Herod and these Jews? They can imagine and yield John risen from the dead, that never did miracle, and rose not; whereas Christ, who did infinite miracles, and rose from the dead by his almighty power, is not yielded by them to have risen. Their over-bountiful misconceit of the servant is not so injurious as their niggardly infidelity to the Master. Both of them shall convince and confound them before the face of God. But, O yet more blockish Herod! thy conscience affrights thee with John's resurrection, and flies in thy face for the cruel murder of so great a saint: yet where is thy repentance for so foul a fact? who would not have expected that thou shouldst hereupon have humbled thyself for thy sin, and have laboured to make thy peace with God and him? The greater the fame and power was of him whom thou supposedst recovered from thy slaughter, the more should have been thy penitence. Impiety is wont to besot men, and turn them senseless of their own safety and welfare. One would have thought, that our first grandsire Adam, when he found his heart to strike him for his disobedience, should have run to meet God upon his knees, and sued for pardon of his offence: instead of that, he runs to hide his head among the bushes. The case is still ours: we inherit both his sin and his senselessness. Besides the infinite displeasure of God, wickedness makes the heart incapable of grace, and impregnable to the means of conversion.

Even the very first act of Herod's cruelty was heinous. He was foul enough with other sins: " He added this above all, that he shut up John in prison." The violence offered to God's messengers is branded for notorious. The sanctity and austere carriage of the man won him honour justly from the multitude, and aggravated the sin: but whatever his person had been, his mission was sacred: " He shall send his messenger;" the wrong redounds to the God that sent him. It is the charge of God, " Touch not mine anointed, nor do my prophets any harm." The precept is perhaps one, for even prophets were anointed; but, at least, next to violation of majesty, is the wrong to a prophet. But what? do I not hear the Evangelist say, that " Herod heard John gladly?" How is it then? did John take the ear and heart of Herod, and doth Herod bind the hands and feet of John? doth he wilfully imprison whom he gladly heard? How inconsistent is a carnal heart to good resolutions! how little trust is to be given to the good motions of unregenerate persons! We have known when even mad dogs have fawned upon their master, yet he hath been too wise to trust them but in chains. As a true friend loves always, so a gracious heart always affects good, neither can be altered with change of occurrences. But the carnal man, like a hollow parasite or a fawning spaniel, flatters only for his own turn: if that be once either served or crossed, like a churlish cur, he is ready to snatch us by the fingers. Is there a worldly-minded man that lives in some known sin, yet makes much of the preacher, frequents the church, talks godly, looks demurely, carries fair? Trust him not: he will prove, after his pious fits, like some resty horse, which

JOHN BAPTIST BEHEADED.

goes on some paces readily and eagerly, but anon either stands still, or falls to flinging and plunging, and never leaves till he hath cast his rider.

What then might be the cause of John's bonds, and Herod's displeasure? "For Herodias' sake, his brother Philip's wife." That woman was the subject of Herod's lust, and exciter of his revenge. This light housewife ran away with her husband's brother; and now doting upon her incestuous lover, and finding John to be a rub in the way of her licentious adultery, is impatient of his liberty, and will not rest till his restraint. Resolved sinners are mad upon their lewd courses, and run furiously upon their gainsayers. A bear robbed of her whelps is less impetuous. Indeed, those that have determined to love their sins more than their souls, whom can they care for? Though Herod was wicked enough, yet, had it not been upon Herodias' instigation, he had never imprisoned John. Importunity of lewd solicitors may be of dangerous consequence, and many times draws greatness into those ways, which it either would not have thought of, or abhorred. In the removal of the wicked is the establishment of the throne.

Yet still is this dame called the wife of Philip. She had utterly left his bed, and was solemnly coupled to Herod; but all the ritual ceremonies of her new nuptials cannot make her other than Philip's wife. It is a sure rule, that which is originally faulty can never be rectified. The ordination of marriage is one for one: "They twain shall be one flesh." There cannot be two heads to one body, nor two bodies to one head. Herod was her adulterer; he was not her husband: she was Herod's harlot, Philip's wife. Yet how doth Herod dote on her, that for her sake he loads John with irons! Whither will not the fury of inordinate lust transport a man? Certainly John was of late in Herod's favour. That rough-hewn preacher was for a wilderness, not for a court: Herod's invitation drew him thither; his reverence and respects encouraged him there. Now the love of his lust carried him into a hate of God's messenger. That man can have no hold of himself, or care of others, who hath given the reins to his unruly concupiscence. He that hath once fixed his heart upon the face of a harlot, and hath beslaved himself to a bewitching beauty, casts off at once all fear of God, respect to laws, shame of the world, regard of his estate, care of wife, children, friends, reputation, patrimony, body, soul. So violent is this beastly passion where it takes; neither ever leaves, till it have hurried him into the chambers of death.

Herodias herself had first plotted to kill the Baptist; her murderers were suborned, her ambushes laid; the success failed, and now she works with Herod for his durance. O marvellous hand of the Almighty! John was a mean man for estate; solitary, guardless, unarmed, impotent: Herodias a queen, so great, that she swayed Herod himself; and not more great than subtile, and not more great and subtile than malicious; yet Herodias laid to kill John, and could not. What an invisible and yet sure guard there is about the poor servants of God, that seem helpless and despicable in themselves! There is over them a hand of divine protection, which can be no more opposed than seen. Malice is not so strong in the hand as in the heart. The devil is stronger than a world of men; a legion of devils stronger than fewer spirits: yet a legion of devils cannot hurt one swine without a permission. What can bands of enemies, or gates of hell, do against God's secret ones? "It is better to trust in the Lord, than to trust in princes."

It is not more clear who was the author, than what was the motive of this imprisonment — the free reproof of Herod's incest: "It is not lawful," &c. Both the offenders were nettled at this bold reprehension. Herod knew the reputation that John carried; his conscience could not but suggest the foulness of his own fact; neither could he but see how odious it would seem to persecute a prophet for so just a reproof. For the colour, therefore, of so tyrannical an act, he brands John with sedition. These presumptuous taxations are a disgrace and disparagement to authority. It is no news with tyrants, to cloak their cruelty with pretences of justice. Never was it other than the lot of God's faithful servants to be loaded with unjust reproaches in the conscionable performance of their duties. They should speed too well in the opinion of men, if they might but appear in their true shape.

The fact of Herod was horrible and prodigious, to rob his own brother of the partner of his bed, to tear away part of his flesh, yea, his body from his head; so as here was at once, in one act, adultery, incest, violence. Adultery, that he took another's wife; incest, that he took his brother's; violence, that he thus took her in spite of her husband. Justly, therefore, might John say, "It is not lawful for thee." He baulked not one of Herod's sins, but reproved him of all the evils that he had done; though more eminently of this, as that which more filled the eye of the world. It was not the crown or awful sceptre of Herod that could daunt the homely but faithful messenger of God: as one that came in the spirit of Elias, he fears no faces, spares no wickedness. There must meet in God's ministers courage and impartiality: impartiality, not to make difference of persons; courage, not to make spare of the sins of the greatest. It is a hard condition that the necessity of our calling casts upon us, in some cases, to run upon the pikes of displeasure. Prophecies were no burdens, if they did not expose us to these dangers. We must connive at no evil: every sin unreproved becomes ours.

Hatred is the daughter of truth, Herod is inwardly vexed with so peremptory a reprehension: and now he seeks to kill the author. And why did he not? "He feared the people." The time was, when he feared John no less than now he hates him: he once reverenced him as a just and holy man, whom now he heartburns as an enemy: neither was it any counterfeit respect; sure the man was then in earnest. What shall we say then? Was it that his inconstant heart was now fetched off by Herodias, and wrought to a disaffection? or was it with Herod, as with Solomon's sluggard, that at once would and would not? His thoughts are distracted with a mixed voluntary contradiction of purposes: as a holy man, and honoured of the people, he would not kill John: he would kill him as an enemy to his lust. The worst part prevaileth: appetite oversways reason and conscience; and now, were it not for fear of the people, John should be murdered. What a self-conflicting and prodigious creature is a wicked man left over to his own thoughts, while on the one side he is urged by his conscience, on the other by his lustful desires, and by the importunity of Satan! "There is no peace, saith my God, to the wicked:" and after all his inward broils, he falls upon the worst, so as his yieldance is worse than his fight. When God sees fit, Herod's tyranny shall effect that which the wise providence of the Almighty hath decreed for his servant's glory. In the meanwhile, rubs shall be cast in his way; and this for one, "He feared the people." What an absurd and sottish thing is hypocrisy! Herod fears the people, he fears not God. Tell me then, Herod, what could the people do at the worst? Perhaps mutiny against thee, raise arms and tumults, disturb the government — it may be, shake it off.

What could God do? yea, what not? Stir up all his creatures to plague thee, and when he hath done, tumble thee down to hell, and there torment thee everlastingly. O fond Herod, that fearest where no fear was, and fearest not where there is nothing but terror!

How God fits lewd men with restraints! If they be so godless as to regard his creature above himself, he hath external bugs to affright them withal; if bashful, he hath shame; if covetous, losses; if proud, disgrace: and by this means the most wise Providence keeps the world in order. We cannot better judge of our hearts, than by what we most fear.

No man is so great as to be utterly exempted from fear. The Jews feared Herod, Herod feared the Jews: the healthful fear sickness, the free servitude: the people fear a tyrant's oppression and cruelty; the tyrant fears the people's mutiny and insurrection. If there have been some so great as to be above the reach of the power and machinations of inferiors, yet never any that have been free from their fears and suspicions. Happy is he that fears nothing but what he should — God.

Why did Herod fear the people? "They held John for a prophet." And this opinion was both common and constant: even the Scribes and Pharisees durst not say, his baptism was from men. It is the wisdom and goodness of God, ever to give his children favour somewhere. If Jezebel hate Elias, Ahab shall for the time honour him; and if Herod hate the Baptist, and would kill him, yet the people reverence him. Herod's malice would make him away; the people's reputation keeps him alive. As wise princes have been content to maintain a faction in their court or state for their own purposes, so here did the God of heaven contrive and order differences of judgment and affection betwixt Herod and his subjects, for his own holy ends; else certainly, if all wicked men should conspire in evil, there could be no being upon earth; as, contrarily, if evil spirits did not accord, hell could not stand. O the unjust and fond partiality of this people! They all generally applaud John for a prophet, yet they receive not his message. Whose prophet was John, but of the Highest? what was his errand, but to be the way-maker unto Christ? what was he, but the voice of that eternal Word of his Father? what was the sound of that voice, but, "Behold the Lamb of God: he that comes after me is greater than I, whose shoe-latchet I am not worthy to unloose?" Yet they honour the servant, and reject the Master: they contemn that prince whose ambassador they reverence. How could they but argue— "John is a prophet: he speaks from God; his words must be true: he tells us, this is the Lamb of God, the Messias that should come to redeem the world; this must needs be he, we will look for no other." Yet this perverse people receive John, and reject Jesus. There is ever an absurdity in unbelief, while it separates those relations and respects which can never in nature be disjoined. Thus it readily apprehends God as merciful in pardoning, not as just in punishing; Christ as a Saviour, not as a Judge. Thus we ordinarily, in a contrariety to these Jews, profess to receive the Master, and contemn the servants, while he hath said, who will make it good, "He that despiseth you, despiseth me."

That which Herod in policy durst not, in wine he dares do: and that which God had restrained till his own time, now in his own time he permits to be done. The day was, as one of the evangelists styles it, "convenient;" if for the purpose of Herodias, I am sure for God's, who, having determined to glorify himself by John's martyrdom, will cast it upon a time when it may be most notified, Herod's birthday. All the peers of the country, perhaps of the neighbour nations, are now assembled. Herodias could not have found out a time more fit to blazon her own shame and cruelty, than in such a confluence. The wise providence of God many times pays us with our own choice; so as when we think to have brought about our own ends to our best content, we bring about his purposes to our own confusion.

Herod's birthday is kept, and so was Pharaoh's; both of them with blood. These personal stains cannot make the practice unlawful. Where the man is good, the birth is memorable.

What blessing have we, if life be none? and if our life be a blessing, why should it not be celebrated? Excess and disorder may blemish any solemnity, but that cleaves to the act, not to the institution.

Herod's birthday was kept with a feast, and this feast was a supper. It was fit to be a night-work: this festivity was spent in works of darkness, not of the light; it was a child of darkness that was then born, not of the day.

"Those that are drunken, are drunk in the night." There is a kind of shame in sin, even where it is committed with the stiffest resolution; at least there was wont to be: if now sin be grown impudent, and justice bashful, woe be to us!

That there might be perfect revels at Herod's birthday, besides the feast there is music and dancing, and that by Salome the daughter of Herodias. A meet daughter for such a mother, bred according to the disposition of so immodest a parent. Dancing, in itself, as it is a set, regular, harmonious motion of the body, cannot be unlawful, more than walking or running: circumstances may make it sinful. The wanton gesticulations of a virgin, in a wild assembly of gallants warmed with wine, could be no other than riggish and unmaidenly. It is not so frequently seen, that the child follows the good qualities of the parent; it is seldom seen that it follows not the evil. Nature is the soil, good and ill qualities are the herbs and weeds; the soil bears the weeds naturally, the herbs not without culture. What with traduction, what with education, it were strange if we should miss any of our parents' misdispositions.

Herodias and Salome have what they desired. The dance pleased Herod well: those indecent motions that would have displeased any modest eye (though what should a modest eye do at Herod's feast?) overpleased Herod. Well did Herodias know how to fit the tooth of her paramour and had therefore purposely so composed the carriage and gesture of her daughter, as it might take best, although doubtless the same action could not have so pleased from another. Herod saw in Salome's face and fashion, the image of her whom he doted on; so did she look, so did she move; besides that his lavish cups had predisposed him to wantonness, and now he cannot but like well that which so pleasingly suited his inordinate desire. All humours love to be fed, especially the vicious, so much more as they are more eager and stirring. There cannot be a better glass, wherein to discern the face of our hearts, than our pleasures; such as they are, such are we, whether vain or holy.

What a strange transportation was this! "Whatsoever thou shalt ask:" half a kingdom for a dance! Herod, this pastime is over-paid for; there is no proportion in this remuneration; this is not bounty, it is prodigence. Neither doth this pass under a bare promise only, but under an oath, and that solemn and (as it might be in wine) serious. How largely do sensual men both proffer and give for a little momentary and vain contentment! How many censure Herod's gross impotence, and yet second it with a worse, giving away their precious souls for a short pleasure of sin! What is half a kingdom, yea, a whole world, to a soul? So much therefore is their madness greater, as their loss is more.

So large a boon was worthy of deliberation. Salome consults with her mother upon so ample and ratified a promise. Yet so much good nature and filial respect was in this wanton damsel, that she would not carve herself of her option, but takes her mother with her. If Herodias were infamously lewd, yet she was her parent, and must direct her choice. Children should have no will of their own: as their flesh is their parents', so should their will be. They do justly unchild themselves, that in main elections dispose of themselves without the consent of those which gave them being. It is both unmannerly and unnatural in the child to run before, without, against, the will of the parent.

O that we could be so officious to our good and heavenly Father, as she was to an earthly and wicked mother; not to ask, not to undertake, aught, without his allowance, without his directions! that, when the world shall offer us whatsoever our heart desires, we could run to the oracles of God for our resolution, not daring to accept what he doth not both license and warrant!

O the wonderful strength of malice! Salome was offered no less than half the kingdom of Herod, yet chooses to ask the head of a poor preacher. Nothing is so sweet to a corrupt heart as revenge, especially when it may bring with it a full scope to a dear sin. All worldlings are of this diet: they had rather sin freely for a while, and die, than refrain and live happily eternally. What a suit was this! "Give me here in a charger the head of John Baptist." It is not enough for her to say, Let John's head be cut off; but, "Give me it in a charger." What a service was here to be brought into a feast, especially to a woman! a dead man's head, swimming in blood!— How cruel is a wicked heart, that can take pleasure in those things which have most horror!

O the importunity of a galled conscience! Herodias could never think herself safe till John was dead: she could never think him dead till his head were off; she could not think his head was off, till she had it brought her in a platter: a guilty heart never thinks it hath made sure enough. Yea, even after the head was thus brought, they thought him alive again. Guiltiness and security could never lodge together in one bosom.

Herod was sorry, and no doubt in earnest, in the midst of his cups and pleasance.

I should rather think his jollity counterfeited than his grief. It is true, Herod was a fox, but that subtle beast dissembles not always; when he runs away from the dogs, he means as he does: and if he were formerly willing to have killed John, yet he was unwillingly willing; and so far as he was unwilling to kill him as a prophet, as a just man, so far was he sorry that he must be killed. Had Herod been wise, he had not been perplexed. Had he been so wise as to have engaged himself lawfully, and within due limits, he had not now been so entangled as to have needed sorrow: The folly of sinners is guilty of their pain, and draws upon them a late and unprofitable repentance.

But here the act was not past, though the word were past. It was his misconceived entanglement that caused this sorrow; which might have been remedied by flying off. A three-fold cord tied him to the performance: the conscience of his oath, the respect to his guests, a loathness to discontent Herodias and her daughter. Herod had so much religion as to make scruple of an oath; not so much as to make scruple of a murder. No man casts off all justice and piety at once, but, while he gives himself over to some sins, he sticks at others. It is no thank to lewd men, that they are not universally vicious. All God's several laws cannot be violated at once: there are sins contrary to each other; there are sins disagreeing with the lewdest dispositions. There are oppressors that hate drunkenness, there are unclean persons which abhor murder, there are drunkards which hate cruelty. One sin is enough to damn the soul, one leak to drown the vessel.

But O fond Herod, what needed this unjust scrupulousness? Well and safely might thou have shifted the bond of thine oath with a double evasion: one, that this generality of thy promise was only to be construed of lawful acts and motions; that only can we do, which we can justly do; unlawfulness is in the nature of impossibility: the other, that had this engagement been so meant, yet might it be as lawfully rescinded as it was unlawfully made. A sinful promise is ill made, worse performed. Thus thou mightst, thou shouldst, have come off fair; where now, holding thyself by an irreligious religion, tied to thy foolish and wicked oath, thou only goest away with this mitigation, that thou art a scrupulous murderer.

In the meanwhile, if an Herod made such conscience in keeping an unlawful oath, how shall he, in the day of judgment, condemn those Christians which make no conscience of oaths lawful, just, necessary? Woe is me! one sells an oath for a bribe, another lends an oath for favour, another casts it away for malice. I fear to think it may be a question, whether there be more oaths broken, or kept. O God! I marvel not, if being implored as a witness, as an avenger of falsehood, thou hold him not guiltless that thus dares take thy name in vain.

Next to his oath, is the respect to his honour. His guests heard his deep engagement, and now he cannot fall off with reputation. It would argue levity and rashness to say and not to do; and what would the world say? The misconceits of the points of honour have cost millions of souls. As many a one doth good only to be seen of men, so many a one doth evil only to satisfy the humour and opinion of others. It is a damnable plausibility so to regard the vain approbation or censure of the beholders, as in the meantime to neglect the allowance or judgment of God. But how ill guests were these! how well worthy of a Herod's table! Had they had but common civility, finding Herod perplexed, they had acquitted him by their dissuasions, and disclaimed the expectation of so bloody a performance: but they rather, to gratify Herodias, make way for so slight and easy a condescent. Even godly princes have complained of the iniquity of their heels: how much more must they needs be ill attended, that give encouragements and examples of lewdness!

Neither was it the least motive, that he was loath to displease his mistress. The damsel had pleased him in her dance; he would not discontent her in breaking his word. He saw Herodias in Salome: the suit, he knew, was the mother's, though in the daughter's lips: both would be displeased in falling off; both would be gratified in yielding. O vain and wicked Herod! he cares not to offend God, to offend his conscience; he cares to offend a wanton mistress. This is one means to fill hell, loathness to displease.

A good heart will rather fall out with all the world than with God, than with his conscience.

The misgrounded sorrow of worldly hearts doth not withhold them from their intended sins. It is enough to vex, not enough to restrain them. Herod was sorry, but he sends the executioner for John's head. One act hath made Herod a tyrant, and John a martyr. Herod a tyrant, in that, without all legal proceedings, without so much as false witnesses, he takes off the head of a man, of a prophet. It was lust that carried Herod into murder. The proceedings of sin are more hardly avoided than the entrance. Whoso gives himself leave to be wicked, knows not where he shall stay. John a martyr, in dying for bearing witness to the truth; truth in life, in judgment, in doctrine. It was the holy purpose of God, that he which had baptized with water, should now be baptized with blood. Never did God mean that his best children should dwell always upon earth: should they stay here, wherefore hath he provided glory above? Now would God have John delivered from a double prison, of his own, of Herod's, and placed in the glorious liberty of his Son's. His head shall be taken off, that it may be crowned with glory. " Precious in the sight of the Lord is the death of his saints."

O happy birthday (not of Herod, but) of the Baptist! Now doth John enter into his joy; and in this name is this day ever celebrated of the church. This blessed forerunner of Christ saith of himself, " I must decrease." He is decreased, indeed, and now grown shorter by the head; but he is not so much decreased in stature, as increased in glory. For one minute's pain, he is possessed of endless joy; and as he came before his Saviour into the world, so is he gone before him into heaven.

The head is brought in a charger. What a dish was here for a feast! How prodigiously insatiable is the cruelty of a wicked heart! O blessed service, fit for the table of heaven! It is not for thee, O wicked Herod, not for thee, malicious and wanton Herodias: it is a dish precious and pleasing to the God of heaven, to the blessed angels, who looked upon that head with more delight in his constant fidelity, than the beholders saw it with horror, and Herodias with contentment of revenge.

It is brought to Salome, as the reward of her dance: she presents it to her mother, as the dainty she had longed for. Methinks I see how that chaste and holy countenance was tossed by impure and filthy hands; that true and faithful tongue, those sacred lips, those pure eyes, those mortified cheeks, are now insultingly handled by an incestuous harlot, and made a scorn to the drunken eyes of Herod's guests.

O the wondrous judgments and incomprehensible dispositions of the holy, wise Almighty God! He that was sanctified in the womb, born and conceived with so much note and miracle, " What manner of child shall this be?" lived with so much reverence and observation, is now, at midnight, obscurely murdered in a close prison, and his head brought forth to the insultation and irrision of harlots and ruffians. O God, thou knowest what thou hast to do with thine own. Thus thou sufferest thine to be misused and slaughtered here below, that thou mayest crown them above. It should not be thus, if thou didst not mean that their glory should be answerable to their depression.

CONTEMPLATION V. — THE FIVE LOAVES AND TWO FISHES.

What flocking there was after Christ, which way soever he went! how did the kingdom of heaven suffer a holy violence in these his followers! Their importunity drove him from the land to the sea. When he was upon the sea of Tiberias, they followed him with their eyes, and when they saw which way he bent, they followed him so fast on foot, that they prevented his landing. Whether it were that our Saviour staid some while upon the water (as that which yielded him more quietness and freedom of respiration), or whether the foot passage, as it oft falls out, were the shorter cut, by reason of the compasses of the water, and the many elbows of the land, I inquire not; sure I am, the wind did not so swiftly drive on the ship, as desire and zeal drove on these eager clients. Well did Christ see them all the way; well did he know their steps, and guided them; and now he purposely goes to meet them whom he seemed to fly. Nothing can please God more than our importunity in seeking him: when he withdraws himself, it is that he may be more earnestly inquired for. Now then he comes to find them whom he made show to decline: " And seeing a great multitude, he passes from the ship to the shore." That which brought him from heaven to earth, brought him also from the sea to land; his compassion on their souls, that he might teach them; compassion on their bodies, that he might heal and feed them.

Judea was not large, but populous: it could not be but there must be, amongst so many men, many diseased: it is no marvel if the report of so miraculous and universal sanations drew customers. They found three advantages of cure, above the power and performance of any earthly physician; certainty, bounty, ease: certainty, in that all comers were cured without fail; bounty, in that they were cured without charge; ease, in that they were cured without pain. Far be it from us, O Saviour, to think that thy glory hath abated of thy mercy: still and ever thou art our assured, bountiful, and perfect Physician, who healest all our diseases, and takest away all our infirmities. O that we could have our faithful recourse to thee in all our spiritual maladies! it were as impossible we should want help, as that thou shouldst want power and mercy.

That our Saviour might approve himself every way beneficent, he, that had filled the souls of his auditors with spiritual repast, will now fill their bodies with temporal; and he, that had approved himself the universal Physician of his church, will now be known to be the great householder of the world, by whose liberal provision mankind is maintained. He did not more miraculously heal, than he feeds miraculously.

The disciples, having well noted the diligent and importune attendance of the multitude, now towards evening come to their Master, in a care of their repast and discharge: " This is a desert place, and the time is now past; send the multitude away, that they may go into the villages and buy themselves victuals." How well it becomes even spiritual guides to regard the bodily necessities of God's people! This is not directly in our charge, neither may we leave our sacred ministration to serve tables. But yet, as the bodily father must take care for the soul of his child, so must the spiritual have respect to the body. This is all that the world commonly looks after, measuring their pastors more by their dishes than by their doctrine or conversation, as if they had the charge of their bellies, not of their souls; if they have open cellars, it matters not whether their mouths be open. If they be sociable in their carriage, favourable and indulgent to their recreations, full in their cheer, how easily doth the world dispense with either their negligence or enormities! as if the souls of these men lay in their weasand, in their gut. But surely they have reason to expect from their teachers a due proportion of hospitality. An unmeet parsimony is here not more odious than sinful; and where ability wants, yet care may not be wanting. Those preachers, which are so intent upon their spiritual work, that in the meantime they overstrain the weaknesses of their people, holding them in their devotions longer than human frailty will permit, forget not themselves more than their pattern, and must be sent to school to these compassionate disciples, who, when evening was come, sue to Christ for the people's dismission.

The place was desert, the time evening.

Doubtless our Saviour made choice of both these, that there might be both more use and more note of his miracle. Had it been in the morning, their stomach had not been up, their feeding had been unnecessary: had it been in the village, provision either might have been made, or at least would have seemed made by themselves. But now that it was both desert and evening, there was good ground for the disciples to move, and for Christ to work their sustentation. Then only may we expect, and crave help from God, when we find our need. Superfluous aid can neither be heartily desired, nor earnestly looked for, nor thankfully received from the hands of mercy. "Cast thy burden upon the Lord, and he shall sustain thee." If it be not a burden, it is no casting it upon God. Hence it is, that divine aid comes ever in the very upshot and exigence of our trials, when we have been exercised, and almost tired with long hopes, yea, with despairs of success; that it may be both more longed for ere it come, and, when it comes, more welcome!

O the faith and zeal of these clients of Christ! they not only follow him from the city into the desert, from delicacy to want, from frequence to solitude, but forget their bodies in pursuit of the food of their souls.

Nothing is more hard for a healthful man to forget than his belly: within few hours this will be sure to solicit him, and will take no denials. Yet such sweetness did these hearers find in the spiritual repast, that they thought not on the bodily: the disciples pitied them; they had no mercy on themselves. By how much more a man's mind is taken up with heavenly things, so much less shall he care for earthly. What shall earth be to us, when we are all spirit? and in the meantime, according to the degrees of our intellectual elevations shall be our neglect of bodily contentments.

The disciples think they move well: "Send them away, that they may buy victuals." Here was a strong charity, but a weak faith; a strong charity, in that they would have the people relieved; a weak faith, in that they supposed they could not otherwise be so well relieved. As a man who, when he sees many ways lie before him, takes that which he thinks both fairest and nearest, so do they: this way of relief lay openest to their view, and promised most. Well might they have thought, It is as easy for our Master to feed them, as to heal them; there is an equal facility in all things to a supernatural power: yet they say, "Send them away." In all our projects and suits, we are still ready to move for that which is most obvious, most likely, when sometimes that is less agreeable to the will of God.

The All-wise and Almighty arbiter of all things hath a thousand secret means to honour himself in his proceedings with us. It is not for us to carve boldly for ourselves; but we must humbly depend on the disposal of his wisdom and mercy.

Our Saviour's answer gives a strange check to their motion: "They need not depart." Not need! They had no victuals; they must have; there was gone to be had. What more need could be? He knew the supply which he intended, though they knew it not. His command was therefore more strange than his assertion, "Give ye them to eat." Nothing gives what it hath not. Had they had victuals, they had not called for a dismission; and not having, how should they give? It was thy wisdom, O Saviour, thus to prepare thy disciples for the intended miracle: thou wouldst not do it abruptly, without an intimation both of the purpose of it, and the necessity. And how modestly dost thou undertake it, without noise, without ostentation! I hear thee not say, I will give them to eat; but, "Give ye:" as if it should be their act, not thine. Thus sometimes it pleaseth thee to require of us what we are not able to perform; either that thou mayest show us what we cannot do, and so humble us; or that thou mayest erect us to a dependence upon thee, which canst do it for us. As when the mother bids the infant come to her, which hath not yet the steady use of his legs, it is that he may cling the faster to her hand or coat for supportation.

Thou biddest us impotent wretches to keep thy royal law. Alas! what can we sinners do? there is no one letter of those thy ten words that we are able to keep. This charge of thine intends to show us not our strength, but our weakness. Thus thou wouldst turn our eyes both back to what we might have done, to what we could have done; and upwards to thee in whom we have done it, in whom we can do it. He wrongs thy goodness and justice that misconstrues these thy commands, as if they were of the same nature with those of the Egyptian taskmasters, requiring the brick, and not giving the straw. But in bidding us do what we cannot, thou enablest us to do what thou biddest. Thy precepts, under the gospel, have not only an intimation of our duty, but an habilitation of thy power: as here, when thou badest the disciples to give to the multitude, thou didst mean to supply unto them what thou commandedst to give.

Our Saviour hath what he would — an acknowledgment of their insufficiency: "We have here but five loaves and two fishes." A poor provision for the family of the Lord of the whole earth. Five loaves, and those barley; two fishes, and those little ones. We well know, O Saviour, that the beasts were thine on a thousand mountains, all the corn thine that covered the whole surface of the earth, all the fowls of the air thine; it was thou that providedst those drifts of quails that fell among the tents of thy rebellious Israelites, that rainedst down those showers of manna round about their camp: and dost thou take up, for thyself and thy household, with "five barley loaves and two little fishes?" Certainly this was thy will, not thy need; to teach us that this body must be fed, not pampered. Our belly may not be our master, much less our god; or if it be, the next world is, "whose glory is their shame, whose end damnation." It is noted as the crime of the rich glutton, that "he fared deliciously every day." I never find that Christ entertained any guests but twice, and that was only with loaves and fishes. I find him sometimes feasted by others more liberally. But his domestical fare, how simple, how homely is it! The end of food is to sustain nature. Meat was ordained for the belly, the belly for the body, the body for the soul, the soul for God: we must still look through the subordinate ends to the highest. To rest in the pleasure of the meat, is for those creatures which have no souls. O the extreme delicacy of these times! What conquisition is here of all sorts of curious dishes from the furthest seas and lands, to make up one hour's meal! what broken cookery! what devised mixtures! what nice sauces! what feasting, not of the taste only, but of the scent! Are we the disciples of him that took up with the loaves and fishes, or the scholars of a Philoxenus, or an Apicius, or Vitellius, or those other monsters of the palate — the true sons of those first parents that killed themselves with their teeth?

Neither was the quality of these victuals more coarse than the quantity small. They make a "but" of five loaves and two fishes; and well might, in respect of so many thousand mouths. A little food to a hungry stomach doth rather stir up appetite than satisfy it; as a little rain upon a droughty soil doth rather help to scorch than refresh it. When we look with the eye of sense or reason upon any object, we shall see an impossibility of those effects which faith can easily apprehend, and divine power more easily produce. Carnal minds are ready to measure all our hopes by human possibilities, and, when they fail, to despair of success, where true faith measures them by divine power, and therefore can never be disheartened. This grace is for things not seen, and whether beyond hope, or against it.

The virtue is not in the means, but in the agent: "Bring them hither to me." How much more easy had it been for our Saviour to fetch the loaves to him, than to multiply them! The hands of the disciples shall bring them, that they might more fully witness both the Author, and manner of the instant miracle. Had the loaves and fishes been multiplied without this bringing, perhaps they might have seemed to have come by the secret provision of the guests; now there can be no question either of the act, or of the agent. As God takes pleasure in doing wonders for men, so he loves to be acknowledged in the great works that he doth. He hath no reason to part with his own glory: that is too precious for him to lose, or for his creature to embezzle. And how justly didst thou, O Saviour, in this, mean to teach thy disciples, that it was thou only who feedest the world, and upon whom both themselves and all their fellow-creatures must depend for their nourishment and provision; and that, if it came not through thy hands, it could not come to theirs!

There need no more words. I do not hear the disciples stand upon the terms of their own necessity: Alas, Sir, it is too little for ourselves; whence shall we then relieve our own hunger? give leave to our charity to begin at home. But they willingly yield to the command of their Master, and put themselves upon his providence for the sequel. When we have a charge from God, it is not for us to stand upon self-respects; in this case there is no such sure liberty as in a self-contempt. O God, when thou callest to us for our five loaves, we must forget our own interest; otherwise, if we be more thrifty than obedient, our good turns evil; and much better had it been for us to have wanted that which we withhold from the owner.

He that is the Master of the feast marshals the guests: "He commanded the multitude to sit down on the grass." They obey, and expect. O marvellous faith! so many thousands sit down, and address themselves to a meal, when they saw nothing but five poor barley loaves, and two small fishes! None of them say, Sit down to what? here are the mouths, but where is the meat? we can soon be set, but whence shall we be served? ere we draw our knives, let us see our cheer. But they meekly and obediently dispose themselves to their places, and look up to Christ for a miraculous purveyance. It is for all, that would be Christ's followers, to lead the life of faith; and, even where means appear not, to wait upon that merciful hand. Nothing is more easy than to trust God when our barns and coffers are full; and to say, "Give to us our daily bread," when we have it in our cupboard. But when we have nothing, when we know not how or whence to get anything, then to depend upon an invisible bounty, this is a true and noble act of faith. To cast away our own, that we may immediately live upon divine Providence, I know no warrant. But when the necessity is of God's making, we see our refuge; and happy are we, if our confidence can fly to it, and rest in it. Yea, fulness should be a curse, if it should debar us from this dependence: at our best, we must look up to this great Householder of the world, and cannot but need his provision. If we have meat, perhaps not appetite; if appetite, it may be not digestion; or, if that, not health and freedom from pain; or, if that, perhaps from other occurrence, not life.

The guests are set, full of expectation. He, that could have multiplied the bread in absence, in silence takes it and blesses it: that he might at once show them the Author and the means of this increase. It is thy blessing, O God, that maketh rich. What a difference do we see in men's estates! Some languish under great means, and enjoy not either their substance or themselves; others are cheerful and happy in a little. Second causes may not be denied their work; but the overruling power is above. The subordinateness of the creature doth not take away from the right, from the thank of the first mover.

He could as well have multiplied the loaves whole; why would he rather do it in the breaking? Was it to teach us, that in the distribution of our goods we should expect his blessing, not in their entireness and reservation? "There is that scattereth, and yet increaseth," saith Solomon: yea, there is no man but increaseth by scattering. It is the grain thrown into the several furrows of the earth, which yields the rich interest unto the husbandman: that which is tied up in his sack, or heaped in his granary, decreaseth by keeping. "He that soweth liberally, shall reap liberally."

Away with our weak distrust! If wealth came by us, giving were the way to want: now that God gives to the giver, nothing can so sure enrich us as our beneficence.

He multiplied the bread, not to keep, but to give: "He gave it to the disciples." And why not rather by his own hand to the multitude, that so the miracle and thank might have been more immediate? Wherefore was this, O Saviour, but that thou mightest win respect to thy disciples from the people? as great princes, when they would ingratiate a favourite, pass no suits but through his hands. What an honour was this to thy servants, that as thou wert Mediator betwixt thy Father and man, so thou wouldst have them, in some beneficial occasion, mediate betwixt men and thee! How fit a type is this of thy spiritual provision, that thou who couldst have fed the world by thine immediate word, wouldst, by the hands of thy ministers, divide the bread of life to all hearers! likeas it was with the law; well did the Israelites see and hear that thou couldst deliver that dreadful message with thine own mouth, yet, in favour of their weakness, thou wouldst treat with them by a Moses. Use of means derogates nothing from the efficacy of the principal agent, yea, adds to it. It is a strange weakness of our spiritual eyes, if we can look but to the next hand. How absurd had these guests been, if they had terminated the thanks in the servitors, and had said, We have it from you; whence ye had it, is no part of our care: we owe this favour to you; if you owe it to your master, acknowledge your obligations to him, as we do unto you. But since they well knew that the disciples might have handled this bread long enough ere any such effect could have followed, they easily find to whom they are beholden. Our Christian wisdom must teach us, whosoever be the means, to reserve our main thanks for the Author of our good.

He gave the bread then to his disciples, not to eat, not to keep, but to distribute. It was not their particular benefit he regarded in this gift, but the good of many.

In every feast, each servitor takes up his dish, not to carry it aside into a corner for his own private repast, but to set it before the guests, for the honour of his master: when they have done, his cheer begins. What shall we say to those injurious waiters, who fatten themselves with those concealed messes which are meant to others? Their table is made their snare, and these stolen morsels cannot but end in bitterness.

Accordingly, the disciples set this fare before the guests. I do not see so much as Judas reserve a share to himself, whether out of hunger or distrust. Had not our Saviour commanded so free a distribution, their self-love would easily have taught them where to begin. Nature says, First thyself, then thy friends: either extremity or particular charge gives grace occasion to alter the case. Far be it from us to think we have any claim in that which the owner gives us merely to bestow.

I know not now whether more to wonder at the miraculous eating, or the miraculous leaving. Here were a whole host of guests, five thousand men; and, in all likelihood, no fewer women and children. Perhaps some of these only looked on: nay, they did all eat. Perhaps every man a crumb, or a bit: nay, they did all eat to satiety; "All were satisfied." So many must needs make clean work: of so little, there could be left nothing. Yea, there were fragments remaining; perhaps some crumbs or crusts, hardly to be discerned, much less gathered: nay, "Twelve baskets full;" more remained than was first set down. Had they eaten nothing, it was a just miracle that so much should be left; had nothing remained, it was no less miracle that so many had eaten, and so many satisfied; but now that so many bellies and so many baskets were filled, the miracle was doubled. O work of a boundless Omnipotency! Whether this were done by creation or by conversion, uses to be questioned, but needs not: while Christ multiplies the bread, it is not for us to multiply his miracles. To make aught of nothing, is more than to add much unto something. It was therefore rather by turning of a former matter into these substances, than by making these substances of nothing.

Howsoever, here is a marvellous provision made, a marvellous bounty of that provision, a no less marvellous extent of that bounty.

Those that depend upon God, and busy themselves in his work, shall not want a due purveyance in the very desert. Our strait and confined beneficence reaches so far as to provide for own: those of our domestics, which labour in our service, do but justly expect and challenge their diet; whereas, day-labourers are ofttimes at their own finding. How much more will that God, who is infinite in mercy and power, take order for the livelihood of those that attend him! We see the birds of the air provided for by him: how rarely have we found any of them dead of hunger; yet, what do they, but what they are carried unto by natural instinct? how much more, where, besides propriety, there is a rational and willing service. Shall the Israelites be fed with manna, Elijah by the ravens, the widow by her multiplied meal and oil, Christ's clients in the wilderness with loaves and fishes? O God, while thou dost thus promerit us by thy providence, let not us wrong thee by distrust.

God's undertakings cannot but be exquisite: those whom he professes to feed must needs have enough. The measure of his bounty cannot but run over. Doth he take upon him to prepare a table for his Israel in the desert? the bread shall be the food of angels; the flesh shall be the delicates of princes, manna and quails. Doth he take upon him to make wine for the marriage-feast of Cana? there shall be both store and choice; the vintage yields poor stuff to this. Will he feast his auditors in the wilderness? if they have not dainties, they shall have plenty; "They were all satisfied." Neither, yet, O Saviour, is thy hand closed. What abundance of heavenly doctrine dost thou set before us! how are we feasted, yea, pampered with thy celestial delicacies! not according to our meanness, but according to thy state, are we fed. Thrifty and niggardly collations are not for princes. We are full of thy goodness: O let our hearts run over with thanks!

I do gladly wonder at this miracle of thine, O Saviour, yet so as that I forget not mine own condition. Whence is it that we have our continual provision? one and the same munificent hand doth all. If the Israelites were fed with manna in the desert, and with corn in Canaan, both were done by the same power and bounty. If the disciples were fed by the loaves multiplied, and we by the grain multiplied, both are the act of one Omnipotence. What is this but a perpetual miracle, O God, which thou workest for our preservation? Without thee there is no more power in the grain to multiply, than in the loaf: it is thou that "givest it a body at thy pleasure, even to every seed his own body;" it is thou that "givest fulness of bread and cleanness of teeth." It is no reason thy goodness should be less magnified, because it is universal.

One or two baskets could have held the five loaves and two fishes; not less than twelve can hold the remainders. The divine munificence provides not for our necessity only, but for our abundance, yea superfluity. Envy and ignorance, while they make God the author of enough, are ready to impute the surplusage to another cause; as we commonly say of wine, that the liquor is God's, the excess Satan's.

Thy table, O Saviour, convinces them, which had more taken away than set on: thy blessing makes an estate not competent only, but rich. I hear of barns full of plenty, and presses bursting out with new wine, as the rewards of those that honour thee with their substance. I hear of heads anointed with oil, and cups running over. O God, as thou hast a free hand to give, so let us have a free heart to return thee the praise of thy bounty.

Those fragments were left behind. I do not see the people, when they had filled their bellies, cramming their pockets, or stuffing their wallets; yet the place was desert, and some of them doubtless had far home.

It becomes true disciples to be content with the present, not too solicitous for the future. O Saviour, thou didst not bid us beg bread for to-morrow, but for to-day: not that we should refuse thy bounty when thou pleasest to give, but that we should not distrust thy Providence for the need we may have.

Even these fragments, though but of barley-loaves and fish-bones, may not be left in the desert, for the compost of that earth whereon they were increased; but, by our Saviour's holy and just command, are gathered up. The liberal housekeeper of the world will not allow the loss of his orts: the children's bread may not be given to dogs; and if the crumbs fall to their share, it is because their smallness admits not of a collection. If those who out of obedience or due thrift have thought to gather up crumbs, have found them pearls, I wonder not: surely, both are alike the good creatures of the same Maker, and both of them may prove equally costly to us in their wilful mispending. But O, what shall we say, that not crusts and crumbs, not loaves and dishes and cups, but whole patrimonies, are idly lavished away, not merely lost — this were more easy — but ill spent in a wicked riot, upon dice, drabs, drunkards. O the fearful account of these unthrifty bailiffs, which shall once be given in to our great Lord and Master, when he shall call us to a strict reckoning of all our talents! He was condemned that increased not the sum concredited to him: what shall become of him that lawlessly impairs it?

Who gathered up these fragments, but the twelve apostles, every one his basket full? They were the servitors that set on this banquet; at the command of Christ, they waited on the tables, they took away.

It was our Saviour's just care that those offals should not perish; but he well knew that a greater loss depended upon those scraps, a loss of glory to the omnipotent Worker of that miracle. The feeding of the multitude was but the one half of the work, the other half was in the remnant. Of all other it most concerns the successors of the apostles to take care, that the marvellous works of their God and Saviour may be improved to the best; they may not suffer a crust or crumb to be lost, that may yield any glory to that Almighty agent.

Here was not any morsel or bone that was not worthy to be a relic, every the least parcel whereof was no other than miraculous. All the ancient monuments of God's supernatural power and mercy were in the keeping of Aaron and his sons. There is no servant in the family but should be thriftily careful for his master's profit; but most of all the steward, who is particularly charged with this oversight. Woe be to us, if we care only to gather up our own scraps, with neglect of the precious morsels of our Maker and Redeemer!

CONTEMPLATION VI.—THE WALK UPON THE WATERS.

ALL elements are alike to their Maker. He that had well approved his power on the land, will now show it in the air and the waters; he that had preserved the multitude from the peril of hunger in the desert, will now preserve his disciples from the peril of the tempest in the sea.

Where do we ever else find any compulsion offered by Christ to his disciples? He was like the good centurion: he said to one, " Go, and he goeth." When he did but call them from their nets, they came; and when he sent them by pairs into the cities and country of Judea, to preach the gospel, they went. There was never errand whereon they went unwillingly; only now he constrained them to depart. We may easily conceive how loath they were to leave him, whether out of love or common civility. Peter's tongue did but (when it was) speak the heart of the rest: " Master, thou knowest that I love thee." Who could choose but be in love with such a Master? and who can willingly part from what he loves? But had the respects been only common and ordinary, how unfit might it seem to leave a master, now towards night, in a wild place, amongst strangers, unprovided of the means of his passage! Where otherwise, therefore, he needed but to bid, now he constrains: O Saviour, it was ever thy manner to call all men unto thee: " Come to me, all that labour and are heavy laden." When didst thou ever drive any one from thee? Neither had it been so now, but to draw them closer unto thee, whom thou seemedst for the time to abdicate. In the meanwhile, I know not whether more to excuse their unwillingness, or to applaud their obedience. As it shall be fully above, so it was proportionably here below: "In thy presence," O Saviour, "is the fulness of joy." Once, when thou askedst these thy domestics, whether they also would depart, it was answered thee by one tongue for all: "Master, whither should we go from thee? thou hast the words of eternal life." What a death was it, then, to them to be compelled to leave thee! Sometimes it pleaseth the divine goodness to lay upon his servants such commands as savour of harshness and discomfort, which yet, both in his intention and in the event, are no other than gracious and sovereign. The more difficulty was in the charge, the more praise was in the obedience. I do not hear them stand upon the terms of capitulation with their Master, nor pleading importunately for their stay; but instantly, upon the command, they yield and go. We are never perfect disciples till we can depart from our reason, from our will; yea, O Saviour, when thou biddest us, from thyself.

Neither will the multitude be gone without a dismission. They had followed him while they were hungry; they will not leave him now they are fed. Fain would they put that honour upon him, which to avoid, he is fain to avoid them; gladly would they pay a kingdom to him, as their shot for their late banquet: he shuns both it and them. O Saviour, when the hour of thy passion was now come, thou couldst offer thyself readily to thine apprehenders; and now, when the glory of the world presses upon thee, thou runnest away from a crown. Was it to teach us, that there is less danger in suffering than in outward prosperity? What! do we doat upon that worldly honour which thou heldest worthy of avoidance and contempt?

Besides this reservedness, it was devotion that drew Jesus aside: he went alone up to the mountain to pray. Lo, thou, to whom the greatest throng was a solitude, in respect of the fruition of thy Father; thou, who wert incapable of distraction from him with whom thou wert one, wouldst yet so much act man, as to retire for the opportunity of prayer; to teach us, who are nothing but wild thoughts and giddy distractedness, to go aside when we would speak with God. How happy is it for us that thou prayedst! O Saviour, thou prayedst for us, who have not grace enough to pray for ourselves, not worth enough to be accepted when we do pray. Thy prayers, which were most perfect and impetrative, are they by which our weak and unworthy prayers receive both life and favour. And now, how assiduous should we be in our supplications, who are empty of grace, full of wants: when thou who wert a God of all power, prayedst for that which thou couldst command! Therefore do we pray, because thou prayedst: therefore do we expect to be graciously answered in our prayers, because thou didst pray for us here on earth, and now intercedest for us in heaven.

The evening was come. The disciples looked long for their Master, and loath they were to have stirred without him: but his command is more than the strongest wind to fill their sails; and they are now gone. Their expectation made not the evening seem so long, as our Saviour's devotion made it seem short to him; he is on the mount, they on the sea; yet, while he was on the mount praying, and lifting up his eyes to his Father, he fails not to cast them about upon his disciples tossed on the waves. Those all-seeing eyes admit of no limits: at once he sees the highest heavens, and the midst of the sea; the glory of his Father, and the misery of his disciples. Whatever prospects present themselves to his view, the distress of his followers is ever most noted.

How much more dost thou now, O Saviour, from the height of thy glorious advancement, behold us, thy wretched servants, tossed on the unquiet sea of this world, and beaten with the troublesome and threatening billows of affliction! Thou foresawest their toil and danger ere thou dismissedst them, and purposely sendedst them away that they might be tossed. Thou, that couldst prevent our sufferings by thy power, wilt permit them in thy wisdom, that thou mayest glorify thy mercy in our deliverance, and confirm our faith by the issue of our distresses.

How do all things now seem to conspire to the vexing of the poor disciples! The night was sullen and dark, their Master was absent, the sea was boisterous, the winds were high and contrary. Had their Master been with them, howsoever the elements had raged, they had been secure; had their Master been away, yet, if the sea had been quiet, or the winds fair, the passage might have been endured. Now both season, and sea, and wind, and their Master's desertion, had agreed to render them perfectly miserable. Sometimes the Providence of God hath thought good so to order it, that to his best servants there appeareth no glimpse of comfort, but so absolute vexation, as if heaven and earth had plotted their full affliction. Yea, O Saviour, what a dread night, what a fearful tempest, what an astonishing dereliction was that, wherein thou thyself criedst out 'n the bitterness of thine anguished soul, "My God! my God! why hast thou forsaken me?" Yet, in all these extremities of misery, our gracious God intends nothing but his greater glory and ours; the triumph of our faith, the crown of our victory.

All that longsome and tempestuous night must the disciples wear out in danger and horror, as given over to the winds and waves; but in the fourth watch of the night, when they were wearied out with toils and fears, comes deliverance.

At their entrance into the ship, at the rising of the tempest, at the shutting in of the evening, there was no news of Christ: but when they have been all the night long beaten, not so much with storms and waves, as with their own thoughts, now in the fourth watch, which was near to the morning, Jesus came unto them, and purposely not till then, that he might exercise their patience, that he might inure them to wait upon divine Providence in cases of extremity, that their devotions might be more whetted by delay, that they might give gladder welcome to their deliverance. O God, thus thou thinkest fit to do still. We are by turns in our sea; the winds bluster, the billows swell, the night and thy absence heighten our discomfort; thy time and ours is set: as yet it is but midnight with us; can we but hold out patiently till the fourth watch, thou wilt surely come and rescue us. O let us not faint under our sorrows, but wear out our three watches of tribulation, with undaunted patience and holy resolution!

O Saviour, our extremities are the seasons of thine aid. Thou camest at last, but yet so as that there was more dread than joy in thy presence: thy coming was both miraculous and frightful.

Thou, God of elements, passedst through the air, walkedst upon the waters. Whether thou meantest to terminate this miracle in thy body, or in the waves which thou troddest upon, whether so lightening the one, that it should make no impression in the liquid waters, or whether so consolidating the other, that the pavemented waves yielded a firm causeway to thy sacred feet to walk on, I neither determine nor inquire: thy silence ruleth mine: thy power was in either miraculous, neither know I in whether to adore it more. But withal, give me leave to wonder more at thy passage than at thy coming. Wherefore camest thou but to comfort them? and wherefore, then, wouldst thou pass by them as if thou hadst intended nothing but their dismay? Thine absence could not be so grievous as thy preterition: that might seem justly occasioned; this could not but seem willingly neglective. Our last conflicts have wont ever to be the sorest; as when after some dripping rain it pours down most vehemently, we think the weather is changing to serenity.

O Saviour, we may not always measure thy meaning by thy semblance: sometimes what thou most intendest, thou showest least. In our afflictions thou turnest thy back upon us, and hidest thy face from us, when thou most mindest our distresses. So Jonathan shot the arrows beyond David, when he meant them to him: so Joseph calls for Benjamin into bonds, when his heart was bound to him in the strongest affection: so the tender mother makes as if she would give away her crying child, whom she hugs so much closer in her bosom.

If thou pass by us while we are struggling with the tempest, we know it is not for want of mercy. Thou canst not neglect us: O let us not distrust thee!

What object should have been so pleasing to the eyes of the disciples as their Master, and so much the more as he showed his divine power in this miraculous walk? But lo, contrarily, "they are troubled;" not with his presence, but with this form of presence. The supernatural works of God, when we look upon them with our own eyes, are subject to a dangerous misprision. The very sunbeams, to which we are beholden for our sight, if we eye them directly, blind us. Miserable men! we are ready to suspect truths, to run away from our safety, to be afraid of our comforts, to misknow our best friends.

And why are they thus troubled? "They had thought they had seen a spirit." That there have been such apparitions of spirits, both good and evil, hath ever been a truth undoubtedly received of Pagans, Jews, and Christians; although in the blind times of superstition, there was much collusion mixed with some verities: crafty men, and lying spirits, agreed to abuse the credulous world; but even where there was not truth, yet there was horror. The very good angels were not seen without much fear; their sight was construed to bode death: how much more the evil, which in their very nature are harmful and pernicious! We see not a snake or a toad, without some recoiling of blood, and some sensible reluctation;

although those creatures run away from us: how much more must our hairs stand upright, and our senses boggle, at the sight of a spirit, whose nature and will both are contrary to ours, and professedly bent to our hurt!

But say it had been what they mistook it for, a spirit: why should they fear? Had they well considered, they had soon found, that evil spirits are nevertheless present when they are not seen, and nevertheless harmful or malicious when they are present unseen. Visibility adds nothing to their spite or mischief: and could their eyes have been opened, they had, with Elisha's servant, seen "more with them than against them;" a sure, though invisible guard of more powerful spirits, and themselves under the protection of the God of spirits: so as they might have bidden a bold defiance to all the powers of darkness. But, partly their faith was yet but in the bud, and partly the presentation of this dreadful object was sudden, and without the respite of a recollection and settlement of their thoughts.

O the weakness of our frail nature, who, in the want of faith, are affrighted with the visible appearance of those adversaries whom we profess daily to resist and vanquish, and with whom we know the decree of God hath matched us in an everlasting conflict! Are not these they that ejected devils by their command? are not these of them that could say, "Master, the evil spirits are subject to us?" Yet now, when they see but an imagined spirit, they fear. What power there is in the eye to betray the heart!

While Goliah was mingled with the rest of the Philistine host, Israel camped boldly against them; but when that giant stalks out single between the two armies, and fills and amazes their eyes with his hideous stature, now they run away for fear. Behold, we are committed with legions of evil spirits, and complain not: let but one of them give us some visible token of his presence, we shriek and tremble, and are not ourselves.

Neither is our weakness more conspicuous than thy mercy, O God, in restraining these spiritual enemies from these dreadful and ghastly representations of themselves to our eyes. Might those infernal spirits have liberty to appear, how and when, and to whom they would, certainly not many would be left in their wits, or in their lives. It is thy power and goodness to frail mankind, that they are kept in their chains, and reserved in the darkness of their own spiritual being, that we may both oppugn and subdue them unseen.

But, O the deplorable condition of reprobate souls! If but the imagined sight of one of these spirits of darkness can so daunt the heart of those which are free from their power, what a terror shall it be to live perpetually in the sight, yea, under the torture, of thousands, of legions, of millions of devils! O the madness of wilful sinners, that will needs run themselves headily into so dreadful a damnation!

It was high time for our Saviour to speak: what with the tempest, what with the apparition, the disciples were almost lost with fear. How seasonable are his gracious redresses! Till they were thus affrighted, he would not speak; when they were thus affrighted, he would not hold his peace. If his presence were fearful, yet his word was comfortable: "Be of good cheer, it is I:" Yea, it is his word only which must make his presence both known and comfortable. He was present before: they mistook him and feared: there needs no other erection of their drooping hearts, but "It is I." It is cordial enough to us, in the worst of our afflictions, to be assured of Christ's presence with us. Say but "It is I," O Saviour, and let evils do their worst; thou needest not say more. Thy voice was evidence enough; so well were thy disciples acquainted with the tongue of thee their Master, that "It is I," was as much as a hundred names. Thou art the good Shepherd: we are not of thy flock, if we know thee not by thy voice from a thousand. Even this one is a great word, yea, an ample style: "It is I." The same tongue that said to Moses, "I am hath sent thee," saith now to the disciples, "It is I;" I your Lord and Master, I the Commander of winds and waters, I the sovereign Lord of heaven and earth, I the God of spirits. Let heaven be but as one scroll, and let it be written all over with titles, they cannot express more than "It is I." O sweet and seasonable word of a gracious Saviour! able to calm all tempests, able to revive all hearts! Say but so to my soul, and in spite of hell, I am safe.

No sooner hath Jesus said "I," than Peter answers, "Master." He can instantly name him that did not name himself. Every little hint is enough to faith. The church sees her beloved as well through the lattice, as through the open window. Which of all the followers of Christ gave such pregnant testimonies, upon all occasions, of his faith, of his love to his Master, as Peter? The rest were silent, while he both owned his

Master, and craved access to him in that liquid way. Yet what a sensible mixture is here of faith and distrust! It was faith that said, "Master;" it was distrust, as some have construed it, that said, "If it be thou." It was faith that said, "Bid me come to thee;" implying that his word could as well enable as command; it was faith that durst step down upon that watery pavement; it was distrust, that upon the sight of a mighty wind feared; it was faith, that he walked; it was distrust that he sunk; it was faith that said, "Lord, save me!" O the imperfect composition of the best saint upon earth, as far from pure faith as from mere infidelity! If there be pure earth in the centre, all upward is mixed with the other elements: contrarily, pure grace is above in the glorified spirits; all below is mixed with infirmity, with corruption. Our best is but as the air, which never was, never can be at once fully enlightened; neither is there in the same region one constant state of light. It shall once be noon with us, when we shall have nothing but bright beams of glory: now it is but the dawning, wherein it is hard to say whether there be more light than darkness. We are now fair as the moon, which hath some spots in her greatest beauty; we shall be pure as the sun, whose face is all bright and glorious. Ever since the time that Adam set his tooth in the apple, till our mouth be full of mould, it never was, it never can be other with us. Far be it from us to settle willingly upon the dregs of our infidelity! far be it from us to be disheartened with the sense of our defects and imperfections! "We believe, Lord, help our unbelief."

While I find some disputing the lawfulness of Peter's suit, others quarrelling his "If it be thou," let me be taken up with wonder at the faith, the fervour, the heroical valour of this prime apostle, that durst say, "Bid me come to thee upon the waters." He might have suspected that the voice of his Master might have been as easily imitated by that imagined spirit as his person; he might have feared the blustering tempest, the threatening billows, the yielding nature of that devouring element: but, as despising all these thoughts of misdoubt, such is his desire to be near his Master, that he says, "Bid me come to thee upon the waters." He says not, Come thou to me: this had been Christ's act, and not his. Neither doth he say, Let me come to thee: this had been his act, and not Christ's. Neither doth he say, Pray that I may come to thee, as if this act had been out of the power of either but, "Bid me come to thee." I know thou canst command both the waves and me: me to be so light, that I shall not bruise the moist surface of the waves; the waves to be so solid, that they shall not yield to my weight: " All things obey thee: Bid me come to thee upon the waters."

It was a bold spirit that could wish it, more bold that could act it. No sooner hath our Saviour said, "Come," than he sets his foot upon the unquiet sea, not fearing either the softness or the roughness of that uncouth passage. We are wont to wonder at the courage of that daring man who first committed himself to the sea in a frail bark, though he had the strength of an oaken plank to secure him: how valiant must we needs grant him to be, that durst set his foot upon the bare sea, and shift his paces! Well did Peter know, that he who bade him, could uphold him; and therefore he both sues to be bidden, and ventures to be upholden. True faith tasks itself with difficulties, neither can be dismayed with the conceits of ordinary impossibilities: it is not the scattering of straws, or casting of mole-hills, whereby the virtue of it is described, but removing of mountains: like some courageous leader, it desires the honour of a danger, and sues for the first onset: whereas, the worldly heart freezes in a lazy or cowardly fear, and only casts for safety and ease.

Peter sues, Jesus bids. Rather will he work miracles, than disappoint the suit of a faithful man. How easily might our Saviour have turned over this strange request of his bold disciple, and have said, What my omnipotence can do is no rule for thy weakness: it is no less than presumption in a mere man, to hope to imitate the miraculous works of God and man. Stay thou in the ship, and wonder, contenting thyself in this, that thou hast a Master to whom the land and water is alike. Yet I hear not a check, but a call, "Come." The suit of ambition is suddenly quashed in the mother of the Zebedees. The suits of revenge prove no better in the mouth of the two fiery disciples. But a suit of faith, though high, and seemingly unfit for us, he hath no power to deny. How much less, O Saviour, wilt thou stick at those things which lie in the very road of our Christianity! Never man said, Bid me come to thee in the way of thy commandments, whom thou didst not both bid and enable to come.

True faith rests not in great and good desires, but acts and executes accordingly. Peter doth not wish to go, and yet stand still; but his foot answers his tongue, and instantly chops down upon the waters. To sit still, and wish, is for sluggish and cowardly spirits.

Formal volitions, yea, velleities of good, while we will not so much as step out of the ship of our nature to walk unto Christ, are but the faint motions of vain hypocrisy. It will be long enough ere the gale of good wishes can carry us to our haven. "Ease slayeth the foolish." O Saviour, we have thy command to come to thee out of the ship of our natural corruption: let no sea affright us, let no tempest of temptation withhold us. No way can be but safe, when thou art the end.

Lo! Peter is walking upon the waves! Two hands uphold him, the hand of Christ's power, the hand of his own faith: neither of them would do it alone. The hand of Christ's power laid hold on him; the hand of his faith laid hold on the power of Christ commanding. Had not Christ's hand been powerful, that faith had been in vain: had not that faith of his strongly fixed upon Christ, that power had not been effectual to his preservation. While we are here in the world, we walk upon the waters; still the same hands bear us up. If he let go his hold of us, we drown; if we let go our hold of him, we sink and shriek as Peter did here, who, when he saw the wind boisterous, was afraid, and, "beginning to sink, cried, saying, Lord, save me."

When he wished to be bidden to walk unto Christ, he thought of the waters; "Bid me come to thee on the waters:" he thought not on the winds which raged on those waters; or if he thought of a stiff gale, yet that tempestuous and sudden gust was out of his account and expectation. Those evils that we are prepared for have not such power over us as those that surprise us. A good waterman sees a dangerous billow coming towards him, and cuts it, and mounts over it with ease; the unheedy is overwhelmed. O Saviour, let my haste to thee be zealous, but not improvident; ere I set my foot out of the ship, let me foresee the tempest; when I have cast the worst, I cannot either miscarry or complain.

So soon as he began to fear, he began to sink: while he believed, the sea was brass; when once he began to distrust, those waves were water. He cannot sink, while he trusts the power of his Master; he cannot but sink when he misdoubts it. Our faith gives us, as courage and boldness, so success too; our infidelity lays us open to all dangers, to all mischiefs.

It was Peter's improvidence not to foresee; it was his weakness to fear, it was the effect of his fear to sink; it was his faith that recollects itself, and breaks through his infidelity, and, in sinking, could say, "Lord, save me." His foot could not be so swift in sinking, as his heart in imploring: he knew who could uphold him from sinking, and, being sunk, deliver him; and therefore he says, "Lord, save me."

It is both a notable sign and effect of true faith, in sudden extremities, to ejaculate holy desires, and, with the wings of our first thoughts, to fly up instantly to the throne of grace for present succour. Upon deliberation, it is possible for a man, that hath been careless and profane, by good means to be drawn to holy dispositions: but on the sudden, a man will appear as he is; whatever is most rife in the heart, will come forth at the mouth. It is good to observe how our surprisals find us: the rest is but forced, this is natural: "Out of the abundance of the heart the mouth speaketh." O Saviour, no evil can be swifter than my thought; my thought shall be upon thee ere I can be seized upon by the speediest mischief: at least, if I overrun not evils, I shall overtake them.

It was Christ his Lord whom Peter had offended in distrusting; it is Christ his Lord to whom he sues for deliverance. His weakness doth not discourage him from his refuge. O God, when we have displeased thee, when we have sunk in thy displeasure, whither should we fly for aid, but to thee whom we have provoked? Against thee only is our sin, in thee only is our help. In vain shall all the powers of heaven and earth conspire to relieve us, if thou withhold from our succour. As we offend thy justice daily by our sins, so let us continually rely upon thy mercy by the strength of our faith: "Lord, save us!"

The mercy of Christ is at once sought and found: "Immediately Jesus stretched forth his hand, and caught him." He doth not say, hadst thou trusted me, I would have safely preserved thee, but, since thou wilt needs wrong my power and care with a cowardly diffidence, sink and drown: but rather, as pitying the infirmity of his fearful disciple, he puts out the hand for his relief. That hand hath been stretched forth for the aid of many a one that never asked it: never any asked it to whose succour it hath not been stretched. With what speed, with what confidence, should we fly to that sovereign bounty, from which never any suitor was sent away empty!

Jesus gave Peter his hand, but withal he

gave him a check: "O thou of little faith, why doubtest thou?" As Peter's faith was not pure, but mixed with some distrust, so our Saviour's help was not clear and absolute, but mixed with some reproof; a reproof, wherein there was both a censure and an expostulation; a censure of his faith, an expostulation for his doubt; both of them sore and heavy.

By how much more excellent and useful a grace faith is, by so much more shameful is the defect of it; and by how much more reason here was of confidence, by so much more blameworthy was the doubt. Now Peter had a double reason of his confidence: the command of Christ, the power of Christ; the one in bidding him to come, the other in sustaining him while he came. To misdoubt him whose will he knew, whose power he felt, was well worth a reprehension.

When I saw Peter stepping forth upon the waters, I could not but wonder at his great faith; yet behold, ere he can have measured many paces, the Judge of hearts taxes him for little faith. Our mountains are but motes to God. Would my heart have served me to dare the doing of this that Peter did? durst I have set my foot where he did? O Saviour, if thou foundest cause to censure the weakness and poverty of his faith, what mayest thou well say to mine! They mistake that think thou wilt take up with anything. Thou lookest for firmness and vigour in those graces, which thou wilt allow in thy best disciples, no less than truth.

The first steps were confident, there was fear in the next. O the sudden alteration of our affections, of our dispositions! one pace varies our spiritual condition. What hold is there of so fickle creatures, if we be left never so little to ourselves? As this lower world, wherein we are, is the region of mutability, so are we, the living pieces of it, subject to a perpetual change. It is for the blessed saints and angels above to be fixed in good: while we are here, there can be no constancy expected from us, but in variableness.

As well as our Saviour loves Peter, yet he chides him. It is the fruit of his favour and mercy that we escape judgment, not that we escape reproof. Had not Peter found grace with his Master, he had been suffered to sink in silence; now he is saved with a check. There may be more love in frowns than in smiles: "Whom he loves he chastises." What is chiding but a verbal castigation? and what is chastisement but a real chiding? "Correct me, O Lord, yet in thy judgment, not in thy fury." "O let the righteous God smite me, when I offend, with his gracious reproofs; these shall be a precious oil that shall not break my head."

CONTEMPLATION VII.—THE BLOODY ISSUE HEALED.

THE time was, O Saviour, when a worthy woman offered to touch thee, and was forbidden: now a meaner touches thee with approbation and encouragement. Yet as there was much difference in that body of thine which was the object of that touch, being now mortal and passible, then impassible and immortal, so there was in the agents: this a stranger, that a familiar; this obscure, that famous.

The same actions vary with time and other circumstances; and accordingly receive their dislike or allowance.

Doubtless thou hadst herein no small respect to the faith of Jairus, unto whose house thou wert going. That good man had but one only daughter, which lay sick in the beginning of his suit; ere the end, lay dead; while she lived, his hope lived; her death disheartened it. It was a great work that thou meantest to do for him; it was a great word that thou saidst to him: "Fear not, believe, and she shall be made whole." To make this good, by the touch of the verge of thy garment, thou revivedst one from the verge of death. How must Jairus needs now think, He who, by the virtue of his garment, can pull this woman out of the paws of death, which hath been twelve years dying, can as well, by the power of his word, pull my daughter, who hath been twelve years living, out of the jaws of death, which hath newly seized on her. It was fit the good ruler should be raised up with this handsel of thy divine power, whom he came to solicit.

That thou mightest lose no time, thou curedst in thy passage. The sun stands not still to give his influences, but diffuses them in his ordinary motion. How shall we imitate thee, if we suffer our hands to be out of use with good? Our life goes away with our time: we lose that which we improve not.

The patient laboured of an issue of blood; a disease that had not more pain than shame, nor more natural infirmity than legal impurity. Time added to her grief; twelve long years had she languished under this woful complaint. Besides the tediousness, diseases must needs get head by continuance, and so much more both weaken nature and strengthen themselves, by how much longer they afflict us. So it is in the soul, so in the state: vices which are the sicknesses of both, when they grow inveterate, have a strong plea for their abode and uncontrollableness.

Yet more, to mend the matter, poverty, which is another disease, was superadded to her sickness; "she had spent all she had upon physicians." While she had wherewith to make much of herself, and to procure good tendance, choice diet, and all the succours of a distressing languishment, she could not but find some mitigation of her sorrow: but now want began to pinch her no less than her distemper, and helped to make her perfectly miserable.

Yet could she have parted from her substance with ease, her complaint had been the less. Could the physicians have given her, if not health, yet relaxation and painlessness, her means had not been misbestowed; but now, "she suffered many things from them;" many an unpleasing potion, many tormenting incisions and divulsions did she endure from their hands; the remedy was equal in trouble to the disease.

Yet had the cost and pain been never so great, could she have thereby purchased health, the match had been happy; all the world were no price for this commodity: but alas, her estate was the worse, her body not the better; her money was wasted, not her disease. Art could give her neither cure nor hope. It were injurious to blame that noble science, for that it always speeds not. Notwithstanding all those sovereign remedies, men must, in their times, sicken and die. Even the miraculous gifts of healing could not preserve the owners from disease and dissolution.

It were pity but that this woman should have been thus sick; the nature, the durableness, cost, pain, incurableness of her disease, both sent her to seek Christ, and moved Christ to her cure. Our extremities drive us to our Saviour; his love draws him to be most present and helpful to our extremities. When we are forsaken of all succours and hopes, we are fittest for his redress. Never are we nearer to help, than when we despair of help. There is no fear, no danger, but in our own insensibleness.

This woman was a stranger to Christ; it seems she had never seen him. The report of his miracles had lifted her up to such a confidence of his power and mercy, as that she said in herself, "If I may but touch the hem of his garment, I shall be whole." The shame of her disease stopt her mouth from any verbal suit. Had her infirmity been known, she had been shunned and abhorred, and disdainfully put back of all the beholders, as doubtless, where she was known, the law forced her to live apart. Now she conceals both her grief, and her desire, and her faith; and only speaks where she may be bold, within herself: "If I may but touch the hem of his garment, I shall be whole."

I seek not mysteries in the virtue of the hem, rather than of the garment. Indeed, it was God's command to Israel, that they should be marked, not only in their skin, but in their clothes too: those fringes and ribands upon the borders of their garments were for holy memorials of their duty, and God's law. But that hence she supposed to find more virtue and sanctity in the touch of the hem than of the coat, I neither dispute nor believe; it was the sight, not the signification that she intimated; not as of the best part, but the utmost. In all likelihood, if there could have been virtue in the garment, the nearer to the body the more. Here was then the praise of this woman's faith, that she promiseth herself cure from the touch of the utmost hem. Whosoever would look to receive any benefit from Christ, must come in faith: it is that only which makes us capable of any favour. Satan, the common ape of the Almighty, imitates him also in this point: all his charms and spells are ineffectual without the faith of the user, of the receiver.

Yea, the endeavour and issue of all, both human and spiritual things, depends upon our faith. Who would commit a plant or seed to the earth, if he did not believe to have it nursed in that kindly bosom? What merchant would put himself upon the guard of an inch-board in a furious sea, if he did not trust to the faithful custody of that plank? Who would trade, or travel, or war, or marry, if he did not therein surely trust he should speed well? What benefit can we look to carry from a divine exhortation, if we do not believe it will edify us? from a sacramental banquet, the food of angels, if we do not believe it will nourish our souls? from our best devotions, if we do not persuade ourselves they will fetch down blessings? O our vain and heartless services, if we do not say, May I drink but one drop of that heavenly nectar, may I taste but one crumb of that bread of life, may I hear but one word from the mouth of Christ, may I send up but one hearty sigh or ejaculation of a holy desire to my God, I shall be whole!

According to her resolution is her practice. She touched, but she came behind to touch; whether for humility, or her secrecy rather, as desiring to steal a cure unseen, unnoted. She was a Jewess, and therefore well knew that her touch was, in this case, no better than a pollution, as hers, perhaps, but not of him. For, on the one side, necessity is under no positive law; on the other, the Son of God was not capable of impurity. Those may be defiled with a touch, that cannot heal with a touch; he, that was above law is not comprised in the law: be we never so unclean, he may heal us; we cannot infect him. O Saviour, my soul is sick and foul enough with the spiritual impurities of sin; let me, by the hand of faith, lay hold but upon the hem of thy garment (thy righteousness is thy garment), it shall be both clean and whole.

Who would not think but a man might lade up a dish of water out of the sea unmissed? Yet that water, though much, is finite; those drops are within number: that art, which hath reckoned how many corns of sand would make up a world, could more easily compute how many drops of water would make up an ocean; whereas the mercies of God are absolutely infinite, and beyond all possibility of proportion: and yet this bashful soul cannot steal one drop of mercy from this endless, boundless, bottomless sea of divine bounty, but it is felt and questioned: "And Jesus said, Who touched me?"

Who can now say that he is a poor man that reckons his store, when that God, who is rich in mercy, doth so? He knows all his own blessings, and keeps just tallies of our receipts; delivered so much honour to this man, to that so much wealth; so much knowledge to one, to another so much strength. How carefully frugal should we be in the notice, account, usage of God's several favours, since his bounty sets all his gifts upon the file! Even the worst servant in the gospel confessed his talents, though he employed them not. We are worse than the worst, if either we misknow, or dissemble, or forget them.

Who now can forbear the disciple's reply? Who touched thee, O Lord? the multitude. Dost thou ask of one, when thou art pressed by many? In the midst of a throng, dost thou ask, "Who touched me?"

Yea, but yet, "some one touched me:" all thronged me; but one touched me. How riddle-like soever it may seem to sound, they that thronged me touched me not; she only touched me that thronged me not, yea, that touched me not. Even so, O Saviour, others touched thy body with theirs; she touched thy hem with her hand, thy divine power with her soul.

Those two parts whereof we consist, the bodily, the spiritual, do in a sort partake of each other. The soul is the man, and hath those parts, senses, actions, which are challenged as proper to the body. This spiritual part hath both a hand, and a touch; it is by the hand of faith that the soul toucheth; yea, this alone both is and acts all the spiritual senses of that immaterial and divine part: this sees, hears, tasteth, toucheth God; and without this, the soul doth none of these. All the multitude then pressed Christ: he took not that for a touch, since faith was away; only she touched him that believed to receive virtue by his touch. Outward fashionableness comes into no account with God; that is only done which the soul doth. It is no hoping that virtue should go forth from Christ to us, when no hearty desires go forth from us to him. He that is a spirit, looks to the deportment of that part which resembleth himself: as, without it, the body is dead; so without the actions thereof, bodily devotions are but carcasses.

What reason had our Saviour to challenge this touch? "Somebody touched me." The multitude, in one extreme, denied any touch at all: Peter, in another extreme, affirmed an over-touching of the multitude. Betwixt both, he who felt it can say, "Somebody touched me." Not all, as Peter; not none, as the multitude; but somebody. How then, O Saviour, how doth it appear that somebody touched thee? "For I perceive virtue is gone out from me." The effect proves the act; virtue gone out evinces the touch. These two are in thee convertible: virtue cannot go out of thee but by a touch, and no touch can be of thee, without virtue going out from thee. That which is a rule in nature, that every agent works by a contract, holds spiritually too: then dost thou, O God, work upon our souls, when thou touchest our hearts by the Spirit; then do we re-act upon thee, when we touch thee by the hand of our faith and confidence in thee; and, in both these, virtue goes out from thee to us; yet goes not so out, as that there is less in thee. In all bodily emanations, whose powers are but finite, it must needs follow, that the more is sent forth, the less is reserved: but as it is in the sun, which gives us light, yet loseth none ever the more, the luminosity of it being no whit impaired by that perpetual emission of lightsome beams, so much more is it in thee, the Father of lights. Virtue could not go out of thee without thy knowledge, without thy sending. Neither was it in a dislike, or in a grudging exprobration, that thou saidst, "Virtue is gone out from me." Nothing could please thee better, than to feel virtue fetched out from thee by the faith of the receiver. It is the nature and praise of good to be communicative: none of us would be other than liberal of our little, if we did not fear it would be lessened by imparting. Thou, that knowest thy store so infinite, that participation doth only glorify and not diminish it, canst not but be more willing to give, than we to receive. If we take but one drop of water from the sea, or one corn of sand from the shore, there is so much, though insensibly, less: but were we capable of worlds of virtue and benediction from that munificent hand, our enriching could no whit impoverish thee. Thou which wert wont to hold it much "better to give than to receive," canst not but give gladly. Fear not, O my soul, to lade plentifully at this well, this ocean of mercy, which, the more thou takest, overflows the more.

But why then, O Saviour, why didst thou thus inquire, thus expostulate? Was it for thy own sake, that the glory of the miracle might thus come to light, which otherwise had been smothered in silence? was it for Jairus' sake, that his depressed heart might be raised to a confidence in thee, whose mighty power he saw proved by this cure, whose omniscience he saw proved by the knowledge of the cure? or, was it chiefly for the woman's sake, for the praise of her faith, for the securing of her conscience?

It was within herself that she said, "If I may but touch:" none could hear this voice of the heart, but he that made it. It was within herself that the cure was wrought: none of the beholders knew her complaint, much less her recovery; none noted her touch, none knew the occasion of her touch. What a pattern of powerful faith had we lost, if our Saviour had not called this act to trial! as her modesty hid her disease, so it would have hid her virtue. Christ will not suffer this secrecy. O the marvellous but free dispensation of Christ! One while he enjoins a silence to his re-cured patients, and is troubled with their divulgation of his favour; another while, as here, he will not lose the honour of a secret mercy, but fetches it out by his inquisition, by his profession: "Who hath touched me? for I perceive virtue is gone out from me." As we see in the great work of his creation, he hath placed some stars in the midst of heaven, where they may be most conspicuous; others he hath set in the southern obscurity, obvious to but few eyes: in the earth he hath planted some flowers and trees in the famous gardens of the world; others, no less beautiful, in untracked woods or wild deserts, where they are either not seen, or not regarded.

O God, if thou hast intended to glorify thyself by thy graces in us, thou wilt find means to fetch them forth into the notice of the world; otherwise our very privacy shall content us, and praise thee.

Yet even this great faith wanted not some weakness. It was a poor conceit in this woman, that she thought she might receive so sovereign a remedy from Christ without his heed, without his knowledge. Now that she might see she had trusted to a power which was not more bountiful than sensible, and whose goodness did not exceed his apprehension, but one that knew what he parted with, and willingly parted with that which he knew beneficial to so faithful a receiver, he can say, "Somebody hath touched me, for I perceive virtue is gone out from me." As there was an error in her thought, so in our Saviour's words there was a correction. His mercy will not let her run away with that secret offence. It is a great favour of God to take us in the manner, and to shame our closeness. We scour off the rust from a weapon that we esteem, and prune the vine we care for. O God, do thou ever find me out in my sin, and do not pass over my least infirmities without a feeling controlment!

Neither doubt I, but that herein, O Saviour, thou didst graciously forecast the securing of the conscience of this faithful, though overseen, patient, which might well have afterwards raised some just scruples, for the filching of a cure, for unthankfulness to the Author of her cure; the continuance whereof she might have good reason to misdoubt, being surreptitiously gotten, ungratefully concealed. For prevention of all these dangers, and the full quieting of her troubled heart, how fitly, how mercifully, didst thou bring forth this close business to the light, and clear it to the bottom! It is thy great mercy to foresee our perils, and to remove them ere we can apprehend the fear of them: as some skilful physician, who, perceiving a fever or phrenzy coming, which the distempered patient little misdoubts, by seasonable applications anticipates that grievous malady, so as the sick man knows his safety, ere he can suspect his danger.

Well might the woman think, He who can thus cure, and thus know his cure, can as well know my name, and descry my person and shame, and punish my ingratitude. With a pale face, therefore, and a trembling foot, she comes and falls down before him, and humbly acknowledges what she had done, what she had obtained: "But the woman finding she was not hid," &c.

Could she have perceived that she might have slily gone away with the cure, she had not confessed it: so had she made God a loser of glory, and herself an unthankful receiver of so great a benefit.

Might we have our own wills, we should be injurious both to God and ourselves. Nature lays such plots as would be sure to befool us, and is witty in nothing but deceiving herself. The only way to bring us home, is to find we are found, and to be convinced of the discovery of all our evasions: as some unskilful thief, that finds the owner's eye was upon him in his pilfering, lays down his stolen commodity with shame. Contrarily, when a man is possessed with a conceit of secrecy, and cleanly escapes, he is emboldened in his lewdness. The adulterer chooses the twilight, and says, "No eye shall see me;" and joys in the sweetness of his stolen waters. O God! in the deepest darkness, in my most inward retiredness, where none sees me, when I see not myself, yet let me then see thine all-seeing eye upon me; and if ever mine eyes shall be shut, or held with a prevailing temptation, check me with a speedy reproof, that, with this abashed patient, I may come in, and confess my error, and implore thy mercy.

It is no unusual thing for kindness to look sternly for the time, that it may endear itself more when it lists to be discovered. With a severe countenance did our Saviour look about him, and ask, "Who touched me?" When the woman comes in trembling, and confessing both her act and success, he clears up his brows, and speaks comfortably to her: "Daughter, be of good cheer, thy faith hath made thee whole; go in peace." O sweet and seasonable word, fit for those merciful and divine lips, able to secure any heart, to dispel any fears! Still, O Saviour, thou dost thus to us: when we fall down before thee in an awful dejectedness, thou rearest us up with a cheerful and compassionate encouragement; when thou findest us bold and presumptuous, thou lovest to take us down; when humbled, it is enough to have prostrated us. Like as that lion of Bethel worries the disobedient prophet, guards the poor ass that stood quaking before him; or like some mighty wind that bears over a tall elm or cedar with the same breath that it raiseth a stooping reed: or like some good physician, who, finding the body obstructed and surcharged with ill humours, evacuates it, and when it is sufficiently pulled down, raises it up with sovereign cordials: and still do thou so to my soul! If at any time thou perceivest me stiff and rebellious, ready to face out my sin against thee, spare me not; let me smart till I relent. But a broken and contrite heart thou wilt not, O Lord! O Lord, do not reject!

It is only thy word which gives what it requires, comfort and confidence. Had any other shaken her by the shoulder, and cheered her up against those oppressive passions, it had been but waste wind. No voice but his, who hath power to remit sin, can secure the heart from the conscience of sin, from the pangs of conscience. In the midst of the sorrows of my heart, thy comforts, O Lord, thy comforts only, have power to refresh my soul. Her cure was Christ's act, yet he gives the praise of it to her: "Thy faith hath made thee whole." He had said before, "Virtue is gone out from me;" now he acknowledges a virtue inherent in her. It was his virtue that cured her, yet he graciously casts this work upon her faith: not that her faith did it by way of merit, by way of efficiency, but by way of impetration. So much did our Saviour regard that faith which he had wrought in her, that he will honour it with the success of her cure. Such and the same is still the remedy of our spiritual diseases, our sins: "By faith we are justified, by faith we are saved." Thou only, O Saviour, canst heal us; thou wilt not heal us but by our faith; not as it issues from us, but as it appropriates thee. The sickness is ours, the remedy is ours; the sickness is our own by nature, the remedy ours by thy grace, both working and accepting it. Our faith is no less from thee, than thy cure is from our faith.

O happy dismission, "Go in peace!" How unquiet had this poor soul formerly been! she had no outward peace with her neighbours, they shunned and abhorred her presence in this condition, yea they must do so. She had no peace in body, that was pained and vexed with so long and foul a disease; much less had she peace in her mind, which was grievously disquieted with sorrow for her sickness, with anger and discontentment at her torturing physicians, with fear of the continuance of so bad a guest. Her soul, for the present, had no peace, from the sense of her guiltiness in the carriage of this business, from the conceived displeasure of him to whom she came for comfort and redress. At once now doth our Saviour calm all these storms; and, in one word and act, restores her to peace with her neighbours, peace in herself, peace in body, in mind, in soul: " Go in peace." Even so, Lord, it was for thee only, who art the Prince of Peace, to bestow thy peace where thou pleasest. Our body, mind, soul, estate, is thine, whether to afflict or ease. It is a wonder if all of us do not ail somewhat. In vain shall we speak peace to ourselves, in vain shall the world speak peace to us, except thou say to us, as thou didst to this distressed soul, " Go in peace."

CONTEMPLATION VIII. — JAIRUS AND HIS DAUGHTER.

How troublesome did the people's importunity seem to Jairus! That great man came to sue unto Jesus for his dying daughter; the throng of the multitude intercepted him. Every man is most sensible of his own necessity. It is no straining courtesy in the challenge of our interest in Christ; there is no unmannerliness in our strife for the greatest share in his presence and benediction.

That only child of this ruler lay a-dying when he came to solicit Christ's aid, and was dead while he solicited it. There was hope in her sickness; in her extremity there was fear; in her death despair, and impossibility, as they thought, of help: " Thy daughter is dead, trouble not the Master." When we have to do with a mere finite power, this word were but just. He was a prophet no less than a king, that said, " While the child was yet alive, I fasted and wept; for I said, Who can tell whether God will be gracious to me, that the child may live? but now he is dead, wherefore should I fast? Can I bring him back again? I shall go to him, but he shall not return to me." But since thou hast to do with an omnipotent agent, know now, O thou faithless messenger, that death can be no bar to his power. How well would it have become thee to have said, " Thy daughter is dead!" But who can tell whether thy God and Saviour will not be gracious to thee, that the child may revive? cannot he, in whose hands are the issues of death, bring her back again?

Here were more manners than faith: " Trouble not the Master." Infidelity is all for ease, and thinks every good work tedious. That which nature accounts troublesome, is pleasing and delightful to grace. Is it any pain for a hungry man to eat? O Saviour, it was thy "meat and drink to do thy Father's will;" and his will was, that thou shouldst bear our griefs, and take away our sorrows. It cannot be thy trouble which is our happiness, that we must still sue to thee.

The messenger could not so whisper his ill news, but Jesus heard it. Jairus hears that he feared, and was now heartless with so sad tidings. He that resolved not to trouble the Master, meant to take so much more trouble to himself, and would now yield to a hopeless sorrow. He whose work it is to comfort the afflicted, rouseth up the dejected heart of that pensive father: " Fear not; believe only, and she shall be made whole." The word was not more cheerful than difficult: " Fear not." Who can be insensible of so great an evil? Where death hath once seized, who can but doubt he will keep his hold? No less hard was it not to grieve for the loss of an only child, than not to fear the continuance of the cause of that grief.

In a perfect faith there is no fear: by how much more we fear, by so much less we believe. Well are these two then coupled: " Fear not; believe only." O Saviour, if thou didst not command us somewhat beyond nature, it were no thank to us to obey thee. While the child was alive, to believe that it might recover, it was no hard task; but now that she was fully dead, to believe she should live again, was a work not easy for Jairus to apprehend, though easy for thee to effect: yet must that be believed, else there is no capacity of so great a mercy. As love, so faith, is stronger than death, making those bonds no other than, as Samson did his withes, like threads of tow. How much natural impossibility is there in the return of these bodies from the dust of their earth, into which, through many degrees of corruption, they are at the last mouldered! Fear not, O my soul! believe only: it must, it shall be done.

The sum of Jairus' first suit was for the health, not for the resuscitation of his daughter: now, that she was dead, he would, if he durst, have been glad to have asked her life. And now, behold, our Saviour bids him expect both her life and her health: " Thy daughter shall be made whole;" alive from her death, whole from her disease.

Thou didst not, O Jairus, thou daredst not ask so much as thou receivedst. How glad wouldst thou have been, since this last news, to have had thy daughter alive, though weak and sickly! now thou shalt receive her, not living only, but sound and vigorous. Thou dost not, O Saviour, measure thy gifts by our petitions, but by our wants and thine own mercies.

This work might have been as easily done by an absent command; the power of Christ was there, while himself was away: but he will go personally to the place, that he might be confessed the author of so great a miracle. O Saviour, thou lovest to go to the house of mourning; thy chief pleasure is the comfort of the afflicted. What a confusion there is in worldly sorrow! The mother shrieks, the servants cry out, the people make lamentation, the minstrels howl and strike dolefully, so as the ear might question whether the ditty or the instrument were more heavy. If ever expressions of sorrow sound well, it is when death leads the choir. Soon doth our Saviour charm this noise, and turns these unseasonable mourners, whether formal or serious, out of doors: not that he dislikes music, whether to condole or comfort; but that he had life in his eye, and would have them know, that he held these funeral ceremonies to be too early, and long before their time: "Give place, for the maid is not dead, but sleepeth." Had she been dead, she had but slept; now she was not dead, but asleep, because he meant this nap of death should be so short, and her awakening so speedy. Death and sleep are alike to him, who can cast whom he will into the sleep of death, and awake when and whom he pleaseth out of that deadly sleep.

Before, the people and domestics of Jairus held Jesus for a prophet; now they took him for a dreamer. "Not dead, but asleep!" They that came to mourn cannot now forbear to laugh. Have we piped at so many funerals, and seen and lamented so many corpses, and cannot we distinguish betwixt sleep and death? The eyes are set, the breath is gone, the limbs are stiff and cold? Who ever died, if she do but sleep? How easily may our reason or sense befool us in divine matters! Those that are competent judges in natural things, are ready to laugh God to scorn when he speaks beyond their compass, and are by him justly laughed to scorn for their unbelief. Vain and faithless men! as if that unlimited power of the Almighty could not make good his own word, and turn either sleep into death, or death into sleep, at pleasure. Ere many minutes, they shall be ashamed of their error and incredulity.

There were witnesses enough of her death; there shall not be many of her restoring. Three choice disciples, and the two parens, are only admitted to the view and testimony of this miraculous work.

The eyes of those incredulous scoffers were not worthy of this honour. Our infidelity makes us incapable of the secret favours and the highest counsels of the Almighty.

What did these scorners think and say, when they saw him putting the minstrels and people out of doors? Doubtless the maid is but asleep; the man fears lest the noise shall awake her: we must speak and tread softly, that we disquiet her not. What will he and his disciples do the while? Is it not to be feared, they will startle her out of her rest? Those that are shut out from the participation of God's counsels, think all his words and projects no better than foolishness. But art thou, O Saviour, ever the more discouraged by the derision and censure of these scornful unbelievers? because fools jeer thee, dost thou forbear thy work! Surely I do not perceive that thou heedest them, save for contempt; or carest more for their words than their silence. It is enough that thine act shall soon honour thee, and convince them: "He took her by the hand, and called, saying, Maid, arise; and her spirit came again, and she arose straightway."

How could that touch, that call, be other than effectual? He, who made that hand, touched it; and he, who shall once say, "Arise, ye dead," said now, "Maid, arise." Death cannot but obey him who is the Lord of life. The soul is ever equally in his hand who is the God of spirits; it cannot but go and come at his command. When he says, "Maid, arise," the now dissolved spirit knows his office, his place, and instantly re-assumes that room which, by his appointment, it had left.

O Saviour, if thou do but bid my soul to arise from the death of sin, it cannot lie still: if thou bid my body to arise from the grave, my soul cannot but glance down from her heaven, and animate it. In vain shall my sin, or my grave, offer to withhold me from thee.

The maid revives; not now to languish for a time upon her sickbed, and by some faint degrees to gather an insensible strength; but at once she rises from her death, and from her couch; at once she puts off her fever with her dissolution: she finds her life and her feet at once; at once she finds her feet and her stomach: "He commanded to give her meat." Omnipotency doth not use to go the pace of nature. All God's immediate works are, like himself, perfect. He that raised her supernaturally, could have so fed her. It was never the purpose of his power to put ordinary means out of office.

2 L

CONTEMPLATION IX. — THE MOTION OF THE TWO FIERY DISCIPLES REPELLED.

The time drew on wherein Jesus must be received up; he must take death in his way; Calvary is in his passage to mount Olivet: he must be lifted up to the cross, thence to climb into his heaven. Yet this comes not into mention, as if all the thought of death were swallowed up in this victory over death. Neither, O Saviour, is it otherwise with us, the weak members of thy mystical body: we must die, we shall be glorified. What if death stand before us? we look beyond him, at that transcendent glory. How should we be dismayed with that pain which is attended with a blessed immortality?

The strongest receipt against death is the happy estate that follows it: next to that, is the fore-expectation of it, and resolution against it: " He stedfastly set his face to go to Jerusalem." Jerusalem, the nest of his enemies, the amphitheatre of his conflicts, the fatal place of his death. Well did he know the plots and ambushes that were there laid for him, and the bloody issue of those designs: yet he will go, and goes resolved for the worst. It is a sure and wise way to send our thoughts before us, to grapple with those evils which we know must be encountered; the enemy is half overcome that is well prepared for. The strongest mischief may be outfaced with a seasonable fore-resolution. There can be no greater disadvantage, than the suddenness of a surprisal. O God, what I have not the power to avoid, let me have the wisdom to expect.

The way from Galilee to Judea lay through the region of Samaria, if not the city. Christ, now towards the end of his preaching, could not but be attended with a multitude of followers: it was necessary there should be purveyors and harbingers, to procure lodgings and provisions for so large a troop. Some of his own retinue are addressed to this service; they seek not for palaces and delicates, but for house-room and victuals. It was he whose the earth was, and the fulness thereof; whose the heavens are, and the mansions therein: yet he, who could have commanded angels, sues to Samaritans; he, that filled and comprehended heaven, sends for shelter in a Samaritan cottage. It was thy choice, O Saviour, to take upon thee the shape, not of a prince, but of a servant. How can we either neglect means, or despise homeliness, when thou, the God of all the world, wouldst stoop to the suit of so poor a provision?

We know well on what terms the Samaritans stood with the Jews; so much more hostile, as they did more symbolize in matters of religion: no nations were mutually so hateful to each other. A Samaritan's bread was no better than swine's flesh: their very fire and water was not more grudged than infectious: the looking towards Jerusalem was here cause enough of repulse. No enmity is so desperate as that which arises from matter of religion. Agreement in some points, when there are differences in the main, doth but advance hatred the more.

It is not more strange to hear the Son of God sue for a lodging, than to hear him repelled. Upon so churlish a denial, the two angry disciples return to their Master on a fiery errand: " Lord, wilt thou that we command fire to come down from heaven and consume them, as Elias did ?"

The sons of thunder would be lightning strait: their zeal, whether as kinsmen or disciples, could not brook so harsh a refusal. As they were naturally more hot than their fellows, so now they thought their piety bade them be impatient.

Yet they dare not but begin with leave: " Master, wilt thou ?" His will must lead theirs; their choler cannot drive their wills before his: all their motion is from him only. True disciples are like those artificial engines, which go no otherwise than they are set; or like little children, that speak nothing but what they are taught. O Saviour, if we have wills of our own, we are not thine: do thou set me as thou wouldst have me go; do thou teach me what thou wouldst have me say or do.

A mannerly preface leads in a faulty suit: " Master, wilt thou that we command fire to come down from heaven, and consume them ?" faulty, both in presumption, and in desire of private revenge. I do not hear them say, Master, will it please thee, who art the sole Lord of the heavens and the elements, to command fire from heaven upon these men? but, " Wilt thou that we command?" As if, because they had power given them over diseases and unclean spirits, therefore heaven and earth were in their managing. How easily might they be mistaken! Their large commission had the just limits. Subjects, that have munificent grants from their princes, can challenge nothing beyond the words of their patent; and if the fetching down fire from heaven were less than the dispossessing of devils, since the devil shall enable the beast to do thus much, yet how possible is it to do the greater, and stick at the less, where both depend upon a delegated power! The magicians of Egypt could bring forth frogs and blood; they could not bring lice. Ordinary corruption can do that which they could not.

It is the fashion of our bold nature, upon an inch given to challenge an ell; and, where we find ourselves graced with some abilities, to flatter ourselves with the faculty of more.

I grant, faith hath done as great things as ever presumption undertook; but there is great difference in the enterprises of both. The one hath a warrant, either by instinct or express command; the other none at all. Indeed, had these two disciples either meant, or said, Master, if it be thy pleasure to command us to call down fire from heaven, we know thy word shall enable us to do what thou requirest; if the words be ours, the power shall be thine; this had been but holy, modest, faithful: but if they supposed there needed nothing save a leave only, and that, might they be but let loose, they could go alone, they presumed, they offended.

Yet had they thus overshot themselves in some pious and charitable motion, the fault had been the less. Now the act had in it both cruelty and private revenge. Their zeal was not worthy of more praise, than their fury of censure. That fire should fall down from heaven upon men, is a fearful thing to think of, and that which hath not been often done. It was done in the case of Sodom, when these five unclean cities burned with the unnatural fire of hellish lust: it was done two several times at the suit of Elijah; it was done, in a height of trial, to that great pattern of patience. I find it no more, and tremble at these I find.

But besides the dreadfulness of the judgment itself, who can but quake at the thought of the suddenness of this destruction, which sweeps away both body and soul, in a state of unpreparation, of unrepentance; so as this fire should but begin a worse, this heavenly flame should but kindle that of hell?

Thus unconceivably heavy was the revenge but what was the offence? We have learned not to think any indignity light, that is offered to the Son of God; but we know these spiritual affronts are capable of degrees. Had these Samaritans reviled Christ and his train, had they violently assaulted him, had they followed him with stones in their hands, and blasphemies in their mouths, it had been a just provocation of so horrible a vengeance: now the wrong was only negative; "They received him not;" and that, not out of any particular quarrel or dislike of his person, but of his nation only: the men had been welcome, had not their country distasted. All the charge that I hear our Saviour give to his disciples, in case of their rejection, is, "If they receive you not, shake off the dust of your feet:" yet this was amongst their own, and when they went on that sacred errand of publishing the gospel of peace. These were strangers from the commonwealth of Israel: this measure was not to preachers, but to travellers, only a mere inhospitality to misliked guests; yet no less revenge will serve them than fire from heaven.

I dare say for you, ye holy sons of Zebedee, it was not your spleen, but your zeal, that was guilty of so bloody a suggestion. Your indignation could not but be stirred to see the great Prophet and Saviour of the world so unkindly repelled: yet all this will not excuse you from a rash cruelty, from an inordinate rage.

Even the best heart may easily be miscarried with a well-meant zeal: no affection is either more necessary or better accepted. Love to any object cannot be severed from hatred of the contrary: whence it is, that all creatures, which have the concupiscible part, have also the irascible adjoined unto it. Anger and displeasure is not so much an enemy, as a guardian and champion of love: whoever, therefore, is rightly affected to his Saviour, cannot but find much regret at his wrongs. O gracious and divine zeal, the kindly warmth and vital temper of piety, whither hast thou withdrawn thyself from the cold hearts of men? or is this according to the just constitution of the old and decrepit age of the world into which we are fallen? How many are there that think there is no wisdom but in a dull indifference, and choose rather to freeze than burn! How quick and apprehensive are men in cases of their own indignities! how insensible of their Saviour's!

But there is nothing so ill as the corruption of the best. Rectified zeal is not more commendable and useful, than inordinate and misguided is hateful and dangerous. Fire is a necessary and beneficial element, but if it be once misplaced, and have caught upon the beams of our houses, or stacks of our corn, nothing can be more direful.

Thus sometimes zeal turns to murder: " They that kill you shall think they do God service;" sometimes frenzy, sometimes rude indiscretion. Wholesome and blessed is that zeal that is well grounded, and well governed; grounded upon the word of truth, not upon unstable fancies; governed by wisdom and charity; wisdom to avoid rash ness and excess; charity, to avoid just offence.

No motion can want a pretence: Elias did so, why not we? He was a holy prophet: the occasion, the place, abludes not much: there wrong was offered to a servant, here to his Master; there to a man, here to a God and man. If Elias then did it, why not we? There is nothing more perilous than to draw all the actions of holy men into examples, for, as the best men have their weaknesses, so they are not privileged from letting fall unjustifiable actions. Besides that, they may have have had, perhaps, peculiar warrants signed from heaven, whether by instinct or special command, which we shall expect in vain. There must be much caution used in our imitation of the best patterns, whether in respect of persons or things; else we shall make ourselves apes, and our acts sinful absurdities.

It is a rare thing for our Saviour to find fault with the errors of zeal, even where have appeared sensible weaknesses. If Moses, in a sacred rage and indignation, broke the tables written with God's own hand, I find him not checked. Here our meek Saviour turns back and frowns upon his furious suitors, and takes them up roundly: "Ye know not of what spirit ye are." The faults of uncharitableness cannot be swallowed up in zeal. If there were any colour to hide the blemishes of this misdisposition, it should be this crimson dye. But he that needs not our lie, will let us know he needs not our injury, and hates to have a good cause supported by the violation of our charity. We have no reason to disclaim our passions; even the Son of God chides sometimes, yea, where he loves. It offends not that our affections are moved, but that they are inordinate.

It was a sharp word, "Ye know not of what spirit ye are:" another man would not perhaps have felt it; a disciple doth. Tender hearts are galled with that which the carnal mind slighteth. The spirit of Elias was that which they meant to assume and imitate; they shall now know their mark was mistaken. How would they have hated to think, that any other but God's spirit had stirred them up to this passionate motion! now they shall know it was wrought by that ill spirit whom they professed to hate.

It is far from the good spirit of God to stir up any man to private revenge, or thirst of blood. Not an eagle, but a dove, was the shape wherein he chose to appear: neither wouldst thou, O God, be in the whirlwind, or in the fire, but in the soft voice. O Saviour, what do we seek for any precedent but thine, whose name we challenge? Thou camest to thine own, thine own received thee not. Didst thou call for fire from heaven upon them? didst thou not rather send down water from thy compassionate eyes, and weep for them by whom thou must bleed? Better had it been for us never to have had any spirit, than any but thine. We can be no other than wicked, if our mercies be cruelty.

But is it the name of Elias, O ye zealots, which ye pretend for a colour of your impotent desire? Ye do not consider the difference betwixt his spirit and yours: his was extraordinary and heroical, besides the instinct or secret command of God for this act of his; far otherwise is it with you, who, by a carnal distemper, are moved to this furious suggestion. Those that would imitate God's saints in singular actions, must see they go upon the same grounds. Without the same spirit, and the same warrant, it is either a mockery or a sin to make them our copies. Elias is no fit pattern for disciples, but their Master: "The Son of man came not to destroy men's lives, but to save them."

Then are our actions and intentions warrantable and praiseworthy, when they accord with his. O Saviour, when we look into those sacred acts and monuments of thine, we find many a life which thou preservedst from perishing: some that had perished by thee recalled; never any by thee destroyed; only one poor fig-tree, as the real emblem of thy severity to the unfruitful, was blasted and withered by thy curse. But to man, how wert thou ever favourable and indulgent! So repelled as thou wert, so reviled, so persecuted, laid for, sold, betrayed, apprehended, arraigned, condemned, crucified, yet what one man didst thou strike dead for these heinous indignities? Yea, when one of thine enemies lost but an ear in that ill quarrel, thou gavest that ear to him who came to take life from thee. I find some whom thou didst scourge and correct, as the sacrilegious moneychangers; none whom thou killedst. Not that thou either lovest not, or requirest not the duly severe execution of justice. Whose sword is it that princes bear but thine? Offenders must smart and bleed. This is a just sequel, but not the intention of thy coming; thy will, not thy drift.

Good princes make wholesome laws for the well-ordering of their people: there is no authority without due coercion. The violation of these good laws is followed with death, whose end was preservation, life, order; and this not so much for revenge of an offence past, as for prevention of future mischief.

How can we then enough love and praise thy mercy, O thou Preserver of men! How should we imitate thy saving and beneficent disposition towards mankind! as knowing, the more we can help to save, the nearer we come to thee that camest to save all; and the more destructive we are, the more we resemble him who is Abaddon, a murderer from the beginning.

CONTEMPLATION X. — THE TEN LEPERS.

THE Samaritans were tainted, not with schism, but heresy, yea, paganism; our Saviour yet baulks them not, but makes use of the way as it lies, and bestows upon them the courtesy of some miracles. Some kind of commerce is lawful, even with those without: terms of entireness, and leagues of inward amity, are here unfit, unwarrantable, dangerous; but civil respects, and wise uses of them for our convenience or necessity, need not, must not, be forborne.

Ten lepers are here met. Those that are excluded from all other society, seek the company of each other; fellowship is that we all naturally affect, though even in leprosy; even lepers will flock to their fellows; where shall we find one spiritual leper alone? Drunkards, profane persons, heretics, will be sure to consort with their matches: why should not God's saints delight in a holy communion? why is it not our chief joy to assemble in good?

Jews and Samaritans could not abide one another; yet here in leprosy they accord. Here was one Samaritan leper with the Jewish: community of passion hath made them friends, whom even religion disjoined: what virtue there is in misery, that can unite even the most estranged hearts!

I seek not mystery in the number. These ten are met together, and all meet Christ, not casually, but upon due deliberation: they purposely waited for this opportunity; no marvel if they thought no attendance long, to be delivered from so loathsome and miserable a disease. Great Naaman could be glad to come from Syria to Judea, in hope of leaving that hateful guest behind him: we are all sensible enough of our bodily infirmities. O that we could be equally weary of the sicknesses and deformities of our better part: surely our spiritual maladies are no less than mortal, if they be not healed: neither can they heal alone; these men had died lepers, if they had not met with Christ.

O Saviour, give us grace to seek thee, and patience to wait for thee, and then we know thou wilt find us, and we remedy.

Where do these lepers attend for Christ but in a village? and that not in the street of it, but in the entrance, in the passage to it: the cities, the towns, were not for them: the law of God had shut them out from all frequence, from all conversation: care of safety, and fear of infection, was motive enough to make their neighbours observant of this piece of the law. It is not the body only that is herein respected by the God of spirits: those that are spiritually contagious must be still and ever avoided; they must be separated from us, we must be separated from them; they from us by just censures, or, if that be neglected, we from them by a voluntary declination of their familiar conversation. Besides the benefit of our safety, wickedness would soon be ashamed of itself, if it were not for the encouragement of companions. Solitariness is the fittest antidote for spiritual infection. It were happy for the wicked man, if he could be separated from himself.

These lepers that came to seek Christ, yet finding him, stand afar off: whether for reverence, or for security, God had enacted this distance. It was their charge, if they were occasioned to pass through the streets, to cry out, "I am unclean." It was no less than their duty to proclaim their own infectiousness: there was not danger only, but sin, in their approach.

How happy were it, if in those wherein there is more peril, there were more remoteness, less silence! O God, we are all lepers to thee, overspread with the loathsome scurf of our own corruptions: it becomes us well, in the conscience of our shame and vileness, to stand afar off. We cannot be too awful of thee, too much ashamed of ourselves.

Yet these men, though they be far off in the distance of place, yet they are near in respect of the acceptance of their prayer: "The Lord is near unto all that call upon him in truth." O Saviour, while we are far off from thee, thou art near unto us. Never dost thou come so close to us, as when in a holy bashfulness we stand farthest off. Justly dost thou expect we should be at once bold and bashful. How boldly should we come to the throne of grace, in respect of the grace of that throne! how fearfully, in respect of the awfulness of the majesty of that throne, and that unworthiness which we bring with us into that dreadful presence!

He that stands near may whisper, but

he that stands afar off must cry aloud; so did these lepers: yet not so much distance as passion strained their throats. That which can give voice to the dumb, can much more give loudness to the vocal.

All cried together: these ten voices were united in one sound, that their conjoined forces might expugn that gracious ear. Had every man spoken singly for himself, this had made no noise, neither yet any show of a fervent importunity: now, as they were all affected with one common disease, so they all set out their throats together, and (though Jews and Samaritans) agree in one joint supplication. Even where there are ten tongues, the word is but one, that the condescent may be universal. When we would obtain common favours, we may not content ourselves with private and solitary devotions, but must join our spiritual forces together, and set upon God by troops. Two are better than one; because they have a good reward for their labour. No faithful prayer goes away unrecompensed: but, where many good hearts meet, the retribution must needs be answerable to the number of the petitioners. O holy and happy violence that is thus offered to heaven! how can we want blessings, when so many cords draw them down upon our heads?

It was not the sound, but the matter, that carried it with Christ: if the sound were shrill, the matter was faithful: "Jesu, Master, have mercy upon us!" No word can better become the mouth of the miserable. I see not where we can meet with fitter patterns. Surely they were not verier lepers than we: why do we not imitate them in their actions, who are too like them in our condition? Whither should we seek but to our Jesus? How should we stand aloof in regard of our own wretchedness! How should we lift up our voice in the fervour of our supplications! What should we rather sue for than mercy! " Jesu, Master, have mercy upon us!"

O gracious prevention of mercy, both had and given ere it can be asked! Jesus, when he saw them, said, " Go, show yourselves to the priests." Their disease is cured ere it can be complained of: their showing to the priest pre-supposes them whole; whole in his grant, though not in their own apprehension. That single leper that came to Christ before (Matt. viii. Luke v.) was first cured in his own sense, and then was bid to go to the priest for approbation of the cure. It was not so with these, who are sent to the judges of leprosy, with an intention they shall in the way find themselves healed. There was a different purpose in both these: in the one, that the perfection of the cure might be convinced, and seconded with a due sacrifice; in the other, that the faith of the patients might be tried in the way; which, if it had not held as strong in the prosecution of their suit as in the beginning, had, I doubt, failed of the effect. How easily might these lepers think, Alas! to what purpose is this? Show ourselves to the priests! what can their eyes do? they can judge whether it be cured, which we see yet it is not; they cannot cure it. This is not now to do: we have been seen enough and loathed. What can their eyes see more than our own? We had well hoped that Jesus would have vouchsafed to call us to him, and to lay his hands upon us, and to have healed us. These thoughts had kept them lepers still. Now shall their faith and obedience be proved by their submission both to this sudden command, and that divine ordination.

That former leper was charged to show himself to the chief priest, these to the priests. Either would serve: the original command runs, either to Aaron or to one of his sons. But why to them? leprosy was a bodily sickness: what is this to spiritual persons? wherefore serve physicians, if the priests must meddle with diseases? We never shall find those sacred persons to pass their judgment upon fevers, dropsies, palsies, or any other bodily distemper: neither should they on this, were it not that this affection of the body is joined with a legal uncleanness: not as a sickness, but as an impurity, must it come under their cognizance; neither this, without a farther implication. Who but the successors of the legal priesthood are proper to judge of the uncleanness of the soul? whether an act be sinful, or in what degree it is such; what grounds are sufficient for the comfortable assurance of repentance, of forgiveness; what courses are fittest to avoid the danger of relapses; who is so like to know, so meet to judge, as our teachers? Would we, in these cases, consult oftener with our spiritual guides, and depend upon their faithful advices and well-grounded absolutions, it were safer, it were happier for us. O the dangerous extremity of our wisdom! Our hoodwinked progenitors would have no eyes but in the heads of their ghostly fathers: we think ourselves so quick-sighted, that we pity the blindness of our able teachers; none but ourselves are fit to judge of our own leprosy.

Neither was it only the peculiar judgment of the priest that was here intended, but the thankfulness of the patient: that, by the sacrifice which he should bring with him, he might give God the glory of his sanation. O God, whomsoever thou curest of this spiritual leprosy, it is reason he should present thee with the true evangelical sacrifices, not of his praises only, but of himself, which are reasonable and living. We are still leprous, if we do not first see ourselves foul, and then find ourselves thankfully serviceable.

The lepers did not, would not go of themselves, but are sent by Christ: "Go, and show yourselves." And why sent by him? Was it in obedience to the law? was it out of respect to the priesthood? was it for prevention of cavils? was it for conviction of gainsayers? or was it for confirmation of the miracle? Christ, that was above the law, would not transgress it: he knew this was his charge by Moses. How justly might he have dispensed with his own? but ne will not: though the law doth not bind the Maker, he will voluntarily bind himself. He was within the ken of his *consummatum est;* yet would not anticipate that approaching end, but holds the law on foot till his last pace. This was but a branch of the ceremonial; yet would he not slight it, but in his own person gives example of a studious observation.

How carefully should we submit ourselves to the royal laws of our Creator, to the wholesome laws of our superiors, while the Son of God would not but be so punctual in a ceremony!

While I look to the persons of those priests, I see nothing but corruption, nothing but professed hostility to the true Messiah. All this cannot make thee, O Saviour, to remit any point of the observance due to their places. Their function was sacred, whatever their persons were: though they have not the grace to give thee thy due, thou wilt not fail to give them theirs. How justly dost thou expect all due regard to thine evangelical priesthood, who gavest so curious respect to the legal! It were shame the synagogue should be above the church; or that priesthood, which thou didst mean speedily to abrogate, should have more honour than that which thou meanest to establish and perpetuate.

Had this duty been neglected, what clamours had been raised by his emulous adversaries? what scandals? though the fault had been the patient's, not the physician's. But they that watched Christ so narrowly, and were apt to take so poor exceptions at his Sabbath cures, at the unwashen hands of his disciples, how much more would they have calumniated him, if by his neglect the law of leprosy had been palpably transgressed! Not only evil must be avoided, but offence; and that not on our parts, but on others'. That offence is ours, which we might have remedied.

What a noble and irrefragable testimony was this to the power, to the truth of the Messiah! How can these Jews but either believe, or be made inexcusable in not believing? When they shall see so many lepers come at once to the temple, all cured by a secret will, without word or touch, how can they choose but say, This work is supernatural; no limited power could do this: How is he not God, if his power be infinite? Their own eyes shall be witnesses and judges of their own conviction.

The cure is done by Christ more exquisitely than by art or nature; yet it is not publicly assured and acknowledged, till, according to the Mosaical law, certain subsequent rites be performed. There is no admittance into the congregation, but by sprinkling of blood. O Saviour, we can never be ascertained of our cleansing from that spiritual leprosy wherewith our souls are tainted, but by the sprinkling of thy most precious blood: wash us with that, and we shall be whiter than snow. This act of showing to the priest, was not more required by the law, than prerequired of these lepers by our Saviour, for the trial of their obedience. Had they now stood upon terms with Christ, and said, "We will first see what cause there will be to show ourselves to the priests; they need not see our leprosy, we shall be glad they should see our cure; do thou work that which we shall show, and bid us show what thou hast wrought; till then excuse us: it is our grief and shame to be seen too much;" they had been still lepers.

It hath been ever God's wont, by small precepts to prove men's dispositions. Obedience is as well tried in a trifle as in the most important charge; yea, so much more, as the thing required is less: for ofttimes those, who would be careful in main affairs, think they may neglect the smallest. What command soever we receive from God, or our superiors, we must not scan the weight of the thing, but the authority of the commander. Either difficulty or slightness is a vain pretence for disobedience.

These lepers are wiser; they obeyed, and went. What was the issue? As they went, they were healed." Lo! had they stood still, they had been lepers; now they went, they are whole. What haste the blessing makes to overtake their obedience! This walk was required by the very law, if they should have found themselves healed: what was it to prevent the time a little, and to do that sooner upon hopes, which upon sense they must do after? The horror of the disease adds to the grace of the cure; and that is so much more gracious as the task is easier: it shall cost them but a walk. It is the bounty of that God whom we serve, to reward our worthless endeavours with infinite requitals. He would not have any proportion betwixt our acts and his remunerations.

Yet, besides this recompense of obedience, O Saviour, thou wouldst herein have respect to thine own just glory. Had not these lepers been cured in the way, but in the end of their walk, upon their showing to the priests, the miracle would have lost much light: perhaps the priests would have challenged it to themselves, and have attributed it to their prayers: perhaps, the lepers might have thought it was thy purpose to honour the priests as the instruments of that marvellous cure. Now there can be no colour of any other's participation, since the leprosy vanishes in the way. As thy power, so thy praise, admits of no partners.

And now, methinks, I see what an amazed joy there was amongst these lepers, when they saw themselves thus suddenly cured: each tells other what a change he feels in himself; each comforts other with the assurance of his outward cleanness; each congratulates other's happiness, and thinks, and says, How joyful this news will be to their friends and families. Their society now serves them well to applaud and heighten their new felicity.

The miracle, indifferently wrought upon all, is differently taken. All went forward according to the appointment, towards the priests; all were obedient; one only was thankful: all were cured; all saw themselves cured; their sense was alike, their hearts were not alike. What could make the difference but grace? and who could make the difference of grace, but he that gave it? He that wrought the cure in all, wrought the grace not in all, but in one. The same act, the same motives, are not equally powerful to all; where the ox finds grass, the viper poison. We all pray, all hear; one goes away bettered, another cavils. Will makes the difference; but who makes the difference of wills, but he that made them? He that creates the new heart, leaves a stone in one bosom, puts flesh into another. "It is not in him that willeth, nor in him that runneth, but in God that hath mercy:" O God, if we look not up to thee, we may come, and not be healed: we may be healed, and not be thankful.

This one man breaks away from his fellows to seek Christ. While he was a leper, he consorted with lepers: now that he is healed, he will be free. He saith not, I came with these men, with them I will go; if they will return, I will accompany them; if not, what should I go alone? As I am not wiser than they, so I have no more reason to be more thankful. There are cases wherein singularity is not lawful only, but laudable: "Thou shalt not follow a multitude to do evil. I and my house will serve the Lord." It is a base and unworthy thing for a man so to subject himself to others' examples, as not sometimes to resolve to be an example to others. When either evil is to be done, or good neglected, how much better is it to go the right way alone, than to err with company!

O noble pattern of thankfulness! What speed of retribution is here! No sooner doth he see his cure, than he hastes to acknowledge it; the benefit shall not die nor sleep in his hand. Late professions of our obligations savour of dulness and ingratitude. What a laborious and diligent officiousness is here! he stands not still, but puts himself to the pains of a return. What a hearty recognition of a blessing! his voice was not more loud in his suit than in his thanks. What an humble reverence of his benefactor! he falls down at his feet; as acknowledging at once beneficence and unworthiness. It were happy for all Israel, if they could but learn of this Samaritan.

This man is sent with the rest to the priests. He well knew this duty a branch of the law of ceremonies, which he meant not to neglect: but his heart told him there was a moral duty of professing thankfulness to his benefactor, which called for his first attendance. First therefore he turns back, ere he will stir forward. Reason taught this Samaritan, and us in him, that ceremony must yield to substance, and that main points of obedience must take place of all ritual compliments.

It is not for nothing that note is made of the country of this thankful leper: "He was a Samaritan;" the place is known and branded with the infamy of a paganish misreligion. Outward disadvantage of place of parentage cannot block up the way of God's grace and free election; as contrarily, the privileges of birth and nature avail us nothing in spiritual occasions.

How sensible wert thou, O Saviour, of thine own beneficence! "Were there not ten cleansed? but where are the nine?"

The trooping of these lepers together did not hinder thy reckoning. It is both justice and wisdom in thee to keep a strict account of thy favours. There is a wholesome and useful art of forgetfulness in us men, both of benefits done and of wrongs offered. It is not so with God: our injuries indeed he soon puts over, making it no small part of his style, that he "forgives iniquities:" but for his mercies, there is no reason he should forget them; they are worthy of more than our memory. His favours are universal, over all his works; there is no creature that tastes not of his bounty; his sun and rain are for others besides his friends, but none of his good turns escape either his knowledge or record. Why should not we, O God, keep a book of our receipts from thee, which, agreeing with thine, may declare thee bounteous, and us thankful?

Our Saviour doth not ask this by way of doubt, but of exprobration. Full well did he count the steps of those absent lepers: he knew where they were; he upbraids their ingratitude, that they were not where they should have been. It was thy just quarrel, O Saviour, that while one Samaritan returned, nine Israelites were healed and returned not. Had they been all Samaritans, this had been faulty; but now they were Israelites, their ingratitude was more foul than their leprosy. The more we are bound to God, the more shameful is our unthankfulness. There is scarce one in ten that is careful to give God his own: this neglect is not more general than displeasing. Christ had never missed their presence, if their absence had not been hateful and injurious.

CONTEMPLATION XI. — THE POOL OF BETHESDA.

To the Reader.

THE reader may be pleased to understand, that my manner hath still been, first to pass through all these Divine Histories by way of Sermons; and then after, to gather the quintessence of those larger discourses into these forms of Meditations, which he sees: only, I have thought good, upon these two following heads, for some good reasons, to publish the Sermons in their own shape, as they were delivered, without alteration. It seemed not amiss, that some of those metals should be shown in the ore, whereof so great a quantity was presented in the wedge.

A Sermon preached at the Court, before King James.

OTHERWHERE ye may look long, and see no miracle; but here behold two miracles in one view: the former, of the angel curing diseases; the latter, of the God of angels, Christ Jesus, preventing the angel in his cure. Even the first, Christ wrought by the angel, the second immediately by himself. The first is incomparable; for, as Montanus truly observes, there is no one *miraculum perpetuum* but this one, in the whole book of God. Be content to spend this hour with me in the porches of Bethesda, and consider with me the topography, the aitiology, the chronography of this miracle: these three limit our speech and your patient attention. The chronography, which is first in place and time, offers us two heads: 1. A feast of the Jews; 2. Christ going up to the feast.

The Jews were full of holidays, both of God's institution and the church's. Of God's, both weekly, monthly, anniversary. Weekly, that one of seven, which I would to God we had learned of them to keep better. In this regard it was that Seneca said, the Jews did *septimam ætatis partem perdere;* "lose the seventh part of their life." Monthly, the new moons: Numb. xxviii. Anniversary, Easter, Pentecost, and the September feasts. The church's, both the Purim by Mordocheus, and the Encenia by Judas Maccabeus, which yet Christ honoured by his solemnization; John x. Surely God did this for the cheerfulness of his people in his service; hence the church hath laudably imitated this example. To have no feasts, is sullen; to have too many, is Paganish and superstitious. Neither would God have cast the Christian Easter upon the just time of the Jewish Pasch, and their Whitsuntide upon the Jewish Pentecost, if he would not have had these feasts continued. And why should the Christian church have less power than the Jewish synagogue? Here was not a mere feriation, but a feasting; they must appear before God *cum muneribus*, "with gifts." The tenth part of their increase must be spent upon the three solemn feasts, besides their former tithes to Levi; Deut. xiv. 23. There was no holiday wherein they feasted above six hours; and in some of them, tradition urged them to their quantities of drink; and David, when he would keep holiday to the ark, allows every Israelite a cake of bread, a piece of flesh, a bottle of wine; not a dry dinner, *prandium caninum;* not a mere drinking of wine with out meat, but to make up a perfect feast, bread, flesh, wine; 2 Sam. vi. 19. The true purims of this island, are those two feasts of August and November. He is no true Israelite that keeps them not, as the days which the Lord hath made. When are joy and triumphs seasonable, if not at feasts? but not excess. Pardon me; I know not how feasts are kept at the court, but, as Job, when he thought of the banquets of his sons, says, "It may be they have sinned:" so let me speak at peradventures. If sensual immoderation should have set her foot into these Christian feasts, let me at least say with indulgent Eli, *non est bona fama, filii,* "It is no good report, my sons." Do ye think that St. Paul's rule, *non in commessationibus et ebrietate,* "not in surfeiting and drunkenness," was for work-days only? The Jews had a conceit, that on their Sabbath and feast days, the devils fled from their cities, *ad montes umbrosos,* "to the shady mountains." Let it not be said, that on our Christian feasts they should *e montibus aulam petere;* and that he seeks, and finds not, *loca arida,* but *madida.* God forbid that Christians should sacrifice to Bacchus, instead of the everliving God! and that on the day when you should have been blown up by treacherous fire from earth to heaven, you should fetch down the fire of God's anger from heaven upon you by swilling and surfeits! God forbid! God's service is *unum necessarium,* "the one thing necessary," saith Christ. *Homo ebrius superflua creatura,* "a drunken man is a superfluous creature," saith Ambrose. How ill do those two agree together! This I have been bold to say out of caution, not of reproof.

Thus much, that there was a feast of the Jews. Now, what feast it was is questionable: whether the Pasch, as Ireneus, and Beza with him, thinks, upon the warrant of John iv. 35, where our Saviour had said, "Yet four months, and then cometh the harvest;" or whether Pentecost, which was fifty days from the shaking of the sheaf, that was Easter Sunday, as Cyril, Chrysostom, Theophylact, Euthymius, and some later; or whether one of the September feasts, as some others. The excellency of the feast makes for Easter; the feast κατ' ἐξοχὴν, the number of interpreters for Pentecost, the number of feasts for September. For as God delighted in the number of seven, the seventh day was holy, the seventh year, the seventh seven year; so he showed it in the seventh month, which reserves his number still, September; the first day whereof was the sabbath of trumpets, the tenth *dies expiationum,* and on the fifteenth began the feast of tabernacles for seven days. It is an idleness to seek that which we are never the better when we have found. What if Easter? what if Tabernacles? what if Pentecost? what loss, what gain is this? *Magna nos molestia Johannes liberasset si unum adjecisset verbum,* "John had eased us of much trouble, if he had added but one word," saith Maldonat. But for us, God give them sorrow that love it: this is one of St. Paul's διαπαρατριβαὶ, "vain disputations," that he forbids his Timothy: yea (which is the subject thereof) one of them which he calls μωρὰς καὶ ἀπαιδεύτους ζητήσεις, "foolish and unlearned questions;" 2 Tim. ii. 23. *Quantum mali facit nimia subtilitas,* "how much mischief is done by too much subtility!" saith Seneca. These are some idle cloisterers that have nothing to do but to pick straws in divinity; like to Appian the grammarian, that with long discourse would pick out of Homer's first verse of his Iliad, and the first word μῆνιν, the number of the books of Iliad and Odyssey; or like Didymus χαλκέντερος, that spent some of his four thousand books, about which was Homer's country, who was Æneas's true mother, what the age of Hecuba, how long it was betwixt Homer and Orpheus; or those wise critics of whom Seneca speaks, that spent whole volumes whether Homer or Hesiod were the elder: *Non profuturam scientiam tradunt,* "they vent an unprofitable skill," as he said. Let us be content with the learned ignorance of what God hath concealed, and know, that what he hath concealed will not avail us to know.

Rather let us inquire why Christ would go up to the feast. I find two silken cords that drew him up thither: 1. His obedience; 2. His desire of manifesting his glory.

First, it was a general law, all males must appear thrice a-year before the Lord. Behold, he was the God whom they went up to worship at the feast, yet he goes up to worship. He began his life in obedience, when he came in his mother's belly to Bethlehem at the taxation of Augustus, and so he continues it. He knew his due: "Of whom do the kings of the earth receive tribute? of their own or of strangers? then their sons are free." Yet he that would pay tribute to Cæsar, will also pay this tribute of obedience to his Father. He that was above the law, yields to the law: *Legi satisfacere voluit, etsi non sub lege,* "He would satisfy the law, though he were not under the law." The Spirit of God says, "He learned obedience, in that he suffered";

Surely also he taught obedience, in that he did. This was his πρέπον ἐστὶ to John Baptist: " It becomes us to fulfil all righteousness." He will not abate his Father one ceremony. It was dangerous to go up to that Jerusalem which he had left before for their malice; yet now he will up again. His obedience drew him up to that bloody feast, wherein himself was sacrificed: how much more now that he might sacrifice? What can we plead to have learned of Christ, if not his first lesson, obedience? The same proclamation that Gideon made to Israel, he makes still to us: " As ye see me do, so do ye." Whatsoever, therefore, God enjoins us, either immediately by himself, or mediately by his deputies, if we will be Christians, we must so observe, as those that know themselves bound to tread in his steps, that said, " In the volume of thy book it is written of me, I desired to do thy will, O God;" Psal. xl. 6. " I will have obedience (saith God), and not sacrifice;" but where sacrifice is obedience, he will have obedience in sacrificing: therefore Christ went up to the feast.

The second motive was the manifestation of his glory. if we be the light of the world, which are so much snuff, what is he that is the Father of lights? It was not for him to be set under the bushel of Nazareth, but upon the table of Jerusalem: thither, and then, was the confluence of all the tribes. Many a time had Christ passed by this man before, when the streets were empty (for there he lay many years) yet heals him not till now. He, that sometimes modestly steals a miracle with a *vide ne cui dixeris*, " see thou tell no man," that no man might know it, at other times does wonders upon the scaffold of the world, that no man might be ignorant, and bids proclaim it on the house-tops. It was fit the world should be thus publicly convinced, and either won by belief, or lost by inexcusableness. Good, the more common it is, the better: "I will praise thee" (saith David) *in ecclesia magna,* " in the great congregation." Glory is not got in corners: no man, say the envious kinsmen of Christ, keeps close and would be famous; no, nor that would have God celebrated. The best opportunities must be taken in glorifying him. He, that would be crucified at the feast, that his death and resurrection might be more famous, will, at the feast, do miracles, that his divine power might be approved openly. Christ is *flos campi, non horti,* " the flower of the field, and not of the garden," saith Bernard. God cannot abide to have his graces smothered in us.

" I have not hid thy righteousness within my heart," saith the Psalmist. Absalom, when he would be *insigniter improbus*, " notoriously wicked," does his villany publicly in the eyes of the sun, under no curtain but heaven. He that would do notable service to God, must do it conspicuously. Nicodemus gained well by Christ, but Christ got nothing by him, so long as, like a night-bird, he never came to him but with owls and bats. Then he began to be a profitable disciple, when he durst oppose the Pharisees in their condemnation of Christ, though indefinitely: but most, when in the night of his death the light of his faith brought him openly to take down the sacred corpse before all the gazing multitude, and to embalm it. When we confess God's name, with the Psalmist, before kings; when kings, defenders of the faith, profess their religion in public and everlasting monuments to all nations, to all times, this is glorious to God, and in God to them. It is no matter how close evils be, nor how public good is.

This is enough for the chronography: the topography follows. I will not here stand to show you the ignorance of the vulgar translation, in joining *probatica* and *piscina* together, against their own fair Vatican copy, with other ancient: nor spend time to discuss whether ἀγορὰ or πύλη be here understood for the substantive of προβατική· it is most likely to be that sheepgate spoken of in Ezra: nor to show how ill *piscina* in the Latin answers the Greek κολυμβήθρα· ours turn it a pool, better than any Latin word can express it: nor to show you, as I might, how many public pools were in Jerusalem: nor to discuss the use of this pool, whether it were for washing the beasts to be sacrificed, or to wash the entrails of the sacrifice, whence I remember Jerome fetches the virtue of the water, and in his time thought he discerned some redness, as if the blood spilt four hundred years before could still retain its first tincture in a liquid substance: besides, that it would be a strange swimming pool that were brewed with blood, and this was κολυμβήθρα. This conceit arises from the error of the construction, in mismatching κολυμβήθρα with προβατική. Neither will I argue whether it should be Bethsida, or Bethzida, or Bethsheda, or Bethesda. If either you or myself knew not how to be rid of time, we might easily wear out as many hours in this pool, as this poor impotent man did years. But it is edification that we affect, and not curiosity. This pool had five porches. Neither will I run here with St. Austin into allegories, that this pool was the people of the Jews, *aquæ multæ populus multus;* and these five porches, the Law in the five books of Moses; nor stand to confute Adricomius, which, out of Josephus, would persuade us, that these five porches were built by Solomon, and that this was *stagnum Solomonis* for the use of the temple. The following words show the use of the porches: for the receipt of "impotent, sick, blind, halt, withered, that waited for the moving of the water." It should seem it was walled about to keep it from cattle, and these five vaulted entrances were made by some benefactors for the more convenience of attendance. Here was the mercy of God seconded by the charity of men: if God will give cure, they will give harbour. Surely it is a good matter to put our hands to God's, and to further good works with conveniency of enjoying them.

Jerusalem was grown a city of blood, to the persecution of the prophets, to a wilful despite of what belonged to her peace, to a profanation of God's temple, to a mere formality in God's services: and yet here were public works of charity in the midst of her streets. We may not always judge of the truth of piety by charitable actions: Judas disbursed the money for Christ; there was no traitor but he. The poor traveller that was robbed and wounded betwixt Jerusalem and Jericho, was passed over, first by the Priest, then by the Levite, at last the Samaritan came and relieved him: his religion was naught, yet his act was good; the Priest's and Levite's religion good, their uncharity ill. Novatus himself was a martyr, yet a schismatic. Faith is the soul, and good works are the breath, saith St. James: but as you see in a pair of bellows, there is a forced breath without life, so in those that are puffed up with the wind of ostentation, there may be charitable works without faith. The church of Rome, unto her four famous orders of Jacobins, Franciscans, Augustines, and Carmelites, hath added a fifth of Jesuits; and, like another Jerusalem, for those five leprous and lazarly orders, hath built five porches, that if the water of any state be stirred, they may put in for a share. How many cells and convents hath she raised for these miserable cripples! and now she thinks, though she exalt herself above all that is called God, though she dispense with and against God, though she fall down before every block and wafer, though she kill kings, and equivocate with magistrates, she is the only city of God. *Digna est, nam struxit synagogam,* "She is worthy, for she hath built a synagogue." Are we more othodox, and shall not we be as charitable? I am ashamed to think of rich noblemen and merchants, that die and give nothing to our five porches of Bethesda. What shall we say? have they made their mammon their God, instead of making friends with their mammon to God? Even when they die, will they not, like Ambrose's good usurers, part with that which they cannot hold, that they may get that which they cannot lose? Can they begin their will, *In Dei nomine, Amen,* and give nothing to God? Is he only a witness, and not a legatee? Can we bequeath our souls to Christ in heaven, and give nothing to his limbs on earth? And if they will not give, yet will they not lend to God? "He that gives to the poor," *fæneratur Deo,* "lends to God." Will they put out to any but God? and then, when instead of giving security, he receives with one hand, and pays with another, receives our bequest and gives us glory! O damnable niggardness of vain men, that shames the gospel, and loses heaven! Let me show you a Bethesda that wants porches. What truer house of effusion than the church of God, which sheds forth waters of comfort, yea, of life! Behold some of the porches of this Bethesda, so far from building, that they are pulled down. It is a wonder if the demolished stones of God's house have not built some of yours, and if some of you have not your rich suits guarded with souls. There were wont to be reckoned three wonders of England, *ecclesia, fœmina, lana,* "the churches, the women, the wool." *Fœmina* may pass still, who may justly challenge wonder for their vanity, if not their person. As for *lana,* if it be wonderful alone, I am sure it is illjoined with *ecclesia:* the church is fleeced, and hath nothing left but a bare pelt upon her back. And as for *ecclesia,* either men have said with the Babylonians, "Down with it, down with it, even to the ground;" or else, in respect of the maintenance with Judas, *ut quid perditio hæc?* "why was this waste?" How many remorseful souls have sent back, with Jacob's sons, their money in their sack's mouth! How many great testators have, in their last will, returned the anathematized peculium of impropriations to the church, choosing rather to impair their heir, than to burden their souls? *Dum times ne pro te patrimonium tuum perdas, ipse pro patrimonio tuo peris,* saith Cyprian; "While thou fearest to lose thy patrimony for thy own good, thou perishest with thy patrimony." Ye great men, spend not all your time in building castles in the air, or houses on the sand;

but set your hands and purses to the building of the porches of Bethesda. It is a shame for a rich Christian to be like a Christmas box, that receives all, and nothing can be got out till it be broken in pieces: or like unto a drowned man's hand, that holds whatsoever it gets. "To do good, and to distribute, forget not; for with such sacrifices God is well pleased."

This was the place: what was the use of it? All sorts of patients were at the bank of Bethesda: where should cripples be but at the spital? The sick, blind, lame, withered, all that did either *morbo laborare,* or *vitio corporis,* "complain of sickness or impotency," were there. In natural course, one receipt heals not all diseases, no, nor one agent; one is an oculist, another a bone-setter, another a chirurgeon; but all diseases are alike to the supernatural power of God.

Hippocrates, though the prince of physicians, yet swears by Esculapius, he will never meddle with cutting for the stone. There is no disease that art will not meddle with; there are many that it cannot cure. The poor hæmorrhoissa was eighteen years in the physician's hands, and had purged away both her body and her substance. Yea, some it kills instead of healing: whence one Hebrew word signifies both physicians and dead men. But behold, here all sicknesses cured by one hand, and by one water! O all ye that are spiritually sick and diseased, come to the pool of Bethesda, the blood of Christ! Do ye complain of the blindness of your ignorance? here ye shall receive clearness of sight: of the distemper of passions? here ease: of the superfluity of your sinful humours? here evacuation: of the impotency of your obedience? here integrity: of the dead witheredness of good affections? here life and vigour. Whatsoever your infirmity be, come to the pool of Bethesda, and be healed.

All these may be cured; yet shall be cured at leisure: all must wait, all must hope in waiting. Methinks I see how enviously these cripples look one upon another, each thinking other a let, each watching to prevent other, each hoping to be next; like emulous courtiers, that gape and vie for the next preferment, and think it a pain to hope, and a torment to be prevented. But Bethesda must be waited on: he is worthy of his crutches that will not wait God's leisure for his cure: there is no virtue, no success, without patience. Waiting is a familiar lesson with courtiers, and here we have all need of it: one is sick of an overflowing of the gall, another of a tumour of pride, another of the tentigo of lust, another of the vertigo of inconstancy, another of the choking squinancy of curses and blasphemies; one of the boulimy of gluttony, another of the pleuritical stitches of envy; one of the contracting cramp of covetousness, another of the atrophy of unproficiency: one is hidebound with pride, another is consumed with emulation, another rotten with corrupt desires; and we are so much the sicker, if we feel not these distempers. O that we could wait at the Bethesda of God, attend diligently upon his ordinances: we could no more fail of cure, than now we can hope for cure. We wait hard, and endure much for the body. *Quantis laboribus agitur ut longiore tempore laboretur! multi cruciatus suscipiuntur certi, ut pauci dies adjiciantur incerti,* "What toil do we take that we may toil yet longer! we endure many certain pains for the addition of a few uncertain days," saith Austin. Why will we not do thus for the soul? Without waiting, it will not be. The cripple (Acts iii. 4) was bidden βλίψον εἰς ἡμᾶς, "look up to us:" he looked up; it was cold comfort that he heard: "Silver and gold have I none;" but the next clause made amends for all, *Surge et ambula,* "Rise and walk;" and this was, because ἔτυχεν προσδοκῶν, "he attended expecting," ver. 5. Would we be cured, it is not for us to snatch at Bethesda, as a dog at Nilus; nor to draw water and away, as Rebecca; nor to set us a while upon the banks, as the Israelites by the rivers of Babylon: but we must dwell in God's house, wait at Bethesda. But what shall I say to your courtiers, but even as St. Paul to his Corinthians, "Ye are full, ye are rich, ye are strong without us?" Many of you come to this place, not as to Bethel the house of God, or Bethesda the house of effusion, but as to Bethaven, the house of vanity. If ye have not lost your old wont, there are more words spoken in the outer closet by the hearers, than in the chapel by the preacher; as if it were closet *quasi* close set, in an Exchange, like communication of news. What do ye think of sermons? As matters of formality, as very superfluities, as your own idle compliments, which either ye hear not, or believe not? What do ye think of yourselves? Have ye only a postern to go to heaven by yourselves, wherethrough ye can go, besides the foolishness of preaching? Or do ye sing that old Pelagian note, *Quid nunc mihi opus est Deo?* "What need have I of God?" What should I say to this but *increpa domine?* As for our household sermons, our auditors are like the fruit of a tree in an unseasonable year, or like a wood new felled, that hath some few spires left for standers some poles distance; or like tythe sheaves in a field when the corn is gone, *εἷς, δύο, τρεῖς*, &c. as he said. It is true, ye have more sermons, and more excellent than all the courts under heaven put together; but as Austin said well, *Quid mihi proderit bona res non utenti bene?* "What am I the better for a good thing, if I use it not well?" Let me tell you, all these forcible means, not well used, will set you the further off from heaven. If the chapel were the Bethesda of promotion, what thronging would there be into it? yea, if it were but some maskhouse, wherein a glorious, though momentary show were to be presented, neither white staves nor halberts could keep you out: behold here, ye are offered the honour to be, by this seed of regeneration, the sons of God. The kingdom of heaven, the crown of glory, the sceptre of majesty, in one word, eternal life is here offered, and performed to you: O let us not so far forget ourselves, as in the ordinances of God to contemn our own happiness! but let us know the time of our visitation, let us wait reverently and intentively upon this Bethesda of God, that when the angel shall descend and move the water, our souls may be cured, and, through all degrees of grace, may be carried to the full height of their glory!

CONTEMPLATION XII. — THE FIRST PART OF THE MEDITATIONS UPON THE TRANSFIGURATION OF CHRIST.

A Sermon preached at Havering Bower, before King James.

THERE is not in all divinity a higher speculation than this of Christ transfigured: suffer me therefore to lead you up by the hand into mount Tabor, for nearer to heaven ye cannot come while ye are upon earth, that you may see him glorious upon earth, the region of his shame and abasement, who is now glorious in heaven, the throne of his majesty. He that would not have his transfiguration spoken of till he were raised, would have it spoken of all the world over, now that he is raised and ascended, that by this momentary glory we may judge of the eternal. The circumstances shall be to us as the skirts of the hill, which we will climb up lightly: the time, place, attendants, company; the time, after six days the place, a high hill apart; the attendants, Peter, James, John; the company, Moses and Elias; which when we have passed, on the top of the hill shall appear to us that sight which shall once make us glorious, and in the meantime happy.

All three Evangelists accord in the *terminus a quo*, that it was immediately after those words, "There be some of them that stand here, which shall not taste of death till they have seen the Son of man come in his kingdom." Wherein, methinks, the act comments upon the words. Peter, James, and John, were these some; they tasted not of death, till they saw this heavenly image of the royalty of Christ glorified. But the *terminus quo* disagrees a little. Matthew and Mark say, after six; Luke, *post fere octo*, which, as they are easily reconciled by the usual distinction of inclusive and exclusive, necessary for all computations; and Luke's about eight, so methinks, seems to intimate God's seventh day, the Sabbath: why should there be else so precise mention of six days after, and about eight, but to imply that day which was betwixt the sixth and eighth? God's day was fittest for so divine a work; and well might that day, which imported God's rest and man's glory, be used for the clear representation of the rest and glory of God and man. But in this conjecture, for aught I know, I go alone; I dare not be too resolute: certainly it was the seventh, whether it were that seventh, the seventh after the promise of the glory of his kingdom exhibited; and this perhaps not without a mystery: "God teacheth both by words and acts (saith Hilary), that after six ages of the world should be Christ's glorious appearance, and our transfiguration with him." But I know what our Saviour's farewell was, *οὐχ ὑμῶν γνῶναι*, "it is not for us to know;" but if we may not know, we may conjecture; yet not above that we ought, saith St. Paul; we may not *super sapere*, as Tertullian's phrase is.

For the place, tradition hath taken it still for Tabor. I list not to cross it without warrant; this was a high hill indeed: thirty furlongs high, saith Josephus; *mira rotunditate sublimis*, saith Hierom; and so steep, that some of our English travellers, that have desired to climb it of late, have been glad to give it up in the midway, and to measure the rest with their eyes. Doubtless this hill was a symbol of heaven, being near it, as in situation, so in resemblance. Heaven is expressed usually by the name of God's hill: and nature, or this appellation, taught the heathens to figure it by their Olympus. All divine affairs, of any magnificence, were done on hills: on the hill of

CONT. XII.] TRANSFIGURATION OF CHRIST.

Sinai was the law delivered; on the hill of Moriah was Isaac to be sacrificed; whence Abraham's posie is, *In monte providebitur.* On the hill of Rephidim stood Moses with the rod of God in his stretched hand, and figured him crucified upon the hill, whom Joshua figured victorious in the valley; on the hills of Ebal and Gerizim were the blessings and curses; on Carmel was Elijah's sacrifice; the phrontisteria, schools, or universities of the prophets were still Ramath and Gibeah, *excelsa*, " high places." Who knows not that on the hill of Sion stood the temple? " I have looked up to the hills," saith the Psalmist; and idolatry, in imitation, had its hill altars. On the Mount of Olives was Christ wont to send up his prayers, and sent up himself: and here, Luke saith, he went up to a high hill to pray; not for that God makes difference of places, to whose immensity heaven itself is a valley: it was a heathenish conceit of those Aramites, that God is *Deus montium*, "the God of the mountains:" but because we are commonly more disposed to good by either the freedom of our scope to heaven, or the awfulness or solitary silence of places, which (as one saith) strikes a kind of adoration into us; or by our local removal from this attractive body of the earth: howsoever, when the body sees itself above the earth, the eye of the mind is more easily raised to her heaven. It is good to take all advantage of place, setting aside superstition, to further our devotion; Aaron and Hur were in the mountain with Moses, and held up his hands; Aaron, say some allegorists, is mountainous; Hur, fiery: heavenly meditation and the fire of charity, must lift up our prayers to God. As Satan carried up Christ to a high hill, to tempt him, so he carries up himself, to be freed from temptation and distraction: if ever we would be transfigured in our dispositions, we must leave the earth below, and abandon all worldly thoughts, *venite, ascendamus, &c.* " O come, let us climb up to the hill, where God sees," or is seen (saith devout Bernard); " O all ye cares, distractions, thoughtfulness, labours, pains, servitudes, stay me here with this ass, my body, till I with the boy, that is, my reason and understanding, shall worship and return," saith the same father, wittily alluding to the journey of Abraham for his sacrifice.

Wherefore then did Christ climb up this high hill? not to look about him, but, saith St. Luke, προσεύξασθαι, " to pray ;" not for prospect, but for devotion, that his thoughts might climb up yet nearer to heaven. Behold how Christ entered upon all his great works with prayers in his mouth. When he was to enter into that great work of his humiliation in his passion, he went into the garden to pray: when he is to enter into this great work of his exaltation in his transfiguring, he went up into the mountain to pray; he was taken up from his knees to both. O noble example of piety and devotion to us! He was God that prayed: the God that he prayed to, he might have commanded; yet he prayed, that we men might learn of him to pray to him. What should we men dare to do without prayers, when he that was God would do nothing without them? The very heathen poet could say, *A Jove principium:* and which of those verse-mongers ever durst write a ballad, without imploring of some deity? which of the heathens durst attempt any great enterprise, *insalutato numine*, " without invocation and sacrifice?" Saul himself would play the priest, and offer a burnt-offering to the Lord, rather than the Philistines should fight with him unsupplicated; as thinking any devotion better than none; and thinking it more safe to sacrifice without a priest, than to fight without prayers. " Ungirt, unblessed," was the old word; as not ready till they were girded, so not till they had prayed. And how dare we rush into the affairs of God or the state? how dare we thrust ourselves into actions, either perilous or important, without ever lifting up our eyes and hearts unto the God of heaven? except we would say, as the devilish malice of Surius slanders that zealous Luther, *Nec propter Deum hæc res cœpta, est nec propter Deum finietur, &c.* " This business was neither begun for God, nor shall be ended for him." How can God bless us, if we implore him not? how can we prosper if he bless us not? How can we hope ever to be transfigured from a lump of corrupt flesh, if we do not ascend and pray? As the Samaritan woman said weakly, we may seriously. The well of mercies is deep: if thou hast nothing to draw with, never look to taste of the waters of life. I fear the worst of men, Turks, and the worst Turks, the Moors, shall rise up in judgment against many Christians, with whom it is a just exception against any witness by their law, that he hath not prayed six times in each natural day. Before the day-break they pray for day; when it is day, they give God thanks for day; at noon they thank God for half the day past; after that they pray for a good sun-set; after that they thank God for the day past; and, lastly, pray for a good night after their day. And we Christians suffer so many suns and moons to rise and set upon our heads, and never lift up our hearts to their Creator and ours, either to ask his blessing or to acknowledge it. Of all men under heaven, none had so much need to pray as courtiers. That which was done but once to Christ, is always done to them. They are set upon the hill, and see the glory of the kingdoms of the earth. But I fear it is seen of them as it is with some of the mariners, the more need, the less devotion.

Ye have seen the place; see the attendants. He would not have many, because he would not have it yet known to all: hence was his intermination, and sealing up their mouths with a *nemini dicite*, "tell no man." Not none, because he would not have it altogether unknown; and afterwards would have it known to all. Three were a legal number: *in ore duorum aut trium*, " in the mouth of two or three witnesses." He had eternally possessed the glory of his Father without any witnesses; in time the angels were blessed with that sight; and after that, two bodily yet heavenly witnesses, were allowed, Enoch and Elias. Now, in his humanity, he was invested with glory, he takes but three witnesses, and those earthly and weak, Peter, James, John. And why these? We may be too curious: Peter, because the eldest; John, because the dearest; James, because, next Peter, the zealousest: Peter, because he loved Christ most; John, because Christ most loved him; James, because, next to both, he loved, and was loved most. I had rather to have no reason, but *quia complacuit*, " because it so pleased him." Why may we not as well ask why he chose these twelve from others, as why he chose three out of the twelve? If any Romanists will raise from hence any privilege to Peter, (which we would be well content to yield, if that would make them ever the honester men) they must remember that they must take company with them, which these Pompeian spirits cannot abide. As good no privilege as any partners. And withal, they must see him more taxed for his error in this act, than honoured by his presence at the act; whereas the beloved disciple saw and erred not. These same three, which were witnesses of his transfiguration in the mount, were witnesses of his agony in the garden; all three, and these three alone, were present at both; but both times sleeping. These were *arietes gregis*, "the bell-wedders of the flock," as Austin calls them. O weak devotion of three great disciples! These were Paul's three pillars, οἱ στύλοι δοκοῦντες, Gal. ii. 9. Christ takes them up twice; once to be witnesses of his greatest glory, once of his greatest extremity; they sleep both times. The other was in the night, more tolerable; this by day, yea, in a light above day. Chrysostom would fain excuse it to be an amazedness, not a sleep, not considering that they slept both at that glory, and after in the agony. To see that master praying, one would have thought should have fetched them on their knees; especially to see those heavenly affections look out at his eyes; to see his soul lifted up in his hands, in that transported fashion, to heaven. But now the hill hath wearied their limbs, their body clogs their soul, and they fall asleep. While Christ saw divine visions, they dreamed dreams; while he was in another world, ravished with the sight of his Father's glory, yea, of his own, they were in another world, a world of fancies, surprised with the cousin of death, sleep. Besides so gracious an example, their own necessity, *quia incessanter pecco*, " because I continually sin," Bernard's reason might have moved them to pray, rather than their Master; and behold, instead of fixing their eyes upon heaven, they shut them; instead of lifting up their hearts, their heads fell down upon their shoulders; and shortly, here was snoring instead of sighs and prayers. This was not Abraham's or Elihu's ecstatical sleep (Job xxxiii.); not the sleep of the church, a waking sleep, but the plain sleep of the eyes; and that not a slumbering sleep, which David denies to himself (Psal. cxxxii.) but a sound sleep, which Solomon forbids (Prov. vi. 4); yea, rather the dead sleep of Adam or Jonas; and, as Bernard had wont to say when he heard a monk snore, they did *carnaliter seu seculariter dormire*. Prayer is an ordinary receipt for sleep. How prone are we to it, when we should mind divine things! Adam slept in Paradise and lost a rib: but this sleep was of God's giving, and this rib was of God's taking. The good husbandman slept, and found tares. Eutychus slept, and fell. While Satan lulls us asleep, as he doth always rock the cradle when we sleep in our devotions, he ever takes some good from us, or puts some evil in us, or endangers us a deadly fall. Away with this spiritual lethargy! Bernard had wont to say, that those which sleep are dead to men, those that are dead are asleep to God. But, I say, those that sleep at church are dead to God: so we preach their funeral sermons instead of hortatory. And as he was wont to say, he lost no time so much as that wherein he slept; so let me add, there is no loss of time so desperate as of holy time. Think that Christ saith to thee at every sermon, as he did to Peter, *Etiam Petre dormis?* "Sleepest thou, Peter? couldst thou not wake with me one hour?" A slumbering and a drowsy heart does not become the business and presence of him that keepeth Israel, and slumbers not.

These were the attendants: see the companions of Christ. As our glory is not consummate without society, no more would Christ have his; therefore his transfiguration hath two companions, Moses, Elias. As St. Paul says of himself, "Whether in the body or out of the body, I know not, God knows;" so say I of these two. Of Elias there may seem less doubt, since we know that his body was assumed to heaven, and might as well come down for Christ's glory, as go up for his own; although some grave authors, as Calvin, Œcolampadius, Bale, Fulk, have held this body with Enoch's resolved into their elements. *Sed ego non credulus illis, Enoch translatus est in carne, et Elias carneus raptus est in cœlum, &c.* "Enoch was translated in the flesh, and Elias, being yet in the flesh, was taken into heaven," saith Jerom, in his epistle *ad Pammachium.*

And for Moses, though it be rare and singular, and Austin makes much scruple of it, yet why might not he after death return in his body to the glory of Christ's transfiguration, as well as afterwards many of the saints did to the glory of his resurrection? I cannot therefore, with the gloss, think there is any reason why Moses should take another, a borrowed body, rather than his own. Heaven could not give two fitter companions, more admirable to the Jews for their miracles, more gracious with God for their faith and holiness; both of them admitted to the conference with God in Horeb; both of them types of Christ; both of them fasted forty days; both of them for the glory of God suffered many perils; both divided the waters; both the messengers of God to kings; both of them marvellous, as in their life so in their end. A chariot of angels took away Elias; he was sought by the prophets, and not found. Michael strove with the devil for the body of Moses; he was sought for by the Jews and not found, and now both of them are found here together on Tabor. This Elias shows himself to the royal prophet of his church; this Moses shows himself to the true Michael. Moses the publisher of the law, Elias the chief of the prophets, show themselves to the God of the law and prophets. *Alter populi informator aliquando, alter reformator quandoque,* " one the informer once of the people, the other the reformer sometimes," saith Tertull. *in 4. adver. Marcionem. Alter initiator Veteris Testamenti, alter consummator Novi,* "one the first register of the Old Testament, the other the shutter up of the New." I verily think with Hilary, that these two are pointed at as the forerunners of the second coming of Christ, as now they were the foretellers of his departure: neither doubt I that these are the two witnesses which are alluded to in the Apocalypse, howsoever divers of the fathers have thrust Enoch into the place of Moses. Look upon the place, Apoc. xi. 5, who but Elias can be he of whom it is said, " If any man will hurt him, fire proceedeth out of his mouth and devoureth his enemies?" alluding to 2 Kings i. Who but Elias, of whom it is said, " He hath power to shut the heaven, that it rain not in the days of his prophesying?" alluding to 1 Kings xviii. Who but Moses, of whom it is said, " He hath power to turn the waters into blood, and smite the earth with all manner of plagues?" alluding to Exodus vii. 8. But take me aright, let me not seem a friend to the publicans of Rome, an abettor of those Alcoran-like fables of our Popish doctors, who, not seeing the wood for trees, do *hærere in cortice,* "stick in the bark;" taking all concerning that Antichrist according to the letter, *Odi et arceo.* So shall Moses and Elias come again in those witnesses, as Elias is already come in John Baptist: their spirits shall be in these witnesses, whose bodies and spirits were witnesses both of the present glory and future passion of Christ. Doubtless many thousand angels saw this sight, and were not seen; these two both saw and were seen. O how great a happiness was it for these two great prophets, in their glorified flesh to see their glorified Saviour, who before his incarnation had spoken to them! To speak to that Man-God, of whom they were glorified, and to become prophets not to men, but to God! And if Moses' face so shone before, when he spoke to him without a body in mount Sinai, in the midst of the flames and clouds, how did it shine now, when himself glorified speaks to him a man, in Tabor, in light and majesty! Elias hid his face before with a mantle when he passed by him in the rock; now with open face he beholds him present, and in his own glory adores his. Let that impudent Marcion, who ascribes the law and prophets to another god, and devises a hostility betwixt Christ and them, be ashamed to see Moses and Elias not only *in colloquio,* but *in consortio claritatis,* " not only in conference, but in a partnership of brightness," as Tertullian speaks, with Christ whom, if he had misliked, he had his choice of all the choir of heaven ; and now choosing them, why were they not *in sordibus et tenebris*, " in rags and darkness ?" *Sic in alienos demonstrat illos dum secum habet ; sic relinquendos docet quos sibi jungit ; sic destruit quos de radiis suis exstruit.* " So doth he show them far from strangeness to him, whom he hath with him ; so doth he teach them to be forsaken, whom he joins with himself ; so doth he destroy those whom he graces with his beams of glory," saith that father. His act verifies his word, " Think not that I come to destroy the law or the prophets ; I am not come to destroy, but to fulfil them," Matth. v. 17. O what consolation, what confirmation was this to the disciples, to see such examples of their future glory ! such witnesses and adorers of the eternal Deity of their Master : They saw, in Moses and Elias, what they themselves should be. How could they ever fear to be miserable, that saw such precedents of their ensuing glory ? how could they fear to die, that saw in others the happiness of their own change ? The rich glutton pleads with Abraham, that " if one came to them from the dead, they will amend :" Abraham answers, " They have Moses and the prophets, let them hear them." Behold, here is both Moses and the prophets, and these too come from the dead: how can we now but be persuaded of the happy state of another world, unless we will make ourselves worse than the damned ? See and consider that the saints of God are not lost, but departed ; gone into a far country with their Master, to return again richer and better than they went. Lest we should think this the condition of Elias only, that was rapt into heaven, see here Moses matched with him, that died and was buried. And is this the state of these two saints alone ? shall none be seen with him in the Tabor of heaven, but those which have seen him in Horeb and Carmel? O thou weak Christian, wilt only one or two limbs of Christ's body glorious in the transfiguration, or the whole ? he is the head, we are the members. If Moses and Elias were more excellent parts, tongue or hand, let us be but heels or toes ; his body is not perfect in glory without ours. " When Christ, which is our life, shall appear, then shall we also appear with him in glory," Colos. iii. 4. How truly may we say to death, " Rejoice not, mine enemy ; though I fall, yet shall I rise ; yea, I shall rise in falling." We shall not all sleep, we shall be " changed," saith St. Paul to his Thessalonians. Elias was changed, Moses slept :

both appeared ; to teach us, that neither our sleep nor change can keep us from appearing with him. When therefore thou shalt receive the sentence of death on mount Nebo, or when the fiery chariot shall come and sweep thee from this vale of mortality, remember thy glorious re-apparition with thy Saviour, and thou canst not but be comforted, and cheerfully triumph over that last enemy, outfacing those terrors with the assurance of a blessed resurrection to glory. To the which, &c.

CONTEMPLATION XIII.—THE SECOND PART OF THE MEDITATIONS UPON THE TRANSFIGURATION OF CHRIST.

A Sermon preached at Whitehall, before King James.

IT falls out with this discourse as with mount Tabor itself, that it is more easily climbed with the eye than with the foot. If we may not rather say of it, as Josephus did of Sinai, that it doth not only *ascensus hominum*, but *aspectus fatigare*, " weary not only the steps, but the very sight of men." We had thought not to spend many breaths, in the skirts of the hill, the circumstances: and it hath cost us one hour's journey already ; and we were glad to rest us ere we can have left them below us. One pause more, I hope, will overcome them, and set us on the top. No circumstance remains undiscussed but this one, what Moses and Elias did with Christ in their apparition ? For they were not, as some sleepy attendants, like the three disciples in the beginning, to be there and see nothing; nor, as some silent spectators, mute witnesses, to see and say nothing: but, as if their glory had no whit changed their profession, they are prophets still, " and foretold his departure," as St. Luke tells us. Foretold, not to him which knew it before, yea, which told it them ; they could not have known it but from him ; he was ὁ λόγος, " the word" of his Father : they told but that which he before had told his disciples, and now these heavenly witnesses tell it over again, for confirmation. Like as John Baptist knew Christ before ; he was *vox clamantis,* " the voice of a crier :" the other, *verbum Patris,* " the word of his Father :" there is great affinity betwixt *vox* and *verbum,* yea, this voice had uttered itself clearly, *Ecce agnus Dei,* " Behold the Lamb of God ;" yet he sends his disciples with an " Art thou he?" that he might confirm to them by him, that which he both knew and had said of him. So our Saviour follows his forerunner in this, that what he knew and told his disciples, the other Elias, the typical John Baptist, and Moses, must make good to their belief.

This ἔξοδος, "departure of Christ," was σκληρὸς λόγος, a word both hard and harsh; hard to believe, and harsh in believing. The disciples thought of nothing but a kingdom; a kingdom restored magnificently, interminably; and two of these three witnesses had so swallowed this hope, that they had put in for places in the state, to be his chief peers. How could they think of a parting? The throne of David did so fill their eyes, that they could not see his cross; and if they must let down this pill, how bitter must it needs be? His presence was their joy and life: it was their death to think of his loss. Now, therefore, that they might see that his sufferings and death were not of any sudden impotence, but predetermined in heaven, and revealed to the saints, two of the most noted saints in heaven shall second the news of his departure, and that in the midst of his transfiguration: that they could not choose but think, He that can be thus happy, needs not be miserable; that passion which he will undergo, is not out of weakness, but out of love. It is wittily noted by that sweet Chrysostom, that Christ never lightly spake of his passion, but immediately before and after he did some great miracle. And here, answerably, in the midst of his miraculous transfiguration, the two saints speak of his passion. A strange opportunity! in his highest exaltation to speak of his sufferings; to talk of Calvary in Tabor; when his head shone with glory, to tell him how it must bleed with thorns; when his face shone like the sun, to tell him it must be blubbered and spit upon; when his garments glistered with that celestial brightness, to tell him they must be stripped and divided; when he was adored by the saints of heaven, to tell him how he must be scorned by the basest of men; when he was seen between two saints, to tell him how he must be seen between two maléfactors: in a word, in the midst of his divine Majesty, to tell him of his shame; and, while he was transfigured in the mount, to tell him how he must be disfigured upon the cross. Yet these two heavenly prophets found this the fittest time for this discourse: rather choosing to speak of his sufferings in the height of his glory, than of his glory after his sufferings. It is most seasonable in our best, to think of our worst estate; for both that thought will be best digested when we are well, and that change will be best prepared for when we are the farthest from it. You would perhaps think it unseasonable for me, in the midst of all your court jollity, to tell you of the days of mourning, and, with that great king, to serve in a death's-head amongst your royal dishes, to show you coffins in the midst of your triumphs; yet these precedents, above exception, show me, that no time is so fit as this. Let me therefore say to you, with the Psalmist, " I have said, ye are gods:" if ye were transfigured in Tabor, could ye be more? "but ye shall die like men:" there is your ἔξοδος. It was a worthy and witty note of Jerome, that amongst all trees the cedars are bidden to praise God, which are the tallest: and yet *dies Domini super omnes cedros Libani*, " the day of the Lord shall be upon all the cedars of Lebanon," Isaiah ii. Ye gallants, whom a little yellow earth, and the webs of that curious worm, have made gorgeous without, and perhaps proud within, remember that, ere long, as one worm decks you without, so another worm shall consume you within, and that both' the earth that you prank up, and that earth wherewith you prank it, is running back into dust. Let not your high estate hide from you your fatal humiliation: let not your purples hide from you your winding-sheet, but even on the top of Tabor think of the depth of the grave; think of your departure from men, while ye are advanced above men.

We are now ascended the top of the hill, let us therefore stand, and see, and wonder at this great sight: as Moses, to see the "bush flaming and not consumed;" so we, to see the humanity continuing itself in the midst of these beams of glory. Christ was ἐν μορφῇ δούλου, saith St. Paul, "in the form of a servant;" now for the time he was truly μεταμορφώθεις, "transformed:" that there is no cause why Maldonat should so inveigh against some of ours, yea of his own, as Jansenius, who translates it transformation: for what is the external form but the figure? and their own Vulgate (as hotly as he takes it) reads it, Philip. ii. 7. μορφὴν δούλου, "*formam servi accipiens*," "taking the form of a servant." There is no danger in this ambiguity; not the substantial form but the external fashion of Christ was changed: he having three forms (as Bernard distinguishes), *Contemptam, splendidam, divinam*, " the despised, the resplendent, the divine," changeth here the first into the second: this is one of the rarest occurrences that ever befell the Saviour of the world. I am wont to reckon up these four principal wonders of his life; incarnation, temptation, transfiguration, and agony: the first, in the womb of the virgin; the second, in the wilderness; the third, in the mount; the fourth, in the garden. The first, that God should become man; the second, that God and man should be tempted, and transported by Satan; the third, that man should be glorified upon earth; the last, that he which was man and God should sweat blood, under the sense of God's wrath for man: and all these either had the angels for witnesses, or the immediate voice of God. The first had angels singing; the second angels ministering; the third the voice of God thundering; the fourth the angels comforting; that it may be no wonder, the earth marvels at those things, whereat the angels of heaven stand amazed. Bernard makes three kinds of wonderful changes; *sublimitas in humilitatem*, "height to lowliness," when the Word took flesh; *contemptibilitas in majestatem*, when Christ transformed himself before his disciples; *mutabilitas in eternitatem*, when he arose again, and ascended to heaven to reign for ever: ye see this is one of them; and as Tabor did rise out of the valley of Galilee, so this exaltation did rise out of the midst of Christ's humiliation. Other marvels do increase his dejection, this only makes for his glory; and the glory of this is matchable with the humiliation of all the rest. That face, wherein before (saith Isaiah) there was no form nor beauty, now shines as the sun: that face, which men hid their faces from in contempt, now shines so, that mortal eyes could not choose but hide themselves from the lustre of it, and immortal receive their beams from it: He had ever in *vultu sidereum quiddam*, as Jerome speaks, a "certain heavenly majesty and port in his countenance," which made his disciples follow him at first-sight, but now here was the perfection of super-celestial brightness. It was a miracle in the three children, that they were so delivered from the flames, that their very garments smelt not of the fire: it is no less miracle in Christ, that his very garments were dyed celestial, and did savour of his glory. Like as Aaron was so anointed on his head and beard, that his skirts were all perfumed: his clothes therefore shined as snow, yea, (that were but a waterish white), as the light itself, saith St. Mark and Matthew, in the most Greek copies: that seamless coat, as it had no welt, so it had no spot. The king's son is all fair, even without. O excellent glory of his humanity! the best diamond or carbuncle is hid with a case: but this brightness pierceth through all his garments, and makes them lightsome in him, which use to conceal light in others:

Herod put him on in mockage ἐσθῆτα λαμπρὰν, (Luke xxiii.) not a white, but a bright robe (the ignorance whereof makes a show of disparity in the evangelists); but God the Father, to glorify him, clothes his very garments with heavenly splendour. "Behold, thou art fair, my beloved; behold, thou art fair; and there is no spot in thee. Thine head is as fine gold, thy mouth is as sweet things, and thou art wholly delectable. Come forth, ye daughters of Sion, and behold king Solomon, with the crown wherewith his father crowned him, in the day of the gladness of his heart!" O Saviour, if thou wert such in Tabor, what art thou in heaven? if this were the glory of thy humanity, what is the presence of thy Godhead. Let no man yet wrong himself so much, as to magnify this happiness as another's; and to put himself out of the participation of this glory. Christ is our head, we are his members; as we all were in the first Adam, both innocent and sinning; so are we in the second Adam, both shining in Tabor, and bleeding sweat in the garden: and as we are already happy in him, so shall we be once in ourselves, by and through him. He shall change our vile bodies, that they may be like his glorious body: behold our pattern, and rejoice! like his glorious body. These very bodies, that are now cloudy like the earth, shall once be bright as the sun; and we, that now see clay in one another's faces, shall then see nothing but heaven in our countenances; and we, that now set forth our bodies with clothes, shall then be clothed upon with immortality, out of the wardrobe of heaven: and if ever any painted face should be admitted to the sight of this glory, (as I much fear it, yea, I am sure God will have none but true faces in heaven), they would be ashamed to think, that ever they had faces to daub with these beastly pigments, in comparison of this heavenly complexion. Let us therefore look upon this flesh, not so much with contempt of what it was, and is, as with a joyful hope of what it shall be; and when our courage is assaulted with the change of these bodies from healthful to weak, from living to dead, let us comfort ourselves with the assurance of this change, from dust to incorruption. We are not so sure of death, as of transfiguration; all the days of our appointed time we will, therefore, wait till our changing shall come.

Now, from the glory of the Master, give me leave to turn your eyes to the error of the servant, who having slept with the rest, and now suddenly awaking, knoweth not whether he slept still. To see such a light about him, three so glittering persons before him, made him doubt now, as he did after, when he was carried by the angel through the iron gate, whether it were a pleasing dream, or a real act. All slept, and now all waked; only Peter slept waking, and I know not whether more erred in his speech, or in his sleep. It was a shame for a man to sleep in Tabor, but it is a more shame for a man to dream with his eyes open. Thus did Peter, " Master, it is good for us to be here; let us make us three tabernacles." I could well say with Optatus, on this or any other occasion, *Ipsius sancti Petri beatitudo veniam tribuat, dubito dicere peccasse tantam sanctitatem,* " Let blessed Peter pardon me, I fear to say so great holiness offended." Yet, since our adversaries are so over-partial to this worthy saint, in whom they have as little as they boast much, that they can be content his praise should blemish the dignity of all the rest, yea, that God himself is in danger to be a loser by the advancement of so dear a servant; give me leave to lay my finger a little upon this blot. God would never have recorded that which it should be uncharitable for us to observe. It was the injurious kindness of Marcion, in honour of Peter, to leave out the story of Malchus, as Epiphanius notes. It shall be our blame, if we do not so note, that we benefit ourselves even by his imperfections. St. Mark's gospel is said to be Peter's; O blessed apostle, can it be any wrong to say of thee, that which thou hast written of thyself, not for insultation, not for exprobration: God forbid but that men may be ashamed to give that to him which he hath denied to himself. Let me, therefore, not doubt to say (with reverence to so great a saint), that as he spake most, so he is noted to have erred most. Not to meddle with his sinking, striking, judaizing, one while we find him carnally insinuating, another while carnally presuming; one while weakly denying, another while rashly misconstruing; carnally insinuating, " Master, favour thyself." Which, though some parasites of Rome would fain smooth up, that he, in this, showed his love to Christ, as before his faith, out of St. Jerome and St. Austin; yet it must needs be granted, which Bernard saith, *diligebat spiritum carnaliter,* "he loved the spirit in a carnal fashion." Let them choose whether they will admit Christ to have chid unjustly, or Peter worthy of chiding: except, perhaps, with Hilary, they will stop where they should not; *vade post me,* "follow me," spoken to Peter in approbation; *Satana, non sapis quæ Dei sunt,*

" Satan, thou savourest not the things that are of God," spoken to Satan in objurgation: carnally presuming, " though all men, yet not I." If he had not presumed of his strength to stand, he had not fallen. And as one yawning makes many open mouths, so did his vain resolution draw on company; " Likewise said the other disciples." For his weak denial, ye all know his simple negation, lined with an oath, faced with an imprecation. And here, that no man may need to doubt of an error, the Spirit of God saith, " He knew not what he said;" not only τί λαλήση, as Mark, " what he should say," but, ὀλίγη, saith Luke, " what he did speak:" whereof St. Mark gives the reason, ἦσαν ἔκφοβοι, " they were amazedly affrighted." Amazedness may abate an error of speech, it cannot take it away. Besides astonishment, here was a fervour of spirit, a love to Christ's glory, and a delight in it; a fire, but misplaced in the top of the chimney, not on the hearth; *præmatura devotio,* as Ambrose speaks, "a devotion, but rash and heedy." And, if it had not been so, yet it is not in the power of a good intention to make a speech good. In this the matter failed; for what should such saints do in earthly tabernacles, in tabernacles of his making? And if he could be content to live there without a tent (for he would have but three made), why did he not much more conceive so of those heavenly guests? And if he spoke this to retain them, how weak was it to think their absence would be for want of house-room? or how could that at once be which Moses and Elias had told him, and that which he wished? for, how should Christ both depart at Jerusalem, and stay in the mount? or if he would have their abode there, to avoid the sufferings at Jerusalem, how did he yet again sing over that song for which he had heard before, " Come behind me, Satan?" Or if it had been fit for Christ to have staid there, how weakly doth he, which Chrysostom observes, equalize the servant with the Master; the saints with God? In a word, the best and the worst that can be said here of Peter is, that which the Psalmist saith of Moses, *effutiit labiis,* " he spake unadvisedly with his lips;" Psal. cvi. 33.

Yet if any earthly place or condition might have given warrant to Peter's motion, this was it. Here was a hill, the emblem of heaven; here were two saints, the epitome of heaven; here was Christ, the God of heaven: and if Peter might not say so of this, how shall we say of any other place, *Bonum est esse hic?* " It is good to be here?" Will ye say of the country, *Bonum est esse hic?* there is melancholy, dulness, privacy, toil. Will ye say of the court, *bonum est esse hic?* there dwells ambition, secret undermining, attendance, serving of humours and times. Will ye say of the city, *Bonum est esse hic?* there you find continual tumult, usury, cozenage in bargains, excess, and disorder. Get you to the wilderness, and say, It is good to be here; even there evils will find us out. *In nemore habitat lupus,* saith Bernard, "in the wood dwells the wolf:" weariness and sorrow dwell everywhere. The rich man wallows amongst his heaps, and when he is in his counting-house, beset with piles of bags, he can say, *Bonum est esse hic:* he worships these molten images; his gold is his god, his heaven is his chest; not thinking of that which Tertullian notes, *aurum ipsum quibusdam gentibus ad vincula servire,* " that some countries make their very fetters of gold:" yea, so doth he, whilst he admires it, making himself the slave to his servant, *damnatus ad metalla,* "condemned to the mines," as the old Roman punishment was. *Coacta servitus miserabilior, affectata miserior,* "forced bondage is more worthy of pity, affected bondage is more miserable." And if God's hand touch him never so little, can his gold bribe a disease, can his bags keep his head from aching, or the gout from his joints? or doth his loathing stomach make a difference betwixt an earthen and silver dish? O vain desires, and impotent contentments of men, who place happiness in that which doth not only not save them from evils, but help to make them miserable! Behold, their wealth feeds them with famine, recreates them with toil, cheers them with cares, blesses them with torments, and yet they say, *Bonum est esse hic.* How are their sleeps broken with cares! how are their hearts broken with losses! Either riches have wings, which, in the clipping or pulling, fly away, and take them to heaven; or else their souls have wings, *stulte hac nocte,* "thou fool, this night," and fly from their riches to hell. *Non dominus, sed colonus,* saith Seneca, "not the lord, but the farmer:" so that here are both perishing riches, and a perishing soul. Uncertainty of riches (as St. Paul to his Timothy) and certainty of misery: and yet these vain men say, *Bonum est esse hic.*

The man of honour, that I may use Bernard's phrase, that hath Ahasuerus' proclamation made before him, which knows he is not only τις μέγας, "a certain great man," as Simon affected, but ὁ αὐτὸς, "the man which Demosthenes was proud of, that sees all heads bare, and all knees bent to him, that finds himself out of the reach of envy, on the pitch of admiration, says, *Bonum est esse hic.*" Alas! how little thinks he of that which that good man said to his Eugenius, *Non est quod blandiatur celsitudo, ubi solicitudo major,* "What care we for the fawning of that greatness, which is attended with more care?" King Henry VII.'s emblem in all his buildings, in the windows, was still a crown in a bush of thorns: I know not with what historical allusion; but sure, I think, to imply, that great places are not free from great cares. Saul knew what he did, when he hid himself among the stuff. No man knoweth the weight of a sceptre, but he that swayeth it. As for subordinate greatness, it hath so much less worth as it hath more dependence. How many sleepless nights, and restless days, and busy shifts, doth their ambition cost them that affect eminence! Certainly, no men are so worthy of pity, as they whose height thinks all other worthy of contempt. High places are slippery; and as it is easy to fall, so the ruin is deep, and the recovery difficult. *Altiorem locum sortitus es, non tutiorem, subliniorem, sed non securiorem,* saith Bernard, "Thou hast got an higher place, but not a safer; a loftier, but not more secure." *Aulæ culmen lubricum,* "The slippery ridge of the court," was the old title of honour. David's curse was, *Fiat via eorum tenebræ et lubricum,* "Let their way be made dark and slippery." What difference is there betwixt his curse and the happiness of the ambitious, but this, that the way of the one is dark and slippery, the way of the other lightsome and slippery: that dark, that they may fall; this light, that they may see and be seen to fall? Please yourselves then, ye great ones, and let others please you in the admiration of your height; but if your goodness do not answer your greatness, *Sera querela est quoniam elevans allisisti me,* "It is a late complaint, thou hast lift me up to cast me down." Your ambition hath but set you up a scaffold, that your misery might be more notorious. And yet these clients of honour say, *Bonum est esse hic.*

The pampered glutton, when he seeth his table spread with full bowls, with costly dishes, and curious sauces, the dainties of all three elements, says, *Bonum est esse hic.* And yet eating hath a satiety, and satiety a weariness: his heart is never more empty of contentment, than when his stomach is fullest of delicates. When he is empty, he is not well till he be filled; when he is full, he is not well till he have got a stomach. *Et momentanea blandimenta gulæ stercoris fine condemnat*, saith Jerome; "And condemns all the momentary pleasures of his maw to the dunghill." And when he sits at his feasts of marrow and fat things (as the prophet speaks), his table, according to the Psalmist's imprecation, is made his snare: a true snare every way. His soul is caught in it with excess; his estate with penury; his body with diseases. Neither doth he more plainly tear his meat in pieces with his teeth, than he doth himself: and et this vain man says, *Bonum est esse hic.*

The petulant wanton thinks it the only happiness, that he may have his full scope to filthy dalliance. Little would he so do, if he could see his strumpet as she is: her eyes the eyes of a cockatrice, her hair snakes, her painted face the visor of a fury, her heart snares, her hands bands, and her end wormwood; consumption of the flesh, destruction of the soul, and the flames of lust ending in the flames of hell. Since, therefore, neither pleasures, nor honour, nor wealth, can yield any true contentment to their best favourites, let us not be so unwise as to speak of this vale of misery, as Peter did of the hill of Tabor, *Bonum est esse hic.*

And if the best of earth cannot do it, why will ye seek it in the worst? how dare any of you great ones seek to purchase contentment with oppression, sacrilege, bribery, outfacing innocence and truth with power, damning your own souls for but the humouring of a few miserable days? "*Filii hominum, quousque gravi corde? ad quid diligitis vanitatem et quæritis mendacium?*" "O ye sons of men, how long," &c. But that which moved Peter's desire (though with imperfection) shows what will perfect our desire and felicity: for if a glimpse of this heavenly glory did so ravish this worthy disciple, that he thought it happiness enough to stand by and gaze upon it, how shall we be affected with the contemplation, yea fruition, of the divine presence! Here was but Tabor, there is heaven; here were but two saints, there many millions of saints and angels; here was Christ transfigured, there he sits at the right hand of Majesty; here he was a representation, there a gift and possession of blessedness. O that we could now forget the world, and fixing our eyes upon this better Tabor, say, *Bonum est esse hic.* Alas! this life of ours, if it were not short, yet it is miserable; and if it were not miserable, yet it is short. Tell me, ye that have the greatest command on earth, whether this vile world hath ever afforded you any sincere contentation.— The world is your servant: if it were your parasite, yet, could it make you heartily merry? Ye delicatest courtiers, tell me if pleasure itself hath not an unpleasant tediousness hanging upon it, and more sting than honey? And whereas all happiness, even here below, is in the vision of God; how is our spiritual eye hindered, as the body is, from its object, by darkness, by false light, by aversion! Darkness, he that doth sin is in darkness; false light, while we measure eternal things by temporary; aversion, while, as weak eyes hate the light, we turn our eyes from the true and immutable good, to the fickle and uncertain. We are not on the hill, but the valley, where we have tabernacles, not of our own making, but of clay; and such as wherein we are witnesses of Christ, not transfigured in glory, but blemished with dishonour, dishonoured with oaths and blasphemies, recrucified with our sins; witnesses of God's saints, not shining in Tabor, but mourning in darkness, and, instead of that heavenly brightness, clothed with sackcloth and ashes. Then and there we shall have "tabernacles not made with hands, eternal in the heavens," where we shall see how sweet the Lord is: we shall see the triumphs of Christ; we shall hear and sing the hallelujahs of saints: "*Quæ nunc nos angit vesaniæ vitiorum sitire absinthium,*" &c. saith that devout father. O how hath our corruption bewitched us, to thirst for this wormwood, to affect the shipwrecks of this world, to dote upon the misery of this fading life! and not rather to fly up to the felicity of saints, to the society of angels, to that blessed contemplation wherein we shall see God in himself, God in us, ourselves in him! There shall be no sorrow, no pain, no complaint, no fear, no death. There is no malice to rise against us, no misery to afflict us, no hunger, thirst, weariness, temptation to disquiet us. There, O there, one day is better than a thousand! there is rest from our labours, peace from our enemies, freedom from our sins! How many clouds of discontentment darken the sunshine of our joy while we are here below! *Væ nobis qui vivimus plangere quæ pertulimus, dolere quæ sentimus, timere quæ expectamus!* Complaint of evils past, sense of present, fear of future, have shared our lives amongst them. Then shall we be *semper læti, semper satiati*, "always joyful, always satisfied," with the vision of that God, "in whose presence there is fulness of joy, and at whose right hand are pleasures for evermore." Shall we see that heathen Cleombrotus abandoning his life, and casting himself down from the rock, upon an uncertain noise of immortality; and shall not we Christians abandon the wicked superfluities of life, the pleasures of sin, for that life which we know more certainly than this? What stick we at, my beloved? Is there a heaven, or is there none? have we a Saviour there, or have we none? We know there is a heaven, as sure as that there is an earth below us; we know we have a Saviour there, as sure as there are men that we converse with upon earth; we know there is happiness, as sure as we know there is misery and mutability upon earth. O our miserable sottishness and infidelity, if we do not contemn the best offers of the world, and lifting up our eyes and hearts to heaven, say, *Bonum est esse hic!*

"Even so, Lord Jesus, come quickly." To Him that hath purchased and prepared this glory for us, together with the Father and blessed Spirit, one incomprehensible God, be all praise for ever! Amen.

CONTEMPLATION XIV. — THE PROSECUTION OF THE TRANSFIGURATION.

BEFORE, the disciples' eyes were dazzled with glory: now, the brightness of that glory is shaded with a cloud. Frail and feeble eyes of mortality cannot look upon a heavenly lustre. That cloud imports both majesty and obscuration. Majesty; for it was the testimony of God's presence of old: the cloud covered the mountain, the tabernacle, the oracle. He that makes the clouds his chariot, was in a cloud carried up into heaven. Where have we mention of any divine representation but a cloud is one part of it? what comes nearer to heaven, either in place or resemblance? Obscuration; for as it showed there was a majesty, and that divine, so it showed them, that the view of that majesty was not for bodily eyes. Like as when some great prince walks under a canopy, that vail shows there is a great person under it, but withal restrains the eye from a free sight of his person; and if the cloud were clear, yet it shaded them. Why then was this cloud interposed betwixt that glorious vision and them, but for a check of their bold eyes?

Had they too long gazed upon this resplendent spectacle, as their eyes had been blinded, so their hearts had perhaps grown to an over-bold familiarity with that heavenly object: how seasonably doth the cloud intercept it! The wise God knows our need of these vicissitudes and allays. If we have a light, we must have a cloud; if a light to cheer us, we must have a cloud to humble us.

It was so in Sinai, it was so in Sion, it saw so in Olivet; it shall never be but so. The natural day and night do not more duly interchange, than this light and cloud. Above we shall have the light without the cloud, a clear vision and fruition of God, without all dim and sad interpositions; below we cannot be free from these mists and clouds of sorrow and misapprehension.

But this was a bright cloud. There is difference betwixt the cloud in Tabor, and that in Sinai: this was clear, that darksome; there is darkness in the law, there is light in the grace of the gospel: Moses was there spoken to in darkness, here he was spoken with in light. In that dark cloud there was terror, in this there was comfort: though it were a cloud then, yet it was bright; and though it were bright, yet it was a cloud: with much light there was some shade. God would not speak to them concerning Christ out of darkness; neither yet would he manifest himself to them in an absolute brightness: all his appearances have this mixture. What need I other instance, than in these two saints? Moses spake oft to God, mouth to mouth; yet not so immediately, but that there was ever somewhat drawn, as a curtain, betwixt God and him; either fire in Horeb, or smoke in Sinai; so as his face is not more vailed from the people, than God's from him. Elias shall be spoken to by God, but in the rock, and under a mantle. In vain shall we hope for any revelation from God, but in a cloud. Worldly hearts are in utter darkness; they see not so much as the least glimpse of these divine beams, not a beam of that inaccessible light: the best of his saints see him here but in a cloud, or in a glass. Happy are we, if God has honoured us with these divine representations of himself; once in his light, we shall see light.

I can easily think with what amazedness these three disciples stood compassed in that bright cloud, expecting some miraculous event of so heavenly a vision, when suddenly they might hear a voice sounding out of that cloud, saying, " This is my beloved Son, in whom I am well pleased; hear him," They need not be told whose that voice was: the place, the matter evinced it; no angel in heaven could or durst have said so. How gladly doth Peter afterwards recount it! for he received from God the Father honour and glory, when there came such a voice to him from the excellent glory, "This is my beloved Son, in whom I am well pleased; hear him."

It was only the ear that was here taught, not the eye: as of Horeb, so of Sinai, so of Tabor, might God say, Ye saw no shape, nor image, in that day that the Lord spake unto you. He that knows our proneness to idolatry, avoids those occasions which we might take to abuse our own fancies.

Twice hath God spoken these words to his own Son from heaven; once in his baptism, and now again in his transfiguration: here not without some oppositive comparison; not Moses, not Elias, but this. Moses and Elias were servants, this a Son: Moses and Elias were sons, but of grace and choice; this is that Son, the Son by nature. Other sons are beloved as of favour and free election; this is the Beloved, as in the unity of his essence. Others are so beloved, that he is pleased with themselves; this so beloved, that in him and for him, he is pleased with mankind. As the relation betwixt the Father and the Son is infinite, so is the love: we measure the intenseness of love by the extension: the love that rests in the person affected alone, is but strait; true love descends, like Aaron's ointment, from the head to the skirts, to children, friends, allies. O incomprehensibly large love of God the Father to the Son, that, for his sake, he is pleased with the world! O perfect and happy complacence! Out of Christ, there is nothing but enmity betwixt God and the soul; in him there can be nothing but peace: when the beams are met in one centre, they do not only heat, but burn. Our weak love is diffused to many; God hath some, the world more, and therein wives, children, friends; but this infinite love of God hath all the beams of it united in one only object, the Son of his love; neither doth he love any thing, but in the participation of his love, in the derivation from it. O God, let me be found in Christ, and how canst thou but be pleased with me?

This one voice proclaims Christ at once the Son of God, the Reconciler of the world, the Doctor and Lawgiver of his Church. As the Son of God he is essentially interested in his love : as he is the Reconciler of the world in whom God is well pleased, he doth most justly challenge our love and adherence: as he is the Doctor and Lawgiver, he doth justly challenge our audience, our obedience. Even so, Lord, teach us to hear and obey thee as our Teacher; to love thee, and believe in thee as our Reconciler: and as the eternal Son of thy Father, to adore thee.

The light caused wonder in the disciples,-but the voice astonishment; they are all fallen down upon their faces. Who can blame a mortal man to be thus affected with the voice of his Maker? yet this word was but plausible and hortatory. O God, how shall flesh and blood be other than swallowed up with the horror of thy dreadful sentence of death? The lion shall roar, who shall not be afraid! How shall those, that have slighted the sweet voice of thine invitations, call to the rocks to hide them from the terror of thy judgments!

The God of mercies pities our infirmities: I do not hear our Saviour say, Ye lay sleeping one while upon the earth; now ye lie astonished: ye could neither wake to see, nor stand to hear; now lie still and tremble: but he graciously touches and comforts them, " Arise, fear not." That voice, which shall once raise them up out of the earth, might well raise them up from it; that hand, which by the least touch restored sight, limbs, life, might well restore the spirits of the dismayed. O Saviour, let that sovereign hand of thine touch us, when we lie in the trances of our griefs, in the bed of our securities, in the grave of our sins, and we shall arise.

" They looking up saw no man, save Jesus alone," and that, doubtless, in his wonted form; all was now gone — Moses, Elias, the cloud, the voice, the glory. Tabor itself cannot be long blessed with that divine light, and those shining guests; heaven will not allow to earth any long continuance of glory; only above is constant happiness to be looked for and enjoyed, where we shall ever see our Saviour in his unchangeable brightness, where the light shall never be either clouded or varied.

Moses and Elias are gone; only Christ is left: the glory of the law and the prophets was but temporary, yea, momentary, that only Christ may remain to us entire and conspicuous: they came but to give testimony to Christ; when that is done, they are vanished.

Neither could these raised disciples find any miss of Moses and Elias, when they had Christ still with them. Had Jesus been gone, and left either Moses or Elias, or both, in the mount with his disciples, that presence, though glorious, could not have comforted them; now that they are gone, and he is left, they cannot be capable of discomfort. O Saviour, it matters not who is away, while thou art with us : thou art God all-sufficient; what can we want, when we want not thee? Thy presence shall make Tabor itself a heaven; yea, hell itself cannot make us miserable with the fruition of thee.

CONTEMPLATION XV.—THE WOMAN TAKEN IN ADULTERY.

What a busy life was this of Christ's! He spent the night in the Mount of Olives, the day in the temple; whereas the night is for a retired repose, the day for company: his retiredness was for prayer, his companionableness was for preaching. All night he watches in the mount; all the morning he preaches in the temple. It was not for pleasure that he was here upon earth: his whole time was penal and toilsome: how do we resemble him, if his life were all pain and labour, ours all pastime?

He found no such fair success the day before: the multitude was divided in their opinion of him; messengers were sent, and suborned to apprehend him, yet he returns to the temple. It is for the sluggard or the coward to plead a lion in the way; upon the calling of God, we must overlook and contemn all the spite and opposition of men: even after an ill harvest we must sow, and after denials, we must woo for God.

This Sun of righteousness prevents that other, and shines early with wholesome doctrines upon the souls of his hearers; the auditory is both thronged and attentive, yet not all with the same intentions. If the people came to learn, the Scribes and Pharisees came to cavil and carp at his teaching; with what a pretence of zeal and justice yet do they put themselves into Christ's presence! As lovers of chastity and sanctimony, and haters of uncleanness, they bring to him a woman taken in the flagrance of her adultery.

And why the woman rather, since the man's offence was equal, if not more; because he should have had more strength of resistance, more grace not to tempt? Was it out of necessity? perhaps the man, knowing his danger, made use of strength to shift away, and violently break from his apprehenders. Or was it out of cunning, in that they hoped for more likely matter to accuse Christ, in the case of the woman than of the man? for that they supposed his merciful disposition might more probably incline to compassionate her weakness rather than the stronger vessel? Or was it rather out of partiality? was it not then, as now, that the weakest soonest suffers, and impotency lays us open to the malice of an enemy? Small flies hang in the webs, while wasps break through without control; the wand and the sheet are for poor offenders, the great either out-face or out-buy their shame: a beggarly drunkard is haled to the stocks, while the rich is chambered up to sleep out his surfeit.

Out of these grounds is the woman brought to Christ: not to the Mount of Olives, not to the way, not to his private lodging, but to the temple; and that not to some obscure angle, but into the face of the assembly.

They pleaded for her death: the punishment which they would onwards inflict, was her shame; which must needs be so much more, as there were more eyes to be witnesses of her guiltiness. All the brood of sin affects darkness and secrecy, but this more properly: the twilight, the night, is for the adulterer. It cannot be better fitted than to be dragged out into the light of the sun, and to be proclaimed with hootings and basins. O the impudence of those men who can make merry professions of their own beastliness, and boast of the shameful trophies of their lust!

Methinks I see this miserable adulteress, how she stands confounded amidst that gazing and disdainful multitude! how she hides her head, how she wipes her blubbered face and weeping eyes! In the meantime, it is no dumb-show that is here acted by these Scribes and Pharisees; they step forth boldly to her accusation: "Master, this woman was taken in adultery, in the very act." How plausibly do they begin! Had I stood by and heard them, should I not have said, What holy, honest, conscionable men are these! what devout clients of Christ! with what reverence they come to him! with what zeal of justice! when he that made and ransacks their bosom tells me, "All this is done but to tempt him." Even the falsest hearts will have the plausiblest mouths: like to Solomon's courtezan, "Their lips drop as an honeycomb, and their mouth is smoother than oil; but their end is bitter as wormwood."

False and hollow Pharisees! he is your Master whom ye serve, not he whom ye tempt: only in this shall he be approved your Master, that he shall pay you your wages, and give you your portion with hypocrites.

The act of adultery was her crime: to be taken in the very act, was no part of her sin, but the proof of her just conviction; yet her deprehension is made an aggravation of her shame. Such is the corrupt judgment of the world: to do ill, troubles not men, but to be taken in doing it; unknown filthiness passes away with ease; it is the notice that perplexes them, not the guilt. But, O foolish sinners, all your packing and secrecy cannot so contrive it, but that ye shall be taken in the manner; your conscience takes you so, the God of heaven takes you so; and ye shall once find, that your conscience is more than a thousand witnesses, and God more than a thousand consciences.

They that complain of the act, urge the punishment: "Now Moses in the law commanded us that such should be stoned." Where did Moses bid so? Surely the particularity of this execution was without the book? Tradition and custom enacted it, not the law.

Indeed, Moses commanded death to both the offenders, not the manner of death to either. By analogy it holds thus: it is flatly commanded in the case of a damsel betrothed to a husband, and found not to be a virgin; in the case of a damsel betrothed, who being defiled in the city, cried not: tradition and custom made up the rest; obtaining out of this ground, that all adulterers should be executed by lapidation. The ancienter punishment was burning; death always, though in divers forms. I sname to think, that Christians should slight that sin which both Jews and Pagans held ever deadly.

What a mis-citation is this! "Moses commanded." The law was God's, not Moses's. If Moses were employed to mediate betwixt God and Israel, the law is never the more his: he was the hand of God to reach the law to Israel, the hand of Israel to take it from God. We do not name the water from the pipes, but from the spring. It is not for a true Israelite to rest in the second means, but to mount up to the supreme original of justice. How reverent soever an opinion was had of Moses, he cannot be thus named without a shameful undervaluing of the royal law of his Maker. There is no mortal man whose authority may not grow into contempt: that of the everliving God cannot but be ever sacred and inviolable. It is now with the gospel, as it was then with the law: the word is no other than Christ's, though delivered by our weakness;—whosoever be the crier, the proclamation is the King of heaven's. While it goes for ours, it is no marvel if it lie open to despite.

How captious a word is this! Moses said thus, "What sayest thou?" If they be not sure that Moses said so, why do they affirm it? and if they be sure, why do they question that which they know decided? They would not have desired a better advantage, than a contradiction to that received lawgiver. It is their profession, "We are Moses' disciples," and "we know that God spake to Moses." It had been quarrel enough to oppose so known a prophet. Still I find it the drift of the enemies of truth, to set Christ and Moses together by the ears, in the matter of the Sabbath, of circumcision, of marriage and divorce; of the use of the law, of justification by the law, of the sense and extent of the law, and where not? but they shall never be able to effect it: they two are fast and indissoluble friends on both parts for ever; each speaks for other, each establishes other; they are subordinate, they cannot be opposite; Moses faithful as a servant, Christ as a son. A faithful servant cannot but be officious to the Son. The true use we make of Moses is, to be our schoolmaster to teach us, to whip us unto Christ; the true use we make of Christ is, to supply Moses: "By him all that believe are justified from all things, from which they could not be justified by the law of Moses." Thus must we hold in with both, if we will have our part in either: so shall Moses bring us to Christ, and Christ to glory.

Had these Pharisees, out of simplicity, and desire of resolution in a case of doubt, moved this question to our Saviour, it had been no less commendable, than now it is blameworthy.

O Saviour, whither should we have recourse, but to thine oracle? thou art the Word of the Father, the Doctor of the church: while we hear from others, what say fathers? what say councils? let them hear from us, "What sayest thou?"

But here it was far otherwise: they came not to learn, but to tempt, and to tempt that they might accuse like their father the devil, who solicits to sin that he may plead against us for yieldance. Fain would these colleaguing adversaries draw Christ to contradict Moses, that they might take advantage of his contradiction.

On the one side they saw his readiness to tax the false glosses which their presumptuous doctors had put upon the law, with an "I say unto you;" on the other, they saw his inclination to mercy and commiseration in all his courses, so far as to neglect even some circumstances of the law as to touch the leper, to heal on the Sabbath, to eat with known sinners, to dismiss an infamous but penitent offender, to select and countenance two noted publicans; and hereupon they might perhaps think that his compassion might draw him to cross this Mosaical institution.

What a crafty bait is here laid for our Saviour! such as he cannot bite at, and not be taken. It seems to them impossible he should avoid a deep prejudice either to his justice or mercy. For thus they imagine: either Christ will second Moses in sentencing this woman to death, or else he will cross Moses in dismissing her unpunished. If he commands her to be stoned, he loses the honour of his clemency and mercy; if he appoints her dismission, he loses the honour of his justice. Indeed, strip him of either of these, and he can be no Saviour.

O the cunning folly of vain men, that hope to beguile Wisdom itself!

Silence and neglect shall first confound those men, whom after his answer will send away convicted. Instead of opening his mouth, our Saviour bows his body; and instead of returning words from his lips, writes characters on the ground with his finger. O Saviour, I had rather silently wonder at thy gesture, than inquire curiously into the words thou wrotest, or the mysteries of thus writing; only herein I see thou meanest to show a disregard to these malicious and busy cavillers. Sometimes taciturnity and contempt are the best answers. Thou that hast bidden us "Be wise as serpents," givest us this noble example of thy prudence. It was most safe that these tempters should be thus kept fasting with a silent disrespect, that their eagerness might justly draw upon them an ensuing shame.

The more unwillingness they saw in Christ to give his answer, the more pressing and importunate they were to draw it from him. Now, as forced by their so zealous irritation, our Saviour rouseth up himself and gives it them home, with a reprehensory and stinging satisfaction: "He that is without sin among you, let him first cast a stone at her;"—as if his very action had said, I was loath to have shamed you, and therefore could have been willing not to have heard your ill-meant motion; but since you will needs have it, and by your vehemence force my justice, I must tell you, there is not one of you but is as faulty as she whom you accuse; there is no difference, but that your sin is smothered in secrecy, hers is brought forth into the light. Ye had more need to make your own peace by an humble repentance, than to urge severity against another. I deny not but Moses hath justly from God imposed the penalty of death upon such heinous offences, but what then would become of you? if death be her due, yet not by those your unclean hands; your hearts know you are not honest enough to accuse.

Lo, not the bird, but the fowler, is taken. He says not, Let her be stoned; this had been against the course of his mercy: he says not, Let her not be stoned; this had been against the law of Moses. Now he so answers, that both his justice and mercy are entire; she dismissed, they shamed.

It was the manner of the Jews, in those heinous crimes that were punished with lapidation, that the witnesses and accusers should be the first that should lay hands upon the guilty: well doth our Saviour, therefore, choke these accusers with the conscience of their so foul incompetency. With what face, with what heart, could they stone their own sin in another person?

Honesty is too mean a term. These Scribes and Pharisees were noted for extraordinary and admired holiness: the outside of their lives was not only inoffensive, but saint-like and exemplary. Yet that all-seeing eye of the Son of God, which "found folly in the angels," hath much more found wickedness in these glorious professors. It is not for nothing, that "his eyes are like a flame of fire." What secret is there which he searches not? Retire yourselves, O ye foolish sinners, into your inmost closets, yea, (if you can) into the centre of the earth: his eye follows you, and observes all your carriages; no bolt, no bar, no darkness, can keep him out. No thief was ever so impudent as to steal in the very face of the judge; O God, let me see myself seen by thee, and I shall not dare to offend.

Besides, notice, here is exprobration. These men's sins, as they had been secret, so they were forgotten. It is long since they were done; neither did they think to have heard any more news of them. And now, when time and security had quite worn them out of thought, he, that shall once be their Judge, calls them to a back-reckoning.

One time or other shall that just God lay our sins in our dish, and make us possess the sins of our youth. "These things thou didst, and I kept silence, and thou thoughtst that I was like unto myself; but I will reprove thee, and set them in order before thee." The penitent man's sin lies before him for his humiliation; the impenitent's, for his shame and confusion.

The act of sin is transient; not so the guilt; that will stick by us, and return upon us, either in the height of our security, or the depth of our misery, when we shall be least able to bear it. How just may it be with God to take us at advantages, and then to lay his arrest upon us when we are laid up upon a former suit!

THE WOMAN TAKEN IN ADULTERY.

It is but just there should be a requisition of innocence in them that prosecute the vices of others. The offender is worthy of stoning, but who shall cast them: how ill would they become hands as guilty as her own! what do they but smite themselves, who punish their own offences in other men? Nothing is more unjust or absurd, than for the beam to censure the mote, the oven to upbraid the kiln. It is a false and vagrant zeal that begins not first at home.

Well did our Saviour know how bitter and strong a pill he had given to these false justiciaries: and now he will take leisure to see how it wrought. While, therefore, he gives time to them to swallow it, and put it over, he returns to his old gesture of a seeming inadvertency. How sped the receipt?

I do not see any of them stand out with Christ, and plead his own innocency; and yet these men, which is very remarkable, placed the fulfilling or violation of the law only in the outward act. Their hearts misgave them, that if they should have stood out in contestation with Christ, he would have utterly shamed them, by displaying their old and secret sins; and have so convinced them by undeniable circumstances, that they should never have clawed off the reproach; and therefore, "when they heard it, being convicted by their own conscience, they went out one by one, beginning at the eldest, even unto the last."

There might seem to be some kind of mannerly order in this guilty departure; not all at once, lest they should seem violently chased away by this charge of Christ; now their slinking away "one by one," may seem to carry a show of a deliberate and voluntary discession. The eldest first: the ancienter is fitter to give than take example; and the younger could think it no shame to follow the steps of a grave foreman.

O wonderful power of conscience! man can no more stand out against it, than it can stand out against God. The Almighty, whose substitute is set in our bosom, sets it on work to accuse. It is no denying, when that says we are guilty; when that condemns us, in vain are we acquitted by the world. With what bravery did these hypocrites come to set upon Christ! with what triumph did they insult upon that guilty soul! Now they are thunder-struck with their own conscience, and drop away confounded; and well is he that can run away farthest from his own shame. No wicked man needs to seek out of himself for a judge, accuser, witness, tormentor.

No sooner do these hypocrites hear of their sins from the mouth of Christ, than they are gone. Had they been sincerely touched with a true remorse, they would have rather come to him upon their knees, and have said, Lord, we know and find that thou knowest our secret sins; this argues thy divine omniscience. Thou that art able to know our sins, art able to remit them. O pardon the iniquities of thy servants! Thou that accusest us, do thou also acquit us! But now, instead hereof, they turn their back upon their Saviour, and haste away.

An impenitent man cares not how little he hath, either of the presence of God, or of the mention of his sins. O fools! if ye could run away from God, it were somewhat; but, while ye move in him, what do ye? whither go ye? ye may run from his mercy; ye cannot but run upon his judgment.

Christ is left alone; alone in respect of these complainants, not alone in respect of the multitude. There yet stands the mournful adulteress: she might have gone forth with them, nobody constrained her stay; but that which sent them away, staid her — conscience. She knew her guiltiness was publicly accused, and durst not be by herself denied: as one that was therefore fastened there by her own guilty heart, she stirs not till she may receive a dismission.

Our Saviour was not so busy in writing, but that he read the while the guilt and absence of those accusers; he that knew what they had done, knew no less what they did, what they would do. Yet, as if the matter had been strange to him, "he lifts up himself, and says, Woman, where are thy accusers?"

How well was this sinner to be left there! Could she be in a safer place than before the tribunal of a Saviour? might she have chosen her refuge, whither should she rather have fled? O happy we, if, when we are convinced in ourselves of our sins, we can set ourselves before that Judge who is our Surety, our Advocate, our Redeemer, our Ransom, our Peace!

Doubtless, she stood doubtful betwixt hope and fear: hope, in that she saw her accusers gone; fear, in that she knew what she had deserved: and now, while she trembles in expectation of a sentence, she hears, "Woman, where are thy accusers?"

Wherein our Saviour intends the satisfaction of all the hearers, of all the beholders, that they might apprehend the guiltiness, and therefore the unfitness of the accusers; and might well see there was no warrantable ground of his farther proceeding against her.

Two things are necessary for the execution of a malefactor — evidence, sentence; the one from witnesses, the other from the judge. Our Saviour asks for both. The accusation and proof must draw on the sentence; the sentence must proceed upon the evidence of the proof: "Where are thy accusers? hath no man condemned thee?" Had sentence passed legally upon the adulteress, doubtless our Saviour would not have acquitted her: for, as he would not intrude upon others' offices, so he would not cross or violate the justice done by others. But now, finding the coast clear, he says, "Neither do I condemn thee."

What, Lord! dost thou then show favour to foul offenders? art thou rather pleased that gross sins should be blanched, and sent away with a gentle connivancy? Far, far be this from the perfection of thy justice. He that hence argues adulteries not punishable by death, let him argue the unlawfulness of dividing of inheritances; because, in the case of the two wrangling brethren, thou saidst, "Who made me a divider of inheritances?" thou declinedst the office, thou didst not dislike the act, either of parting lands, or punishing offenders. Neither was here any absolution of the woman from a sentence of death, but a dismission of her from thy sentence, which thou knewest not proper for thee to pronounce. Herein hadst thou respect to thy calling, and to the main purpose of thy coming into the world, which was neither to be an arbiter of civil causes, nor a judge of criminal, but a Saviour of mankind: not to destroy the body, but to save the soul. And this was thy care in this miserable offender: "Go, and sin no more." How much more doth it concern us to keep within the bounds of our vocation, and not to dare to trench upon the functions of others! How can we ever enough magnify thy mercy, who takest no pleasure in the death of a sinner? who so camest to save, that thou challengest us of unkindness for being miserable: "Why will ye die, O house of Israel?"

But, O Son of God, though thou wouldst not then be a judge, yet thou wilt once be: thou wouldst not in thy first coming judge the sins of men, thou wilt come to judge them in thy second. The time shall come, when upon that just and glorious tribunal thou shalt judge every man according to his works. That we may not one day hear thee say, "Go, ye cursed," let us now hear thee say, "Go, sin no more."

CONTEMPLATION XVI. — THE THANKFUL PENITENT.

ONE while I find Christ invited by a publican, now by a Pharisee. Wherever he went, he made better cheer than he found, in a happy exchange of spiritual repast for bodily.

Who knows not the Pharisees to have been the proud enemies of Christ; men over-conceited of themselves, contemptuous of others, severe in show, hypocrites in deed, strict sectaries, insolent justiciaries; yet here one of them invites Christ, and that in good earnest. The man was not, like his fellows, captious, not ceremonious: had he been of their stamp, the omission of washing the feet had been mortal. No profession hath not yielded some good: Nicodemus and Gamaliel were of the same strain. Neither is it for nothing that the Evangelist, having branded this sect for despising the counsel of God against themselves, presently subjoins this history of Simon the Pharisee, as an exempt man. O Saviour, thou canst find out good Pharisees, good publicans, yea, a good thief upon the cross; and that thou mayest find, thou canst make them so.

At the best, yet he was a Pharisee, whose table thou here refusedst not. So didst thou, in wisdom and mercy, attemper thyself, as to "become all things to all men, that thou mightst win some." Thy harbinger was rough; as in clothes, so in disposition, professedly harsh and austere: thyself wert mild and sociable: so it was fit for both. He was a preacher of penance, thou the author of comfort and salvation: he made way for grace, thou gavest it. Thou hast bidden us to follow thyself, not thy forerunner. That, then, which politics and time-servers do for earthly advantages, we will do for spiritual; frame ourselves to all companies, not in evil, but in good, yea, in indifferent things. What wonder is it, that thou, who camest down from heaven to frame thyself to our nature, shouldst, whilst thou wert on earth, frame thyself to the several dispositions of men? Catch not at this, O ye licentious hypocrites, men of all hours, that can eat with gluttons, drink with drunkards, sing with ribalds, scoff with profane scorners, and yet talk holily with the religious, as if ye had hence any colour of your changeable conformity to all fashions. Our Saviour never sinned for any man's sake, though for our sakes he was sociable, that he might keep us from sinning. Can ye so converse with lewd good-fellows, as that ye repress their sins, redress their exorbitances, win them to God? now, ye walk in the steps of him that stuck not to sit down in the Pharisee's house.

There sat the Saviour, and, "behold, a woman in the city that was a sinner." I marvel not that she is led in with a note of wonder; wonder, both on her part, and on Christ's. That any sinner, that a sensual sinner, obdured in a notorious trade of evil, should, voluntarily, out of a true remorse for her lewdness, seek to a Saviour, it is worthy of an accent of admiration. The noise of the gospel is common; but where is the power of it? it hath store of hearers, but few converts. Yet were there no wonder in her, if it were not with reference to the power and mercy of Christ; his power that thus drew the sinner, his mercy that received her. O Saviour, I wonder at her, but I bless thee for her, by whose only grace she was both moved and accepted.

A sinner! Alas! who was not? who is not so? not only "in many things we sin all," but in all things we let fall many sins. Had there been a woman not a sinner, it had been beyond wonder. One man there was that was not a sinner, even he that was more than a man, that God and man, who was the refuge of this sinner; but never woman that sinned not. Yet he said not, a woman that had sinned, but, "that was a sinner." An action doth not give denomination, but a trade. Even the wise charity of Christians, much more the mercy of God, can distinguish between sins of infirmity, and practice of sin, and esteem us not by a transient act, but by a permanent condition.

The woman was noted for a luxurious and incontinent life. What a deal of variety there is of sins! that which faileth cannot be numbered. Every sin continued, deserves to brand the soul with this style. Here one is picked out from the rest: she is not noted for murder, for theft, for idolatry; only her lust makes her "a woman that was a sinner." Other vices use not to give the owner this title, although they should be more heinous than it.

Wantons may flatter themselves in the indifferency or slightness of this offence: their souls shall need no other conveyance to hell than this, which cannot be so pleasing to nature, as it is hateful to God, who so speaks of it, as if there were no sins but it; "a woman that was a sinner."

She was a sinner, now she is not; her very presence argues her change. Had she been still in her old trade, she would no more have endured the sight of Christ, than that devil did which cried out, "Art thou come to torment me?" Her eyes had been lamps and fires of lust, not fountains of tears; her hairs had been nets to catch foolish lovers, not a towel for her Saviour's feet; yet still she carries the name of what she was: a scar still remains after the wound healed. Simon will be ever the leper, and Matthew the publican. How carefully should we avoid those actions which may ever stain us!

What a difference there is betwixt the carriage and proceedings of God and men! The mercy of God, as it "calleth those things that are not, as if they were," so it calleth those things that were, as if they were not: "I will remember your iniquities no more;" as some skilful chirurgeon so sets the bone, or heals the sore, that it cannot be seen where the complaint was. Man's word is, that which is done cannot be undone: but the omnipotent goodness of God doth, as it were, undo our oncecommitted sins: "Take away my iniquity, and thou shalt find none." What we were in ourselves, we are not to him, since he hath changed us from ourselves.

O God, why should we be niggardly where thou art liberal? why should we be reading those lines which thou hast not only crossed, but quite blotted, yea, wiped out?

It is a good word, "she was a sinner." To be wicked, is odious to God, angels, saints, men; to have been so, is blessed and glorious. I rejoice to look back and see my Egyptians lying dead upon the shore, that I may praise the Author of my deliverance and victory. Else, it matters not what they were, what I was. O God, thou, whose title is, "I am," regardest the present. He befriends and honours us, that says, "Such ye were, but ye are washed."

The place adds to the heinousness of the sin: "in the city." The more public the fact is, the greater is the scandal. Sin is sin, though in a desert: others' eyes do not make the act more vile in itself, but the offence is multiplied by the number of beholders.

I hear no name of either the city or the woman: she was too well known in her time. How much better is it to be obscure than infamous! Herein, I doubt not, God meant to spare the reputation of a penitent convert. He who hates not the person, but the sin, cares only to mention the sin, not the person. It is justice to prosecute the vice; it is mercy to spare the offender. How injurious a presumption is it for any man to name her whom God would have concealed; and to cast this aspersion on those whom God hath noted for holiness!

The worst of this woman is past—" She was a sinner;" the best is to come—" She sought out Jesus;" Where? in the house of a Pharisee. It was the most inconvenient place in the world for a noted sinner to seek Christ in.

No men stood so much upon the terms of their own righteousness; no men so scornfully disdained an infamous person. The touch of an ordinary, though honest Jew, was their pollution: how much more the presence of a strumpet? What a sight was a known sinner to him, to whom his holiest neighbour was a sinner! How doth he, though a better Pharisee, look awry to see such a piece in his house, while he dares think, " If this man were a prophet, he would surely know what manner of woman this is!" Neither could she fore-imagine less, when she ventured to press over the threshold of a Pharisee. Yet not the known austerity of a man, and her miswelcome to the place, could affright her from seeking her Saviour even there. No disadvantage can defer the penitent soul from a speedy recourse to Christ. She says not, If Jesus were in the street, or in the field, or in the house of some humble publican, or anywhere save with a Pharisee, I would come to him : now, I will rather defer my access, than seek him where I shall find scorn and censure; but, as not fearing the frowns of that overly host, she thrusts herself into Simon's house to find Jesus. It is not for the distressed to be bashful; it is not for a believer to be timorous. O Saviour, if thy spouse miss thee, she will seek thee through the streets; the blows of the watch shall not daunt her. If thou be on the other side of the water, a Peter will leap into the sea and swim to thee; if on the other side of the fire, thy blessed martyrs will run through those flames to thee. We are not worthy of the comfort of thy presence, if, wheresoever we know thou art, whether in prison or in exile, or at the stake, we do not hasten thither to enjoy thee.

The place was not more unfit than the time : a Pharisee's house was not more improper for a sinner, than a feast was for humiliation. Tears at a banquet are as jigs at a funeral. There is a season for all things. Music had been more apt for a feast than mourning.

The heart that hath once felt the sting of sin, and the sweetness of remission, hath no power to delay the expressions of what it feels, and cannot be confined to terms of circumstance.

Whence then was this zeal of her access? Doubtless she had heard from the mouth of Christ, in those heavenly sermons of his, many gracious invitations of all troubled and labouring souls; she had observed how he vouchsafed to come under the roofs of despised publicans, of professed enemies; she had noted all the passages of his power and mercy, and now deep remorse wrought upon her heart for her former viciousness. The pool of her conscience was troubled by the descending angel, and now she steps in for a cure. The arrow stuck fast in her soul, which she could not shake out; and now she comes to this sovereign dittany to expel it. Had not the Spirit of God wrought upon her ere she came, and wrought her to come, she had never either sought or found Christ. Now she comes in, and finds that Saviour whom she sought; she comes in, but not empty-handed; though debauched, she was a Jewess. She could not but have heard that she ought " not to appear before the Lord empty." What, then, brings she? It was not possible she could bring to Christ a better present than her own penitent soul; yet, to testify that, she brings another, delicate both for the vessel and the contents, " a box of alabaster;" a solid, hard, pure, clear marble, fit for the receipt of so precious an ointment : the ointment pleasant and costly : a composition of many fragrant odours, not for medicine, but delight.

The soul that is truly touched with the sense of its own sin, can think nothing too good, too dear for Christ. The remorsed sinner begins first with the tender of " burntofferings, and calves of a year old;" thence he ascends to hecatombs, " thousands of rams;" and above that yet, to " ten thousand rivers of oil;" and, yet higher, could be content to " give the first fruit of his body," to expiate " the sin of his soul." Any thing, every thing, is too small a price for peace. O Saviour, since we have tasted how sweet thou art, lo! we bring thee the daintiest and costliest perfumes of our humble obediences; yea, if so much of our blood, as this woman brought ointment, may be useful or pleasing to thy name, we do most cheerfully consecrate it unto thee. If we would not have thee think heaven too good for us, why should we stick at any earthly retribution to thee in lieu of thy great mercies?

Yet here I see more than the price. This odoriferous perfume was that wherewith she had wont to make herself pleasing to her wanton lovers, and now she comes purposely to offer it up to her Saviour.

As her love was turned another way,

from sensual to divine, so shall her ointment also be altered in the use: that which was abused to luxury, shall now be consecrated to devotion. There is no other effect in whatsoever true conversion: "As we have given our members servants to iniquity to commit iniquity, so shall we now give our members servants unto righteousness in holiness." If the dames of Israel, that thought nothing more worth looking on than their own faces, have spent too much time at their glasses, now they shall cast in those metals to make a laver, for the washing off their uncleannesses. If I have spent the prime of my strength, the strength of my wit, upon myself and vanity, I have bestowed my alabaster-box amiss: O now teach me, my God and Saviour, to improve all my time, all my abilities, to thy glory. This is all the poor recompense can be made thee for those shameful dishonours thou hast received from me.

The woman is come in, and now she doth not boldly face Christ, but, as unworthy of his presence, she stands behind. How could she, in that sight, wash his feet with her tears? Was it that our Saviour did not sit at the feast after our fashion, but, according to the then Jewish and Roman fashion, lay on the one side? or was it that this phrase doth not so much import posture as presence? Doubtless it was bashfulness and shame, arising from the conscience of her own former wickedness, that placed her thus. How well is the case altered! She had wont to look boldly in the face of her lovers; now she dares not behold the awful countenance of her Saviour. She had wont to send her alluring beams forth into the eyes of her wanton paramours; now she casts her dejected eyes to the earth, and dares not so much as raise them up to see those eyes for which she desired commiseration. It was a true inference of the prophet, "Thou hast a whore's forehead, thou canst not blush:" there cannot be a greater sign of whorishness than impudence. This woman can now blush: she hath put off the harlot, and is turned true penitent. Bashfulness is both a sign and effect of grace. O God! could we but bethink how wretched we are in nature, how vile through our sins, how glorious, holy, and powerful a God thou art, before whom the brightest angels hide their faces, we could not come but with a trembling awfulness into thy presence!

Together with shame, here is sorrow; a sorrow testified by tears, and tears in such abundance, that she washes the feet of our Saviour with those streams of penitence:

"She began to wash his feet with tears." We hear when she began; we hear not when she ended. When the grapes are pressed, the juice runs forth; so, when the mind is pressed, tears distil the true juice of penitence and sorrow. These eyes were not used to such clouds, or to such showers: there was nothing in them formerly but sunshine of pleasure, beams of lust; now they are resolved into the drops of grief and contrition. Whence was this change, but from the secret working of God's Spirit? "He caused his wind to blow, and the waters flowed; he smote the rock, and the waters gushed out." O God! smite thou this rocky heart of mine, and the waters of repentance shall burst forth in abundance.

Never were thy feet, O Saviour, bedewed with more precious liquor than this of remorseful tears. These cannot be so spent, but that thou keepest them in thy bottle, yea, thou returnest them back with interest of true comfort: "They that sow in tears shall reap in joy. Blessed are they that mourn." Lo! this wet seed-time shall be followed with a harvest of happiness and glory.

That this service might be complete, as her eyes were the ewer, so her hair was the towel for the feet of Christ. Doubtless, at a feast, there was no want of the most curious linen for this purpose. All this was nothing to her: to approve her sincere humility, and hearty devotion to Christ, her hair shall be put to this glorious office. The hair is the chief ornament of womanhood; the feet, as they are the lowest part of the body, so the meanest for account, and homeliest for employment; and, lo! this penitent bestows the chief ornament of her head on the meanest office, to the feet of her Saviour. That hair, which she was wont to spread as a net to catch her amorous companions, is honoured with the employment of wiping the beautiful feet of him that brought the glad tidings of peace and salvation; and might it have been any service to him to have licked the dust under those feet of his, how gladly would she have done it! Nothing can be mean that is done to the honour of a Saviour.

Never was any hair so preferred as this. How I envy those locks that were graced with the touch of those sacred feet, but much more those lips that kiss them! Those lips that had been formerly inured to the wanton touches of her lascivious lovers, now sanctify themselves with the testimony of her humble homages and dear respects to the Son of God. Thus her ointment, hands, eyes, hair, lips, are now consecrated to the service of Christ her Saviour, whom she had offended. If our satisfaction be not in some kind proportionable to our offence, we are no true penitents.

All this while, I hear not one word fall from the mouth of this woman. What need her tongue speak, when her eyes spake, her hands spake? Her gesture, her countenance, her whole carriage, was vocal. I like this silent speaking well, when our actions talk, and our tongues hold their peace. The common practice is contrary; men's tongues are busy, but their hands are still. All their religion lies in their tongue; their hands either do nothing, or ill, so as their profession is but wind, as their words. Wherefore are words, but for expression of the mind? if that could be known by the eye or by the hand, the language of both were alike. There are no words amongst spirits, yet they perfectly understand each other. "The heavens declare the glory of God." All tongues cannot speak so loud as they that have none. Give me the Christian that is seen and not heard. The noise that our tongue makes in a formality of profession, shall, in the silence of our hands, condemn us for hypocrites.

The Pharisee saw all this, but with an evil eye. Had he not had some grace, he had never invited such a guest as Jesus; and if he had grace enough, he had never entertained such a thought as this of the guest he invited: "If this man were a prophet, he would have known what manner of woman it is that toucheth him, for she is a sinner."

How many errors in one breath! Justly, O Simon, hath this one thought lost thee the thank of thy feast. Belike, at the highest, thou judgedst thy guest but a prophet; and now thou doubtest whether he were so much. Besides this undervaluation, how unjust is the ground of this doubt! Every prophet knew not every thing; yea, no prophet ever knew all things. Elisha knew the very secrets of the Assyrian privy-chamber; yet he knew not the calamity of his worthy hostess. The finite knowledge of the ablest seer reaches but so far as it will please God to extend it. Well might he therefore have been a prophet, and, in the knowledge of greater matters, not have known this.

Unto this, how weakly didst thou, because of Christ's silent admission of the woman, suppose him ignorant of her quality! as if knowledge should be measured always by the noise of expression. Stay but a-while, and thou shalt find that he well knew both her life and thy heart. Besides, how injuriously dost thou take this woman for what she was? not conceiving, as well thou mightest, were not this woman a convert, she would never have offered herself into this presence. Her modesty and her tears bewray her change; and if she be changed, why is she censured for what she is not?

Lastly, How strongly did it savour of the leaven of thy profession, that thou supposedst, were she what she was, that it could not stand with the knowledge and holiness of a prophet to admit of her least touch, yea, of her presence; whereas, on the one side, outward conversation in itself makes no man unclean or holy, but according to the disposition of the patient; on the other, such was the purity and perfection of this thy glorious guest, that it was not possibly infectible, nor any way obnoxious to the danger of others' sin. He, that said once, "Who touched me?" in regard of virtue issuing from him, never said, whom have I touched? in regard of any contagion incident unto him. We sinful creatures, in whom the prince of this world finds too much, may easily be tainted with other men's sins. He, who came to take away the sins of the world, was incapable of pollution by sin. Had the woman then been still a sinner, thy censure of Christ was proud and unjust.

The Pharisee spake, but it was within himself; and now, behold, "Jesus answering, said."

What we think, we speak to our hearts, and we speak to God; and he equally hears, as if it came out of our mouths. Thoughts are not free. Could men know and convince them, they would be no less liable to censure, than if they came forth clothed with words. God, who hears them, judges of them accordingly. So here, the heart of Simon speaks, "Jesus answers."

Jesus answers him, but with a parable. He answers many a thought with judgment; the blasphemy of the heart, the murder of the heart, the adultery of the heart, are answered by him with a real vengeance. For Simon, our Saviour saw his error was either out of simple ignorance, or weak mistaking; where he saw no malice, then it is enough to answer with a gentle conviction. The convictive answer of Christ is by way of parable. The wisdom of God knows how to circumvent us for our gain; and can speak that pleasingly, by a prudent circumlocution, which downright would not be digested. Had our Saviour said in plain terms, Simon, whether dost thou or this sinner love me more? the Pharisee could not for shame but have stood upon his reputation, and, in a scorn of the comparison, have protested his exceeding respects to Christ. Now, ere he is aware, he is fetched in to give sentence against himself, for her whom he condemned. O Saviour, thou hast made us fishers of men: how should we learn of thee so to bait our hooks, that they may be most likely to take! Thou, the great householder of thy church, hast provided victuals for thy family, thou hast appointed us to dress them: if we do not so cook them, as that they may fit the palates to which they are intended, we do both lose our labour and thy cost. The parable is of two debtors to one creditor; the one owed a lesser sum, the other a greater; both are forgiven. It was not the purpose of him that propounded it, that we should stick in the bark: God is our creditor, our sins our debts; we are all debtors, but one more deep than another. No man can pay this debt alone: satisfaction is not possible; only remission can discharge us. God doth in mercy forgive as well the greatest as the least sins. Our love to God is proportionable to the sense of our remission. So then the Pharisee cannot choose but confess, that the more and greater the sin is, the greater mercy in the forgiveness; and the more mercy in the forgiver, the greater obligation and more love in the forgiven.

Truth, from whose mouth soever it falls, is worth taking up: our Saviour praises the true judgment of a Pharisee. It is an injurious indiscretion in those who are so prejudiced against the persons, that they reject the truth. He, that would not quench the smoking flax, encourages even the least good. As the careful chirurgeon strokes the arm ere he strikes the vein, so did Christ here: ere he convinces the Pharisee of his want of love, he graceth him with a fair approbation of his judgment; yet the while turning both his face and his speech to the poor penitent, as one that cared more for a true humiliation for sin, than for a false pretence of respect and innocence.

With what a dejected and abashed countenance, with what earth-fixed eyes, do we imagine the poor woman stood, when she saw her Saviour direct his face and words to her.

She that durst but stand behind him, and steal the falling of some tears upon his feet, with what a blushing astonishment doth she behold his sidereal countenance cast upon her! While his eyes were turned towards this penitent, his speech was turned to the Pharisee concerning that penitent, by him mistaken: "Seest thou this woman?" He who before had said, "If this man were a prophet, he would have known what manner of woman this is," now hears, "Seest thou this woman?" Simon saw but her outside; Jesus lets him see that he saw her heart, and will thus convince the Pharisee that he is more than a prophet, who knew not her conversation only, but her soul. The Pharisee, that went all by appearance, shall by her deportment see the proof of her good disposition: it shall happily shame him, to hear the comparison of the wants of his own entertainments, with the abundance of hers.

It is strange that any of this formal sect should be defective in their lotions. Simon had not given water to so great a guest; she washes his feet with her tears. By how much the water of the eye was more precious than the water of the earth, so much was the respect and courtesy of this penitent above the neglected office of the Pharisee. What use was there of a towel, where was no water? she, that made a fountain of her eyes, made precious napery of her hair: that better flax shamed the linen in the Pharisee's chest.

A kiss of the cheek had wont to be pledge of the welcome of their guests: Simon neglects to make himself thus happy; she redoubles the kisses of her humble thankfulness upon the blessed feet of her Saviour. The Pharisee omits ordinary oil for the head; she supplies the most precious and fragrant oil to his feet.

Now the Pharisee reads his own taxations in her praise, and begins to envy where he had scorned.

It is our fault, O Saviour, if we mistake thee. We are ready to think, so thou have the substance of good usage, thou regardest not the compliments and ceremonies: whereas now we see thee to have both meat and welcome in the Pharisee's house, and yet hear thee glance at his neglect of washing, kissing, anointing. Doubtless, omission of due circumstances in thy entertainment may deserve to lose our thanks. Do we pray to thee? do we hear thee preach to us? now we make thee good cheer in our house: but if we perform not these things with the fit decency of our outward carriages, we give thee not thy water, thy kisses, thy oil. Even meet ritual observances are requisite for thy full welcome.

Yet how little had these things been regarded, if they had not argued the woman's thankful love to thee, and the ground of that love, sense of her remission, and the Pharisee's default in both!

Love and action do necessarily evince each other. True love cannot lurk long unexpressed; it will be looking out at the eyes, creeping out of the mouth, breaking out at the fingers' ends, in some actions of dearness, especially those wherein there is pain and difficulty to the agent, profit or pleasure to the affected. O Lord, in vain shall we profess to love thee, if we do nothing for thee! Since our goodness cannot reach up unto thee, who art our glorious head, O let us bestow upon thy feet, thy poor members here below, our tears, our hands, our ointment, and whatever of our gifts or endeavours may testify our thankfulness and love to thee in them.

O happy word! "Her sins, which are many, are forgiven her." Methinks I see how this poor penitent revived with this breath; how new life comes into her eyes, new blood into her cheeks, new spirits into her countenance, like unto our mother earth, when, in that first confusion, "God said, Let the earth bring forth grass, the herb that beareth seed, and the fruit-tree yielding fruit;" all runs out into flowers, and blossoms, and leaves, and fruit. Her former tears said, "Who shall deliver me from this body of death?" now her cheerful smiles say, "I thank God, through Jesus Christ my Lord."

Seldom ever do we meet with so perfect a penitent; seldom do we find so gracious a dismission. What can be wished of any mortal creature but remission, safety, faith, peace? all these are here met, to make a contrite soul happy; remission the ground of her safety, faith the ground of her peace, safety and salvation the issue of her remission, peace the blessed fruit of her faith.

O woman, the perfume that thou broughtst is poor and base, in comparison of those sweet savours of rest and happiness that are returned to thee! Well was that ointment bestowed, wherewith thy soul is sweetened to all eternity.

CONTEMPLATION XVII.—MARTHA AND MARY.

WE may read long enough ere we find Christ in a house of his own. "The foxes have holes, and the birds have nests:" he that had all, possessed nothing. One while I see him in a publican's house, then in a Pharisee's; now I find him at Martha's. His last entertainment was with some neglect, this with too much solicitude. Our Saviour was now in his way; the sun might as soon stand still as he.

The more we move, the liker we are to heaven, and to this God that made it. His progress was to Jerusalem, for some holy feast. He, whose devotion neglected not any of those sacred solemnities, will not neglect the due opportunities of his bodily refreshing: as not thinking it meet to travel and preach harbourless, he diverts (where he knew his welcome) to the village of Bethany. There dwelt the two devout sisters, with their brother, his friend Lazarus: their roof receives him. O happy house, into which the Son of God vouchsafed to set his foot! O blessed women, that had the grace to be the hostesses to the God of heaven! How should I envy your felicity herein, if I did not see the same favour, if I be not wanting to myself, lying open to me! I have two ways to entertain my Saviour; in his members, and in himself: in his members, by charity and hospitableness: "What I do to one of these his little ones, I do to him;" in himself by faith: "If any man open, he will come in and sup with him."

O Saviour, thou standest at the door of our hearts, and knockest by the solicitations of thy messengers, by the sense of thy chastisements, by the motions of thy Spirit: if we open to thee by a willing admission and faithful welcome, thou wilt be sure to take up our souls with thy gracious presence, and not to sit with us for a momentary meal, but to dwell with us for ever. Lo! thou didst but call in at Bethany; but here shall be thy rest for everlasting.

Martha, it seems, as being the eldest sister, bore the name of the housekeeper: Mary was her assistant in the charge. A blessed pair! sisters not more in nature than grace, in spirit no less than in flesh. How happy a thing is it when all the parties in a family are jointly agreed to entertain Christ!

No sooner is Jesus entered into the house, than he falls to preaching; that no time may be lost, he stays not so much as till his meat be made ready, but, while his bodily repast was in hand, provides spiritual food for his hosts. It was his meat and drink to do the will of his Father: he fed more upon his own diet than he could possibly upon theirs; his best cheer was, to see them spiritually fed. How should we, whom he hath called to this sacred function, "be instant in season and out of season!" We are, by his sacred ordination, the lights of the world. No sooner is the candle lighted, than it gives that light which it hath, and never intermits till it be wasted to the snuff.

Both the sisters, for a time, sat attentively listening to the words of Christ. Household occasions call Martha away; Mary sits still at his feet, and hears. Whether shall we more praise her humility or her docility? I do not see her take a stool and sit by him, or a chair and sit above him; but, as desiring to show her heart was as low as her knees, she sits at his feet. She was lowly set, richly warmed with those heavenly beams. The greater submission, the more grace. If there be one hollow in the valley lower than another, thither the waters gather.

Martha's house is become a divinity school: Jesus, as the doctor, sits in the chair; Martha, Mary, and the rest, sit as disciples at his feet. Standing implies a readiness of motion; sitting, a settled composedness to this holy attendance.

Had these two sisters provided our Saviour never such delicates, and waited on his trencher never so officiously, yet, had they not listened to his instruction, they had not bidden him welcome; neither had he so well liked his entertainment.

This was the way to feast him; to feed their ears by his heavenly doctrine: his best cheer is our proficiency, our best cheer is his word. O Saviour, let my soul be thus feasted by thee, do thou thus feast thyself by feeding me: this mutual diet shall be thy praise and my happiness.

Though Martha was for the time an attentive hearer, yet now her care of Christ's entertainment carries her into the kitchen; Mary sits still. Neither was Mary more devout than Martha busy: Martha cares to feast Jesus; Mary to be feasted of him. There was more solicitude in Martha's active part; more piety in Mary's sedentary attendance: I know not in whether more zeal. Good Martha was desirous to express her joy and thankfulness for the presence of so blessed a guest, by the actions of her careful and plenteous entertainment. I know not how to censure the holy woman for her excess of care to welcome her Saviour. Sure she herself thought she did well: and, out of that confidence, fears not to complain to Christ of her sister.

I do not see her come to her sister, and whisper in her ear the great need of her aid; but she comes to Jesus, and in a kind of unkind expostulation of her neglect, makes her moan to him: "Lord, dost thou not care that my sister hath left me to serve alone?" Why did she not rather make her first address to her sister? was it for that she knew Mary was so tied by the ears with those adamantine chains that came from the mouth of Christ, that, until his silence and dismission, she had no power to stir? or was it out of an honour and respect to Christ, that, in his presence, she would not presume to call off her sister without his leave?

Howsoever, I cannot excuse the holy woman from some weaknesses. It was a fault to measure her sister by herself, and, apprehending her own act to be good, to think her sister could not do well if she did not so too; whereas goodness hath much latitude. Ill is opposed to good, not good to good. Neither in things lawful nor indifferent are others bound to our examples. Mary might hear, Martha might serve, and both do well. Mary did not censure Martha for her rising from the feet of Christ to prepare his meal: neither should Martha have censured Mary for sitting at Christ's feet to feed her soul. It was a fault, that she thought an excessive care of a liberal outward entertainment of Christ was to be preferred to a diligent attention to Christ's spiritual entertainment of them. It was a fault, that she durst presume to question our Saviour of some kind of unrespect to her toil: "Lord, dost thou not care?" What sayest thou, Martha? dost thou challenge the Lord of heaven and earth of incogitancy and neglect? dost thou take upon thee to prescribe unto that infinite wisdom, instead of receiving directions from him? It is well thou mettest with a Saviour, whose gracious mildness knows how to pardon and pity the errors of our zeal.

Yet I must needs say, here wanted not fair pretences for the ground of this thy expostulation. Thou, the elder sister, workest; Mary, the younger, sits still; and what work was thine but the hospitable receipt of thy Saviour and his train? Had it been for thine own paunch, or for some carnal friends, it had been less excusable; now it was for Christ himself, to whom thou couldst never be too obsequious.

But all this cannot deliver thee from the just blame of this bold subincusation: "Lord, dost thou not care?" How ready is our weakness, upon every slight discontentment, to quarrel with our best friend, yea, with our good God! and the more we are put to it, to think ourselves the more neglected, and to challenge God for our neglect! Do we groan on the bed of our sickness, and, languishing in pain, complain of long hours and weary sides? Straight we think, Lord, dost thou not care that we suffer? Doth God's poor church go to wreck, while the ploughers, ploughing on her back, make long furrows? "Lord, dost thou not care?" But know, O thou feeble and distrustful soul, the more thou dost, the more thou sufferest, the more thou art cared for: neither is God ever so tender over his church, as when it is most exercised. Every pang, and stitch, and gird is first felt of him that sends it. O God, thou knowest our works, and our labour, and our patience: we may be ignorant and diffident, thou canst not but be gracious.

It could not but trouble devout Mary to hear her sister's impatient complaint: a complaint of herself to Christ, with such vehemence of passion, as if there had been such strangeness betwixt the two sisters, that the one would do nothing for the other, without an external compulsion from a superior. How can she choose but think, If I have offended, why was I not secretly taxed for it in a sisterly familiarity? what if there had been some little omission? must the whole house ring of it before my Lord, and all his disciples? is this carriage beseeming a sister? is my devotion worthy of a quarrel? Lord, dost thou not care that I am injuriously censured? Yet I hear not a word of reply from that modest mouth. O holy Mary, I admire thy patient silence: thy sister blames thee for thy piety; the disciples afterwards blame thee for thy bounty and cost: not a word falls from thee in a just vindication of thine honour and innocence, but, in a humble taciturnity, thou leavest thine answer to thy Saviour. How should we learn of thee, when we are complained of for well-doing, to seal up our lips, and to expect our righting from above!

And how sure, how ready art thou, O Saviour, to speak in the cause of the dumb! "Martha, Martha, thou art careful and troubled about many things, but one thing is needful, and Mary hath chosen the better part."

What needed Mary to speak for herself, when she had such an advocate? Doubtless, Martha was, as it were, divided from herself with the multiplicity of her careful thoughts: our Saviour therefore doubles her name in his compellation, that, in such distraction, he may both find and fix her heart. The good woman made full account, that Christ would have sent away her sister with a check, and herself with thanks; but now her hopes fail her; and though she be not directly reproved, yet she hears her sister more approved than she: "Martha, Martha, thou art careful and troubled about many things." Our Saviour received courtesy from her in her diligent and costly entertainment; yet he would not blanch her error, and smooth her up in her weak misprision. No obligations may so enthral us, as that our tongues should not be free to reprove faults where we find them. They are base and servile spirits that will have their tongue tied to their teeth.

This glance towards a reproof implies an an opposition of the condition of the two sisters: themselves were not more near in nature, than their present humour and estate differed. One is opposed to many, necessary to superfluous, solicitude to quietness: "Thou art careful and troubled about many things, one thing is necessary." How far then may our care reach to these earthly things? On the one side, O Saviour, thou hast charged us to "take no thought what to eat, drink, put on;" on the other, thy chosen vessel hath told us, that "he that provides not for his family hath denied the faith, and is worse than an infidel." We may, we must, care for many things, so that our care be for good, and well; for good, both in kind and measure; well, so as our care be free from distraction, from distrust; from distraction, that it hinder us not from the necessary duties of our general calling; from distrust, that we misdoubt not God's providence, while we employ our own. We cannot care for thee, unless we thus care for ourselves, for ours.

Alas! how much care do I see everywhere, but how few Marthas! Her care was for her Saviour's entertainment; ours for ourselves. One finds perplexities in his estate, which he desires to extricate; another beats his brains for the raising of his house: one busies his thoughts about the doubtful condition, as he thinks, of the times, and casts in his anxious head the imaginary events of all things, opposing his hopes to his fears; another studies how to avoid the cross blows of an adversary. "Martha, Martha, thou art careful and troubled about many things." Foolish men! why do we set our hearts upon the rack, and need not? why will we endure to bend under that burden, which more able shoulders have offered to undertake for our ease?

Thou hast bidden us, O God, to cast our cares upon thee, with promise to care for us. We do gladly unload ourselves upon thee: O let our care be to depend upon thee, as thine is to provide for us.

Whether Martha be pitied or taxed for her sedulity, I am sure Mary is praised for her devotion: "One thing is necessary." Not by way of negation, as if nothing were necessary but this; but by way of comparison, as that nothing is so necessary as this. Earthly occasions must vail to spiritual. Of those three main grounds of all our actions, necessity, convenience, pleasure, each transcends other: convenience carries it away from pleasure, necessity from convenience, and one degree of necessity from another. The degrees are according to the conditions of the things necessary. The condition of these earthly necessaries is, that without them we cannot live temporally; the condition of the spiritual, that without them we cannot live eternally. So much difference, then, as there is betwixt temporary and eternal, so much there must needs be betwixt the necessity of these bodily actions and these spiritual: both are necessary in their kinds; neither must here be an opposition, but a subordination. The body and soul must be friends, not rivals; we may not so ply the Christian, that we neglect the man.

O the vanity of those men, who, neglecting that one thing necessary, affect many things superfluous! Nothing is needless with worldly minds but this one, which is only necessary, the care of their souls. How justly do they lose that they cared not for, while they over-care for that which is neither worthy nor possible to be kept!

Neither is Mary's business more allowed than herself: "She hath chosen the good part." It was not forced upon her, but taken up by her election. Martha might have sat still as well as she: she might have stirred about as well as Martha. Mary's will made this choice, not without the inclination of him who both gave this will, and commends it. That will was before renewed: no marvel if it choose the good; though this were not in a case of good and evil, but of good and better. We have still this holy freedom, through the inoperation of him that hath freed us. Happy are we, if we can improve this liberty to the best advantage of our souls.

The stability or perpetuity of good, adds much to the praise of it. Martha's part was soon gone; the thank and use of a little outward hospitality cannot long last: " but Mary's shall not be taken away from her." The act of her hearing was transient, the fruit permanent; she now hears that which shall stick by her for ever.

What couldst thou hear, O holy Mary, from those sacred lips, which we hear not still? that heavenly doctrine is never but the same, not more subject to change than the Author of it. It is not impossible that the exercise of the gospel should be taken from us; but the benefit and virtue of it is as inseparable from our souls as their being. In the hardest times that shall stick closest to us, and till death, in death, after death, shall make us happy.

CONTEMPLATION XVIII.—THE BEGGAR THAT WAS BORN BLIND, CURED.

THE man was born blind. This cure requires not art, but power; a power no less than infinite and divine. Nature presupposeth a matter, though formless; art looks for matter formed to our hands; God stands not upon either. Where there was not an eye to be healed, what could an oculist do? It is only a God that can create. Such are we, O God, to all spiritual things; we want not sight but eyes; it must be thou only that canst make us capable of illumination.

The blind man sat begging. Those that have eyes, and hands, and feet of their own, may be able to help themselves; those that want these helps must be beholden to the eyes, hands, feet of others. The impotent are cast upon our mercy; happy are we, if we can lend limbs and senses to the needy. Affected beggary is odious; that which is of God's making, justly challengeth relief.

Where should this blind man sit begging, but near the temple? At one gate sits a cripple, a blind man at another. Well might these miserable souls suppose that piety and charity dwelt close together: the two tables were both of one quarry. Then are we best disposed to mercy towards our brethren, when we have either craved or acknowledged God's mercy towards ourselves. If we go thither to beg of God, how can we deny mites, when we hope for talents?

Never did Jesus move one foot but to purpose. He passed by, but so as that his virtue stayed; so did he pass by that his eye was fixed. The blind man could not see him; he sees the blind man. His goodness prevents us, and yields better supplies to our wants. He saw compassionately, not shutting his eyes, nor turning them aside, but bending them upon that dark and disconsolate object. That which was said of the sun, is much more true of him that made it: " Nothing is hid from his light:" but of all other things, miseries, especially of his own, are most intentively eyed of him. Could we be miserable unseen, we had reason to be heartless. O Saviour, why should we not imitate thee in this merciful improvement of our senses! Woe be to those eyes that care only to gaze upon their own beauty, bravery, wealth; not abiding to glance upon the sores of Lazarus, the sorrows of Joseph, the dungeon of Jeremy, the blind beggar at the gate of the temple!

The disciples see the blind man too, but with different eyes: our Saviour for pity and cure, they for expostulation: "Master, who did sin, this man or his parents, that he is born blind?" I like well that whatsoever doubt troubled them, they straight vent it into the ear of their Master. O Saviour, while thou art in heaven, thy school is upon earth. Wherefore serve thy "priests' lips" but to "preserve knowledge?" What use is there of the tongue of the learned, but to speak a word in season? Thou teachest us still, and still we doubt, and ask, and learn.

In one short question, I find two truths and two falsehoods; the truths implied, the falsehoods expressed. It is true, that commonly man's suffering is for sin; that we may justly, and do, often suffer even for the sins of our parents; it is false, that there is no other reason of our suffering but sin, that a man could sin actually before he was, or was before his being, or could beforehand suffer for his after sins. In all likelihood, that absurd conceit of the transmigration of souls possessed the very disciples. How easily, and how far, may the best be miscarried with a common error! We are not thankful for our own illumination, if we do not look with charity and pity upon the gross mis-opinions of our brethren.

Our Saviour sees, and yet will wink at so foul a misprision of his disciples. I hear neither chiding nor conviction. He that could have enlightened their minds, as he did the world, at once, will do it by due leisure; and only contents himself here with a mild solution: "Neither this man nor his parents." We learn nothing of thee, O Saviour, if not meekness. What a sweet temper should be in our carriage towards the weaknesses of others' judgment! how should we instruct them without bitterness, and, without violence of passion, expect the meet seasons of their better information? The tender mother or nurse doth not rate her little one for that he goes not well, but gives him her hand that he may go better. It is the spirit of lenity that must restore and confirm the lapsed.

The answer is direct and punctual; neither the sin of the man nor of his parents bereaved him of his eyes: there was a higher cause of this privation, the glory that God meant to win to himself by redressing it. The parents had sinned in themselves, the man had sinned in his first parents; it is not the guilt of either that is guilty of this blindness. All God's afflictive acts are not punishments; some are for the benefit of the creature, whether for probation, or prevention, or reformation: all are for the praise, whether of his divine power, or justice, or mercy.

It was fit that so great a work should be ushered in with a preface. A sudden and abrupt appearance would not have beseemed so glorious a demonstration of omnipotence. The way is made; our Saviour addresses himself to the miracle; a miracle not more in the thing done, than in the form of doing it.

The matter used was clay. Could there be a meaner? could there be aught more unfit? O Saviour, how oft hadst thou cured blindnesses by thy word alone! how oft by thy touch! how easily couldst thou have done so here! Was this to show thy liberty, or thy power? liberty, in that thou canst at pleasure use variety of means, not being tied to any; power, in that thou couldst make use of contraries. Hadst thou pulled out a box, and applied some medicinal ointment to the eyes, something had been ascribed to thy skill, more to the natural power of thy receipt; now thou madest use of clay, which had been enough to stop up the eyes of the seeing; the virtue must be all in thee, none in the means. The utter disproportion of this help to the cure, adds glory to the worker.

How clearly didst thou hence evince to the world, that thou who of clay couldst make eyes, wert the same who of clay hadst made man! Since there is no part of the body that hath so little analogy to clay as the eye; this clearness is contrary to that opacity. Had not the Jews been more blind than the man whom thou curedst, and more hard and stiff than the clay which thou mollifiedst, they had, in this one work, both seen and acknowledged thy Deity.

What could the clay have done without thy tempering? It was thy spittle that made the clay effectual; it was that sacred mouth of thine that made the spittle medicinal: the water of Siloam shall but wash off that clay which this inward moisture made powerful. The clay, thus tempered, must be applied by the hand that made it, else it avails nothing.

What must the blind man needs think when he felt the cold clay upon the holes of his eyes? or, since he could not conceive what an eye was, what must the beholders needs think, to see that hollowness thus filled up? Is this the way to give either eyes or sight? why did not the earth see with this clay as well as the man? what is there to hinder the sight, if this make it?

Yet with these contrarieties must faith be exercised, where God intends the blessing of a cure.

It was never meant that this clay should dwell upon those pits of the eyes: it is only put on to be washed off, and that not by every water; none shall do it but that of Siloam, which signifies Sent; and if the man had not been sent to Siloam, he had been still blind. All things receive their virtue from divine institution. How else should a piece of wheaten bread nourish the soul? how should spring-wate wash off spiritual filthiness? how should the foolishness of preaching save souls? how should the absolution of God's minister be more effectual than the breath of an ordinary Christian? Thou, O God, hast set apart these ordinances; thy blessing is annexed to them: hence is the ground of all our use, and their efficacy. Hadst thou so instituted, Jordan would as well have healed blindness, and Siloam leprosy.

That the man might be capable of such a miracle, his faith is set on work; he must be led, with his eyes daubed up, to the pool of Siloam. He washes and sees. Lord, what did this man think when his eyes were now first given him? what a new world did he find himself now come into! how did he wonder at heaven and earth, and the faces and shapes of all creatures, the goodly varieties of colours, the cheerfulness of the light, the lively beams of the sun, the vast expansion of the air, the pleasant transparence of the water! at the glorious piles of the temple and stately palaces of Jerusalem! Every thing did not more please than astonish him. Lo! thus shall we be affected, and more, when, the scales of our mortality being done away, we shall see as we are seen; when we shall behold the blessedness of that other world, the glory of the saints and angels, the infinite majesty of the Son of God, the incomprehensible brightness of the all-glorious Deity. O my soul, that thou couldst be taken up beforehand with the admiration of that which thou canst not as yet be capable of foreseeing!

It could not be but that many eyes had been witnesses of this man's want of eyes. He sat begging at one of the temple gates; not only all the city, but all the country, must needs know him: thrice a-year did they come up to Jerusalem; neither could they come to the temple and not see him: his very blindness made him noted. Deformities and infirmities of body do more easily both draw and fix the eye, than an ordinary symmetry of parts.

Besides his blindness, his trade made him remarkable; the importunity of his begging drew the eyes of the passengers; but, of all other, the place most notified him. Had he sat in some obscure village of Judea, or in some blind lane of Jerusalem, perhaps he had not been heeded of many; but now, that he took up his seat in the heart, in the head, of the chief city, whither all resorted from all parts, what Jew can there be that knows not the blind beggar at the temple gate? Purposely did our Saviour make choice of such a subject for his miracle; a man so poor, so public: the glory of the work could not have reached so far, if it had been done to the wealthiest citizen of Jerusalem. Neither was it for nothing that the act and the man is doubted of, and inquired into by the beholders: "Is not this he that sat begging? some said, It is he; others said, It is like him." No truths have received so full proofs as those that have been questioned. The want, or the sudden presence, of an eye, much more of both, must needs make a great change in the face; those little balls of light, which no doubt were more clear than nature could have made them, could not but give a new life to the countenance. I marvel not if the neighbours, who had wont to see this dark visage led by a guide, and guided by a staff, seeing him now walking confidently alone out of his own inward light, and looking them cheerfully in the face, doubted whether this were he. The miraculous cures of God work a sensible alteration in men, not more in their own apprehension than in the judgment of others. Thus in the redress of the spiritual blindness, the whole habit of the man is changed. Where, before, his face looked dull and earthly, now there is a sprightly cheerfulness in it, through the comfortable knowledge of God and heavenly things; whereas, before, his heart was set upon worldly things, now he uses them, but enjoys them not; and that use is because he must, not because he would: where, before, his fears and griefs were only for pains of body, or loss of estate or reputation, now they are only spent upon the displeasure of his God, and the peril of his soul. So as now the neighbours can say, "Is this the man?" others, "It is like him, It is not he."

The late blind man hears, and now sees himself questioned, and soon resolves the doubt: "I am he." He that now saw the light of the sun, would not hide the light of truth from others. It is an unthankful silence to smother the works of God in an affected secrecy. To make God a loser by his bounty to us, were a shameful injustice. We ourselves abide not those spunges that suck up good turns unknown. O God, we are not worthy of our spiritual eye-sight, if we do not publish thy mercies on the house-top, and praise thee in the great congregation.

Man is naturally inquisitive: we search studiously into the secret works of nature, we pry into the reasons of the witty inventions of art; but if there be any thing that transcends art and nature, the more high and abstruse it is, the more busy we are to seek into it. This thirst after hidden, yea, forbidden knowledge, did once cost us dear; but, where it is good and lawful to know, inquiry is commendable; as here in these Jews: "How were thine eyes opened?" The first improvement of human reason is inquisition, the next is information and resolution; and if the meanest events pass us not without a question, how much less those that carry in them wonder and advantage!

He that was so ready to profess himself the subject of the cure, is no niggard of proclaiming the Author of it: "A man that is called Jesus made clay, and anointed mine eyes, and sent me to Siloam to wash, and now I see." The blind man knew no more than he said, and he said what he apprehended: "A man." He heard Jesus speak, he felt his hand; as yet he could look no farther: upon his next meeting he saw God in this man. In matter of knowledge we must be content to creep ere we can go. As that other recovered blind man saw first men walk like trees, after like men; so no marvel if this man saw, first this God only as a man, after this man as God also. Onwards he thinks him a wonderful man, a mighty prophet. In vain shall we either expect a sudden perfection in the understanding of divine matters, or censure those that want it.

How did this man know what Jesus did? He was then stone-blind; what distinction could he yet make of persons, of actions? True, but yet the blind man never wanted the assistance of others' eyes; their relation hath assured him of the manner of his cure: besides the contribution of his other senses, his ear might perceive the spittle to fall, and hear the enjoined command; his feeling perceived the cold and moist clay upon his lids; all these conjoined, gave sufficient warrant thus to believe, thus to report. Our ear is our best guide to a full apprehension of the works of Christ. The works of God the Father, his creation and government, are best known by the eye: the works of God the Son, his redemption and mediation, are best known by the ear. O Saviour! we cannot personally see what thou hast done here. What are the monuments of thine apostles and evangelists, but the relations of the blind man's guide, what and how thou has wrought for us? On these we strongly rely, these we do no less confidently believe, than if our very eyes had been witnesses of what thou didst and sufferedst upon earth. There were no place for faith, if the ear were not worthy of as much credit as the eye.

How could the neighbours do less than ask, where he was that had done so strange a cure? I doubt yet with what mind; I fear, not out of favour. Had they been but indifferent, they could not but have been full of silent wonder, and inclined to believe in so omnipotent an agent. Now, as prejudiced to Christ, and partial to the Pharisees, they bring the late blind man before those professed enemies unto Christ.

It is the preposterous religion of the vulgar sort to claw and adore those which have tyrannically usurped upon their souls; though with neglect, yea, with contempt, of God, in his word, in his works. Even unjust authority will never want soothing up in whatsoever courses, though with disgrace and opposition to the truth. Base minds, where they find possession, never look after right.

Our Saviour had picked out the Sabbath for this cure. It is hard to find out any time wherein charity is unseasonable. As mercy is an excellent grace, so the works of it are fittest for the best day. We are all born blind; the font is our Siloam: no day can come amiss, but yet God's day is the properest for our washing and recovery.

This alone is quarrel enough to those scrupulous wranglers, that an act of mercy was done on that day wherein their envy was but seasonable.

I do not see the man beg any more when he once had his eyes: no burgher in Jerusalem was richer than he. I hear him stoutly defending that gracious Author of his cure against the cavils of the malicious Pharisees: I see him, as a resolute confessor, suffering excommunication for the name of Christ, and maintaining the innocence and honour of so blessed a benefactor: I hear him read a divinity lecture to them that sat in Moses' chair, and convincing them of blindness, who punished him for seeing.

How cannot I but envy thee, O happy man, who, of a patient, provest an advocate for thy Saviour! whose gain of bodily sight made way for thy spiritual eyes! who hast lost a synagogue, and hast found heaven! who, being abandoned of sinners, art received of the Lord of Glory!

CONTEMPLATION XIX.—THE STUBBORN DEVIL EJECTED.

How different, how contrary, are our conditions here upon earth! While our Saviour is transfigured on the mount, his disciples are perplexed in the valley. Three of his choice followers were with him above, ravished with the miraculous proofs of his Godhead; nine other were troubled with the business of a stubborn devil below.

Much people met to attend Christ, and there they will stay till he come down from Tabor. Their zeal and devotion brought them thither; their patient perseverance held them there. We are not worthy the name of his clients, if we cannot painfully seek him, and submissively wait his leisure.

He that was now awhile retired into the mount to confer with his Father, and to receive the attendance of Moses and Elias, returns into the valley to the multitude. He was singled out a while for prayer and contemplation; now he was joined with the multitude for their miraculous cure and heavenly instruction. We that are his spiritual agents, must be either preparing in the mount, or exercising in the valley; one while in the mount of meditation, in the valley of action another; alone to study, in the assembly to preach: here is much variety, but all is work.

Moses, when he came down from the hill, heard music in the valley; Christ, when he came down from the hill, heard discord. The scribes, it seems, were setting hard upon the disciples: they saw Christ absent; nine of his train left in the valley, those they fly upon. As the devil, so his imps, watch close for all advantages. No subtile enemy but will be sure to attempt that part where is likelihood of least defence, most weakness. When the spouse misses him whom her soul loveth, every watchman hath a buffet for her. O Saviour, if thou be never so little stepped aside, we are sure to be assaulted with powerful temptations.

They that durst say nothing to the Master, so soon as his back is turned, fall foul upon his weakest disciples. Even at the first hatching, the serpent was thus crafty to begin at the weaker vessel: experience and time hath not abated his wit. If he still work upon "silly women laden with divers lusts," upon rude and ungrounded ignorants, it is no other than his old wont.

Our Saviour, upon the skirts of the hill, knew well what was done in the plain, and therefore hastes down to the rescue of his disciples. The clouds and vapours do not sooner scatter upon the sun's breaking forth, than these cavils vanish at the presence of Christ; instead of opposition, they are straight upon their knees; here are now no quarrels, but humble salutations, and if Christ's question did not force theirs, the scribes had found no tongue.

Doubtless, there were many eager patients in this throng; none made so much noise as the father of the demoniac. Belike upon this occasion it was that the scribes held contestation with the disciples. If they wrangled, he sues, and that from his knees. Whom will not need make both humble and eloquent? The case was woful and accordingly expressed. A son is a dear name, but this was his only son. Were his grief ordinary, yet the sorrow were the less; but he is a fearful spectacle of judgment, for he is lunatic. Were this lunacy yet merely from a natural distemper, it were more tolerable; but this is aggravated by the possession of a cruel spirit, that handles him in a most grievous manner. Yet were he but in the rank of other demoniacs, the discomfort were more easy; but lo! this spirit is worse than all other his fellows; others are usually dispossessed by the disciples, this is beyond their power: "I besought thy disciples to cast him out, but they could not; therefore, Lord, have thou mercy on my son." The despair of all other helps sends us importunately to the God of power.—Here was his refuge: the strong man had gotten possession; it was only the stronger than he that could eject him. O God, spiritual wickednesses have naturally seized upon our souls: all human helps are too weak; only thy mercy shall improve thy power to our deliverance.

What bowels could choose but yearn at the distress of this poor young man? Phrensy had taken his brain; that disease was but health, in comparison of the tyrannical possession of that evil spirit, wherewith it was seconded. Out of hell there could not be a greater misery: his senses are either bereft, or else left to torment him; he is torn and racked so as he foams and gnashes; he pines and languishes; he is cast sometimes into the fire, sometimes into the water. How that malicious tyrant rejoices in the mischief done to the creature of God! Had earth had anything more pernicious than fire and water, thither had he been thrown, though rather for torture than despatch. It was too much favour to die at once. O God, with how deadly enemies hast thou matched us! Abate thou their power, since their malice will not be abated.

How many think of this case with pity and horror, and, in the meantime, are insensible of their own fearfuller condition!

It is but oftentimes that the devil would cast this young man into a temporary fire: he would cast the sinner into an eternal fire, whose everlasting burnings have no intermissions. No fire comes amiss to him; the fire of affliction, the fire of lust, the fire of hell. O God, make us apprehensive of the danger of our sin, and secure from the fearful issue of sin.

All these very same effects follow his spiritual possession. How doth he tear and rack them whom he vexes and distracts with inordinate cares and sorrows! how do they foam and gnash whom he hath drawn to an impatient repining at God's afflictive hand! how do they pine away, who hourly decay and languish in grace!

O the lamentable condition of sinful souls, so much more dangerous, by how much less felt!

But all this while, what part hath the moon in this man's misery? How comes the name of that goodly planet in question? Certainly these diseases of the brain follow much the course of this queen of moisture. That power which she hath in humours is drawn to the advantage of the malicious spirit; her predominancy is abused to his despite. Whether it were for the better opportunity of his vexation, or whether for the drawing of envy and discredit upon so noble a creature, it is no news with that subtile enemy, to fasten his effects upon these secondary causes, which he usurps to his own purposes. Whatever be the means, he is the tormentor. Much wisdom needs to distinguish betwixt the evil spirit abusing the good creature, and the good creature abused by the evil spirit.

He that knew all things asks questions: "How long hath he been so?" not to inform himself,—(that devil could have done nothing without the knowledge, without the leave of the God of spirits)—but that, by the confession of the parent, he might lay forth the woful condition of the child, that, the thank and glory of the cure might be so much greater, as the complaint was more grievous: "He answered, from a child."

O God, how I adore the depth of thy wise, and just, and powerful dispensation! Thou that couldst say, "I have loved Jacob, and Esau have I hated, ere the children had done good or evil," thoughtst also good, ere this child could be capable of good or evil, to yield him over to the power of that evil one. What need I ask for any other reason than that which is the rule of all justice—thy will? Yet even these weak eyes can see the just grounds of thine actions. That child, though an Israelite, was conceived and born in that sin, which both could and did give Satan an interest in him; besides, the actual sins of the parents deserved this revenge upon that piece of themselves. Rather, O God, let me magnify this mercy, that we and ours escape this judgment, than question thy justice, that some escape not. How just might it have been with thee, that we, who have given way to Satan in our sins, should have way and scope given to Satan over us in our punishments! It is thy praise, that any of us are free; it is no quarrel that some suffer.

Do I wonder to see Satan's bodily possession of this young man from a child, when I see his spiritual possession of every son of Adam from a longer date; not from a child, but from the womb, yea, in it? Why should not Satan possess his own? We are all by nature the sons of wrath. It is time for us to renounce him in baptism, whose we are till we be regenerate. He hath right to us in our first birth; our new birth acquits us from him, and cuts off all his claim. How miserable are they that have nothing but nature! better it had been to have been unborn, than not to be born again.

And if this poor soul, from an infant, were thus miserably handled, having done none actual evil, how just cause have we to fear the like judgments, who, by many foul offences, have deserved to draw this executioner upon us! O my soul, thou hast not room enough for thankfulness to that good God, who hath not delivered thee up to that malignant spirit.

The distressed father sits not still, neglects not means: "I brought him to thy disciples." Doubtless, the man came first to seek for Christ himself; finding him absent, he makes suit to the disciples. To whom should we have recourse, in all our spiritual complaints, but to the agents and messengers of God? The noise of the like cures had surely brought this man, with much confidence, to crave their succour; and now, how cold was he at the heart, when he found that his hopes were frustrated! "They could not cast him out." No doubt the disciples tried their best; they laid their wonted charge upon this dumb spirit, but all in vain. They that could come with joy and triumph to their Master, and say, "The devils are subject to us," find now themselves matched with a stubborn and refractory spirit. Their way was hitherto smooth and fair; they met with no rub till now: and now, surely, the father of the demoniac was not more troubled at this event than themselves. How could they choose but fear, lest their Master had, with himself, withdrawn that spiritual power which they had formerly exercised! Needs must their heart fail them with their success.

The man complained not of their impotence; it were fondly injurious to accuse them for that which they could not do. Had the want been in their will, they had well deserved a querulous language; it was no fault to want power: only he complains of the stubbornness, and laments the invincibleness of that evil spirit.

I should wrong you, O ye blessed followers of Christ, if I should say, that as Israel, when Moses was gone up into the mount, lost their belief with their guide, so that ye, missing your Master, who was now ascended up to his Tabor, were to seek for your faith. Rather the wisdom of God saw reason to check your over-assured forwardness, and both to pull down your hearts by a just humiliation, in the sense of your own weakness, and to raise up your hearts to new acts of dependence upon that sovereign power from which your limited virtue was derived.

What was more familiar to the disciples than ejecting of devils? In this only it is denied them. Our good God sometimes finds it requisite to hold us short in those abilities whereof we make least doubt, that we may feel whence we had them. God will be no less glorified in what we cannot do, than in what we can do. If his graces were always at our command, and ever alike, they would seem natural, and soon run into contempt: now, we are justly held in an awful dependence upon that gracious hand, which so gives as not to cloy us, and so denies as not to discourage us.

Who could now but expect that our Saviour should have pitied and bemoaned the condition of this sad father and miserable son, and have let fall some words of comfort upon them? Instead whereof, I hear him chiding and complaining, "O faithless and perverse generation, how long shall I be with you? how long shall I suffer you?" complaining, not of that woful father and more woful son—it was not his fashion to add affliction to the distressed, to break such bruised reeds; but of those Scribes, who, upon the failing of the success of this suit, had insulted upon the disability of the followers of Christ, and depraved his power; although, perhaps, this impatient father, seduced by their suggestion, might slip into some thoughts of distrust.

There could not be a greater crimination than "faithless and perverse:" faithless in not believing; perverse in being obstinately set in their unbelief. Doubtless, these men were not free from other notorious crimes; all were drowned in their infidelity. Moral uncleannesses or violences may seem more heinous to men, none are so odious to God as these intellectual wickednesses.

What a happy change is here in one breath of Christ! "How long shall I suffer you? bring him hither to me." The one is a word of anger, the other of favour. His just indignation doth not exceed or impeach his goodness. What a sweet mixture there is in the perfect simplicity of the divine nature! "In the midst of judgment he remembers mercy," yea, he acts it: his sun shines in the midst of this storm. Whether he frown, or whether he smile, it is all to one purpose, that he may win the incredulous and disobedient. Whether should the rigour of all our censures tend, but to edification, and not to destruction? We are physicians, we are not executioners; we give purges to cure, and not poisons to kill. It is for the just Judge to say one day to reprobate souls, "Depart from me;" in the meantime, it is for us to invite all that are spiritually possessed to the participation of mercy, "Bring him hither to me."

O Saviour, distance was no hinderance to thy work. Why should the demoniac be brought to thee? was it, that this deliverance might be the better evicted, and that the beholders might see it was not for nothing that the disciples were opposed with so refractory a spirit? or was it, that the scribes might be witnesses of that strong hostility that was betwixt thee and that foul spirit, and be ashamed of their blasphemous slander? or was it, that the father of the demoniac might be quickened in that faith, which now, through the suggestion of the scribes, began to droop; when he should hear and see Christ so cheerfully to undertake and perform that whereof they had bidden him despair?

The possessed is brought; the devil is rebuked and ejected. That stiff spirit which stood boldly out against the commands of the disciples, cannot but stoop to the voice of the Master: that power which did at first cast him out of heaven, easily dispossesses him of a house of clay: "The Lord rebuke thee, Satan," and then thou canst not but flee.

The disciples, who were not used to these affronts, cannot but be troubled at their mis-success: "Master, why could we not cast him out?" Had they been conscious of any defect in themselves, they had never asked the question: little did they think to hear of their unbelief. Had they not had great faith, they could not have cast out any devils; had they not had some want of faith, they had cast out this. It is possible for us to be defective in some graces, and not to feel it.

Although not so much their weakness is guilty of this unprevailing, as the strength of that evil spirit: "This kind goes not out but by prayer and fasting." Weaker spirits were wont to be ejected by a command; this devil was more sturdy and boisterous. As there are degrees of statures in men, so there are degrees of strength and rebellion in spiritual wickednesses. Here, bidding will not serve; they must pray, and praying will not serve without fasting. They must pray to God that they may prevail; they must fast to make their prayer more fervent, more effectual: we cannot now command; we can fast and pray. How good is our God to us, that while he hath not thought fit to continue to us those means which are less powerful for the dispossessing of the powers of darkness, yet hath he given us the greater! While we can fast and pray, God will command for us, Satan cannot prevail against us.

CONTEMPLATION XX.—THE WIDOW'S MITES.

THE sacred wealth of the temple was either in stuff or in coin; for the one, the Jews had a house; for the other, a chest. At the concourse of all the males to the temple thrice a-year, upon occasion of the solemn feasts, the oblations of both kinds were liberal. Our Saviour, as taking pleasure in the prospect, sets himself to view those offerings, whether for holy uses or charitable.

Those things we delight in, we love to behold; the eye and the heart will go together. And can we think, O Saviour, that thy glory hath diminished aught of thy gracious respects to our beneficence? or, that thine acceptance of our charity was confined to the earth? Even now, that thou sittest at the right hand of thy Father's glory, thou seest every hand that is stretched out to the relief of thy poor saints here below. And if vanity have power to stir up our liberality, out of a conceit to be seen of men, how shall faith encourage our bounty in knowing that we are seen of thee, and accepted by thee? Alas! what are we the better for the notice of those perishing and impotent eyes, which can only view the outside of our actions; or for that waste wind of applause which vanisheth in the lips of the speaker? Thine eye, O Lord, is piercing and retributive. As to see thee is perfect happiness, so to be seen of thee is true contentment and glory.

And dost thou, O God, see what we give thee, and not see what we take away from thee? are our offerings more noted than our sacrileges? Surely thy mercy is not more quick-sighted than thy justice. In both kinds our actions are viewed, our account is kept; and we are as sure to receive rewards for what we have given, as vengeance for what we have defaulked. With thine eye of knowledge thou seest all we do; but what we do well, thou seest with an eye of approbation. So didst thou now behold these pious and charitable oblations. How well wert thou pleased with this variety! Thou sawest many rich men give much, and one poor widow give more than they in lesser room.

The Jews were now under the Roman pressure: they were all tributaries, yet many of them rich, and those rich men were liberal to the common chest. Hadst thou seen those many rich give little, we had heard of thy censure; thou expectest a proportion betwixt the giver and the gift, betwixt the gift and the receipt; where that fails, the blame is just. That nation, though otherways faulty enough, was in this commendable. How bounteously open were their hands to the house of God! Time was when their liberality was fain to be restrained by proclamation; and now it needed no incitement; the rich gave much, the poorest gave more: "He saw a poor widow casting in two mites." It was misery enough that she was a widow. The married woman is under the careful provision of a husband; if she spend, he earns: in that estate, four hands work for her; in her widowhood, but two. Poverty added to the sorrow of her widowhood. The loss of some husbands is supplied by a rich jointure: it is some allay to the grief, that the hand is left full, though the bed be empty. This woman was not more desolate than needy; yet this poor widow gives; and what gives she? an offering like herself—"two mites;" or, in our language, two half-farthing-tokens. Alas! good woman, who was poorer than thyself? wherefore was that corban but for the relief of such as thou? who should receive, if such give? Thy mites were something to thee, nothing to the treasury. How ill is that gift bestowed, which disfurnisheth thee, and adds nothing to the common stock! some thrifty neighbour might;

perhaps, have suggested this probable discouragement. Jesus publishes and applauds her bounty: " He called his disciples, and said unto them, Verily I say unto you, this woman hath cast in more than they all." While the rich put in their offerings, I see no disciples called; it was enough that Christ noted their gifts alone: but when the widow comes with her two mites, now the domestics of Christ are summoned to assemble, and taught to admire this munificence; a solemn preface makes way to her praise, and her mites are made more precious than the others' talents: " She gave more than they all;" more, not only in respect of the mind of the giver, but of the proportion of the gift as hers. A mite to her was more than pounds to them: pounds were little to them, two mites were all to her; they gave out of their abundance, she out of her necessity. That which they gave left the heap less, yet a heap still; she gives all at once, and leaves herself nothing. So as she gave not more than any, but "more than they all." God doth not so much regard what is taken out, as what is left. O Father of mercies! thou lookest at once into the bottom of her heart, and the bottom of her purse, and esteemest her gift according to both. As thou seest not as man, so thou valuest not as man: man judgeth by the worth of the gift, thou judgest by the mind of the giver, and the proportion of the remainder. It were wide with us, if thou shouldst go by quantities. Alas! what have we but mites, and those of thine own lending? It is the comfort of our meanness, that our affections are valued, and not our presents: neither hast thou said, " God loves a liberal giver, but a cheerful." If I had more, O God, thou shouldst have it; had I less, thou wouldst not despise it, who " acceptest the gift according to that a man hath, and not according to that he hath not."

Yea, Lord, what have I but two mites, a soul and a body? mere mites, yea, not so much, to thine infiniteness. O that I could perfectly offer them up unto thee, according to thine own right in them, and not according to mine. How graciously wouldst thou be sure to accept them! how happy shall I be in thine acceptation!

CONTEMPLATION XXI.—THE AMBITION OF THE TWO SONS OF ZEBEDEE.

HE who has his own time and ours in his hand, foreknew and foretold the approach of his dissolution. When men are near their end, and ready to make their will, then is it seasonable to sue for legacies.

Thus did the mother of the two Zebedees; therein well approving both her wisdom and her faith: wisdom in the fit choice of her opportunity; faith, in taking such an opportunity.

The suit is half obtained that is seasonably made. To have made this motion, at the entry into their attendance, had been absurd, and had justly seemed to challenge a denial. It was at the parting of the angel that Jacob would be blessed. The double spirit of Elijah is not sued for till his ascending.

But O the admirable faith of this good woman! When she heard the discourse of Christ's sufferings and death, she talks of his glory; when she hears of his cross, she speaks of his crown. If she had seen Herod come and tender his sceptre unto Christ, or the elders of the Jews come upon their knees with a submissive proffer of their allegiance, she might have had some reason to entertain the thoughts of a kingdom: but now, while the sound of betraying, suffering, dying, was in her ear, to make account of, and sue for a room in his kingdom, it argues a belief able to triumph over all discouragements.

It was nothing for the disciples, when they saw him after his conquest of death, and rising from the grave, to ask him — " Master, wilt thou now restore the kingdom unto Israel?" but for a silly woman to look through his future death and passion, at his resurrection and glory, it is no less worthy of wonder than praise.

To hear a man in his best health and vigour to talk of his confidence in God, and assurance of divine favour, cannot be much worth: but if in extremities we can believe above hope, against hope, our faith is so much more noble as our difficulties are greater.

Never sweeter perfume arose from any altar than that which ascended from Job's dunghill: " I know that my Redeemer liveth."

What a strange style is this that is given to this woman! It had been as easy to have said, the wife of Zebedee, or the sister of Mary or of Joseph, or, as her name was, plain Salome; but now, by an unusual description, she is styled " The Mother of Zebedee's children." Zebedee was an obscure man; she, as his wife, was no better: the greatest honour she ever had, or could have, was to have two such sons as James and John; these give a title to both their parents. Honour ascends as well as descends. Holy children dignify the loins and wombs from whence they proceed, no less than their parents traduce honour unto them. Salome might be a good wife, a good housewife, a good woman, a good neighbour; all these cannot ennoble her so much as the " The Mother of Zebedee's children."

What a world of pain, toil, care, cost, there is in the birth and education of children! Their good proof requites all with advantage: next to happiness in ourselves, is to be happy in a gracious issue.

The suit was the sons', but by the mouth of their mother: it was their best policy to speak by her lips. Even these fishermen had already learned craftily to fish for promotion. Ambition was not so bold in them as to show her own face: the envy of the suit shall thus be avoided, which could not but follow upon their personal request. If it were granted, they had what they would; if not, it was but the repulse of a woman's motion, which must needs be so much more pardonable, because it was of a mother for her sons.

It is not discommendable in parents to seek the preferment of their children. Why may not Abraham sue for an Ishmael? so it be by lawful means, in a moderate measure, in due order, this endeavour cannot be amiss. It is the neglect of circumstances that makes the desire sinful. O the madness of those parents that care not which way they raise a house; that desire rather to leave their children great than good; that are more ambitious to have their sons lords on earth, than kings in heaven! Yet I commend thee, Salome, that thy first plot was to have thy sons disciples of Christ; then after to prefer them to the best places of that attendance. It is the true method of divine prudence, O God, first to make our children happy with the honour of thy service, and then to endeavour their meet advancement upon earth.

The mother is put upon this suit by her sons; their heart was in her lips. They were not so mortified by their continual conversation with Christ, hearing his heavenly doctrine, seeing his divine carriage, but that their minds were yet roving after temporal honours: pride is the inmost coat which we put off last, and which we put on first. Who can wonder to see some sparks of weak and worldly desires in their holiest teachers, when the blessed apostles were not free from some ambitious thoughts, while they sat at the feet, yea, in the bosom of their Saviour?

The near kindred this woman could challenge of Christ, might seem to give her just colour of more familiarity; yet now, that she comes upon a suit, she submits herself to the lowest gesture of suppliants. We need not be taught, that it is fit for petitioners to the great, to present their humble supplications upon their knees. O Saviour, if this woman, so nearly allied to thee according to the flesh, coming but upon a temporal occasion to thee, being as then compassed about with human infirmities, adored thee ere she durst sue to thee, what reverence is enough for us, that come to thee upon spiritual suits, sitting now in the height of heavenly glory and majesty? Say then, thou wife of Zebedee, what is it that thou cravest of thine omnipotent kinsman? " A certain thing." Speak out, woman! what is this certain thing that thou cravest? How poor and weak is this supplicatory anticipation to Him that knew thy thoughts ere thou utteredst them, ere thou entertainedst them! We are all in this tune: every one would have something, such perhaps as we are ashamed to utter. The proud man would have a certain thing—honour in the world; the covetous would have a certain thing too—wealth and abundance; the malicious would have a certain thing—revenge on his enemies; the epicure would have pleasure and long life; the barren, children; the wanton, beauty. Each one would be humoured in his own desire, though in variety, yea, contradiction to other; though in opposition not more to God's will than our own good.

How this suit sticks in her teeth, and dares not freely come forth, because it is guilty of its own faultiness! What a difference there is betwixt the prayers of faith, and the motions of self-love and infidelity! Those come forth with boldness, as knowing their own welcome, and being well assured both of their warrant and acceptation; these stand blushing at the door, not daring to appear, like to some baffled suit, conscious to its own unworthiness and just repulse. Our inordinate desires are worthy of a check: when we know that our requests are holy, we cannot come with too much confidence to the throne of grace.

He that knew all their thoughts afar off, yet, as if he had been a stranger to their purposes, asks, " What wouldst thou?" Our infirmities do then best shame us, when they are fetched out of our own mouths; likeas our prayers also serve not to acquaint God with our wants, but to make us the more capable of his mercies.

The suit is drawn from her; now she must speak: " Grant that these my two sons

THE SONS OF ZEBEDEE.

may sit, one on thy right hand, the other on thy left, in thy kingdom;" it is hard to say whether out of more pride or ignorance. It was as received as erroneous a conceit among the disciples of Christ, that he should raise up a temporal kingdom over the now tributary and enslaved people of Israel. The Romans were now their masters; their fancy was, that their Messias should shake off this yoke, and reduce them to their former liberty. So grounded was this opinion, that the two disciples, in their walk to Emmaus, could say, " We trusted it had been he that should have delivered Israel;" and when, after his resurrection, he was walking up Mount Olivet towards heaven, his very apostles could ask him, if he would now restore that long expected kingdom. How should we mitigate our censures of our Christian brethren, if either they mistake, or know not some secondary truths of religion, when the domestic attendants of Christ, who heard him every day till the very point of his ascension, misapprehended the chief cause of his coming into the world, and the state of his kingdom! If our charity may not bear with small faults, what do we under his name that connived at greater! Truth is, as the sun, bright in itself; yet there are many close corners into which it never shined. O God, if thou open our hearts, we shall take in those beams: till thou do so, teach us to attend patiently for ourselves, charitably for others.

These fishermen had so much courtship to know, that the right hand and the left of any prince were the chief places of honour. Our Saviour had said, that his twelve followers should sit upon twelve thrones, and judge the twelve tribes of Israel. This good woman would have her two sons next to his person, the prime peers of his kingdom. Every one is apt to wish the best to his own. Worldly honour is neither worth our suit, nor unworthy our acceptance. Yea, Salome, had thy mind been in heaven, hadst thou intended this desired pre-eminence of that celestial state of glory, yet I know not how to justify thine ambition. Wouldst thou have thy sons preferred to the "father of the faithful," to the blessed mother of thy Saviour? That very wish were presumptuous. For me, O God, my ambition shall go so high as to be a saint in heaven, and to live as holily on earth as the best: but for precedency of heavenly honour, I do not, I dare not, affect it. It is enough for me, if I may lift up my head amongst the heels of thy blessed ones.

The mother asks; the sons have the answer. She was but their tongue; they shall be her ears. God ever imputes the acts to the first mover, rather than to the instrument.

It was a sore check, " Ye know not what ye ask." In our ordinary communication, to speak idly is sin; but, in our suits to Christ, to be so inconsiderate as not to understand our own petitions, must needs be a foul offence. As faith is the ground of our prayers, so knowledge is the ground of our faith. If we come with indigested requests, we profane that name we invoke.

To convince their unfitness for glory, they are sent to their impotency in suffering; " Are ye able to drink of the cup whereof I shall drink, and to be baptized with the baptism wherewith I am baptized?" O Saviour, even thou, who wert one with thy Father, hadst a cup of thine own: never potion was so bitter as that which was mixed for thee. Yea, even thy draught is stinted: it is not enough for thee to sip of this cup; thou must drink it up to the very dregs. When the vinegar and gall were tendered to thee by men, thou didst but kiss the cup; but when thy Father gave into thine hands a potion infinitely more distasteful, thou, for our health, didst drink deep of it, even to the bottom, and saidst, " It is finished." And can we repine at those unpleasing draughts of affliction that are tempered for us sinful men, when we see thee, the Son of thy Father's love, thus dieted? We pledge thee, O blessed Saviour, we pledge thee, according to our weakness, who hast begun to us in thy powerful sufferings. Only do thou enable us, after some sour faces made in our reluctation, yet at last willingly to pledge thee in our constant sufferings for thee.

As thou must be drenched within, so must thou be baptized without. Thy baptism is not of water, but of blood; both these came from thee in thy passion: we cannot be thine, if we partake not of both. If thou hast not grudged thy precious blood to us, well mayest thou challenge some worthless drops from us.

When they talk of thy kingdom, thou speakest of thy bitter cup, of thy bloody baptism. Suffering is the way to reigning. "Through many tribulations must we enter into the kingdom of heaven." There was never wedge of gold that did not first pass the fire; there was never pure grain that did not undergo the flail. In vain shall we dream of our immediate passage, from the pleasures and jollity of earth, to the glory of heaven. Let who will hope to walk upon roses and violets to the throne of heaven: O Saviour, let me trace thee by the track of thy blood, and by thy red steps follow thee to thine eternal rest and happiness!

I know this is no easy task, else thou hadst never said, "Are ye able?" Who should be able, if not they that had been so long blessed with thy presence, informed by thy doctrine, and, as it were, beforehand possessed of their heaven in thee? Thou hadst never made them judges of their power, if thou couldst not have convinced them of their weakness. Alas! how full of feebleness is our body, and our mind of impatience! If but a bee sting our flesh, it swells; and if but a tooth ache, the head and heart complain. How small trifles make us weary of ourselves! What can we do without thee? without thee, what can we suffer? If thou be not, O Lord, strong in my weakness, I cannot be so much as weak, I cannot so much as be. O do thou prepare me for my day, and enable me to my trials! "I can do all things through thee that strengthenest me."

The motion of the two disciples was not more full of infirmity than their answer, "We are able:" out of an eager desire of the honour, they are apt to undertake the condition. The best men may be mistaken in their own powers. Alas! poor men! when it came to the issue, they ran away, and, I know not whither, one without his coat. It is one thing to suffer in speculation, another in practice. There cannot be a worse sign, than for a man, in a carnal presumption, to vaunt of his own abilities. How justly doth God suffer that man to be foiled purposely, that he may be ashamed of his own self-confidence. O God, let me ever be humbly dejected in the sense of mine own insufficiency; let me give all glory to thee, and take nothing to myself but my infirmities.

O the wonderful mildness of the Son of God! He doth not rate the two disciples, either for their ambition in suing, or presumption in undertaking; but, leaving the worst, he takes the best of their answer, and omitting their errors, encourages their good intentions: "Ye shall drink indeed of my cup, and be baptized with my baptism; but to sit on my right hand and my left, is not mine to give, but to them for whom it is prepared of my Father." I know not whether there be more mercy in the concession, or satisfaction in the denial. Were it not a high honour to drink of thy cup, O Saviour, thou hadst not fore-promised it as a favour. I am deceived, if what thou grantest were much less than that which thou deniest. To pledge thee in thine own cup, is not much less dignity and familiarity than to sit by thee: "If we suffer with thee, we shall also reign together with thee." What greater promotion can flesh and blood be capable of, than a conformity to the Lord of glory? Enable thou me to drink of thy cup, and then set me where thou wilt.

But, O Saviour, while thou dignifiest them in thy grant, dost thou disparage thyself in thy denial? "Not mine to give!" whose is it, if not thine? If it be thy Father's, it is thine. Thou, who art truth, hath said, "I and my Father are one." Yea, because thou art one with the Father, it is not thine to give to any save those for whom it is prepared of the Father. The Father's preparation was thine, his gift is thine: the decree of both is one. That eternal counsel is not alterable upon our vain desires. The Father gives these heavenly honours to none but by thee: thou givest them to none but according to the decree of thy Father. Many degrees there are of celestial happiness. Those supernal mansions are not all of a height. That Providence which hath varied our stations upon earth, hath pre-ordered our seats above. O God, admit me within the walls of thy new Jerusalem, and place me wheresoever thou pleasest

CONTEMPLATION XXII. — THE TRIBUTE-MONEY PAID.

ALL these other histories report the power of Christ: this shows both his power and obedience; his power over the creature, his obedience to civil powers. Capernaum was one of his own cities; there he made his chief abode in Peter's house: to that host of his, therefore, do the toll-gatherers repair for the tribute. When that great disciple said, "We have left all," he did not say, We have abandoned all, or sold, or given away all; but we have left, in respect of managing, not of possession; not in respect of right, but of use and present fruition; so left, that, upon just occasion, we may resume; so left, that it is our due, though not our business. Doubtless, he was too wise to give away his own, that he might borrow of a stranger. His own roof gave him shelter for the time, and his Master with him. Of him, as the householder, is the tribute required; and by and for him is it also paid. I inquire not either into the occasion, or the sum. What need we make this exaction sacrilegious; as if that half-shekel, which was appointed by God to be paid by every Israelite to the use of the tabernacle and temple, were now diverted to the Roman exchequer. There was no necessity that the Roman lords should be tied to the Jewish reckonings; it was free for them to impose what payments they pleased upon a subdued people: when great Augustus commanded the world to be taxed, this rate was set. The mannerly collectors demand it first of him with whom they might be more bold: "Doth not your Master pay tribute?" All Capernaum knew Christ for a great Prophet: his doctrine had ravished them; his miracles had astonished them; yet when it comes to a money matter, his share is as deep as the rest. Questions of profit admit no difference. Still the sacred tribe challength reverence: who cares how little they receive, how much they pay? yet no man knows with what mind this demand was made; whether in a churlish grudging at Christ's immunity, or an awful compellation of the servant rather than the master.

Peter had it ready what to answer. I hear him not require their stay till he should go in and know his Master's resolution; but, as one well acquainted with the mind and practice of his Maker, he answers, Yes.

There was no truer paymaster of the king's dues, than he that was King of kings. Well did Peter know that he did not only give, but preach tribute. When the Herodians laid twigs for him, as supposing that so great a Prophet would be all for the liberty and exemption of God's chosen people, he chokes them with their own coin, and told them the stamp argued the right: "Give unto Cæsar the things that are Cæsar's."

O Saviour, how can thy servants challenge that freedom which thyself had not? Who, that pretends to be from thee, can claim homage from those to whom thou gavest it? If thou, by whom kings reign, forbearest not to pay tribute to a heathen prince, what power under thee can deny it to those that rule for thee?

That demand was made without doors. No sooner is Peter come in, than he is prevented by his Master's question, "What thinkest thou, Simon? of whom do the kings of the earth receive tribute? of their own children, or of strangers?" This very interrogation was answer enough to that which Peter meant to move: he, that could thus know the heart, was not, in true light, liable to human exactions.

But, O Saviour, may I presume to ask, what this is to thee? Thou hast said, "My kingdom is not of this world:" how doth it concern thee what is done by the kings of the earth, or imposed upon the sons of earthly kings? Thou wouldst be the son of an humble virgin, and choosest not a royal state, but a servile. I dispute not thy natural right to the throne, by thy lineal descent from the loins of Judah and David: what should I plead that which thou wavest? It is thy divine royalty and sonship which thou here justly urgest: the argument is irrefragable and convictive. If the kings of the earth do so privilege their children, that they are free from all tributes and impositions, how much more shall the king of heaven give this immunity to his only and natural Son? so as in true reason, I might challenge an exemption for me and my train. Thou mightst, O Saviour, and no less, challenge a tribute of all the kings of the earth to thee, by whom all powers are ordained: reason cannot mutter against this claim; the creature owes itself, and whatsoever it hath, to the Maker; he owes nothing to it. "Then are the children free." He that hath right to all, needs not pay anything, else there should be a subjection in sovereignty, and men should be debitors to themselves. But this right was thine own peculiar, and admits no partners: why dost thou speak of children, as of more, and, extending this privilege to Peter, sayest, "Lest we scandalize them?" Was it for that thy disciples, being of thy robe, might justly seem interested in the liberties of their Master: surely no otherwise were they children, no otherwise free. Away with that fanatical conceit, which challenges an immunity from secular commands and taxes, to a spiritual and adoptive sonship: no earthly saintship can exempt us from tribute to whom tribute belongeth. There is a freedom, O Saviour, which our Christianity calls us to affect; a freedom from the yoke of sin and Satan, from the servitude of our corrupt affections: we cannot be sons, if we be not thus free. O free thou us, by thy free spirit, from the miserable bondage of our nature, so shall the children be free. But as to these secular duties, no man is less free than the children: O Saviour, thou wert free, and wouldst not be so; thou wert free by natural right, wouldst not be free by voluntary dispensation, "Lest an offence might be taken." Surely had there followed an offence, it had been taken only, and not given. "Woe be to the man by whom the offence cometh!" it cometh by him that gives it, it cometh by him that takes it, when it is not given: no part of this blame could have cleaved unto thee either way. Yet such was thy goodness, that thou wouldst not suffer an offence unjustly taken, at that which thou mightst justly have denied. How jealous should we be even of others' perils! how careful so to moderate our power in the use of lawful things, that our charity may prevent others' scandals! to remit of our own right for another's safety! O the deplorable condition of those wilful men, who care not what blocks they lay in the way to heaven, not forbearing, by a known lewdness, to draw others into their own damnation!

To avoid the unjust offence, even of very publicans, Jesus will work a miracle. Peter is sent to the sea, and that not with a net, but with a hook. The disciple was now in his own trade. He knew a net might inclose many fishes, a hook could take but one: with that hook must he go angle for the tribute-money. A fish shall bring him a stater in her mouth; and that fish that bites first. What an unusual bearer is here! what an unlikely element to yield a piece of ready coin!

O that omnipotent power, which could command the fish to be both his treasurer to keep his silver, and his purveyor to bring it! Now whether, O Saviour, thou causedst this fish to take up that shekel out of the bottom of the sea, or whether by thine almighty word thou madest it in an instant in the mouth of that fish, it is neither possible to determine, nor necessary to inquire: I rather adore thine infinite knowledge and power, that couldst make use of unlikeliest means; that couldst serve thyself of the very fishes of the sea, in a business of earthly and civil employment. It was not out of need that thou didst this; though I do not find that thou ever affectedst a full purse— what veins of gold, or mines of silver, did not lie open to thy command?—but out of a desire to teach Peter, that while he would be tributary to Cæsar, the very fish of the sea was tributary to him. How should this encourage our dependence upon that omnipotent hand of thine, which hath heaven, earth, sea, at thy disposing! Still thou art the same for thy members, which thou wert for thyself, the Head. Rather than offence shall be given to the world by a seeming neglect of thy dear children, thou wilt cause the very fowls of heaven to bring them meat, and the fish of the sea to bring them money. O let us look up ever to thee by the eye of our faith, and not be wanting in our dependence upon thee, who canst not be wanting in thy providence over us.

CONTEMPLATION XXIII.—LAZARUS DEAD.

O THE wisdom of God in penning his own story! The disciple whom Jesus loved comes after his fellow evangelists, that he might glean up those rich ears of history which the rest had passed over; that eagle soars high, and towers up by degrees. It was much to turn water into wine; but it was more to feed five thousand with five loaves. It was much to restore the ruler's son; it was more to cure him that had been thirty-eight years a cripple. It was much to cure him that was born blind; it was more to raise up Lazarus that had been so long dead. As a stream runs still the stronger and wider, the nearer it comes to the ocean whence it was derived; so didst thou, O Saviour, work the more powerfully the nearer thou drewest to thy glory. This was, as one of thy last, so of thy greatest, miracles: when thou wert ready to die thyself, thou raisedst him to life who smelt strong of the grave. None of all the sacred histories is so full and punctual as this, in the report of all circumstances. Other miracles do not more transcend nature, than this transcends other miracles.

This alone was a sufficient eviction of thy Godhead, O blessed Saviour! None but an infinite power could so far go beyond nature, as to recall a man four days dead, from not a mere privation, but a settled corruption. Earth must needs be thine, from which thou raisest his body; heaven must needs be thine, from whence thou fetchest his spirit. None but he that created man, could thus make him new.

Sickness is the common preface to death; no mortal nature is exempted from this complaint; even Lazarus, whom Jesus loved, is sick. What can strength of grace or dearness of respect prevail against disease, against dissolution?

It was a stirring message that Mary sent to Jesus: " He whom thou lovest is sick:" as if she would imply, that his part was no less deep in Lazarus than hers. Neither doth she say, He that loves thee is sick; but, " He whom thou lovest:" not pleading the merit of Lazarus's affection to Christ, but the mercy and favour of Christ to him. Even that other reflection of love had been no weak motive; for, O Lord, thou hast said, " Because he hath set his love upon me, therefore will I deliver him." Thy goodness will not be behind us for love, who professest to love them that love thee. But yet the argument is more forcible from thy love to us, since thou hast just reason to respect everything of thine own, more than aught that can proceed from us. Even we weak men, what can we stick at where we love? Thou, O infinite God, art love itself. Whatever thou hast done for us is out of thy love; the ground and motive of all thy mercies is within thyself, not in us, and if there be aught in us worthy of thy love, it is thine own, not ours; thou givest what thou acceptest. Jesus well heard the first groan of his dear Lazarus; every short breath he drew, every sigh that he gave, was upon account; yet this Lord of life lets his Lazarus sicken, and languish, and die; not out of neglect or impotence, but out of power and resolution: "This sickness is not to death." He to whom the issues of death belong, knows the way both into it and out of it. He meant that sickness should be to death, in respect of the present condition, not to death in respect of the event; to death, in the process of nature, not to death in the success of his divine power, "that the Son of God might be glorified thereby." O Saviour, thy usual style is the Son of Man; thou that wouldst take up our infirmities, wert willing thus to hide thy Godhead under the coarse weeds of our humanity; but here thou sayest, "That the Son of God might be glorified." Though thou wouldst hide thy divine glory, yet thou wouldst not smother it. Sometimes thou wouldst have thy sun break forth in bright gleams, to show that it hath no less light even while it seems kept in by thy clouds. Thou wert now near thy passion: it was most seasonable for thee at this time to set forth thy just title. Neither was this an act that thy humanity could challenge to itself, but far transcending all finite powers. To die was an act of the Son of man, to raise from death was an act of the Son of God.

Neither didst thou say merely that God, but "That the Son of God might be glorified." God cannot be glorified, unless the Son be so. In very natural relations, the wrong or disrespect offered to the child reflects upon the father; as, contrarily, the parent's upon the child: how much more, where the love and respect is infinite! where the whole essence is communicated with the entireness of relation!

O God, in vain shall we tender our devotions to thee indefinitely, as to a glorious and incomprehensible Majesty, if we kiss not the Son, who hath most justly said, "Ye believe in the Father, believe also in me."

What a happy family was this! I find none upon earth so much honoured: "Jesus loved Martha, and her sister, and Lazarus." It is no standing upon terms of precedency: the Spirit of God is not curious in marshalling of places. Time was when Mary was confessed to have chosen the better part; here Martha is named first, as most interested in Christ's love; for aught appears, all of them were equally dear. Christ had familiarly lodged under their roof. How fit was that to receive him, whose indwellers were hospitable, pious, unanimous! hospitable, in the glad entertainment of Jesus and his train; pious, in their devotions; unanimous, in their mutual concord. As, contrarily, he baulks and hates that house which is taken up with uncharitableness, profaneness, contention.

But, O Saviour, how doth this agree? thou lovedst this family, yet, hearing of their distress, thou heldest off two days more from them. Canst thou love those thou regardest not? canst thou regard them from whom thou willingly absentest thyself in their necessity? Behold, thy love, as it is above ours, so it is oft against ours. Even out of every affection art thou not seldom absent. None of thine but have sometimes cried, "How long, Lord?" What need we instance, when thine eternal Father did purposely estrange his face from thee, so as thou criedst out of forsaking?

Here thou wouldst knowingly delay, whether for the greatening of the miracle, or for the strengthening of thy disciples' faith.

Hadst thou gone sooner, and prevented the death, who had known, whether strength of nature, and not thy miraculous power, had done it? hadst thou overtaken his death by this quickening visitation, who had known, whether this had been only some qualm or ecstacy, and not a perfect dissolution? Now this large gap of time makes thy work both certain and glorious.

And what a clear proof was this beforehand to thy disciples, that thou wert able to accomplish thine own resurrection on the third day, who wert able to raise up Lazarus on the fourth! The more difficult the work should be, the more need it had of an omnipotent confirmation.

He that was Lord of our times and his own, can now, when he found it seasonable, say, "Let us go into Judea again." Why left he it before? was it not upon the heady violence of his enemies? Lo! the stones of the Jews drove him thence; the love of Lazarus and the care of his divine glory drew him back thither.

We may, we must be wise as serpents for our own preservation; we must be careless of danger, when God calls us to the hazard. It is far from God's purpose to give us leave so far to respect ourselves, as that we should neglect him. Let Judea be all snares, all crosses: O Saviour, when thou callest us, we must put our lives into our hands, and follow thee thither.

This journey thou hast purposed and contrived: but what needest thou to acquaint thy disciples with thine intent? where didst thou ever, besides this, make them of counsel with thy voyages? Neither didst thou say, How think you if I go? but, " Let us go." Was it for that thou, who knewest thine own strength, knewest also their weakness? Thou wert resolute, they were timorous; they were sensible enough of their late peril, and fearful of more: there was need to forearm them with an expectation of the worst, and preparation for it. Surprisal with evils may endanger the best constancy. The heart is apt to fail, when it finds itself entrapped in a sudden mischief.

The disciples were dearly affected to Lazarus; they had learned to love where their Master loved; yet now, when our Saviour speaks of returning to that region of peril, they pull him by the sleeve, and put him in mind of the violence offered unto him: " Master, the Jews of late sought to stone thee, and goest thou thither again?"

No less than thrice, in the foregoing chapter, did the Jews lift up their hands to murder him by a cruel lapidation. Whence was this rage and bloody attempt of theirs? only for that he taught them the truth concerning his divine nature, and gave himself the just style of the Son of God. How subject carnal hearts are to be impatient of heavenly verities! Nothing can so much fret that malignant spirit which rules in those breasts, as that Christ should have his own. If we be persecuted for his truth, we do but suffer with him with whom we shall once reign.

However, the disciples pleaded for their Master's safety, yet they aimed at their own: they well knew their danger was inwrapped in his. It is but a cleanly colour that they put upon their own fear. This is held but a weak and base passion; each one would be glad to put off the opinion of it from himself, and to set the best face upon his own impotency.

Thus, white-livered men, that shrink and shift from the cross, will not want fair pretences to evade it. One pleads the peril of many dependents, another the disfurnishing the church of succeeding abettors: each will have some plausible excuse for his sound skin. What error did not our Saviour rectify in his followers! Even that fear, which they would have dissembled, is graciously dispelled by the just consideration of a sure and inevitable Providence: " Are there not twelve hours in the day," which are duly set, and proceed regularly for the direction of all the motions and actions of men? so in this course of mine, which I must run on earth, there is a set and determined time wherein I must work, and do my Father's will. The sun, that guides these hours, is the determinate counsel of my Father, and his calling to the execution of my charge: while I follow that, I cannot miscarry, no more than a man can miss his known way at high noon: this while in vain are either your dissuasions or the attempts of enemies; they cannot hurt, ye cannot divert me.

The journey then holds to Judea; his attendants shall be made acquainted with the occasion. He that had formerly denied the deadliness of Lazarus's sickness, would not suddenly confess his death, neither yet would he altogether conceal it; so will he therefore confess it, as that he will shadow it out in a borrowed expression: " Lazarus our friend sleepeth." What a sweet title is here, both of death and of Lazarus! death is a sleep, Lazarus is our friend. Lo, he says not, my friend, but ours; to draw them first into a gracious familiarity and communion of friendship with himself; for what doth this import, but, " ye are my friends," and Lazarus is both my friend and yours? " our friend."

O meek and merciful Saviour, that disdainest not to stoop so low, as that, while thou "thoughtst it no robbery to be equal unto God," thou thoughtst it no disparagement to match thyself with weak and wretched men! " Our friend Lazarus!" There is a kind of parity in friendship. There may be love where is the most inequality, but friendship supposes pairs: yet the Son of God says of the sons of men, " Our friend Lazarus." O what a high and happy condition is this for mortal men to aspire unto, that the God of heaven should not be ashamed to own them for friends! Neither saith he now abruptly, Lazarus our friend is dead; but, " Lazarus our friend sleepeth."

O Saviour, none can know the estate of life or death so well as thou that art the Lord of both. It is enough that thou tellest us death is no other than sleep; that which was wont to pass for the cousin of death, is now itself. All this while, we have mistaken the case of our dissolution: we took it for an enemy, it proves a friend: there is pleasure in that wherein we supposed horror.

Who is afraid, after the weary toils of the day, to take his rest by night? or what is more refreshing to the spent traveller than a sweet sleep? It is our infidelity, our impreparation, that makes death any other than advantage. Even so, Lord, when thou seest I have toiled enough, let me sleep in peace; and when thou seest I have slept enough, awake me, as thou didst thy Lazarus: "But I go to awake him." Thou saidst not, Let us go to awake him: those whom thou wilt allow companions of thy way, thou wilt not allow partners of thy work; they may be witnesses, they cannot be actors. None can awake Lazarus out of this sleep, but he that made Lazarus. Every mouse or gnat can raise us up from that other sleep; none but an omnipotent power from this. This sleep is not without a dissolution. Who can command the soul to come down and meet the body, or command the body to piece with itself, and rise up to the soul, but the God that created both? It is our comfort and assurance, O Lord, against the terrors of death and tenacity of the grave, that our resurrection depends upon none but thine omnipotence.

Who can blame the disciples if they are loath to return to Judea? Their last entertainment was such as might justly dishearten them. Were this as literally taken, all the reason of our Saviour's purpose of so perilous a voyage, they argued not amiss: "If he sleep, he shall do well." Sleep in sickness is a good sign of recovery, for extremity of pain bars our rest; when nature, therefore, finds so much respiration, she justly hopes for better terms. Yet it doth not always follow, "If he sleep, he shall do well:" how many have died of lethargies! how many have lost, in sleep, what they would not have foregone waking! Adam slept, and lost his rib; Samson slept, and lost his strength; Saul slept, and lost his weapon; Ishbosheth and Holofernes slept, and lost their heads: in ordinary course it holds well; here they mistook and erred. The misconstruction of the words of Christ led them into an unseasonable and erroneous suggestion. Nothing can be more dangerous than to take the speeches of Christ according to the sound of the letter; one error will be sure to draw on more, and if the first be never so slight, the last may be important.

Wherefore are words but to express meanings? why do we speak but to be understood? Since, then, our Saviour saw himself not rightly construed, he delivers himself plainly, "Lazarus is dead." Such is thy manner, O thou eternal Word of thy Father, in all thy sacred expressions. Thine own mouth is thy best commentary: what thou hast more obscurely said in one passage, thou interpretest more clearly in another. Thou art the sun, which givest us that light whereby we see thyself.

But how modestly dost thou discover thy deity to thy disciples! not upon the first mention of Lazarus's death, instantly professing thy power and will of his resuscitation; but contenting thyself only to intimate thy omniscience, in that thou couldst, in that absence and distance, know and report his departure: they shall gather the rest, and cannot choose but think, We serve a Master that knows all things; and he that knows all things, can do all things.

The absence of our Saviour from the deathbed of Lazarus was not casual, but voluntary; yea, he is not only willing with it, but glad of it: "I am glad, for your sakes, that I was not there." How contrary may the affections of Christ and ours be, and yet be both good! The two worthy sisters were much grieved at our Saviour's absence, as doubting it might savour of some neglect: Christ was glad of it, for the advantage of his disciples' faith. I cannot blame them, that they were thus sorry; I cannot but bless him, that he was thus glad. The gain of their faith, in so divine a miracle, was more than could be countervailed by their momentary sorrow. God and we are not alike affected with the same events: he laughs where we mourn; he is angry where we are pleased.

The difference of the affections arises from the difference of the objects, which Christ and they apprehend in the same occurrence. Why are the sisters sorrowful? because, upon Christ's absence, Lazarus died. Why was Jesus glad he was not there? for the benefit which he saw would accrue to their faith. There is much variety of prospect in every act, according to the several intentions and issues thereof; yea, even in the very same eyes. The Father sees his Son combating in a duel for his country: he sees blows and wounds on the one side, he sees renown and victory on the other; he grieves at the wounds, he rejoices in the honour. Thus doth God in all our afflictions: he sees our tears, and hears our groans, and pities us; but withal, he looks upon our patience, our faith, our crown, and is glad that we are afflicted.

O God, why should not we conform our diet unto thine? When we lie in pain and extremity, we cannot but droop under it; but, do we find ourselves increased in true mortification, in patience, in hope, in a constant reliance on thy mercies? why are we not more joyed in this, than dejected with the other, since the least grain of the increase of grace is more worth than can be equalled with whole pounds of bodily vexation?

O strange consequence! "Lazarus is dead;" nevertheless, "let us go unto him." Must they not needs think, what should we do with a dead man? what should separate, if death cannot? Even those, whom we loved dearliest, we avoid once dead; now we lay them aside under the board, and thence send them out of our houses to their grave. Neither hath death more horror in it than noisomeness; and if we could entreat our eyes to endure the horrid aspect of death, in the face we loved, yet can we persuade our scent to like that smell that arises up from their corruption? "O love stronger than death!" behold here, a friend whom the very grave cannot sever.

Even those that write the longest and most passionate dates of their amity, subscribe but, "Your friend till death;" and if the ordinary strain of human friendship will stretch out a little further, it is but to the brim of the grave; thither a friend may follow us, and see us bestowed in this house of our age, but there he leaves us to our worms and dust. But for thee, O Saviour, the grave-stone, the earth, the coffin, are no bounders of thy dear respects; even after death, and burial, and corruption, thou art graciously affected to those thou lovest. Besides the soul (whereof thou sayest not, let us go to it, but, let it come to us), there is still a gracious regard to that dust, which was, and shall be a part of an undoubted member of that mystical body whereof thou art the head. Heaven and earth yield no such friend but thyself. O make me ever ambitious of this love of thine, and ever unquiet, till I feel myself possessed of thee!

In the mouth of a mere man, this word had been incongruous: "Lazarus is dead, yet let us go to him;" in thine, O Almighty Saviour, it was not more loving than seasonable, since I may justly say of thee, thou hast more to do with the dead than the living; for both they are infinitely more, and have more inward communion with thee, and thou with them: death cannot hinder either our passage to thee, or thy return to us. I joy to think the time is coming, when thou shalt come to every of our graves, and call us up out of our dust, and we "shall hear thy voice, and live."

CONTEMPLATION XXIV.—LAZARUS RAISED.

GREAT was the opinion that these devout sisters had of the power of Christ, as if death durst not show his face to him: they suppose his presence had prevented their brother's dissolution; and now the news of his approach begins to quicken some late hopes in them. Martha was ever the more active; she, that was before so busily stirring in her house to entertain Jesus, was now as nimble to go forth of her house to meet him; she, in whose face joy had wont to smile upon so blessed a guest, now salutes him with the sighs, and tears, and blubbers, and wrings of a disconsolate mourner. I know not whether the speeches of her greeting had in them more sorrow or religion. She had been well catechized before; even she also had sat at Jesus' feet; and can now give good account of her faith, in the power and Godhead of Christ, in the certainty of a future resurrection. This conference hath yet taught her more, and raised her heart to an expectation of some wonderful effect. And now she stands not still, but hastes back into the village to her sister, carried thither by the two wings of her own hopes and her Saviour's commands. The time was, when she would have called off her sister from the feet of that divine Master, to attend the household occasions; now she runs to fetch her out of the house to the feet of Christ.

Doubtless, Martha, was much affected with the presence of Christ; and as she was overjoyed with it herself, so she knew how equally welcome it would be to her sister; yet she doth not ring it out aloud in the open hall, but secretly whispers these pleasing tidings in her sister's ear: "The Master is come, and calleth for thee." Whether out of modesty or discretion, it is not fit for a woman to be loud and clamorous: nothing beseems that sex better than silence and bashfulness; as not to be too much seen, so not to be heard too far. Neither did modesty more charm her tongue than discretion, whether in respect to the guests, or to Christ himself. Had those guests heard of Christ's being there, they had, either out of fear or prejudice, withdrawn themselves from him; neither durst they have been witnesses of that wonderful miracle, as being overawed with that Jewish edict which was out against him; or perhaps they had withheld the sisters from going to him, against whom they knew how highly their governors were incensed. Neither was she ignorant of the danger of his own person, so lately before assaulted violently by his enemies at Jerusalem. She knew they were within the smoke of that bloody city, the nest of his enemies; she holds it not therefore fit to make open proclamation of Christ's presence, but rounds her sister secretly in the ear. Christianity doth not bid us abate anything of our wariness and honest policies; yea, it requires us to have no less of the serpent than of the dove

There is a time when we must preach Christ on the house-top: there is a time when we must speak him in the ear, and, as it were, with our lips shut. Secrecy hath no less use than divulgation. She said enough: "The Master is come, and calleth for thee." What a happy word was this which was here spoken! what a high favour is this that is done, that the Lord of life should personally come and call for Mary! Yet such as is not appropriated to her: thou comest to us still, O Saviour, if not in thy bodily presence, yet in thy spiritual; thou callest us still, if not in thy personal voice, yet in thine ordinances. It is our fault, if we do not, as this good woman, arise quickly, and come to thee. Her friends were there about her, who came purposely to condole with her; her heart was full of heaviness; yet so soon as she hears mention of Christ, she forgets friends, brother, grief, cares, thoughts, and hastes to his presence.

Still was Jesus standing in the place where Martha left him. Whether it be noted to express Mary's speed, or his own wise and gracious resolutions, his presence in the village had perhaps invited danger, and set off the intended witnesses of the work; or it may be, to set forth his zealous desire to despatch the errand he came for; that as Abraham's faithful servant would not receive any courtesy from the house of Bethuel, till he had done his master's business concerning Rebecca; so thou, O Saviour, wouldst not so much as enter into the house of these two sisters in Bethany, till thou hadst effected this glorious work which occasioned thee thither. It was thy " meat and drink to do the will of thy Father;" thy best entertainment was within thyself. How do we follow thee, if we suffer either pleasures or profits to take the wall of thy services?

So good women were well worthy of kind friends. No doubt Bethany, being not two miles distant from Jerusalem, could not but be furnished with good acquaintance from the city: these knowing the dearness, and hearing of the death of Lazarus, came over to comfort the sad sisters. Charity, together with the common practice of that nation, calls them to this duty. All our distresses expect these good offices from those that love us; but, of all others, death, as that which is the extremest of evils, and makes the most fearful havoc in families, cities, kingdoms, worlds. The complaint was grievous: "I looked for some to comfort me, but there was none." It is some kind of ease to sorrow to have partners, as a burden is lightened by many shoulders, or as clouds, scattered into many drops, easily vent their moisture into air. Yea, the very presence of friends abates grief. The peril that arises to the heart from passion is the fixedness of it, when, like a corrosive plaster, it eats into the sore. Some kind of remedy it is, that it may breathe out in good society.

These friendly neighbours, seeing Mary hasten forth, make haste to follow her. Martha went forth before; I saw none go after her: Mary stirs; they are at her heels. Was it that Martha, being the elder sister, and the housewife of the family, might stir about with less observation? or was it that Mary was the more passionate, and needed the more heedy attendance? However, their care and intentiveness is truly commendable; they came to comfort her, they do what they came for. It contents them not to sit still and chat within doors, but they wait on her at all turns. Perturbations of mind are diseases: good keepers do not only tend the patient in bed, but when he sits up, when he tries to walk; all his motions have their careful assistance. We are no true friends if our endeavours of the redress of distempers in them we love be not assiduous and unwearyable.

It was but a loving suspicion: " She is gone to the grave to weep there." They well knew how apt passionate minds are to take all occasions to renew their sorrow: every object affects them. When she saw but the chamber of her dead brother, straight she thinks, there Lazarus was wont to lie, and then she wept afresh; when the table, there Lazarus was wont to sit, and then new tears arise; when the garden, there Lazarus had wont to walk, and now again she weeps. How much more do these friends suppose the passions would be stirred with the sight of the grave, when she must needs think, There is Lazarus! O Saviour, if the place of the very dead corpse of our friend have power to draw our hearts thither, and to affect us more deeply, how should our hearts be drawn to and affected with heaven, where thou sittest at the right hand of thy Father? there, O thou, "which wert dead and art alive," is thy body and thy soul present, and united to thy glorious Deity. Thither, O thither, let our access be; not to mourn there, where is no place for sorrow, but to rejoice with joy unspeakable and glorious, and more and more to long for that thy beatifical presence.

Their indulgent love mistook Mary's errand; their thoughts, how kind soever, were much too low: while they supposed she went to a dead brother, she went to a living Saviour. The world hath other conceits of the action and carriage of the regenerate than are truly intended, setting such constructions upon them as their own carnal reason suggests: they think them dying, when behold, they live; sorrowful, when they are always rejoicing; poor, while they make many rich. How justly do we appeal from them as incompetent judges, and pity those misinterpretations which we cannot avoid!

Both the sisters met Christ; not both in one posture: Mary is still noted, as for more passion, so for more devotion; she that before sat at the feet of Jesus, now falls at his feet. That presence had wont to be familiar to her, and not without some outward homeliness; now it fetches her upon her knees in an awful veneration: whether out of a reverent acknowledgment of the secret excellency and power of Christ, or out of a dumb intimation of that suit concerning her dead brother, which she was afraid to utter; the very gesture itself was supplicatory. What position of body can be so fit for us, when we make our address to our Saviour? it is an irreligious unmannerliness for us to do less. Where the heart is affected with an awful acknowledgment of majesty, the body cannot but bow.

Even before all her neighbours of Jerusalem, doth Mary thus fall down at the feet of Jesus; so many witnesses as she had, so many spies she had, of that forbidden observance. It was no less than excommunication for any body to confess him; yet good Mary, not fearing the informations that might be given by those Jewish gossips, adores him; and, in her silent gesture, says as much as her sister had spoken before: "Thou art the Christ, the Son of God." Those, that would give Christ his right, must not stand upon scrupulous fears. Are we naturally timorous? why do we not fear the denial, the exclusion of the Almighty? "Without shall be the fearful."

Her humble prostration is seconded by a lamentable complaint: "Lord, if thou hadst been here, my brother had not died." The sisters are both in one mind, both in one speech; and both of them, in one speech, bewray both strength and infirmity: strength of faith, in ascribing so much power to Christ, that his presence could preserve from death; infirmity, in supposing the necessity of a presence for this purpose. Why, Mary, could not thine omnipotent Saviour, as well in absence, have commanded Lazarus to live? Is his hand so short, that he can do nothing but by contraction? If his power were finite, how could he have forbidden the seizure of death? if infinite, how could it be limited to place, or hindered by distance? It is a weakness of faith to measure success by means, and means by presence, and to tie effects to both, when we deal with an Almighty agent. Finite causes work within their own sphere; all places are equally near, and all effects equally easy to the infinite. O Saviour, while thou now sittest gloriously in heaven, thou dost no less impart thyself unto us, than if thou stoodst visibly by us, than if we stood locally by thee! no place can make difference of thy virtue and aid.

This was Mary's moan: no motion, no request sounded from her to her Saviour. Her silent suit is returned with a mute answer: no notice is taken of her error. O that marvellous mercy that connives at our faulty infirmities! All the reply that I hear of, is a compassionate groan with himself. O blessed Jesu, thou, that wert free from all sin, wouldst not be free from strong affections. Wisdom and holiness should want much work, if even vehement passions might not be quitted from offence. Mary wept; her tears drew on tears from her friends; all their tears united, drew groans from thee. Even in thine heaven, thou dost no less pity our sorrows: thy glory is free from groans, but abounds with compassion and mercy: if we be not sparing of our tears, thou canst not be insensible of our sorrows. How shall we imitate thee, if, like our looking-glass, we do not answer tears, and weep on them that weep on us!

Lord, thou knewest (in absence) that Lazarus was dead, and dost thou not know where he was buried? Surely thou wert further off when thou sawest and reportedst his death, than thou wert from the grave thou inquiredst of: thou, that knewest all things, yet askest what thou knowest: "Where have ye laid him?" not out of need, but out of will; that as in thy sorrow, so in thy question, thou mightst depress thyself in the opinion of the beholders for the time, that the glory of thine instant miracle might be the greater, the less it was expected. It had been all one to thy omnipotence to have made a new Lazarus out of nothing; or, in that remoteness, to have commanded Lazarus, wheresoever he was, to come forth: but thou wert neither willing to work more miracle than was requisite, nor yet unwilling to fix the minds of the people upon the expectation of some marvellous thing that thou meantest to work; and therefore askest, "Where have you laid him?"

They are not more glad of the question, than ready for the answer: "Come and see." It was the manner of the Jews, as likewise of those Egyptians among whom they had sojourned, to lay up the dead bodies of their friends with great respect: more cost was wont to be bestowed on some of their graves than on their houses; as neither ashamed, then, nor unwilling to show the decency of their sepulture, they say, "Come and see." More was hoped for from Christ than a mere view; they meant and expected, that his eye should draw him on to some further action. O Saviour, while we desire our spiritual resuscitation, how should we labour to bring thee to our grave! how should we lay open our deadness before thee, and bewray to thee our impotence and senselessness! Come, Lord, and see what a miserable carcass I am; and, by the power of thy mercy, raise me from the state of my corruption.

Never was our Saviour more submissively dejected than now, immediately before he would approve and exalt the majesty of his Godhead. To his groans and inward grief he adds his tears. Anon they shall confess him a God; these expressions of passions shall onwards evince him to be a man. The Jews construe this well: "See how he loved him." Never did anything but love fetch tears from Christ. But they do foully misconstrue Christ in the other: "Could not he, that opened the eyes of him that was born blind, have caused that even this man should not have died?" Yes, know ye, O vain and importune questionists, that he could have done it with ease. To open the eyes of a man born blind, was more than to keep a sick man from dying: this were but to uphold and maintain nature from decaying; that were to create a new sense, and to restore a deficiency in nature. To make an eye, was no whit less difficult than to make a man: he that could do the greater might well have done the less. Ye shall soon see this was not for want of power. Had ye said, Why would he not? why did he not? the question had been fairer, and the answer no less easy — For his own greater glory. Little do ye know the drift, whether of God's acts or delays; and ye know as much as you are worthy. Let it be sufficient for you to understand, that he, who can do all things, will do that which shall be most for his own honour.

It is not improbable that Jesus, who before groaned in himself for compassion of their tears, now groaned for their incredulity. Nothing could so much afflict the Saviour of men as the sins of men. Could their external wrongs to his body have been separated from offence against his divine person, their scornful indignities had not so much affected him. No injury goes so deep as our spiritual provocations of our God. Wretched men! why should we grieve the good Spirit of God in us? why should we make him groan for us, that died to redeem us?

With these groans, O Saviour, thou camest to the grave of Lazarus. The door of that house of death was strong and impenetrable: thy first word was, "Take away the stone." O weak beginning of a mighty miracle! If thou meantest to raise the dead, how much more easy had it been for thee to remove the grave-stone! One grain of faith in thy very disciples was enough to remove mountains, and dost thou say, "Take away the stone?" I doubt not but there was a greater weight that lay upon the body of Lazarus than the stone of his tomb — the weight of death and corruption: a thousand rocks and hills were not so heavy a load as this alone; why then didst thou stick at this shovel-full? Yea, how easy had it been for thee to have brought up the body of Lazarus through the stone, by causing that marble to give way by a sudden rarefaction! But thou thoughtst best to make use of their hands rather, whether for their own more full conviction; for had the stone been taken away by thy followers, and Lazarus thereupon walked forth, this might have appeared to thy malignant enemies to have been a set match betwixt thee, the disciples, and Lazarus; or whether for the exercise of our faith, that thou mightst teach us to trust thee under contrary appearances. Thy command to remove the stone seemed to argue an impotence; straight that seeming weakness breaks forth into an act of omnipotent power. The homeliest shows of thine human infirmity are ever seconded with some mighty proofs of thy Godhead: and thy miracle is so much more wondered at, by how much it was less expected.

It was ever thy just will that we should do what we may. To remove the stone, or to untie the napkin, was in their power;

this they must do: to raise the dead was out of their power; this therefore thou wilt do alone. Our hands must do their utmost ere thou wilt put to thine.

O Saviour, we are all dead and buried in the grave of our sinful nature: the stone of obstination must be taken away from our hearts, ere we can hear thy reviving voice. We can no more remove this stone, than dead Lazarus could remove his; we can add more weight to our graves. O let thy faithful agents, by the power of thy law, and the grace of thy gospel, take off the stone, that thy voice may enter into the grave of miserable corruption.

Was it a modest kind of mannerliness in Martha, that she would not have Christ annoyed with the ill scent of that stale carcass? or was it out of distrust of reparation, since her brother had passed all the degrees of corruption, that she says, " Lord, by this time he stinketh, for he hath been dead four days?" He that understood hearts, found somewhat amiss in that intimation; his answer had not endeavoured to rectify that which was utterly faultless. I fear, the good woman meant to object this as a likely obstacle to any further purposes or proceedings of Christ. Weak faith is still apt to lay blocks of difficulties in the way of the great works of God.

Four days were enough to make any corpse noisome. Death itself is not unsavoury: immediately upon dissolution the body retains the wonted sweetness: it is the continuance under death that is thus offensive. Neither is it otherwise in our spiritual condition: the longer we lie under our sin, the more rotten and corrupt we are. He who, upon the fresh commission of his sin, recovers himself by a speedy repentance, yields no ill scent to the nostrils of the Almighty. The candle that is presently blown in again, offends not; it is the snuff, which continues choked with its own moisture, that sends up unwholesome and odious fumes. O Saviour, thou wouldst yield to death, thou wouldst not yield to corruption; ere the fourth day, thou wert risen again. I cannot but receive many deadly foils; but O, do thou raise me up again, ere I shall pass the degrees of rottenness in my sins and trespasses!

They that laid their hands to the stone, doubtless held now still awhile, and looked one while on Christ, another while upon Martha, to hear what issue of resolution would follow upon so important an objection; when they find a light touch of taxation to Martha: " Said I not to thee, that if thou wouldst believe, thou shouldst see the glory of God?" That holy woman had before professed her belief, as Christ had professed his great intentions: both were now forgotten; and now our Saviour is fain to revive both her memory and faith: "Said I not to thee?" The best of all saints are subject to fits of unbelief and oblivion, the only remedy whereof must be the inculcation of God's merciful promises of their relief and supportation. O God, if thou hast said it, I dare believe; I dare cast my soul upon the belief of every word of thine " Faithful art thou which hast promised, who wilt also do it."

In spite of all the unjust discouragements of nature, we must obey Christ's command. Whatever Martha suggests, they remove the stone, and may now see and smell him dead, whom they shall soon see revived. The scent of the corpse is not so unpleasing to them as the perfume of their obedience is sweet to Christ. And now, when all impediments are removed, and all hearts ready for the work, our Saviour addresses to the miracle.

His eyes begin; they are lift up to heaven. It was the malicious mis-suggestion of his enemies, that he looked down to Beelzebub; the beholders shall now see whence he expects and derives his power, and shall by him learn whence to expect and hope for all success. The heart and the eye must go together; he that would have aught to do with God, must be sequestered and lifted up from earth.

His tongue seconds his eye: " Father." Nothing more stuck in the stomach of the Jews, than that Christ called himself the Son of God; this was imputed to him for a blasphemy, worthy of stones. How seasonably is this word spoken in the hearing of these Jews, in whose sight he will be presently approved so! How can ye now, O ye cavillers, except at that title which ye shall see irrefragably justified? Well may he call God Father, that can raise the dead out of the grave. In vain shall ye snarl at the style, when ye are convinced of the effect.

I hear of no prayer, but a thanks for hearing. While thou saidst nothing, O Saviour, how doth thy Father hear thee? Was it not with thy Father and thee, as it was with thee and Moses? Thou saidst, " Let me alone, Moses," when he spake not. Thy will was thy prayer. Words express our hearts to men, thoughts to God. Well didst thou know, out of the self-sameness of thy will with thy Father's, that if thou didst but think in thine heart that Lazarus should rise, he was now raised. It was not for thee to pray vocally and audibly, lest those captious hearers should say, thou didst all by entreaty, nothing by power. Thy thanks overtake thy desires; ours require time and distance: our thanks arise from the echo of our prayers resounding from heaven to our hearts; thou, because thou art at once in earth and heaven, and knowest the grant to be of equal paces with the request, most justly thankest in praying.

Now ye cavilling Jews are thinking straight, Is there such distance betwixt the Father and the Son? is it so rare a thing for the Son to be heard, that he pours out his thanks for it as a blessing unusual? Do ye not now see that he who made your heart knows it, and anticipates your fond thoughts with the same breath? "I knew that thou hearest me always, but I said this for their sakes, that they might believe."

Merciful Saviour, how can we enough admire thy goodness, who makest our belief the scope and drift of thy doctrine and actions! Alas! what wert thou the better, if they believed thee sent from God? what wert thou the worse, if they believed it not? Thy perfection and glory stand not upon the slippery terms of our approbation or dislike, but is real in thyself; and that infinite, without possibility of our increase or diminution. We, we only are they that have either the gain or loss in thy receipt or rejection; yet so dost thou affect our belief, as if it were more thine advantage than ours.

O Saviour, while thou spakest to thy Father, thou liftedst up thine eyes; now thou art to speak unto dead Lazarus, thou liftedst up thy voice, and criedst aloud, "Lazarus, come forth." Was it that the strength of the voice might answer to the strength of the affection? since we faintly require what we care not to obtain, and vehemently utter what we earnestly desire: was it, that the greatness of the voice might answer to the greatness of the work? was it, that the hearers might be witnesses of what words were used in so miraculous an act — no magical incantations, but authoritative and divine commands? was it to signify, that Lazarus' soul was called from far? the speech must be loud that shall be heard in another world: was it in relation to the estate of the body of Lazarus, whom thou hadst reported to sleep? since those that are in a deep and dead sleep cannot be awaked without a loud call: or was it in a representation of that loud voice of the last trumpet, which shall sound into all graves, and raise all flesh from their dust?

Even so still, Lord, when thou wouldst raise a soul from the death of sin, and grave of corruption, no easy voice will serve. Thy strongest commands, thy loudest denunciations of judgments, the shrillest and sweetest promulgations of thy mercies, are but enough.

How familiar a word is this, "Lazarus, come forth!" no other than he was wont to use while they lived together. Neither doth he say, Lazarus, revive; but, as if he supposed him already living, "Lazarus, come forth: to let them know, that those who are dead to us, are to and with him alive; yea, in a more entire and feeling society, than while they carried their clay about them. Why do I fear that separation which shall more unite me to my Saviour?

Neither was the word more familiar than commanding: "Lazarus, come forth." Here is no suit to his Father, no adjuration to the deceased, but a flat and absolute injunction, "Come forth." O Saviour, that is the voice that I shall once hear sounding into the bottom of my grave, and raising me up out of my dust; that is the voice that shall pierce the rocks and divide the mountains, and fetch up the dead out of the lowest depths. Thy word made all, thy word shall repair all. Hence, all ye diffident fears! He whom I trust is omnipotent.

It was the Jewish fashion to enwrap the corpse in linen, to tie the hands and feet, and to cover the face of the dead. The fall of man, besides weakness, brought shame upon him. Ever since, even while he lives, the whole body is covered; but the face, because some sparks of that extinct majesty remain there, is wont to be left open. In death, all those poor remainders being gone, and leaving deformity and ghastliness in the room of them, the face is covered also.

There lies Lazarus, bound in double fetters: one almighty word hath loosed both, and now, "he that was bound came forth." He whose power could not be hindered by the chains of death, cannot be hindered by linen bands; he that gave life, gave motion, gave direction; he that guided the soul of Lazarus into the body, guided the body of Lazarus without his eyes, moved the feet without the full liberty of his regular paces: no doubt, the same power slackened those swathing bands of death, that the feet might have some little scope to move, though not with that freedom that followed after. Thou didst not only, O Saviour, raise the body of Lazarus, but the faith of the beholders. They cannot deny him dead, whom they saw rising: they see the signs of death, with the proofs of life; those very swathes convinced him to be the man that was raised. Thy less miracle confirms the greater; both confirm the faith of the beholders. O clear and irrefragable example of our resuscitation! Say now, ye shameless Sadducees, with what face can ye deny the resurrection of the body, when ye see Lazarus, after four days' death, rising up out of his grave? And if Lazarus did thus start up at the bleating of this Lamb of God, that was now every day preparing for the slaughter-house, how shall the dead be roused up out of their graves, by the roaring of that glorious and immortal Lion, whose voice shall shake the powers of heaven, and move the very foundations of the earth!

With what strange amazedness do we think that Martha and Mary, the Jews, and the disciples, looked to see Lazarus come forth in his winding sheet, shackled with his linen fetters, and walk towards them? Doubtless fear and horror strove in them, whether should be for the time more predominant. We love our friends dearly; but to see them again after their known death, and that in the very robes of the grave, must needs set up the hair in a kind of uncouth rigour. And now, though it had been most easy for him that brake the adamantine fetters of death, to have broke in pieces those linen ligaments wherewith his raised Lazarus was encumbered, yet he will not do it but by their hands. He that said, "Remove the stone," said, "Loose Lazarus." He will not have us expect his immediate help, in that we can do for ourselves. It is both a laziness, and a presumptuous tempting of God, to look for an extraordinary and supernatural help from God, where he hath enabled us with common aid.

What strange salutations do we think there were betwixt Lazarus and Christ that had raised him; betwixt Lazarus and his sisters, and neighbours, and friends! what amazed looks! what unusual compliments! for Lazarus was himself at once: here was no leisure of degrees to reduce him to his wonted perfection, neither did he stay to rub his eyes, and stretch his benumbed limbs, nor take time to put off that dead sleep wherewith he had been seized; but instantly he is both alive, and fresh, and vigorous; if they do but let him go, he walks so as if he had ailed nothing, and receives and gives mutual gratulations. I leave them entertaining each other with glad embraces, with discourses of reciprocal admiration, with praises and adorations of that God and Saviour that had fetched him into life.

CONTEMPLATION XXV.—CHRIST'S PROCESSION TO THE TEMPLE.

NEVER did our Saviour take so much state upon him as now, that he was going towards his passion: other journeys he measured on foot, without noise or train; this with a princely equipage and loud acclamation. Wherein yet, O Saviour, shall I more wonder at thy majesty, or thine humility; that divine majesty which lay hid under so humble appearance, or that sincere humility which veiled so great a glory? Thou, O Lord, whose chariots are twenty-thousand, even thousands of angels, wouldst make choice of the silliest of beasts to carry thee in thy last and royal progress. How well is thy birth suited with thy triumph! even that very ass whereon thou rodest was prophesied of; neither couldst thou have made up those vatical predictions without this conveyance. O glorious, and yet homely pomp!

Thou wouldst not lose aught of thy right; thou, that wast a king, wouldst be proclaimed so: but that it might appear thy kingdom was not of this world, thou that couldst have commanded all worldly magnificence, thoughtst fit to abandon it.

Instead of the kings of the earth, who, reigning by thee, might have been employed in thine attendance, the people are thine heralds; their homely garments are thy foot-cloth and carpets; their green boughs the strewings of thy way; those palms, which were wont to be borne in the hands of them that triumph, are strewed under the feet of thy beast. It was thy greatness and honour to contemn those glories which worldly hearts were wont to admire.

Justly did thy followers hold the best ornaments of the earth worthy of no better than thy treading upon; neither could they ever account their garments so rich, as when they had been trampled upon by thy carriage. How happily did they think their back disrobed for thy way! how gladly did they spend their breath in acclaiming thee! "Hosanna to the Son of David! blessed is he that cometh in the name of the Lord!" Where now are the great masters of the synagogue, that had enacted the ejection of whosoever should confess Jesus to be the Christ? Lo, here bold and undaunted clients of the Messiah, that dare proclaim him in the public road, in the open streets. In vain shall the impotent enemies of Christ hope to suppress his glory: as soon shall they with their hand hide the face of the sun from shining to the world, as withhold the beams of his divine truth from the eyes of men, by their envious opposition. In spite of all Jewish malignity, his kingdom is confessed, applauded, blessed.

"O thou fairer than the children of men, in thy majesty ride prosperously, because of truth, and meekness, and righteousness: and thy right hand shall teach thee terrible things."

In this princely, and yet poor and despicable pomp, doth our Saviour enter into the famous city of Jerusalem; Jerusalem, noted of old for the seat of kings, priests, prophets: of kings, for there was the throne of David; of priests, for there was the temple; of prophets, for there they delivered their errands, and left their blood. Neither know I whether it were more wonder for a prophet to perish out of Jerusalem, or to be safe there. Thither would Jesus come as a king, as a priest, as a prophet: acclaimed as a King, teaching the people, and foretelling the woful vastation of it as a prophet; and as a priest, taking possession of his temple, and vindicating it from the foul profanations of Jewish sacrilege. Oft before had he come to Jerusalem without any remarkable change, because without any semblance of state: now that he gives some little glimpse of his royalty, "the whole city was moved." When the sages of the East brought the first news of the king of the Jews, " Herod was troubled, and all Jerusalem with him:" and now that the King of the Jews comes himself, though in so mean a port, there is a new commotion. The silence and obscurity of Christ never trouble the world; he may be an underling without any stir: but if he do but put forth himself never so little, to bear the least sway amongst men, now their blood is up, the whole city is moved: neither is it otherwise in the private economy of the soul. O Saviour, while thou dost, as it were, hide thyself, and lie still in the heart, and takest all terms contentedly from us, we entertain thee with no other than a friendly welcome; but when thou once beginnest to ruffle with our corruptions, and to exercise thy spiritual power in the subjugation of our vile affections, now all is in a secret uproar, all the angles of the heart are moved.

Although, doubtless, this commotion was not so much of tumult, as wonder. As when some uncouth sight presents itself in a populous street, men run, and gaze, and throng, and inquire; the feet, the tongue, the eyes walk; one spectator draws on another; one asks and presses another; the noise increases with the concourse; each helps to stir up others' expectation: such was this of Jerusalem.

What means this strangeness? Was not Jerusalem the spouse of Christ? had he not chosen her out of all the earth? had he not begotten many children of her, as the pledges of their love? How justly mayest thou now, O Saviour, complain with that mirror of patience, "My breath was grown strange to my own wife, though I entreated her for the children's sake of my own body!" Even of thee is that fulfilled, which thy chosen vessel said of thy ministers, thou art " made a gazing-stock to the world, to angels, and to men."

As all the world was bound to thee for thy incarnation and residence upon the face of the earth, so especially Judea, to whose limits thou confinedst thyself, and therein, above all the rest, three cities, Nazareth, Capernaum, Jerusalem, on whom thou bestowedst the most time and cost of preaching, and miraculous works: yet in all three thou receivedst not strange entertainment only, but hostile. In Nazareth they would have thee cast down headlong from the mount; in Capernaum they would have bound thee; in Jerusalem they crucified thee at last, and now are amazed at thy presence. Those places and persons that have the greatest helps and privileges afforded them, are not always the most answerable in the return of their thankfulness. Christ's being amongst us, doth not make us happy, but his welcome. Every day may we hear him in our streets, and yet be as new to seek as these citizens of Jerusalem; "Who is this?"

Was it a question of applause, or of contempt, or of ignorance? Applause of his abettors, contempt of the Scribes and Pharisees, ignorance of the multitude. Surely his abettors had not been moved at this sight the Scribes and Pharisees had rather envied than contemned; the multitude, doubtless, inquired seriously, out of a desire of information. Not that the citizens of Jerusalem knew not Christ, who was so ordinary a guest, so noted a prophet amongst them. Questionless, this question was asked of that part of the train which went before this triumph, while our Saviour was not yet in sight, which, ere long, his presence had resolved. It had been their duty to have known, to have attended Christ, yea, to have published him to others: since this is not done, it is well yet that they spend their breath in an inquiry. No doubt there were many that would not so much as leave their shop-board, and step to their doors, or their windows, to say, "Who is this?"

as not thinking it could concern them who passed by, while they might sit still. Those Greeks were in some way to good, that could say to Philip, "We would see Jesus." O Saviour, thou hast been so long amongst us, that it is our just shame if we know thee not. If we have been slack hitherto, let our zealous inquiry make amends for our neglect. Let outward pomp and worldly glory draw the hearts and tongues of carnal men after them: O let it be my care and happiness, to ask after nothing but thee.

The attending disciples could not be to seek for an answer; which of the prophets have not put it into their mouths, " Who is this?" Ask Moses, and he shall tell you, " The seed of the woman that shall break the serpent's head." Ask our father Jacob, and he shall tell you, " The Shiloh of the tribe of Judah." Ask David, and he shall tell you, " The King of glory." Ask Isaiah, he shall tell you, " Immanuel, Wonderful, Counsellor, the Mighty God, the Everlasting Father, the Prince of Peace." Ask Jeremiah, and he shall tell you, ".The Righteous Branch." Ask Daniel, he shall tell you, " The Messiah." Ask John the Baptist, he shall tell you, " The Lamb of God." If ye ask the God of the prophets, he hath told you, " This is my beloved Son, in whom I am well pleased." Yea, if all these be too good for you to consult with, the devils themselves have been forced to say, " I know who thou art, even that Holy One of God." On no side hath Christ left himself without a testimony; and accordingly the multitude here have their answer ready, " This is Jesus, the prophet of Nazareth in Galilee."

Ye undervalue your Master, O ye well-meaning followers of Christ: " A prophet, yea, more than a prophet!" John Baptist was so, yet was but the harbinger of this Messiah. This was that God by whom the prophets were both sent and inspired. " Of Nazareth," say you? ye mistake him: Bethlehem was the place of his birth, the proof of his tribe, the evidence of his Messiahship. If Nazareth were honoured by his preaching, there was no reason he should be dishonoured by Nazareth. No doubt, he whom you confessed, pardoned the error of your confession. Ye spake but according to the common style. The two disciples in their walk to Emmaus, after the death and resurrection of Christ, gave him no other title. This belief passed current with the people, and thus high even the vulgar thoughts could then rise: and, no doubt, even thus much was for that time very acceptable to the Father of mercies.

If we make profession of the truth according to our knowledge, though there be much imperfection in our apprehension and delivery, the mercy of our good God takes it well; not judging us for what we have not, but accepting us in what we have. Shouldst thou, O God, stand strictly upon the punctual degrees of knowledge, how wide would it go with millions of souls! for, besides much error in many, there is more ignorance. But herein do we justly magnify and adore thy goodness, that, where thou findest diligent endeavour of better information, matched with an honest simplicity of heart, thou passest by our unwilling defects, and crownest our well-meant confessions.

But O the wonderful hand of God, in the carriage of this whole business! The people proclaimed Christ first a king, and now they proclaim him a prophet. Why did not the Roman bands run into arms upon the one? why did not the Scribes and Pharisees, and the envious priesthood, mutiny upon the other? They had made decrees against him, they had laid wait for him; yet now he passes in state through their streets, acclaimed both a King and a Prophet, without their reluctation. What can we impute this unto, but to the powerful and overruling arm of his Godhead? He that restrained the rage of Herod and his courtiers, upon the first news of a king born, now restrains all the opposite powers of Jerusalem, from lifting up a finger against this last and public avouchment of the regal and prophetical office of Christ. When flesh and blood have done their worst, they can be but such as he will make them. If the legions of hell combine with the potentates of the earth, they cannot go beyond the reach of their tether. Whether they rise or sit still, they shall, by an insensible ordination, perform that will of the Almighty which they least think of, and most oppose.

With this humble pomp and just acclamation, O Saviour, dost thou pass through the streets of Jerusalem to the temple. Thy first walk was not to Herod's palace, or to the market places or burses of that populous city, but to the temple; whether it were out of duty, or out of need: as a good son, when he comes from far, his first alighting is at his father's house; neither would he think it other than preposterous to visit strangers before his friends, or friends before his father. Besides that the temple had more use of thy presence; both there was the most disorder, and from thence, as from a corrupt spring, it issued forth into all the channels of Jerusalem. A wise physician inquires first into the state of the head, heart, liver, stomach, the vital and chief parts, ere he asks after the petty symptoms of the meaner and less-concerning members. Surely all good or evil begins at the temple. If God have there his own, if men find there nothing but wholesome instruction, holy example, the commonwealth cannot want some happy tincture of piety, devotion, sanctimony; as that fragrant perfume from Aaron's head sweetens his utmost skirts; contrarily, the distempers of the temple cannot but affect the secular state. As, therefore, the good husbandman, when he sees the leaves grow yellow, and the branches unthriving, looks presently to the root; so didst thou, O holy Saviour, upon sight of the disorders spread over Jerusalem and Judea, address thyself to the rectifying of the temple.

No sooner is Christ alighted at the gate of the outer court of his Father's house, than he falls to work: reformation was his errand; that he roundly attempts. That holy ground was profaned by sacrilegious barterings: within the third court of that sacred place was a public mart held; here was a throng of buyers and sellers, though not of all commodities; the Jews were not so irreligious, only of those things which were for the use of sacrifice. The Israelites came many of them from far; it was no less from Dan to Beersheba than the space of a hundred and threescore miles; neither could it be without much inconvenience for them to bring their bullocks, sheep, goats, lambs, meal, oil, and such other holy provision with them up to Jerusalem. Order was taken by the priests, that these might, for money, be had close by the altar, to the ease of the offerer, and for the benefit of the seller, and perhaps no disprofit to themselves. The pretence was fair, the practice unsufferable. The great Owner of the temple comes to vindicate the reputation and rights of his own house; and, in an indignation at that so foul abuse, lays fiercely about him, and, with his three-stringed scourge, whips out those sacrilegious chapmen, casts down their tables, throws away their baskets, scatters their heaps, and sends away their customers with smart and horror.

With what fear and astonishment did the repining offenders look upon so unexpected a justicer, while their conscience lashed them more than those cords, and the terror of that meek chastiser more affrighted them than his blows! Is this that mild and gentle Saviour that came to take upon him our stripes, and to undergo the chastisements of our peace? Is this that quiet Lamb, which before his shearers openeth not his mouth? See now how his eyes sparkle with holy anger, and dart forth beams of indignation in the faces of these guilty money-changers: see how his hands deal strokes and ruin. Yea, thus, thus it became thee, O thou gracious Redeemer of men, to let the world see that thou hast not lost thy justice in thy mercy; that there is not more lenity in thy forbearances, than rigour in that just severity; that thou canst thunder, as well as shine.

This was not thy first act of this kind; at the entrance of thy public work thou begannest so, as thou now shuttest up, with purging thine house. Once before had these offenders been whipped out of that holy place, which now they dare again defile. Shame and smart are not enough to reclaim obdured offenders. Gainful sins are not easily checked, but less easily mastered. These bold flies, where they are beaten off, will alight again: " He that is filthy, will be filthy still."

Oft yet had our Saviour been, besides this, in the temple, and often had seen the same disorder; he doth not think fit to be always whipping. It was enough thus twice to admonish and chastise them before their ruin. That God, who hates sin always, will not chide always, and strikes more seldom; but he would have those few strokes perpetual monitors; and if those prevail not, he smites but once. It is his uniform course, first the whip, and, if that speed not, then the sword.

There is a reverence due to God's house for the Owner's sake, for the service's sake. Secular and profane actions are not for that sacred roof, much less uncivil and beastly. What but holiness can become that place which is the " beauty of holiness?"

The fairest pretences cannot bear out a sin with God. Never could there be more plausible colours cast upon any act; the convenience, the necessity of provisions for the sacrifice: yet through all these do the fiery eyes of our Saviour see the foul covetousness of the priests, the fraud of the money-changers, the intolerable abuse of the temple. Common eyes may be cheated with easy pretexts; but he that looks through the heart at the face, justly answers our apologies with scourges.

None but the hand of public authority must reform the abuses of the temple. If all be out of course there, no man is barred from sorrow: the grief may reach to all, the power of reformation only to those whom it concerneth. It was but a just question, though ill propounded, to Moses, "Who made thee a judge, or a ruler?" We must all imitate the zeal of our Saviour; we may not imitate his correction. If we strike uncalled, we are justly stricken for our arrogance, for our presumption. A tumultuary remedy may prove a medicine worse than the disease.

But what shall I say of so sharp and imperious an act from so meek an agent? Why did not the priests and Levites, whose this gain partly was, abet these money-changers, and make head against Christ? why did not those multitudes of men stand upon their defence, and wrest that whip out of the hand of a seemingly weak and unarmed prophet, but instead thereof run away like sheep from before him, not daring to abide his presence, though his hand had been still? Surely, had these men been so many armies, yea, so many legions of devils, when God will astonish and chase them, they cannot have the power to stand and resist. How easy is it for him that made the heart, to put either terror or courage into it at pleasure! O Saviour, it was none of thy least miracles, that thou didst thus drive out a world of able offenders, in spite of their gain and stomachful resolutions! their very profit had no power to stay them against thy frowns. "Who hath resisted thy will?" Men's hearts are not their own: they are, they must be such as their Maker will have them.

CONTEMPLATION XXVI. — THE FIG-TREE CURSED.

WHEN in this state, our Saviour had rode through the streets of Jerusalem, that evening he lodged not there. Whether he would not, that, after so public an acclamation of the people, he might avoid all suspicion of plots or popularity (even unjust jealousies must be shunned; neither is there less wisdom in the prevention, than in the remedy of evils), or whether he could not, for want of an invitation. Hosanna was better cheap than an entertainment; and perhaps the envy of so stomached a reformation discouraged his hosts. However, he goes that evening supperless out of Jerusalem. O unthankful citizens! do ye thus part with your no less meek than glorious King? His title was no more proclaimed in your streets than your own ingratitude. If he hath purged the temple, yet your hearts are foul. There is no wonder in men's unworthiness; there is more than wonder in thy mercy, O thou Saviour of men, that wouldst yet return thither where thou wert so palpably disregarded. If they gave thee not thy supper, thou givest them their breakfast: if thou mayest not spend the night with them, thou wilt with them spend the day. O love to unthankful souls, not discourageable by the most hateful indignities, by the basest repulses? What burden canst thou shrink under, who canst bear the weight of ingratitude?

Thou that givest food to all things living, art thyself hungry. Martha, Mary, and Lazarus, kept not so poor a house, but that thou mightst have eaten something at Bethany. Whether thy haste outran thine appetite, or whether on purpose thou forbarest repast, to give opportunity to thine ensuing miracle, I neither ask nor resolve. This was not the first time that thou wast hungry. As thou wouldst be a man, so thou wouldst suffer those infirmities that belong to humanity. Thou camest to be our high-priest; it was thy act and intention, not only to intercede for thy people, but to transfer unto thyself, as their sins, so their weaknesses and complaints. Thou knowest to pity what thou hast felt. Are we pinched with want? we endure but what thou didst, we have reason to be patient · thou enduredst what we do, we have reason to be thankful.

But what shall we say to this thine early hunger? The morning, as it is privileged from excess, so from need; the stomach is not wont to rise with the body. Surely, as thine occasions were, no season was exempted from thy want: thou hadst spent the day before in the holy labour of thy reformation; after a supperless departure, thou spentest the night in prayer; no meal refreshed thy toil. What! do we think much to forbear a morsel, or to break a sleep for thee, who didst thus neglect thyself for us?

As if meat were no part of thy care, as if anything would serve to stop the mouth of hunger, thy breakfast is expected from the next tree. A fig-tree grew by the wayside, full-grown, well-spread, thick-leaved, and such as might promise enough to a remote eye: thither thou camest to seek that which thou foundest not; and, not finding what thou soughtest, as displeased with thy disappointment, cursedst that plant which deluded thy hopes. Thy breath instantly blasted that deceitful tree; it did (no otherways than the whole world must needs do) wither and die with thy curse.

O Saviour, I had rather wonder at thine actions than discuss them. If I should say, that as a man thou either knewest not, or consideredst not of this fruitlessness, it could no way prejudice thy divine omniscience; this infirmity were no worse than thy weariness or hunger: it was no more disparagement to thee to grow in knowledge than in stature; neither was it any more disgrace to thy perfect humanity, that thou, as man, knewest not all things at once, than that thou wert not in thy childhood at thy full growth. But herein I doubt not to say, it is more likely thou camest purposely to this tree, knowing the barrenness of it answerable to the season, and fore-resolving the event, that thou mightst hence ground the occasion of so instructive a miracle; likeas thou knewest Lazarus was dying, was dead, yet wouldst not seem to take notice of his dissolution, that thou mightst the more glorify thy power in his resuscitation. It was thy willing and determined disappointment, for a greater purpose.

But why didst thou curse a poor tree for the want of that fruit which the season yielded not? If it pleased thee to call for that which it could not give, the plant was innocent; and if innocent, why cursed? O Saviour, it is fitter for us to adore than to examine. We may be saucy in inquiring after thee, and fond in answering for thee.

If that season were not for a ripe fruit, yet for some fruit it was. Who knows not the nature of the fig-tree to be always bearing? That plant, if not altogether barren, yields a continual succession of increase: while one fig is ripe, another is green; the same bough can content both our taste and hope. This tree was defective in both, yielding nothing but an empty shade to the mis-hoping traveller.

Besides that, I have learned that thou, O Saviour, wert wont not to speak only, but to work parables; and what was this other than a real parable of thine? All this while hadst thou been in the world; thou hadst given many proofs of thy mercy (the earth was full of thy goodness), none of thy judgments; now, immediately before thy passion, thou thoughtest fit to give this double demonstration of thy just austerity. How else should the world have seen, thou canst be severe as well as meek and merciful? and why mightst not thou, who madest all things, take liberty to destroy a plant for thine own glory? Wherefore serve thy best creatures, but for the praise of thy mercy and justice? What great matter was it, if thou, who once saidst, " Let the earth bring forth the herb yielding seed, and the tree yielding the fruit of its own kind," shouldst now say, " Let this fruitless tree wither?" All this yet was done in figure: in this act of thine I see both an emblem, and a prophecy. How didst thou herein mean to teach thy disciples how much thou hatest an unfruitful profession, and what judgments thou meantst to bring upon that barren generation! Once before hadst thou compared the Jewish nation to a fig-tree in the midst of thy vineyard, which, after three years' expectation and culture, yielding no fruit, was by thee, the Owner, doomed to a speedy excision; now thou actest what thou then saidst. No tree abounds more with leaf and shade, no nation abounded more with ceremonial observations and semblances of piety. Outward profession, where there is want of inward truth and real practice, doth but help to draw on and aggravate judgment. Had this fig-tree been utterly bare and leafless, it had perhaps escaped the curse. Hear this, ye vain hypocrites, that care only to show well; never caring for the sincere truth of a conscionable obedience; your fair outside shall be sure to help you to a curse.

That which was the fault of this tree, is the punishment of it, fruitlessness: " Let no fruit grow on thee henceforward for ever." Had the boughs been appointed to be torn down, and the body split in pieces, the doom had been more easy, and that juicy plant might yet have recovered, and have lived to recompense this deficiency; now it shall be what it was, fruitless. Woe be to that church or soul that is punished with her own sin. Outward plagues are but favour, in comparison of spiritual judgments.

That curse might well have stood with a long continuance; the tree might have lived long, though fruitless: but no sooner is the word passed, than the leaves flag and turn yellow, the branches wrinkle and shrink, the bark discolours, the root dries, the plant withers.

O God, what creature is able to abide the blasting of the breath of thy displeasure? even the most great and glorious angels of heaven could not stand one moment before thine anger, but perished under thy wrath everlastingly. How irresistible is thy power! how dreadful are thy judgments! Lord! chastise my fruitlessness, but punish it not; at least, punish it, but curse it not, lest I wither and be consumed!

CONTEMPLATION XXVII.—CHRIST BETRAYED.

Such an eye-sore was Christ that raised Lazarus, and Lazarus whom Christ raised, to the envious priests, scribes, elders of the

Jews, that they consult to murder both: while either of them lives, neither can the glory of that miracle die, nor the shame of the oppugners.

Those malicious heads are laid together in the parlour of Caiaphas. Happy had it been for them if they had spent but half those thoughts upon their own salvation, which they mis-employed upon the destruction of the innocent. At last this results, that force is not their way; subtility and treachery must do that which should be vainly attempted by power.

Who is so fit to work this feat against Christ as one of his own? There can be no treason, where is not some trust. Who so fit among the domestics as he that bare the bag, and over-loved that which he bare? That heart, which hath once enslaved itself to red and white earth, may be made anything. Who can trust to the power of good means, when Judas, who heard Christ daily, whom others heard to preach Christ daily, who daily saw Christ's miracles, and daily wrought miracles in Christ's name, is, at his best, a thief, and ere long a traitor? That crafty and malignant spirit, which presided in that bloody council, hath easily found out a fit instrument for this hellish plot. As God knows, so Satan guesses, who are his, and will be sure to make use of his own. If Judas were Christ's domestic, yet he was Mammon's servant: he could not but hate that Master whom he formally professed to serve, while he really served that Master which Christ professed to hate. He is but in his trade, while he is bartering even for his Master: "What will ye give me, and I will deliver him unto you?" Saidst thou not well, O Saviour, "I have chosen you twelve, and one of you is a devil?" Thou, that knewest to distinguish betwixt men and spirits, callest Judas by his right name. Lo, he is become a tempter to the worst of evils.

Wretched Judas! whether shall I more abhor thy treachery, or wonder at thy folly? What will they, what can they, give thee valuable to that head which thou profferest to sale? Were they able to pay, or thou capable to receive, all those precious metals that are laid up in the secret cabins of the whole earth, how were this price equivalent to the worth of him that made them! Had they been able to fetch down those rich and glittering spangles of heaven, and to have put them into thy fist, what had this been to weigh with a God? How basely therefore dost thou speak of chaffering for him whose the world was? "What will ye give me?" Alas, what were they? what had they, miserable men, to pay for such a purchase? The time was, when he that set thee on work, could say, "All the kingdoms of the earth, and the glory of them, are mine, and I give them to whom I please; all these will I give thee." Had he now made that offer to thee in this woful bargain, it might have carried some colour of a temptation: and even thus it had been a match ill made; but for thee to tender a trade of so invaluable a commodity to these pelting petty chapmen, for thirty poor silverlings, it was no less base than wicked!

How unequal is this rate! Thou that valuedst Mary's ointment, which she bestowed upon the feet of Christ, at three hundred pieces of silver, sellest thy Master, on whom that precious odour was spent, at thirty. Worldly hearts are penny-wise, and pound-foolish: they know how to set high prices upon the worthless trash of this world; but for heavenly things, or the God that owns them, these they shamefully undervalue.

"And I will deliver him unto you." False and presumptuous Judas! it was more than thou couldst do; thy price was not more too low than the undertaking was too high. Had all the powers of hell combined with thee, they could not have delivered thy Master into the hands of men. The act was none but his own; all that he did, all that he suffered, was perfectly voluntary. Had he pleased to resist, how easily had he, with one breath, blown thee and thy accomplices down into their hell! It is no thank to thee that he would be delivered. O Saviour, all our safety, all our comfort, depends not so much upon thine act as upon thy will: in vain should we have hoped for the benefit of a forced redemption.

The bargain is driven, the price paid. Judas returns, and looks no less smoothly upon his Master and fellows, than as if he had done no disservice. What cares he? his heart tells him he is rich, though it tells him he is false. He was not now first a hypocrite. The passover is at hand; no man is so busy to prepare for it, or more devoutly forward to receive it, than Judas.

O the sottishness and obdurateness of this son of perdition! How many proofs had he formerly of his Master's omniscience! There was no day wherein he saw not, that thoughts and things absent came familiar under his cognizance, yet this miscreant dares plot a secret villany against his person, and face it: if he cannot be honest, yet he will be close. That he may be notoriously impudent, he shall know he is descried: while he thinks fit to conceal his treachery, our Saviour thinks not fit to conceal the knowledge of that treacherous conspiracy: " Verily I say unto you, that one of you shall betray me." Who would not think but that discovered wickedness should be ashamed of itself? Did not Judas (think we) blush, and grow pale again, and cast down his guilty eyes, and turn away his troubled countenance at so galling an intimation? Custom of sin steels the brow, and makes it incapable of any relenting impressions. Could the other disciples have discerned any change in any one of their faces, they had not been so sorrowfully affected with the charge. Methinks I see how intentively they bent their eyes upon each other, as if they would have looked through those windows down into their bosom; with what self-confidence, with what mutual jealousy, they perused each others' foreheads; and now, as rather thinking fit to distrust their own innocence than their Master's assertion, each trembles to say, " Lord, is it I?" It is possible, there may lurk secret wickedness in some blind corner of the heart, which we know not of: it is possible that time and temptation, working upon our corruption, may at last draw us into some such sin as we could not fore-believe. Whither may we not fall, if we be left to our own strength? It is both wise and holy to misdoubt the worst: " Lord, is it I?"

In the meantime, how fair hath Judas, all this while, carried with his fellows! Had his former life bewrayed any falsehood or misdemeanour, they had soon found where to pitch their just suspicion: now Judas goes for so honest a man, that every disciple is rather ready to suspect himself than him. It is true he was a thief; but who knows that besides his Maker? The outsides of men are no less deceitful than their hearts. It is not more unsafe to judge by outward appearances, than it is uncharitable not to judge so.

O the headstrong resolutions of wickedness, not to be checked by any opposition! Who would not but have thought, if the notice of an intended evil could not have prevented it, yet that the threats of judgment should have affrighted the boldest offender? Judas can sit by, and hear his Master say, " Woe be to the man by whom the Son of Man is betrayed! it had been better for that man never to have been born," and is no more blanked than very innocence; but thinks, what care I? I have the money; I shall escape the shame: the fact shall be close, the match gainful: it will be long ere I shall get so much by my service; if I fare well for the present, I shall shift well enough for the future. Thus secretly he claps up another bargain; he makes a covenant with death, and with hell an agreement. O Judas, didst thou ever hear aught but truth fall from the mouth of that thy divine Master? canst thou distrust the certainty of that dreadful menace of vengeance? how then durst thou persist in the purpose of so flagitious and damnable a villany? Resolved sinners run on desperately in their wicked courses, and have so bent their eyes upon the profit or pleasure of their mischievous projects, that they will not see hell lie open before them in the way.

As if that shameless man meant to outbrave all accusations, and to outface his own heart, he dares asks it too, " Master, is it I?" No disciple shall more zealously abominate that crime than he that fosters it in his bosom. Whatever the Searcher of hearts knows, by him is locked up in his own breast; to be perfidious is nothing, so he may be secret: his Master knows him for a traitor; it is not long that he shall live to complain: his fellows think him honest; all is well while he is well esteemed. Reputation is the only care of false hearts, not truth of being, not conscience of merit; so they may seem fair to men, they care not how foul they are to God.

Had our Saviour only had this knowledge at the second-hand, this boldness had been enough to make him suspect the credit of the best intelligence: who could imagine that a guilty man dared thus browbeat a just accusation? Now he, whose piercing and unfailing eyes see things as they are, not as they seem, can peremptorily convince the impudence of this hollow questionist, with a direct affirmation: " Thou hast said." Foolish traitor! couldst thou think that those blear eyes of thine would endure the beams of the sun, or that counterfeit slip, the fire? was it not sufficient for thee to be secretly vicious, but thou must presume to contest with an omniscient accuser? Hast thou yet enough? Thou supposedst thy crime unknown: to men it was so; had thy Master been no more, it had been so to him; now his knowledge argues him divine. How dost thou yet resolve to lift up thy hand against him, who knows thine offence, and can either prevent or revenge it? As yet the charge was private, either not heard, or not observed by thy fellows: it shall be at first whispered to one, and at last known to all. Bashful and penitent sinners are fit to be concealed; shame is meet for those that have none.

Curiosity of knowledge is an old disease

of human nature; besides, Peter's zeal would not let him dwell under the danger of so doubtful a crimination; he cannot but sit on thorns, till he know the man. His signs ask what his voice dare not. What law requires all followers to be equally beloved? why may not our favours be freely dispensed where we like best, without envy, without prejudice? None of Christ's train could complain of neglect. John is highest in grace: blood, affection, zeal, diligence have endeared him above his fellows. He, that is dearest in respect, is next in place: in that form of side-sitting at the table, he leaned on the bosom of Jesus. Where is more love, there may be more boldness. This secrecy and entireness privilege John to ask that safely, which Peter might not without much inconvenience and peril of a check. The beloved disciple well understands this silent language, and dares put Peter's thought into words. Love shutteth out fear. O Saviour, the confidence of thy goodness emboldens us not to shrink at any suit. Thy love, shed abroad in our hearts, bids us ask that which in a stranger were no better than presumption. Once, when Peter asked thee a question concerning John, "What shall this man do?" he received a short answer, "What is that to thee?" Now, when John asks thee a question, no less seemingly curious, at Peter's instance, "Who is it that betrays thee?" however thou mightst have returned him the same answer, since neither of their persons was any more concerned, yet thou condescendest to a mild and full, though secret, satisfaction. There was not so much difference in the men, as in the matter of the demand. No occasion was given to Peter of moving that question concerning John: the indefinite assertion of treason amongst the disciples was a most just occasion of moving John's question for Peter and himself. That which therefore was timorously demanded, is answered graciously: "He it is to whom I shall give a sop, when I have dipped it: and he gave the sop to Judas." How loath was our Saviour to name him whom he was not unwilling to design! All is here expressed by dumb signs; the hand speaks what the tongue would not. In the same language wherein Peter asked the question of John, doth our Saviour shape an answer to John: what a beck demanded, is answered by a sop.

O Saviour, I do not hear thee say, Look on whomsoever I frown, or to whomsoever I do a public affront, that is the man; but "to whomsoever I shall give a sop." Surely a by-stander would have thought this man deep in thy books, and would have construed this act as they did thy tears for Lazarus: "See how he loves him." To carve a man out of thine own dish, what could it seem to argue but a singularity of respect? yet, lo, there is but one whom thou hatest, one only traitor at thy board; and thou givest him a sop. The outward gifts of God are not always the proofs of his love; yea, sometimes are bestowed in displeasure. Had not he been a wise disciple that should have envied the great favour done to Judas, and have stomached his own preterition? So foolish are they, who, measuring God's affection by temporal benefits, are ready to applaud prospering wickedness, and to grudge outward blessings to them which are incapable of any better.

"After the sop, Satan entered into Judas." Better had it been for that treacherous disciple to have wanted that morsel: not that there was any malignity in the bread, or that the sop had any power to convey Satan into the receiver, or that, by a necessary concomitance, that evil spirit was in or with it. Favours ill used make the heart more capable of farther evil. That wicked spirit commonly takes occasion, by any of God's gifts, to assault us the more eagerly. After our sacramental morsel, if we be not the better, we are sure the worse. I dare not say, yet I dare think, that Judas, comparing his Master's words, and John's whisperings, with the tender of this sop, and finding himself thus denoted, was now so much the more irritated to perform what he had wickedly purposed. Thus Satan took advantage by the sop of a farther possession. Twice before had that evil spirit made a palpable entry into that lewd heart. First, in his covetousness and theft; those sinful habits could not be without that author of ill: then in his damnable resolution and plot of so heinous a conspiracy against Christ. Yet now, as if it were new to begin, "After the sop, Satan entered." As in every gross sin which we entertain, we give harbour so that evil spirit; so, in every degree of growth in wickedness, new hold is taken by him of the heart. No sooner is the foot over the threshold, than we enter into the house; when we pass thence into the inner rooms, we make still but a perfect entrance. At first, Satan entered to make the house of Judas's heart his own, now he enters into it as his own. The first purpose of sin opens the gates to Satan, consent admits him into the entry, full resolution of sin gives up the keys to his hands, and puts him into absolute possession. What a plain difference there is be twixt the regenerate and evil heart! Satan lays siege to the best by his temptations, and sometimes, upon battery and breach made, enters; the other admits him by willing composition. When he is entered upon the regenerate, he is entertained with perpetual skirmishes, and, by a holy violence, at last repulsed; in the other, he is plausibly received, and freely commandeth. O the admirable meekness of this Lamb of God! I see not a frown, I hear not a check, but, "What thou dost, do quickly." Why do we startle at our petty wrongs, and swell with anger, and break into furious revenges upon every occasion, when the Pattern of our patience lets not fall one harsh word upon so foul and bloody a traitor? Yea, so fairly is this carried, that the disciples as yet can apprehend no change: they innocently think of commodities to be bought, when Christ speaks of their Master sold, and, as one that longs to be out of pain, hastens the pace of his irreclaimable conspirator: "What thou dost, do quickly." It is one thing to say, Do what thou intendest, and another to say, Do quickly what thou dost. There was villany in the deed: the speed had no sin; the time was harmless, while the man and the act were wicked. O Judas, how happy had it been for thee, if thou hadst never done what thou perfidiously intendedst! but since thou wilt needs do it, delay is but a torment.

That steely heart yet relents not. The obfirmed traitor knows his way to the high priest's hall, and to the garden: the watchword is already given, "Hail, Master, and a kiss." Yet more hypocrisy; yet more presumption upon so overstrained a lenity! How knewest thou, O thou false traitor, whether that sacred cheek would suffer itself to be defiled with thine impure touch? Thou well foundest thy treachery was unmasked; thine heart could not be so false to thee as not to tell thee how hateful thou wert. Go, kiss and adore those silverlings which thou art too sure of; the Master whom thou hast sold is not thine. But, O the impudence of a deplored sinner! That tongue which hath agreed to sell his Master, dares say, Hail! and those lips, that have passed the compact of his death, dare offer to kiss him whom they had covenanted to kill. It was God's charge of old, "Kiss the Son, lest he be angry." O Saviour, thou hadst reason to be angry with this kiss: the scourges, the thorns, the nails, the spear of thy murderers, were not so painful, so piercing, as this touch of Judas: all these were in this one alone. The stabs of an enemy cannot be so grievous as the skin-deep wounds of a disciple.

CONTEMPLATION XXVIII.—THE AGONY.

WHAT a preface do I find to my Saviour's passion! A hymn, and an agony: a cheerful hymn, and an agony no less sorrowful. A hymn begins, both to raise and testify the courageous resolutions of his suffering; an agony follows, to shew that he was truly sensible of those extremities wherewith he was resolved to grapple. All the disciples bore their part in that hymn: it was fit they should all see his comfortable and divine magnanimity wherewith he entered into those sad lists: only three of them shall be allowed to be the witnesses of his agony, only those three that had been the witnesses of his glorious transfiguration. That sight had well fore-armed and prepared them for this. How could they be dismayed to see his trouble, who there saw his majesty? how could they be dismayed to see his body now sweat, which they had then seen to shine? how could they be daunted to see him now accosted with Judas and his train, whom they then saw attended with Moses and Elias? how could they be discouraged to hear the reproaches of base men, when they had heard the voice of God to him from that excellent glory: "This is my beloved Son, in whom I am well pleased?"

Now, before these eyes this sun begins to be overcast with clouds: "He began to be sorrowful, and very heavy." Many sad thoughts for mankind had he secretly hatched, and yet smothered in his own breast; now his grief is too great to keep in: "My soul is exceeding sorrowful, even unto death." O Saviour, what must thou needs feel, when thou saidst so? Feeble minds are apt to bemoan themselves upon light occasions; the grief must needs be violent, that causeth a strong heart to break forth into a passionate complaint. Woe is me, what a word is this for the Son of God! Where is that Comforter which thou promisedst to send to others? where is that thy Father of all mercies, and God of all comfort, "in whose presence is the fulness of joy, and at whose right hand there are pleasures for evermore?" where are those constant and cheerful resolutions of a fearless walking through the valley of the shadow of death? Alas! if that face were not hid from thee, whose essence could not be disunited, these pangs could not have been. The sun was withdrawn awhile, that there might be a cool, though not a dark night, as in the world, so in thy breast; withdrawn in respect of sight, not of being. It was the hardest piece of thy sufferings that thou must be disconsolate.

But to whom dost thou make this moan, O thou Saviour of men? Hard is that man driven, that is fain to complain to his inferiors. Had Peter, or James, or John, thus bewailed himself to thee, there had been ease to their soul in venting itself; thou hadst been both apt to pity them, and able to relieve them: but now, in that thou lamentest thy case to them, alas! what issue couldst thou expect? They might be astonished with thy grief; but there is neither power in their hands to free thee from those sorrows, nor power in their compassion to mitigate them. Nay, in this condition, what could all the angels of heaven, as of themselves, do to succour thee? what strength could they have but from thee? what creature can help when thou complainest? It must be only the stronger that can aid the weak.

Old and holy Simeon could fore-say to thy blessed mother, that " A sword should pierce through her soul;" but, alas! how many swords at once pierce thine! Every one of these words is both sharp and edged: " My soul is exceeding sorrowful, even unto death." What human soul is capable of the conceit of the least of those sorrows that oppressed thine? It was not thy body that suffered now; the pain of body is but as the body of pain; the anguish of the soul is as the soul of anguish. That, and in that thou sufferedst, where are they that dare so far disparage thy sorrow, as to say thy soul suffered only in sympathy with thy body? not immediately, but by participation? not in itself, but in its partner? Thou best knewest what thou feltest, and thou, that feltest thine own pain, canst cry out of thy soul. Neither didst thou say, My soul is troubled; so it often was, even to tears; but, " My soul is sorrowful:" as if it had been before assaulted, now possessed, with grief. Nor yet this in any tolerable moderation, (changes of passion are incident to every human soul), but "exceeding sorrowful." Yet there are degrees in the very extremities of evils: those, that are most vehement, may yet be capable of a remedy, at least a relaxation; thine was past these hopes: " exceeding sorrowful unto death."

What was it, what could it be, O Saviour, that lay thus heavy upon thy divine soul? Was it the fear of death? was it the forefelt pain, shame, torment, of thine ensuing crucifixion? O poor and base thoughts of the narrow hearts of cowardly and impotent mortality! How many thousands of thy blessed martyrs have welcomed no less tortures with smiles and gratulations, and have made a sport of those exquisite cruelties which their very tyrants thought unsufferable! Whence had they strength but from thee? If their weakness were thus undaunted and prevalent, what was thy power? No, no: it was the sad weight of the sin of mankind; it was the heavy burden of thy Father's wrath for our sin, that thus pressed thy soul, and wrung from thee these bitter expressions.

What can it avail thee, O Saviour, to tell thy grief to men? Who can ease thee, but He of whom thou saidst, " My Father is greater than I?" Lo, to him thou turnest; " O Father, if it be possible, let this cup pass from me."

Was not this thy prayer, O dear Christ, which in the days of thy flesh thou offeredst up with strong crying and tears, to him that was able to save thee from death? Surely this was it. Never was cry so strong; never was God thus solicited. How could heaven choose but shake at such a prayer from the power that made it? how can my heart but tremble to hear this suit from the Captain of our salvation? O thou that saidst, " I and my Father are one," dost thou suffer aught from thy Father but what thou wouldst, what thou determinedst? was this cup of thine either casual or forced? wouldst thou wish for what thou knewest thou wouldst not have possible? Far, far be these misraised thoughts of our ignorance and frailty! Thou camest to suffer, and thou wouldst do what thou camest for: yet since thou wouldst be a man, thou wouldst take all of man, save sin: it is but human, and not sinful, to be loath to suffer what we may avoid. In this velleity of thine, thou wouldst show what that nature of ours, which thou hadst assumed, could incline to wish; but, in thy resolution, thou wouldst show us what thy victorious thoughts, raised and assisted by thy divine power, had determinately pitched upon: " Nevertheless, not as I will, but as thou wilt." As man, thou hadst a will of thine own: no human soul can be perfect without that main faculty. That will, which naturally could be content to incline towards an exemption from miseries, gladly veils to that divine will, whereby thou art designed to the chastisements of our peace. Those pains, which in themselves were grievous, thou embracest as decreed; so as thy fear hath given place to thy love and obedience.

How should we have known these evils so formidable, if thou hadst not, in half a thought, inclined to deprecate them? how could we have avoided so formidable and deadly evils, if thou hadst not willingly undergone them? we acknowledge thine holy fear, we adore thy divine fortitude.

While thy mind was in this fearful agitation, it is no marvel if thy feet were not fixed. Thy place is more changed than thy thoughts: one while thou walkest to thy drowsy attendants, and stirrest up their needful vigilancy; then thou returnest to thy passionate devotions, thou fallest again upon thy face. If thy body be humbled down to the earth, thy soul is yet lower; thy prayers are so much more vehement as thy pangs are: "And being in an agony, he prayed more earnestly, and his sweat was, as it were, great drops of blood falling down to the ground." O my Saviour, what an agony am I in, while I think of thine! What pain, what fear, what strife, what horror was in thy sacred breast! how didst thou struggle under the weight of our sins, that thou thus sweatest, that thou thus bleedest! All was peace with thee; thou wert one with thy co-eternal and co-essential Father; all the angels worshipped thee; all the powers of heaven and earth awfully acknowledged thine infiniteness. It was our person that feoffed thee in this misery and torment; in that thou sustainedst thy Father's wrath, and our curse. If eternal death be unsufferable, if every sin deserve eternal death, what, O! what was it for thy soul, in this short time of thy bitter passion, to answer those millions of eternal deaths, which all the sins of all mankind had deserved from the just hand of thy Godhead! I marvel not if thou bleedest a sweat, if thou sweatest blood: if the moisture of that sweat be from the body, the tincture of it is from the soul. As there never was such another sweat, so neither can there be ever such a suffering. It is no wonder if the sweat were more than natural, when the sufferings were more than human.

O Saviour, so willing was that precious blood of thine to be let forth for us, that it was ready to prevent thy persecutors; and issued forth in those pores, before thy wounds were opened by thy tormentors. O that my heart could bleed unto thee, with true inward compunction, for those sins of mine which are guilty of this thine agony, and have drawn blood of thee, both in the garden and on the cross! Woe is me! I had been in hell, if thou hadst not been in thine agony; I had scorched, if thou hadst not sweat. O! let me abhor my own wickedness, and admire and bless thy mercy.

But, O ye blessed spirits, which came to comfort my conflicted Saviour, how did ye look upon the Son of God, when ye saw him labouring for life under these violent temptations! with what astonishment did ye behold him bleeding, whom ye adored! In the wilderness, after his duel with Satan, ye came and ministered unto him; and now in the garden, while he is in a harder combat, ye appear to strengthen him. O the wise and marvellous dispensation of the Almighty! Whom God will afflict, an angel shall relieve; the Son shall suffer, the servant shall comfort him; the God of angels droopeth, the angel of God strengthens him.

Blessed Jesu! if as man thou wouldest be "made a little lower than the angels," how can it disparage thee to be attended and cheered up by an angel! Thine humiliation would not disdain comfort from meaner hands. How free was it for thy Father to convey seasonable consolations to thine humbled soul, by whatsoever means! Behold, though thy cup shall not pass, yet it shall be sweetened. What if thou see not, for the time, thy Father's face, yet thou shalt feel his hand. What could that spirit have done without the God of spirits? O Father of mercies! thou mayest bring thine into agonies, but thou wilt never leave them there. "In the midst of the sorrows of my heart, thy comforts shall refresh my soul." Whatsoever be the means of my supportation, I know and adore the Author.

CONTEMPLATION XXIX.—PETER AND MALCHUS: OR, CHRIST APPREHENDED.

WHEREFORE, O Saviour, didst thou take those three choice disciples with thee from their fellows, but that thou expectedst some comfort from their presence? A seasonable word may sometimes fall from the meanest attendant; and the very society of those we trust, carries in it some kind of contentment. Alas! what broken reeds are men! While thou art sweating in thine agony, they are snoring securely. Admonitions, threats, entreaties, cannot keep their eyes open. Thou tellest them of danger, they will needs dream of ease; and though twice roused, as if they had purposed this neglect, they carelessly sleep out thy sorrow, and their own peril. What help hast thou of such followers? In the mount of thy transfiguration they slept, and, besides, fell on their faces, when they should behold thy glory, and were not themselves for fear. In the garden of thine agony, they fell upon the ground for drowsiness, when they should compassionate thy sorrow, and lost themselves in a stupid sleepiness.— Doubtless, even this disregard made thy prayers so much more fervent. The less comfort we find on earth, the more we seek above. Neither soughtest thou more than thou foundest: lo! thou wert heard in that which thou fearedst. An angel supplies men: that spirit was vigilant, while thy disciples were heavy; the exchange was happy.

No sooner is this good angel vanished, than that domestic devil appears: Judas comes up, and shows himself in the head of those miscreant troops. He, whose too much honour it had been to be a follower of so blessed a Master, affects now to be the leader of this wicked rabble. The sheep's fleece is now cast off; the wolf appears in his own likeness. He that would be false to his Master, would be true to his chapmen: even evil spirits keep touch with themselves. The bold traitor dare yet still mix hypocrisy with villany; his very salutations and kisses murder. O Saviour, this is no news to thee. All those who, under a show of godliness, practise impiety, do still betray thee thus. Thou, who hadst said, "One of you is a devil," didst not now say, "Avoid, Satan!" but, "Friend, wherefore art thou come?" As yet, Judas, it was not too late: had there been any the least spark of grace yet remaining in that perfidious bosom, this word had fetched thee upon thy knees. All this sunshine cannot thaw an obdurate heart. The sign is given; Jesus is taken. Wretched traitor! why wouldst thou for this purpose be thus attended? And ye foolish priests and elders! why sent you such a band, and so armed, for this apprehension? One messenger had been enough for a voluntary prisoner. Had my Saviour been unwilling to be taken, all your forces, with all the legions of hell to help them, had been too little: since he was willing to be attached, two were too many. When he did but say, "I am he," that easy breath alone routed all your troops, and cast them to the earth, whom it might as easily have cast down into hell. What if he had said, I will not be taken; where had ye been? or what could your swords and staves have done against Omnipotence?

Those disciples, that failed of their vigilance, failed not of their courage: they had heard their Master speak of providing swords, and now they thought it was time to use them: "Shall we smite?" They were willing to fight for him, with whom they were not careful to watch: but of all others, Peter was most forward; instead of opening his lips, he unsheathes his sword; and, instead of, Shall I? smites. He had noted Malchus, a busy servant of the high-priest, too ready to second Judas, and to lay his rude hands upon the Lord of life: against this man his heart rises, and his hand is lift up. That ear, which had too officiously listened to the unjust and cruel charge of his wicked master, is now severed from that worse head which it had mis-served.

I love and honour thy zeal, O blessed disciple! Thou couldst not brook wrong done to thy divine Master: had thy life been dearer to thee than his safety, thou hadst not drawn thy sword upon a whole troop. It was in earnest that thou saidst, "Though all men yet not I;" and, "Though I should die with thee, yet I will not deny thee." Lo! thou art ready to die upon him that should touch that sacred person. What would thy life now have been in comparison of renouncing him. Since thou wert so fervent, why didst thou not rather fall upon that traitor that betrayed him, than that serjeant that arrested him? Surely the sin was so much greater, as the plot of mischief is more than the execution, as a domestic is nearer than a stranger, as the treason of a friend is worse than the forced enmity of an hireling. Was it that the guilty wretch, upon the fact done, subdued himself, and shrouded his false head under the wings of darkness? was it that thou couldst not so suddenly apprehend the odious depth of that villany, and instantly hate him that had been thy old companion? was it that thy amazedness as yet conceived not the purposed issue of this seizure, and astonishedly waited for the success? was it that though Judas was more faulty, yet Malchus was more imperiously cruel? Howsoever, thy courage was awakened with thyself, and thy heart was no less sincere than thine hand was rash. "Put up again thy sword into his place: for all they that take the sword, shall perish with the sword." Good intentions are no warrant for our actions. O Saviour! thou canst at once accept of our meanings, and censure our deeds. Could there be an affection more worth encouragement than the love to such a Master? could there be a more just cause, wherein to draw his sword, than in thy quarrel? yet this love, this quarrel, cannot shield Peter from thy check; thy meek tongue smites him gently, who had furiously smote thine enemy: "Put up thy sword."

It was Peter's sword; but to put up, not to use: there is a sword which Peter may use; but it is of another metal. Our weapons are, as our warfare, spiritual: if he smite not with this, he incurs no less blame than for smiting with the other: as for this material sword, what should he do with it, that is not allowed to strike? When the Prince of Peace bade his followers sell their coat and buy a sword, he meant to insinuate the need of these arms, not their improvement, and to teach them the danger of the time, not the manner of the repulse of the danger. When they therefore said, "Behold, here are two swords," he answered, "It is enough." He said not, "Go, buy more." More had not been enough, if a bodily defence had been intended: David's tower had been too strait to yield sufficient furniture of this kind. When it comes to use, Peter's one sword is too much: "Put up thy sword." Indeed, there is a temporal sword; and that sword must be drawn, else wherefore is it? but drawn by him that bears it; and he bears it, that is ordained to be an avenger, "to execute wrath upon him that doth evil; for he bears not the sword in vain." If another man draw it, it cuts his fingers, and draws so much blood of him that unwarrantably wields it, as that "he who takes the sword shall perish with the sword." Can I choose but wonder how Peter could thus strike unwounded? how he, whose first blow made the fray, could escape hewing in pieces from that band of ruffians? This could not have been, if thy power, O Saviour, had not restrained their rage; if thy seasonable and sharp reproof had not prevented their revenge.

Now, for aught I see, Peter smarts no less than Malchus: neither is Peter's ear less smitten by the mild tongue of his Master, than Malchus' ear by the hand of Peter. Weak disciple! thou hast zeal, "but not according to knowledge:" there is not more danger in this act of thine, than inconsideration and ignorance. "The cup which my Father hath given me, shall I not drink it?" Thou drawest thy sword to rescue me from suffering. Alas! if I suffer not, what would become of thee? what would become of mankind? Where were that eternal and just decree of my Father, wherein I am a "Lamb slain from the beginning of the world?" Dost thou go about to hinder thine own and the whole world's redemption? Did I not once before call thee Satan, for suggesting to me this immunity from my passion? and dost thou now think to favour me with a real opposition to this great and necessary work? Canst thou be so weak as to imagine, that this suffering of mine is not free and voluntary? Canst thou be so injurious to me, as to think I yield, because I want aid to resist? Have I not given to thee and to the world many undeniable proofs of my omnipotence? Didst thou not see how easy it had been for me to have blown away these poor forces of my adversaries? Dost thou not know, that, if I would require it, all the glorious troops of the angels of heaven (any one whereof is more than worlds of men) would presently show themselves ready to attend and rescue me? Might this have stood with the justice of my decree, with the glory of my mercy, with the benefit of man's redemption, it had been done: my power should have triumphed over the impotent malice of my enemies: but now, since that eternal decree must be accomplished, my mercy must be approved, mankind must be ransomed; and this cannot be done without my suffering. Thy well-meant valour is no better than a wrong to thyself, to the world, to Me, to my Father.

O gracious Saviour! while thou thus smitest thy disciple, thou healest him whom thy disciple smote. Many greater miracles hadst thou done; none that bewrayed more mercy and meekness than this last cure: of all other, this ear of Malchus hath the loudest tongue to blazon the praise of thy clemency and goodness to thy very enemies. Wherefore came that man but in a hostile manner to attach thee? Besides his own, what favour was he worthy of for his master's sake? and if he had not been more forward than his fellows, why had not his skin been as whole as theirs? Yet, even amidst the throng of thine apprehenders, in the heat of their violence, in the height of their malice, and thine own instant peril of death, thou healest that unnecessary ear which had been guilty of hearing blasphemies against thee, and receiving cruel and unjust charges concerning thee. O Malchus, could thy ear be whole, and not thy heart broken and contrite with remorse, for rising up against so merciful and so powerful a hand? Could thou choose but say, O blessed Jesus! I see it was thy providence that preserved my head, when my ear was smitten; it is thine Almighty power that hath miraculously restored that ear of mine which I had justly forfeited: this head of mine shall never be guilty of plotting any further mischief against thee; this ear shall never entertain any more reproaches of thy name, this heart of mine shall ever acknowledge and magnify thy tender mercies, thy divine omnipotence? Could thy fellows see such a demonstration of power and goodness with unrelenting hearts? Unthankful Malchus! and cruel soldiers! ye were worse wounded, and felt it not. God had struck your breasts with a fearful obduration, that ye still persist in your bloody enterprise. "And they, that had laid hold on Jesus, led him away," &c.

CONTEMPLATION XXX.—CHRIST BEFORE CAIAPHAS.

That traitor, whom his own cord made soon after too fast, gave this charge concerning Jesus: "Hold him fast." Fear makes his guard cruel; they bind his hands, and think no twist can be strong enough for this Samson. Fond Jews and soldiers! if his own will had not tied him faster than your cords, though those manacles had been the stiffest cables or the strongest iron, they had been but threads of tow.

What eyes can but run over to see those hands, that made heaven and earth, wrung together and bruised with those merciless cords! to see him bound, who came to restore us to the liberty of the sons of God! to see the Lord of life contemptuously dragged through the streets, first to the house of Annas, then from thence to the house of Caiaphas, from him to Pilate, from Pilate to Herod, from Herod back again to Pilate, from Pilate to his Calvary! while, in the meantime, the base rabble and scum of the incensed multitude runs after him with shouts and scorns! The act of death hath not in it so much misery and horror as the pomp of death.

And what needed all this pageant of cruelty? Wherefore was this state and lingering of an unjust execution? Was it for that their malice held a quick dispatch too much mercy? was it for that, while they meant to be bloody, they would fain seem just? A sudden violence had been palpably murderous; now the colour of a legal process gilds over all their deadly spite, and would seem to render them honest, and the accused guilty.

This attachment, this convention of the innocent, was a true night-work: a deed of so much darkness was not for the light. Old Annas, and that wicked bench of grey-headed scribes and elders, can be content to break their sleep to do mischief: envy and malice can make noon of midnight. It is resolved he shall die; and now pretences must be sought that he may be clearly murdered. All evil begins at the sanctuary: the priests and scribes and elders are the first in this bloody scene; they have paid for this head, and now long to see what they shall have for their thirty silverlings. The bench is set in the hall of Caiaphas; false witnesses are sought for, and hired; they agree not, but shame their suborners. Woe is me! what safety can there be for innocence, when the evidence is wilfully corrupted? What state was ever so pure as not to yield some miscreants, that will either sell or lend an oath! What a brand hath the wisdom of God set upon falsehood!—even dissonance and distraction: whereas truth ever holds together, and jars not while it is itself. O Saviour! what a perfect innocence was in thy life, what an exact purity in thy doctrine, that malice itself cannot so much as devise what to slander! It were hard if hell should not find some factors upon earth. At last two witnesses are brought in, that have learned to agree with themselves, while they differ from truth; they say the same, though false: "This fellow said, I am able to destroy the temple of God, and build it again in three days." Perjured wretches! were these the terms that you heard from that sacred mouth? said he formally thus as ye have deposed? It is true, he spake of the temple, of destroying and building, of three days: but did he speak of that temple, of his own destroying of a material building in that space? He said, Destroy ye: ye say, I am able to destroy. He said, This temple of his body; ye say, The temple of God. He said, I will make up this temple of my body in three days: ye say, I am able in three days to build this material temple of God. The words were his, the sentence yours: the words were true, the evidence false: so, while you report the words, and misreport the sense, ye swear a true falsehood, and are truly forsworn. Where the resolutions are fixed, any colour will serve. Had those words been spoken, they contained no crime: had he been such as they supposed him, a mere man, the speech had carried a semblance of ostentation, no semblance of blasphemy. Yet how vehement is Caiaphas for an answer; as if those words had already battered that sacred pile, or the protestation of his ability had been the highest treason against the God of the temple. That infinite wisdom knew well how little satisfaction there could be in answers, where the sentence was determined: "Jesus held his peace." Where the asker is unworthy, the question captious, words bootless, the best answer is silence.

Erewhile, his just and moderate speech to Annas was returned with a buffet on the cheek: now, his silence is no less displeasing. Caiaphas was not more malicious than crafty: what was in vain attempted by witnesses, shall be drawn out of Christ's own mouth; what an accusation could not effect, an adjuration shall: " I adjure you by the living God, that thou tell us, whether thou be the Christ, the Son of God." Yea, this was the way to screw out a killing answer. Caiaphas, thy mouth was impure, but thy charge was dreadful. Now, if Jesus hold his peace, he is cried down for a profane disregarder of that awful name: if he answer, he is ensnared; an affirmation is death; a denial, worse than death. No, Caiaphas, thou shalt well know, it was not fear that all this while stopped that gracious mouth: thou speakest to him that cannot fear those faces he hath made; he that hath charged us to confess him, cannot but confess himself: " Jesus saith unto him, Thou hast said." " There is a time to speak, and a time to keep silence." He, that is the Wisdom of his Father, hath here given us a pattern of both. We may not so speak, as to give advantage to cavils: we may not be so silent as to betray the truth. Thou shalt have no more cause, proud and insulting Caiaphas, to complain of a speechless prisoner: now thou shalt hear more than thou demandest: " Hereafter shall ye see the Son of Man sitting on the right hand of power, and coming in the clouds of heaven." There spake my Saviour; " the voice of God, and not of man." Hear now, insolent high-priest, and be confounded. That Son of Man, whom thou seest, is the Son of God, whom thou canst not see: that Son of Man, that Son of God, that God and Man, whom thou now seest standing despicably before thy consistorial seat, in a base dejectedness, him shalt thou once, with horror and trembling, see majestically sitting on the throne of heaven, attended with thousand thousands of angels, and coming in the clouds to that dreadful judgment, wherein thyself, amongst other damned malefactors, shall be presented before that glorious tribunal of his, and adjudged to thy just torments.

Go now, wretched hypocrite, and rend thy garments; while, in the meantime, thou art worthy to have thy soul rent from thy body, for thy spiteful blasphemy against the Son of God. Onwards thy pretence is fair, and such as cannot but receive applause from thy compacted crew: " What need have we of witnesses? behold, now ye have heard his blasphemy. What think ye? And they answered and said, He is guilty of death."

What heed is to be taken of men's judgment? so light are they upon the balance, that one dram of prejudice or forestalment turns the scales. Who were these but the grave benchers of Jerusalem, the synod of the choice Rabbis of Israel? yet these pass sentence against the Lord of life: sentence of that death of his, whereby, if ever, they shall be redeemed from the murder of their sentence.

O Saviour! this is not the last time wherein thou hast received cruel dooms from them that profess learning and holiness. What wonder is it if thy weak members suffer that which was endured by so perfect a head? what care we to be judged by man's day, when thou, who art the righteous Judge of the world, wert thus misjudged by men? Now is the fury of thy malignant enemies let loose upon thee: what measure can be too hard for him that is denounced worthy of death? Now those foul mouths defile thy blessed face with their impure spittle, the venomous froth of their malice: now those cruel hands are lifted up to buffet thy sacred cheeks: now scorn and insultation triumph over thine humble patience: " Prophesy unto us, thou Christ, who it is that smote thee." O dear Jesu, what a beginning is here of a passion! There thou standest bound, condemned, spit upon, buffeted, derided by malicious sinners. Thou art bound, who camest to loose the bands of death; thou art condemned, whose sentence must acquit the world; thou art spit upon, who art " fairer than the sons of men;" thou art buffeted, " in whose mouth there was no guile;" thou art derided, " who art clothed with glory and majesty."

In the meanwhile, how can I enough wonder at thy infinite mercy, who, in the midst of all these woful indignities, couldst find a time to cast thine eyes back upon thy frail and ungrateful disciple, and in whose gracious ear Peter's cock sounded louder than all these reproaches? O Saviour! thou, who, in thine apprehension, couldst forget all thy danger, to correct and heal his over-lashing, now in the heat of thy arraignment and condemnation, canst forget thy own misery, to reclaim his error: and, by that seasonable glance of thine eye, to strike his heart with a needful remorse. He that was lately so valiant to fight for thee, now, the next morning, is so cowardly as to deny thee: he shrinks at the voice of a maid, who was not daunted with the sight of a band. O Peter, had thy slip been sudden, thy fall had been more easy; premonition aggravates thy offence: that stone was foreshowed thee whereat thou stumbledst; neither did thy warning more add to thy guilt, than thine own fore-resolution. How didst thou vow, though thou shouldst die with thy Master, not to deny him! Hadst thou said nothing, but answered with a trembling silence, thy shame had been the less. Good purposes, when they are not held, do so far turn enemies to the entertainer of them, as that they help to double both his sin and punishment.

Yet a single denial had been but easy: thine, I fear to speak it, was lined with swearing and execration. Whence then, O whence, was so vehement and peremptory disclamation of so gracious a Master? What such danger had attended thy profession of his attendance? One of thy fellows was known to the high-priest for a follower of Jesus, yet he not only came himself into that open hall, in view of the bench, but treated with the maid that kept the door to let thee in also. She knew him for what he was, and could therefore speak to thee, as brought in by his mediation: "Art not thou also one of this man's disciples?" Thou also supposest the first acknowledged such; yet what crime, what danger, was urged upon that noted disciple? What could have been more to thee? Was it that thy heart misgave thee thou mightst be called to account for Malchus? It was no thank to thee that that ear was healed; neither did there want those that would think how near that ear was to the head. Doubtless, that busy fellow himself was not far off, and his fellows and kinsmen would have been apt enough to follow thee, besides thy discipleship, upon a bloodshed, a riot, a rescue. Thy conscience hath made thee thus unduly timorous: and now, to be sure, to avoid the imputation of that affray, thou renouncest all knowledge of him in whose cause thou foughtest. Howsoever, the sin was heinous. I tremble at such a fall of so great an apostle. It was thou, O Peter, that buffetedst thy Master more than those Jews; it was to thee that he turned the cheek from them, as to view him by whom he most smarted: he felt thee afar off, and answered thee with a look; such a look as was able to kill and revive at once. Thou hast wounded me, mayst thou now say, O my Saviour! "Thou hast wounded my heart with one of thine eyes;" that one eye of thy mercy hath wounded my heart with a deep remorse for my grievous sin, with an indignation at my unthankfulness; that one glance of thine hath resolved me into the tears of sorrow and contrition.— O that mine eyes were fountains, and my cheeks channels that shall never be dried! "And Peter went out and wept bitterly."

CONTEMPLATION XXXI. — CHRIST BEFORE PILATE.

WELL worthy were these Jews to be tributary: they had cast off the yoke of their God, and had justly earned this Roman servitude. Tiberius had befriended them too well with so favourable a governor as Pilate. Had they had the power of life and death in their hands, they had not been beholden to a Heathen for a legal murder. I know not whether they more repine at this slavery, or please themselves to think how cleanly they can shift off this blood into another's hand. These great masters of Israel flock from their own consistory to Pilate's judgment-hall. The sentence had been theirs, the execution must be his; and now they hope to bear down Jesus with the stream of that frequent confluence.

But what ails you, O ye rulers of Israel, that ye stand thus thronging at the door? why do ye not go in to that public room of judicature, to call for that justice ye came for? Was it for that ye would not defile yourselves with the contagion of a Heathen roof? Holy men! your consciences would not suffer you to yield to so impure an act; your Passover must be kept, your persons must be clean: while ye expect justice from the man, ye abhor the pollution of the place. Woe to you priests, scribes, elders, hypocrites! can there be any roof so unclean as that of your own breasts? Not Pilate's walls, but your hearts, are impure. Is murder your errand, and do ye stick at a local infection? "God shall smite you, ye whited walls." Do ye long to be stained with blood, with the blood of God? and do ye fear to be defiled with the touch of Pilate's pavement? Doth so small a gnat stick in your throats, while ye swallow such a camel of flagitious wickedness? Go out of yourselves, ye false dissemblers, if ye would not be unclean. Pilate, onwards, hath more cause to fear, lest his walls should be defiled with the presence of so prodigious monsters of impiety.

That plausible governor condescends to humour their superstition: they dare not come into him; he yields to go forth to them. Even Pilate begins justly: "What accusation bring you against this man?" It is no judging of religion by the outward demeanour of men; there is more justice amongst Romans than amongst Jews. These malicious Rabbis thought it enough, that they had sentenced Jesus; no more was now expected but a speedy execution. "If he were not a malefactor, we would not have delivered him up unto thee." Civil justice must be their hangman. It is enough conviction that he is delivered up to the secular powers: themselves have judged, these other must kill. Pilate and Caiaphas have changed places: this pagan speaks that law and justice which that highpriest should have done; and that highpriest speaks those murdering incongruities which would better have beseemed the mouth of a pagan. "What needs any new trial? Dost thou know, Pilate, who we are? Is this the honour that thou givest to our sacred priesthood? is this thy valuation of our sanctity? Had the basest of the vulgar complained to thee, thou couldst but have put them to a review. Our place and holiness looked not to be distrusted. If our scrupulous consciences suspect thy very walls, thou mayest well think, there is small reason to suspect our consciences. Upon a full hearing, ripe deliberation, and exquisitely judicial proceeding, we have sentenced this malefactor to death: there needs no more from thee but thy command of execution." O monsters, whether of malice or injustice! Must he then be a malefactor whom ye will condemn? is your bare word ground enough to shed blood? whom did ye ever kill but the righteous? by whose hands perished the prophets? The word was but mistaken: ye should have said, If we had not been malefactors, we had never delivered up this innocent man unto thee.

It must needs be notoriously unjust, which very nature hath taught pagans to abhor. Pilate sees and hates this bloody suggestion and practice. Do ye pretend holiness, and urge so injurious a violence? If he be such as ye accuse him, where is his conviction? if he cannot be legally convicted, why should he die? Do ye think I may take your complaint for a crime? If I must judge for you, why have ye judged for yourselves? Could ye suppose that I would condemn any man unheard? If your Jewish laws yield you this liberty, the Roman laws yield it not to me; it is not for me to judge after your laws, but after our own. Your prejudgment may not sway me; since ye have gone so far, be ye your own carvers of justice: "Take ye him and judge him according to your law."

O Pilate, how happy had it been for thee, if thou hadst held thee there! thus thou hadst washed thy hands more clean than in all thy basons. Might law have been the rule of this judgment, and not malice, this blood had not been shed. How palpably doth their tongue bewray their heart! "It is not lawful for us to put any man to death." Pilate talks of judgment, they talk of death. This was their only aim: law was but a colour, judgment was but a ceremony; death was their drift, and without this nothing. Blood-thirsty priests and elders! it is well that this power of yours is restrained: no innocence could have been safe, if your lawless will had had no limits. It were pity this sword should be in any but just and sober hands. Your fury did not always consult with law: what law allowed your violence to Stephen, to Paul and Barnabas, and your deadly attempts against this blessed Jesus, whom ye now persecute? How lawful was it for you to procure that death which ye could not inflict? It is all the care of hypocrites to seek umbrages and pretences for their hateful purposes, and to make no other use of laws, whether divine or human, but to serve turns.

Where death is fore-resolved, there cannot want accusations. Malice is not so barren as not to yield crimes enough: "And they began to accuse him, saying, We found this fellow perverting the nation, and forbidding to give tribute unto Cæsar, saying, that he himself is Christ and king."

What accusations, saidst thou, O Pilate? heinous and capital: thou mightst have believed our confident intimation; but, since thou wilt needs urge us to particulars, know, that we come furnished with such an indictment as shall make thine ears glow to hear it. Besides that blasphemy whereof he hath been condemned by us, this man is a seducer of the people, a raiser of sedition, an usurper of sovereignty. O impudent suggestion! What marvel is it, O Saviour, if thine honest servants be loaded with slanders, when thy most innocent person escaped not so shameful criminations? Thou a perverter of the nation, who taughtst the way of God truly!—thou a forbidder of tribute, who paidst it, who prescribedst it, who provedst it to be Cæsar's due!—thou a challenger of temporal sovereignty, who avoidedst it, who renouncedst it, who professedst to come to serve! O the forehead of malice! Go, ye shameless traducers, and swear that truth is guilty of all falsehood, justice of all wrong; and that the sun is the only cause of darkness, fire of cold.

Now Pilate startles at the charge. The name of tribute, the name of Cæsar, is in mention; these potent spells can fetch him back to the common hall, and cull Jesus to the bar. There, O Saviour, standest thou meekly to be judged, who shall once come to judge the quick and the dead: then shall he, before whom thou stoodst guiltless and dejected, stand before thy dreadful Majesty, guilty and trembling.

The name of a king, of Cæsar, is justly tender and awful; the least whisper of a usurpation or disturbance is entertained with a jealous care. Pilate takes this intimation at the first bound: " Art thou then the King of the Jews?" He felt his own freehold now touched; it was time for him to stir. Daniel's weeks were now famously known to be near expiring. Many arrogant and busy spirits, as Judas of Galilee, Theudas, and that Egyptian seducer, taking that advantage, had raised several conspiracies, set up new titles to the crown, gathered forces to maintain their false claims. Perhaps Pilate supposed some such business now on foot, and therefore asks so curiously, " Art thou the King of the Jews?"

He, that was no less wisdom than truth, thought it not best either to affirm or deny at once. Sometimes it may be extremely prejudicial to speak all truths. To disclaim that title suddenly, which had been of old given him by the prophets, at his birth by the Eastern sages, and now lately at his procession by the acclaiming multitude, had been injurious to himself; to profess and challenge it absolutely, had been unsafe, and needlessly provoking. By wise and just degrees, therefore, doth he so far affirm this truth, that he both satisfies the inquirer, and takes off all peril and prejudice from his assertion. Pilate shall know him a King, but such a King as no king needs to fear, as all kings ought to acknowledge and adore: " My kingdom is not of this world." It is your mistaking, O ye earthly potentates, that is guilty of your fears. Herod hears of a King born, and is troubled; Pilate hears of a King of the Jews, and is incensed. Were ye not ignorant, ye could not be jealous; had he learned to distinguish of kingdoms, these suspicions would vanish.

There are secular kingdoms, there are spiritual: neither of these trenches upon other: your kingdom is secular, Christ's is spiritual; both may, both must stand together. His laws are divine, yours civil: his reign is eternal, yours temporal: the glory of his rule is inward, and stands in the graces of sanctification, love, peace, righteousness, joy in the Holy Ghost; yours in outward pomp, riches, magnificence: his enemies are the devil, the world, and the flesh; yours are bodily usurpers, and external peace-breakers: his sword is the power of the Word and Spirit, yours material; his rule is over the conscience, yours over bodies and lives; he punishes with hell, ye with temporal death or torture. Yea, so far is he from opposing your government, that, " by him ye kings reign:" your sceptres are his; but to maintain, not to wield, not to resist. O the unjust fears of vain men! He takes not away your earthly kingdoms, who gives you heavenly; he discrowns not the body, who crowns the soul; his intention is not to make you less great, but more happy.

The charge is so fully answered, that Pilate acquits the prisoner. The Jewish masters stand still without: their very malice dares not venture their pollution in going in to prosecute their accusation. Pilate hath examined him within, and now comes forth to these eager complainants, with a cold answer to their over-hot expectation: " I find in him no fault at all." O noble testimony of Christ's innocence, from that mouth which afterwards doomed him to death! What a difference there is betwixt a man as he is himself, and as he is the servant of others' wills! It is Pilate's tongue that says, " I find in him no fault at all:" it is the Jews' tongue in Pilate's mouth, that says, " Let him be crucified." That cruel sentence cannot blot him, whom this attestation cleareth. Neither doth he say, I find him not guilty in that whereof he is accused; but gives a universal acquittance of the whole carriage of Christ— " I find in him no fault at all." In spite of malice, innocence shall find abettors. Rather than Christ shall want witnesses, the mouth of Pilate shall be opened to his justification. How did these Jewish blood-suckers stand thunder-stricken with so unexpected a word! His absolution was their death, his acquittal their conviction. " No fault," when we have found crimes? " no fault at all," when we have condemned him for capital offences? How palpably doth Pilate give us the lie! how shamefully doth he affront our authority, and disparage our justice! So ingenuous a testimony, doubtless, exasperated the fury of these Jews: the fire of their indignation was seven-fold more intended with the sense of their repulse.

I tremble to think how just Pilate as yet was, and how soon after depraved; yea, how merciful, together with that justice. How fain would he have freed Jesus, whom he found faultless! Corrupt custom, in memory of their deliverance from Egyptian bondage, allowed to gratify the Jews with the free delivery of some one prisoner. Tradition would be encroaching: the Paschal lamb was monument enough of that happy rescue; men affect to have something of their own. Pilate was willing to take this advantage of dismissing Jesus. That he might be the more likely to prevail, he proposeth him with the choice and nomination of so notorious a malefactor-as he might justly think incapable of all mercy; Barabbas, a thief, a murderer, a seditionary, infamous for all, odious to all. Had he propounded some other innocent prisoner, he might have feared the election would be doubtful; he cannot misdoubt the competition of so prodigious a malefactor:— "Then they all cried again, Not him, but Barabbas."

O malice, beyond all example shameless and bloody! Who can but blush to think, that a heathen should see Jews so impetuously unjust, so savagely cruel? He knew there was no fault to be found in Jesus; he knew there was no crime that was not to be found in Barabbas: yet he hears, and blushes to hear them say, "Not him, but Barabbas." Was not this, think we, out of similitude of condition? Every thing affects the like to itself; every thing affects the preservation of that it liketh. What wonder is it, then, if ye Jews, who profess yourselves the murderers of that just One, favour Barabbas? O Saviour, what a killing indignity was this for thee to hear from thine own nation! Hast thou refused all glory, to put on shame and misery for their sakes? hast thou disregarded thy blessed self, to save them? and do they refuse thee for Barabbas? Hast thou said, not heaven, but earth; not sovereignty, but service; not the Gentile, but the Jew? and do they say, "Not him, but Barabbas?" Do ye thus requite the Lord, O ye foolish people and unjust? Thus were thine ears and thine eyes first crucified, and through them was thy soul wounded, even to death, before thy death, while thou sawest their rage and heardest their noise of "Crucify! crucify!"

Pilate would have chastised thee. Even that had been a cruel mercy from him; for what evil hadst thou done? But that cruelty had been true mercy to this of the Jews, whom no blood would satisfy but that of thy heart. He calls for thy fault, they call for thy punishment; as proclaiming thy crucifixion is not intended to satisfy justice, but malice, " They cried the more, Crucify him! Crucify him!"

As their clamour grew, so the president's justice declined. Those graces that lie loose and ungrounded, are easily washed away with the first tide of popularity. Thrice had that man proclaimed the innocence of him whom he now inclines to condemn, "willing to content the people." O the foolish aims of ambition! Not God, not his conscience, come into any regard, but the people. What a base idol doth the proud man adore! even the vulgar, which a base man despiseth. What is their applause but an idle wind? what is their anger but a painted fire? O Pilate, where now is thyself and thy people? whereas a good conscience would have stuck by thee for ever, and have given thee boldness, before the face of that God which thou and thy people shall never have the happiness to behold.

The Jews have played their first part; the Gentiles must now act theirs. Cruel Pilate, who knew Jesus was "delivered for envy," accused falsely, maliciously pursued, hath turned his proffered chastisement into scourging: "Then Pilate took Jesus and scourged him." Woe is me! dear Saviour! I feel thy lashes, I shrink under thy painful whippings, thy nakedness covers me with shame and confusion! That tender and precious body of thine is galled and torn with cords! Thou, that didst of late water the garden of Gethsemane with the drops of thy bloody sweat, dost now bedew the pavement of Pilate's hall with the showers of thy blood! How fully hast thou made good thy word, "I gave my back to the smiters, and my cheeks to them that plucked off the hair; I hid not my face from shame and spitting!" How can I be enough sensible of my own stripes? These blows are mine; both my sins have given them, and they give remedies to my sins: "He was wounded for our transgressions, he was bruised for our iniquities, the chastisement of our peace was upon him, and with his stripes are we healed." O blessed Jesu! why should I think strange to be scourged with tongue or hand, when I see thee bleeding? what lashes can I fear either from heaven or earth, since thy scourges have been borne for me, and have sanctified them to me? Now, dear Jesu, what a world of insolent reproaches, indignities, tortures, art thou entering into! To an ingenuous and tender disposition, scorns are torment enough; but here pain helps to perfect thy misery, their despite.

Who should be actors in this whole bloody execution but grim and barbarous soldiers, men inured to cruelty, in whose faces were written the characters of murder, whose very trade was killing, and whose looks were enough to prevent their hands! These, for the greater terror of their concourse, are called together, and whether by the connivance or the command of their wicked governor, or by the instigation of the malicious Jews, conspire to anticipate his death with scorns, which they will after inflict with violence.

O my blessed Saviour! was it not enough that thy sacred body was stripped of thy garments, and torn with bloody stripes, but that thy person must be made the mocking-stock of thine insulting enemies, thy back disguised with purple robes, thy temples wounded with a thorny crown, thy face spit upon, thy cheeks buffeted, thy head smitten, thy hand sceptred with a reed, thyself derided with wry mouths, bended knees, scoffing acclamations! Insolent soldiers! whence is all this jeering and sport, but to flout majesty? All these are the ornaments and ceremonies of a royal inauguration, which now in scorn ye cast upon my despised Saviour. Go on, make yourselves merry with this jolly pastime. Alas! long ago ye now feel whom ye scorned. Is he a king, think you, whom you thus played upon? Look upon him with gnashing and horror, whom ye looked at with mockage and insultation. Was not that head fit for your thorns, which ye now see crowned with glory and majesty? was not that hand fit for a reed, whose iron sceptre crushes you to death? was not that face fit to be spit upon, from the dreadful aspect whereof ye are ready to desire the mountains to cover you?

In the meantime, whither, O whither dost thou stoop, O thou co-eternal Son of thine eternal Father! whither dost thou abase thyself for me! I have sinned, and thou art punished; I have exalted myself, and thou art dejected; I have clad myself with shame, and thou art stripped; I have made myself naked, and thou art clothed with robes of dishonour; my head hath devised evil, and thine is pierced with thorns; I have smitten thee, and thou art smitten for me; I have dishonoured thee, and thou, for my sake, art scorned; thou art made the sport of men, for me that have deserved to be insulted on by devils!

Thus disguised, thus bleeding, thus mangled, thus deformed, art thou brought forth, whether for compassion, or for a more universal derision to the furious multitude, with an *Ecce homo*, " Behold the man!" Look upon him, O ye merciless Jews! see him in his shame, in his wounds and blood, and now see whether ye think him miserable enough! Ye see his face black and blue with buffeting, his eyes swoln, his cheeks beslabbered with spittle, his skin torn with scourges, his whole body bathed in blood, and would ye yet have more? " Behold the man!" the man whom ye envied for his greatness, whom ye feared for his usurpation: doth he not look like a king? is he not royally dressed? See whether his magnificence do not command reverence from you. Would ye wish a finer king? are ye not afraid he will wrest the sceptre out of Cæsar's hand? " Behold the man!"

Yea, and behold him well, O thou proud Pilate! O ye cruel soldiers! O ye insatiable Jews! Ye see him base, whom ye shall see glorious: the time shall surely come wherein ye shall see him in another dress. He shall shine, whom ye now see to bleed; his crown cannot be now so ignominious and painful, as it shall be once majestical and precious. Ye, who now bend your knees to him in scorn, shall see all knees, both in heaven and earth, and under the earth, to bow before him in an awful adoration; ye, that now see him with contempt, shall behold him with horror.

What an inward war do I yet find in the breast of Pilate! His conscience bids him spare, his popularity bids him kill. His wife, warned by a dream, warns him to have no hand in the blood of that just man; the importunate multitude presses him for a sentence of death. All shifts have been tried to free the man whom he hath pronounced innocent: all violent motives are urged to condemn that man whom malice pretends guilty.

In the height of this strife, when conscience and moral justice were ready to sway Pilate's distracted heart to a just dismission, I hear the Jews cry out, " If thou let this man go, thou art not Cæsar's friend." There is the word that strikes it dead. It is now no time to demur any more. In vain shall we hope, that a carnal heart can prefer the care of his soul to the care of his safety and honour, God to Cæsar. Now Jesus must die: Pilate hastes into the judgment-hall; the sentence sticks no longer in his teeth: " Let him be crucified."

Yet, how foul soever his soul shall be with this fact, his hands shall be clean: " He took water, and washed his hands before the multitude, saying, I am innocent of the blood of this just person; see ye to it." Now all is safe: I doubt not but this is expiation enough; water can wash off blood; the hands can cleanse the heart: protest thou art innocent, and thou canst not be guilty. Vain hypocrite! canst thou think to escape so? is murder of no deeper dye? canst thou dream waking, thus to avoid the charge of thy wife's dream? is the guilt of the blood of the Son of God to be wiped off with such ease? What poor shifts do foolish sinners make to beguile themselves! anything will serve to charm the conscience, when it lists to sleep.

But, O Saviour! while Pilate thinks to wash off the guilt of thy blood with water, I know there is nothing that can wash off the guilt of this his sin but thy blood. O do thou wash my soul in that precious bath, and I shall be clean! O Pilate, if that very blood which thou sheddest do not wash off the guilt of thy bloodshed, thy water doth but more defile thy soul, and intend that fire wherewith thou burnest.

Little did the desperate Jews know the weight of that blood, which they were so forward to wish upon themselves and their children. Had they deprecated their interest in that horrible murder, they could not so easily have avoided the vengeance; but now, that they fetch it upon themselves by a willing execration, what should I say, but that they long for a curse; it is pity they should not be miserable. And have ye not felt, O nation worthy of plagues! have ye not now felt what blood it was whose guilt ye affected? Sixteen hundred years are now passed since you wished yourselves thus wretched: have ye not been ever since the hate and scorn of the world? did ye not live, many of you, to see your city buried in ashes, and drowned in blood? to see yourselves no nation? Was there ever people under heaven that was made so famous a spectacle of misery and desolation? Have ye yet enough of that blood which ye called for upon yourselves and your children? Your former cruelties, uncleannesses, idolatries, cost you but some short captivities: God cannot but be just. This sin, under which ye now lie groaning and forlorn, must needs be so much greater than these, as your vastation is more; and what can that be other than the murder of the Lord of life! Ye have what ye wished: be miserable, till ye be penitent.

CONTEMPLATION XXXII.—THE CRUCIFIXION.

THE sentence of death is passed: and now, who can with dry eyes behold the sad pomp of my Saviour's bloody execution? All the streets are full of gazing spectators, waiting for this rueful sight. At last, O Saviour, there thou comest out of Pilate's gate, bearing that which shall soon bear thee. To expect thy cross, was not torment enough: thou must carry it. All this while, thou shalt not only see, but feel, thy death before it come, and must help to be an agent in thine own passion. It was not out of favour that those scornful robes being stripped off, thou art led to death in thine own clothes. So was thy face besmeared with blood, so swoln and discoloured with buffetings, that thou couldst not have been known but by thy wonted habit. Now thine insulting enemies are so much more imperiously cruel, as they are more sure of their success. Their merciless tormentings have made thee half dead already; yet now, as if they had done nothing, they begin afresh and will force thy weakened and fainting nature to new tasks of pain. The transverse of thy cross, at least, is upon thy shoulder: when thou canst scarce go, thou must carry. One kicks thee with his foot, another strikes thee with his staff, another drags thee hastily by thy cord, and more than one spur on thine unpitied weariness with angry commands of haste. O true form and 'state of a servant! All thy former actions, O Saviour, were, though painful, yet free; this, as it is in itself servile, so it is tyrannously enforced; enforced yet more upon thee, by thine own love to mankind, than by their power and despite. It was thy Father that " laid upon thee the iniquity of us all:" it was thine own mercy that caused thee to bear our sins upon the cross, and to bear the cross with the curse annexed to it, for our sins. How much more voluntary must that needs be in thee, which thou requirest to be voluntarily undertaken by us! It was thy charge, " If any man will come after me, let him deny himself, and take up his cross, and follow me." Thou didst not say, Let him bear his cross, as forcibly imposed by another; but, " Let him take up his cross," as his free burden; free in respect of his heart, not in respect of his hand: so free, that he shall willingly undergo it, when it is laid upon him; not so free as that he shall lay it upon himself unrequired. O Saviour, thou didst not snatch the cross out of the soldiers' hands, and cast it upon thy shoulder, but when they laid it upon thy neck, thou underwentest it. The constraint was theirs, the will was thine. It was not so heavy to them, or to Simon, as it was to thee; they felt nothing but the wood, thou feltest it clogged with the load of the sins of the whole world. No marvel if thou faintedst under that sad burden; thou, that bearest up the whole earth by thy word, didst sweat, and pant, and groan under this unsupportable carriage. O blessed Jesu! how could I be confounded in myself to see thee, after so much loss of blood and overtoiledness of pain, languishing under that fatal tree! And yet why should it more trouble me to see thee sinking under thy cross now, than to see thee anon hanging upon thy cross? In both thou wouldst render thyself weak and miserable, that thou mightst so much the more glorify thy infinite mercy in suffering.

It is not out of any compassion of thy misery, or care of thine ease, that Simon of Cyrene is forced to be the porter of thy cross; it was out of their own eagerness of thy dispatch; thy feeble paces were too slow for their purpose; their thirst after thy blood made them impatient of delay. If thou have wearily struggled with the burden of thy shame all along the streets of Jerusalem, when thou comest once past the gates, a helper shall be deputed to thee: the expedition of thy death was more sweet to them than the pain of a lingering passage. What thou saidst to Judas, they say to the executioner: "What thou doest, do quickly." While thou yet livest, they cannot be quiet, they cannot be safe: to hasten thine end, they lighten thy carriage.

Hadst thou done this out of choice, which thou didst out of constraint, how I should have envied thee, O Simon of Cyrene, as too happy in the honour to be the first man that bore that cross of thy Saviour, wherein millions of blessed martyrs have, since that time, been ambitious to succeed thee? Thus to bear thy cross for thee, O Saviour, was more than to bear a crown for thee. Could I be worthy to be thus graced by thee, I should pity all other glories.

While thou thus passest, O dear Jesu! the streets and ways resound not all with one note. If the malicious Jews and cruel soldiers insulted upon thee, and either haled or railed thee on with a bitter violence, thy faithful followers were no less loud in their moans and ejulations. neither would they endure, that the noise of their cries and lamentations should be drowned with the clamour of those reproaches: but especially thy blessed mother, and those other zealous associates of her own sex, were most passionate in their wailings. And why should I think that all that devout multitude which so lately cried Hosanna in the streets, did not also bear their part in these public condolings? Though it had not concerned thyself, O Saviour, thine ears had been still more open to the voice of grief than of malice; and so thy lips also are open to the one, shut to the other: "Daughters of Jerusalem, weep not for me, but weep for yourselves and for your children." Who would not have thought, O Saviour, that thou shouldst have been wholly taken up with thine own sorrows? The expectation of so bitter a death had been enough to have overwhelmed any soul but thine: yet even now can thy gracious eye find time to look beyond thine own miseries, at theirs; and to pity them, who, insensible of their own ensuing condition, mourned for thine now present. They see thine extremity; thou foreseest theirs: they pour out their sorrow upon thee; thou divertest it upon themselves. We, silly creatures, walk blindfolded in this vale of tears, and little know what evil is towards us: only what we feel we know; and while we feel nothing, can find leisure to bestow our commiseration on those who need it, perhaps, less than ourselves. Even now, O Saviour, when thou wert within the view of thy Calvary, thou canst foresee and pity the vastation of thy Jerusalem, and givest a sad prophecy of the imminent destruction of that city, which lately had cost thee tears, and now shall cost thee blood. It is not all the indign cruelty of men that can rob thee of thy mercy.

Jerusalem could not want malefactors, though Barabbas was dismissed. That all this execution might seem to be done out of the zeal of justice, two capital offenders, adjudged to their gibbet, shall accompany thee, O Saviour, both to thy death and in it. They are led manacled after thee, as less criminal: no stripes had disabled them from bearing their own crosses. Long ago was this unmeet society foretold by thine evangelical seer: "He was taken from prison and from judgment; he was cut off out of the land of the living; he made his grave with the wicked." O blessed Jesu! it had been disparagement enough to thee to be sorted with the best of men, since there is much sin in the perfectest, and there could be no sin in thee; but to be matched with the scum of mankind, whom vengeance would not let live, is such an indignity as confounds my thoughts. Surely there is no angel in heaven, but would have been proud to attend thee; and what could the earth afford worthy of thy train? Yet malice hath suited thee with company next to hell, that their viciousness might reflect upon thee, and their sin might stain thine innocence. Ye are deceived, O ye fond judges! this is the way to grace your dying malefactors; this is not the way to disgrace him whose guiltlessness and perfection triumphed over your injustice: his presence was able to make your thieves happy: their presence could no more blemish him than your own. Thus guarded, thus attended, thus accompanied, art thou, blessed Jesu, led to that loathsome and infamous hill, which now thy last blood shall make sacred;

now thou settest thy foot upon that rising ground which shall prevent thine Olivet, whence thy soul shall first ascend into thy glory.

There, while thou art addressing thyself for thy last act, thou art presented with that bitter and farewell-potion wherewith dying malefactors were wont to have their senses stupified, that they might not feel the torments of their execution. It was but the common mercy of men to alleviate the death of offenders; since the intent of their last doom is not so much pain as dissolution.

That draught, O Saviour, was not more welcome to the guilty, than hateful unto thee. In the vigour of all thine inward and outward senses, thou wouldst encounter the most violent assaults of death, and scornedst to abate the least touch of thy quickest apprehension. Thou well knewest that the work thou wentest about would require the use of all thy powers: it was not thine ease that thou soughtest, but our redemption; neither meantst thou to yield to thy last enemy, but to resist and to overcome him: which, that thou mightst do the more gloriously, thou challengedst him to do his worst; and, in the meantime, wouldst not disfurnish thyself of any of thy powerful faculties. This greatest combat that ever was shall be fought on even hand; neither wouldst thou steal that victory which now thou achievedst over death and hell. Thou didst but touch at this cup: it is a far bitterer than this, that thou art now drinking up to the dregs. Thou refusedst that which was offered thee by men, but that which was mixed by thine eternal Father, though mere gall and wormwood, thou didst drink up to the last drop. And therein, O blessed Jesu! lies all our health and salvation. I know not, whether I do more suffer in thy pain, or joy in the issue of thy suffering.

Now, even now, O Saviour, art thou entering into those dreadful lists, and now art thou grappling with thy last enemy: as if thou hadst not suffered till now, now thy bloody passion begins; a cruel expoliation begins that violence. Again do these grim and merciless soldiers lay their rude hands upon thee, and strip thee naked; again are those bleeding weals laid open to all eyes; again must thy sacred body undergo the shame of an abhorred nakedness. Lo! thou that clothest man with raiment, beasts with hides, fishes with scales and shells, earth with flowers, heaven with stars, art despoiled of clothes, and standest exposed to the scorn of all beholders. As the first Adam entered into his Paradise, so dost thou, the second Adam, into thine, naked; and as the first Adam was clothed with innocence when he had no clothes, so wert thou, the second, too: and more than so; —thy nakedness, O Saviour, clothes our souls, not with innocence only, but with beauty. Hadst not thou been naked, we had been clothed with confusion. O happy nakedness, whereby we are covered from shame! O happy shame, whereby we are invested with glory! All the beholders stand wrapped with warm garments; thou only art stripped to tread the wine-press alone. How did thy blessed mother now wish her veil upon thy shoulders! and that disciple, who lately ran from thee naked, wished in vain that his loving pity might do that for thee, which fear forced him to do for himself!

Shame is succeeded with pain. O the torment of the cross! Methinks I see and feel, how, having fastened the transverse to the body of that fatal tree, and laid it upon the ground, they racked and strained thy tender and sacred limbs, to fit the extent of their fore-appointed measure; and having tentered out thine arms beyond their natural reach, how they fastened them with cords, till those strong iron nails, which were driven up to the head through the palms of thy blessed hands, had not more firmly than painfully fixed thee to the gibbet. The tree is raised up, and now, not without a vehement concussion, settled in the mortise. Woe is me! how are thy joints and sinews torn, and stretched till they crack again, by this torturing distension! How doth thine own weight torment thee, while thy whole body rests upon this forced and dolorous hold, till thy nailed feet bear their part in a no less afflictive supportation! How did the rough iron pierce thy soul, while, passing through those tender and sensible parts, it carried thy flesh before it, and as it were rivetted it to that shameful tree!

There now, O dear Jesu! there thou hangest between heaven and earth, naked, bleeding, forlorn, despicable, the spectacle of miseries, the scorn of men! Be abashed, O ye heavens and earth! and all ye creatures, wrap up yourselves in horror and confusion, to see the shame and pain and curse of your most pure and omnipotent Creator! How could ye subsist, while he thus suffers, in whom ye are? O Saviour, didst thou take flesh for our redemption, to be thus indignly used, thus mangled, thus tortured? Was this measure fit to be offered to that sacred body, that was conceived by the Holy Ghost, of the pure substance of an immaculate virgin? Woe is me! that which was unspotted with sin is all blemished with human cruelty, and so wofully disfigured, that the blessed mother that bore thee could not now have known thee: so bloody were thy temples, so swoln and discoloured was thy face, so was the skin of thy whole body streaked with red and blue stripes, so did thy thorny diadem shade thine heavenly countenance, so did the streams of thy blood cover and deform all thy parts! The eye of sense could not distinguish thee, O dear Saviour! in the nearest proximity to thy cross: the eye of faith sees thee in all this distance; and by how much more ignominy, deformity, pain, it finds in thee, so much more it admires the glory of thy mercy. Alas! is this the head that is decked by thine eternal Father with a crown of pure gold, of immortal and incomprehensible majesty, which is now bushed with thorns? Is this the eye that saw the heavens opened, and the Holy Ghost descending upon that head, that saw such resplendence of heavenly brightness on mount Tabor, which now begins to be over-clouded with death? Are these the ears that heard the voice of thy Father owning thee out of heaven, which now tingle with buffetings, and glow with reproaches, and bleed with thorns? Are these the lips that "spake as never man spake, full of grace and power," that called out dead Lazarus, that ejected the stubbornest devils, that commanded the cure of all diseases, which now are swoln with blows, and discoloured with blueness and blood? Is this the face that should be " fairer than the sons of men," which the angels of heaven so desired to see, and can never be satisfied with seeing, that is thus foul with the nasty mixtures of sweat and blood, and spittings on? Are these the hands that " stretched out the heavens as a curtain," that by their touch healed the lame, the deaf, the blind, which are now bleeding with the nails? Are these the feet which walked lately upon the liquid pavement of the sea, before whose footstool all the nations of the earth are bidden to worship, that are now so painfully fixed to the cross? O cruel and unthankful mankind, that offered such measure to the Lord of life! O infinitely merciful Saviour, that wouldst suffer all this for unthankful mankind! That fiends should do these things to guilty souls, it is, though terrible, yet just; but that men should do thus to the blessed Son of God, it is beyond the capacity of our horror!

Even the most hostile dispositions have been only content to kill; death hath sated the most eager malice: thine enemies, O Saviour, held not themselves satisfied, unless they might enjoy thy torment. Two thieves are appointed to be thy companions in death: thou art designed to the midst, as the chief malefactor; on whether hand soever thou lookest, thine eye meets with a hateful partner. But, O blessed Jesu! how shall I enough admire and celebrate thy infinite mercy, who madest so happy a use of this Jewish despite, as to improve it to the occasion of the salvation of one, and the comfort of millions! Is not this, as the last, so the greatest speciality of thy wonderful compassion, to convert that dying thief? with those nailed hands to snatch a soul out of the mouth of hell? Lord, how I bless thee for this work! How do I stand amazed at this above all other the demonstrations of thy goodness and power! The offender came to die; nothing was in his thoughts but his guilt and torment: while he was yet in his blood, thou saidst, This soul shall live. Ere yet the intoxicating potion could have time to work upon his brain, thy Spirit infuses faith into his heart. He, that before had nothing in his eye but present death and torture, is now lifted up above his cross in a blessed ambition: " Lord, remember me when thou comest into thy kingdom." Is this the voice of a thief, or of a disciple? Give me leave, O Saviour, to borrow thine own words ; " Verily, I have not found so great faith, no not in all Israel." He saw thee hanging miserably by him, and yet styles thee Lord; he saw thee dying, yet talks of thy kingdom; he felt himself dying, yet talks of a future remembrance. O faith stronger than death; that can look beyond the cross at a crown! beyond dissolution, at a remembrance of life and glory! Which of thine eleven was heard to speak so gracious a word to thee in these thy last pangs? After thy resurrection, and knowledge of thine impassible condition, it was not strange for them to talk of thy kingdom; but, in the midst of thy shameful death, for a dying malefactor to speak of thy reigning, and to implore thy remembrance of himself in thy kingdom, it is such an improvement of faith as ravisheth my soul with admiration. O blessed thief, that hast thus happily stolen heaven! How worthy hath thy Saviour made thee to be a partner of his sufferings, a pattern of undauntable belief, a spectacle of unspeakable mercy! " This day shalt thou be with me in Paradise." Before, I wondered at thy faith; now, I envy at thy felicity. Thou cravedst a remembrance; thy

Saviour speaks of a present possession—"This day:" thou suedst for remembrance, as a favour to the absent; thy Saviour speaks of thy presence with him: thou speakest of a kingdom; thy Saviour of Paradise. As no disciple could be more faithful, so no saint could be happier. O Saviour, what a precedent is this of thy free and powerful grace! Where thou wilt give, what unworthiness can bar us from mercy? when thou wilt give, what time can prejudice our vocation? who can despair of thy goodness, when he, that in the morning was posting towards hell, is in the evening with thee in Paradise? Lord, he could not have spoken this to thee, but by thee, and from thee. What possibility was there for a thief to think of thy kingdom, without thy Spirit? That good Spirit of thine breathed upon this man, breathed not upon his fellow: their trade was alike, their sin was alike, their state alike, their cross alike; only thy mercy makes them unlike: one is taken, the other is refused. Blessed be thy mercy in taking one! blessed be thy justice in leaving the other! Who can despair of that mercy? who can but tremble at that justice?

Now, O ye cruel priests and elders of the Jews, ye have full leisure to feed your eyes with the sight ye so much longed for: there is the blood ye purchased, and is not your malice yet glutted? is not all this enough, without your taunts, and scoffs, and sports, at so exquisite a misery? The people, the passengers, are taught to insult where they should pity. Every man hath a scorn ready to cast at a dying innocent. A generous nature is more wounded with the tongue than with the hand. O Saviour, thine ear was more painfully pierced than thy brows, or hands, or feet. It could not but go deep into thy soul, to hear these bitter and girding reproaches from them thou camest to save.

But, alas! what flea-bitings were these, in comparison of those inward torments which thy soul felt in the sense and apprehension of thy Father's wrath, for the sins of the whole world, which now lay heavy upon thee for satisfaction! This, O this was it, that pressed thy soul, as it were, to the nethermost hell. While thine eternal Father looked lovingly upon thee, what didst thou, what neededst thou, to care for the frowns of men or devils? but when he once turned his face from thee, or bent his brows upon thee, this, this was worse than death. It is no marvel now, if darkness were upon the face of the whole earth, when thy Father's face was eclipsed from thee by the interposition of our sins. How should there be light in the world without, when the God of the world, the Father of lights, complains of the want of light within? That word of thine, O Saviour, was enough to fetch the sun down out of heaven, and to dissolve the whole frame of nature, when thou criedst, "My God, my God, why hast thou forsaken me?" O what pangs were these, dear Jesu, that drew from thee this complaint! Thou well knewest, nothing could be more cordial to thine enemies than to hear this sad language from thee: they could see but the outside of thy sufferings; never could they have conceived so deep an anguish of thy soul, if thy own lips had not expressed it. Yet, as not regarding their triumph, thou thus pouredst out thy sorrow; and, when so much is uttered, who can conceive what is felt?

How is it then with thee, O Saviour, that thou thus astonishest men and angels with so woful a quiritation? Had thy God left thee? Thou not long since saidst, "I and my Father are one;" are ye now severed? Let this thought be as far from my soul, as my soul from hell. No more can thy blessed Father be separated from thee, than from his own essence. His union with thee is eternal; his vision was intercepted; he could not withdraw his presence, he would withdraw the influence of his comfort. Thou, the second Adam, stoodst for mankind upon this tree of the cross, as the first Adam stood and fell for mankind under the tree of offence. Thou barest our sins; thy Father saw us in thee, and would punish us in thee, thee for us: how could he but withhold comfort, where he intended chastisement? Herein, therefore, he seems to forsake thee for the present, in that he would not deliver thee from that bitter passion which thou wouldst undergo for us. O Saviour, hadst thou not been thus forsaken, we had perished; thy dereliction is our safety: and, however our narrow souls are not capable of the conceit of thy pain and horror, yet we know there can be no danger in the forsaking, while thou canst say, "My God." He is so thy God, as he cannot be ours; all our right is by adoption, thine by nature; thou art one with him in eternal essence, we come in by grace and merciful election: yet, while thou shalt enable me to say, "My God," I shall hope never to sink under thy desertions.

But, while I am transported with the sense of thy sufferings, O Saviour, let me not forget to admire those sweet mercies of thine which thou pouredst out upon thy persecutors. They rejoice in thy death, and triumph in thy misery, and scoff at thee in both. Instead of calling down fire from heaven upon them, thou heapest coals of fire upon their heads: "Father, forgive them, for they know not what they do." They blaspheme thee, thou prayest for them; they scorn, thou pitiest; they sin against thee, thou prayest for their forgiveness; they profess their malice, thou pleadest their ignorance. O compassion without example, without measure, fit for the Son of God, the Saviour of men! Wicked and foolish Jews! ye would be miserable, he will not let you; ye would fain pull upon yourselves the guilt of his blood, he deprecates it; ye kill, he sues for your remission and life. His tongue cries louder than his blood, "Father, forgive them." O Saviour, thou couldst not but be heard. Those, who out of ignorance and simplicity thus persecuted thee, find the happy issue of thine intercession. Now I see whence it was, that three thousand souls were converted soon after, at one sermon. It was not Peter's speech, it was thy prayer, that was thus effectual. Now they have grace to know and confess whence they have both forgiveness and salvation, and can recompense their blasphemies with thanksgiving. What sin is there, Lord, whereof I can despair of the remission? or what offence can I be unwilling to remit, when thou prayest for the forgiveness of thy murderers and blasphemers?

There is no day so long but hath his evening. At last, O blessed Saviour, thou art drawing to an end of these painful sufferings; when spent with toil and torment, thou criest out, "I thirst." How shouldst thou do other, O dear Jesu, how shouldst thou do other than thirst? The night thou has spent in watching, in prayer, in agony, in thy conveyance from the garden to Jerusalem, from Annas to Caiaphas, from Caiaphas to Pilate: in thy restless answers, in buffetings and stripes; the day in arraignments, in haling from place to place, in scourgings, in stripping, in robing and disrobing, in bleeding, in tugging under thy cross, in woundings and distention, in pain and passion: no marvel if thou thirstedst. Although there was more in this drought than thy need, it was no less requisite thou shouldst thirst, than that thou shouldst die; both were upon the same predetermination, both upon the same prediction. How else should that word be verified, (Psal. xxii. 14, 15), "All my bones are out of joint, my heart is like wax, it is melted in the midst of my bowels; my strength is dried up like a potsherd, and my tongue cleaveth to my jaws; and thou hast brought me into the dust of death?" Had it not been to make up taht word, whereof one jot cannot pass, though thou hadst felt this thirst, yet thou hadst not bewrayed it. Alas! what could it avail to bemoan thy wants to insulting enemies, whose sport was thy misery? how should they pity thy thirst, that pitied not thy bloodshed? It was not their favour that thou expectedst herein, but their conviction. O Saviour, how can we, thy sinful servants, think much to be exercised with hunger and thirst, when we hear thee thus complain?

Thou, that not long since proclaimedst in the temple, "If any man thirst, let him come to me, and drink: He that believeth in me, out of his belly shall flow rivers of living waters," now thyself thirstest. Thou, in whom we believe, complainest to want some drops: thou hadst the command of all the waters, both above the firmament and below it, yet thou wouldst thirst. Even so, Lord, thou, that wouldst die for us, wouldst thirst for us. O give me to thirst after those waters which thou promisest, whatever become of those waters which thou wouldst want. The time was, when, craving water of the Samaritan, thou gavest better than that thou askedst. O give me to thirst after that more precious water! and so do thou give me of that water of life, that I may never thirst again!

Blessed God how marvellously dost thou contrive thine own affairs! Thine enemies, while they would despite thee, shall unwittingly justify thee, and convince themselves. As thou foresaidst, "In thy thirst, they gave thee vinegar to drink." Had they given thee wine, thou hadst not taken it: the night before, thou hadst taken leave of that comfortable liquor, resolving to drink no more of that sweet juice, till thou shouldst drink it new with them in thy Father's kingdom. Had they given thee water, they had not fulfilled that prediction, whereby they were self-condemned. I know not now, O dear Jesu, whether this last draught of thine were more pleasing to thee, or more distasteful: distasteful in itself, for what liquor could be equally harsh; pleasing, in that it made up those sufferings thou wert to endure, and those prophecies thou wert to fulfil.

Now there is no more to do: thy full consummation of all predictions, of all types and ceremonies, of all sufferings, of all satisfactions, is happily both effected and proclaimed: nothing now remains but a voluntary, sweet, and heavenly resignation of thy blessed soul into the hands of thine eternal Father, and a bowing of thine head for the change of a better crown, and a peaceable obdormition in thy bed of ease and honour, and an instant entrance into rest, triumph, glory.

And now, O blessed Jesu, how easily have carnal eyes all this while mistaken the passages and intentions of this thy last and most glorious work! Our weakness could hitherto see nothing here but pain and ignominy; now my better enlightened eyes see, in this elevation of thine, both honour and happiness. Lo! thou that art the Mediator betwixt God and man, the Reconciler of heaven and earth, art lift up betwixt earth and heaven, that thou mightest accord both. Thou, that art the great Captain of our salvation, the Conqueror of all the adverse powers of death and hell, art exalted upon this triumphal chariot of the cross, that thou mightest trample upon death, and drag all those infernal principalities manacled after thee. Those arms, which thine enemies meant violently to extend, are stretched forth for the embracing of all mankind that shall come in, for the benefit of thine all-sufficient redemption. Even while thou sufferest, thou reignest. O the impotent madness of silly men! they think to disgrace thee with wry faces, with tongues put out, with bitter scoffs, with poor wretched indignities; when, in the mean time, the heavens declare thy righteousness, O Lord, and the earth shows forth thy power. The sun pulls in his light, as not abiding to see the sufferings of his Creator; the earth trembles under the sense of the wrong done to her Maker; the rocks rend, the veil of the temple tears from the top to the bottom; shortly all the frame of the world acknowledges the dominion of that Son of God, whom man despiseth.

Earth and hell have done their worst. O Saviour! thou art in thy Paradise, and triumphest over the malice of men and devils: the remainders of thy sacred person are not yet free. The soldiers have parted thy garments, and cast lots upon thy seamless coat. those poor spoils cannot so much enrich them as glorify thee, whose scriptures are fulfilled by their barbarous sortitions. The Jews sue to have thy bones divided, but they sue in vain. No more could thy garments be whole, than thy body could be broken: one inviolable decree overrules both. Foolish executioners! ye look up at that crucified body, as if it were altogether in your power and mercy; nothing appears to you but impotence and death: little do ye know what an irresistible guard, there is upon that sacred corpse, such as, if all the powers of darkness shall band against, they shall find themselves confounded. In spite of all the gates of hell, that word shall stand: "Not a bone of him shall be broken."

Still the infallible decree of the Almighty leads you on to his own ends, through your own ways. Ye saw him already dead whom ye came to dispatch; those bones therefore shall be whole, which ye had no power to break. But yet, that no piece, either of your cruelty, or of divine prediction, may remain unsatisfied, he, whose bones may not be impaired, shall be wounded in his flesh; he, whose ghost was yielded up, must yield his last blood: "One of the soldiers with a spear pierced his side, and forthwith there came out blood and water." Malice is wont to end with life; here it overlives it. Cruel man! what means this so late wound? what commission hadst thou for this bloody act? Pilate had given leave to break the bones of the living, he gave no leave to gore the side of the dead? What wicked supererogation is this! what a superfluity of maliciousness! To what purpose did thy spear pierce so many hearts in that one? why wouldst thou kill a dead man? Methinks the blessed Virgin, and those other passionate associates of hers, and the disciple whom Jesus loved, together with the other of his fellows, the friends and followers of Christ, and especially he that was so ready to draw his sword upon the troop of his Master's apprehenders, should have work enough to contain themselves within the bounds of patience at so savage a stroke; their sorrow could not choose but turn to indignation, and their hearts could not but rise, as even mine doth now, at so impertinent a villany. How easily could I rave at that rude hand! But, O God, when I look up to thee, and consider how thy holy and wise providence so overrules the most barbarous actions of men, that, besides their will, they turn beneficial, I can at once hate them, and bless thee. This very wound hath a mouth to speak the Messiahship of my Saviour, and the truth of thy Scripture; "They shall look at him whom they have pierced." Behold now the second Adam sleeping, and out of his side formed the mother of the living, the evangelical church! Behold the Rock which was smitten, and the waters of life gushed forth! Behold the Fountain that is set open to the house of David, for sin and for uncleanness; a fountain not of water only, but of blood too! O Saviour, by thy water we are washed, by thy blood we are redeemed. Those two sacraments, which thou didst institute alive, flow also from thee dead, as the last memorials of thy love to thy church; the water of baptism, which is the laver of regeneration; "The blood of the New Testament shed for remission of sins;" and these, together with the Spirit that gives life to them both, are the three witnesses on earth, whose attestation cannot fail us. O precious and sovereign wound, by which our souls are healed! Into this cleft of the rock let my dove fly and enter, and there safely hide herself from the talons of all the birds of prey.

It could not be but that the death of Christ, contrived and acted at Jerusalem in so solemn a festival, must needs draw a world of beholders: the Romans, the centurion and his band, were there as actors, as supervisors of the execution. Those strangers were no otherwise engaged, than as they that would hold fair correspondence with the citizens where they were engarrisoned; their freedom from prejudice rendered them more capable of an ingenuous construction of all events: "Now, when the centurion, and they that were with him that watched Jesus, saw the earthquake, and the things that were done, they feared greatly, and glorified God, and said, Truly this was the Son of God."

What a marvellous concurrence is here of strong irrefragable conviction! Meekness in suffering, prayer for his murderers, a faithful resignation of his soul into the hands of his heavenly Father, the sun eclipsed, the heavens darkened, the earth trembling, the graves open, the rocks rent, the veil of the temple torn: who could go less than this, "Truly this was the Son of God?" He suffers patiently; this is through the power of grace: many good men have done so through his enabling. The frame of nature suffers with him; this is proper to the God of nature, the Son of God.

I wonder not that these men confessed thus; I wonder that any spectator confessed it not: these proofs were enough to fetch all the world upon their knees, and to nave made all mankind converts. But all hearts are not alike; no means can work upon the wilfully obdured. Even after this, the soldier pierced that blessed side; and while pagans relented, Jews continued impenitent. Yet, even of that nation, those beholders, whom envy and partiality had not interested in this slaughter, were stricken with just astonishment, and smote their breasts, and shook their heads, and, by passionate gesture, spake what their tongues durst not. How many must there needs be, in this universal concourse, of them whom he had healed of diseases, or freed from devils, or miraculously fed, or some way obliged in their persons or friends! These, as they were deeply affected with the mortal indignities which were offered to their acknowledged Messiah, so they could not but be ravished with wonder at those powerful demonstrations of the Deity of him in whom they believed, and strangely distracted in their thoughts, while they compared those sufferings with that Omnipotence. As yet their faith and knowledge were but in the bud, or in the blade. How could they choose but think, Were he not the Son of God, how could these things be? And if he were the Son of God, how could he die? His resurrection, his ascension, should soon after perfect their belief; but, in the meantime, their hearts could not but be conflicted with thoughts hard to be reconciled. Howsoever, they glorify God, and stand amazed at the expectation of the issue

But, above all other, O thou blessed Virgin, the holy mother of our Lord, how many swords pierced thy soul, while, standing close by his cross, thou sawest thy dear son and Saviour thus indignly used, thus stripped, thus stretched, thus nailed, thus bleeding, thus dying, thus pierced! How did thy troubled heart now recount what the angel Gabriel had reported to thee from God, in the message of thy blessed conception of that Son of God! How didst thou think of the miraculous formation of that thy divine burden by the power of the Holy Ghost! How didst thou recall those prophecies of Anna and Simeon concerning him, and all those supernatural works of his, the irrefragable proofs of his Godhead! and, laying all these together, with the miserable infirmities of his passion, how wert thou crucified with him! The care that he took for thee in the extremity of his torments, could not choose but melt thy heart into sorrow: but O, when in the height of his pain and misery, thou heardst him cry out, "My God, my God, why hast thou forsaken me?" what a cold horror possessed thy soul! I cannot now wonder at thy qualms and swoonings; I could rather wonder that thou survivedst so sad an hour. But when, recollecting thyself, thou sawest the heavens to bear a part with thee in thy mourning, and feltest the earth to tremble no less than thyself, and foundest that the dreadful concussion of the whole frame of nature proclaimed the Deity of him that would thus suffer and die, and rememberedst his frequent predictions of drinking this bitter cup, and of being baptized thus in blood; thou begannest to take heart, and to comfort thyself with the assured expectation of the glorious issue. More than once had he foretold thee this his victorious resurrection. He, who had openly professed Jonas for his type, and had fore-promised in three days to raise up the ruined temple of his body, had doubtless given more full intimation unto thee, who hadst so great a share in that sacred body of his. "The just shall live by faith." Lo! that faith of thine in his ensuing resurrection, and in his triumph over death, gives thee life, and cheers up thy drooping soul, and bids it, in a holy confidence, to triumph over all thy fears and sorrows; and him, whom thou seest dead and despised, represents unto thee living, immortal, glorious.

CONTEMPLATION XXXIII. THE RESURRECTION.

Grace doth not ever make show where it is. There is much secret riches both in the earth and sea, which never eye saw. I never heard any news till now of Joseph of Arimathea; yet was he eminently both rich and wise and good; a worthy, though close, disciple of our Saviour. True faith may be wisely reserved, but will not be cowardly. Now he puts forth himself, and dares beg the body of Jesus. Death is wont to end all quarrels. Pilate's heart tells him he hath done too much already, in sentencing an innocent to death: no doubt that centurion had related unto him the miraculous symptoms of that passion. He, that so unwillingly condemned innocence, could rather have wished that just man alive, than have denied him dead. The body is yielded and taken down; and now that which hung naked upon the cross is wrapped in fine linen; that which was soiled with sweat and blood is curiously washed and embalmed. Now even Nicodemus comes in for a part, and fears not the envy of a good profession. Death hath let that man loose, whom the law formerly overawed with restraint. He hates to be a night-bird any longer, but boldly flies forth, and looks upon the face of the sun, and will be now as liberal in his odours as he was before niggardly in his confession. O Saviour! the earth was thine, and the fulness of it: yet as thou hadst not a house of thine own while thou livedst, so thou hadst not a grave when thou wert dead. Joseph, that rich counsellor, lent thee his; lent it so as it should never be restored: thou tookst it but for a while; but that little touch of that sacred corpse of thine made it too good for the owner.

O happy Joseph, that hadst the honour to be landlord of the Lord of life! how well is thy house-room repaid with a mansion not made with hands, eternal in the heavens! Thy garden and thy tomb were hard by Calvary, where thou couldst not fail of many monitions of thy frailty. How oft hadst thou seasoned that new tomb with sad and savoury meditations; and hadst oft said within thyself, Here I shall once lie down to my last rest, and wait for my resurrection. Little didst thou then think to have been disappointed by so blessed a guest; or that thy grave should be again so soon empty, and in that emptiness uncapable of any mortal indweller. How gladly dost thou now resign thy grave to him in whom thou livest, and who liveth for ever, whose soul is in Paradise, whose Godhead everywhere! Hadst thou not been rich before, this gift alone had enriched thee, and more ennobled thee than all thine earthly honour. Now great princes envy thy bounty, and have thought themselves happy to kiss the stones of that rock which thou thus hewedst, thus bestowedst.

Thus purely wrapped, and sweetly embalmed, lies the precious body of our Saviour in Joseph's new vault. Are ye now also at rest, O ye Jewish rulers? is your malice dead and buried with him? hath Pilate enough served your envy and revenge? Surely it is but a common hostility that can die; yours surviveth death, and puts you upon a further project: "The chief priests and Pharisees came together unto Pilate, saying, Sir, we remember that this deceiver said, while he was yet alive, After three days I will rise again; command, therefore, that the sepulchre be made sure till the third day, lest his disciples come by night, and steal him away, and say to the people, he is risen."

How full of terrors and inevitable perplexities, is guiltiness! These men were not more troubled with envy at Christ alive, than now with fear of his resurrection. And what can now secure them? Pilate had helped to kill him; but who shall keep him from rising? Wicked and foolish Jews! how fain would ye fight against God, and your own hearts! how gladly would ye deceive yourselves, in believing him to be a deceiver, whom your consciences knew to be no less true than powerful! Lazarus was still in your eye: that man was no phantasm; his death, his reviving was undeniable; the so fresh resuscitation of that dead body, after four days' dissolution, was a manifest conviction of omnipotence. How do ye vainly wish, that he could deceive you in the fore-reporting of his own resurrection! Without a divine power, he could have raised neither Lazarus nor himself: with, and by it, he could as well raise himself as Lazarus. What need we other witnesses than your own mouths? that which he would do, ye confess he foretold; that the truth of his word might answer the power of this deed, and both of them might argue him the God of truth and power, and yourselves enemies to both. And now what must be done? the sepulchre must be secured, and you with it; a huge stone, a strong guard must do the deed; and that stone must be sealed, that guard of your own designing. Methinks I hear the soldiers and busy officers, when they were rolling that other weighty stone, for such we probably conceive, to the mouth of the vault, with much toil, and sweat, and breathlessness, how they bragged of the sureness of the place, and unremovableness of that load: and when that so choice a watch was set, how they boasted of their valour and vigilance, and said, they would make him safe from either rising or stealing. O the madness of impotent men, that think, by either wile or force, to frustrate the will and designs of the Almighty! How justly doth that wise and powerful Arbiter of the world laugh them to scorn in heaven, and befool them in their own vain devices! O Saviour, how much evidence had thy resurrection wanted, if these enemies had not been thus maliciously provident! how irrefragable is thy rising made, by these bootless endeavours of their prevention!

All this while the devout Maries keep close, and silently spend their Sabbath in a mixture of grief and hope. How did they wear out those sad hours in bemoaning themselves each to other, in mutual relations of the patient sufferings, of the happy expiration of their Saviour, of the wonderful events both in the heavens and earth, that accompanied his crucifixion, of his frequent and clear predictions of his resurrection? and now they have gladly agreed, so soon as the time will give them leave, in the dawning of the Sunday morning, to visit that dear sepulchre. Neither will they go empty handed: she, that had bestowed that costly alabaster box of ointment upon their Saviour alive, hath prepared no less precious odours for him dead.

Love is restless and fearless. In the dark of night, these good women go to buy their spices, and, ere the day break, are gone out of their houses, towards the tomb of Christ, to bestow them. This sex is commonly fearful: it was much for them to walk alone in that unsafe season: yet, as despising all fears and dangers, they thus spend the night after their Sabbath. Might they have been allowed to buy their perfumes on the Sabbath, or to have visited that holy tomb sooner, can we think they would have staid so long? can we suppose they would have cared more for the Sabbath than for the "Lord of the Sabbath," who now kept his Sabbath in the grave? Sooner they might not come, later they would not, to present their last homage to their dead Saviour. Had these holy women known their Jesus to be alive, how had they hasted, who made such speed to do their last offices to his sacred corpse! for us, we "know that our Redeemer liveth," we know where he is. O Saviour, how cold and heartless is our love to thee, if we do not haste to find thee in thy word and sacraments, if our souls do not fly up to thee, in all holy affections, into thy heaven!

Of all the women, Mary Magdalene is first named, and in some Evangelists alone; she is noted above her fellows. None of them were so much obliged, none so zealously thankful. Seven devils were cast out of her by the command of Christ. That heart which was freed from Satan, by that powerful dispossession, was now possessed with a free and gracious bounty to her deliverer. Twice, at the least, hath she poured out her fragrant and costly odours upon him. Where there is a true sense of favour and beneficence, there cannot but be a fervent desire of retribution. O blessed Saviour, could we feel the danger of every sin, and the malignity of those spiritual possessions from which thou hast freed us, how should we pour out ourselves into thankfulness unto thee!

Every thing here had horror. The place both solitary and a sepulchre; nature abhors, as the visage, so the region of death and corruption. The time, night; only the moon gave them some faint glimmering, for this being the seventeenth day of her age, afforded some light to the latter part of the night. The business, the visitation of a dead corpse. Their zealous love hath easily overcome all these. They had followed him in his sufferings, when the disciples left him; they attended him to his cross weeping; they followed him to his grave, and saw how Joseph laid him; even there they leave him not, but, ere it be day-light, return to pay him the last tribute of their duty. How much stronger is love than death! O blessed Jesu, why should not we imitate thy love to us? Those, " whom thou lovest, thou lovest to the end," yea in it, yea after it: even when we are dead, not our souls only, but our very dust is dearly respected of thee. What condition of thine should remove our affections from thy person in heaven, from thy limbs on earth?

Well did these worthy women know what Joseph of Arimathea, and Nicodemus had done to thee; they saw how curiously they had wrapped thee, how preciously they had embalmed thee: yet as not thinking others' beneficence could be any just excuse of theirs, they bring their own odours to thy sepulture, to be perfumed by the touch of thy sacred body. What thank is it to us, that others are obsequious to thee, while we are slack or niggardly? We may rejoice in others' forwardness, but if we rest in it, how small joy shall it be to us to see them go to heaven without us?

When on the Friday evening they attended Joseph to the entombing of Jesus, they marked the place, they marked the passage, they marked that inner grave-stone, which the owner had fitted to the mouth of that tomb, which all their care is now to remove: "Who shall roll away the stone?" That other more weighty load wherewith the vault was barred, the seal, the guard set upon both, came not perhaps into their knowledge; this was the private plot of Pilate and the priests, beyond the reach of their thoughts.

I do not hear them say, How shall we recover the charges of our odours? or how shall we avoid the envy and censure of our angry elders, for honouring him whom the governors of our nation have thought worthy of condemnation? The only thought they now take is, "Who shall roll away the stone?" Neither do they stay at home and move this doubt, but when they are well forward on their way, resolving to try the issue. Good hearts cannot be so solicitous for anything under heaven, as for removing those impediments, which lie between them and their Saviour. O blessed Jesu! thou, who art clearly revealed in heaven, art yet still both hid and sealed up from too many here on earth: neither is it some thin veil that is spread between thee and them, but a huge stone, even a true stone of offence, lies rolled upon the mouth of their hearts. Yea, if a second weight were superadded to thy grave here, no less than three spiritual bars are interposed betwixt them and the above; idleness, ignorance, unbelief. Who shall roll away these stones, but the same power that removed thine? O Lord, remove our ignorance, that we may know thee; our idleness, that we may seek thee; our unbelief, that we may find and enjoy thee.

How well it succeeds when we go faithfully and conscionably about our work, and leave the issue to God! Lo, now God hath removed the cares of these holy women; together with the grave-stone. To the wicked, that falls out which they feared; to the godly, that which they wished and cared for, yea more.

Holy cares ever prove well; the worldly dry the bones and disappoint the hopes. Could these good visitants have known of a greater stone sealed, of a strong watch set, their doubts had been doubled. Now God goes beyond their thoughts, and at once removes that which both they did, and might have feared. The stone is removed, the seal broken, the watch fled. What a scorn doth the Almighty God make of the impotent designs of men! they thought, the stone shall make the grave sure, the seal shall make the stone sure, the guard shall make both sure; now, when they think all safe, God sends an angel from heaven above, the earth quakes beneath, the stone rolls away, the soldiers stand like carcases, and, when they have got heart enough to run away, think themselves valiant! the tomb is opened, Christ is risen, they confounded. O the vain projects of silly men! as if, with one shovel-full of mire, they would dam up the sea; or, with a clout hanged forth, they would keep the sun from shining. O these spiders' webs, or houses of cards, which fond children have, as they think, skilfully framed, which the least breath breaks and ruins! Who are we, sorry worms, that we should look, in any business, to prevail against our Creator; what creature is so base, that he cannot arm against us to our confusion! The lice and frogs shall be too strong for Pharaoh, the worms for Herod. "There is no wisdom nor counsel against the Lord."

O the marvellous pomp and magnificence of our Saviour's resurrection! The earth quakes, the angel appears, that it may be plainly seen that this divine person, now rising, had the command both of earth and heaven. At the dissolution of thy human nature, O Saviour, was an earthquake; at the re-uniting of it, is an earthquake: to tell the world, that the God of nature then suffered, and had now conquered. While thou layest still in the earth, the earth was still; when thou camest to fetch thine own, "The earth trembled at the presence of the Lord, at the presence of the God of Jacob." When thou, our true Samson, awakedst and foundst thyself tied with these Philistine cords, and rousedst up, and breakedst those hard and strong twists with a sudden power, no marvel if the room shook under thee.

Good cause had the earth to quake, when the God that made it powerfully calls for his own flesh from the usurpation of her bowels; good cause had she to open her graves, and yield up her dead, in attendance to the Lord of life, whom she had presumed to detain in that cell of her darkness. What a seeming impotency was here, that thou, who art the true Rock of thy church, shouldst lie obscurely shrouded in Joseph's rock! thou, that art the true corner-stone of thy church, shouldst be shut up with a double stone, the one of thy grave, the other of thy vault! thou, " by whom we were sealed to the day of our redemption, should be sealed up in a blind cavern of earth. But now, what a demonstration of power doth both the world and I see, in thy glorious resurrection! the rocks tear, the graves open, the stones roll away, the dead rise and appear, the soldiers flee and tremble, saints and angels attend thy rising. O Saviour, thou liest down in weakness, thou risest in power and glory; thou liest down like a man, thou risest like a God.

What a lively image hast thou herein given me of the dreadful majesty of the general resurrection, and thy second appearance! Then not the earth only, but " the powers of heaven shall be shaken:" not some few graves shall be open, and some saints appear, but all the bars of death shall be broken, and " all that sleep in their graves shall awake, and stand up from the dead," before thee. Not some one angel shall descend, but thou, " the great angel of the covenant," attended with thousand thousands of those mighty spirits. And if these stout soldiers were so filled with terror, at the feeling of an earthquake, and the sight of an angel, that they had scarce breath left in them, for the time, to witness them alive; where shall thine enemies appear, O Lord, in the day of thy terrible appearance, when the earth shall reel and vanish, and the elements shall be on a flame about their ears, and the heavens shall wrap up as a scroll.

O, God, thou mightst have removed this stone by the force of thine earthquake, as well as rive other rocks; yet thou wouldst rather use the ministry of an angel; or thou, that gavest thyself life, and gavest being both to the stone and to the earth, couldst more easily have removed the stone than moved the earth: but it was thy pleasure to make use of an angel's hand. And now he, that would ask why thou wouldst do it rather by an angel than by thyself, may as well ask why thou dost not rather give thy law by thine own immediate hand, than by the ministration of angels; why by an angel thou struckest the Israelites with plagues, the Assyrians with the sword; why an angel appeared to comfort thee after thy temptation and agony, when thou wert able to comfort thyself; why thou usest the influences of heaven to fruiten the earth ; why thou employest second causes in all events, when thou couldst do all things alone? It is good reason thou shouldst serve thyself of thine own: neither is there any ground to be required, whether of their motion or rest, besides thy will.

Thou didst raise thyself, the angels removed the stone. They that could have no hand in thy resurrection, yet shall have a hand in removing outward impediments; not because thou needst, but because thou wouldst: like as thou alone didst raise Lazarus, thou badest others let him loose. Works of omnipotency thou reservest to thine own immediate performance; ordinary actions thou dost by subordinate means.

Although this act of the angels was not merely with respect to thee; but partly to those devout women, to ease them of their care, to manifest unto them thy resurrection. So officious are those glorious spirits, not only to thee their Maker, but even to the meanest of thy servants, especially in the furtherance of all their spiritual designs. Let us bring our odours, they will be sure to roll away the stone. Why do not we imitate them in our forwardness to promote each other's salvation? we pray to do thy will here, as they do in heaven; if we do not act our wishes, we do but mock thee in our devotions.

How glorious did this angel of thine appear! the terrified soldiers saw his face like lightning; both they and the women saw his garments shining bright and white as snow; such a presence became his errand. It was fit, that as in thy passion the sun was darkened, and all creatures were clad with heaviness, so, in thy resurrection, the best of thy creatures should testify their joy and exultation in the brightness of their habit; that, as we on festival days put on our best clothes, so thine angels should celebrate this blessed festivity with a meet representation of glory. They could not but enjoy our joy, to see the work of man's redemption thus fully finished; and if there be " mirth in heaven at the conversion of one sinner," how much more when a world of sinners is perfectly ransomed from death, and restored to salvation? Certainly, if but one or two appeared, all rejoiced, all triumphed. Neither could they but be herein sensible of their own happy advantage, who by thy mediation are confirmed in their glorious estate; since thou, by the blood of thy cross, and power of thy resurrection, hast "reconciled things not in earth only, but in heaven."

But, above all other, the love of thee, their God and Saviour, must needs heighten their joy, and make thy glory theirs. It is their perpetual work to praise thee: how much more now, when such an occasion was offered as never had been since the world began, never could be after! when thou the God of Spirits hadst vanquished all the spiritual powers of darkness! when thou, the Lord of life, hadst conquered death for thee and all thine, so as they may now boldly insult over their last enemy!— "O death, where is thy sting? O grave, where is thy victory?"

Certainly, if heaven can be capable of an increase of joy and felicity, never had those blessed spirits so great a cause of triumph and gratulation as in this day of thy glorious resurrection. How much more, O dear Jesu, should we men, whose flesh thou didst assume, unite, revive; for whose sakes, and in whose stead, thou didst vouchsafe to suffer and die; whose arrearages thou paidst in death, and acquittedst in thy resurrection; whose souls are discharged, whose bodies shall be raised by the power of thy rising; how much more should we think we have cause to be overjoyed with the happy memory of this great work of thy divine power and inconceivable mercy!

Lo now, how weak soever I am in myself, yet, in the confidence of this victorious resurrection of my Saviour, I dare boldly challenge and defy you, O all ye adverse powers! Do the worst ye can to my soul; in despite of you, it shall be safe.

Is it sin that threatens me? Behold, this resurrection of my Redeemer publishes my discharge. My surety was arrested, and cast into the prison of his grave; had not the utmost farthing of mine arrearages been paid, he could not have come forth: he is come forth; the sum is fully satisfied. What danger can there be of a discharged debt?

Is it the wrath of God? Wherefore is that but for sin? If my sin be defrayed, that quarrel is at an end: and if my Saviour suffered it for me, how can I fear to suffer it in myself? That infinite justice hates to be twice paid. He is risen, therefore he hath satisfied: "Who is he that condemneth? It is Christ that died; yea, rather that is risen."

Is it death itself? Lo! my Saviour, that overcame death by dying, hath triumphed over him in his resurrection. How can I now fear a conquered enemy? what harm is there in the serpent, but for his sting? "The sting of death is sin:" that is pulled out by my powerful Redeemer; it cannot now hurt me; it may refresh me to carry this cool snake in my bosom.

O then, my dear Saviour! I bless thee for thy death; but I bless thee more for thy resurrection. That was a work of wonderful humility, of infinite mercy; this was a work of infinite power: in that was human weakness; in this divine omnipotence: in that thou didst "die for our sins;" in this thou didst "rise again for our justification."

And now how am I conformable to thee, if, when thou art risen, I lie still in the grave of my corruptions? How am I a limb of thy body, if, while thou hast that perfect dominion over death, death hath dominion over me? if, while thou art alive and glorious, I lie rotting in the dust of death? I know the locomotive faculty is in the head: by the power of the resurrection of thee, our head, all we, thy members, cannot but be raised. As the earth cannot hold my body from thee in the day of the second resurrection, so cannot sin withhold my soul from thee in the first. How am I thine, if I be not risen? and if I be risen with thee, why do I not seek the things above, where thou sittest at the right hand of God?

The vault or cave, which Joseph had hewn out of the rock, was large, capable of no less than ten persons: upon the mouth of it, eastward, was that great stone rolled; within it, at the right hand, in the north part of the cave, was hewn out a receptacle for the body, three handfuls high from the pavement; and a stone was accordingly fitted for the cover of that grave.

Into this cave the good women, finding the stone rolled away, descended to seek the body of Christ, and in it saw the angels. This was the goal to which Peter and John ran, finding the spoils of death, the graveclothes wrapped up, and the napkin that was about the head folded up together, and laid in a place by itself; and as they came in haste, so they returned with wonder.

I marvel not at your speed, O ye blessed disciples, if, upon the report of the woman, ye ran, yea flew upon the wings of zeal, to see what was become of your Master. Ye had wont to walk familiarly together in the attendance of your Lord: now society is forgotten; and, as for a wager, each tries the speed of his legs, and, with neglect of other, vies who shall be first at the tomb.

Who would not but have tried masteries with you in this case, and have made light touches of the earth to have held paces with you? Your desire was equal; but John is the younger; his limbs are more nimble, his breath more free: he first looks into the sepulchre, but Peter goes down first. O happy competition who shall be more zealous in the inquiry after Christ! Ye saw enough to amaze you, not enough to settle your faith. How well might you have thought, Our Master is not subduced, but risen. Had he been taken away by other's hands, this fine linen had not been left behind: had he not himself risen from this bed of earth, he had not thus wrapped up his night-clothes, and laid them sorted by themselves. What can we doubt, when he foretold us he would rise? O blessed Jesu, how wilt thou pardon our errors? how should we pardon and pity the errors of each other on lesser occasions, when as yet thy prime and dearest disciples, after so much divine instruction, "knew not the Scriptures, that thou must rise again from the dead?" They went away more astonished than confident; more full of wonder, as yet, than of belief.

There is more strength of zeal, where it takes, in the weaker sex. Those holy women, as they came first, so they staid last: especially devout Mary Magdalene stands still at the mouth of the cave weeping. Well might those tears have been spared, if her knowledge had been answerable to her affection, her faith to her fervour. Withal, as our eye will be where we love, she stoops, and looks down into that dear sepulchre.

Holy desires never but speed well. There she sees two glorious angels, the one sitting "at the head, the other at the feet, where the body of Jesus had lain." Their shining brightness showed them to be no mortal creatures: besides, that Peter and John had but newly come out of the sepulchre, and both found and left it empty in her sight, which was now suddenly filled with those celestial guests. That white linen, wherewith Joseph had shrouded the sacred body of Jesus, was now shamed with a brighter whiteness.

Yet do I not find the good woman aught appalled with that unexpected glory. So was her heart taken up with the thought for her Saviour, that she seemed not sensible of whatsoever other objects. Those tears, which she did let drop into the sepulchre, send up back to her the voice of those angels, "Woman, why weepest thou?" God and his angels take notice of every tear of our devotion. The sudden wonder hath not dried her eyes, nor charmed her tongue: she freely confesseth the cause of her grief to be the missing of her Saviour: "They have taken away my Lord, and I know not where they have laid him." Alas! good Mary, how dost thou lose thy tears! of whom dost thou complain, but of thy best friend? who hath removed thy Lord, but himself? who, but his own Deity, hath taken away that human body out of that region of death? neither is he now laid any more; he stands by thee, whose removal thou complainest of. Thus many a tender and humble soul afflicts itself with the want of that Saviour whom it hath, and feeleth not.

Sense may be no judge of the bewailed absence of Christ. Do but turn back thine eye, O thou religious soul, "and see Jesus standing by thee," though "thou knewest not that it was Jesus." His habit was not his own. Sometimes it pleases our Saviour to appear unto his not like himself: his holy disguises are our trials. Sometimes he will seem a stranger, sometimes an enemy; sometimes he offers himself to us in the shape of a poor man, sometimes of a distressed captive. Happy is he that can discern his Saviour in all forms. Mary took him for a gardener. Devout Magdalene, thou art not much mistaken. As it was the trade of the first Adam to dress the garden of Eden, so was it the trade of the second to tend the garden of his church. He digs up the soil by seasonable afflictions, he sows in it the seeds of grace, he plants it with gracious motions, he waters it with his word, yea, with his own blood, he weeds it by wholesome censures. O blessed Saviour! what is it that thou neglectest to do for this selected inclosure of thy church? As in some respect thou art the true Vine, and thy Father the Husbandman, so also in some other we are the vine, and thou art the Husbandman. O be thou such to me as thou appearedst unto Magdalene! break up the fallow of my nature, implant me with grace, prune me with meet corrections, bedew me with the former and latter rain! do what thou wilt to make me fruitful!

Still the good woman weeps, and still complains, and passionately inquires of thee, O Saviour, for thyself. How apt are we, if thou dost never so little vary from our apprehensions, to misknow thee, and to wrong ourselves by our misopinions! All this while hast thou concealed thyself from thine affectionate client; thou sawest her tears, and heardest her importunities and inquiries; at last (as it was with Joseph, that he could no longer contain himself from the notice of his brethren) thy compassion causes thee to break forth into a clear expression of thyself, by expressing her name unto herself, "Mary." She was used, as to the name, so to the sound, to the accent. Thou spakest to her before, but in the tone of a stranger; now of a friend, of a master. Like a good Shepherd, "thou callest thy sheep by their name, and they know thy voice." What was thy call of her, but a clear pattern of our vocation?

As her, so thou callest us: first, familiarly, effectually. She could not begin with thee otherwise than in the compellation of a stranger; it was thy mercy to begin with her. That correction of thy Spirit is sweet and useful: "Now after ye have known God, or rather, are known of him." We do know thee, O God, but our active knowledge is after our passive: first we are known of thee, then we know thee that knewest us. And as our knowledge, so is our calling. so is our election; thou beginnest to us in all, and most justly sayest, "You have not chosen me, but I have chosen you." When thou wouldst speak to this devout client as a stranger, thou spakest aloof: "Woman, whom seekest thou?" now, when thou wouldst be known to her, thou callest her by her name, "Mary." General invitations and common mercies are for us as men; but where thou givest grace as to thine elect, thou comest close to the soul, and winnest us with dear and particular intimations.

That very name did as much as say, Know him of whom thou art known and beloved, and turns her about to thy view and acknowledgment. "She turned herself, and saith unto him, Rabboni, which is to say, Master." Before, her face was towards the angels; this word fetches her about, and turns her face to thee, from whom her misprision had averted it. We do not rightly apprehend thee, O Saviour, if any creature in heaven or earth can keep our eyes and our hearts from thee. The angels were bright and glorious; thy appearance was homely, thy habit mean: yet, when she heard thy voice, she turns her back upon the angels, and salutes thee with a Rabboni, and falls down before thee, in a desire of an humble amplexation of those sacred feet, which she now rejoices to see past the use of her odours.

Where there was such familiarity in the mutual compellation, what means such strangeness in the charge, "Touch me not, for I am not yet ascended to my Father?" Thou wert not wont, O Saviour, to make so dainty of being touched: it is not long since these very same hands touched thee in thine anointing: the bloody-fluxed woman touched thee; the thankful penitent in Simon's house touched thee. What speak I of these? the multitude touched thee, the executioners touched thee; and, even after thy resurrection, thou didst not stick to say to thy disciples, "Touch me, and see," and to invite Thomas to put his fingers into thy side; neither is it long after this before thou sufferest the three Maries to touch and hold thy feet. How then sayest thou, "Touch me not?" Was it in a mild taxation of her mistaking? as if thou hadst said, "Thou knowest not that I have now an immortal body, but so demeanest thyself towards me, as if I were still in my wonted condition: know now that the case is altered; howsoever indeed I have not yet ascended to my Father, yet this body of mine, which thou seest to be real and sensible, is now impassible, and qualified with immortality, and therefore worthy of a more awful veneration than heretofore. Or was it a gentle reproof of her dwelling too long in this dear hold of thee, and fixing her thoughts upon thy bodily presence; together with an implied direction of reserving the height of her affection for thy perfect glorification in heaven? Or, lastly, was it a light touch of her too much haste and eagerness in touching thee, as if she must use this speed in preventing thine ascension, or else to be endangered to be disappointed of her hopes? as if thou hadst said, Be not so passionately forward and sudden in laying hold of me, as if I were instantly ascending; but know, that I shall stay some time with you upon earth, before my going up to my Father. O Saviour, even our well-meant zeal in seeking and enjoying thee may be faulty; if we seek thee where we should not, on earth; how we should not, unwarrantably. There may be a kind of carnality in spiritual actions. "If we have heretofore known thee after the flesh, henceforth know we thee so no more." That thou livedst here in this shape, that colour, this stature, that habit, I should be glad to know: nothing that concerns thee can be unuseful. Could I say, here thou satest, here thou layest, here and thus thou wert crucified, here buried, here settest thy last foot; I should with much contentment see and recount these memorials of thy presence: but if I shall so fasten my thoughts upon these, as not to look higher to the spiritual part of thine achievements, to the power and issue of thy resurrection, I am never the better.

No sooner art thou risen, than thou speakest of ascending: as thou didst lie down to rise, so didst thou rise to ascend; that is the consummation of thy glory, and ours in thee. Thou, that forbadest her touch, enjoinedst her errand: "Go to my brethren, and say, I ascend unto my Father and your Father, to my God and your God."

The annunciation of thy resurrection and ascension is more than a private fruition: this is for the comfort of one, that for the benefit of many. To sit still and enjoy, is more sweet for the present; but to go and tell, is more gainful in the sequel. That great angel thought himself, as he well might, highly honoured, in that he was appointed to carry the happy news unto the blessed Virgin, thy holy mother, of her conception of thee her Saviour: how honourable must it needs be to Mary Magdalene, that she must be the messenger of thy second birth, thy resurrection, and instant ascension! How beautiful do the feet of those deserve to be, who bring the glad tidings of peace and salvation! What matter is it, O Lord, if men despise where thou wilt honour?

To whom then dost thou send her? "Go tell my brethren." Blessed Jesu! who are these? were they not thy followers? yea, were they not thy forsakers? yet still thou stylest them thy brethren. O admirable humility! O infinite mercy! How dost thou raise their titles with thyself! At first they were thy servants, then disciples; a little before thy death, they were thy friends; now, after thy resurrection, they were thy brethren. Thou, that wert exalted infinitely higher from mortal to immortal, descendedst so much lower to call them brethren, who were before friends, disciples, servants. What! do we stand upon the terms of our poor inequality, when the Son of God stoops so low as to call us brethren? But, O mercy without measure! why wilt thou, how canst thou, O Saviour, call them brethren, whom, in their last parting, thou foundest fugitives? Did they not run from thee? did not one of them rather leave his inmost coat behind him, than not be quit of thee? did not another of them deny thee, yea, abjure thee? and yet thou sayest "Go, tell my brethren." It is not in the power of the sins of our infirmity to unbrother us: when we look at the acts themselves, they are heinous; when at the persons, they are so much more faulty as more obliged: but when we look at the mercy of thee who hast called us, now, " Who shall separate us?" when we have sinned, thy dearness hath reason to aggravate our sorrows; but when we have sorrowed, our faith hath no less reason to uphold us from despairing: even yet we are brethren; brethren in thee, O Saviour, who art ascending for us; in thee, who hast made thy Father ours, thy God our God. He is thy Father by eternal generation, our Father by his gracious adoption; thy God by unity of essence, our God by his grace and election.

It is this propriety wherein our life and happiness consisteth: they are weak comforts that can be raised from the apprehension of thy general mercies. What were I the better, O Saviour, that God were thy Father, if he be not mine? O do thou give me a particular sense of my interest in thee, and thy goodness to me; bring thou thyself home to me, and let me find that I have a God and Saviour of my own.

It is fit I should mark thy order: first, my Father, then yours. Even so, Lord, he is first thine, and in thine only right ours. It is in thee that we are adopted, it is in thee that we are elected; without thee, God is not only a stranger, but an enemy to us. Thou only canst make us free, thou only canst make us sons. Let me be found in thee, and I cannot fail of a Father in heaven.

With what joy did Mary receive this errand! with what joy did the disciples welcome it from her! Here was good news from a far country, even as far as the utmost regions of death.

Those disciples, whose flight scattered them upon their Master's apprehension, are now, at night, like a dispersed covey, met together by their mutual call: their assembly is secret; when the light was shut in, when the doors were shut up. Still were they fearful, still were the Jews malicious. The assured tidings of their Master's resurrection and life hath filled their hearts with joy and wonder. While their thoughts and speech are taken up with so happy a subject, his miraculous and sudden presence bids their senses be witnesses of his reviving and their happiness. "When the door were shut, where the disciples were assembled, for fear of the Jews, came Jesus and stood in the midst, and said, Peace be unto you." O Saviour, how thou camest in thither, I wonder, I inquire not: I know not what a glorified body can do; I know there is nothing that thou canst not do. Had not thine entrance been recorded for strange and supernatural, why was thy standing in the midst noted before thy passage into the room? why were the doors said to be shut while thou camest in? why were thy disciples amazed to see thee ere they heard thee? Doubtless, they that once before took thee for a spirit when thou didst walk upon the waters, could not but be astonished to see thee, while the doors were barred, without any noise of thine entrance to stand in the midst: well might they think, thou couldst not thus be there, if thou wert not the God of spirits. There might seem more scruple of thy reality than of thy power; and therefore, after thy wonted greeting, thou showedst them thy hands and thy feet, stamped with the impressions of thy late sufferings. Thy respiration shall argue the truth of thy life. Thou breathest on them as a man, thou givest them thy Spirit as a God; and as God and man thou sendest them on the great errand of thy gospel.

All the mists of their doubts are now dispelled; the sun breaks out clear: "They were glad when they had seen the Lord." Had they known thee for no other than a mere man, this re-appearance could not but have affrighted them, since till now by thine almighty power this was never done, that the long-since dead rose out of their graves, and appeared unto many: but when they recounted the miraculous works that thou hadst done, and thought of Lazarus so lately raised, thine approved Deity gave them confidence, and thy presence joy.

We cannot but be losers by our absence from holy assemblies. Where wert thou, O Thomas, when the rest of that sacred family were met together? Had thy fear put thee to so long a flight, that as yet thou wert not returned to thy fellows? or didst thou suffer other occasions to detain thee from this happiness? Now, for the time, thou missedst that divine breath which so comfortably inspired the rest; now thou art suffered to fall into that weak distrust which thy presence had prevented. They told thee, "We have seen the Lord." Was not this enough? would no eyes serve thee but thine own? were thy ears to no use for thy faith? "Except I see in his hands the print of the nails, and put my finger into the print of the nails, and thrust my hand into his side, I will not believe." Suspicious man! who is the worse for that? whose is the loss if thou believe not? is there no certainty but in thine own senses? why were not so many and so holy eyes and tongues as credible as thine own hands and eyes? how little wert thou yet acquainted with the ways of faith! "Faith comes by hearing:" these are the tongues that must win the whole world to an assent, and dost thou the first man detract to yield? Why was that word so hard to pass? Had not that thy divine Master foretold thee with the rest that he must be crucified, and the third day rise again? Is anything related to be done, but that which was fore-promised? anything beyond the sphere of divine omnipotence? Go then, and please thyself in thine over-wise incredulity, while thy fellows are happy in believing.

It is a whole week that Thomas rests in this sullen unbelief; in all which time, doubtless, his ears were beaten with the many constant assertions of the holy women, the first witnesses of the resurrection, as also of the two disciples walking to Emmaus, whose hearts, burning within them, had set their tongues on fire, in a zealous relation of those happy occurrences, with the assured reports of the rising and reappearance of many saints, in attendance of the Lord and Giver of life: yet still he struggles with his own distrust, and stiffly suspends his belief to that truth, whereof he cannot deny himself enough convinced. As all bodies are not equally apt to be wrought upon by the same medicine, so are not all souls by the same means of faith: one is refractory, while others are pliable. O Saviour! how justly mightest thou have left this man to his own pertinacity! whom could he have thanked, if he had perished in his unbelief? But, O thou good Shepherd of Israel, that couldst be content to leave the ninety and nine, to go fetch one stray in the wilderness, how careful wert thou to reduce this straggler to his fellows! Right so were thy disciples re-assembled; such was the season, the place the same, so were the doors shut up, when that unbelieving disciple, being now present with the rest, thou so camest in, so stoodst in the midst, so showedst thy hands and feet, and singling out thy incredulous client, invitedst his eyes to see, and his fingers to handle thine hands, and his hand to be thrust into thy side, that he might not be faithless, but faithful.

Blessed Jesu! how thou pitiest the errors and infirmities of thy servants! even when we are froward in our misconceits, and worthy of nothing but desertion, how thou followest us, and overtakest us with mercy! and, in thine abundant compassion, wilt reclaim and save us, when either we meant not, or would not! By how much more unworthy those eyes and hands were to see and touch that immortal and glorious body by so much more wonderful was thy goodness, in condescending to satisfy that curious infidelity. Neither do I hear thee so much as to chide that weak obstinacy. It was not long since thou didst sharply take up the two disciples that walked to Emmaus: "O fools, and slow of heart to believe all that the prophets have spoken!" but this was under the disguise of an unknown traveller upon the way, when they were alone; now thou speakest with thine own tongue, before all thy disciples; instead of rebuking, thou only exhortest: "Be not faithless, but faithful."

Behold, thy mercy no less than thy power, hath melted the congealed heart of thy unbelieving follower: "Then Thomas answered and said unto him, My Lord, and my God." I do not hear, that when it came to the issue, Thomas employed his hands in this trial: his eyes were now sufficient assurance; the sense of his Master's omniscience, in this particular challenge of him, spared, perhaps, the labour of a further disquisition. And now how happily was that doubt bestowed, which brought forth so faithful a confession, "My Lord! my God!"

I hear not such a word from those that believed. It was well for us, it was well for thee, O Thomas, that thou distrustedst, else neither had the world received so perfect an evidence of that resurrection whereon all our salvation dependeth, neither hadst thou yielded so pregnant and divine an astipulation to thy blessed Saviour. Now thou dost not only profess his resurrection, but his Godhead too, and thy happy interest in both. And now, if they be blessed that have not seen, and yet believed; blessed art thou also, that, having seen, hast thus believed: and blessed be thou, O God, who knowest how to make advantage of the infirmities of thy chosen, for the promoting of their salvation, the confirmation of thy church, the glory of thine own name. *Amen.*

CONTEMPLATION XXXIV.—THE ASCENSION.

It stood not with thy purpose, O Saviour, to ascend immediately from thy grave into heaven: thou meantst to take the earth in thy way, not for a sudden passage, but for a leisurely conversation. Upon thine Easter-day, thou spakest of thine ascension; but thou wouldst have forty days interposed. Hadst thou merely respected thine own glory, thou hadst instantly changed thy grave for thy Paradise: for so much the sooner hadst thou been possessed of thy Father's joy. We would not continue in a dungeon, when we might be in a palace; but thou, who for our sakes vouchsafedst to descend from heaven to earth, wouldst now, in the upshot, have a gracious regard to us in thy return.

Thy death had troubled the hearts of many disciples, who thought that condition too mean to be compatible with the glory of the Messiah: and thoughts of diffidence were apt to seize upon the holiest breasts. So long, therefore, wouldst thou hold footing upon earth, till the world were fully convinced of the infallible evidences of thy resurrection; of all which time thou only canst give an account. It was not for flesh and blood to trace the ways of immortality; neither was our frail, corruptible, sinful nature, a meet companion for thy now glorified humanity: the glorious angels of heaven were now thy fittest attendants. But yet, how oft did it please thee graciously to impart thyself this while unto men; and not only to appear unto thy disciples, but to renew unto them the familiar forms of thy wonted conversation, in conferring, walking, eating with them! And now, when thou drewest near to thy last parting, thou who hadst many times showed thyself before to thy several disciples, thoughtest meet to assemble them all together, for an universal valediction.

Who can be too rigorous in censuring the ignorance of well-meaning Christians, when he sees the domestic followers of Christ, even after his resurrection, mistake the main end of his coming in the flesh? "Lord, wilt thou, at this time, restore again the kingdom to Israel?" They saw their Master now out of the reach of all Jewish envy: they saw his power illimited and irresistible; they saw him stay so long upon earth, that they might imagine he meant to fix his abode there; and what should he do there but reign? and wherefore should they be now assembled, but for the choice and distribution of offices, and for the ordering of the affairs of that state which was now to be vindicated? O weak thoughts of well-instructed disciples! What should a heavenly body do in an earthly throne? How should a spiritual life be employed in secular cares? How poor a business is the temporal kingdom of Israel for the King of heaven? And even yet, O blessed Saviour, I do not hear thee sharply control this erroneous conceit of thy mistaken followers: thy mild correction insists rather upon the time, than the misconceited substance, of that restoration. It was thy gracious purpose, that thy Spirit should by degrees rectify their judgments, and illuminate them with thy divine truths: in the meantime, it was sufficient to raise up their hearts to an expectation of that Holy Ghost, which should shortly lead them into all needful and requisite verities. And now, with a gracious promise of that spirit of thine, with a careful charge renewed unto thy disciples for the promulgation of thy gospel, with a heavenly benediction of all thine acclaiming attendance, thou takest leave of the earth: " When he had spoken these things, while they beheld, he was taken up, and a cloud received him out of their sight."

O happy parting, fit for the Saviour of mankind, answerable to that divine conversation, to that succeeding glory! O blessed Jesu! let me so far imitate thee, as to depart hence with a blessing in my mouth! let my soul, when it is stepping over the threshold of heaven, leave behind it a legacy of peace and happiness!

It was from the mount of Olives that thou tookst thy rise into heaven. Thou mightst have ascended from the valley; all the globe of earth was alike to thee; but since thou wert to mount upward, thou wouldst take so much advantage as that stair of ground would afford thee; thou wouldst not use the help of a miracle in that wherein nature offered her ordinary service. What difficulty had it been for thee to have soared up from the very centre of earth? But, since thou hadst made hills so much nearer unto heaven, thou wouldst not neglect the benefit of thy own creation. Where we have common helps, we may not depend upon supernatural provisions; we may not strain the divine Providence to the supply of our negligence, or the humouring of our presumption. Thou that couldst always have walked on the sea, wouldst walk so but once, when thou wantedst shipping; thou, to whom the highest mountains were but valleys, wouldst walk up a hill, to ascend thence into heaven. O God! teach me to bless thee for means, when I have them, and to trust thee for means, when I have them not; yea, to trust to thee without means, when I have no hope of them.

What hill was this thou chosest, but the mount of Olives? thy pulpit, shall I call it, or thine oratory? the place from whence thou hadst wont to shower down thine heavenly doctrine upon the hearers; the place whence thou hadst wont to send up thy prayers unto thy heavenly Father; the place that shared with the temple for both: in the day-time thou wert preaching in the temple, in the night praying in the mount of Olives. On this very hill was the bloody sweat of thine agony; now is it the mount of thy triumph. From this mount of Olives did flow that oil of gladness, wherewith thy church is everlastingly refreshed. That God, that uses to punish us in the same kind wherein we have offended, retributes also to us in the same kind and circumstances wherein we have been afflicted. To us also, O Saviour, even to us thy unworthy members, dost thou seasonably vouchsafe to give a proportionable joy to our heaviness, laughter to our mourning, glory to contempt and shame. Our agonies shall be answered with exaltation.

Whither then, O blessed Jesu! whither didst thou ascend? whither but home into thine heaven? From the mountain wert thou taken up, and what but heaven is above the hills? Lo! these are those mountains of spices which thy spouse the church long since desired thee to climb. Thou hast now climbed up that infinite steepness, and hast left all sublimity below thee. Already hadst thou approved thyself the Lord and commander of earth, of sea, of hell. The earth confessed thee her Lord, when at thy voice she rendered thee thy Lazarus; when she shook at thy passion, and gave up her dead saints. The sea acknowledged thee, in that it became a pavement to thy feet, and, at thy command, to the feet of thy disciple; in that it became thy treasury for thy tribute money. Hell found and acknowledged thee, in that thou conqueredst all the powers of darkness; even him that had the power of death, the devil. It now only remained, that, as the Lord of the air, thou shouldst pass through all the regions of that yielding element; and as Lord of heaven, thou shouldst pass through all the glorious contignations thereof, that so " every knee might bow to thee, both in heaven, and in earth, and under the earth."

Thou hadst an everlasting right to that heaven that should be; an undoubted possession of it ever since it was; yea, even while thou didst cry and sprawl in the manger, while thou didst hang upon the cross, while thou wert sealed up in thy grave; but thine human nature had not taken actual possession of it till now. Like as it was in thy true type, David, he had right to the kingdom of Israel immediately upon his anointing; but yet many a hard brunt did he pass ere he had the full possession of it, in his ascent to Hebron. I see now, O blessed Jesu! I see where thou art; even far above all heavens, at the right hand of thy Father's glory! This is the far country into which the nobleman went to receive for himself a kingdom; far off to us, to thee near, yea intrinsical. O do thou raise up my heart thither to thee! place thou my affections upon thee above, and teach me therefore to love heaven because thou art there!

How then, O blessed Saviour, how didst thou ascend? "While they beheld, he was taken up, and a cloud received him out of their sight." So wast thou taken up, as that the act was thine own, the power of the act none but thine. Thou that descendedst wast the same that ascendedst; as in thy descent there was no use of any power or will but thine own, no more was there in thine ascent. Still and ever wert thou the master of thine own acts. Thou laidst down thy own life, no man took it from thee; thou raisedst up thyself from death, no hand did or could help thee; thou carriedst up thine own glorified flesh, and placedst it in heaven. The angels did attend thee, they did not aid thee: whence had they their strength but from thee? Elias ascended to heaven, but he was fetched up in a chariot of fire; that it might appear hence, that man had need of other helps, who else could not of himself so much as lift up himself to the airy heaven, much less to the empyreal. But thou, our Redeemer, neededst no chariot, no carriage of angels: thou art the Author of life and motion; they move in and from thee. As thou therefore didst move thyself upward, so, by the same divine power, thou wilt raise us up to the participation of thy glory. "These vile bodies shall be made like to thy glorious body, according to the working whereby thou art able to subdue all things unto thyself."

Elias had but one witness of his rapture into heaven; St Paul had none, no not himself; for "whether in the body, or out of the body," he knew not. Thou, O blessed Jesu! wouldst neither have all eyes witnesses of thine ascension, nor yet too few. As, after thy resurrection, thou didst not set thyself upon the pinnacle of the temple, nor yet publicly show thyself within it, as making thy presence too cheap; but madest choice of those eyes whom thou wouldst bless with the sight of thee; thou wert seen indeed of five hundred at once, but they were brethren: so in thine ascension, thou didst not carry all Jerusalem promiscuously forth with thee, to see thy glorious departure, but only that selected company of thy disciples which had attended thee in thy life. Those who immediately upon thine ascension returned to Jerusalem, were a hundred and twenty persons: a competent number of witnesses, to verify that thy miraculous and triumphant passage into thy glory. Lo! those only were thought worthy to behold thy majestic ascent, which had been partners with thee in thy humiliation. Still thou wilt have it thus with us, O Saviour, and we embrace the condition; if we will converse with thee in thy lowly estate here upon earth, wading with thee through contempt and manifold afflictions, we shall be made happy with the sight and communion of thy glory above.

O my soul, be thou now, if ever, ravished with the contemplation of this comfortable and blessed farewell of thy Saviour. What a sight was this! how full of joyful assurance, of spiritual consolation! Methinks I see it still with their eyes, how thou, my glorious Saviour, didst leisurely and insensibly rise up from thine Olivet, taking leave of thine acclaiming disciples now left below thee, with gracious eyes, with heavenly benedictions. Methinks I see how they followed thee with eager and longing eyes, with arms lifted up, as if they had wished them winged, to have soared up after thee. And if Elijah gave assurance to his servant Elisha, that if he should behold him in that rapture, his Master's spirit should be doubled upon him, what an accession of the spirit of joy and confidence must needs be to thy happy disciples in seeing thee thus gradually rising up to thy heaven! O how unwillingly did their intentive eyes let go so blessed an object! — how unwelcome was that cloud that interposed itself betwixt thee and them, and, closing up itself, left only a glorious splendour behind it, as the bright track of thine ascension! Of old, here below, the glory of the Lord appeared in the cloud, now afar off in the sky; the cloud intercepted this heavenly glory, if distance did not rather do it than that bright meteor. Their eyes attended thee on thy way so far as their beams would reach; when they could go no farther, the cloud received thee. Lo! yet even that very screen, whereby thou wert taken off from all earthly view, was no other than glorious: how much rather do all the beholders fix their sight upon that cloud, than upon the best piece of the firmament! Never was the sun itself gazed on with so much intention. With what long looks, with what astonished acclamations, did these transported beholders follow thee, their ascending Saviour. as if they would have looked through that cloud, and that heaven, that hid thee from them!

But, O what tongue of the highest archangel of heaven can express the welcome of thee, the King of glory, into these blessed regions of immortality? Surely the empyreal heaven never resounded with so much joy: God ascended with jubilation, and the Lord with the sound of the trumpet. It is not for us, weak and finite creatures, to wish to conceive those incomprehensible, spiritual, divine gratulations, that the glorious Trinity gave to the victorious and now glorified human nature. Certainly, if, when he brought his only-begotten Son into the world, he said, "Let all the angels worship him;" much more now that he "ascends on high, and hath led captivity captive, hath he given him a name above all names, that at the name of JESUS all knees should bow." And if the holy angels did so carol at his birth, in the very entrance into that state of humiliation and infirmity, with what triumph did they receive him, now returning from the perfect achievement of man's redemption? and if, when his type had vanquished Goliah, and carried the head into Jerusalem, the damsels came forth to meet him with dances and timbrels, how shall we think those angelical spirits triumphed, in meeting of the great Conqueror of hell and death? How did they sing, "Lift up your heads, ye gates! and be lifted up, ye everlasting doors, and the King of glory shall come in!"

Surely, as he shall come, so he went; and, "Behold, he shall come with thousands of his holy ones; thousand thousands ministered unto him, and ten thousand thousands stood before him;" from all whom, methinks I hear that blessed applause, "Worthy is the Lamb that was killed, to receive power, and riches, and wisdom, and strength, and honour, and glory, and praise: praise, and honour, and glory, and power, be to Him that sitteth upon the throne, and to the Lamb for evermore." And why dost not thou, O my soul, help to bear thy part with that happy choir of heaven? Why art not thou rapt out of my bosom, with an ecstasy of joy, to see this human nature of ours exalted above all the powers of heaven, adored of angels, archangels, cherubim, seraphim, and all those mighty and glorious spirits, and sitting there crowned with infinite glory and majesty?

Although little would it avail thee, that our nature is thus honoured, if the benefit of this ascension did not reflect upon thee. How many are miserable enough in themselves, notwithstanding the glory of their human nature in Christ! None but those that are found in him, are the happier by him: who but the members are the better for the glory of the head? O Saviour, how should our weakness have ever hoped to climb into heaven, if thou hadst not gone before, and made way for us? It is for us, that thou the forerunner art entered in. Now thy church hath her wish: "Draw me, and I will run after thee." Even so, O blessed Jesu, how ambitiously should we follow thee with the paces of love and faith, and aspire towards thy glory! Thou, that art "the way," hast made the way to thyself and us: "Thou didst humble thyself, and become obedient to the death, even the death of the cross: therefore hath God also highly exalted thee;" and upon the same terms will not fail to advance us. We see thy track before us, of humility and obedience: O teach me to follow thee in the roughest ways of obedience, in the bloody paths of death, that I may at last overtake thee in those high steps of immortality.

Amongst those millions of angels that attended this triumphant ascension of thine, O Saviour, some are appointed to this lower station, to comfort thine astonished disciples, in the certain assurance of thy no less glorious return: "Two men stood by them in white apparel." They stood by them, they were not of them; they seemed men, they were angels; men for their familiarity; two, for more certainty of testimony; in white, for the joy of thine ascension.

The angels formerly celebrated thy nativity with songs; but we do not find they appeared then in white: thou wert then to undergo much sorrow, many conflicts; it was the vale of tears into which thou wert come down. So soon as thou wert risen, the women saw an angel, in the form of a young man clothed in white; and now, so soon as thou art ascended, two men clothed in white stand by thy disciples: thy task was now done, thy victory achieved, and nothing remained but a crown, which was now set upon thy head. Justly, therefore, were those blessed angels suited with the robes of light and joy. And why should our garments be of any other colour? why should oil be wanting to our heads, when the eyes of our faith see thee thus ascended? It is for us, O Saviour, that thou art gone to prepare a place in those celestial mansions; it is for us that thou sittest at the right hand of Majesty. It is a piece of thy divine prayer to thy Father, that "those whom he hath given thee, may be with thee." To every bleeding soul thou sayest still, as thou didst to Peter, "Whither I go thou canst not follow me now, but thou shalt follow me hereafter." In assured hope of this glory, why do I not rejoice, and beforehand walk in white with thine angels, that at the last I may walk with thee in white?

Little would the presence of these angels have availed, if they had not been heard as well as seen. They stand not silent therefore, but directing their speech to the amazed beholders, say, "Ye men of Galilee, why stand ye gazing into heaven?" What a question was this! Could any of those two hundred and forty eyes have power to turn themselves off to any other object than that cloud and that point of heaven where they left their ascended Saviour? Surely every one of them were so fixed, that had not the speech of these angels called them off, there they had set up their rest till the darkness of night had interposed. Pardon me, O ye blessed angels! had I been there with them, I should also have been unwilling to have had mine eyes pulled off from that dear prospect and diverted unto you. Never could they have gazed so happily as now. If but some great man be advanced to honour over our heads, how apt we are to stand to gaze, and to eye him as some strange meteor; let the sun but shine a little upon these dials, how are they looked at by all passengers! yet, alas! what can earthly advancement make us other than we are, dust and ashes, which the higher it is blown, the more it is scattered! O how worthy is the king of glory to command our eyes, now in the highest pitch of his heavenly exaltation! Lord, I can never look enough at the place where thou art; but what eye could be satisfied with seeing the way that thou wentst?

It was not the purpose of these angels to check the long looks of these faithful disciples after their ascended Master: it was only a change of eyes that they intended; of carnal for spiritual, of the eye of sense for the eye of faith. "This same Jesus, which is taken up from you into heaven, shall so come in like manner as ye have seen him go into heaven." Look not after him, O ye weak disciples, as so departed that ye shall see him no more; if he be gone, yet he is not lost; those heavens that received him shall restore him; neither can those blessed mansions decrease his glory. Ye have seen him ascend upon the chariot of a bright cloud; and, in the clouds of heaven, ye shall see him descend again to his last judgment. He is gone; can it trouble you to know you have an Advocate in heaven? Strive not now so much to exercise your bodily eyes in looking after him, as the eyes of your souls in looking for him.

Ye cannot, O ye blessed spirits, wish other than well to mankind. How happy a diversion of eyes and thoughts is this that you advise! If it be our sorrow to part with our Saviour, yet, to part with him into heaven, it is our comfort and felicity; if his absence could be grievous, his return shall be happy and glorious.

Even so, Lord Jesus, come quickly! In the meanwhile, it is not heaven that can keep thee from me: it is not earth that can keep me from thee: raise thou up my soul to a life of faith with thee: let me ever enjoy thy conversation, whilst I expect thy return.

THE END.

www.ingramcontent.com/pod-product-compliance
Lightning Source LLC
Chambersburg PA
CBHW052040290426
44111CB00011B/1568